NUMBER TEN IN THE

Amerind Foundation, Inc.
Archaeology Series

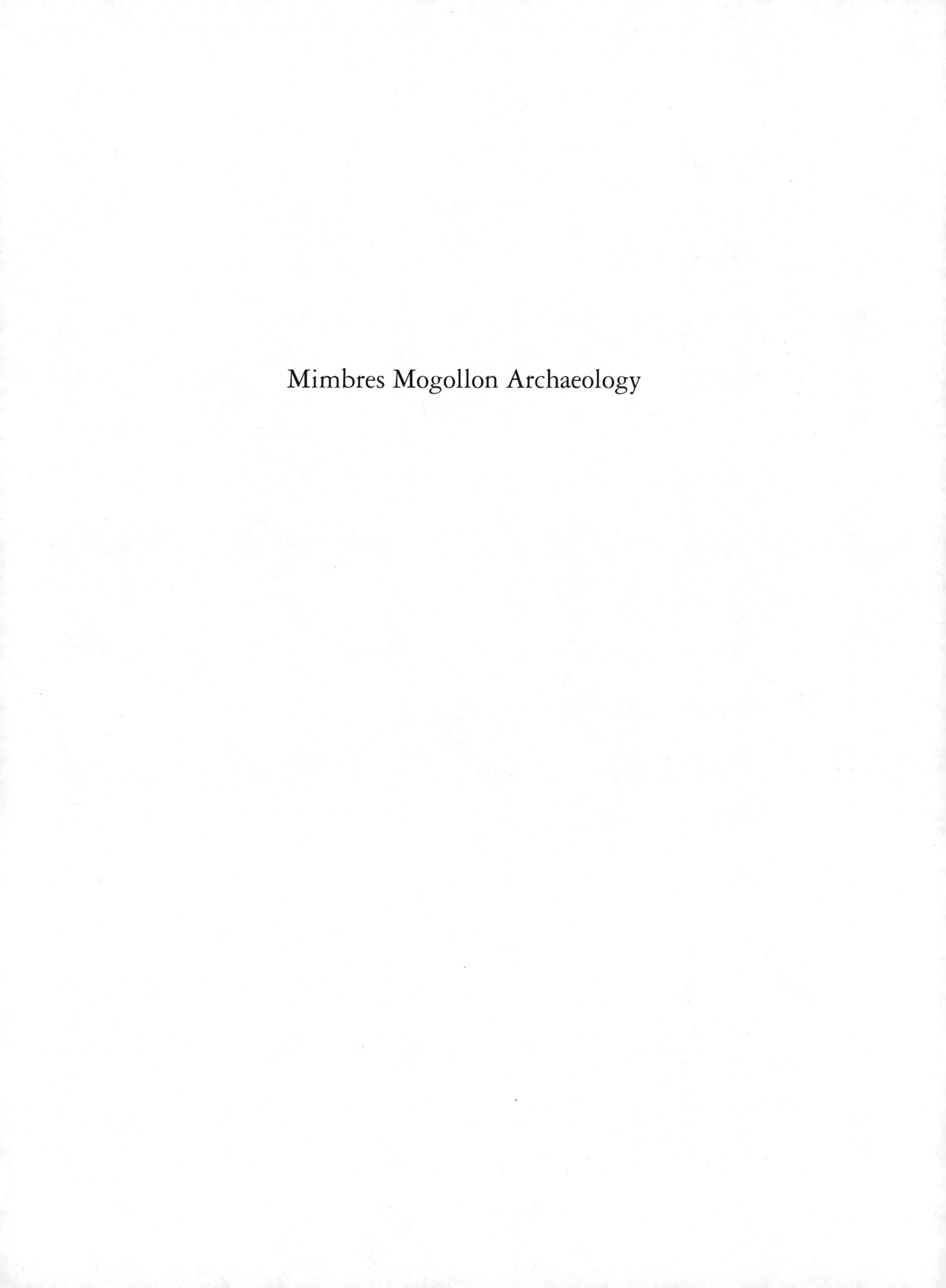

Mimbres Mogollon Archaeology

MIMBRES MOGOLLON ARCHAEOLOGY

Charles C. Di Peso's Excavations at Wind Mountain

Anne I. Woosley and Allan J. McIntyre

An Amerind Foundation Publication
Dragoon, Arizona

UNIVERSITY OF NEW MEXICO PRESS
ALBUQUERQUE

Contributors

Madeleine J. M. Hinkes
Gerald K. Kelso
Charmion R. McKusick
Charles H. Miksicek and Patricia L. Fall
Sandra J. Olsen and John W. Olsen
Edward J. Pasahow
Robert S. Sternberg and Randall H. McGuire
James B. Stoltman

Illustrations by Ronald J. Beckwith
Photographs by Robin Stancliff

First edition

Library of Congress Cataloging-in-Publication Data

Woosley, Anne I.
Mimbres mogollon archaeology : Charles C. Di Peso's excavations at Wind Mountain / Anne I. Woosley and Allan J. McIntyre.—1st ed.
p. cm.—(Amerind Foundation, Inc. archaeology series; no. 10)
1. Wind Mountain Site (N.M.).
2. Mimbres culture—Gila River Region (N.M. and Ariz.).
3. Indians of North America—Commerce—Gila River Region (N.M. and Ariz.).
4. Indians of North America—Gila River Region (N.M. and Ariz.)—Antiquities.
5. Excavations (Archaeology)—Gila River Region (N.M. and Ariz.).
6. Gila River Region (N.M. and Ariz.)—Antiquities.
I. McIntyre, Allan J. II. Title. III. Series.
E99.M76W66 1996
979.1'7—dc20 95—4395
CIP

Our understanding is not an illusion: it is ambiguous.
This ambiguity is present in all our views of works from other civilizations
and even when we contemplate works from our own past.
We are not Greeks, Chinese, or Arabs; yet neither can we say
that we fully comprehend Romanesque or Byzantine sculpture.
We are condemned to translate, and each of these translations,
whether it be of Gothic or Egyptian art,
is a metaphor,
a transmutation of the original.

—OCTAVIO PAZ, *The Art of Mexico: Material and Meaning*

Contents

List of Figures

List of Tables

Acknowledgments

More than 15 years have elapsed since the Wind Mountain site was excavated. Enough time, in other words, for a great many changes to have taken place. Numerous individuals involved with the project, among them Charles C. Di Peso (1920–1982), who initiated it, have since passed away. Others originally associated with fieldwork, in laboratory analysis, or who provided various forms of support and encouragement have retired or are now affiliated with different institutions and agencies. Attempting to identify and properly thank all those who assisted Amerind Foundation staff has proved to be surprisingly difficult. Charles Di Peso's handwritten notes offer some guidance for the period up to 1982; in many cases, however, Di Peso simply recorded the first names or initials of persons he knew well. For those of us responsible for the Wind Mountain study who are not familiar with these friends, reconstructing certain names has been a little like solving a mystery whose clues are scattered throughout the margins of notebooks. Every effort has been made to recognize those who participated; inadvertent omissions are deeply regretted.

Excavations at the Wind Mountain site were supported by a National Science Foundation grant (BNS 682545). Di Peso was especially grateful to Mary Greene, then Associate Program Director for Anthropology, for her interest and assistance. Additional contribution was made by Mr. and Mrs. Jack Lambert of Santa Fe, New Mexico. Importantly, the Board of Directors of the Amerind Foundation, Inc. must be acknowledged for allocating substantial foundation resources throughout the entire course of fieldwork, data analysis, manuscript preparation, and publication.

Several individuals helped Di Peso during the early days of the project. Longtime friends, Jack and Vera Mills, first showed him the site in April of 1975. Ben H. Ormand of the Pacific Western Land Company, together with Edward H. Michaelsen and A. E. Himebaugh, both of the Phelps Dodge Corporation, granted permission to excavate and facilitated fieldwork at the site. John J. Higbie, also of the Phelps Dodge Corporation, recounted the local history of the Azure Mine, including accounts of prehistoric turquoise mining. John Kolessar educated Di Peso about the geology of the Big and Little Burro Mountains. Joe Janes, Gila Forest Archaeologist, shared his extensive knowledge of the regional prehistory.

Di Peso was indebted to many people from the Silver City, New Mexico, vicinity who extended their friendship and hospitality to Amerind staff while the site was being excavated. He gratefully recalled Mary "Aggie" Agnes, Tink Burris, Red Ellison, Jack Hamilton, Mr. and Mrs. Joe E. Haymes, Mr. and Mrs. Clint Johnson, Mr. and Mrs. John King, Mr. and Mrs. James Tanzola, Chino and Jack Whetten, and the membership of the Grant County Archaeological Society. Longtime acquaintance Eddie Gilmore furnished logistical support at various times during the field season.

Excavations were ably directed by Bruce G. Harrill from the Fourth of July 1977 until 27 October 1978. Harrill's excellent, comprehensive field records greatly promoted completion of the manuscript. After Harrill left the project, Carlos F. Caraveo served as field archaeologist from 31 October 1978 to 28 December 1979. Arnold Withers assisting in the field and Malcolm Withers participating in the laboratory were warmly remembered by Di Peso. On Amerind Foundation premises, Gloria J. Fenner supervised the Wind Mountain laboratory during the project's first year. She was succeeded by Carol Ann Rolen, who took on the responsibility for processing and cataloguing artifacts as they were received from the field.

Amerind Foundation staff who assisted in various capacities over the years are many. Special appreciation is extended to Monte L. Bingham, George Brandt, Janet Brooks, Linda Carey, Melissa J. Fulton, Patricia A. Gilman, Mario Klimiades, Vicki L. Kramm, Faye E. Regner, Mary A. Sherry, Jose S. Tapia, and Malcolm Withers.

Ronald J. Beckwith drafted most of the figures, and Robin Stancliff is responsible for the artifact photographs that illustrate this volume. Andrea R. Johnson aided in evaluating and reorganizing the extensive data tables and served as research assistant.

Maureen O'Neill produced the final manuscript. It is with profound gratitude that we acknowledge her exceptional effort to assemble the complicated manuscript throughout its various permutations.

Di Peso and the Wind Mountain staff benefitted from the professional participation of other individuals whom we wish to thank: Walter H. Birkby, Peter Brown, Bruce Bryan, Dan Eichler, Kathryn Elsesser, Robert C. Euler, Arthur J. Jelinek, Alden C. Hayes, LaVerne Herrington, Ellen A. Kelley, J. Charles Kelley, Harold W. Krueger, Clement W. Meighan, Richard Myers, Richard A. Pailes, Stewart Peckham, Michael Pitt, William J. Robinson, Robert J. Salzer, Albert H. Schroeder, Albert C. Spaulding, Willard Van Asdall, Phil C. Weigand, Alice Wesche, Joe Ben Wheat, and Hugh Wilson.

The authors are warmly appreciative to friends and colleagues for their helpful advice and encouragement in bringing the study to conclusion. Emil W. Haury spent many generous hours in worthwhile discussion about Mogollon archaeology, looked at countless sherds, and acted as a "sounding board" for our ideas. He was a consistent source of inspiration and motivation, especially on the days when Wind Mountain seemed "overwhelmingly unfinished." Although Emil reviewed a final draft version, it is with profound sadness that we were unable to present him with the Wind Mountain publication. Both Roger Anyon and R. Gwinn Vivian provided useful commentary on ceramics. The former instructed us on the revised Mimbres typology and the latter on intrusive Anasazi wares. William H. Doelle and Henry D. Wallace graciously examined the Hohokam material. Jeffrey S. Dean is cordially thanked for calibrating the Wind Mountain radiocarbon dates and advising us on chronological issues. Julian Hayden, George J. Gumerman, and Stephen Charnas provided archaeological and other kinds of wise counsel. Gay Kinkade was generous with lending analytical equipment. Michael V. O'Neill provided technical assistance in unraveling our computer and word processing problems. Linda S. Cordell and Stephen H. Lekson offered welcomed, critical review, and their suggestions have strengthened our effort. We express our sincere thanks to Beth Hadas and Barbara Guth of the University of New Mexico Press, who have been unfailing in their support of the Wind Mountain publication.

The generosity and goodwill of two individuals, R. Preston Nash and Joseph A. Hester, are highly valued and deserve special mention. Their contribution greatly assisted in this volume's publication.

The continued patronage of past and present members of the Amerind Foundation Board of Directors is recognized with genuine gratitude: Wm. Duncan Fulton, Peter L. Formo, Michael W. Hard, Elizabeth F. Husband, Samuel J. Campbell, George W. Chambers, Marilyn Fulton, George J. Gumerman, Emil W. Haury, Thomas B. Husband, Peter Johnson, Clay Lockett, Sharline Reedy, William Secor Jr., Lawrence Schiever, and Frank M. Votaw. These individuals were firm in their support of the Wind Mountain study, and without them it could never have been completed.

Finally, had Charles Di Peso lived, his dedication would have read, "To my parents, who have gone to show me the way."

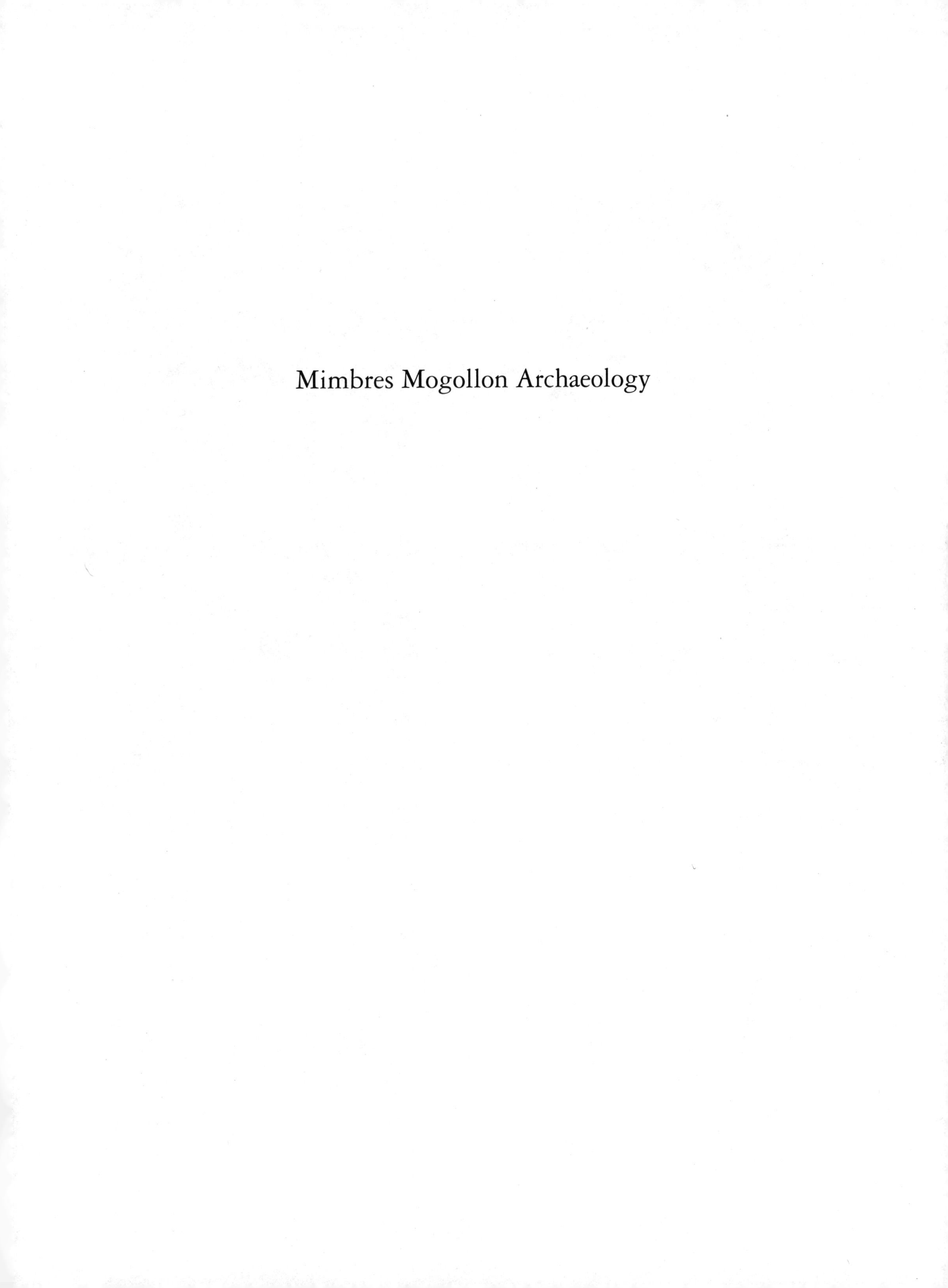

Mimbres Mogollon Archaeology

Introduction

The Wind Mountain site was Charles Di Peso's last archaeological project. With the analysis largely unfinished at the time of his death, this volume represents the cooperative effort of its authors and contributors to bring Di Peso's work on an Upper Gila Mimbres Mogollon settlement to fruition.

For those unfamiliar with the work of Charles Di Peso, it is not an overstatement to say that he never thought along simple lines. He did not deal with the lilliputian but with the grand; he was not interested in activities on a single mesa top or localized in a valley but in their position relative to far reaching interactive networks. The American Southwest and northern Mexico were, for instance, participating subareas within a much broader region he preferred to call the Gran Chichimeca. His approach to explaining prehistory was, in effect, heroic, and the results lasting in their provocation within the field of archaeological research.

Working as director of the privately funded and rurally located Amerind Foundation in Dragoon, Arizona, Di Peso (1974; Di Peso et al. 1974) shook the academic and, to his mind, the provincially entrenched Southwestern archaeological community with the publication of his eight volume magnum opus on the prehistoric Chihuahuan town of Casas Grandes. Espousing radical theories and Mesoamerican perspectives, he forged a new dimension of intellectual discussion that aided in establishing a school of borderlands research. He introduced Mesoamerican gods, elites, traders, economic hierarchies, and social donors and recipients into such geographically remote areas as Chaco Canyon, Mesa Verde, and the Mimbres Valley. Virtually any place where complex prehistoric Southwest systems emerged, Di Peso saw the footprints of influential Mesoamericans. Whether or not his ideas concerning Mesoamerican dominance were correct (and there is ample evidence that he overstated his case), Di Peso opened new avenues of inquiry and generated innovative thoughts and dialogue into Mesoamerican-Southwestern interactions. After the introduction of Di Peso's theories, the perplexing problem of the role played by Mesoamerica in the affairs of the prehistoric Southwest could no longer be a matter of simplistic speculation followed by a quick dismissal. To argue contrary to Di Peso's theories required an amplitude of data possessed by few individuals. Ever after, if archaeologists were to argue successfully with Di Peso, it would be necessary to be knowledgeable about a multitude of regions, cultures, and even disciplines. It was insufficient merely to be competent in Anasazi or Hohokam pottery styles—one was required to know intimately the Mogollon, as well as the styles of the Valley of Mexico, West Mexico, Chihuahua and Sonora, West Texas, and so forth. Pottery, of course, was only the thin gloss to understanding the total scheme of things. Fluency was required in various architectural styles, lithic industries, and associated temporal frameworks. Familiarity with Mesoamerican cosmologies or the literature of economic and social theory was highly recommended, if not actually demanded, to refute (or intelligently discuss) Di Peso's hypothesis of Mesoamerican-Southwest interaction. And finally, Di Peso not only relied on archaeological data, but applied his vast knowledge of historiography to reconstruct prehistoric processes.

This combination of talents coupled with an individualistic literary style created a formidable stream of fresh and intriguing ideas. Many archaeologists working in the Southwest found his concepts controversial, but Di Peso believed that expansion of his earlier research would prove his assertions. Thus, in 1977 Di Peso ventured into the New Mexican Mimbres Mogollon.

Wind Mountain and the Gran Chichimeca

Di Peso's entry into the Mimbres Mogollon region is understandable in light of his ideas concerning prehistoric culture change as shaped by economic enterprise (Di Peso 1968a, 1968b, 1983a). Central to this view was his belief in the existence of a dynamic mercantile system, originating out of a Mesoamerican hearth but operating in the large geographic expanse called the Gran Chichimeca (Figure 1). Within this broad region, Di Peso proposed that areas of exploitable resources were linked by satellite procurement sites and market centers which redistributed commodities. As this network of centers and satellites was established in territories occupied by indigenous Southwestern peoples, their attendant cultural patterns were fundamentally altered through the intervention of southern traders. Di Peso believed that the site of Casas Grandes in Chihuahua functioned as a pivotal market place within the Gran Chichimecan mercantile system (Di Peso 1974:58–59, 299–309, 620–622) and perceived its merchants as implementors of culture change. In looking northward, Di Peso wished to identify sites allied economically with, but subordinate to, the Casas Grandes hub.

He was excited by Wind Mountain's potential to confirm his economic theories for a number of reasons. Its location placed it on a north-south corridor linking Mexico (Di Peso 1979b:4–5), particularly Casas Grandes, with distant areas of the northern Gran Chichimeca. Of significance was the settlement's proximity to the mineral rich deposits, particularly turquoise, and other useful materials, including azurite, hematite, and limonite, found in the Big and Little Burro Mountains. Prehistoric exploitation of nearby turquoise deposits in the historic mines of Azure and Parker had long been reported (Jones 1904). Di Peso remarked on a lack of archaeological investigation in such mining areas and suggested that Wind Mountain inhabitants may have exploited this resource for trade (Di Peso 1979a:21). Di Peso also believed in a causal relationship between the Perros Bravos phase of the Viejo period in Chihuahua and the emergence of a Mimbres occupation at the Wind Mountain site c. A.D. 950–1060 (Di Peso 1974:179–252; 1977:20). Because the Wind Mountain site contained both Mimbres Mogollon Pit House period and Pueblo surface components, Di Peso felt it would provide data to chart long term socioeconomic developments. Finally, he was aware of the extreme vandalism that characterized many Mimbres sites, commenting on the desirability of excavating a relatively undisturbed Mimbres locality (Di Peso 1977:13).

Cultural Dynamics in an Economic Framework

Di Peso's ideas about culture change blended his notions of the impact on northern populations by southern *pochteca* overlords within the framework of world systems concepts developed by Wallerstein (1974). The merchant adventurers, or pochteca (spelled "puchteca" by Di Peso; see Riley 1993), who controlled the mercantile system were viewed as donors. These intruders directly affected the sociopolitical fabric of the exploited indigenous, or recipient, populations. Di Peso characterized this process as a donor-recipient pattern of culture conquest, with merchants consciously implanting Mesoamerican technologies and ideologies into the indigenous "Mogollon Chichimec" culture (Di Peso 1977:21–28). Within the context of an expanding long distance marketing system, trade was judged the prime mover of culture change. The cultural changes at Wind Mountain, from the Pit House period to Mimbres times, were seen as the result of intrusive merchant conquest (Di Peso 1977: Figure 4).

The indigenous Wind Mountain residents, identified by Di Peso as Mogollon Chichimecs, were described as products of a long-lived, uninterrupted cultural sequence that began with Paleo-Indian peoples and their successors, Archaic hunter-gatherers (Di Peso 1977:14, 1979b:1). By the Formative period, or A.D. 1, local patterns began to undergo slight change due to the introduction of southern based innovations and ideas, especially those relating to maize agriculture and ceramic technologies. At Wind Mountain, Formative period events were suggested to correspond with the early Pit House occupations of the site, which were compared to the Viejo period in Chihuahua (Di Peso 1974:179–252), with Loma San Gabriel of the Chalchihuites (Kelley and Kelley 1975), and with the San Juan and San Luis cultures of San Luis Potosi (Braniff 1975; Di Peso 1977:14–19; 1979a:14). From c. A.D. 950 to 1060, however, the indigenous culture pattern was said to alter dramatically as the Wind Mountain people were dominated by Viejo period pochtecas and became an intrinsic component of the Gran Chichimecan mercantile system (Di Peso 1977:22, Figure 4).

Di Peso theorized that between c. A.D. 950 and 1060, traders, described as merchant adventurers supported by a hungry Mesoamerican heartland, established Casas Grandes as a foreign port of trade or entrepot. Because the hinterland was the source of new exploitable raw materials, once Casas Grandes was operational, merchants could push farther into the north to found satellite markets. Wind Mountain, given its proximity to important minerals, was believed by Di Peso to be a likely candidate as one of these trade satellites or "gleaning centers" (Di Peso 1977:20 and 22, Figure 4).

Di Peso pursued several lines of evidence to support his hypothesis that elite traders precipitated significant culture change at Wind Mountain. He wanted first to define precisely the Mogollon Chichimecs, presumably represented by the earlier deposits of the site. Having reconstructed the original indigenous pattern, he could then seek evidence for the donor culture complex identified by Mesoamerican-inspired materials and symbolic expressions. In the case of the material inventory, Di Peso anticipated a preponderance of trade

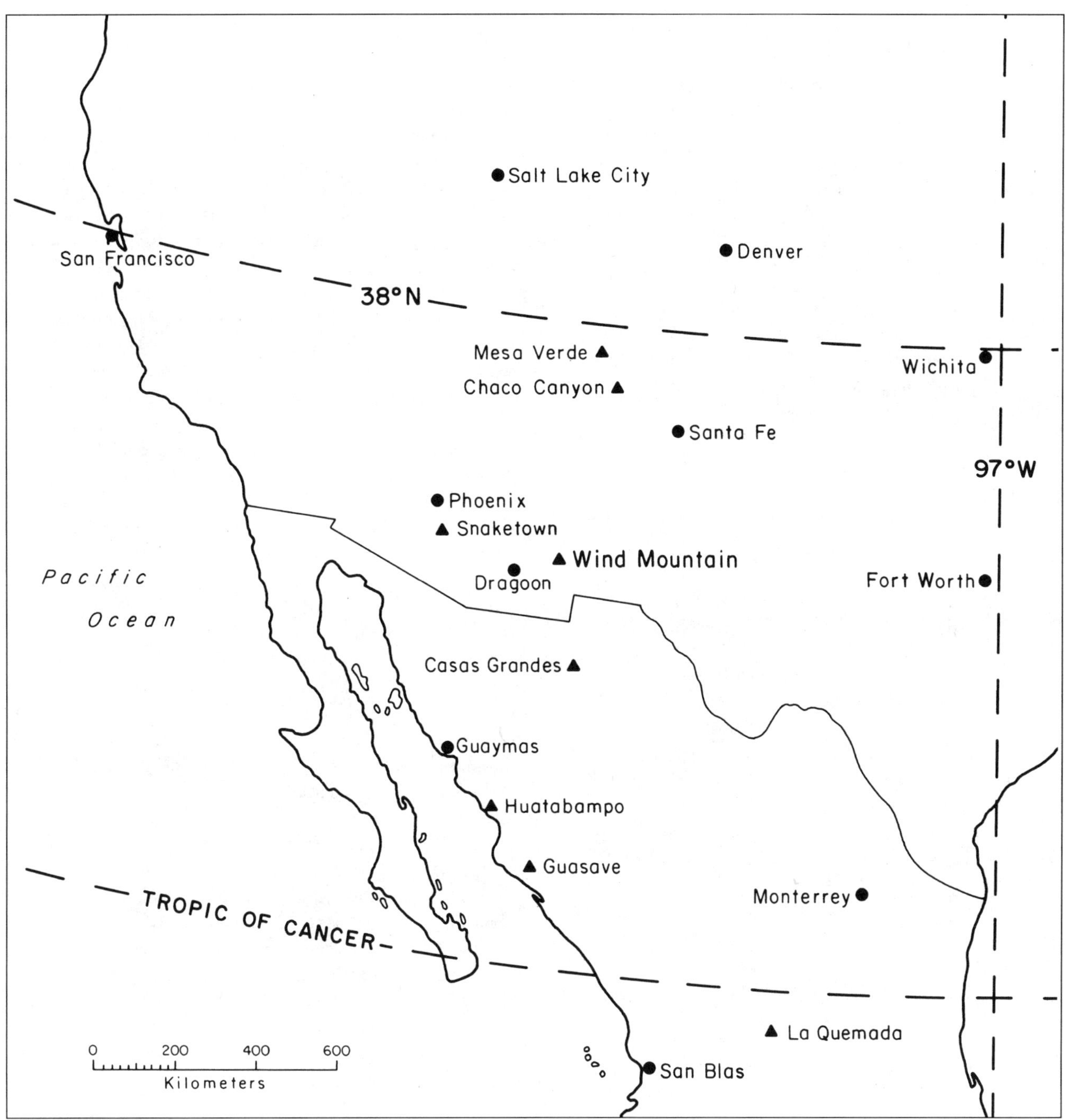

FIGURE 1. The Gran Chichimeca as defined by Di Peso (1974:53) bordered on the south by the Tropic of Cancer, on the north by the 38° northern latitude, on the east by the 97° western longitude, and on the west by the Pacific Ocean.

goods, either as raw materials or finished commodities. These would be unevenly distributed across the site, because such items were expected to be contained in the settlement's public warehouses. Moreover, if Wind Mountain was primarily a trade satellite responsible for commodity procurement/production—mainly turquoise and other minerals—economically valued objects were predicted to occur in far greater quantities than ordinary, utilitarian materials. Additionally, important Mesoamerican iconographic elements (e.g., plumed serpents, macaws, or the "smoking man" motif) and numerous socioreligious artifacts (e.g., ritual pipes and figurines) would corroborate the presence or ideology of a southern elite. In this regard, direct comparisons were sought between Wind Mountain and Casas Grandes (Di Peso 1977:20–21). The existence of elites and formalized external trade would be further tested by examining the site's specific architectural units (domestic vs. public structures), internal spatial organization, and burials (e.g., high status graves; Di Peso 1977:22, Figure 4).

History of Work

Di Peso viewed the Upper Gila as virtually untouched, a proving ground in which to test his theories of socioeconomic development and attendant culture change within the context of Mimbres Mogollon archaeology. He recognized that only a large and diverse data base could address such broad issues. Consequently, Di Peso employed a field strategy based on whole-scale exposure of all site deposits. Excavations were planned for two 12 month seasons, to be succeeded by two years of laboratory analyses, followed by a final stage of work in which the Wind Mountain publication would be prepared (Di Peso 1977:29–37). By the end of the second field season, however, the extent and complexity of the site was fully appreciated and the need to allow additional time was clear (Di Peso 1979a:1). Analysis of the data recovered and any thought of completing the project on schedule was cut short by Di Peso's premature death.

Fieldwork began in July of 1977 with vegetation stripping and excavation. Provenience control was maintained by overlaying a master 10 m grid on the Wind Mountain locus and a 5 m grid on the Ridout locus (for site maps, refer to Figures 4.1 and 4.2). By the end of 1979, most of the deposits from both loci had been completely uncovered. This strategy exposed 83 pit houses, more than had been excavated from any other Mimbres Mogollon site up to that point, as well as 16 surface rooms. The architectural data provided a wealth of information spanning the period from c. A.D. 250 to 1150/1200. To identify the full range of cultural patterns of the site (e.g., storage facilities, specialized work localities, and burial practices), Di Peso investigated surface areas between structures, not merely the architectural units themselves. Analysis of the accompanying material inventory strove to determine prehistoric activities, as well as the diversity and distribution of artifacts produced by the inhabitants of Wind Mountain.

Volume Organization

Di Peso (1968a, 1968b, 1979c, 1983a) wrote and lectured widely on the concept of the Gran Chichimeca and his theoretical position regarding the cultural dynamics believed to have occurred in this geographic macroregion. Prior to his death, he devoted a great deal of energy to reiterating his theories of economic enterprise and his conviction that Wind Mountain was a component of the Gran Chichimecan sphere. Unhappily, Di Peso's untimely death not only interrupted the process of analysis but left many questions about the precise mechanisms that linked the Wind Mountain site with other sites and regions unanswered. Nonetheless, every effort has been made to retain as many of Di Peso's ideas as possible. We have also preserved his strong conviction that detailed descriptive data presentation was an essential element in any archaeological report presentation. What we identify as the "Di Peso format" (refer especially to Di Peso et al. 1974) was followed in many instances throughout the volume. In terms of actual analysis, Di Peso's notes, though sparse, on the stone tool assemblage are perhaps his most complete assessment of any specific Wind Mountain data set. These thoughts have been incorporated into the Wind Mountain lithic discussion. Di Peso had also developed a material classification scheme, which is included in its entirety. Although he was able to classify and count the individual objects that comprised his various data sets, the time left him was too short and little was ultimately accomplished in the way of interpretation. Only scant, cryptic notations remain which describe the majority of data recovered during the Wind Mountain excavations.

Due to the confused status of all Wind Mountain data, a necessary reanalysis was undertaken. The authors assumed this responsibility which included inspection of pertinent information from Di Peso's project diary, notes, correspondence, funding proposals and, in certain cases, previous publications. Field notes and photographs, laboratory inventory lists, catalogue cards, together with material collections and the results of technical analyses form the basis for the Wind Mountain study. Inevitably, because we were responsible for much of the analysis, our interpretations (and biases) and our position regarding many topics, especially those of temporal placement and cultural relationships, are our own and, we presume, would diverge from those of Di Peso had he lived to write the Wind Mountain volume himself. We, for instance, paid particular attention to unraveling the chronology of the site. In part, we were concerned about the internal spatial complexity of a multicomponent settlement whose activities were circumscribed by the topography of a restricted ridge top. We felt that the internal timing of the various occupations was essential to understanding the Wind Mountain site and, therefore, its relationship to other sites. Important, too, when making associations between Wind Mountain and other areas is a recent revision of the Casas Grandes chronology (Dean and Ravesloot 1993). Reevaluation of the Casas Grandes sequence has far reaching implications for much of Di Peso's thinking about the politics and economics of the Gran Chichimeca, in which Wind Mountain ostensibly participated.

The volume is separated into 11 chapters and nine technical appendices. The first two chapters provide historical and physical context for the site. Chapter 1 summarizes explorations and archaeological work in the Mangas Valley of the Upper Gila, and Chapter 2 places the Wind Mountain site in its physical setting. The chapters that follow present data recovered during the course of excavations and are meant to be interactive and to involve the reader in the site interpretation. We begin with the chronology of the site in Chapter 3. Wind Mountain's internal period and phase sequence, the chronometric techniques that proved informative as well as those that failed, and ancillary data are examined. The Wind Mountain site chronology is further compared with regional Mogollon temporal frameworks for correlations and divergences. Chapter 4 explores Wind Mountain architecture, one of the site's most extensive data sets. The chapter is organized into two parts, the first of which discusses architectural trends characterizing the site's multiple occupations. Part 2, in keeping with Di Peso's admonition to present all available data, describes each structure, its internal stratigraphy, and associated features. The Wind Mountain typological framework is introduced in Chapter 5 with a short discussion of Di Peso's approach to classification schemes. As mentioned above, Di Peso spent a great deal of time in developing a comprehensive typological vocabulary, which he felt would aid in interpreting Chichimec culture patterns. In addition to the usual ceramic or lithic categories, the typology extends to classes such as house and hearth types. The Wind Mountain ceramic tradition, including its component types and evolution, is explored in Chapter 6. Chapter 7 presents the lithic assemblage and represents our most complete use of Di Peso's typological system. Chapter 8 describes and examines socioreligious objects that were felt to be indicative of Mesoamerican-inspired transformations of indigenous Mogollon Chichimec culture patterns. Treatment of the Wind Mountain dead is investigated in Chapter 9, and Chapter 10 is devoted to the animal burials uncovered at the site. Chapter 11 offers closing thoughts on the Wind Mountain site and perspectives on Mogollon prehistory.

The subsequent appendix section provides additional, technical information about Wind Mountain pit house architecture, Di Peso's complex taxonomic designations, as well as the results of specialized studies, including archaeomagnetic, ceramic petrographic, faunal, macrobotanical, osteological, and palynological analyses.

1

Background to Research
Explorations and Archaeological Investigations

Although archaeological investigations into the region of the Upper Gila River and its tributaries did not begin until the turn of the twentieth century, the Upper Gila has been explored since the middle 1700s. In addition to describing the countryside through which they traveled, some early historians also noted the surviving traces of the area's prehistoric inhabitants.

Early Explorations

The Spanish military, in campaigns mounted against the Apache and their allies, conducted the first forays into the Upper Gila (for an in-depth historical overview, see Kessell 1971:133–160). In 1747 Viceroy Conde de Revillagigedo launched a force to vanquish the Tcihene (aka, Gila, Warm Spring or Warm Springs, and Mimbres Apache), a band of the eastern Chiricahua, and secure the frontier for Spanish colonization. Bernardo de Miera y Pacheco, an engineer who accompanied the military, mapped the expedition's course past present day Silver City, and possibly journeyed through the Mangas Valley on route to the Gila River.

A decade later the Apache remained undaunted, and the Spanish initiated another punitive campaign. Led by Captain Bernardo Antonio de Bustamante y Tagle and Captain Gabriel de Vildosola, this attempt was no more successful than the others. However, a chronicle of the expedition written by the Jesuit Fr. Bartolome Sáenz survives and provides useful information about the region.

After establishing their base camp at Todos Santos, near the modern town of Cliff, the Spaniards ventured through the Mangas Valley. Fr. Sáenz described the valley and Ojo de Santa Lucia (now called Mangas Springs) as one of the few locations in the region with good water and arable land suitable for Spanish settlements. He noted an abundance of deer, pronghorn antelope, rabbits, and quail. He also observed beaver along stream banks and two types of fish in the Gila River. It is highly probable he passed by the Wind Mountain site, though it is impossible to determine if any of the party searched either Whitewater or Deadman Canyon, which border the site. Fr. Sáenz (Kessell 1971:147) was intrigued by the evidence of earlier human inhabitants (probably sites belonging to the Pueblo period):

> From Todos Santos on, one begins to see ruins of ancient buildings with square patios, as well as other vestiges of earthenware jugs, ollas, and pots decorated with a variety of colors of paints. On the ground I also saw clearly that they had brought an irrigation ditch which carried water to their fields.

Spanish efforts to quell the Apache continued unsuccessfully until the 1780s, the decade marking the demise of Spain's colonial empire. By century's end, the Spanish military and religious presence was replaced by fur trappers pushing westward. During the early 1820s, the colorful James Ohio Pattie trapped beaver along the Gila and its tributaries. He wrote letters home indicating, erroneously, that he was the first white man to explore the region (Flint 1984:70–71), and his accounts do not expand on Fr. Sáenz's earlier descriptions. Following the American takeover of New Mexico Territory in 1848, expeditions were again sent to conquer the Apache in the 1850s (e.g., those led by Col. Dixon S. Miles and Col. W. W. Loring), but it was not until the late 1870s and 1880s that the Apache were finally subdued. It was only with the expulsion of the Apache from the area and the introduction of the railroad that permanent settlements were established.

Adolph F. Bandelier, who journeyed extensively throughout the Southwest and Mexico, observing and recording as he traveled, bridged the era of early explorations and expeditions and the era of modern archaeological research (Bandelier 1890, 1892). He was in the Upper Gila and Mangas Valley region in January of 1884 (Lange and Riley 1970:193–203), the final years of Apache activity and still an exceedingly unsettled time. He explored cliff dwellings near the town of Cliff and described a large cave at Mangas Springs that contained bows, arrows, sandals, and other materials similar to Mogollon inventories later recovered from caves in the nearby Reserve area (Martin et al. 1952) and in the Winchester Mountains of southeastern Arizona (Fulton 1941). On 24 January 1884, Bandelier recounted exploring the Whitewater country southwest of the Burro Sierra and noted that its spring was not permanent. This is Whitewater Canyon and its ephemeral stream. Bandelier's trek undoubtedly took him directly past the Wind Mountain site.

With cessation of Apache hostilities, the modern history of the Upper Gila and its tributaries began. Bordering the Mangas Valley to the west and east, the Big and Little Burro Mountains and their mineral resources beckoned miners (for a complete synopsis of mining operations and ownership, see Gillerman 1964). The arable valley floodplain and adjacent grasslands invited ranchers and farmers. The resources that had appealed to Spanish colonists and the prehistoric Mogollon people now summoned another community of settlers.

Archaeological Work of the Upper Gila Region

Compared with other regions of the Southwest, relatively little archaeological work has been conducted in the Upper Gila and even less in the Mangas drainage, location of the Wind Mountain site (Figure 1.1; refer to Figure 2.1). Early surveys or limited excavations, for example, Editha Watson (1927, 1929) and the Cosgroves (Cosgrove 1947) working out of Silver City between 1926 and 1930, tended to focus on nearby caves and cliff dwellings, some of which had been visited by Bandelier. The more systematic investigations of the 1930s were, at least in part, precipitated by research supported through Gila Pueblo, and were directed toward establishing the diversity and extent of prehistoric Southwest cultures (Gladwin and Gladwin 1934). With Haury's development of the Mogollon concept (1936a, 1936b), field studies were initiated not only to test its viability as a taxonomic designation but also to determine the geographic distribution of Mogollon culture.

In the Mangas drainage, John R. Paul's (1938) reconnaissance and modest excavation stand out as the incipient effort to interpret the area's Mimbres Mogollon archaeology. He recorded 18 prehistoric localities, six of which were large sites: Lucky Lode Ruin, a pit house site; Pit Ruin, Thompson Ruin, and C-F Ruin, with pit house and Mimbres components; Pollack Ruin, a Salado site; and Saddle Rock Ruin, a site of unknown time period. Paul also excavated a single room at C-F Ruin from which he recovered Three Circle Red-on-white ceramics. Following Paul's initial investigations, the next 20 years were virtually barren of archaeological research.

With the exception of Danson (1957), work did not continue in the Upper Gila until the 1960s, when a growing number of contract archaeology projects accompanied highway construction programs. During the course of the Cliff Highway Salvage Project, for example, the Dinwiddie site (two small room blocks and two masonry pit structures) and the Lee site (50 rectangular and circular pit structures) were excavated (Hammack et al. 1966). This fieldwork was succeeded by the Upper Gila Project and the Upper Gila Water Supply Study, which remain two of the most ambitious archaeological investigations undertaken in the region (Fitting et al. 1982a, 1982b). Because the Upper Gila was so imperfectly understood, Fitting's first objective was to determine the baseline cultural sequence for the area (Fitting 1972b). Between 1967 and 1972, he combined large scale survey with excavation along the Gila River and several secondary tributaries, including Mangas Creek, as well as in the Big Burro Mountains country and a number of its side canyons (Fitting 1972a, 1972b, 1973a, 1973b, 1974). Fitting and his colleagues documented the regional prehistoric sequence from Archaic through Salado. Among other sites, they excavated the Archaic period Eaton site (Fitting 1974; Hemphill 1983), early pit houses at Winn Canyon (Fitting 1973a), late pit structures at MC 110 in the foothills of the Burro Mountains (Fitting 1971), Burro Springs sites 1 and 2, also in the Burro Mountains (Fitting 1973b), and portions of the Saige-McFarland site located on the confluence of Duck Creek and the Gila River (Fitting et al. 1971; Klinger and Lekson 1973; Lekson 1990).

As noted in the Introduction, Di Peso came to the Mangas drainage wishing to test his theories of prehistoric economic interaction and associated cultural change by intensively investigating a large multicomponent site. Wind Mountain fulfilled his requirements and was the focus of excavations from mid-1977 through 1979. Since that time, little additional work has been undertaken in the Mangas drainage or adjacent mountain foothills. In the larger region, however, Chapman and his colleagues (1985) conducted survey and excavation in the Cliff vicinity and southern San Francisco River drainage. Lekson (1990) completed analysis of previously excavated Saige-McFarland, a site showing distinct similarities with Wind Mountain. These studies form the primary data base for Upper Gila prehistory in general and the Mangas drainage in particular.

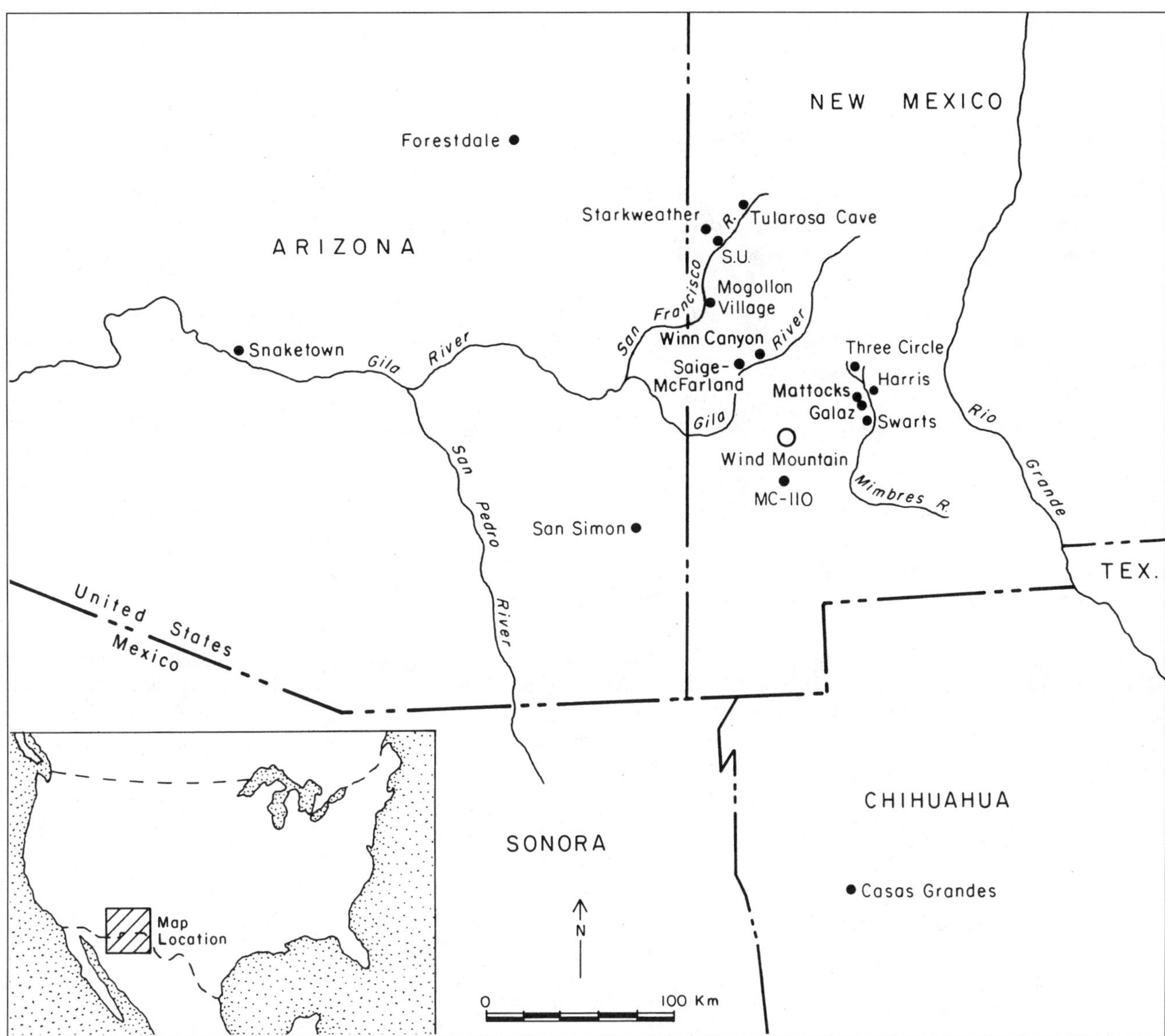

FIGURE 1.1. The Wind Mountain site in relation to other sites in the Southwest and northern Mexico.

The Upper Gila in Relation to Nearby Regions

Although the Upper Gila Wind Mountain site is considered part of the Mimbres Mogollon (represented by the Early and Late Pit House periods through the Mimbres phase of the Pueblo period; see Martin 1979:63, Figure 1), a major portion of the research that defines Mogollon culture and its temporal sequencing has been conducted elsewhere. Most work has focused on the Forestdale and Reserve areas to the north or in the Mimbres Valley to the east. As already noted, archaeological investigations came to the Upper Gila and Mangas Valley following the emergence of the Mogollon concept, first proposed by Haury in the late 1930s. Haury (1936a) identified the Mogollon culture based on his 1933 summer work at Mogollon Village on the San Francisco River and his 1934 field season at the slightly later occurring Harris Village in the Mimbres Valley (Haury was never happy with the taxonomic value of "Mogollon" in areas other than those he originally cited; see Haury 1986, 1988). Excavations by other researchers at localities such as the SU site (Martin 1940, 1943; Martin and Rinaldo 1947) served to validate Haury's concept. Not surprisingly, the Upper Gila, which is located between the Mimbres and San Francisco/Reserve Valleys, was also explored, if only sporadically until the 1960s.

To a certain extent, research into the earlier periods of Mogollon culture, which were often characterized by small pit house sites, lagged behind excavations of large, later surface settlements. By the time Haury (1936a) provided a framework for Mogollon archaeology, much work had already been directed toward Mimbres sites. Primarily associated with the Mimbres Valley, these surface pueblos, dramatic in their size, had been mined for their distinctive black-on-white pottery from the turn of the century (Fewkes 1914). Early research oriented archaeologists frequently had to compete for sites with pot hunters seeking collectable or saleable ceramic vessels—a condition that exists to this day. During the first decades of Mimbres archaeology, notable projects included excavations at Cameron Creek Village (Bradfield 1931), Mattocks Ruin (Nesbitt 1931), Galaz Ruin (Bryan 1931a, 1931b, 1931c), Swarts Ruin (Cosgrove and Cosgrove 1932), and Starkweather Ruin (Nesbitt 1938).

Mimbres phase surface archaeology took precedence over Mogollon pit house sites, not only because of a fascination with complex sites and their appealing material inventories but also because of the extreme, persistent looting that was rapidly destroying such settlements. A resurgence in research aimed at interpreting regional developments over the long term has resulted in the instigation of more balanced studies that comprise all phases of the Mogollon sequence. The Mimbres Foundation attempted to follow this approach (LeBlanc and Whalen 1980), and, more recently, Shafer initiated multiyear excavations at the Mimbres NAN Ranch site (1982, 1983, 1986, 1987, 1988, 1990, 1991a, 1991b; Shafer and Taylor 1986). Outside the Mimbres Valley, Lekson's (1978a) survey of the Red Rock Valley (to the west of the Mangas drainage) provided additional comparative information pertinent to Mogollon interpretations.

Wind Mountain and Mogollon Archaeology

The Wind Mountain site spans the entire Mimbres Mogollon sequence from the Early Pit House period to its final Pueblo period occupation, a small Mimbres phase surface component. Wind Mountain chronicles a long developmental sequence of Mogollon culture as yet unknown for other single site locations in the Upper Gila. The settlement exhibits strong correlations with the San Francisco/Reserve region, the Mimbres Valley, and, not surprisingly, certain other Upper Gila sites. There are interregional similarities in the pit structures reported from Mogollon Village, Harris Village, and the SU site, among others, and parallels in the ceramic assemblages of sites from all three regions. For instance, the Alma Plain, San Francisco Red, and Mogollon Red-on-brown wares recovered from Wind Mountain correspond to the same types in the inventories at Mogollon Village and Harris Village. The Wind Mountain Three Circle Red-on-white component conforms to ceramics from the Saige-McFarland site in the Upper Gila near Duck Creek. During the Mimbres phase, there are obvious analogies between the Boldface Black-on-white (Styles I and II) ceramics identified at Harris Village, Saige-McFarland, and Wind Mountain. Pottery from these sites also show similarities with the Mimbres Classic Black-on-white (Style III) pottery from Galaz Ruin in the Mimbres Valley.

By way of a contrasting view, Di Peso's approach to interpreting Mogollon culture patterns was on the order of the macroregion, not specific river valleys. He incorporated the Upper Gila, the San Francisco/Reserve area, and Mimbres Valley into the Gran Chichimeca, referring to the inhabitants of these subareas as Mogollon Chichimecs. Cultural dynamics operated in a vast arena, and relationships were not defined on the basis of neighboring regions but, rather, in the context of donor-recipient interactions, especially between northern frontiers and southern centers.

Whatever the geographic extent, the inherent diversity of Mogollon culture as expressed in terms of numerous regional (or macroregional) manifestations has long been recognized (Haury 1936a, 1936b; Wheat 1955). Though the Upper Gila and Mangas Valley were believed to constitute part of the physical distribution of Mogollon people, little work was forthcoming in the area. Data recovered from the Wind Mountain site, together with Lekson's Saige-McFarland analysis and Fitting's survey and excavations, now form the basis for a more complete understanding of Mogollon prehistory in the Upper Gila. Wind Mountain, albeit on a limited scale, also extends our knowledge of Mimbres phase archaeology beyond the confines of the Mimbres Valley.

2

Wind Mountain and Its Environs

The Wind Mountain site was once located atop a ridge, at an elevation of about 1,730 m (5,680 feet), between western Whitewater and eastern Deadman Canyons in the Mangas Creek drainage of the Upper Gila River (Figure 2.1). To the west the Big Burro Mountains created a major barrier, with Big Burro Peak reaching 2,451 m (8,041 feet). The Mangas Valley and the Little Burro Mountains, with a maximum elevation of 1,922 m (6,306 feet), bordered the site on the east (Figure 2.2). The settlement consisted of two loci, the Wind Mountain locus and the Ridout locus (pronounced "ride out"), separated by a shallow saddle of land 40 m (130 feet) wide (Figure 2.3). The Wind Mountain locus (Amerind Foundation site designation NM:Y:7:1) occupied the northern portion of the ridge, approximately 5 m lower than the Ridout locus (Amerind Foundation site designation NM:Y:7:3) to the south. The combined loci are known as the Wind Mountain site, which covered about 9,500 m^2 (2.3 acres) of the ridge top (Figure 2.4). After excavations were completed, subsequent mining activities removed all traces of the site.

Geology

Wind Mountain was situated in a mining area known as the Deadman-California Gulch-Whitewater Canyon districts. Big Burro Peak formed a granite upthrust southwest of the site ridge. Coarsely porphyritic, andesite and basalt plugs intrude the granite formations of the Big Burro Mountains (Hewitt 1958). The primary materials characterizing these highly mineralized mountains date to the Late Cretaceous and Early Tertiary periods and contain chalcopyrite, bornite, pyrite, molybdenite, specular hematite, magnetite, gold fluorite, quartz, barite, and calcite as well as secondary minerals such as chalcocite, malachite, azurite, turquoise, cuprite, native copper, limonite, other hydrous iron oxides, and chalcedony (Gillerman 1964:33–41, 1970). Turquoise, nuggets of red hematite, and limonite usually occur in either the granite or quartz monzonite porphyry deposits (Jones 1904; Sterrett 1908:829).

To the east the Little Burro Mountains constitute part of the Precambrian tilted Mangas fault block (Gillerman 1964:111). This exposure includes several nonmetallic deposits, such as Colorado shale and pink or white tuffs, which are associated with the clays of Redrock Canyon some 3 km (2 miles) from the site. These clay deposits, a variety of lithic materials, and diverse minerals were exploited by the prehistoric inhabitants of Wind Mountain (Figure 2.5).

Soils

Soil configurations associated with Wind Mountain were complex, given the settlement's position on a ridge and its proximity to lower elevation stream channels and alluvial fans. The Soil Conservation Service conducted detailed soil mapping in the region, and the following discussion draws heavily from this work (Parham et al. 1983:20–21, 30–31, 40). The site terrace can be described generally as an Encierro-Rock outcrop complex. Encierro soil is shallow and well drained with slow water permeability resulting in a moderate degree of water erosion and problems with blowing soil. It is formed in residuum derived primarily from limestone. The rock outcrop, if exposed, is barren or nearly barren. Piñon, juniper, and grasses are the principal native plants of this complex.

In the vicinity of the Encierro-Rock outcrop complex and sometimes intermingled with it are two other soil complexes, both well suited to farming. The first, Manzano-Paymaster-Ellicott soils (from 0 to 5 percent slope), occurs on

FIGURE 2.1. The Wind Mountain site ridge looking southward. The settlement is visible in the upper middle view (Neg. No. WM 103–20F).

floodplains, on alluvial fans, and in old stream channels. Composed of sandy loam, gravelly sand, and loam, this soil complex is deep and well drained with rapid to slow permeability, depending on edaphic conditions. Effective plant rooting is measured at 152 plus cm (60 plus inches). Runoff is slow, so water erosion and blowing soil hazards are negligible. Native vegetation consists mainly of grasses.

The second complex, Lonti-Manzano-Ustorthents soils (1 to 60 percent slope), is associated with nearby hills and terraces. These soils form predominately in alluvium derived from conglomerate and other sources and contain a component of gravelly loam. Such soils are generally deep and well drained with effective plant rooting at 152 plus cm (60 or more inches). Permeability is slow to moderately slow, resulting in rapid runoff, so that water erosion and blowing soil can cause problems. Grasses are the predominate form of native vegetation.

Climate

Climate records, primarily precipitation and temperature data, have been maintained for much of New Mexico since 1931. The information presented here (compiled from Houghton in Parham et al. 1983:1–2) is based on a 29 year study (1931–1960) from Fort Bayard, the weather station nearest the Wind Mountain site, located about 20 km (12 miles) to the east. Annual precipitation during this period measured between 31 and 48 cm (12 and 19 inches), most of the rain falling as summer thunderstorms between July and September. Spring and fall were generally dry, and additional precipitation often occurred as winter snowfall. On the average, temperatures ranged between 8° and 19° C (47° to 57° F) with a record low of minus 24° C (minus 12° F, Silver City, January 1913) and a record high of 40° C (103° F, Silver City, July 1958). Maximum summer temperatures measured about 27° C (in the 80° F range), with an average of only 27 days per year on which they exceeded 32° C (90° F).

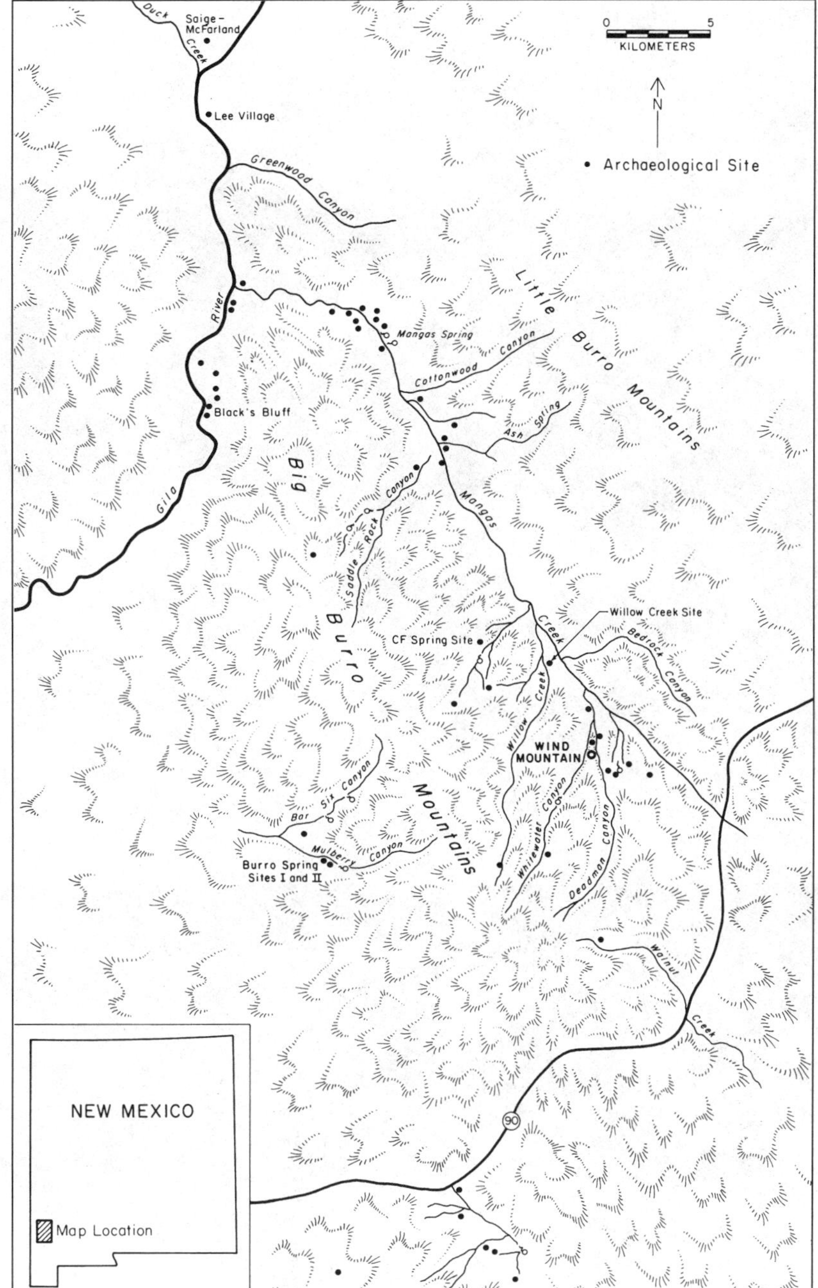

FIGURE 2.2. Location of the Wind Mountain site relative to selected sites in the upper Gila drainage.

Temperatures in excess of 38° C (100° F) were said to be rare. Winter months were relatively mild, with much sunshine and daytime temperatures registering about 10° C (in the 50° F range). Below freezing temperatures were uncommon, occurring on the average of twice a year. Freezing temperatures were recorded between November and March. The growing season was estimated at 150 to 180 days, or from mid-April to mid-October (for additional climatic data, see Appendix 4 in this volume).

These precipitation and temperature data can be misleading, however, because both are greatly affected by elevation. Elevations in the immediate site vicinity range from less than 1,525 m (5,000 feet) to in excess of 2,135 m (7,000 feet), and nearby mountain peaks are even higher at 2,440 m

FIGURE 2.3. Overview of the Wind Mountain site. The Wind Mountain locus is on the northern (left), the Ridout locus on the southern (right), portion of the ridge (Neg. No. WM 103–19F).

FIGURE 2.4. Low overview of the site in which the Wind Mountain locus room blocks (lower left), one of its largest pit structures, House X, and excavation trenches are clearly apparent (Neg. No. WM 103–0F).

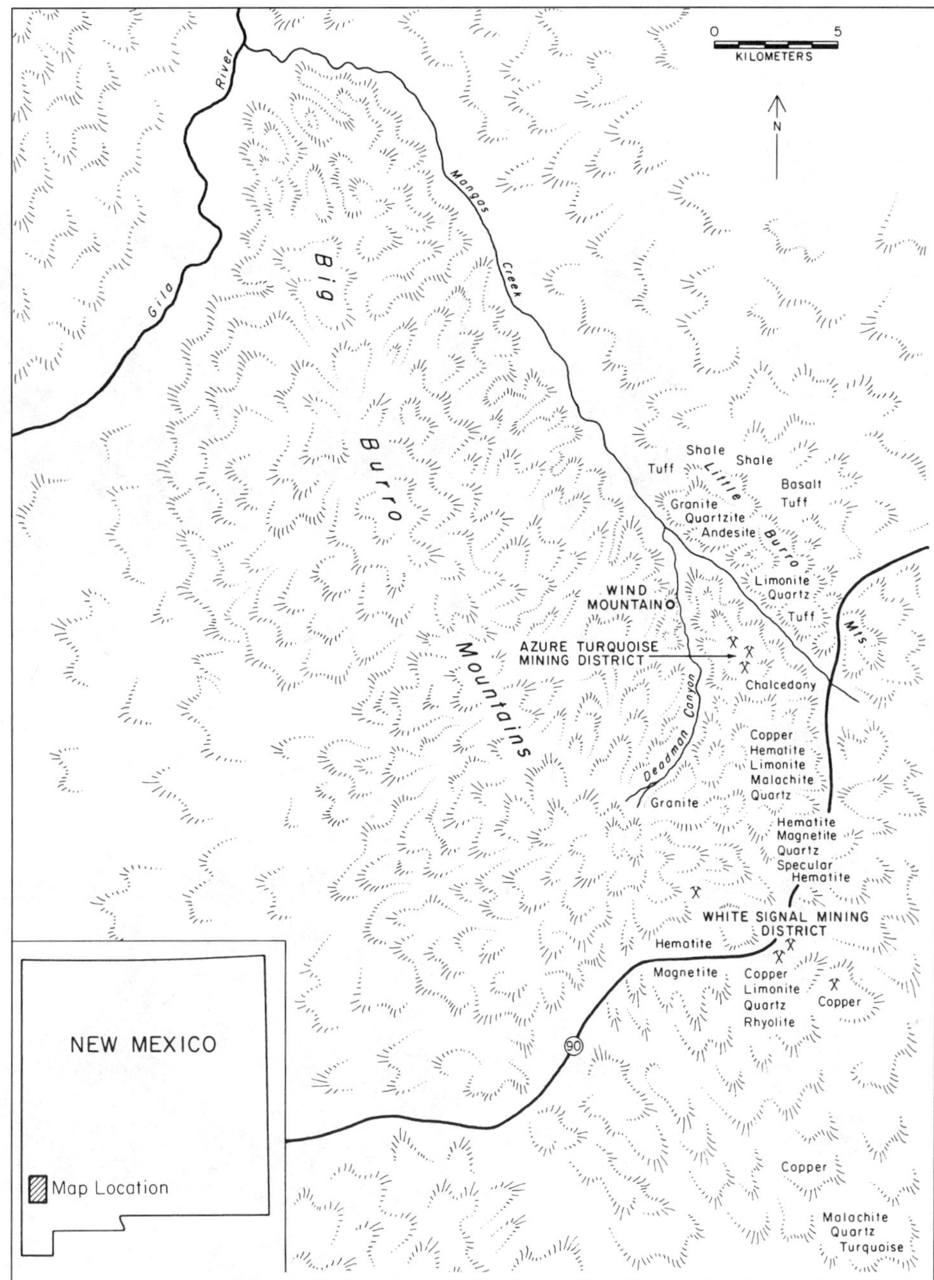

FIGURE 2.5. Distribution of selected stone and mineral deposits within an approximate 10 km radius of the Wind Mountain site.

(8,000 plus feet). As elevation increases, temperatures drop markedly and rainfall tends to increase. Whatever climatic vicissitudes the residents of Wind Mountain confronted, farming and other subsistence endeavors under semiarid conditions would have proved difficult at times.

Water Resources

It is difficult to reconstruct the surface water resources available to the prehistoric inhabitants of Wind Mountain due to large scale mining operations, the damming of water courses, and modern irrigation technology, which have fundamentally altered local stream flow patterns. All evidence

FIGURE 2.6. Typical vegetation colonizing the Wind Mountain site prior to excavation. Yucca, cacti, and grasses predominated (Neg. No. WM 3–15F).

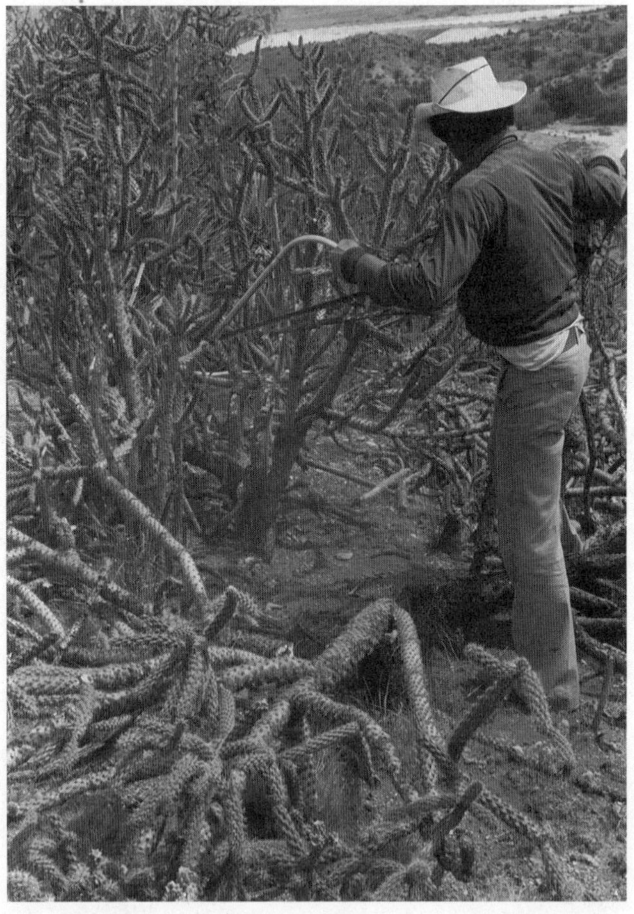

FIGURE 2.7. Clearing a cholla thicket from the site prior to excavation (Neg. No. WM 5–4F).

suggests that prehistoric water conditions were relatively favorable, certainly more so than is the case today. Located in the greater Mangas Creek drainage, the Mangas Valley opens up a scant 1 km (.6 miles) to the north of the site. Two secondary drainages, Whitewater Canyon on the west and Deadman Canyon/California Gulch on the east, channel natural precipitation runoff from nearby higher mountain slopes as well as spring fed water down their courses, which border either side of the settlement ridge. Wind Mountain was situated only about 35 m (just over 100 feet) above these drainages. Though numerous springs are now dry, many still flow in the area. Using a combination of stream diversion and dry farming, Wind Mountain farmers could have satisfactorily supported their crops.

Vegetation

The Wind Mountain site falls into the piñon-juniper belt generally associated with elevations between 1,373 and 1,983 m (4,500 to 6,500 feet; Elmore 1976:5). Both types of trees, but particularly juniper, dot the landscape adjacent the Wind Mountain settlement ridge. The slopes of the ridge support a mixed vegetation of piñon, juniper, oak, some mesquite, and bear grass. An extensive agave community thrives at the base of the ridge on its southern and eastern sides. Prior to excavation, dense growths of cholla cactus and yucca covered the prehistoric settlement, that is, an area principally delineated by architectural remains (Figures 2.6 and 2.7). Below the site ridge, rich riparian communities once bordered nearby stream channels, but only remnants, in the form of cottonwoods, survive today. Nearby mountains are forested with ponderosa pines and other conifers. Botanical transects were run in the vicinity of the site to provide a more specific view of the modern vegetation in the area. This data was later compared to stratigraphic botanical profiles from prehistoric site contexts in an attempt to reconstruct prehistoric biotic conditions (refer to Appendixes 1 and 2 in this volume).

Fauna

Modern land and water manipulation have also altered animal communities native to the Mangas Creek drainage by reducing or obliterating their native habitats. Reptiles, amphibians, and fishes were especially vulnerable to the effects of mining and irrigation activities that changed local hydrological schemes. Most of these species have disappeared from the region entirely (Janes and Rogers 1974c). Large indigenous mammals such as mule and white-tailed deer, bear, and mountain lion, still survive, though in greatly reduced populations (Janes and Rogers 1974b). In contrast, all birds identified in the Wind Mountain prehistoric site deposits (excluding a single scarlet macaw) continue to inhabit the Mangas Creek Valley (Janes and Rogers 1974a; refer to Appendixes 8 and 9 in this volume).

3

Chronological Considerations

Chronological analysis demonstrated a lengthy period of recurrent occupations at the Wind Mountain site, extending from the Mogollon Pit House period into Mimbres times. As a preview to the data presented in this chapter, it is useful to outline, in advance, our conclusions regarding the Wind Mountain occupation sequence. The chronology begins with limited use of the site ridge during the Early Pit House period (c. A.D. 250–550), but the sparsity of evidence from this early habitation precludes assigning phase designations. In contrast, the Late Pit House period (c. A.D. 550–950) is extremely well documented at Wind Mountain and is represented by numerous dated structures. Good chronometric data support the Georgetown phase (c. A.D. 550–650), the San Francisco phase (c. A.D. 650–800), and the Three Circle phase (c. A.D. 800–950). Following the Late Pit House period, the Wind Mountain chronology continues with a Pueblo period, which consists of a transitional Mangas phase (c. A.D. 950–1000/1050) and the Mimbres phase (c. A.D. 1000–1150/1200). Although the succeeding Animas (var. Black Mountain) and Salado (var. Cliff) phases have been proposed for the Pueblo period of the region (LeBlanc 1980), these manifestations were not apparent at the site. The final stage is reflected in a small Mimbres phase community, the last observable use of the ridge as a settlement.

Sixty chronometric determinations make Wind Mountain one of the most thoroughly dated Mimbres Mogollon sites in the Upper Gila. Yet the chronological interpretations were not without their difficulties. Though radiocarbon and archaeomagnetic techniques were successful, their date ranges generally overlapping, tree-ring and obsidian hydration assays were inconclusive. The Wind Mountain site was, moreover, stratigraphically complex; multiple construction episodes greatly affected the temporal reconstruction of the settlement's habitation sequence (Figure 3.1).

Unraveling the Wind Mountain site chronology depended not only on absolute dating methods but also on several collateral data sets. For example, the stratigraphic order of architectural features was established (Chapter 4, Part 2) and correlated with date ranges. The relative relationships of temporally associated ceramics (Chapter 6) and, to a lesser extent, house types (Chapter 4, Part 1) were also compared with dates. This cross-correlation of complementary data sets improved the accuracy of numerous absolute dates. Such comparisons assisted in the selection of some dates over others in cases in which a single feature yielded multiple date ranges.

An important consideration in assessing the applicability of the Wind Mountain time frame to other contexts is scale. Is a single site chronology compatible with regional sequences? A lack of consensus regarding the specifics of the Mogollon progression (e.g., Di Peso 1979c; Anyon et al. 1981; Fitting et al. 1982b; LeBlanc 1986; Lekson 1990) suggests that chronology building for the Mogollon, especially at the regional level, remains to be done. Consequently, we review the principal Mogollon time schemes from the Upper Gila, the Mimbres Valley, and the neighboring San Francisco/Reserve region. By way of contrast, we discuss Di Peso's ideas concerning Gran Chichimecan prehistory on a macroregional scale. Against these broad-based Mogollon chronologies derived from the data of numerous sites, we appraise, examining both parallels and divergences, the Wind Mountain results.

Tree-Ring Analysis

Although Wind Mountain is located near forests, and abundant quantities of post and roof beam materials were recov-

FIGURE 3.1. The Wind Mountain locus, in the vicintiy of House G and Room 3, graphically illustrating how multiple construction episodes may have affected the temporal reconstruction of the site's occupations (Neg. No. WM 17–31F).

ered from its structures, tree-ring results were disappointing. Some 260 samples were analyzed (Tree-Ring Laboratory, University of Arizona), with no data forthcoming (Table 3.1). Most wood samples lacked a sufficient number of rings, averaging less than 25, to correlate with the existing dendrochronological sequence. Much of the building materials used by Wind Mountain residents to construct their houses consisted of cottonwood, juniper, and piñon pine, which did not provide dates. A contributing factor to the absence of dates was the preponderance of complacent trees, which, because of their proximity to water, produced rings at irregular rates. The only temporal information gathered from the Wind Mountain tree-ring analysis determined that one cutting date from Wind Mountain locus House E occurred 59 years later than another in Wind Mountain locus House X (Jeffrey S. Dean, personal communication 1987).

Obsidian Hydration Results

Of the 26 obsidian samples submitted to the Obsidian Hydration Laboratory (University of California, Los Angeles), 23 produced hydration values (Table 3.2). Obsidian hydration data were interpreted by C. W. Meighan, who determined that the small sample size prevented their correlation with radiocarbon dates (Meighan and Russell 1981:85).

Meighan (1981) also compared hydration values with house types to establish a sequence of architectural forms at the site. He associated round (or early) structures with an average 3.03 micron reading, rectangular (or intermediate) houses with an average 2.96 microns, and surface rooms (or late) with an average 2.77 microns. Though the differences between obsidian hydration measures were extremely small, Meighan cautiously proposed that the results supported a round to rectangular to surface construction sequence at Wind Mountain (Meighan and Russell 1981:85). The distribution of round Type I and Type II structures does not, however, confirm this progression (Table 3.2). Specifically, of the six round and presumably early structures (Types I, II, and B), four fall into the lower ranking, or that portion of the hydration table representing most recent values. Similarly, Type IV rectangular structures occur randomly from early to late throughout the entire table. As a dating technique, obsidian hydration analysis was not successful in either contributing to the absolute chronology of the region or establishing internal trends at the site.

TABLE 3.1. Tree Types Represented by Wind Mountain Dendrochronological Samples

Tree Type	Samples Analyzed WM Locus	Samples Analyzed RO Locus	Total Number of Samples	Percent of Total
Piñon pine	143	1	144	55
Juniper	93	2	95	37
Ponderosa pine	10	–	10	4
Non-coniferous	8	–	8	3
Oak	3	–	3	1
Totals	257	3	260	100

TABLE 3.2. Obsidian Hydration Data

Lab No.	Feature	Type	Cultural Context	Artifact Form	Micron Value	Date Range A.D.
5812	Pit 25	II	Fill	Shatter	5.4	–
5823	House Z	IV	Floor fill	Primary raw flake	5.3	–
5820	House R	II	Floor fill	Shatter	3.8	680–980
5814	House ZZ	IV	Floor	Secondary raw flake	3.8	–
5815	House B	IV	Floor fill	Secondary raw flake	3.4	–
5825	House X	B	Floor fill	Primary raw flake	3.4	800–940
5804	House XX	C	Floor fill	Shatter	3.4	778–1030
5830	House PP	IV	Strat-Test Unit C	Primary raw flake	3.3	–
5829	House PP	IV	Strat-Test Unit C	Primary raw flake	3.2	–
5803	House XX	C	Floor fill	Shatter	3.2	778–1030
5822	Room 13	V	Floor fill	Secondary raw flake	3.2	–
5817	House H	IV	Floor fill	Primary raw flake	3.1	900–1070
5827	House KK	II	Floor fill	Primary raw flake	3.1	–
5821	House T	II	Floor fill	Shatter	2.8	–
5824	House CC	VI	Floor fill	Secondary raw flake	2.8	–
5835	House QQ	II	Floor fill	Shatter	2.8	–
5819	House K	IV	Floor fill	Primary raw flake	2.7	–
5826	House HH	I	Floor fill	Primary raw flake	2.6	640–730
5816	Room 4	V	Floor fill	Primary raw flake	2.6	–
5828	House NN	III	Floor fill	Shatter	2.5	766–1020
5833	House PP	IV	Floor fill	Primary raw flake	2.3	–
5832	House PP	IV	Floor fill	Primary raw flake	2.1	–
5818	Room 9	V	Floor fill	Secondary raw flake	2.1	–

Radiocarbon Dating

Happily, radiocarbon analysis proved more successful, as Wind Mountain structures produced 31 date ranges (Table 3.3).

Radiocarbon samples were submitted to Geochron Laboratories (Cambridge, Massachusetts), where they were processed and the raw dates determined (analysis conducted between 1978 and 1980). These raw dates were subsequently calibrated by Jeffrey S. Dean (personal communication 1991) using the CALIB Program (Stuiver and Reimer 1987).

Wind Mountain radiocarbon dates, unless otherwise stated, were plotted using calibrated date ranges to one standard deviation (Figure 3.2). The distribution of radiocarbon date-ranges is heavily redundant (58 percent) for the period spanning c. A.D. 540 to 1030. Specifically, Wind Mountain locus Houses E, J, N, R, FF, NN, WW, XX, AE, AI, AK, AM, AO, and AQ, and Ridout locus Houses A, C, J, and K, date within this time interval (refer to Figures 4.1 and 4.2 for house locations). Although the beginning date ranges of several other Wind Mountain locus structures, Houses H, AA, OO, AF, and AL, overlap this group, their concluding dates extend into the c. A.D. 1100–1200 range. The terminal radiocarbon ranges of yet another set of structures, Wind Mountain locus Houses D, DD, and AG, and Ridout locus House B, persisted to c. A.D. 1200–1300.

The two earliest radiocarbon date ranges obtained from the settlement derived from Ridout locus House I (390 B.C.-A.D. 4), and Wind Mountain locus House AN (A.D. 255–560). The two latest date ranges were secured from Wind Mountain locus Houses E (A.D. 1233–1398) and X (A.D. 1260–1410).

Archaeomagnetic Date Ranges

The archaeomagnetic analysis of hearths, as well as floor and wall plaster from the settlement's structures, produced 47 date ranges from 28 proveniences (Figure 3.3, Table 3.4; Appendix 3). One additional date range was obtained from Cremation 2. Individual archaeomagnetic samples often yielded one or more temporal ranges, each of which required evaluation. At Wind Mountain, 18 archaeomagnetic samples generated more than one range. The degree of confidence in archaeomagnetic dates is said to increase when ranges can be combined with other chronometric and diagnostic material culture data (Randall H. McGuire, personal communication 1990). Such data comparisons were made using the results of chronological and material analyses.

TABLE 3.3. Wind Mountain Radiocarbon Data

Geochron Sample No.	Field Sample No. WM(c)/	Provenience	Cultural Context	Depth (cm)	Sample Material	Sample Weight (gm)	Geochron Ages B.P.	Calibrated Ages A.D.* 1σ Range
		WM locus						
GX-6900	92	House AN	Floor	80	Charcoal	190.5	1625±135	255–560
GX-6561	56	House AI	Floor fill	80–98	Charcoal	153.1	1385±135	540–770
GX-6899	86	House AM	Floor	90	Charcoal	135.0	1335±135	582–855
GX-6558	44	House AE	Floor	100	Charcoal	5.1	1310±135	604–872
GX-6903	100	House AQ	Floor	170	Charcoal	443.0	1295±125	640–876
GX-5487	7	House N	Floor fill	80–95	Charcoal–roof and/or walls	77.4	1255±140	640–944
GX-6902	99	House AO	Floor	160	Charcoal	191.0	1230±135	650–980
GX-6556	27	House WW	Floor, Pit 1	30–68	Charcoal	87.3	1180±130	680–990
GX-5488	8	House R	Floor & Floor fill	45–55	Maize–Charcoal	28.3	1180±115	680–980
GX-6554	20	House FF	Hearth 2	120–136	Charcoal and Ash	27.6	1155±130	687–1000
GX-5485	4	House E	Floor fill	95–105	Charcoal–roof and/or walls	10.0	1125±135	694–1020
GX-5484	3	House E	Floor fill	95–105	Thatch–charcoal	12.0	680±115	1233–1398
GX-5483	2	House J	Floor	125	Charcoal–roof and/or walls	10.4	1115±135	733–1020
GX-6555	21	House NN	Floor, Post hole 1	–	Post–Charcoal	43.2	1105±120	766–1020
GX-7462	68	House AK	Entry fill under floor of House AD	–	Charcoal	?	1090±125	778–1030
GX-6557	39	House XX	Floor, Post hole 18	–	Charcoal	27.0	1090±125	778–1030
GX-6898	85	House AL	Floor, Post hole 8	–	Charcoal	22.0	1055±120	783–1150
GX-5482	1	House H	Floor	150	Thatch–Charcoal	4.0	1025±160	782–1190
GX-6553	18	House OO	Floor	120	Beam–Charcoal	59.7	1020±130	890–1160
GX-5489	9	House AA	Floor fill	105–120	Charcoal	33.1	980±125	903–1207
GX-6560	54	House AF	Floor fill	110–112	Charcoal	40.4	935±120	990–1220
GX-5486	6	House D	Floor fill	90–110	Charcoal–roof and/or walls	67.7	905±125	1000–1260
GX-6559	52	House AG	Floor	126	Charcoal	144.9	885±130	1000–1275
GX-6552	15	House DD	Floor fill	140–160	Charcoal–Log	46.3	840±120	1030–1280
GX-5490	10	House X	Floor fill	140–160	Thatch–Charcoal	11.6	645±115	1260–1410
		RO locus						
GX-6906	110	House I	Floor	90	Charcoal	26.0	2165±135	390B.C.–A.D.4
GX-6904	108	House J	Floor fill	120–130	Charcoal	42.0	1415±125	540–758
GX-6897	79	House A	Floor, Post hole 1	–	Charcoal	30.0	1355±130	570–798
GX-6901	98	House C	Floor	160	Charcoal	131.0	1340±120	600–799
GX-6905	109	House K	Floor	135	Charcoal	17.0	1135±135	692–1019
GX-7224	75	House B	Floor, Post hole 8 entry	–	Wood–Minor charring	15.5	885±130	1000–1275

*Calibrated by J. S. Dean using the CALIB Program (Stuiver and Reimer, 1987).

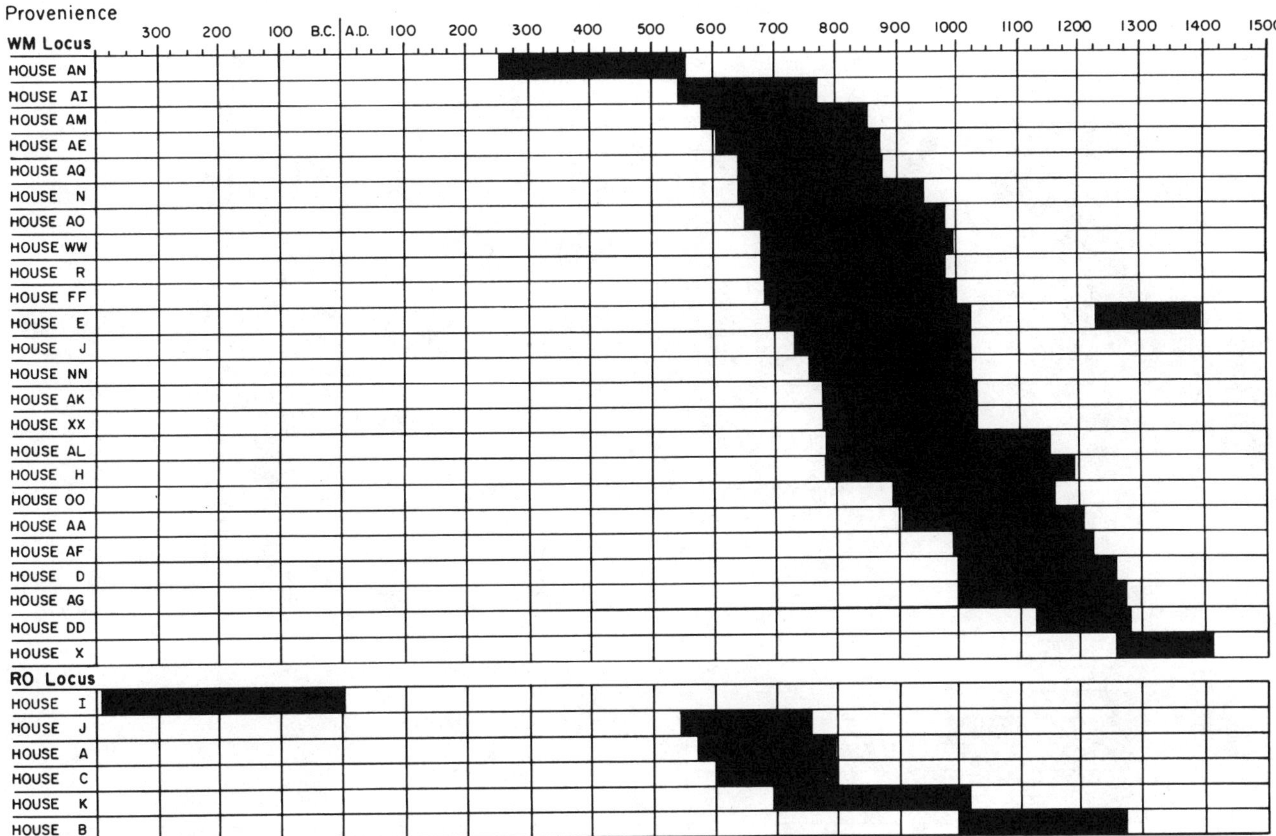

FIGURE 3.2. Wind Mountain site radiocarbon date ranges calibrated to one standard deviation.

Initial findings show that Wind Mountain archaeomagnetic date ranges form two main groups, the first extending from c. A.D. 620–1070 and the second from c. A.D. 1000–1260 (Figure 3.3, Table 3.4). A third group, consisting of four ranges obtained from Wind Mountain locus House M and Rooms 7, 15, and 16, dates between A.D. 1000 and 1260, or the Pueblo period of the site. A fourth group of date ranges, derived from Wind Mountain locus Houses V and W and Ridout locus House F, extends either partially or completely beyond A.D. 1300, or after the suggested abandonment of the ridge. Viewed as a single chronometric data set, the settlement's archaeomagnetic ranges fall principally between c. A.D. 600 and 1100, a temporal distribution similar to that observed for the radiocarbon ranges.

Evaluating the Temporal Placement of Structures

In an effort to establish the chronological sequence for the settlement and to associate date ranges with specific structures, all chronometric results were evaluated against collateral data. For example, 12 structures produced both archaeomagnetic and radiocarbon date ranges. While their temporal ranges often overlapped, viewed in isolation from other corroborative evidence, their dates merely implied generalized and, at times, contradictory trends. After evaluating the reliability of individual date ranges in terms of sample content and stratigraphic positioning, they were compared with associated diagnostic ceramics (Tables 6.1, 6.2, 6.4, and 6.5) and architectural types (Chapter 4). Taking this multiple data set approach, those date ranges best accommodating all available complementary lines of evidence were then selected as most accurately representing the ages of structures. In-depth analysis of supplementary data is presented in the following chapters.

Early Date Ranges

As previously noted, the earliest date ranges produced by the settlement were obtained by radiocarbon assay from Ridout locus House I (390 B.C.-A.D. 4) and House AN (A.D. 255–560) at the Wind Mountain locus. These radiocarbon determinations were assumed to have derived from roof fall

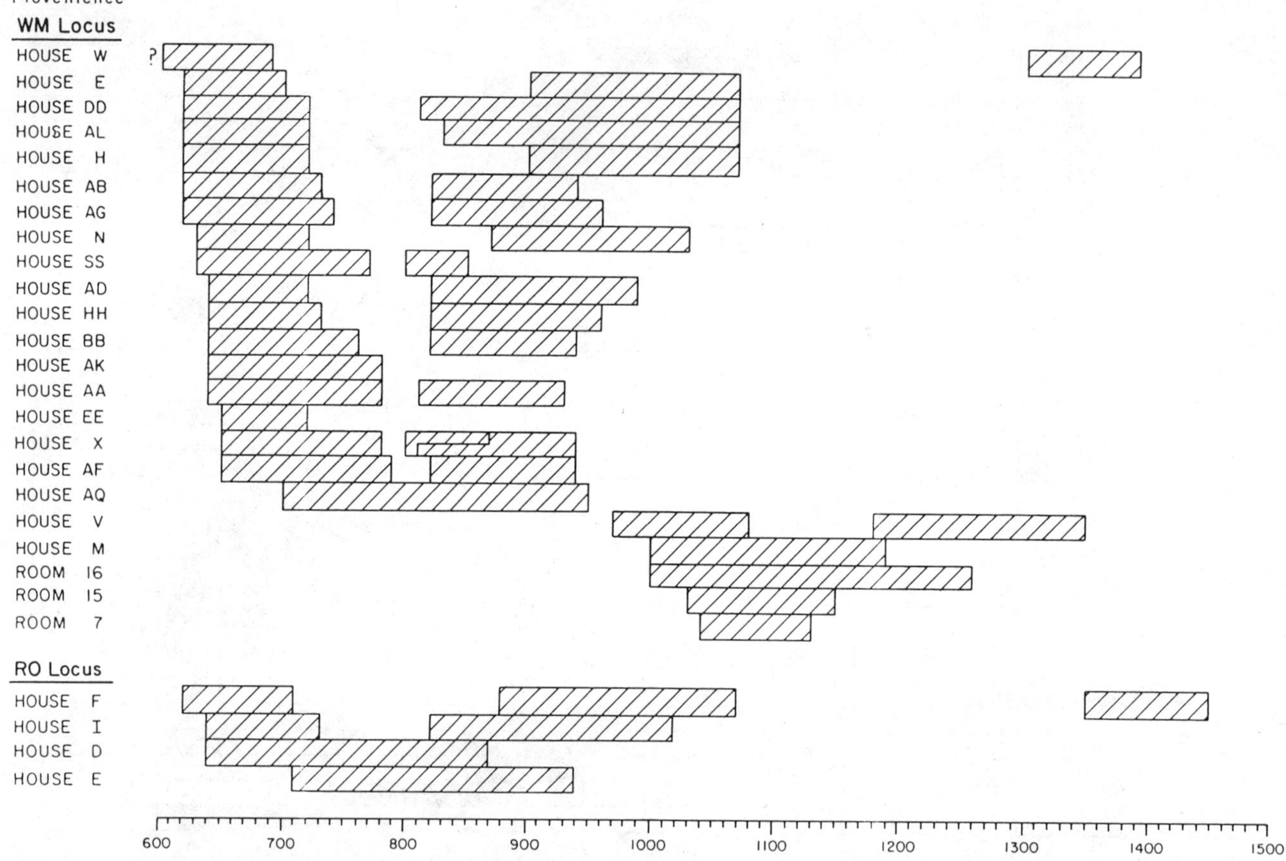

FIGURE 3.3. Wind Mountain site archaeomagnetic date ranges.

material in each structure. Both houses are Type I structures and are, therefore, theoretically associated with the beginning stages of Mimbres Mogollon architecture. Unfortunately, the early chronological placement of House I conflicts with two late archaeomagnetic date ranges (A.D. 640–730 or A.D. 820–1020) obtained from its hearth. Ceramics that might have refined this temporal range were not recovered from the house floor. Erosion and intrusive construction episodes also impacted the structure. Some clarification of temporal positioning may be forthcoming by examining the stratigraphic order of two nearby structures in relation to House I.

House I intruded into Ridout locus House E, which was dated using the archaeomagnetic method (A.D. 710–940). Though it produced no date ranges, House G superimposed House I. The construction sequence, then, would begin with House E, continue with House I, and end with House G, presumably the most recent of the three structures. Stratigraphy and available date ranges would seem to suggest an A.D. 640–730 or A.D. 820–1020 occupation for House I and an A.D. 710–940 use for House E. Important, however, were two archaeomagnetic samples analyzed from House G that could not be plotted against established archaeomagnetic curves. Because present archaeomagnetic techniques are informative only for the period A.D. 600 and later (Appendix 3), House G might well date prior to A.D. 600. Because it was the last structure of the three to be built, Houses E and I may have early occupations that present analytical techniques are unable to detect. All three structures may occur early in the life of the site, during the Early Pit House period, as hinted at by the House I radiocarbon date range (390 B.C.-A.D. 4). Certainly the round Type I floor plans of the houses imply the early stages of the Mimbres Mogollon sequence rather than a post-A.D. 700 date. It should be remembered that disturbances in the vicinity of Ridout locus Houses E, G, and I were extreme and that chronometric interpretations of these structures must be viewed with caution. By itself, Ridout locus House I cannot with confidence provide an absolute beginning date for the Wind Mountain settlement. The combined data of architectural house type and radiocarbon assays, however, suggest a placement during the Early Pit House period for Houses E, G, and I.

A second early date range comes from Wind Mountain locus House AN (A.D. 255–560), a structure not impacted by later building activities. An Alma Plain jar was recovered

TABLE 3.4. Archaeomagnetic Age Ranges

Sample No.	Provenience	Cultural Context	Ranges A.D.*
	WM locus		
8	House W	Hearth	?–690 or 1300–1390
3	House E	Hearth	620–700 or 900–1070
17	House DD	Floor plaster	620–720 or 810–1070
37	House AL	Wall plaster	620–720 or 830–1070
4	House H	Hearth	620–720 or 900–1070
26	House AB	Hearth	620–730 or 820–940
29	House AG	Wall plaster	620–740 or 820–960
2	House N	Hearth	630–720 or 870–1030
22	House SS	Wall plaster	630–770 or 800–860
43	House AD	Hearth	640–720 or 820–990
21	House HH	Hearth	640–730 or 820–960
9	House BB	Hearth	640–760 or 820–940
20	House AK	Floor plaster	640–780
10	House AA	Hearth	640–780 or 810–930
14	House EE	Floor plaster	650–720
16	House X	Floor plaster	650–780 or 810–940
15	House X	Hearth	800–870
19	House AF	Hearth	650–790 or 820–940
24	Cremation 2	Wall plaster	670–860
38	House AQ	Wall plaster	700–950
11	House V	Hearth	970–1080 or 1180–1350
6	House M	Hearth	1000–1190
13	Room 16	Floor plaster	1000–1260
12	Room 15	Hearth	1030–1150
7	Room 7	Hearth	1040–1130
	RO Locus		
30	House F	Hearth	620–710 or 880–1070 or 1350–1450
34	House I	Hearth	640–730 or 820–1020
41	House D	Hearth	640–870
40	House E	Wall plaster	710–940

*Dates from A.D. 600–960 derived from Eighmy et al. 1982, and dates from A.D. 1000–1500 are derived from Sternberg and McGuire 1990.

from its floor, with additional Alma plainware sherds collected from floor fill contexts. House AN is the only surviving dated structure (besides the problematical Ridout locus House I) likely to represent an Early Pit House period occupation at the site.

Late Date Ranges

The pair of latest possible radiocarbon date ranges from the settlement were procured from Houses E (A.D. 1233–1398) and X (A.D. 1260–1410) at the Wind Mountain locus. Both were determined from roofing thatch. They do not agree with either archaeomagnetic (from hearths and floor plaster; Table 3.4) or other radiocarbon date ranges (roof and wall beams; Table 3.3) secured from the same structures. House E, for instance, produced a radiocarbon range of A.D. 694–1020 from floor fill as well as an archaeomagnetic range of A.D. 620–700 or A.D. 900–1070. These ranges, combined with floor and floor fill ceramics consisting of Alma series pottery, San Francisco Red ware, Three Circle Red-on-white, Boldface, and Mimbres Classic Black-on-white (the black-on-white wares may be intrusive from superimposed Room 10) suggest a use period between c. A.D. 620 and 1070, a span obtained by combining the two archaeomagnetic date ranges comprising the earliest and latest dates possible. The ceramic assemblage and architectural stratigraphic positioning supports a House E occupation toward the end of the archaeomagnetic range, A.D. 900–1070, but certainly not as late as A.D. 1233–1398.

Similarly, a late radiocarbon date range for House X (A.D. 1260–1410) would seem unlikely given the alternative archaeomagnetic ranges of A.D. 650–780, A.D. 800–870, or A.D. 810–940. Ceramic sherds on the floor of House X, which included brown and red plainwares (the Alma series and San

Francisco Red), Mogollon Red-on-brown, Three Circle Red-on-white, and Boldface Black-on-white pottery, indicate an estimate of the structure's use life between A.D. 800 and 940. The presence of alternative date ranges, supported by ceramic data, eliminates the possibility of a post-A.D. 1300 occupation for Houses E and X and for the community as a whole. It is possible that these late date ranges may be the result of ephemeral intrusive disturbances after A.D. 1200–1300.

Three archaeomagnetic date ranges were also late, extending beyond A.D. 1300. These ranges, from Wind Mountain locus Houses V (A.D. 1180–1350) and W (A.D. 1300–1390) as well as from Ridout locus House F (A.D. 1350–1450), were rejected based on the lack of corroborating floor ceramics, architectural style, and/or stratigraphic positioning (refer to individual structure discussions below).

Suggested Temporal Placement of Wind Mountain Structures

The majority of Wind Mountain date ranges occurred roughly between c. A.D. 550/600 and 1150/1200. The specific date ranges selected for individual structures often incorporated radiocarbon and/or archaeomagnetic results (Tables 3.3 and 3.4), as well as the relative dates associated with pottery, stratigraphic order, and, to a lesser extent, architecture. Date ranges representing the "best fit" of all available evidence are presented after each house. The organization of data generally follows a progression based on the earliest beginning date ranges for the A.D. 500s, 600s, 700s, 800s, 900s, and post 1000 period. It should be noted that the beginning date is used only for the convenience of data presentation and discussion. Beginning dates are not intended to imply that they reflect either a definite commencement for the construction of individual houses or their precise temporal ordering at the site. Similarly, selected date ranges are not meant to suggest absolute occupation ranges. They merely propose the range of probability in which a structure was used. The date range may be inclusive of the entire use life of the house or, perhaps, capture only its early (if at the late end of the range) or terminal (if at the early end of the date range) activities.

Several of the settlement's structures have date ranges beginning in the A.D. 500s. These include Ridout locus Houses J (A.D. 540–758) and A (A.D. 570–798) and Wind Mountain locus Houses AI (A.D. 540–770) and AM (A.D. 582–855). All are Type IV structures. Radiocarbon ranges from these structures are considered reliable; none were disturbed by later intrusive construction or other invasive activities. Floor and floor fill ceramic assemblages, dominated by Alma series, San Francisco Red, and Three Circle Neck Corrugated wares, support the date ranges. Painted pottery was restricted to Mogollon Red-on-brown, Three Circle Red-on-white, and traces of Boldface Black-on-white sherds.

Eighteen structures show beginning ranges in the A.D. 600s. Ridout locus House C (A.D. 600–799), an undisturbed Type IV structure, reveals a date range supported by Alma series (n = 7) and San Francisco Red (n = 2) vessels recovered from its floor (Chapter 6; Tables 6.1 and 6.4). Ridout locus House F (A.D. 620–710), a relatively undisturbed Type A community structure, contained an early plainware floor assemblage that corroborated the associated date range.

In contrast, House AE (A.D. 604–872), a Type IV structure, occurred in a portion of the Wind Mountain locus characterized by multiple building episodes. Even so, its radiocarbon range conforms to the stratigraphic order of nearby structures. House AE intruded into House AB (archaeomagnetic date ranges A.D. 620–730 or 820–940), a Type B community structure. The construction of House AE postdates House AB, a circumstance used to support the earlier date range (A.D. 620–730) of the latter.

Wind Mountain locus House E (A.D. 620–1070) initially produced contradictory date ranges, the latest of which was rejected. The sparse floor and floor fill ceramic assemblage (Tables 6.1 and 6.2) and its Type IV architecture accommodate the archaeomagnetic date ranges. In addition, House E related chronologically to House X (A.D. 800–940) by tree-rings. A cutting date for House E was determined to be 59 years later than a cutting date from House X. The House E occupation would, then, logically have to postdate House X.

Another Type IV Wind Mountain locus structure, House SS (A.D. 630–860) produced two archaeomagnetic ranges (A.D. 630–770 or 800–860). Its placement is relatively straightforward with floor ceramics supporting the combined date range. The Alma series and San Francisco Red dominate, though smaller amounts of Three Circle Neck Corrugated, Mogollon Red-on-brown, Three Circle Red-on-white, and Boldface Black-on-white sherds were also collected. A few Mimbres Corrugated sherds were noted in the floor fill.

Wind Mountain locus Type IV House N (A.D. 630–1030) yielded both radiocarbon (A.D. 640–944) and archaeomagnetic ranges (A.D. 630–720 or 870–1030). The ceramic floor assemblage, consisting mainly of Alma series and San Francisco Red sherds with some Three Circle Neck Corrugated materials, suggests a pre-A.D. 1000 date. This placement is bolstered by the absence of black-on-white ceramics. Stratigraphic order argues for a House N occupation before A.D. 1000. The structure is superimposed by House E (A.D. 620–1070) and Rooms 7 (A.D. 1040–1130) and 10, from which no absolute date was available, though it was presumed to represent the post-A.D. 950 Mangas phase surface community.

Marginally overlapping radiocarbon (A.D. 778–1030) and archaeomagnetic (A.D. 640–780) ranges assisted in approximating the date of Wind Mountain locus House AK (A.D. 640–780), a Type D community structure. Floor and floor fill ceramics were sparse and intermixed with intrusive materials from overlying House AF. House AF (A.D. 820–940) superimposed House AK, tending to mutually confirm both date ranges.

House HH produced two archaeomagnetic date ranges (A.D. 640–730 or 820–960). A Type I structure, House HH was situated in a highly disturbed area of the Wind Mountain locus. The overlying construction of House DD (A.D. 810–1070) with its later date range lends credibility to the earlier archaeomagnetic date range of A.D. 640–730 for House HH (a pre-A.D. 600 date is possible based on its Type I architecture; refer to Early Date Ranges section in this chapter; Chapter 4). Floor and floor fill ceramics were redeposited, the result of later intrusive activities.

Ridout locus House D (A.D. 640–870), a Type IV structure located in an area free from disturbances, yielded a reliable archaeomagnetic date range. Alma series and San Francisco Red sherds, and a Mogollon Red-on-brown spindle whorl recovered from the house floor substantiate the date range.

House BB (A.D. 640–940), a Type IV structure at the Wind Mountain locus, displays a combined archaeomagnetic range (A.D. 640–760 or 820–940) corroborated by floor and floor fill ceramics and stratigraphic order. The usual plain brown and red pottery types were prevalent with some Mogollon Red-on-brown, Three Circle Red-on-white, Three Circle Neck Corrugated, Boldface Black-on-white, Mimbres Classic Black-on-white, and Mimbres Corrugated wares represented in low numbers. House BB was superimposed by Room 13, a presumed post-A.D. 1000 Mimbres phase surface structure.

Type II Wind Mountain locus House EE (A.D. 650–720) exhibited a date range that fits well with the floor and floor fill ceramics. Exclusive of one Mimbres Corrugated sherd in the floor fill, the assemblage was composed entirely of unpainted Alma series and San Francisco Red sherds.

Wind Mountain locus House AO (A.D. 650–980), a Type IV structure, was largely undisturbed except for the limited impact of Pit 71 and Pit Oven 19. Ceramics confirmed the date range and included Alma series, San Francisco Red, Mogollon Red-on-brown, and Three Circle Neck Corrugated sherds. One Mimbres Corrugated sherd was found in the floor fill.

House FF (A.D. 687–1000), a Type IV structure at the Wind Mountain locus, was probably robbed of its superstructure following abandonment (Chapter 4, Part 2). No associated ceramics were found on its floor. House FF does, however, occur under Rooms 15 (A.D. 1030–1150) and 16 (A.D. 1000–1260), thereby presumably dating prior to c. A.D. 1000.

House R (A.D. 680–980) is a Type II structure at the Wind Mountain locus. A combined radiocarbon sample consisting of maize and charcoal recovered from floor and floor fill contexts is too late for the construction period of a Type II house. Taking the calibrated date range to its second standard deviation (A.D. 640–1148) may approximate the estimation for the actual building of House R, that is, c. A.D. 640. The shallow floor (55 cm) probably accounts for the mixed sherd assemblage (Tables 6.1 and 6.2).

Wind Mountain locus House WW (A.D. 680–990), identified as a Type III structure, produced numerous vessels that corroborated the radiocarbon date range. Twelve floor vessels, including two miniatures, represented the Alma series, Three Circle Neck Corrugated, and Boldface Black-on-white types. Fourteen floor fill (within approximately 10 cm of the floor surface) vessels consisted of these types as well as a single Mimbres Classic Black-on-white bowl (Tables 6.4 and 6.5).

Type IV Ridout locus House K (A.D. 692–1019) produced a floor and floor fill ceramic assemblage consisting of Alma series, San Francisco Red, Mogollon Red-on-brown, and Three Circle Red-on-white sherds. Based on the presence of these types and the near absence of black-on-white sherds in direct association with the floor (only one Boldface sherd was observed), occupation of House K apparently occurred during an early stage of the date range.

Wind Mountain locus House W (A.D. ?-690) is a Type IV structure that produced contradictory archaeomagnetic date ranges of A.D. ?-690 and A.D. 1300–1390. The late range is not supported by either its architectural type or, more important, the ceramics located on the floor and in floor fill. Alma series sherds dominated, although numerous Mimbres Corrugated ceramics were recovered from floor fill. Painted pottery consisted of Boldface Black-on-white, Mimbres Classic Black-on-white, and a trace of Mogollon Red-on-brown. Except for three Mimbres Classic Black-on-white sherds on the house floor (presumably intrusive), all other ceramics derived from floor fill (Tables 6.1, 6.2, 6.4, and 6.5).

The date ranges of five structures begin in the A.D. 700s. A suggested use period for House AQ (A.D. 700–950), a Type IV structure, at the Wind Mountain locus is based on overlapping radiocarbon (A.D. 640–876) and archaeomagnetic (A.D. 700–950) ranges. The floor and floor fill ceramics, including primarily the Alma series, San Francisco Red, Mogollon Red-on-brown, Three Circle Red-on-white, and Boldface Black-on-white, support the date range.

The proposed date range for Ridout locus House E (A.D. 710–940) has been previously discussed and seems late in terms of its Type I architecture. Located near Houses G and I, House E was subject to disturbances stemming from intrusive construction episodes. Erosion was extensive in this portion of the Ridout locus. Furthermore, the archaeomagnetic wall plaster sample was reported to be only poorly fired. The reliability of the House E date range is suspect.

House J (A.D. 733–1020), a Type IV structure at the Wind Mountain locus, produced a date range that fits well with other evidence and suggests an occupation toward the early limit of the range. It was superimposed by House H (A.D. 900–1070) and was, therefore, most likely constructed prior to A.D. 900.

Wind Mountain locus Type III structure, House NN (A.D. 766–1020) provided a radiocarbon range extending slightly beyond A.D. 1000. However, floor and floor fill ceramics imply a pre-A.D. 1000 date. Painted pottery is dominated by Boldface Black-on-white and traces of Mimbres Classic Black-on-white (six sherds). Unpainted wares consisted mostly of the Alma series and Three Circle Neck Corrugated, with smaller amounts of San Francisco Red, and minute quantities of Mimbres Corrugated. Interestingly, a portion of a Boldface Black-on-white bowl, one sherd of which was found in the fill of House NN, was collected from the floor of House D (Wind Mountain locus House D discussion below). House NN must be earlier than House D to allow for the accumulation of trash, including the deposition of this broken bowl, after the former structure (i.e., House NN) was abandoned.

The date for community structure Type C, Wind Mountain locus House XX (A.D. 778–1030) provided a radiocarbon range conforming to a ceramic floor assemblage dominated by Alma Plain and San Francisco Red. Boldface Black-on-white was the most common painted pottery observed, while traces of Mogollon Red-on-brown and Mimbres Classic Black-on-white were noted. Stratigraphic order supports the date range. House XX (A.D. 778–1030) was constructed over House AB (A.D. 620–730).

The date ranges of eight structures, all of them at the Wind Mountain locus, begin during the A.D. 800s. As noted previously, House X (A.D. 800–940), a Type B community structure, generated contradictory radiocarbon (A.D. 1260–1410, from thatch charcoal) and archaeomagnetic (A.D. 650–780 and 810–940, from floor plaster, or A.D. 800–870, from a hearth) date ranges. After examining collateral data sets, an A.D. 800–940 conjoined date range was selected as best representing the structure's occupation. Floor and floor fill ceramics reflect a pre-A.D. 1000 assemblage. The presence of small quantities of painted wares (Mogollon Red-on-brown, Three Circle Red-on-white, and Boldface Black-on-white) does not provide convincing argument for an occupation during the earliest portion of the archaeomagnetic range (i.e., A.D. 650–780). Moreover, Room 14 was built over House X. Construction of the settlement's surface rooms is suggested to begin c. A.D. 950 (during the Mangas phase) or slightly later in the Mimbres phase. A cutting date associated with House E (A.D. 620–1070) was reported to have occurred 59 years after a separate cutting date from House X. The construction of House X must, therefore, predate House E.

Type IV House AA (A.D. 810–930) had multiple date ranges, though its radiocarbon and archaeomagnetic ranges slightly overlapped. Floor ceramics (two Alma Plain bowls and one Three Circle Neck Corrugated jar) indicate a pre-A.D. 1000 occupation.

House DD (A.D. 810–1070), a Type IV structure, exhibited somewhat overlapping radiocarbon (A.D. 1030–1280) and archaeomagnetic (A.D. 620–720 or 810–1070) ranges. Its date range is confirmed by associated ceramics, which consisted of early and late plainwares such as the Alma series and Mimbres Corrugated. Early and later occurring painted pottery, including Mogollon Red-on-brown, Boldface Black-on-white, and Mimbres Classic Black-on-white, was also collected. House DD superimposed House HH (A.D. 640–730), with the date ranges of both structures mutually corroborating the building progression.

Type IV structure House AF superimposed House AK. One radiocarbon (A.D. 990–1220) and two archaeomagnetic (A.D. 650–790 or 820–940) date ranges were recovered from House AF. The radiocarbon range is late for a floor ceramic assemblage of Mogollon Red-on-brown, Three Circle Red-on-white, and Boldface Black-on-white pottery with no Mimbres Classic Black-on-white material. Moreover, the earlier archaeomagnetic range does not agree with the observed stratigraphic order of structures. House AF (A.D. 820–940) was constructed after House AK (A.D. 640–780).

A Type IV structure, House AG (A.D. 820–960) superimposed Houses AF and AK. The use life of House AG must, therefore, occur later than House AF. House AG also provided one earlier archaeomagnetic date range (A.D. 620–740) as well as a late radiocarbon range (A.D. 1000–1275). This last range was rejected. The structure contained no post-A.D. 1000 ceramics, though Three Circle Red-on-white and Boldface Black-on-white ceramics (four sherds each) were recovered from the house floor.

House AD (A.D. 820–990), a Type IV structure, yielded two archaeomagnetic ranges (A.D. 640–720 or 820–990), the later of which agrees with a pottery assemblage dominated by Boldface Black-on-white and the Alma series. San Francisco Red, Mogollon Red-on-brown, and Three Circle Red-on-white sherds were recovered. Traces of Mimbres Classic Black-on-white and Mimbres Corrugated ceramics were noted (Table 6.2). House AD construction impacted earlier House AE (A.D. 604–872). Both House AE and House XX (A.D. 778–1030) intruded into House AB (A.D. 620–730). Consequently, the structures in this portion of the settlement chart multiple superimposed construction episodes.

The Type IV House AL (A.D. 830–1070) date range was determined from partly overlapping radiocarbon (A.D. 783–1150) and archaeomagnetic ranges (A.D. 620–720 or 830–1070). Floor and floor fill ceramics include the Alma series and Three Circle Neck Corrugated sherds, as well as a Boldface Black-on-white worked sherd and spindle whorl fragments, thereby corroborating the date range.

The radiocarbon range for House OO (A.D. 890–1160), a Type IV structure, agrees with associated floor fill ceramics, which consisted primarily of Alma series and Boldface Black-on-white sherds. Some Mimbres Corrugated and Mimbres Classic Black-on-white pottery was collected. No other building activity occurred in the vicinity of House OO.

Only two structures exhibited beginning date ranges in the A.D. 900s. Wind Mountain locus Type IV structure House H (A.D. 900–1070) included both radiocarbon (A.D. 782–1190) and archaeomagnetic (A.D. 620–720 or 900–1070) ranges. Floor pottery indicated a pre-A.D. 1000 use date for the structure. In addition, House H occurred under Rooms 4 and 5, further supporting a pre-A.D. 1000 construction. As demonstrated by dates from Rooms 7, 15, and 16, Wind Mountain surface rooms did not appear until after c. A.D. 950. Stratigraphic order, augmented by date ranges, indicates building activities in this part of the settlement were initiated with House J, followed by House H, and ended with the construction of surface Rooms 4 and 5.

Wind Mountain locus House V (A.D. 970–1080), a Type F community structure, produced archaeomagnetic ranges (A.D. 970–1080 or 1180–1350). Associated floor fill sherds agree with the earlier range. Unpainted brownwares and redwares, Mogollon Red-on-brown, Three Circle Red-on-white, Boldface Black-on-white, and Mimbres Classic Black-on-white comprise the pottery assemblage. House V is superimposed by Room 12, a stratigraphic order supportive of the earlier date range.

The date ranges of three pit structures and three surface rooms begin c. A.D. 1000. The Type IV Wind Mountain locus House M (A.D. 1000–1190) archaeomagnetic range agrees with the stratigraphic order of nearby structures. It is superimposed by Rooms 5, 6, and 11, all presumably either of the Mangas or Mimbres phase. House M intruded into Houses J (A.D. 733–1020) and Q (no absolute date available). Although not abundant, black-on-white (n = 13) and Mimbres Corrugated (n = 1) sherds from the floor and fill correlate with the House M date range.

The Type IV Wind Mountain locus House D (A.D. 1000–1260) radiocarbon range, when compared with the ceramic floor assemblage, may be a little late for this structure. Four Boldface Black-on-white vessels, one Alma Plain jar, and an Alma Rough ladle were recovered from the house floor together with sherds from floor and floor fill contexts. Most sherds represented pre-A.D. 1000 types with only a trace of either Mimbres Classic Black-on-white or Mimbres Corrugated material. A slightly earlier date range is supported by the presence of a large Boldface Black-on-white sherd on the House D floor. As mentioned earlier, most of this broken vessel was recovered from the fill of House NN (A.D. 766–1020), an earlier occurring structure. Consequently, the House D occupation may be slightly earlier than the radiocarbon date range indicates.

Type IV Ridout locus House B (A.D. 1000–1275) produced a radiocarbon date range somewhat late to accommodate its floor and floor fill ceramics. Alma series, San Francisco Red, Mogollon Red-on-brown, and Three Circle Red-on-white sherds occurred in floor fill and floor associations. No Boldface or Mimbres Classic Black-on-white or Mimbres Corrugated types were found. The radiocarbon sample was reported to show only minor charring, and the resultant date range was, therefore, rejected.

Archaeomagnetic ranges for all three Wind Mountain locus Type V surface structures, Room 16 (A.D. 1000–1260), Room 15 (A.D. 1030–1150), and Room 7 (A.D. 1040–1130), fit well with the known origin of Mimbres surface pueblo architecture c. A.D. 1000. Excluding Room 3, which was aberrantly deep (120 cm), the mean depth of all other Wind Mountain surface rooms was 50 cm (mean = 49.33 cm). Ceramic associations were sparse, disturbed, and generally unhelpful in untangling the chronological sequencing of these rooms (Tables 6.1, 6.2, 6.4, and 6.5). The surface rooms appear to have been the final primary architectural units constructed on the ridge top; they were not intruded by later structures.

Period and Phase Designations

Chronological analysis of the Wind Mountain site suggests that the principal sequence of occupations lasted approximately 700 to 900 years, or beginning c. A.D. 250 and terminating c. A.D. 1150/1200. Date ranges from a few structures indicate that the site may have been occupied even earlier, possibly between 390 B.C. and A.D. 4. Although the ridge was most likely intermittently inhabited, the entire Mimbres Mogollon sequence, including both Early and Late Pit House periods through the succeeding Mimbres phase of the Pueblo period, is represented.

As the site evolved and one occupation followed another, several developmental phases transpired. These phases conform in appearance, though not always in precise temporal placement, to established Mogollon chronologies (Figure 3.4). Mogollon phase designations are a useful means of discussing changing trends in the whole of the Wind Mountain occupation. They should not be mistaken, however, as discrete units of time characterized by specific cultural attributes contained by strict temporal boundaries. The Wind Mountain chronological sequence and its phase designations relied on the combined evidence of absolute dating, stratigraphic positioning, and ceramics. Some date ranges deriving from structures (especially if they integrated multiple archaeomagnetic and radiocarbon assays) were extremely broad. However, by using comparative stratigraphic information and diagnostic ceramic data, it was possible to refine such ranges to a more precise estimate of structure use life. Those structures displaying the most persuasive sets of complementary data formed the basis for determining the settlement's phase chronology (Table 3.5).

Temporal estimations could be made for all but 17 structures from the Wind Mountain locus. Specifically, House RR, a Type II structure (Chapter 4), is proposed to date to the Georgetown phase. Unfortunately, the failure to recover tem-

TABLE 3.5. Dated Structures Providing the Wind Mountain Site's Period/Phase Chronology

	House	Structure Type	Date Range A.D.
Early Pit House period ?–A.D. 550	RO–I	I	390 B.C.–A.D. 4
	WM-AN	I	255–560
	WM–HH	I	640–730*
	RO–E	I	710–940*
Late Pit House period Georgetown phase A.D. 550–650	WM–R	II	640–1148
	WM–EE	II	650–720
San Francisco phase A.D. 650–800	WM–W	IV	?–690
	RO–J	IV	540–758
	WM–AI	IV	540–770
	RO–A	IV	570–798
	RO–C	IV	600–799
	WM–AE	IV	604–872
	RO–F	A	620–710
	WM–AB	B	620–730
	WM–AK	D	640–780
	RO–D	IV	640–870
	WM–AO	IV	650–980
	RO–K	IV	692–1019
	WM–AQ	IV	700–950
	RO–B	IV	1000–1275*
Three Circle phase A.D. 800–950	WM–AM	IV	582–855
	WM–E	IV	620–1070
	WM–SS	IV	630–860
	WM–N	IV	630–1030
	WM–BB	IV	640–940**
	WM–FF	IV	687–1000
	WM–J	IV	733–1020
	WM–XX	C	778–1030
	WM–X	B	800–940
	WM–AA	IV	810–930
	WM–DD	IV	810–1070
	WM–AF	IV	820–940
	WM–AG	IV	820–960
	WM–AL	IV	830–1070
	WM–H	IV	900–1070
Pueblo period Mangas phase A.D. 950–1050	WM–WW	III	680–990
	WM–NN	III	766–1020
	WM–AD	IV	820–990
	WM–OO	IV	890–1160
	WM–V	F	970–1080
	WM–M	IV	1000–1190
	WM–D	IV	1000–1260
Mimbres phase A.D. 1000–1150	WM–16	V	1000–1260
	WM–15	G	1030–1150
	WM–7	E	1040–1130

*Rejected date, phase designation stands.
**Phase designation is problematical.

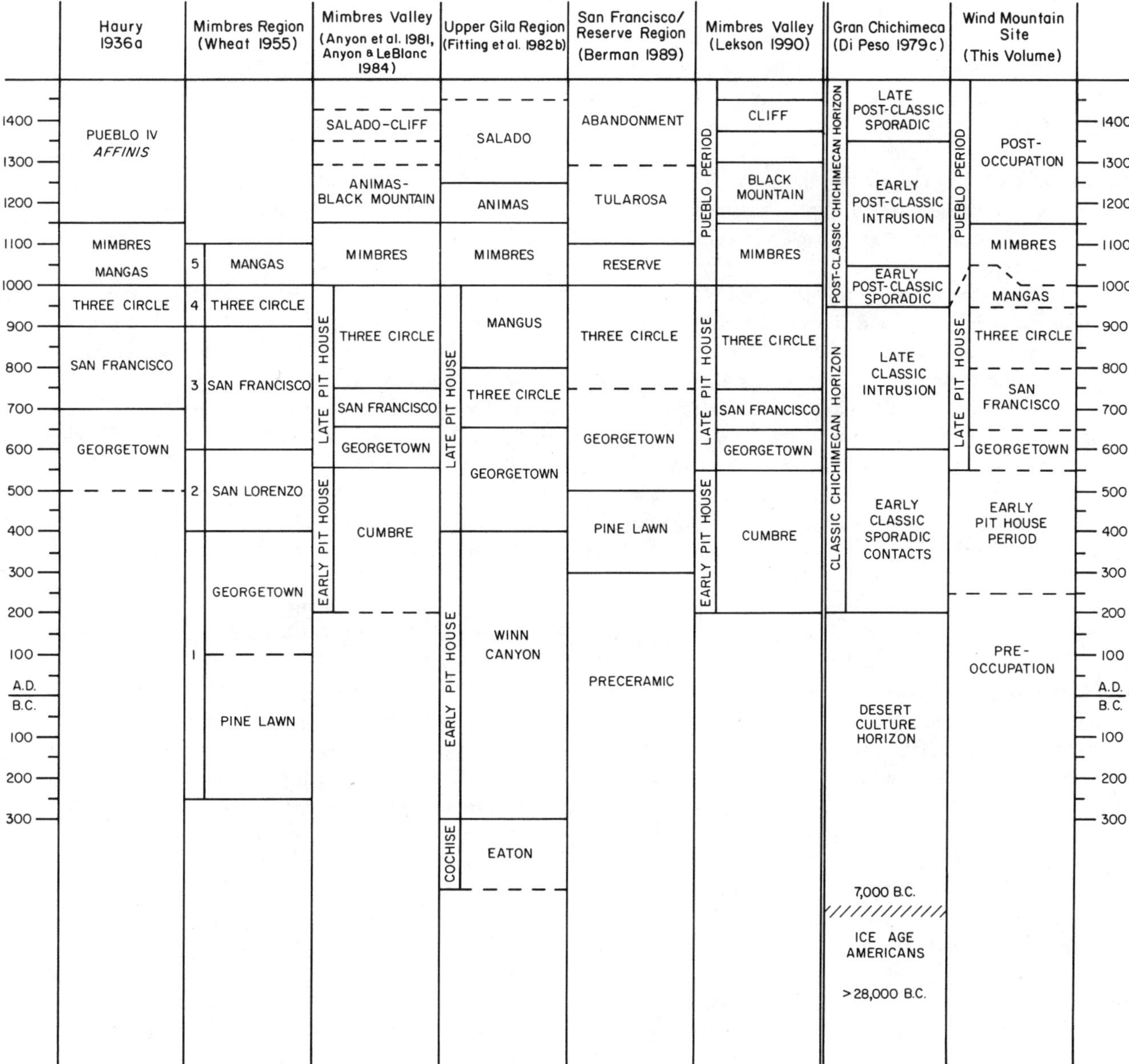

FIGURE 3.4. Comparison of regional chronological frameworks established for the Mogollon.

porally sensitive material in floor contexts renders its chronological placement problematical. Several Type IV houses were also difficult to place due to a lack of supporting data. The Type IV architectural plan of Houses A, B1, C, L, P1, Z, UU, VV, and AC suggests that they fall into either the San Francisco or Three Circle phase. Community structures House O (Type A), House U, and House Y (both Type C) were enigmatic. Based on architectural type, these structures may belong to the San Francisco or Three Circle phases. Finally, four indeterminate Type VI structures, including Houses F, I, CC, and AH, survived only as remnants, precluding their chronological assignment.

The Early Pit House Period

The Wind Mountain settlement may have been established by A.D. 255, as indicated by a radiocarbon determination from the floor of House AN (A.D. 255–560). Ridout locus House I (390 B.C.–A.D. 4), as previously noted, produced an earlier but problematical date range and does not provide proof for the origination of the site. In contrast, Wind Mountain locus House AN, with its Alma Plain ceramic assemblage and Mimbres Mogollon Type I floor plan, provides evidence for an Early Pit House period occupation. Even so, House AN may not reflect the incipient Wind Mountain habitation. Additional early structures at the site may have been destroyed by later building activities. In several areas of the settlement, remnant structures possibly dating to the Early Pit House period (e.g., Wind Mountain locus Houses LL and MM or Ridout locus Houses E and G) were observed. Later archeomagnetic date ranges were derived from Wind Mountain locus House HH (A.D. 640–730 or 820–960) and Ridout locus House E (A.D. 710–940). As discussed earlier, however, technological limitations in the analytical method would have failed to assay dates before A.D. 600. Based on their Type I architectural form, we believe these structures relate to the Early Pit House period. There is a high probability that the earliest occupations of the Wind Mountain site were erased by construction activities conducted during the Late Pit House period. In the absence of additional dated structures with compelling early material associations, however, phase designations were not attempted for the Early Pit House period.

The Late Pit House Period

Though the Early Pit House period is sparsely represented, the occupation of the Wind Mountain site throughout the Late Pit House period was extensive and is well documented. Date ranges from numerous structures, as well as associated ceramic floor and floor fill assemblages form the basis for distinguishing tentative habitation phases. Ceramics served as relative temporal indicators, their use as phase markers being well established (e.g., Haury 1936a; Anyon 1980; Anyon and LeBlanc 1984). First defined for other regions of the Mogollon, the Wind Mountain settlement phases and their suggested date ranges for the Late Pit House period include: Georgetown (c. A.D. 550–650), San Francisco (c. A.D. 650–800), and Three Circle (c. A.D. 800–950).

The Wind Mountain Georgetown occupation (c. A.D. 550–650) is represented by Wind Mountain locus House R (A.D. 640–1148 to the second standard deviation) and House EE (A.D. 650–720). House EE contained a typical Georgetown ceramic assemblage consisting mainly of unpainted Alma series pottery with smaller quantities of San Francisco Red. No painted wares are identified for the Georgetown phase, and only scant quantities of intrusive sherds were observed on the floor or in the floor fill of these structures. The House R sherd assemblage consisted primarily of Alma Plain and some San Francisco Red, though a trace of painted material (n = 6) was found. Other structures that most likely dated to the Georgetown phase included Wind Mountain locus Houses Q, S, and QQ. No date ranges were derived from these houses, but they contained characteristic Georgetown phase ceramics. In some cases, minute amounts of later occurring ceramic types were found. These inclusions were likely the result of disturbances related to prehistoric building as house pits were excavated or due to noncultural activities (e.g., rodent burrowing, ant colonies, and the root systems of plants). Although associated ceramics were sparse, Wind Mountain locus Houses T, GG, II, JJ, and KK may also belong to the Georgetown phase. The virtual absence of floor ceramics in these structures is possibly the product of later invasive house construction. These structures, as well as Wind Mountain locus House RR, all displayed the early Mogollon floor plan (i.e., round to oval) equated with Georgetown phase architecture.

The San Francisco phase (A.D. c. 650–800) coincides with the appearance of Mogollon painted pottery. Mogollon Red-on-brown emerged first and was closely followed by Three Circle Red-on-white. Production of Alma series plain and textured wares, as well as San Francisco Red, continued in large quantities. A shift in the predominant secular domestic house shape from round (Types I and II) to rectangular (Type IV) was evident. Wind Mountain locus House AB (A.D. 620–730) and House AK (A.D. 640–780), as well as Ridout locus House J (A.D. 540–758), House D (A.D. 640–870), and House K (A.D. 692–1019) floor and floor fill assemblages exhibited the newly occurring painted pottery types. Ridout locus House C (A.D. 600–799) and House F (A.D. 620–710) are assumed San Francisco phase structures, although they contained no painted pottery. Several of the vessels recovered from the floor of House C were identified as Alma Rough, a somewhat later appearing variety (as compared with Alma Plain) of the Alma series (Rinaldo's discussion in Martin 1940:78, 1943:238, 264–265). House F, at the Ridout locus, contained brownwares and red plainwares. Other structures with standard San Francisco phase pottery included Ridout locus House A (A.D. 570–798) and House B (A.D. 1000–1275; a rejected date), as well as House AI (A.D. 540–770), House AE (A.D. 604–872), House AO (A.D. 650–980), and House AQ (A.D. 700–950) at the Wind Mountain locus. With the exception of Ridout locus House B, date ranges for these structures overlap portions of regional San Francisco phase chronologies. The Ridout locus House B ceramic assemblage (and its house plan) are characteristic of the San Francisco phase, though the date range is far too late, probably due to the poor, only "slightly charred" wood sample submitted for radiocarbon analysis. Wind Mountain locus House W (A.D. ?-690) produced little in the way of diagnostic floor ceramics and is placed in the San Francisco phase based on the best estimate of two archaeomagnetic date ranges (the second range, A.D. 1300–1390, is beyond the projected occupation for the site). Neither Ridout locus Houses H and K nor Wind Mountain locus Houses G, K, YY, AJ, and AP produced date ranges, but they contained San Francisco phase ceramics and hypothetically belong in this phase. The floor of Wind Mountain locus House K, for example, produced a Mogollon Red-on-brown bowl, a San Francisco Red bowl, and an Alma Neck Banded jar—type associations typical of a San Francisco phase definition.

Three Circle (c. A.D. 800–950) is the final phase of the Late Pit House period. It is characterized by the emergence of Boldface Black-on-white (alternatively Style I and Style II) pottery, as well as a new unpainted textured ware, Three Circle Neck Corrugated. Both the Alma series and San Francisco Red endured as common components of the Wind Mountain ceramic assemblage. Mogollon Red-on-brown and Three Circle Red-on-white continued in small but consistent quantities. The date range from Wind Mountain locus House AM (A.D. 582–855), as well as a pottery collection favoring Alma and San Francisco Red together with small amounts of Boldface Black-on-white and Three Circle Neck Corrugated materials, may reflect an occupation at the end of the San Francisco phase and the onset of the Three Circle phase. Structures that best document the settlement's Three Circle phase with converging date ranges and ceramics are Wind Mountain locus House XX (A.D. 778–1030), House X (A.D. 800–940), House AA (A.D. 810–930), House DD (A.D. 810–1070), House AF (A.D. 820–940), House AG (A.D. 820–960), House AL (A.D. 830–1070), and House H (A.D. 900–1070). Other structures with Three Circle phase ceramics and overlapping, albeit broadly spanning, date ranges include Wind Mountain locus House E (A.D. 620–1070), House SS (A.D. 630–860), House N (A.D. 630–1030), and House FF (A.D. 687–1000). Wind Mountain locus House J (A.D. 733–1020), which occurred under House H (A.D. 900–1070), contained no diagnostic floor ceramics to aid in establishing a phase designation. House J was assigned to the Three Circle phase based on its relationship to House H and its Type IV architecture. A few structures with no absolute date ranges but displaying ceramics typical of the phase are Wind Mountain locus Houses PP, TT, and ZZ.

Pit House to Pueblo Transition: The Mangas Phase

After c. A.D. 950, Wind Mountain reflects a material culture in transition. Occupations combine long established patterns in architecture and ceramics with newly developing forms. The transition from the Late Pit House period to the Mimbres phase of the Pueblo period is termed the Mangas phase (c. A.D. 950–1000/1050) at Wind Mountain. While recently losing adherents (especially LeBlanc and Whalen 1980; LeBlanc 1986:303), historically the Mangas phase was used to describe small surface pueblos, often associated with concurrently occupied pit houses, and a preponderance of Boldface Black-on-white over Mimbres Classic Black-on-white pottery (Gladwin and Gladwin 1934; for a taxonomic discussion of the viability of the Mangas phase, see Lekson 1988; 1990:91–92).

The earliest evidence for near surface architecture comes from Wind Mountain locus House WW (A.D. 680–990) and House NN (A.D. 766–1020). Originally defined as Type III houses, both appear similar to surface structures with depressed floors rather than pit houses (Chapter 4). Both contained a distinctive Mangas phase ceramic assemblage. On the floor and in the floor fill of House WW, for instance, numerous vessels consisting of Three Circle Neck Corrugated jars together with Boldface Black-on-white bowls and a single Mimbres Classic Black-on-white bowl were found. In terms of floor fill sherd counts, Boldface outnumbered Mimbres Classic Black-on-white by 173 to 2. At House NN, although the pottery collection was meager, a similar trend in the frequency of black-on-white types was observed. This tendency was also apparent in the ceramic distributions in floor fill at Wind Mountain locus House V (A.D. 970–1080), where Boldface Black-on-white was the most common painted pottery type. House V is of further interest because it greatly resembles a suggested Mangas phase structure, Pit House 3, at the Saige-McFarland site (Lekson 1990:33–34, 91). Both the Wind Mountain and Saige-McFarland structures are extremely deep rectangular houses with ventilators. Other Wind Mountain locus pit structures with Mangas phase ceramics included House AD (A.D. 820–990), House OO (A.D. 890–1160), House M (A.D. 1000–1190), and House D (A.D. 1000–1260).

In addition, several Wind Mountain locus surface rooms may have belonged to the Mangas phase. Floor, floor fill, and fill assemblages in Rooms 1, 10, 11, and 14 consisted of either approximately equal or larger amounts of Boldface Black-on-white versus Mimbres Classic Black-on-white materials. Sherd counts were modest, but ceramics recovered from these rooms, with their minute quantities of Mimbres Classic Black-on-white and Mimbres Corrugated wares, do not suggest a decisive Mimbres phase pottery assemblage.

The Mimbres Phase

The Wind Mountain Mimbres occupation was represented by a scant dozen rooms. Rooms 16 (A.D. 1000–1260), 15 (A.D. 1030–1150), and 7 (A.D. 1040–1130) provide the temporal range for dated Mimbres structures. Preservation and context was excellent for Rooms 7 and 15, enhancing the reliability of their affiliated date ranges. Room 16 was greatly disturbed, and its temporal position must be viewed with circumspection. The chronological placement of Room 6 remains problematical because no diagnostic materials were recovered from its fill, floor fill, or floor. Room 6 is, however, adjacent to Rooms 5 and 8, so that an architectural relationship suggests it, too, is a Mimbres phase structure. In contrast to the Mangas phase, 11 rooms from the Mimbres phase

(Wind Mountain locus Rooms 2, 3, 4, 5, 7, 8, 9, 12, 13, 15, 16) clearly demonstrate that Mimbres Classic Black-on-white was the most commonly associated painted pottery type. In addition, Mimbres Polychrome sherds were recovered from the floor fill of Room 8 (n = 4). Two rectangular pit structures, Wind Mountain locus Houses B2 and P2, may belong to a Mangas phase or early Mimbres phase occupation. In both pit houses, Mimbres Classic Black-on-white was the most frequently occurring painted ware. The House P2 floor also produced two St. Johns Black-on-red sherds. Given the limited numbers of floor sherds, however, it is difficult to do more than acknowledge their presence and tentatively suggest that these structures were in use coincidentally with surface rooms.

Evidence from structures and ceramics indicates the Wind Mountain Mimbres occupation was extremely small. Even in rooms where Mimbres Classic Black-on-white pottery predominated, Boldface Black-on-white still occurred in comparatively large amounts. In only one room, Room 9, does Mimbres Classic Black-on-white far outnumber Boldface Black-on-white (43 to 4 sherds). No room with whitewares contained only Mimbres Classic Black-on-white. Painted wares of the Late Pit House period, Mogollon Red-on-brown and Three Circle Red-on-white, occur sporadically in floor and floor fill contexts in a majority of those surface rooms that contain pottery. This mix of early and late painted ceramic types is probably a function of depositional disturbances.

The relative quantities of Boldface Black-on-white to Mimbres Classic Black-on-white pottery at Wind Mountain raises an interesting point of discussion. The number of whole and partial Boldface to Mimbres Classic vessels from all site contexts is about even, 17 to 16. Yet total sherd counts from structures and other architectural features are approximately 8,200 for Boldface (76 percent) and 2,600 for Mimbres Classic (24 percent), or about three-fourths Boldface Black-on-white to one-fourth Mimbres Classic Black-on-white (floor and floor fill counts are approximately 1,330 Boldface, 78 percent; to 365 Mimbres Classic sherds, 22 percent). Not only do these numbers suggest a limited Mimbres occupation, but they lend support to the validity of a transition (i.e., the Mangas phase) between the Late Pit House period and the Mimbres phase. Indeed, a fully developed Mimbres phase settlement never materialized. Even after c. A.D. 1000, the traditional beginning date for Mimbres in the Mimbres Valley and the Upper Gila, Wind Mountain continues to look much like a Mangas phase site. In other words, the settlement conforms to the Mangas phase taxonomy (a small surface pueblo, some pit house structures, and pottery in amounts of about 60 to 80 percent early black-on-white to 20 to 40 percent classic black-on-white types; see Lekson 1990:91–92; Fitting et al. 1971). These associations recall Haury's (1936a:123) proposal of a Mangas to Mimbres progression and concur with the temporal transition phase suggested by others (Fitting et al. 1982b; Lekson 1990). Evidence for a post-A.D. 1000 Wind Mountain occupation reinforces the reality of the small pueblo as a fundamental unit of Mimbres architecture (Lekson 1990:78; 1992; for an opposing view, LeBlanc 1983; Blake et al. 1986). A small Wind Mountain surface pueblo continued for some time, with the combination of date ranges and ceramic associations indicating that the occupation did not extend much beyond c. A.D. 1150/1200. The infrequent occurrence of intrusive late period ceramic types (refer to Chapter 6) indicates that sporadic activity may have taken place on the ridge top following the Mimbres phase occupation. It is worth noting that of the intrusive types identified, none have an origination date beyond the suggested terminal Wind Mountain occupation at c. A.D. 1200.

Regional Mogollon Chronologies

The chronological framework proposed for the Wind Mountain site rests on regional phase sequences primarily derived from work centered in the San Francisco/Reserve and Mimbres Valleys (for historical summaries, see LeBlanc and Whalen 1980; Berman 1989). Both regions have been the subject of intensive archaeological investigations, ostensibly beginning in the 1930s (Cosgrove and Cosgrove 1932; Haury 1936a). Research in the Upper Gila has been erratic and slow to develop, though a chronology for the area was outlined by the 1970s (Fitting et al. 1982b). These temporal reconstructions have not only contributed to a definition of *Mogollon* but also attempted to chart Mogollon transformations over time. Any effort to correlate the Wind Mountain settlement, which represents one of the largest data bases from the Upper Gila, to a generalized Mogollon or, more specifically, to a Mimbres phase phenomenon, demands a closer look at regional chronological schemes (refer to Figure 3.3). In comparison, Di Peso's interpretations of events at Wind Mountain were shaped by his view of the Gran Chichimeca as a macroregion dominated by large-scale economic interaction among its various inhabitants. His ideas about the changing Wind Mountain settlement from this broader perspective are presented below.

The San Francisco/Reserve Region

The San Francisco/Reserve region, which includes the far reaches of the San Francisco River (and tributaries of the Gila River) northward to the edge of the Colorado Plateau, is often called the Cibola or Reserve Branch of the Mogollon (Martin 1979:63). Haury (1936a, 1936b) originally defined the Mogollon concept from evidence recovered at Mogollon Village in the San Francisco Valley (and from the Harris Village in the Mimbres Valley). After these initial Mogollon studies, a clearer understanding of Mogollon manifestations in the San Francisco/Reserve region emerged with the work of others. Recently, Berman (1989:75–128) reexamined Mogollon research, proposing a modified chronology for the region.

Berman concluded that a series of radiocarbon dates from Tularosa Cave, which had earlier led Martin and his colleagues (1952:483, 492) to set the beginning of Cibola Branch ceramics during the Pine Lawn phase at c. 200 B.C., derived from mixed deposits. Relying on tree-ring dates, Berman (1989:85) proposed a range of A.D. 300–500 for the Pine Lawn phase. Dates from the SU site (Martin 1940, 1943; Martin and Rinaldo 1947), as well as from other suggested Pine Lawn phase sites, were reevaluated using dendrochronological analysis (Ahlstrom 1985:99–101). Tree-ring data again indicated a later range for the phase. At the SU site, for example, the Pine Lawn phase was placed in the A.D. 400s. In the Wind Mountain chronology, the Pine Lawn phase would overlap the Early Pit House period of the settlement.

Investigations by Martin (1959) and others (e.g., Bluhm 1960:539–540) demonstrated that Pine Lawn phase sites were situated in upland locations, including ridge tops, mesas, and the benches above streams, a setting duplicated by the Wind Mountain locality. Associated structures consisted of round pit dwellings and large community or ceremonial houses. When ceramics occurred, they were either Alma Plain and textured types or San Francisco Red.

The succeeding phases were defined as Georgetown and San Francisco, c. A.D. 500–700 and c. A.D. 700–900, respectively (Haury 1936a; Martin et al. 1952), both sparsely represented by excavated sites. Bluhm (1960:543) suggested population stagnation between the Pine Lawn and Georgetown phases, whereas Berman (1989:88–94) advanced the notion of depopulation throughout both phases to account for the paucity of sites. In any event, these phases remain imperfectly understood. Both the Georgetown and San Francisco phases at Wind Mountain are partially contemporary with their counterparts in the San Francisco/Reserve region. At Wind Mountain, the Georgetown phase starts later (c. A.D. 550), while the San Francisco phase ends earlier (c. A.D. 800).

In the San Francisco/Reserve region a beginning date of c. A.D. 750 is proposed for the Three Circle phase based on the correlation of tree-rings, architecture, and painted ceramics (Berman 1989:95). Ahlstrom's (1985:121–126) reassessment of dendrochronological data places the onset of the phase c. A.D. 780–800, a range that corresponds with the inception of the Three Circle phase at Wind Mountain. This timing generally conforms to the San Francisco to Three Circle phase transition (c. A.D. 750–800) in the Mimbres Valley proposed by Anyon and his associates (1981:217). Material remains associated with the San Francisco/Reserve region include rectangular pit structures and the addition of a new painted pottery type, Boldface Black-on-white (Berman 1989:96).

The Reserve phase, c. A.D. 1000–1100 (Martin and Rinaldo 1950b), overlapping in part both the Mimbres phase in the Mimbres Valley, where it is commonly termed the Classic Mimbres period (LeBlanc 1986), and at Wind Mountain, marks the first use of surface masonry architecture in the region. Besides small surface room blocks consisting of no more than 30 rooms, pit structures continue to be built though, at many sites, the large community house does not appear (Peckham et al. 1956; Martin et al. 1957; Berman 1989:102). Settlement location exhibits greater variability than was observed during the preceding Three Circle phase. Reserve phase ceramics include Reserve Black-on-white and Reserve textured wares. Reserve Black-on-white has no equivalent at Wind Mountain, where Boldface and Mimbres Classic Black-on-white constitute the locally produced painted whiteware ceramics. A small quantity of intrusive Reserve textured sherds (Reserve Incised Corrugated and Reserve Punched Corrugated) were collected at Wind Mountain.

The Tularosa phase begins c. A.D. 1100 with the abandonment of numerous San Francisco/Reserve secondary stream tributaries in favor of primary drainages (Bluhm 1950; Rice 1975; Accola 1981). Tularosa phase sites can be large, consisting of as many as 100 rooms, presumably the result of population aggregation (Neely 1978a, 1978b). Most sites contain community or ceremonial structures. The associated ceramic assemblage is varied, including Tularosa Black-on-white, Tularosa White-on-red, Tularosa Fillet Rim, and Tularosa Patterned Corrugated, as well as St. Johns Polychrome (Martin et al. 1952; Rinaldo and Bluhm 1956; Berman 1989:121–122). Some Tularosa phase textured wares occur as trade pottery in the Wind Mountain settlement. After c. A.D. 1300, the Mogollon Reserve/Tularosa sequence draws to a close with the evident abandonment of the region.

The Mimbres Valley

The chronology of the Mimbres Valley is based on excavations conducted during the early decades of the twentieth century (Bradfield 1928; Nesbitt 1931; Cosgrove and Cosgrove 1932; Haury 1936a, 1936b), and revised by investigations in the 1970s and 1980s (LeBlanc and Whalen 1980; Anyon et al. 1981; Shafer 1991b). Anyon and his associates (1981) suggested a hierarchic chronological system of periods and phases in which the former represented major adaptive shifts by the valley's inhabitants and the latter signified alterations in their material culture.

The first of these, the Early Pit House period, c. A.D. 200–550 (Anyon et al. 1981:213–214), was characterized by small sites located atop high knolls (LeBlanc 1986:300). Pit structures were circular or oval in plan, and the associated ceramic inventory included plain brown pottery and a redware, either unpolished or carrying a fugitive wash or thin slip.

The shift from the Early to the Late Pit House period was identified with a move away from upland localities to river terraces (LeBlanc 1986:301). Indeed, river terraces remained the preferred locale throughout Mimbres times until c. A.D. 1150. Between c. A.D. 550 and 1000, adjustments in dominant architectural forms and ceramic styles/types define three phases within the Late Pit House period. First, the Georgetown phase, c. A.D. 550–650, was characterized by circular and D-shaped house floor plans (Anyon et al. 1981:212, 214–216) with Alma Plain and San Francisco Red pottery (Haury 1936a:96–97). Second, the San Francisco phase, c. A.D. 650–750 (Anyon et al. 1981:216–217), added Mogollon Red-on-brown and Three Circle Red-on-white (Haury 1936a:96), and pit structures assumed a rectangular floor plan. Third, the Three Circle phase, c. A.D. 750–900, exhibited the valley's initial black-on-white pottery (Haury 1936a:96), Boldface Black-on-white (syn. Style I). It is suggested that earlier painted pottery types, such as Mogollon Red-on-brown and Three Circle Red-on-white, disappeared toward the end of the Three Circle phase (Haury 1936a:97–98; Anyon and LeBlanc 1984:158–161). Rectangular floor plans were typical of pit houses.

After the close of the Late Pit House period, c. A.D. 1000, significant adaptational change was postulated with a move out of pit structures to contiguous surface masonry room blocks. This shift in principal domestic architecture marks the appearance of the Classic Mimbres period, c. A.D. 1000–1150 (Anyon et al. 1981:212; LeBlanc 1986). Pit structures continued to be used as ceremonial or community houses (Anyon and LeBlanc 1984:97, 115). The painted pottery associated with this period consisted of an early transitional or Style II (also Boldface Black-on-white in the traditional classification scheme) black-on-white ware, which soon gave way to the well known Style III or Mimbres Classic Black-on-white (LeBlanc 1982b; see also Haury 1936b).

The Wind Mountain occupation sequence concurs with many aspects of Mimbres Valley chronology. The Early Pit House period generally corresponds with a terminal date of A.D. 550 for both. The Late Pit House period basically agrees, although the internal phase boundaries (i.e., Georgetown, San Francisco, and Three Circle) differ somewhat. The major point of disagreement between the two is the addition at Wind Mountain of a Mangas phase between the Three Circle phase and the Mimbres phase. Though LeBlanc (1986:303) deleted the Mangas phase from the Mimbres Valley chronology, evidence argues for its inclusion at Wind Mountain. The end of the Mimbres phase in the Mimbres Valley coincides with the final occupation proposed for the Wind Mountain community and the abandonment of the ridge top.

The post-Mimbres chronology in the Mimbres Valley proceeds with the Black Mountain phase (suggested to have affinities with Medio period Casas Grandes), tentatively dated c. A.D. 1150–1300 (Anyon and LeBlanc 1984:24–25). Black Mountain phase sites are concentrated in the southern portion of the Mimbres Valley drainage and the Deming Plain (for a discussion of contemporaneous regional phase designations, see Lekson 1992:19). With the exception of the Galaz Ruin, these late villages do not appear to occur over Late Pit House period or Mimbres occupations (Anyon and LeBlanc 1984:143–148). Contiguous surface room blocks characterize Black Mountain settlements, which were constructed of adobe on slab footings rather than of cobble walls set in adobe mortar (Anyon and LeBlanc 1984:24). Associated ceramics are diverse, dominated by plain and textured wares. Playas Red, possibly of local production, Chupadero Black-on-white, Three Rivers Red-on-terracotta, as well as several Chihuahuan polychrome types and El Paso Polychrome are also reported. Some of these ceramic types were recovered in low quantities from Wind Mountain, where their presence is probably associated with the final occupation at the site.

Following a hypothetical hiatus, a Salado or Cliff phase occupation is suggested to begin c. A.D. 1350–1450 (Anyon and LeBlanc 1984:25–26; Nelson and LeBlanc 1986). The Salado phase of the Mimbres Valley is modest, and only three sites are presently known. These are represented as small adobe walled pueblos having mostly plain and textured pottery. Gila Polychrome is the most commonly encountered painted ware, although traces of El Paso and Chihuahuan polychromes occur. No Salado equivalent, either resembling that reported for the Mimbres Valley or from other sites in the Upper Gila, was observed at Wind Mountain.

The Upper Gila

During the late 1960s and early 1970s, extensive documentation of the Upper Gila's prehistoric settlements was initiated (Fitting et al. 1982a, 1982b). The Upper Gila Project, including survey, testing, and excavation, represented the first systematic effort to establish the cultural development of the region. Fitting's field research and resultant radiocarbon and archaeomagnetic dates form the basis of an Upper Gila regional chronology. Like other Mogollon schemes, Fitting's temporal framework incorporates primary period and secondary phase designations (Fitting et al. 1982b).

The Late Archaic stages of the Upper Gila chronology were defined at the Eaton site, which was located on the Gila River (Fitting 1974; Hemphill 1983). The site, extending over some 40 acres, contained two possible shallow pit structures and a large inventory of chipped stone. A median radiocarbon date of 310 B.C. (a range of 390–230 B.C., Japan Radio Isotope Association; recalibrated by Lekson 1990:88–89 to 401–208 B.C.) was obtained from a pit exposed in an arroyo wall. Investigators proposed a terminal date of 300 B.C. for the preceramic Eaton phase (Fitting et al. 1982b:35).

Dating the Upper Gila preceramic period is confused by two radiocarbon dates reported from the Archaic Red Rock 1 site on the Lower Gila River (Laumbach 1980:40). Feature

A, a shallow, circular pit structure, produced a date range of A.D. 205–515 (UGa-2939), whereas Feature D, a roasting pit with fire cracked rock, fragmentary charcoal, and corn, dated earlier, at A.D. 160–380 (UGa-2940). Clearly, additional work will be necessary to sort out the Upper Gila Archaic. None of the deposits at Wind Mountain were temporally equivalent to the Eaton phase.

The ensuing Winn Canyon phase (c. 300 B.C.-A.D. 400) was originally defined at the Winn Canyon site (Fitting 1973a; Fitting et al. 1982b). The site's temporal boundaries were based on two radiocarbon determinations, although contextual problems existed and, as a result, the Winn Canyon phase chronology remains confused. Fitting derived his earliest date range (520–180 B.C.; N-1555) from a feature he described as a hearth (Feature 10) from beneath the floor of Room 2 (mistakenly identified as Room 1 in Fitting et al. 1982b:37, 40), a large, roughly circular community structure. The second radiocarbon range (A.D. 235–385; N-1556) was recovered from a charcoal sample found in fill above collapsed ceiling debris of Room 6 (Fitting et al. 1982b:37, 40). Lekson (1990:88–89) recalibrated the Winn Canyon site date ranges following Stuiver and Reimer (1986). According to his reevaluation, sample N-1555 (which Lekson 1990: Table 5.3, erroneously associates with Room 6 instead of Room 2) tenders a 757–135 B.C. date range, and sample N-1556 shows an A.D. 262–532 interval. The long temporal range suggests that the legitimacy of the Winn Canyon phase should remain suspect until corroborated by additional data. Noting the presence of Alma Plain and San Francisco Red wares and the absence of painted ceramics at the Winn Canyon site, Fitting correlated the site (and the corresponding Winn Canyon phase) with the Pine Lawn phase of the San Francisco/Reserve region and the Early Pit House period of the Mimbres Valley. Comparing the architecture of the Winn Canyon site with Wind Mountain seems to indicate that Rooms 1, 3, 4, 5, and 6 of the former compare favorably with Type II structures at the latter. Winn Canyon Room 2 may be similar to Wind Mountain Type A structures. The description of the Winn Canyon site appears to compare with the early Late Pit House period, and possibly the Georgetown phase, of the Wind Mountain site. The Winn Canyon phase, together with the succeeding Georgetown, Three Circle, and Mangas phases, define Fitting's Early Ceramic Horizon (Fitting et al. 1982b:36–41) or Berman's (1989:28–43) Formative period.

Fitting and his associates (1982b) observed no discrete Georgetown phase sites, but believed that these localities would occur in the Upper Gila and proposed a range A.D. 400–650. They also questioned the existence of a San Francisco phase in the Upper Gila, suggesting instead that the elusive Georgetown phase would be characterized by Mogollon Red-on-brown, plain brown and redwares, in association with rectangular pit houses (Fitting et al. 1982b:40). Others have noted the difficulty in discerning Upper Gila Georgetown phase sites (Gossett 1985:144–145). Evidence supporting the Georgetown phase at Wind Mountain was forthcoming from several structures, though the onset of the phase is placed much later than is postulated by Fitting (refer to Figure 3.3). Terminal dates for the Georgetown phase in both the Upper Gila regional and Wind Mountain site chronologies are estimated c. A.D. 650. Georgetown phase ceramics were limited to unpainted wares; round houses were observed. In contrast to Fitting's conclusions (1982a, 1982b), evidence supports the presence of a succeeding San Francisco phase at the Wind Mountain site. Mogollon Red-on-brown and Three Circle Red-on-white ceramics as well as rectangular pit structures were associated with Wind Mountain's San Francisco phase.

By omitting the San Francisco phase, the chronology proposed by Fitting and his colleagues (1982b:40) proceeds directly to the Three Circle phase, which they characterized as having "more complex" rectangular domestic pit houses and community structures associated with Three Circle Red-on-white and Boldface Black-on-white ceramics. Fitting (1973a) defined the Upper Gila Three Circle phase at the MC-110 site and Burro Springs site 2. Based on a radiocarbon range of A.D. 490–750 and a single archaeomagnetic assay of A.D. 726–794 from the MC-110 site, the phase was tentatively dated to c. A.D. 650–800 (Fitting et al. 1982b:40). The Three Circle phase was also documented at the Saige-McFarland site (Lekson 1990:82) and in the Mimbres Valley (Anyon et al. 1981), although the beginning of the phase there was placed later, c. A.D. 750. At Wind Mountain, the temporal boundaries suggested to describe the settlement's San Francisco phase occupation correspond with Fitting's Three Circle phase.

The terminal date for the Three Circle phase in the Upper Gila is suggested c. A.D. 800 (Fitting et al. 1982b:40)—precisely when it is believed to begin in the Wind Mountain chronology. A Mangas (spelled Mangus by Fitting) phase is suggested for c. A.D. 800–1000 from deposits at Black's Bluff, Dark Thunder Canyon site 1, Villareal II, and Lee Village. The Mangas phase chronology is derived from four dates, including three radiocarbon ranges: A.D. 665–815 from Black's Bluff, A.D. 765–915 from Dark Thunder Canyon site 1, A.D. 890–1050 from Villareal II, and an archaeomagnetic date of c. A.D. 950 (range not published) from Lee Village (Fitting et al. 1982b:40). Additional analyses, including ceramics, have caused Lekson (1984:56; 1990:89) to suggest that Villareal II more accurately reflects the Mimbres phase. At Wind Mountain the Mangas phase is proposed to begin c. A.D. 950, persisting into the Mimbres phase after A.D. 1000. The Mangas phase has also been identified at other Upper Gila sites (Chapman et al. 1985; Lekson 1990), and in the nearby Redrock Valley (Lekson 1988).

The Upper Gila chronology continues with a Late Ceramic

Horizon or Classic period, c. A.D. 1000–1300, which is divided into three phases: Mimbres, Animas, and Salado (Fitting et al. 1982b:41–50). A modest Mimbres phase occupation (12 of 16 surface rooms) is the only portion of the Wind Mountain sequence that overlaps Fitting's proposed Classic period. The final occupation of Wind Mountain does not extend as late as the range of sites Fitting identified through survey and excavation (i.e., Animas and Salado).

Although large pueblos (e.g., Woodrow Ruin in the Cliff Valley) on the order of 300 rooms are known (Lekson 1990:89), most Upper Gila Mimbres sites are relatively small (Chapman et al. 1985:38). Wind Mountain certainly agrees with this pattern. Other Upper Gila sites with Mimbres components include Saige-McFarland (Fitting et al. 1971; Lekson 1990), Heron Ruin (Burns 1972), the Riverside site (Baker 1971), the Clark site (Sanburg 1976), Burro Springs No. 1 (Fitting 1973b), and Villareal II (Lekson 1990:89).

Supporting Mimbres phase dates come from the Riverside site, where archaeomagnetic ranges fall between A.D. 1131–1179 (Oklahoma Lab No. 664) and A.D. 1152–1198 (Oklahoma Lab No. 665) (Fitting et al. 1982b:48–49). Pit House 1 at Villareal II produced a radiocarbon range of A.D. 984–1157 (Lekson 1990:89). At Saige-McFarland, a Mimbres deposit (Room 6) yielded a tree-ring date of A.D. 1126 vv (Lekson 1990:89). Most radiocarbon and archaeomagnetic ranges or tree-ring dates from the Upper Gila place the Mimbres phase (syn. period) c. A.D. 1000–1150, thereby generally agreeing with the Mimbres Valley chronology (Anyon et al. 1981). Mimbres Classic Black-on-white is the predominant associated painted pottery type.

The final phases of the Upper Gila regional chronology consist of an Animas phase, c. A.D. 1200–1300, and a presently undated Salado phase, suggested to begin c. A.D. 1300 (Fitting et al. 1982b:49–50). The CF Spring site (Fitting 1973b) and Villareal II (Lekson and Klinger 1973b; Lekson 1978b, 1984:56) both contained Animas phase components. Animas associations in the Upper Gila consisted of cobbled wall surface rooms and a diverse ceramic assemblage including El Paso Polychrome and Chupadero Black-on-white. Mimbres Classic Black-on-white is reported in small quantities, presumably occurring either at the beginning of the phase or in a mixed Mimbres-Animas context.

The little understood Salado, the final prehistoric phase of the Upper Gila, is known from several localities, such as the Ormand site (Hammack et al. 1966), the Dinwiddie site on Duck Creek (Mills and Mills 1972), the Kwilleylekia site (cited in Fitting et al. 1982b:50), and the Willow Creek site (Fitting 1973b). These Salado occupations are characterized by multistoried pueblos surrounded by small "farmsteads" (Baker 1971). The painted ceramic assemblage is dominated by typical Salado polychromes (Colton and Hargrave 1937; Haury 1945a). No Pinto, Gila, or Tonto Polychromes were recovered at Wind Mountain.

Di Peso's Gran Chichimecan Time Horizon

Di Peso's Horizon framework for Mogollon prehistory was inexorably linked to his concept of the Gran Chichimeca. He did not wish to consider Mogollon culture in terms of regional manifestations in the Upper Gila, San Francisco/Reserve, or Mimbres Valley. Instead, the indigenous Mogollon Chichimecs were perceived to develop within a larger geographic expanse, where, at various times, local culture patterns were reshaped by southern intruders motivated by the potential for economic gain. His ideas were set forth in several publications (Di Peso 1968a, 1968b, 1974, 1983a) and in Wind Mountain research proposals (Di Peso 1977, 1979a), but Di Peso's most comprehensive statement of Gran Chichimecan cultural, spatial, and temporal dynamics was published posthumously in Spanish by the Academia Nacional de la Historia de Venezuela (1983b). It provides the substance for the following discussion of Mogollon chronology and culture process. Di Peso's descriptive language is used throughout.

With the end of the Pleistocene epoch, native Chichimecs slowly evolved into the long-lived Desert Culture Horizon, 7,000 B.C.-A.D. 200 (Di Peso 1979c:30–39). These groups occupied the whole of the Gran Chichimecan region and, although local variants were apparent, all were believed to share many common attributes. Di Peso identified them as nonsedentary indigenes, loosely organized into bands, who subsisted by hunting and gathering. Their material inventory included the atlatl and the mano/metate. By the beginning of the Christian era, these Desert Horizon people cultivated squashes, bottle gourds, and some maize. Essentially, they represented a relatively static culture, the native stock from which the Mogollon Chichimecs developed.

True Mogollon Chichimec culture emerged with the Classic Chichimecan Horizon, A.D. 200–950, which Di Peso (1979c:39–71) separated into two periods, Early Classic Sporadic Contacts, A.D. 200–600, and Late Classic Intrusion, A.D. 600–950. During the first few centuries of this Horizon, Mogollon Chichimecs were thought to live relatively settled lives, though some sporadic contact with southern centers occurred. The influence of Mesoamerica on the northern portions of the Gran Chichimeca was believed to be reflected with the advent of plain brown and red pottery production (or buffwares in the Hohokam Chichimec area). Additional contact was inferred from the firm establishment of a maize based agricultural economy, A.D. 500. In addition, Di Peso (1979c:52) identified certain socioreligious forms, such as effigy whistles, which were evident in Mogollon material culture, that he equated with southern based rituals.

The time of sporadic contact gave way to marked intrusions, beginning with the early Late Classic, A.D. 600–700, when southern traders intensively searched the north for turquoise, copper, salt, selenite, iron pigments, crystals, pyrites, and other natural resources. Di Peso saw dramatic changes in indigenous Mogollon culture patterns (including Wind Mountain) as southerners introduced decorated pottery, architectural forms, and cotton. Specifically, he identified Chupicuaro ceramics and a pottery making center in Colima (Chapter 6 in this volume) to be the sources for certain painted wares occurring among the Mogollon, Anasazi, and Hohokam Chichimecs (Di Peso 1979c:49, 64). Between A.D. 600 and 700, Di Peso felt that southern centers gave rise to La Plata Black-on-white, Abajo Red-on-orange, Kiatuthlanna Black-on-white, Snaketown Red-on-buff, Mogollon Red-on-brown, Wind Mountain Black-on-white (i.e., Boldface Black-on-white), and other painted wares (Di Peso 1979c:49).

Di Peso (1979a, 1979b) believed the Late Classic to represent the first substantial southern intrusion into the Wind Mountain area, a time when merchants implanted many Mesoamerican cultural patterns concomitant with their quest for minerals in the nearby Big and Little Burro Mountains. Toward the end of the Late Classic Intrusion period, A.D. 900–950, he suggested additional economic related contact resulting from the founding of Casas Grandes (itself tied to the Durango/Zacatecas area and the Chalchihuites) as the operative mercantile center responsible for consolidating northern procurement satellites (Di Peso 1979c:69–73). Wind Mountain was designated a procurement satellite (for further discussion of a Wind Mountain-Casas Grandes relationship see Chapter 11 in this volume).

The succeeding stage of the Di Peso chronology was broadly defined as the post-Classic Chichimecan Horizon, A.D. 950–1520. It was separated into three periods termed the Early post-Classic Sporadic, A.D. 950–1050; the Early post-Classic Intrusion, A.D. 1050–1350; and the Late post-Classic Sporadic, A.D. 1350–1520 (Di Peso 1979c:58–111). During the initial period, the influence of Mesoamerican traders was said to bring about major changes, one of which was translated into the rise of Mimbreño culture. Di Peso (1979a, 1979b) proposed that mining activities controlled by southern traders intensified in the vicinity of the Wind Mountain site as the demand for turquoise by Mesoamerican markets increased. He identified the attendant changes in Mimbres architecture to include development of load bearing walls, multistoried pueblos arranged in compounds, and public buildings (1979c:68–72). Casas Grandes was seen as the immediate source of many cultural inspirations, which were infused into both Mogollon and Hohokam areas. Parenthetically, at least in the context of architecture and the above cited developments, load bearing walls and possibly simple compounds associated with the few surface rooms were evident in the Wind Mountain Mimbres community.

Di Peso regarded southern merchants, in competition with one another for exploitable resources, as cultural "donors" who gained control over various northern Chichimec "recipients" occupying the Gran Chichimeca along the Upper Gila, in the San Francisco/Reserve and Mimbres Valleys, and further afield in Chaco Canyon and Mesa Verde (Di Peso 1979c:82). Economically inspired donor-recipient relationships were particularly conspicuous among the Mimbreños, where turquoise and other minerals were exchanged for *Conus* tinklers, copper crotals, and macaws. Mimbres pottery was believed to be an important northern trade commodity transported to the south, though Di Peso suggested such exchange to cease after A.D. 1060 (Di Peso 1979c:86–87).

Summary Remarks

Di Peso (1977) expected to find evidence to support the Gran Chichimecan Horizon chronology in the Wind Mountain material assemblage and from dated structures. Early in 1975, as he developed his Wind Mountain research strategy, Di Peso presented fundamentally the same progression of events, albeit using alternative labels. The A.D. 1–1000 interval was described as the Formative period, which was followed by a Mimbreño period, A.D. 1000–1300. He appeared to sympathize with Graybill (1973a:100, 1973b) that all Mogollon phase names were mired in confusion. Until discrete chronological phases could be clearly defined, a single Formative period seemed to represent a cautious and conservative course. By the end of the Wind Mountain excavations in December of 1979, however, Di Peso had clarified his position. He did not necessarily disagree with other Mogollon chronologies, but he felt that they were too limiting, too provincial. Di Peso suggested that "localized regional" chronologies should be incorporated into a more comprehensive scheme that described important formative events in the Gran Chichimeca macroregion. This broader temporal framework would then allow the inclusion of diverse southern influences, originating from various Mesoamerican hearths, that shaped Mogollon Chichimec culture. The applicability of Di Peso's scheme to Wind Mountain chronology in particular and Mogollon prehistory in general hinges on the intensity, nature, and timing of Mesoamerican influence on peoples and cultures to the north.

Based on date ranges derived from the settlement's structures, augmented by the supplementary information of stratigraphic order and associated ceramics, the primary Wind Mountain occupations are surmised to have occurred between c. A.D. 250 and 1150/1200. The Wind Mountain site spans both the Pit House and Pueblo periods. Not surprisingly, its temporal sequence compares favorably with established regional Mogollon chronologies, especially for the Late Pit House period, which includes the Georgetown, San Francisco, and Three Circle phases, suggested for the San Francisco/Reserve and the Mimbres regions. The Wind Mountain site sequence reveals many similarities with the Upper Gila and corroborates the presence of a Georgetown phase, which had been proposed but not demonstrated up to this time. During the Three Circle and Mangas phases, Wind Mountain compares favorably with another excavated Upper Gila site, Saige-McFarland. Both sites provide support for the Mangas transitional phase between the Late Pit House period and Mimbres phase of the Pueblo period. The legitimacy of the Mangas phase as indicative of a slow Mogollon transformation, from pit houses to surface structures, should be seriously considered given the evidence from Wind Mountain and Saige-McFarland.

The emerging profile of the Wind Mountain occupational sequence with its proposed phase designations illustrates the progression of Early to Late Pit House periods to Mimbres phase developments at one site in the Upper Gila. More generally, Wind Mountain's long chronology aids in establishing the temporal framework for Mimbres Mogollon cultural evolution.

4

Wind Mountain Architecture

Part 1
Definition and Detail

Wind Mountain architecture demonstrates a developmental sequence of house forms that includes the shift from subterranean to surface structures. Pit houses mainly represented the Early and Late Pit House periods, whereas near surface and surface rooms reflected a small Pueblo period occupation. Ninety-nine whole and fragmentary structures were excavated, many of them (n = 44) associated with radiocarbon and/or archaeomagnetic date ranges. Excavation illustrated the site's intermittent settlement history spanning some 700–900 years (Figures 4.1 [map insert] and 4.2).

Di Peso classified Wind Mountain architecture according to primary and secondary categories. Primary architectural classes referred only to structures; secondary classes included hearths, pits, stone pavements, and ancillary features. Structures were separated into functions and types based on attributes of floor plan, interior surface area, and entries. In his final architectural classification scheme, Di Peso defined a series of domestic and community structures. All primary and secondary categories and their attendant types are summarized in the discussions that follow. Detailed descriptive architectural data for individual structures and their stratigraphic relationships are presented in Part 2 of this chapter. Where appropriate, the Wind Mountain structure types recognized by Di Peso are compared to descriptions of Mogollon pit houses and surface architecture from other sites and regions (e.g., Haury 1936a; Wheat 1955:35–56; Bullard 1962; Di Peso 1974:135–141; Fitting et al. 1982b; Lekson 1990).

The Wind Mountain architectural assemblage, including its primary and secondary components, is appraised to identify potential internal culture patterns. Architectural data is used to establish intrasite relationships in order to infer, at least in part, possible social arrangements that characterized the communities, as well as some of the activities in which the settlement's residents were involved. For example, functional house types are examined as indicators of community organization. Similarly, secondary features are considered as potential indices of subsistence related endeavors and as clues to tasks conducted by the inhabitants of the settlement.

Di Peso viewed the evolution of Wind Mountain architectural forms in terms of donor-recipient cultural processes within the Gran Chichimeca. In particular, he identified several "historical events," the result of southern intrusions, that he believed shaped the Wind Mountain architectural tradition. The Wind Mountain data is, therefore, discussed from Di Peso's perspective of foreign influences, which were considered to have effected architectural change at the site.

Secular Domestic Structures

Domestic structures were described as the domiciles in which the residents of Wind Mountain lived. Di Peso originally proposed that secular domestic structures were distinguished from most community houses by their smaller floor size, which was assumed to measure 30 m^2 or less. However, scrutiny of floor areas indicated that the living spaces of most Wind Mountain domestic structures were usually less than 20 m^2, and often under 15 m^2. Di Peso defined six secular house type classifications: pit houses (Types I-IV), surface rooms (Type V), and indeterminate structures (Type VI). The principal criteria used in determining types included floor plan (round or rectangular), entry (absent or present), and subterranean or surface wall construction. These are the only features to exhibit discernable change over time. Sec-

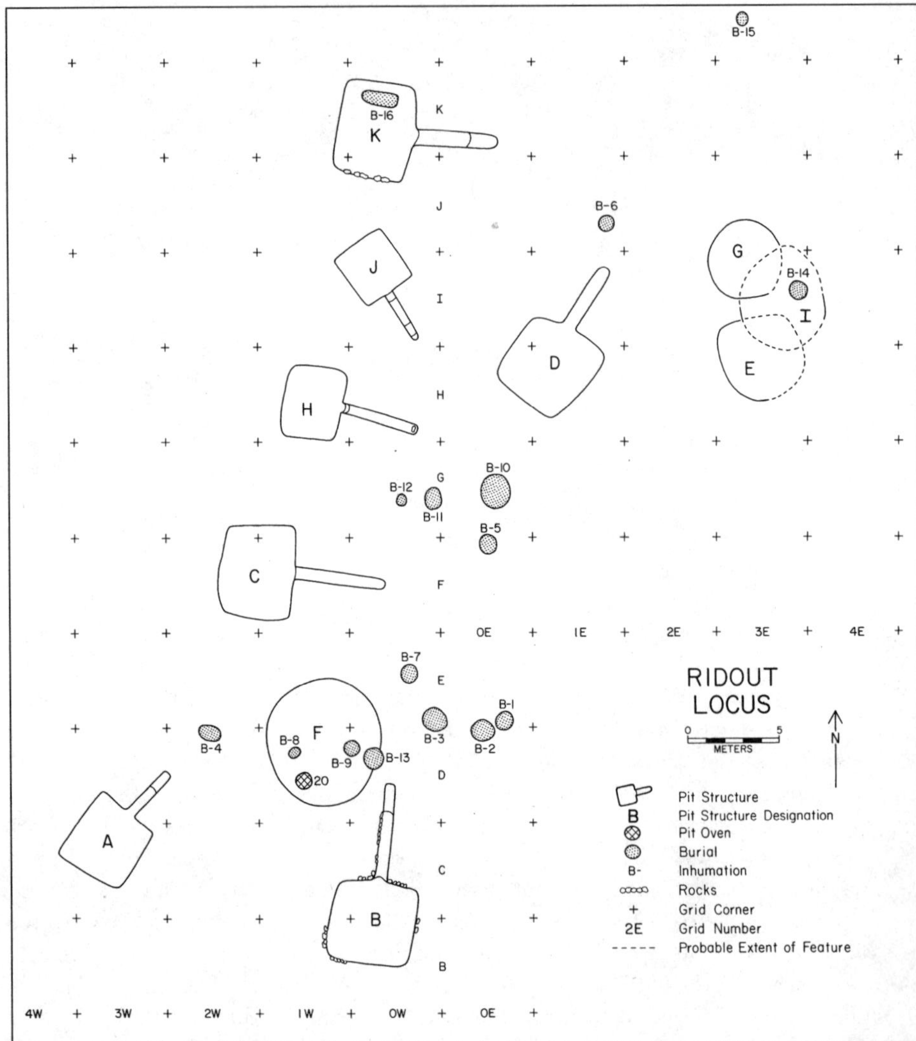

FIGURE 4.2. Site plan of the Ridout locus, illustrating excavation blocks, primary and secondary architectural features, and inhumations.

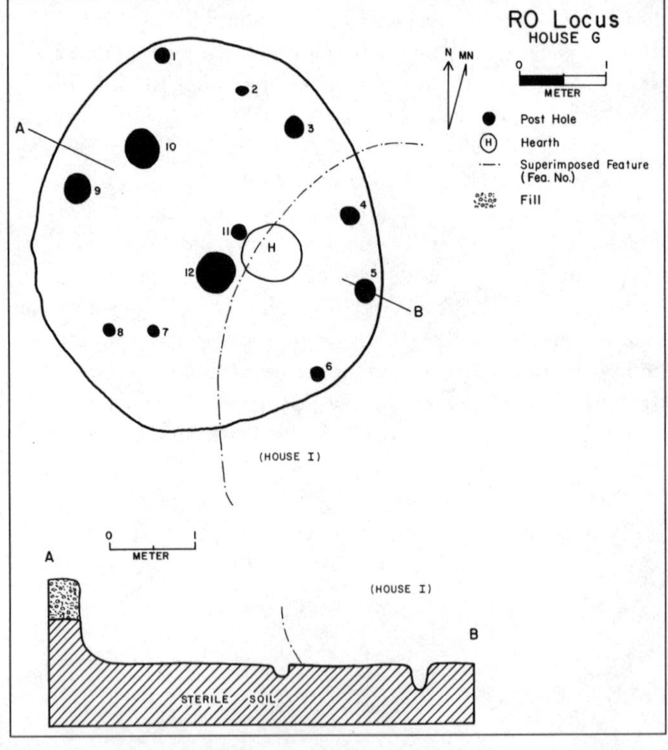

FIGURE 4.3. Plan view and profile of Ridout locus House G, a Type I domestic structure identified by a circular plan, central post roof support, and an absence of a lateral entry.

TABLE 4.1. Dimensions of Type I Structures

Provenience	Length (m)	Width (m)	Area (m²)
WM locus House			
GG	4.00	3.15	10.49
HH	5.20	4.70+	16.71[r]
II	2.90+	2.35+	5.40[r]
JJ	2.90+	2.50+	4.91[r]
LL	3.05+	2.80+	7.35[r]
MM	2.80+	2.45+	3.36[r]
AN	4.20	3.30	11.24
RO locus House			
E	3.90+	4.20+	11.31[r] 15.16[e]
G	4.20	4.00+	10.38[r] 13.49[e]
I	5.50+	4.80+	19.82[r] 20.56[e]

[e]Estimated area.
[r]Remnant area.

TABLE 4.2. Dimensions of Type II Structures

Provenience WM locus House	Length (m)	Width (m)	Area (m²)
Q	3.50	3.20+	9.50[r] 11.88[e]
R	3.10	2.90	6.97
S	3.10	2.50	6.72
T	4.25	3.20+	10.46[r] 12.60[e]
EE	3.80	3.70	11.28
KK	3.30	3.20	8.04
QQ	3.00	2.55	6.44
RR	2.80	2.15	4.99

[e]Estimated area.
[r]Remnant area.

ondary associated attributes such as hearth form, floor pits, hard packed earthen versus plastering of either the floors and walls of pit houses or surface rooms are consistent only in their variability.

Type I House

Type I domestic houses are identified by their circular plan, central post roof support, and the absence of a lateral entry (Figure 4.3). Ten Type I houses were detected, seven at the Wind Mountain locus and three at the Ridout locus (Table 4.1). All but one of the Wind Mountain locus Type I houses cluster in the northeast portion of the settlement. The remaining structure, House AN, occurs toward the southern edge of the Wind Mountain locus, in proximity to Type I Ridout locus houses. Type I structures, with the exception of House AN, were heavily impacted by later construction episodes. It is believed that these structures represent the Wind Mountain occupation during the Early Pit House period with a marginal extension into the Georgetown phase (c. A.D. 550–650) of the Late Pit House period. Thus, the boundaries between earlier, Type I, versus later, Type II, houses are not sharply delineated as both round forms may have persisted coevally.

Wind Mountain Type I houses are equivalent to circular pit structures in the San Francisco/Reserve region, where Wheat (1955:40) noted a 41.4 percent incidence of this house form in the Pine Lawn phase. At Wind Mountain this type represented 16 percent of the domestic pit houses. Seven such structures were excavated at the SU site (Wheat 1955, Table 2). Haury (1936a:52, Figure 16) excavated a similar structure (House 34) associated with the Georgetown phase at Harris Village. Sayles (1945:20) reported a comparable pit house in the early levels of San Simon Village.

Type I structures at the site include Wind Mountain locus Houses GG, HH, II, JJ, LL, MM, and AN as well as Houses E, G, and I at the Ridout locus.

Type II House

Type II structures are viewed as developing out of Type I houses. At Wind Mountain, Type II domestic structures were circular in plan and had central and peripheral roof supports, but, unlike their Type I predecessors, exhibited lateral entries (Figures 4.4 and 4.5). These entries ranged from 100 to 200+ cm in length and were 30–70 cm in width. For the most part, the orientation of Type II house entries was in an easterly direction (Appendix 4: Figure 2). Eight Type II houses were excavated at Wind Mountain, representing 13 percent of the identifiable secular domestic pit structures (Table 4.2).

Wind Mountain Type II houses correspond to the majority of house forms at Mogollon Village (e.g, House 10) and Harris Village (e.g., Houses 24, 25, 29, and 32), which Haury (1936b:10, 52) designated Type 1 Georgetown phase structures. Wheat (1955:40-43) considered the round pit house with a side entry in his discussion of Mogollon 1 architecture in the San Francisco/Reserve region and in the Mimbres Valley. In addition to houses excavated at Mogollon and Harris Villages, Wheat (1955: Figure 2) cites other examples of this form at sites in the San Francisco/Reserve region, including 12 structures from the SU site. He describes their floor plans as "roundish" to "ovoid."

Several of these pit houses were excavated in the Upper Gila, including five from the Winn Canyon site (Fitting

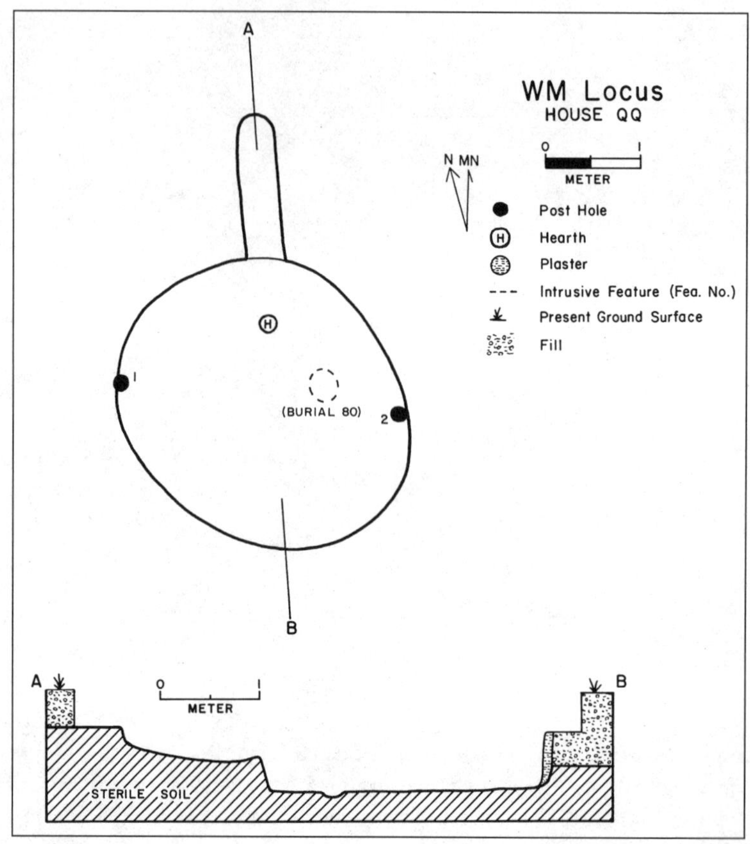

FIGURE 4.4. Plan view and profile of Wind Mountain locus House QQ, a Type II domestic structure identified by a circular plan, peripheral roof supports, and a lateral entry.

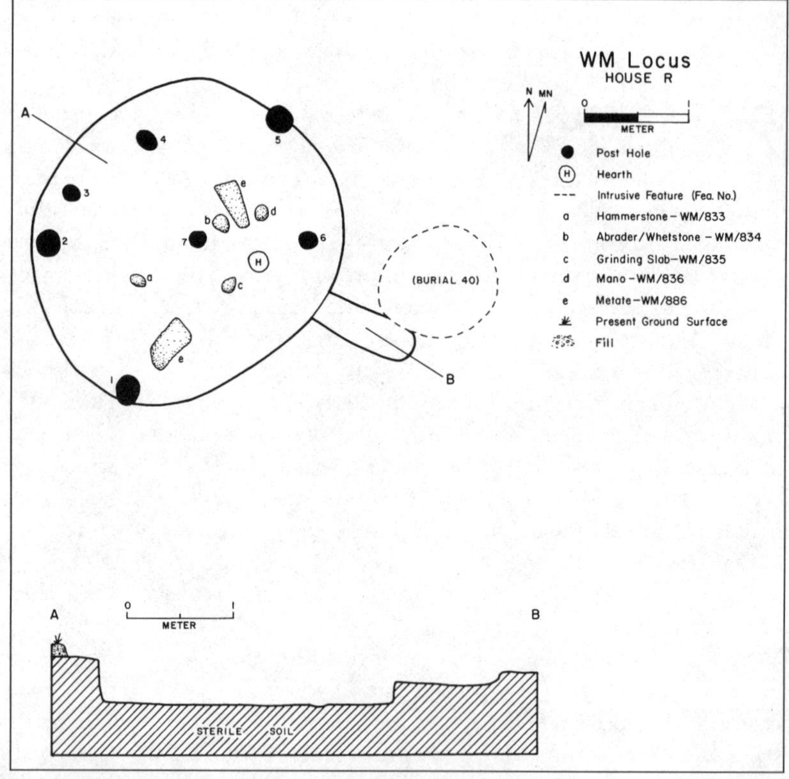

FIGURE 4.5. Plan view and profile of Wind Mountain locus House R, a Type II domestic structure distinguished by a lateral entry.

1973a), where they were considered a diagnostic attribute of the Winn Canyon phase (Fitting et al. 1982b:37). One oval structure (Pit House 4), possibly a Wind Mountain Type I or Type II house, was excavated at the Saige-McFarland site (Lekson 1990:26). Di Peso believed the round Wind Mountain Type II structures to be comparable to House K at the Convento site during the Convento phase (A.D. 650/750-900) of the Viejo period (Di Peso et al. 1974:4:151). The Convento site House K, however, also described as a "house-in-pit," featured a series of post holes ringing its exterior circumference. This element was lacking from the exterior walls of Type II structures at Wind Mountain.

The Type II structures at the Wind Mountain settlement are associated with the Georgetown phase (e.g., Wind Mountain locus House EE, A.D. 650-720), though they may continue into the San Francisco phase (e.g., Wind Mountain locus House R, A.D. 680-980). Unlike the Mimbres Valley, where they are reported for the Cumbre phase (LeBlanc and Whalen 1980:119), there is no evidence from Wind Mountain that round houses with lateral entries occurred during the Early Pit House period. This situation may well be the result of disturbances caused by building episodes which greatly impacted earlier occupation stages. Alternatively, it may indicate that their use was restricted to the early Late Pit House period.

All Type II structures identified at the settlement are located in the Wind Mountain locus and include Houses Q, R, S, T, EE, KK, QQ, and RR.

Type III House

Type III structures were recognized by their rectangular floor plans and lack of entries (Figure 4.6). Di Peso apparently viewed the Type III structure as an evolutionary stage between Type II and Type IV houses. It seems illogical, however, that a developmental process that moved from round structures with lateral entries (Type II) to rectangular structures with lateral entries (Type IV) would be interrupted by a rectangular structure minus a lateral entry (Type III). Rather, the design trend in Wind Mountain Mogollon house construction more than likely progressed from the Type II to the Type IV structure.

The so-called Type III structures at the settlement are of interest, because they may represent an early experimentation with near surface architecture. Only two Type III structures, Wind Mountain locus Houses NN (A.D. 766-1020) and WW (A.D. 680-990), were identified (Table 4.3). Both displayed interior post holes, depressed floors, and possible jacal architecture. Their construction supports the idea of a developmental progression from subterranean to surface architecture associated with the suggested transitional Mangas phase (c. A.D. 950-1000/1050) of the early Pueblo period.

TABLE 4.3. Dimensions of Type III Structures

Provenience WM locus House	Length (m)	Width (m)	Area (m^2)
NN	3.75	2.70	8.88[r] 9.82[e]
WW	3.55	3.25	10.67

[e]Estimated area.
[r]Remnant area.

Type IV House

Clearly representative of the San Francisco and Three Circle phases of the Late Pit House period, Type IV structures were the most commonly encountered houses at the Wind Mountain settlement (Figures 4.7-4.10). Forty-six such structures were excavated, representing 72 percent of all secular domestic pit houses (Table 4.4). Type IV structures were characterized by their rectangular floor plan, a variable post pattern supporting either flat or gabled roofs, and lateral entries, at least half of which had entrance or exit steps. The length of entries ranged between 70 and 510 cm (the mean entry length at the Wind Mountain locus was 238 cm; 394 cm at the Ridout locus). Their widths ranged between 30 and 85 cm (a mean width of 54 cm for structures at both the Wind Mountain and Ridout loci). Structure entries tended to be oriented in an easterly direction, although an entire range of orientations occurred between north/northwest (Wind Mountain locus House D at 346°) and south/southwest (Wind Mountain locus House AC at 208°). Virtually no Type IV structure was oriented between 208° and 346° (Appendix 4: Figure 3). Wheat (1955:54–55) suggests that the shift from round to rectangular house forms was accompanied by an increase in the size of the floor surface area. At Wind Mountain, Type II structure floor area averaged about 9 m^2 (based on seven floor surfaces, mean = 9.13 m^2), whereas Type IV structure surface area averaged between 14 and 15 m^2 (based on 40 floor surfaces, mean = 14.22 m^2). This trend seemingly supports an increase in floor living surfaces from Wind Mountain round Type II structures to rectangular Type IV houses. Besides the small samples comprising all but Type IV structures, it should be noted that the variability of individual Type IV houses was great. The smallest Type IV structure, House AJ at the Wind Mountain locus, measured a scant 3.5 m^2, with the largest, Wind Mountain locus House N, a comparative giant, measuring almost 21 m^2. Furthermore, when the floor areas and date ranges of Type IV structures are compared, size is randomly distributed from early to late (see discussion below). Consequently, any conclusions about increases in living surface area over time should be viewed with caution.

Relating to considerations of surface floor area, additional comment on atypical Type IV structures is useful. In the case

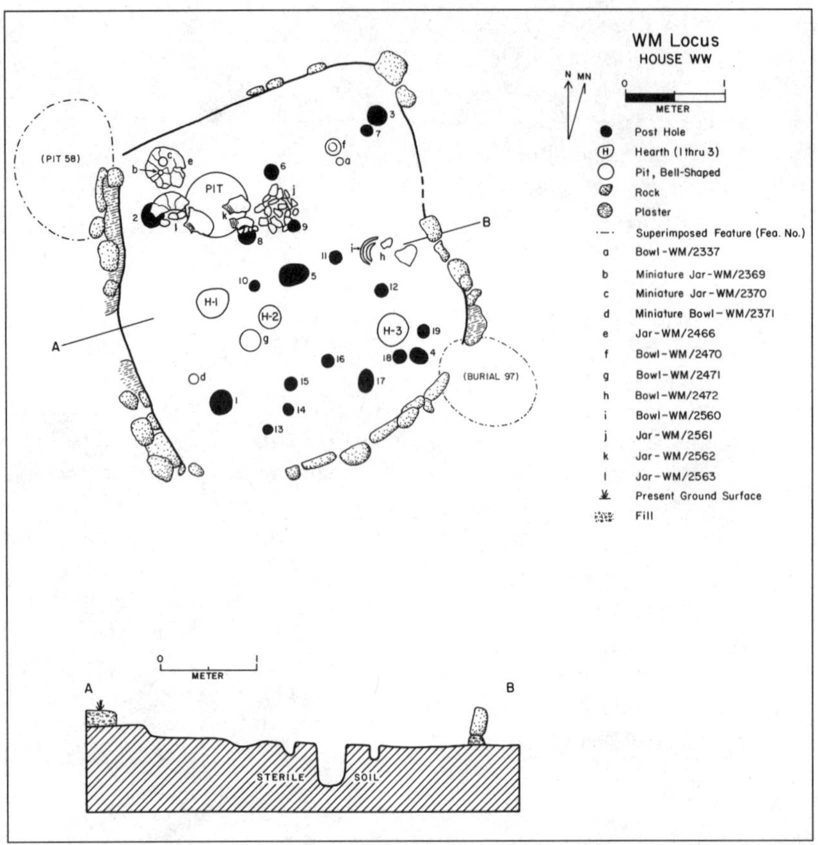

FIGURE 4.6. Plan view and profile of Wind Mountain locus House WW, one of two Type III domestic structures at the site. Type III houses were characterized by their rectangular plan and lack of entry. They may represent Mangas phase experimentation with surface architecture by the residents of Wind Mountain.

of House AJ at the Wind Mountain locus, it is implausible that the extremely limited floor area (3.5 m^2) served as a domestic living space. The house must have had some other function. Haury (1976:68) describes small structures at Snaketown and suggests that they may have been utilized as menstrual huts. Isolating women in special rooms or facilities during menstruation is reported in historic Southwest contexts (Parsons 1970:47). In another prehistoric context, Shafer (1991b:5–6) reported a small structure designated Room 71 (albeit a circular room, unlike Type IV House AJ) at NAN Ranch Ruin of unknown, but presumed specialized, function. The contents of an ash pit indicated extensive use of this room, and he speculated it may have served as a menstrual hut, a place to give birth or, perhaps, a space used by priests or initiates during certain rituals. Shafer cited Convento phase structures excavated by Di Peso (1974:106–110) as being of similar architectural style. It is, of course, impossible to positively determine such specialized function for House AJ, but some purpose other than domestic house use is likely.

Wind Mountain locus House M (A.D. 1000–1190) is another aberrant Type IV structure. Its narrow, elongated floor plan and other interior secondary features distinguish it from the majority of Type IV Houses. Rather than representing a Late Pit House period structure, House M may be indicative of an architectural hybrid associated with the Mangas/Mimbres occupation at Wind Mountain.

Wind Mountain Type IV houses compare with Haury's (1936a:10, 52) Type III San Francisco phase structures at Mogollon Village (e.g., Houses 1, 2, 4, 5B, 7, 8, and 9) and at Harris Village (e.g., Houses 1, 11, 18, 20, 22, and 28), as well as the Type IV structures identified at Harris Village (e.g., Houses 2–7, 9, 13, 15, 16, 19, 21), which were dated to the Three Circle phase. Haury's Type III and Type IV distinctions are based on a more uniform, squared construction, which he associated with the Three Circle phase, in contrast to the rounded walls noted in San Francisco phase houses. Wheat (1955) makes the same observation in his review of Mogollon 3 and 4 structures. In spite of these differences, both house types maintain a generally rectangular floor plan, a post support pattern suggesting an earth covered, semigabled roof, and long lateral entries that correspond to Di Peso's Type IV Wind Mountain structures.

Type IV structures at Wind Mountain probably obtained

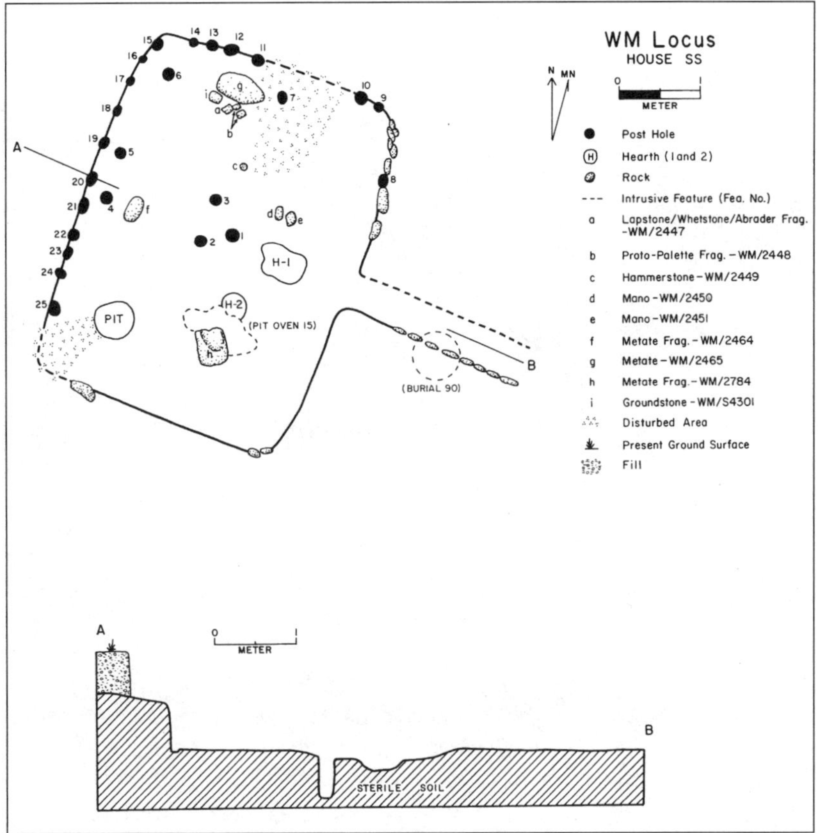

FIGURE 4.7. Plan view and profile of Wind Mountain locus House SS, a Type IV domestic structure. Type IV houses, the most common architectural form at the site, were characterized by their near rectangular plan and lateral entry; roof support patterns were variable. In the case of House SS, a peripheral post arrangement is obvious.

their greatest currency during the San Francisco and Three Circle phases. At the Wind Mountain locus, Type IV structures include Houses A, B (B1 and B2), C, D, E, G, H, J, K, L, M, N, P1, W, Z, AA, BB, DD, FF, OO, PP, SS, TT, UU, VV, ZZ, AC, AD, AE, AF, AG, AI, AJ, AL, AM, AO, AP, and AQ. Type IV structures uncovered at the Ridout locus were Houses A, B, C, D, H, J, and K.

Type V House

Type V domestic structures were identified as rectangular contiguous surface or semisubterranean rooms (Figures 4.11 and 4.12). The appearance of Type V surface architectur traditionally marks the terminus of the Late Pit House period and the emergence of the Pueblo period, C. A.D. 1000. At the Wind Mountain settlement, pit house structures and surface rooms were coincidentally constructed during both the Mangas phase (House M) and possibly the early Mimbres phase (Houses B2 and P2). Three room blocks or, as Di Peso termed them, house units, were excavated (Figure 4.13). Room Unit 1 contained Rooms 1–3, Room Unit 2 consisted of Rooms 4–13, and Room Unit 3 included Rooms 14–16 (for further definition of a Room or House Unit, see Appendix 5). Di Peso assigned 13 rooms to the secular domestic Type V structure classification (Table 4.5). The walls of Type V structures were usually low coursed, square cornered, and constructed of rubble and jacal. Few interconnecting doorways, exterior openings, or obvious architectural elaborations were noted. Room size was variable, ranging from 6 m^2 in Room 6 to an estimated 26 m^2 in Room 10. Such variability in size was also observed in the eight surface rooms excavated in Room Blocks A and B at the Saige-McFarland site (Lekson 1990:7–26).

All Type V structures, identified as Rooms 1, 2, 4, 5, 6, 8, 9, 10, 11, 12, 13, 14, and 16, were located in the Wind Mountain locus.

Type VI House

Houses so fragmentary and poorly preserved that it was impossible to determine their floor plans were assigned to an Unclassified Domestic Type VI structure category. Di Peso

TABLE 4.4. Dimensions of Type IV Structures

Provenience	Length (m)	Width (m)	Area (m²)
WM locus House			
A	3.70	3.40	12.58
B1	–	–	.51[r]
B2	3.60	3.75	13.23
C	3.75	3.60	12.30
D	3.90	3.15	11.95
E	3.10	2.60	8.06
G	4.20	4.00	7.73[r] 15.78[e]
H	3.95	3.90	14.65
J	4.90	4.08	5.31[r] 19.36[e]
K	4.35	3.95	15.36
L	4.10	3.35	12.83
M	5.75	2.30	13.23
N	5.05	4.50	20.68
P1	5.05	3.80	20.04
W	4.25	4.20	17.45
Z	3.70	3.50	11.92
AA	5.05	3.55	15.64
BB	3.60	3.60	12.31
DD	4.55	3.40	15.23
FF	4.80	3.90	17.26
OO	4.10	3.80	15.37
PP	5.05	3.75	17.39
SS	4.35	3.50	14.49
TT	3.90	2.90	10.60
UU	3.70	3.35	8.03[r] 12.44[e]
VV	3.05	2.90	8.07
ZZ	4.55	4.00	14.72
AC	4.20	4.40	17.33
AD	3.90	4.10	15.06
AE	–	3.40	3.58r
AF	4.35	4.40	18.15[e]
AG	3.70	3.60	11.27
AI	4.49	4.30	17.55
AJ	1.90	1.90	3.46
AL	4.78	4.00	16.94
AM	3.85	3.50	12.64
AO	3.90	3.70	13.86
AP	3.15	3.00	8.67
AQ	4.10	3.60	13.31
RO locus House			
A	3.60	3.90	13.48
B	4.25	4.50	18.31
C	5.20	4.20	20.61
D	4.50	4.30	18.23
H	4.00	3.50	13.39
J	3.10	3.00	9.53
K	4.20	5.00	19.75

[e]Estimated area.
[r]Remnant area.

assumed such remnants to represent domestic domiciles, as compared to community houses. Only seven Type VI structures were observed during excavations. These were identified as Houses F, I, CC, YY, and AH, as well as portions of the entries of two structures located under Houses H and J. All Type VI structures occurred at the Wind Mountain locus.

Community Structures

The Mogollon architectural tradition is well known for its community structures. In contrast to domestic dwellings, these structures are suggested to provide a focal point for the activities of all members of the community. Community structures, in other words, are the architectural units that serve to integrate the settlement as a whole. Often given a "ceremonial" function (Bullard 1962:123), they may not only reflect the settlement's ritual activities, but provide an organizational center for community gatherings.

As is true for the classification of Mogollon domestic structures, the typology of community houses and their distribution have been described at length (Wheat 1955:56–62; Di Peso 1974:145–152; Anyon and LeBlanc 1980; LeBlanc and Whalen 1980).

Di Peso defined seven types of community houses at Wind Mountain: Types A, B, C, D, F, G (pit structures) and Type E (surface rooms). He suggested that community structure Types A-E could be identified by their large size, which was assumed to exceed 30 m^2. In contrast, the floor areas of Types F and G were described as measuring less than 30 m^2. Of the 13 community structures distinguished at Wind Mountain, five (38 percent) were larger than 30 m^2 (Wind Mountain locus Houses U, X, AB, and Room 7; Ridout locus House F). Community structures, from the smallest floor surface of 8.96 m^2 (Wind Mountain locus Room 15) to the largest measuring 70.50 m^2 (Wind Mountain locus House X), exhibited a mean area dimension of 29.93 m^2. As noted earlier in the secular domestic house discussion, a reassessment of the floor areas of all structure types indicates that the size boundary separating domestic from community houses is near 25 m^2, although most domestic structures are much smaller.

Some community structures displayed architectural elaborations, including ventilators, niches, and floor grooves (possible foot drums). Secondary features such as hearths, floor pits, and wall or floor plastering were nondiagnostic for purposes of determining community structure type. Such features were found to occur indiscriminately in a variety of forms and associations throughout the settlement's occupation sequence. At Wind Mountain the community structure as an architectural unit apparently does not occur until after the Georgetown phase. In part, this may be due to the way in which such structures have been subjectively defined,

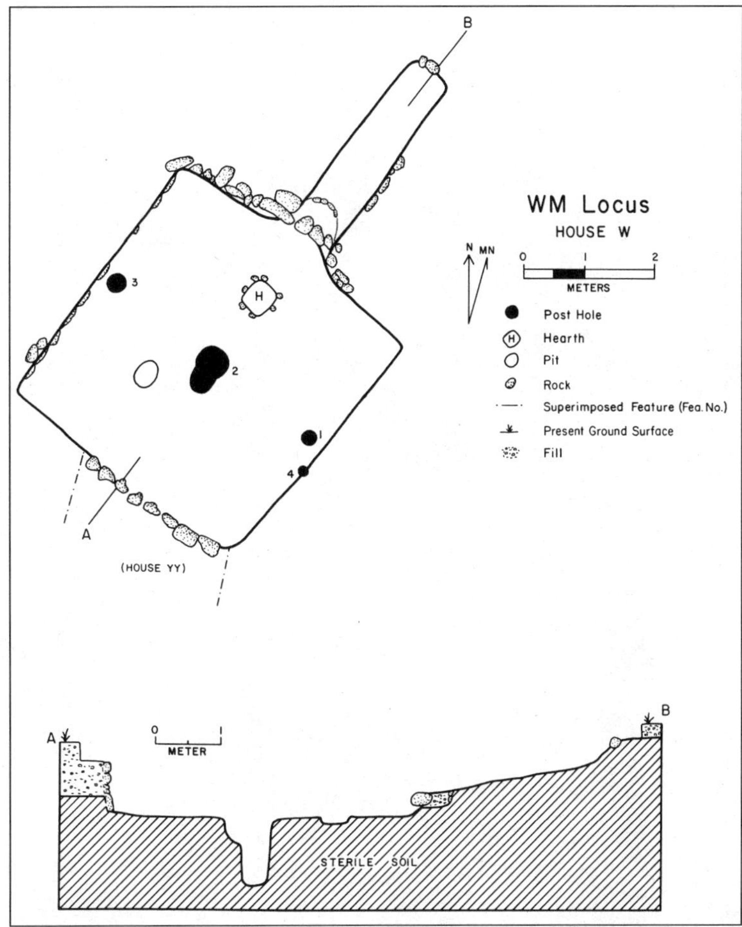

FIGURE 4.8. Plan view and profile of Wind Mountain locus House W, a Type IV domestic structure with a central post support. A hearth, located between the central post support and the entrance ramp, was a common feature of Type IV structures.

namely, by their size. Nondomestic habitation structures functioning for community centered activities may indeed have existed earlier, but remain unrecognized because they failed to attain a large enough dimension.

Type A Community Structure

Di Peso identified Type A Wind Mountain community structures based on their size, subsurface circular floor plan, and an absence of lateral entries (Figure 4.14). Two Type A structures were excavated, Ridout locus House F and Wind Mountain locus House O (Table 4.6). The occurrence of internal features, such as the configuration of support posts, was variable. House F displayed a central post and a number of peripheral post holes, possibly indicating a conical or peaked roof. House O, although heavily impacted by the construction of House N, suggested a quadrilateral post pattern reminiscent of a flat roof (see Bullard 1962: Figure 28a).

Room 2 at Winn Canyon (Fitting 1973a:11–16) resembles a Wind Mountain Type A community structure with its circular plan (8 m diameter) and lack of side entry. Though Fitting initially dated the structure to the Archaic, c. 520–180 B.C. (Fitting et al. 1982b:37, 40), this temporal range is probably far too early (refer to Chapter 3). Room 2 most likely dates to the late Early Pit House period. Another structure, House 5 at the Black's Bluff site in the Forestdale Valley, was also identified as a circular community structure without lateral entry (Haury 1985:299–300). Two Black's Bluff site tree-ring dates, A.D. 320 ± 5 and A.D. 318, place House 5 in the Early Pit House period. Although both these structures at the Winn Canyon and Black's Bluff sites are morphologically similar to Wind Mountain Type A houses, the latter date considerably later than is proposed for either of the former. No Wind Mountain community structure can be dated with confidence to the Early Pit House period, possibly because these houses (if they existed) were destroyed or impacted by later construction. Of the Type A structures identified, Wind

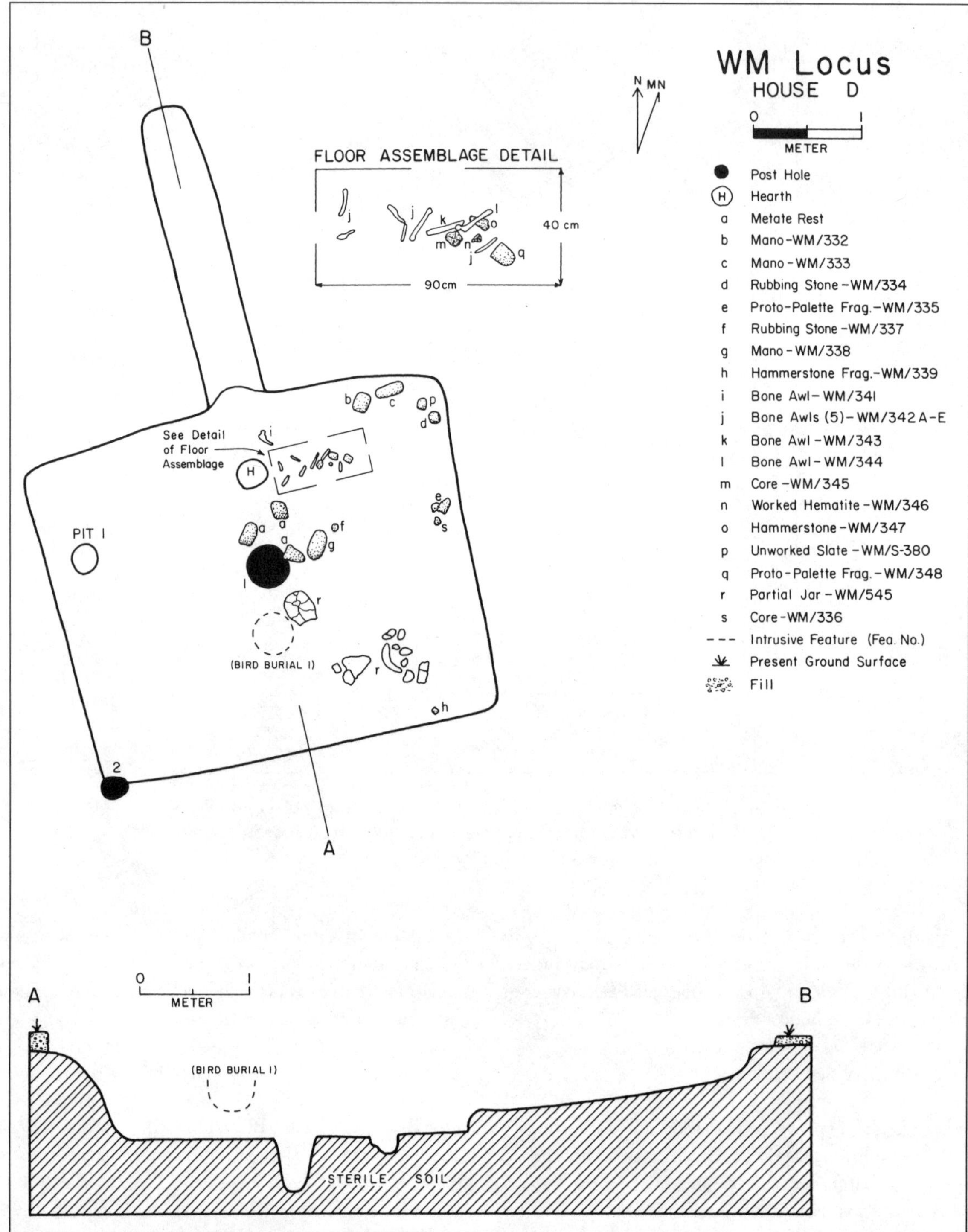

FIGURE 4.9. Plan view and profile of Wind Mountain locus House D, a Type IV domestic structure with a central post support. Utilitarian bone and stone tools were recovered from the House D floor.

FIGURE 4.10. Wind Mountain locus House D (Neg. No. WM 21-6F).

Mountain locus House A can be assigned to the San Francisco or early Three Circle phase age, while Ridout locus House F dates c. A.D. 620–710. House F, a San Francisco phase structure and one of the site's earliest community houses, is suggested to occur contemporaneously with Type IV domestic dwellings during the Late Pit House period (Figure 4.15).

Type B Community Structure

Wind Mountain's Type B community houses were subsurface, circular structures with central and peripheral post supports and lateral entries. Two Type B structures, Wind Mountain locus House X and House AB, were excavated (Table 4.6). House X was the larger, measuring 70.50 m^2 (Figure 4.16). It exhibited several interesting elaborations. House X contained a wall niche, a shelf, a massive central post hole, and two floor grooves (possible foot drums, Figure 4.17; refer to Figure 4.56). These features, plus the absence of floor storage pits, distinguish it from the secular domestic structures of the settlement.

Wind Mountain Type B community structures compare with Haury's (1936a:10, 52) Type II San Francisco phase ceremonial structures at Mogollon Village (e.g., Houses 3 and 5A) and Harris Village (e.g., House 8). At Wind Mountain, however, Type B community structures were apparently constructed not only in the San Francisco phase (House AB, A.D. 620–730) but also during the Three Circle phase (House X, A.D. 800–940). These Wind Mountain structures were seen by Di Peso (1974:110–113) to parallel Convento phase community structures (e.g., Community House 1) at the Convento site, c. A.D. 650/750 to 900. Di Peso considered the Type B community house type to be widely distributed throughout the northern Gran Chichimeca, especially from the Casas Grandes Valley to points north (Di Peso 1974:113; for a comparison of floor plans, see Figures 4.16 and 4.82 in this volume and Di Peso et al. 1974:4:156).

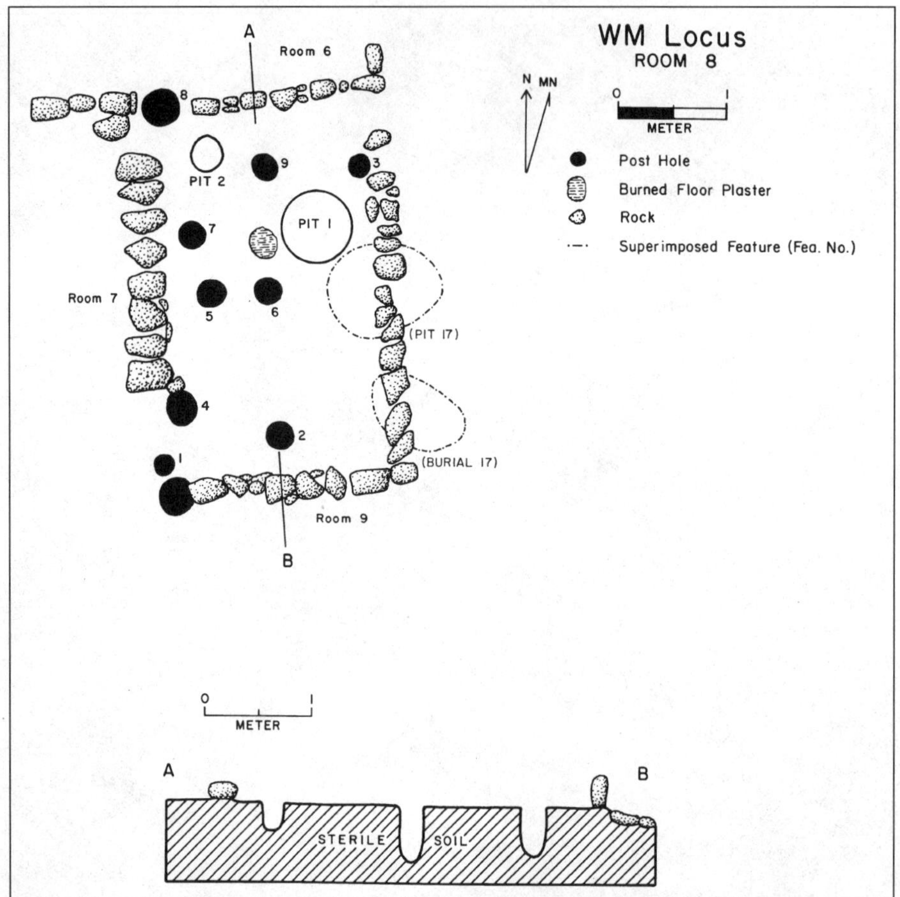

FIGURE 4.11. Plan view and profile of Wind Mountain locus Room 8, a Type V domestic structure. Type V structures were identified as rectangular surface or near surface (semisubterranean) rooms.

Type C Community Structure

Type C community houses were defined as subsurface structures with rectangular floor plans and lateral entries with a support post configuration that suggested a gabled roof (Figures 4.18). Three Type C community structures, Wind Mountain locus Houses U, Y, and XX, were excavated (Table 4.6).

Wind Mountain Type C structures conform to Bullard's large, deep pit houses (Bullard 1962:118, 125). They are also similar to Three Circle phase Type IV ceremonial structures at Harris Village, where House 10 exhibited the large size, side entry, and associated support post pattern (Haury 1936a:52). In the Upper Gila at the Saige-McFarland site, Pit House 1 (A.D. 645–770), a large structure (approximately 58 m^2 and 170 cm deep), was also assigned to the Three Circle phase (Lekson 1990:91). Originally identified as a great kiva based on its size, Pit House 1 was comparable with Type C Wind Mountain or Type IV Harris Village community structures. The ceremonial function of Pit House 1 was supported by the presence of floor vaults and niches, as well as two caches, one of calcite pendants and the other of mica pieces, a quartz crystal, and shell bracelet fragments placed in its post holes (Lekson 1990:31). Comparable structures at Wind Mountain include House XX (c. A.D. 778–1030), House U, and House Y. Although these Type C community structures occur during the Three Circle phase, at the Wind Mountain site they may also be associated with the San Francisco phase.

Type D Community Structure

Type D community structures were defined as subsurface, rectangular houses with a lateral entry. A quadrilateral support post pattern with peripheral posts along the interior wall suggests that these structures might have had flat roofs and possibly interior screens (Figures 4.19 and 4.20). Only one Type D community structure, Wind Mountain locus House AK, was identified (Table 4.6). The morphology of House AK led Di Peso to identify it as a Hohokam house type, specifically Type P3, which dated to the Pioneer period at Snaketown (Haury 1976:74). It is not improbable that contact between

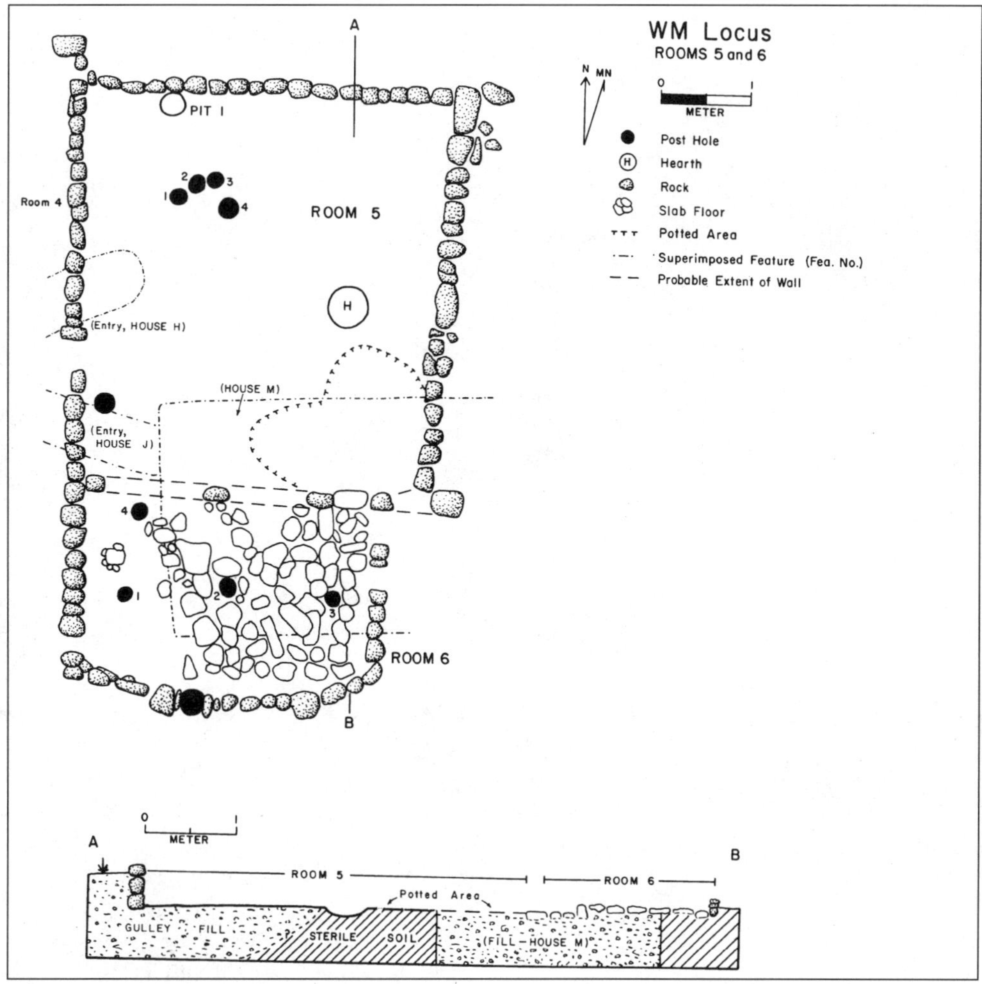

FIGURE 4.12. Plan view and profile of Wind Mountain locus Rooms 5 and 6, both Type V domestic structures.

the Hohokam and Mimbres Mogollon areas, reflected in part by the construction of House AK at Wind Mountain and by imported shell and ceramics, occurred during the Late Pit House period (for further discussion of Hohokam-Mimbres Mogollon interaction, see Chapter 11 in this volume).

No other structures with this support post pattern have been excavated in Mimbres Mogollon contexts (Bullard 1962: Figure 28). House AK (c. A.D. 640–780) would postdate the Pioneer period (300 B.C. to A.D. 550) Snaketown house type following Haury's (1976:338) long Hohokam chronology. In a revised Hohokam phase chronology (Dean 1991:90), however, both the Sweetwater (A.D 600s) and Snaketown (A.D. 700s) phases of the Pioneer period overlap the San Francisco phase House AK date range at Wind Mountain.

Type E Community Structure

The Type E community structure was defined as contiguous surface architecture, distinguished from secular domestic rooms on the basis of its larger floor area (Figures 4.21 and 4.22). No specialized secondary features such as a ventilator or wall niches were located, but Room 7 (A.D. 1040–1130), by virtue of its floor area, which measured almost 38 m^2, was identified as a Type E Mimbres phase community structure (Table 4.6).

Large surface rooms similar to Wind Mountain locus Room 7, but associated with sites in the Mimbres Valley, have also been interpreted as community structures (Anyon and LeBlanc 1980:270). Such Mimbres phase surface rooms and coincidental large pit houses were believed to be mutually exclusive, though each was presumed to have ceremonial (or communal) functions. At the Galaz Ruin, four surface rooms originally reported by Jenks (1929–1931) were given community structure status based on an average 37 m^2 floor area, a dimension twice the size of domestic rooms (Anyon and LeBlanc 1980:271: Table 6). Lekson (1990:76–78) has proposed that certain large surface rooms were set apart for special community use. The seven domestic surface rooms

TABLE 4.5. Dimensions of Type V Structures

Provenience	Length (m)	Width (m)	Area (m²)
WM locus			
1	3.25	2.15	6.99
2	4.20	3.30	7.80[r] 12.86[e]
4	6.90	3.95	24.56
5	4.10	3.95	15.64
6	2.10	3.10	6.00
8	3.25	1.90	6.22
9	4.30	2.80	12.21
10	8.70	3.05	26.00[e]
11	4.10	4.10	17.01
12	3.85	3.95	15.21
13	5.60	4.10	18.70[r] 21.53[e]
14	5.00	4.70	23.50
16	4.00	3.25	10.94[e]

[e]Estimated area.
[r]Remnant area.

TABLE 4.6. Dimensions of Community Structures

Provenience	Type	Length (m)	Width (m)	Area (m²)
WM House O	A	5.90	5.60	9.80[r] 28.24[e]
RO House F	A	6.90	6.60	35.84
WM House X	B	10.10	8.70	70.50
WM House AB	B	7.50	6.50+	37.88[r] 40.50[e]
WM House U	C	6.45	5.65	36.90
WM House Y	C	5.70	5.50	15.92[r] 29.84[e]
WM House XX	C	5.70	4.85	27.95
WM House AK	D	5.70	5.40	28.12[r] 29.85[e]
WM Room 7	E	8.20	4.70	37.90
WM House V	F	4.90	3.10	15.27
WM House P2	G	4.85	3.80	18.24
WM Room 3	G	3.30	3.10	9.06
WM Room 15	G	3.25	2.80	8.96

[e]Estimated area.
[r]Remnant area.

and one community room observed in Room Unit 2 (Rooms 4–9, 12 and 13) at Wind Mountain may be comparable to the 10 or 12 residential rooms and one community room of Block B at Saige-McFarland.

Type F Community Structure

The Type F community structure was represented by a single, curious example. Wind Mountain locus House V was unusual in its extreme depth (220 cm) and small floor area (15.27 m²). The structure exhibited a rectangular floor plan, ventilator, and vertical interior wall grooves, which probably indicated the placement of roof support posts (Figures 4.23 and 4.24, Table 4.6). It was constructed in the fill of earlier House U, a Type C community structure with a lateral entry. House V had no lateral entry, and access was most likely achieved through the roof.

House V (A.D. 970–1080) is associated with the Mangas phase (c. A.D. 950–1000/1050) at Wind Mountain. It shows no clear parallels with structures at sites in neighboring regions (see Wheat 1955; Bullard 1962). Anyon and LeBlanc (1980:268, Table 5) report several small Mimbres pit structures they term "kivas," which may be reminiscent of House V, but these do not exhibit a similar wall construction and they are not nearly as deep.

Type G Community Structure

Type G community structures were defined as small, rectangular pit houses or semisubterranean rooms associated with contiguous surface room blocks (Figure 4.25). Three Type G structures, Wind Mountain locus House P2 (Mangas phase/Mimbres phase), Room 3 (Mimbres phase), and Room 15 (A.D. 1030–1150; Mimbres phase), were excavated (Table 4.6). Rooms 3 and 15 were attached to room blocks; House P2 was a detached, remodelled Type IV pit house structure whose original (i.e., House P1) lateral entry was replaced by a ventilator.

Pit House 3 at Saige-McFarland, which Lekson (1990:33) believed to be associated with a room block, has similarities with both Type F and Type G community houses at Wind Mountain. A rectangular structure at the Dinwiddie site (Hammack et al. 1966) resembles both community house types. Comparable structures have been described as semisubterranean kivas in Mimbres Valley sites (Anyon and LeBlanc 1980:266–267, Table 5). Like their Wind Mountain Type G counterparts, these shallow Mimbres Valley community structures are sometimes attached to room blocks or may appear separately, renovated within earlier pit houses. In the absence of obvious ceremonial elaborations (e.g., foot drums or niches), Di Peso at Wind Mountain (evident from criteria used to define structure types), and Anyon and LeBlanc in the Mimbres Valley (1980:266–270, Table 5), suggest that the presence of ventilator shafts distinguished communal structures from either residential or storage structures. Why

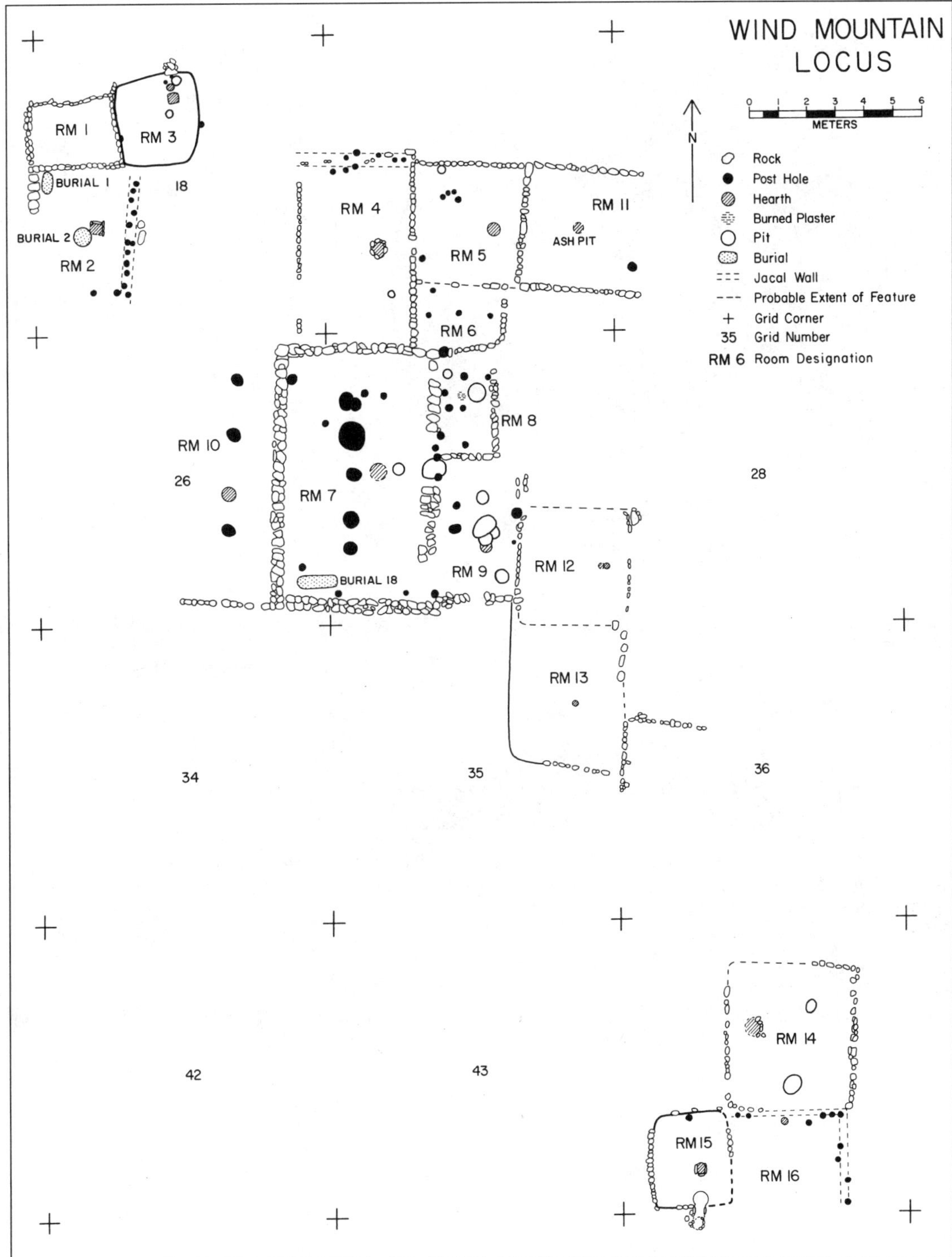

FIGURE 4.13. Plan view of the Wind Mountain site room blocks or house units dating to Mangas and Mimbres phase occupations.

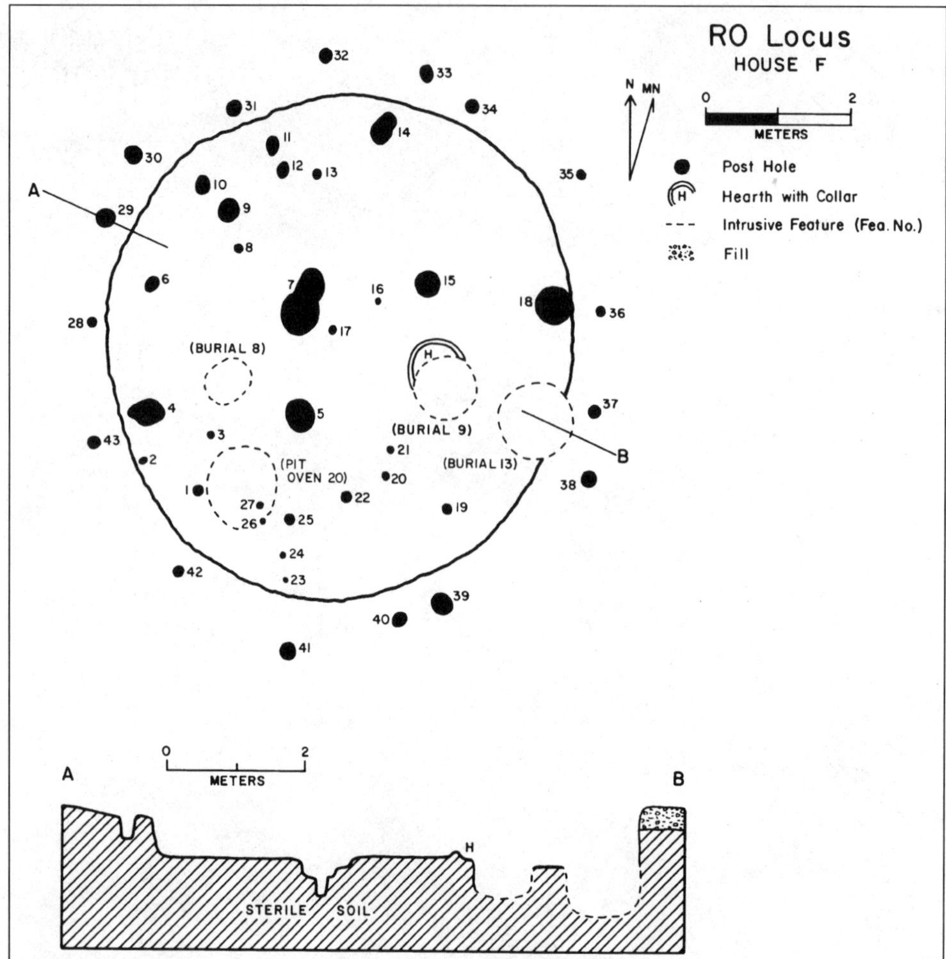

FIGURE 4.14. Plan view and profile of Ridout locus House F, a Type A community structure. Type A structures were determined by their circular plan, lack of lateral entries, and size.

the presence of ventilators should identify the former and be absent in the latter is nowhere explained. It seems plausible to hypothesize that the ventilator was a limited, but accepted, late architectural feature used in both residential and community structures.

Secondary Architectural Features

In addition to primary architectural categories, Di Peso defined secondary or ancillary features that were also subsumed under the broad heading of architecture. Secondary architectural features included classes of hearths, pits, work areas, stone pavements, and miscellaneous elements, each of which was further separated into a series of subtypes. These type descriptions are summarized below (for locational information and details, refer to Figures 4.1 and 4.2 and Part 2 of this chapter). Secondary architectural features do not appear to be chronologically sensitive; nevertheless, they do provide useful insights into the range of activities undertaken by the inhabitants of Wind Mountain.

Hearths

Hearths were generally defined as depressions exhibiting controlled, enclosed burning found inside structures. Ninety hearths were uncovered, distributed throughout 67 pit house structures and 13 surface rooms of the settlement (see individual floor plan figures in this chapter for details). Most structures contained a single hearth, although five pit houses and two surface rooms contained two each. In one instance only (Wind Mountain locus, Mangas phase, House WW), three hearths were discovered on a floor.

In general, Wind Mountain hearths do not show much variability. Based on plan shape, Di Peso identified three primary hearth types (for a complete hearth typology refer to Appendix 5). Type I hearths were irregular in plan, Type II were round to oval, and Type III consisted of rectangular forms. Type IV, or unclassified, hearths included those of indiscernible plan, either the result of some sort of disturbance or due to a lack of distinguishing characteristics. Excluding two "unclassified" Type IV hearths, the division of hearth types was as follows: Type I hearths, 32 percent (n = 28); Type II, 59 percent (n = 52); and Type III, 9 percent (n = 8).

Hearths were usually simply constructed by scooping a depression in the floor of a structure. The walls of many consisted of sterile soil that had become burned or fire hardened through use. Some were elaborated with the addition of a clay lining or thin plaster coat. In a few cases, including, for example, the circular hearth of Wind Mountain locus House V, a clay collar formed the rim. Occasionally, as observed in Wind Mountain locus House ZZ, unmodified stones were irregularly inset around the hearth rims. A few hearths, notably the rectangular types found in Wind Mountain Mimbres phase Rooms 2 and 3, were partially lined with stone slabs. Rectangular hearths in Wind Mountain locus Houses P2, W, and AG incorporated small cobbles and plaster into their construction. In Wind Mountain locus Houses M and AC, no stones were used, but the associated hearths were clay lined. Unlike other forms, rectangular hearths were restricted to Type IV domestic pit houses and surface rooms, thereby representing a Late Pit House period (San Francisco phase and later) addition to the architectural menu of secondary features.

Circular hearths were frequently accompanied by a hearthstone set into or adjacent the rim. In most instances hearthstones were positioned on the hearth edge facing the entry of the structure. Hearthstones were observed in domestic Type IV Wind Mountain locus Houses G, K, L, N, TT, UU, AF, AI, AL, and possibly Z and AG; as well as in Ridout locus Houses B, C, D, H, and K. They also appeared in all three Type C community structures (Wind Mountain locus Houses U, Y, and XX), as well as in one Type B structure (Wind Mountain locus House AB). Haury (1936a) reported them in nine houses at Harris Village (e.g., Houses 8, 20, 32), and they were noted at Swarts Ruin (Cosgrove and Cosgrove 1932), Mattocks Ruin (Nesbitt 1931), and Cameron Creek Village (Bradfield 1931). Bullard (1962:181) associated hearthstones with so-called fireplaces in the structures of sites found in the southern Mimbres region.

The precise function of these stones is conjectural, but it seems likely that their surface area, occurring as it does adjacent a hearth fire, must have been used in conjunction with food preparation. Perhaps they facilitated parching or roasting of food stuffs or helped to heat the contents of vessels by indirect exposure to the hearth fire. If hearthstones served as some form of pot rest, the small depression adjacent the hearth in Wind Mountain locus House T (a Type II structure) may represent a less formalized predecessor of this feature.

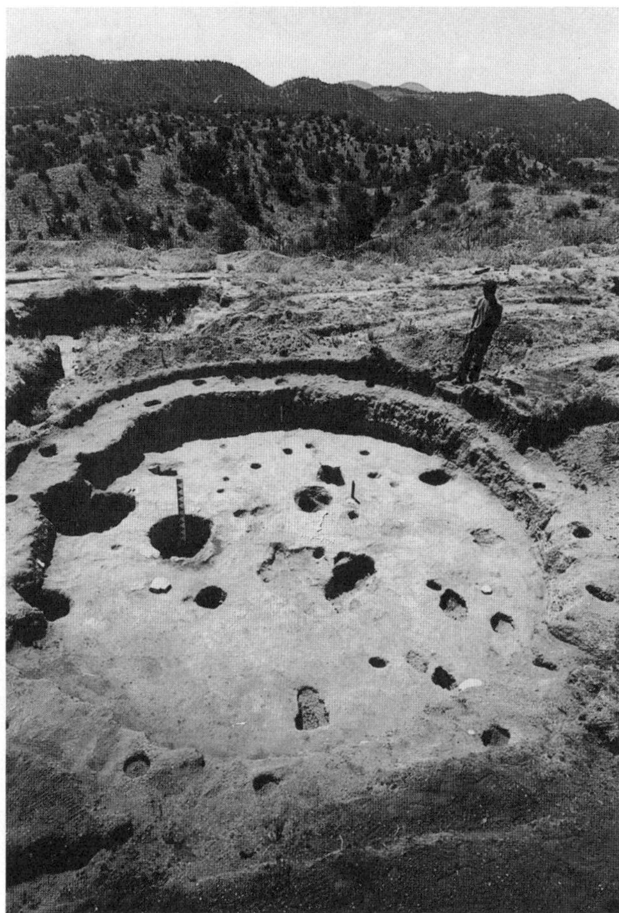

FIGURE 4.15. Ridout locus House F. The Type A community structure is suggested to occur concurrently with Type IV domestic structures during the San Francisco phase (Neg. No. WM 98–31F).

None of the Wind Mountain hearths were particularly large or deep. In Wind Mountain locus pit houses (63 cases) the range of hearth depths measured between 1 and 31 cm with a mean of 12.5 cm; Ridout locus pit house hearths (11 cases) measured between 1 and 20 cm deep with a mean of 9.4 cm. The range of hearth depths in Wind Mountain locus surface rooms (15 cases) measured between 1 and 20 cm with a mean of 11.4 cm. Some hearths appeared only as a shallow, burned smudge on the structure's floor, indicating infrequent, low combustion use. During much of the year, residents probably preferred open air ramada type structures to the dark enclosed spaces of a pit house. Consequently, many interior hearths do not seem to have been heavily used. Small hearths were probably desirable and adequate to heat the pit house living space without endangering the inhabitants. As wooden superstructures dried, fire would have posed an increasing and distinct threat to the occupants of houses.

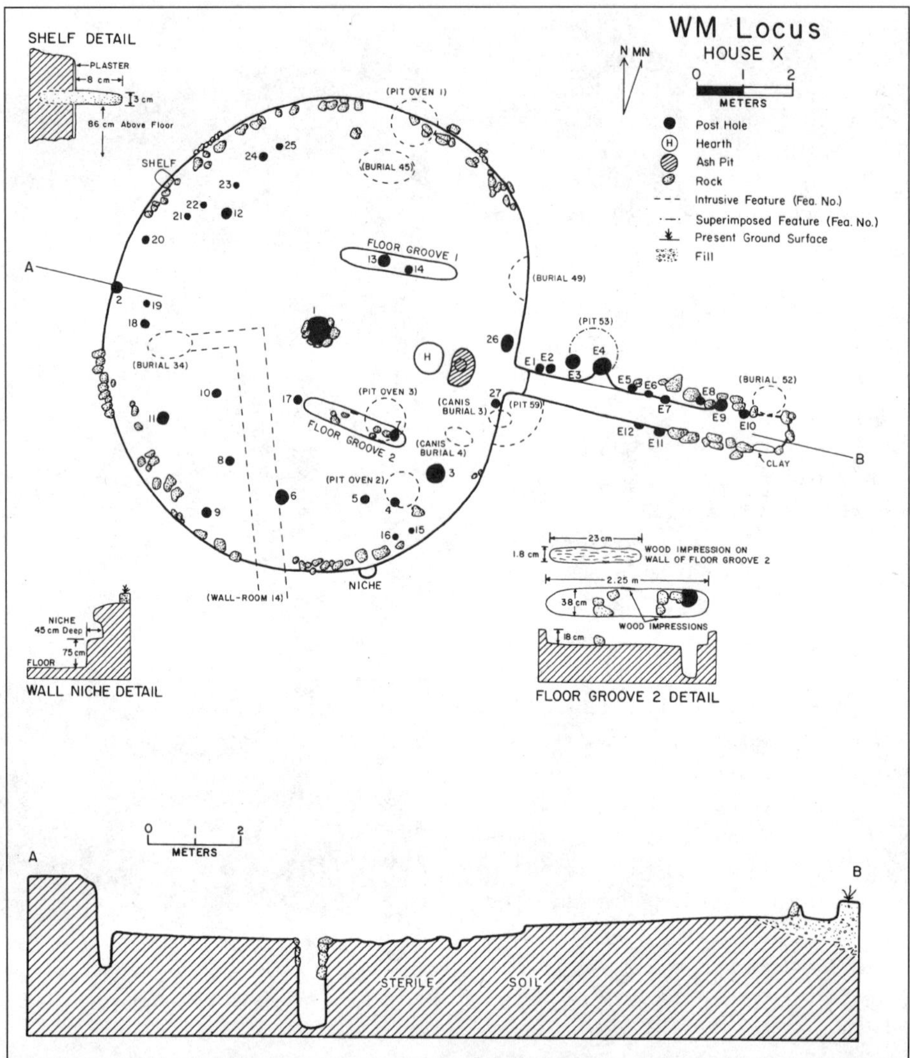

FIGURE 4.16. Plan view and profile of Wind Mountain locus House X, a Type B community structure. Type B structures were characterized by a round plan and lateral entry. House X was the largest pit structure uncovered at the site.

Pits

An absence of burning distinguished pits from hearths. Di Peso determined pit types by their plan shape and profile: Type I, circular to oval with undercut walls (syn. bell-shaped); Type II, circular to oval with straight walls; Type III, rectangular with straight walls; Type IV, stone lined cyst; Type V, collared; Type VI, figure-eight plan; Type VII, modern. The Type V or collared form referred to a pit in which the lower portion was a small circular pit set inside a larger circular pit—a small Type II pit contained in a large Type II pit. The so-called figure-eight plan, or Type VI, may actually have consisted of two juxtapositioned pits. The Type VII or modern pit was most likely a recent pot hunter hole excavated during the last 60 to 70 years.

Seventy-four extramural pits (Table 4.7) were exposed throughout the Wind Mountain settlement (refer to Figure 4.1). Type II pits were the most common by far (56 examples). A few Type I (seven examples), Type III (six examples), and Type V (two examples) were recorded. The remaining types were represented by a single instance only. With the exception of a single stone cyst (Pit 18), pit walls consisted of compacted soil. None were slab, cobble, clay, or plaster lined. Extramural pit features appear to have been randomly excavated into sterile soil or were intrusive into the fill of abandoned houses with need rather than style dictating their placement and manner of construction.

Most pits (86 percent or n = 64) were empty, showing little indication of the materials they originally contained. Some undoubtedly served to store foods for the community's inhabitants (Appendix 1). A few contained artifacts in direct

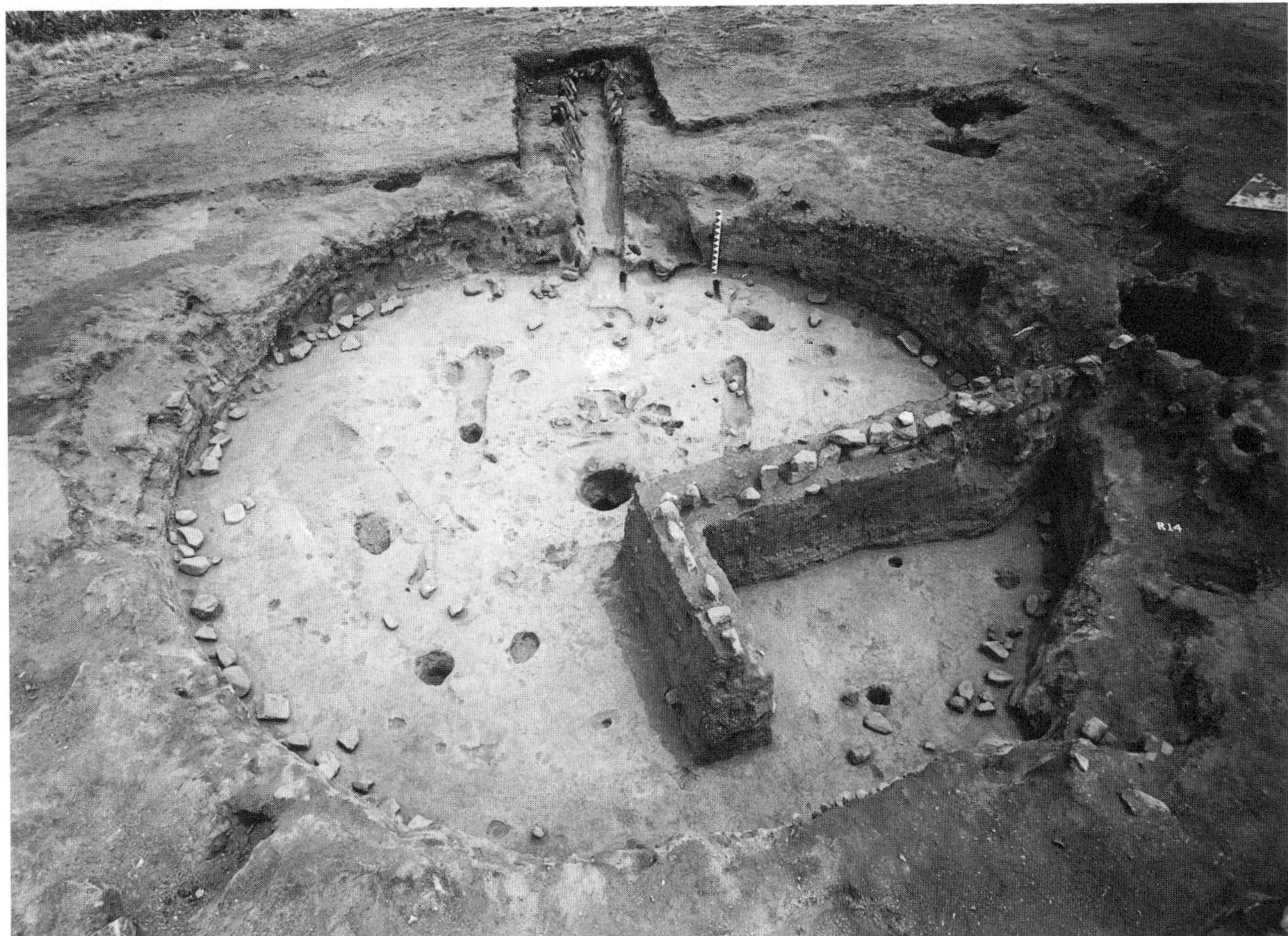

FIGURE 4.17. Wind Mountain locus House X, revealing a large central post hole, floor grooves, and wall niche in right upper view. The L-shaped projection is a balk supporting the remnant walls of Room 14 (Neg. No. WM 57–24A/F).

association with their floors. For example, a notched grinding slab and two stone balls were recovered from Pit 10. A grinding slab and hammerstone, as well as two handstones were recovered from Pits 33 and 34 respectively. Pit 41 contained a slab metate and a bone tool (Appendix 9: Table 3, WM 1886). Large sized fragments of Mimbres Classic Black-on-white and Alma series sherds, two Mimbres Classic Black-on-white bowls (Table 6.5), together with a Mogollon Red-on-brown jar cover were collected near the floor of Pit 27. These ceramics were either directly related to the pit or represent depositional fill.

Five pits were interpreted as containing caches. A stone pipe (WM 791), a flake tool located under a mano fragment, two red ocher nodules, a core, and a drill (WM 790) were recovered from Pit 8. The objects may be the remains of a pipe manufacturing kit, or evidence of ritual smoking. A cache of tools consisting of small manos or rubbing stones, two showing traces of red ocher on their grinding surfaces, were collected from Pit 42 (Figure 4.26). Four Mimbres Classic Black-on-white bowls were cached in Pit 54 (Figure 4.27; Table 6.5). Pit 55 contained one whole and one fragmentary stone bowl, a stone pipe (WM 2034), three quartzite grinding slabs, three small clear quartz crystals, a fragmentary shell bracelet, an iron mineral (magnetite) nodule, two hammerstones, two cores, a flake, and a shale palette-like fragment. A stone pipe cache was discovered in Pit 56 (Figure 4.28; Table 8.4). Clearly, both utilitarian (ground stone tools and ceramic vessels) and nonutilitarian objects (crystals, pipes, and pigments) were cached. Stone pipes, crystals, and pigments seem to represent the most likely glimpse into the ritual life of the Wind Mountain settlement.

Pit Ovens

Pit ovens were cobble lined features (frequently incorporating worn out handstones and metate fragments) usually excavated into extramural areas of the site or into the fill of abandoned pit houses (Figure 4.1). Di Peso defined three pit oven types: Type I, circular to oval with sloping sides; Type II, rectangular with straight sides; Type III, circular with un-

TABLE 4.7. Pits Uncovered in Extramural Contexts

Pit	Type	Size (cm)	Depth* (cm)
1	II	130x120	85
2	II	120x120	45
3	I	235x200	120
4	II	90x85	80
5	II	48x40	28
6	II	215x175	75
7	VII	180x180	?
8	II	50x45	33
9	II	110x65	145
10	II	125x95	80
11	III	120x90	120
12	II	50x45	40
13	II	60x40	55
14	III	80x60	100
15	II	170x115	45
16	II	135x65+	75
17	II	125x65	65
18	IV	41x38	15
19	I	130x115	125
20	II	145x145	70
21	II	210x150	65
22	II	140x80	75
23	II	90x80	60
24	I	95+x80+	65
25	II	115+x85	45
26	II	190+x80+	105
27	II	270x100	95
28	III	225+x95+	60
29	II	165+x90	45
30	II	140x115	90
31	I	150x190	140
32	II	185x95	70
33	II	75x75	75
34	I	95x80	65
35	III	80x65	55
36	II	115x115	95
37	II	130x130	90
38	II	105x90	65
39	II	85x75	65
40	II	160x145	80
41	VI	240x145	200
42	II	105x95	85
43	V	80x80	85
44	V	160x140	115
45	II	105x90	60
46	II	155x80	50
47	II	110x110	70
48	II	150x55	75
49	II	95x85	50
50	II	55x55	65
51	II	105x95	30
52	I	90x90	30
53	II	95+x85+	45
54	II	50x45	40
55	II	35x35	15
56	II	30x?	10
57	II	145x145	65
58	II	135x100	55
59	I	110+x80+	125
60	II	170x142	95
61	II	162+x110+	68
62	III	120x50	40
63	II	138x133	68
64	II	80x75	52
65	II	62x69	58
66	II	140x120	75
67	III	75x45	70
68	II	90x85	73
69	II	79x75	46
70	II	355x145	99
71	II	150x150	82
72	II	81x65	78
73	II	60x50	137
74	II	125x100	70

*Depth is below present day surface.

dercut sides. All but two of the 20 pit ovens identified were assigned a Type I classification (Table 4.8). One rectangular Type II feature, Pit Oven 2, was located. Pit Oven 18 (classified as a Type III structure) was probably not originally designed as an oven. Its size and interior four support post patterning (under cut at a 20–25° angle) suggest it may have first served as a structure of specialized function that was destroyed by fire. After the fire, the abandoned pit was converted and apparently used as a large pit oven.

Wind Mountain pit ovens contained either one or two layers of thermally altered rock (10 cm to 20 cm deep), which were often associated with ash or charcoal fill (Figure 4.29). Presumably, pit ovens were used to roast, parch, or otherwise prepare foods by enclosing them within layers of heated rock. Evidence for some of the plant foods, such as corn and agave, utilized by the site's residents was recovered in the form of macrobotanical remains (Appendix 1).

Pit ovens may have been used for purposes other than cooking, including, for example, pottery firing. Sherds were recovered from Pit Ovens 10 and 12, which may indicate their function as kilns. However, sherds could also have derived from pottery vessels shattered near the ovens and incorporated into the pit fill as trash. In addition, ovens might have served in the production of lithic tools, either to thermally treat raw stone or to temper finished implements. Pit Ovens 5, 10, and 11 yielded chipped stone debris and a projectile point.

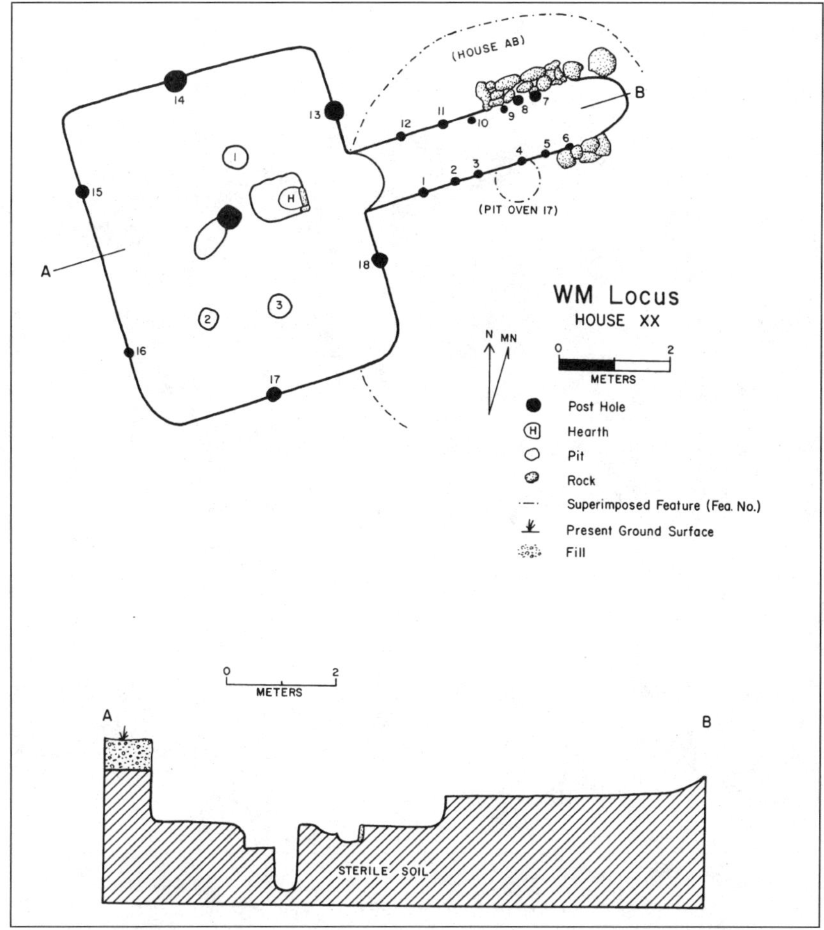

FIGURE 4.18. Plan view and profile of Wind Mountain locus House XX, a Type C community structure associated with the Three Circle phase and possibly the San Francisco phase occupations of the site. Type C structures were defined by their rectangular plan, lateral entry, and size.

Puddling Pits

Three shallow pits yielding a fine, dark gray clay were exposed at the Wind Mountain locus. Puddling Pit 1 (100 cm x 50 cm; depth 20 cm) was located under the floor of Room 5, Puddling Pit 2 (70 cm x 70 cm; depth 5 cm) occurred in the fill of House Q, and Puddling Pit 3 (95 cm x 55 cm; depth 15 cm) was uncovered between Rooms 12 and 13.

Puddling pits were interpreted as shallow depressions in which adobe clay was slaked in preparation for house construction. Clay mixed with water became the plaster coat used to cover house walls, floors, and hearth interiors. Alternatively, such pits may have served as mixing basins for the manufacture of ceramic vessels.

Work Areas

Work areas consisted of compacted surfaces associated with hearths or other features and material remains suggestive of processing activities. Two work areas, numbered 1 and 3, were exposed at the Wind Mountain locus (Figure 4.1). Work Area 2 was deleted during field excavations when it became apparent that it was not a distinct and separate surface but part of Room 16.

Work Area 1 was found in the fill of House L at an approximate depth of 80–90 cm (Figure 4.30). It consisted of a light gray clay surface (measuring approximately 2 m x 2 m) strewn with a layer of broken vessels. Related features included a hearth (35 cm x 25 cm; depth 10 cm) adjacent a small stone circle (pot rest?; diameter 15 cm). A heavily worn Boldface Black-on-white bowl (WM 462; Style II) and five plainware utility jars (three Three Circle Neck Corrugated, WM 1950, WM 2344, WM 2420; and two Alma series vessels, WM 1951, WM 2209) were located. Carbonized corn kernels and beans were recovered from the work surface (Appendix 1 in this volume).

Work Area 3 was located in the fill of House TT, 55 cm

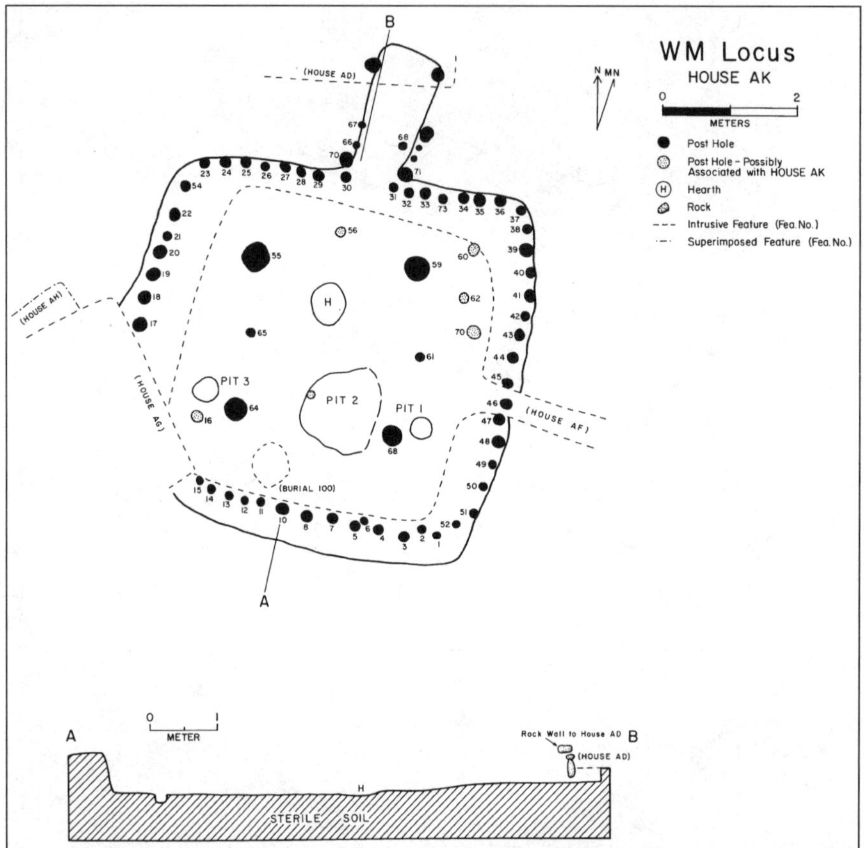

FIGURE 4.19. Plan view and profile of Wind Mountain locus House AK, the only Type D community structure identified at the site. Type D structures were characterized by a rectangular plan, quadrilateral support post pattern, and a lateral entry (see Figure 4.86 for details of House AF).

below present ground surface. Similar in appearance to Work Area 1, it consisted of a compacted surface of trash laden fill measuring approximately 3 m x 4 m. A circular-shaped portion (107 cm x 87 cm) of the work surface was burned; some ash remained. Two associated rock clusters were uncovered. Though analogous in plan and construction to shallow roasting pits, none of the cobbles were fire cracked. A worked Boldface Black-on-white sherd scoop as well as some handstones and cores were collected near the clusters.

Although it is certain that many daily activities took place outside structures, their traces do not often survive. The two Wind Mountain work areas, containing hearths, utility tools, and carbonized plant remains, provide some evidence for subsistence tasks conducted by the community's inhabitants. Vestiges of post holes indicate that they may have been covered. Such ramada-like features with associated pits and hearths, protected from the sun and rain, are known from other sites in upland settings (Woosley 1980b:27–28). At Wind Mountain, the work areas most likely represent localities in the settlement where a diverse assortment of daily activities occurred.

Stone Pavements

Four stone pavements constructed of cobbles, stone slabs, and a few metate fragments were uncovered at the Wind Mountain locus (Figure 4.1). Stones as small as 5 cm x 5 cm to slabs as large as 20 cm x 30 cm were closely positioned to create a flat, paved surface. Pavement 1 (150 cm x 120 cm) was discovered in the vicinity of Room 2; Pavement 2 (250 cm x 220 cm) was located near House K (Figure 4.30); Pavement 3 (210 cm x 190 cm) was exposed during the excavation of Block 28–D; and Pavement 4 (195 cm x 170 cm) was found close to House EE. Only Pavement 2 was associated with a support post, which may indicate the presence of a covered structure. Although their function is difficult to determine, pavements were generally small, perhaps suggesting their use as drying surfaces.

Architectural Elements

Di Peso defined a final class of secondary architectural elements (Appendix 5). This class included (1) stationary stone

FIGURE 4.20. Wind Mountain locus House AK, a Type D community structure, suggested to have affinities with Hohokam Pioneer period houses (Neg. No. WM 91-19F).

elements: Paving Slabs (Reference No. 375), Grinding Slabs (Reference No. 376), Cooking Slabs (Reference No. 377), Step Treads (Reference No. 378); (2) miscellaneous-shaped stone elements: Slabs (Reference No. 379), Pebbles (Reference No. 380), Cobbles (Reference No. 381), Boulders (Reference No. 382); and (3) jacal/adobe: Wood Framing Casts (Reference No. 383), Matting Casts (Reference No. 384), Wall Plaster (Reference No. 385).

Stationary stone elements consisted of artifacts used in architecture, even if their original and primary function may have been something quite different. For example, a grinding slab or metate that was incorporated into a pit house structure to help shore up a wall would be assigned an Architectural Element type. Worn out grinding slabs or metates once used for food processing became architectural elements when used as paving slabs, step treads, or as wall reinforcement in house construction and renovation. Lastly, literally hundreds of jacal fragments and casts were collected from the settlement. The frequency of mud casts was principally due to the numerous house fires, which baked the superstructures, thereby preserving the jacal architecture.

Discussion and Interpretations

The Wind Mountain settlement extended across a ridge top that, due to the presence of a shallow saddle, Di Peso separated into two loci, the Wind Mountain locus and the Ridout locus. Both contained houses dating to the earliest occupation (refer to Figures 4.1 and 4.2 for locations of structures; Chapter 3). By the Three Circle phase, house construction occurred on only the northern portion of the ridge, the Wind Mountain locus. Architectural remains, augmented by absolute date ranges and ceramics, indicate that Wind Mountain was inhabited intermittently over a span of approximately 700 to 900 years. Although the site was not continuously occupied, Wind Mountain architecture typifies the Mogollon sequence of the Upper Gila region.

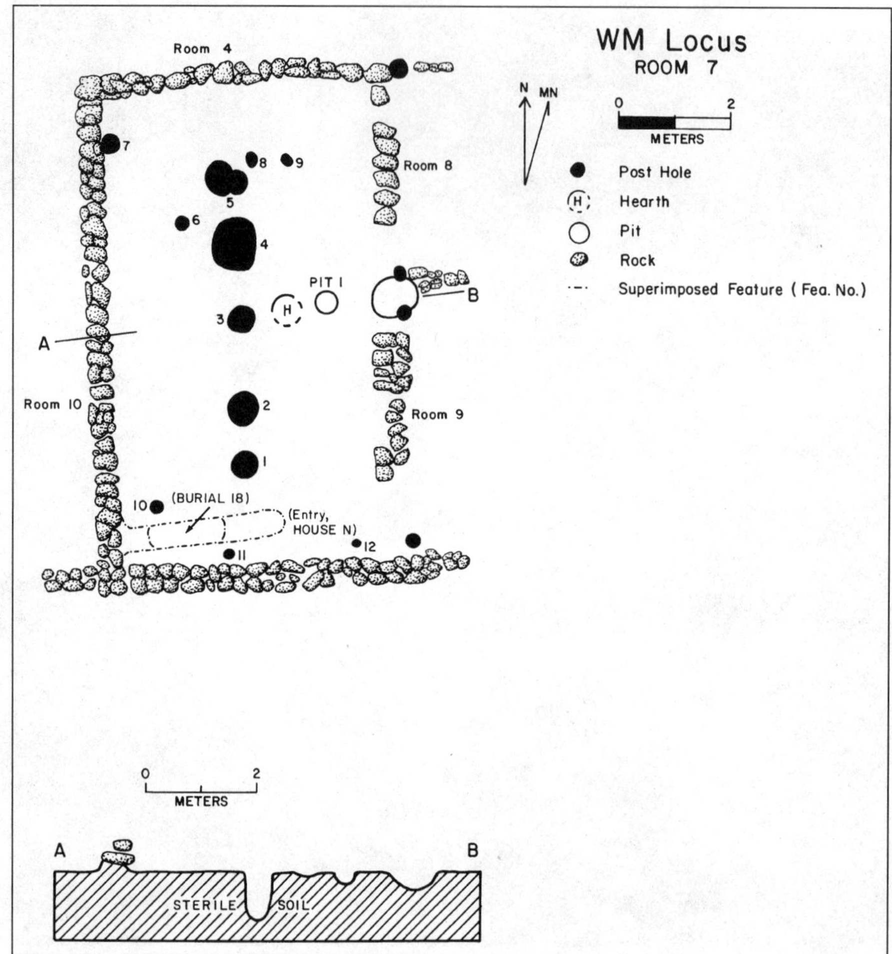

FIGURE 4.21. Plan view and profile of Wind Mountain locus Room 7, a Type E community structure characterized as contiguous surface architecture. Type E community structures were distinguished from contemporaneous domestic rooms by their larger size.

Architectural Trends

Developmental trends in Mimbres Mogollon architecture may be characterized by the early appearance of pit house structures modeled on a round floor plan, which were later superseded by houses with rectangular plans. Subterranean architecture was eventually largely supplanted by the construction of surface rooms (Haury 1936a, 1985; Wheat 1955; Anyon and LeBlanc 1984). This progression of forms was similarly evident at the Wind Mountain site, where the architectural sequence encompassed both domestic and community pit houses representing the early and middle stages of the settlement. Following a Mangas phase transition, the Mimbres phase was characterized by small surface room blocks indicative of the settlement's final occupation.

At Wind Mountain, for instance, some of the community's earliest domestic structures, which typify the Early Pit House period (e.g., Wind Mountain locus Type I House AN) and the Georgetown phase of the Late Pit House period (e.g., Wind Mountain locus Type II House T), conform to a round floor plan. Early Mogollon pit structures reportedly lack interior hearths (Rice 1980:465; Stafford 1980:48–49), a condition evident in House AN. Later rectangular structures are associated with the San Francisco phase (e.g., Wind Mountain locus Houses AE and AI, both Type IV; Ridout locus House A and D, both Type IV) and the Three Circle phase (e.g., Wind Mountain locus Houses AA, AF, and AG, all Type IV). Experimentation with domestic surface architecture begins with the transitional Mangas phase of the Pueblo period (e.g., Wind Mountain locus Type III House WW, Figure 4.31; refer to Figure 4.6), and the majority of surface rooms (e.g., Rooms 9 and 16, both Type V) are illustrative of a Mimbres phase settlement.

Wind Mountain community structures comply with the general trend of round to rectangular pit houses followed by surface room construction (Figure 4.1). The stratigraphic relationship of Wind Mountain locus Houses XX and AB af-

FIGURE 4.22. Type E community structure, Room 7 exhibiting a row of large support post holes (Neg. No. WM 34–29F).

fords a clear case of a rectangular plan structure (Type C Three Circle phase House XX, A.D. 778–1030) built over an earlier round plan structure (Type B San Francisco phase House AB, A.D. 620–730).

As noted by Haury (1985:180), however, Mogollon pit houses of round or rectangular shape may occur at any time in the Late Pit House period. Haury's observation has relevance at Wind Mountain. Though traditional Mogollon architectural developments characterized by pit houses to surface rooms (Wheat 1955; Bullard 1962) were obvious, there were some exceptions. For example, Wind Mountain locus House R (A.D. 680–980), a Georgetown phase Type II structure, may have persisted into the San Francisco phase when rectangular Type IV structures are assumed predominant. Similarly, Ridout locus House F (A.D. 620–710), a large, round Type C community structure, was constructed during the San Francisco phase.

Alternatively, some Type IV rectangular domestic pit houses including Wind Mountain locus Houses D (A.D. 1000–1260) and OO (A.D. 890–1160), as well as Type F community structure House V (A.D. 970–1080), were probably built coincidentally with surface architecture associated with either the Mangas or Mimbres phases. Evidence from Wind Mountain suggests that round community structures and rectangular domestic forms developed concurrently and that round domestic pit houses continued to be built even as rectangular floor plans became the norm.

Furthermore, pit houses and surface architecture also occurred together during the final occupation stages. Although particular house designs dominated at certain times (and in certain phases), the inhabitants of Wind Mountain were apparently flexible in the types of surface or subterranean architecture they constructed throughout the lifetime of the settlement.

Two final observations relating to Wind Mountain architectural trends, one concerning pit house plans and the other, area of living space, are offered. With regard to pit house shape, three distinct developmental stages have been suggested (Haury 1936a:82–83; LeBlanc 1983:61). As noted above, round pit houses were succeeded by rectangular structures. In his original discussion of architecture at Mogollon and Harris Villages, Haury (1936a) also identified an inter-

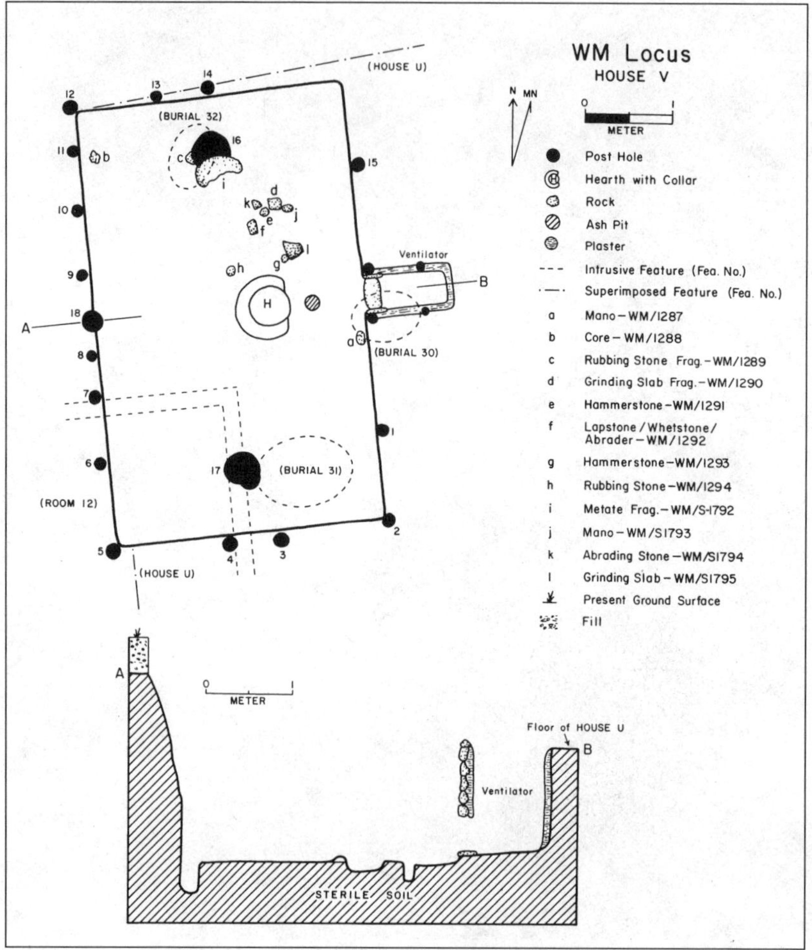

FIGURE 4.23. Plan view and profile of Wind Mountain locus House V, a Type F community structure defined by a rectangular plan, probable roof entry, and a ventilator.

mediary or subrectangular form between round and rectangular structures. In the evolution of Mogollon pit houses, the round house has been associated with the Georgetown phase, and the subrectangular structure (rectangular houses with fully rounded corners), representing a transitional architectural stage during the San Francisco phase, developed into the more fully rectangular houses of the Three Circle phase. This developmental trend was not observed at the Wind Mountain site. Wind Mountain pit houses can be characterized as either round or rectangular in plan, with an intermediary subrectangular stage lacking. The reported subrectangular to rectangular pit house continuum may be more a product of archaeological classification than distinctive prehistoric design.

Minor differences in the pit houses of Wind Mountain can easily be ascribed to such factors as diversity in the surrounding soils into which structures were excavated, postoccupational erosion, variation in materials used in post and crosstie fabrication, or the inherent vicissitudes of human behavior during the process of house construction (and archaeological excavation).

In addition, one other house plan, the D-shaped pit house structure, has been described for some areas of the Mogollon during the earlier stages of the temporal sequence (Wheat 1955:40, 44; Martin 1979:66–67; Anyon et al. 1981:212). Wheat (1955: Table 2) cites such structures at Cave Creek, Crooked Ridge, and Harris Village. No D-shaped floor plans were observed for any Wind Mountain pit house.

Turning to the subject of Mogollon house size, the tendency toward an increase in available living space from early to late in the sequence has been proposed (Wheat 1955:41). A sample (n = 21, 46 percent) of rectangular, Type IV structures representing occupation at Wind Mountain from the San Francisco phase into the Mangas phase was examined for variation in pit house size through time. No evidence supporting an increase in the area of living surfaces was indicated by these structures (Table 4.9). In fact, size ranges were found to vary throughout the habitation sequence. This data

FIGURE 4.24. Wind Mountain locus House V, the site's single Type F community structure. A vertical, interior wall groove is visible in the upper left view. The collared hearth and ventilator are apparent in the middle view (Neg. No. WM 41–30F).

agrees with observations at Galaz Ruin, where size variability over time was great (Anyon and LeBlanc 1984:93).

Orientation of Structures

The overwhelming majority of Wind Mountain structures with entry ramps were oriented in an easterly direction (Appendix 4). Of 61 structures with entries, 52, or 85 percent (seven Type II and 40 Type IV domestic houses; five community structures), faced eastward between 1° and 179°. Only House KK (a Type II structure exhibiting two entry ramps), Houses D, M, Z, AA, OO, and AC (Type IV structures), and a single community structure, House Y (Type C), all at the Wind Mountain locus, were oriented between 180° and 360°.

The prehistoric pit house inhabitants of Wind Mountain positioned their houses for a variety of reasons that crosscut both environmental and cultural considerations. A southeasterly orientation of structures on the ridge top would provide maximum exposure to morning sun during the winter months. Such exposure must have been beneficial to pit house occupants from the standpoint of light and morning warmth. In addition, the location of hearths in line with entries suggests that the purposeful positioning of houses in relation to prevailing wind direction may have been another factor in their orientation.

How the orientation of domestic and community structures related to the beliefs and world view shared by Wind Mountain's inhabitants is a mystery. However, the importance of the rising sun and sun symbolism to historic and contemporary Native American groups in the Southwest (Ortiz 1969:95, 102–107) implies that prehistoric placement of structures facing east was not simply practical, but may also have had religious significance. The importance of watching the sunrise or eastern horizon in the context of ceremonies at Hopi was reported by Alexander Stephen (1969:39). Both sun and cardinal directional symbolism are known key elements in the way in which sedentary agriculturalists order their universe as expressed, for example, in the schedule of their ritual calendar or the placement of

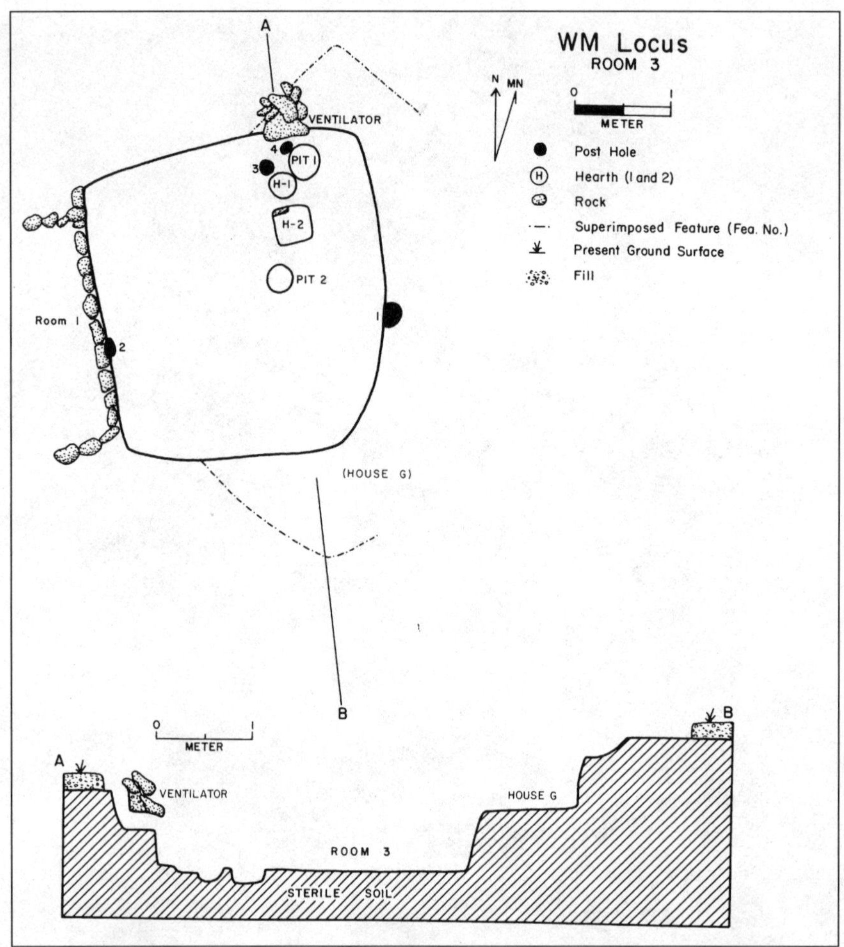

FIGURE 4.25. Plan view and profile of Wind Mountain locus Room 3, a Type G community structure. Type G structures were identified as small, rectangular subterranean pit houses or semisubterranean rooms associated with domestic surface architecture.

shrines (Ortiz:1969:20–21; Stephen 1969:1190; Dozier 1970:204–209). In this regard, as important as the solstices are to modern Pueblo peoples, and apparently to their prehistoric predecessors, it is of interest that no Wind Mountain structure was aligned to the summer solstice (near 60°). Three Wind Mountain locus structures were, however, aligned in close approximation to the winter solstice (near 117°), including House T (Type II), House UU (Type IV), and House AB (Type B).

Intrasite Variability: Domestic versus Community Structures

The two primary classes of Wind Mountain architecture, domestic and community structures, were previously described by type. In the following discussion, some implications of this architecture to the lifeways of the settlement's occupants are examined.

Principally distinguished by their smaller size, secular domestic structures were thought to represent individual Wind Mountain households. Community structures, in comparison, were related to the religious and secular life of the community as a whole—their large size indicative of communal rather than domestic household needs (refer to Appendix 5: Table 3 for typological definition).

Community house status was assigned to 13 structures. Nine of these (Types A-E) were significantly larger (range 27.95 to 70.50 m^2) than their domestic counterparts: San Francisco phase Ridout locus House F and Wind Mountain locus House O (both Type A); San Francisco phase Wind Mountain locus Houses AB (Type B) and AK (Type D); two Three Circle phase Wind Mountain locus Houses, XX (Type C) and X (Type B); Mimbres phase Room 7 (Type E); temporally less secure (San Francisco phase or Three Circle phase) Wind Mountain locus House U and House Y (both Type C). The remaining four structures (Types F and G) were desig-

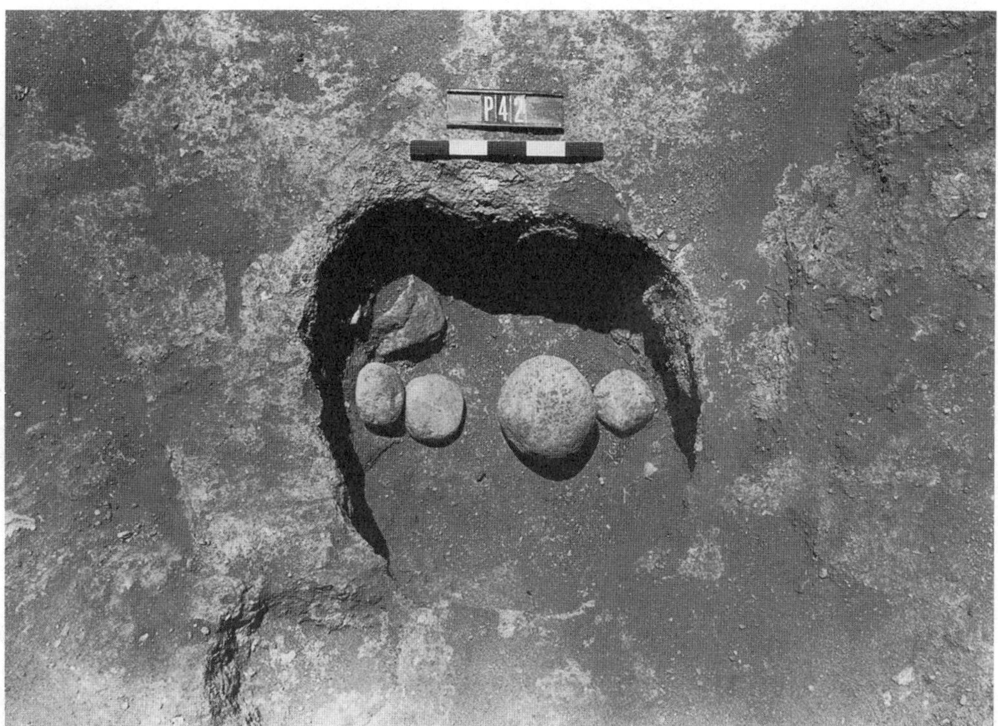

FIGURE 4.26. Pit 42, a secondary architectural feature at the Wind Mountain locus, in which ground stone tools were cached (WM 1945, WM 1946, WM 1947, WM 1948; Neg. No. WM 71–2F).

FIGURE 4.27. Pit 54, uncovered at the Wind Mountain locus, contained the sherds of four Mimbres Classic Black-on-white bowls (WM 2443, WM 2444, WM 2445, and WM 2446) and fragments of an unnumbered Mimbres Corrugated jar (Neg. No. WM 75–17F).

FIGURE 4.28. The stone pipe cache discovered in Pit 56 at the Wind Mountain locus (WM 2277, WM 2278, WM 2279; Neg. No. WM 76–4F).

FIGURE 4.29. Pit Oven 12, cleared at the Wind Mountain locus, represents a secondary architectural feature characterized by thermally altered rock and burned soil (Neg. No. WM 79–3F).

TABLE 4.8. Pit Ovens Uncovered in Extramural Contexts

Provenience	Type	Approximate Dimensions (cm)	Depth* (cm)
WM locus			
1	I	110x105	85
2	II	75x75	55
3	I	90x55	90
4	I	60x35	80
5	I	80x75	45
6	I	90x55	55
7	I	75x45	70
8	I	90x80	50
9	I	80+x75	25
10	I	110x80	60
11	I	125x90	30
12	I	55x50	55
13	I	75x40	28
14	I	80x78	40
15	I	100x75	26
16	I	75x71	50
17	I	55+x60	90
18	III	195x185	90
19	I	80x80	140
RO locus			
20	I	70x70	30

*Depth is below present day surface.

TABLE 4.9. Floor Area (m²) of Type IV Pit Houses (n = 21) by Phase

Provenience	San Francisco n = 6	Three Circle n = 11	Mangas n = 4
RO House J	9.53		
WM House AI	17.55		
RO House A	13.48		
RO House C	20.61		
RO House D	18.23		
WM House AO	13.86		
	mean = 15.50 m²		
WM House AM		12.64	
WM House E		8.09	
WM House SS		14.49	
WM House N		20.68	
WM House FF		17.26	
WM House H		14.65	
WM House AA		15.64	
WM House DD		15.23	
WM House AF		18.15	
WM House AG		11.27	
WM House AL		16.97	
		mean = 15.00 m²	
WM House AD			15.06
WM House OO			15.37
WM House M			13.19
WM House D			11.95
			mean = 13.90 m²

Note: Structures are ordered earliest to latest.

nated community houses even though they were small (range 8.96 to 18.24 m^2), their sizes falling into the range of residential pit houses or rooms (less than 30 m^2). Di Peso felt they exhibited specialized elaborations not present in domestic structures. Small community houses, all occurring at the Wind Mountain locus, included: House V (Type F), associated with the Mangas phase; Mangas phase/Mimbres phase House P2 as well as Mimbres phase Rooms 15 (A.D. 1030–1150) and 3 (all Type G). The few associated ceramics together with their stratigraphic positioning suggest the latter two structures were in use after c. A.D. 1000.

Turning first to the large community structures representative of the Pit House period occupations (Types A-D), it seems logical to assume that such specialized architecture was intended to integrate the members of a community. Community religious architecture has also been the subject of much discussion among archaeologists working with the Hohokam (Haury 1976:78–94; Wilcox and Sternberg 1983; Gregory and Nials 1985; Fish and Fish 1991), although there it took different directions that incorporated ballcourts and mounds. In any event, community level architecture was probably a conventional element of most, if not all, prehistoric agrarian settlement organizations. The Wind Mountain settlement, then, falls into a pan-Southwestern architectural tradition that includes the construction of religious/community structures.

Both their large size and limited occurrence are strong indicators of the integrative nature of these structures to the Wind Mountain occupants. The approximate 1 to 8 ratio of large community houses (eight examples) to smaller, presumed secular domestic pit house structures (64 examples) underscores the potential communal function such specialized architecture signified at Wind Mountain during the Pit House period. Many of the Wind Mountain community structures are fairly simple in their architectural elaboration, a characteristic that extends generally to all Mogollon architecture. When compared with Anasazi religious architecture of comparable age, certain features are suggestive of ritual. Wind Mountain locus House X, a Three Circle phase structure, may provide the most persuasive evidence for ceremonial architecture at the settlement. It is not only the largest structure at the site, but it also contains two floor grooves (possibly foot drums), a niche, and a shelf. The House X ma-

FIGURE 4.30. Two secondary architectural features, Work Area 1 and Pavement 2, uncovered at the Wind Mountain locus. Work Area 1 consisted of a hard packed use surface; Pavement 2 was characterized by a layer of cobbles (Neg. No. WM 27–4F).

FIGURE 4.31. Wind Mountain locus House WW, perhaps indicative of experimentation with surface architecture associated with the Mangas phase. Note the abundant floor ceramics (Neg. No. WM 76–32F).

terial assemblage included exotic shell, both *Glycymeris gigantea* and *Oliva spicata,* beads near one floor groove, a stone animal effigy pendant, fragments of bone tubes and stone pipes, sherd counters/disks, and quartz crystals. The fill of the central post hole contained a perforated stone disk and a drill. No ceramic vessels, stone utility artifacts, or storage pits were observed on the house floor.

House X was situated in a relatively central position on the settlement ridge, undisturbed by the construction of other pit house structures. Domestic structures were concentrated to the north and south and, to a somewhat lesser extent, to the east and west (a covarying factor with the configuration of the ridge). The physical separation of House X from other structures gives rise to the idea of the "middle place" among historic Southwestern Pueblo peoples (Ortiz 1969:20–21). In Western Pueblo symbolism, the center or middle of the cosmos is conceptualized with the sipapu, the placement of shrines, and in the arrangement of domestic houses and religious structures or plazas (Ortiz 1972:142). Possibly, the location of House X reflects a similar world view held by the inhabitants of Wind Mountain. In fact, it can be argued that most of Wind Mountain's large community structures are in a central location relative to domestic structures.

In a less speculative vein and in keeping with its temporal association with the Three Circle phase, House X was not impacted by construction activities until Mangas phase Room 14 was built. If, as is proposed, House X was important to the religious life of the community during the Three Circle phase, it probably would not have been encroached upon by other houses. It is likely that a "respectful distance" was preserved. If House X was strongly identified with ritual or sacred use, it may have been associated with prohibitions against intrusions for some time after its abandonment. The huge depression created by House X would, in any event, have rendered its immediate location unsuitable for other construction until some in filling had occurred. In fact, no new building activities were discernable until after the onset of the Mangas phase. Wind Mountain locus House U also exhibits this lack of disturbance. House U was only intruded into at a later date by House V, a Mangas phase structure.

House AK is a unique community structure that also warrants individual mention. Di Peso identified it as a Type D structure based on its large size and atypical construction. House AK is reminiscent of Hohokam structures with four central support posts and screen posts running along its interior walls. Hohokam contact or influence is a possible explanation for its presence at Wind Mountain. The subject of Hohokam interaction with the Mimbres Mogollon inhabitants of Wind Mountain will be addressed subsequently, but it suffices to point out here that House AK, while possibly functioning as a communal structure, may also indicate an active relationship between two regions. Such interaction may have involved the exchange of material objects, ideas, and motivating influences responsible for the construction design of House AK.

In another example of a large structure given the community classification, Room 7 is the only Mimbres phase surface room with a floor area greater than 30 m^2. It displays a complete lack of any distinguishing features—bench, niche, cached material remains—that might be associated with specialized or nondomestic functions. If size is the principal attribute determining community related use, then Room 7 appropriately falls into the community structure class. If, on the other hand, the presence of additional attributes distinguish communal from domestic architecture, the classification of Room 7 as one of Wind Mountain's Mimbres phase community structures is questionable.

Before continuing the discussion with the remaining smaller structures, it is worthwhile to consider the term *community structure* as it is applied to Mogollon architecture. The community appellation immediately removes these large structures from the realm of a family domestic house and suggests their communal use. Lip service is paid to both a ritual *and* secular function; in reality, however, the ceremonial aspect of these structures is consistently emphasized. This tendency is clearly shown by using labels such as "ceremonial structures" (Wheat 1955) or by borrowing the kiva and great kiva taxonomy of Anasazi, that is, Northern Pueblo, ceremonial architecture (Lightfoot and Feinman 1982; LeBlanc 1983:66–71; Haury 1985:175–179, 186–188). Others have suggested that Anasazi terminology is inappropriate for Mogollon architecture (Anyon and LeBlanc 1984:115; Lekson 1990:75), a view that can be extended to Wind Mountain.

The concept of the kiva traditionally defines religious structures via a strict set of features (e.g., sipapu, bench, niche, and pilaster, among others). Individual kivas, such as those in the Rio Grande cultural milieu versus others in the San Juan sphere, do not necessarily have to contain all these definitive kiva attributes, but they usually contain a majority of them (for an in-depth discussion see Smith 1990:59–75). In fact, these features constitute the diagnostic constants of Anasazi ceremonial architecture—constants that should not be extended gratuitously to the Mimbres Mogollon. No such codified set of architectural expressions existed at Wind Mountain.

With the possible exception of their large size, Wind Mountain community structures were not standardized and displayed no universal, definitive features. Only two community structures exhibited wall niches (one each in Houses U and X) and none contained benches or sipapus. Incidentally, Wind Mountain locus House Z (a domestic Type IV) also contained a corner niche. These were the only niches observed in Wind Mountain structures. As noted, House X with its floor grooves is the sole example of a structure with specialized "ritual" architectural elaborations. The notion of an explicitly defined ceremonial architecture consisting of an identifiable set of repeated features (presumably indicative of a conceptualized world view) is not apparent at Wind Mountain specifically or for the Mimbres Mogollon in general. The term *community structure* eliminates inappropriate cultural comparisons or symbolism raised by *kiva* and emphasizes the more desirable communal, encompassing both secular and religious, functions of these structures.

In addition to the eight large pit house structures and one large surface room discussed above, four small structures (Houses P2 and V, Rooms 3 and 15) were designated as community structures (Types F-G). Although comparable in size to many domestic houses and rooms, Di Peso felt that they exhibited specialized features exclusive of domestic structures. For example, all four contained ventilator shafts. Access to House V, an extremely deep pit house structure, and House P2 was probably achieved through a roof entry. Rooms 3 and 15 were semisubterranean in relation to nearby surface rooms. Depth, roof entry, and the presence of ventilators were, therefore, believed to represent specialized attributes not found in domestic structures but illustrative of ceremonial architecture. Perhaps, these rarely occurring (in relation to the Wind Mountain architectural milieu as a whole) attributes do signify a nondomestic function. Their small size, however, argues against defining them as community structures. Size alone may suggest domestic or household rather than communal use.

Though the term kiva has been assigned to other small Mogollon ceremonial structures (Anyon and LeBlanc 1980:266–268), the absence of standardized kiva features argues against its parallel application in Mogollon ritual architecture. Indeed, kiva terminology is entirely unsuited to describing any Wind Mountain structure. In answer to Wat Smith's (1990) earlier query—"When is a kiva not a kiva?"—one response must be, when it is a Mimbres Mogollon structure (or we could just call it a duck . . . Why a duck? see Lekson 1990:92).

If these small structures did, in fact, function in a nonresidential capacity at the settlement then two forms of specialized, ritual architecture existed at Wind Mountain. One category is represented by large community structures (primarily associated with the Late Pit House period), with a presumed function emphasizing various communally oriented activities. The second category, in contrast, characterized by smaller structures (primarily associated with the Mangas phase and secondarily with the Late Pit House period), may have consisted of sacred and secular activities involving a limited number of individuals. Evidence consisting of small floor areas, ventilator features, and possible roof access is, unfortunately, too sparse to reach a definitive conclusion. Alternatively, some might contend that the occurrence of ventilators in these temporally late structures suggests a Northern Pueblo influence on Mogollon architecture (Haury 1986:451–456). As noted above, the manner in which kiva is defined within the Anasazi domain does not correlate easily with architectural organization at Wind Mountain. Though kivas and domestic rooms are set apart structurally in many Anasazi contexts, at Wind Mountain such obvious differentiation is generally not possible.

Architectural Development and Donor-Recipient Contact

Di Peso viewed the architectural developments at Wind Mountain as part of the larger phenomenon of donor-recipient contact within the Gran Chichimeca. He believed that with the beginning of the A.D. era, the northern frontier, populated with recipient cultures, became sporadically but consistently shaped by foreign Mesoamerican forces, or donor cultures, taking the form of long distance traders. Di Peso identified the first milestone in this time of Mesoamerican and Mogollon Chichimec contact at the end of the Early Pit House period (his Early Classic Sporadic Contacts stage, c. A.D. 200–600), the end of which coincided with the appearance of Wind Mountain Type IV domestic structures. He associated Type B and C community houses with Type IV residences at Wind Mountain and drew parallels between the former and Convento phase structures in Chihuahua (Di Peso et al. 1974:4:144–145) and felt the latter were analogous to the Type P3 structures found at Snaketown (Haury 1976:68; Di Peso Wind Mountain files, Amerind Foundation).

Di Peso (1974:84–85, 90–91) theorized that gabled roofs were characteristic of rectangular Type IV houses (a roof construction that may or may not have occurred at the site), and illustrated it as one example of an array of southern traits that came northward into the Mogollon homeland via western Mexico, particularly from the Loma San Gabriel and Huatabampo areas. Interestingly, Bullard (1962:133), too, suggested that the gabled roof came first to the Hohokam, and from there to the Mogollon, arising out of southern sources as part of a wave of other imports. Di Peso (1977, 1979a, 1979b) proposed that some of these imports included hybrid corn varieties adapted to higher elevations, painted pottery (possibly out of Colima and Zacatecas) as well as closed trough metates (perhaps from Chametla in Sinaloa). These intrusive elements were incorporated into the local Mogollon Chichimec culture pattern as by-products of the first exploratory ventures into the north by southern merchants seeking minerals and other trade commodities. Besides this southern intervention, Di Peso also recognized the possibility of contact between the Hohokam and Mogollon Chichimecs, citing a Hohokam style house

(House AK at Wind Mountain locus) as evidence of such interaction.

Di Peso's second suggested milestone of southern influences over the indigenous Mogollon Chichimecs occurred during the transition from the Late Classic Intrusion period, c. A.D. 900, to the incipient Early post-Classic Sporadic period, c. A.D. 950–1050 (Di Peso 1979c:58–71). This later interval corresponds with the emergence of surface architecture (i.e., Type V structures at Wind Mountain) in the Upper Gila. Di Peso described the internal Wind Mountain site arrangement at this time as domestic surface house clusters with associated community houses oriented around plazas. He found similarities at other Upper Gila sites, particularly the room blocks reported for the Luna Valley (Hough 1907). This conjectured formalized community organization, as compared to the dispersed, random placement of pit houses characterizing the Late Pit House period Wind Mountain occupation, was related to similar developments seen at the Perros Bravos Village of the Convento site (Di Peso 1974: 190–193). Indeed, Di Peso saw strong connections between Casas Grandes merchant traders and the mineral rich regions of the Gran Chichimeca in which Wind Mountain figured as a prominent Casas Grandes procurement or gleaning satellite. The origins of a Wind Mountain surface village is suggested as the direct result of southern intervention by economically motivated Casas Grandes merchants and their greatly expanded mining activities. Turquoise, hematite, and other exploitable minerals were the object of these incursions. Di Peso identifies alterations in architectural form and configuration as clues to the Casas Grandes-Wind Mountain connection, and also cites the appearance of a new ceramic trade complex, a surge in trade commodities (e.g., ricolite, turquoise, shell), and the presence of southern ritual imports (e.g., the scarlet macaw and figurine cult).

Part 2
Architectural Units of the Wind Mountain Site

Descriptions and Primary Internal Stratigraphy

As previously stated, excavation of the Wind Mountain site brought to light 99 prehistoric structures. The remains of 70 Mimbres Mogollon pit houses (recorded as Houses A-Z, AA-ZZ, and AB-AQ), two remnant pit house entries (recorded as entrances E and W), as well as 16 surface or semisubterranean units (recorded as Rooms 1–16) relating to a small Mangas phase/Mimbres phase occupation were explored within the boundaries of the Wind Mountain locus. This brought the number of whole or partial structures uncovered at the Wind Mountain locus to 88. Another 11 pit structures (recorded as Houses A-K) were excavated at the Ridout locus.

For the most part, descriptions of Wind Mountain architecture derive from the Amerind Mimbres Project field form developed by Amerind Foundation staff. To promote uniformity of data recording, the form outlined those specifics an excavator was required to define and measure. In brief, the project form requested provenience; photo number; excavation date; excavator; stratigraphy; house form; dimension; depth; as well as wall, floor, and entry construction, along with any other associated features. Plan view and profile illustrations were also expected for each structure.

The content of the following discussion draws heavily on this recorded information. Field notes recorded primarily by Bruce Harrill and augmented by Carlos Caraveo, Charles Di Peso, and Arny Withers provided useful comments about complex stratigraphic situations and architecture. In absence of the written word, field photos supplied information otherwise lacking (e.g., the specifics of floor surfaces or wall construction). In several instances, neglected architectural details were identified and interpreted by photo analysis.

Organization of Data

Architectural data is organized around six basic categories: (1) illustrations, (2) structure definition and dimensions, (3) contextual placement, (4) internal stratigraphy, (5) house features and dimensions, and (6) general comments.

Individual structure types are based on Di Peso's architecture typology (refer to Part 1 in this chapter; Appendix 5). House types remain essentially as Di Peso defined them. The only modification to Di Peso's typological scheme was the reclassification of two Type IV houses (Houses CC and YY) as Type VI, that is, indeterminate structures.

Structural dimensions of houses and rooms (length and width) were determined in the field and tend to reflect measurements taken through the midpoint of each structure. The area of living surfaces (m^2) was determined by the authors using a digital planimeter and field generated floor plans. Because one aspect of Di Peso's typological definition relied on floor area as a diagnostic indicator (e.g., to separate domestic from communal houses), it was felt that a planimeter would provide the most accurate measurement of floor areas.

The orientation of structure entries (House Types II and IV, Community Structures B, C, and D) was calculated by determining a midpoint axis line through the center of a house entry and orienting this line to a compass azimuth point coordinated to true north. In several cases, either due to archaeological disturbances, compass discrepancies, or individual error, house illustrations (field plan views) were at variance with the master site map (field plan view). If this discrepancy was in error > 3° on either side of the mean axis line, then the master site map was considered to represent the final word regarding house entry orientation; azimuth

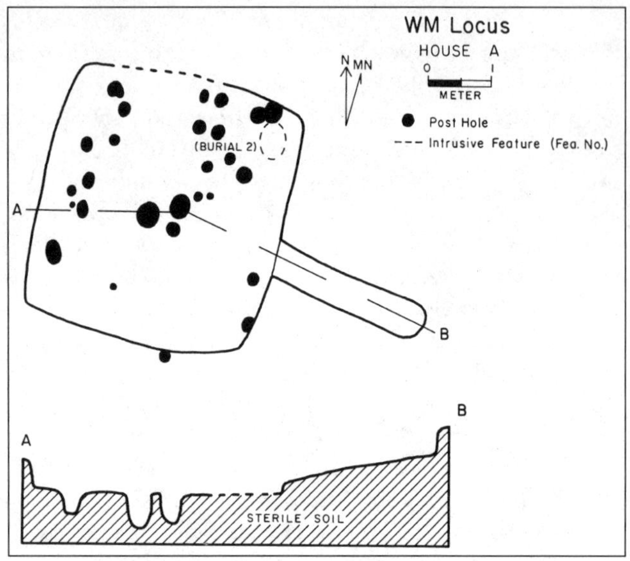

FIGURE 4.32. Plan view and profile of Wind Mountain locus House A, a Type IV structure.

readings were derived from that source (refer to Appendix 4 in this volume).

A clear understanding of the positioning of individual structures was extremely important to the overall interpretation of Wind Mountain architecture and chronology. Contextual placement of primary and secondary architectural features was often difficult on the restricted ridge top. Superpositioning and intrusion by structures, burials, and pits rendered many areas of the site a stratigraphic nightmare. For instance, parts or all of the following features were observed in Block 21, a 10 m x 10 m square, located in the northeast corner of the Wind Mountain locus: Houses S, T, DD, HH, II, JJ, and LL; Burials 26, 27, 28, 29, 42, 59, 61, and 62; Pit Ovens 4, 5, 8, and 9; Pits 8, 36, 40, and 48; and Bird Burial 7.

The internal stratigraphy of individual structures was defined by three stratigraphic events: fill, floor fill, and floor. Delineation of stratigraphic levels was based primarily on observable (visually distinctive) changes in stratigraphy. However, on occasion, stratigraphic levels were determined arbitrarily. Floor fill most commonly comprised the final 10 cm of fill occurring immediately above the floor surface. Not infrequently, however, floor fill extended 15 to 20 cm above floor surfaces. Generally, floor fill was a convenience for later artifact analysis, enabling the relationship between near floor items and in situ floor artifacts to be resolved. House floors (living surfaces) were usually compacted or plastered and easily detected during excavation. In several cases, however, floors extended over or into the loose fill of earlier abandoned structures, thereby losing their structural integrity. Secondary architectural classes, including an inventory of hearth types (Appendix 5 in this volume) and other house features together with their dimensions, are incorporated in the descriptions of individual structures.

Pit Structures of the Wind Mountain Locus

House A (Figure 4.32)

Type IV structure; length 3.70 m, width 3.40 m; area of living surface 12.53 m^2; mean orientation of entry 115°.

House A was superimposed by the construction of Room 2. Burial 2 was intrusive into the house fill, which was badly disturbed by modern pot hunting activities.

Level 1 (range 0–105 cm), was composed of a loose, recently disturbed, homogeneous, gray-brown pebbly soil, intermixed with cultural debris and rock from fallen walls. Level 2 (depth 105 cm), the house floor, consisted of a level, smoothly packed, red sterile soil. Pot hunting activity was extensive as evidenced by the presence of a metal bottle cap on the house floor, as well as the scars of picks and shovels on its surface. The sides of the pit house excavated during prehistoric construction were smooth and vertical but unplastered. Its hearth was apparently destroyed, presumably the result of a pot hunter's pit. The house entry (area 1.15 m^2) was a long (240 cm), narrow (55 cm), stepped incline that allowed access to the house through the midsection of the east wall. House A was probably destroyed by fire. Field notes indicate that the structure may have been completely emptied by pot hunters and was refilled at a later time. If so, Burial 2, which was recovered from the disturbed fill, represents redeposited human remains rather than a primary interment.

House B (B1 and B2) (Figures 4.33 and 4.34)

Type IV structures; House B1, length and width indeterminate; surviving area of living surface .51 m^2; mean orientation of entry 62°. House B2, length 3.60 m, width 3.75 m; area of living surface 13.23 m^2; mean orientation of entry 64°.

House B1 was possibly larger and earlier than House B2. Pit 74 intruded into the entries of both houses.

Level 1 (range 0–70 cm) comprised a dark gray, pebbly silt. Level 2 (range 70–80 cm, floor fill) was composed of a dark brown, pebbly, cultural debris laden silt. The house floor (depth 80 cm) consisted of a smoothed, use compacted, plastered surface excavated into sterile soil. Unplastered house walls used the near vertical sides of the original pit house. Rock, placed no higher than one or two courses and varying in width from 15 to 40 cm, was piled up along the southwest wall, two-thirds of the southeast wall, and one-quarter of the northwest wall. The rock lined northeast wall (north of the entry) was probably associated with House B1. The southern portion of the same wall lacked stone, but numerous rocks found in the immediate area may be the remnants of stone facing. Remodeling of House B1 into B2 was most

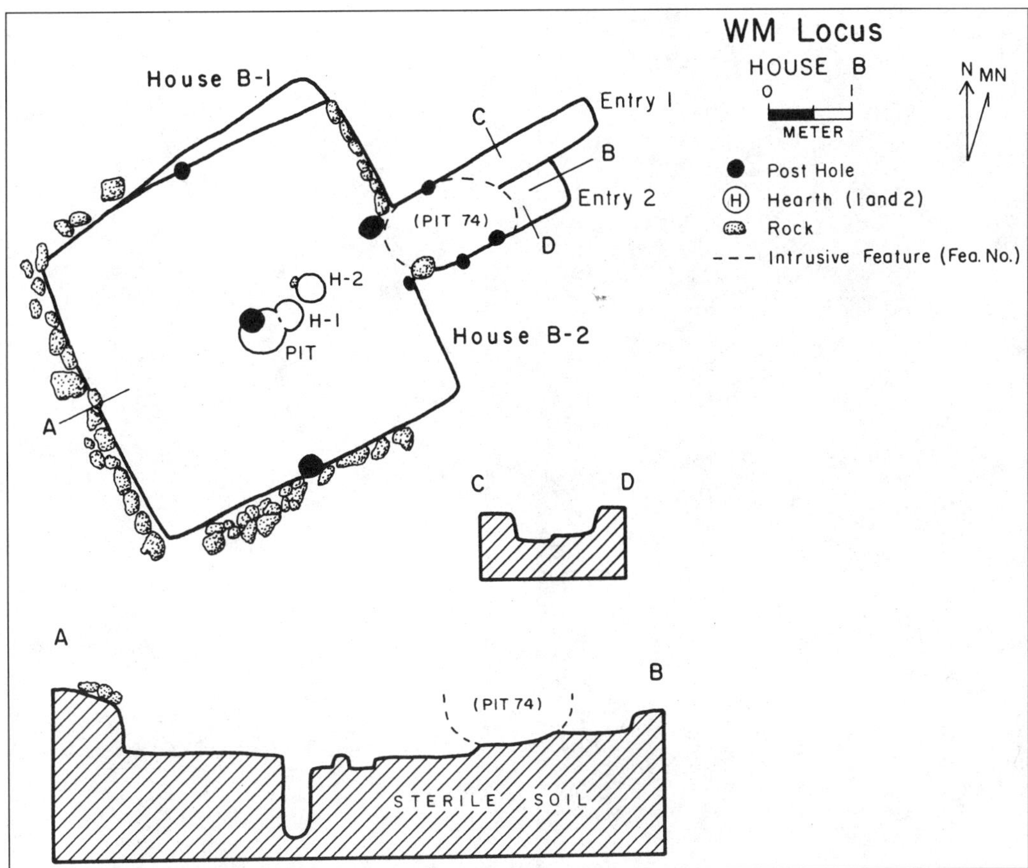

FIGURE 4.33. Plan view and profile of Wind Mountain locus House B, comprised of two superimposed Type IV structures, Houses B1 and B2.

apparent along the northwest wall, where the B1 wall projected out and away from the later B2 wall, and by the presence of two distinct entrances. Two hearths, both slightly to the east of the house center, probably relate to the separate occupation phases of the structure(s). Hearth 1 (Type IIA; diameter 34 cm, depth 17 cm), circular with sloping sides, clay lined (0.5 cm thick) with a concave floor, belonged to House B1. An oval, clay lined floor pit (length 45 cm, width 20 cm, depth 25 cm) was exposed adjacent this hearth. Both Hearth 1 and the floor pit were filled in at some point and sealed over with a 3 cm thick layer of clay. Hearth 2 (Type IIIC1; length 35 cm, width 30 cm, depth 14 cm) described an oval plan with nearly straight sides, lined in small rocks plastered over with a smooth layer of clay and having a flat floor, was associated with House B2. Entry 1 (estimated area 1.00 m^2) was a long (265 cm), narrow (40 cm), and level feature identified with House B1. Entry 2 (estimated area 1.13 m^2) was shorter (210 cm), having an estimated width of 85 cm. Both entries were excavated into sterile soil and allowed access to their respective houses through the northeast wall. As suggested by remnant floor plaster visible in the profile of the central post hole, remodeling occurred during occupation (while the post was still in place). Because House B2 was excavated deeper than the earlier house, the House B1 floor was virtually obliterated. However, a remnant impression of the original House B1 floor was preserved along the northeastern wall, approximately 8 cm above the more deeply dug House B2 floor.

House C (Figure 4.35)

Type IV structure; length 3.75 m, width 3.60 m; area of living surface 12.30 m^2; mean orientation of entry 26°.

No architectural superpositioning was apparent though other disturbances were observed.

Level 1 (range 0–50 cm) comprised a dark gray, gravel laden deposit of undifferentiated loam and sand. Level 2 (range 50–70 cm) was similar, but light gray in color and contained some ash. Level 3 (range 70–90 cm) consisted of a gray-brown, undifferentiated gravelly loam. Level 4 (range 90–100 cm, floor fill) contained a dark gray, pebbly silt with less gravel than the upper levels. The House C floor (depth 100 cm) described a leveled, unplastered, use compacted surface. Walls were badly eroded and difficult to distinguish.

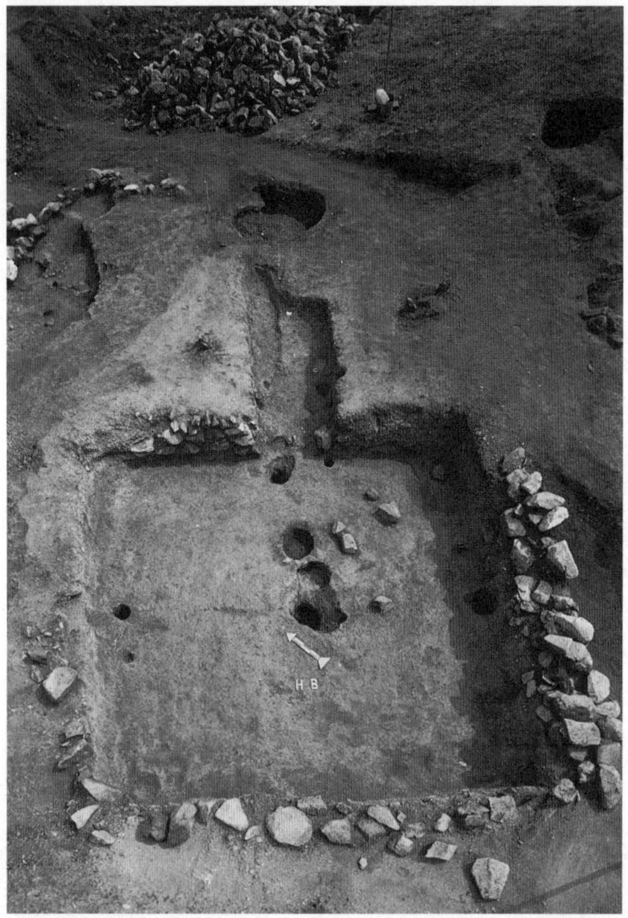

FIGURE 4.34. Wind Mountain locus Houses B1 and B2, two superimposed houses, most clearly visible in the overlapping lateral entries. Compare with Figure 4.33 (Neg. No. WM 14–5F).

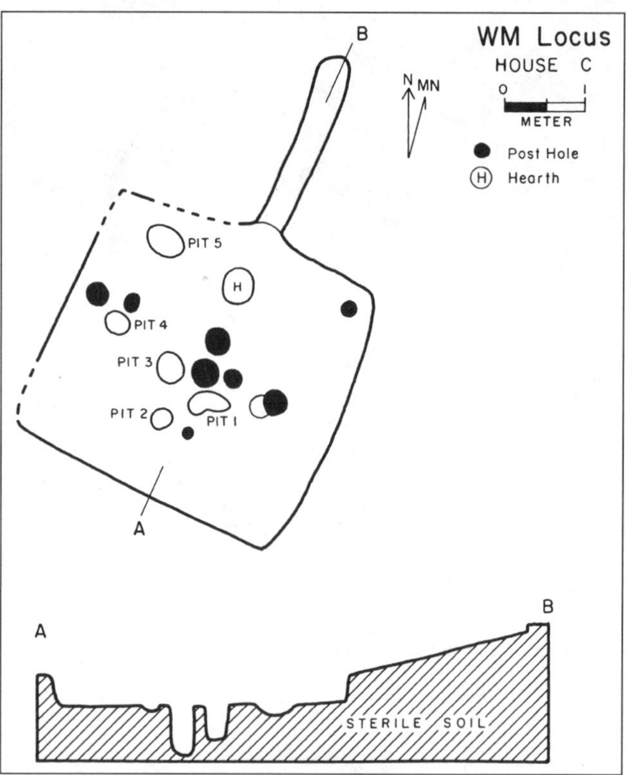

FIGURE 4.35. Plan view and profile of Wind Mountain locus House C, a Type IV structure.

Such extensive wall erosion might suggest that the house was stripped of its superstructure for reuse elsewhere at the site. The unprotected pit house was then exposed to the elements and susceptible to degradation. The hearth (Type IIB; diameter 45 cm, depth 8 cm) was defined as a shallow, ash filled circular depression cut into sterile subsoil. Five pits of varying size and shape were scattered across the midsection of the house. Pit 1 (length 60 cm, width 25 cm, depth 30 cm,), crescent-shaped; Pit 2 (length 24 cm, width 18 cm, depth 15 cm), an oval bowl with sloping sides and a concave floor; Pit 3 (diameter 40 cm, depth 27 cm), a circular depression with sloping sides and a concave floor; Pit 4 (length 35 cm, width 30 cm, depth 20 cm), an oval basin with straight sides and a concave floor; Pit 5 (length 41 cm, width 28 cm, depth 25 cm), an oval feature with straight sides and a concave floor. None of these floor pits were clay lined. Field notes caution that Pit 1 and adjacent features (post holes and other floor pits) may be the product of rodent activity. The entry (area .79 m^2) to House C was characterized as a long (210 cm), narrow (30–45 cm), stepped incline (12°) that joined to the structure at the midpoint of the north wall. The entry was excavated into sterile soil.

House D (refer to Figures 4.9 and 4.10)

Type IV structure; length 3.90 m, width 3.15 m; area of living surface 11.95 m^2; mean orientation of entry 346°.

Bird Burial 1, interred sometime after its abandonment, was the only intrusion observed in House D.

Level 1 (range 0–70 cm) consisted of a uniformly gray, compacted, gravelly, silty sand. Level 2 (range 70–90 cm) comprised a gray-brown fill similar to Level 1. Level 3 (range 90–110, floor fill) differed from Levels 1 and 2 only by the presence of charcoal fragments. Both the floor fill and the house floor surface were littered with the burned clay impressions of building materials derived from house walls, the roof, or both. This material contained the casts of reed segments, agave stalks, and yucca leaves. The house floor (depth 110 cm) described a leveled, use compacted, sterile soil. The floor surface had been fire blackened in several areas, presumably the result of burning structural debris. One C^{14} sample (GX-5486), collected from the floor fill, was analyzed (Chapter 3). House walls were vertical to slightly sloping, smoothed and unplastered with squared corners. The south wall exhibited an exaggerated inward incline from floor to wall. The hearth (Type IIB; length 28 cm, width 24 cm, depth 11 cm) was described as a small circular to slightly oval pit with an irregular base and straight sides. Pit 1, located within the western half of the house, delineated a circular depression (diameter 30 cm, depth 15 cm) with sloping sides and a concave floor. The long (270 cm) and narrow (50 cm) house entry (area 1.36 m^2) with a stepped incline (6°) joined the house near the midpoint of the north wall. Entry sides were vertical, verging onto a slightly rounded (concave) floor. Sections of burned beams, burned wall plaster, and charcoal indicate the house burned.

House E (Figures 4.36 and 4.37)

Type IV structure; length 3.10 m, width 2.60 m; area of living surface 8.09 m^2; mean orientation of entry 128°.

House E was superimposed by the construction of Room 10 and was intrusive into earlier Houses N and O.

Level 1 (range 0–40 cm) was partially comprised of the fill from overlying Room 10, which cut into the deposit by about 30 cm. This fill was composed of a dark gray, trash laden, pebbly silt intermixed with rock from wall fall. Level 2 (range 40–95 cm) differed from Level 1 by the relatively abundant addition of stone. This rock material either derived from wall fall or from in filling and leveling activities associated with the construction of Room 10. The soil matrix of Level 2 was similar in composition to Level 1. Level 3 (range 95–105 cm, floor fill) lacked the stone fill of upper levels, although its composition was otherwise comparable. Two C^{14} samples, GX-5484 (charred thatch, possible roofing material) and GX-5485, were recovered from Level 3 (Chapter 3). The floor (depth 105 cm) consisted of a leveled, use compacted, unplastered surface, which became fire hardened when House E burned. House walls were smooth, vertical and unplastered. The loose fill of Houses N and O, both underlying the southern corner of House E, left the walls in this portion of the structure ill-defined and badly preserved. The hearth (Type IIA; diameter 20 cm, depth 8 cm) was defined as a small, circular, clay lined basin that still contained ash. One archaeomagnetic sample (No. 003) was removed from the hearth (Chapter 3). A circular, unlined, basin-shaped floor pit (diameter 30 cm, depth 10 cm) occurred south of the hearth. The entry (width 50 cm), positioned along the east side of the house, consisted of a plastered ramp incline (4°) constructed within the loose fill of Houses N and O (surviving area .30 m^2). Beyond approximately 40 cm, the entry proved impossible to discern, losing its structural integrity in the disturbed soil of underlying features. A groove (length 40 cm, width 10 cm), observed in the floor at the juncture of entry shaft and house, may have held a log step since rotted away. Side entry walls were indistinguishable from the surrounding soils.

House F (Figure 4.38)

Type VI structure; length 3.80+ m, width 3.20 m; area of living surface 9.85 m^2.

House F was impacted by floor Pits 1 and 2, as well as occupation and postoccupational activities.

Level 1 (range 0–80 cm) was described as a dark gray, pebbly silt, containing a few lenses of sterile, red-brown, pebbly silt. Level 2 (range 80–90 cm, floor fill) was comparable. The floor (depth 90 cm) was leveled, moderately compacted by use, and unplastered. House F walls were vertical and smooth but otherwise nonelaborated. The eastern wall represented the only surviving intact wall surface. Due to erosion, northwestern, southwestern, and western walls were almost completely absent. Only a remnant 5 cm high ridge along the west side of the house delineated an original wall. Two pits were exposed on the house floor. Pit 1 (length 155 cm, width 115 cm, depth 55 cm) described an irregular oval pit with vertical sides and a flat floor. Extensive rodent activity was apparent. Pit 2 (length 100 cm, width 75 cm, depth 10 cm) defined a shallow, nearly oval depression with vertical sides and a flat floor. The fill of both pits contained abundant cultural and faunal debris. The House F entry did not survive, though it was probably a lateral side access. Prehistoric construction and modern vandalism greatly impacted House F, obliterating its hearth, central post hole, and any other feature originally associated with the structure.

House G (Figure 4.39)

Type IV structure; length 4.20 m, width 4.00 m; estimated area of living surface 15.78 m^2; mean orientation of entry 39°.

House G was superimposed on Pit 3, and was intruded into by Room 3 construction, Burial 8, and Pit 4.

Level 1 (range 0–60 cm) was composed of a dark gray, pebbly silt overlying what appeared to be eroded sterile wall material of a red-orange, pebbly silt (varying in thickness from 1 to 20 cm), that included burned wall plaster. Level 2 (range 60–70 cm, floor fill) consisted of a dark gray silt, less pebbly than Level 1, intermixed with burned plaster and site refuse. The house floor (depth 70 cm) was characterized as a leveled, use compacted sterile soil. A few areas of burned floor plaster (about 1 mm thick) were observed. House walls were near vertical, excavated into sterile soil. Remnant patches of a single layer of plaster were observed on all but the south house wall. Rock reinforcement was apparent along the east corner of the house, where it intruded into Pit 3. The hearth (Type IB2; length 65 cm, width 45 cm, depth from 10 to 16 cm), located near the house entrance, consisted of an irregularly shaped depression. A mano hearthstone was plastered into and defined the hearth's north rim. The southern edge of the hearth was enhanced by a deeper bowl-shaped pit (diameter 18 cm, depth 16 cm) whose interior walls were burned

FIGURE 4.36. Plan view and profile of Wind Mountain locus House E, a Type IV structure.

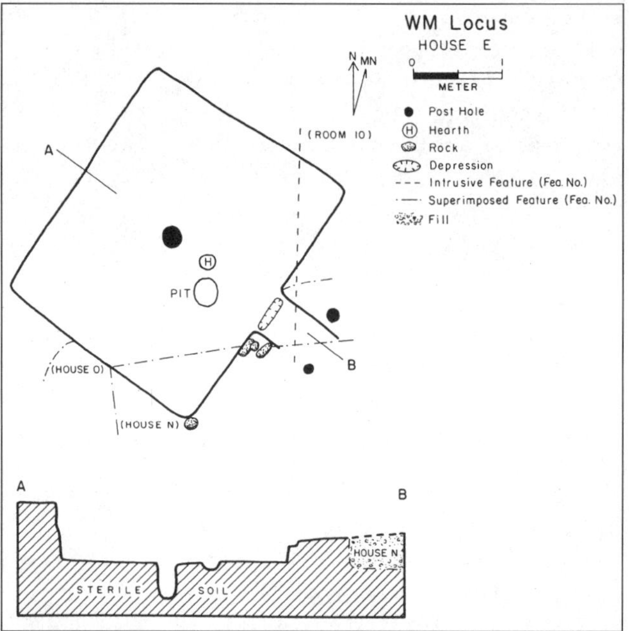

FIGURE 4.37. Wind Mountain locus House E in the middle view and its relation to superimposed Room 10. Room 7 is visible in the upper left (Neg. No. WM 33–22F).

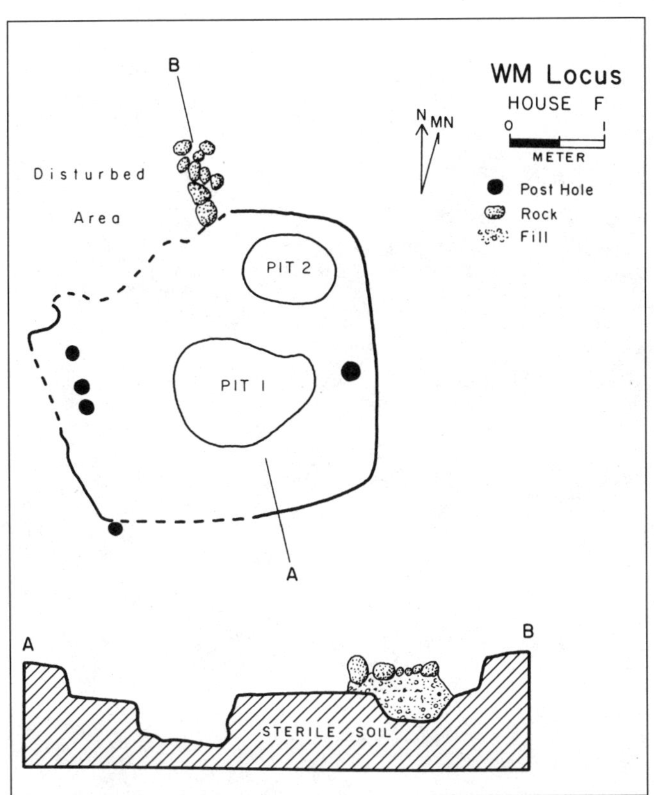

FIGURE 4.38. Plan view and profile of Wind Mountain locus House F, a Type IV structure.

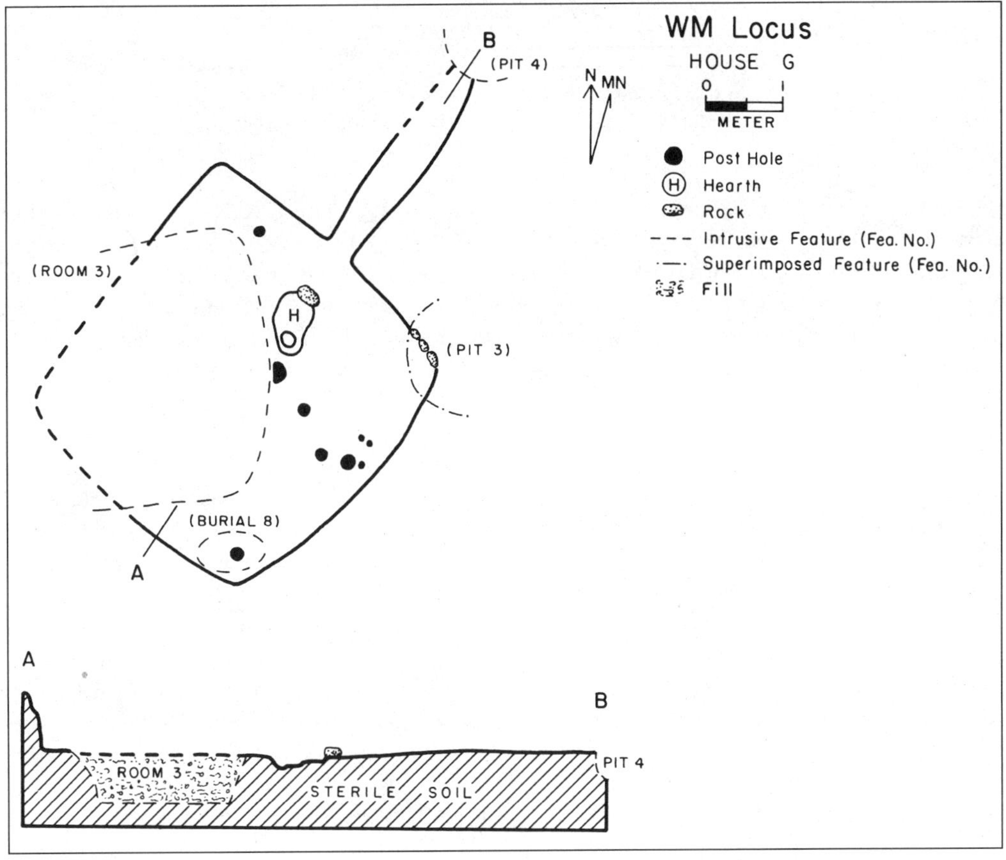

FIGURE 4.39. Plan view and profile of Wind Mountain locus House G, a Type IV structure.

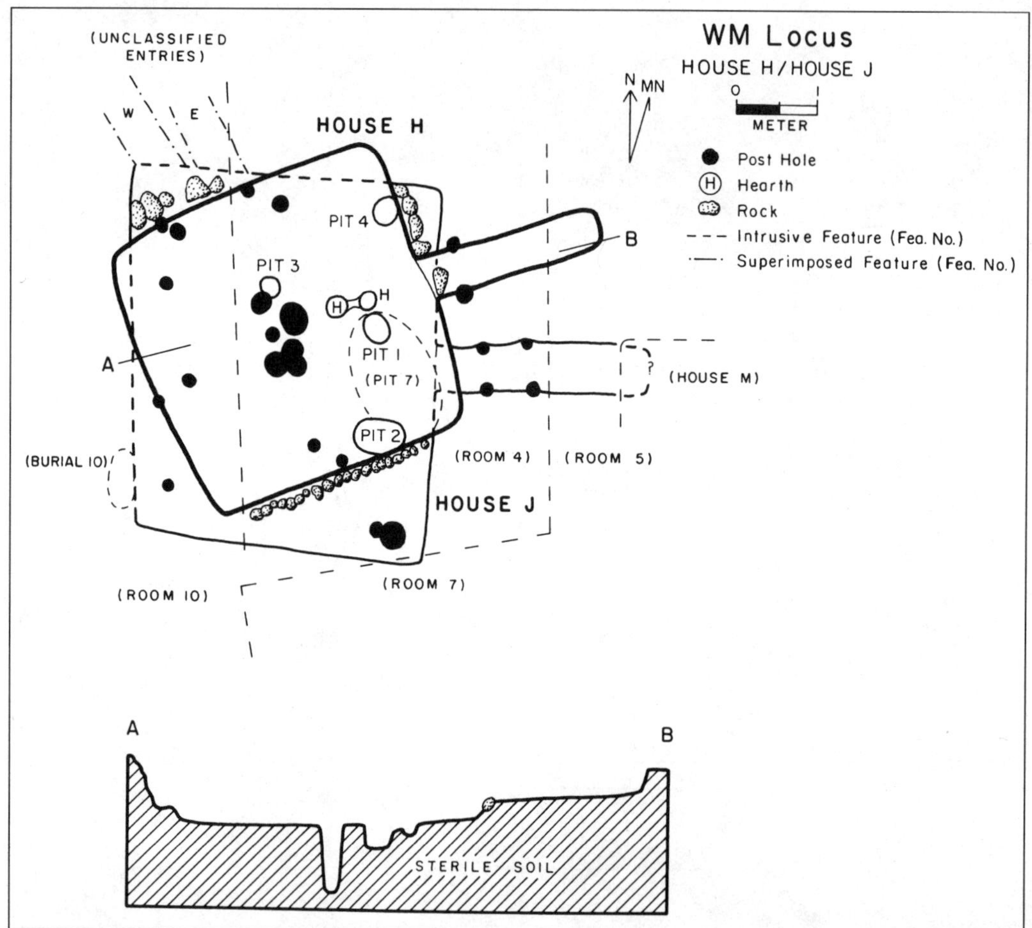

FIGURE 4.40. Plan views and profile of Wind Mountain locus Houses H and J, both Type IV structures. The House H vicinity is an example of the complex cultural stratigraphy found at the site.

and contained a white ash. The unplastered house entry (surviving area 1.30 m²), excavated into sterile soil, described a narrow (range 35–55 cm), almost level shaft that permitted access to the house through the midpoint of the northeast wall. Pit 4 intruded into and terminated the northern end of the entry.

House H (Figure 4.40)

Type IV structure; length 3.95 m², width 3.90 m²; area of living surface 14.65 m²; mean orientation of entry 75°.

House H intruded into House J and was superpositioned by Rooms 4, 5, and 10. Pit 7 cut into the fill.

Level 1 (range 0–85 cm), intruded by the later construction of Room 4, consisted of fill characterized as a homogeneous, dark brown pebbly soil with some rock wall fall. Level 2 (range 85–140 cm) defined primarily a dark gray, pebbly silt intermixed with occupation debris. A slight color change (lighter gray) was noted at about the 115–120 cm level. Level 3 (range 140–150 cm, floor fill) comprised a light gray, pebbly silt. One C^{14} sample (GX-5482) was analyzed from the floor (Chapter 3). The floor (depth 150 cm) represented a leveled, use compacted surface displaying patches of burned plaster. In places, burned plaster extended down the wall and across the floor. For the most part, however, floor plaster was only irregularly preserved. House H was intrusive into and positioned slightly off center from earlier House J. House H had been built over House J with construction extending into sterile soil. House H walls were vertical to slightly sloping. Rock reinforcement had been added along the south, east, and north walls, where it cut through the loose fill of House J. Wall plastering was observed on all four walls, ranging in height (measured from the floor) from 30 cm on the west wall to 5 cm on the east wall. Generally, wall plaster did not survive (or was not applied) on those areas above the rock retaining wall. Two circular, clay lined hearths filled with ash and connected by a narrow channel some 12 cm wide and 8 cm deep were exposed. Both hearths exhibited straight to slightly sloping walls with concave floors. The dimensions of Hearth 1 (Type IIA3) measured 26 cm in diameter and 18

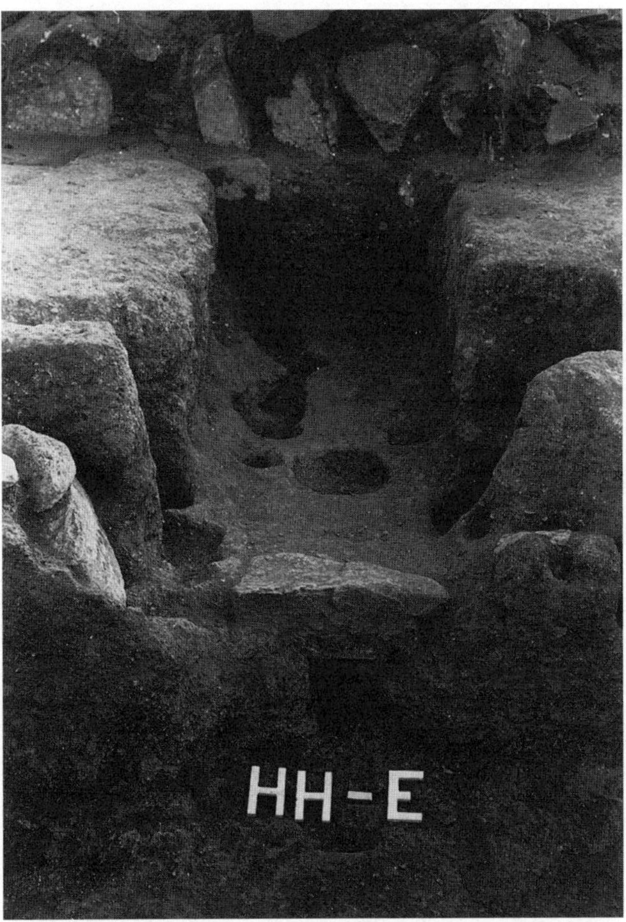

FIGURE 4.41. A stone step discovered in the entry ramp of House H (Neg. No. WM 26–29F).

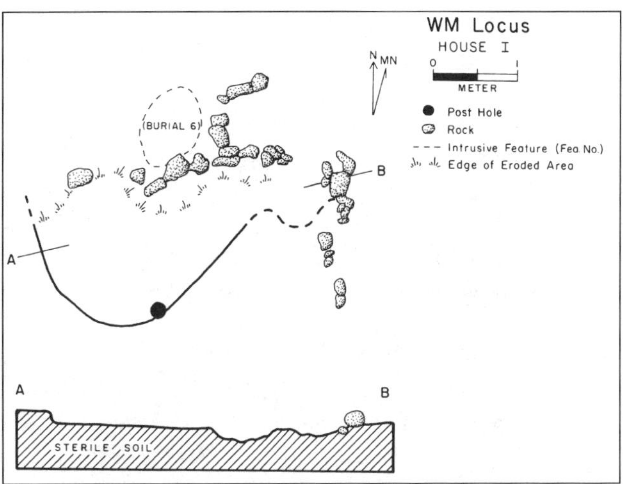

FIGURE 4.42. The remnant of Wind Mountain locus House I, classified as a Type VI structure due to its poor state of preservation.

cm deep and Hearth 2 (Type IIA3) measured 33 cm long, 26 cm wide, and 31 cm deep. One archaeomagnetic sample (No. 004) was taken from the rim of Hearth 2 (Chapter 3). Four floor pits were located. Pit 1 (length 44 cm, width 39 cm, depth 27 cm) and Pit 2 (length 66 cm, width 42 cm, depth 21 cm) were oval-shaped depressions with straight sides and concave floors. Pit 3 (diameter 30 cm, depth 14 cm) and Pit 4 (diameter 35 cm, depth 30 cm) displayed circular plans with vertical sides and flat floors. The House H entry (area 1.28 m^2), excavated into sterile soil, disclosed a long (235 cm) and narrow (55 cm) stepped incline (2°) that joined the house at the midpoint of the east wall. A rock step was placed near the union of entry ramp and house (Figure 4.41). Two post holes flanking either side of the entry were partially set into its walls. Field notes comment that Houses H and J may have superimposed and disturbed two earlier, poorly preserved houses represented only as fragmentary entries. These remnant entries are designated as "unclassified entries" "W" and "E." Entry W (width 47 cm), slightly inclined (1°) and terminated by the construction of House G, occurred about 28 cm above the floor of House J. Entry E (width 50 cm), primarily intruded into by Pit 3, was situated about 31 cm above the floor of House J. In profile both entries displayed concave floors excavated into sterile soil.

House I (Figure 4.42)

Type VI structure; length 2.50 m, width 1.75 m; remaining area of living surface 3.54 m^2.

House I was extensively disturbed as downslope erosion slowly destroyed the northern portion of the structure. Burial 6 intruded into its floor surface.

Level 1 (range 0–15 cm) consisted of a dark gray, trash laden, pebbly silt. Level 2 (range 15–30 cm, floor fill) compared with Level 1. The unplastered house floor (depth 30 cm) was represented by a smooth, level surface excavated into sterile soil. House walls were barely discernable, extending upward a mere 30 cm along the east wall, and found to be completely absent along the north and west sides. No trace of a hearth or entrance survived.

House J (refer to Figure 4.40)

Type IV structure; length 4.90 m, width 4.08 m; estimated area of living surface 19.36 m^2; mean orientation of entry 92°.

House J, intruded by the later construction of Houses H and M, was superimposed by Rooms 4, 5, and 10. Burial 10 was uncovered along the exterior of House J's western edge.

Level 1 (range 0–85 cm) contained the fill of Rooms 4, 5, and 10 and was characterized as a homogeneous, dark brown, pebbly silt intermixed with rock wall fall. Level 2 (range 85–115 cm) consisted of a dark gray, pebbly silt mixed with site debris. Level 3 (range 115–125 cm, floor fill) compared with Level 2. Preserved remnants of the unplastered floor surface (depth 125 cm) indicated it was level, smooth, and excavated into sterile soil. One C^{14} sample (GX-5483) removed from a beam or support post was analyzed (Chapter 3). Intact, but ill-defined, walls were vertical and unplastered. Many of the post holes are confused as to their original association (whether belonging to House J or House H). The unplastered House J entry (estimated area 1.51 m^2, width 60 cm), excavated into sterile soil, was located near the midpoint of the east wall. Two pairs of post holes partially inset into the north and south walls of the entry probably represent the remains of a roof support. The eastern extreme of the entry ramp was terminated by the later construction of House M. No hearth was observed, doubtlessly due to the subsequent construction of House H. Stone visible in the northeast and northwest corners of House J fill defines wall reinforcement associated with House H.

House K (Figure 4.43)

Type IV structure; length 4.35 m, width 3.95 m; area of living surface 15.36 m^2; mean orientation of entry 111°.

House K was partly overlain by Pavement 2. Two burials were placed in the house fill following its abandonment. Burial 20 intruded into its entry, and Burial 11 extended into the northeast corner of the structure.

Level 1 (range 0–60 cm) described a uniformly dark gray, pebbly silt intermixed with rock and occupation debris. Level 2 (range 60–70 cm, floor fill) was analogous to Level 1. The house floor (depth 70 cm) consisted of a level, smooth surface that showed evidence of burning. Burned floor plaster (2–4 mm thick) lay in patches across the surface. The structure's northeast corner was partially built over a dense deposit of refuse and the remaining portion over sterile soil. House walls were smooth and vertical. Two upright stones, secured by mortar (located along the southeast wall, north of the entry), represented the only section of wall to survive in those areas constructed over fill. The south wall was plastered (1–5 mm thick), reaching a height (measured from the floor) of 85 cm. The hearth (Type IIB1; diameter 23 cm, depth 10 cm), a circular, unlined, basin-shaped pit, contained a gray ash. Two stones were set into the hearth, one on its eastern and the other on its western edge. A third stone was placed in the hearth fill, and a fourth was located about 10 cm to the northwest. These stones may have served as pot rests to raise cooking vessels above hot coals. Two floor pits, Pit 1 (diameter 50 cm, depth 45 cm) near the southwest corner and Pit 2 (diameter 33 cm, depth 22 cm) near the north wall, were noted. Both pits defined circular, straight sided depressions with flat floors. The House K entry (length 230 cm, width 55 cm) displayed an irregularly leveled, clay plastered floor surface (area 1.26 m^2); no evidence of walls remained.

House L (Figure 4.44)

Type IV structure; length 4.10 m, width 3.35 m; area of living surface 12.83 m^2; mean orientation of entry 87°.

House L was intruded into by Work Area 1.

Level 1 fill (range 0–80 cm) was deeply intruded by the construction of Work Area 1. Level 2 (range 80–95 cm), a pebbly, trash laden gray silt, included a portion of Work Area 1 intermixed with house fill material. Level 3 (range 95–140 cm) was similar to Levels 1 and 2, but appeared to be less disturbed. Level 4 (range 140–150 cm, floor fill) compared with the upper levels. The unplastered house floor (depth 150 cm) consisted of a leveled, use compacted surface. The western two-thirds of the house was constructed over sterile soil; the eastern third was laid over compacted fill. Level 5 (range 150–175 cm, subfloor) analogous in composition to Level 4, exhibited a compacted fill under the eastern one-third of the house, most likely the result of floor leveling prior to construction. The eastern one-third of the house may have been built over a gully, thus accounting for the use of fill in that area. Where the walls of the house cut into sterile soil, they appeared smooth and unplastered. In places where house walls were excavated into fill, they were reinforced with upright stone slabs set with adobe mortar (Figure 4.45). The hearth (Type IIB1; diameter 40 cm, depth 10 cm) was a circular, unlined, ash filled basin. A mano hearthstone was plastered into its eastern edge. An ash pit (diameter 22 cm, depth 14 cm), probably also serving as a hearth as indicated by the fire altered soil lining its interior, occurred northwest of the primary hearth. It was defined by a circular plan, had vertical sides with a concave floor, and contained a gray-white ash. A small Alma Plain storage jar (WM 481) had been plastered into the house floor with its rim extending a slight 1 cm above the floor surface. The jar was placed about 45 cm south of the central post hole. The long (295 cm), narrow (65 cm), and level House L entry (area 2.07 m^2) joined the structure at the midpoint of its east wall. The entry had been excavated into loose fill and was partially lined with upright slabs along its southern side. The eastern end of the entrance floor was plastered with a thick (5 cm) clay coating.

House M (Figure 4.46)

Type IV structure; length 5.75 m, width 2.30 m; area of living surface 13.19 m^2; mean orientation of entry 183°.

House M had been superimposed by the construction of Rooms 5, 6, and 11. It intruded into portions of earlier Houses J and Q.

Level 1 (range 0–20 cm) was greatly disturbed by the construction of Rooms 5, 6, and 11. Level 2 (range 20–75 cm) consisted of a uniformly light gray, pebbly silt, intermixed with rock, clods of sterile soil, and wall or roof clay. Level 3 (range 75–90 cm, floor fill) compared with Level 2. The plas-

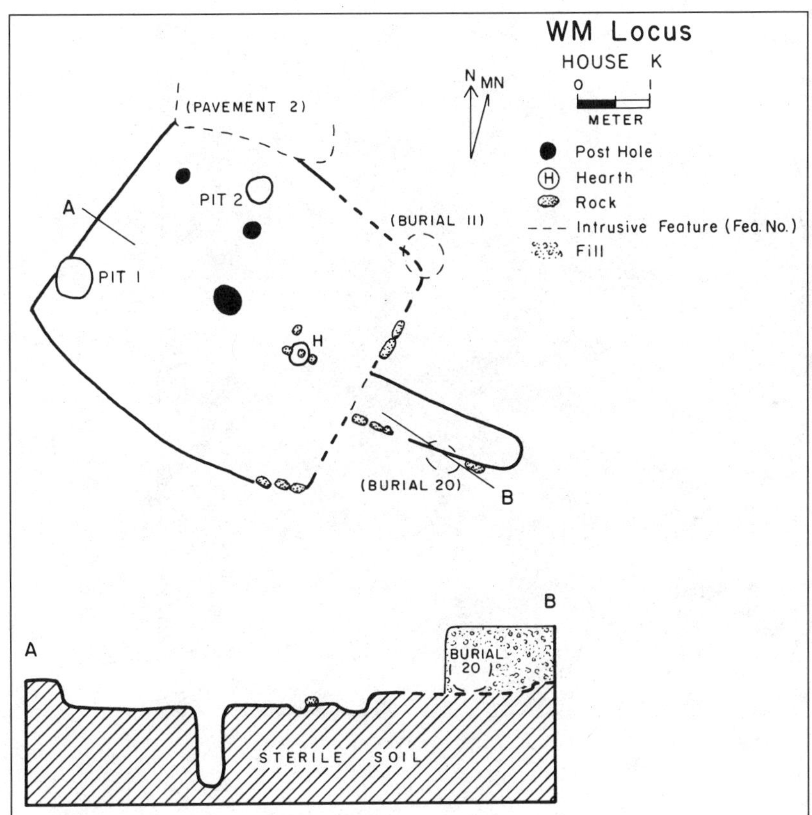

FIGURE 4.43. Plan view and profile of Wind Mountain locus House K, a Type IV structure.

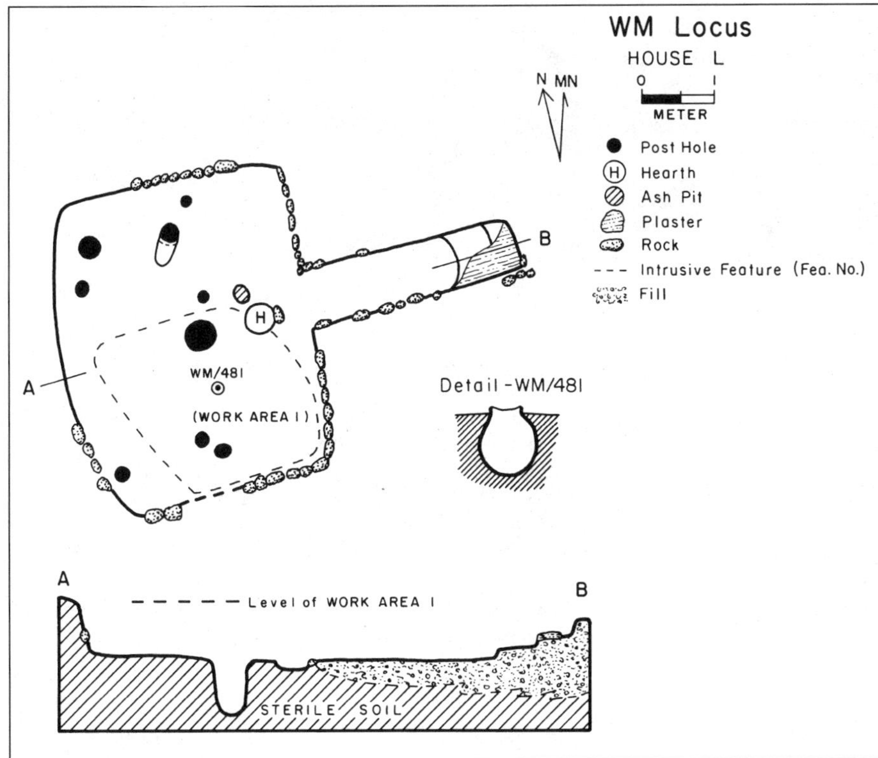

FIGURE 4.44. Plan view and profile of Wind Mountain locus House L, a Type IV structure.

FIGURE 4.45. The east wall of Wind Mountain locus House L, which was reinforced by upright stone slabs (Neg. No. WM 32–10F).

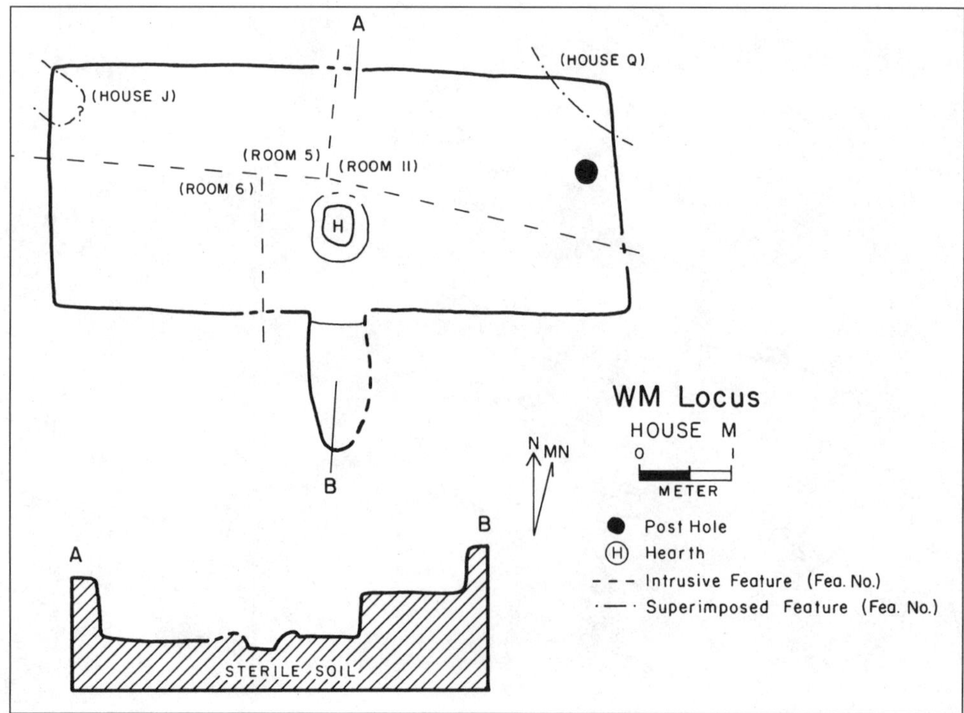

FIGURE 4.46. Plan view and profile of Wind Mountain locus House M, an aberrant Type IV structure.

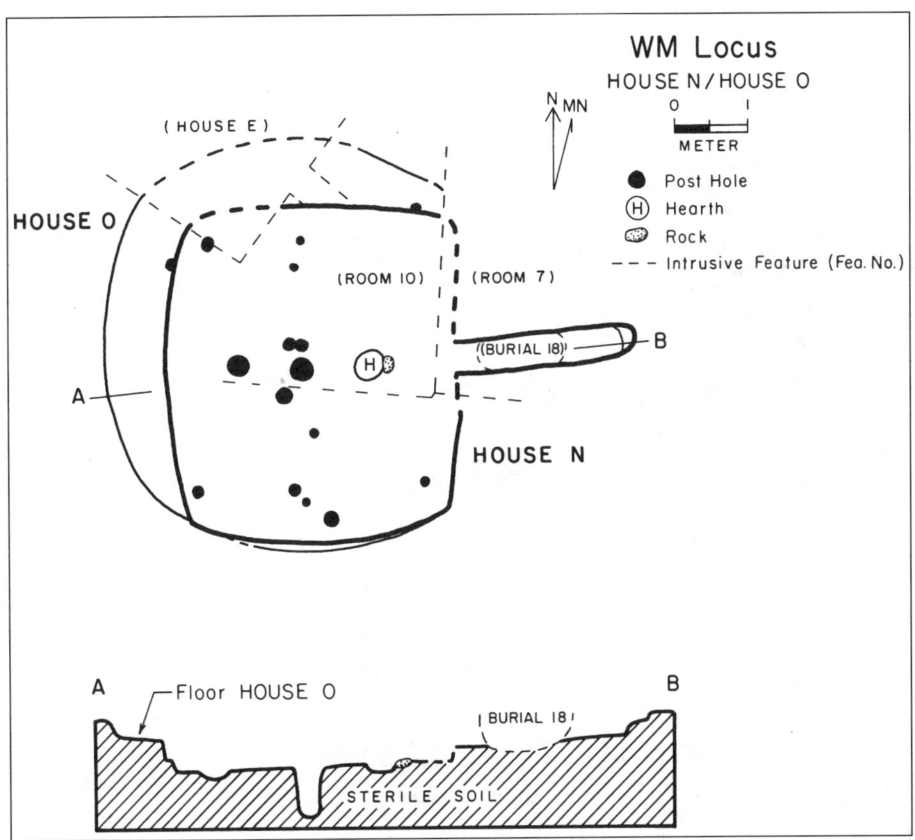

FIGURE 4.47. Plan view and profile of Type IV House N, which intruded into Type A community structure House O, both at the Wind Mountain locus.

tered house floor (depth 90 cm) had been excavated into a sterile, reddish orange sand. The southwest corner of the house retained a remnant patch (thickness 3.5 cm) of floor plaster. The walls of House M represented the smooth vertical sides of the house pit originally excavated during the structure's construction. A light gray plaster (approximately 1 mm thick) covered all four walls and ranged in height (measured from the floor) from 70 cm on the east wall to 90 cm on the west. A subrectangular, clay lined hearth (Type IIIA1; diameter 32 cm, depth 15 cm) having vertical sides and a slightly concave floor occurred near the house entry. Its rim extended slightly (5 cm) above the floor surface. One archaeomagnetic sample (No. 006) was taken from the House M hearth (Chapter 3). A stepped, unplastered entry (estimated area .64 m^2, length 120 cm, width 55 cm) with vertical walls joined the house at the middle of the south wall.

House N (Figure 4.47)

Type IV structure; length 5.05 m, width 4.50 m; area of living surface 20.68 m^2; mean orientation of entry 83°.

House N intruded into House O. It was superimposed by Rooms 7 and 10, and House E. Burial 18 was placed within the entry fill.

Level 1 (range 0–40 cm) was determined arbitrarily and measured from the floor of Room 10. Fill consisted of a uniformly dark gray, pebbly silt intermixed with small rocks. Level 2 (range 40–80 cm) compared with Level 1. Level 3 (range 80–95 cm, floor fill) was similar to the upper levels but contained more rock. One C^{14} sample (GX-5487) was analyzed from floor fill (Chapter 3). The house floor (depth 95 cm) was level and compacted from use. In general, house walls were smooth and vertical but unplastered. In two places, however (the northeast corner under Room 10 and the southwest corner, where House N cuts through House O), clay patching (thickness 4 cm) was used as wall reinforcement in an apparent attempt to retain loose fill. The hearth (Type IIA1; diameter 43 cm, depth 12 cm) was a circular, ash filled, clay lined pit with sloping sides and a concave floor. Its lining had been fired to a reddish hue, and a subrectangular hearthstone (28 cm x 15 cm x 4 cm) was plastered into its eastern edge. An archaeomagnetic sample (No. 002) was removed from the House N hearth (Chapter 3). The entry (area 1.35 m^2), a long (290 cm) and narrow (45 cm) stepped incline (5°), joined the structure at the midpoint of the east wall. Entry walls were vertical, well smoothed, and unplastered.

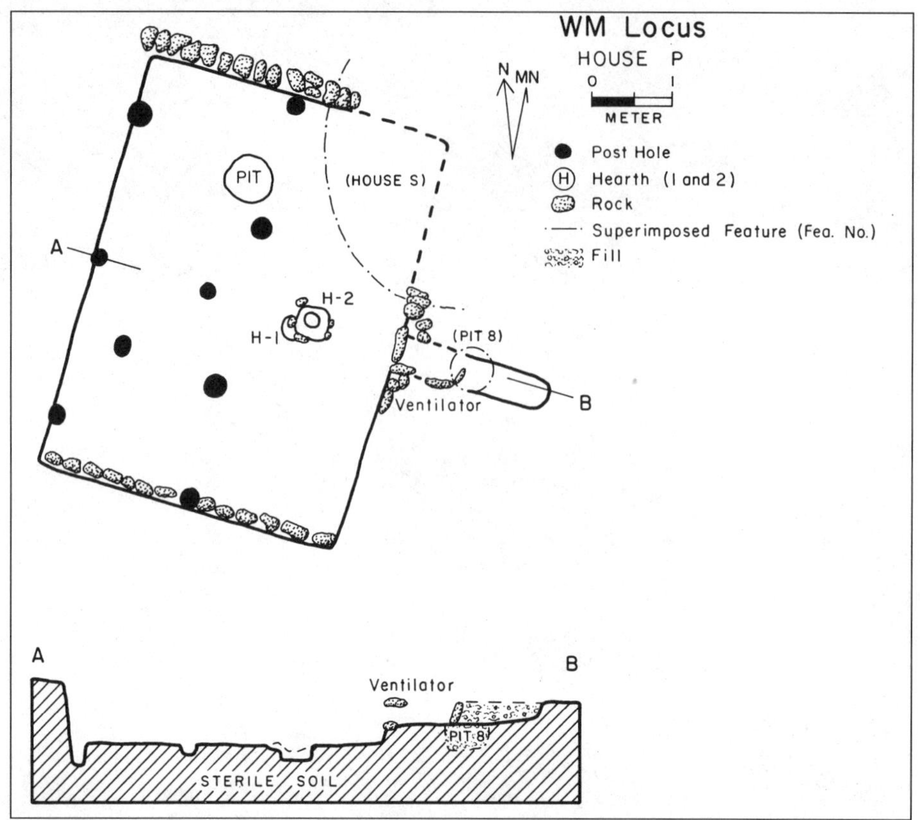

FIGURE 4.48. Plan view and profile of Wind Mountain locus Houses P1 and P2, consisting of P1, a Type IV structure, and P2, a Type G community structure. See text for explanation.

House O (Figure 4.47)

Type A structure; length 5.90 m, width 5.60 m; estimated area of living surface 28.24 m^2.

House O was impacted by several building episodes. Houses N and E disturbed at least 80 to 90 percent of House O, leaving only its southern edge and sections of the western and northern perimeter. Rooms 7 and 10 were later superimposed on these structures.

Level 1 (range 0–20 cm) was disturbed by the construction of Houses E and N as well as Rooms 7 and 10. Level 2 floor fill (range 20–55 cm) was composed of a dark gray, pebbly silt with scattered rock and site debris intermixed within the fill of House N. The floor, Level 3 (depth 55 cm), consisted of a use compacted surface overlying sterile soil. What little remained of house walls exhibited the unplastered, vertical to slightly sloping sides of the house pit originally excavated into sterile soil during its construction. No evidence of a hearth or entry was found.

House P (P1 and P2) (Figure 4.48)

Type IV structure: House P1, length 5.05 m, width 3.80 m; area of living surface 20.04 m^2; orientation of entry 113°.

Type G structure: House P2, length 4.85 m, width 3.80 m; area of living surface 18.24 m^2.

House P was superimposed on House S. House P displayed a two phase construction sequence changing its typological definition from a Type IV (House P1) to a Type G (House P2) structure. The House P1 entry superimposed Pit 8.

Level 1 (range 0–85 cm) consisted of a dark gray, trash laden, pebbly silt disturbed by pot hunters. Level 2 (range 85–95 cm, floor fill) was similar to Level 1, although disturbances were less extensive. Level 3, (depth 95 cm) the house floor (House P2), described a leveled, use compacted sterile soil showing evidence of burning. The initial construction (House P1) defined a Type IV house, characterized by a rectangular plan and lateral side entry. Subsequent remodeling modified the structure into a Type G community house with a rectangular plan, roof entry, and a ventilator shaft (House P2). The presence of burned plaster and replastered walls indicate episodes of remodeling/reuse. The north end of the east wall was destroyed by pot hunting, but the remaining two-thirds represented the intact vertical wall of the original pit excavation. A few stones placed on either side of the P1 house entry (later the ventilator of House P2) were evidently employed to reinforce loose fill. The south wall of

House P1 was plastered with a light gray, sandy clay that showed evidence of burning over its surface. The south wall of House P2 was built of masonry construction (thickness 20 cm), cemented into place with a dark gray, pebbly silt. The western wall of both houses displayed a smooth vertical surface. The western two-thirds of the north wall was constructed of rough masonry set with gray pebbly silt mortar—a necessity because the wall was built in an area of loose, unconsolidated fill. The eastern section of this wall was destroyed by pot hunting. All four walls of House P2 exhibited plastering in the form of clay repairs (thickness 2–3 mm) across their surfaces. Two hearths were located. Hearth 1 (Type IIA; diameter 25 cm, depth 10 cm) of House P1 defined a small, circular, clay lined pit containing gray ash. It was superimposed by Hearth 2 (Type IIIB1; length 40 cm, width 38 cm, depth 10 cm) associated with House P2. Hearth 2 was characterized as a rectangular plan with slightly curving sides and a stone and plaster lined rim. A smaller, distinctive basin-shaped feature (diameter 20 cm, depth 10 cm), interpreted as a secondary hearth, was noted in the center of Hearth 2. Another circular, unlined basin (diameter 60 cm, depth 70 cm) having vertical sides and a concave floor located in the northern half of the structure was identified as a floor pit. The lateral entry (area .75 m^2) to House P1 defined a long (175 cm), narrow (40 cm), level passageway that joined the house through the midsection of its east wall. The entry's north wall was destroyed by pot hunting. Later, House P2 modification took advantage of the preexisting entry channel by building a ventilator within this lateral entrance (Figure 4.49). The ventilator sill (length 71 cm, width 12 cm, thickness 5 cm) was set some 18 cm above the house floor. The ventilator's north wall was destroyed by the same pot hunting incident that impacted House P1's north entry wall. A large in situ vertically placed stone slab (length 42 cm, height 40 cm, width 37 cm) on the south side of the ventilator was probably one of a pair originally flanking the ventilator (vandals having removing the north side slab). The ventilator vent (height 38 cm, width 38 cm) extended about 85 cm laterally (horizontally) away from the house. The ascending ventilator outlet (vertical) rose 77 cm in height and measured between 35 and 38 cm in diameter.

House Q (Figure 4.50)

Type II structure; length 3.50 m, width 3.20+ m; estimated area of living surface 11.88 m^2; mean orientation of entry 77°.

House Q was intruded by Room 11, House M, Puddle Pit 2, and Burial 24. House Q superpositioned Pit 10.

Level 1 (range 0–30 cm) was disturbed by Room 11 construction and other subsequent occupational activities. Level 2 (range 30–90 cm) consisted of a uniformly dark gray, pebbly silt intermixed with rock and charcoal. Level 3 (range 90–100 cm, floor fill) compared with Level 2. The unplastered House Q floor (depth 100 cm) described a level, use compacted surface. The northern and northeastern walls of House Q, constructed into the loose fill of an upward slope, were nearly indiscernible. A clay patch (1–2 cm thick) on the northwestern wall was the only surviving evidence of a prepared wall. A small area of burned floor plaster (25 cm x 30 cm) 1 m west of the entry may have been a hearth. However, because it occurs in fill, situated over an earlier oval floor pit (length 72 cm, width 53 cm, depth 30 cm), no definite conclusion could be drawn. This possible hearth (Type IV) superimposed a thin layer (2 cm) of ash that was plastered over, perhaps indicating a remodeling event. The House Q entry (estimated area .60 m^2) was a narrow (60 cm), stepped incline (4°) that entered the house through its eastern wall. Entry walls were vertical and unplastered. The eastern end of the entry was indistinguishable, disappearing into loose, trash laden fill.

House R (refer to Figure 4.5)

Type II structure; length 3.10 m, width 2.90 m; area of living surface 6.97 m^2; mean orientation of entry 123°.

Level 1 (range 0–20 cm) consisted of a uniformly gray-brown, pebbly silt. Level 2 (range 20–45 cm) was similar in composition, but contained numerous fragments of charred corn and beans. Burned adobe, apparently from roof fall, was also noted. Level 3 (range 45–55 cm, floor fill) compared in composition to Level 2. The unplastered house floor (depth 55 cm) described a leveled, use compacted surface. Vertical house walls had been excavated into sterile soil. A few small patches of wall plaster occurred along the western side of the house. Upper wall sections were apparently constructed of jacal composed of mud and rock packed against a wood and brush framework. Many jacal impressions were preserved in the form of burned adobe casts, which were recovered from house fill. The hearth (Type IB; diameter 20 cm, depth 4 cm) appeared as a shallowly depressed burned area. The short (100 cm), narrow (30 cm), and stepped entry was excavated into sterile soil (area .33 m^2). Based on the large quantity of charred plant remains (corn and beans) recovered through fine screening, and the presence of burned vegetal impressed adobe (reeds or small sticks), House R was most likely destroyed by fire. One C^{14} sample (GX-5488), collected from the house floor and floor fill, was analyzed (Chapter 3). Some disturbance, the result of rodent activity, was observed near the southwestern margin of the house.

House S (Figure 4.51)

Type II structure; length 3.10 m, width 2.50 m; area of living surface 6.72 m^2; mean orientation of entry 90°.

House S superimposed the western edge of House T. It was moderately impacted by the later intrusions of House P and

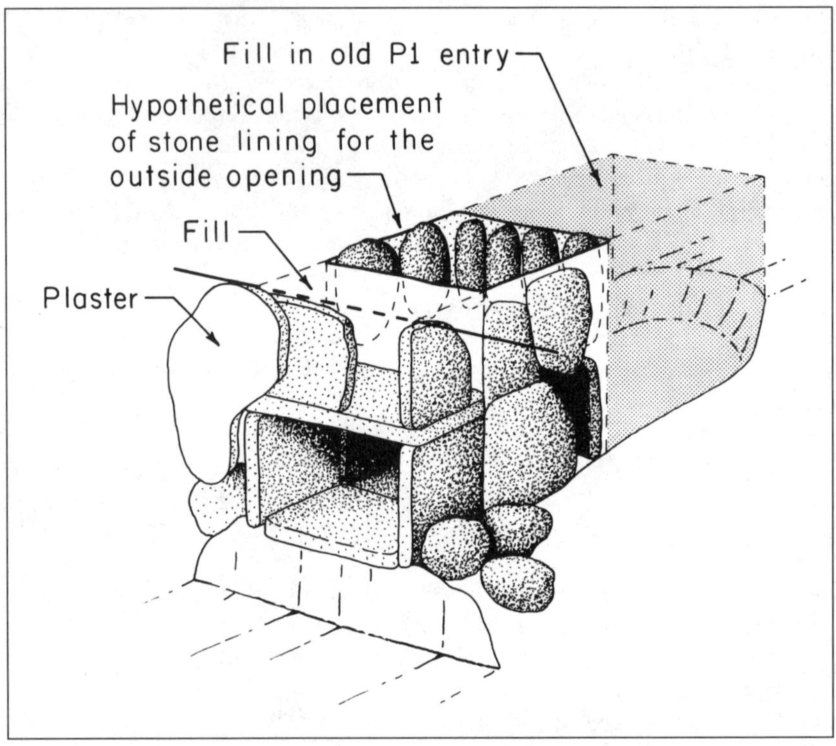

FIGURE 4.49. The ventilator of Type G House P2, which was constructed in the lateral entry of the earlier Type IV House P1.

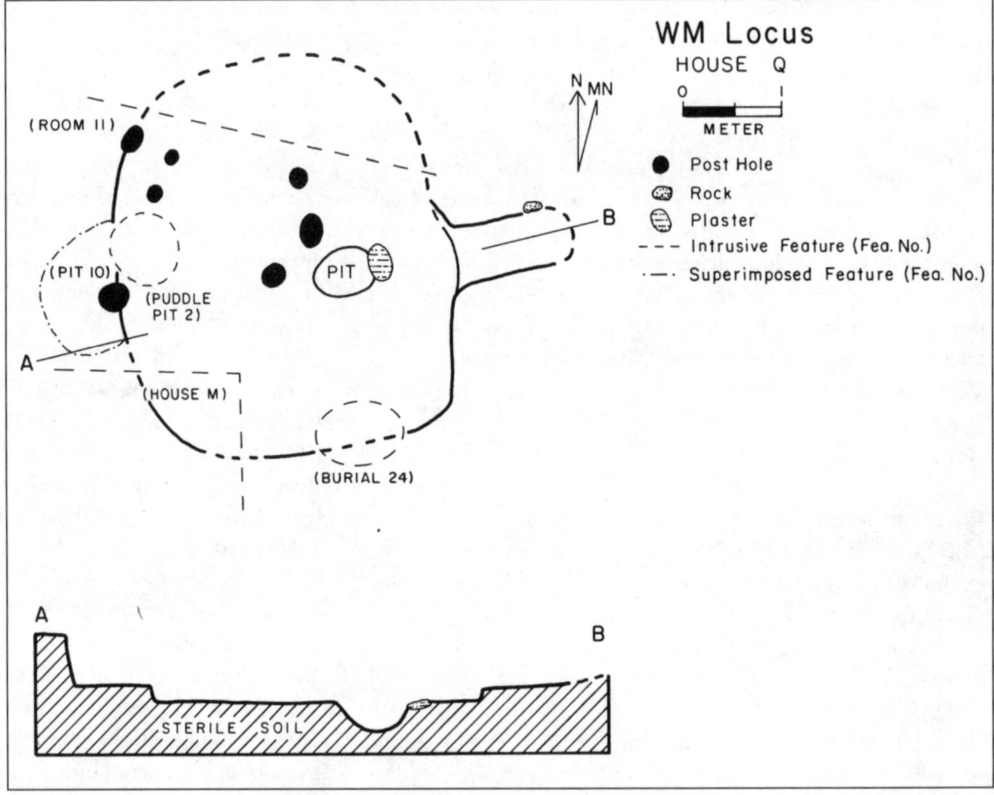

FIGURE 4.50. Plan view and profile of Wind Mountain locus House Q, a Type II structure.

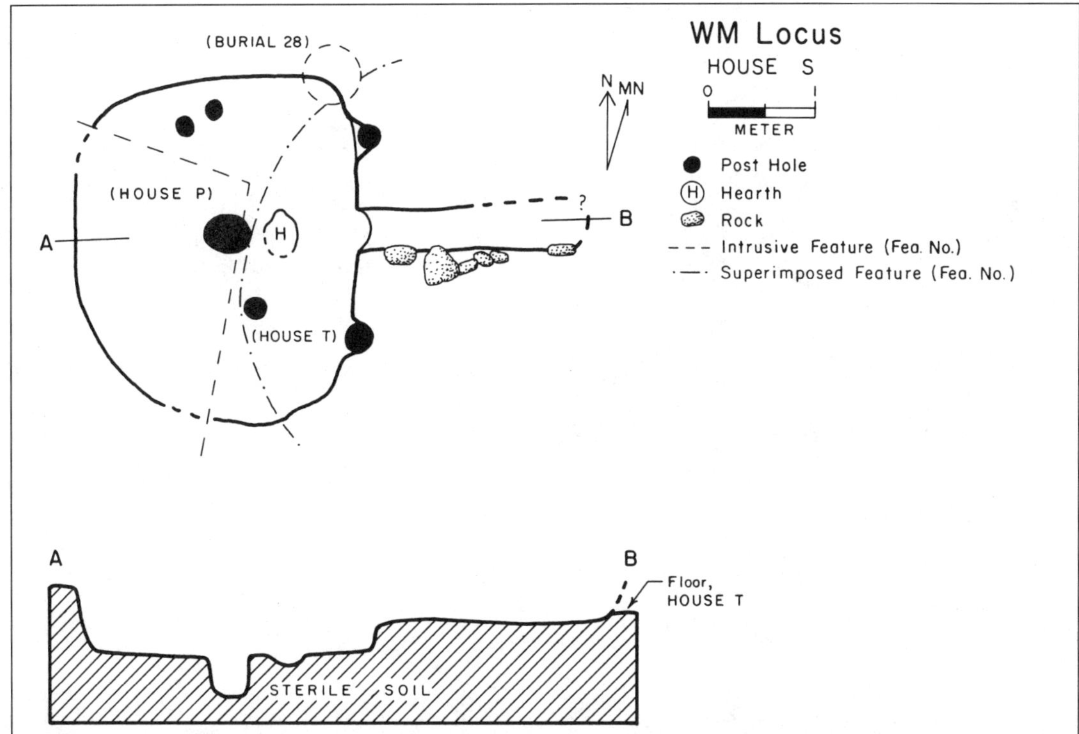

FIGURE 4.51. Plan view and profile of Wind Mountain locus House S, a Type II structure.

moderately impacted by the later intrusions of House P and Burial 28.

Level 1 (range 0–120 cm), heavily disturbed by pot hunting, consisted of a uniformly dark gray, pebbly silt with numerous rocks. Level 2 (range 120–130 cm, floor fill) was comparable to Level 1 except for a higher density of rocks. The unplastered House S floor (depth 130 cm) described an irregularly leveled, use compacted surface that may have been disturbed by pot hunting. House walls, excavated into sterile soil, appeared smooth and unplastered. In places where the House S floor cut through House T, a small 10 cm clay lip was noted, which presumably acted to contain loose fill. The hearth (Type IB; approximate length 45 cm, width 30 cm, depth 8 cm) was an irregularly shaped depression defined by heat reddened soil and ash. Two post holes located along the eastern wall of the house and apparently set into the house wall may have belonged to the superstructure of earlier House T. Field observations were inconclusive. The House S entrance (estimated area .76 m^2), rock lined on its south side, was long (200+ cm), narrow (35 cm), and level. Its eastern extent was lost within the loose fill of House T.

House T (Figure 4.52)

Type II structure; length 4.25 m, width 3.20+ m; estimated area of living surface 12.60 m^2; mean orientation of entry 117°.

The west side of House T was impacted by the construction of House S. Burials 26–29 were intrusive into House T fill.

Level 1 (range 0–60 cm) comprised a dark gray, pebbly silt with some loose rock. Level 2 (range 60–85 cm) consisted of a dark gray, pebbly silt with numerous large pieces of burned plaster and earth. Level 3 (range 85–95 cm, floor fill) was composed of a dark gray, pebbly, trash laden silt intermixed with burned plaster. The House T floor (depth 95 cm) was a leveled, use compacted surface. Surviving walls showed evidence of plastering (e.g., 3–5 cm thick on the north wall). Field notes discussed a large slab of burned plaster found slumped against the eastern wall, suggesting to the excavators that the original wall was at least 95 cm high. Wall plaster was characterized as a thick gray clay, reddened on its interior surface by an intense fire. Field observations also indicated that Burial 26, located along the southern margin of the house, may originally have been interred behind the wall plaster (i.e., outside of the house). However, wall slumping, a result of fire, may have relocated the burial inward toward the house interior. The unplastered House T hearth (Type IB; length 40 cm, width 28 cm, depth 15 cm) exhibited an irregular plan with sloping sides and a concave floor. A small depression (width 15 cm, depth 3–5 cm), found immediately east of the hearth, was interpreted as a pot rest. Two floor pits were located. Pit 1 (length 40 cm, width 38 cm, depth 15 cm) and Pit 2 (length 42 cm, width 38 cm, depth 25 cm)

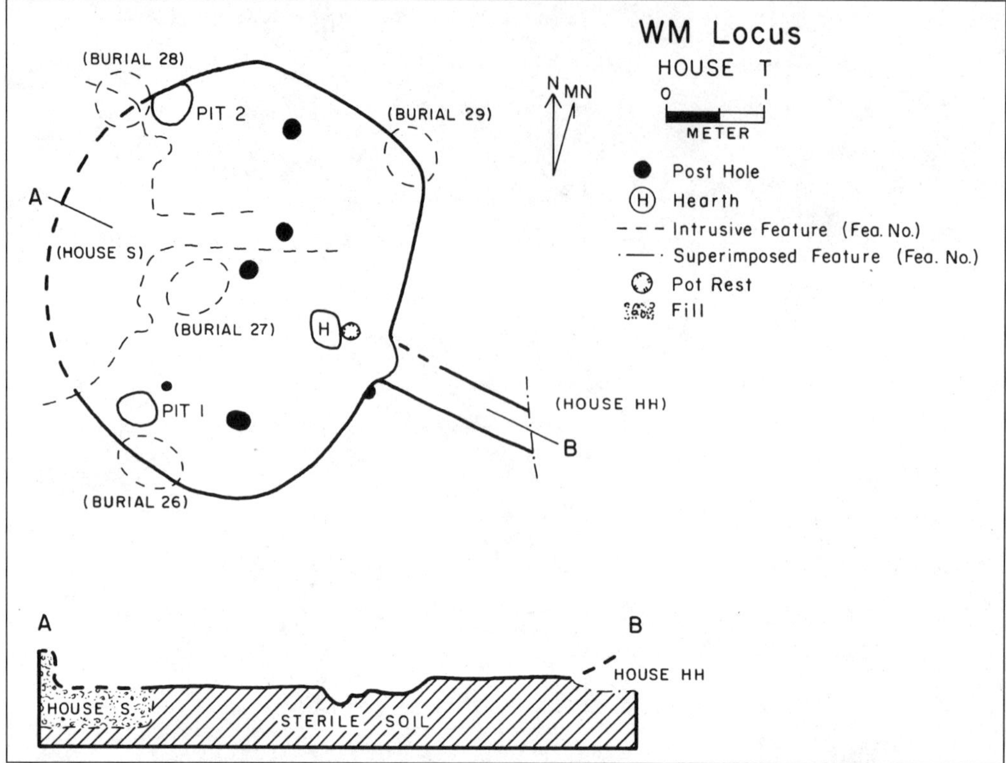

FIGURE 4.52. Plan view and profile of Wind Mountain locus House T, a Type II structure.

described oval plans with sloping sides and concave floors. The lateral entry shaft (surviving area .59 m^2) was a level, narrow (width 40 cm), stepped feature with vertical walls that joined the house through the middle of its eastern wall. The entry's north wall, excavated into fill, was plastered with an orange clay (thickness 2–4 cm). Its unplastered south wall was dug into sterile soil. The eastern end of the entry lost its structural integrity in the loose fill of House HH.

House U (Figure 4.53)

Type C structure; length 6.45 m, width 5.65 m; area of living surface 36.90 m^2; mean orientation of entry 85°.

House U was intruded by House V, which greatly disturbed its northwest corner. Room 12 superimposed both Houses U and V. The House U entry superpositioned Pit 15 and was intruded by Pit 16.

Level 1 (range 0–20 cm) consisted of a dark gray, pebbly silt with occasional fragments of sterile soil and rock. Level 2 (range 20–85 cm) was similar to Level 1. Level 3 (range 85–100 cm, floor fill) compared with Levels 1 and 2. The unplastered House U floor (depth 100 cm) appeared as a use compacted, leveled surface, though a large portion (approximately 15 m^2, 41 percent) of it had been disrupted by the construction of House V. Walls were poorly preserved, having slumped in several locations. A small amount of fire reddened wall plaster noted near the southeastern corner suggested House U may have burned. An unplastered niche (height 30 cm, width 55 cm, depth 20 cm) was identified in the west wall. Located 35 cm above the floor, its base consisted of a recessed ledge; the sides, back, and top were concave. A clay lined, roughly circular hearth (Type IIA1; measuring approximately, length 42 cm, width 38 cm, depth 20 cm) containing ash was uncovered near the house entrance. A flat, irregularly shaped hearthstone (length 45 cm, width 20 cm, thickness 8 cm) had been set into the east side of the hearth and protruded about 6 cm above the floor. The House U entry (area 1.82 m^2) was a long (390 cm), narrow (width 45 cm) incline that joined the structure at the midpoint of its east wall. Upright stone slabs had been placed at uneven intervals along the vertical and unplastered entry walls, evidently in an effort to shore up loose fill.

House V (refer to Figures 4.23 and 4.24)

Type F structure; length 4.90 m, width 3.10 m; area of living surface 15.27 m^2.

House V was built almost entirely within the northwestern half of House U. Room 12 partially superimposed House V, and Burials 30–32 intruded into its fill.

Level 1 (range 0–85 cm), similar in composition to fill found in House U, was described as a dark gray, pebbly silt

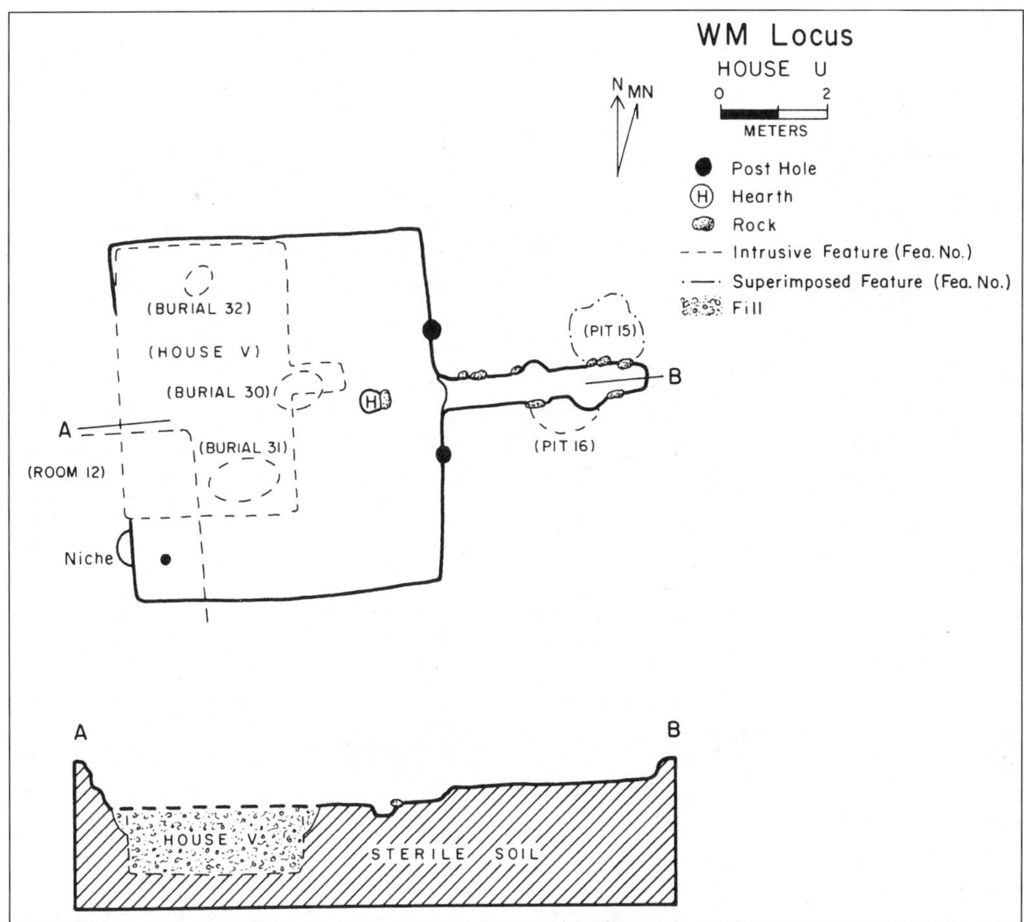

FIGURE 4.53. Plan view and profile of Wind Mountain locus House U, a Type C community structure.

mixed with rock and site debitage. Level 2 (range 85–115 cm) was analogous to Level 1. Level 3 (range 115–210 cm) compared to Levels 1 and 2 with the addition of sloping lenses of ash and sand, as well as and considerable evidence of rodent activity. Level 4 (range 210–220 cm, floor fill) corresponded to Level 3. The House V floor (depth 220 cm) consisted of a level, plastered surface (thickness 2–3 mm). Both floor and wall plaster (a gray clay) were alike in appearance. All four vertical interior walls had been smoothed and plastered. Fifteen vertical wall grooves, ranging in diameter from 9 to 20 cm (a mean diameter of approximately 14 cm), were discovered. The longest wall grooves were noted in the southwest corner of House V, extending upward from its floor to the floor of superimposed Room 12, a distance of 220 cm. In other areas, excessive erosion eliminated the possibility for determining the length of additional grooves. Wall grooves were evidently constructed to secure vertical roof supports in place. Partially inset into the surrounding walls, these roof beam uprights may have supplied greater structural support than if they had been left free standing. Moreover, increased usable living area was obtained by placing interior posts closer to the house wall, away from the interior surface of the room. A thin veneer of plaster (thickness 2–5 mm) coated both the grooves and the sterile soil comprising house walls. The ventilator (height 40 cm, width 55 cm, depth 105 cm), located in the middle of the east wall, was positioned about 10 cm above the floor (Figure 4.54). It was supported in part by four upright wooden posts, set into the north and south walls (two near the front and two placed laterally approximately 70 cm into the vent). Both the walls of the vent and all four support posts were covered with a layer of clay (5–10 cm). A shaped stone sill (length 40 cm, width 18 cm, thickness 4 cm), placed into the floor of the vent opening, braced two upright shaped stone slabs (each approximately 38 cm high, 20 cm wide, and 4 cm deep). The header beam to the vent opening was originally a small wooden log, still visible in the form of a clay impression. A thin masonry wall (thickness 15 cm), immediately above the header, extended upward 90 cm from the beam along the interior house wall. This masonry wall was built against the loose fill found above the vent. A clay lined circular hearth (Type IIA2; width 45 cm, depth 8 cm) bordered by a plastered U-shaped collar was also

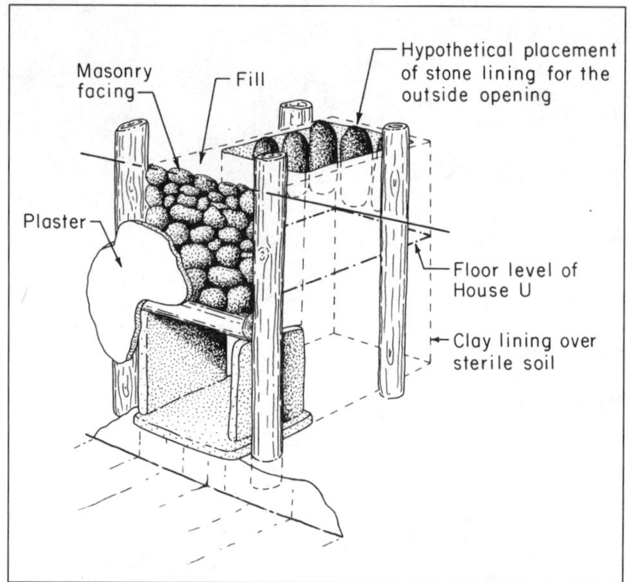

FIGURE 4.54. The ventilator constructed into the east wall of Wind Mountain locus House V, a Type F community structure.

noted. One archaeomagnetic sample (No. 001) was taken from this hearth (Chapter 3). A small ash pit (diameter 16 cm, depth 21 cm) with fire reddened walls and containing white ash, was exposed just in front of the hearth. A note appended to field notes indicated that Di Peso gave some passing thought to interpreting this feature as a sipapu.

House W (Figure 4.55; refer to Figure 4.8)

Type IV structure; length 4.25 m, width 4.20 m; area of living surface 17.45 m²; mean orientation of entry 37°.

House W was superimposed over the northern end of House YY.

Level 1 (range 0–30 cm) comprised a mostly uniform dark gray, pebbly silt. Level 2 (range 30–130 cm) was similar to Level 1, but contained alternating bands of sand, gravel, and rock, the latter probably derived from wall fall. Level 3 (range 130–140 cm, floor fill) compared with Level 2. The unplastered house floor (depth 140 cm) described a level, use compacted surface. Walls were vertical and tended to be reinforced with stone in areas characterized by layers of unconsolidated sand and gravel. The east wall showed evidence of plaster in two small patches (thickness 1 mm). Approximately two-thirds of the southern wall was faced with large upright stone slabs set along the lower perimeter; smaller rock was placed along the upper margin. The eastern and western walls were constructed of rock and secured with a black mortar or mud. The hearth (Type IIIB1; length 45 cm, width 42 cm, depth 10 cm), a rectangular, clay lined box with rounded corners that contained a thin layer of ash (thickness 3–4 cm), exhibited vertical sides and a flat floor. Its lip was constructed flush with the house floor. Small stones were embedded in the clay sides and then plastered over. One archaeomagnetic sample (No. 008) was taken from the House W hearth (Chapter 3). The central post hole (length 48 cm, width 45 cm, depth 92 cm) was rock lined, presumably a device to brace the post in place. A smaller and shallower sloping hole contiguous to the central post hole may have been dug to aid in positioning the central post. A small oval floor pit (length 42 cm, width 30 cm, depth 20 cm) with uniform sides sloping towards a concave floor was uncovered west of the central post hole. The House W entrance (area 2.27 m²) consisted of a long (300 cm), moderately narrow (80 cm), stepped incline (10°) with vertical sides. Entry walls were unplastered but used some rock as a lining material. Entry remodeling was apparent at the juncture of the ramp with the northeast house wall. A small semicircular depression located at the lowest section of the entry ramp was filled in with rock and mortar, a condition that modified its original construction. Neither the original construction nor the intent of the modification is understood. Two patches of burned wall plaster suggest House W burned.

House X (Figure 4.56; refer to Figures 4.16 and 4.17)

Type B structure; length 10.10 m, width 8.70 m; area of living surface 70.50 m²; mean orientation of entry 102°.

House X was located under Room 14. Burials 34, 45, 49, and 52; *Canis* Burials 3 and 4; Pit Ovens 1–3; and Pit 59 intruded into House X fill.

Level 1 (range 0–30 cm) was defined as a "very consolidated," uniformly dark gray, pebbly silt. Level 2 (range 30–120 cm) was less consolidated, consisting of a homogeneous, light gray pebbly silt with some rock. Level 3 (range 120–140 cm) was composed of layers and patches of tan, pebbly silt intermixed with a light gray, pebbly, unconsolidated silt. Level 3 contained relatively more charcoal, rocks, and rodent activity when compared with the upper levels. Level 4 (range 140–160 cm, floor fill) was analogous to Level 3. One C^{14} sample (GX-5490) was analyzed from the floor level (Chapter 3). The House X floor (depth 160 cm), showing sporadic traces of plaster, described a level, use compacted surface. Due to intense burning, the floor in the structure's southwest quadrant near its north wall was well preserved. In contrast, extreme rodent activity between the house entry and the central post hole disrupted the floor in that portion of the house. The hearth (Type IIb; length 70 cm, width 65 cm, depth 9 cm), an oval basin with sloping sides, a flat floor, and a lip set flush with the floor surface, was located roughly halfway between the house entrance and its central post hole. Two archaeomagnetic samples were collected, one from the House X hearth (No. 015) and the other from its plastered floor (No. 016) (Chapter 3). Two floor grooves were exposed

FIGURE 4.55. Wind Mountain locus House W, a Type IV structure, showing details of reinforced stone walls and large central post support (Neg. No. WM 43–25F).

to the north and south of the hearth and central post hole (Figure 4.56). Floor Groove 1 (length 245 cm, maximum width 40 cm, depth 16 cm) displayed parallel sides, rounded ends, slightly sloping sides converging on a flat floor, and a lip flush with the house floor. The general description of Floor Groove 2 (length 225 cm, maximum width 38 cm, depth 18 cm) was similar. Several rocks occurred in Floor Groove 2 together with impressions of log or wooden plank fragments. One impression (width about 1.8 cm) on the south wall of Groove 2 began 4 cm below floor level and extended about 23 cm east to west. A second impression (width about 2.2 cm) in the groove's north wall appeared about 2 cm below the floor and continued for approximately 20 cm. A roughly D-shaped ash pit (length 70 cm, width 50 cm, depth 15 cm) with sloping sides and a flat floor was located between the hearth and entry. Another smaller depression (diameter 18 cm) with vertical sides that descended 15 cm below the base of the larger ash pit was also noted. Both features contained a white ash. Many intramural post holes (numbered 15–25) were only shallowly dug (depths ranged from 3 cm to 7 cm) into the subfloor and may not have figured into the post hole patterning associated with House X architecture. These may be the remains of internal screens or some feature(s) not related to the superstructure of the house. Vertical house walls were excavated into a sterile soil. Wall reinforcement, consisting of stone placed individually or in courses, was added to the structure at intervals around its circumference. Rocks found on the house floor probably fell from sections of an upper wall. Wall plaster occurred in a thin layer on the northwest wall (thickness 4 mm) and also on the southeast side in a "paper thin layer." Some wall areas were burned. An unlined niche (height 45 cm, width 40 cm, maximum depth 45 cm) was located along the south wall. Positioned 75 cm above the floor, its plan described an irregular arch with a concave interior and a flat sill. A stone shelf (length 16 cm, width 19 cm, thickness 3 cm) fashioned from a flat grinding stone, placed 86 cm above the floor, and protruding 8 cm out from the wall, occurred in the wall opposite the niche. The central post hole was extremely large (diameter range 40 to 65 cm), extending 190 cm below the

FIGURE 4.56. Wind Mountain locus House X, a Type B community structure, showing floor details, including possible foot drums (Neg. No. WM 59–21A/F).

house floor surface. It was lined with stone, which evidently was intended to serve as a wedge to hold the post in place. The House X entry ramp (area 3.30 m^2; inclined at 4°) was long (560 cm), narrow (55 cm), and joined the house at its easternmost point. Its eastern end was irregularly lined with stone set on edge or end and secured with a tan mortar and a dark gray silt. Twelve post holes (diameters ranged from the smallest at 10 cm to the largest, an oval feature, measuring length 30 cm, width 20 cm), ten along the north wall and two in the south wall, were inset into or back from the entry walls. It is particularly interesting to note that, given the large floor area of House X (area 70.50 m^2), not one floor storage pit was located. If an argument can be made that House X was a "community structure" perhaps the absence of utilitarian features as well as the presence of such unusual factors as floor grooves is proof of a function other than residential.

House Y (Figures 4.57 and 4.58)

Type C structure; length 5.70 m, width 5.50 m; estimated area of living surface 29.84 m^2; mean orientation of entry 188°.

House Y was intruded by House AA; Pit 73; and Burials 35, 36, and 38. House Y superimposed Pit 24.

Level 1 (range 0–90 cm) consisted of a homogeneous, dark gray, pebbly silt intermixed with loose rock and occasional remnants of burned wall plaster. Some fill from intrusive House AA occurred in this level. Level 2 (range 90–112 cm, floor fill) compared with Level 1. The unplastered House Y floor (depth 112 cm) described a level, use compacted surface. In general, walls were smooth vertical faces, although most of the north wall was destroyed during the construction of House AA. Stone reinforcement was employed at intervals along the western and southern walls. A thin, patchy layer (thickness 2–3 mm) of burned plaster was observed on the eastern, southern, and western walls. Plaster height (measured from the floor) extended some 35–55 cm from the

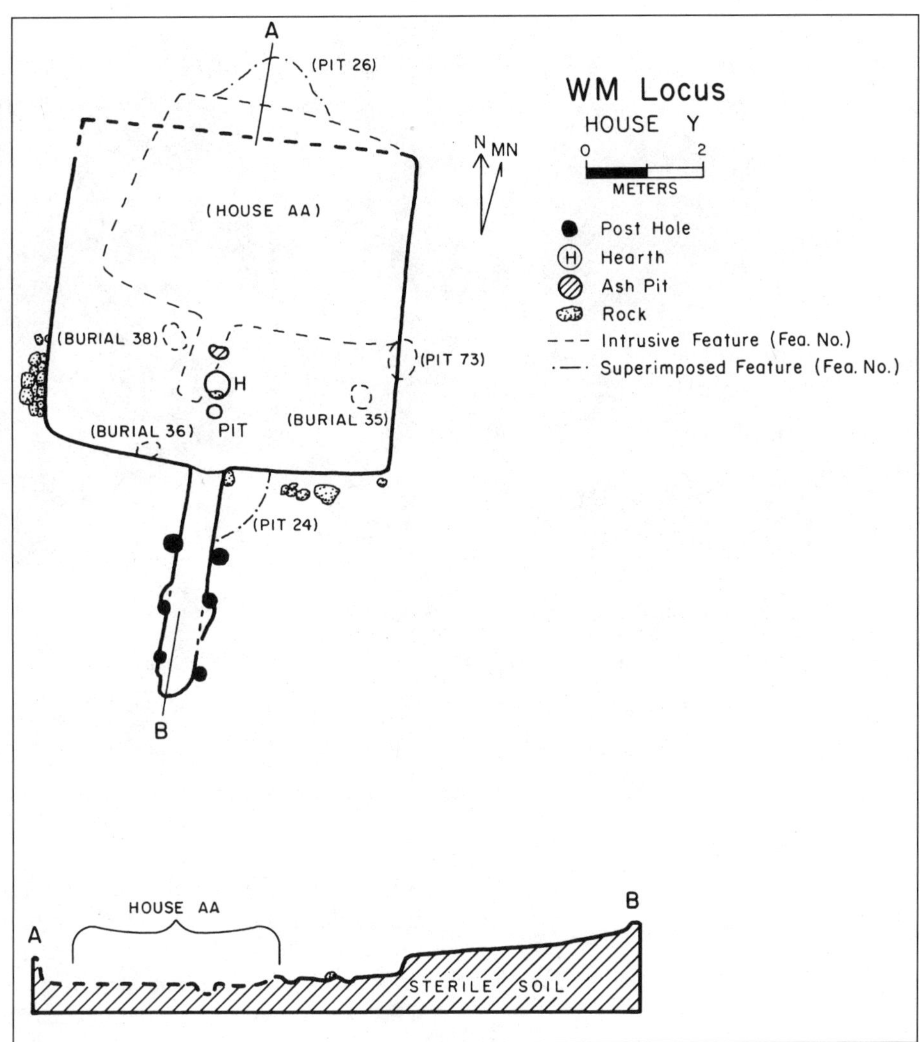

FIGURE 4.57. Plan view and profile of Wind Mountain locus House Y, a Type C community structure.

living surface. A clay lined, circular, basin-shaped hearth (Type IIA1; diameter 38 cm, depth 10 cm), its lip set flush with the house floor, was uncovered. A flat hearthstone (length 20 cm, width 12 cm, depth 4 cm) was set into the hearth's southern edge. A small, irregularly shaped pit, still containing ash, with vertical sides and a flat floor was located 20 cm north of the hearth. Another pit (diameter 22 cm, depth 8 cm), a basin-shaped circular depression with unlined vertical sides, was exposed 20 cm to the south of the main hearth. Its fill corresponded to the House Y floor fill. The entry (area 1.96 m^2) consisted of vertical, smooth walls, and a long (375 cm), narrow (60 cm), stepped incline (5°) that joined the house at the center point of its south wall. Its floor surface was flat to slightly concave. Three pairs of post holes flanked the house entry.

House Z (Figure 4.59)

Type IV structure; length 3.70 m, width 3.50 m; area of living surface 11.92 m^2; mean orientation of entry 190°.

Level 1 (range 0–110 cm) was composed of a uniformly dark gray, pebbly silt with some loose rock. Level 2 (range 110–120 cm, floor fill) was similar to Level 1 but contained a larger quantity of charcoal. The unplastered House Z floor (depth 120 cm) consisted of an irregularly leveled, use compacted surface. The floor was not well preserved, due to rodent activity, loose sand, and underlying gravel, factors that aided in destroying the architectural integrity of this feature. Unplastered house walls were vertical to slightly sloping. Some stone located along the south wall near the house entrance may represent wall reinforcement. A wall niche (height 45 cm, width 45 cm) with a flat sill, extending 40 cm back from the house wall and 32 cm above the floor sur-

FIGURE 4.58. Wind Mountain locus House Y, revealing its extremely long and narrow entry (Neg. No. WM 45–31F).

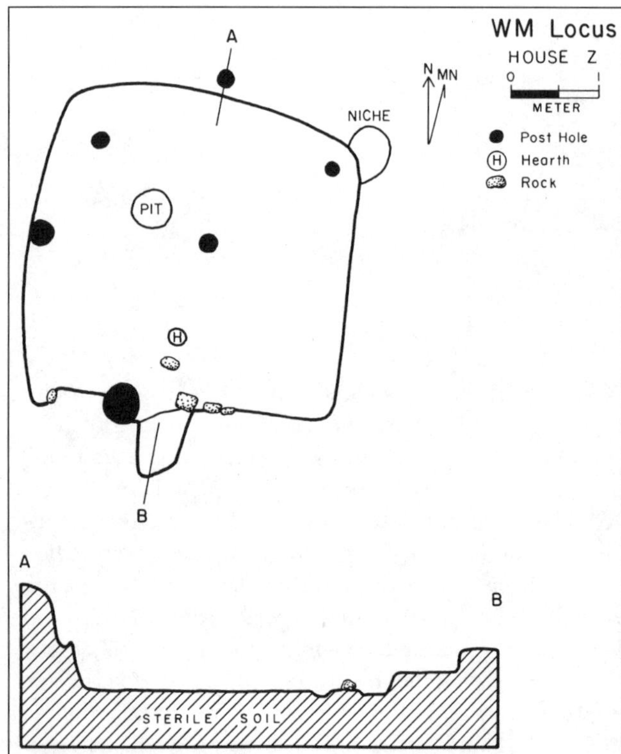

FIGURE 4.59. Plan view and profile of Wind Mountain locus House Z, a Type IV structure.

face, was uncovered in the northwest corner of the structure. The hearth (Type IIA; diameter 17 cm, depth 8 cm), a small, clay lined basin set with its lip flush with the house floor, contained a small quantity of ash. An oval-shaped rock located on the house floor between the hearth and the entry may have been a hearthstone. It was not, however, plastered into either the hearth or floor, and its exact function remains problematical. An unplastered circular floor pit (diameter 45 cm, depth 24 cm) with sloping sides and a concave floor occurred 40 cm northwest of the central post hole. The House Z entry was narrow (45 cm), extremely short (70 cm), and stepped. It displayed unplastered vertical walls, a level floor, and had been excavated into sterile soil (area .31 m^2). A burned patch of house floor in the northeast corner and quantities of charcoal in the floor fill indicate the house burned.

House AA (Figure 4.60; refer to Figure 4.58)

Type IV structure; length 5.05 m, width 3.55 m; area of living surface 15.64 m^2; mean orientation of entry 201°.

House AA superpositioned House Y and Pit 26. Pit 73 slightly impacted the southeast corner of House AA.

Before House AA was detected, Level 1 (range 0–90 cm) was identified and removed as part of House Y fill. Level 2 (range 90–105 cm) consisted of a dark gray, pebbly silt intermixed with rock. Level 3 (range 105–120 cm, floor fill) compared with Level 2, but had a higher incidence of fragmentary charcoal. One C^{14} sample (GX-5489) was analyzed

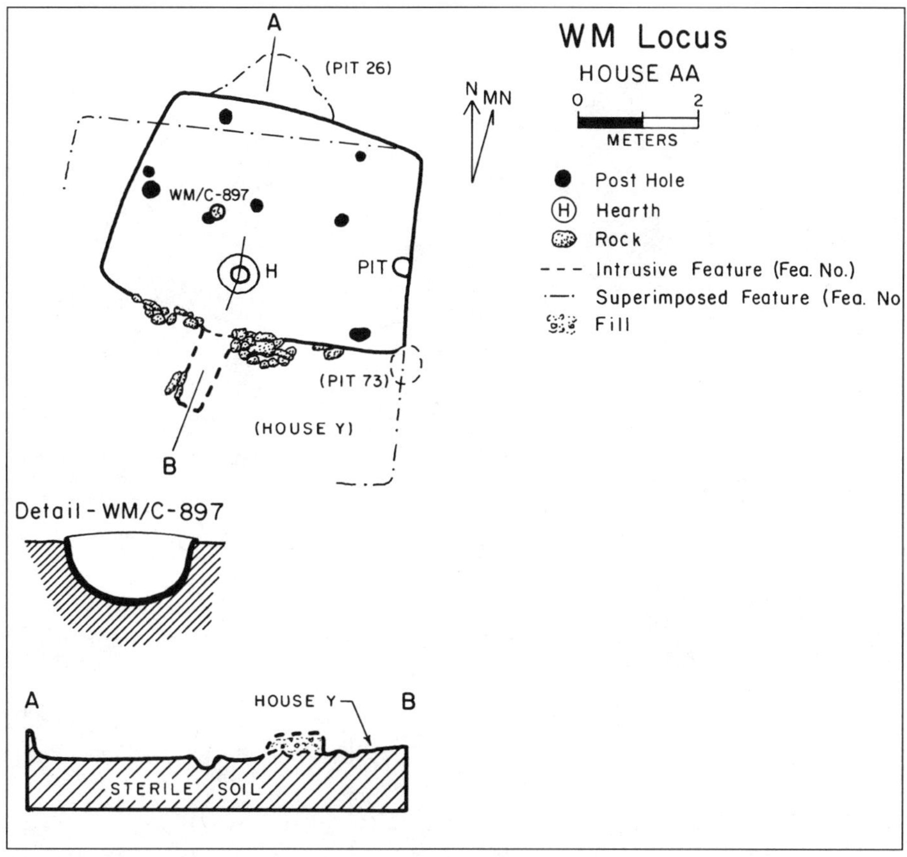

FIGURE 4.60. Plan view and profile of Wind Mountain locus House AA, a Type IV structure. The base of an Alma Plain bowl (WM/C 897) was inset into the house floor (see detail).

from Level 3 (Chapter 3). Level 4, the unplastered, level house floor (depth 120 cm) appeared as a use compacted surface. House walls were smooth and vertical. The east wall of House AA incorporated the earlier House Y wall into its construction. The structure's south wall was reinforced with a rough masonry. A thin layer of plaster (thickness 3–5 mm) was noted on the east, south, and north walls. The height of plaster (measured from the floor) ranged from 20 cm on the south wall to 85 cm along the north wall. The clay lined hearth (Type IIA2; diameter 30 cm, depth 20 cm), circular with a concave floor, was encircled by a low clay collar (height 5 cm, width 20 cm). No evidence of ash was observed. One archaeomagnetic sample (No. 010) was taken from the House AA hearth (Chapter 3). An oval pit (length 26 cm, width 22 cm, depth 10 cm) with vertical sides, occurred near the east wall. A bowl (WM/C 897, Alma Plain), buried up to its rim, was found in the northeast quadrant of the house floor. The House AA entry (estimated area .60 m^2, width 40–50 cm), built into the loose fill of House Y, was difficult to define. It appeared to have been constructed slightly off center from the midpoint of the south wall. The entry was coated with a thin layer of clay plaster.

House BB (Figure 4.61)

Type IV structure; length 3.60 m, width 3.60 m; area of living surface 12.31 m^2; mean orientation of entry 115°.

House BB intruded into House CC. It was later intruded by Room 13, and Pits 28 and 30.

Level 1 (range 0–45 cm) was composed of floor fill from Room 13 (see Room 13 description). Level 2 (range 45–75 cm, floor fill) included a dark gray, pebbly silt intermixed with cultural debris. The unplastered floor (depth 75 cm) was leveled and compacted through use. House walls appeared smooth, unplastered, and vertical. A circular, basin-shaped, clay lined hearth (Type IIA; diameter 28 cm, depth 10 cm) was exposed near the house entrance. It exhibited a low clay ridge on its southern and eastern edges, evidently the result of remodeling and replastering. One archaeomagnetic sample (No. 009) was taken from the House BB hearth (Chapter 3). The unplastered house entry (estimated area .96 m^2) was a moderately long (160 cm) and narrow (55 cm) ramp (8°) with a shallow 10 cm step at its lower end.

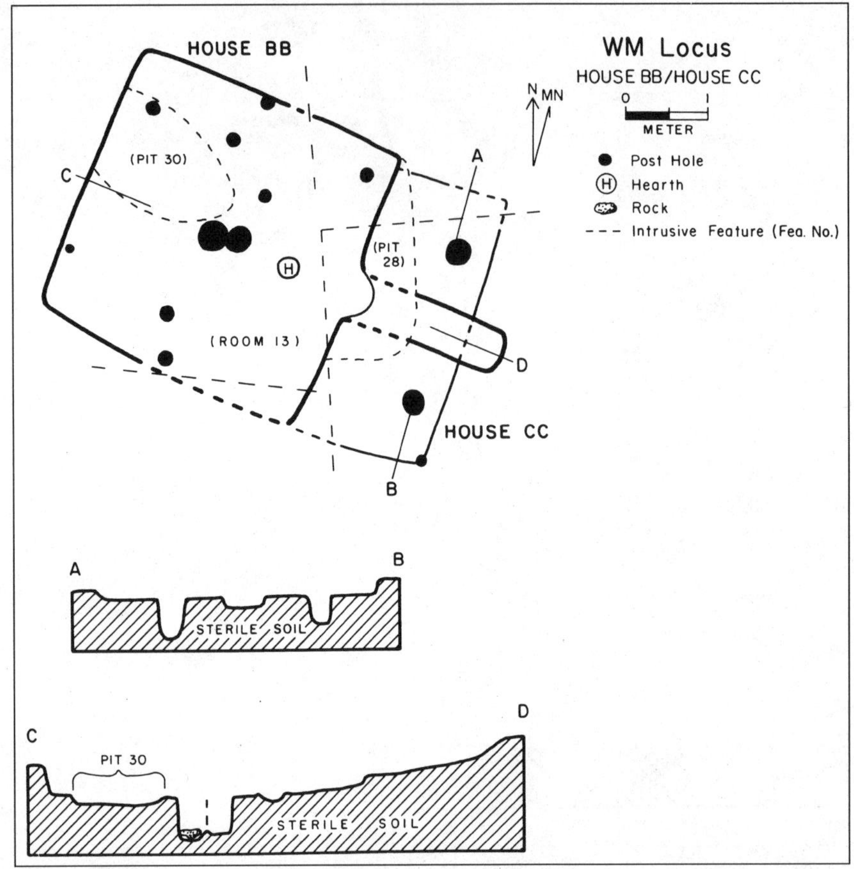

FIGURE 4.61. Plan view and profiles of Wind Mountain locus House BB, a Type IV structure, superimposed on House CC, another Type IV structure.

House CC (Figure 4.61)

Type VI structure; length 3.30 m, width 1.50+ m; remaining area of living surface 4.99 m^2.

House CC was greatly disturbed by both the construction of House BB and excavation of Pit 28.

Level 1 (range 0–20 cm) consisted of a gray, trash laden fill that had been significantly impacted by later occupation activities. Level 2 (range 20–30 cm) was composed of a sterile (apparently alluviated) orange fill containing a large quantity of gravel. Level 3 (range 30–35 cm, floor fill) included a dark gray, pebbly silt intermixed with site debris. The house floor (depth 35 cm), overlying sterile soil, was leveled by use. Unplastered house wall fragments were vertical. Neither the west wall, the house entry, nor a hearth were found.

House DD (Figure 4.62)

Type IV structure; length 4.55 m, width 3.40 m; area of living surface 15.23 m^2; mean orientation of entry 179°.

House DD superpositioned Houses HH and II. Pit Oven 4 intruded into the House DD fill.

Level 1 (range 0–140 cm) comprised a uniformly dark gray, pebbly silt. Fragments of wall plaster and scattered rock were noted at the lowest levels of this stratum. Level 2 (range 140–160 cm, floor fill) was similar in appearance to Level 1, with the addition of burned plaster, rock, wood, and fragmentary charcoal. One C^{14} sample (GX-6552) was analyzed (Chapter 3). The partially plastered (thickness 8 cm) House DD floor (depth 160 cm) appeared as a leveled surface. Floor plastering was most obvious near the southeast corner where burned plaster extended down the vertical wall and out onto the floor, covering an area of about .25 m^2. House walls were vertical and had been plastered with a sandy clay (thickness 1–5 mm). The plaster height (measured from the floor) ranged from 55 cm on the south wall to 70 cm on the north and east walls. The exterior downsloping area outside the north wall had been reinforced with loosely coursed rock and soil, which retained a maximum height above sterile soil of 45 cm. The hearth (Type IB; diameter approximately 36 cm, depth 15 cm), an ephemeral irregularly shaped depression, was located between the entry and central post hole. An unlined, and apparently unburned, ash pit (diameter 35 cm, depth 12 cm) containing a white ash was found northeast of the hearth. The House DD entry (area 1.65 m^2) described a long

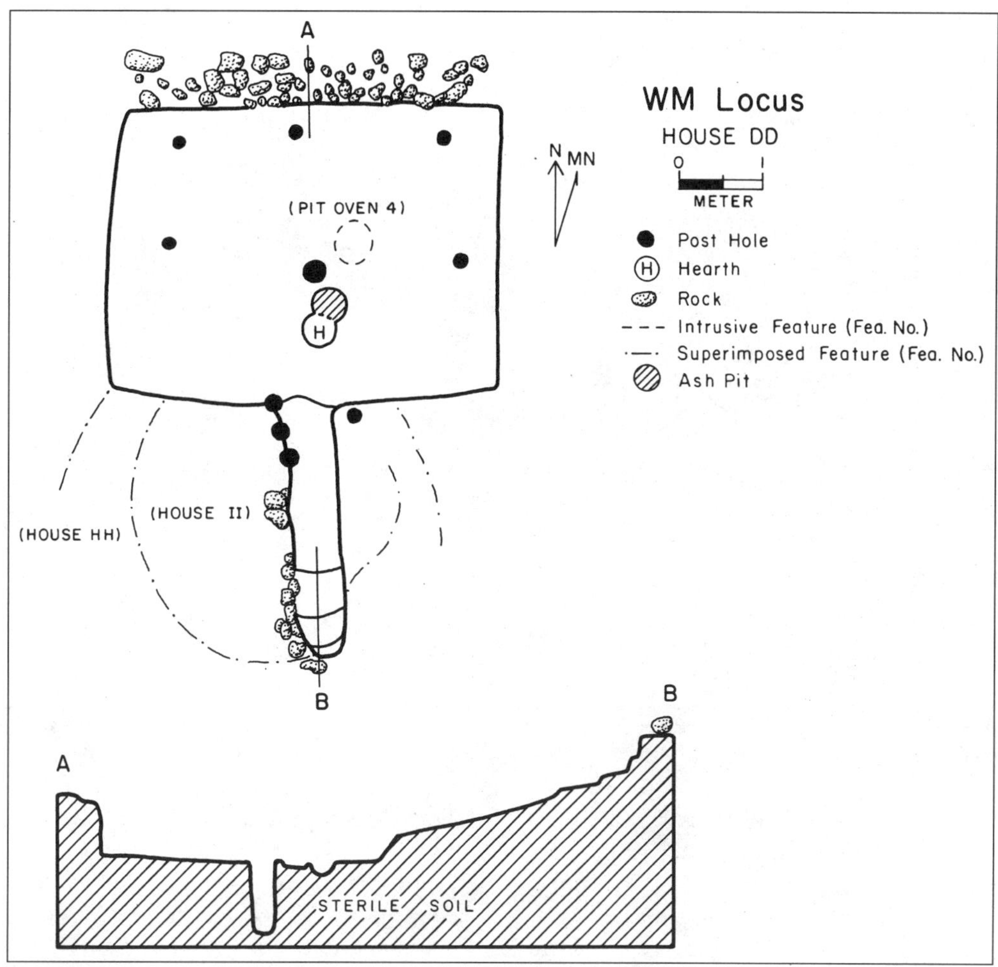

FIGURE 4.62. Plan view and profile of Wind Mountain locus House DD, a Type IV structure.

(290 cm), narrow (55 cm), and stepped ramp (14°) that joined the house at the center of the south wall. Rocks located along the west side of the entry served to retain the loose fill of House II. A concentration of burned material on the House DD floor suggests that it was destroyed by fire. One archaeomagnetic sample (No. 017) was taken from the plastered floor (Chapter 3).

House EE (Figure 4.63)

Type II structure; length 3.80 m, width 3.70 m; area of living surface 11.28 m²; mean orientation of entry 94°.

The northwestern edge of House EE was overlain by Pavement 4 and was slightly intruded by Burial 44.

Level 1 (range 0–10 cm) was characterized by a dark gray, consolidated, pebbly silt. Level 2 (range 10–30 cm) consisted of a uniformly dark gray, pebbly silt with some rock. Level 3 (range 30–40 cm, floor fill) compared with Level 2. The floor (depth 40 cm) was roughly leveled and compacted by use. One small segment of floor plaster (area .25 m²) survived south of the central post hole. An archaeomagnetic sample (No. 014) was taken from the House EE plastered floor (Chapter 3). Slightly sloping house walls had been excavated into sterile soil. A trace of burned plaster (thickness 1 mm) occurred on the west wall. Two stones placed together in the south wall appeared to fill a hole (possibly a rodent burrow), or an unstable spot in the house wall. The hearth (Type IB; length 25 cm, width 20 cm, depth 8 cm), an irregularly shaped basin containing a thin layer of ash was located midway between the central post hole and the house entry. The central post hole (diameter 30 cm, depth 15 cm) held a rectangular stone slab set into the floor of the post socket. Another stone slab was recovered from the south side of the post hole. Stone probably once lined this entire feature, but pot hunting activity had disrupted this portion of the house. The entry (surviving area .64 m²), exposed along the midpoint of the east wall of the house, varied in width (range 35 cm to 70 cm). Entry length was difficult to distinguish beyond approximately 1 m from the house wall, where it disappeared into sterile soil. Three floor pits in the western portion of the

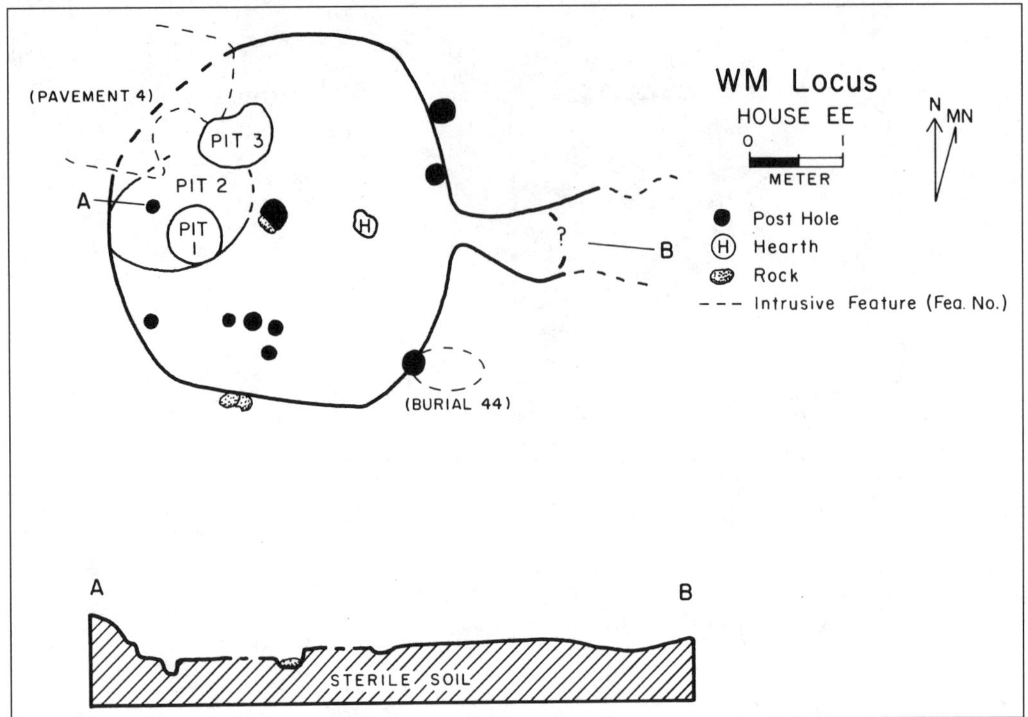

FIGURE 4.63. Plan view and profile of Wind Mountain locus House EE, a Type II structure.

house, evidently excavated while the house was occupied, greatly disturbed the integrity of the original living surface. Pit 1 (diameter 55 cm, depth 50 cm) displayed a circular plan with straight sides and concave floor. Pit 2 (maximum diameter 140 cm, minimum diameter 100 cm, depth 12 cm) consisted of a shallow ovoid pit with sloping sides and a flat floor. Pit 3 (length 80 cm, width 60 cm, depth 60 cm), an irregular oval feature, was slightly disturbed by pot hunting.

House FF (Figure 4.64)

Type IV structure; length 4.80 m, width 3.90 m; area of living surface 17.26 m^2; mean orientation of entry 129°.

House FF was superimposed by Rooms 15 and 16. Burials 47, 48, 50, and 51 intruded into the house fill.

During excavation, House FF was divided into two halves (southeast and northwest). Each half was dug in discrete increments. Level 1 (range 0–55 cm) of the southeast half consisted of Room 16 fill (see Room 16 description). Level 2 (range 55–110 cm) was defined as a dark gray, pebbly silt with a thin layer of a reddish tan clay. Level 1 (range 0–20 cm) of the northwest half was composed of fill from Rooms 15 and 16 (see Rooms 15 and 16 descriptions). Level 2 (range 20–110 cm) included a mixed dark gray, pebbly silt with some horizontal banding of what appeared to be melted adobe. The House FF floor fill, Level 3 (range 110–120 cm), the same in both the southeast and the northwest excavation halves, comprised a dark gray, pebbly soil intermixed with "chunky" sterile soil, rock, and melted adobe. The house floor (depth 120 cm), though level, appeared gravelly and unconsolidated. Unplastered house walls were vertical to slightly sloping. The walls seemed to have deteriorated prior to in filling, suggesting the structure was robbed of its superstructure, which left the house pit vulnerable to erosion. Two hearths were found midway between the house entry and the central post hole. Hearth 1 (Type IA; length 55 cm, width 45 cm) described a shallow basin with a bulging extension (length 20 cm, width 25 cm) along its east side. Both hearth and protrusion were lined with a thin layer of clay and attained a depth of about 10 cm. Hearth 2 (Type IB; length 60 cm, width 25–30 cm, depth 16 cm) exhibited an irregular shape with sloping sides and a concave floor. Hearth 2 predated Hearth 1, which partially overlapped it. One C^{14} sample (GX-6554) was analyzed from Hearth 2. Two pits had been excavated into the House FF floor. Pit 1 (length 110 cm, width 65 cm, depth 45 cm) showed an irregular plan with vertical sides and a concave floor. Pit 2 (length 70 cm, width 60 cm, depth 45 cm) was oval with vertical sides and a concave floor. The House FF entry (area 1.13 m^2), a long (245 cm) and narrow (40 cm) inclined feature, occurred at the center point of the southeast wall. The entry ramp sloped upward at about a 3° angle for its first 160 cm, increasing the acuity of its angle to 18° for the remaining length. It was lined with upright stone slabs, metate fragments, crude masonry, and adobe mud.

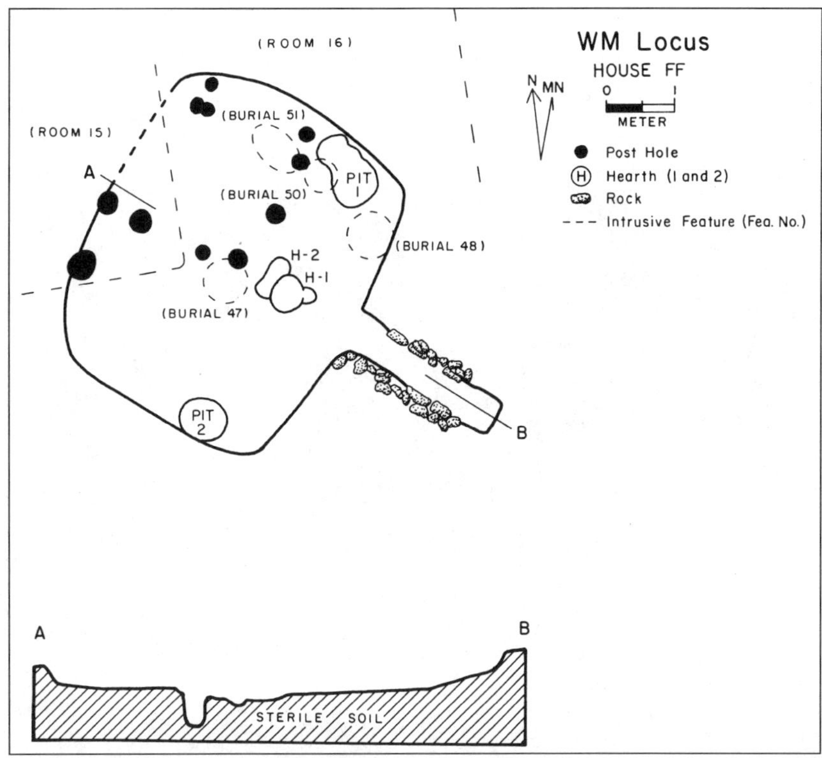

FIGURE 4.64. Plan view and profile of Wind Mountain locus House FF, a Type IV structure.

House GG (Figures 4.65 and 4.66)

Type I structure; length 4.00 m, width 3.15 m; estimated area of living surface 10.49 m².

House GG predated House NN, which cut into the structure on its southeastern edge. Pit Ovens 6, 7, and 20 intruded into the House GG fill. Pit 46 partially impacted its northern side.

Level 1 (range 0–25 cm) was removed as Excavation Unit Block 29–A/B/C/D during a probe for subsurface features. Level 2 (range 25–50 cm) consisted of a homogeneous, dark gray, pebbly silt. Level 3 (range 50–60 cm, floor fill) compared with Level 2. The house floor (depth 60 cm) described a level, use compacted gravelly sterile soil that had been disturbed by either rodents or vandals. Unplastered house walls were vertical to slightly sloping and had been excavated into sterile soil. The hearth (Type IB; length 50 cm, width 30 cm, depth 18 cm) exhibited an irregular plan with sloping sides and a concave floor. No house entry was found.

House HH (Figure 4.67)

Type I structure; length 5.20 m, width 4.70+ m; remaining area of living surface 16.71 m².

House HH intruded into the northern edge of House JJ. House II and the entries of Houses T, DD, and possibly Entry 1 of House KK intruded into House HH. Bird Burial 7 and Burials 59, 61, and 62 intruded into the floor and fill of House HH. Pits 36 and 48 and Pit Ovens 8 and 9 also impacted the structure.

Level 1 (range 0–45 cm) consisted of a homogeneous, dark gray, pebbly silt that was removed as Excavation Unit Block 21–C/D. Level 2 (range 45–65 cm) was composed of a uniform dark gray, pebbly silt intermixed with rock. Rodent disturbance was apparent. Level 3 (range 65–80 cm, floor fill) compared with Level 2. The house floor (depth 80 cm), excavated primarily into sterile soil (exclusive of sections penetrating House JJ) appeared as a level, use compacted surface. A thin veneer of plaster covered the house floor. Surviving walls were vertical and unplastered. The northern walls of House HH were absent due to erosion and the construction of other later structures. A clay lined, basin-shaped hearth (Type IIA; approximate diameter 30 cm, depth 15 cm), partially demolished (50 percent) by the construction of the House DD entry, was exposed. The hearth lip or edge was level with the house floor surface. One archaeomagnetic sample (No. 021) was taken from the House HH hearth (Chapter 3). A fire altered section of floor (26 cm wide) extended 14 cm to the east of the hearth edge. An oval floor pit (length 48 cm, width 38 cm, depth 28 cm) with vertical undercut sides and a flat floor was located near the center of the house. No evidence of a house entry was noted.

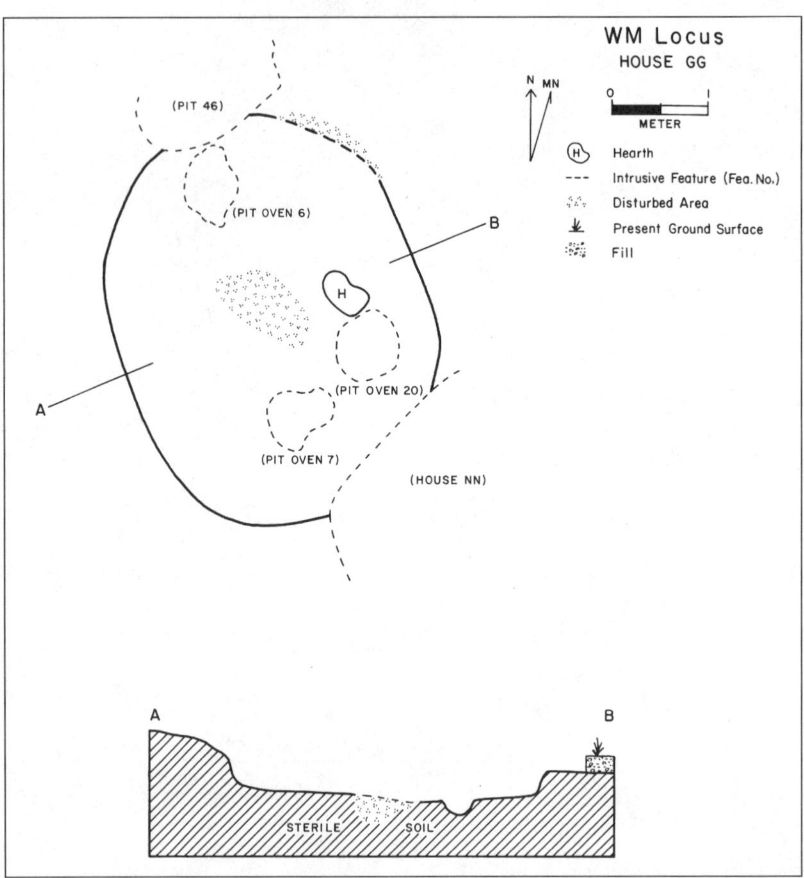

FIGURE 4.65. Plan view and profile of Wind Mountain locus House GG, a Type I structure.

FIGURE 4.66. Wind Mountain locus House GG, indicating its relationship to House NN. Intrusive Pit Ovens 6, 7, and 20 (cf. Figure 4.65) are clearly visible (Neg. No. WM 70–28F).

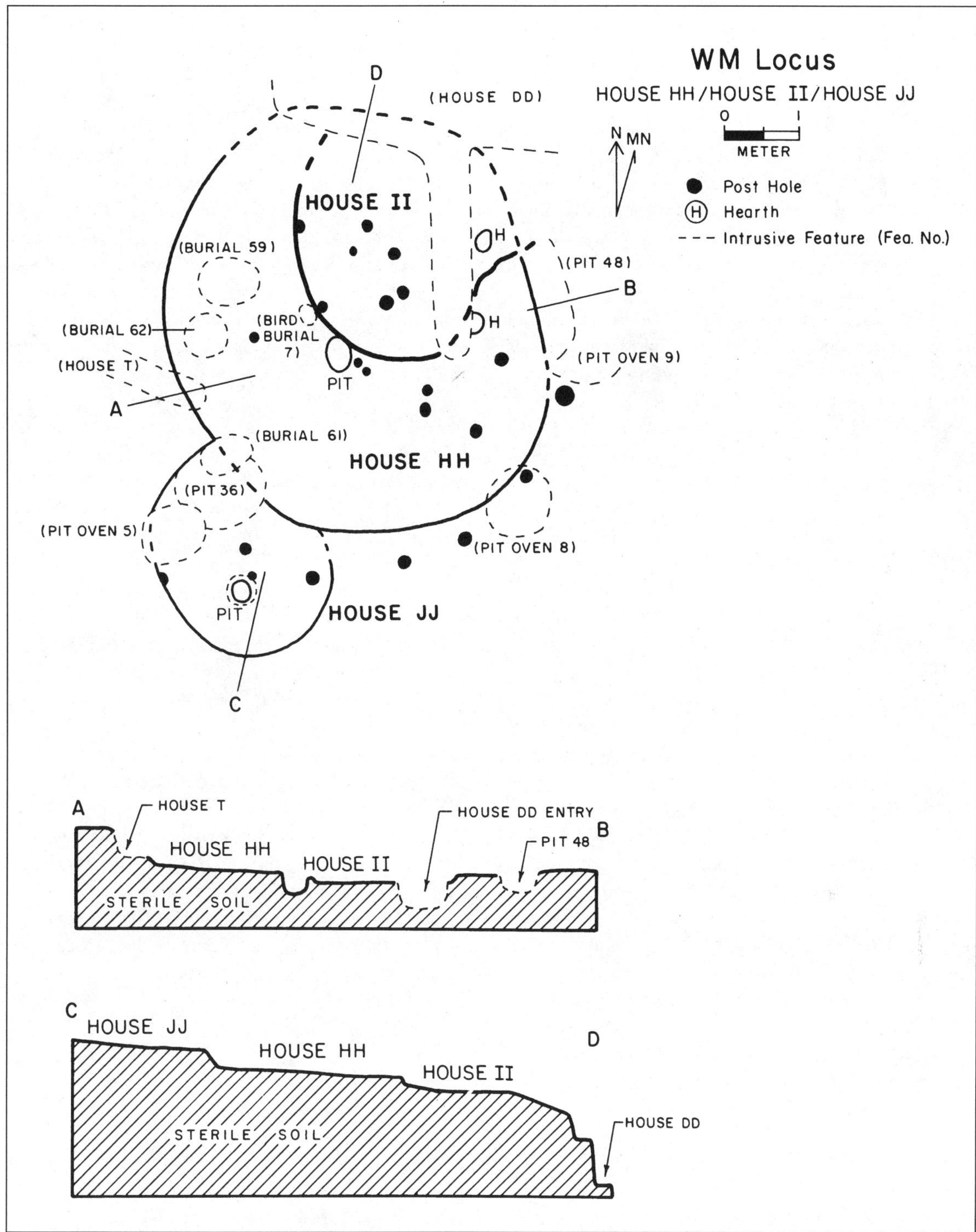

FIGURE 4.67. Plan views and profiles of superimposed Type I structures, Wind Mountain locus Houses HH, II (the least well preserved), and JJ. These houses are another example of the complex stratigraphic positioning of many of the Wind Mountain site's architectural units.

House II (Figure 4.67)

Type I structure; length 2.90+ m, width 2.35+ m; remaining area of living surface 5.41 m^2.

House II intruded into House HH and was, in turn, intruded by House DD.

Level 1 (range 0–45 cm) consisted of a homogeneous, dark gray, pebbly silt that was removed as Excavation Unit Block 21–D. Level 2 (range 45–80 cm) was described as a uniformly dark gray, pebbly silt, with a few rocks and some rodent disturbance. Level 3 (range 80–90 cm, floor fill) compared with Level 2. The floor (depth 90 cm) appeared level and compacted by use, with patches of burned plaster (thickness <1 mm). Walls were slightly sloping and unplastered. Less than 50 percent of House II survived, destroyed by the intrusion of House DD and erosion. A possible hearth (Type IV; diameter 28 cm) identified only as a burned patch of floor plaster was uncovered. No evidence of an entry was located.

House JJ (Figure 4.67)

Type I structure; length 2.90+ m, width 2.50+ m; remaining area of living surface 4.91 m^2.

House JJ was intruded by House HH. Pit 36, Pit Oven 5, and Burial 61 intruded into the house.

Level 1 (range 0–45 cm), including most of the house fill and floor fill, was removed as Excavation Unit Block 20–A before House JJ was recognized as a structure. Level 2 (range 45–55 cm, floor fill) consisted of homogeneous, dark gray, pebbly silt. The unplastered house floor (depth 55 cm) was leveled and compacted by use. Slightly sloping unplastered house walls had been excavated into sterile soil. Approximately one-third of the wall periphery was obliterated by the construction of House HH. House JJ wall remnants reached a height (measured from the floor) of 15 cm. A slightly undercut floor pit (surface diameter 30 cm, maximum diameter 40 cm, depth 30 cm) with a concave floor occurred at the southern end of the house. Due to the poor state of preservation, neither a hearth nor entry was located.

House KK (Figure 4.68)

Type II structure; length 3.30 m, width 3.20 m; area of living surface 8.04 m^2; mean orientation of Entry 1, 303°; mean orientation of Entry 2, 200°.

House KK superimposed Houses LL and MM. It was intruded by Pits 40 and 48, Pit Oven 9, and Burial 68.

Level 1 (range 0–40 cm) was removed as Excavation Unit Block 22–C. Level 2 (range 40–50 cm, floor fill) consisted of a dark gray silt. The house floor (depth 50 cm) was compacted by use, although some rocks and cobbles protruded from the underlying sterile soil. Two hearths were defined. Hearth 1 (Type IA; diameter 32 cm, depth 13 cm) was partly coated with a thin layer of mud or plaster, had sloping sides, a concave floor, and was excavated into sterile soil. A small area of plastered floor survived along its east side. Hearth 2 (Type IIB; diameter 40 cm, depth 20 cm) was circular with sloping sides, a concave floor, and had been excavated into a sterile bed of rocks and cobbles. The edges or lips of both hearths were flush with the house floor surface. A small ash pit (diameter 18 cm, depth 9 cm) occurred midway between Hearth 2 and Entry 2. House KK included two unplastered entries. Entry 1 (surviving area .39 m^2, width 40 cm), on the house's west side, retained a length of 110 cm. Its western end was terminated by the intrusion of Pit 48. Entry 2 (estimated area .72 m^2, length approximately 120 cm, width of surviving section 35 cm), on the structure's south side, was impacted by Pit 40. The existence of two entries and two hearths suggests House KK was remodeled, though the temporal order of these features is unclear.

House LL (Figure 4.69)

Type I structure; length 3.05+ m, width 2.80+ m; estimated area of living surface 7.40 m^2.

House LL intruded into House MM and was impacted by House KK, Pit 40, Pit Oven 8, and Burial 68.

Level 1 (range 0–45 cm) was removed in Excavation Units comprising Blocks 21–D, 22–C, 29–B, and 30–A during subsurface testing. Level 2 (range 45–50 cm, floor fill) was composed of a homogeneous, dark gray, pebbly silt. The unplastered floor (depth 50 cm) was leveled and compacted by use. Remaining house walls were vertical to slightly sloping and unplastered. Erosion and the intrusion of other structures destroyed more than 50 percent of House LL. Pit 40, for instance, which occurred roughly in the center of the house, displaced approximately 1.90 m^2 of floor space. No floor features or house entry were located.

House MM (Figure 4.69)

Type I structure; length 2.80 m, width 2.45+ m; remaining area of living surface 3.36 m^2.

House MM was intruded by House LL, the entry of House KK, and Burial 67.

Level 1 (range 0–45 cm) was removed as Excavation Unit Block 30–A during a subsurface test for features. The house floor, Level 2, (depth 45 cm) was composed of loose dirt, intermixed with materials from upper levels. The surviving floor was level and unplastered, much of it, however, destroyed by downslope erosion. The only intact wall (a remnant) occurred along the upslope, western portion of the house. This wall fragment retained a residual maximum height of 40 cm (measured from the floor). A partially plastered circular hearth (Type IIA; diameter 33 cm, depth 15

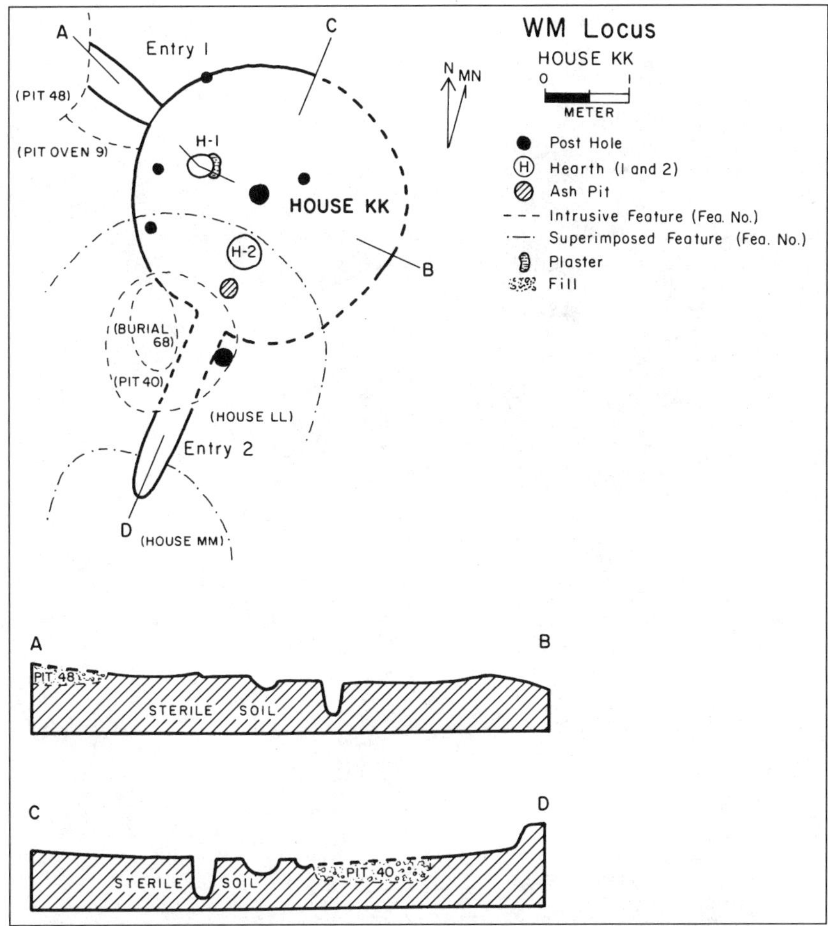

FIGURE 4.68. Plan view and profiles of Wind Mountain locus House KK, a Type II structure.

cm) with sloping sides and concave floor was constructed in sterile soil. Its lip was set flush with the surrounding house floor surface. No evidence of an entrance was found.

House NN (Figure 4.70)

Type III structure; length 3.75 m, width 2.70 m; estimated area of living surface 9.82 m^2.

House NN was superimposed on House GG and was intruded by Pit 45 and Bird Burial 8.

Level 1 (range 0–20 cm) was removed as Excavation Unit Block 29–D during a subsurface test for features. Level 2 (range 20–40 cm) and Level 3 (range 40–60 cm, floor fill) consisted of a dark gray, pebbly silt, littered throughout with burned adobe fragments. Wall, or possibly roof fall, material was observed within the north half of the house. This debris rested on about 20 cm of fill, indicating to the excavators that the house was partially filled in prior to the collapse of its superstructure. The material was composed of a mixture of rock, unburned adobe, and plaster. The plaster displayed numerous clues about house construction and the perishable substances used (Figure 4.71).

Impressions in the clay described a series of vertical beams spaced at 21.6, 23.2, and 27.1 cm intervals. These beams were interpreted as wall posts, their diameters ranging from 0.6 cm (two specimens) to 0.9 cm (one specimen). Field notes make reference to fibrous ties wrapped around the post circumferences. At right angles to the posts "sticks" had been spaced at the following intervals: 7.6, 9.5, 9.6, 9.9, 10.3, and 10.8 cm. Clay impressions suggest that, generally, these sticks (diameters measuring 0.7, 0.8, 0.9, 1.0 (2), 1.1, 1.2 (2), and 1.3 cm) were set in pairs. In the case of a single stick being used, the diameter measured 1.3 cm. A separate and incomplete cast measuring 1.5 cm may or may not have been set as a pair. A composite material of reeds and grasses, (reed diameters were 0.2 (2), 0.3 (7), 0.4 (18), 0.5 (27), 0.6 (20), 0.7 (15), 0.8 (6), and 0.9 (2) cm) occurred parallel to the posts. The house floor (depth 60 cm) was constructed on leveled, sterile soil retaining sufficient structural integrity to determine that it was at one time plastered with a sandy clay (ap-

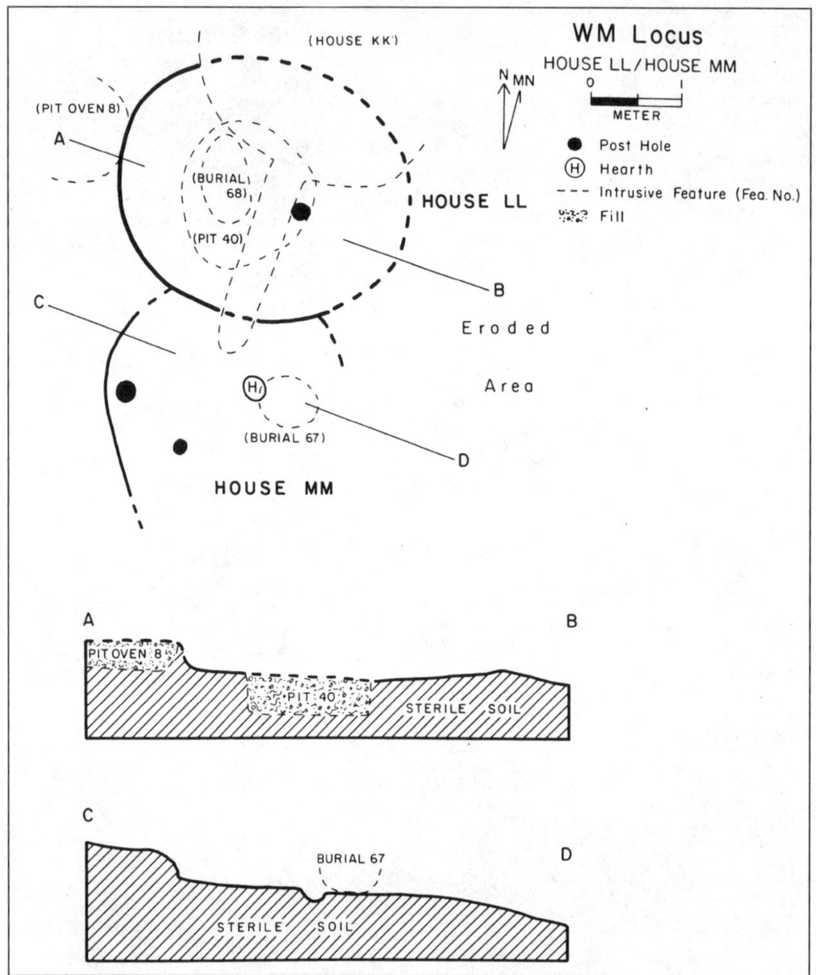

FIGURE 4.69. Plan views and profiles of Wind Mountain locus Houses LL and MM, both Type I structures.

proximate thickness 2 mm). Some portions of the floor displayed evidence of burning, although the entire house was apparently not destroyed by fire. One C^{14} sample (GX-6555) recovered from a partially burned support post was analyzed (Chapter 3). House walls were vertical and originally plastered. The existing wall plaster (measured from the floor) ranged from a height of 20 cm on the west wall to 25 cm on the south wall. Two hearths were located on the floor of House NN. Hearth 1 (Type IIB; diameter 18 cm, depth 5 cm) described a roughly circular, shallow, ash filled depression. Hearth 2 (Type IIB; diameter 30 cm, depth 3 cm) was visible only as a thin ash lens. No entry was located.

House OO (Figures 4.72 and 4.73)

Type IV structure; length 4.10 m, width 3.80 m; area of living surface 15.37 m^2; mean orientation of entry 353°.

The entry to House OO was intruded by *Canis* Burials 7 and 8, as well as by Burial 75.

Level 1 (range 0–100 cm) was composed of a uniformly dark gray, pebbly silt intermixed with pieces of burned plaster and rock. Level 2 (range 100–120 cm, floor fill) compared with Level 1 but showed a slight increase in fragmentary charcoal. The house floor (depth 120 cm) consisted of a level, use compacted surface with patches of burned plaster. One C^{14} sample (GX-6553 was recovered from the House OO floor (Chapter 3). Plastered house walls were vertical to slightly sloping. Plaster extended to all four walls and ranged in height (measured from the floor) from 60 cm on the south wall to 90 cm on the north wall. A portion of the west wall had been heavily reinforced with randomly set stone, secured in place by a tan colored mortar. A circular, basin-shaped hearth (Type IIB; diameter 38 cm, depth 18 cm), its rim level with the floor surface, was located just inside the house entry. A shallow, circular pit (diameter 42 cm, depth 5 cm) occurred near the west wall. The entry (area 2.63 m^2, length 400 cm, width 80 cm) ramp (incline 2–3°) was stepped and allowed access to the house at the midpoint of its north wall.

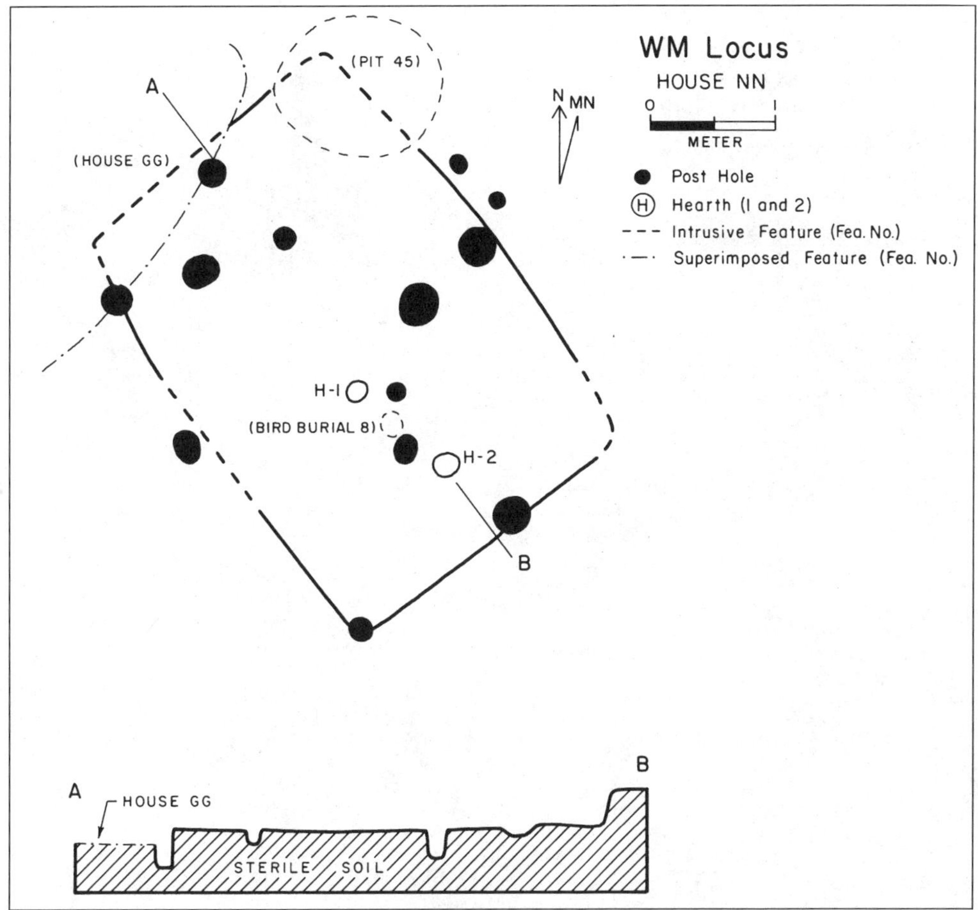

FIGURE 4.70. Plan view and profile of Wind Mountain locus House NN, a Type III structure.

A step situated in the entry way, just outside the living area proper, retained the impression of a log (diameter 9 cm) that had been positioned as a step edge. The southeast corner of House OO was destroyed by pot hunting.

House PP (Figure 4.74)

Type IV structure; length 5.05 m, width 3.75 m; area of living surface 17.39 m²; mean orientation of entry 102°.

Level 1 (range 0–30 cm) comprised a uniformly dark gray, pebbly silt. Level 2 (range 30–100 cm) consisted of a uniform light gray, loosely consolidated pebbly silt. Several ash lenses were observed in the lower portion of this fill. Level 3 (range 100–130 cm) was composed of a uniform light gray, loosely compacted pebbly silt intermixed with some charcoal flecks and adobe fragments of architectural origin. Level 4 (range 130–140 cm, floor fill) compared with to Level 3. The unplastered house floor (depth 140 cm) was level and compacted by use. House walls were near vertical and had been lined with a tan pebbly clay (thickness 2–10 cm). Plaster height (measured from the floor) ranged from 70 cm on the south wall to 100 cm on the north wall. Large stones set into clay, presumably to reinforce the eastern half of the north wall, stabilized loose fill extensive in that area of the site. A shallow, clay lined, basin-shaped hearth (Type IIA; length 53 cm, width 41 cm, depth 13 cm), its lip flush with the house floor, occurred between the central post hole and the house entry. A small post hole (diameter 8 cm, depth 13 cm), located between the central post hole and the west wall, was suggested to mimic the form and placement of a sipapu. Three floor pits, arranged along a north-south axis through the house, were exposed. Pit 1 (length 44 cm, width 38 cm, depth 85 cm) was defined as an irregularly shaped feature with a concave floor and slightly undercut sides. Pit 2 (length 25 cm, width 23 cm, length 15 cm) described an oval-shaped depression with vertical sides and a concave floor. Pit 2 was covered with a slab, the remnant of a grinding stone (WM 2169). Pit 3 (length 53 cm, maximum width 24 cm, depth 31 cm), irregular in plan, contained a cache of stone artifacts, including three manos, three hammerstones, an axe/maul, a scraper, and a small Alma Plain jar (WM 2170). The narrow (35 cm), stepped House PP entry (estimated area 1.36 m²)

FIGURE 4.71. Detail of plaster, wood, and cordage construction of Wind Mountain locus House NN. Reconstruction was based on the analysis of burned daub recovered from house fill.

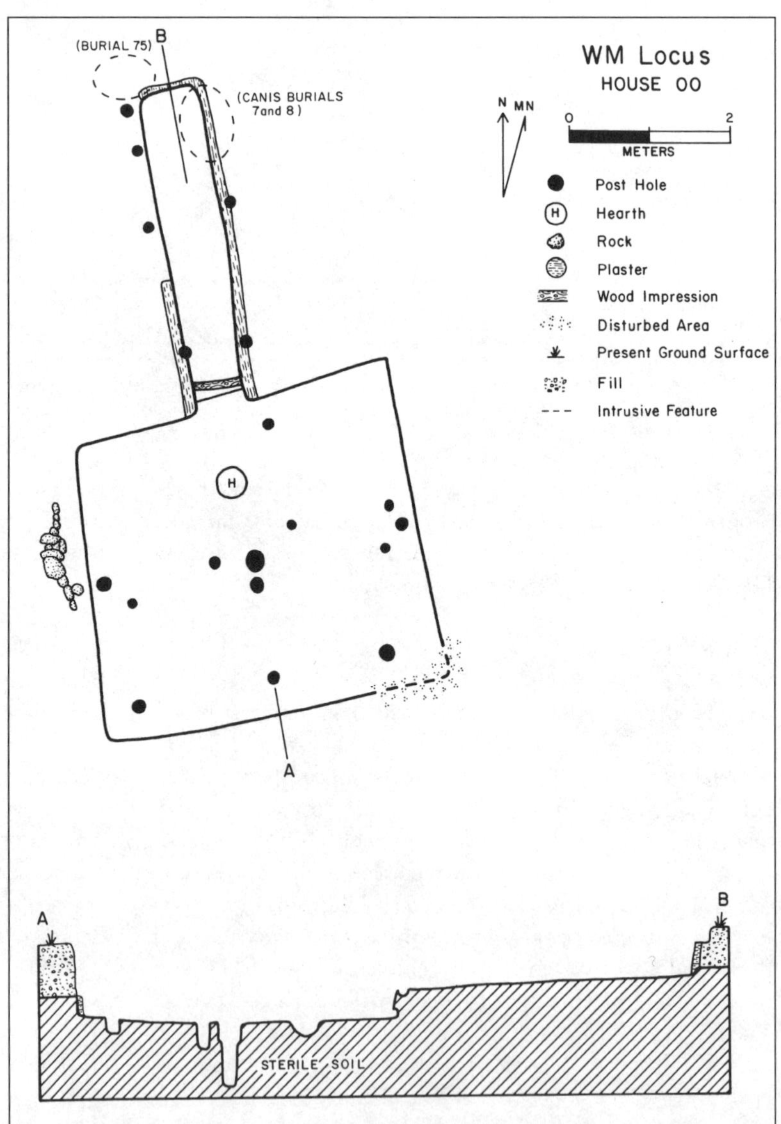

FIGURE 4.72. Plan view and profile of Wind Mountain locus House OO, a Type IV structure.

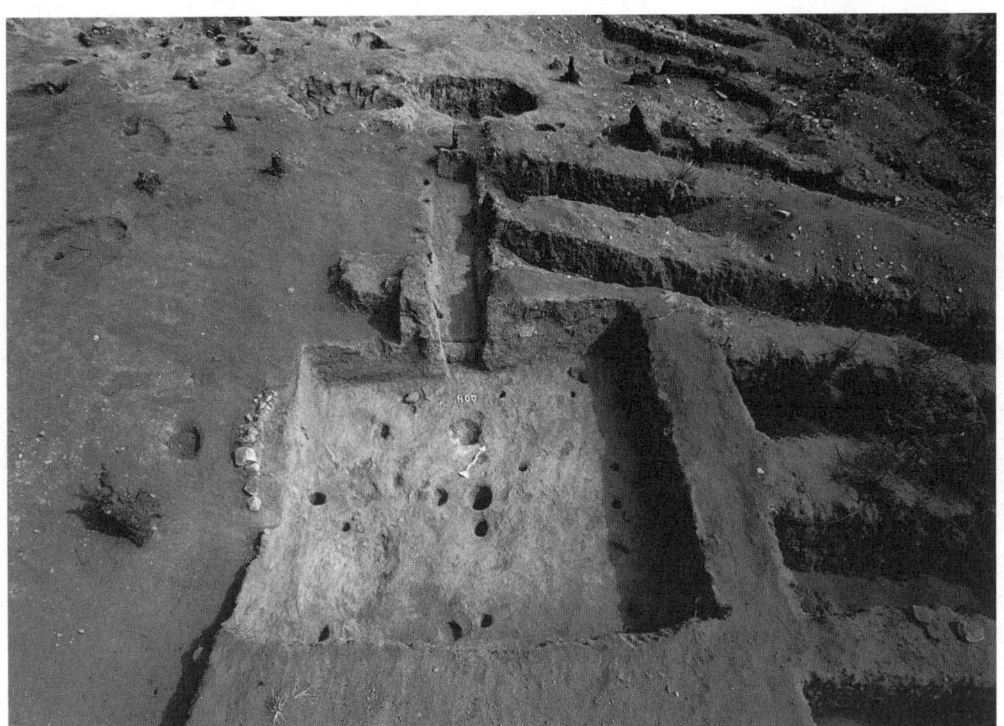

FIGURE 4.73. Wind Mountain locus House OO, exhibiting the structure's long entry. A step is visible at the entry's juncture with the house (Neg. No. WM 72–21A/F).

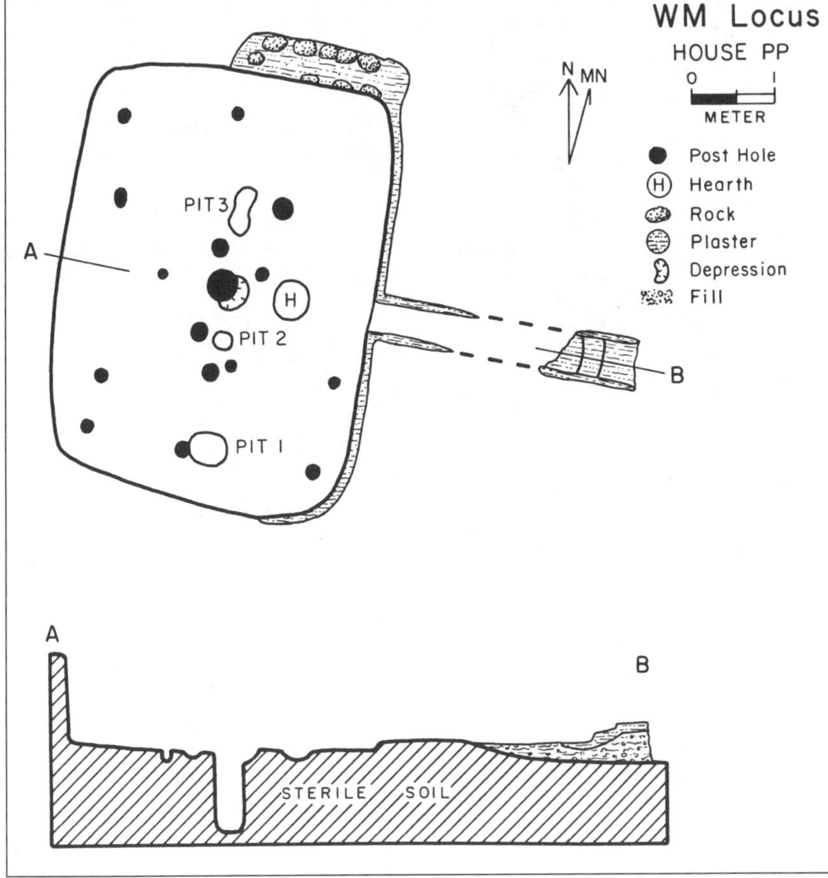

FIGURE 4.74. Plan view and profile of Wind Mountain locus House PP, a Type IV structure.

was uncovered at the midpoint of the east wall. Charring noted along the southern and western walls suggests that the house burned.

House QQ (Figure 4.75; refer to Figure 4.4)

Type II structure; length 3.00 m, width 2.55 m; area of living surface 6.44 m^2; mean orientation of entry 12°.

The fill of House QQ was intruded by Burial 80.

Level 1 (range 0–90 cm) was characterized as a homogeneous, dark gray, pebbly silt. Level 2 (range 90–100 cm, floor fill) compared with Level 1. The house floor (depth 100 cm) described a well smoothed, level surface that showed signs of having been burned in a house fire. Vertical house walls were excavated through site fill into underlying sterile soil. The walls exhibited traces of plastering (thickness 5–30 mm), primarily along the southern side of the house. A small, circular, basin-shaped hearth (Type IIB; diameter 15 cm, depth 3 cm) occurred near the house entry. The House QQ entry (area .50 m^2) consisted of a short (145 cm) and narrow (38 cm) ramp (6°), that joined the structure on its northern side.

House RR (Figure 4.76)

Type II structure; length 2.80 m, width 2.15 m; remaining area of living surface 4.99 m^2; mean orientation of entry 72°.

Level 1 (range 0–60 cm) was composed of a homogeneous, dark gray, pebbly silt intermixed with rock. Level 2 (range 60–70 cm, floor fill) compared with Level 1. The level house floor (depth 70 cm) was compacted by use. House RR walls were not easily distinguishable, but appear to have been vertical. The hearth (Type IIB; diameter 38 cm, depth 10 cm) was a shallow, circular basin, its rim flush with the house floor. The narrow (width 50 cm) house entry (existing area .18 m^2), built into loose fill along its eastern side, was not well preserved. All that survived were two small patches of pebbly clay, extending for approximately 25 cm, flanking the entry on both sides.

House SS (refer to Figure 4.7)

Type IV structure; length 4.35 m, width 3.50 m; area of living surface 14.49 m^2; mean orientation of entry 113°.

House SS was slightly intruded by Pit Oven 15 and Burial 90.

Level 1 (range 0–100 cm) described a loosely compacted, dark gray pebbly silt mixed with cultural debris. Level 2 (range 100–110 cm, floor fill) was generally analogous to Level 1, but contained more rock and burned plaster. Field notes failed to describe the House SS floor (depth 110 cm), although photographs reveal a nonlevel surface covered with rock. Some compaction of the floor undoubtedly occurred through use. House walls were not well preserved, but the north half of the east wall had been rock lined, and its south half was plastered. One archaeomagnetic sample (No. 022) was taken from the plastered House SS wall (Chapter 3). Posts (their diameters ranging from 6 cm to 25 cm) were partially inset into the north and west walls of the house. Two hearths were exposed. Hearth 1 (Type IB; length 60 cm, width 35 cm, depth 15 cm) irregular in plan, occurred between the house entry and post hole 1. Hearth 2 (Type IIA; diameter 30 cm, depth 9 cm) was defined as a shallow, circular, basin-shaped depression with a thin clay lining (5 mm). A straight sided oval floor pit (length 50 cm, width 45 cm, depth 55 cm) with a flat floor was uncovered in the southwestern portion of the house. The narrow (45 cm), apparently level House SS entry (estimated area .98 m^2) joined the structure at the midpoint of its southeast wall. The entry's south wall was rock lined. Its north wall had been destroyed by pot hunting.

House TT (Figure 4.77)

Type IV structure; length 4.35 m, width 3.50 m; area of living surface 10.60 m^2; mean orientation of entry 92°.

House TT intruded into the eastern end of the House AF entry. House TT fill was disturbed by the construction of Work Area 3. Burial 91 was uncovered beneath the structures living surface.

The northeast half of House TT was excavated independently from the southwestern half. Level 1, the northeast portion, extended from 0–95 cm (equivalent to Levels 1, 2, and 3 of the southwest section). Level 1 (range 0–55 cm) was described as a dark gray, well compacted pebbly silt. Level 2 had been disturbed by the construction of Work Area 3. Level 3 (range 55–95 cm) consisted of a loosely consolidated light gray, pebbly silt. Level 4 (range 95–105 cm, floor fill) compared with to Level 3, though it contained a higher concentration of fragmentary charcoal. The unplastered house floor (depth 105 cm) had been graveled and compacted by use. Plastered house walls were vertical. Plaster height (measured from the floor) ranged from 50 cm on the east wall to 80 cm on the north wall. A circular, basin-shaped hearth (Type IIB1; length 38 cm, width 32 cm, depth 12 cm), with sloping sides and a concave floor, occurred just inside the house entry. A flat, unworked hearthstone (length 30 cm, width 15 cm, thickness 8 cm) was found to the east of the hearth's rim. The house entry (surviving area 1.56 m^2) was a narrow (range 45–60 cm) ramp (20° for the first 40 cm and 4° thereafter) that entered the house at the midpoint of the east wall. The eastern end of the entry disappeared into loose fill. House TT was apparently destroyed in a fire.

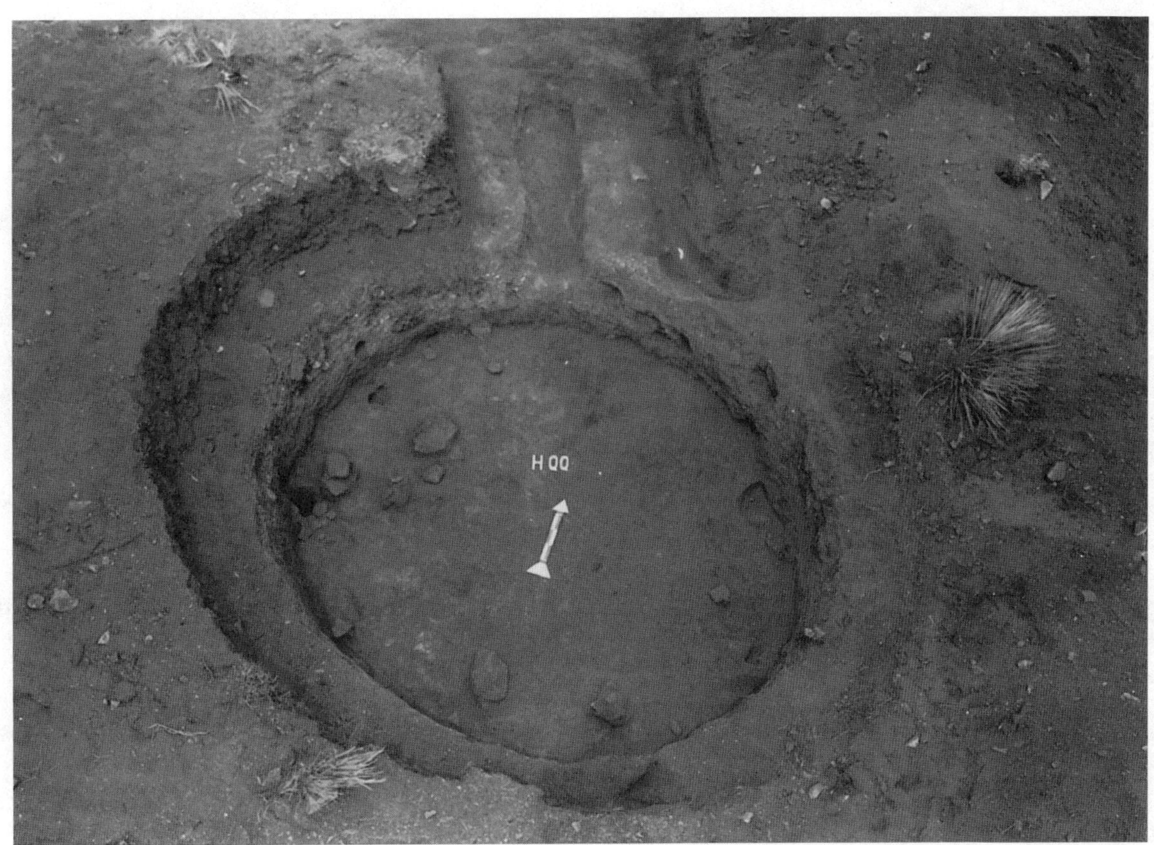

FIGURE 4.75. Wind Mountain locus House QQ, a Type II structure (Neg. No. WM 74–22F).

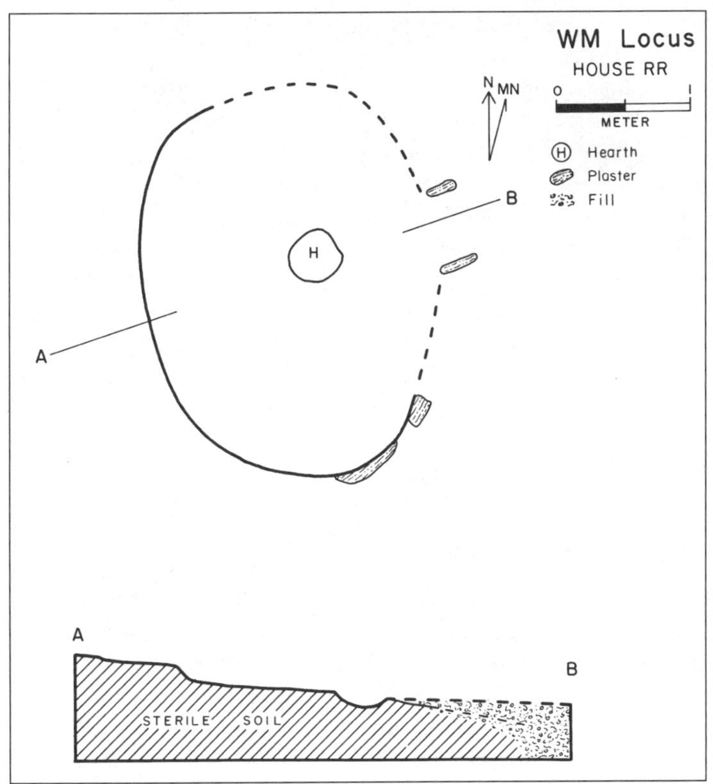

FIGURE 4.76. Plan view and profile of Wind Mountain locus House RR, a Type II structure.

House UU (Figure 4.78)

Type IV structure; length 3.90 m, width 2.90 m; estimated area of living surface 12.44 m^2; mean orientation of entry 117°.

House UU was intruded by House VV and Pit Oven 12. The House UU entry superimposed Pit 60.

Level 1 (range 0–85 cm) comprised a dark gray, pebbly silt and included some House VV fill. Level 2 (range 85–105 cm, floor fill) compared with Level 1. The house floor (depth 105 cm) was smooth and level on the western side, becoming more irregular and 10 cm deeper toward the structure's eastern half. Surviving walls were vertical and smooth, but unplastered. Most of the north wall and a section of the east wall were destroyed by the construction of House VV. The unplastered hearth (Type IB1; diameter 45 cm, depth 15 cm) was described as an irregularly shaped basin with sloping sides and a concave floor, its lip or edge set flush with the house floor. A hearthstone (length 22 cm, width 8 cm, thickness 8 cm) was placed on its southeastern edge. A floor pit (length 36 cm, width 33 cm, depth 45 cm) was exposed near the southern perimeter of the house. The narrow (40 cm), slightly inclined (1°) entry (surviving area 1.16 m^2) permitted access to the structure at the midpoint of its east wall. A patch of burned soil on the house's west wall suggests House UU burned.

House VV (Figure 4.79)

Type IV structure; length 3.70 m, width 3.35 m; area of living surface 8.07 m^2; mean orientation of entry 131°.

House VV intruded into House UU and superimposed Pit 60. Pit Oven 12 intruded into the fill of Houses UU and VV.

Level 1 (range 0–85 cm) was composed of a dark gray, pebbly silt that was removed as House UU fill. Level 2 (range 85–95 cm, floor fill) compared with Level 1. Level 3 (range 95–105 cm) consisted of a subfloor excavation into the shallow depression discovered on the structure's east side. Level 3 fill described a dark gray, pebbly silt. The level unplastered house floor (depth 95 cm) had been compacted by use. The walls on the north side of House VV descended to sterile soil. Walls along the structure's southern section had been cut into the loose fill of House UU. The House VV south wall was plastered with a tan, pebbly clay (8–12 cm thick). A circular, basin-shaped hearth (Type IIB; diameter 50 cm, depth 10 cm) occurred near the entry. The hearth was unlined and its rim set flush with the house floor. A floor pit (diameter 45 cm, depth 55 cm) was exposed just southwest of the central post hole. The House VV entry (surviving area .71 m^2; width 40 cm) joined the house near the midpoint of its southeast wall. Three stone slabs, presumably an attempt to contain loose fill, were found along the entry's north wall. House VV was not recognized as a discrete structure until the fill from its southwestern half was removed during the excavation of House UU.

House WW (refer to Figures 4.6 and 4.31)

Type III structure; length 3.55 m, width 3.25 m; area of living surface 10.67 m^2.

House WW moderately superimposed Pit 58 and Burial 97.

Level 1 (range 0–30 cm) consisted of a well consolidated dark gray, pebbly silt that contained rock and the fragmentary remains of structural adobe derived from burned walls and roofing plaster. A large number of pottery sherds was found intermixed with this material. It was assumed that these sherds represented vessels, either placed on the roof or suspended from "ceiling" beams, which crashed down during a house fire. Burned adobe fragments retained the impressions of what appeared to include beams, cross-beams, reeds, and grass. The house floor, Level 2 (depth 30 cm), was described as a level, use compacted surface that had been burned in several places. House walls were not well preserved. Upright stones (their long axes set vertically) were mortared into place around the house's perimeter, presumably to shore up the walls against loose external fill. Mud plaster was also used extensively around the perimeter. Three hearths were found. Hearth 1 (Type IIA; length 35 cm, width 30 cm, depth 8 cm) was characterized as an oval basin, lined with a thin layer of burned clay (thickness <1 mm), its rim set flush with the house floor. Hearth 2 (Type IIA; diameter 22 cm, depth 17 cm), a circular pit with steep sloping sides, a concave floor, its lip set flush with the house floor, was lined with a thin plaster veneer and appeared only partially burned. While the house was occupied, Hearth 2 had been filled in with a red sterile soil, smoothed over at floor level. Hearth 3 (Type IIB; diameter 30 cm, depth 6 cm) described a shallow, circular basin with its lip set flush with the house floor. Floor Pit 1 (diameter at floor 60 cm, maximum interior diameter 80 cm, depth 38 cm), a large circular depression with undercut sides and a slightly concave floor, occurred in the northwest quadrant of the house. One C^{14} sample (GX-6556) was recovered from Pit 1 (Chapter 3). No evidence of a house entry was observed. It is possible that House WW represented a covered work area, and did not function as a domestic structure.

House XX (refer to Figure 4.18)

Type C structure; length 5.70 m, width 4.85 m; area of living surface 27.95 m^2; mean orientation of entry 66°.

House XX superimposed House AB and Pit Oven 17.

Level 1 (range 0–60 cm) consisted of a dark black, humus-like soil intermixed with numerous sherds. Level 2 (range 60–130 cm) was composed of a light brown, compacted soil with less site debris than Level 1. Level 3 (range 130–148 cm) compared with Level 2, but contained less cultural ma-

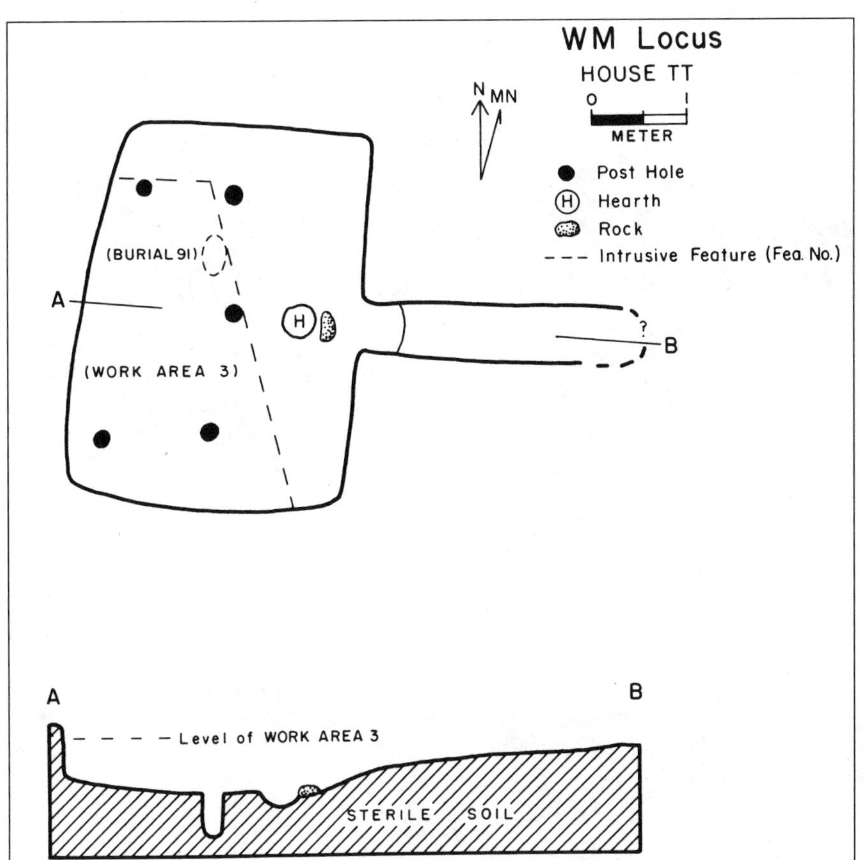

FIGURE 4.77. Plan view and profile of Wind Mountain locus House TT, a Type IV structure.

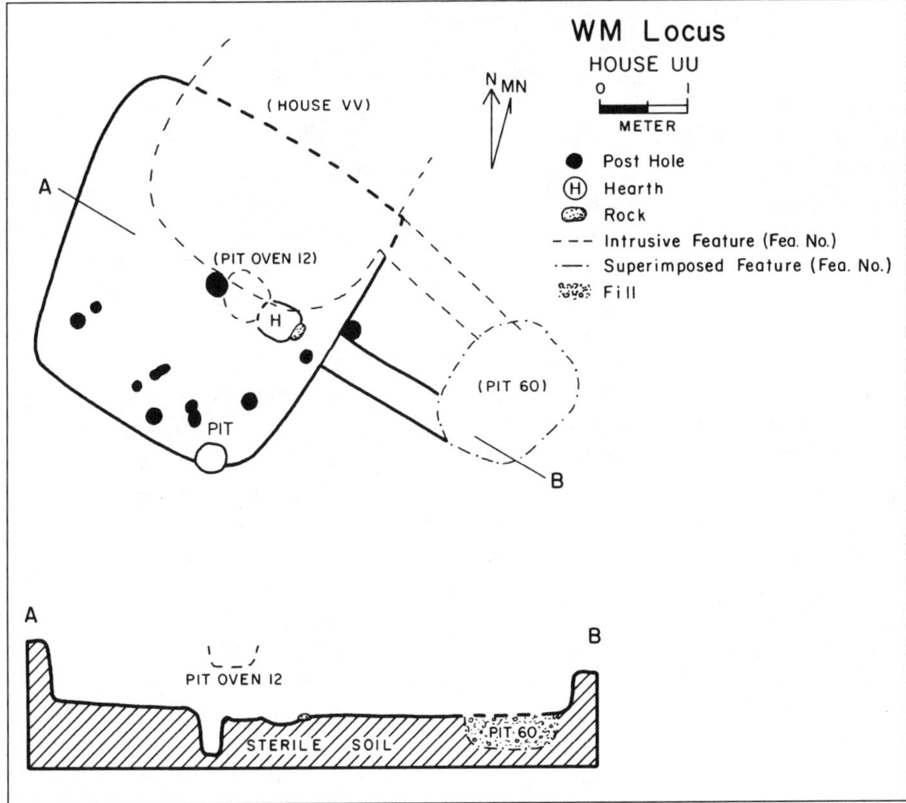

FIGURE 4.78. Plan view and profile of Wind Mountain locus House UU, a Type IV structure.

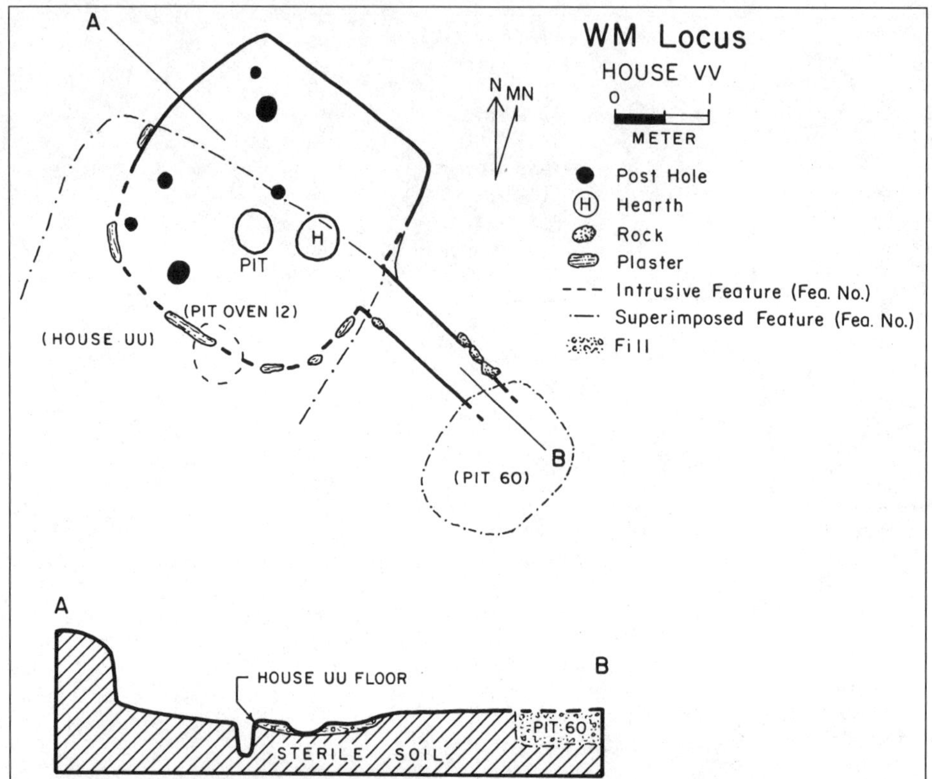

FIGURE 4.79. Plan view and profile of Wind Mountain locus House VV, a Type IV structure.

terial. Level 4 (range 148–158 cm, floor fill) was analogous to Level 3, although large stones, probably derived from wall fall, were noted. The house floor (depth 158 cm) described a level, use compacted surface. Vertical house walls had been excavated into sterile soil. Six post holes ringing the house interior were partially inset into supporting walls. One C^{14} sample (GX-6557), collected from a post hole, was analyzed (Chapter 3). The House XX hearth (Type IA3; length approximately 90 cm, width 60 cm, depth 20 cm) was large, shallow, and enclosed a smaller, deeper depression (depth 30 cm). Two stones, one of them a mano, were set into its eastern edge. Three floor pits were exposed. Pit 1 (diameter 47 cm, depth 35 cm) and Pit 3 (diameter 45 cm, depth 13 cm) were circular basins with polished clay linings, while Pit 2 (diameter 35 cm, depth 10 cm) was described only as a small depression (diameter 35 cm, depth 10 cm). The central post hole was offset by a shallow, oval-shaped depression (40 cm), possibly a remnant feature for aiding in the placement of the original support post. The House XX entry (area 3.07 m^2) was extremely long (507 cm), moderately narrow (70 cm), and stepped in three locations. It gave access to the structure at the midpoint of its east wall. Six post holes, partially inset into the entry walls, were aligned along each side of the entry ramp.

House YY (Figure 4.80)

Type VI structure; length 2.94+ m, width 2.28+ m; remaining area of living surface 6.09 m^2.

House YY was greatly impacted on its northern side by the construction of House W.

Level 1 (range 0–80 cm) comprised a loose gray-black, ashy soil with patches of red clay dispersed throughout. Level 2 (range 80–90 cm, floor fill) compared to Level 1. The level house floor (depth 90 cm) had been compacted by use. The structure's north wall and portions of its east and west walls were completely destroyed by the construction of House W. Surviving walls were vertical and had been excavated into sterile soil. Two small patches of wall plaster, one at the center of the south wall and one on the west wall, were noted. No hearth or entry were observed.

House ZZ (Figure 4.81)

Type IV structure; length 4.55 m, width 4.00 m; area of living surface 14.72 m^2; mean orientation of entry 89°.

Level 1 (range 0–85 cm) consisted of a dark gray silt intermixed with stone. Level 2 (range 85–95 cm, floor fill) differed from Level 1 by the addition of charcoal fragments. The uneven house floor (depth 95 cm) had been excavated into sterile soil. Unplastered house walls were vertical. The southern end of the east wall had been constructed in loose fill and was reinforced with stone. A large, irregularly shaped hearth (Type IB1; length 117 cm, width 85 cm, depth 10 cm), partially outlined with stones, was uncovered between the central post hole and the house entry. A floor pit (diameter at floor 43 cm, maximum diameter 48 cm, depth 37 cm) with undercut sides and a concave floor, was found in the northeast quadrant of the house. The house (area 1.01 m^2, length 170 cm, width 75 cm) was positioned near the middle of the east wall. Both north and south sides of the inclined (15°) entry ramp, where they joined the house, were lined with large, vertically placed stones. One of these included a worn, discarded metate.

House AB (Figure 4.82)

Type B structure; length 7.50 m, width 6.50+ m; estimated area of living surface 40.50 m^2; mean orientation of entry 117°.

House AB was intruded by House XX, House AE, Burial 96, as well as Pit Ovens 14 and 17. Pit 68 cut into the southeastern end of the House AB entry ramp.

Level 1 (range 0–40 cm) was composed of a dark humuslike soil mixed with numerous rocks. Level 2 (range 40–60 cm) and Level 3 (range 60–70 cm) compared with Level 1. Level 4 (range 70–80 cm, floor fill) was similar in composition to Levels 1, 2, and 3. The level house floor (depth 80 cm) had been coated with a layer of plaster (5 cm). Unplastered, vertical walls were excavated into sterile soil. Walls had been reinforced with rock on the structure's northeast and southeast sides. A small, irregularly shaped unlined hearth (Type IIIA; length 18 cm, width 15 cm, depth 20 cm) containing ash was found roughly midway between the house entrance and the central post hole. A hearthstone had been set into the southeast edge of the fire pit. One archaeomagnetic sample (No. 026) was taken from the hearth (Chapter 3). The narrow (50 cm) house entry ramp (surviving area .41+ m^2, incline 8°) had been excavated into sterile soil.

House AC (Figure 4.83)

Type IV structure; length 4.20 m, width 4.40 m; area of living surface 17.33 m^2; mean orientation of entry 208°.

House AC was intruded by Pits 61 and 63, Burial 94, Cremation 2, *Canis* Burial 11, and Animal Burial 1 (Figure 4.84).

Level 1 (range 0–50 cm) comprised a dark humuslike soil, intermixed with large amounts of burned adobe near the center of the house and collapsed wall fall adjacent the south wall. Level 2 (range 50–90 cm) consisted of a black soil with site debris throughout. Level 3 (range 90–100 cm, floor fill) compared with Level 2. The level house floor (depth 100 cm) had been compacted by use. House walls had been partially excavated into sterile soil and loose disturbed fill. The southeastern corner of the house was destroyed by the intrusions of Pit 63 and Burial 94. House AC's north wall was reinforced with stone, presumably to contain loose fill. The hearth (Type IIIA; length 78 cm, width 50 cm, depth 6 cm) was a rectangular, clay lined basin, its lip set level with the floor. The House AC entry (area 1.65 m^2) was characterized as a moderately long (240 cm) and narrow (70 cm) ramp (8°) that joined the structure midway along its southwest wall. It had been excavated into sterile soil. The presence of burned adobe in the upper fill was not associated with the occupation of House AC, but probably reflects later activities.

House AD (Figure 4.85)

Type IV structure; length 3.90 m, width 4.10 m; area of living surface 15.06 m^2; mean orientation of entry 93°.

House AD was superimposed on House AE and the entry to House AK.

Level 1 (range 0–40 cm) consisted of a dark humuslike, pebbly silt. Level 2 (range 40–70 cm) and Level 3 (range 70–90 cm) compared with Level 1. Level 4 (range 90–110 cm, floor fill) was similar to Levels 1–3, differing only in a decrease in the quantity of sherds. The level house floor (depth 110 cm) had been compacted by use. House walls were partially excavated into sterile soil. The north wall and the north end of the west wall were constructed in the fill of House AE. Stone observed along the northern wall served to contain loose fill. The hearth (Type IIA; diameter 40 cm, depth 12 cm) was a round, clay lined depression containing a white ash. One archaeomagnetic sample (No. 043) was taken from the hearth (Chapter 3). A long (320 cm), narrow (75 cm), stepped (10°) entry ramp (area 2.29 m^2) allowed access to the structure through the middle of its east wall. This unplastered, rounded (concave in cross section) entry had been excavated into sterile soil.

House AE (Figure 4.85)

Type IV structure; length indeterminate, width 3.40 m; remaining area of living surface 3.58 m^2; mean orientation of entry 76°.

House AE was intruded by House AD but superpositioned the south wall of House AB. The entry of House AE was disturbed by Burial 99.

Level 1 (range 0–80 cm) consisted of a dark humuslike soil intermixed with site debris. Level 2 (range 80–100 cm, floor fill) compared with Level 1. The level, use compacted House AE floor (depth 100 cm) had been excavated into sterile soil. One C^{14} sample (GX-6558) recovered from the floor was analyzed (Chapter 3). The majority of House AE was destroyed by the construction of House AD. The only intact surviving wall occurred on its northern side, where it had been faced

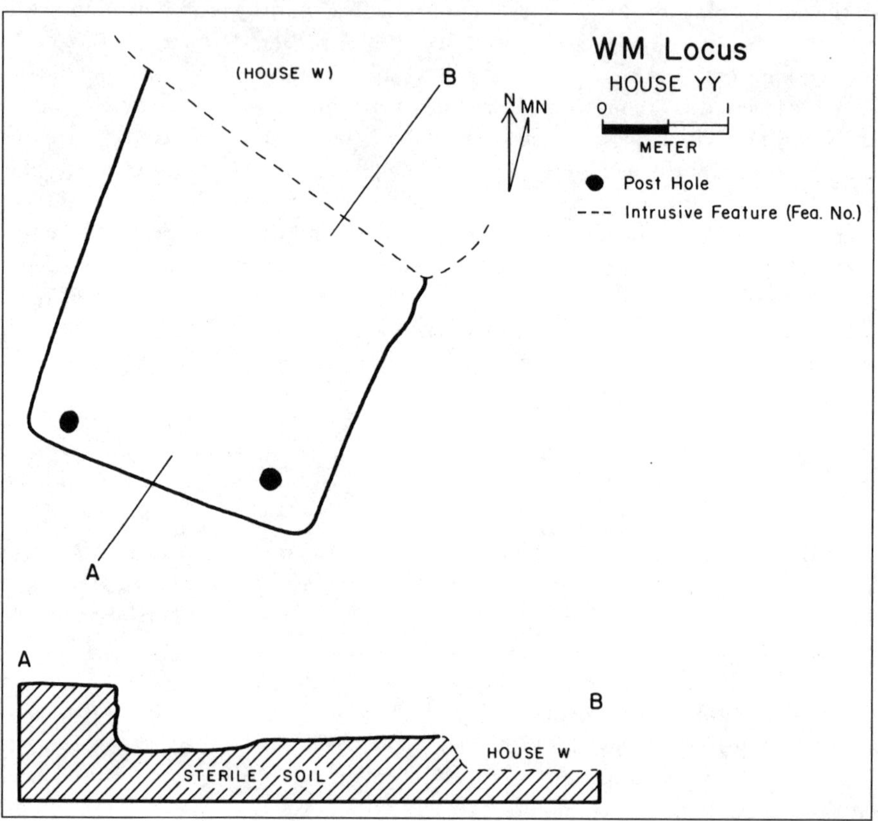

FIGURE 4.80. Plan view and profile of heavily disturbed Wind Mountain locus House YY, a Type VI structure.

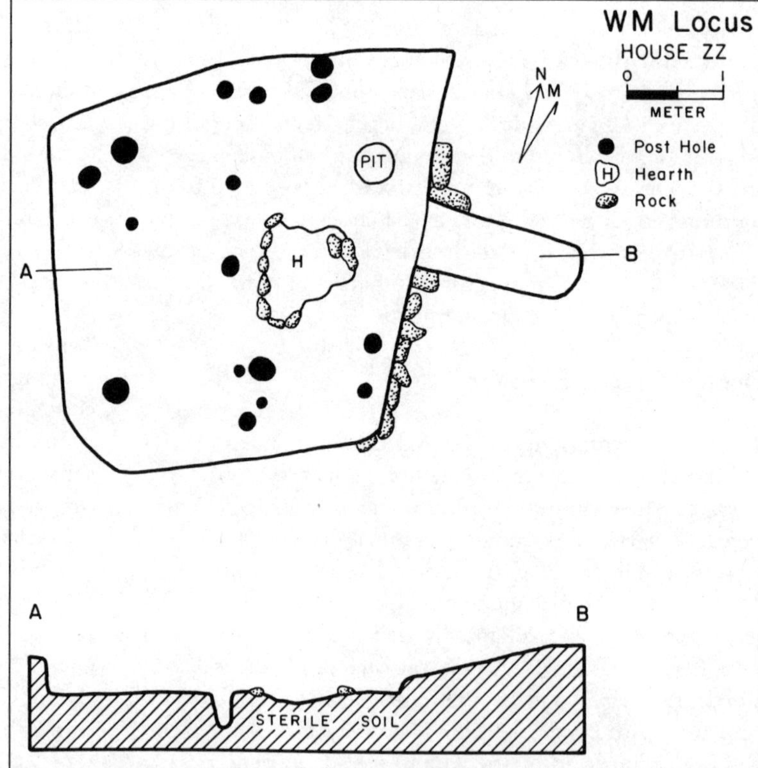

FIGURE 4.81. Plan view and profile of Wind Mountain locus House ZZ, a Type IV structure, showing an irregular hearth and entry.

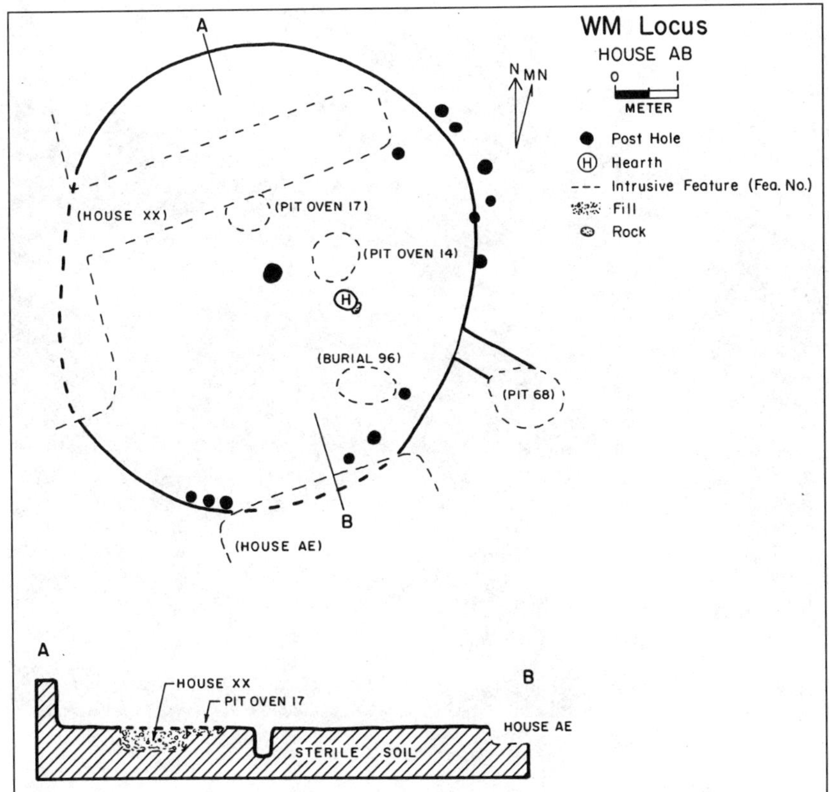

FIGURE 4.82. Plan view and profile of Wind Mountain locus House AB, a Type B community structure.

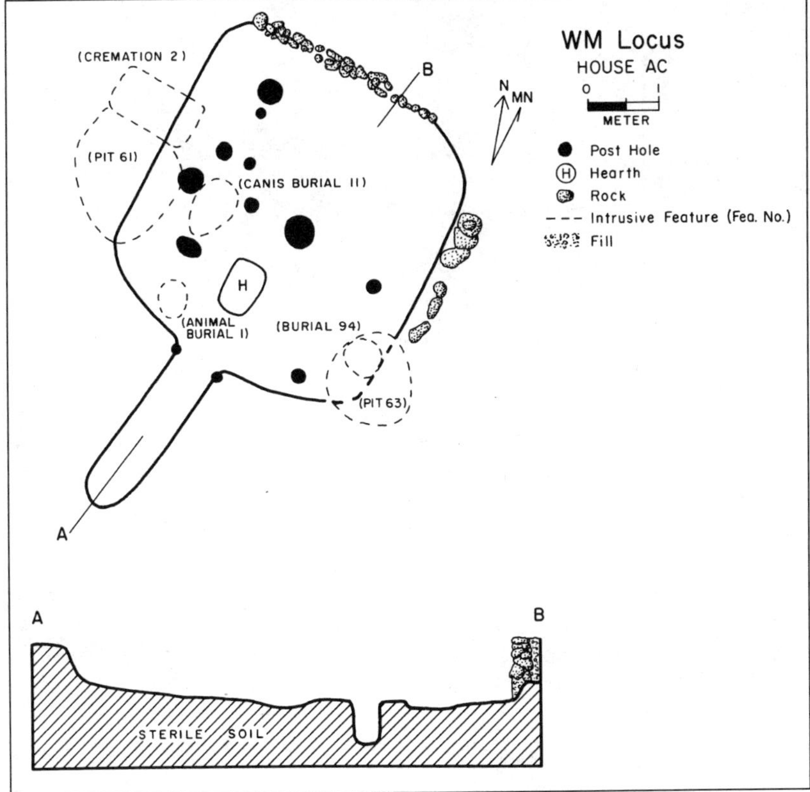

FIGURE 4.83. Plan view and profile of Wind Mountain locus House AC, a Type IV structure.

FIGURE 4.84. House AC showing the upper (1) and lower (2) fill levels, the floor (3), as well as *Canis* Burial 11 (Neg. No. WM 82–33F).

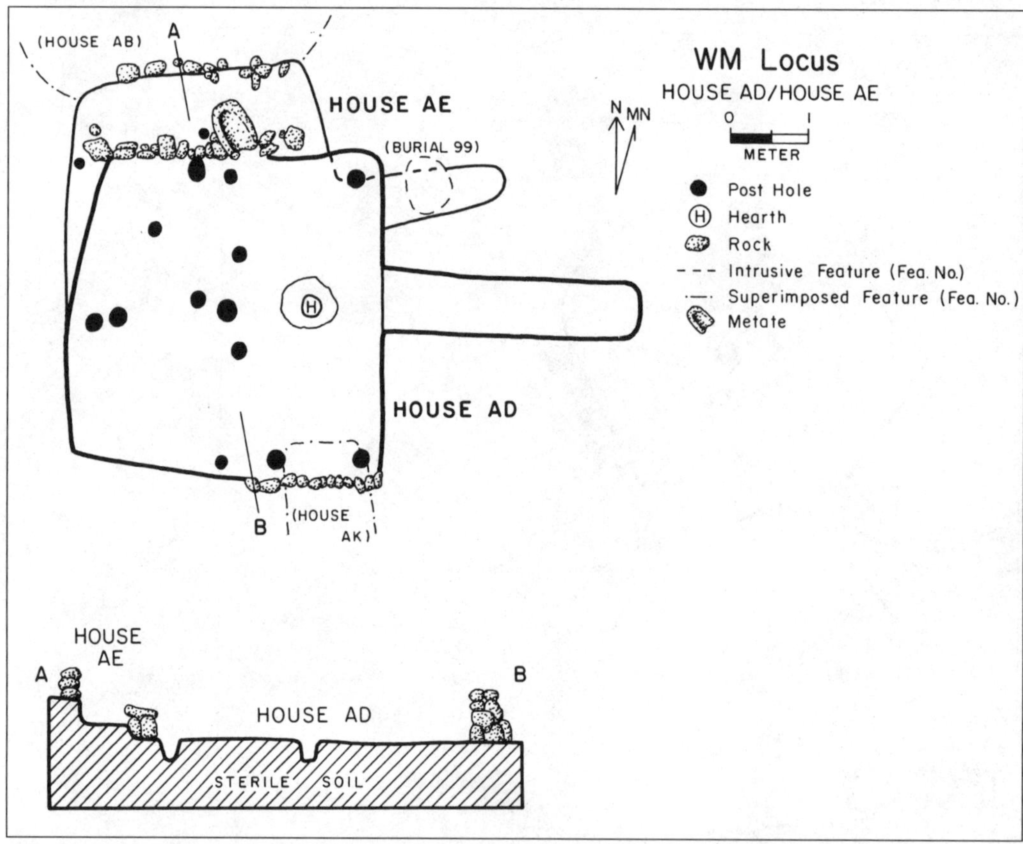

FIGURE 4.85. Plan views and profile of Wind Mountain locus House AD and House AE, two Type IV structures.

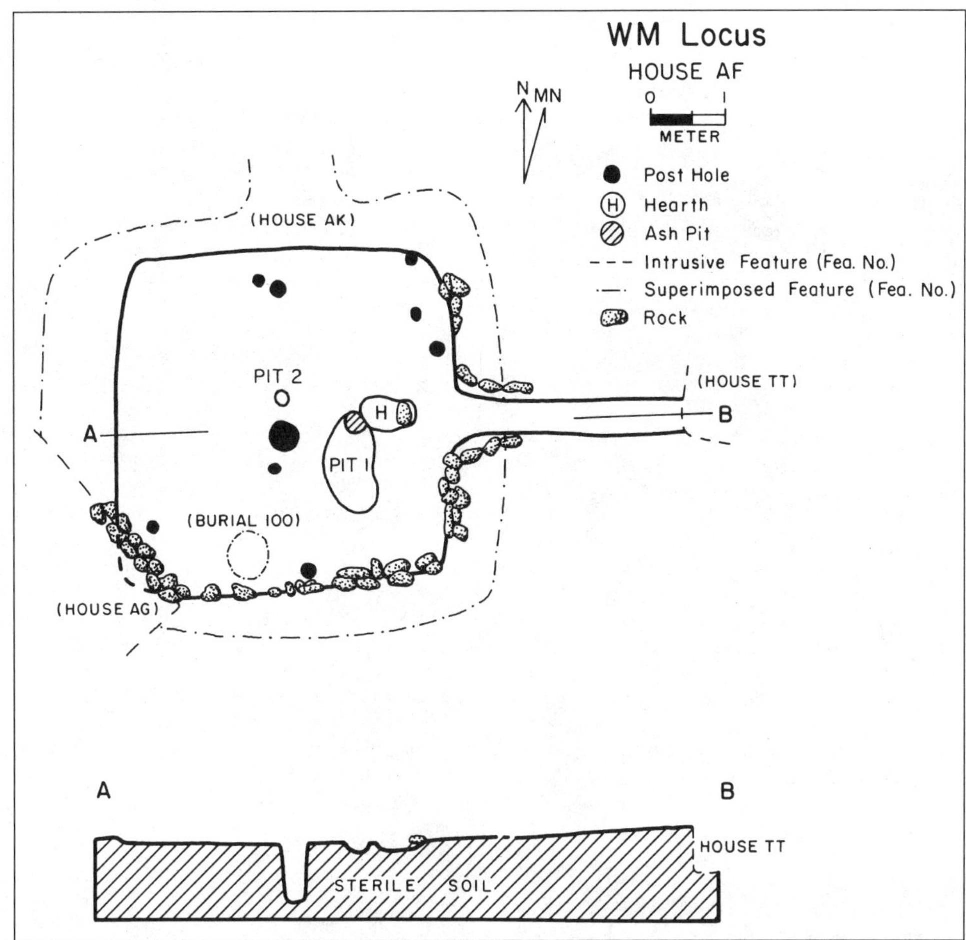

FIGURE 4.86. Plan view and profile of Wind Mountain locus House AF, a Type IV structure (see Figure 4.19 for details of House AK).

with stone, presumably an attempt to shore up the loose fill of House AB. Unplastered and fragmentary remnants of the east and west walls indicate they were originally dug into sterile soil. No hearth was observed. The House AE entry (surviving area .83 m^2) identified a narrow (approximately 50–60 cm) incline that joined the structure along its east wall and had been excavated into sterile soil.

House AF (Figure 4.86)

Type IV structure; length 4.35 m, width 4.40 m; estimated area of living surface 18.15 m^2; mean orientation of entry 91°.

Except for a portion of its entry, House AF was constructed entirely inside the margins of earlier House AK (Figures 4.87 and 4.88). Its southwest corner was intruded by the construction of House AG. The most eastern end of the House AF entry was destroyed by the construction of House TT. Burial 100 was found under the structure's floor.

Level 1 (range 0–50 cm) consisted of a dark humuslike soil intermixed with stone and cultural debris. Level 2 (range 50–100 cm) was similar to Level 1. Level 3 (range 100–112 cm, floor fill) compared with Levels 1 and 2. One C^{14} sample (GX-6560) was recovered from Level 3, between 110–112 cm (Chapter 3). House AF and House AK were excavated simultaneously. Definition of the outer walls of House AK occurred first, and the presence of two discrete houses recognized as excavation progressed. The use compacted floor (depth 112 cm) was slightly concave, sloping gradually inward from all four walls. House AF walls were complex in their construction—composed of grinding stone fragments, unworked stone, and mud mortar—all needed to reinforce the loose fill from the encircling House AK. Indeed, the fill of House AK eventually won out over the reinforced House AF walls and, at some time during the postabandonment period, collapsed inward onto the House AF floor. The hearth (Type IB1; length 55 cm, width 50 cm, depth 15 cm) was defined as an irregularly shaped, unlined basin from which one archaeomagnetic sample (No. 019) was removed (Chapter 3). A hearthstone (length 40 cm, width 30 cm, thickness 8 cm), exposed along the east side of the hearth, was set flush

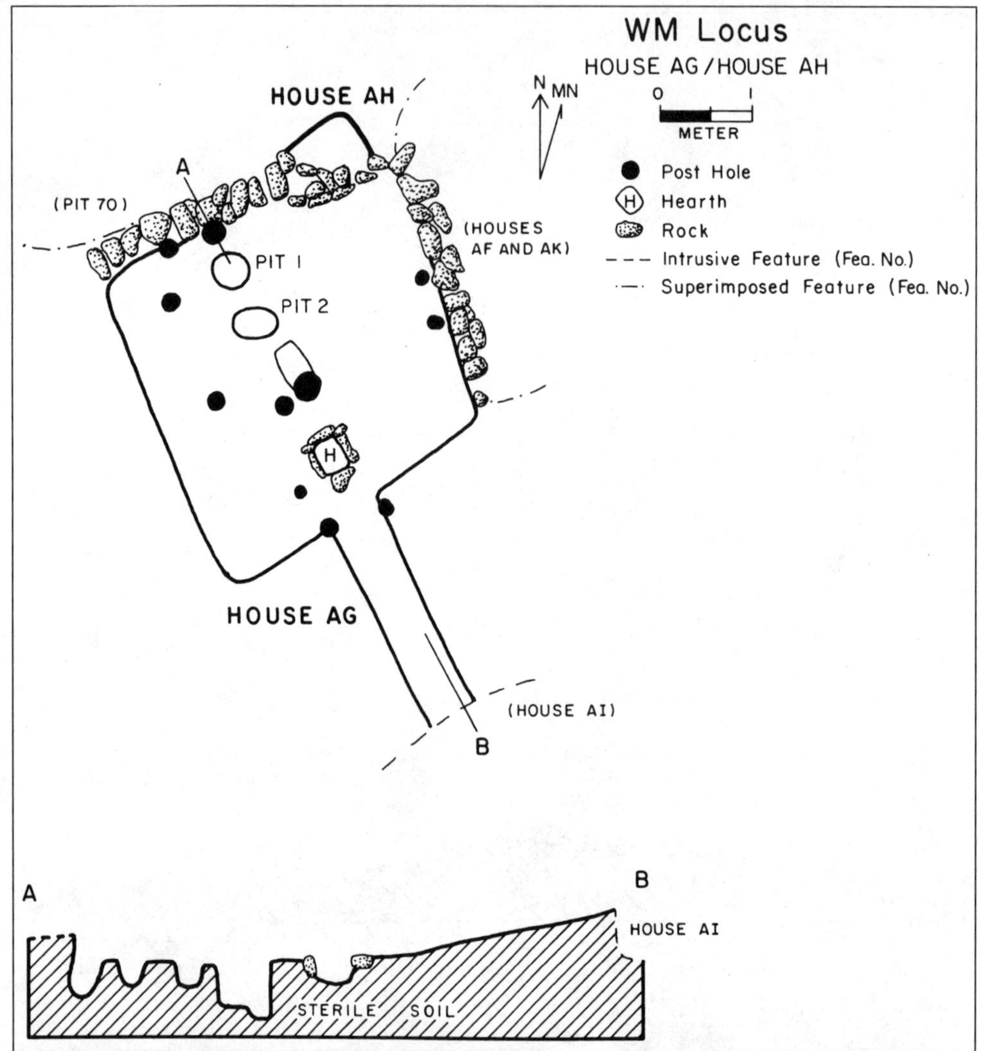

FIGURE 4.87. Plan view and profile of Wind Mountain locus House AG, a Type IV structure, as well as the surviving corner of Type VI House AH.

with the house floor surface. A small ash pit immediately southwest of the hearth still contained ash. Two floor pits were uncovered. Large and irregularly shaped, Pit 1 (length 92 cm, width 54 cm, depth 50 cm) was discovered immediately next to the hearth. Pit 2 (diameter 24 cm, depth 20 cm), a small depression, was located slightly north of the central post hole. The House AF entry (surviving area 1.22 m^2) described a long (300+ cm) and narrow (45 cm) incline (10°) that permitted access to the structure midway along its east wall. Both north and south entry walls were reinforced with unworked stones and metate fragments.

House AG (Figures 4.87 and 4.88)

Type IV structure; length 3.70 m, width 3.60 m; area of living surface 11.27 m^2; mean orientation of entry 156°.

House AG was superimposed on portions of Houses AF, AH, and AK, as well as on Pit 70. The southeastern end of the entry was indistinguishable, disappearing into the loose fill of House AI.

Level 1 (range 0–80 cm) consisted of a dark humuslike soil intermixed with site debris. Level 2 (range 80–110 cm) compared with Level 1. Level 3 (range 110–126 cm, floor fill) was analogous to Levels 1 and 2. The house floor (depth 126 cm), described as an uneven surface, was compacted by use and excavated into sterile soil. One C^{14} sample (GX-6559) was recovered from the house floor (Chapter 3). House walls along the north and east sides were stone lined, presumably to contain the loose fill associated with House AH, House AK, and Pit 70. South and west walls had been excavated into sterile soil. A plaster remnant (thickness 3 mm) from which an archaeomagnetic sample (No. 029) was taken

(Chapter 3) was exposed on the south wall. The hearth (Type IIIB2; length 70 cm, width 65, depth 29 cm) occurred as a rectangular pit, lined on all four sides with stones. A large flat slab, possibly a hearthstone, was found on its southeastern side. Two floor pits were uncovered. Pit 1 (diameter 40 cm, depth 29 cm), circular in plan, had unplastered, tapering sides and a concave floor. Pit 2 (length 47 cm, width 34 cm, depth 29 cm) was oval with unplastered straight sides converging on a concave floor. A depression immediately adjacent the central post hole on its northwest side probably facilitated the original positioning of this roof support. The House AG entry (surviving area 1.44 m^2) was a moderately narrow (60 cm) incline (16°) that gave access to the structure through the midpoint of its southeast wall. The entry's southeastern end was lost within the loose fill of earlier House AI.

House AH (Figures 4.87 and 4.88)

Type VI structure; length .90 m, width .50 m; remaining area of living surface .39 m^2.

All but the northern corner of House AH was destroyed by the construction of Houses AF, AG, and AK.

Level 1 (range 0–50 cm) was removed as the fill of House AG. Level 2 (range 50–80 cm) consisted of a dark humuslike fill. Level 3 (range 80–88 cm, floor fill) compared with Level 2. Surviving portions of the house floor (depth 88 cm) indicated a level, use compacted surface. Only fragments of the structure's north and east walls survived. Both walls had once been plastered with a thick layer (2 cm) of tan colored adobe. No evidence of either a hearth or an entry was found.

House AI (Figure 4.89)

Type IV structure; length 4.49 m, width 4.30 m; area of living surface 17.55 m^2; mean orientation of entry 91°.

The northwest corner of House AI impacted the extreme southeastern end of House AG's entry. Burial 101 intruded into the fill and floor of House AI.

Level 1 (range 0–50 cm) comprised a dark humuslike soil described as "highly mixed." Collapsed wall fall was apparent in the southeast corner. Level 2 (range 30–65 cm) compared with Level 1, minus the wall stones. Level 3 (range 80–98 cm, floor fill) consisted of a black sandy soil. One C^{14} sample (GX-6561) was recovered from the House AI floor fill (Chapter 3). The house floor (depth 98 cm) was described as "unstable" and compacted by use. Walls had been excavated into sterile soil. One remnant patch of plaster (1 cm thick) was noted on the north wall. The hearth (Type IIA1; diameter 70 cm, depth 15 cm) was a roughly circular, adobe lined basin with a hearthstone set into its eastern edge. The central post hole was positioned immediately adjacent another large subfloor depression, perhaps indicative of a construction feature used to place the central support. The house entry (estimated area .83 to 1.67 m^2) occurred as a short (135 cm), moderately narrow (60 cm), stepped ramp (5°) that joined the house at the midpoint of its east wall.

House AJ (Figure 4.90)

Type IV structure; length 1.90 m, width 1.90 m; area of living surface 3.46 m^2; mean orientation of entry 9°.

Level 1 (range 0–65 cm) and Level 2 (range 65–75 cm, floor fill) were comparable, composed of a dark humuslike soil intermixed with small amounts of site debris. Level 3, the unplastered floor, had been heavily impacted by rodent activity. Soil under the house was described as unstable and sandy, a condition that may account for the failure to locate post holes, hearth, or any other floor feature. The plastered (thickness 5 mm) vertical walls sloped gently inward toward the floor, which had been excavated into sterile soil. Plaster height (measured from the floor) ranged from 22 cm on the west wall to 31 cm on the south wall. The House AJ entry (estimated area .58 to .76 m^2) was a short (110 cm), narrow (50 cm) incline (5°) allowing access to the structure at the midpoint of the north wall. The entry side walls were vertical and its floor level. The northern end was destroyed during excavation by a test trench.

House AK (refer to Figures 4.19, 4.20, and 4.88)

Type D structure; length 5.70 m, width 5.40 m; estimated area of living surface 29.85 m^2; mean orientation of entry 15°.

House AK was intruded by Houses AD, AF, and AG. House AK was superimposed on House AH.

House AK was excavated concurrently with House AF (for a description of its stratigraphic levels see House AF). House AK's plastered floor was disturbed by the later construction of House AF. One archaeomagnetic sample (No. 020) was taken from a section of the surviving floor (Chapter 3). An oval-shaped hearth (Type IIB; length 60 cm, width 50 cm, depth 5 cm) occurred in line with the house entry. Three floor pits were exposed. Pit 1 (diameter 35 cm, depth 17 cm), a small round depression, was found in the southeastern quadrant of the house. Pit 2 (length 115 cm, width 77+ cm, depth 25 cm), large and irregular in plan, was encountered immediately beneath Pit 1, in the floor of House AF. Excavators felt these floor pits represented two distinct features, each associated with a separate house floor. Pit 3 (diameter 40 cm, depth 16 cm), another small depression, was situated in the structure's southwestern quadrant. The House AK perimeter was composed of 52 closely spaced post holes (ranging in diameter from 10 cm to 25 cm and from 10 cm to 40 cm in depth) that originally were part of its superstructure. Four interior post holes (ranging in diameter from 32 cm to 44 cm) were observed at the approximate midpoint of each quarter section of the house. The moder-

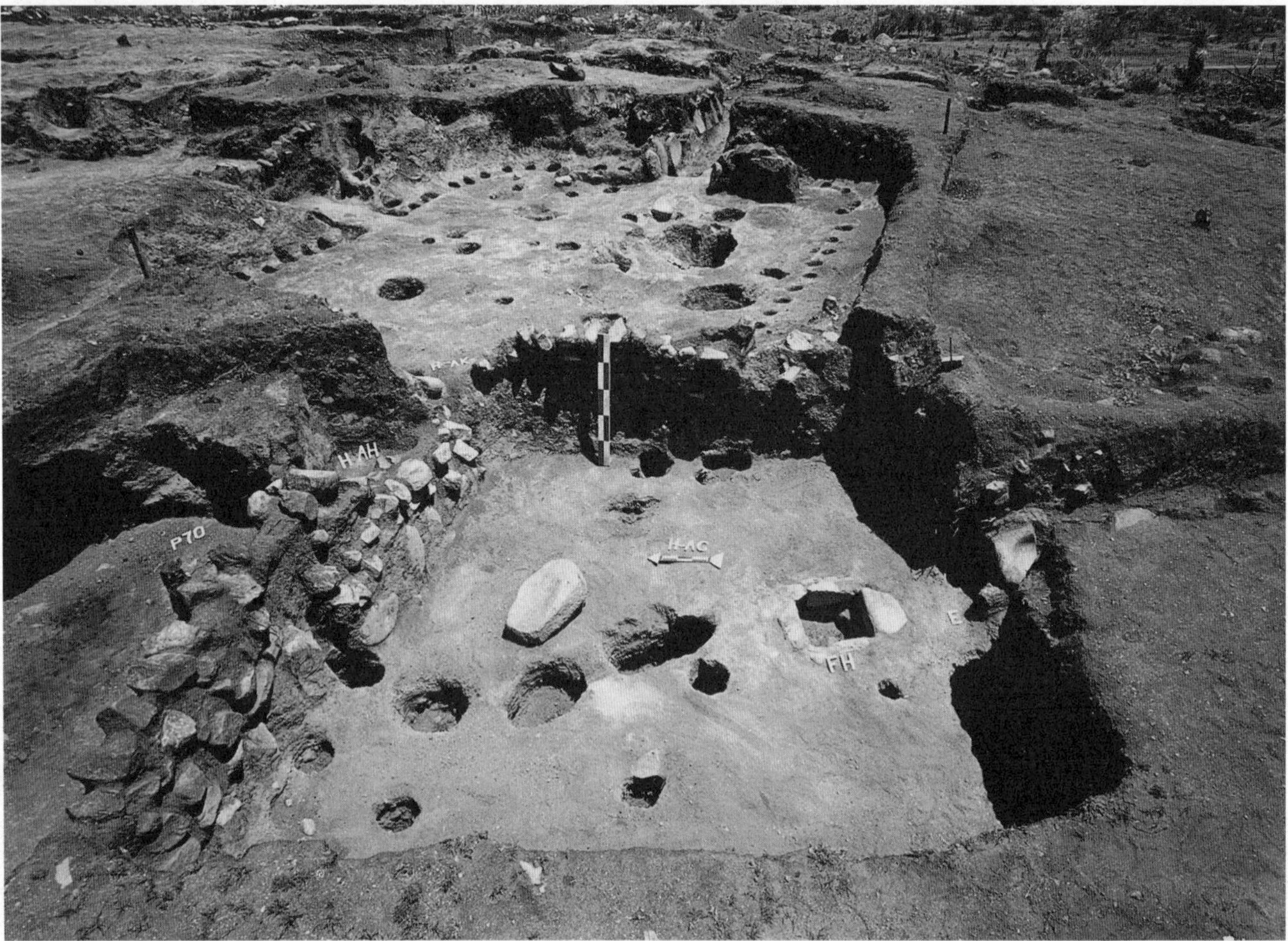

FIGURE 4.88. Wind Mountain locus House AG showing its relationship to remnant Houses AF, AH, and AK. The slab lined hearth, post holes, floor pits, and a large floor metate are clearly apparent. (Neg. No. WM 91–5F).

ately wide entry (width 70–90 cm, estimated area 1.61 m^2) was long (200 cm) and only slightly ramped (2°), joining the structure at the midsection of its north wall. One C^{14} sample (GX-7462) was recovered from the entry ramp, underneath the floor of House AD (Chapter 3).

House AL (Figure 4.91)

Type IV structure; length 4.78 m, width 4.00 m; area of living surface 16.94 m^2; mean orientation of entry 116°.

The fill of House AL was slightly intruded by Pit 72 and Burial 102.

Level 1 (range 0–50 cm) was composed of a homogeneous, dark soil intermixed with site debris. Level 2 (range 50–100 cm) and Level 3 (range 100–140 cm) compared with Level 1. Level 4 (range 140–150 cm, floor fill) was similar to the upper levels, but exhibited a higher incidence of stone. The unplastered house floor (depth 150 cm) was compacted by use and excavated into sterile soil. One C^{14} sample (GX-6898) was recovered from the House AL floor (Chapter 3). Vertical walls were plastered with a dark sandy clay (thickness 2 to 6 mm). Plaster height (measured from the floor) ranged from 42 cm on the west wall to 74 cm on the south wall. One archaeomagnetic sample (No. 037) was taken from wall plaster (Chapter 3). The northwest and southwest corners of the house were reinforced with stones and boulders placed on end (long axis vertical). The hearth (Type IIB1; diameter 45 cm, depth 18 cm), a rounded, basin-shaped depression, occurred midway between the house entry and the central post hole. A hearthstone had been plastered into the rim on its eastern edge. A single floor pit (diameter at floor 25 cm, maximum interior diameter 40 cm, depth 25 cm) was uncovered in the structure's northwest quadrant. The pit sides were undercut to its midsection, then tapered to an almost pointed base. The house entry (area 1.54 m^2) consisted of a long (285 cm), moderately narrow (40–65 cm), stepped ramp (11°) allowing access through the house's eastern wall. The second step of the entry ramp was inset with a large mano that served as a stair tread.

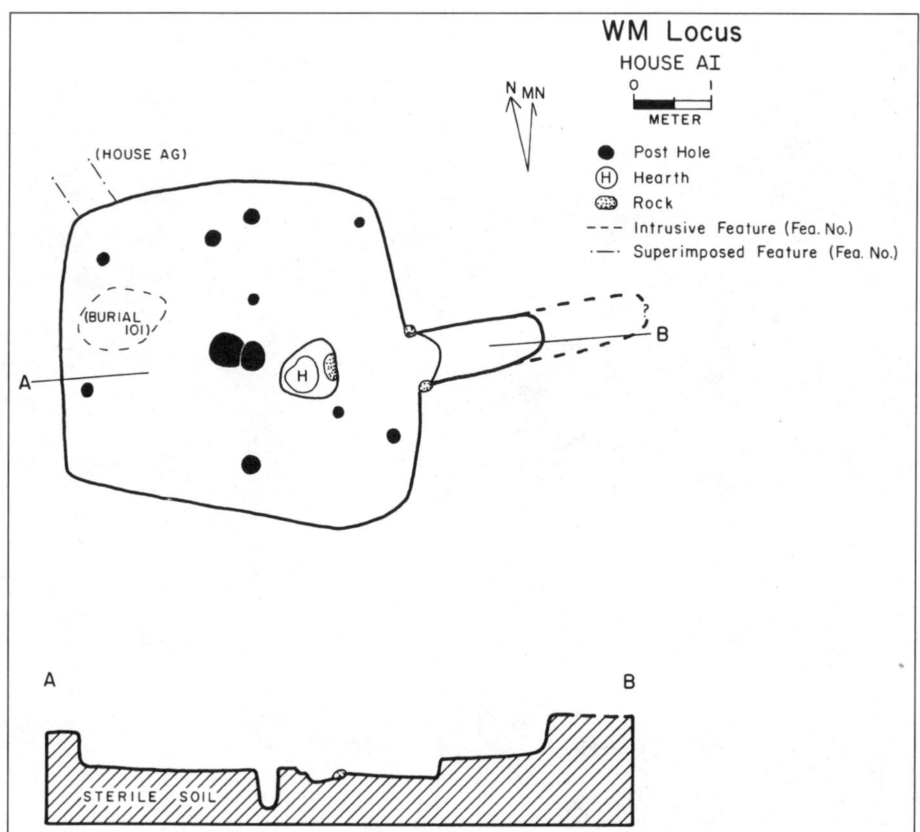

FIGURE 4.89. Plan view and profile of Wind Mountain locus House AI, a Type IV structure.

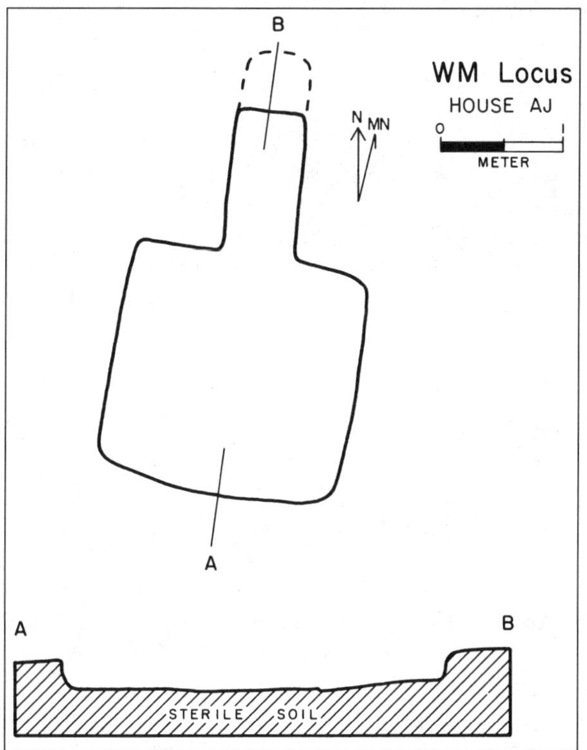

FIGURE 4.90. Plan view and profile of Wind Mountain locus House AJ, a Type IV structure.

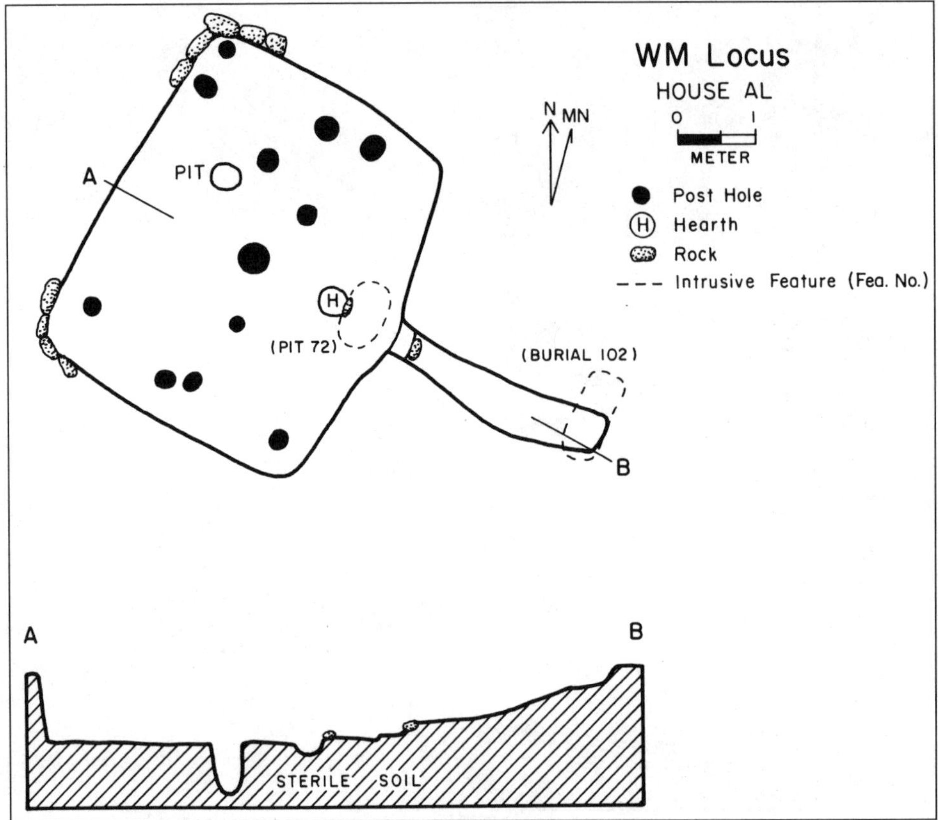

FIGURE 4.91. Plan view and profile of Wind Mountain locus House AL, a Type IV structure.

House AM (Figure 4.92)

Type IV structure; length 3.85 m, width 3.50 m; area of living surface 12.64 m^2; mean orientation of entry 86°.

Burials 103–105 intruded into the fill of House AM.

Level 1 (range 0–80 cm) consisted of a loosely consolidated dark soil intermixed with site debris. Level 2 (range 80–90 cm, floor fill) compared with Level 1, but exhibited a higher concentration of stone. The level, use compacted house floor (depth 90 cm) had been excavated into sterile soil. One C^{14} sample (GX-6899) was recovered from this floor (Chapter 3). The hearth (Type IB; length 55 cm, width 45 cm, depth 12 cm), an irregular, basin-shaped depression, was situated midway between the entry and central post hole. House walls were vertical and plastered. Plaster (thickness 3 to 6 mm) survived on three walls and ranged in height (measured from the floor) from 45 cm on the north wall to 55 cm on the east and south walls. The plaster was burned. The entry of House AM (area 1.04 m^2) described a long (215 cm), narrow (50 cm), stepped incline (6°). It joined the structure near the midpoint of the east wall and had been excavated into sterile soil.

House AN (Figure 4.93)

Type I structure; length 4.20 m, width 3.30 m; area of living surface 11.24 m^2.

Level 1 (range 0–40 cm) and Level 2 (range 40–70 cm) were composed of a dark, humic, trash laden fill. Level 3 (range 70–80 cm, floor fill) compared with Levels 1 and 2. The level house floor (depth 80 cm) had been compacted by use. One C^{14} sample (GX-6900) was recovered from the house floor (Chapter 3). Unplastered house walls rounded inward at the wall-floor contact. No floor features or entry were observed.

House AO (Figure 4.94)

Type IV structure; length 3.90 m, width 3.70 m; area of living surface 13.86 m^2; mean orientation of entry 40°.

House AO was intruded by Pit Oven 19 and Pit 71.

Level 1 (range 0–80 cm), Level 2 (range 80–150 cm), and Level 3 (range 150–160 cm, floor fill) were all described as a dark, alluviated soil intermixed with site debris. The house floor (depth 160 cm) had been heavily disturbed by rodent activity, although surviving portions revealed a level surface compacted by use. One C^{14} sample (GX-6902) was recov-

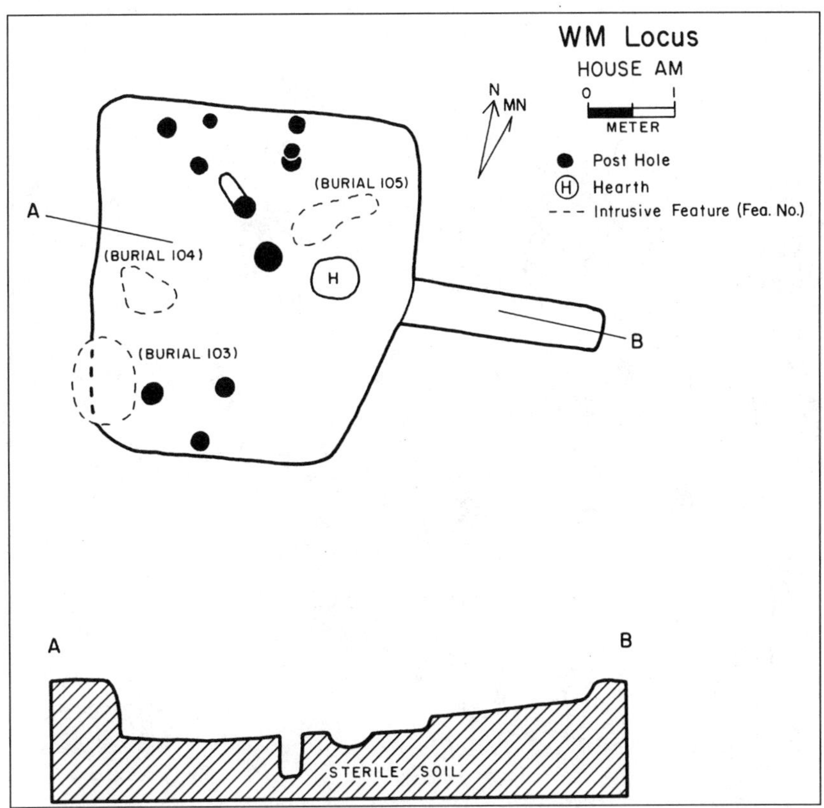

FIGURE 4.92. Plan view and profile of Wind Mountain locus House AM, a Type IV structure.

ered from the floor (Chapter 3). Unplastered house walls were vertical and inwardly rounded at the wall-floor juncture. A circular hearth (Type IIB; length 55 cm, width 45 cm, depth 10 cm) was found near the entry. One irregularly shaped pit (diameter 70 cm, depth 35 cm) was exposed in the northeastern corner of the structure. The entry (area 1.54 m^2) consisted of a long (330 cm) and narrow (50 cm) incline (7°) that gave access to the house at the midsection of its north wall. It had been excavated into sterile soil.

House AP (Figure 4.95)

Type IV structure; length 3.15 m, width 3.00 m; area of living surface 8.67 m^2; mean orientation of entry 101°.

Level 1 (range 0–50 cm), Level 2 (range 50–80 cm), and Level 3 (range 80–90 cm, floor fill) were described as a dark, alluviated soil intermixed with site debris. The level house floor (depth 90 cm) had been plastered (thickness 5 mm). Unplastered house walls were vertical. The hearth (Type IB; length 65 cm, width 40 cm, depth 27 cm), an irregular, unlined depression, still contained ash. At some point after the hearth was constructed, a post (diameter 22 cm, depth 17 cm) was placed in its center, apparently an aid for supporting the structure. The entry (area 1.29 m^2) was a long (285

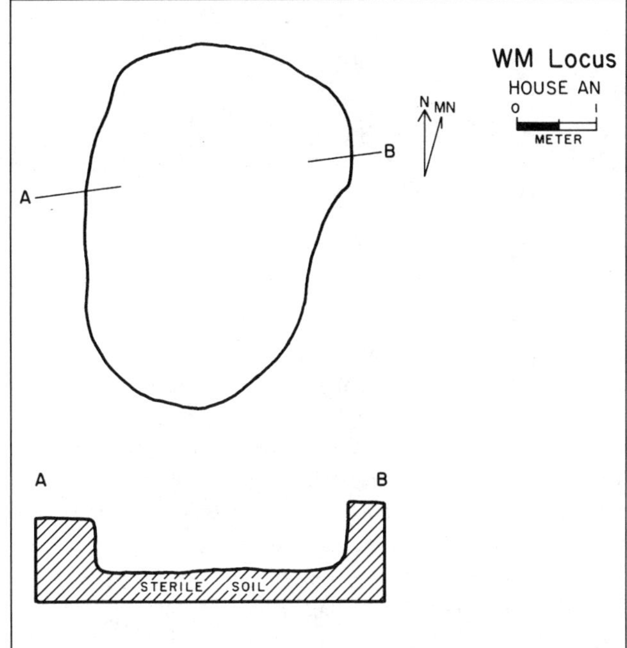

FIGURE 4.93. Plan view and profile of Wind Mountain locus House AN, a Type I structure.

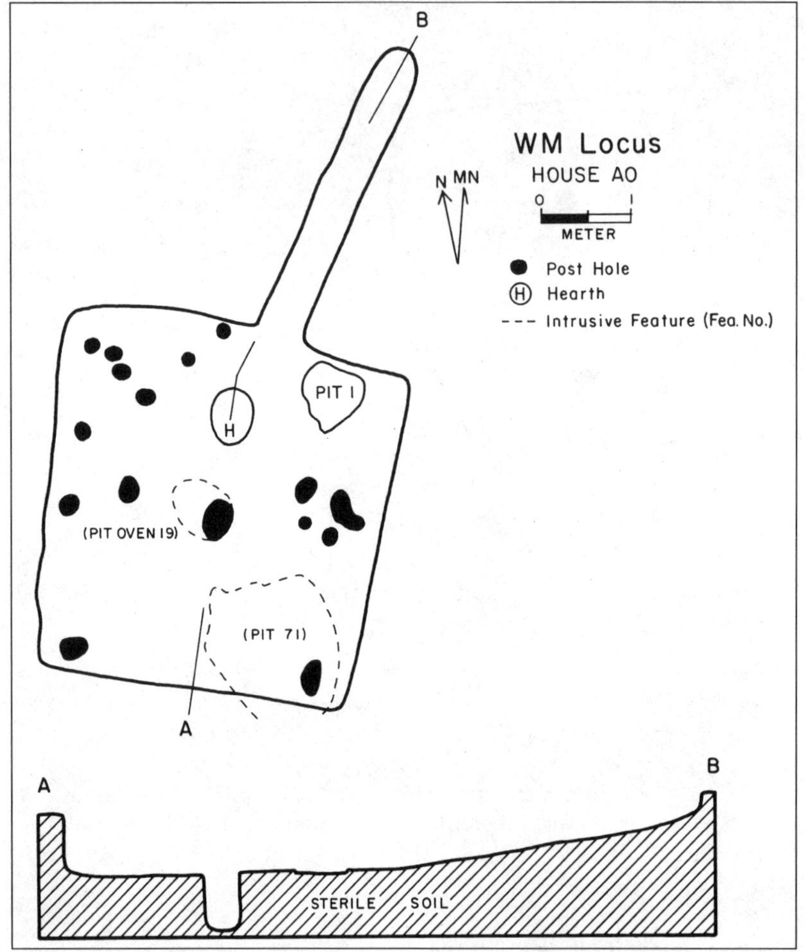

FIGURE 4.94. Plan view and profile of Wind Mountain locus House AO, a Type IV structure.

cm), narrow (55 cm), stepped incline (8°) that enabled access to the house through the east wall. The ramp was unplastered and concave in cross section.

House AQ (Figure 4.96)

Type IV structure; length 4.10 m, width 3.60 m; area of living surface 13.31 m^2; mean orientation of entry 121°.

Level 1 (range 0–100 cm), Level 2 (range 100–160 cm), and Level 3 (range 160–170 cm, floor fill) were composed of a dark, loose fill containing site debris (redeposited from upslope). Stones were scattered throughout the various levels but tended to concentrate toward the center of the house and its lower levels. The level, unplastered floor (depth 170 cm) had been compacted by use. One C^{14} sample (GX-6903) was recovered from the floor (Chapter 3). The north, south, and east walls were reinforced with stones. No reinforcement was observed on the west wall. The west and north walls had been plastered with a thin layer of red clay. One archaeomagnetic sample (No. 038) was taken from the wall plaster (Chapter 3). The hearth (Type IB; length 86 cm, width 50 cm, depth 10 cm), an irregular depression that contained a white ash, was situated midway between the entry and the central post hole. The entry (area 1.45 m^2) described a long (325 cm), narrow (45 cm) incline (10° for approximately the first 150 cm and 20° thereafter) that gave access to the house through the midsection of the east wall.

Surface (and Semisubterranean) Rooms of the Wind Mountain Locus

Rooms 1–16 were surface or, in a few cases, semisubterranean constructions interpreted as Room Units. A Room Unit was defined as one or more contiguously joined surface domestic rooms in association with one community structure. Three such room units were identified at Wind Mountain. Room Unit 1 included Rooms 1–3; Room Unit 2 contained Rooms 4–13; Room Unit 3 consisted of Rooms 14–16.

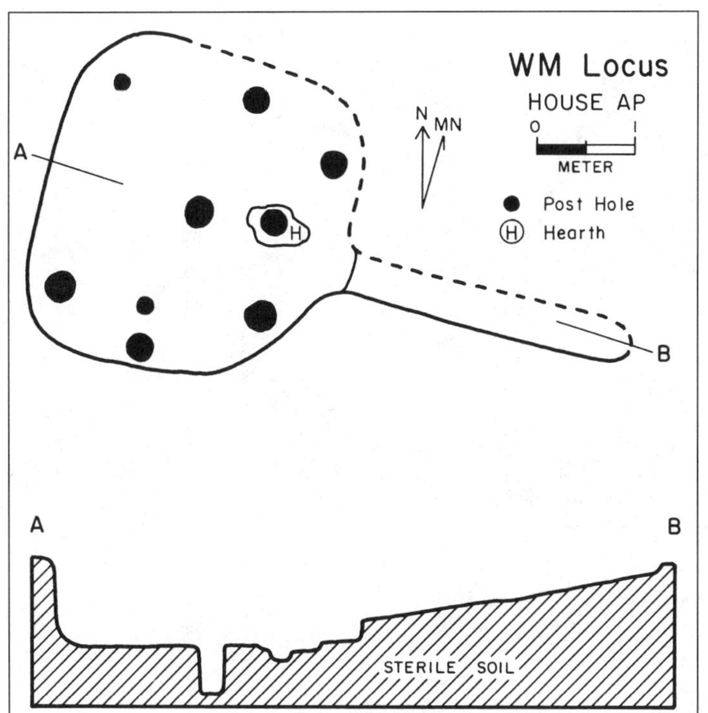

FIGURE 4.95. Plan view and profile of Wind Mountain locus House AP, a Type IV structure.

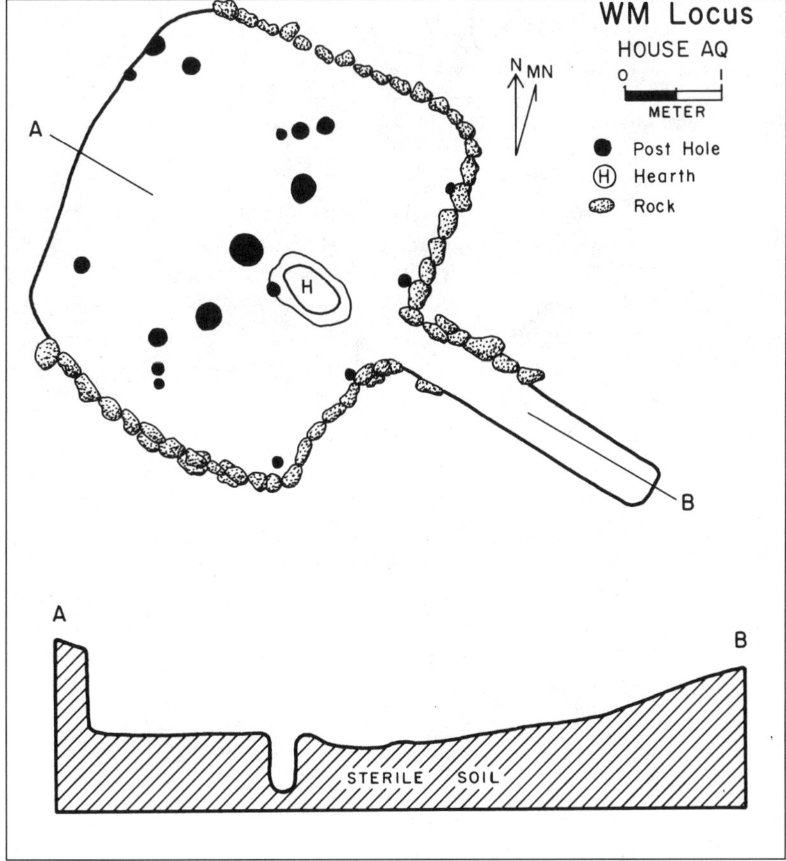

FIGURE 4.96. Plan view and profile of Wind Mountain locus House AQ, a Type IV structure.

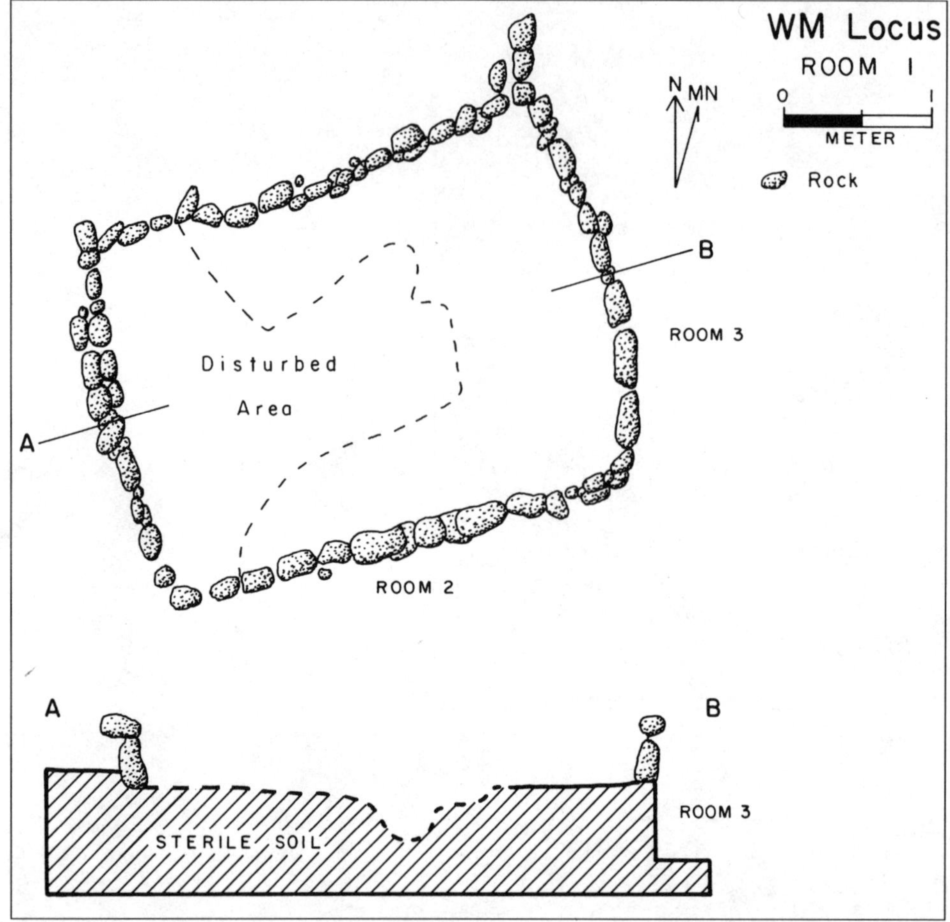

FIGURE 4.97. Plan view and profile of Wind Mountain locus Room 1, a Type V structure.

Room 1 (Figures 4.97 and 4.98)

Type V structure; length 3.25 m, width 2.15 m; area of living surface 6.97 m^2.

Level 1 (range 0–40 cm) was described as a compacted, dark brown soil intermixed with site debris. Level 2 (range 40–50 cm, floor fill) overlay a bed of sterile, graveled soil. The smooth Room 1 floor (depth 50 cm) was a use compacted surface cut 15 cm into sterile soil. Room walls were constructed of stone cobbles and irregularly shaped boulders that retained a height (measured from the floor) of 35–50 cm along the east wall and 50–70 cm along the south wall. Rocks were usually set on end (long axis vertical) and positioned with their flattest surface facing toward the house interior. No floor features or room entries were noted. Evidence of pot hunting was extensive and impacted approximately 2.85 m^2 (41 percent) of the Room 1 living surface.

Room 2 (Figure 4.99)

Type V structure; length 4.20 m, width 3.30 m; estimated area of living surface 12.86 m^2.

Room 2 was superimposed on House A and Pit 6. Burials 1 and 2 were interred beneath the room floor.

Level 1 (range 0–40 cm) comprised a loosely consolidated but homogeneous, dark, pebbly silt. Level 2 (range 40–50 cm, floor fill) compared with Level 1. The level room floor (depth 50 cm) was partially constructed over sterile soil and the loose fill of House A and Pit 6. Room walls consisted of masonry (possibly the stone footings of a puddled adobe wall) along the north, west, and south sides. Jacal construction, suggested by post hole impressions, was evident along the east wall. The hearth (Type IIIB1; length 40 cm, width 35 cm, depth 18 cm) was described as a rectangular, stone lined pit in which the north, east, and south sides were composed of stone slabs that extended about 3–5 cm above the floor surface. The hearth's west side was clay lined and unslabbed. No evidence of a roof or entry was observed.

Room 3 (Figure 4.100; refer to Figure 4.25)

Type G structure; length 3.30 m, width 3.10 m; area of living surface 9.06 m^2.

FIGURE 4.98. Wind Mountain locus Room 1 showing the cobble wall construction. Modern pot hunting is apparent by the hole (center view) dug into the room and through its floor (Neg. No. WM 5–15F).

Room 3 was a semisubterranean construction that superimposed the western half of House G.

Level 1 (range 0–100 cm) was composed of a dark gray, pebbly silt intermixed with site debris and stone fallen from the east wall of Room 1. The upper 60 cm of Level 1 had been heavily disturbed by pot hunting. Level 2 (range 100–120 cm, floor fill) compared with Level 1. The level, use compacted Room 3 floor (depth 120 cm) exhibited traces of plaster across its surface. Vertical room walls had been excavated into sterile soil. Plastering was evident on the south, west, and north walls, ranging in height (measured from the floor) from 35 cm on the west wall to 55 cm on the north wall. The north interior corner of the west wall was reinforced (buttressed) with stone that covered an area of about 70 cm by 80 cm (Figure 4.101). A ventilator (height 22 cm, width 36 cm, depth 40 cm) located in the north wall was not centrally positioned, but set 45 cm west from the east wall (Figure 4.102). It was placed about 30 cm above the room floor. A stone support or header (length about 44 cm, thickness about 10 cm) secured the mass of the rock in place (see profile illustration). Two hearths occurred on the floor. Hearth 1 (Type IIB; diameter 30 cm, depth 12 cm) described a circular, unlined basin. Hearth 2 (Type IIIB1; length 38 cm, width 36 cm, depth 14 cm) consisted of a rectangular, clay lined pit with a concave floor. A small stone slab set vertically along the northwest side of Hearth 2 suggests that it may have been partially slab lined. Two floor pits were exposed. Pit 1 (diameter at floor level 30 cm, maximum interior diameter 45 cm, depth 46 cm) was circular with undercut sides. Pit 2 (diameter at floor level 23 cm, maximum interior diameter 35 cm, depth 38 cm) was similarly constructed but contained fill composed of numerous rocks. No room entry was observed; access was possibly attained through the roof.

Room 4 (Figure 4.103)

Type V structure; length 6.90 m, width 3.95 m; area of living surface 24.56 m^2.

Room 4 was superimposed on Houses H and J. Pit 7 intruded into the fill of Room 4.

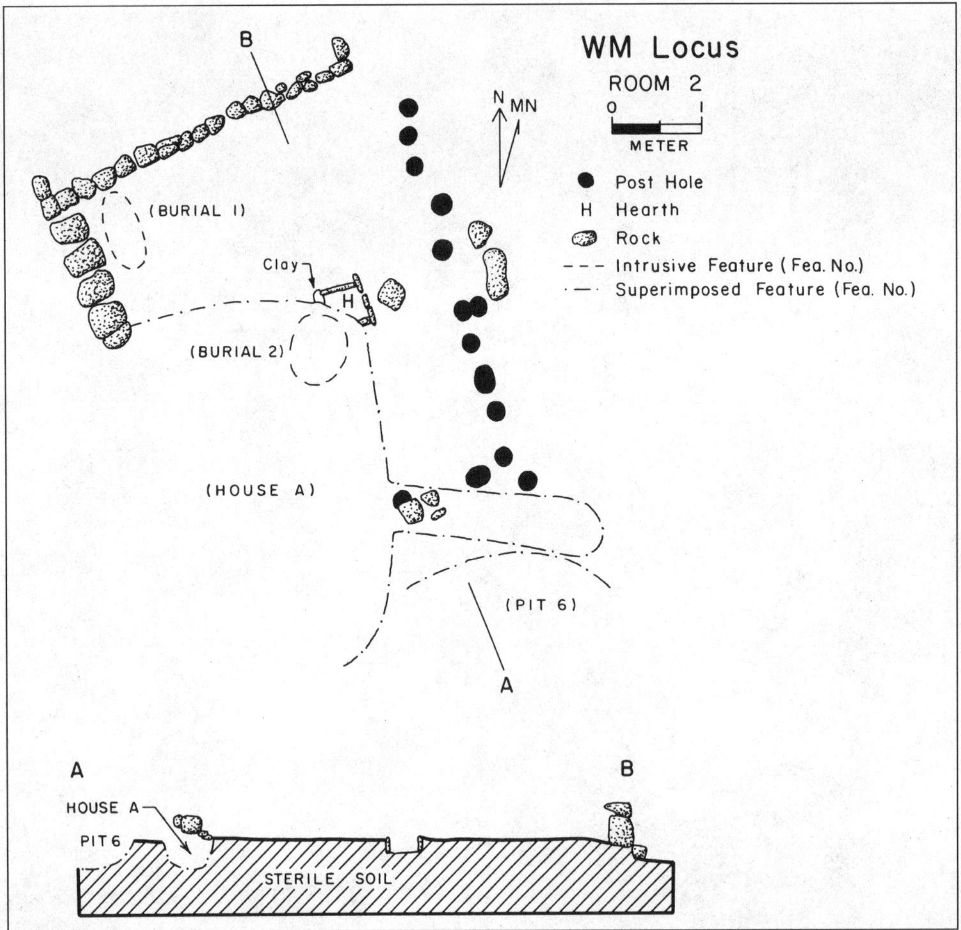

FIGURE 4.99. Plan view and profile of the surviving portions of Wind Mountain locus Room 2, a Type V structure.

Level 1 (range 0–65 cm) was described as a dark, homogeneous, pebbly silt intermixed with rock from wall fall. Level 2 (range 65–80 cm, floor fill) was analogous to Level 1. The level room floor (depth 80 cm) had been plastered (3 cm thick) and was partially constructed over sterile soil and over the loose fill of Houses H and J. The east, south, and west walls were built of stone (possibly wall footings), whereas the northern wall was apparently constructed of jacal. Masonry walls (measured from the room floor) retained a maximum height of 65 cm along the south wall and a minimum height of 25 cm along the west wall. In general, masonry consisted of large blocky stones set on end (long axis vertical) with a tendency for the smoothest surface to face the room interior. No wall plastering was noted. The hearth (Type IIC2; length 50 cm, width 45 cm, depth 15 cm), a basin-shaped oval, was partly enclosed by rock. Besides the hearth, the only other floor feature included a small pit (diameter 20 cm, depth 5 cm) near the east wall. The entry to Room 4 may have been through the midsection of its east wall.

Room 5 (Figures 4.104 and 4.105; refer to Figure 4.12)

Type V structure; length 4.10 m, width 3.95 m; area of living surface 15.64 m^2.

Room 5 superimposed the northwest corner of House M and the entries to Houses J and H. Puddling Pit 1, under the floor of Room 5, was discovered during subfloor testing.

Level 1 (range 0–20 cm) consisted of a dark gray, debris laden, pebbly silt. A considerable amount of rock from wall fall was noted. Level 2 (range 20–30 cm, floor fill) compared with Level 1, differing only in consistency as the fill became more compacted closer to the floor surface. The level room floor (depth 30 cm) had been compacted by use. Room 5 walls were constructed of masonry, reaching a maximum height (measured from the floor) of 60 cm along the north wall and a minimum height of 30 cm along the south wall. Metate fragments were used in constructing both eastern and western walls. No plastering was noted. The hearth (Type IIB; diameter 45 cm, depth 10 cm) appeared as a circular, shallow basin. A floor pit (diameter 25 cm, depth 25 cm) was ex-

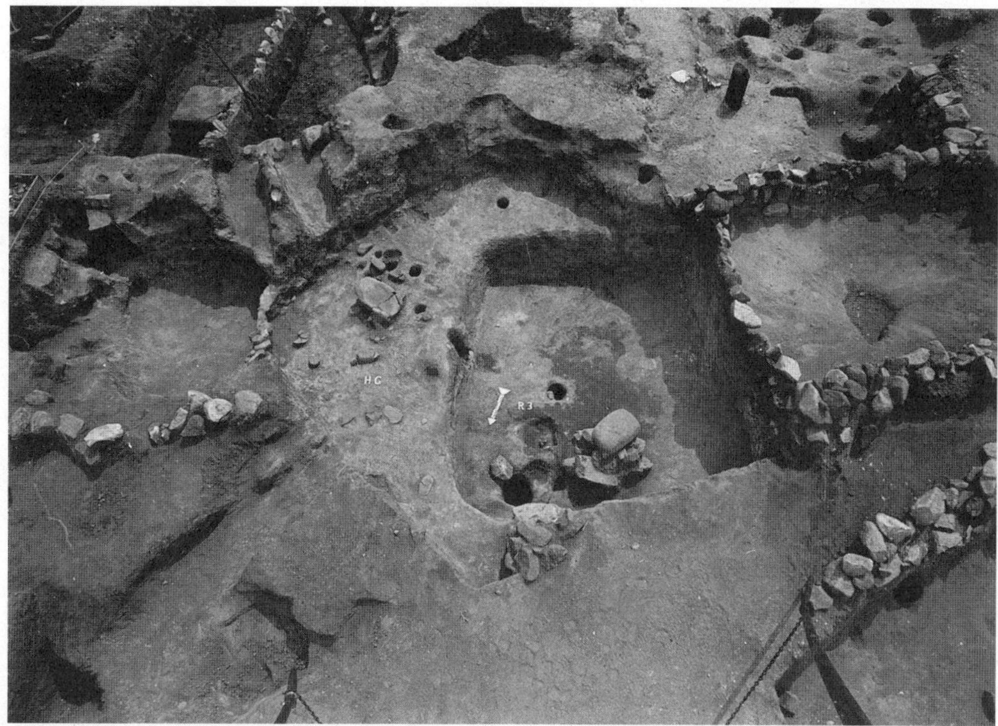

FIGURE 4.100. Wind Mountain locus Room 3, a Type G community structure. Room 3 was a subterranean structure, constructed into House G (Neg. No. WM 15–5F).

FIGURE 4.101. The stone reinforced corner wall of Wind Mountain locus Room 3 (Neg. No. WM 15–31F).

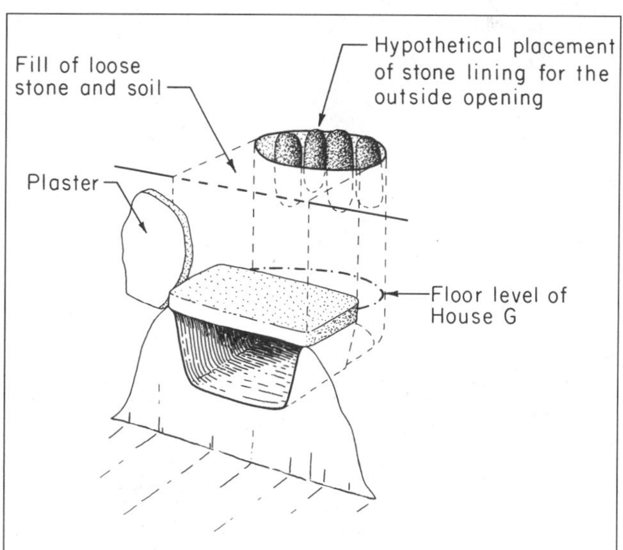

FIGURE 4.102. The Wind Mountain locus Room 3 ventilator.

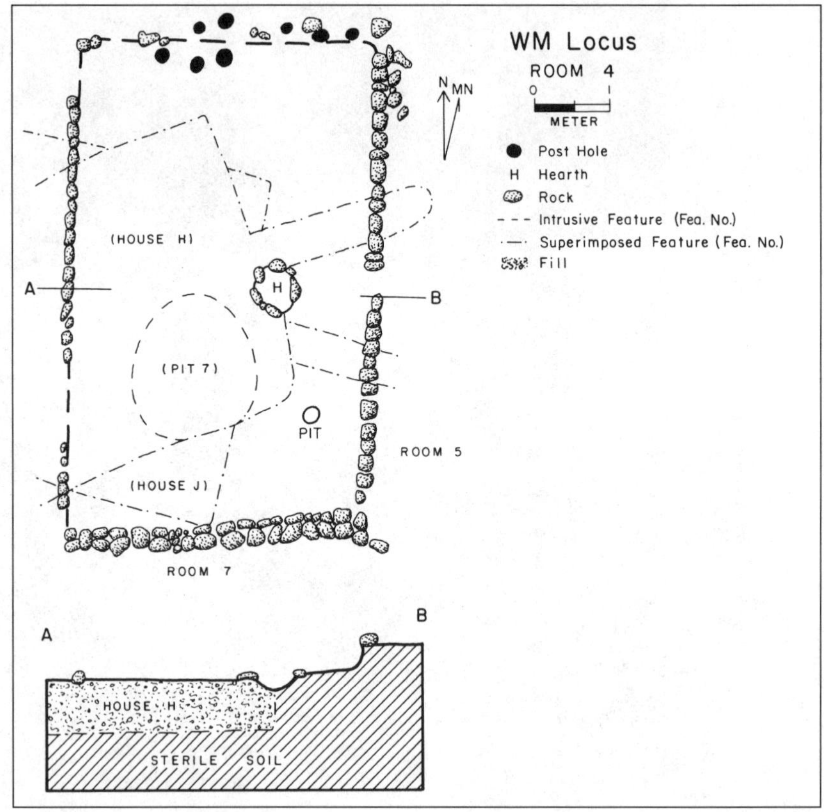

FIGURE 4.103. Plan view and profile of Wind Mountain locus Room 4, a Type V structure.

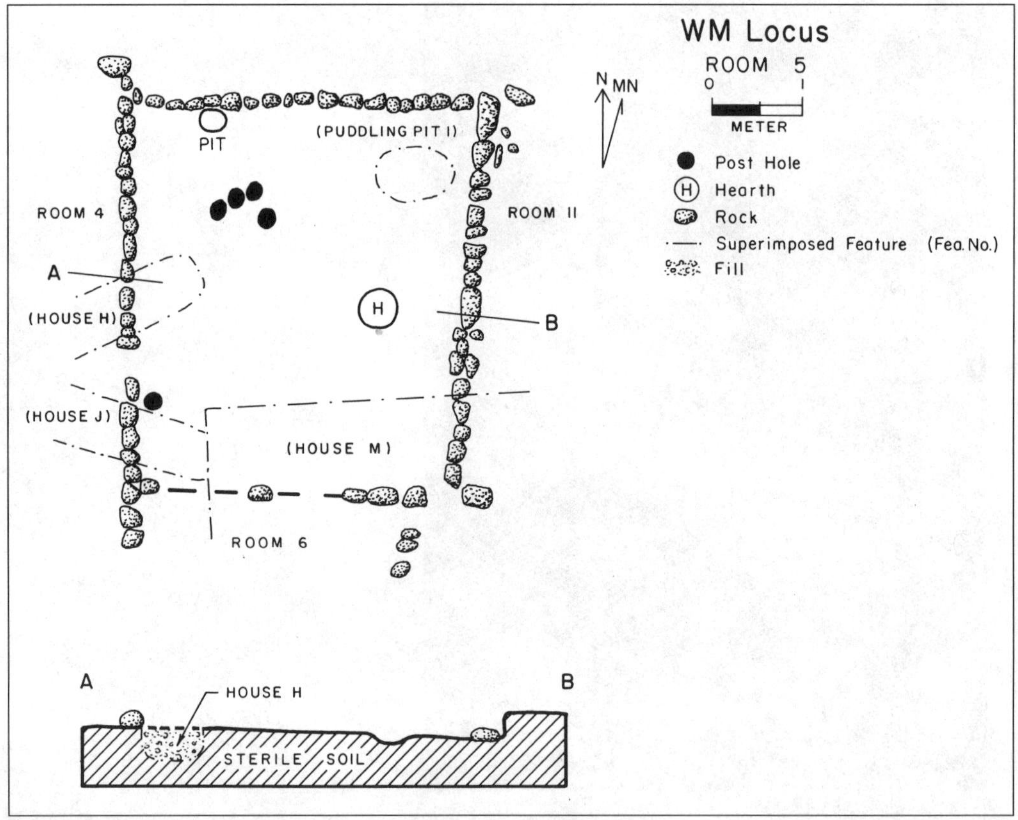

FIGURE 4.104. Plan view and profile of Wind Mountain locus Room 5, a Type V structure.

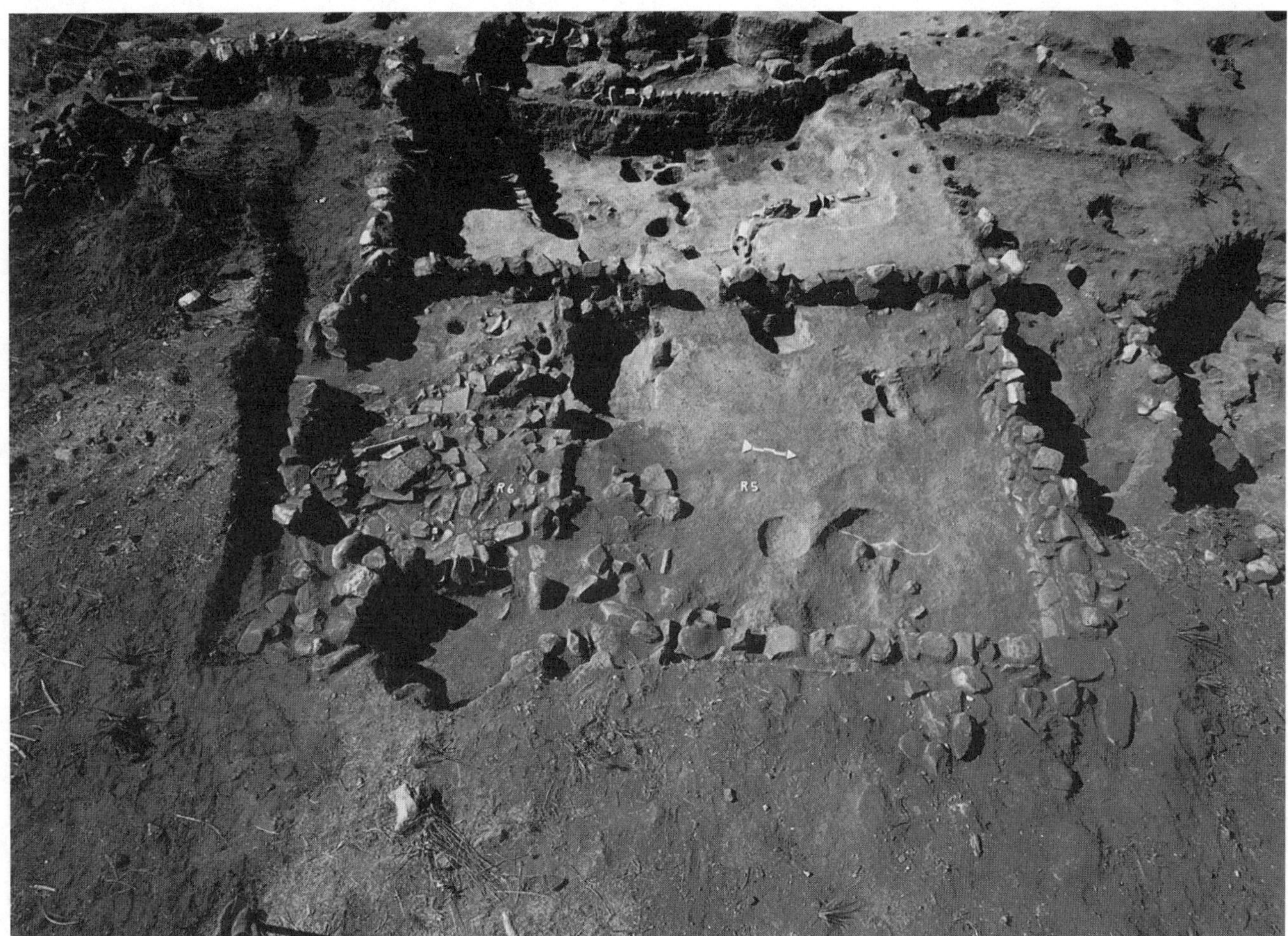

FIGURE 4.105. Wind Mountain locus Rooms 5 and 6, two Type V structures. Room 5 floor features included a shallow, circular hearth and a deep floor pit. Stone slabs paved the floor of Room 6 (Neg. No. WM 29–14F).

posed near the room's north wall. No evidence of a roof was found. Access may have been achieved through the midsection of the east wall, where a large stone slab (length 50 cm, width 22 cm, thickness 10 cm) indicates the presence of a step entry. A gap in the western wall suggests a possible doorway into Room 4. A subfloor test in the northeast corner of the room uncovered Puddling Pit 1, a feature apparently associated with an earlier site occupation.

Room 6 (Figures 4.105 and 4.106; refer to Figure 4.12)

Type V structure; length 3.10 m, width 2.10 m; area of living surface 6.00 m^2.

Room 6 superimposed the southwestern corner of House M.

Level 1 (range 0–25 cm) consisted of a uniformly dark gray, trash laden, pebbly silt. The fill contained a considerable amount of stone wall fall, melted adobe, and charcoal. Level 2 (range 25–35 cm, floor fill) compared with Level 1. The floor of Room 6 (depth 35 cm) was probably once paved with stone slabs. Stone slabs had been set into the eastern two-thirds of the floor. The unpaved, unplastered western third was compacted by use. Room walls were constructed of a crudely coursed masonry that incorporated heavy, blocky stones placed on end intermixed with smaller, irregularly shaped rocks. The southwest corner of the room was excavated 10 cm into sterile soil; masonry work began above this point. Other than four post hole impressions, no floor features were noted. The room entry may have been achieved through either of two gaps in the east wall. Room 6 apparently burned.

Room 7 (refer to Figures 4.21 and 4.22)

Type E structure; length 8.20 m, width 4.70 m; area of living surface 37.90 m^2.

The northern wall of Room 7 was superimposed upon the southeast corner of House J. Its southwestern corner superimposed the entry of House N. Burial 18 was found under the Room 7 floor, interred within the entry of House N.

Level 1 (range 0–25 cm) was composed of a homogeneous, dark gray, pebbly silt (or silty clay) intermixed with a con-

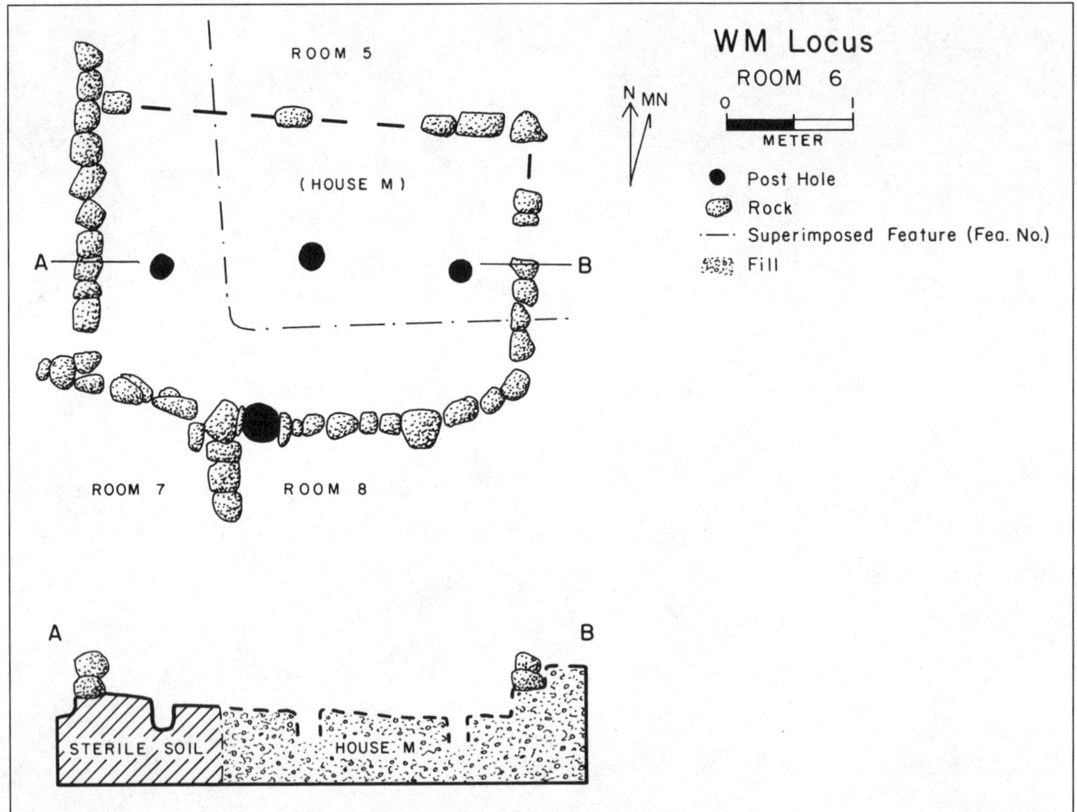

FIGURE 4.106. Plan view and profile of Wind Mountain locus Room 6, a Type V structure.

siderable amount of wall fall. Level 2 (range 25–35 cm, floor fill) consisted of a dark gray, densely consolidated, pebbly silt. The level room floor (depth 35 cm) was compacted by use. The eastern wall of Room 7 consisted of a discontinuous line of stones set one course high (average height 25 cm). Its southern and western walls were made of roughly coursed stone set into a dark gray, pebbly mortar. Three courses survived (average height 55–60 cm), but rock fall suggested a wall twice that height. The north wall, one or two courses wide, was crudely constructed, partially laid on sterile soil and on loose fill. The hearth (Type IB; approximate diameter 50 cm, depth 10 cm), an irregularly shaped, unlined depression of heat altered soil, was disturbed by a mesquite root. One archaeomagnetic sample (No. 007) was taken from this hearth (Chapter 3). A circular pit (diameter 35 cm, depth 20 cm) with sloping sides and a concave floor was exposed just to the east of the hearth. Entry may have been achieved through any of the openings along the room's eastern wall. A floor pit, located in the middle of the east wall between two post holes, probably represents an earlier feature (see Room 9, Pit 6).

Room 8 (Figure 4.107; refer to Figure 4.11)

Type V structure; length 3.25 m, width 1.90 m; area of living surface 6.22 m^2.

Room 8 superimposed Pit 17 and Burial 17.

Level 1 (range 0–50 cm) consisted of a dark gray, pebbly silt intermixed with stone, the result of wall fall. Level 2 (range 15–20 cm, floor fill) compared with Level 1. The floor (depth 20 cm) was described as an unplastered, level, use compacted surface. Room 8 walls were constructed of unworked boulders laid in rough alignment. Their maximum height along the north wall was 40 cm. Walls never attained a height greater than one course of stone and may represent the remains of wall footings. No wall plaster was noted. The hearth (Type IB; diameter 20 cm) occurred as a burned patch on the floor. Two floor pits, both circular- and basin-shaped, were found: Pit 1 (diameter 65 cm, depth 30 cm) and Pit 2 (diameter 30 cm, depth 30 cm). No form of room entry was observed.

FIGURE 4.107. Wind Mountain locus Room 8, a Type V structure. Its masonry walls were constructed of unshaped boulders (Neg. No. WM 38–12F).

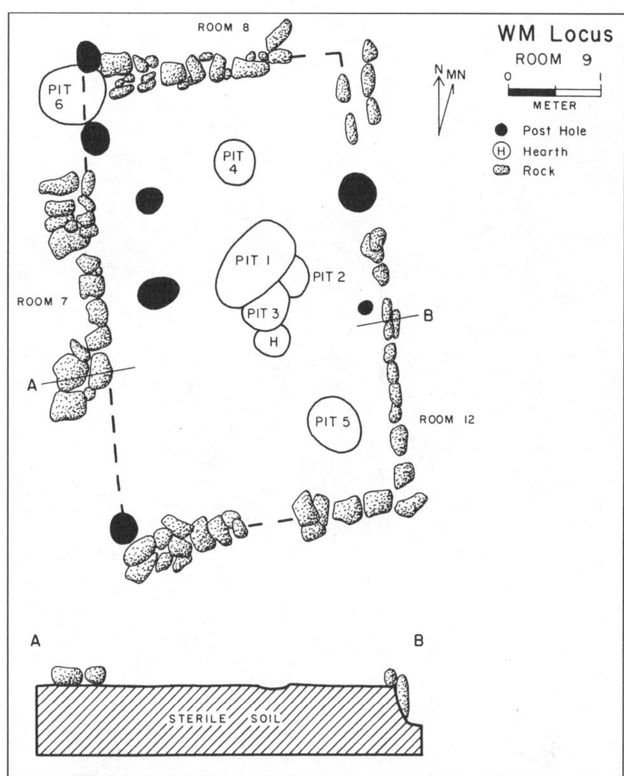

FIGURE 4.108. Plan view and profile of Wind Mountain locus Room 9, a Type V structure.

Room 9 (Figure 4.108)

Type V structure; length 4.30 m, width 2.80 m; area of living surface 12.21 m^2.

Level 1 (range 0–30 cm) consisted of a dark, consolidated, trash laden silt intermixed with a considerable amount of stone from fallen walls. Level 2 (range 30–40 cm, floor fill) was composed of a dark gray, consolidated, trash laden silt that acquired greatest density near the floor. The level unplastered floor (depth 40 cm) was compacted by use. Room 9 walls were constructed of stone and loosely bordered the living surface. Walls were incomplete in many places, no more than one course of stone high, and may indicate the remains of wall footings. The hearth (Type IB; length 30 cm, width 25 cm) was an irregularly shaped burned patch on the room floor. Six floor pits were located: Pit 1 (length 100 cm, width 65 cm, depth 35 cm) was oval-shaped with slightly undercut sides and a flat floor; Pit 2 (diameter 40 cm, depth 15 cm) was irregularly shaped with sloping sides and a round base; Pit 3 (diameter 50 cm, depth 20 cm) was irregularly shaped with sloping sides and a flat floor; Pit 4 (diameter at floor level 45 cm, diameter at base 60 cm, depth 30 cm) was circular with undercut sides and a flat floor; Pit 5 (diameter 50 cm, depth 25 cm) was irregularly shaped with sloping sides and a concave floor; Pit 6 (length 85 cm, width 70 cm, depth 30 cm) was incompletely described. Notes briefly mention the presence of Pit 6 and infer that it may represent a feature associated with earlier activities than those of either Rooms 7 or 9.

Room 10 (Figure 4.109)

Type V structure; length 8.70 m, width 3.05 m; estimated area of living surface 26.00 m^2.

Room 10 superimposed Houses E, N, and O.

Level 1 (range 0–30 cm) consisted of a dark gray, trash laden, pebbly silt with rocks from wall fall. Level 2 (range 30–55 cm) and Level 3 (range 55–65 cm, floor fill) compared with Level 1. The room floor (depth 65 cm) survived only as a small remnant plaster patch between the hearth and the east wall. Room walls (for a description of the Room 10 east wall, see Room 7 west wall) were extant only along the eastern and southern sides. The western and northern walls were missing and possibly never existed. The southern wall comprised a single alignment of upright rocks (long axis vertical), possi-

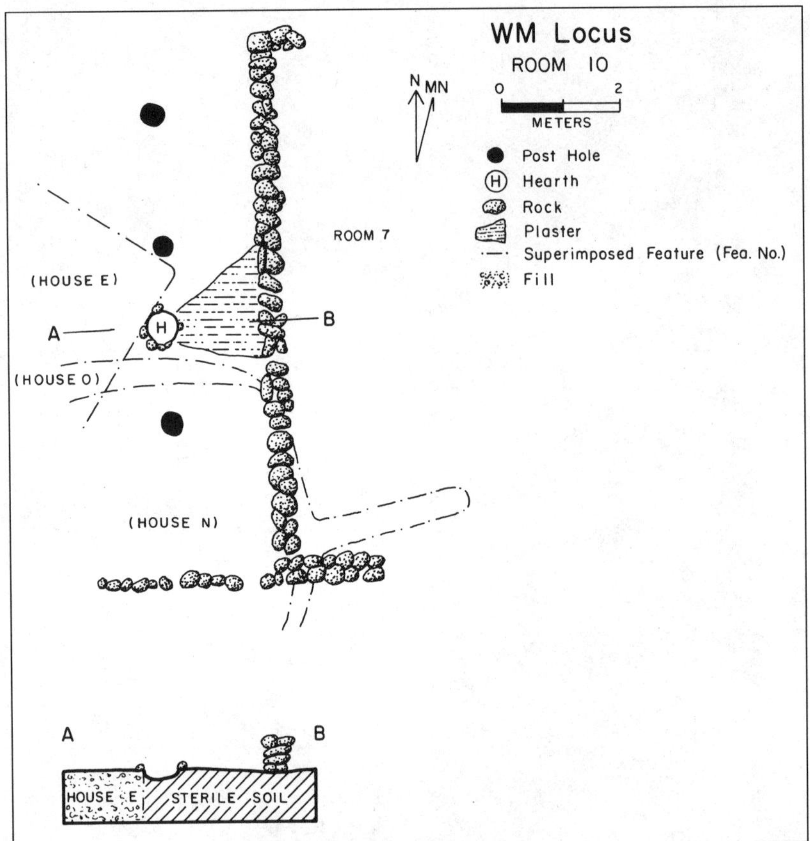

FIGURE 4.109. Plan view and profile of the surviving portions of Wind Mountain locus Room 10, a Type V structure.

bly footing material, one course high. The hearth (Type IIA1; diameter 55 cm, depth 20 cm) was described as a circular, clay lined pit with a crescent-shaped rim along its eastern edge.

Room 11 (Figure 4.110)

Type V structure; length 4.10 m, width 4.10 m; area of living surface 17.01 m^2.

Room 11 superimposed portions of House M, House Q, Burial 24, Puddling Pit 2, and Pit 10.

Level 1 (range 0–30 cm, room fill) consisted of a dark gray, debris laden silt (the upper strata of Level 1 was interpreted as the fill of Houses M and Q). The room floor was not found, but thought to have occurred at about the 30 cm level. The inability to locate a floor was due, in part, to the loose fill characterizing Houses M and Q. Estimation of the floor level was based on averaging the depth of several stones found in the wall construction. However, many of the wall stones extended beneath the assumed floor level, which subsided into loose underlying fill. Three of the Room 11 walls (south, west, and north) were constructed of crude masonry. The south and west walls were represented by several stone courses, attaining a maximum height (measured from the floor) of 40 cm. The north wall was indicated by a single course, and the east wall was missing entirely. No hearth was found, but an ash pit or ash scatter was located near the center of the room. The only other floor feature observed included a fragmentary stone lined post hole (diameter 17 cm, depth 55 cm) in the southeastern quadrant of the room.

Room 12 (Figure 4.111)

Type V structure; length 3.95 m, width 3.85 m; area of living surface 15.22 m^2.

Room 12, a semisubterranean construction, intruded into Room 13, partially superimposing Houses U and V, as well as the northern edge of Puddling Pit 3.

Level 1 (range 0–50 cm) comprised a dark gray pebbly silt, intermixed with a large number of stones and site debris. The stones were assumed to derive from the common wall belonging to Room 9 and Room 12. Level 2 (range 50–60 cm, floor fill) compared with Level 1. The room floor was located at the 60 cm level. The western two-thirds of the floor consisted of a level, use compacted surface. Its eastern third disappeared into the loose fill of House U and House V. Room 12's east-

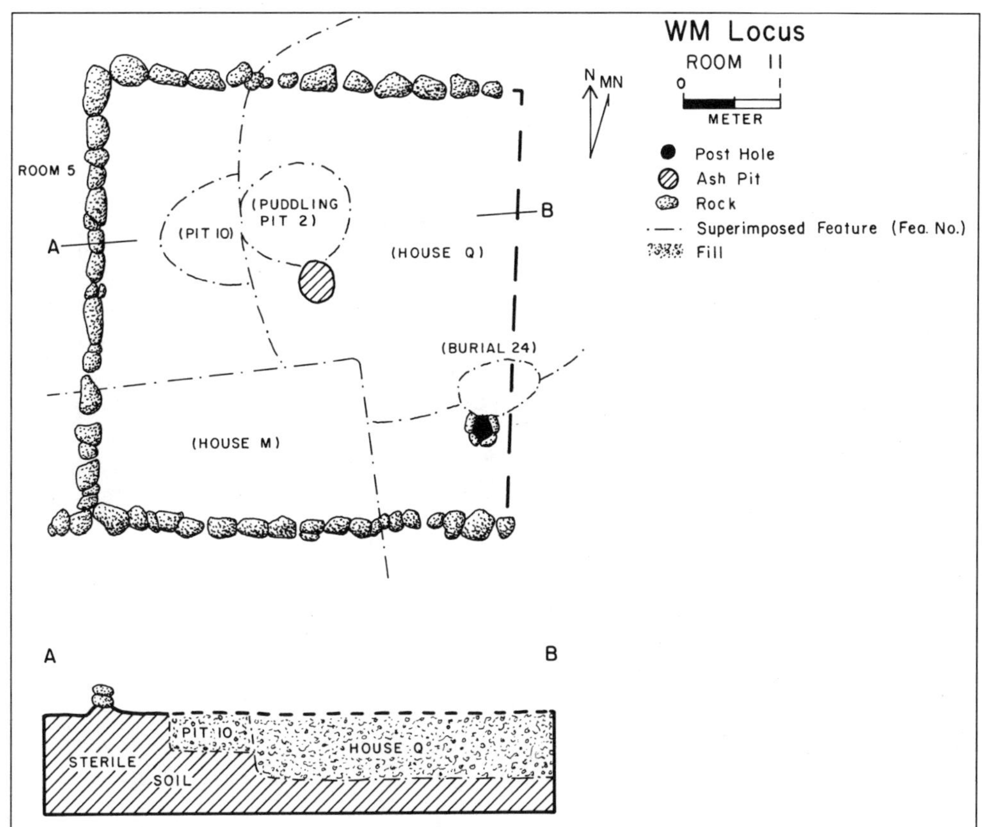

FIGURE 4.110. Plan view and profile of Wind Mountain locus Room 11, a Type V structure.

ern and western walls were inset with stone boulders that served as a lining for this slightly subterranean room. The southern and northern walls were unlined, exhibiting only a handful of stones along their margins. Two hearths were exposed. Hearth 1 (Type IIA; diameter 23 cm, depth 10 cm) occurred as a circular, clay lined pit located west of and partly impacted by Hearth 2. Hearth 2 (Type IIA; diameter 20 cm, depth 12 cm), constructed after Hearth 1, was a circular, clay lined depression, its lip set flush with the house floor. Each hearth contained a small quantity of ash. Puddling Pit 3 was found under the floors of Rooms 12 and 13 and predates their construction.

Room 13 (Figure 4.112)

Type V structure; length 5.60 m, width 4.10 m; estimated area of living surface 21.53 m^2.

Room 13 was intruded by Room 12 but superimposed House BB, House CC, Pit 30, and Puddling Pit 3.

Level 1 (range 0–35 cm) consisted of a dark gray, pebbly silt intermixed with site debris. Level 1 was removed and recorded as Excavation Unit Block 35–B before Room 13 was recognized as a discrete architectural feature. Level 2 (range 35–45 cm, floor fill) compared with Level 1. Where Room 13 superimposed House BB, its floor was not clearly discernable. Over time its deposits were intermixed with those of House BB. The remaining floor area (45 cm) exhibited a use compacted surface. All four Room 13 walls were constructed of low (range 25–45 cm), crudely aligned stone masonry that was interrupted at intervals by gaps. A poorly preserved, unlined circular hearth (Type IIB; diameter 20 cm, depth 10 cm) was noted. A small ash pit (diameter 20 cm, depth 8 cm) occurred immediately southeast of the hearth. Excavation demonstrated that Room 13 was constructed slightly before Room 12 as the latter intruded into the former.

Room 14 (Figure 4.113)

Type V structure; length 5.00 m, width 4.70 m; area of living surface 23.00 m^2.

Room 14 superimposed House X, Burial 34, and Pit 20.

Level 1 (range 0–50 cm) was removed as Excavation Unit Block 44–A/B/C/D, which investigators originally identified as a plaza area (i.e., Plaza 1). The notion of formal Wind Mountain plazas was later rejected and the term removed from the architectural lexicon of the site. Pot hunting activity was prevalent in this area of the site. Level 1 fill consisted of a dark gray, uniform, pebbly silt, intermixed with large rocks.

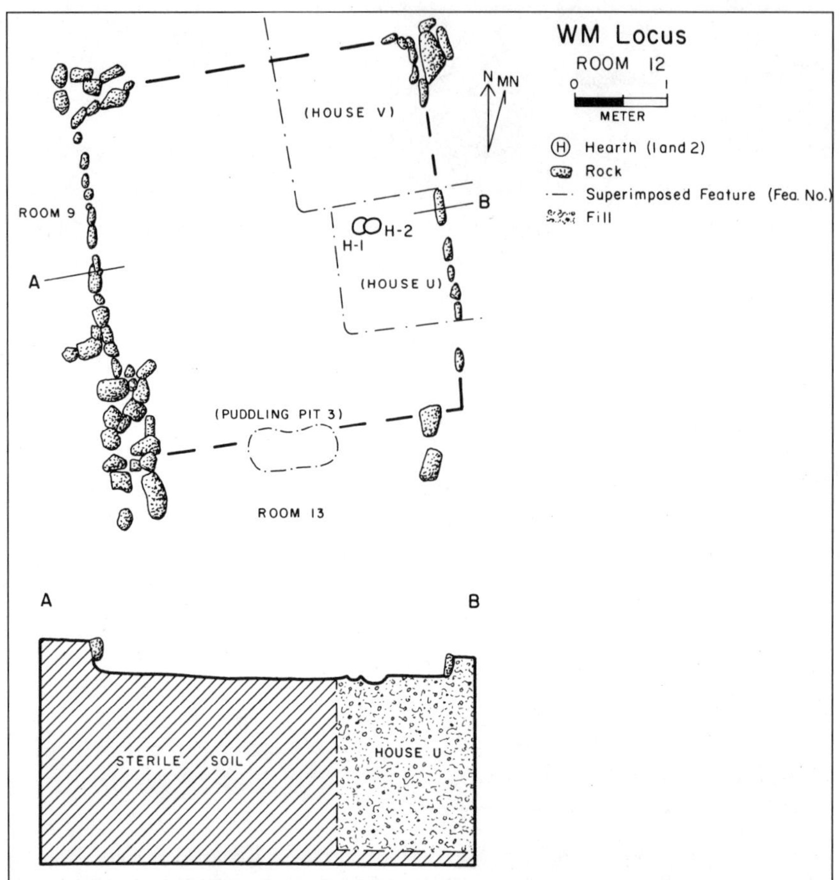

FIGURE 4.111. Plan view and profile of Wind Mountain locus Room 12, a Type V structure.

Level 2 (range 50–65 cm, floor fill) compared with Level 1, but contained more stones, presumably representing wall fall. The unplastered house floor (depth 65 cm) described an uneven surface. That portion of the house floor overlying House X had settled somewhat, subsiding into the loose fill of the feature beneath. A few patches of floor were, however, still distinguishable. The east, west, and north walls were made of blocky stones (approximately 30 cm x 20 cm x 15 cm) set upright (long axis vertical) with the smooth surface facing the room interior. Stones were secured with a dark gray, pebbly mortar. The Room 14 south wall was indicated by four vertical stones set into sterile soil. These attained a maximum height of 10 cm above ground level. The hearth (Type IIC2; depth 12 cm) was a poorly defined, circular, heat altered section of floor. A curving line of burned stone formed its eastern edge. An unlined oval pit (length 70 cm, width 60 cm, depth 40 cm) with sloping sides and a concave floor occurred near the southern margin of Room 14. A second pit was discovered under the floor in the room's northeastern quadrant. Definition of its plan and shape was not possible due to the unstable nature of the underlying loose fill. Its existence was established by a cache of three miniature vessels; WM 1930, WM 1285, and WM 1286.

Room 15 (Figure 4.114)

Type G structure; length 3.25 m, width 2.80 m; area of living surface 8.96 m^2.

Room 15 partly superimposed the northwestern portion of House FF.

Level 1 (range 0–30 cm) consisted of a dark gray, pebbly silt intermixed with site debris and rock. Level 1 was removed as Excavation Unit Block 44–C. Level 2 (range 30–65 cm) and Level 3 (range 65–80 cm) were analogous to Level 1. Floor fill and floor components were mixed. The room floor (depth 80 cm) described a use compacted surface, graveled over most of its area. The majority of the south and east walls had been excavated into the loose fill of House FF; the northern and western walls and the western portion of the south wall were dug into sterile soil. Walls were reinforced with upright boulders (long axis vertical) set into gray silty mortar. The unplastered Room 15 north wall cut directly into

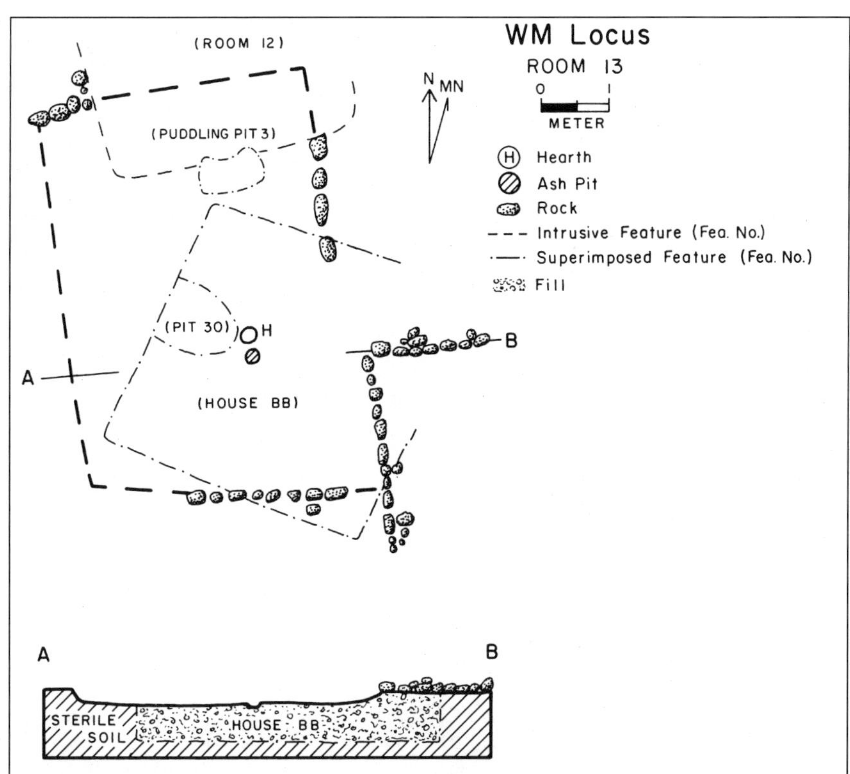

FIGURE 4.112. Plan view and profile of Wind Mountain locus Room 13, a Type V structure.

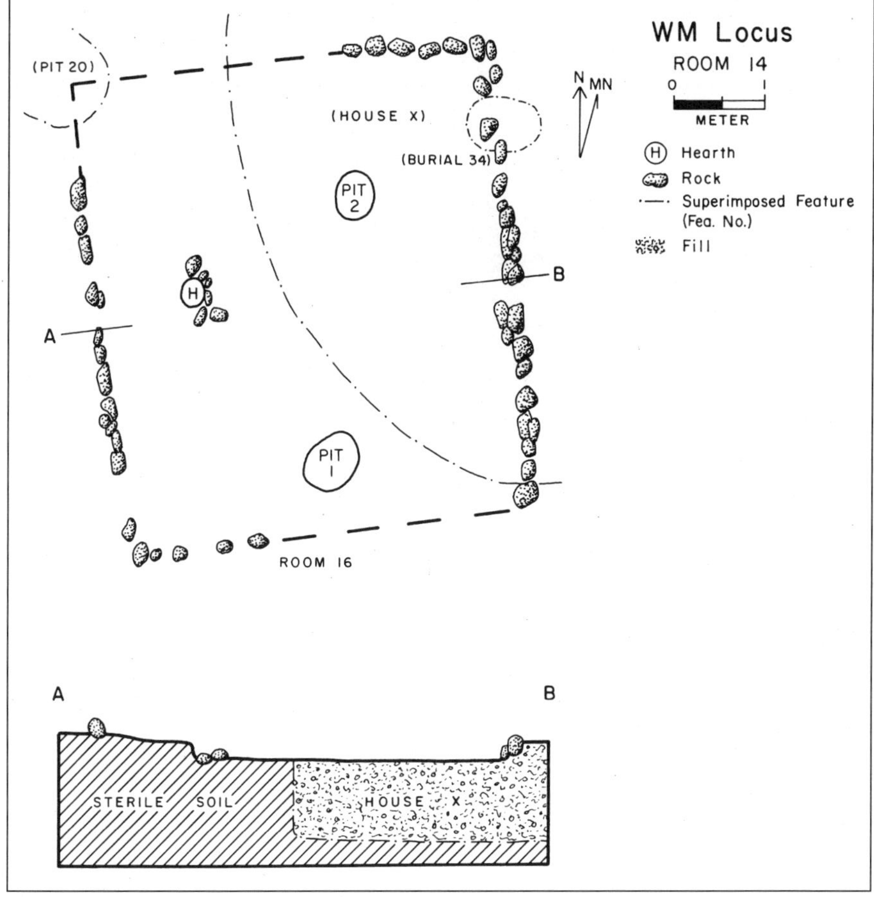

FIGURE 4.113. Plan view and profile of Wind Mountain locus Room 14, a Type V structure.

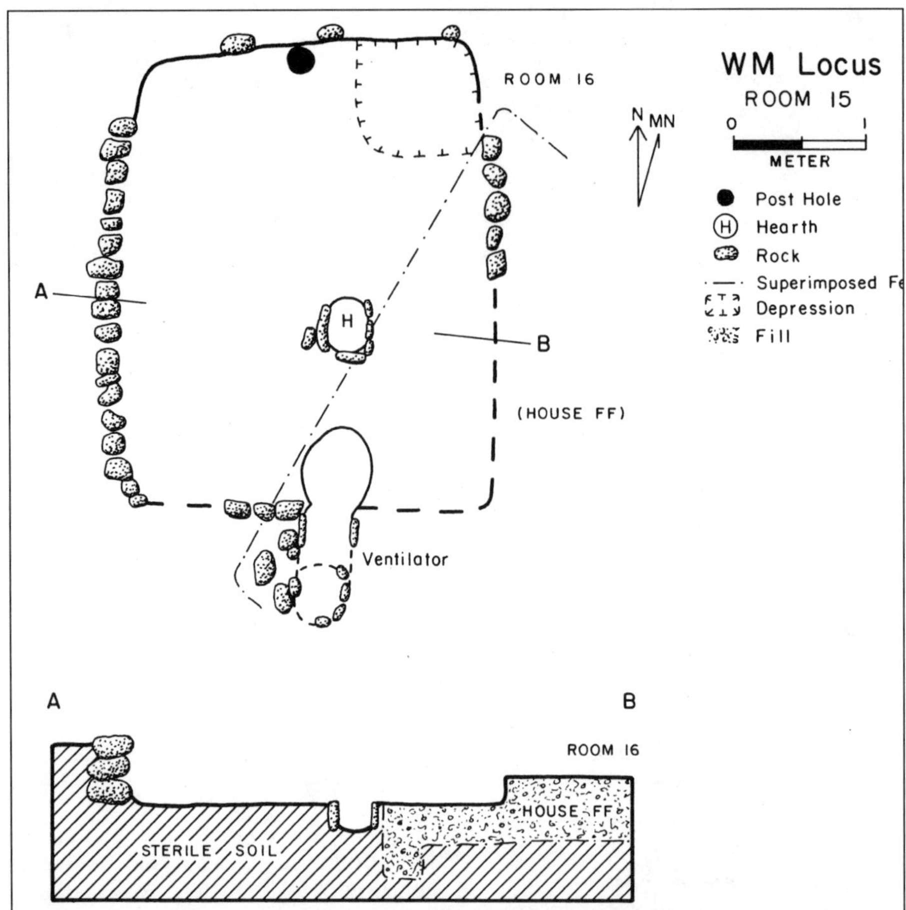

FIGURE 4.114. Plan view and profile of Wind Mountain locus Room 15, a Type G community structure.

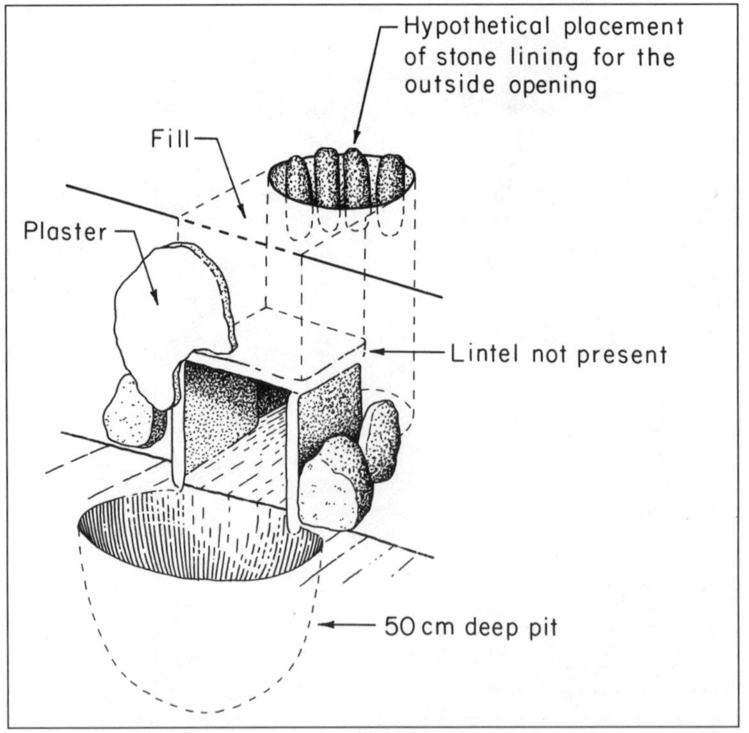

FIGURE 4.115. The Room 15 ventilator.

sterile soil. A few stones lying atop this vertical surface were all that defined the north wall. A ventilator (with an interior area of approximately .32 m^2) was observed near the midsection of the south wall (Figure 4.115). It exhibited a rectangular opening (width 35 cm, approximate height 35 cm) set flush with the house floor. Two vertical slabs (approximate thickness 2–4 cm) positioned about 30 cm into the side walls formed the interior lateral sides of the ventilator. No upper support stone or header was found. A semicircular stone feature buried in the loose fill of adjacent House FF may have formed the ventilator shaft. A round, 50 cm deep floor pit occurred directly in front of the ventilator opening. Excavation of House FF appears to have disturbed this feature. The hearth (Type IIIB1; length 38 cm, width 30 cm, depth 20 cm) was described as a rectangular, partially stone lined depression that contained gray ash. Though not slab lined, its north wall and base were plastered (thickness 1–3 mm). One archaeomagnetic sample (No. 012) was taken from the hearth (Chapter 3). A depression (depth 10 cm) of unknown function was noted in the room's northeast corner.

Room 16 (Figure 4.116)

Type V structure; length 4.00 m, width 3.25 m; estimated area of living surface 10.94 m^2.

Room 16 partially superimposed House FF. Burials 47, 48, 50, and 51 were all located under the floor of Room 16 (i.e., in the fill of House FF).

Level 1 (range 0–55 cm) was composed of a dark gray, pebbly silt intermixed with site debris and rock. A clearly defined floor surface was not found but was estimated to have occurred at about 55 cm. Where observable, the room floor appeared as a use compacted gravel surface constructed atop sterile soil. The portion of the floor overlying House FF consisted of a patchy red-orange gravelly silt, varying in thickness from 1 to 10 cm. Room 16 walls were mostly lacking. Except for a single stone alignment near the northwest corner, no other possible load bearing walls were noted. A few scattered post holes were identified, although as mentioned in the field records, they may not have belonged to Room 16. A fragmentary circular hearth (Type IIA; diameter 20 cm) was exposed near the north end of the room. It was a thinly plastered (< 1 mm), slightly depressed (depth 6 cm) burned surface with a sparse layer of ash. One archaeomagnetic sample (No. 013) was taken from the hearth area (Chapter 3). At some point in the early investigation of Room 16, the term "Work Area 2" was assigned (as compared with "room"). The "Work Area" definition was later abandoned in favor of reassigning the original appellation of Room 16.

Pit Structures of the Ridout Locus

House A (Figure 4.117)

Type IV structure; length 3.90 m, width 3.60 m; area of living surface 13.48 m^2; mean orientation of entry 47°.

Level 1 (range 0–150 cm) consisted of a black humuslike soil intermixed with site debris. Level 2 (range 150–160 cm, floor fill) compared with Level 1. The house floor (depth 160 cm) was not well preserved, possibly due to poor drainage. Disruption of the living surface was most apparent along the structure's east wall, where the floor was described as a "sandy pool." House A walls were not reinforced with stone, but had been excavated directly into sterile soil. An oval-shaped, ephemeral hearth (Type IB; length 70 cm, width 45 cm, depth 7 cm) occurred near the entry. One C^{14} sample (GX-6897), recovered from the fill of the central post hole, was analyzed (Chapter 3). The lateral entry (area 1.37 m^2) allowed access into the structure through the midsection of its northeast wall. The entry ramp, a long (295 cm) and narrow (50 cm) incline (10° for the first 150 cm and 24° thereafter), had been excavated into sterile soil. A small patch of light brown plaster (thickness 1.5 cm) was noted along its southeastern wall.

House B (Figure 4.118)

Type IV structure; length 4.50 m, width 4.25 m; area of living surface 18.31 m^2; mean orientation of entry 6°.

Level 1 (range 0–110 cm) and Level 2 (range 110–150 cm) were composed of dark humuslike soils intermixed with site debris. Level 3 (range 150–160 cm, floor fill) compared with Levels 1 and 2, although an increased number of ceramic sherds was observed. The level house floor (depth 160 cm) was compacted by use and appeared to have been lightly plastered. Unplastered house walls were reinforced with stone at various points along their periphery. The hearth (Type IA1; length 75 cm, width 60 cm, depth 12 cm) was an irregularly shaped, adobe lined basin with a hearthstone set into its north edge. Three floor pits were exposed. Pit 1 (diameter 30 cm, depth 27 cm), a circular, clay lined basin, was found on the structure's western side. Pit 2 (diameter 20 cm, depth 10 cm) was a small basin-shaped feature located immediately north of Pit 1. Pit 3 (diameter 15 cm, depth 5 cm) occurred as a shallow floor depression on the eastern side of the house. Its entry (area 3.19 m^2) was an extremely long (510 cm) and narrow (60 cm), stepped incline (2°) that allowed access to the house through the midsection of its north wall. The use compacted entry floor had been excavated into sterile soil. A number of stones lined the western wall of the entry ramp, acting as reinforcement to contain loose fill. One C^{14} sample (GX-7224) was recovered from an entry post hole (Chapter 3).

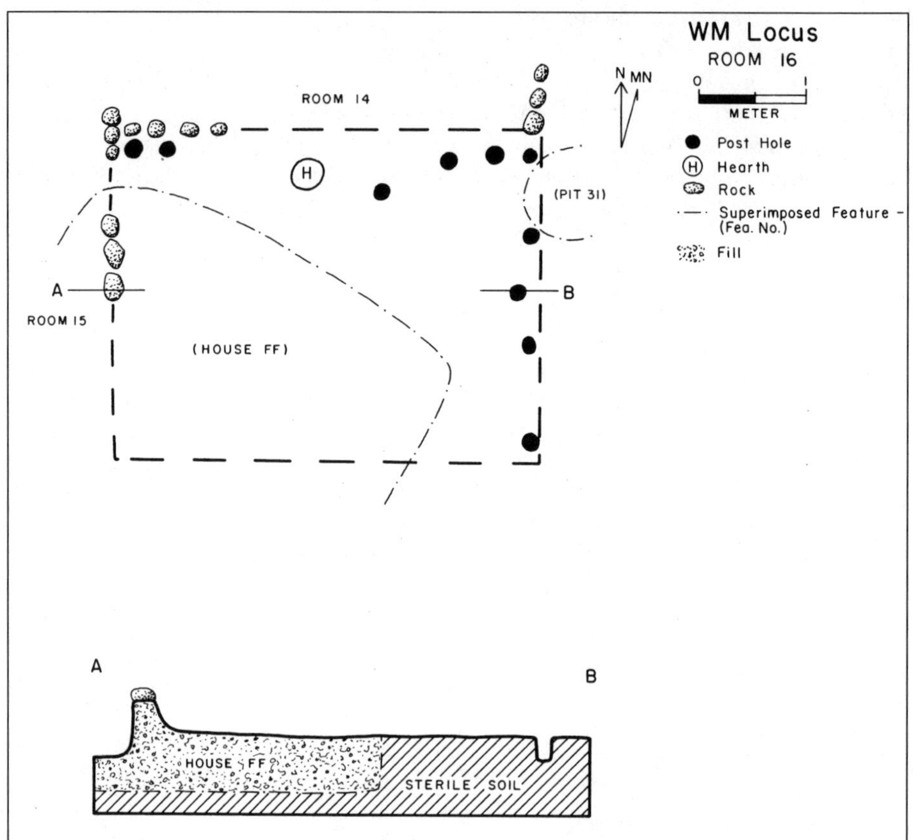

FIGURE 4.116. Plan view and profile of Wind Mountain locus Room 16, a Type V structure.

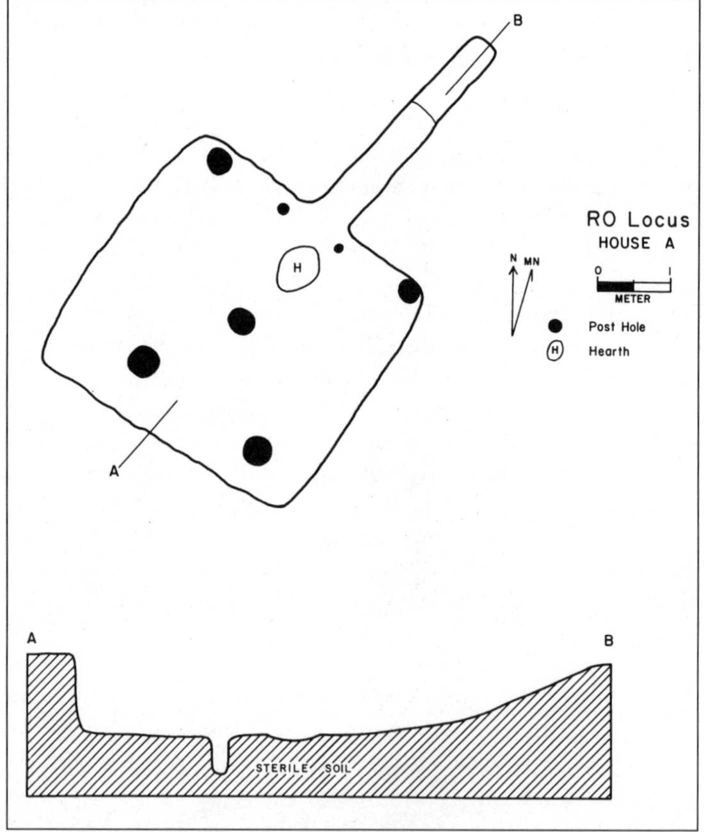

FIGURE 4.117. Plan view and profile of Ridout locus House A, a Type IV structure.

House C (Figures 4.119 and 4.120)

Type IV structure; length 5.20 m, width 4.20 m; area of living surface 20.61 m²; mean orientation of entry 95°.

Level 1 (range 0–100 cm) represented a dark humuslike soil. Level 2 (range 100–150 cm) was analogous to Level 1. Level 3 (range 150–160 cm, floor fill) contained quantities of adobe fragments, possibly the result of collapsed roofing material. The unplastered house floor (depth 160 cm) was an uneven surface of use compacted soil. One C^{14} sample (GX-6901) was recovered from the floor. Vertical house walls had been excavated into sterile soil. The House C north wall was plastered (approximate thickness 1.2 cm) and attained a maximum height (measured from the floor) of 60 cm. The circular hearth (Type IIB1; diameter 40 cm, depth 15 cm) was an unplastered, basin-shaped depression with a hearthstone set into its eastern edge. The entry consisted of a long (330 to 470 cm), narrow (45 cm) ramp (8°) joining the structure near the midsection of its east wall. The entry ramp (area 2.13 m²), its floor flat in cross section, had been excavated into sterile soil.

House D (Figure 4.121)

Type IV structure; length 4.50 m, width 4.30 m; area of living surface 18.23 m²; mean orientation of entry 31°.

Level 1 (range 0–120 cm) was composed of a dark humuslike soil intermixed with site debris. Level 2 (range 120–130 cm, floor fill) compared with Level 1. The house floor (depth 130 cm) was described as an uneven surface heavily impacted by various features, including post holes, pits, and a hearth, as well as postoccupational disturbance (i.e., rodents). Unplastered house walls were vertical. The hearth (Type IB1; length 85 cm, width 60 cm, depth 10 cm) consisted of an irregularly shaped, unlined depression with a hearthstone set into its north edge. One archaeomagnetic sample (No. 041) was taken from the hearth (Chapter 3). A small circular ash pit (diameter 17 cm, depth 15 cm), still containing ash, occurred immediately adjacent the hearth. Two floor pits were located. Pit 1 (diameter 65 cm, depth 55 cm), a circular, unlined depression, was exposed in the southeastern quadrant of House D. Pit 2 (diameter 30 cm, depth 35 cm), also circular and unlined, was found near the central post hole. The entry (area 1.83 m²) joined the structure through the midsection of its north wall. It was a long (390 cm), relatively narrow (65 cm), slightly inclined ramp (3°) that had been excavated into sterile soil.

House E (Figure 4.122)

Type I structure; length 4.20 m, width 3.90 m; estimated area of living surface 15.16 m².

House E was superimposed by later House I.

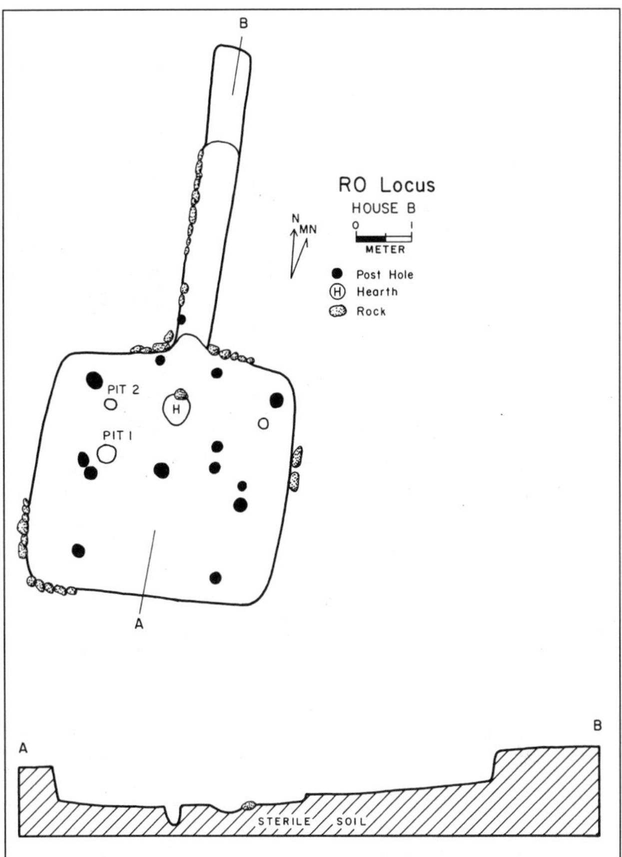

FIGURE 4.118. Plan view and profile of Ridout locus House B, a Type IV structure.

Level 1 (range 0–60 cm) and Level 2 (range 60–135 cm) were composed of dark, humuslike soil intermixed with site debris. It was believed that downslope erosion from the vicinity of House D was responsible for much of the cultural debris and fill found in Houses E, G, and I. Level 3 (range 135–140 cm, floor fill) compared in composition and origin to Levels 1 and 2. The level floor (depth 140 cm) was compacted by use. A small discoloration on the floor adjacent the hearth may represent the surviving traces of a thin plaster wash. An area of floor-wall contact along the structure's north wall appeared to have been lightly plastered. One archaeomagnetic sample from the aforementioned location (No. 040) was taken 15 cm above the house floor (Chapter 3). A possible hearth (Type IB; approximate length 45 cm, width 30 cm) occurred in the structure's northwest quadrant. Only marginally identifiable, it was impacted by the construction of House I. It should be noted that the overlapping floors of Houses E and I made the identification of associated post holes virtually impossible. Any correlation of post holes to houses in this vicinity is suspect.

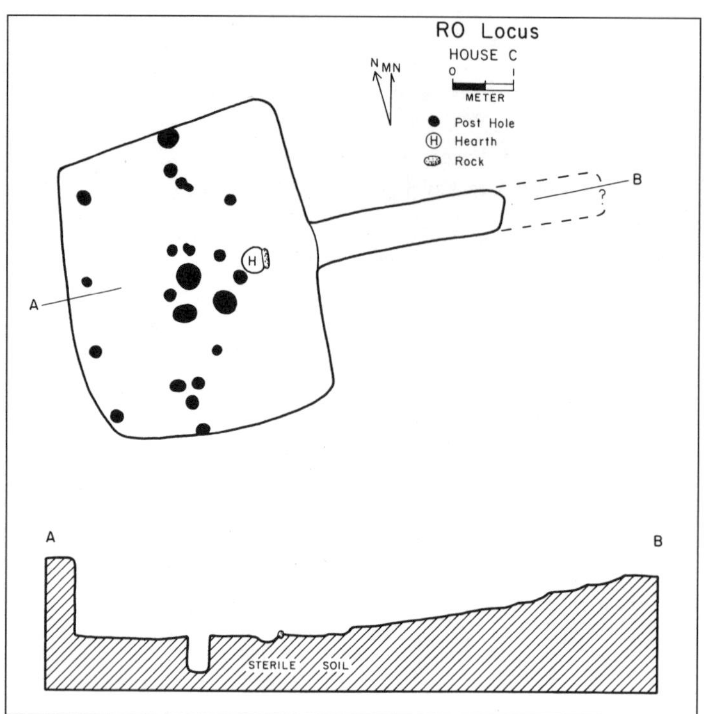

FIGURE 4.119. Plan view and profile of Ridout locus House C, a Type IV structure.

FIGURE 4.120. Ridout locus House C showing floor features and artifacts. Note its long, narrow entry, an attribute common to numerous Type IV structures at the site (Neg. No. WM 98–12F).

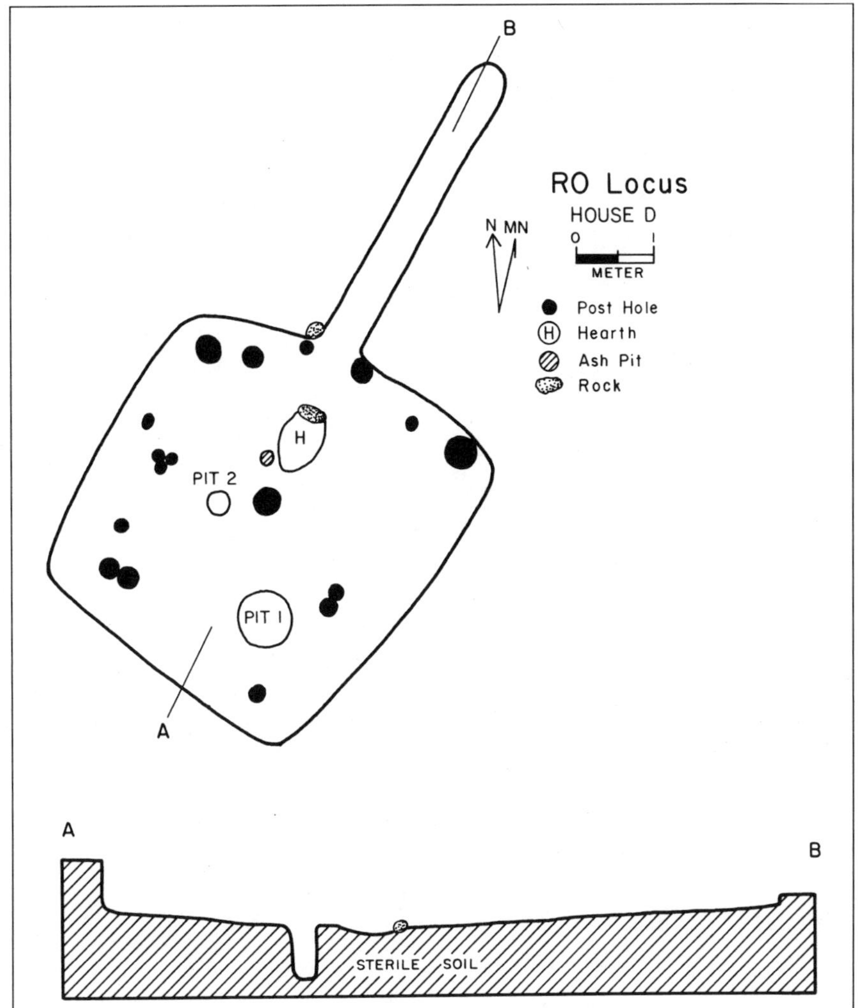

FIGURE 4.121. Plan view and profile of Ridout locus House D, a Type IV structure.

House F (refer to Figure 4.15)

Type A structure; length 6.90 m, width 6.60 m; area of living surface 35.84 m^2.

House F was intruded by Burials 8, 9, and 13, as well as by Pit Oven 20.

Level 1 (range 0–107 cm) was a compacted, dark, humuslike soil intermixed with site debris. Level 2 (range 107–117 cm, floor fill) compared with Level 1. The level House F floor (depth 117 cm) was described as a compacted, plastered surface. Unplastered walls were excavated directly into sterile soil. The 16 post holes (diameter ranges: 15 cm to 30 cm; depth ranges: 4 cm to 37 cm) ringing the structure represent the remains of main load bearing walls. The House F hearth (Type IIA2; diameter 65 cm, depth 9 cm) had been partially destroyed by Burial 9. The surviving hearth fragment revealed a circular, clay lined basin containing ash that was encircled by an 8 cm high clay collar. One archaeomagnetic sample (No. 030) was taken from the hearth (Chapter 3).

House G (refer to Figures 4.3 and 4.122)

Type I structure; length 4.20 m, width 4.00+ m; estimated area of living surface 13.49 m^2.

House G superimposed the northwestern edge of House I.

Level 1 (range 0–45 cm) consisted of a black humuslike soil intermixed with site debris. Level 2 (range 45–80 cm) compared with Level 1. Level 3 (range 80–90 cm, floor fill) was similar to Levels 1 and 2 with the addition of burned adobe fragments. The House G floor (depth 90 cm), though badly eroded, may have been plastered. Walls ranged in height (measured from the floor) from 65 cm on the east to 100 cm on the south. Surviving wall plaster (thickness 1 mm) extended from 20 cm on the east wall to 50 cm on the south.

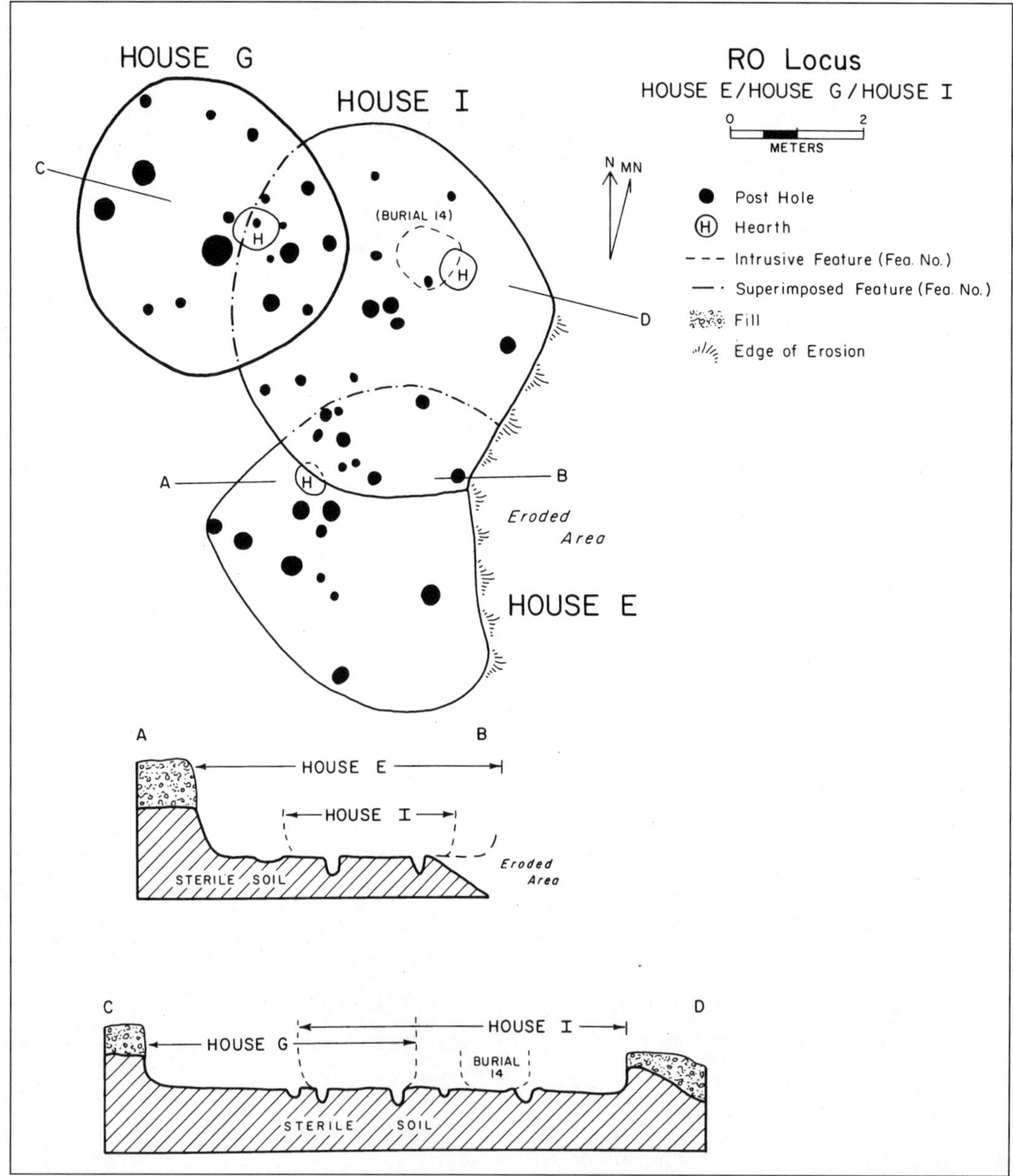

FIGURE 4.122. Plan views and profiles of Ridout locus Houses E, G, and I, three Type I structures.

An area of burned floor was interpreted as the hearth (Type IB; diameter 70 cm, depth 5 cm).

House H (Figure 4.123)

Type IV structure; length 4.00 m, width 3.50 m; area of living surface 13.39 m^2; mean orientation of entry 107°.

Level 1 (range 0–80 cm) and Level 2 (range 80–155 cm) were composed of a dark humuslike soil intermixed with site debris. Level 3 (range 155–165 cm, floor fill) was analogous to Levels 1 and 2, with the addition of some large stones incorporated throughout the fill. The level house floor (depth 165 cm) was a use compacted surface excavated into sterile soil. House walls were vertical and reinforced with stone along a short section (30 cm) of the north wall, which had also been plastered with a light brown, fine sandy clay (thickness 5 mm). The unplastered hearth (Type IB1; length 40 cm, width 35 cm, depth 20 cm), an irregularly shaped pit, occurred between the house entrance and the central post hole. A hearthstone was set in the east rim of the fire pit. A floor pit (diameter 18 cm, depth 16 cm) was exposed on the structure's south side. The entry (area 2.17 m^2) consisted of a long (410 cm), narrow (50 cm), stepped ramp (16°) that joined the house through the midsection of its eastern wall. The

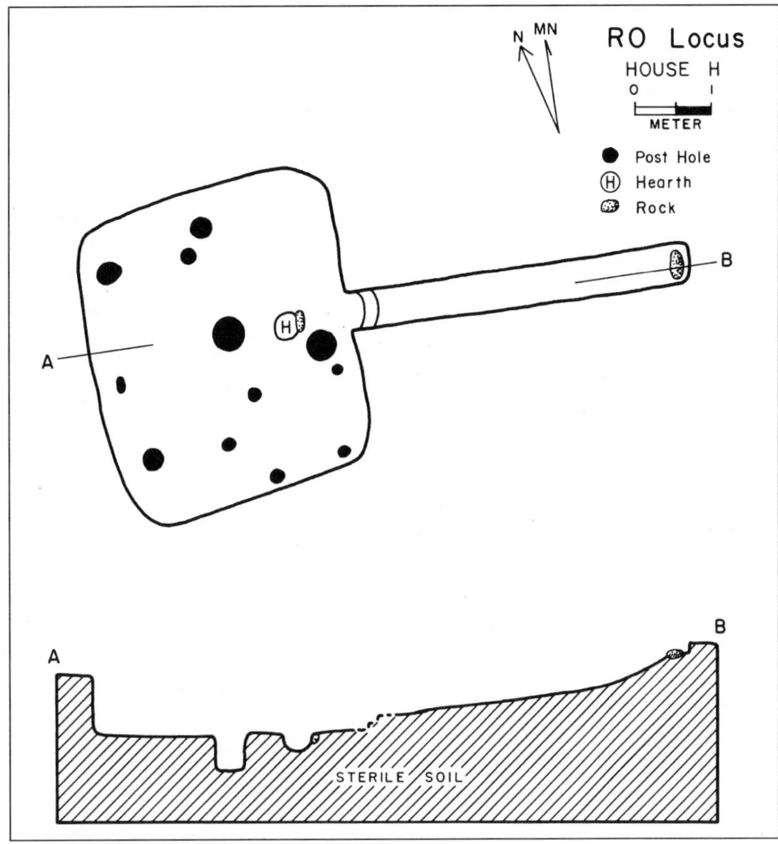

FIGURE 4.123. Plan view and profile of Ridout locus House H, a Type IV structure.

ramp floor was compacted by use and had been excavated into sterile soil.

House I (refer to Figure 4.122)

Type I structure; length 5.50 m, width 4.80 m; estimated area of living surface 20.56 m^2.

House I was superimposed by the southeastern edge of House G, and superimposed the northern edge of earlier House E. Burial 14 intruded into the House I fill.

Level 1 (range 0–22 cm) and Level 2 (range 22–80 cm) were composed of a dark black, humuslike soil intermixed with site debris. Level 3 (range 80–90 cm, floor fill) compared with Levels 1 and 2. The House I floor (depth 90 cm) was described as an uneven plastered surface. Unplastered House I walls extended to a maximum height of 65 cm above the floor. One C^{14} sample (GX-6906) was recovered from the floor (Chapter 3). The hearth (Type IIA; diameter 32 cm, depth 15 cm) occurred as a circular, clay lined basin. One archaeomagnetic sample (No. 034) was taken from the House I hearth (Chapter 3). As was the case for adjoining Houses E and G, downslope movement of soil and trash was responsible for a majority of the fill in this structure.

House J (Figure 4.124)

Type IV structure; length 3.10 m, width 3.00 m; area of living surface 9.53 m^2; mean orientation of entry 146°.

Level 1 (range 0–80 cm) and Level 2 (range 80–120 cm) were composed of a black, humuslike soil intermixed with fragments of wall fall, plaster, and charred corn. Level 3 (range 120–130 cm, floor fill) compared with Levels 1 and 2. The unplastered house floor (depth 130 cm) consisted of a level, use compacted surface that had been excavated into sterile soil. One C^{14} sample (GX-6904) was recovered from the House J floor fill (Chapter 3). Remnants of wall plaster in the form of light brown clay fragments about 5 mm thick, were found in the structure's northeast corner. The hearth (Type IIA; diameter 33 cm, depth 10 cm) occurred as a round, clay lined pit. The entry (area 1.37 m^2) was a long (300 cm), narrow (40 cm), stepped ramp allowing access to the house through the midsection of its southeast wall. Unplastered entry steps had been excavated into sterile soil.

House K (Figure 4.125)

Type IV structure; length 5.00 m, width 4.20 m; area of living surface 19.75 m^2; mean orientation of entry 96°.

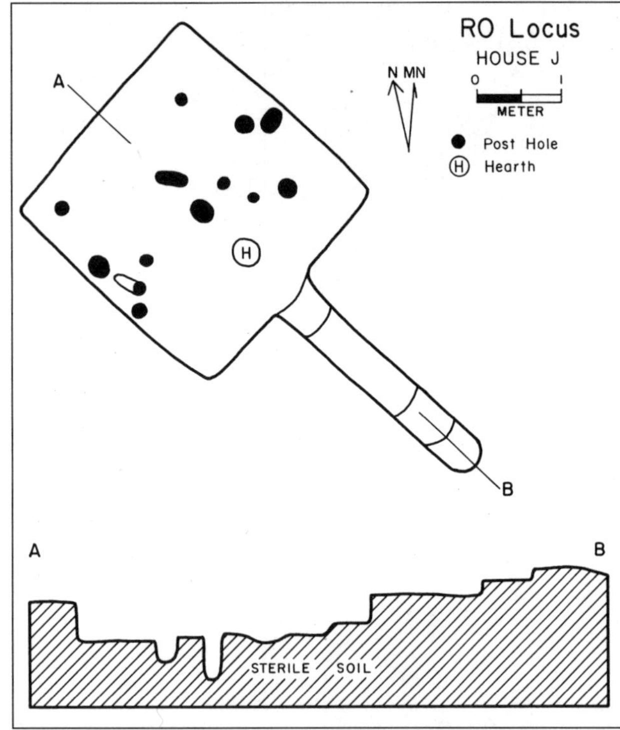

FIGURE 4.124. Plan view and profile of Ridout locus House J, a Type IV structure.

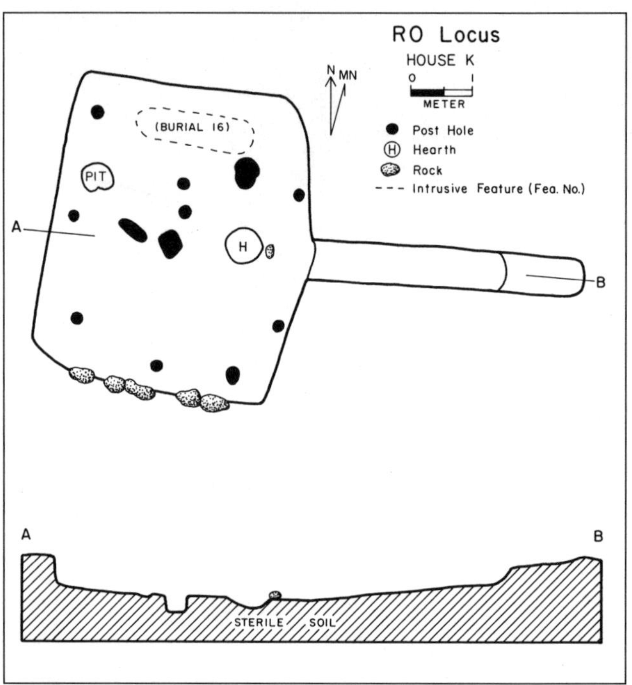

FIGURE 4.125. Plan view and profile of Ridout locus House K, a Type IV structure.

The floor of House K was intruded by Burial 16.

Level 1 (range 0–90 cm) and Level 2 (range 90–125 cm) were composed of a black humuslike soil intermixed with wall fall and site debris. Level 3 (range 125–135 cm) consisted of floor fill. The house floor (depth 135 cm) was a level, use compacted surface that appeared to have been plastered. One C^{14} sample (GX-6905) was recovered from the house floor (Chapter 3). The southern wall of House K had been reinforced with stone in several places. The house walls were vertical, unplastered, and had been excavated into sterile soil. The hearth (Type IIB1; diameter 60 cm, depth 17 cm) was a circular, unlined basin containing ash with a hearthstone set into its eastern edge. A floor pit (diameter 53 cm, depth 13 cm) occurred near the structure's western wall. The entry (area 2.91 m^2) was a long (455 cm), narrow (65 cm), stepped incline (5° for the first 320 cm, 2° thereafter) that allowed access to the structure through the midsection of its east wall. The unplastered ramp had been excavated into sterile soil.

5

Introduction to Material Culture
Approach to Typology

Throughout his career, Di Peso was concerned with the development and refinement of archaeological taxonomic systems. He frequently noted the degree to which Brew's (1946:44–66) seminal discussion of systematics as applied to archaeology influenced his own efforts to classify material objects. Di Peso concurred with Brew's (1946:46) assertion that only by identifying multiple attributes could artifact classes be accurately ordered and types assigned. From Di Peso's perspective, accuracy in classification was unequivocally linked to artifact function. This conviction formed the basis for his approach to ordering the Wind Mountain material inventory, and departed radically from most other typological systems, which stressed form over function (e.g., Ford 1938; McKern 1939; Spaulding 1953). The classification framework developed for Wind Mountain was, moreover, a continuation of previous methods of artifact organization and typological development initiated at Casas Grandes (see esp. Di Peso et al. 1974:6 and 7).

In setting forth his artifact typology for Wind Mountain, Di Peso described those components he felt represented the site's total material assemblage and organized them into a single system that relied on three primary discriminant criteria: functional attributes, method of manufacture, and object morphology. This precedence of function over other attributes was also evident in the analysis of the Casas Grandes material culture (e.g., Di Peso et al. 1974:7:17–20, 49–56). In that instance, the method in which stone implements were used (e.g., specific food processing tasks or ritual) was ranked first, succeeded by a discussion of how tools were produced (e.g., by grinding or chipping), followed by a description of morphological differences (e.g., shape, size, or secondary edge modification). Di Peso's emphasis on a functional definition as the initial step toward classification differs from traditional typological constructs in which artifacts were separated according to raw material (stone, clay, bone, and others) or stylistic treatments (e.g., design elements or texturing on pottery).

In an unfinished discussion of lithic implements (Di Peso Wind Mountain files, Amerind Foundation), it is clear that he intended to introduce his new typological concept to the archaeological community using the stone tools recovered from Wind Mountain by way of example or instruction. Unfortunately, the typological concepts and his justifying arguments were not fully developed. The following short summation must stand in an absence of other notes addressing the issue of material classification:

> Utilitarian (practical) forms have been separated from nonutilitarian (ornamental) goods, and these from unworked raw materials on the basis of implied use. The morphology of manufacture, i.e., pecked and ground versus percussion, is a second important observation and in this ordering it takes precedence over observed design, such as is the case in regard to two-piece fitted pulverizers having reciprocal or rotary action. The old use terminology (trough metates, mortars, palettes, etc.) is referred to as an aid to the reader to more easily understand this proposed morphological classification.
>
> Hopefully, some classificatory confusion (Woodbury 1954:vi-vii) will be eliminated as this system comes to be understood, as it also can accommodate the application of various sets of analytical standards and procedures (Di Peso et al. 1974:7:1–16).
>
> This morphological classification of stone tools reflects descriptive terms derived from observable features rather than implied use. At times it is more cumbersome than the use terminology, but in the overall view it is a better arrangement of identifiable features that can be touched and measured and compared with common understanding.

> The second purpose of this study format is to facilitate a time-tracing tool that will ascertain which tool designs were of indigenous Chichimecan origin, i.e., produced locally prior to A.D. 550, and which were brought into the area subsequent to this date when it is assumed that several strong Mesoamerican cultural impacts were made upon the northern frontier cultures.
>
> To do this is to begin to create a history of the area by presupposing that certain Chichimecan historical events are reflected in the various local material culture inventories of the time, and that foreign or alien influences can be ascertained by temporal shifts in the designs of food production tools, housing, ceramic decorations, etc.
>
> The third aspect of this type of study arrangement is to utilize the summary data to ascertain the sociopolitical structure of the associated producers by determining the percentage of basic or essential artifact categories (i.e., utilitarian tools) as compared to the number of nonessential categories (i.e., personal ornamentation and socioreligious categories). These comparative figures should reflect exiguous communal drives of a soil member subsistence economy, as compared to an ordered subsistence economy of full or part-time dry farming soil parasites and a stratified market economy of a soil exploiter group.

In essence, Di Peso is defining a shorthand terminology equivalent in practice to a mathematical definition, a system in which terms and objects are reduced to a series of numbers, letters, and symbols producing a data set terminology similar to algebraic formulae. Through this system, fact and understanding remain inherent in a process in which pure artifact definition is possible and semantic obfuscation is reduced to a minimum. In truth, Di Peso's system expects too much. It implies a concordance of agreement with regard to the manner in which any object is perceived by any typologist—a conceptual universality that seems beyond the boundaries of human possibility.

When viewing the material culture of Wind Mountain in terms of the Di Peso classification system (refer to Appendix 5), five broad functional artifact categories or classes are recognizable: utilitarian objects, socioreligious items, personal ornamentation, architectural elements, and raw materials (refer to the Typology Summary Outline, Table 5.1, this chapter; the complete Wind Mountain classification system is presented in Appendix 5: Table 1). Function was determined on the basis of commonly held assumptions. For example, because projectile points were produced for the hunt, they were considered utility objects. Alternatively, ethnographic analogy was employed to assign function to ambiguous cases. Based on the extensive corpus of ethnographic information depicting ritual smoking among Native American peoples, Wind Mountain pipes and tubes were placed in the socioreligious category. Following the Di Peso classification system, then, any one of the five principal artifact classes might contain objects made of ceramic, stone, bone, or any other raw material. All objects interpreted as necessary to daily subsistence were subsumed under the utilitarian category. In comparison, artifacts not essential to rudimentary survival but indicative of social ranking and wealth or ceremony were incorporated either into the socioreligious or the personal ornamentation object classes. The category of architectural elements consisted of modified materials used in construction or in structure maintenance. For instance, it is this category, not the utilitarian artifact class, that contained metates or grinding slabs employed to help shore up house walls. Finally, all unworked substances, such as ceramic or architectural clay, as well as raw stone, minerals, and bone, were included in the raw material category. Di Peso believed that these five principal artifact classes comfortably accommodated the full range of artifacts expressed by the Wind Mountain material assemblage. Once objects were assigned to their appropriate functional category, they were organized according to ceramic, stone, bone, or any other raw material from which they were manufactured in the customary manner.

Di Peso proposed that these functional categories accurately reflected how individual artifacts were actually used by the prehistoric inhabitants of Wind Mountain. Anticipating criticism to the contrary, he asserted that specific function was established objectively (not based on a priori assumptions) by examining visible attributes such as the grinding patterns or surface use area observed on ground stone implements. Extremely careful scrutiny was demanded to demonstrate precisely what substances were processed and, by logical extension, the function of a particular artifact. Di Peso exhorted archaeologists to pay closer attention to what he viewed as the attributes of morphology in order to come to a clearer understanding of artifact classification. The multiple attribute focus would, he suggested, eliminate the confusion surrounding existing functional interpretations he felt characterized much of the archaeological literature. This position explains the great descriptive detail and hierarchical complexity that typifies Di Peso's classification system (refer to Appendix 5: Table 1) and is especially apparent in his ordering of lithics (Chapter 7 in this volume).

The Di Peso method of artifact classification might best be illustrated by applying his system of typology to a mano. Based on the visible morphological attributes occurring on the artifact, augmented by inferences about prehistoric plant processing and comparative ethnographic data, a mano would be placed in the primary functional class of utilitarian object. Proceeding through all descriptive levels, the mano is further defined by its method of manufacture (whether pecked or ground), as a one or two hand implement, and a series of additional traits, all of which eventually combine to distinguish its specific "type" (refer to Appendix 5: Tables 1 and 2).

TABLE 5.1. Summary Outline of the Di Peso Classification System

- I. Utilitarian Tool Morphology
  - A. Stone tools
    1. Pecked and/or ground manufacture
    2. Percussion and/or flaked manufacture
  - B. Bone tools
    1. Pointed piercing tools
    2. Spatula tip tools
    3. Antler tine
  - C. Ceramic tools
    1. Finger manipulated hollow formed receptacles
    2. Sherd tools
    3. Solid modeled forms
- II. Socioreligious Tool Morphology
  - A. Stone
    1. Pecked and/or ground stone
    2. Percussion and/or flaked stone
  - B. Bone
    1. Odocoileus antlers
    2. Artiodactyl femurs
    3. Artiodactyl scapula
    4. *Chelonia* plastron
    5. Aves femurs
  - C. Ceramic
    1. Unperforated solid modeled figurines
    2. Unperforated sherd figurines
    3. Finger manipulated ceramics
- III. Personal Ornamentation Morphology
  - A. Stone
    1. Pecked and/or ground manufacture
  - B. Shell
    1. Marine mollusc
    2. Fresh water mollusc
  - C. Bone
    1. Artiodactyl femurs
  - D. Ceramic
    1. Edge perforated sherd suspension; pendant
    2. Perforated modeled sphere; bead
- IV. Architectural Elements Morphology
  - A. Architectural stone elements
    1. Pecked and/or ground
  - B. Architectural ceramic element
    1. Jacal casts
- V. Raw Material Morphology
  - A. Raw stone/mineral material
    1. Paint pigments; mineral
    2. Andesite
    3. Aragonite
    4. Biotite schist
    5. Breccia
    6. Calcite
    7. Concretion
    8. Copper
    9. Dacite
    10. Dolomite
    11. Felsite slickenside
    12. Fluorite
    13. Fossil
    14. Granite
    15. Gypsum
    16. Limestone
    17. Mica
    18. Obsidian
    19. Opaline
    20. Pumice
    21. Quartz
    22. Rhyolite
    23. Ricolite
    24. Sandstone
    25. Shale
    26. Slag
    27. Steatite
    28. Travertine
    29. Tuff
    30. Turquoise
    31. Vesicular basalt
  - B. Raw bone material
    1. Artiodactyl femur
    2. Artiodactyl metapodial
    3. Artiodactyl costa
    4. Artiodactyl cranium
    5. Aves femur
  - C. Raw ceramic material
    1. Fillet; rod
    2. Modeled clay lump
    3. Incised sherd
    4. Sawed sherd

Integral to his classification system, Di Peso devised a particularistic terminology, which he deemed necessary to explicitly identify artifact function. A mano, for example, was termed the upper half of a set of two piece fitted pulverizers with coincident parts used in reciprocal action on a flat surface (the nether stone). This, instead of the simplistic and generalized mano or handstone terminology, was believed to properly and completely describe its specific function—to process substances by grinding. According to Di Peso's classification scheme, when additional attributes of size, cross section, and surface wear were added, a complete mano type designation might read IA1a(1a)2'a'1"a", which would describe a utilitarian tool, made of stone, of pecked and/or ground manufacture, identified as a two piece fitted pulverizer with coincident parts in contact, used in a reciprocal action and having a flat surface. The numerical/letter nomenclature describes a handstone (or mano) used in one hand, measuring less than 16 cm long with a tapered cross section that is unifacially worn (refer to Appendix 5: Table 1). This final type appellative consists of individual digits and letters, each signifying a discrete descriptive level in the classification. Because the magnitude of detail is difficult to follow, use, or verbalize easily, reference numbers were eventually assigned as a shorthand method for identifying the complicated sets of descriptive attributes comprising the specific artifact "types" (refer to Appendix 5: Table 2).

Although many archaeologists would be uncomfortable using such a complicated and lengthy system, it is important to understand Di Peso's underlying rationale. Simply put, the artifact classification lays the foundation for many of his interpretations relating to the effects of prehistoric economic interaction as perceived through changes in material culture. Di Peso's emphasis on functional artifact classes is closely intertwined with his ideas of prehistoric donor-recipient relationships, as well as the historic anthropological milieu in which he matured. Di Peso firmly believed that in the minutiae of typological detail, as yet undisclosed facets of prehistoric culture were waiting to be interpreted. It was not that typology was a feeble tool for explaining the past, but rather, that the forms of typology being employed were inadequate. Di Peso felt that important cultural information was lost in typologies that were too coarse grained in their resolution and that a fine grained approach was the only solution to interpreting material culture and, by extension, prehistoric culture systems.

It is not the intention here to replay the development of American archaeology in the 1970s. Suffice it to say that in the 1970s Southwestern archaeology was in turmoil as archaeologists argued about the role of archaeology, its aims, and its methodological procedures. In the context of the times, then, when various theories (many overburdened in mere wordspeak) and their adherents gained prominence, certain postulates of what had been considered normative archaeological practice came under attack. In general, cultural history, chronology building, and artifact classification schemes were considered nonessential (if not outright archaic) manifestations of a failed pseudo-scientific approach to explaining prehistoric lifeways. Into the middle of the 1970s enters Di Peso's eight volume Casas Grandes study, which had taken some 15 years to produce (1959–1974, from beginning of fieldwork to final publication). These volumes, loaded with individualistic thinking, multiple eccentric hypotheses, and new raw data, were acknowledged by Di Peso's peers with mixed praise. The volumes presented, in effect, everything that archaeology and archaeologists had once demanded. But something had changed, and the age of the "New Archaeology" was upon the scene. What was previously held to be good archaeology was now considered arcane or provincial. Research emphasizing typology as an incisive explanatory method was passé. Au courant were discussions of philosophical matters and theory building, which were deemed more significant to a field that had become moribund with nonstringent scientific process and a propensity for description. Di Peso's reaction to this new social and political trend in the discipline was to reject it. He fervently maintained that artifact typologists in America were a dying breed and, importantly, that the teaching of typology at the university level had vastly deteriorated. Thus, even while the tide of consensus regarding archaeological method and theory was against him, he kept faith with a system of archaeology in which he believed. A telling reproach of some of his young colleagues is documented in Di Peso's Wind Mountain Site Daily Log, dated 4 May 1978, on attending the Forty-third Annual Society for American Archaeology meeting in Tucson:

> Symposium was an all day affair on Hohokam. Very repetitive and filled with papers by young people who had dreams of models and paradigms bouncing about in their heads. Somewhere and somehow I felt alien to these young rebels who quite openly state that I cannot think. I suppose my logic may be antiquated as that of Socrates and Plato, but then the concepts upon which they pose their thought processes is equally as old—but newly discovered.

Di Peso, consequently, endorsed the study of material culture as a means for studying prehistoric interactions using involved classification systems characterized by numerous, specific attributes. It was only by such attention to detail that the material remains of prehistoric people would come to provide informative data with which to elucidate the past. Certainly, the classification scheme he developed for Wind Mountain is in keeping with this credo.

6

Ceramics

The Wind Mountain settlement yielded more than 270,000 sherds, 213 whole and fragmentary vessels, as well as other miscellaneous ceramic artifacts from its houses, features, and bulk fill. Wind Mountain ceramics chart the sequence of Mimbres Mogollon pottery production from early brownwares and redwares through the black-on-white Mimbres tradition in the Mangas Creek drainage. Locally made Mimbres Mogollon pottery dominated the collection, although small quantities of various exogenous pottery types were noted. Because a large area of Wind Mountain was excavated and screened (Figure 4.1), there exists a high degree of confidence that the ceramics recovered accurately reflect the proportions of types manufactured, traded, and used throughout the various occupations of the site.

In making sense of Wind Mountain's ceramic assemblage, floor and floor fill artifacts were considered to be most informative. These assemblages, many derived from dated structures, were believed to best represent those site contexts free from excessive disturbances. Specific interpretations relating to ceramic developments, such as the chronological placement of new types or the persistence of established wares, relied primarily on floor and floor fill whole and fragmentary vessels and sherds. Ceramics from bulk fill deposits were viewed as indicative of the general range of pottery either locally produced or imported into Wind Mountain during its multiple occupations.

The Wind Mountain pottery assemblage is described according to widely accepted type names (San Francisco Red, Mogollon Red-on-brown, etc.). Care is taken to specify any points of departure Wind Mountain ceramics may have taken from previously designated traditional Mogollon type definitions (refer to Haury 1936b). Types are presented in order of their presumed origination dates, beginning with the earliest unpainted Mogollon wares, Alma Plain and San Francisco Red, and continuing through Mimbres Classic Black-on-white. This arrangement established the temporal progression of types and identified those, whether painted or unpainted, that occurred as companion wares at Wind Mountain. Once described, the ceramic assemblage is viewed in terms of its spatial and temporal distribution at the site. Exogenous (possible commerce) ceramics are discussed in terms of their frequency and point of origin. The chapter concludes with an examination of the nature of Wind Mountain's ceramic tradition from both a site specific and regional perspective.

Origin of Mogollon Ceramics

From dated contexts at Tularosa Cave, Martin and others (1952:483, 496) originally suggested that Mogollon pottery (in the form of Alma Plain) may have emerged as early as 300 B.C., and certainly by at least 150 B.C. Soon after the occurrence of Alma Plain, two other types, Alma Rough and San Francisco Red, appeared. These three types constituted the Pine Lawn phase pottery assemblage from 150 B.C. to A.D. 500 (Martin et al. 1952:55). More recently, LeBlanc (1982a, 1982b) revised upward the onset of Mogollon pottery making and suggested a A.D. 200–300 threshold for the beginning of all Southwest ceramic manufacture.

Whatever their actual starting dates, early Mogollon plainwares were described as technologically fully developed and far beyond any incipient or experimental stage of pottery production (Martin 1959:80). The question then arises as to the origin of Mogollon ceramics. Previous investigators have postulated Mexico as the probable source for the prehistoric Southwest's knowledge of pottery making (Martin 1959:80; Haury 1976:223). They point to numerous attributes displayed by Mogollon brown and red plainwares (the result of an oxidizing atmosphere when firing) that also describe many earlier Mexican wares distributed over a geographically wide region from Chihuahua and Sonora in the north to Colima, Durango, and Zacatecas in the south. Current studies (Wilson 1992; Wilson et al. 1993) indicate, however, that while Mogollon ceramics were fired in a neutral to slightly oxidizing atmosphere, their brown or red appearance is due less to the firing technology employed than to the locally available clays that were selected for the manufacture of pottery vessels (Kohler 1993). This does not alter the generally held belief that ceramics were first produced in the south and were later adapted in the prehistoric Southwest.

Although the precise routes of transmission remain ambiguous, a pathway along the eastern flanks of the Sierra Madre de Occidental is suggested for the dispersion of brown and red pottery out of Mexico that eventually emerged as the Alma brown series and San Francisco Red of the Mogollon (Lister 1946, 1958; Martin 1959:79–81; Haury 1976:223). In Di Peso's (1979c) view, both the Alma brownware series and San Francisco Red exhibited common morphological elements illustrative of other pottery types found throughout the Gran Chichimeca, including, among others, Vahki Red, Gila Plain, Adamana Brown, Rio de Flag Brown, Dragoon Red, Trincheras Red, Casas Grandes Plainware, and Convento Red. Their origins were all suggested to develop out of southern or Mesoamerican ceramic traditions.

Wind Mountain Pottery

The earliest reported Mogollon ceramics, Alma Plain and textured varieties as well as San Francisco Red, are presumed to be those types that should be observed in the settlement's earliest structures. This would include houses predating c. A.D. 550 in the Early Pit House period as well as the Georgetown phase, c. A.D. 550–650, of the Late Pit House period. Unfortunately, as illustrated by Tables 6.1 and 6.4, such precise associations between ceramics and structures do not survive at a site in which the earliest deposits are also the most disturbed due to a long history of multiple occupations. After the onset of the San Francisco phase at Wind Mountain (c. A.D. 650–800), the first painted pottery type appears in the form of Mogollon Red-on-brown, followed by Three Circle Red-on-white (e.g., Tables 6.2 and 6.5; floor/floor fill assemblages in Wind Mountain locus Houses G, K, and R; Ridout locus Houses A, B, H, and K). During the Three Circle phase (c. A.D. 800–950), a third painted ware, Boldface Black-on-white (syn. Style I and Style II), makes its appearance and continues through the Mangas phase of the Pueblo period (e.g., Tables 6.2 and 6.5; Wind Mountain locus Houses H, NN, TT, WW, ZZ, and AF). A new ware, Three Circle Neck Corrugated, probably produced by the end of the San Francisco phase but becoming more abundant during the Three Circle phase, represents another form of unpainted surface design technique alongside the textured treatments of the Alma series (e.g., Tables 6.1 and 6.4; Wind Mountain locus Houses AA, and WW). After c. A.D. 950/1000, which would include Mangas phase and Mimbres phase occupations, Mimbres Classic Black-on-white (syn. Style III) and Mimbres Corrugated wares are added to the Wind Mountain ceramic inventory (e.g., Tables 6.2 and 6.5; Wind Mountain locus Rooms 2, 4, 7, 9, 14, 15; Burials 1, 24, 27, 32).

The unpainted brownware and redware pottery together with the painted ceramics cited above constitute those types believed to have been manufactured by the residents of Wind Mountain. Individual types are reviewed and compared below. Type descriptions and idiosyncratic traits peculiar to the Wind Mountain pottery assemblage are examined.

A small assemblage inclusive of ceramics assumed to be exogenous or "commerce" ceramics was recovered, mainly from extramural excavation contexts and from one structure (Wind Mountain locus House P2), as well as from two pits (Pits 21 and 27). These intrusives are treated separately, and their implications for possible interregional contact between the people of Wind Mountain and other regions are evaluated.

Alma series (Haury 1936b:32–34, 35, 38–40; Martin 1940, 1943).

The unpainted Alma brownware series refers to one well represented class of utility vessels recovered from the Wind Mountain site. The series comprises Alma Plain (Figures 6.1 and 6.2), the principal type, and its known variations, including Alma Rough (Figure 6.3), Alma Scored, Alma Tool Punched, Alma Incised (Figure 6.4), Alma Neck Banded (Figure 6.5), and Alma Black Burnished. The Wind Mountain Alma series inventory generally conforms to existing descriptions of the unslipped brownware characterized by tool smoothing or polishing marks, some interior smudging, and in rare cases, appliqué. The broken edges of sherds exhibited diversity in tempering materials—large pieces of crushed quartz, granite, and other pulverized minerals—which had been added by ceramists during production (Appendix 6 in this volume). Some Wind Mountain Alma Plain vessels contained quantities of mica and biotite schist, giving them the appearance of a micaceous ware. These "micaceous" vessels are viewed as variations within the Alma series and are not believed to constitute a separate type. Jars and bowls were the most common forms recovered (Figures 6.6–6.8). Jars (n = 68) outnumbered bowls (n = 33) two to one. Many of these represented miniature vessels (Table 6.4; 40 jars and 20 bowls). The two to one ratio of miniature Alma series jars to bowls paralleled their standard sized counterparts. Several ladles (n = 8) and one shallow dish form were also collected.

TABLE 6.1. Sherd Counts of Unpainted Ceramics in Wind Mountain Structures and Features

WM locus	Context	Alma Plain	Alma Rough	Alma Black Burnished	Alma Scored	Alma Incised	Alma Tool Punched	Alma Neck Banded	San Francisco Red*	Three Circle Neck Corrugated	Mimbres Corrugated	Mimbres Rubbed Corrugated	Totals
House A	Fill	1,031	11	13	7	23	2	11	182	33	6	231	1,550
	Floor fill	–	–	–	–	–	–	–	–	–	–	–	–
	Floor	–	–	–	–	–	–	–	–	–	–	–	–
House B2	Fill	493	12	6	4	–	3	23	64	10	11	134	760
	Floor fill	139	–	3	5	1	–	–	29	4	–	22	203
	Floor	29	–	3	1	–	–	–	4	–	2	17	56
House C	Fill	675	23	4	7	2	1	6	–	9	21	533	1,281
	Floor fill	101	4	–	1	–	–	3	–	1	–	29	139
	Floor	10	–	1	1	–	–	–	–	–	1	2	15
House D	Fill	548	4	–	8	1	5	3	83	16	21	99	788
	Floor fill	111	–	–	–	–	–	–	12	2	5	15	145
	Floor	1	–	–	–	–	–	–	–	–	–	1	2
House E	Fill	322	9	–	2	–	–	–	45	22	1	45	446
	Floor fill	18	–	–	–	–	–	–	4	–	–	–	22
	Floor	4	–	–	–	–	–	–	–	–	–	–	4
House F	Fill	1,015	31	13	7	4	3	6	107	10	78	349	1,623
	Floor fill	188	7	1	–	–	–	1	19	9	19	35	279
	Floor	4	–	–	1	–	–	–	–	–	–	–	5
House G	Fill	159	1	8	5	4	–	–	24	–	–	22	223
	Floor fill	77	–	3	–	–	–	–	7	–	1	3	91
	Floor	20	–	–	3	–	–	–	–	–	–	–	23
House H	Fill	1,118	4	8	12	1	5	2	139	15	53	137	1,494
	Floor fill	155	–	–	–	–	–	1	12	2	2	6	178
	Floor	7	–	–	1	–	–	–	5	–	–	3	16
House I	Fill	–	–	–	–	–	–	–	–	–	–	–	–
	Floor fill	100	–	–	1	–	–	2	4	6	–	3	116
	Floor	82	–	–	–	–	–	–	1	1	–	–	84
House J	Fill	146	2	–	1	–	–	–	–	–	–	36	185
	Floor fill	68	–	–	–	–	–	–	–	–	–	5	73
	Floor	–	–	–	–	–	–	–	–	–	–	–	–
House K	Fill	1,850	31	22	13	1	4	15	304	27	13	661	2,941
	Floor fill	175	3	1	3	–	–	1	29	–	–	20	232
	Floor	22	1	–	1	–	–	–	4	–	–	4	32
House L	Fill	2,314	41	10	26	6	5	17	304	99	2	349	3,173
	Floor fill	167	1	4	2	–	–	1	14	4	2	9	204
	Floor	35	–	–	–	–	–	1	7	–	–	2	45
House M	Fill	362	13	5	5	4	2	–	38	11	6	68	514
	Floor fill	110	4	–	1	1	1	2	19	4	–	1	143
	Floor	–	–	–	–	–	–	–	–	–	–	–	–

Table 6.1. *(continued)*

WM locus	Context	Alma Plain	Alma Rough	Alma Black Burnished	Alma Scored	Alma Incised	Alma Tool Punched	Alma Neck Banded	San Francisco Red*	Three Circle Neck Corrugated	Mimbres Corrugated	Mimbres Rubbed Corrugated	Totals
House N	Fill	2,325	29	7	43	14	9	2	436	29	20	190	3,104
	Floor fill	184	2	1	1	3	1	–	82	–	–	1	275
	Floor	257	–	1	4	55	2	–	72	25	1	13	430
House O	Fill	–	–	–	–	–	–	–	–	–	–	–	–
	Floor fill	–	–	–	–	–	–	–	–	–	–	–	–
	Floor	57	3	–	2	–	–	–	9	–	–	–	71
House P2	Fill	557	15	15	7	–	–	14	130	10	23	197	968
	Floor fill	–	–	–	–	–	–	–	–	–	–	–	–
	Floor	114	4	1	1	1	–	1	21	5	13	38	199
House Q	Fill	716	15	4	10	2	–	3	91	13	3	79	936
	Floor fill	–	–	–	–	–	–	–	–	–	–	–	–
	Floor	92	2	5	3	–	–	–	12	1	–	3	118
House R	Fill	221	23	3	2	–	–	–	53	3	5	30	340
	Floor fill	–	–	–	–	–	–	–	–	–	–	–	–
	Floor	110	1	–	1	–	–	–	21	1	–	2	136
House S	Fill	577	17	2	12	9	4	2	130	10	18	82	863
	Floor fill	89	1	1	1	–	–	–	25	–	–	9	126
	Floor	9	–	–	–	–	–	–	–	–	–	–	9
House T	Fill	1,515	44	14	29	1	6	9	310	35	44	193	2,200
	Floor fill	47	–	–	–	–	–	–	8	–	–	–	55
	Floor	12	1	–	–	–	–	–	6	–	–	–	19
House U	Fill	3,585	136	43	73	64	28	43	897	52	188	498	5,607
	Floor fill	–	–	–	–	–	–	–	–	–	–	–	–
	Floor	–	–	–	–	–	–	–	–	–	–	–	–
House V	Fill	3,085	120	30	101	26	32	55	523	79	471	220	4,742
	Floor fill	144	4	2	13	–	1	–	36	7	7	–	214
	Floor	3	–	–	–	–	–	–	1	–	1	–	5
House W	Fill	1,118	44	20	18	8	25	10	118	57	126	319	1,863
	Floor fill	102	11	8	2	–	5	–	6	2	39	20	195
	Floor	–	–	–	–	–	–	–	–	–	–	–	–
House X	Fill	14,474	828	201	300	41	191	327	2,921	642	186	310	20,421
	Floor fill	1,311	67	15	82	7	16	47	446	39	16	–	2,046
	Floor	35	–	3	1	–	–	1	65	–	4	–	109
House Y	Fill	3,575	116	77	74	5	37	9	405	187	98	388	4,971
	Floor fill	–	–	–	–	–	–	–	–	–	–	–	–
	Floor	9	–	–	–	–	–	–	–	–	–	–	9

TABLE 6.1. *(continued)*

WM locus	Context	Alma Plain	Alma Rough	Alma Black Burnished	Alma Scored	Alma Incised	Alma Tool Punched	Alma Neck Banded	San Francisco Red*	Three Circle Neck Corrugated	Mimbres Corrugated	Mimbres Rubbed Corrugated	Totals
House Z	Fill	881	42	9	13	6	24	6	116	40	100	155	1,392
	Floor fill	132	1	1	–	–	2	1	25	7	1	2	172
	Floor	10	–	–	–	–	–	–	–	–	2	4	16
House AA	Fill	834	36	23	14	3	8	5	133	31	5	18	1,110
	Floor fill	385	28	9	8	2	2	6	52	11	–	14	517
	Floor	8	–	–	–	–	–	–	–	–	–	1	9
House BB	Fill	1	–	–	–	–	–	–	–	–	–	–	1
	Floor fill	182	9	5	–	1	1	1	10	15	9	26	259
	Floor	30	1	2	–	–	–	–	1	6	1	4	45
House CC	Fill	–	–	–	–	–	–	–	–	–	–	–	–
	Floor fill	6	–	2	–	–	–	–	1	2	–	10	21
	Floor	–	–	–	–	–	–	–	–	–	–	–	–
House DD	Fill	1,692	110	60	40	18	10	4	438	36	62	264	2,734
	Floor fill	–	–	–	–	–	–	–	–	–	–	–	–
	Floor	363	12	1	12	–	1	–	131	–	7	10	537
House EE	Fill	413	–	3	–	–	–	1	41	3	4	9	474
	Floor fill	127	2	–	–	–	–	–	7	–	1	–	137
	Floor	55	–	–	–	–	–	–	–	–	–	–	55
House FF	Fill	564	20	–	20	13	4	4	324	18	24	6	997
	Floor fill	3	6	–	–	2	–	5	70	–	3	–	89
	Floor	–	–	–	–	–	–	–	–	–	–	–	–
House GG	Fill	579	75	22	11	3	2	2	122	58	27	41	942
	Floor fill	65	8	1	1	–	–	–	18	1	1	2	97
	Floor	–	–	–	–	–	–	–	–	–	–	–	–
House HH	Fill	340	29	3	1	6	–	1	67	16	11	15	489
	Floor fill	178	21	4	1	–	–	–	23	2	7	1	237
	Floor	25	3	1	–	–	–	–	11	–	1	2	43
House II	Fill	–	–	–	–	–	–	–	–	–	–	–	–
	Floor fill	111	3	10	3	1	1	–	30	–	13	4	176
	Floor	–	–	–	–	–	–	–	–	–	–	–	–
House JJ	Fill	–	–	–	–	–	–	–	–	–	–	–	–
	Floor fill	23	3	1	1	–	–	1	10	2	3	2	46
	Floor	–	–	–	–	–	–	–	–	–	1	–	1
House KK	Fill	–	–	–	–	–	–	–	–	–	–	–	–
	Floor fill	33	3	–	–	1	–	–	9	2	6	3	57
	Floor	1	1	–	–	–	–	–	2	–	–	–	4
House LL	Floor	–	–	–	–	–	–	–	–	–	–	–	–
	Floor fill	9	–	1	–	–	–	1	12	–	1	1	25
	Floor	–	–	–	–	–	–	–	–	–	–	–	–

TABLE 6.1. *(continued)*

WM locus	Context	Alma Plain	Alma Rough	Alma Black Burnished	Alma Scored	Alma Incised	Alma Tool Punched	Alma Neck Banded	San Francisco Red*	Three Circle Neck Corrugated	Mimbres Corrugated	Mimbres Rubbed Corrugated	Totals
House MM	Fill	–	–	–	–	–	–	–	–	–	–	–	–
	Floor fill	17	–	2	–	–	–	–	1	–	–	4	24
	Floor	–	–	–	–	–	–	–	–	–	–	–	–
House NN	Fill	–	–	–	–	–	–	–	–	–	–	–	–
	Floor fill	235	6	9	1	–	–	–	46	17	10	4	328
	Floor	–	–	–	–	–	–	–	–	75	–	–	75
House OO	Fill	1,993	276	23	27	1	45	14	264	159	130	34	2,966
	Floor fill	301	15	4	–	–	3	4	29	23	18	6	403
	Floor	–	–	–	–	–	–	–	–	–	–	–	–
House PP	Fill	5,008	402	99	171	40	29	22	1,605	97	212	152	7,837
	Floor fill	390	40	–	12	2	–	2	146	6	–	–	598
	Floor	20	2	–	–	–	–	–	6	–	–	–	28
House QQ	Fill	1,368	49	5	54	3	6	12	211	42	10	12	1,772
	Floor fill	–	–	–	–	–	–	–	–	–	–	–	–
	Floor	227	3	–	1	–	–	–	21	2	–	–	254
House RR	Fill	192	13	–	2	2	–	3	35	7	5	5	264
	Floor fill	22	2	–	1	–	1	–	7	–	1	–	34
	Floor	–	–	–	–	–	–	–	–	–	–	–	–
House SS	Fill	3,063	227	17	68	15	31	30	733	89	54	21	4,348
	Floor fill	422	9	–	11	1	4	4	95	3	5	4	558
	Floor	52	5	1	–	–	–	2	12	1	–	–	73
House TT	Fill	753	56	4	13	3	19	14	129	58	15	6	1,070
	Floor fill	–	–	–	–	–	–	–	–	–	–	–	–
	Floor	157	9	4	1	1	4	–	9	6	6	–	197
House UU	Fill	1,966	157	16	60	7	21	39	633	41	14	7	2,961
	Floor fill	250	14	1	10	1	2	1	74	–	2	–	355
	Floor	–	–	–	–	–	–	–	–	–	–	–	–
House VV	Fill	4	–	–	–	–	–	–	1	–	–	–	5
	Floor fill	235	17	17	4	–	3	3	44	1	–	–	324
	Floor	5	–	–	–	–	1	–	3	–	–	–	9
House WW	Fill	–	–	–	–	–	–	–	–	–	–	–	–
	Floor fill	853	13	4	8	–	24	5	79	293	31	3	1,313
	Floor	–	–	–	–	–	–	–	–	–	–	–	–
House XX	Fill	1,913	151	9	35	3	37	12	351	137	418	40	3,106
	Floor fill	358	20	9	6	–	8	–	46	27	18	–	492
	Floor	87	14	1	–	–	1	3	15	5	–	1	127
House YY	Fill	269	12	–	1	–	1	–	29	5	2	2	321
	Floor fill	–	–	–	–	–	–	–	–	–	–	–	–
	Floor	228	4	–	–	–	–	–	21	3	–	–	256

TABLE 6.1. *(continued)*

WM locus	Context	Alma Plain	Alma Rough	Alma Black Burnished	Alma Scored	Alma Incised	Alma Tool Punched	Alma Neck Banded	San Francisco Red*	Three Circle Neck Corrugated	Mimbres Corrugated	Mimbres Rubbed Corrugated	Totals
House ZZ	Fill	767	61	6	10	2	12	20	141	60	55	17	1,151
	Floor fill	174	13	–	7	–	–	–	33	17	3	–	247
	Floor	80	3	–	2	1	3	1	18	–	–	–	108
House AB	Fill	894	45	3	19	4	6	1	220	37	69	36	1,334
	Floor fill	57	3	2	–	–	–	–	10	1	1	1	75
	Floor	–	1	–	–	–	–	–	2	–	–	–	3
House AC	Fill	1,114	117	20	23	–	21	4	194	78	44	9	1,624
	Floor fill	485	16	9	4	–	3	7	80	16	12	7	639
	Floor	27	2	–	–	–	–	1	8	1	–	1	40
House AD	Fill	1,280	76	3	23	3	9	8	192	60	44	13	1,711
	Floor fill	403	16	7	8	3	4	6	53	17	15	1	533
	Floor	190	7	7	8	–	–	1	26	12	8	1	260
House AE	Fill	–	–	–	–	–	–	–	–	–	–	–	–
	Floor fill	78	3	10	1	–	–	1	26	–	–	3	122
	Floor	1	–	–	–	–	–	–	1	–	–	–	2
House AF	Fill	3,922	232	86	71	10	53	62	651	206	76	33	5,402
	Floor fill	303	20	20	4	2	2	9	51	7	–	–	418
	Floor	245	19	19	1	2	1	6	65	–	–	–	368
House AG	Fill	1,163	56	13	20	4	20	46	193	90	10	7	1,622
	Floor fill	317	15	8	4	–	1	–	36	23	–	–	404
	Floor	72	3	3	1	–	1	–	6	2	–	–	88
House AH	Fill	18	3	–	–	–	–	–	4	2	–	–	27
	Floor fill	–	–	1	–	–	1	–	–	–	–	–	2
	Floor	–	–	–	–	–	–	–	–	–	–	–	–
House AI	Fill	1,191	66	11	28	3	9	7	377	31	13	8	1,744
	Floor fill	244	16	–	10	1	2	–	64	4	–	–	341
	Floor	7	1	–	–	–	–	–	1	–	–	–	9
House AJ	Fill	187	13	–	1	–	–	6	31	9	2	–	249
	Floor fill	–	–	–	–	–	–	–	–	–	–	–	–
	Floor	18	1	–	–	–	–	19	7	–	–	–	45
House AK	Fill	–	–	–	–	–	–	–	–	–	–	–	–
	Floor fill	–	–	–	–	–	–	–	–	–	–	–	–
	Floor	65	1	1	1	–	1	6	10	1	–	–	86
House AL	Fill	1,472	72	22	30	4	87	13	–	156	23	43	1,922
	Floor fill	238	9	1	3	1	2	2	–	22	–	–	278
	Floor	67	–	–	–	–	1	–	–	9	–	–	77
House AM	Fill	673	25	2	6	–	2	4	96	21	2	4	835
	Floor fill	142	3	2	–	–	–	1	33	3	–	1	185
	Floor	3	–	–	–	–	–	–	–	–	–	–	3
House AN	Fill	166	4	1	–	1	1	1	–	17	2	2	195
	Floor fill	127	4	–	–	–	1	–	–	4	2	–	138
	Floor	–	–	–	–	–	–	–	–	–	–	–	–

Table 6.1. *(continued)*

WM locus	Context	Alma Plain	Alma Rough	Alma Black Burnished	Alma Scored	Alma Incised	Alma Tool Punched	Alma Neck Banded	San Francisco Red*	Three Circle Neck Corrugated	Mimbres Corrugated	Mimbres Rubbed Corrugated	Totals
House AO	Fill	1,478	60	18	26	4	4	19	277	10	8	7	1,911
	Floor fill	14	–	–	2	–	–	–	4	–	–	–	20
	Floor	57	1	1	3	–	–	–	8	1	–	–	71
House AP	Fill	2,165	97	14	37	6	7	17	456	39	12	28	2,878
	Floor fill	–	–	–	–	–	–	–	–	–	–	–	–
	Floor	16	–	–	–	–	–	–	1	–	–	–	17
House AQ	Fill	2,987	249	24	85	20	14	48	1,003	56	8	8	4,502
	Floor fill	299	14	–	15	3	–	5	69	3	1	–	409
	Floor	15	–	–	–	–	–	–	5	–	–	–	20
Room 1	Fill	112	4	6	2	2	–	1	25	3	1	29	185
	Floor fill	–	–	–	–	–	–	–	–	–	–	–	–
	Floor	–	–	–	–	–	–	–	–	–	–	–	–
Room 2	Fill	84	1	1	–	–	–	–	22	1	–	34	143
	Floor fill	62	3	–	2	–	–	1	5	2	3	44	122
	Floor	6	–	1	–	–	–	–	4	–	–	3	14
Room 3	Fill	149	5	8	1	–	1	1	12	1	23	60	261
	Floor fill	59	2	1	–	–	–	–	8	2	3	37	112
	Floor	18	–	–	–	–	–	1	1	–	–	4	24
Room 4	Fill	346	6	–	–	2	–	–	50	20	23	127	574
	Floor fill	119	2	1	2	–	–	–	18	1	13	43	199
	Floor	6	–	–	–	–	–	–	–	–	–	3	9
Room 5	Fill	201	9	–	–	–	–	–	30	4	7	90	341
	Floor fill	110	–	–	1	3	–	–	16	1	1	48	180
	Floor	6	–	–	–	–	–	–	–	–	–	3	9
Room 7	Fill	859	6	2	6	2	1	1	100	15	10	922	1,924
	Floor fill	137	2	1	4	1	–	–	17	4	3	197	366
	Floor	4	–	–	2	–	–	–	1	–	–	23	30
Room 8	Fill	–	–	–	–	–	–	–	–	–	–	–	–
	Floor fill	79	–	–	5	1	1	1	10	1	1	51	150
	Floor	4	–	–	–	–	–	–	–	–	–	–	4
Room 9	Fill	2	–	–	–	–	–	–	–	–	–	1	3
	Floor fill	229	–	–	–	3	3	–	22	4	–	134	395
	Floor	–	–	–	–	–	–	–	–	–	–	–	–
Room 10	Fill	–	–	–	–	–	–	–	–	–	–	–	–
	Floor fill	225	5	–	–	1	–	–	42	7	3	58	341
	Floor	–	–	–	–	–	–	–	–	–	–	–	–
Room 11	Fill	213	9	3	2	6	1	2	36	5	2	148	427
	Floor fill	–	–	–	–	–	–	–	–	–	–	–	–
	Floor	–	–	–	–	–	–	–	–	–	–	–	–

TABLE 6.1. *(continued)*

WM locus	Context	Alma Plain	Alma Rough	Alma Black Burnished	Alma Scored	Alma Incised	Alma Tool Punched	Alma Neck Banded	San Francisco Red*	Three Circle Neck Corrugated	Mimbres Corrugated	Mimbres Rubbed Corrugated	Totals
Room 12	Fill	97	3	–	1	1	–	–	13	3	–	58	176
	Floor fill	–	–	–	–	–	–	–	–	–	–	–	–
	Floor	1	–	–	–	–	–	–	–	–	–	–	1
Room 13	Fill	15	1	1	–	–	–	–	2	1	1	5	26
	Floor fill	105	4	3	1	1	–	–	9	5	12	24	164
	Floor	–	–	–	–	–	–	–	–	–	–	–	–
Room 14	Fill	106	2	–	1	–	2	1	12	2	7	14	147
	Floor fill	123	9	5	2	–	1	–	19	–	7	25	191
	Floor	–	–	–	–	–	–	–	–	–	–	–	–
Room 15	Fill	–	–	–	–	–	–	–	–	–	–	–	–
	Floor fill	122	3	1	–	2	8	–	37	5	22	28	228
	Floor	–	–	–	–	–	–	–	–	–	–	–	–
Room 16	Fill	58	–	–	1	–	1	1	24	1	–	2	88
	Floor fill	–	–	–	–	–	–	–	–	–	–	–	–
	Floor	–	–	–	–	–	–	–	–	–	–	–	–
Work Area 1	Fill	906	17	1	7	6	2	3	105	24	78	199	1,348
Work Area 3	Fill	8	–	–	–	–	1	–	–	–	–	–	9
Pavement 1	Fill	62	–	1	1	–	–	1	6	2	5	34	112
	Floor	–	–	–	–	–	–	–	–	–	2	–	2
Pavement 2	Fill	8	–	–	–	–	–	–	1	–	–	2	11
	Floor	4	–	–	–	–	–	–	–	–	–	5	9
RO locus													
House A	Fill	705	30	45	7	–	–	12	161	1	–	–	961
	Floor fill	55	5	4	1	–	–	1	7	–	–	–	73
	Floor	81	–	–	1	–	–	–	18	–	–	–	100
House B	Fill	637	59	5	9	–	–	14	305	–	–	–	1,029
	Floor fill	507	16	9	7	–	1	8	115	–	–	–	663
	Floor	41	2	–	–	–	–	1	26	–	–	–	70
House C	Fill	938	61	27	12	–	–	37	235	–	–	–	1,310
	Floor fill	185	4	2	3	–	–	5	67	–	–	–	266
	Floor	81	1	–	1	–	–	–	21	–	–	–	104
House D	Fill	1,043	33	20	25	2	–	56	263	1	–	–	1,443
	Floor fill	–	–	–	–	–	–	–	–	–	–	–	–
	Floor	19	–	8	–	–	–	1	6	–	–	–	34
House E	Fill	1,015	52	2	27	–	1	62	223	1	–	–	1,383
	Floor fill	–	–	–	–	–	–	–	–	–	–	–	–
	Floor	–	–	–	–	–	–	–	–	–	–	–	–

Table 6.1. *(continued)*

RO locus	Context	Alma Plain	Alma Rough	Alma Black Burnished	Alma Scored	Alma Incised	Alma Tool Punched	Alma Neck Banded	San Francisco Red*	Three Circle Neck Corrugated	Mimbres Corrugated	Mimbres Rubbed Corrugated	Totals
House F	Fill	398	65	9	7	–	–	6	109	–	–	–	594
	Floor fill	50	1	2	–	–	–	–	8	–	–	–	61
	Floor	14	–	–	–	–	–	–	2	–	–	–	16
House G	Fill	870	115	3	14	–	2	43	150	–	–	–	1,197
	Floor fill	–	–	–	–	–	–	–	–	–	–	–	–
	Floor	31	–	–	–	–	–	–	4	–	–	–	35
House H	Fill	827	23	15	24	–	–	49	238	1	–	–	1,177
	Floor fill	240	7	5	7	–	–	10	51	–	–	–	320
	Floor	15	1	–	–	–	–	–	3	–	–	–	19
House I	Fill	234	1	1	8	–	–	11	48	–	–	–	303
	Floor fill	149	5	2	8	–	–	4	34	–	–	–	202
	Floor	–	–	–	–	–	–	–	–	–	–	–	–
House J	Fill	728	64	30	2	2	–	16	121	–	–	–	963
	Floor fill	54	4	–	–	–	–	–	5	–	–	–	63
	Floor	–	–	–	–	–	–	–	–	–	–	–	–
House K	Fill	514	38	14	24	2	–	30	147	–	–	–	769
	Floor fill	624	31	49	29	4	–	22	131	–	–	–	890
	Floor	46	–	2	–	–	–	1	1	–	–	–	50
Total	Fill	94,226	5,004	1,215	1,856	425	856	1,329	18,809	3,164	3,012	7,897	137,793
	Floor fill	13,738	559	264	309	49	105	175	2,666	641	323	966	19,795
	Floor	3,420	109	66	54	60	16	56	705	157	50	150	4,843
	Total	111,384	5,672	1,545	2,219	534	977	1,560	22,180	3,962	3,385	9,013	162,431

*Counts include San Francisco Red Patterned.

TABLE 6.2 Sherd Counts of Painted Ceramics in Wind Mountain Structures and Features

WM locus	Context	Mogollon R/Br	Three Circle R/W	Boldface B/W*	Mimbres Classic B/W**	Mimbres Poly	Indet. White Wares	Totals
House A	Fill	152	17	51	61	–	30	311
	Floor fill	–	–	1	–	–	–	1
	Floor	–	–	–	–	–	–	–
House B2	Fill	17	23	40	34	–	20	134
	Floor fill	13	6	4	7	–	1	31
	Floor	3	3	6	8	–	3	23
House D	Fill	9	68	58	25	–	7	167
	Floor fill	3	2	9	5	–	3	22
	Floor	1	–	4	–	–	–	5
House E	Fill	8	19	24	12	–	9	72
	Floor fill	–	3	1	2	–	–	6
	Floor	–	–	2	1	–	–	3
House F	Fill	10	11	81	79	–	69	250
	Floor fill	5	–	10	11	–	2	28
	Floor	–	–	1	–	–	–	1
House G	Fill	17	4	2	6	–	1	30
	Floor fill	7	–	1	–	–	–	8
	Floor	–	–	–	–	–	–	–
House H	Fill	49	18	45	25	–	–	137
	Floor fill	6	4	5	3	–	–	18
	Floor	–	1	3	–	–	–	4
House I	Fill	–	–	–	–	–	–	–
	Floor fill	2	1	1	–	–	–	4
	Floor	–	–	–	–	–	–	–
House K	Fill	48	25	223	135	–	51	482
	Floor fill	3	1	6	5	–	2	17
	Floor	2	–	–	1	–	–	3
House L	Fill	61	33	166	134	1	43	437
	Floor fill	2	3	14	3	–	–	22
	Floor	–	3	1	1	–	–	5
House M	Fill	8	6	12	18	–	27	71
	Floor fill	–	1	4	3	–	5	13
	Floor	–	–	–	1	–	–	1
House N	Fill	16	8	15	54	–	31	124
	Floor fill	1	2	–	–	–	–	3
	Floor	1	1	–	–	–	1	3
House P2	Fill	12	16	44	67	–	19	158
	Floor fill	–	–	–	–	–	–	–
	Floor	2	5	6	10	–	3	26
House Q	Fill	7	6	50	10	–	7	80
	Floor fill	–	–	–	–	–	–	–
	Floor	6	2	7	1	–	–	16
House R	Fill	–	19	7	12	–	7	45
	Floor fill	–	–	–	–	–	–	–
	Floor	–	4	3	1	–	2	10
House S	Fill	30	33	23	36	–	12	134
	Floor fill	5	2	1	3	–	–	11
	Floor	2	–	–	1	–	–	3
House T	Fill	44	94	77	69	–	5	289
	Floor fill	1	–	1	2	–	–	4
	Floor	–	–	2	–	–	–	2

TABLE 6.2 *(continued)*

WM locus	Context	Mogollon R/Br	Three Circle R/W	Boldface B/W*	Mimbres Classic B/W**	Mimbres Poly	Indet. White Wares	Totals
House U	Fill	173	170	267	144	1	47	801
	Floor fill	–	–	–	–	–	–	–
	Floor	–	–	–	–	–	–	–
House V	Fill	169	156	360	95	–	49	829
	Floor fill	7	5	12	6	–	2	32
	Floor	–	1	–	–	–	–	1
House W	Fill	11	18	60	27	1	51	167
	Floor fill	2	–	11	5	–	8	26
	Floor	–	–	–	3	–	–	3
House X	Fill	796	888	1,578	133	–	142	3,537
	Floor fill	71	59	52	7	–	2	191
	Floor	6	4	6	–	–	–	16
House Y	Fill	75	43	376	145	–	81	720
	Floor fill	–	–	–	–	–	–	–
	Floor	–	–	–	–	–	–	–
House Z	Fill	19	13	156	78	–	32	298
	Floor fill	2	3	21	8	–	1	35
	Floor	–	–	2	2	–	–	4
House AA	Fill	19	6	72	3	–	12	112
	Floor fill	13	2	33	4	–	3	55
	Floor	–	–	–	–	–	–	–
House BB	Fill	–	–	1	–	–	–	1
	Floor fill	2	1	28	18	–	4	53
	Floor	1	–	3	–	–	1	5
House CC	Fill	–	–	–	–	–	–	–
	Floor fill	–	–	3	1	–	3	7
	Floor	–	–	–	–	–	–	–
House DD	Fill	41	19	92	98	–	34	284
	Floor fill	–	–	–	–	–	–	–
	Floor	14	1	7	7	–	–	29
House EE	Fill	–	3	7	9	–	6	25
	Floor fill	–	–	–	–	–	–	–
	Floor	–	–	–	–	–	–	–
House FF	Fill	3	5	8	6	–	8	30
	Floor fill	1	–	2	–	–	–	3
	Floor	–	–	–	–	–	–	–
House GG	Fill	12	14	55	89	–	24	194
	Floor fill	1	1	1	1	–	4	8
	Floor	–	–	–	–	–	–	–
House HH	Fill	7	12	12	20	–	4	55
	Floor fill	3	1	1	5	–	2	12
	Floor	–	–	–	4	–	2	6
House II	Fill	–	–	–	–	–	–	–
	Floor fill	1	3	11	10	–	4	29
	Floor	–	–	–	–	–	–	–
House JJ	Fill	–	–	–	–	–	–	–
	Floor fill	1	3	4	3	–	3	14
	Floor	–	–	–	–	–	–	–

Table 6.2 *(continued)*

WM locus	Context	Mogollon R/Br	Three Circle R/W	Boldface B/W*	Mimbres Classic B/W**	Mimbres Poly	Indet. White Wares	Totals
House KK	Fill	–	–	–	–	–	–	–
	Floor fill	–	1	6	3	–	–	10
	Floor	–	–	–	–	–	–	–
House LL	Fill	–	–	–	–	–	–	–
	Floor fill	–	1	–	2	–	3	6
	Floor	–	–	–	–	–	–	–
House MM	Fill	–	–	–	–	–	–	–
	Floor fill	–	1	1	1	1	3	6
	Floor	–	–	–	–	–	–	–
House NN	Fill	–	–	–	–	–	–	–
	Floor fill	2	–	36	6	–	15	59
	Floor	–	–	1	–	–	–	1
House OO	Fill	25	34	349	160	–	95	663
	Floor fill	3	4	54	9	–	9	79
	Floor	–	–	1	–	–	–	1
House PP	Fill	67	59	151	41	–	48	366
	Floor fill	–	1	4	2	–	–	7
	Floor	–	–	–	–	–	–	–
House QQ	Fill	16	31	91	7	–	13	158
	Floor fill	–	–	–	–	–	–	–
	Floor	2	–	10	–	–	–	12
House RR	Fill	–	3	25	–	–	5	33
	Floor fill	1	1	7	–	–	–	9
	Floor	–	–	–	–	–	–	–
House SS	Fill	202	195	160	10	–	5	572
	Floor fill	24	9	15	–	–	2	50
	Floor	2	1	1	–	–	–	4
House TT	Fill	24	13	178	17	–	32	264
	Floor fill	–	–	–	–	–	–	–
	Floor	9	5	46	–	–	2	62
House UU	Fill	118	53	81	9	–	9	270
	Floor fill	1	–	3	–	–	–	4
	Floor	–	–	–	–	–	–	–
House VV	Fill	–	–	–	–	–	–	–
	Floor fill	16	1	3	–	–	–	20
	Floor	1	–	–	–	–	–	1
House WW	Fill	–	–	–	–	–	–	–
	Floor fill	16	15	173	2	–	13	219
	Floor	–	–	–	–	–	–	–
House XX	Fill	31	42	270	63	–	22	428
	Floor fill	17	–	55	9	–	4	85
	Floor	1	–	171	1	–	–	173
House YY	Fill	1	1	6	2	–	–	10
	Floor fill	–	–	–	–	–	–	–
	Floor	–	–	6	–	–	2	8
House ZZ	Fill	13	15	88	4	–	25	145
	Floor fill	10	4	39	1	–	1	55
	Floor	1	6	37	1	–	1	46

TABLE 6.2 *(continued)*

WM locus	Context	Mogollon R/Br	Three Circle R/W	Boldface B/W*	Mimbres Classic B/W**	Mimbres Poly	Indet. White Wares	Totals
House AB	Fill	6	20	80	15	–	36	157
	Floor fill	–	2	2	–	–	1	5
	Floor	–	–	–	–	–	–	–
House AC	Fill	45	40	194	–	–	13	292
	Floor fill	22	11	66	1	–	1	101
	Floor	1	2	1	–	–	–	4
House AD	Fill	32	27	97	18	–	25	199
	Floor fill	15	5	65	7	–	6	98
	Floor	5	5	24	6	–	4	44
House AE	Fill	–	–	–	–	–	–	–
	Floor fill	1	2	6	–	–	–	9
	Floor	–	–	–	–	–	–	–
House AF	Fill	150	265	555	1	–	54	1,025
	Floor fill	20	31	19	–	–	2	72
	Floor	24	21	17	–	–	–	62
House AG	Fill	14	38	152	1	–	27	232
	Floor fill	3	6	39	–	–	8	56
	Floor	–	4	4	–	–	1	9
House AH	Fill	–	–	2	–	–	1	3
	Floor fill	–	–	–	–	–	–	–
	Floor	–	–	–	–	–	–	–
House AI	Fill	35	–	59	6	–	22	122
	Floor fill	7	1	6	–	–	2	16
	Floor	2	–	–	–	–	3	5
House AJ	Fill	3	1	16	–	–	11	31
	Floor fill	2	–	–	–	–	–	2
	Floor	–	–	1	–	–	–	1
House AK	Fill	–	–	–	–	–	–	–
	Floor fill	–	–	–	–	–	–	–
	Floor	2	6	8	–	–	–	16
House AL	Fill	–	–	1	–	–	–	1
	Floor fill	–	–	–	–	–	–	–
	Floor	–	–	–	–	–	–	–
House AM	Fill	3	–	12	1	–	–	16
	Floor fill	–	–	8	–	–	–	8
	Floor	–	–	–	–	–	–	–
House AO	Fill	58	12	19	4	–	8	101
	Floor fill	–	–	–	–	–	–	–
	Floor	5	–	–	–	–	–	5
House AP	Fill	72	31	31	1	–	39	174
	Floor fill	–	–	–	–	–	–	–
	Floor	–	–	–	–	–	–	–
House AQ	Fill	133	49	88	–	–	18	288
	Floor fill	14	2	8	–	–	–	24
	Floor	–	1	–	–	–	–	1

Table 6.2 *(continued)*

WM locus	Context	Mogollon R/Br	Three Circle R/W	Boldface B/W*	Mimbres Classic B/W**	Mimbres Poly	Indet. White Wares	Totals
Room 1	Fill	5	2	12	13	1	2	34
	Floor fill	–	–	–	–	–	–	–
	Floor	–	–	–	–	–	–	–
Room 2	Fill	1	2	2	5	–	4	14
	Floor fill	1	1	3	6	–	6	17
	Floor	–	–	–	–	–	–	–
Room 3	Fill	7	3	8	13	–	–	31
	Floor fill	1	1	3	7	–	–	12
	Floor	2	1	–	2	–	–	5
Room 4	Fill	6	1	20	56	–	20	103
	Floor fill	3	4	11	16	–	–	34
	Floor	–	–	–	1	–	–	1
Room 5	Fill	2	1	14	36	–	16	69
	Floor fill	2	2	5	11	–	3	23
	Floor	2	–	1	2	–	–	5
Room 7	Fill	1	3	49	81	–	95	229
	Floor fill	3	5	11	10	–	10	39
	Floor	–	–	–	2	–	2	4
Room 8	Fill	–	–	–	–	–	–	–
	Floor fill	1	–	11	14	4	11	37
	Floor	–	–	–	–	–	–	–
Room 9	Fill	–	–	–	–	–	–	–
	Floor fill	1	2	4	43	–	20	70
	Floor	–	–	–	–	–	–	–
Room 10	Fill	–	–	–	–	–	–	–
	Floor fill	2	3	14	10	–	18	47
	Floor	–	–	–	–	–	–	–
Room 11	Fill	2	5	26	14	–	11	58
	Floor fill	–	–	–	–	–	–	–
	Floor	–	–	–	–	–	–	–
Room 12	Fill	2	3	10	17	–	7	39
	Floor fill	–	–	–	–	–	–	–
	Floor	–	–	–	–	–	–	–
Room 13	Fill	–	3	6	3	–	1	13
	Floor fill	–	1	7	13	–	10	31
	Floor	–	–	–	–	–	–	–
Room 14	Fill	3	2	21	7	–	–	33
	Floor fill	–	6	19	3	–	3	31
	Floor	–	–	–	–	–	–	–
Room 15	Fill	–	–	–	–	–	–	–
	Floor fill	2	2	15	23	–	5	47
	Floor	–	–	–	–	–	–	–
Room 16	Fill	1	1	1	6	–	1	10
	Floor fill	–	–	–	–	–	–	–
	Floor	–	–	–	–	–	–	–

TABLE 6.2 *(continued)*

WM locus	Context	Mogollon R/Br	Three Circle R/W	Boldface B/W*	Mimbres Classic B/W**	Mimbres Poly	Indet. White Wares	Totals
Work Area 1	Fill	14	14	61	35	–	12	136
Work Area 3	Fill	–	–	7	–	–	–	7
Pavement 1	Fill	1	2	–	4	–	4	11
	Floor	–	–	–	–	–	–	–
Pavement 4	Fill	–	–	–	1	–	–	1
	Floor	–	–	–	–	–	–	–
RO locus								
House A	Fill	13	8	–	–	–	–	21
	Floor fill	1	–	–	–	–	–	1
	Floor	1	1	–	–	–	–	2
House B	Fill	2	22	–	–	–	–	24
	Floor fill	7	27	–	–	–	–	34
	Floor	–	4	–	–	–	–	4
House C	Fill	7	14	–	–	–	–	21
	Floor fill	–	1	–	–	–	–	1
	Floor	–	–	–	–	–	–	–
House D	Fill	60	81	–	–	–	–	141
	Floor fill	–	–	–	–	–	–	–
	Floor	–	–	–	–	–	–	–
House E	Fill	39	128	1	–	–	–	168
	Floor fill	–	–	–	–	–	–	–
	Floor	–	–	–	–	–	–	–
House F	Fill	3	1	–	–	–	–	4
	Floor fill	–	1	–	–	–	–	1
	Floor	–	–	–	–	–	–	–
House G	Fill	20	28	–	–	–	–	48
	Floor fill	–	–	–	–	–	–	–
	Floor	–	–	–	–	–	–	–
House H	Fill	33	43	–	–	–	–	76
	Floor fill	14	–	–	–	–	–	14
	Floor	4	–	–	–	–	–	4
House I	Fill	10	20	–	–	–	–	30
	Floor fill	1	9	–	–	–	–	10
	Floor	–	–	–	–	–	–	–
House J	Fill	3	6	–	–	–	–	9
	Floor fill	–	–	–	–	–	–	–
	Floor	–	–	–	–	–	–	–
House K	Fill	20	22	–	–	–	–	42
	Floor fill	33	47	1	–	–	–	81
	Floor	4	1	–	–	–	–	5
Total	Fill	3,116	3,091	6,905	2,275	4	1,509	16,900
	Floor fill	398	313	956	311	5	205	2,188
	Floor	106	83	382	56	–	27	654
	Total	3,620	3,487	8,243	2,642	9	1,741	19,742

*Boldface Black-on-white includes Styles I and II.
**Classic Mimbres Black-on-white is equivalent to Style III.

FIGURE 6.1. Alma Plain bowl (WM 2470) recovered from the floor of House WW. For context and dimensions of all vessels refer to Tables 6.4 and 6.5 (Neg. No. WM 149–36L).

FIGURE 6.2. Example of an Alma Plain jar (WM 1728), one of the largest Alma series vessels recovered from the site (Neg. No. WM 148–31L).

FIGURE 6.3. Alma Rough jar (WM 1954) from Burial 65 (Neg. No. WM 150–28L).

FIGURE 6.4. Alma Incised jar (WM 1923) from Burial 65. The incising on Alma Incised vessels may be either finely or crudely executed (Neg. No. WM 150–29L).

FIGURE 6.5. Alma Neck Banded jar (WM 471) from the floor of House K (Neg. No. WM 150–27L).

FIGURE 6.7. Shallow Alma Plain bowl (WM 1208) from Burial 35 (Neg. No. WM 149–36A/L).

FIGURE 6.8. An Alma Plain vessel (WM 1244) from the floor of House AA in a simple avian form or "duck pot" style. This is an infrequent vessel form in the Alma series inventory from Wind Mountain (Neg. No. WM 145–3A/L).

FIGURE 6.6. Bilobed Alma Plain jar (WM 2452) from the floor of House TT. The bilobed form is rare when compared with the more common globular jar form (Neg. No. WM 150–31L).

TABLE 6.3. Unpainted and Painted Sherds Recovered from Wind Mountain Excavation Blocks and Extramural Features

	Excavation Blocks	Pits	Pit Ovens
Unpainted Types			
Alma Plain	44,958	1,954	124
Alma Rough	2,519	97	3
Alma Black Burnished	553	55	2
Alma Scored	673	47	2
Alma Incised	213	5	1
Alma Tool Punched	429	15	1
Alma Neck Banded	369	15	1
San Francisco Red*	7,878	286	11
Three Circle Neck Corrugated	1,787	103	7
Mimbres Corrugated	3,017	130	4
Mimbres Rubbed Corrugated	7,235	306	2
Vesiculated	56	1	–
Painted Types			
Mogollon R/Br	853	51	3
Three Circle R/W	1,065	44	2
Boldface B/W	3,886	196	12
Mimbres Classic B/W	3,326	165	1
Indet. whitewares	1,866	59	6
Mimbres Polychrome	2	1	–
Totals	80,685	3,530	182

*Includes San Francisco Red Patterned.

TABLE 6.4. Unpainted Vessels Recovered from All Contexts of the Wind Mountain Site

WM locus	Context	Catalogue No.	Reference No.	Di Peso Type	Revised Type	Vessel Form	Rim Diameter (cm)	Body Diameter (cm)	Height (cm)	Thickness (cm)	Weight (gm)	Estimated Volume (ml)
House A	Fill	WM 1	251	AR	AR	J*	0.5	2.9	2.6	0.3	14.4	–
House A	Fill	WM 41	259	API	AI	J*	1.3	3.2	2.1	0.5	17.6	1.5
House A	Fill	WM 1929	251	AR	AR	J*	4.2	7.3	5.5	0.5	15.4	77
House D	Floor	WM/C 101	254	AR	AR	L*	2.4+	3.1+	1.2	0.4	5.8	–
House D	Floor	WM 545	243	AP	AP	J	15.9	31.0	28.5+	0.7	2995+	9400
House E	Fill	WM/C 198	247	AR	AR	L*	1.5+	2.1+	1.2+	0.3	5.5	–
House K	Floor	WM 471	257	ANB	ANB	J	13.4	18.4	19.7	0.4	850	2800
House K	Floor	WM 472	270	SFR	SFR	B	22.1	23.2	9.5	0.8	580.4	1900
House K	Fill	WM/C 115B	253	AR	AR	B*	1.7+	4.0+	3.6+	0.8	6.2	–
House K	Fill	WM 289	251	AR	AR	J*	1.8	6.5	5.0	0.7	117.6	11
House K	Fill	WM 290	251	AR	AR	J*	1.3	3.9	3.9	1.0	49.2	4
House K	Fill	WM 291	251	AR	AR	J*	2.3	4.9	5.7	0.5	45	22
House K	Fill	WM 374	251	AR	AR	J*	0.5	1.6	1.1	0.3	2.4	–
House K	Fill	WM 387	252	AR	AP	D	12.7+ x 6.9+	13.7+ x 7.7+	3.4	0.6	150.6+	220
House L	Floor	WM 481	243	AP	AP	J	13.1	23.0	22.5	0.5	1640	4700
House L	Fill	WM 306	253	AR	AR	J*	4.8	7.7	5.7	0.8	56	83
House L	Fill	WM 1728	243	AP	AP	J	19.6	43.4	38.1	0.5	5250	22400
House N	Fill	WM 520	251	AR	AP	J*	2.5	5.3	5.5	0.7	62.4	24
House N	Fill	WM/C 1407	251	AR	AR	J*	1.9	4.4+	4.8	0.5	52.4	–
House Q	Floor	WM 803	272	WMR	SFR	B	24.6	25.1	10.0	0.5	735	2900
House Q	Floor	WM 804	271	WMR	SFR	J	6.2	15.0	13.0	0.3	402	1200
House Q	Floor	WM 1020	243	AP	AP	J	11.7	20.5	23.5	0.4	948	4900
House Q	Floor	WM 1161	243	AP	AP	J	13.5	30.6	36.0	0.5	2450	12750
House T	Floor	WM 1169	269	SFR	SFR	J*	3.5	5.9	5.3	0.4	79.4	44
House T	Floor	WM 1229	243	AP	AP	J	17.7	28.7	33.4	0.4	2680	10250
House U	Fill	WM 865	254	AP	AP	L*	1.8	3.1	2.7	0.4	19.8+	–
House W	Fill	WM/C 428	254	AR	AR	L*	1.6	2.6	2.1	0.6	14.5	–
House X	Fill	WM 1553	251	AR	AR	J*	2.8	5.5	6.1	0.3	67.4	44
House Y	Fill	WM 1113	251	AR	AR	J*	2.4	4.7	3.5	0.5	39.8	22
House Y	Fill	WM 1114	244	AP	AP	J*	1.8	5.6	4.2	0.4	61	24
House Y	Fill	WM 1115	251	AR	AR	J*	1.4	3.9	2.5	0.4	26.4	4
House Z	Fill	WM 1047	246	AP	AP	J*	2.1	3.6	3.5	0.5	23.8	11
House Z	Fill	WM 1048	253	AR	AR	B*	3.3	4.9	3.6	0.4	36.8	12
House AA	Floor	WM/C 897	245	AP	AP	B	18.1	19.5	11.5+	0.5	508	–
House AA	Floor	WM 1244	245	AP	AP	B	13.0 x 8.4	14.6 x 10.3	7.0	0.7	316+	375

TABLE 6.4. *(continued)*

WM locus	Context	Catalogue No.	Reference No.	Di Peso Type	Revised Type	Vessel Form	Rim Diameter (cm)	Body Diameter (cm)	Height (cm)	Thickness (cm)	Weight (gm)	Estimated Volume (ml)
House AA	Floor/ Floor fill	WM 1243	264	3 Cir NC	3 Cir NC	J	7.6	12.9	12.5	0.4	470	800
House CC	Floor fill	WM/C 32	244	AP	AP	J*	–	2.7+	2.9	0.5	7	–
House DD	Floor	WM 1752	253	AR	AR	B*	2.9	3.7	1.5	0.5	12	4
House DD	Entry fill	WM 1385	244	AP	AP	J*	1.8	3.4	3.1	0.4	18.4	7
House EE	Fill	WM/C 905	285	AP	AP	J	10.8	19.0+	14.6+	0.5	272	–
House NN	Floor fill	WM 2132	262	ATP	ATP	J*	5.1	8.3	7.7	0.5	129.8	165
House PP	Floor Pit 3	WM 2170	243	AP	AP	J	5.9	9.2	10.3	0.4	210	330
House PP	Fill	WM/C 862	253	AR	AR	B*	1.0	3.5	2.3	1.4	13	–
House SS	Floor fill	WM 2440	270	SFR	SFR	B	17.8	18.6	8.0	0.5	390	1050
House SS	Fill	WM/C 945	251	AR	AR	J*	1.4+	2.5	2.2+	0.4	7.2	–
House SS	Fill	WM 2235	253	AR	AR	B*	2.4	3.2	1.4	0.5	8.8	2
House SS	Fill	WM 2442	264	3 Cir NC	ANB	J	6.5	11.3	11.9	0.4	234	550
House TT	Floor	WM/C 1066	252	AP	AP	B	10.5	11.3	4.5	0.5	93	–
House TT	Floor	WM 2452	243	AP	AP	J	6.3	12.4	14.5	0.4	435	975
House UU	Floor	WM/C 1074	255	AR	AR	J	–	6.4	2.1	0.3	30.8	–
House UU	Floor fill	WM/C 1040	246	AP	AP	B*	6.3	7.2	4.1+	0.5	74.2	–
House UU	Fill	WM/C 985	254	AR	AR	L*	2.2	2.5	1.4	0.4	8.3	–
House UU	Fill	WM 2318	270	SFR	SFR	B	12.7	13.3	6.5	0.5	193.2	400
House WW	Floor	WM 2369	251	AR	AR	J*	2.8	6.4	5.7	0.5	80	44
House WW	Floor	WM 2370	251	AR	AR	J*	1.9	5.2	4.3	0.5	67	21
House WW	Floor	WM 2466	264	3 Cir NC	3 Cir NC	J	14.9	32.0	30.8	0.5	3120	10200
House WW	Floor	WM 2470	245	AP	AP	B	11.4	15.9	10.9	0.5	470	1200
House WW	Floor	WM 2561	264	3 Cir NC	3 Cir NC	J	17.8	27.0	24.1	0.6	2310	7000
House WW	Floor	WM 2562	264	3 Cir NC	3 Cir NC	J	20.3	41.0	40.2+	0.6	3500+	–
House WW	Floor	WM 2563	264	3 Cir NC	3 CIr NC	J	15.9	26.7	27.8	0.5	2250	7000
House WW	Floor fill	WM/C 1290	264	3 Cir NC	3 Cir NC	J	17.8	33.2	23.5+	0.5	1900	–
House WW	Floor fill	WM/C 1291	264	3 Cir NC	3 Cir NC	J	18.8+	–	–	0.8	2700	–
House WW	Floor fill	WM/C 1295	264	3 Cir NC	3 Cir NC	J	–	–	–	–	1200	–
House WW	Floor fill	WM/C 1296	264	3 Cir NC	3 Cir NC	J	15.3+	19.0+	28.8+	0.6	1550	–
House WW	Floor fill	WM/C 1297	264	3 Cir NC	3 Cir NC	J	15.3+	26.5+	26.0+	0.6	1400	–
House WW	Floor fill	WM/C 1298	264	3 Cir NC	3 Cir NC	J	15.2+	–	–	0.7	2300	–
House WW	Floor fill	WM/C 1299	264	3 Cir NC	3 Cir NC	J	25.5+	35.0+	29.5+	0.6	3400	–
House WW	Floor fill	WM/C 1383	264	3 Cir NC	3 Cir NC	J	–	–	–	–	1300	–
House WW	Floor fill	WM 2467	264	3 Cir NC	3 Cir NC	J	7.8	12.6	11.5	0.5	296	700
House WW	Floor fill	WM 2557	264	3 Cir NC	3 Cir NC	J	13.8	22.2	20.5	0.5	1380	3400
House WW	Floor fill	WM 2558	264	3 Cir NC	3 Cir NC	J	10.3	19.0	21.0	0.5	1042	2200
House ZZ	Floor	WM 2576	253	AR	AR	B*	3.8	4.5	1.9	0.3	15.4	13
House ZZ	Floor	WM 2575	253	AR	AR	B*	3.3	4.3	2.1	0.4	15.6	11

TABLE 6.4. *(continued)*

WM locus	Context	Catalogue No.	Reference No.	Di Peso Type	Revised Type	Vessel Form	Rim Diameter (cm)	Body Diameter (cm)	Height (cm)	Thickness (cm)	Weight (gm)	Estimated Volume (ml)
House AD	Floor	WM 2775	244	AP	AP	J*	4.5	8.5	6.5	0.4	95.2	165
House AF	Floor	WM 2780	251	AR	AR	J*	3.6	6.3	6.2	0.4	89.6	77
House AF	Floor fill	WM 2851	252	AR	AR	B	7.0	8.4	7.2+	0.6	120+	220+
House AI	Floor	WM 2837	251	AR	AR	J*	4.1	7.8	9.1	0.6	180.2	165
House AI	Floor	WM 2876	243	AP	AP	J*	3.9, 3.6	5.7	8.4	0.5	125	88
House AI	Floor	WM 2877	251	AR	AR	J*	2.1	4.6	4.2	0.5	47.6	24
House AI	Floor fill	WM 2875	246	AP	AP	B*	7.5	8.5	4.1	0.4	75	138
House AI	Fill	WM 2808	253	AR	AR	B*	5.9	7.0	4.2	0.8	85.8	46
House AK	Floor	WM 3125	243	AP	AP	J	29.0	30.5	23.0+	0.5	1350+	–
House AM	Floor	WM 3127	243	AP	AP	J	13.3	23.2	25.0	0.5	1695+	5000
House AM	Floor fill	WM/C 1385	243	AP	AP	J	–	26.7+	14.0+	0.8	1397	–
House AN	Floor	WM 3087	243	AP	AP	J	10.6	18.8	22.7	0.4	1170	3000
House AP	Fill	WM/C 1332		AR	AR	J*	–	–	–	–	29.0	–
House AP	Fill	WM 3009	245	AP	AP	B	17.1	18.0	8.5	0.5	400	1050
House AQ	Fill	WM/C 1345	253	AR	AR	B*	3.1	3.9	1.2	0.7	10.2	–
Room 2	Floor fill	WM/C 1394	266	MRC	MC	J	–	38.5+	39.0+	0.7	1450	–
Room 3	Floor fill	WM/C 134	253	AR	AR	B*	4.2	5.1	2.5	0.6	28	–
Room 14	Subfloor pit	WM 1930	265	MC	MC	J*	4.0	8.7	7.6	0.6	165	165
Room 14	Floor fill	WM/C 1393	266	MC	MC	J	18.2	30.3+	29.0+	0.6	700	–
Work Area 1	Bl. 11-D	WM 1950	264	3 Cir NC	3 Cir NC	J	11.3	20.4	20.0	0.4	1210+	3200
Work Area 1	Bl. 11-D	WM 1951	261	ATP	ATP	J	7.7	12.6	12.7	0.5	510	850
Work Area 1	Bl. 11-D	WM 2209	261	ATP	ATP	J	18.9+	36.0+	35.0+	0.7	3900	–
Work Area 1	Bl. 11-D	WM 2344	264	3 Cir NC	3 Cir NC	J	27.7	45.2	47.0	0.6	7650	36000
Work Area 1	Bl. 11-D	WM 2420	264	3 Cir NC	3 Cir NC	J	17.8	28.0	26.5	0.8	2800	7000
Burial 1	Room 2 Subfloor pit	WM 1952	266	MRC	MC	J	8.5	13.1	12.5	0.8	538	550
Burial 3	Bl. 2-D	WM 198	243	AP	AP	J	10.7	17.5	19.7	0.7	1180	2150
Burial 4	Bl. 11-A	WM 199	272	WMR	SFR	B	25.8	27.0	10.1	0.5	760	2900
Burial 7	Pit 2	WM 1953	253	AR	AR	B*	7.6	8.5	5.2	0.5	109.4	121
Burial 12	Bl. 26-A	WM 461	270	SFR	SFR	B	18.3	19.0	9.0	0.4	410	1400
Burial 25	Bl. 28-B	WM/C 332	253	AR	AR	B*	7.6	8.6	3.0	0.8	83.4	–
Burial 26	H-T fill	WM 805	271	WMR	SFR	J	12.0	16.7	13.2	0.6	490	1600
Burial 32	H-V fill	WM 962	267	MRC	AP	B	14.2	15.2	7.0	0.6	364.2	550
Burial 32	H-V fill	WM 963	246	AP	AP	B*	7.5	8.2	3.2	0.4	68.4	77
Burial 32	H-V fill	WM 1164	266	MRC	MC	J	8.8	15.6	15.0	0.6	670	1300
Burial 35	H-Y fill	WM 1208	263	ABB	AP	B	12.6	13.4	7.0	0.5	255	400
Burial 59	H-HH fill	WM 1790	270	SFR	SFR	B	15.0	15.8	7.2	0.5	297+	700
Burial 62	H-HH fill	WM 1817	245	AP	AP	B	10.6	13.0	8.0	0.4	250	600
Burial 65	Bl. 30-D	WM 1922	270	SFR	SFR	B	9.9	10.7	6.3	0.5	135	300

TABLE 6.4. *(continued)*

WM locus	Context	Catalogue No.	Reference No.	Di Peso Type	Revised Type	Vessel Form	Rim Diameter (cm)	Body Diameter (cm)	Height (cm)	Thickness (cm)	Weight (gm)	Estimated Volume (ml)
Burial 65	Bl. 30-D	WM 1923	258	API	AI	J	9.1	12.2	13.5	0.4	353	800
Burial 65	Bl. 30-D	WM 1954	250	AR	AR	J	10.0	15.3	16.0	0.5	622	1400
Burial 82	Bl. 62-C	WM/C 918	244	AP	AP	J*	3.3+	8.0	8.2	0.6	85.6	–
Burial 82	Bl. 62-C	WM/C 919	248	AP	AP	J*	–	9.4	4.4+	0.4	77.8	–
Burial 82	Bl. 62-C	WM/C 920	272	WMR	SFR	B	10.2	10.9	7.0	0.5	103.2	–
Burial 85	Bl. 62-D	WM 2216	270	SFR	SFR	B	18.6	19.4	7.0	0.5	405	1100
Burial 86	Bl. 62-D	WM 2217	273	WMR	SFR	B*	11.0	11.5	3.6	0.3	107.1	125
Burial 89	Bl. 54-A	WM 2281	272	WMR	SFR	B	18.5	19.3	8.9	0.5	420	1350
Burial 94	H-AC Floor/Fill	WM 2777	272	WMR	SFR	B	18.5	19.3	9.0	0.4	435	1500
Burial 95	Bl. 54-A	WM 2679	272	WMR	SFR	B	12.1	14.9	11.3	0.4	500	1200
Burial 96	H-AB Floor/Fill	WM 2669	245	AP	AP	B	12.7	12.8	8.0	0.4	290	600
Burial 96	H-AB Floor/Fill	WM 2670	272	WMR	SFR	B	17.8	18.5	7.0	0.5	395+	1000
Burial 99	H-AE Fill	WM 2778	252	AR	AR	B	13.5	14.5	5.5	0.6	235+	300
Burial 101	H-AI Floor/Fill	WM 2836	245	AP	AP	B	12.0	12.5	6.4	0.5	205	404
Burial 103	H-AM fill	WM 3083	272	WMR	SFR	B	16.2	17.0	8.9	0.4	410	1000
Burial 103	H-AM fill	WM 3126	270	SFR	SFR	B	24.4	25.3	9.0	0.4	500	2200
Block 10-D	–	WM 543	268	SFR	SFR	J	7.5+	10.8+	7.5+	0.5	102+	250+
Block 10-D	–	WM 544	256	AS	AS	J	7.0	11.9	14.4	0.5	384.2	650
Block 18-D	–	WM 2064	266	MRC	MC	J	27.5	41.3+	41.0	0.7	3500	34000
Block 26-A	–	WM 372	246	AR	AR	B*	1.0	1.9	1.4	0.3	4.2	–
Block 28-A	–	WM 693	253	AR	AR	B*	1.4	2.1	1.4	0.3	3.0	–
Block 28-A	–	WM/C 1408	244	AP	AP	J*	3.1	7.9+	5.6+	0.5	22.8	–
Block 30-D	–	WM 1955	266	MRC	MC	J	7.4	14.3	11.0	0.6	500	800
Block 34-C	–	WM/C 483	254	AR	AR	L*	1.2+	2.0+	1.4+	0.5	8.6	–
Block 36-C	–	WM/C 675	262	ATP	AP	J*	1.5	4.7	3.6	0.6	25.2	–
Block 36-C	–	WM 760	272	WMR	SFR	B	11.0+	11.2+	8.6	0.5	217+	500+
Block 44-B	–	WM/C 1411	253	AR	AR	B*	2.4+	3.5+	2.9	0.5	10.1	–
Block 45-D	–	WM 2008	251	AR	AR	J*	2.3	6.3	4.7	0.6	63.2	44
Block 48-B	–	WM/C 797	(?)	AR	AR	J*	–	–	–	–	4.0	–
Block 53-B	–	WM/C 1016	254	AR	AR	L*	2.5	3.2+	1.7	0.5	7.0	–
Block 53-B	–	WM 2376	244	AP	AP	J*	2.5	6.0	4.7	0.3	72	44
Block 54-D	–	WM 2139	267	MRC	AP	B	12.7	14.0	7.1	0.6	385.4	500
Block 61-D	–	WM/C 1024	253	AR	AR	J*	1.2	2.5+	2.5	0.6	5.6	–
Block 62-D	–	WM/C 1409	244	AP	AR	J*	3.1+	6.3+	7.3+	0.5	33.8	–

TABLE 6.4. *(continued)*

RO locus	Context	Catalogue No.	Reference No.	Di Peso Type	Revised Type	Vessel Form	Rim Diameter (cm)	Body Diameter (cm)	Height (cm)	Thickness (cm)	Weight (gm)	Estimated Volume (ml)
House A	Floor	RO 23	256	AS	AS	J	5.0	8.9	11.2	0.5	230	250
House C	Floor	RO/C 37	251	AR	AR	J*	2.6+	4.2	4.5	0.6	34.6	–
House C	Floor	RO/C 85	243	AP	AP	J	16.9+	37.1+	30.5+	0.5	1598.2	–
House C	Floor	RO 83	251	AR	AR	J*	1.9	5.0+	3.0+	0.3	187.8	–
House C	Floor	RO 85	270	SFR	SFR	B	14.0	14.6	6.0	0.4	157.8	425
House C	Floor	RO 86	270	SFR	SFR	B	12.1+	13.1+	6.0	0.6	150+	325+
House C	Floor	RO 87	244	AR	AR	J*	2.7	5.6+	6.4+	0.5	39.2	–
House C	Floor	RO 88	243	AP	AP	J	5.4	9.1	10.1	0.5	230	255
House C	Floor	RO 89	249	AP	AP	J	10.4	15.0	16.9	0.5	540	1700
House C	Floor	RO 245	257	ANB	ANB	J	22.0	43.0	47.0	0.5	4450	29000
House F	Floor/ Subfloor	RO 220	272	WMR	SFR	B	23.8	24.5	7.8	0.5	525	1900
House F	Fill	RO 205	252	AR	AP	B	12.1	12.8	6.0	0.5	165+	500+
House F	Fill	RO 206	272	WMR	SFR	B	20.3	21.1	8.0	0.6	390	1300
House F	Fill	RO/C 86	243	AR	AR	J	13.8+	22.7+	15.5+	0.5	321.2	–
House F	Fill	RO/C 87	249	AR	AR	J	12.5	13.6+	7.0+	0.4	166.2	–
House J	Fill	RO 171	246	AP	AP	B*	4.9	5.4	1.8	0.3	22.4	–
House K	Floor fill	RO/C 80	254	AR	AR	L*	3.0	3.7	2.7+	0.5	13.4	–
Burial 9	H-F Floor/Fill	RO 219	272	WMR	SFR	B	13.7	14.4	7.8	0.5	260	625
Burial 9	H-F Floor/Fill	RO 220	272	WMR	SFR	B	24.5	24.5	7.8	0.6	525	1900
Burial 9	H-F Floor/Fill	RO 221	270	SFR	SFR	B	14.5	15.3	8.0	0.5	265	800
Burial 9	H-F Floor/Fill	RO 222	272	WMR	SFR	B	23.0	23.7	7.6	0.5	540	1500
Burial 10	Bl. G0E	RO 227	272	WMR	SFR	B	13.1	13.8	8.0	0.5	255	600
Burial 10	Bl. G0E	RO 228	270	SFR	SFR	B	13.0	13.5	9.0	0.4	285	800
Burial 13	H-F Floor/Fill	RO 229	270	SFR	SFR	B	12.0	12.7	5.4	0.5	195	225

*Miniature vessels.

Note: ABB = Alma Black Burnished, AI = Alma Incised, ANB = Alma Neck Banded, AP = Alma Plain, API = Alma Pattern Incised, AR = Alma Rough, AS = Alma Scored, ATP = Alma Tool Punched, MC = Mimbres Corrugated, MRC = Mimbres Rubbed Corrugated, SFR = San Francisco Red, 3 Cir NC = Three Circle Neck Corrugated, WMR = Wind Mountain Red, B = Bowl, D = Dish, J = Jar, L = Ladle.

TABLE 6.5. Painted Vessels Recovered from All Contexts of the Wind Mountain Site

WM locus	Context	Catalogue No.	Reference No.	Di Peso Type	Revised Type	Vessel Form	Rim Diameter (cm)	Body Diameter (cm)	Height (cm)	Thickness (cm)	Weight (gm)	Estimated Volume (ml)
House D	Floor	WM/C 154	281	Man B/W	Style I/II	B	18.2+	19.5+	13.1+	0.6	229.5	–
House D	Floor	WM/C 155	279	Man B/W	Style II	B	18.5+	19.5+	14.8+	0.5	267.2	–
House D	Floor	WM/C 156	280	Man B/W	Style I	B*	8.1+	9.0+	5.0	0.6	61.4	–
House D	Floor	WM/C 1414	277	WM B/W	Style I	J	10.8+	21.7+	10.8+	0.5	238.7	
House G	Floor fill	WM 441	275	M R/Br	M R/Br	E	10.4 l	6.1 w	8.0+	0.4	133+	165
House G	Floor fill	WM/C 1386	274	M R/Br	M R/Br	B	18.0+	19.1+	10.0	0.4	247	–
House K	Floor	WM 470	274	M R/Br	M R/Br	B	17.1	18.0	5.8	0.5	323+	700
House K	Fill	WM/C 1378	274	M R/Br	M R/Br	B	32.5+	34.0+	13.5+	0.7	591.8	–
House P2	Floor fill	WM 2695	276	3 Cir R/W	3 Cir R/W	B	23.3+	24.0+	8.5+	0.5	230+	–
House U	Fill	WM 966	287	ind. poly	ind. poly	B	14.5+	15.2+	5.0	0.5	169+	400+
House X	Fill	WM/C 704	286	Red Mesa B/W	Cibola WW	B	17.0+	18.0+	7.0	0.4	160.4	–
House X	Fill	WM 1704	283	M B/W	Early Style III	B	24.8	26.1	12.0	0.6	531	2400
House Y	Fill	WM/C 465	280	WM B/W	Style I	B*	6.0+	6.8+	2.1	0.6	31.6	–
House NN	Floor fill/ Floor	WM 3131	279	WM B/W	Late Style I	B	30.0	31.0	12.5	0.6	953+	4900
House SS	Fill	WM 2441	276	3 Cir R/W	3 Cir R/W	B	17.2+	18.5+	16.5+	0.5	540+	–
House WW	Floor	WM 2337	282	Man B/W	Style I	B*	6.8	7.5	3.3	0.4	56.8	66
House WW	Floor	WM 2371	282	Man B/W	Style I	B*	9.7	10.6	3.6	0.5	117.4	121
House WW	Floor	WM 2471	281	Man B/W	Style I	B	22.2	23.0	8.8	0.6	610	1700
House WW	Floor	WM 2472	279	WM B/W	Style I	B	29.1	30.2	11.8	0.6	1049	3800
House WW	Floor	WM 2560	279	WM B/W	Style I	B	34.2	35.0	14.3	0.5	1520	7100
House WW	Floor fill	WM 2468	283	M B/W	Style II/III	B	17.1	16.0	6.8	0.4	225	700
House WW	Floor fill	WM 2469	278	WM B/W	Style I	J*	3.2	7.2	7.2	0.4	96.8	121
House WW	Floor fill	WM 2492	281	Man B/W	Late Style I	B	26.2	27.2	8.5	0.5	780	1100
House AF	Fill	WM 2743	276	3 Cir R/W	3 Cir R/W	B	11.0	12.1	7.1	0.5	187	400
Room 14	Subfloor pit	WM 1285	284	M B/W	Style II/III	B*	9.0	9.7	4.0	0.4	76.8	165

Table 6.5. *(continued)*

WM locus	Context	Catalogue No.	Reference No.	Di Peso Type	Revised Type	Vessel Form	Rim Diameter (cm)	Body Diameter (cm)	Height (cm)	Thickness (cm)	Weight (gm)	Estimated Volume (ml)
Room 14	Subfloor pit	WM 1286	284	Man B/W	Style III	B*	8.2	8.9	3.6	0.7	90.4	66
Work Area 1	Bl. 11-D	WM 462	281	Man B/W	Style II	B	24.5	25.5	10.2	0.5	834	2600
Pit 27	Bl. 35-D	WM/C 1384	283	Man B/W	Style III	B	26.5+	28.7+	17.2	0.8	886	–
Pit 27	Bl. 35-D	WM 1397	283	M B/W	Style III	B	22.8	23.7	11.6	0.6	767.2	2500
Pit 54	Bl. 54-A	WM 2443	283	M B/W	Style III	B	18.1	19.1	8.3	0.6	415	1200
Pit 54	Bl. 54-A	WM 2444	283	M B/W	Style III	B	25.7	26.0	12.5	0.6	795	3400
Pit 54	Bl. 54-A	WM 2445	283	M B/W	Style III	B	23.4	24.7	12.5	0.8	905	2875
Pit 54	Bl. 54-A	WM 2446	283	M B/W	Style III	B	28.1	29.5	11.1	0.7	1070	3800
Burial 1	Room 2 Subfloor pit	WM 90	283	M B/W	Style III	B	26.2	27.1	13.7	0.5	1235	4600
Burial 1	Room 2 Subfloor pit	WM 91	283	M B/W	Style III	B	21.9	22.9	9.3	0.6	714	1800
Burial 3	Bl. 2-D	WM 200	283	M B/W	Style II	B	29.0	24.3	12.0	0.6	878	3150
Burial 24	H-Q fill	WM 716	283	M B/W	Style III	B	22.1	23.1	10.1	0.6	697	2050
Burial 27	H-T fill	WM 788	283	M B/W	Style III	B	23.5	24.7	12.0	0.8	1060	2850
Burial 30	H-V fill	WM 1162	281	Man B/W	Style II/III	B	27.3	28.5	14.3	0.8	1025	4700
Burial 32	H-V fill	WM 1163	283	M B/W	Style III	B	19.2	20.7	9.5	0.8	565	1550
Burial 99	H-AE fill	WM 2779	274	M R/Br	3 Cir R/W	B	14.8+	14.8+	7.8	0.4	137.2+	–
Block 30-A	Fill	WM 2009	296	Man B/W	Late Style I	B	31.4	32.8	12.0	0.7	910+	–
Blocks 30-A, 29-B	Fill	WM 3130	276	3 Cir R/W	3 Cir R/W	B	27.0	28.0	12.5+	0.5	500+	–
Block 37-A	Fill	WM 3124	280	WM B/W	Style I	B*	9.0	10.0	4.7	0.7	89+	132

*Miniature vessel.

Note: Cibola WW = Cibola whiteware, M B/W = Mimbres Classic Black-on-white, M R/Br = Mogollon Red-on-brown, Man B/W = Mangas Black-on-white, WM B/W = Wind Mountain Black-on-white, 3 Cir R/W = Three Circle Red-on-white, B = Bowl, E = Eccentric, J = Jar.

FIGURE 6.9. Examples of San Francisco red bowls in their characteristic hemispherical form. Clockwise from extreme left: WM 2836, RO 227, WM 3083, WM 1922, WM 2217 (Neg. No. WM 145–10A/L).

Of the 110 complete or substantially complete examples belonging to the Alma series recovered from the site, 47 were classified as Alma Plain, and burnished or textured varieties accounted for the remaining pieces.

San Francisco Red (Haury 1936b 28–31; Colton and Hargrave 1937:48–49); syn. Wind Mountain Red, Ridout Red (Di Peso Wind Mountain files, Amerind Foundation).

Along with the Alma series pottery, San Francisco Red constitutes the only other early unpainted utility ware associated with Georgetown phase and possibly even some Early Pit House period structures at the site (Figure 6.9). Vessels and large sherds compare with published descriptions of the type with some minor variation. Temper frequently consists of finely divided (as contrasted with the coarsely tempered Alma brownwares) angular quartz, granite, mica, or biotite schist, crushed minerals, and sand. As was noted for the Alma series, some San Francisco Red fragments contained large amounts of mica, more than is usually described for the type at other Mogollon sites. Wind Mountain potters had access to mica bearing deposits (stone sources and possibly clays) and obviously made use of these. Mica rich vessels are, in fact, common components of the Wind Mountain ceramic tradition. San Francisco Red vessels were well polished, demonstrating distinct polishing marks with or without finger indenting. Interior smudging of bowls is not uncommon. Many of Wind Mountain's San Francisco Red vessels were extremely thin walled and stone polished to a high luster. In contrast, other pieces lacked careful polishing and displayed only indifferent surface finishing treatments. The diminished quality in San Francisco Red manufacture may correlate with the increased production of corrugated utility wares toward the end of the Late Pit House period. Bowls (n = 29, including one miniature) far outnumber jars (n = 4, including one miniature) in the whole and fragmentary vessel inventory (Table 6.4), but the remains of many additional jars are indicated by the extensive sherd collection (n = 30,355; Figures 6.10 and 6.11; Tables 6.1 and 6.3).

FIGURE 6.11. San Francisco Red jar (WM 805) with an outcurving rim from Burial 26. Jar forms are less common than bowls in the San Francisco Red type (Neg. No. WM 145–9A/L).

FIGURE 6.10. San Francisco Red jar (WM 804) from the floor of House Q (Neg. No. WM 145–9A/L).

Di Peso distinguished Wind Mountain Red and Ridout Red types from San Francisco Red. These distinctions seem to have been made on the basis of varying surface treatments observed within the redware inventory from the site. At least half of Wind Mountain's redware bowls and sherds fail to exhibit the exterior surface "dimpling" caused by finger indenting, an attribute often believed characteristic of the San

FIGURE 6.12. Exterior of San Francisco Red bowl (WM 461) displaying finger "dimpling," a characteristic of some vessels belonging to the type (Neg. No. WM 145–8A/L).

FIGURE 6.13. Exterior of San Francisco Red bowl (WM 2216) displaying the red slip manipulated into a simple cross band design. An uncommon example of red pigment employed as painted decoration rather than the overall slip customary to most San Francisco Red vessels (Neg. No. WM 145–6A/L).

Francisco Red type (Figure 6.12). Moreover, slip color ranges from a highly polished rich, almost brick red to a dull brownish red. Casual incising is apparent on some vessels. In one instance, the exterior of a shallow bowl with outcurving sides was unslipped but decorated with a simple crossing band design using the pigment customarily applied as an overall slip (Figure 6.13). Manipulation of the slip in this manner may represent an early experimentation with painted designs. With the possible exception of this bowl, the Wind Mountain redware material falls into the accepted variation described for the type.

Fifty years after he first defined San Francisco Red, Haury (personal communication 1989) expressed his opinion that greater variability existed within the type (including the presence or absence of surface dimpling and a range of slipping or polishing techniques) than was indicated in his original type description (Haury 1936b). Both Wind Mountain and Ridout Red wares are, therefore, subsumed under the San Francisco Red classification.

San Francisco Red Patterned (proposed new type).

Six hundred thirty-five textured redware sherds were recovered mainly from bulk fill contexts of the Wind Mountain site. A limited number of these patterned sherds were also found in architectural features (n = 1 sherd each from the floor fill of Wind Mountain locus Houses K, M, and R as well as in Pits 27 and 41; n = 2 sherds from Pit 21; n = 3 sherds from the floor fill of Houses P2, PP, and Room 9; n = 4 sherds from House B floor fill; n = 6 sherds in Room 7 floor and floor fill contexts). These examples mimic San Francisco Red with their thin walls and finely polished or smoothed matte red slip, as well as with their comparable tempering agents and paste. Rim sherds represented bowl and jar forms. Textured designs included parallel bands of cord impressions beginning at the shoulder and incised line and tool punched motifs alone or in combination (Figures 6.14 and 6.15). In approximately half the collection, the textured pattern was cord impressed or etched directly into the damp clay fabric prior to firing. In the remainder, the red hematite, San Francisco Red like slip was applied after texturing, thereby partially filling in the pattern.

Obvious comparisons exist between the Wind Mountain incised redware component and the textured varieties of the Alma series, especially Alma Tool Punched and Alma Incised. There are also similarities with Playas Red Incised from Chihuahua, perhaps best known from Casas Grandes (Di Peso et al. 1974:6:151–152). Undoubtedly, decorative motifs incorporating textured surface treatments had a wide distribution throughout the Southwest and most of northern Mexico. Among the Hohokam, for instance, patterned incising is seen in Estrella Red-on-gray and Sweetwater Red-on-gray, where texturing is combined with painting (Haury 1976:220, 226, 228). However, the emphasis on surface texturing, as compared to painted decoration, was particularly character-

FIGURE 6.14. San Francisco Red Patterned bowl and jar sherds. In these examples the characteristic San Francisco Red slip was applied over the incised or impressed design (Neg. No. WM 147–5L).

FIGURE 6.15. San Francisco Red Patterned bowl and jar sherds. In these examples the surface textured design was incised or impressed after the application of a red slip (Neg. No. WM 147–6L).

FIGURE 6.16. Mogollon Red-on-brown bowl (WM 470) from the floor of House K. Refer to Figure 6.17a (Neg. No. WM 146-15L).

istic of Mogollon ceramics from the initial stages of pottery production. The textured redware examples from Wind Mountain may well have developed from San Francisco Red (possibly inspired by the textured Alma varieties or even indirectly by Playas Incised) and were made locally at the settlement.

Mogollon Red-on-brown (Haury 1936b:10–17; Colton and Hargrave 1937:47–48).

Mogollon Red-on-brown, the first painted pottery to appear in the Mogollon ceramic sequence and at Wind Mountain, coincides with the San Francisco phase of the Late Pit House period (Figure 6.16). Haury (1976:223) noted that the use of a slip is a technical antecedent to creating patterns. The longstanding familiarity with mixing crushed hematite to produce the San Francisco Red slip eventually evolved into the red painted designs seen on Mogollon Red-on-brown vessels (Haury 1976:223). At Wind Mountain, Mogollon Red-on-brown is a small component of the ceramic assemblage, beginning sometime during the San Francisco phase after c. A.D. 650 and extending into the late Three Circle phase.

Crushed quartz, granite, and sherds were commonly used tempering agents. Both quartz and hematite sources, employed in the manufacture of Mogollon Red-on-brown and several other Wind Mountain Mogollon pottery types, occur in proximity to the settlement. Bowl exteriors were slipped with a hematite based pigment (also used in the execution of surface designs) and stone polished. Like San Francisco Red, the exteriors of some Mogollon Red-on-brown bowls and sherds exhibited surface dimpling. The interior design layout was quartered in rectilinear geometrics and solid pendent triangles (Figure 6.17). The practice of overpolishing the design field produced a slight blurring of the line work. Some Mogollon Red-on-brown ceramics exhibited a purple hue in their red painted motifs, somewhat reminiscent of Encinas Red-on-brown of the San Simon series at Cave Creek (Sayles 1945:43–44). All red-on-brown pottery from Wind Mountain displayed those attributes expected for Mogollon Red-on-brown, including a quartered design layout and elements consisting primarily of broad and narrow lines, solid triangles, and painted rims. Vessels with the purple pigmented designs may simply reflect experimentation with locally available minerals.

FIGURE 6.17. Reconstruction of designs on four Mogollon Red-on-brown bowls. Note the quartered design layout, parallel lines, as well as the pendant triangle motifs characteristic of this type.

Three Circle Red-on-white (Haury 1936b 18–21; Martin and Rinaldo 1950a:362–369).

Shortly after the appearance of Mogollon Red-on-brown, Three Circle Red-on-white began to be produced at Wind Mountain, probably during the San Francisco phase (Figure 6.18). Three Circle Red-on-white signified a departure from the previous Mogollon ceramic theme, which focused solely on the production of brown and redwares. Haury (1936b:20) suggested that Three Circle Red-on-white was a transitional ceramic type which bridged early Mogollon wares with the later occurring Mimbres black-on-white series. At Wind Mountain, Three Circle Red-on-white was represented mainly by sherd material (n = 4,598; Tables 6.2 and 6.3) from structures, features, and excavation blocks. Only one complete and four fragmentary vessels (all bowls) were recovered from the site (Table 6.5). Even so, the inventory provides sufficient information to make several observations.

As is the case for other Wind Mountain ceramic types, Three Circle Red-on-white generally corresponds to published descriptions. Temper was finely divided and consisted primarily of crushed minerals and quartz. Interior bowl slips were chalky, often heavily applied. If the slip was thick, its surface appeared "crackled." Exterior surfaces were slipped and polished, often exhibiting scraping marks, dimpling, or alternatively, vessels were left rough and unslipped. Bowl forms were most common, though some jars were made as evidenced by the presence of several large rim sherds (Figure 6.19).

The quartered design layout of Three Circle Red-on-white was reminiscent of Mogollon Red-on-brown, as were the predominant design motifs, which included solid, pendent triangles and checkerboards combined with parallel lines (Figure 6.20). Scroll elements were not uncommon (Figure 6.21). If present, overpolishing did not blur the painted decorative designs.

Three Circle Neck Corrugated (Haury 1936b:36–37).

Three Circle Neck Corrugated refers to a textured pottery type that emerged slightly later than Three Circle Red-on-white (Figures 6.22 and 6.23). The type has clear affinities with, and probably develops out of, Alma Neck Banded utility ware (Figure 6.24). Three Circle Neck Corrugated vessels display multiple, closely spaced narrow bands on the rims of jars. The final band is often, but not always, elaborated with indenting or pinching (Figure 6.25). Three Circle Neck Corrugated was represented by sherd material (n = 5,859; Tables 6.1 and 6.3) recovered from structures, features, and excavation blocks and complete or fragmentary jars (n = 19; Table 6.4). Petrographic studies of several vessels indicate that granite was the preferred tempering material (Appendix 6 in this volume). Three Circle Neck Corrugated continued the characteristic Mogollon practice of surface texturing unpainted ceramics which was initiated with the earlier Alma series.

Boldface Black-on-white (Cosgrove and Cosgrove 1932:76; Haury 1936b:22–27); syn. Mangus Black-on-white (Gladwin and Gladwin 1934:18); New Type (proposed), Wind Mountain Black-on-white (Di Peso Wind Mountain files, Amerind Foundation); Revised, Style I and Style II (Scott 1983; Anyon and LeBlanc 1984).

For the Mogollon, black-on-white ceramic types begin with Boldface Black-on-white, a name assigned by the Cosgroves (1932) from their work at Swarts Ruin in the Mimbres Valley. Surface treatment consists of black-on-white painted designs and the continued use of a white slipped background initiated earlier with Three Circle Red-on-white.

In classifying the black-on-white pottery from Wind Mountain, Di Peso employed the Mangas Black-on-white type name developed from "Mangus" assigned by the Gladwins (1934), an appellation that never gained widespread acceptance and was eventually superseded by the term Boldface. In addition, Di Peso assigned a new type name, Wind Mountain Black-on-white, which he felt preceded Mangas Black-on-white. Unfortunately, the criteria he developed to distinguish these types do not survive and are essentially nonreplicable. Comparisons of vessels and sherds identified as either Wind Mountain or Mangas Black-on-white agree with the traditional published descriptions of Boldface Black-on-white; the latter type name is used in subsequent ceramic discussions.

Archaeologists working in the Mimbres Valley have recently revised the 1930s Mimbres type names, replacing them with a Style I, Style II, and Style III classification. These classes are believed to represent a set of temporally discrete, sequentially ordered types (LeBlanc 1983:114; Anyon and LeBlanc 1984:159; Shafer and Taylor 1986; Shafer 1987, 1988). Style I is viewed as the earliest occurring black-on-white ware, Style II represents a chronological transition said to combine the geographic motifs of Style I with the layout and some designs (e.g., life forms) common to Style III, and Style III is the final black-on-white type in the Mimbres series. Style I and Style II are equivalent to the Boldface Black-on-white designation, and Style III corresponds to Mimbres Classic Black-on-white. The revised classification also allows for transitional designations such as Style I/II and II/III (Table 6.5).

The Wind Mountain black-on-white wares are discussed using the widely recognized original type names: Boldface Black-on-white and Mimbres Classic Black-on-white. The former was comparable to Di Peso's Wind Mountain and Mangas Black-on-white types as well as to the Style I and Style II appellations. The latter conformed to the Style III designation. In presenting the whole and fragmentary vessels from the site (Table 6.5), however, Di Peso's type assignments, together with the recently developed designations, are provided. The whole and partial vessels from Wind Mountain were classified according to the Style I, II, and III system by Roger Anyon (at the Amerind Foundation, 1987). These distinctions were not attempted with the Wind Mountain sherd assemblage.

Turning specifically to the Boldface Black-on-white material (including Styles I and II), 15 whole and fragmentary bowls and two jars (Table 6.5), as well as numerous sherds (n = 12,337; Tables 6.2 and 6.3) were recovered from the structures, features, and excavation blocks of the site (Figures 6.26 and 6.30). Temper was frequently coarse, containing large quantities of crushed granite (Appendix 6 in this volume). Bowls were usually large and often warped, presumably an undesired by-product of firing. Interlocking scrolls and spirals, wavy opposed lines, linear and cross hachures, solid elements, and scalloped borders were evident in much of the material. Designs extended to the rim, a practice reminiscent of Mogollon Red-on-brown painting. Some life forms were observed.

FIGURE 6.18. Three Circle Red-on-white bowl (WM 2743). Refer to Figure 6.20b (Neg. No. WM 147–32L).

FIGURE 6.19. Fragments of Three Circle Red-on-white jars. Jar forms are less frequent than bowls in the type (Neg. No. WM 146–20L).

Mimbres Classic Black-on-white (Cosgrove and Cosgrove 1932:72–76); syn. Classic Mimbres Black-on-white (Gladwin and Gladwin 1931); Revised, Style III (Scott 1983; Anyon and LeBlanc 1984).

Mimbres Classic Black-on-white was represented by 16 bowls (Table 6.5) and a quantity of sherds (n = 6,134; Tables 6.2 and 6.3). Technology, form, and designs correspond to published descriptions. The Mimbres Classic Black-on-white material from Wind Mountain displays complex geometric fine line hachure elements in combination with solids (Figures 6.31–6.33). Execution is variable, ranging from crisp design work utilizing dense black paint to watery brown motifs with casual brush work. Life forms were rarely encountered and limited to bat, mountain sheep, inchworm (?), and stylized bird motifs on whole vessels (Figures 6.34–6.37). Life forms were observed on a handful of sherds (possibly comprising both Styles II and III). Although certain zoomorphic designs are reminiscent of Hohokam motifs, particularly some bird forms (Haury 1976:230–233), most represent animals that would have been familiar to the Wind Mountain residents. Mountain lions, big-horned sheep, lizards, birds, and fish were indicative of the forested upland and local riparian environments near the settlement. A fragment of an intriguing human face or possibly a mask depiction was noted (Figure 6.38).

Mimbres Polychrome (Cosgrove and Cosgrove 1932:79).

A handful (n = 12 sherds) of Mimbres Polychrome material was recovered in bulk screening (Tables 6.2 and 6.3). Mimbres Polychrome is an undoubted variant of Mimbres Classic Black-on-white, showing many similarities in design, composition, and layout. The Wind Mountain sherds display a fine white to cream slip decorated by black line work in combination with dark and light brown or red-brown painted solids.

Mimbres Corrugated (Cosgrove and Cosgrove 1932:83–85; Hawley 1936:64).

The textured pottery ware accompanying the painted black-on-white ceramics at Wind Mountain is classified as Mimbres Corrugated (Figures 6.39 and 6.40). In the Wind Mountain assemblage, corrugations cover most or all of the vessel body and are left plain or are smoothed, rubbed or polished, sometimes to a high sheen (Figure 6.41). Whole jars and sherds indicate that the corrugations of numerous vessels are indented. Tempering materials (including large pieces of angular quartz and biotite schist) are clearly visible, protruding from exterior and interior surfaces as well as the edges of sherds. Seven jars (Table 6.4) in addition to numerous sherds (n = 23,092; Tables 6.1 and 6.3) were recovered from Wind Mountain structures, features, and excavation blocks. Haury (1936b:36–37) suggested that the textured surface treat-

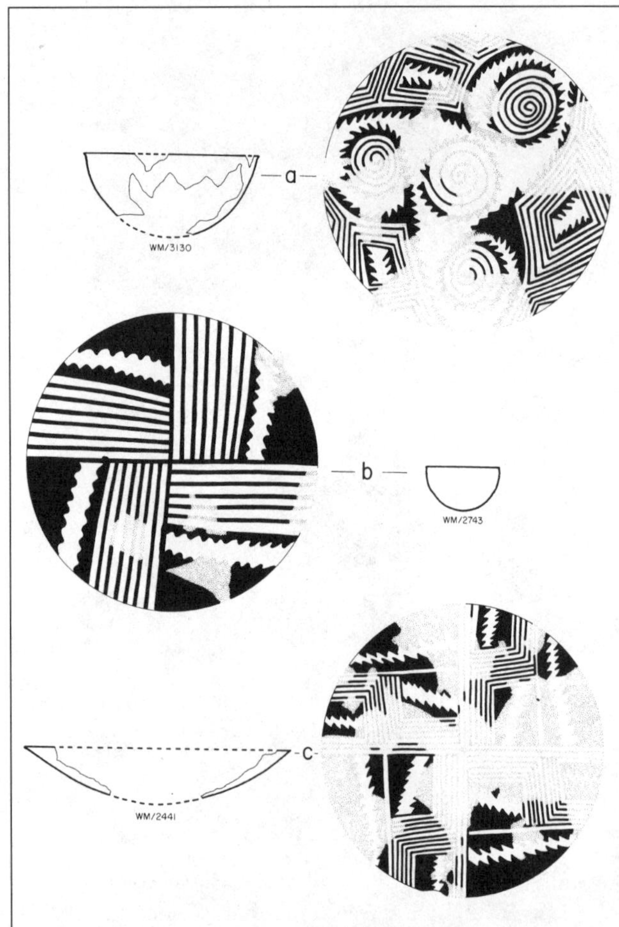

FIGURE 6.20. Reconstruction of designs on Three Circle Red-on-white bowls. Note the continuation of the quartered design layout first observed in Mogollon painted ceramics with Mogollon Red-on-brown. Three Circle Red-on-white displays more complex design combinations and a wider variety of motifs (see view "a"). Designs generally decorate the interior surfaces of bowls.

FIGURE 6.21. Scroll or spiral motifs on Three Circle Red-on-white sherds. Spirals, a new addition to the Mogollon painted design repertoire, were a frequently executed motif on Three Circle Red-on-white pottery from Wind Mountain (Neg. No. WM 145–29L).

FIGURE 6.22. Three Circle Neck Corrugated jar (WM 2466) from the floor of House WW. Three Circle Neck Corrugated has clear affinities with Alma Neck Banded (refer to Figure 6.5) and may have developed out of the former type (Neg. No. WM 147–34L).

ments characterizing Mimbres Corrugated ceramics developed from earlier Mogollon Three Circle Neck Corrugated.

The Wind Mountain Sherd Assemblage

The Wind Mountain sherd assemblage is useful for establishing general trends in the manufacture of ceramics at the site. Sherds from the fill, floor fill, and the floors of structures (Tables 6.1 and 6.2), together with fragmentary ceramic materials from extramural features and excavation blocks (Table 6.3), provide information about the percentages of unpainted versus painted types as well as the comparative frequencies of locally produced, individual pottery types.

The total sherd count representing all site contexts and local ceramic types numbers 267,262 fragments. This sherd total breaks down into 235,925 unpainted, 27,608 painted, and another 3,729 unidentifiable fragments. The latter consisted of indeterminate whitewares (n = 3,672 sherds) and vesiculated pottery (n = 57 sherds). Di Peso's vesiculated ce-

FIGURE 6.23. Three Circle Neck Corrugated pitchers with single strap handles having a twisted or braided appearance. Clockwise from upper left: WM 1950, recovered from Work Area 1; WM 2558 and WM 2467, both from the floor fill of House WW. Note the indenting on the bottom coil of WM 2558, a trait characteristic of some vessels belonging to this type (Neg. No. WM 147–33L).

FIGURE 6.24. Pitchers. Left: Three Circle Neck Corrugated pitcher (WM 1243) from the floor and floor fill of House AA. Right: Alma Tool Punched pitcher (WM 1951) from Work Area 1. Note the similarities between the two types as illustrated by these vessels; also WM 2558 (Figure 6.23) and the jars in Figures 6.5 and 6.22 (Neg. No. WM 150–32L).

FIGURE 6.25. Three Circle Neck Corrugated rim sherds. The bottom corrugation is often elaborated by pinching or indenting (Neg. No. WM 147–4L).

FIGURE 6.26. Boldface Black-on-white or Style I bowl (WM 2471) from the floor of House WW. The interior black-on-white design rising to the rim, quartered patterning, and the sawtooth line defining a solid element are common Style I motifs (Neg. No. WM 150–8L).

ramics from Wind Mountain were sherds that had been burned, probably in a house fire. Subjected to conditions of intense heat, they were so highly fired that they have the appearance of a volcanic pumice. Some organic tempering material and less dense clay fraction had been burned out, rendering the sherds porous and extremely light in weight. Most, if not all, of the vesiculated sherds represented locally made Mogollon types.

Clearly, Wind Mountain ceramists produced much more unpainted (88 percent) as compared to painted (12 percent) pottery. Alma Plain (158,420 sherds) was the most common ceramic type, whether plain or painted, produced at Wind Mountain. It and its textured relatives in the Alma series, including Alma Rough (n = 8,291 sherds), Alma Scored (n = 2,941 sherds), Alma Neck Banded (n = 1,945 sherds), Alma Black Burnished (n = 2,155 sherds), Alma Tool Punched (n = 1,422 sherds), and Alma Incised (n = 753 sherds), accounted for 175,927 sherds, or 75 percent, of the unpainted wares and 66 percent of the total sherd assemblage. San Francisco Red, the next most frequently recovered

FIGURE 6.27. Boldface Black-on-white or Style I bowl (WM 2472) from the floor of House WW. The use of spirals as filler within bands is common to Style I ceramics (Neg. No. WM 150–9L).

FIGURE 6.29. Boldface Black-on-white or late Style II bowl (WM 200) from Burial 3. A single thick rim band above a parallel band from which design elements are suspended is obvious in this example. The use of scroll motifs continues in late Style II ceramics. A hint at the origin of later figurative Style III design work may be implied with the clover motif (Neg. No. WM 150–6L).

FIGURE 6.28. Boldface Black-on-white or Style II bowl (WM 462) from Work Area 1. Style II ceramics exhibit a quartered design layout, and employ fine line elements outlined by thicker lines. The use of solid flags or pendants near bowl rims is a frequently occurring motif (Neg. No. WM 150–7L).

FIGURE 6.30. Boldface Black-on-white or Style II/III bowl (WM 2468) from the floor fill of House WW. The refinement of fine hachures in the absence of heavy framing lines is one step closer in the development of true Style III pottery (Neg. No. WM 150–23L).

FIGURE 6.31. Mimbres Classic Black-on-white or Style II/III bowl (WM 1162) from Burial 30. The absence of an interior rim band, with the design ascending to the edge of the rim is indicative of Style II ceramics. However, the apparent experimentation with stylized motifs is expressive of Style III Mimbres phase pottery. Note the absence of a kill hole (Neg. No. WM 149–7L).

FIGURE 6.32. Mimbres Classic Black-on-white or Style III bowl (WM 788) from Burial 27. In Style III bowls, designs ascend to an interior band painted below the rim. Hachures are no longer confined by heavy outlines (Neg. No. WM 150–2L).

FIGURE 6.33. Mimbres Classic Black-on-white or Style III bowl (WM 2446) from Pit 54 (Neg. No. WM 148–35L).

FIGURE 6.34. Mimbres Classic Black-on-white or Style III miniature bowl (WM 1286) decorated with a double bat motif recovered from a subfloor pit in Room 14 (Neg. No. WM 150–10L).

FIGURE 6.35. Mimbres Classic Black-on-white or Style III bowl (WM 2443) decorated with a mountain sheep life form uncovered in Pit 54. Refer to Figure 6.33 (Neg. No. WM 150–3L).

FIGURE 6.36. Mimbres Classic Black-on-white or Style III bowl (WM 1163) adorned with an inchworm motif from Burial 32 (Neg. No. WM 150–4L).

FIGURE 6.37. Mimbres Classic Black-on-white or Style III bowl (WM 2444) discovered in Pit 54 (refer to Figures 6.33 and 6.35). Note that the stylized birds are equipped with fishlike tails (Neg. No. WM 150–25L).

FIGURE 6.38. Examples of figurative motifs on Mimbres Classic Black-on-white (Style II and Style III) sherds. Identified life forms include a possible mountain sheep, human, fish, bird, rabbit, and lizard motifs (Neg. No. WM 150–11L).

FIGURE 6.39. Mimbres Corrugated jar (WM 2064). Note that the textured treatment, unlike the decorations characterizing earlier Alma Neck Banded or Three Circle Neck Corrugated types, covers the entire jar surface (Neg. No. WM 148–32L).

FIGURE 6.40. Mimbres Corrugated pitchers with braided or twisted stirrup handles. Left: WM 1955 and Right: WM 1164 from Burial 32. Refer to Figure 6.36 (Neg. No. WM 149–16L).

FIGURE 6.41. Mimbres Corrugated sherds. Corrugations may be left plain or smoothed, rubbed, or polished (Neg. No. WM 149–13L).

type, was a distant second with 30,355 sherds (plus an additional 635 San Francisco Red Patterned sherds), Mimbres Corrugated types numbered 23,092 sherds, and Three Circle Neck Corrugated was relatively rare, accounting for only 5,859 sherds.

Among painted types, sherds identified as Boldface Black-on-white (n = 12,337 sherds) were most profuse, followed by Mimbres Classic Black-on-white (n = 6,134 sherds), Three Circle Red-on-white (n = 4,598 sherds), Mogollon Red-on-brown (n = 4,527 sherds), and a scant trace of Mimbres Polychrome (n = 12 sherds). Definite identification of another 3,672 whiteware sherds was indeterminate due to a lack of painted decoration, but their slip and surface treatment indicate they probably belonged to one of the site's black-on-white Mimbres types.

When examining the entire Wind Mountain sherd assemblage, not only do plainwares far outnumber their painted counterparts, but those types associated with a pre-A.D. 1000 date are much more common than those placed at or post-A.D. 1000. Of the ceramics presumed to be produced locally, only Mimbres Classic Black-on-white and Mimbres Polychrome (and perhaps some forms of Mimbres Corrugated) occur c. A.D. 1000 and later. Time ranges for the manufacture of other types, at least for their primary period of production, end by c. A.D. 1000. The temporal propensity expressed by the Wind Mountain sherd assemblage is a pre-A.D. 1000 emphasis with a limited extension into the thirteenth century.

A comparison of sherd counts in various structure contexts, that is, fill, floor fill, and floors, also suggests that when abandoned, many houses and rooms were emptied of ceramics. For example, though numerous sherds were recovered in the fill of Wind Mountain locus Houses A, F, U, and W, as well as from Ridout locus Houses E and J, virtually none were found on their respective house floors. Only as house pits were filled in did cultural debris accumulate; the living surfaces associated with the occupied structures were often devoid of material.

Abandoned pit house or room depressions must have represented convenient repositories for domestic refuse. Broken pottery was incorporated into the fill of many structures, a by-product of trash disposal. Both fill and floor fill may contain mixed refuse of varying ages which accumulated after structures were actually inhabited.

Alternatively, sherds may also have been deposited through roof fall. The superstructures of pit houses are presumed to have consisted of a wooden and brush framework over which an earthen fill was packed (for a discussion of pit house/earthen lodge construction and disintegration see Ahlstrom 1985:82–90). If this earthen matrix included accumulated cultural fill, possibly reflecting multiple occupations at the site, sherd material would have been incorporated into the house superstructure. Upon abandonment, the collapse of this matrix would result in the mixing of any remaining floor artifacts with those contained in the fallen superstructure.

That some movement of sherds occurred within structures is indicated by the presence of Mimbres Classic Black-on-white material on the floor of an early house, probably dating to the Georgetown phase. House Q, a Wind Mountain locus Type II structure, exhibited four floor vessels (a San Francisco Red bowl and a jar; two Alma Plain jars). Both architecture and the floor vessel assemblage denote an early house (A.D. 550–650). Yet a Mimbres Classic Black-on-white sherd (A.D. 1000–1150) was recovered from the House Q floor (100 cm below ground surface). Similarly, San Francisco phase Wind Mountain locus House K, a Type IV structure, contained three floor vessels (an Alma Neck Banded jar, a San Francisco Red bowl, and a Mogollon Red-on-brown bowl). Mimbres Classic Black-on-white sherds were also found (Table 6.2), in this case possibly the result of disturbances caused by Burials 11 and 20. Other structures with date ranges in the Late Pit House period (e.g., Wind Mountain locus Houses R, AB, BB, DD, and XX) displayed small quantities of Mimbres Classic Black-on-white sherds in either floor fill or floor contexts. This sort of depositional mixing is not surprising given the disruptions observed at the site. The small ridge top experienced intensive construction activities throughout its prehistoric occupation. Leveling old surfaces, redepositing cultural fill, or clearing out old house pits for new structures all served to transport small, mobile objects such as sherds. A certain amount of artifact redeposition also occurred as a result of animal burrowing and recent pot hunting. Consequently, although the sherd assemblage is extremely useful for assessing the relative quantities of individual ceramic types produced, it must be remembered that sherds, especially those incorporated into the settlement's trash, are more susceptible to movement than whole vessels and even large vessel fragments. In general, ceramic fragments must be viewed with caution when addressing questions of temporal and spatial comparability.

Whole and Fragmentary Vessels from Wind Mountain

The Wind Mountain vessel assemblage, representing the full spectrum of Mogollon pottery types believed to have been produced at the site, numbered 213 whole and fragmentary vessels (Tables 6.4 and 6.5). Fragmentary vessels (20–95 percent complete) were those for which form could be determined and measurements estimated. Vessels were associated with primary and secondary architectural features (n = 101), burials (n = 45), and the mixed fill deposits of structures and excavation blocks (n = 67). The type and frequency distributions of whole and fragmentary vessels closely corresponds to patterns evident in the sherd assemblage. Unpainted pottery greatly outnumbered painted ceramics, 169 to 44 examples, or 79 percent to 21 percent. The Alma series (47 Alma Plain examples and 63 of its textured relatives) occurred most commonly, accounting for 110 vessels representing 65 percent of unpainted types and 52 percent of all types recovered from the site. Other unpainted types include 33 examples of San Francisco Red (20 percent of unpainted wares and 16 percent of all types), 19 Three Circle Neck Corrugated jars (11 percent of unpainted and 9 percent of total), and seven Mimbres Corrugated jars (4 percent of unpainted and 3 percent of total).

Of the painted wares, Boldface Black-on-white (syn. Style I and Style II) with 17 examples (39 percent of painted types and 8 percent of all types) barely surpasses Mimbres Classic Black-on-white (syn. Style III) represented by 16 bowls (36 percent of painted types and just under 8 percent of all types) as the most common type encountered. In addition to the above black-on-white types, five Three Circle Red-on-white bowls (representing 11 percent of painted types and 2 percent of all types) and four Mogollon Red-on-brown bowls (representing 9 percent of painted types and 2 percent of all types) were found. Of the two remaining vessels from the site, one was so badly weathered that no determination could be made, and the other was a Cibola whiteware of indeterminate type.

Comparing the progression of common to rare types noted in vessel and sherd assemblages (Tables 6.1 through 6.5) demonstrates the similitude of both. Unpainted vessels greatly outnumbered painted types, almost four to one. The Alma series was by far the most dominant type represented. The order of types in diminishing frequency revealed some differences between vessel and sherd assemblages. San Francisco Red was the second most frequent type observed in each, though Three Circle Neck Corrugated was better represented as whole vessels (n = 19) than sherds (n = 5,859) when compared with Mimbres Corrugated.

Whereas Three Circle Red-on-white and Mogollon Red-on-brown scarcely occurred in other than sherd form (n = 4,598 and n = 4,527, respectively), Boldface and Mimbres Classic Black-on-white types were somewhat more abundant as whole vessels. In part these discrepancies may be the result of earlier houses being subjected to intense intrusions from later construction. At Wind Mountain (and probably at most sites) the degree to which houses were disturbed probably covaries with age. One caveat with the Mimbres phase rooms, however, is that these late constructions were the direct object of vandals seeking Mimbres Classic Black-on-white bowls. Other factors that may have enhanced the survival potential for some types of ceramics include the curation practice of Wind Mountain inhabitants in caching vessels in pits and the inclusion of ceramics as funerary accompaniments. But no matter the context, the trends displayed by both whole and fragmentary vessels and sherd assemblages are comparable.

Vessels Associated with Structures

Whatever the exact mechanism, the majority of Wind Mountain structures appear to have been emptied upon abandonment. Roughly one-third (n = 30) yielded ceramic material from floor (61 vessels) and near floor (28 vessels) contexts (Tables 6.4 and 6.5). Many of these structures contained a single vessel, but there were exceptions. For instance, Wind Mountain locus House WW (A.D. 680–990, Mangas phase), with the highest number of vessels of any structure at the site, deserves special mention. Fourteen vessels, including 11 Three Circle Neck Corrugated jars, two Boldface Black-on-white bowls, and one Mimbres Classic Black-on-white bowl, were discovered near the floor. Another dozen vessels, consisting of four Three Circle Neck Corrugated jars, two Alma Rough jars, and an Alma Plain bowl, as well as five Boldface Black-on-white bowls, were found in direct contact with the floor. Field notes indicate that House WW was burned and that the near floor vessels may have represented roof top storage (alternatively, vessels stored on or hanging from interior beams) that collapsed onto the house floor when the structure was destroyed.

Ridout locus House C (A.D. 600–799, San Francisco phase) and Wind Mountain locus House D (A.D. 1000–1260, Mangas phase) each yielded nine floor ceramics. In House C seven Alma series jars and two San Francisco Red bowls were recovered, and three Boldface Black-on-white bowls and one jar, as well as an Alma series ladle and a jar were found in House D. Field notes suggest that both structures were destroyed by fire. Several structures contained four vessels each, including Wind Mountain House Q (Georgetown phase) with two Alma Plain jars and two San Francisco Red bowls; House AI (A.D. 540–770, San Francisco phase) with three Alma series jars and one bowl; and the floor pit of Room 14 with two Mimbres Classic Black-on-white bowls and two Mimbres Corrugated jars. Wind Mountain locus Houses K and AA contained three vessels each, and Houses G, T, NN, TT, UU, ZZ, AF, and AM had two each. One vessel was recovered from the floors of the remaining 14 structures. Consequently, of the structures with floor and near floor vessels, 47 percent had a single example, 27 percent had two, 6 percent contained three, 10 percent had four, and 10 percent yielded more than six. It is worth noting that no Ridout locus house produced any whole or fragmentary painted vessel. For that matter, painted sherds occurred only rarely (Table 6.2). Of the 742 painted sherds recovered from Ridout locus structures, only 15 (or 2 percent) came from floors. The other 727 sherds were discovered in mixed fill and floor fill deposits. This virtual absence of painted wares suggests that the Ridout locus occupation occurred before the advent of painted Mogollon ceramics, that is, Mogollon Red-on-brown. Though Houses E, G, and I are probably associated with the Georgetown phase or earlier, the seven remaining Type IV structures clustered around a Type A community house, together with their plainware pottery assemblage, are indicative of a Ridout locus occupation dating primarily to the earlier stages of the San Francisco phase and before.

Vessels in Secondary Features

A dozen vessels were recovered from secondary architectural features. For example, four Mimbres Classic Black-on-white bowls were recovered from Pit 54 (located in Excavation Block 54–A) and another two bowls derived from Pit 27 (located in Excavation Block 35–D), both in the Wind Mountain locus. Neither was associated with any discernable structure, but both pits may represent the caching of vessels during the Mimbres phase. These ceramic caches are similar to other pits and features at the site which contained ground stone, pipes, and manufacturing equipment.

Another secondary feature that contained vessels is Work Area 1 (located in Excavation Block 11–D) at the Wind Mountain locus. The work area was identified by its hard packed surface on which three Three Circle Neck Corrugated jars, two Alma Tool Punched jars, and a Boldface Black-on-white bowl were found. In addition to these vessels, the work surface exhibited ground and chipped stone implements intermixed with ash, charcoal, and macrobotanical material (Appendix 1).

Vessels Accompanying Burials

Forty-five whole or fragmentary vessels were recovered from 28 burials (Tables 6.2 and 6.4; Chapter 9: Table 9.2). As was the case for vessels and sherds from other site contexts, unpainted wares (n = 37 or 82 percent) were far more common than painted types (n = 8 or 18 percent). Only San Francisco Red vessels accompanied burials at the Ridout locus (Burials 9, 10, and 13). In fact, San Francisco Red appeared to be the preferred ceramic funerary accompaniment of the site, numbering 21 vessels (47 percent). The Alma series was well represented (14 vessels, or 31 percent), although Boldface Black-on-white (one bowl) and Mimbres Classic Black-on-white (six bowls) occurred relatively infrequently. Mimbres Corrugated (n = 2) and Three Circle Red-on-white (n = 1) vessels were also represented. In another 11 burials, a single sherd or sherds were placed, presumably purposefully, adjacent the human remains on their interment. San Francisco Red sherds were found in four burials (Wind Mountain locus

FIGURE 6.42. Examples of Wind Mountain burial vessels. Upper center: Mimbres Classic Black-on-white or Style III bowl (WM 90) from Burial 1. Lower left: Mimbres Classic Black-on-white or Style III bowl (WM 716) from Burial 24. Lower right: Mimbres Classic Black-on-white or Style III bowl (WM 91) from Burial 1. It was not uncommon for vessels accompanying burials to display use wear. This appears to suggest that previous assumptions relating to the manufacture of a discrete class of Mimbres mortuary ceramics require reevaluation. Both WM 90 and WM 91 illustrate the heavy use each received prior to their placement in a burial context. Note the lack of kill holes (Neg. No. WM 150–13L).

Burials 5, 8, 10, and 13), Alma Plain in another four (Wind Mountain locus Burials 12, 14, 49, and 86), Boldface Black-on-white in two (Wind Mountain locus Burials 11 and 36), and both Boldface Black-on-white and Mimbres Classic Black-on-white in another (Wind Mountain locus Burial 18). If the presence of Mimbres Classic Black-on-white material is indicative of burials belonging to the Mimbres settlement, then five or six (Wind Mountain locus Burials 1, 18, 24, 27, 32, and possibly 30) date to this phase. Following this criterion all other burials (n = 117) are suggestive of the Pit House period.

Burial vessels were examined for absence or presence of wear marks. If it is assumed that a specific class of mortuary vessels was manufactured, then these might be recognized by a lack of abrasions caused by use. With one exception (a Boldface Black-on-white bowl in Wind Mountain locus Burial 30, WM 1162), however, all vessels from Wind Mountain burials are heavily worn, implying they first functioned in some utilitarian capacity and were only secondarily employed as grave goods (Figure 6.42). It does not appear that Wind Mountain potters, in any phase or period, produced ceramics of a mortuary specific function.

One final observation concerns the so-called killed vessels often associated with burials, particularly those of the Mimbres phase. Only three Wind Mountain burial vessels (a San Francisco Red bowl, RO 222, in Ridout locus Burial 9; a Boldface Black-on-white bowl, WM 200, in Wind Mountain locus Burial 3; and a Mimbres Classic Black-on-white bowl, WM 788, in Wind Mountain locus Burial 27) were killed, a hole deliberately punched through their bases. Intriguingly, some killed vessels were found on house floors (e.g., Wind Mountain locus House WW) or in caches (e.g., Pits 27 and 54). These vessels may be indicative of burial preparation activities prior to an actual interment, the abandonment of a house, or the dissolution of a household.

Miniature Vessels

Miniatures, including bowls, jars, and ladles, were recovered from the floors of structures and secondary features (n = 25), burials (n = 6), in bulk settlement fill (n = 46), and accounted for 36 percent of the whole and fragmentary ceramic artifact inventory (Tables 6.4 and 6.5). Following the Cosgroves (1932:80–82) and Wheat (1955:104), Di Peso defined a miniature as having a volume measuring less than 165 ml. The Wind Mountain miniatures display the same type distribution as standard vessels with a preponderance of unpainted (n = 69; 90 percent) over painted (n = 8; 10 percent) types. The majority belong to the Alma series (n = 66; Figures 6.43–6.45). Other types were only rarely represented, limited to a San Francisco Red bowl and a jar, one Mimbres Corrugated jar, five bowls and one jar identified as Boldface Black-on-white, as well as two Mimbres Classic Black-on-white bowls.

The intent of miniature ceramic manufacture is problematic. Perhaps, miniatures were made to store a valued personal ornament such as a carved pendant? Some were placed in burials (e.g., with the infant in Wind Mountain locus Burial 7) or were cached (e.g., vessels in the floor pit of Room 14). Certain miniatures are skillfully manufactured objects, clearly the products of a knowledgeable ceramist; the miniature form was obviously the intended finished product (Figures 6.46 and 6.47, see Figure 6.31). In contrast, others appear to be "practice" pieces, conceivably produced by children learning the craft of pottery making (Figures 6.48 and 6.49). Whatever their functions, miniature ceramic vessels and ladles are definite expressions of the Wind Mountain ceramic tradition.

Miscellaneous Ceramic Objects

Di Peso differentiated several categories of miscellaneous ceramics which included a hollow modeled effigy, worked sherds, and solid modeled artifacts. He considered these to

FIGURE 6.43. Examples of Alma series miniature vessels. Left to right: Alma Rough jar (WM 1047), Alma Rough bowl (WM 1752) from the floor of House DD, Alma Rough bowl (WM 2576) from the floor of House ZZ, Alma Plain jar (WM 1385) (Neg. No. WM 149–24L).

FIGURE 6.44. Alma Plain miniature vessels. Left: Alma Plain bowl (WM 963) from Burial 32 (refer to Figures 6.36 and 6.40). Right: Alma Plain seed jar (WM 1114) (Neg. No. WM 150–19L).

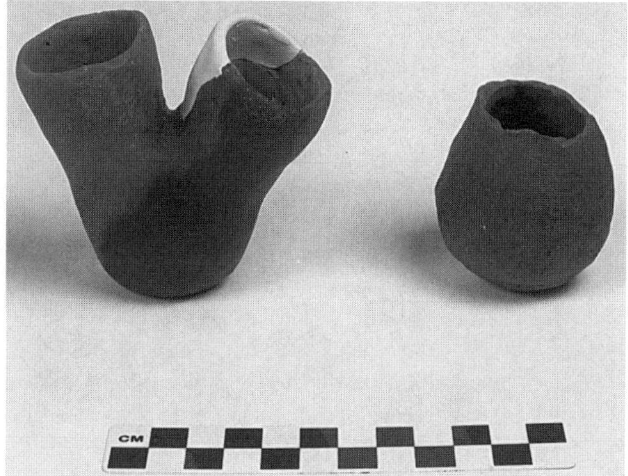

FIGURE 6.45. Miniature vessels. Left: Double spouted Alma Plain jar (WM 2876) from the floor of House AI. Right: Alma Rough jar (WM 1553) (Neg. No. WM 149–19L).

FIGURE 6.46. Miniature vessels. Left to right: Alma Rough jar (WM 2837) from the floor of House AI (refer to Figure 6.45); Mimbres Corrugated pitcher with braided handle (WM 1930) from a subfloor pit in Room 14 (refer to Figure 6.34); Alma Plain jar (WM 2170) from a subfloor pit in House PP. Note the difference in quality of manufacture among the three vessels (Neg. No. WM 149–18L).

have utilitarian function, as compared with ceramic figurines or cornucopias which were assigned to the socioreligious classes (Chapter 8).

Modeled Effigy

A single hollow effigy (WM 441, Figure 6.50; Table 6.5) was recovered from the floor fill of Wind Mountain locus House G (San Francisco phase). Identified as a bear though its head is missing, the effigy belonged to the Mogollon Red-on-brown type. Although not found with the frequency characterizing Hohokam ceramic assemblages, hollow effigies are not uncommon in Mogollon sites (Cosgrove and Cosgrove 1932:75–76). It is unclear why Di Peso subsumed this animal effigy under a utilitarian heading (IC1c1', Reference No. 275) instead of including it in the Type II category (socioreligious). Instead, he assigned the effigy to the ceramic tool subdivision as a finger manipulated hollow form receptacle.

Worked Sherds

Most of Wind Mountain's worked sherds (n = 1,675) were scattered throughout the bulk fill of its structures and extramural contexts. Di Peso separated worked sherds into several specific categories based on shape and proposed function (Table 6.6). These included jar cover/counter (Reference No. 288, Figure 6.51), spindle whorl/bead (Reference No. 289, Figure 6.52), and a series of eccentric forms identified as spoons, scrapers, and scoops (Reference Nos. 290–298, Figure 6.53). An unclassified worked sherd category (Reference No. 299) was also assigned (refer to Appendix 5: Table 2).

FIGURE 6.47. Miniature Mimbres Classic Black-on-white or Style II/III bowl (WM 1285) from a subfloor pit in Room 14 (see Figures 6.46 and 6.34). One of the few painted miniature vessels recovered at the site (Neg. No. WM 149–11L).

FIGURE 6.49. Miniature vessels. Left to right: Alma Rough jar (WM 2369) from the floor of House WW; Alma Rough pinch pot (WM 1048); San Francisco Red jar (WM 1169) from the floor of House T (Neg. No. WM 149–20L).

FIGURE 6.48. Miniature pinch pots. Left to right: Alma Rough bowl (WM 372), Alma Rough jar (WM 1), Alma Rough bowl (WM 693) (Neg. No. WM 149–125L).

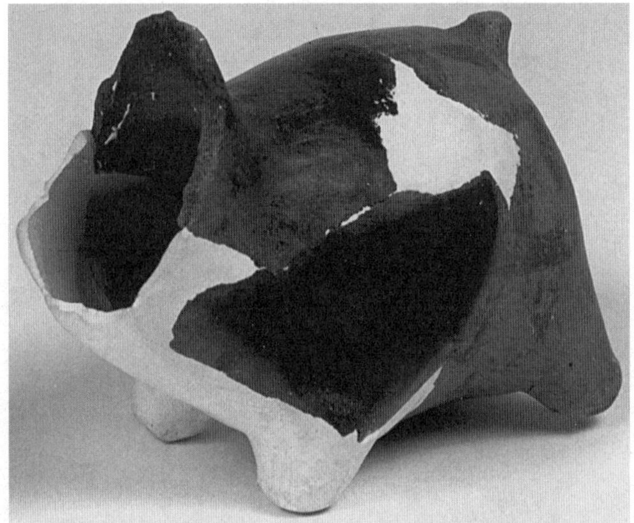

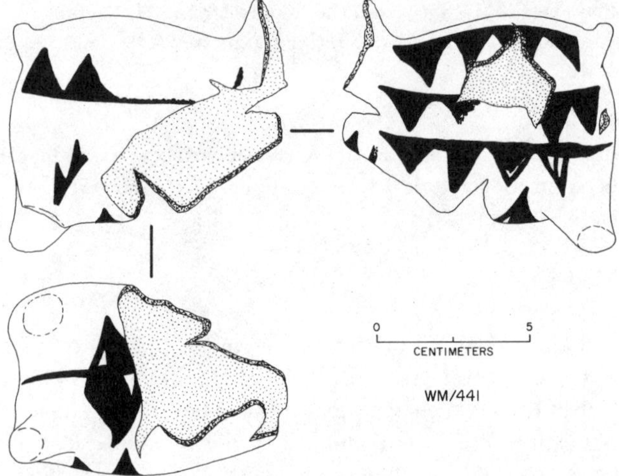

FIGURE 6.50. Modeled effigy (WM 441). Upper view: fragment of a hollow zoomorphic figure from the floor fill of House G. Lower view: illustration detailing the Mogollon Red-on-brown solid pendant triangle design (Neg. No. WM 149–15L).

TABLE 6.6. Worked Sherds Recovered from the Wind Mountain Site

Local Pottery	Jar Cover/ Counter Reference No. 288	Spindle Whorl/ Bead Reference No. 289	Rectanguloid Spoon/Scraper/ Eccentric Reference Nos. 290, 291	Trapezoidal Spoon/Eccentric/ Scraper Reference Nos. 292, 293	Trianguloid Scraper/Eccentric Reference No. 294	Ovoid Spoon/ Scraper/ Eccentric/ Scoop Reference Nos. 295, 296	Irregular Spoon/ Scraper/Scoop Reference Nos. 297, 298	Unclassified Fragment Reference No. 299	Total
Alma Plain	142	125	122	1	6	17	11	139	563
Alma Incised	4	–	1	–	–	–	–	1	6
Alma Neck Banded	2	–	1	–	–	–	–	1	4
San Francisco Red	79	125	49	2	2	2	4	46	309
Incised Redware	2	–	1	–	–	–	–	–	3
Mogollon Red-on-brown	14	18	10	–	–	2	1	13	58
Three Circle Red-on-white	50	81	56	2	–	1	2	17	209
Three Circle Neck Corrugated	1	1	–	–	–	–	–	3	5
Mimbres black-on-white series	138	136	101	6	3	13	11	81	489
Mimbres Polychrome	–	–	–	–	–	–	–	1	1
Mimbres Corrugated	–	1	–	–	–	–	–	–	1
Mimbres Rubbed Corrugated	16	2	2	–	–	–	1	–	21
Intrusive Pottery									
Tularosa Patterned Corrugated	–	–	–	–	–	–	–	1	1
Tularosa Fillet Rim	1	–	–	–	–	–	–	–	1
St. Johns Black-on-red	3	–	1	–	–	–	–	–	4
Total	452	489	344	11	11	35	30	303	1,675

FIGURE 6.51. Worked sherds identified as the jar cover/counter class, Reference No. 288. Worked sherds include Alma Plain, Mimbres Corrugated, Boldface Black-on-white, and St. Johns Black-on-red (upper right) types. Diameter of largest jar cover/counter measures 11.7 cm (Neg. No. WM 148–25L).

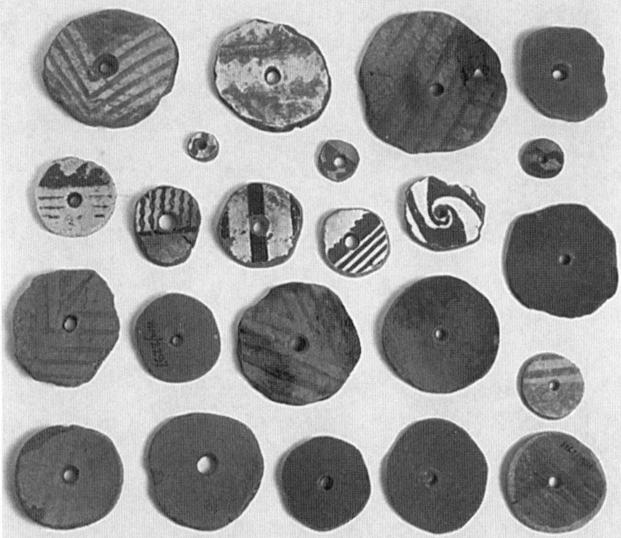

FIGURE 6.52. Worked sherds identified as the spindle whorl/bead class, Reference No. 289. Includes the Alma series, Mogollon Red-on-brown, Three Circle Red-on-white, and Boldface Black-on-white types. Diameter of the largest example measures about 7 cm (Neg. No. WM 147–28L).

Worked sherds primarily reflect pottery types made locally by Wind Mountain ceramists. Only six examples were made from intrusive types comprised of Tularosa Patterned Corrugated, Tularosa Fillet Rim, and St. Johns Black-on-red. Interestingly, though unpainted types (912 worked sherds or 55 percent) outnumber painted varieties (757 worked sherds or 45 percent), the relative amount of each is much closer than was observed in either the vessel or unworked sherd assemblages. Wind Mountain residents apparently preferred to retain the decorative motifs on their spindle whorls, scrapers, and ceramic scoops. Plain brownwares were, moreover, used almost exclusively for the largest jar covers. The dimensionally greater body sherds from large, unpainted storage jars were probably better suited for sealing wide-mouthed vessels than the more delicate, thin-walled redware or painted bowls.

TABLE 6.7. Solid Modeled Artifacts

	Cultural Context	Catalogue No.	Reference No.	Material	Type	Length (cm)	Width (cm)	Thickness (cm)
WM locus								
House K	Floor	WM/C 168	300	Burned clay	Plug	–	–	3.5*
House K	Floor	WM/C 169	300	Burned clay	Plug	–	–	3.2*
House L	Fill	WM 477	302	Alma Rough	Spindle whorl	5.0	4.7	1.0
House X	Fill	WM/C 612	300	Adobe	Jar cover	3.8+	2.4+	1.6
House X	Fill	WM/C 644	300	Adobe	Jar cover	3.9+	3.6+	1.7
House Y	Floor fill	WM/C 469	300	Burned clay	Jar cover	7.6	7.1	1.9
House AI	Fill	WM/C 1279	300	Burned clay	Jar cover	10.8	7.1+	3.7
Block 11-D	Extramural	WM 392	301	Burned clay	Plug	7.6	7.3	5.4
RO locus								
House J	Fill	RO/C 59	300	Burned clay	Jar cover	8.0	6.0+	2.0
House J	Floor fill	RO/C 61A	300	Burned clay	Jar cover	8.2+	7.2+	2.5
House J	Floor fill	RO/C 61B	300	Burned clay	Jar cover	6.0	5.0	1.7
House K	Floor fill	RO/C 81	300	Burned clay	Jar cover	8.0	7.7	2.7

*Diameter

FIGURE 6.53. Worked sherds identified as spoon/scraper/scoop classes, Reference Nos. 290–298 (refer to Table 6.6). Types include Alma Plain and Boldface Black-on-white. Length of largest example is about 21 cm (Neg. No. WM 147–31L).

FIGURE 6.54. Reserve Incised Corrugated and Reserve Punched Corrugated (lower row, second from right) sherds. It is suggested that this intrusive ceramic material came to Wind Mountain from the San Francisco/Reserve region (Neg. No. WM 147–7L).

Solid Modeled Artifacts

In contrast to worked sherds, Di Peso used this class to describe roughly modeled clay objects (Table 6.7). Most were shaped of raw, sun-dried or burned clay. Di Peso identified 12 solid modeled artifacts (Reference Nos. 300–302) that he believed were used mainly as plugs or to seal containers. Eight were classified as jar covers, three as plugs, and one as a chipped edge spindle whorl (the only fired artifact in this category).

Pottery Making Objects

Di Peso classified four types of objects that he suggested were indicative of the manufacture of ceramic vessels (Table 6.8). Incised (Reference No. 449) and sawed (Reference No. 450) sherds were presumably used to smooth vessel surfaces prior to firing. Clay fillets (Reference No. 451) represented prepared coils of raw clay from which jars and bowls were constructed. Lumps (Reference No. 452) were assumed to be the remains of unused potters' clay. These pottery making objects, together with the site's puddling or clay mixing basins, were considered evidence for ceramic production at Wind Mountain.

Exogenous Ceramics

Exogenous, trade, or, as Di Peso would have termed them, commerce wares, accounted for only a small fraction (n = 493 sherds representing all types) of the total ceramic material recovered from Wind Mountain. Painted types (n = 264 or 54 percent) slightly outnumbered plainware types (n = 229 or 46 percent). These intrusive wares were mainly represented in sherd form, though a partially complete Cibola whiteware bowl (WM/C 704) was removed from the fill of House X (Table 6.5). Only a trace (12 sherds) was recovered in direct association with architectural features (in Wind Mountain locus House P2; in Pits 21 and 27).

Despite their occurrence in only small quantities, and probably never constituting a substantial trade commodity, some commerce pottery was nevertheless transported to the site. Limited amounts of foreign material came to Wind Mountain from the San Francisco/Reserve (n = 229 sherds), from the Middle Gila (n = 15 sherds), from the Little Colorado

TABLE 6.8. Objects Used in the Manufacture of Pottery

Material	Incised Sherd Reference No. 449	Sawed Sherd Reference No. 450	Fillet Reference No. 451	Lump Reference No. 452	Total
Alma Plain	2	–	–	–	2
San Francisco Red	1	1	–	–	2
Mimbres Black-on-white series	2	–	–	–	2
Potter's clay	–	–	10	28	38
Total	5	1	10	28	44

FIGURE 6.55. Tularosa Fillet Rim sherds. Tularosa Fillet Rim was an intrusive pottery type found at Wind Mountain. Its origin of manufacture was probably in the San Francisco/Reserve region (Neg. No. WM 147–8L).

FIGURE 6.57. Hohokam style sherds. A handful of sherd material was either copied by Wind Mountain ceramists or represented true intrusive Hohokam ceramics possibly made in the vicinity of Safford, Arizona (Emil W. Haury, personal communication 1991) (Neg. No. WM 147-13L).

and Chaco (n = 107 sherds), Mesa Verde (n = 12 sherds), and the Jornada region (n = 130 sherds).

The San Francisco/Reserve Region

Four types of textured pottery from the San Francisco/Reserve region found their way into the Wind Mountain settlement, presumably during the Mangas and Mimbres phases. Approximately 83 highly textured, Reserve Incised Corrugated (Rinaldo and Bluhm 1956:155–169) c. A.D. 950–1125 and Reserve Punched Corrugated (Rinaldo and Bluhm 1956:155–169) c. A.D. 1000–1150, sherds were recovered (Figure 6.54). Another 123 examples of Tularosa Fillet Rim (Martin et al. 1952:63, 65) c. A.D. 1100–1300 were also collected (Figure 6.55). Rim sherds displayed the characteristic two or three narrow indented fillets, brown smoothed exteriors, and the hematite converted to magnetite glossy black interior walls (Lyon 1988; Peckham 1990:39). Twenty-three Tularosa Patterned Corrugated sherds (Rinaldo and Bluhm 1956:169–171), c. A.D. 1050 to 1250, with exterior surfaces showing an almost basketlike textured effect, were also recovered (Figure 6.56).

FIGURE 6.56. Tularosa Patterned Corrugated sherds. In addition to other intrusive textured wares (refer to Figures 6.54 and 6.55), Tularosa Patterned Corrugated represents one form of San Francisco/Reserve region ceramics recovered at Wind Mountain (Neg. No. WM 147–10L).

The Reserve and Tularosa textured types occur coincidentally with Mimbres Corrugated varieties made locally at Wind Mountain. These elaborate surface treatments reflect a continued interest by Mogollon people in decorative texturing—techniques that emerged early in the ceramic tradition with the onset of the Alma series.

The Gila Basin or Hohokam Wares

A scant four sherds of Hohokam manufacture were recovered at Wind Mountain. These sherds, originating in the Gila Basin (Emil W. Haury, personal communication 1990), were identified as Snaketown Red-on-buff. They exhibit the mica-schist and quartz temper, light-colored surface wash, and hachure dominated patterns associated with the type (Gladwin et al. 1937:189–192; Haury 1976:214–216). Haury suggested the Snaketown phase to date between c. A.D. 350–575 (1976:338), but more recently Dean (1991) placed it between c. A.D. 650 and 900, with a probable range in the A.D. 700s. Whatever the final resolution of the Hohokam sequence, the Snaketown Red-on-buff material came to Wind Mountain at some stage during the Pit House period.

A handful of sherds (n = 11) not assignable to specific type are also of possible Hohokam manufacture (Figure 6.57). Some may derive from the Safford area of eastern Arizona. The material recalls Sedentary period Hohokam ceramic making. Several sherds are reminiscent of Sacaton Red-on-buff and, perhaps, represent Tucson Basin or Safford area variants. Unlike the Sacaton Red-on-buff materials described at Snake-

FIGURE 6.58. White Mound Black-on-white sherds. One of several black-on-white intrusive ceramic types representing the Little Colorado/Chaco region (Neg. No. WM 147–22L).

FIGURE 6.60. Red Mesa Black-on-white sherds from the little Colorado/Chaco region (Neg. No. WM 147–25L).

town, for instance, at Wind Mountain the Hohokam pastes are not soft, nor do they exhibit surface pores (Haury 1976:205–207). Moreover, the cream background is a true slip (not a fugitive wash) that covers the exterior surfaces completely and bonds well with its base. These Hohokam sherds would have entered the site between either c. A.D. 900–1100 (Haury 1976:338) or c. A.D. 950–1150 (Dean 1991).

Wind Mountain ceramists presumably had some familiarity with Hohokam pottery. Several sherds show Hohokam-like designs, including the swastika and serrated lines, and may be of local manufacture. Temper and paste conform to Mogollon Red-on-brown and Three Circle Red-on-white ceramics. Although the rare occurrence of actual Hohokam pottery indicates it was not important to trade, interaction with the Hohokam is likely, given the quantities of Gulf of California shell observed at the site (Chapter 8 in this volume). Due to their infrequent occurrence, Hohokam vessels appear to have been incidental imports along with other trade goods. The new designs and styles on such imports may have been copied by Wind Mountain potters. A few Sedentary period Hohokam or Hohokam-like sherds have been found elsewhere in the Upper Gila (e.g., the Saige-McFarland site; Lekson 1990:102).

FIGURE 6.59. Kiatuthlanna Black-on-white sherds from the Little Colorado/Chaco region (Neg. No. WM 147–23L)

The Little Colorado/Chaco Region

Wind Mountain deposits yielded several painted wares from the Little Colorado/Chaco region, including White Mound Black-on-white, Kiatuthlanna Black-on-white, Red Mesa Black-on-white, Deadmans Black-on-red, St. Johns Black-on-red, and St. Johns Polychrome.

Six sherds of White Mound Black-on-white (Hawley 1936:23; Gladwin 1943:22, Plate 12), a late Basketmaker III to Early Pueblo I ware were recovered (Figure 6.58). All exhibit the gray paste and flaky white float characteristic of the type. White Mound Black-on-white has been discovered at other Mogollon sites, albeit in low quantities, such as Mogollon Village (Haury 1936a:26) and Tularosa Cave (Martin et al. 1952:67, 69). Haury (1936a:16–17, Figure 6) suggested that Mogollon Red-on-brown influenced the design and layout schemes of both White Mound Black-on-white and the later Kiatuthlanna Black-on-white. There may well be a connection. While Mogollon Red-on-brown displays design arrangements that cover the whole vessel surface, the earliest Basketmaker III wares, such as La Plata Black-on-white pottery, show large open fields (Haury 1936a:16–17, Figure 6). In contrast to La Plata Black-on-white, White Mound Black-on-white exhibits surface in-filling with extensive decorative zones. White Mound Black-on-white dates to c. A.D. 675–900, beginning only slightly later, or possibly even coincidentally, with Mogollon Red-on-brown.

The Wind Mountain trade sherd assemblage also contained 16 sherds of Kiatuthlanna Black-on-white (Roberts 1931:130–145; Hawley 1936:27–28; Gladwin 1943:24). Most sherds belonged to one bowl, though two additional vessels were probably represented (Figure 6.59). All sherds revealed the dense white slip, and sharp black lines associated with this Pueblo I pottery type c. A.D. 825–910. Kiatuthlanna Black-on-white was also reported in limited quantities at Mogollon Village (Haury 1936a:26), and at Tularosa Cave (Martin et al. 1952:67, 69).

Four weathered sherds of Red Mesa Black-on-white (Glad-

FIGURE 6.61. The widely distributed Little Colorado St. Johns Black-on-red pottery type was represented by several dozen sherds at Wind Mountain (Neg. No. WM 147–14L).

FIGURE 6.62. Mancos Black-on-white sherds. The far northern Mesa Verde ceramic tradition was represented by only a few sherds belonging to a single bowl (Neg. No. WM 147–26L).

win 1943:56, Plate 29) were found (Figure 6.60). Red Mesa developed from Kiatuthlanna c. A.D. 850 and extended into the initial stage of the Mimbres phase until c. A.D. 1100. White Mound and Kiatuthlanna were introduced into the Wind Mountain site during the Late Pit House period, and Red Mesa Black-on-white may be a later arrival, co-occurring with the production of Mimbres phase pottery, c. A.D. 1000. Red Mesa Black-on-white was reported at Harris Village (Haury 1936a:66) and at the Saige-McFarland site (Lekson 1990:102).

Little Colorado/Chaco Region pottery was also represented by black-on-red painted types. Only two sherds of Deadmans Black-on-red were identified (Hawley 1936:26, 28; Colton and Hargrave 1937:70–71), but the highly polished red slip and mineral paint were unmistakable. Deadmans Black-on-red dates c. A.D. 800 to 1050 and is, therefore, contemporaneous with the end of the Late Pit House period and beginning of the Pueblo period at Wind Mountain.

Some 64 sherds of St. Johns Black-on-red (Carlson 1970:29–31) and another 15 St. Johns Polychrome (Gladwin and Gladwin 1931:36–37; Carlson 1970:31–41) fragments were recovered (Figure 6.61). Both types date to c. A.D. 1175–1300, though the polychrome form may originate a bit later, c. A.D. 1200 (Carlson 1970:39), and must have appeared at the settlement during its final occupation. Centered in the Little Colorado and Cibola regions, St. Johns Polychrome is one of the most widely distributed of any prehistoric ceramic type. It appears throughout much of the Southwest toward the end of the A.D. 1100s. All the Wind Mountain St. Johns Polychrome sherds are the remains of bowls that retained only traces of their exterior kaolin painted design.

The Mesa Verde Region

Originating far to the north of the settlement, Mesa Verde pottery was represented by 12 sherds belonging to a single Mancos Black-on-white bowl (Hawley 1936:45). Large sherds exhibited the characteristic blue-gray paste and mineral paint design (Figure 6.62). Mancos Black-on-white is a Pueblo II ware, dating c. A.D. 900–1150. It overlaps with Kiatuthlanna Black-on-white (during its final stage) and Red Mesa Black-on-white, as well as with the Three Circle Red-on-white, Boldface Black-on-white, and Mimbres Classic Black-on-white made at Wind Mountain.

FIGURE 6.63. El Paso Polychrome sherds. One of two intrusive polychrome types (with St. Johns Polychrome) recovered from the site. El Paso Polychrome was represented by several dozen sherds (Neg. No. WM 147–19L).

The Jornada Region

The easterly adjacent Jornada region was represented by three post-A.D. 1100 wares. One of two polychromes observed at Wind Mountain, 85 sherds of El Paso Polychrome (Hawley 1936:64–65; Sayles 1936), c. A.D. 1100–1350, were collected (Figure 6.63). The Wind Mountain El Paso Polychrome material displays much variation, a characteristic generally associated with the type. The paint is fugitive, and designs commonly exfoliate. Varying shades of red (from maroon, to brick red, to brown) and black dominate.

TABLE 6.9. Intrusive Pottery Types Identified by Di Peso and Their Revised Classifications

Di Peso Type	Point of Origin	Revised Type
Armadillo Red	Zacatecas	San Francisco Red
Convento Red	Chihuahua	San Francisco Red
Cuchujaqui Red	Sonora	San Francisco Red
Highlands Lake Country Red	Zacatecas	San Francisco Red
Morales Red	Zacatecas	San Francisco Red
Negative A	Durango	indeterminate
Playas Red Standard	Chihuahua	San Francisco Red
Teuchitlan Red	Durango	San Francisco Red
Venedito Brown	Sonora	Alma Plain
Casas Grandes Pattern Incised	Chihuahua	Alma Pattern Incised
Casas Grandes Tool Punched	Chihuahua	Alma Series
Cloverdale Corrugated	Chihuahua	Mimbres Style Corrugated
Convento Pattern Incised	Chihuahua	Alma Pattern Incised
Playas Red Textured	Chihuahua	San Francisco Red Patterned
Anchondo Red-on-brown	Chihuahua	Mogollon Red-on-brown
Chico Red-on-brown	Durango	Mogollon Red-on-brown
Leal Red-on-brown	Chihuahua	Mogollon Red-on-brown
Victoria Red-on-brown Textured	Chihuahua	Alma Pattern Incised with paint
Lolandis Red Rim	Zacatecas	Mogollon Red-on-brown
Pilon Red Rim	Chihuahua	Mogollon Red-on-brown
Corralitos Polychrome	Chihuahua	El Paso Polychrome
Las Ventanas Polychrome	Zacatecas	El Paso Polychrome
Santa Cruz Polychrome	Sonora	El Paso Polychrome
Villa Ahumada Polychrome	Chihuahua	El Paso Polychrome

In contrast, Three Rivers Red-on-terracotta (Mera and Stallings 1931; Hawley 1936:65–66), represented by a mere two sherds, was a finely made ceramic with none of the friable surface tendencies of El Paso Polychrome. Though the red paint is sometimes fugitive, surfaces are well smoothed or polished, and the interior carries a float. Tempering materials contain much sand, and design motifs consist primarily of narrow line and solid band motifs. Three Rivers Red-on-terracotta, c. A.D. 1125–1300, was coexistent with El Paso Polychrome.

FIGURE 6.64. Chupadero Black-on-white sherds. Chupadero Black-on-white is generally intrusive from the east and southeast. Its bold black-on-white designs and interior scoring easily identify the type (Neg. No. WM 147–27L).

Chupadero Black-on-white (Mera 1931; Hawley 1936:67) was the third Jornada type recovered from Wind Mountain, in the form of 43 sherds. As is true of the site's other trade wares, Chupadero Black-on-white was represented by a handful of bowl and jar sherds (Figure 6.64). It was identifiable by the striations that score interior vessel surfaces. These marks probably result from using a corn cob or pine cone to smooth the vessel walls. Design elements include solid black elements in combination with hachures. Chupadero Black-on-white ranges in time between A.D. 1150 and 1550, and thereby constitutes a late arrival in the Wind Mountain occupation. A single Chupadero Black-on-white sherd was reported from Saige-McFarland (Lekson 1990:102).

Intrusive Ceramics from the South

When Di Peso examined the Wind Mountain sherd assemblage, he felt that a variety of types originating in Chihuahua, Sonora, Durango, and Zacatecas had been brought to the site by southern traders (Table 6.9). After careful reanalysis, this sherd component appears to principally reflect the local Mogollon ceramic making tradition and its associated types as well as some intrusives from other regions of the Mogollon. Parenthetically, Di Peso's original taxonomic specimens have been preserved for reference at the Amerind Foundation.

Turning first to the redwares, the entire collection seems to represent San Francisco Red in all the variability (e.g., presence or absence of dimpling; high surface polish versus matte smoothing; among other attributes) expected for the type. A portion of the redware collection exhibited surface texturing. It is believed this textured red pottery was of local manufacture. Paste and temper appear to be equivalent to the San Francisco Red vessels and sherds from the site, and a new type name has been proposed, San Francisco Red Patterned.

The plain brownwares, on the other hand, principally represent the Alma series, including Alma Plain, Alma Black Burnished, and the various Alma textured types. In a few instances, texturing is combined with simple red painted designs. This combination of surface texturing and painting, while uncommon, does persistently occur in Mogollon ceramics. As with the redwares, pastes and tempers conform to the Alma series vessels and sherds. A few brownware textured sherds were, however, of nonlocal production. Though Di Peso located their points of origins to the south, this material more likely represents Reserve textured types from the San Francisco/Reserve region.

Similarly, the red-on-brown painted pottery identified with Chihuahua and Durango corresponds to accepted variability in the Mogollon Red-on-brown type. Particularly, because Di Peso's identifications rely on at most six sherds per designation, it seems incautious to assign the names of distant pottery types when their attributes conform to local Mogollon ceramics.

Finally, all the polychromes Di Peso associated with Chihuahua, Sonora, or Zacatecas are, in fact, the highly variable and ubiquitous El Paso Polychrome.

Wind Mountain Ceramic Assemblage Discussion

Any ceramic assemblage derived from repetitive occupations at a single site over the long term has the potential to illustrate the changing patterns that characterize the tradition, such as the emergence of discrete types and trends in design and form. Specifically, the development of Mogollon brown and red pottery types and the production of whitewares unfold at Wind Mountain. Early unpainted Alma series brown and San Francisco Red plain and textured ceramics, the first painted types identified as Mogollon Red-on-brown and Three Circle Red-on-white, the raised and pinched coils of Three Circle Neck Corrugated, the corrugated decorations of Mimbres Corrugated, as well as Boldface and Mimbres Classic Black-on-white wares constitute the Mogollon sequence. Together these types represent the evolution of the Mogollon ceramic tradition.

In the main, the ceramics recovered from the Wind Mountain site conform to previously published descriptions of Mogollon types (refer to Haury 1936b), though certain departures are apparent. A degree of morphological variability and technical experimentation is to be expected with any long-lived tradition. Diagnostic indicators originally used to distinguish types may predominate, though ancillary attributes may evince localized expressions. For example, the red-on-brown painted pottery from Wind Mountain shows a color range from red to purple to brown. Both redwares and brownwares contain large quantities of mica. Materials used to temper pottery were diverse and included andesite, basalt, quartzite, sand, and possibly biotite schist.

Variability in the physical properties of pottery types is possibly the result of prehistoric ceramists testing and sampling various clay, mineral, and stone sources. Most of the material constituents identified in the Wind Mountain ceramic assemblage were available nearby in the Big and Little Burro Mountains. The use of volcanic glass, the single instance of exotic stone used as a tempering agent, was found in a Mimbres Classic Black-on-white bowl sherd (Appendix 6). This may well reflect the addition of crushed obsidian debitage initially procured for lithic production, not the importation of Mimbres Classic Black-on-white vessels to Wind Mountain.

Variation in the Wind Mountain assemblage was undoubtedly due to the human desires and designs of Wind Mountain potters. During the several hundred years that Alma series ceramics were produced, a few vessels show painting combined with texturing. In the case of San Francisco Red, the red slip was occasionally manipulated as paint to create simple designs which decorate some bowl exteriors. Texturing was added to a component of the San Francisco Red assemblage, opening the way for a new type designation, San Francisco Red Patterned. Over the course of time that San Francisco Red vessels were made, hard and thin, highly polished walls began to be replaced by less well polished, thick-walled pieces. Perhaps, as corrugated pottery became more popular and the demand for San Francisco Red decreased, less attention was paid to finishing this once dominant utility ware.

Design Trends

The temporal and material breadth of the Wind Mountain ceramic assemblage is particularly illustrative for tracing the development of individual pottery types that collectively form the Mimbres Mogollon tradition. The typological continuum in which earlier types are obvious predecessors to later arrivals in the sequence is apparent in both unpainted and painted wares. By way of comparison, Three Circle Neck Corrugated

FIGURE 6.65. Comparisons between Mogollon Red-on-brown and Three Circle Red-on-white designs. The design trends in Mogollon painted pottery are clearly evident when comparing these two bowl fragments. Parallel lines and "squared" central pendant triangle motifs decorate both types. In Mogollon Red-on-brown (left, Neg. No. WM 145–36L) the design is simplified as compared to the more complex Three Circle Red-on-white painting (right, Neg. No. WM 145–33L). In tracking the temporal progression of Mogollon painted types, Mogollon Red-on-brown is a clear precursor to Three Circle Red-on-white.

FIGURE 6.66. Mogollon Red-on-brown (left) and Three Circle Red-on-white (right) design similarities. These two bowl fragments display virtually the same decorative motif. The primary difference is the closed interlocking design element in Three Circle Red-on-white, whereas the Mogollon Red-on-brown motif remains open (Neg. No. WM 146–29L).

has clear affinities with the Alma series, especially Alma Neck Banded and Alma Tool Punched (refer to Figure 6.21). The practice of incising between rim and shoulder, the elaborated indented final band, as well as the predominance of jar shapes over bowls, are common characteristics of both types. In Three Circle Neck Corrugated, however, incising and indenting are usually executed with greater precision and symmetry, while jars achieve greater size, though forms are analogous between the two types.

The developmental relationships among types are, perhaps, of greatest interest when examining painted wares. Compared with plainwares, the ceramist's creativity in terms of approaches to design layout, decorative motifs, and composition are more sophisticated and further ranging. This is not to disparage the technological refinement of unpainted and textured vessels, which was considerable, but painted pottery seems to voice more of a potter's individuality (and cultural connectedness) through graphic expression.

Developing design trends of Mogollon pottery are conspicuous when comparing the influence of Mogollon Red-on-brown on Three Circle Red-on-white. Mogollon Red-on-brown with its quartered design layout is characterized by rectilinear geometric design fields dominated by pendent triangles and parallel lines (Figures 6.65 and 6.66). This decorative treatment is clearly carried over into Three Circle Red-on-white in which interlocking scrolls are added to the line work (Figure 6.67). Other geometric elements are executed in quartered arrangements covering the entire design surfaces of vessels (refer to Figures 6.17 and 6.20). The practice of polishing over painted designs (slightly blurring the motifs) persists from Mogollon Red-on-brown to Three Circle Red-

FIGURES 6.67. Mogollon Red-on-brown and Three Circle Red-on-white designs. Sherds exhibiting a strong design continuum from Mogollon Red-on-brown (left, Neg. No. WM 145–19L) through Three Circle Red-on-white (right, Neg. No. WM 146–24L). Parallel lines and solid triangles are common design elements on both types. In Three Circle Red-on-white, however, these are combined with scrolls and checkerboards — motifs commonly found on the succeeding type, Boldface Black-on-white or Style II ceramics.

on-white. In the latter, however, overpolishing is performed with a lighter hand, so that the edges of the designs remain crisp. In the early Wind Mountain painted ceramics assemblage there are bowls with simple designs ordinarily associated with Mogollon Red-on-brown, yet they have a white slip characteristic of Three Circle Red-on-white. Alternatively, there are red-on- brown vessels decorated with the interlocking scrolls usually attributed to Three Circle Red-on-white.

The primary difference between the two types is the white slip of Three Circle Red-on-white. The composition and decorative motifs of both types (though the early designs are limited to bands and solid triangles with other elements added subsequently) are essentially similar, incorporating a combination of rectilinear geometric decorations which cover the surfaces of each. Haury (1936b:21) has postulated an influence of Anasazi ceramists at this time (C. A.D. 750–950; Pueblo I) on Mogollon potters (late San Francisco phase through Three Circle phase) who adapted the white slip from northern whitewares.

A continuum of decorative styles is evident between Three Circle Red-on-white and its successor, Boldface Black-on-white. The quartered design layout observed in Mogollon Red-on-brown and Three Circle Red-on-white carries over into Boldface Black-on-white. Interlocking geometric elements, as well as newly appearing naturalistic motifs, including flowers, are reminiscent of the paired spiral combinations of Three Circle Red-on-white. Unlike the tendency of earlier Mogollon ceramists to fill all vessel surfaces, design fields are integrated with open zones free of any painted decoration. The use of open fields is evocative of Anasazi ceramics and may, together with the production of whitewares, indicate a growing influence from the north on Mogollon pottery production. Apparently, during a period of overlap when Three Circle Red-on-white was accompanied by Boldface Black-on-white, polishing over the painted designs decreases. There are, however, red-on-white and black-on-white bowls both with and without overpolishing. The characteristic thick, chalky slip common to Three Circle Red-on-white is sometimes applied to vessels that otherwise display all the attributes of Boldface Black-on-white.

With the emergence of Mimbres Classic Black-on-white, geometric motifs are arranged within complex design panels bordered by parallel framing lines. Central design fields are separated by open zones. Compositions do not subscribe to a quartered layout and overpolishing does not occur. Life form motifs are a hallmark of Mimbres Classic Black-on-white. Though Wind Mountain's Mimbres phase ceramic component was small, anthropomorphic and zoomorphic designs were represented.

Viewed in total, the Wind Mountain ceramic assemblage demonstrates the developmental relationship of Mogollon pottery types. The influence of earlier types on later types is clear, perhaps most apparent through transformations of design composition, layout, and surface treatments, including painting, slipping, and texturing.

Vessel Form and Function

Prehistoric Wind Mountain ceramists produced large and small jars, pitchers, bowls, ladles, and scoops among other pottery forms. In determining possible functions of ceramic objects, common sense dictates that vessels were used to cook, serve, and store foods, as water containers, and as all purpose receptacles. Textured and plainware globular, wide-mouthed jars were probably used for dry and liquid storage. Other jars served as cooking pots; sooted exterior bases and sides attested to their association with hearths. Small-mouthed containers could be tightly sealed to prevent rodent or insect infestation and, perhaps, to limit the evaporation of liquids. Bowls may have functioned for short term storage of comestibles or, with some seed jars and miniatures, to keep paint pigments, shells, and small objects. Shallow forms appear better suited to serving individual meals, comparable to modern plate forms. No bowls display the carbon accumulation exhibited by jars, an indication that their primary function may not have been for cooking. Scoops and ladles were undoubtedly utilized to transfer materials from one container to another.

In addition to subsistence related uses, the presence of standard sized and miniature ceramic containers in numerous Wind Mountain burials (Tables 6.4; 9.2) establishes the importance of pottery as a funerary offering. In contrast, some miniatures may not have had a pragmatic use whatsoever, but represent the tokens of children's efforts to copy the ceramic vessels produced by adult potters.

Informal examination of Wind Mountain whole vessels and rim sherds may indicate that bowls and jars of all types tend to increase in size over time. The tendency toward larger vessels has been noted for the Mimbres Mogollon (including the Mimbres phase) ceramics generally (Haury 1936b:22, 28–29; Taylor 1984:72–74, dealing exclusively with funerary vessels). This is not to imply that large vessels superseded small ones, rather that they became more common in the Mimbres Mogollon sequence. At Wind Mountain, for example, the inclination toward larger, deeper bowls is especially noticeable when comparing San Francisco forms to either Boldface or Mimbres Classic Black-on-white vessels.

It has been suggested that increases in vessel size may be linked to the appearance of larger communities and their associated human populations (Haury 1976:226), which may, in turn, be related to a responding need for agricultural intensification (Braun 1980, 1983). For instance, large bowls may reflect the larger social units they serve, and large capacity jars may indicate the presence of greater amounts of stored food and, ergo, increased sedentism. To explore the possibility that changes in the Wind Mountain ceramic assemblage might correlate with alterations in settlement population or subsistence practices, its pottery was assessed in the broader context of the site as a whole.

The bulk of the ceramic inventory recovered from Wind Mountain, consisting of painted and unpainted redwares and brownwares together with Boldface Black-on-white, dates c. A.D. 1000 and earlier. In contrast, the Mimbres phase habitation is represented by a sparse dozen rooms and a comparably small ceramic component. Although the number of structures belonging to the Pit House and Pueblo periods approaches 100, Wind Mountain was probably never a large settlement at any time during its sequence of occupations. Furthermore, nothing in either its material or macrobotanical inventories suggests an increase in agricultural dependence. Instead, subsistence, based on a broad spectrum exploitation of wild plants and animals, plus corn, beans, squash, and agave cultivation, as well as domestic turkeys (and dogs?) is inferred from a multipurpose ceramic and lithic assemblage, charred botanical remains, and faunal data. Interestingly, no increase in the number of storage vessels over time was observed, a tendency which would be expected if larger quantities of agricultural produce were harvested and maintained.

In other words, the move to large vessel manufacture occurs even though no changes in either site size (i.e., inferred population) or increased agricultural product are documented. Though subsistence activities most likely affect vessel size, other factors (probably related to stylistic preferences) contribute to changing vessel capacities. Besides the trend from smaller to larger vessels, increased standardization of size ranges and forms are markedly apparent from early to late at Wind Mountain. Much internal variability characterizes the Alma series. Jars and bowls are asymmetrical, bases can be either flat or rounded, and vessels exhibit idiosyncracies no doubt tied to the skills and care exercised by the individual potter. This variation is absent from San Francisco Red ware in which bowl forms conform to a strict hemispherical form. Though large, medium, and small shallow and deep bowls were manufactured, within these general form and size categories, vessels adhere to formalized modes of production. The conventionalized nature of Mimbres Mogollon ceramics, expressed in the morphological attributes of size, form, and surface treatment, describes all types, including those of the Pueblo period as ceramists established acceptable parameters of pottery production. Size and form variability in Wind Mountain ceramics, therefore, probably relate more to the predilections of those making and using the vessels, than to an expanding population involved in more intensive agriculture.

Wind Mountain Ceramics in Regional Perspective

The limited amount of exogenous or trade pottery collected from the site suggests that Wind Mountain residents relied on locally produced ceramics, and that intrusive vessels never constituted highly desired trade items. Yet Wind Mountain did participate in some type of procurement or exchange network, if only on a low level, as indicted by the presence of a few exotic wares as well as other commodities, including marine shell and obsidian.

Temporally, the exogenous pottery assemblage seems to range from the middle of the San Francisco phase, c. A.D. 700, to the site's final occupation in the Mimbres phase, c. A.D. 1150/1200. Geographically, intrusive ceramic types mainly represent the San Francisco/Reserve region, the Little Colorado and Chaco area, the Hohokam or Middle Gila, Mesa Verde, and the Jornada. A direct relationship between Wind Mountain and northern Mexico is more problematical and cannot be demonstrated with any confidence.

The View North and West

The earliest exogenous pottery at Wind Mountain derives from the Little Colorado and Chaco regions in the form of White Mound Black-on-white (from c. A.D. 675), Deadmans Black-on-red (from c. A.D. 800), and Kiatuthlanna Black-on-white (from c. A.D. 825). Both black-on-white types have been reported from other Mogollon sites (e.g., Tularosa Cave and Mogollon Village) and may support Haury's (1936b:27) early contention that contact between the Mogollon and the Anasazi may be seen in the influence of Mogollon Red-on-brown on the design development of Pueblo I pottery (in this particular instance, Kiatuthlanna Black-on-white A.D. 825–910). In any event, some interaction, apparently limited, between the Mimbres Mogollon and Anasazi during the Late Pit House period is indicated by the presence of northern wares at Wind Mountain.

The precise temporal position of another early intrusive, Snaketown Red-on-buff, is equivocal in light of the revised Hohokam chronology. Haury (1976:338) dated Snaketown Red-on-buff before A.D. 500, although Dean (1991) now places the type in the A.D. 700s. If Haury's date is accurate, Snaketown Red-on-buff would constitute the single earliest—falling into the Early Pit House period—trade ceramic recovered at the site. If Dean is correct, as seems likely, Snaketown Red-on-buff would co-occur with White Mound and Kiatuthlanna Black-on-white.

A slightly later complement of trade wares, associated with a post-A.D. 900 occupation, at Wind Mountain includes Little Colorado-area Red Mesa Black-on-white (from c. A.D. 850), Mancos Black-on-white (from c. A.D. 900) from Mesa Verde, as well as Hohokam Sacaton Red-on-buff (Dean 1991:64), Tucson or Safford varieties. The northern connection continues, but it is impossible to gauge the intensity of the contact from so little data (one fragmentary Mancos Black-on-white bowl and a handful of sherds). Intrusive Sacaton Red-on-buff (and possibly the Wind Mountain copies of Sedentary period Hohokam ceramics) may have come into the site as late as the early A.D. 1100s.

The View North, West, and East

The final group of trade wares extends the geographic range of intrusives beyond the Little Colorado/Chaco and the Hohokam to include the San Francisco/Reserve and the Jornada regions. Ceramics are represented by Reserve textured types (from c. A.D. 1000), Tularosa Fillet Rim (from c. A.D. 1100), Tularosa Patterned Corrugated (from c. A.D. 1050), St. Johns Black-on-red and St. Johns Polychrome (both from c. A.D. 1175), Three Rivers Red-on-terracotta (from c. A.D. 1125), Chupadero Black-on-white (from c. A.D. 1150), and El Paso Polychrome (from c. A.D. 1100). Some of these types, especially St. Johns Polychrome, Chupadero Black-on-white, and El Paso Polychrome were probably introduced to Wind Mountain during the site's final occupation. Others, such as Reserve Incised Corrugated (c. A.D. 950–1125), may have occurred during the transition from the Mangas phase to the Mimbres phase.

The majority of the exogenous types deriving from the San Francisco/Reserve consist of textured, unpainted wares that may have developed out of the principal Mogollon brown pottery, Alma Plain. In keeping with a strong preference for textured pottery—a predilection that characterizes so much of the Mogollon ceramic sequence—most of the intrusive material from this area is of unpainted, patterned types. In contrast, the painted intrusive pottery, with the exception of St. Johns Red-on-black, is represented by only a handful of sherds per type.

The View South

Although exogenous pottery can be assigned directly to northern sources, as well as the Middle Gila to the west, and the Jornada region to the east of Wind Mountain, no trade ceramics recovered from the site were positively attributable to Mexico. Even so, a large portion of Mexico from Zacatecas, Durango, Jalisco, and Colima northward to Chihuahua and Sonora is distinguished by a red and brown ceramic tradition of greater time depth than exists in the American Southwest. The wares of Chupicuaro and the Chalchihuites of Zacatecas are suggested to have contributed to ceramic traditions in the north (Kelley 1966:102). Di Peso (1979c:49) proposed that local Wind Mountain folk played a recipient role c. A.D. 700 by accepting many southern cultural traits, among them painted wares from the Morrett site in Colima—pottery he believed gave rise to his Wind Mountain Black-on-white. Such specific contact is difficult to support with the ceramic data from Wind Mountain, but the likelihood that a *general* relationship existed between Mogollon ceramics and certain northern Mexico types is inescapable.

For example, a red-on-brown painted tradition, though displaying much local variation, occurs throughout most of the southern American Southwest and northern Mexico. In the Mogollon region of central Arizona and New Mexico the red-on-brown ware is subsumed under the Mogollon Red-on-brown type name. In the San Simon Valley of southeastern Arizona, Sayles (1945) identified a series of red-on-brown types, such as Galiuro and Encinas Red-on-brown, among others, associated with San Simon Village. In the San Pedro Valley area, still other types, including Benson Red-on-brown, Cascabel Red-on-brown, Deep Well Red-on-brown, Dragoon Red-on-brown, and Tres Alamos Red-on-brown, have been identified (Tuthill 1947:50–54). In the Casas Grandes Valley of Chihuahua, Mexico, Anchondo Red-on-brown, Fernando Red-on-brown, Leal Red-on-brown, and possibly Pilon Red Rim have many affinities with red-on-brown types of Arizona and New Mexico (Di Peso et al. 1974:6:30–31).

This similarity among pottery types distributed across such a vast region is duplicated by many unpainted, plain or textured redwares and brownwares. San Francisco Red has obvious parallels with Dragoon Red of southern Arizona, as well as Convento Red and Playas Red of Chihuahua. San Francisco Red Patterned from Wind Mountain is reminiscent of the Alma series textured types and Playas Red Incised from Chihuahua. Other textured wares, such as Reserve Incised Corrugated, bear a resemblance not only to the Alma series but also to Convento Pattern Incised Corrugated (Di Peso et al. 1974:6:31). Moreover, rim sherds of Alma Scored are virtually indistinguishable from Convento Scored with vertical patterning recovered from Casas Grandes (Di Peso et al. 1974:6:31). Analogies are also evident between the smoothed, rubbed, and polished corrugated wares accompanying Boldface Black-on-white and Mimbres Classic Black-on-white ceramics and later occurring Cloverdale Corrugated and Casas Grandes Rubbed Corrugated from Chihuahua (Di Peso et al. 1974:6:130–134).

The distribution of so many allied red and brown types indicates the existence across a great geographic expanse of a broad ceramic tradition characterized by many of the same generic attributes. Universal affinities among the wares comprising this "macrotradition" of brown and redwares include similar methods of surface treatment, such as polishing over designs, incising, grooving, painted and textured decorative motifs, coil and scrape manufacturing techniques, and vessel morphology. Resemblances among various ceramic types are so strong as to suggest interaction among the human inhabitants of the region resulting in shared technologies and stylistic expressions. Neither the chronology nor the mechanisms of contact are fully known, but there can be little doubt that, for example, Mogollon Red-on-brown and Anchondo Red-on-brown are local aspects of a developing style that described an enormous region of pottery making. Wind Mountain ceramics represent both localized pottery traditions developing over a period of successive site occupations as well as the participation by generations of ceramists in a geographically wide ranging tradition that emphasized the production of brownwares and redwares.

7

The Lithic Assemblage
Ground and Chipped Stone

Virtually all prehistoric peoples relied on stone as their principal raw material for making tools. In the Wind Mountain material inventory, stone artifacts, either as whole or fragmentary implements or as manufacturing debris, represented (after sherds) the single largest category of objects recovered. The residents of Wind Mountain were fortunate that the stone resources located near their settlement were abundant, diverse, and easily accessible. Cherts and chalcedony were as close as the base of the site ridge. Andesite, basalt, granite, and welded tuff, among other materials, could, with little difficulty, be carried back to the settlement from adjacent mountain slopes. The Wind Mountain inhabitants shaped raw stone into a myriad of large and small objects. In architecture, they used stone for wall reinforcement, hearth liners, support post wedges, shelves, and other features. They crushed stone and minerals for paints and temper. Some stone objects even provide hints into their ritual activities and preferences in items of personal adornment. But by far the major use for stone in the Wind Mountain settlement was in the production of implements to sustain daily life. Ground and chipped stone tools for obtaining, cultivating, and processing food, as well as in the manufacture of other implements, were especially plentiful, outnumbering all other lithic artifact classes defined at the site.

Di Peso viewed all objects associated with domestic tasks as "utilitarian," a broad classification including most classes of ground and chipped stone. The primary utility tools, belonging to each general category, such as nether stone, handstone, or projectile point/knife, are described according to Di Peso's type definitions (refer to Appendix 5).

Ground Stone

Ground stone objects are shaped by pecking, polishing, or purposeful abrasion through usage. At Wind Mountain the classification of multipurpose tools comprises many different types. The inventory includes objects as different as a metate 65 cm in length and weighing more than 58 kg (Catalogue No. WM 2465), to a delicate, miniature stone palette (Catalogue No. WM 2521) measuring less than 6 cm at its greatest dimension. The raw stone used to produce the numerous types of ground stone tools is also variable, reflecting a broad pattern of lithic procurement. Stone, fashioned by the settlement's residents, could be coarse and granular or dense and fine with all gradations between. Although much of the Wind Mountain ground stone assemblage is directly associated with subsistence activities, the presence of many other tasks are implied. Indeed, the lithic assemblage is particularly useful in elucidating the demands of daily living that confronted the occupants of the site.

Nether Stones: Metates and Grinding Slabs

Metates and grinding slabs traditionally associated with processing both organic and inorganic materials constitute a large class of artifacts subsumed under Di Peso's broad nether stone category. A metate, or grinding, slab was described as a nether stone on which some substance was pulverized. Di Peso identified several nether stone types, employing commonly recognized Southwestern ground stone terminology (Figure 7.1).

Following his descriptive terminology, slab metates (Reference Nos. 1 and 2) were characterized by reciprocal (back and forth) grinding wear patterns on a flat surface using an arm stroke of 30 cm or more. They were made from naturally

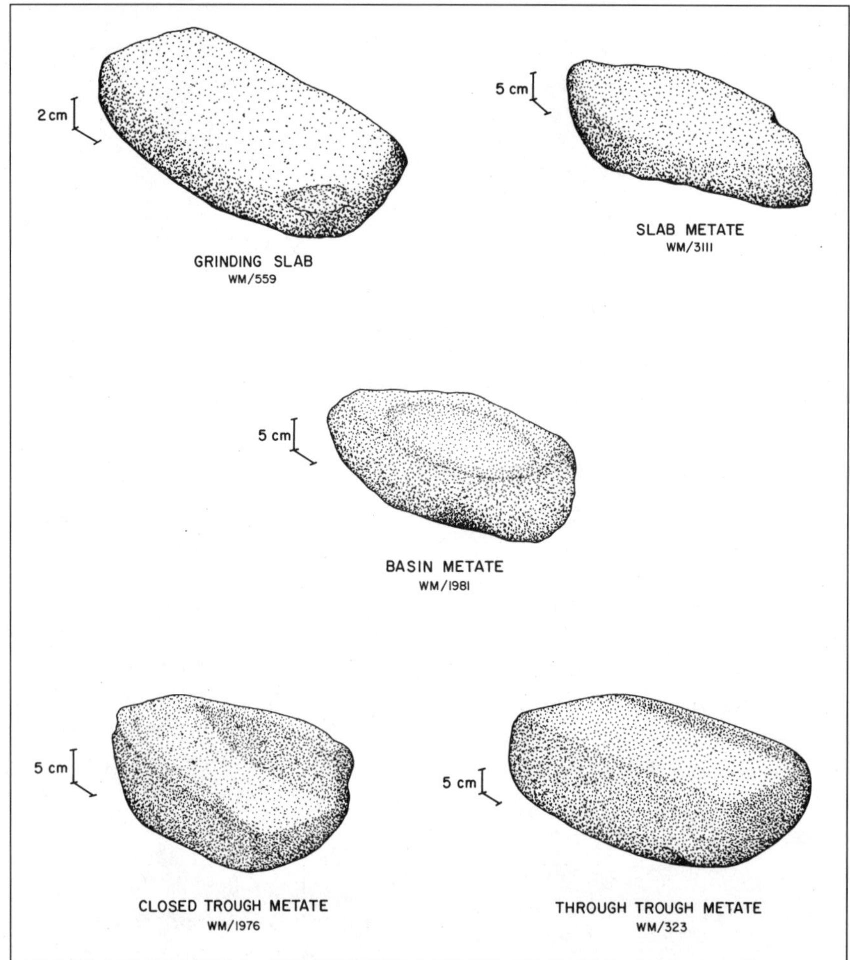

FIGURE 7.1. Examples of nether stone types associated with reference numbers. Grinding slab (WM 559), Reference No. 30; Slab metate (WM 3111), Reference No. 2; Basin metate (WM 1981), Reference No. 81; Closed trough metate (WM 1976), Reference No. 41; Through trough metate (WM 323), Reference No. 44. In Di Peso's classification, nether stones are the stationary lower halves of two piece fitted pulverizers with coincident parts used in reciprocal action.

occurring, fortuitously shaped stone slabs or boulders. Types defined as grinding slabs (Reference Nos. 28–31) exhibited attributes similar to slab metates, except the associated arm stroke measured less than 30 cm. Basin metates, (Reference Nos. 81 and 82) though also made on slabs or boulders, displayed a rotary grinding action that hollowed out the working surface, the result of material processing. The arm stroke on basin metates measured less than 30 cm. Closed trough (Reference Nos. 41 and 42) and through trough (Reference Nos. 43 and 44) metates exhibited reciprocal grinding wear patterns with an arm stroke of more than 30 cm. In addition, three unclassified metate types (Reference Nos. 88, 89, and 89A) were identified. These unclassified types were either produced from boulders and slabs or were indeterminate as to form. Trough metates and grinding slabs tended to be the most elaborate of the nether stone types, often displaying shaping and edge trimming. In contrast, slab and basin metates show little modification but for the pecking used to prepare their processing surfaces (see also Haury 1936a:30–31; Di Peso et al. 1974:7:419–422; Lekson 1990:67).

More than 480 whole or fragmentary metates and grinding slabs were recovered from Wind Mountain structures, features, and extramural excavation blocks. Complete or substantially complete examples were rare; only 105 were found. In comparison, numerous fragments (n = 382) were collected, indicative of the heavy use such implements received. Most fragmentary metates and grinding slabs were obtained either from the trash fill of structures or from extramural contexts at the site. A few metates, exhausted of their original func-

TABLE 7.1. Variation in Nether Stone Types over Time

Nether Stone Type	EPHP	GT	SF	Transitional SF/TC	TC	Mangas	Mimbres	Total
Slab metates Reference Nos. 1 and 2	1	1	1	–	–	–	–	3
Grinding slabs Reference Nos. 28–31	–	2	6	1	7	2	–	18
Closed trough metates Reference Nos. 41 and 42	–	1	4	1	6	–	–	12
Through trough metates Reference Nos. 43 and 44	–	–	–	–	–	–	1	1
Basin metates Reference Nos. 81 and 82	–	1	2	–	6	–	–	9
Unclassified metates Reference Nos. 88–89A	–	–	–	–	1	–	–	1
Total	1	5	13	2	20	2	1	44

Note: Based on examples recovered from the floors of structures. EPHP = Early Pit House period, GT = Georgetown phase, SF = San Francisco phase, TC = Three Circle phase.

tion, were reused architecturally incorporated into house walls or footings and in stone pavements, as well as rock fill for hearths and pits.

The distribution of 44 specimens recovered from floor contexts suggests a temporal progression of certain nether stone types (Table 7.1). Slab metates occurred early during the Early Pit House period and in the Georgetown phase but seem to have disappeared from the inventory sometime during the San Francisco phase. Grinding slabs, closed trough and basin metates appeared during the Georgetown phase and continued throughout the Late Pit House period. Only one example, a through trough metate, was recovered from a Mimbres association. Moreover, the majority of all metate and grinding slab types are concentrated during the San Francisco and Three Circle phases, paralleling the period of presumed greatest activity at the site. Given the relatively low frequency (n = 44) of floor context examples, however, caution must be exercised when drawing temporal type conclusions. In part, discrepancies in the frequencies of metate and grinding slab types may be related to the much larger material inventory associated with the pre-c. A.D. 950/1000 Wind Mountain pit house occupations versus the comparatively sparse and fleeting post-A.D. 1000 Mimbres phase settlement.

Metates and grinding slabs were manufactured from a variety of coarse- and fine-grained stone available in the Big and Little Burro Mountains (Table 7.2; see Figure 2.4). The largest percentage were fashioned either of granite (35 percent) or welded tuff (31 percent). Both lithic materials tend toward a granular consistency, suggesting that stone grit was a generous addition to any substance ground on the metate surface made from them. Dense, fine-grained stone such as andesite (5 percent) and quartzite (3 percent), presumably occurring as smaller nodules, were utilized comparatively infrequently in metate production.

The selection of stone for the manufacture of specific metate types most likely depended on multiple factors including the availability and nature of the raw lithics (e.g., occurring as blocks, boulders, nodules, or tabular blanks in coarse- or fine-grained materials), as well as individual human preference. There must also be a functional relationship between lithic raw material, metate and grinding slab type, and the substance to be processed. Evidence for multiple plant processing stages has been recovered in the form of successive, in situ metates intended to grind corn or other plant seed from coarse to fine meal (Martin 1959:108, 1979:71, Figure 11). Based on observations of ground stone assemblages in the Mimbres Valley, Lancaster (1983:70–74; 1984) suggests such multiple processing stages to produce meal by using a series of metates made of coarse- to fine-grained stone. No such formalized progression was observed in the Wind Moun-

TABLE 7.2. Frequencies of Nether Stone Types Correlated with Lithic Raw Materials

Nether Stone Type	Granite	Welded Tuff	Sandstone	Andesite	Vesicular Basalt	Quartzite	Gabbro	Biotite Schist	Breccia	Total
Slab metates Reference Nos. 1 and 2	4	2	1	–	–	1	–	–	1	9
Grinding slabs Reference Nos. 28–31	3	25	14	4	–	–	–	1	–	47
Closed trough metates Reference Nos. 41 and 42	21	3	–	–	1	–	2	–	–	27
Through trough metates Reference Nos. 43 and 44	3	–	1	–	1	–	–	–	–	5
Basin metates Reference Nos. 81 and 82	6	3	–	1	2	2	–	–	–	14
Unclassified metates Reference Nos. 88–89A	–	–	2	–	1	–	–	–	–	3
Total	37	33	18	5	5	3	2	1	1	105

Note: Comprises complete or substantially complete examples.

tain metate inventory. Even though the structured positioning of nether stones based on lithic material did not occur, common sense dictates that the inhabitants used the appropriate implement for the task set.

Though no formal arrangement of metates existed at Wind Mountain, certain nether stone forms probably did relate to function, particularly with regard to the primary material to be ground. For example, researchers have identified grinding slabs with processing wild plants, whereas the true trough metate is thought to be indicative of corn agriculture and the preparation of corn meal (Haury 1976:282, 1983:162–164; Lancaster 1983, 1984). Slabs or a milling stone type of grinding equipment have a long history throughout the Southwest, first appearing in Archaic contexts in which they were purportedly used to crush wild plant seed (Sayles and Antevs 1941; Haury 1950). Simple slab and basin forms are known from Mogollon Village and Harris Village (Haury 1936a:30–32, 70). Through trough metates are reported from Anasazi sites (Haury 1985:244), but Di Peso suggested that the closed and through trough types were imports into the Gran Chichimecan macroregion (see also Haury 1976:280–281, 300; Martin 1979:71 states that the through trough metate appeared c. A.D. 800). Specifically, Di Peso suggested that the introduction of these two forms occurred concomitantly with hybrid corn out of western Mexico (Di Peso Wind Mountain files, Amerind Foundation). Consequently, as corn was transmitted into the Gran Chichimeca, so too was the technology with which to process it. Heavily dependent on both wild and domestic resources, the residents of Wind Mountain undoubtedly employed metates to prepare a variety of collected and cultivated plant seeds. Moreover, they most likely used grinding stones to pulverize many other nonedible substances.

Manos

A mano is described as the upper, moveable element used in concert with the stationary nether stone. Di Peso identified several mano types, defined on the basis of length, cross section, and plan shape attributes (Figure 7.2). By examining these attributes, along with edge and surface wear patterns, mano types were matched with metates. According to Di Peso's classification system, manos and metates are viewed, therefore, as a single tool or a composite artifact set consisting of two complementary components. This approach to ordering is evident in the type names Di Peso assigned, which include one hand (Reference Nos. 3–14) and two hand manos for slab metates (Reference Nos. 15–27), one (Reference Nos. 45–62) and two hand (Reference Nos. 63–80) manos for trough metates, as well as one hand manos for basin

TABLE 7.3. One and Two Hand Manos Arranged by Plan Shape and Correlated with Lithic Raw Materials

	Rectangular		Oval		Circular		Petaloid		Asymmetric		Trapezoid		Subtotal		
Material	1–h	2–h	1–h	2–h	1–h	2–h	1–h	2–h	1–h	2–h	1–h	2–h	1–h	2–h	Total
Sandstone	10	39	12	9	2	–	–	1	1	1	1	1	26	51	77
Granite	9	16	11	11	3	1	4	3	1	1	–	–	28	32	60
Vesicular basalt	11	13	6	5	5	3	–	–	–	–	–	–	22	21	43
Welded tuff	9	15	3	1	–	1	–	–	–	3	–	1	12	21	33
Andesite	6	4	8	2	3	–	2	1	–	–	–	–	19	7	26
Quartzite	1	2	3	1	1	–	1	–	–	–	–	1	6	4	10
Felsite	1	4	–	2	1	–	–	–	–	–	–	–	2	6	8
Basalt	1	–	1	2	2	–	1	–	–	–	–	–	5	2	7
Biotite schist	2	3	1	–	–	–	–	–	–	–	–	–	3	3	6
Arkose	1	1	–	–	–	–	–	–	–	–	–	–	1	1	2
Gabbro	1	–	–	–	1	–	–	–	–	–	–	–	2	–	2
Rhyolite/ Porphyry	–	–	–	–	–	1	–	–	–	–	–	–	–	1	1
Subtotal	52	97	45	33	18	6	8	5	2	5	1	3	126	149	
Total	149		78		24		13		7		4				275

1–h = one hand; 2–h = two hand.

metates (Reference Nos. 83–87). The total mano count from Wind Mountain numbered 126 one hand (less than 16 cm) and 149 two hand (16 cm or greater) types (Table 7.3).

For the most part, the Wind Mountain mano inventory parallels the metate assemblage in terms of the range of raw stone used in the manufacture of each. Like metates, manos were frequently produced from granite (22 percent). Both sandstone (28 percent) and vesicular basalt (16 percent) occurred more frequently in mano production as compared with metates. Welded tuff (12 percent), andesite (9 percent), as well as small quantities of quartzite (4 percent), felsite (3 percent), basalt (3 percent), and biotite schist (2 percent) were represented. Although noted, arkose, gabbro, and rhyolite/porphyry appeared in less than 1 percent of the mano inventory and never as metates.

One hand manos were usually made from cobbles or nodules, often only unifacially modified and flattened through subsequent use. In addition, single composite upper and nether stone sets were by no means always made from the same material.

One and two hand manos were recovered from all spatial and temporal contexts of the site. They, like their metate counterparts, demonstrate their utility through heavy use wear patterns and breakage.

Rubbing Stones

Rubbing stones (Reference Nos. 32–40) constituted a separate class of handstone, distinctive from the more traditionally employed mano definition. In reality, rubbing stones differed only slightly from manos. Like manos, rubbing stones were circular or rectangular in plan, unifacially or bifacially utilized, and were unshaped or secondarily shaped (Figure 7.2). In the Di Peso classification rubbing stones were distinguished on the basis of their long axis measurement, which was determined to be less than 13 cm. If they measured in excess of 13 cm, they were identified as manos.

Di Peso classified 158 rubbing stones in the Wind Mountain ground stone inventory (Table 7.4). Most were unshaped and separated into rectangular uniface (n = 46, Reference No. 34), circular uniface (n = 26, Reference No. 32), or circular biface (n = 26, Reference No. 37) categories. Rubbing stones made from unshaped (63 percent) lithic materials far outnumbered shaped (37 percent) examples. A slight preference for rectangular (56 percent) over circular (44 percent) plan forms was noted. This trend compares with the plan shapes of manos in which 54 percent were rectangular as compared with 37 percent round to oval forms.

The distribution of raw lithic materials used to produce rubbing stones paralleled that of mano manufacture. Most rubbing stones were made of sandstone (25 percent), granite (19 percent), or welded tuff (12 percent). The only divergence evident was the frequent use of andesite in rubbing stone production (23 percent) which was not apparent in the mano collection (9 percent). In contrast, vesicular basalt occurred infrequently as rubbing stones (5 percent), but more commonly as manos (16 percent).

Rubbing stones were recovered from all site contexts in-

TABLE 7.4. Frequencies of Rubbing Stone Types Correlated with Lithic Raw Materials

Material	Reference No. 32	Reference No. 33	Reference No. 34	Reference No. 35	Reference No. 36	Reference No. 37	Reference No. 38	Reference No. 39	Reference No. 40	Total
Sandstone	5	–	11	4	–	7	3	6	3	39
Andesite	7	1	9	8	3	6	2	1	–	37
Granite	5	3	7	4	3	4	2	2	–	30
Welded tuff	3	1	10	2	1	1	1	–	–	19
Dacite	4	–	3	–	2	2	–	3	–	14
Vesicular basalt	1	2	2	1	–	2	–	–	–	8
Quartzite	1	–	1	–	–	1	–	1	–	4
Pyroxenite	–	–	1	–	–	1	–	–	–	2
Basalt	–	–	–	–	–	–	1	–	–	1
Biotite schist	–	–	1	–	–	–	–	–	–	1
Dolomite	–	–	1	–	–	–	–	–	–	1
Felsite	–	–	–	–	–	1	–	–	–	1
Gabbro	–	–	–	–	–	1	–	–	–	1
Total	26	7	46	19	9	26	9	13	3	158

Note: Refer to Appendix 5 for complete reference number type descriptions.

cluding the floors of structures reflecting a longevity from the Georgetown phase through the Mimbres phase. Together with metates, grinding slabs, and manos, rubbing stones illustrate one of the broad, basic utility tool categories characteristic of the Wind Mountain lithic assemblage, abundant from near the beginning to the end of the site's occupation sequence.

Mortars and Pestles

Mortars (Reference Nos. 91–94, 103) and pestles (Reference Nos. 95–102, 104) represent another composite nether (the mortar) and upper (the pestle) artifact class. Eighteen mortars and 55 pestles were recovered from Wind Mountain. Mortars were made of welded tuff (n = 11), sandstone (n = 5), as well as one example each of dacite and vesicular basalt. Andesite accounted for 42 percent (n = 23) of the pestles. Dacite (n = 16), granite (n = 10), chalcedony (n = 2), together with one example each of basalt, limestone, chert, and quartz were also identified. Mean dimensions are misleading when describing pestles which ranged in size from a fragment 28 cm in length to a complete, small specimen measuring less than 7 cm. Though pestles display abrading marks on their ends, many are highly polished on all surfaces and may have been used as smoothing tools (Figure 7.3).

Mortars, too, are large and small, produced on stone blocks or hand sized, modified nodules (Figure 7.4). Some well shaped, sculpted "mortars" have the appearance of stone bowls (Figure 7.5). Besides the complete samples found, fragments representing at least 24 additional stone bowls were reported, indicating their not infrequent occurrence at the site. Most stone bowls were undecorated, and in rare instances some were embellished by incising and grooving. Large mortars and pestles were generally manufactured of coarse-grained materials such as welded tuff or granite, whereas fine-grained andesite and dacite was employed for their smaller counterparts.

Large mortar/pestle combinations were probably more commonly employed for processing plant seed, and the smaller versions may have been used to crush minerals. Pigment adhering to five small pestles (WM 1678, WM 2417, WM 2719, RO 49, and RO 50) support this conclusion. Only one larger pestle (WM 1947) retained pigment. Of these six pestles with traces of pigment, five were colored red (ocher/hematite); the remaining residue was black.

Palettes and Proto-palettes

Palettes and proto-palettes comprise two other types of nether stone classifications. Di Peso originally identified 56 proto-palettes (Reference No. 113, n = 33 Reference No. 114, n = 23). Proto-palettes were usually made of shale (71 percent) and, to a lesser extent, of welded tuff (21 percent); displayed modified (41 percent by grinding) or unmodified (59 percent) edges; and varied in size from a small specimen of 5.0 cm x 4.5 cm x 0.5 cm (WM 971) to a large fragment measuring 22.2 cm x 14.9 cm x 6.2 cm (WM 502). Many of these examples may represent either blanks intended for later palette production or a shaped but simplified and undecorated precursor (i.e., a proto-palette) of a formalized palette

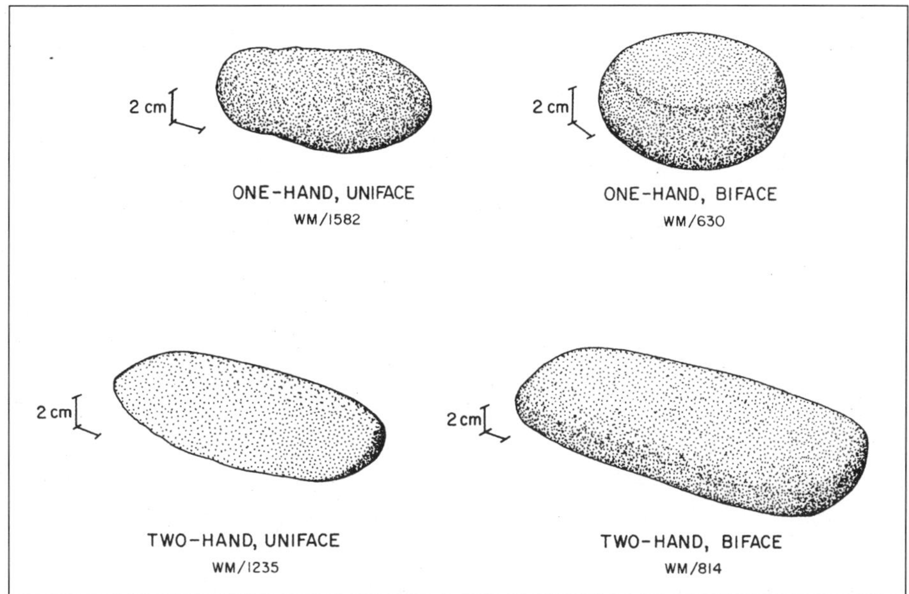

FIGURE 7.2. Examples of mano and rubbing stone types associated with reference numbers. One hand, unifacially worn mano (WM 1582), Reference No. 47; One hand, bifacially worn rubbing stone (WM 630), Reference No. 37; Two hand, unifacially worn mano (WM 1235), Reference No. 15; Two hand, bifacially worn mano (WM 814), Reference No. 23. In Di Peso's classification, manos and rubbing stones are the mobile upper halves of two piece fitted pulverizers with coincident parts used in reciprocal action.

FIGURE 7.3. Pestles, Reference No. 98. Left to right, upper view: WM 1924, WM 173, WM 312; lower view: WM/S 575, WM 1279, WM 2593, WM 308. WM 308 measures 7.3 cm in length (Neg. No. WM 143-2L).

TABLE 7.5. Palettes Recovered from the Wind Mountain Site

Provenience	Context	Catalogue No.	Material	Pigment	Length (cm)	Width (cm)	Thickness (cm)
WM locus							
House B	Fill	WM/S 49	Shale	White	3.1+	1.1+	0.5+
House R	Floor fill	WM/S 930	Shale	–	1.9+	3.7+	0.5
House U	Fill	WM 891	Shale	Yellow	6.5	3.6	0.5
House U	Fill	WM/S 1239	Shale	–	5.3+	3.9+	0.6
House W	Floor fill	WM/S 1468	Shale	–	3.0+	1.8+	0.7
House W	Fill	WM/S 1460	Shale	–	2.8+	2.6+	0.6+
House X	Fill	WM/S 2131	Welded tuff	–	3.6+	1.4+	0.6
House X	Fill	WM/S 1958	Shale	Yellow	4.3+	2.7+	0.6
House X	Fill	WM/S 2244	Pinal schist	–	2.7+	2.1+	1.1+
House Y	Fill	WM 1129	Shale	–	6.6	6.1	1.0
House Y	Fill	WM/S 1634	Shale	–	3.7+	1.8+	0.7
House WW	Fill/Floor fill	WM 2335	Sandstone	–	9.3	4.3	1.5
House WW	Fill/Floor fill	WM/S 1410	Shale	–	2.0+	1.8+	0.8+
House WW	Fill/Floor fill	WM/S 1411	Shale	Red	3.0+	2.9+	0.7
House WW	Fill/Floor fill	WM/S 1412	Shale	Red	6.3+	3.9+	0.6
House XX	Fill	WM/S 4395	Shale	–	3.3+	2.3+	0.7
House ZZ	Floor fill	WM/S 4389	Welded tuff	–	2.9+	4.2+	1.2
House AB	Fill	WM/S 4721	Sandstone	–	2.8+	2.4+	0.6
House AC	Floor fill	WM 2705	Shale	–	3.5+	2.8	0.3
House AE	Floor fill	WM/S 4920	Welded tuff	–	3.7+	2.1+	0.4+
House AF	Fill	WM/S 4951	Shale	–	3.9+	2.2+	0.3
Room 16	Fill	WM/S 2731	Welded tuff	–	3.8+	2.6+	0.7
Pit 25	Fill	WM/S 1738	Welded tuff	–	3.8+	2.5+	0.8
Block 20–D	Extramural	WM/S 836	Sandstone	–	2.8+	2.3+	0.6+
Block 21–D	Extramural	WM/S 2197	Shale	–	6.2+	5.1+	0.7
Block 25–B	Extramural	WM 86	Shale	Yellow	7.3	5.7	0.4
Block 26–A	Extramural	WM 390	Shale	Red	5.9+	6.5	0.8
Block 47–C	Extramural	WM/S 3525	Welded tuff	–	3.9+	3.8+	0.4
Block 52–B	Extramural	WM/S 2960	Welded tuff	–	10.5+	5.9	1.7
Block 52–B	Extramural	WM/S 4315	–	–	–	–	–
Block 53–C	Extramural	WM/S 5688	Shale	–	4.1+	3.9+	0.7
Block 53–D	Extramural	WM 2521	Shale	–	5.8	4.6	0.5
Block 54–A	Extramural	WM/S 4497	Welded tuff	–	5.6+	4.9+	0.8
Block 60–B	Extramural	WM/S 4743	Welded tuff	–	5.1+	3.9+	0.7
RO locus							
House D	Fill	RO/S 193	Shale	–	2.5+	2.1+	0.8

form. Others could just as easily be identified as lapstones, abraders, smoothers, or another sort of nether working surface (Figure 7.6).

As compared with proto-palettes, only 35 true palettes (Reference No. 115) were recovered from the floor fill and fill of Wind Mountain structures or in extramural excavation blocks. With one exception, the Wind Mountain palettes are fragmentary. Most were fashioned of shale (n = 21), although welded tuff (n = 9) and sandstone (n = 3) were also represented (Table 7.5). One palette was made from Pinal schist and the raw material of another, now lost, was not identified. The majority were rectangular or square shaped with straight edges or, less commonly, rounded, concave, or convex. Decorations included simple, linear grooving and incising, or incised ticks that garnished borders (Figure 7.7). Some edges were notched or scalloped (Figures 7.8 and 7.9). In one unusual case, a Wind Mountain locus palette was adorned with opposing lizards carved along its border (Figure 7.10). Typically, however, borders tended to be flush with the adjacent surface, separated only by the incised design. Raised borders were rare. Some palettes had center depressions, but many showed little or no signs of surface grinding or abrading. A few had been burned, possibly an effect of use (Haury 1976:288–289) or as the result of a house fire.

The Wind Mountain palette assemblage is reminiscent of

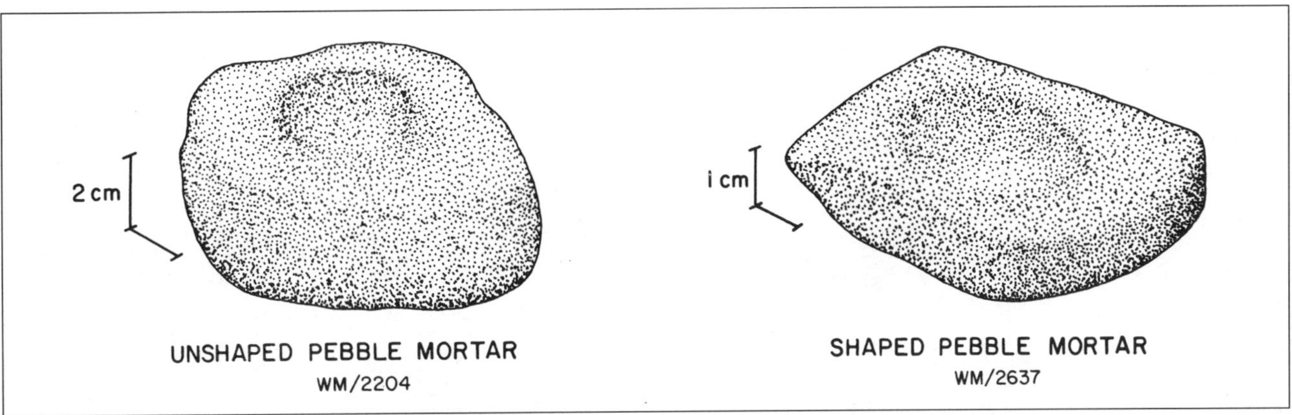

FIGURE 7.4. Examples of pebble mortars. WM 2204, Reference No. 91 and WM 2637, Reference No. 92.

FIGURE 7.5. Mortars or stone bowls. Clockwise from right: RO 213, Reference No. 93; WM 2738, Reference No. 93; WM 578, Reference No. 94; WM 492, Reference No. 94. Diameter of RO 213 measures about 15 cm (Neg. No. WM 144–7L).

FIGURE 7.6. Proto-palettes. Left to right, upper row: WM 1765, WM 1844, WM 335, Reference No. 113; lower row: WM 2336, WM 759, WM 248, Reference No. 114. WM 1765 measures about 13 cm in length (Neg. No. WM 143–5L).

Sedentary period Hohokam types, which are characterized by running incised border designs (Haury 1976:286–289). Haury (1976:286–289) associated sculpted life forms with the Colonial period, Santa Cruz phase. If Wind Mountain palettes were an innovation or, in the case of the Pinal schist palette a direct import from the Hohokam, such contact would date c. A.D. 850/900–950/1000 (Haury 1976:338; Dean 1991:90). Di Peso believed both the Pinal schist and sculpted lizard palettes to be Hohokam trade commodities. Pinal schist occurs in the Pinal Mountains near Globe in eastern Arizona (Wilson 1962), an area Di Peso thought to be part of the Hohokam sphere of influence prior to the dominance of Casas Grandes after c. A.D. 950 (Di Peso 1979b). Anyon and LeBlanc (1984:269–273) in their study of the Galaz Ruin note a possible relationship between Hohokam and Late Pit House period and Mimbres phase palettes. They propose that the palettes of the Mimbres Valley reach their highest frequencies during the Three Circle phase, which coincides with the Colonial period, when Hohokam palettes were most abundant and stylistically varied (Haury 1976:286).

The function of the Wind Mountain palettes remains somewhat enigmatic. Although often associated with mineral pigment grinding (seven Wind Mountain palette fragments revealed traces of red or yellow hematite/ocher or white kaolin residues), many do not even exhibit surface wear patterns. The Wind Mountain palettes are neither large enough to have accommodated censers (Haury 1976:289) nor obviously encrusted with materials that may be the product of incense burning. Though they are not particularly rare at Wind Mountain, their function does not appear to be entirely analogous to Hohokam palettes.

FIGURE 7.7. Palette fragments, Reference No. 115, exhibiting simple incised borders. Upper right: WM/S 1634. Lower left: WM/S 2960. Refer to Table 7.5 for context and dimensions (Neg. No. WM 144–14L).

FIGURE 7.8. Palette fragments, Reference No. 115, exhibiting notched and scalloped edges. Most Wind Mountain palettes were rectangular in form, although a few oval examples were recovered. Clockwise from upper left: WM/S 4497, WM/S 3525, WM/S 4389, WM/S 1460, WM/S 4920, WM/S 1468. Refer to Table 7.5 for context and dimensions (Neg. No. WM 144–15L).

Grooved Abrading Stones

Grooved stone tools were considered by Di Peso to represent another type of one piece nether stone (Reference Nos. 107, 111 and 112). These granular, abrasive tools were apparently used to smooth or sharpen other implements (e.g., arrow shafts or awls) and customarily exhibited from one to five transverse grooves on a modified or unmodified nodule or slab (Figures 7.11 and 7.12). Some abraders were grooved on both sides, suggesting a pragmatic, efficient utilization of raw stone. The complete grooved abrading slabs from Wind Mountain were made of sandstone (n = 3), welded tuff (n = 1),

TABLE 7.6. Grooved Abrading Stone Types

Provenience	Context	Catalogue No.	Reference No.	Material	Length (cm)	Width (cm)	Thickness (cm)
WM locus							
House A	Fill	WM 18	111	Welded tuff	15.6	6.7	2.3
House E	Fill	WM 555	111	Dacite	3.8	2.6	2.3
House N	Floor	WM 820	112	Sandstone	11.8	11.4	2.5
House X	Fill	WM 1451	111	Sandstone	9.0	5.8+	0.8
House X	Fill	WM/S 1961	111	Sandstone	8.3+	8.0+	3.4
House X	Fill	WM/S 2631	111	Welded tuff	8.1+	5.8+	1.6
House Y	Fill	WM/S 1507	111	Sandstone	9.7+	5.2+	3.3+
House Y	Fill	WM/S 1508	111	Sandstone	9.0+	6.8+	0.8+
House SS	Fill	WM/S 4240	111	Sandstone	6.2+	5.5+	1.1+
House AF	Fill	WM 2722	111	Sandstone	7.2+	7.4	1.8
House AL	Floor fill	WM/S 5396	111	Sandstone	3.5+	3.0+	1.0+
Room 16	Fill	WM/S 2728A	111	Sandstone	6.7+	6.2+	2.0+
Block 29-D	Extramural	WM/S 3191A	111	Sandstone	5.0+	4.9+	0.7+
Block 52-B	Extramural	WM/S 2959	112	Welded tuff	7.5+	5.2+	2.2+
Block 62-A	Extramural	WM/S 4275	107	Talc	6.2	4.2	1.8

FIGURE 7.9. Palette fragment (WM 2705), Reference No. 115, with grooved and notched edges. Refer to Table 7.5 for context and dimensions (Neg. No. WM 144–9L).

FIGURE 7.11. Examples of grooved abrading stone types. Clockwise from upper right: WM 820, WM/S 2631, both Reference No. 112; WM 18, Reference No. 111. Abrading stones are suggested to function as tool fashioners or sharpeners. Refer to Table 7.6 for context and dimensions (Neg. No. WM 144–16L).

and dacite (n = 1). All are effective substances for honing tools or for smoothing objects of wood and bone (Table 7.6).

Miscellaneous Nether Stones

Di Peso assigned two additional one piece nether stone types, including whetstone/abrader (Reference Nos. 105, 106, and 108) and lapstone/whetstone/abraders (Reference Nos. 109, 110). Such tools were produced on pebbles, cobbles, or slab blocks and exhibited many similar attributes. Some had prepared surfaces only, while others displayed all over modification. The whetstone/abrader category numbered only five complete artifacts (two of andesite; one each of dacite, welded tuff, and sandstone), although 480 fragments were also noted. Thirty-seven complete lapstone/whetstone/abrader examples (20 welded tuff, 13 sandstone, two dacite, and one each of andesite and pumice) as well as 26 fragments were recovered. Artifacts representing these classes of nether stone provided useful working surfaces for any number of tasks involving the grinding, abrading, polishing, or perforating of substances (Figure 7.13).

FIGURE 7.10. Lizard palette (WM 1129), Reference No. 115. A life form palette similar to Sedentary period Hohokam types, the only such example recovered from the site. Opposing lizards are carved in relief on its borders. Refer to Table 7.5 for context and dimensions (Neg. No. WM 143–8L).

Hammerstones

Multipurpose hammerstones constituted the largest number of hand-held tools identified in the Wind Mountain lithic inventory. Di Peso viewed them as primary pulverizing implements, similar in function to manos and rubbing stones. Consequently, hammerstones were ordered with ground stone categories in the Di Peso classification system rather than including them with chipped stone artifact types in the more traditional manner. He classified hammerstones as one piece,

FIGURE 7.12. Grooved abrading stone fragments, Reference No. 111. Left: WM/S 1961. Right: WM 2722. Many of these abrader types exhibited multiple grooves. Refer to Table 7.6 for context and dimensions (Neg. No. WM 143–16L).

FIGURE 7.13. Examples of miscellaneous nether stones. Clockwise from upper left: WM 244, Reference No. 110; WM 2907, Reference No. 110; WM 556, Reference No. 109; WM 873, Reference No. 110; WM 1127, Reference No. 109. Di Peso's classification included miscellaneous nether stones, which he suggested functioned as lapstones and abraders. WM 873 measures 14.7 cm in length (Neg. No. WM 143–17L).

rounded, unhelved (i.e., unhafted) pulverizers, further separating them on the basis of multidirectional (Reference No. 121), localized (Reference No. 122), and indeterminate or unclassified (Reference No. 123) use wear patterns (Figure 7.14). Like manos or rubbing stones, hammerstones were considered "upper" rather than "nether" utilitarian stone tools. Wind Mountain produced 536 complete or substantially complete hammerstones as well as 124 fragments undifferentiated as to type or lithic material. Manufactured from a variety of raw stone, most examples tended to be produced from quartzite (58 percent), chert (14 percent), or basalt (13 percent) (Table 7.7).

Polishing Stones

Polishing stones, either unshaped (Reference No. 119) or shaped (Reference No. 120), represented another class of hand-held tools. Generally of relatively small size, they were distinguished from other one piece upper pulverizers by their highly polished, glossy surfaces (Figures 7.15 and 7.16). Many were made of dense, fine-grained dacite (n = 32) or andesite (n = 31). The remaining examples were produced from miscellaneous stone: quartzite (n = 7), quartz (n = 4), granite (n = 4), chalcedony (n = 3), ricolite (n = 2), and one each of fluorite, sandstone, and a concretion. Of these materials, ricolite, unavailable from nearby mountain sources, is noteworthy as the only exotic that would have required transport, possibly from the Red Rock area to the west of the site. In addition, 20 polishing stone fragments, undifferentiated by raw material, were reported. In addition to numerous other functions, polishing stones were presumably used to smooth "green" clay vessels prior to firing. Because some polishing stones were made of coarse-grained stone, possible multiple surface smoothing steps in the production of ceramics may be indicated.

Axes and Mauls

Di Peso regarded axes (Reference Nos. 124–128), mauls (Reference Nos. 129–131), and a single axe/maul (Reference No. 132) as one-piece, helved (i.e., hafted), pounding action pulverizers. Relatively few axes (n = 16; Table 7.8), mauls (n = 3; Table 7.9), or axe/mauls (n = 3; Table 7.9) were recovered at Wind Mountain. Except for one axe made of biotite schist, all other Wind Mountain examples were manufactured of dacite (81 percent) and andesite (13 percent), both extremely dense, hard lithic materials. Grooves, either three-quarter (n = 3) or full (n = 2), were pecked with the remaining surface areas finely ground and polished. Similar full and three-quarter grooved mauls are reported from Mogollon Village and Harris Village (Haury 1936a:36, 70). Full grooved axes are known from Mogollon and Harris villages (Haury 1936a:36, 70), from Saige-McFarland (Lekson 1990:68), and Galaz Ruin (Anyon and LeBlanc 1984:279). The three-quarter groove variety is described in assemblages at Galaz (Anyon and LeBlanc:279) and Snaketown (Haury 1976:291). Di Peso suggests that the three-quarter groove axe originated in western Mexico and was introduced into the Gran Chichimeca, possibly via the Hohokam (1979c:42; see also Woodbury 1954).

Due to their heavy use for wood and stone working, axes and mauls usually do not occur in large quantities in the material inventory of sites. When they do survive, as evident in the Wind Mountain collection, most are fragmentary. Secondary modification, such as grinding a worn or broken edge

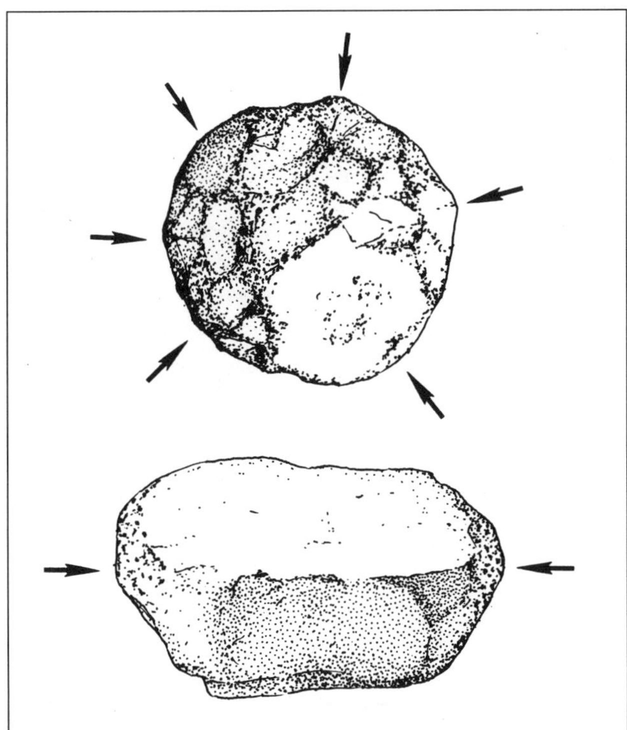

FIGURE 7.14. Hammerstones. Di Peso classified hammerstones with ground stone implements, arguing that both types functioned as pulverizing tools. Types exhibiting multidirectional use wear (upper view, Reference No. 121) and localized use wear (lower view, Reference No. 122) patterns were identified.

FIGURE 7.15. Examples of polishing stones, Reference No. 119. Clockwise from upper left: RO 175, RO/S 287, RO 193. RO 193 diameter measures 4.6 cm (Neg. No. WM 143–18L).

to increase use life, is apparent on some Wind Mountain pieces. One dacite axe (WM 1871) exhibited double three-quarter grooving (Figure 7.17). Apparently, the poll broke off of a simple grooved axe and a new groove was ground enabling it to be rehafted. Alternatively, if axes and mauls were used away from the settlement in farm fields, forests, or for mining stone, such implements would have been discarded off site and would not, therefore, have become incorporated into the settlement's material inventory (Anyon and LeBlanc 1984:276).

TABLE 7.7. Frequencies of Hammerstone Types Correlated with Raw Materials

Material	Multidirectional Use Wear Reference No. 121	Localized Use Wear Reference No. 122	Unclassified Reference No. 123	Total
Quartzite	104	54	154	312
Chert	33	25	19	77
Basalt	12	10	45	67
Dacite	17	15	2	34
Magnetite	1	5	5	11
Chalcedony	1	2	7	10
Andesite	3	4	–	7
Dolomite	3	–	1	4
Granite	–	2	2	4
Quartz	2	–	2	4
Hematite	–	1	2	3
Felsite	1	1	–	2
Pyroxenite	1	–	–	1
Total	178	119	239	536

Miscellaneous Upper Pulverizers

Unhelved (i.e., unhafted) handstone types were assigned to a general class of upper one piece pulverizers. These included abrading/rubbing stone, abrading stone/rasp, and flat abrader categories (Reference Nos. 116–118A). Di Peso identified 47 examples manufactured from welded tuff (n = 19), sandstone (n = 9), andesite (n = 5), dacite (n = 5), granite (n = 4), micaceous schist (n = 2), shale (n = 2), and pyroxenite (n = 1). It is suggested that such hand tools were used by employing a motion, similar to a file or rasp action, against the material to be processed (Figure 7.18).

Disks/Spindle Whorls

Two stone disks/spindle whorls (Reference Nos. 133, 134), both center perforated and shaped from welded tuff, were

TABLE 7.8. Axe Types

Provenience	Context	Catalogue No.	Reference No.	Material	Length (cm)	Width (cm)	Thickness (cm)
WM locus							
House V	Fill	WM/S 1193	126	Dacite	6.6+	4.5+	0.8+
House V	Fill	WM/S 1224	126	Dacite	8.1+	7.1+	3.0+
House X	Fill	WM/S 2240	127	Dacite	5.4+	3.0+	2.2+
House X	Fill	WM/S 2502	126	Andesite	6.9+	4.8+	2.4+
House Y	Fill	WM/S 1510*	125	Dacite	–	–	–
House FF	Fill	WM/S 2700	126	Dacite	4.9+	7.1+	3.0+
House NN	Floor fill	WM 1871*	125	Dacite	12.4	6.7+	4.1
House XX	Fill	WM/S 4418	126	Dacite	2.9+	3.5+	2.7+
House AF	Fill	WM/S 4983C	127	Dacite	3.0+	3.2+	1.8+
House AG	Floor fill	WM/S 5097A	127	Dacite	3.5+	3.0+	1.2+
Block 13–C	Extramural	WM 598	126	Andesite	7.0+	4.8+	2.4
Block 22–C	Extramural	WM/S 1763	128	Dacite	5.9+	4.2+	5.7+
Block 52–D	Extramural	WM/S 4631	128	Dacite	5.9+	3.1+	2.1+
Block 54–A	Extramural	WM/S 4498	127	Dacite	5.0+	3.9+	2.3+
Block 61–A	Extramural	WM/S 4856	127	Dacite	3.8+	4.2+	2.4+
RO locus							
House C	Floor	RO 58	124	Biotite schist	12.1+	10.0	3.9

*Fragments from the same axe. Note: Refer to Appendix 5 for complete reference number type descriptions.

TABLE 7.9. Maul and Axe/Maul Types

Provenience	Context	Catalogue No.	Reference No.	Material	Length (cm)	Width (cm)	Thickness (cm)
WM locus							
House D	Fill	WM/S 388	132	Dacite	3.8+	6.7+	5.4+
House N	Floor	WM 822	131	Dacite	8.8+	8.2+	8.1+
House T	Fill	WM/S 1071	130	Dacite	6.9+	5.9+	2.4+
House EE	Fill	WM/S 1987	132	Dacite	7.3+	7.1	6.6+
House PP	Pit 3, cache	WM 2215	132	Dacite	10.3+	8.5	7.9
RO locus							
House C	Floor	RO 84	129	Dacite	12.5	9.5	7.0

Note: Refer to Appendix 5 for complete reference number type descriptions.

collected. One fragment (WM 556, diameter 9.3 cm) derived from the fill of House E and the other, a complete specimen (WM 1595, diameter 4 cm), was recovered from the central post hole (No. 1) of House X (Figure 7.19). Di Peso noted that he had discovered 30 comparable objects in all stages of manufacture at the Babocomari site in southeastern Arizona (1951:161–164). Disks are also known from the Mimbres Valley where they are considered rare. One was recovered at Galaz Ruin (Anyon and LeBlanc 1984:286). The Galaz disk was equated in size with a Hohokam disk from Snaketown (Haury 1976:290). Both examples from these sites (diameter 17.1 cm at Galaz; diameter 18.4 cm at Snaketown) are about twice as large as the stone disk fragment recovered at Wind Mountain. Haury (1950:329) reported 24 stone disks from deposits at Ventana Cave, many dating to the San Pedro Archaic. In contrast, Di Peso believed disks (or spindle whorls) to be generally late in the American Southwest. He associated them with post-A.D. 1200 sites such as Tres Alamos (Tuthill 1947:72), Casa Grande (Fewkes 1912:129), Los Muertos (Haury 1945a:142), Kinishba (Cummings 1940:54), Jackrabbit Ruin (Scantling 1940:52), Awatovi (Woodbury 1954:185), and Medio period Casas Grandes (Di Peso et al. 1974:7:139–140). Clearly, whatever their antiquity, stone disks have a wide geographic and temporal distribution in the American Southwest and northern Mexico.

FIGURE 7.16. Examples of polishing stones. Clockwise from upper left: RO 184, WM 1730, both Reference No. 119; RO 65, RO 125, both Reference No. 120. RO 125 diameter measures 4 cm (Neg. No. WM 144–22L).

FIGURE 7.17. Axe and maul examples. Clockwise from upper left: Full grooved axe (RO 58), Reference No. 124; double three-quarter grooved axe (WM 1871), Reference No. 125; full grooved maul (RO 84), Reference No. 84. Refer to Tables 7.8 and 7.9 for context and dimensions (Neg. No. WM 143–19L).

Chipped Stone

The Wind Mountain chipped stone assemblage was segregated into principal categories of debitage, cores, and tools made from cores, flakes, and shatter. Debitage accounted for the vast majority of the lithic inventory, consisting of some 20,783 fragments (Table 7.10). In addition to debitage, Di Peso analyzed and classified approximately 2,370 chipped stone tools. Artifacts were identified as tools if they exhibited a retouched or utilized edge. Primary tool classes were separated according to a series of other attributes. For example, if an artifact was placed in the "Flake" category, it was then classified in ever greater detail based on 11 specific worked edge descriptions (Figure 7.20). The final type assignment consisted of the principal class (e.g., core, flake, or shatter tool), together with its particular attributes.

Di Peso's typological definitions were somewhat individualistic because he often dismissed other, more widely used type names (Appendix 5). In the case of "shatter," he defined this class as stone pieces and tools which did not display the characteristics of either cores or flakes. He viewed shatter as representing splinters of stone that served as the raw material from which some tools were made. Di Peso apparently adopted the term from Binford and Quimby (1963:278–279), who used it to describe the lithic debris resulting from heavy percussion techniques or from stone materials which had split along old fracture planes. In other words, shatter was composed of cubical and irregularly shaped fragments *not* suitable for tool manufacture (Binford and Quimby 1963:278–279). Di Peso modified Binford and Quimby's original shatter definition, as well as other lithic terminology, and his usages are retained in the following discussion with appropriate explanation where necessary.

Debitage

The enormous quantity of unmodified, either by use or purposeful retouch, chipped stone was defined as debitage (Reference Nos. 142, 176). Specifically, debitage represented the by-product of flake or shatter tool production. Debitage at Wind Mountain consisted primarily of quartzite (62 percent), basalt (18 percent), chalcedony (13 percent) which, when

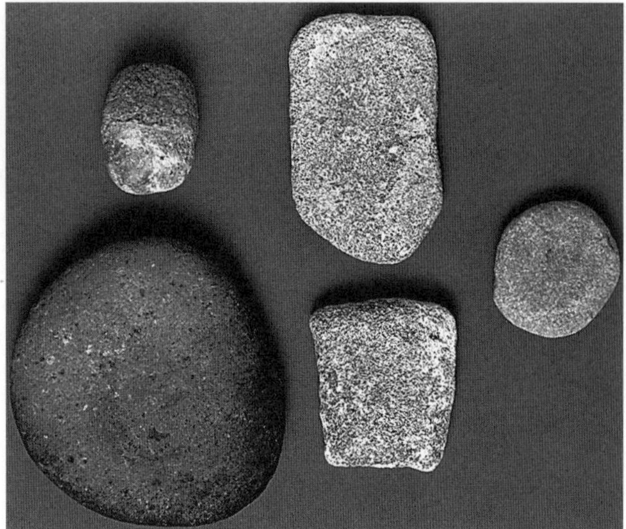

FIGURE 7.18. Examples of miscellaneous upper pulverizers. Several types of hand held abrading stones were identified in the Di Peso classification. Clockwise from upper left: WM 4352, Reference No. 116; WM/S 4693, not classified; WM 1860, Reference No. 116; WM 702, Reference No. 118; WM 65, Reference No. 116. WM 702 measures 5.7 cm in length (Neg. No. WM 143–22L).

FIGURE 7.19. Stone disks/spindle whorls. Left: WM 1595, Reference No. 134, 4 cm diameter. Right: WM 556, Reference No. 133, 9 cm diameter (Neg. No. WM 143–23L).

combined, numbered 19,227 pieces or 93 percent of identified raw materials (Table 7.10). Other lithics well suited to percussion and pressure flaking techniques accounted for the remaining 7 percent of raw materials.

TABLE 7.10. Debitage Frequencies Correlated with Lithic Raw Materials

Material	Flake, Raw Reference No. 142	Shatter, Raw Reference No. 176	Total
Quartzite	4,294	8,647	12,941
Basalt	1,194	2,451	3,645
Chalcedony	493	2,148	2,641
Chert	140	371	511
Dolomite	12	354	366
Obsidian	110	190	300
Granite	1	252	253
Hematite	16	33	49
Opaline	2	23	25
Agate	5	19	24
Magnetite	2	6	8
Quartz	–	8	8
Andesite	1	6	7
Rhyolite	2	–	2
Rock crystal	–	2	2
Turquoise	1	–	1
Total	6,273	14,510	20,783

Cores

Cores (Reference No. 135) were defined as unmodified pieces of stone from which flakes could be struck in order to manufacture tools (see Crabtree 1972:54–56). The Wind Mountain lithic assemblage produced 57 cores including obsidian (n = 41), quartzite (n = 6), chalcedony (n = 5), chert (n = 2), basalt (n = 1), dolomite (n = 1), and magnetite (n = 1). With the exclusion of obsidian, all of these raw materials are available in the immediate vicinity of the community. The frequency of raw cores seems low for a site so completely excavated. Di Peso suggested, however, that most cores had been reduced during the production of other stone tools.

Core Tools

Di Peso employed Webster's dictionary (1952) and Crabtree's (1972:54) definitions to define core tools (Reference Nos. 136–141A), and characterized them generally as pieces of stone from which flakes had been struck. Flake scars occurred at points where flakes were removed. Di Peso identified 29 utilized core tools that were modified primarily by usage (Table 7.11) and 16 unifacially retouched core tools which had been consciously shaped (Table 7.12). Combined core tool frequencies showed a distribution of stone materials similar to that observed for debitage. Local quartzite (42 percent) and imported obsidian (27 percent) were both well represented.

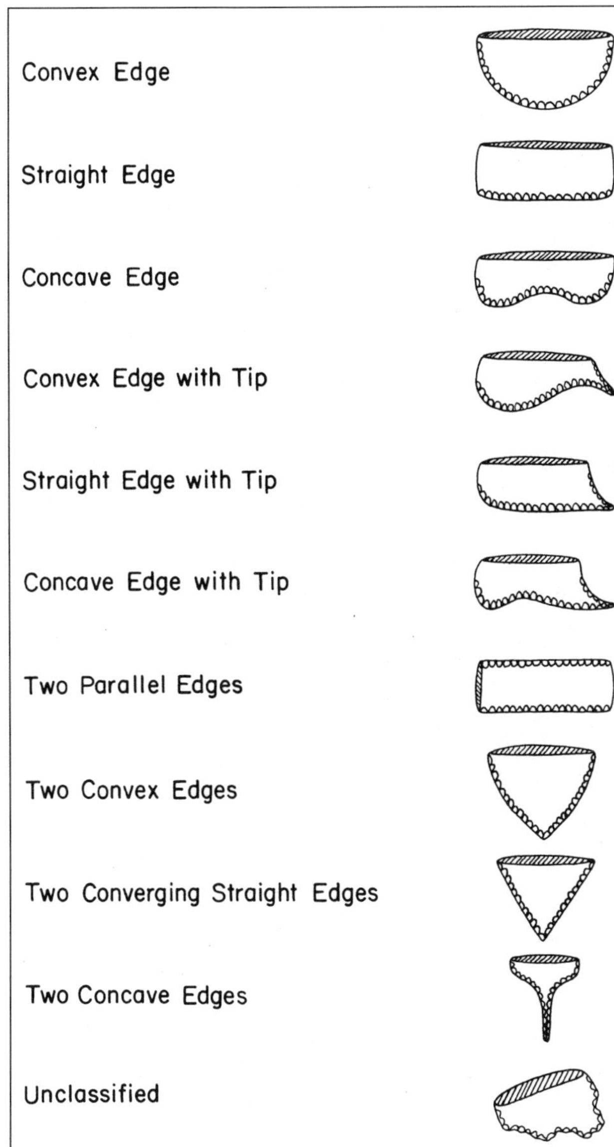

FIGURE 7.20. Edge wear attributes of chipped stone tools. Eleven attributes contributed to the "type" assignment of individual chipped stone artifacts.

Flake Tools

Flake tools refer to artifacts that display a cutting edge and retain a platform, including, in Di Peso's words, a bulb of force and a striking platform. Flake tools (n = 1,550) were distinguished as utilized (n = 1,027; Reference Nos. 143–153), as unifacially (n = 377; Reference Nos. 154–164), or as bifacially (n = 146; Reference Nos. 165–175) retouched. The full range of flake tool types (Tables 7.13, 7.14, and 7.15) identified at Wind Mountain exhibits a similar distribution of raw materials as was evident in the debitage assemblage. Most flake tools were produced of quartzite (60 percent), followed by basalt (21 percent) and chalcedony (8 percent) as compared to values of 62 percent, 18 percent, and 13 percent respectively in debitage. Although imported obsidian represented only 1 percent of the total site lithic inventory, 8 percent of all flake tools recovered were made of this exotic material. The abundant occurrence of flakes in all contexts of the settlement underscores their all purpose utility as cutting and scraping tools.

TABLE 7.11. Frequencies of Utilized Core Tool Types Correlated with Lithic Raw Materials

Material	Chopper Convex Edge Reference No. 136	Scraper Straight Edge Reference No. 137	Scraper Concave Edge Reference No. 138	Unclassified Reference No. 138A	Total
Quartzite	8	2	1	–	11
Obsidian	6	1	–	–	7
Chert	3	–	–	1	4
Basalt	–	1	1	–	2
Magnetite	2	–	–	–	2
Chalcedony	1	–	–	–	1
Dolomite	1	–	–	–	1
Hematite	–	–	1	–	1
Total	21	4	3	1	29

Shatter Tools

Di Peso applied the term *shatter* to implements, not to the chipping debris associated with stone tool production. Shatter tools (n = 491) were manufactured from stone splinters and did not display the characteristics of either cores or flakes. Like flakes, however, they were divided into utilized (n = 364; Reference Nos. 177–184), unifacial (n = 99; Reference Nos. 185–193), or bifacial (n = 28; Reference Nos. 194–200) retouched tools. Di Peso's shatter tool types were also associated with cutting and scraping and could be accommodated by more traditional unifacial or bifacial flake classifications (Tables 7.16, 7.17, and 7.18).

Drills and Projectile Points

Helved (i.e., hafted), bifacially retouched chipped stone tools were classified separately (Figure 7.21; Tables 7.19–7.22). Hafted tools (Reference Nos. 201–228) were primarily identified as drills (n = 22) or projectile points (n = 205), though these designations were sometimes combined as projectile point/knife/drill (e.g., Reference Nos. 201–204; Appendix 5), an effort to accommodate the presumed multipurpose nature of some artifacts. In such cases, the individual responsible for the classification appears to have subjectively assigned a "name" based on the appearance and the assumed primary

TABLE 7.12. Frequencies of Unifacial Edge Retouch Core Tool Types Associated with Lithic Raw Materials

Material	Chopper Convex Edge Reference No. 139	Scraper Convex Edge Reference No. 140	Scraper Two Cutting Edges Reference No. 141	Unclassified Reference No. 141A	Total
Quartzite	8	–	–	–	8
Obsidian	–	4	1	–	5
Andesite	1	–	–	–	1
Quartz	–	–	–	1	1
Unidentified	–	–	–	1	1
Total	9	4	1	2	16

function of the artifact in question. Consequently, a drill may have exactly the same reference number as a projectile point (compare Tables 7.19 and 7.21).

Drills were distinguished from other implements when they exhibited restricted or parallel edges, had blunt tips, and were square or rhomboidal in cross section (Tables 7.19 and 7.20). In contrast to projectile points, drills showed rotary wear marks perpendicular to their long axis and counter cutting of the retouched edge or lip (Figure 7.22).

The stone materials used to make drills and projectile points correspond to those represented by debitage with some interesting differences. Basalt was scarcely used as a drill or projectile point, representing only 3 percent of those tool assemblages. In contrast, hard vitreous stone, including quartz (39 percent) and chalcedony (23 percent), were employed in the manufacture of drills and projectile points (Table 7.23). However if, among other tasks, drills were used to perforate hides or to incise shell and stone ornaments, a durable point would be most desirable. Obsidian, while providing extremely sharp edges suited to cutting soft materials, is not particularly strong when applying direct pressure against a hard object. Thus, dense, fine-grained quartz (59 percent) and chalcedony (18 percent) commonly occur as drills, whereas obsidian was restricted to the manufacture of projectile points. The correlation between various raw materials and specific artifact types has been noted in lithic assemblages analyzed from many sites throughout the Southwest (e.g., Kidder 1932:13; M. Nelson 1981:104–133, 1986; Kelly 1985:133–134).

Di Peso examined the Wind Mountain drills and projectile points from the perspective of those types he believed developed out of a local Archaic tradition as compared with intrusive types. He referred to the long sequence of types reported from Ventana Cave (Haury 1950:290) as indicative of a Desert Chichimec Archaic base, the assumed precursor of the Mogollon Wind Mountain settlement. Reviewing all stemmed and stemless types (see Figure 7.18, Appendix 5), he proposed that most evolved from Desert Archaic roots, but cited two introduced forms (Di Peso Wind Mountain files, Amerind Foundation). The first nonlocal tool cited is an oblique notched, stemmed drill with a convex base (Reference No. 212) whose origin was linked to eastern North America, c. post-A.D. 1000. The second import was described as a laterally notched stemmed point (Reference No. 210, refer to Figure 7.21), which Di Peso related to the Hohokam c. post-A.D. 800 (Haury 1976:297–298). Whatever the development of Wind Mountain drill and projectile point types, the collection is highly reminiscent of other Mimbres Mogollon chipped stone inventories (e.g., Haury 1936a; Fitting et al. 1982b; Anyon and LeBlanc 1984; Lekson 1990).

Another consideration when assessing the Wind Mountain chipped stone assemblage is the overwhelming preponderance of locally available raw materials employed in the manufacture of the settlement's tools. Most stone and minerals were readily obtainable from Deadman and Whitewater Canyons immediately below the site ridge, from the nearby Mangas Creek channel, and from sources in the Big and Little Burro Mountains. Typically, the majority of lithic materials were procured within a distance of 4 km (2.5 miles), certainly less than a day's round trip walk (refer to Figure 2.5). Ricolite and obsidian were the only "exotic" materials noted in the ground and chipped stone tool inventory. The nearest known ricolite source is located in Red Rock Canyon some 30 km (18 miles) to the west. The area between Wind Mountain and the ricolite source consists of rugged mountains, however, so access would not have involved a quick trip there and back. Not surprisingly, ricolite was not abundantly represented in either raw material or finished artifact form. In contrast, obsidian occurred in higher frequencies, especially as projectile points and raw fragments, even though the closest known source is in the Mule Creek area about 60 km (37 miles) northwest of the site.

Discussion and Summary Remarks

The Wind Mountain lithic assemblage, consisting of ground and chipped stone, represents a nonspecialized, multipurpose

TABLE 7.13. Frequencies of Utilized Flake Tool Types Correlated with Lithic Raw Materials

Material	Knife/Scraper Convex Edge Reference No. 143	Knife/Scraper Straight Edge Reference No. 144	Scraper Concave Edge Reference No. 145	Knife/Scraper with Tip Convex Edge Reference No. 146	Knife/Scraper with Tip Straight Edge Reference No. 147	Scraper with Tip Concave Edge Reference No. 148	Knife/Scraper Two Parallel Edges Reference No. 149	Graver/Chisel/ Perforator/Drill Reference No. 150	Knife/Scraper Two Converging Straight Edges Reference No. 151	Scraper Two Concave Edges Reference No. 152	Unclassified Reference No. 153	Total
Quartzite	129	122	70	76	67	20	89	3	29	5	9	619
Basalt	48	39	27	27	23	7	38	4	10	–	2	225
Chalcedony	9	18	5	6	2	4	19	–	9	–	2	74
Obsidian	16	3	11	8	5	2	15	2	2	–	1	65
Chert	7	5	1	3	3	1	6	–	3	–	–	29
Hematite	3	1	1	–	1	–	3	–	–	–	–	9
Magnetite	1	–	–	–	–	–	2	–	–	–	–	3
Porphyry	1	–	–	–	–	–	–	–	–	–	–	1
Agate	–	–	–	–	–	–	1	–	–	–	–	1
Unidentified	–	–	–	–	–	–	–	–	–	–	1	1
Total	214	188	115	120	101	34	173	9	53	5	15	1,027

TABLE 7.14. Frequencies of Unifacial Edge Retouch Flake Tools Correlated with Lithic Materials

Material	Knife/Scraper Convex Edge Reference No. 154	Knife/Scraper Straight Edge Reference No. 155	Scraper Concave Edge Reference No. 156	Knife/Scraper with Tip Convex Edge Reference No. 157	Knife/Scraper with Tip Straight Edge Reference No. 158	Scraper with Tip Concave Edge Reference No. 159	Knife/Scraper Two Parallel Edges Reference No. 160	Graver/Chisel/ Perforator/Drill Reference No. 161	Knife/Scraper Two Converging Straight Edges Reference No. 162	Scraper Two Concave Edges Reference No. 163	Unclassified Reference No. 164	Total
Quartzite	28	69	20	9	14	7	35	8	23	7	14	234
Basalt	15	22	5	7	2	3	13	–	7	2	5	81
Chalcedony	1	3	5	3	1	1	3	1	4	4	7	33
Chert	3	–	–	–	–	1	2	–	3	2	4	15
Obsidian	4	1	–	–	1	1	2	–	–	1	2	12
Hematite	–	–	–	–	–	–	–	–	–	–	1	1
Agate	1	–	–	–	–	–	–	–	–	–	–	1
Total	52	95	30	19	18	13	55	9	37	16	33	377

TABLE 7.15. Frequencies of Bifacial Edge Retouch Flake Tool Types Correlated with Lithic Raw Materials

Material	Knife/Scraper Convex Edge Reference No. 165	Knife/Scraper Straight Edge Reference No. 166	Scraper Concave Edge Reference No. 167	Kife/Scraper with Tip Convex Edge Reference No. 168	Knife/Scraper with Tip Straight Edge Reference No. 169	Scraper with Tip Concave Edge Reference No. 170	Knife/Scraper Two Parallel Edges Reference No. 171	Graver/Chisel/ Perforator/Drill Reference No. 172	Knife/Scraper Two Converging Straight Edges Reference No. 173	Scraper Two Concave Edges Reference No. 174	Unclassified Reference No. 175	Total
Quartzite	7	11	1	10	6	–	15	7	7	5	11	80
Basalt	4	7	2	4	1	–	1	–	1	2	–	22
Chalcedony	–	1	3	–	–	1	1	–	1	5	4	16
Obsidian	1	–	1	–	2	1	4	–	1	2	2	14
Chert	1	–	1	–	–	1	–	2	2	–	2	9
Hematite	–	–	–	–	1	–	1	–	–	–	3	5
Total	13	19	8	14	10	3	22	9	12	14	22	146

TABLE 7.16. Frequencies of Utilized Shatter Tool Types Correlated with Raw Materials

Material	Knife/Scraper Convex Edge Reference No. 177	Knife/Scraper Straight Edge Reference No. 178	Scraper Concave Edge Reference No. 179	Knife/Scraper with Tip Convex Edge Reference No. 180	Knife/Scraper with Tip Straight Edge Reference No. 181	Scraper with Tip Concave Edge Reference No. 182	Scraper Two Concave Edges Reference No. 183	Unclassified Reference No. 184	Total
Quartzite	35	58	27	12	24	16	4	14	190
Basalt	22	22	4	4	6	1	–	5	64
Chalcedony	13	10	4	1	10	2	–	4	44
Obsidian	12	3	5	1	5	1	–	2	29
Chert	7	6	1	1	1	–	–	–	16
Dolomite	1	4	–	–	2	–	–	1	8
Andesite	2	4	–	–	–	–	–	–	6
Hematite	–	3	1	–	–	–	–	–	4
Magnetite	1	–	–	–	–	–	–	–	1
Opaline	1	–	–	–	–	–	–	–	1
Granite	–	1	–	–	–	–	–	–	1
Total	94	111	42	19	48	20	4	26	364

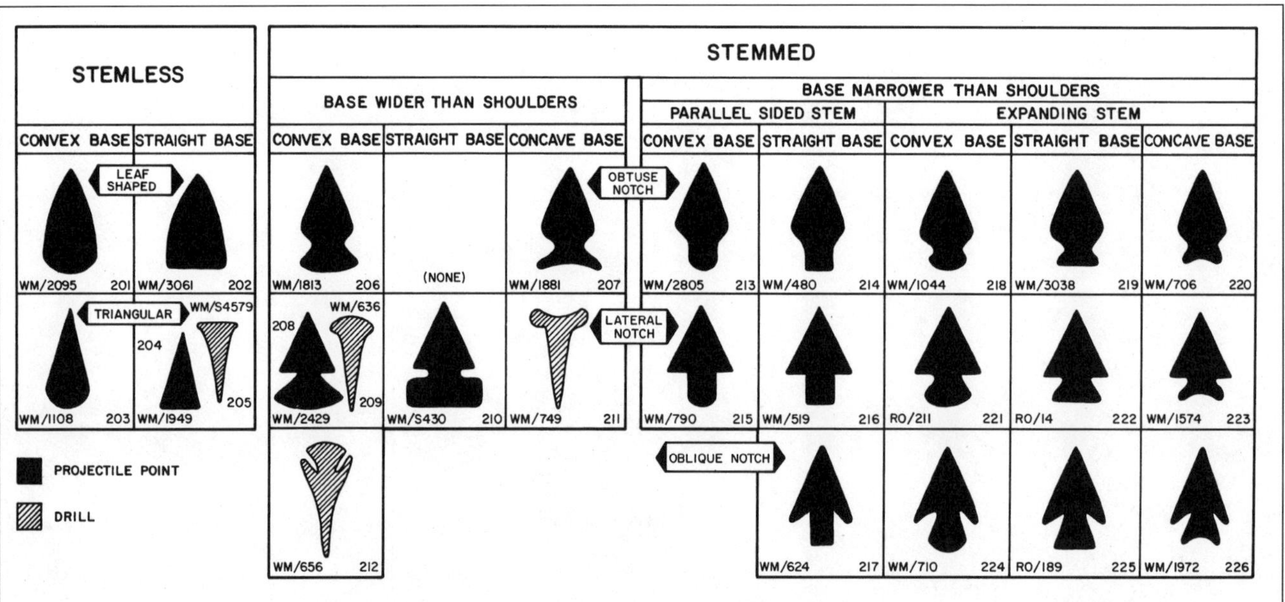

FIGURE 7.21. Projectile point and drill types. The projectile points and drills from Wind Mountain were catalogued according to the above type descriptions.

tool kit suited to diverse tasks. The chronological placement of Wind Mountain substantiates inceptive occupation after agriculture had been established in the Mimbres Mogollon region. Crop plants were important contributors to Wind Mountain's subsistence base, possibly as early as A.D. 250, but certainly by A.D. 450/500. Nether stones and handstones of various sorts, indicative of domestic plant preparation, occur in all contexts, including the earliest structures such as House AN. Charred macrobotanical remains demonstrate that the Wind Mountain agriculturalists cultivated and processed corn, beans, squashes, and agave (Appendixes 1 and 2). Other ground stone implements, including mortars and pestles, as well as basin metates were probably more commonly used to prepare the seeds of wild plant foods. Indeed, the botanical sample suggests that Wind Mountain residents participated in acorn, piñon nut, juniper berry, and possibly walnut harvests.

As is confirmed for many upland settings and, perhaps, for

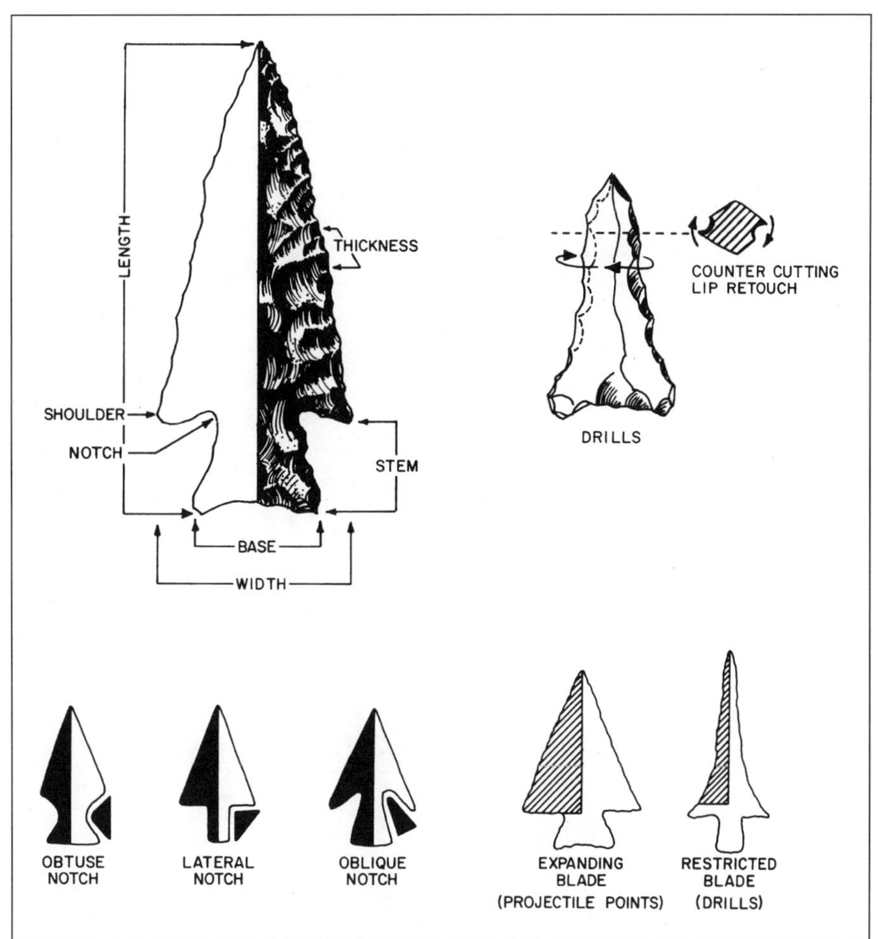

FIGURE 7.22. Projectile point and drill attribute comparisons. Drills exhibited rotary wear marks perpendicular to their long axis and countercutting of the retouched edge.

TABLE 7.17. Frequencies of Unifacial Edge Retouch Shatter Tool Types Correlated with Lithic Raw Materials

Material	Knife/ Scraper Convex Edge Reference No. 185	Knife/ Scraper Grass Knife/ Hoe Straight Edge Reference No. 186	Scraper Concave Edge Reference No. 187	Knife/ Scraper with Tip Convex Edge Reference No. 188	Knife/ Scraper with Tip Straight Edge Reference No. 189	Scraper with Tip Concave Edge Reference No. 190	Knife/ Scraper Two Converging Straight Edges Reference No. 191	Scraper Two Concave Edges Reference No. 192	Unclassified Reference No. 193	Total
Quartzite	7	9	8	3	3	5	10	4	8	57
Basalt	2	1	3	5	–	–	1	–	1	13
Chalcedony	3	3	1	–	–	–	1	–	4	12
Obsidian	–	1	2	1	1	1	–	–	3	9
Chert	2	2	–	–	1	–	–	–	1	6
Hematite	–	1	–	–	–	–	1	–	–	2
Total	14	17	14	9	5	6	13	4	17	99

TABLE 7.18. Frequencies of Bifacial Edge Retouch Shatter Tool Types Correlated with Lithic Raw Materials

Material	Knife/Scraper Convex Edge Reference No. 194	Knife/Scraper/ Grass Knife/Hoe Straight Edge Reference No. 195	Scraper Concave Edge Reference No. 196	Knife/Scraper Two Parallel Edges Reference No. 197	Knife/Scraper Two Converging Straight Edges Reference No. 198	Scraper Two Concave Edges Reference No. 199	Total
Chalcedony	–	1	1	1	1	3	7
Quartzite	–	4	1	–	–	2	7
Obsidian	1	2	–	–	–	1	4
Rhyolite	–	4	–	–	–	–	4
Basalt	1	1	–	–	–	–	2
Chert	–	–	–	–	–	1	1
Shale	–	1	–	–	–	–	1
Welded tuff	–	1	–	–	–	–	1
Crystalline limestone	–	1	–	–	–	–	1
Total	2	15	2	1	1	7	28

Note: Reference No. 200 was defined; however, no shatter tools fitting this category were recovered (see Appendix 5).

TABLE 7.19. Stemless Drill Types Recovered from the Wind Mountain Site

Provenience	Context	Catalogue No.	Reference No.	Material	Shape	Base	Length (cm)	Width (cm)	Thickness (cm)
WM locus									
House V	Fill	WM 1025	204	Quartz	Triangular	Straight	5.7	2.2	0.9
House Y	Fill	WM 1108	203	Quartz	Triangular	Convex	3.3	1.9	0.5
House Z	Fill	WM 1138	204	Quartz	Triangular	Straight	4.3	2.1	0.6
House AC	Fill	WM/S 4579	205	Quartz	Triangular	Straight	3.1+	1.4	0.6
House AD	Fill	WM/S 4899	205	Quartz	Triangular	Straight	2.6+	1.8	0.5
House AF	Fill	WM/S 4928	205	Chalcedony	Triangular	Straight	2.2	1.8	0.7
Block 42-D	Extramural	WM 1157	201	Chert	Leaf	Convex	3.6	2.6	0.7
Block 44-C	Extramural	WM 721	201	Quartz	Leaf	Convex	3.0	1.1	0.6
RO locus									
House H	Fill	RO 146	201	Quartz	Leaf	Convex	4.0	2.1	1.2

TABLE 7.20. Stemmed Drill Types Recovered from the Wind Mountain Site

Provenience	Context	Catalogue No.	Reference No.	Material	Stem	Notches	Base	Length (cm)	Width (cm)	Thickness (cm)
WM locus										
House D	Fill	WM 77	216	Quartz	Parallel	Lateral	Straight	4.3+	1.8	0.9
House E	Fill	WM 551	211	Quartz	Expanding	–	Concave	4.7+	2.2	0.8
House M	Floor fill	WM 656	212	Chalcedony	Expanding	–	Convex	4.4	2.8+	0.5
House R	Floor fill	WM 749	211	Basalt	Expanding	–	Concave	3.6+	1.9	0.6
House T	Fill	WM 851	211	Quartz	Expanding	–	Concave	4.2+	1.3+	0.7+
House V	Fill	WM 937	221	Basalt	Expanding	Lateral	Narrow, convex	4.3+	1.8	0.7
House X	Post hole 1	WM 1594	212	Chert	Expanding	–	Convex	3.9	2.3	0.5
House X	Floor fill	WM 1722	217	Chert	Parallel	Oblique	Straight	3.3	2.0	0.5
House X	Fill	WM 1181	221	Quartz	Expanding	Lateral	Narrow, convex	5.3	2.2	0.9
House X	Fill	WM 1573	221	Chalcedony	Expanding	Lateral	Narrow, convex	3.5	1.9	0.6
Pit 8	Cache	WM 790	215	Quartz	Parallel	Lateral	Convex	12.2	7.3	2.1
Block 20-A	Extramural	WM 636	209	Chalcedony	Expanding	–	Wide, convex	3.6	1.9	0.6
Block 20-B	Extramural	WM 1071	221	Quartz	Expanding	Lateral	Narrow, convex	4.6+	1.9	0.8

prehistoric Southwest agriculture in general (Woosley 1980a, 1986; Wills 1988), neither wild plant gathering or, for that matter, hunting were ever fully replaced by farming and continued to play important roles in the overall economy. At Wind Mountain, the large component of rabbit, deer, and other animal bones with butchering marks (Appendixes 8 and 9) recovered from numerous structures and features provides additional proof for the salience of hunted game as a food resource.

A dependence on both wild and domestic resources and the tools to exploit them is further supported by the diverse nature of the stone inventory and the association of different types of stone tools. In terms of ground stone, the floors of several houses contained nether stone types that have often been associated with either wild or domestic plant preparation. For example, several house floors, including Three Circle Houses H, SS, and AM, yielded closed trough metates (presumably related to processing cultivated corn) and basin metates (for preparing wild plant seeds). Various combinations of basin, closed and through trough metates, slabs, grinding slabs, and in some cases mortars are evident from the floor assemblages of numerous structures (Table 7.24).

Chipped stone, too, argues in favor of a diversified economy. Unifaces and bifaces, projectile points, drills, hammerstones (which Di Peso classified with ground stone), and other chipped stone implements were useful in dispatching and butchering animals, suited to hide scraping, and bone or wood working. Furthermore, heavy chipped stone tools also functioned to fell trees for building materials and in the processing of woody plants.

A movement toward agricultural intensification during the life of the settlement cannot be demonstrated by the Wind Mountain stone tool assemblage (cf. Appendix 1 in this volume). As the site progressed from the Early to the Late Pit House period with the occupation apparently peaking during the Three Circle phase, all aspects of the economy seem

TABLE 7.21. Stemless Projectile Point Types Recovered from the Wind Mountain Site

Provenience	Context	Catalogue No.	Reference No.	Material	Shape	Base	Length (cm)	Width (cm)	Thickness (cm)
WM locus									
House A	Fill	WM 34	204	Rock crystal	Triangular	Straight	3.1+	2.7	1.2
House V	Fill	WM 981	202	Quartz	Leaf	Straight	4.1+	2.4+	0.7
House X	Floor fill	WM 1424	203	Obsidian	Triangular	Convex	1.8	1.3	0.5
House X	Floor fill	WM 1706	204	Chalcedony	Triangular	Straight	2.3+	1.8	0.6
House X	Fill	WM 1507	204	Quartz	Triangular	Straight	2.9+	2.8	1.1
House X	Fill	WM 1523	203	Quartz	Triangular	Convex	3.5+	2.4	0.7
House X	Fill	WM 1714	203	Obsidian	Triangular	Convex	2.0	1.3	0.3
House X	Fill	WM/S 1836	203	Quartz	Triangular	Convex	2.4+	1.9+	0.3
House X	Fill	WM/S 1838	203	Chalcedony	Triangular	Convex	3.6+	2.5+	0.9
House X	Fill	WM/S 2415	201	Quartz	Leaf	Convex	2.6+	1.9	0.4
House X	Fill	WM/S 2416	201	Quartz	Leaf	Convex	2.9+	1.8	0.6
House X	Fill	WM/S 2417	203	Quartz	Triangular	Convex	2.3+	2.7+	0.6
House X	Fill	WM/S 2550	201	Opaline	Leaf	Convex	5.2+	3.4	1.1
House Y	Fill	WM 1185	204	Chalcedony	Triangular	Straight	3.5+	2.5	1.0
House Z	Fill	WM/S 1527	201	Quartz	Leaf	Convex	3.9+	2.7+	0.8
House AA	Floor fill	WM/S 1643	203	Obsidian	Triangular	Convex	2.2+	1.2	0.4
House OO	Fill	WM/S 3424	201	Chert	Leaf	Convex	2.2+	2.7+	0.8
House OO	Fill	WM/S 3535	201	Chalcedony	Leaf	Convex	3.1+	3.1	1.1
House PP	Fill	WM/S 652	201	Quartz	Leaf	Convex	2.2+	2.6+	0.7
House PP	Fill	WM 2069	203	Quartz	Triangular	Convex	3.1+	1.8	0.5
House PP	Fill	WM 2095	201	Quartz	Leaf	Convex	3.5	2.5	0.6
House QQ	Fill	WM/S 3798	203	Chert	Triangular	Convex	2.1+	1.8	0.5
House SS	Fill	WM/S 3925	204	Quartz	Triangular	Straight	2.8+	2.4	0.5
House SS	Fill	WM/S 4233	203	Quartz	Triangular	Convex	2.4+	2.6	0.5
House AC	Fill	WM 2590	203	Obsidian	Triangular	Convex	2.7	1.8	0.4
House AC	Fill	WM/S 4580	203	Quartz	Triangular	Convex	2.6+	2.4	0.5
House AF	Floor fill	WM 2771	201	Quartz	Leaf	Convex	3.7+	2.4	0.9
House AG	Fill	WM/S 5072L	201	Chert	Leaf	Convex	1.9+	2.4+	0.9+
House AI	Fill	WM/S 5140	201	Chalcedony	Leaf	Convex	2.2+	2.4	0.5
House AP	Fill	WM 2997	201	Quartz	Leaf	Convex	3.0+	1.4	0.7
House AQ	Fill	WM 3031	204	Chalcedony	Triangular	Straight	2.1	1.4	0.5
House AQ	Fill	WM 5637	204	Chert	Triangular	Straight	2.1+	1.6	0.5
House AQ	Fill	WM/S 5577	204	Quartz	Triangular	Straight	1.9+	1.9	0.6
Room 7	Floor fill	WM 511	203	Chalcedony	Triangular	Convex	3.7+	2.2	0.7
Room 7	Fill	WM 495	201	Chert	Leaf	Convex	4.0	1.6	0.4
Room 12	Hearth	WM/S 910	204	Obsidian	Triangular	Straight	1.3+	1.4	0.3
Room 13	Floor fill	WM 1087	203	Chert	Triangular	Convex	3.2	1.8	0.8
Pit 57	Extramural	WM/S 4167	203	Quartz	Triangular	Convex	3.4+	1.5+	0.8
Pit Oven 11	Extramural	WM 1949	204	Obsidian	Triangular	Straight	2.0	1.6	0.3
Pit Oven 18	Extramural	WM 3061	202	Quartz	Leaf	Straight	4.0	2.8	1.1
Block 18-C	Extramural	WM 72B	204	Quartz	Triangular	Straight	2.7+	1.4	0.7
Block 25-B	Extramural	WM 75	201	Chert	Leaf	Convex	4.0	2.2	0.5
Block 28-B	Extramural	WM 699	204	Obsidian	Triangular	Straight	1.7+	1.3	0.4
Block 37-D	Extramural	WM 1931	201	Quartz	Leaf	Convex	3.3+	1.9	0.8
Block 37-D	Extramural	WM 1932	201	Opaline	Leaf	Convex	3.1	2.1	0.7
Block 38-D	Extramural	WM 2066	204	Quartz	Triangular	Straight	4.8	3.6	1.0
Block 43-A	Extramural	WM 1158	204	Quartz	Triangular	Straight	3.0	1.8	0.6
Block 44-B	Extramural	WM 726	203	Chalcedony	Triangular	Convex	2.9	1.9	0.4
Block 45-C	Extramural	WM 1734	201	Quartz	Leaf	Convex	4.6+	2.7	1.1
Block 54-A	Extramural	WM 2525	201	Hematite	Leaf	Convex	3.0	1.9+	0.8+
Block 54-B	Extramural	WM/S 3851	203	Chert	Triangular	Convex	2.4+	1.6	0.3
Surface	Extramural	WM 1600	204	Obsidian	Triangular	Straight	1.6	0.9	0.3

TABLE 7.21. *(continued)*

Provenience	Context	Catalogue No.	Reference No.	Material	Shape	Base	Length (cm)	Width (cm)	Thickness (cm)
Surface	Extramural	WM/S 5204	201	Quartz	Leaf	Convex	1.9+	2.2	0.8
Surface	Extramural	WM/S 5769	204	Chalcedony	Triangular	Straight	3.4+	2.7	0.6
RO locus									
House A	Fill	RO/S 7(?)	203	Chalcedony	Triangular	Convex	2.6+	1.7	0.7
House B	Fill	RO/S 77	204	Chalcedony	Triangular	Straight	1.9+	1.6+	0.3
House G	Fill	RO 140	201	Chert	Leaf	Convex	3.7	1.7	0.6
House G	Fill	RO 347	204	Chalcedony	Triangular	Straight	2.8+	2.1+	0.6
House G	Fill	RO/S 359	202	Chalcedony	Leaf	Straight	3.1+	1.8	0.7
House H	Entry fill	RO 149	201	Chalcedony	Leaf	Convex	3.9	2.3	0.7
House H	Floor fill	RO 151	203	Quartz	Triangular	Convex	4.2	1.4	0.6

to expand. This expansion is inferred not only from the lithic collection, but the growth observed in other dimensions of material culture including architecture, as well as macrobotanical and faunal remains. Subsistence endeavors involving the procurement of wild resources and cultigens are presumed to have kept pace with increases in the total economic base and the technologies to exploit them as the Wind Mountain settlement reached its maximum extent. No cataclysmic changes in lithic technology occurred, though some minor trends in implement types are indicated by floor artifacts.

Looking to the nether stone collection from house floors (Table 7.1), for instance, shows that the slab metate type is earliest, appearing in the Early Pit House period as well as during the Georgetown and San Francisco phases, after which the type cannot be associated with a particular house type or temporal placement. In comparison, grinding slabs, basin and closed trough metate types were relatively consistent from the Georgetown phase through the Three Circle phase. Only one through trough metate type was acquired from a floor context (a Mimbres phase structure) at the site (Table 7.24). Consequently, the combination of various types of slabs and metates reinforces the existence of a diversified economy. More tenuous, however, is the certainty that nether stone types are chronologically diagnostic at Wind Mountain. The trends described are based on 44 nether stones recovered from floors, which represent 9 percent of the entire collection (105 whole examples and 382 fragments) from the site. The nether stone sample is somewhat small to make definitive statements about changes of types over time.

Another perspective on determining the magnitude of agricultural intensification involves an analysis of manos. Several studies (Plog 1974; Lancaster 1983, 1986; Hard 1986, 1990; Morris 1990; Schlanger 1991; Nelson and Lippmeier 1993) have attempted to quantify agricultural dependency by demonstrating a correlation with increased ground stone size. Specifically, it has been proposed that mano length, and concomitantly grinding surface area, would increase coevally as agricultural reliance escalated. Hard (1990) has attempted to apply data compiled from Murdock's (1967) *Ethnographic Atlas,* which ranked different cultures with their degree of dependence on cultigens from 0 (none) to 9 (high). Employing data from both ethnographic and archaeological sources, Hard suggested that a mano length of less than 11 cm correlated with none to low (0–15 percent) dependency values; 11–15 cm with none to moderate (0–45 percent); 15–20 cm with moderate to high (35–75 percent); and in excess of 20 cm reflected a high (65 plus percent) dependence on agriculture.

Comparing the data from 111 Wind Mountain site handstones, which included manos and rubbing stones, by phase from pit house and room floor contexts (Table 7.25) against this ranking defines the settlement as moderately to highly dependent on agriculture. The highest values on the scale are associated with the Georgetown, San Francisco, and Mangas phases, the Three Circle and Mimbres phases ranking lowest. The difference in the range of mean mano lengths, randomly distributed for all phases from the site, is a mere 2 cm (13.5 to 15.5 cm). A direct linear correlation between the single variable (length) of one tool type (a mano) to quantity the complex process of agricultural dependency may be inadequate. In reality, when conceptualizing increased reliance on cultigens and the possible codependent development of processing tools, it is highly likely that smaller, as well as larger, implements were created for specialized tasks. We could speculate that the dispersion about the mean might actually broaden with agricultural intensification, leaving the mean virtually unchanged even while the *range* of tool sizes (and types) expands.

Moreover, when reviewing the evidence from botanical and faunal assemblages in addition to the ground stone inventory of the site, the Wind Mountain economy does not appear to have been dominated by agriculture as a primary component. Rather, Wind Mountain subsistence may be properly described as stable and diversified. Cultigens, apparently important early in the life of the settlement (as indicated by the presence of corn kernels and pollen in such structures as Wind Mountain locus Houses R and S and

TABLE 7.22. Stemmed Projectile Point Types Recovered from the Wind Mountain Site

Provenience	Context	Catalogue No.	Reference No.	Material	Stem	Notches	Base	Length (cm)	Width (cm)	Thickness (cm)
WM locus										
House A	Fill	WM 4	222	Chalcedony	Expanding	Lateral	Narrow, straight	2.9+	1.4	0.6
House A	Fill	WM 24	221	Chert	Expanding	Lateral	Narrow, convex	2.5+	2.2	0.6
House A	Fill	WM 45	221	Obsidian	Expanding	Lateral	Narrow, convex	1.2+	0.9	0.2
House B	Fill	WM 46	225	Chalcedony	Expanding	Oblique	Narrow, straight	2.1+	1.6	0.4
House B	Fill	WM 204	214	Quartz	Parallel Sided	Obtuse	Straight	3.8	2.4	0.8
House D	Fill	WM 141	224	Chert	Expanding	Oblique	Narrow, convex	2.9	3.1	0.5
House F	Fill	WM/S 318	222	Quartz	Expanding	Lateral	Narrow, straight	3.8+	2.7	0.7
House L	Floor	WM 480	214	Chert	Parallel Sided	Obtuse	Straight	4.3	2.2	0.6
House L	Floor fill	WM/S 539	219	Obsidian	Expanding	Obtuse	Narrow, straight	2.2+	1.5	0.4
House L	Fill	WM 305	217	Quartz	Parallel Sided	Oblique	Straight	4.2	2.2	0.6
House L	Fill	WM 478	214	Quartz	Parallel Sided	Obtuse	Straight	3.4	1.7	0.5
House P	Fill	WM 708	221	Quartz	Expanding	Lateral	Narrow, convex	4.9+	2.0	0.6
House Q	Floor fill	WM 710	224	Obsidian	Expanding	Oblique	Narrow, convex	3.3	2.0	0.5
House U	Fill	WM 890	224	Chert	Expanding	Oblique	Narrow, convex	3.5+	3.1	0.6
House U	Fill	WM/S 1236	218	Chert	Expanding	Obtuse	Narrow, convex	4.4	1.5+	0.6
House V	Fill	WM 958	206	Chert	Expanding	Obtuse	Wide, convex	2.8+	1.7	0.5
House V	Fill	WM 959	218	Quartz	Expanding	Obtuse	Narrow, convex	3.4	1.6	0.5
House V	Fill	WM 1026	220	Obsidian	Expanding	Obtuse	Narrow, concave	2.4	1.8	0.5
House V	Fill	WM/S 1220	224	Chalcedony	Expanding	Oblique	Narrow, convex	2.6+	2.4	0.6
House W	Fill	WM 1039	218	Chert	Expanding	Obtuse	Narrow, convex	3.1+	1.8	0.7
House X	Fill	WM 1433	218	Quartz	Expanding	Obtuse	Narrow, convex	2.7	1.9	0.5
House X	Floor fill	WM/S 2812	224	Quartz	Expanding	Oblique	Narrow, convex	2.5+	1.7+	0.4
House X	Fill	WM 1044	218	Obsidian	Expanding	Obtuse	Narrow, convex	4.0	1.3	0.4
House X	Fill	WM 1180	216	Obsidian	Parallel Sided	Lateral	Straight	2.6+	1.4	0.4
House X	Fill	WM 1515	224	Quartz	Expanding	Oblique	Narrow, convex	3.3	2.1	0.6
House X	Fill	WM 1574	223	Chert	Expanding	Lateral	Narrow, concave	3.7+	2.2	0.5
House X	Fill	WM 1618	218	Basalt	Expanding	Obtuse	Narrow, convex	2.3	1.5	0.4
House X	Fill	WM 1628	222	Chalcedony	Expanding	Lateral	Narrow, straight	3.1	2.1	0.6
House X	Fill	WM/S 2049	225	Chalcedony	Expanding	Oblique	Narrow, straight	2.8	2.2+	0.4
House X	Fill	WM/S 2271	222	Quartz	Expanding	Lateral	Narrow, straight	1.8+	2.4+	0.5
House X	Fill	WM/S 2495	224	Chalcedony	Expanding	Oblique	Narrow, convex	2.0+	1.9+	0.4
House Y	Fill	WM 1107	223	Obsidian	Expanding	Lateral	Narrow, concave	1.8	0.9	0.3
House Y	Fill	WM 1111	218	Obsidian	Expanding	Obtuse	Narrow, convex	3.9	1.1+	0.4
House Y	Fill	WM/S 1481	224	Chalcedony	Expanding	Oblique	Narrow, convex	2.2+	2.3	0.3
House AA	Floor fill	WM/S 1644	225	Quartz	Expanding	Oblique	Narrow, straight	3.9+	2.5	0.6
House DD	Floor	WM 1753	218	Chert	Expanding	Obtuse	Narrow, convex	1.6	0.7	0.1
House DD	Floor fill	WM 1749	218	Quartz	Expanding	Obtuse	Narrow, convex	3.5	2.0	0.7
House HH	Floor fill	WM 1813	206	Obsidian	Expanding	Obtuse	Wide, convex	2.6	1.7	0.4
House OO	Floor fill	WM/S 3637	224	Quartz	Expanding	Oblique	Narrow, convex	3.4+	2.6	0.8

TABLE 7.22. *(continued)*

Provenience	Context	Catalogue No.	Reference No.	Material	Stem	Notches	Base	Length (cm)	Width (cm)	Thickness (cm)
House OO	Fill	WM 2048	222	Quartz	Expanding	Lateral	Narrow, straight	2.6	1.6	0.5
House OO	Fill	WM 2049	225	Chalcedony	Expanding	Oblique	Narrow, straight	3.0	2.2+	0.5
House OO	Fill	WM 2050	222	Chalcedony	Expanding	Lateral	Narrow, straight	3.2	1.8	0.7
House OO	Fill	WM 2051	221	Chalcedony	Expanding	Lateral	Narrow, convex	5.2	2.0	0.5
House OO	Fill	WM/S 3538	221	Quartz	Expanding	Lateral	Narrow, convex	3.4+	2.1	0.9
House OO	Fill	WM/S 3582	221	Chalcedony	Expanding	Lateral	Narrow, convex	2.4+	1.8	0.6
House PP	Fill	WM/S 3554	219	Quartz	Expanding	Obtuse	Narrow, straight	3.3+	2.9	0.8
House PP	Fill	WM/S 3661	218	Quartz	Expanding	Obtuse	Narrow, convex	2.2+	1.8	0.5
House PP	Fill	WM/S 3662	225	Quartz	Expanding	Oblique	Narrow, straight	2.3+	2.4+	0.5
House SS	Fill	WM 2840	224	Chert	Expanding	Oblique	Narrow, convex	3.4	2.1+	0.7
House TT	Floor fill	WM 2350	218	Obsidian	Expanding	Obtuse	Narrow, convex	3.3	1.9	0.6
House UU	Fill	WM/S 4087	224	Obsidian	Expanding	Oblique	Narrow, convex	4.1	1.9+	0.4
House ZZ	Floor	WM 2571	224	Quartz	Expanding	Oblique	Narrow, convex	3.5	2.0	0.5
House ZZ	Floor fill	WM/S 4410	222	Chalcedony	Expanding	Lateral	Narrow, straight	1.8+	1.9+	0.3
House ZZ	Fill	WM 2503	222	Quartz	Expanding	Lateral	Narrow, straight	3.1	1.8	0.5
House AC	Floor fill	WM 2703	221	Obsidian	Expanding	Lateral	Narrow, convex	2.2	1.5	0.4
House AC	Floor fill	WM 2704	224	Chalcedony	Expanding	Oblique	Narrow, convex	2.6+	1.7	0.4
House AC	Fill	WM/S 4583	218	Quartz	Expanding	Obtuse	Narrow, convex	2.1+	1.4	0.7
House AF	Floor	WM 2852	224	Obsidian	Expanding	Oblique	Narrow, convex	1.8	1.1+	0.3
House AF	Fill	WM/S 4926	225	Quartz	Expanding	Oblique	Narrow, straight	2.3+	2.6	0.5
House AF	Fill	WM/S 4980	221	Chalcedony	Expanding	Lateral	Narrow, convex	3.1+	2.3	0.6
House AG	Fill	WM 2785	221	Chert	Expanding	Lateral	Narrow, convex	3.8	1.9+	0.5
House AI	Floor fill	WM 2834	221	Obsidian	Expanding	Lateral	Narrow, convex	2.2	1.0	0.4
House AI	Fill	WM 2805	213	Quartz	Parallel Sided	Obtuse	Convex	3.3	2.0	0.6
House AL	Fill	WM 2914	224	Chalcedony	Expanding	Oblique	Narrow, convex	4.8	2.3	0.5
House AQ	Fill	WM 3024	213	Chert	Parallel Sided	Obtuse	Convex	2.8	1.8	0.4
House AQ	Fill	WM 3038	219	Chalcedony	Expanding	Obtuse	Narrow, straight	4.1	0.8	0.7
House AQ	Fill	WM/S 5536	218	Basalt	Expanding	Obtuse	Narrow, convex	2.6+	1.7	0.6
Room 2	Floor	WM 47A	207	Obsidian	Expanding	Obtuse	Wide, concave	2.0+	1.0	0.3
Room 2	Floor	WM 47B	207	Obsidian	Expanding	Obtuse	Wide, concave	1.8+	0.7+	0.3
Room 7	Floor fill	WM 512	226	Basalt	Expanding	Oblique	Narrow, concave	2.9	2.6+	0.4
Room 10	Floor fill	WM 519	216	Obsidian	Parallel Sided	Lateral	Straight	2.3	1.7	0.6
Pit 19	Extramural	WM 1069	221	Obsidian	Expanding	Lateral	Narrow, convex	3.3	2.1	0.5
Pit 31	Extramural	WM 1462	221	Chalcedony	Expanding	Lateral	Narrow, convex	5.0	2.9	0.8
Pit Oven 18	Extramural	WM 3059	221	Quartz	Expanding	Lateral	Narrow, convex	3.5	2.2	0.6
Pit Oven 18	Extramural	WM 3060	224	Chalcedony	Expanding	Oblique	Narrow, convex	2.8+	2.1	0.6
Burials 53/54	Extramural	WM 1787	225	Quartz	Expanding	Oblique	Narrow, straight	4.5	2.4	0.8
Burial 62	Extramural	WM 1816	218	Chalcedony	Expanding	Obtuse	Narrow, convex	3.3	1.8	0.6
Burial 94	Extramural	WM 2699	219	Quartz	Expanding	Obtuse	Narrow, straight	7.0	3.1	0.8
Burial 97	Extramural	WM/S 4774	225	Obsidian	Expanding	Oblique	Narrow, straight	2.7	1.7+	0.4

TABLE 7.22. *(continued)*

Provenience	Context	Catalogue No.	Reference No.	Material	Stem	Notches	Base	Length (cm)	Width (cm)	Thickness (cm)
Burial 103	Extramural	WM 3090	224	Obsidian	Expanding	Oblique	Narrow, convex	3.0	1.5+	0.4
Block 11-D	Extramural	WM 389	222	Chert	Expanding	Lateral	Narrow, straight	3.7	1.3	0.4
Block 12-D	Extramural	WM 661	225	Chert	Expanding	Oblique	Narrow, straight	3.0	1.9	0.4
Block 13-C	Extramural	WM 600	218	Quartz	Expanding	Obtuse	Narrow, convex	7.5	2.6	0.9
Block 19-B	Extramural	WM 623	224	Chalcedony	Expanding	Oblique	Narrow, convex	3.0	2.1+	0.5
Block 19-B	Extramural	WM 624	217	Obsidian	Parallel Sided	Oblique	Straight	2.8+	2.3	0.4
Block 20-A	Extramural	WM 635	225	Chalcedony	Expanding	Oblique	Narrow, straight	2.6	1.9	0.4
Block 20-A	Extramural	WM 640	214	Quartz	Parallel Sided	Obtuse	Straight	5.2	2.1	0.6
Block 20-B	Extramural	WM 670	213	Chalcedony	Parallel Sided	Obtuse	Straight	2.4	1.7	0.5
Block 20-C	Extramural	WM 678	218	Quartz	Expanding	Obtuse	Narrow, convex	2.9+	1.6+	0.4
Block 21-C	Extramural	WM/S 2530	221	Quartz	Expanding	Lateral	Narrow, convex	2.9+	1.7+	0.6
Block 21-D	Extramural	WM/S 600	221	Quartz	Expanding	Lateral	Narrow, convex	3.2+	1.9	0.7
Block 21-D	Extramural	WM 1478	219	Obsidian	Expanding	Obtuse	Narrow, straight	2.6	1.8	0.4
Block 21-D	Extramural	WM/S 2015	224	Quartz	Expanding	Oblique	Narrow, convex	2.7+	2.1	0.6
Block 21-D	Extramural	WM/S 2016	224	Quartz	Expanding	Oblique	Narrow, convex	2.4+	2.3+	0.4
Block 25-B	Extramural	WM 74	224	Opaline	Expanding	Oblique	Narrow, convex	3.2+	2.1+	0.6
Block 26-A	Extramural	WM 373	221	Quartz	Expanding	Lateral	Narrow, convex	3.6+	1.9	0.6
Block 26-A	Extramural	WM/S 430	210	Chalcedony	–	Lateral	Straight	1.4+	1.6	0.3
Block 26-D	Extramural	WM 507	224	Quartz	Expanding	Oblique	Narrow, convex	2.5	3.4	0.5
Block 29-D	Extramural	WM 1881	207	Obsidian	Expanding	Obtuse	Wide, concave	2.5	1.9	0.4
Block 30-C	Extramural	WM/S 3221	224	Quartz	Expanding	Oblique	Narrow, convex	2.5+	2.4	0.7
Block 35-A	Extramural	WM 800	221	Obsidian	Expanding	Lateral	Narrow, convex	1.7	0.9	0.2
Block 35-B	Extramural	WM 706	220	Basalt	Expanding	Obtuse	Narrow, concave	3.1	1.7	0.5
Block 35-B	Extramural	WM/S 945	210	Obsidian	–	Lateral	Straight	1.8+	1.0	0.4+
Block 35-D	Extramural	WM 1220	206	Quartz	Expanding	Obtuse	Wide, convex	3.4+	1.8	0.7
Block 36-A	Extramural	WM 755	218	Quartz	Expanding	Obtuse	Narrow, convex	3.0+	1.5	0.4
Block 37-D	Extramural	WM 1936	221	Chalcedony	Expanding	Lateral	Narrow, convex	4.1	1.7	0.6
Block 38-A	Extramural	WM 1963	221	Quartz	Expanding	Lateral	Narrow, convex	3.8	1.9	0.7
Block 38-A	Extramural	WM 1964	221	Obsidian	Expanding	Lateral	Narrow, convex	2.2	1.8	0.4
Block 38-A	Extramural	WM/S 3334	222	Quartz	Expanding	Lateral	Narrow, straight	3.2+	2.1	0.7
Block 45-B	Extramural	WM 1776	225	Quartz	Expanding	Oblique	Narrow, straight	3.6+	2.4	0.4
Block 45-B	Extramural	WM 1917	206	Chalcedony	Expanding	Obtuse	Wide, convex	2.3+	1.5	0.5
Block 45-B	Extramural	WM 1918	206	Quartz	Expanding	Obtuse	Wide, convex	4.3+	1.6+	0.6
Block 45-B	Extramural	WM 1919	224	Obsidian	Expanding	Oblique	Narrow, convex	2.5	1.7+	0.5
Block 47-A	Extramural	WM 1972	226	Quartz	Expanding	Oblique	Narrow, concave	4.1+	2.3	0.6
Block 52-B	Extramural	WM 1779	222	Chalcedony	Expanding	Lateral	Narrow, straight	3.3	1.8	0.4
Block 52-B	Extramural	WM 1780	225	Chalcedony	Expanding	Oblique	Narrow, straight	4.0	2.7	0.4
Block 53-B	Extramural	WM/S 4130	206	Obsidian	–	Obtuse	Wide, convex	1.5+	1.4	0.3
Block 53-D	Extramural	WM 2514	221	Quartz	Expanding	Lateral	Narrow, convex	4.4	2.1	0.6
Block 54-A	Extramural	WM/S 4489	206	Chalcedony	–	Obtuse	Wide, convex	1.9+	1.7	0.4

TABLE 7.22. *(continued)*

Provenience	Context	Catalogue No.	Reference No.	Material	Stem	Notches	Base	Length (cm)	Width (cm)	Thickness (cm)
Block 54-D	Extramural	WM 2429	208	Obsidian	Expanding	Lateral	Wide, convex	2.4	1.9	0.4
Surface	Extramural	WM 14A	221	Obsidian	Expanding	Lateral	Narrow, convex	1.7+	0.9	0.5
Surface	Extramural	WM 14C	218	Obsidian	Expanding	Obtuse	Narrow, convex	2.0	1.3+	0.5
Surface	Extramural	WM/S 53	218	Obsidian	Expanding	Obtuse	Narrow, convex	1.2+	0.9	0.5
Surface	Extramural	WM 155	225	Obsidian	Expanding	Oblique	Narrow, straight	1.6	1.0	0.2
Surface	Extramural	WM 2208	224	Obsidian	Expanding	Oblique	Narrow, convex	1.6	1.0	0.2
Surface	Extramural	WM 3098	221	Obsidian	Expanding	Lateral	Narrow, convex	1.8	1.0	0.4
Surface	Extramural	WM 3099	224	Obsidian	Expanding	Oblique	Narrow, convex	1.6+	1.1	1.1
Surface	Extramural	WM/S 5770	218	Quartz	Expanding	Obtuse	Narrow, convex	3.9+	2.3	1.0
RO locus										
House A	Fill	RO 14	222	Chalcedony	Expanding	Lateral	Narrow, straight	3.4	2.0+	0.5
House D	Floor fill	RO 108	221	Quartz	Expanding	Lateral	Narrow, convex	4.7	2.3+	0.7
House E	Floor	RO 119	224	Quartz	Expanding	Oblique	Narrow, convex	3.5	2.0	0.6
House F	Fill	RO 123	224	Chert	Expanding	Oblique	Narrow, convex	3.7	2.6	0.5
House F	Fill	RO/S 311	218	Opaline	Expanding	Obtuse	Narrow, convex	2.8+	2.0+	0.9
House H	Floor fill	RO 150	225	Quartz	Expanding	Oblique	Narrow, straight	4.5	2.1	0.6
House H	Floor fill	RO 152	222	Quartz	Expanding	Lateral	Narrow, straight	3.4+	2.0	0.6
House H	Fill	RO/S 309	222	Chalcedony	Expanding	Lateral	Narrow, straight	2.8+	1.8	0.6
House H	Fill	RO/S 384	218	Chalcedony	Expanding	Obtuse	Narrow, convex	2.4+	1.5+	0.4
House I	Fill	RO 156	222	Chalcedony	Expanding	Lateral	Narrow, straight	2.2+	2.1	0.5
House J	Floor fill	RO 180	224	Obsidian	Expanding	Oblique	Narrow, convex	4.4	1.7+	0.5
House K	Floor fill	RO 189	225	Chert	Expanding	Oblique	Narrow, straight	4.1	2.5+	0.5
House K	Floor fill	RO 201	225	Basalt	Expanding	Oblique	Narrow, straight	2.5	1.4	0.5
Burial 2	Extramural	RO 211	221	Chalcedony	Expanding	Lateral	Narrow, convex	8.5	3.5	0.8
Surface	Extramural	RO 24	224	Chalcedony	Expanding	Oblique	Narrow, convex	2.7+	2.3	0.4
Surface	Extramural	RO/S 468	224	Quartz	Expanding	Oblique	Narrow, convex	2.2+	1.9+	0.6+

TABLE 7.23. Lithic Materials Used in the Production of Projectile Points and Drills

	Quartz	Chalcedony	Obsidian	Chert	Other	Total
Stemmed projectile points	50	34	37	13	10	144
Stemless projectile points	26	14	8	5	8	61
Subtotal (%)	37	23	22	9	9	
Subtotal	76	48	45	18	18	205
Stemmed drills	6	3	–	1	3	13
Stemless drills	7	1	–	–	1	9
Subtotal (%)	59	18	–	5	18	
Subtotal	13	4	–	1	4	22
Total (%)	39	23	20	8	10	
Total	89	52	45	19	22	227

TABLE 7.24. Nether Stone Types Recovered from the Floors of Dated Structures

Period or Phase	Provenience	Catalogue No.	Type	Reference No.
	WM Locus			
EPHP	House AN	WM 2887	Slab metate	2
GT	House Q	WM 778	Slab metate	2
GT	House Q	WM 780	Grinding slab	29
GT	House Q	WM 885	Closed trough metate	42
GT	House R	WM 835	Grinding slab	29
GT	House R	WM 886	Basin metate	82
SF	House G	WM 352	Grinding slab	29
SF	House G	WM 357	Basin metate	81
SF	House G	WM 358	Grinding slab	29
SF	House K	WM 432	Grinding slab	29
SF	House K	WM 1977	Closed trough metate	41
SF	House AE	WM 2889	Closed trough metate	41
SF	House AI	WM 2883	Grinding slab	29
SF	House AI	WM 2891	Slab metate	1
SF	House AO	WM 3121	Grinding slab	29
Transitional SF/TC	House Y	WM 1234	Grinding slab	29
Transitional SF/TC	House Y	WM 1280	Closed trough metate	41
TC	House H	WM 473	Closed trough metate	42
TC	House H	WM 474	Basin metate	81
TC	House N	WM 810	Grinding slab	29
TC	House N	WM 813	Grinding slab	29
TC	House N	WM 830	Grinding slab	30
TC	House AA	WM 1238	Unclassified metate from slab	89

TABLE 7.24. *(continued)*

Period or Phase	Provenience	Catalogue No.	Type	Reference No.
TC	House DD	WM 1795	Grinding slab	29
TC	House DD	WM 1797	Grinding slab	29
TC	House PP	WM 2168	Basin metate	82
TC	House SS	WM 2464	Closed trough metate	41
TC	House SS	WM 2465	Basin metate	81
TC	House SS	WM 2784	Basin metate	82
TC	House TT	WM 2389	Closed trough metate	41
TC	House TT	WM 2405	Basin metate	82
TC	House XX	WM 2783	Closed trough metate	41
TC	House ZZ	WM 2572	Grinding slab	30
TC	House AG	WM 2862	Closed trough metate	41
TC	House AM	WM 2886	Basin metate	81
TC	House AM	WM 2888	Closed trough metate	41
TC	House AM	WM 2969	Grinding slab	29
Mangas	House V	WM 1290	Grinding slab	29
Mangas	House AD	WM 2845	Grinding slab	29
Mimbres	Room 5/6	WM 492	Mortar	94
Mimbres	Room 15	WM 1980	Through trough metate	43
	RO locus			
SF	House C	RO 3	Basin metate	82
SF	House C	RO 4	Closed trough metate	41
SF	House C	RO 81	Grinding slab	28
SF	House K	RO 8	Closed trough metate	41

EPHP = Early Pit House period, GT = Georgetown phase, SF = San Francisco phase, TC = Three Circle phase.

Ridout locus Houses I and J), were contributors alongside hunted animal resources and gathered wild plants. Consequently, at Wind Mountain mano lengths probably do not represent changes in the economy that involve greater agricultural dependence or intensification but simply reflect size variations common to the manufacture and use of these tools throughout the site's many occupations.

In the case of Wind Mountain, the frequencies of nether stones and handstones escalates over time, reaching their greatest degree and diversity toward the end of the Late Pit House period. Chipped stone artifacts paralleled this tendency. No one subsistence practice intensified substantially over any other. All seemed to expand while sustaining the Late Pit House period occupation. Wind Mountain never developed into a large Mimbres community on the order of a Mattocks, Swarts, or Galaz Ruin whose larger population would have demanded an increased agricultural yield. In contrast, Wind Mountain's economic stability is indicated by the lithic assemblage recovered from the site. Transformations in food procurement and production as indicated by major technological innovations are not apparent and probably did not occur and, indeed, were unnecessary given the magnitude of the Wind Mountain occupation. Some environmental hardship has been suggested for the small Mimbres community (refer to Appendix 2). If environmental stress, whether induced by cultural or natural factors or a combination of the two, affected the final stages of the Wind Mountain habitation, it might explain the eventual abandonment of the settlement ridge.

When considering the functional potential of stone tools, it is important not to lose sight of uses other than those associated with food preparation. For example, the nether stone and handstone combination is extremely efficient for pulverizing clay, sand, or sherds intended for pottery production. Similarly, mortars and pestles may be used to crush minerals for tempering material or pigments. Modern Native

TABLE 7.25. Mean Lengths of Manos and Rubbing Stones from Wind Mountain and Ridout Loci Floor Contexts

	Georgetown	San Francisco	Three Circle	Mangas	Mimbres	Combined Range (All Phases)
Range (cm):						
Length	9.2–21.8	8.1–27.0	4.8–25.6	6.5–26.8	11.4–18.7	4.8–27.0
Width	8.0–16.5	6.7–15.0	4.4–18.7	8.6–16.1	9.5–13.4	4.4–18.7
Thickness	3.1–7.2	2.7–8.0	2.5–9.1	3.5–6.5	3.9–7.7	2.5–9.1
Mean (cm):						
Length	15.3	15.5	13.5	15.3	14.6	13.5–15.5
Width	11.9	11.2	10.0	10.8	11.2	10.0–11.9
Thickness	4.5	4.6	4.5	4.6	5.9	4.5–5.9
Frequency of artifacts used in calculations:						
Manos	8	26	29	4	5	72
Rubbing Stones	3	15	16	4	1	39
Total	11	41	45	8	6	111

American potters are known to salvage prehistoric grinding tools for precisely this purpose. Many Wind Mountain pestles displayed a high sheen on all surfaces suggesting that they doubled as polishers. Tabular proto-palettes were used as abraders, smoothers, and to sharpen awls as indicated by a variety of wear marks. Worn nether stones often found secondary architectural use, for instance, in the repairing of pit house walls. Used handstones were heated and placed in hearths and roasting pits to cook foods. The multiple function of most stone tools is firmly supported by ethnographic data. The Hopi, for instance, utilize hammerstones to crush minerals and seed, to pound hides, and to act as pecking tools (Woodbury 1954:92–93). Very few tool types in prehistoric inventories were exclusively used for one purpose. In all likelihood, all tools served diverse functions.

Finally, the ground and chipped stone assemblage from Wind Mountain reflects the extent and variety of raw materials locally available, especially from the Big and Little Burro Mountains. Workable pebbles, cobbles, and boulders were immediately accessible from the two drainages bordering the site and from nearby Mangas Creek. Clearly, the residents of the Wind Mountain settlement utilized stone that could be obtained locally and found it unnecessary to acquire much lithic material from elsewhere.

8

Southern Inspiration and Economic Enterprise

Three general material classes, including socioreligious objects, articles of personal adornment, and raw materials, are, at first reading, a curious union of categories. However, a reappraisal of Di Peso's view of Mogollon prehistory as only one contributing component to the broad based cultural expressions characterizing the Gran Chichimecan macroregion will clarify this seemingly puzzling association of artifact classes.

A persistent theme in Di Peso's portrayal of cultural dynamics in the Gran Chichimeca is that of economic enterprise as the prime motivator of change (Di Peso 1974, 1983b). At various times and in varying degrees, southern based merchants moved northward out of present day Mexico seeking resources not available in their homelands. Concomitant with economic expansion, these traders imposed Mesoamerican inspired culture patterns on local Chichimec populations. This infusion of foreign conventions was achieved through religious mechanisms, which brought southern cults and symbolism to, among other groups, the Mogollon Chichimecs. Di Peso believed that the mingling of culture patterns could be substantiated by close scrutiny of the material inventory. If, in fact, southern merchants were responsible for the reorganization of northern settlements such as Wind Mountain into trade satellites, he expected "foreign" imports to be common alongside "local" products in the overall Wind Mountain material inventory.

Di Peso's unfailing belief in the existence of the active donor (i.e., Mesoamericans) to passive recipient (i.e., Mogolloñes) relationship—the vehicle that shaped northern Gran Chichimec cultures after c. A.D. 300—strongly influenced his approach to artifact ordering. It is especially apparent when considering the large class of artifacts he termed socioreligious. Though this category contains numerous and diverse types, all are identified with some sort of socioreligious function. Remembering Di Peso maintained that religious mechanisms were a major avenue of foreign cultural imprinting, objects subsumed under this heading were said to carry southern religious symbolism.

With the arrival of sophisticated southern traders, an increase in objects associated with wealth and status, as well as an elaboration in items of personal adornment, was anticipated. Di Peso believed that the stylistic forms expressed by ornaments would reflect the amalgamation of local and foreign attributes. Furthermore, although certain raw materials used in the manufacture of luxury items were locally available (e.g., turquoise, malachite, or amethyst), exotics (shell and possibly copper) would appear in the material inventory that represented more distant centers (linked by a trade network).

Finally, because economic enterprise was the impetus for forming trade satellites, commodities procured for redistribution were expected to occur in large amounts in these subordinate communities. At Wind Mountain, nearby mineral resources were suggested to constitute the settlement's wealth and, for that matter, the determining factor for its inclusion in a southern dominated mercantile system.

In combination, socioreligious objects, articles of personal adornment, and raw resources were judged those elements in Wind Mountain's material inventory to be particularly illustrative of southern donor and northern recipient interactions. Di Peso maintained that these artifact classes were the indicators that would establish the reality of a southern entrepreneurial presence at Wind Mountain. These classes would provide evidence to support the site's role as a resource procurement satellite within a larger Gran Chichimecan trade system. In an admittedly speculative vein, they would also yield hints about the specific religious beliefs brought to Wind Mountain by foreign merchants.

FIGURE 8.1. Zoomorphic figurines modeled of clay, Reference No. 339. Clockwise from left: WM 288, WM 2234, WM 603, WM/C 452, WM 1894. For context and dimensions, refer to Table 8.1 (Neg. No. WM 151–8L).

The Socioreligious Material Inventory

The Wind Mountain socioreligious inventory consisted of objects believed to have ritual or ceremonial connotation. Di Peso identified several artifact types, including figurines, pipes, tubes, fetishes, counters, worked sherds, and cornucopias. These are described below, together with associated religious implications as perceived by Di Peso. A small number of miscellaneous types, each represented in extremely low quantities, but also suggested to have socioreligious functions are combined in a separate discussion.

FIGURE 8.2. Clay hummingbird (RO 235) recovered from the Ridout locus. Reference No. 339 (Neg. No. WM 152–19L).

Figurines

Small human and animal figurines have far-reaching geographic distribution across the prehistoric Southwest. Thirty-seven zoomorphic (Reference No. 339) and 20 anthropomorphic (Reference No. 340) ceramic figurines were recovered at Wind Mountain (Table 8.1). All are made of modeled or pinched clay, which was sometimes, but not always, fired (Figure 8.1).

Figurines were classified as either Alma Plain (n = 40) or Alma Rough (n = 17), generic types that characterize unpainted, often roughly fashioned ceramic forms. With the exception of facial features which are sometimes indicated, for the most part, both animal and human figurines exhibit little detail. Zoomorphic figurines are not recognizable as to specific animal except in rare cases (Figure 8.2). Although the Wind Mountain animal figurines are reminiscent of those reported at Mogollon Village and Harris Village (Haury 1936a:28, 68), no zoomorphic effigies similar to examples reported from other Mogollon contexts (Lekson and Klinger 1973a) were recovered.

All anthropomorphic figurines recovered from the site occurred in fragmentary form; two are clearly female torsos (Figure 8.3). Otherwise, mainly the extremities (e.g., legs) survived. The fragments indicate simply made, highly stylized forms. Only extended, as compared with seated, human figures were represented in the assemblage. The human figurines from Wind Mountain do not exhibit any particular conformity with Hohokam types (Gladwin et al. 1937: Plates 197–207; Haury 1976:255–260), except that they are also unelaborated. Although Southwestern anthropomorphic ceramic figurines are commonly associated with the Hohokam, it has been suggested that all ultimately derived from

TABLE 8.1. Anthropomorphic and Zoomorphic Figurines

Provenience	Context	Catalogue No.	Reference No.	Type	Material	Length (cm)	Width (cm)	Height (cm)
WM locus								
House A	Fill	WM 3	339	Z	AP	2.8+	1.3	1.6+
House B2	Floor	WM/C 26	339	Z	AR	2.7+	1.9+	2.7+
House H	Entry fill	WM 364	339	Z	AP	4.9+	1.8	2.6+
House K	Fill	WM/C 114	340	A	AP	3.6+	1.0	3.6+
House K	Fill	WM 288	339	Z	AP	3.0+	1.6	2.2+
House L	Entry fill	WM/C 159	340	A	AR	2.3+	1.0	2.3+
House N	Fill	WM/C 200	340	A	AP	4.1+	1.6	4.1+
House S	Floor fill	WM/C 324	340	A	AR	2.3+	0.9	2.3+
House S	Fill	WM/C 314	339	Z	AP	3.5+	1.6+	1.8+
House V	Fill	WM/C 351	339	Z	AR	3.0+	2.5+	2.8+
House V	Fill	WM/C 352	339	Z	AR	4.6+	2.3+	2.8+
House X	Fill	WM/C 538	339	Z	AP	4.8+	2.3+	3.0+
House X	Fill	WM/C 616	339	Z	AP	3.8+	1.8+	1.8+
House X	Fill	WM/C 646	340	A	AP	3.5+	1.3	1.3+
House X	Fill	WM/C 688	339	Z	AR	3.1+	1.5+	1.6+
House X	Fill	WM/C 689	339	Z	AP	2.8+	2.1+	2.5+
House X	Fill	WM 1298	340	A	AP	5.9+	2.6	5.9+
House Z	Fill	WM/C 433	340	A	AP	5.0+	3.9+	2.5+
House AA	Fill	WM/C 473	340	A	AR	3.1+	2.3+	1.6+
House DD	Fill	WM/C 481	339	Z	AR	5.6+	3.1	3.0+
House DD	Fill	WM/C 516A	340	A	AP	2.9+	0.8	1.2+
House DD	Fill	WM/C 516B	339	Z	AP	3.2+	2.7+	2.4+
House OO	Fill	WM/C 845	340	A	AP	3.2+	1.3	3.2+
House OO	Fill	WM/C 846	339	Z	AR	2.6+	2.3+	1.4+
House OO	Fill	WM 2039	339	Z	AP	5.3+	1.9+	3.2+
House PP	Floor fill	WM/C 875	339	Z	AP	3.1+	2.0+	2.4+
House PP	Floor fill	WM/C 908	339	Z	AR	4.4+	2.4+	3.0+
House PP	Fill	WM/C 861	339	Z	AP	2.5+	1.6+	2.4+
House SS	Fill	WM/C 944	339	Z	AR	2.9+	1.5+	1.2+
House SS	Fill	WM 2234	339	Z	AP	3.0+	1.5	2.5+
House AF	Fill	WM 2754	339	Z	AP	2.5+	1.4	1.5+
House AQ	Floor fill	WM/C 1361	340	A	AP	2.9+	0.9+	2.9+
House AQ	Floor fill	WM 3055	339	Z	AR	6.2+	2.6+	2.5+
House AQ	Fill	WM/C 1318	339	Z	AP	4.1+	1.9+	2.1+
Room 14	Floor fill	WM/C 452	339	Z	AP	2.5+	1.6	1.8
Room 15	Floor fill	WM/C 571	339	Z	AP	2.7+	2.0+	2.9+
Burial 1	Extramural	WM/C 25	340	A	AP	1.3+	0.7	1.3+
Pit 21	Extramural	WM/C 416	339	Z	AR	3.9+	2.3	3.2+
Block 13-B	Extramural	WM 663	339	Z	AP	4.6+	2.8	4.1+
Block 18-B	Extramural	WM/C 79	340	A	AP	5.4+	2.2	5.4+
Block 18-C	Extramural	WM/C 29	339	Z	AP	3.1+	1.8+	3.1+
Block 19-A	Extramural	WM 603	339	Z	AP	5.0+	1.7	2.4+
Block 20-A	Extramural	WM/C 235	340	A	AP	2.2+	0.8	2.2+
Block 21-D	Extramural	WM/C 608	339	Z	AR	3.7+	2.5	3.2+
Block 25-B	Extramural	WM/C 31	339	Z	AP	4.0+	2.1+	3.1+
Block 28-D	Extramural	WM 705	339	Z	AR	4.7+	1.5+	2.3+
Block 30-A	Extramural	WM/C 753	340	A	AP	2.3+	1.0	2.3+
Block 30-C	Extramural	WM/C 764	339	Z	AR	2.6+	1.8+	1.9+
Block 30-C	Extramural	WM 1894	339	Z	AP	4.1	2.1	2.4+

TABLE 8.1. *(continued)*

Provenience	Context	Catalogue No.	Reference No.	Type	Material	Length (cm)	Width (cm)	Height (cm)
Block 35-A	Extramural	WM/C 403	340	A	AP	3.2+	2.9+	3.2+
Block 37-D	Extramural	WM/C 805	340	A	AP	2.8+	1.2+	2.8+
Block 38-A	Extramural	WM/C 811	340	A	AP	2.4+	0.9	2.4+
Block 38-A	Extramural	WM/C 812	339	Z	AP	4.4+	2.0+	2.5+
Block 44-B	Extramural	WM/C 1412	339	Z	AR	3.1	1.7	2.7
Block 62-A	Extramural	WM/C 1061	340	A	AP	2.1+	0.8+	2.1+
RO locus								
House I	Floor fill	RO/C 54	340	A	AP	2.5+	1.1	2.5+
Block N3E	Extramural	RO 235	339	Z	AP	4.1	1.2	1.4

AP = Alma Plain, AR = Alma Rough, A = Anthropomorphic, Z = Zoomorphic.

Mesoamerican roots (Di Peso 1974:90; Haury 1976:255). Di Peso also proposed that figurines represented a Mesoamerican fertility cult (1974:225).

At Wind Mountain, of the 57 animal and human figurines, only one anthropomorphic form (WM/C 26, House B2) was recovered from a floor. The remaining examples were either recovered from the floor fill or entry fill of structures or from extramural deposits. Interestingly, no figurines were recovered from burial contexts. It would seem, then, that figurines did not have a personal, amulet related function. Moreover, whatever socioreligious role they may have played, Wind Mountain figurines cannot be associated with house shrines. Figurines may have been used in rituals (or buried) outside of structures, and the possibility that some animal or human forms represented nonreligious tokens (e.g., toys) should not be discounted.

FIGURE 8.3. Anthropomorphic figurines of clay, Reference No. 340. Left to right: WM 1298 and WM/C 403. In contrast to zoomorphic forms, few anthropomorphic figures were recovered from the site (Neg. No. WM 151–6L).

Pipes

Ceramic pipes (Reference Nos. 329–332, 334 and 335, Table 8.2), unclassified ceramic pipe/tube fragments (Reference No. 336, Table 8.3), stone pipes (Reference Nos. 307–315, Table 8.4), and bone pipes (Reference Nos. 326 and 327A, Table 8.5) constituted a large class of socioreligious artifacts. The implication of pipes used during ritual smoking will be treated below. At Wind Mountain, most of the 37 ceramic pipes found were undecorated, although one exhibited scoring and another displayed incising on a tapering or funnel form (Figure 8.4). Clay pipes were shaped by hand and pierced before firing. A few were biconically drilled.

Stone pipes (n = 24) were produced primarily from tubular blanks of welded tuff (n = 9), vesicular basalt (n = 7), or biotite schist (n = 7; Figure 8.5). Manufacturing techniques involved pecking and grinding, followed by conical or biconical perforation using a drill (Figures 8.6 and 8.7). As with ceramic forms, most stone pipes were undecorated but a few were embellished with incised designs. One stone pipe was incised and collared (refer to Figure 8.4).

The Wind Mountain pipe inventory also included two examples made of bone (Table 8.5). These may represent the detached stems of a two piece pipe the ceramic "bowls" of which were not recovered (Figure 8.8).

One extramural feature at the site, Pit 8, contained what may have been a cache of pipe manufacturing implements, including an unfinished welded tuff pipe (WM 791, Table 8.4), a drill, a flake tool, a mano fragment, a core, and two pieces of hematite. This complement of tools would have been all that was necessary to shape, perforate, and decorate pipes. The presence of red ocher is intriguing because so few Wind Mountain pipes show any sort of decoration. Perhaps, more

TABLE 8.2. Ceramic Pipes

Provenience	Context	Catalogue No.	Reference No.	Material	Length (cm)	Outside Diameter (cm)	Bowl Diameter (cm)	Stem Hole
WM locus								
House A	Fill	WM/C 14A	335	API	2.7+	1.4+	1.3+	–
House C	Fill	WM/C 40C	334	AR	2.5+	1.9+	0.9+	BC
House C	Fill	WM/C 40D	329	AR	4.7+	3.0+	2.0+	L,S
House C	Fill	WM 117	331	AR	4.3+	4.0	2.9+	Sh,B
House G	Entry fill	WM/C 67	334	AR	4.0	2.7+	2.1+	BC
House K	Fill	WM/C 121	331	AR	6.9	3.6	2.8	Sh,B
House L	Fill	WM/C 92D	329	AR	5.9	2.6+	3.0	L,S
House M	Floor fill	WM/C 228	334	AR	5.0	3.0	2.1	BC
House S	Fill	WM/C 323A	329	AR	5.5	3.0	1.6+	L,S
House U	Fill	WM/C 331	329	AR	2.0+	2.6+	2.0+	L,S
House U	Fill	WM/C 338A	334	AR	5.0	3.3	1.9	BC
House V	Fill	WM/C 374G	331	AR	3.9	2.9	2.2+	Sh,B
House V	Fill	WM/C 1401	334	AR	3.4	2.5	2.1	BC
House W	Floor fill	WM/C 429B	331	AR	4.8	2.3+	1.4+	Sh,B
House W	Fill	WM/C 410A	334	AR	5.0	3.3	1.9	BC
House X	Floor fill	WM/C 685	329	AR	3.5+	2.3+	–	L,S
House X	Fill	WM/C 495	331	AR	4.3	2.4+	2.1+	Sh,B
House X	Fill	WM/C 551A	335	API	4.1+	3.0+	1.9+	–
House X	Fill	WM/C 1396	331	AR	3.0+	2.6+	1.4+	Sh,B
House Y	Fill	WM/C 453A	331	AS	4.0	2.1+	1.5+	Sh,B
House Y	Fill	WM/C 453B	334	AR	4.8	3.6+	2.3+	BC
House PP	Floor fill	WM 2145	330	AR	7.6	4.5	2.2	L,S
House XX	Floor fill	WM/C 1133	331	AR	4.2	2.3+	1.6+	Sh,B
House AQ	Fill	WM/C 1374	329	AP	3.3+	2.8+	–	L,S
Block 13-C	Extramural	WM/C 1400	334	AR	4.2	2.7+	2.0	BC
Block 17-B/D	Extramural	WM/C 15B	331	AR	4.0+	2.9+	2.0+	Sh,B
Block 18-D	Extramural	WM/C 49	329	AR	4.0+	3.3+	1.9	L,S
Block 20-A	Extramural	WM 633	332	AR	1.9+	3.0+	–	Sh,B
Block 21-D	Extramural	WM/C 577A	334	AR	4.1	2.3+	1.5+	BC
Block 21-D	Extramural	WM/C 577B	334	AR	3.4	3.5+	1.5+	BC
Block 21-D	Extramural	WM/C 607	329	AP	5.0	3.5	2.2	L,S
Block 21-D	Extramural	WM 1272	334	AR	4.5	2.9	1.8	BC
Block 22-A	Extramural	WM/C 505	329	AR	2.6+	2.8+	1.9+	L,S
Block 22-C	Extramural	WM/C 533	331	AR	3.4	2.4	1.6+	Sh,B
Block 44-B	Extramural	WM/C 278	331	AR	4.8	3.1+	2.3+	Sh,B
Block 44-B	Extramural	WM/C 354	331	AR	3.4	2.9	1.5	Sh,B
RO locus								
House B	Fill	RO 40	330	AP	5.8	3.6	2.1	L,S

AP = Alma Plain, API = Alma Pattern Incised, AR = Alma Rough, AS = Alma Scored, B = Blunt, BC = Biconical, L = Long, S = Straight, Sh = Short.

pipes were once adorned with mineral paint, but these fugitive pigments did not survive over the long term. A cache of three stone pipes (WM 2277, WM 2278, and WM 2279, Table 8.4) was found in another Wind Mountain extramural context, Pit 56 (refer to Figure 4.28). Such caches have been reported at other Mimbres Mogollon sites, including Galaz Ruin, where two unfinished pipes were associated with stone hoes (Anyon and LeBlanc 1984:289).

Tubes

Tubes (Table 8.6) were produced by modifying bird (Reference No. 325) and mammal (Reference No. 327) bone or by shaping and firing clay cylinders (Reference No. 333). Unclassified ceramic pipe/tube fragments were also noted (Reference No. 336, see Table 8.3). Examples from Wind Mountain were usually undecorated (Figures 8.8 and 8.9). The role

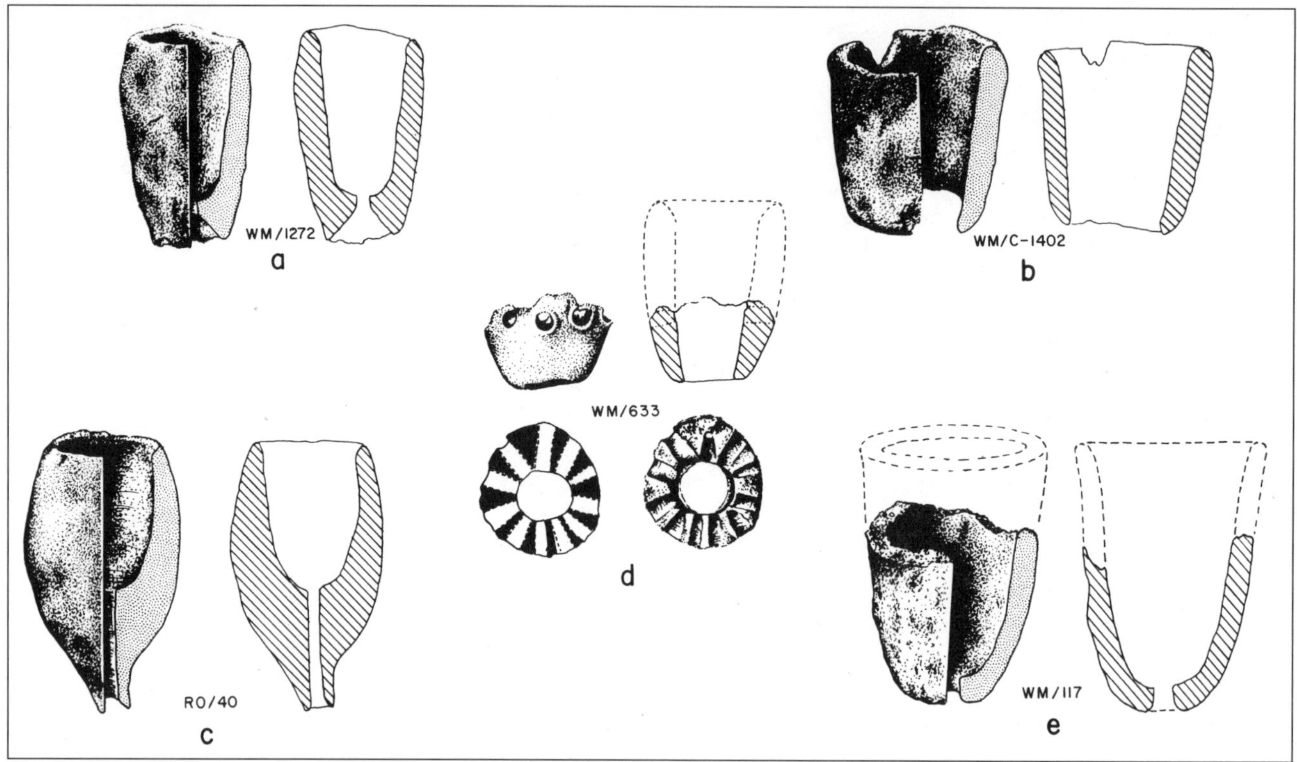

FIGURE 8.4. Examples of ceramic pipes. (a) Reference No. 334; (b) reference number not assigned; (c) Reference No. 330; (d) Reference No. 332; (e) Reference No. 331. Most ceramic pipes were undecorated and may be subsumed under the Alma Plain type. For context and dimensions, refer to Table 8.2.

of tubes in ritual has been widely reported (see below), but their uses could have been more prosaic as drinking tubes, whistles, or tubular bead ornaments (Hodge 1920:121–128; Kidder 1932:267–268).

Di Peso (Wind Mountain files, Amerind Foundation) summarized selected ethnographic sources that describe the ceremonial function of tubes (and pipes) in ritual smoking, cloud production, and the inhalation of powdered narcotics. Both pipes and tubes were used in the latter activity, whereas pipes were mainly associated with smoking, and the tube cloud blower was said to produce ritual smoke. Ethnographic accounts relating to tube and pipe usage comes from the Tohono O'odham (Papago) (Russell 1908:112), from Zuni (Schultes 1972:46–49), and from the Seri (Bowen 1976:74, 101).

Archaeologically, tubes and pipes have great antiquity and are widely distributed. They were recovered in preceramic deposits at Ventana Cave (Haury 1950:329–332), at Mogollon Village, and from Harris Village (Haury 1936a:38, 72, 106). Di Peso (1956:426–430) recovered them from the Paloparado site (aka - San Cayetano) on the Santa Cruz River in southern Arizona and at Casas Grandes (1974:587–588). In the northern Southwest, tubes and pipes have been found at Pecos Pueblo (Kidder 1932:266–268) and at sites in the northern Rio Grande Valley (Woosley 1980b:22).

On the basis of such data, Di Peso interpreted smoking, reflected in the prehistoric material assemblage by pipes and tubes, to purport a priestly cult involving the ceremonial inhalation of hallucinogenics. In the Southwest he cited narcotic plants such as *Datura* or jimson weed (Martin et al. 1956:94–96) and *Nicotiana* or native tobacco (Morris and Jones 1962) that could be used in ceremonies. Smoking rituals were suggested to enhance communication with the gods during ceremonies and for curing. Di Peso quoted both the ethnographic and historical literature for evidence of smoking ceremonies. For instance, Furst (1974:55–57) and Sahagun (1963:129–131) report the use of narcotic plants in Mesoamerica, where smoking was connected with the rain god Tlaloc. Similarly, Roberts (1930:141) noted Puebloan ceremonies in which puffs of smoke blown by priests were intended to represent clouds, thereby enhancing the opportunity for bringing rain. Smoking symbolism associated with pipes and tubes was also wide spread in prehistoric eastern North America (Ford 1969:82–83). Di Peso proposed that ritual smoking customs dispersed into the Gran Chichimeca via west Mexico, especially the Nayarit region, and from other, as yet unidentified origins even further south. The smoker motif, often combined with curing, was widely depicted from Casas Grandes southward (Di Peso 1974:570),

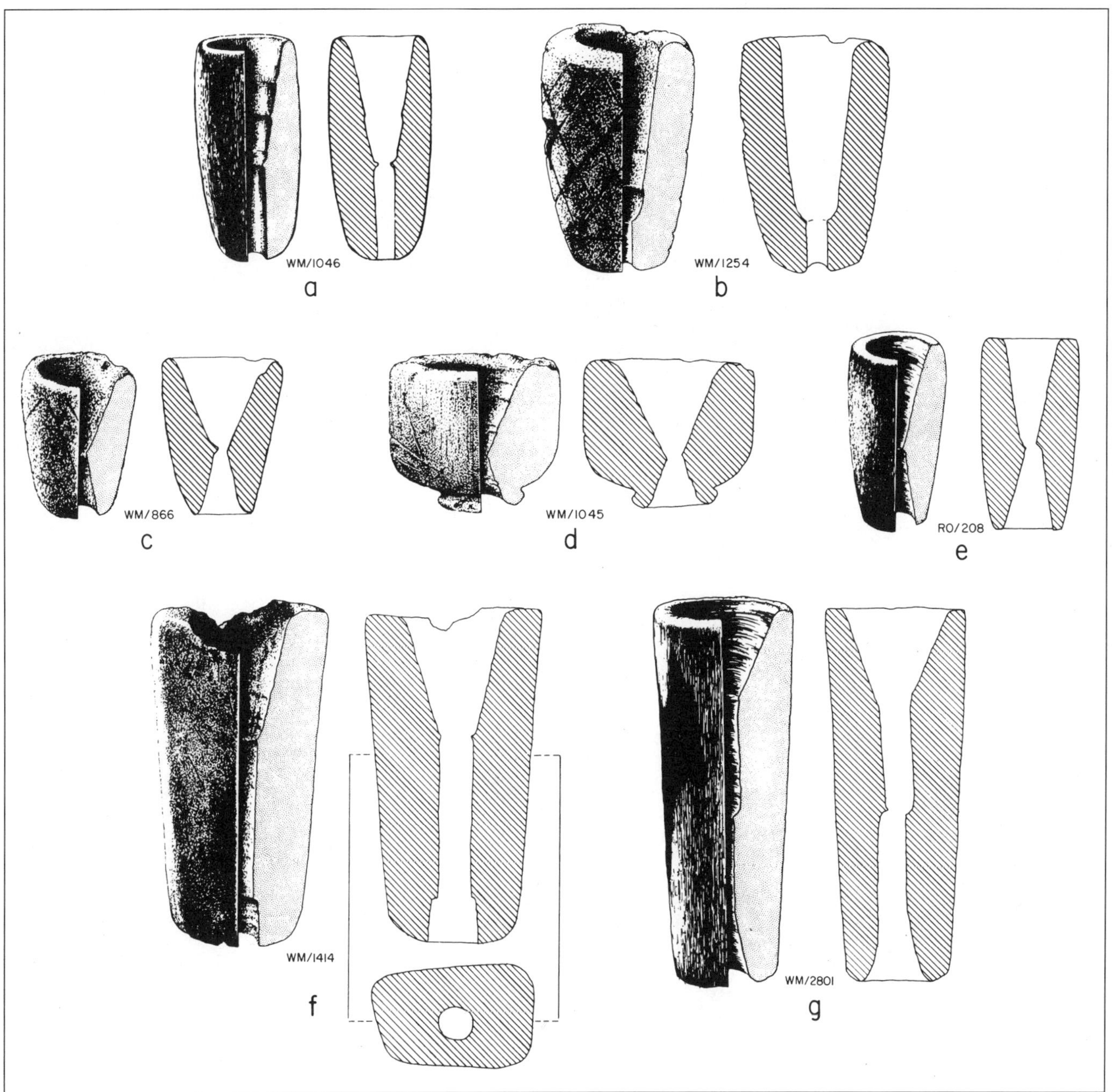

FIGURE 8.5. Examples of stone pipes. (a) Reference No. 309; (b) Reference No. 312; (c) Reference No. 310; (d) Reference No. 313; (e) Reference No. 307; (f) Reference No. 311; (g) Reference No. 308. For context and dimensions, refer to Table 8.4.

and is also known from the Mimbres Valley (Fewkes 1914: Figure 14). Whatever its mode of dispersion, the widespread occurrence of ritual smoking in ethnographic contexts together with the numerous finds of smoking related artifacts in prehistoric sites implies that such ceremony was pandemic to much of the New World. The abundance of pipes and tubes at the Wind Mountain site argues favorably that its inhabitants may have been participants in a long-lived ceremonial tradition.

Stone Fetishes and Counters

Stone fetishes and counters represented another important category of socioreligious objects (Table 8.7). Di Peso identified stone fetishes (n = 11) as either flat (n = 5, Reference No. 305) or round (n = 6, Reference No. 306). They were incised or carved of stone, sometimes merely by modifying naturally occurring concretions of indeterminate forms (Figure 8.10). The Wind Mountain fetish type should not, however, be confused with the more popularly recognized Zuni figures of the

TABLE 8.3. Unclassified Ceramic Pipes/Tubes (Reference No. 336)

Provenience	Context	Catalogue No.	Material	Length (cm)	Outside Diameter (cm)	Bowl Diameter (cm)
WM locus						
House A	Fill	WM/C 148	AR	3.0+	2.2+	1.7+
House C	Fill	WM/C 40A	AR	3.7+	3.5+	5.1+
House C	Fill	WM/C 40B	AR	2.1+	1.8+	1.2+
House E	Fill	WM/C 1398	AR	4.3+	5.4+	5.0+
House K	Fill	WM/C 113A	AR	4.5+	2.4+	1.7+
House K	Fill	WM/C 113B	AR	6.7+	4.2+	3.4
House K	Fill	WM/C 143A	AR	3.7+	3.5+	2.0+
House K	Fill	WM/C 143B	AR	2.8+	2.5+	1.7+
House K	Fill	WM/C 143C	AR	2.9+	1.9+	1.4
House K	Fill	WM/C 143D	AR	3.1+	2.0+	1.6+
House K	Fill	WM/C 143E	AR	3.5+	1.8+	0.7+
House L	Fill	WM/C 92A	AR	4.0+	2.3+	1.9+
House L	Fill	WM/C 92B	AR	4.3+	2.5+	1.4+
House L	Fill	WM/C 92C	AR	4.0+	3.1+	–
House L	Fill	WM/C 170	AS	2.6+	2.9+	2.5
House N	Fill	WM/C 191A	AR	3.3+	2.0+	1.2+
House P2	Fill	WM/C 254B	AR	2.5+	2.0+	–
House S	Fill	WM/C 323B	AR	4.3+	3.0+	2.0+
House U	Fill	WM/C 3388	AP	2.7+	3.0+	3.0+
House U	Fill	WM/C 1395	AR	2.7+	2.5+	–
House V	Fill	WM/C 369A	AR	2.6+	2.2+	1.8+
House V	Fill	WM/C 369B	AR	4.1+	3.5+	2.2+
House V	Fill	WM/C 369C	AR	2.1+	3.4+	3.0+
House V	Fill	WM/C 369D	AR	4.8	2.5+	1.8+
House V	Fill	WM/C 374A	AR	2.9+	1.8+	1.0+
House V	Fill	WM/C 374B	AR	3.2+	2.5+	2.0+
House V	Fill	WM/C 374C	AP	2.9+	2.5+	2.0+
House V	Fill	WM/C 374D	AR	3.2+	3.5+	3.0+
House V	Fill	WM/C 374E	AP	2.5+	2.4+	2.0+
House V	Fill	WM/C 1403	AP	4.1+	5.2+	5.0+
House W	Floor fill	WM/C 429A	AR	2.9+	2.3+	–
House W	Fill	WM/C 410B	AR	2.9+	3.5+	3.0+
House W	Fill	WM/C 410C	AR	4.3+	3.3+	3.0+
House W	Fill	WM/C 410D	API	3.4+	3.3+	3.0+
House W	Fill	WM/C 410E	AR	3.3+	4.0+	3.9+
House W	Fill	WM/C 410F	AP	3.6+	5.0+	2.0+
House X	Fill	WM/C 551C	AR	3.3+	2.6+	–
House Y	Fill	WM/C 1405	AR	3.6+	2.6+	2.0+
House Z	Fill	WM/C 432	AR	3.1+	2.9+	2.0+
House AA	Fill	WM/C 501	AR	4.5+	4.5+	4.0+
House DD	Fill	WM/C 515A	AR	3.0+	5.2+	5.0+
House DD	Fill	WM/C 515B	AR	6.1+	4.5+	3.0+
House II	Floor fill	WM/C 740	AP	2.6+	1.4+	–
House QQ	Fill	WM/C 911	AR	3.4+	3.5+	2.0+
House RR	Fill	WM/C 916	AR	3.1+	2.1+	1.5+
House AF	Fill	WM/C 1217	AR	2.5+	2.6+	2.0+
House AL	Fill	WM/C 1302	AP	3.9+	2.4+	2.0+
House AQ	Fill	WM/C 1339	AP	3.0+	2.5+	2.0+
House AQ	Fill	WM/C 1356	AP	3.1+	2.5+	2.0+
House AQ	Fill	WM/C 1373	AR	3.0+	2.6+	2.0+
Room 3	Floor fill	WM/C 77	AR	2.9+	2.8+	1.8+

TABLE 8.3. *(continued)*

Provenience	Context	Catalogue No.	Material	Length (cm)	Outside Diameter (cm)	Bowl Diameter (cm)
Room 4	Floor fill	WM/C 94A	AR	4.2+	2.0+	1.7+
Room 4	Floor fill	WM/C 94B	AR	2.7+	1.5+	1.1+
Room 4	Floor fill	WM/C 94C	AR	2.3+	1.6+	1.1+
Room 4	Floor fill	WM/C 94D	AR	2.3+	1.9+	1.3+
Pavement 2	Fill	WM/C 167	AP	2.6+	2.6+	4.0
Block 12-D	Extramural	WM/C 229B	AR	3.6+	1.0+	1.0+
Block 17-B/D	Extramural	WM/C 15A	AR	2.7+	3.2+	2.7+
Block 17-B/D	Extramural	WM/C 15C	AR	3.1+	2.7+	1.8+
Block 17-B/D	Extramural	WM/C 15D	AR	3.0+	4.8+	4.0+
Block 17-B/D	Extramural	WM/C 15E	AP	3.2+	2.0+	1.3+
Block 17-B/D	Extramural	WM/C 15F	AR	3.1+	2.0+	1.4+
Block 18-C	Extramural	WM/C 28	AR	2.3+	1.8+	1.7+
Block 20-A	Extramural	WM/C 234B	AR	2.6+	3.2+	2.0+
Block 21-C	Extramural	WM/C 528A	AR	3.6+	3.3+	3.0+
Block 21-C	Extramural	WM/C 528B	AR	2.5+	3.5+	3.0+
Block 21-D	Extramural	WM/C 1404	AR	3.3+	2.7+	2.0+
Block 28-C	Extramural	WM/C 252B	AR	1.9+	4.0+	3.8+
Block 29-B	Extramural	WM/C 745A	AR	2.8+	1.5+	–
Block 30-A	Extramural	WM/C 752	AR	2.1+	2.4+	–
Block 44-B	Extramural	WM/C 1406	AR	2.6+	2.7+	2.0+
Block 44-C	Extramural	WM/C 336	AP	3.5+	1.0+	1.0+
Block 52-A	Extramural	WM/C 507	AR	4.2+	4.0+	2.0+

AP = Alma Plain, API = Alma Pattern Incised, AR = Alma Rough, AS = Alma Scored.

same term that were carved in the round (Cushing 1883). Fetishes similar in style to Wind Mountain forms have been called "medicine" stones (Haury 1976:292) and were, perhaps, imbued with beneficial curing properties or as protective amulets for their owners (Martin 1959:100–101; Di Peso 1974:587–588).

Di Peso defined ground, pecked, or chipped stone counters (n = 3, Reference Nos. 304 and 316, Table 8.7) as socioreligious artifacts, considering these so-called gaming pieces to be a serious part of religious divination (Di Peso 1974:590–592). As one aspect of divination, he cited Mesoamerican folk heros winning games of chance in various Chichimec origin myths. In addition, a suggested shaman's medicine kit at Casas Grandes was found to contain counters together with fetishes and other ritual objects (Di Peso 1974:587). Consequently, Di Peso believed the counters recovered from Wind Mountain to be endowed with similar curing properties (Figure 8.11).

Socioreligious Worked Sherds

These types of nonperforated, modified sherds included zoomorphic (n = 7, Reference No. 337) and eccentric (n = 4, Reference No. 338) forms (Table 8.8). Such sherds were presumed to carry some of the same symbolism as fetishes (Figure 8.12).

Cornucopias

The inhabitants of Wind Mountain also produced clay fired cornucopias (Reference No. 328, Table 8.9). The function of ceramic cornucopias is unknown, though similar objects were found at Mogollon Village and Harris Village (Haury 1936a:28, 68, 103), as well as Pecos (Kidder 1932:141). They are also reported from Basketmaker sites (Morris 1927:156–158).

Miscellaneous Socioreligious Artifacts

Di Peso associated several types of miscellaneous faunal artifacts with ritual function (Table 8.10), thereby including them in the broad socioreligious classification. Unpainted (n = 10, Reference No. 320) and painted (n = 2, Reference No. 321) rectangular bone counters, their possible ceremonial use already discussed, were recovered. In addition bone and antler rasps (n = 3, Reference Nos. 317, 319, and 323), an antler tube/handle (Reference No. 318), and a turtle shell rattle fragment (Reference No. 324, WM 174) were identified. The use of the tube/handle is unclear, but antler and scapula rasps as well as carapace rattles presumably served as rhythm keeping instruments (Figure 8.13). Simple instruments are known from many prehistoric sites, including Casas Grandes, where Di Peso (1974:582–584) equated

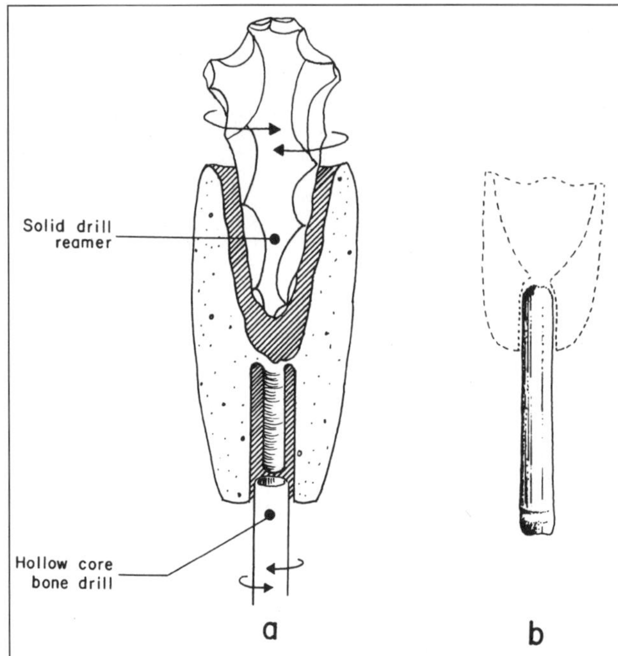

FIGURE 8.6. Reconstruction of a stone pipe manufacturing technique. A solid drill reamer (WM 790) is used to drill the conical bowl end of a stone smoking pipe (WM 791) or both ends of a biconical cloud blower. A hollow core bone drill helps to fashion the mouthpiece of the pipe; the resulting core is snapped off after drilling (a). An organic stem, possibly a reed, or a bone tube is then fitted into the mouthpiece end (b).

FIGURE 8.7. Cross section of a stone pipe (WM 1769), Reference No. 309, revealing both straight and biconical drilling (Neg. No. WM 143–28L).

them with the ceremonial life of the community. Two highly polished, abraded, thin walled sections of bone (Reference No. 322) complete the miscellaneous socioreligious artifact inventory. The function of these objects is unknown, although similarities may exist between the examples from Wind Mountain and bone sections described at Swarts Ruin, where they were interpreted as dice (Cosgrove and Cosgrove 1932:61–62, Figure 11e).

Personal Ornamentation

As previously noted, with the arrival of merchant traders, increases in nonutilitarian artifacts were expected. Objects of personal ornamentation fashioned from stone, shell, and bone were chief among these. Di Peso identified the southern inspiration underlying the creation of many ornament types in terms of their symbolic content and technological innovation. Because ornament artifact types included both those produced from locally available as well as exotic materials, he felt such objects represented components of a functioning trade system. Personal ornamentation is separated into general classes of stone, shell, and bone pendants, beads and bracelets. These principal adornment classes are followed by a short discussion of miscellaneous ornaments.

Ornaments of Stone

Most of the finished Wind Mountain stone ornaments consisted of pendants (n = 32, Reference Nos. 342–345, Table 8.11; Figures 8.14–8.16), turquoise tesserae (n = 177, Reference No. 341) or beads (n = 15, Reference Nos. 346 and 347, Table 8.12).

Indeterminate stone ornament fragments (n = 18, Reference No. 349, Table 8.14), and blanks (n =8, Reference No. 348, Table 8.13) were also noted.

Di Peso affirmed that lapidary arts came out of Mesoamerica into the Chupicuaro area and the west coast of Mexico

TABLE 8.4. Stone Pipes

Provenience	Context	Catalogue No.	Reference No.	Material	Length (cm)	Outside Diameter (cm)	Bowl Diameter (cm)	Drill Hole
WM locus								
House J	Floor fill	WM 386	307	VB	6.0	3.9	1.6	BC
House U	Fill	WM 866	310	VB	5.4	4.2	3.1	BC
House V	Fill	WM/S 1223	315	WT	5.2+	3.6	–	–
House X	Fill	WM 1045	313	BS	5.0	6.0	3.7	BC
House X	Fill	WM 1414	311	WT	10.9	6.0	3.2	BC
House Y	Fill	WM 1046	309	BS	7.7	3.7	2.6	C
House EE	Floor	WM 1254	312	WT	8.1	4.9	2.1	C
House FF	Floor fill	WM 1769	309	WT	8.6	4.7	3.0	C
House FF	Fill	WM/S 2701	315	St	2.6+	1.6	–	–
House OO	Floor fill	WM/S 3639	309	VB	3.4	3.0	1.4	C
House OO	Fill	WM/S 3450	307	VB	3.5+	3.1+	–	BC
House AF	Fill	WM/S 4981	307	VB	3.7+	3.2	1.6	BC
House AI	Fill	WM 2801	308	BS	12.2	4.4	3.4	BC
House AO	Fill	WM/S 5449	309	WT	–	–	–	–
Pit 8	Cache	WM 791	314	WT	15.6	7.1	3.3	–
Pit 55	Cache	WM 2034	314	VB	6.0	3.5	0.9	–
Pit 56	Cache	WM 2277	309	WT	9.2	5.2	3.4	C
Pit 56	Cache	WM 2278	307	BS	6.0	3.8	2.9	BC
Pit 56	Cache	WM 2279	307	WT	6.8	5.2	3.2	BC
Block 47-C	Extramural	WM/S 3358	315	BS	3.1+	3.2+	–	–
Block 61-C	Extramural	WM/S 5192	309	WT	6.4+	4.9	–	C
RO locus								
Burial 1	Extramural	RO 208	307	BS	6.5	3.4	2.1	BC
Burial 2	Extramural	RO 209	307	BS	5.6	3.5	2.1	BC
Burial 8	Extramural	RO 217	307	VB	4.6	3.3	2.0	BC

St = Steatite, VB = Vesicular basalt, WT = Welded tuff, BC = Biconical, BS = Biotite schist, C = Conical.

TABLE 8.5. Bone Pipes

Provenience	Context	Catalogue No.	Reference No.	Material	Length (cm)	Diameter (cm)
WM locus						
Block 20-A	Extramural	WM 634	326	AC	7.5	1.0
Block 30-C	Extramural	WM/B 145	327A	L	5.5	0.8

AC = *Aquila chrysaetos*, L = *Lepus* spp.

TABLE 8.6. Bone and Ceramic Tubes

Provenience	Context	Catalogue No.	Reference No.	Material	Diameter	Length (cm)	Width (cm)	Thickness (cm)
WM locus								
House H	Floor fill	WM 365	327	Lc	0.9	6.1	–	–
House P2	Fill	WM/C 264A	333	AR	3.3+	4.8	–	–
House V	Fill	WM/C 350	333	AR	3.2	4.6	–	–
House V	Fill	WM/C 374H	333	AR	3.7	3.7	–	–
House V	Fill	WM/C 1397	333	AR	2.4+	3.8	–	–
House V	Fill	WM/C 1399	333	AR	2.0+	3.4	–	–
House V	Fill	WM/C 1402	333	AR	–	–	–	–
House X	Unit C	WM/B 106	327	A	2.5+	5.7	–	–
House X	Floor fill	WM/B 121	327	Lc	1.0	4.6+	–	–
House Y	Fill	WM/B 80	327	A	1.4+	3.1	–	–
House DD	Floor fill	WM 1746	325	Mg	–	2.9	1.2	1.2
House HH	Floor fill	WM 1812	327	Lc	0.8	3.8	–	–
House OO	Fill	WM 2038	327	M	0.9	3.6	–	–
House PP	Unit C	WM/B 161	327	Oh	3.5+	5.9	–	–
House AD	Entry fill	WM 2716	327	Cl	1.1	4.0	–	–
House AG	Fill	WM/B 231	325	Av	–	7.5+	0.9+	0.4
Room 2	Floor	WM/C 41	333	AP	1.8+	3.4	–	–
Room 7	Post hole 5	WM/C 179	333	AR	2.3+	3.7	–	–
Burial 9	Extramural	WM/B 4	325	Av	–	1.2+	0.8	0.1
Pit 44	Extramural	WM/B 143	327	Lc	4.0	0.9+	–	–
Block 11-D	Extramural	WM/C 122A	333	AP	5.0	4.6	–	–
Block 11-D	Extramural	WM/C 122B	333	AR	3.1	4.1+	–	–
Block 12-D	Extramural	WM/C 229A	333	AR	3.2+	5.7+	–	–
Block 20-A	Extramural	WM/C 234A	333	AR	3.8	4.1	–	–
Block 27-D	Extramural	WM/C 246	333	AR	3.0+	4.1	–	–
Block 34-C	Extramural	WM/B 93	327	A	2.5+	6.9	–	–
Block 44-C	Extramural	WM/C 361	333	AR	3.4	2.2	–	–
Block 45-B	Extramural	WM 1777	325	Av	–	2.2	1.7	1.3

A= Artiodactyla, AP = Alma Plain, AR = Alma Rough, Av = Aves, Cl = *Canis latrans,* Lc = *Lepus californicus,* M = Mammalia, Mg = *Meleagris gallopavo,* Oh = *Odocoileus hemionus.*

TABLE 8.7. Stone Fetishes and Counters

Provenience	Context	Catalogue No.	Reference No.	Type	Material	Length (cm)	Width (cm)	Thickness (cm)
WM locus								
House X	Fill	WM 1382	306	Fetish	R	3.0	1.4	1.2
House X	Fill	WM 1383	306	Fetish	WT	4.4	4.0	1.2
House X	Fill	WM 1415	306	Fetish	R	3.4	2.1	1.4
House X	Fill	WM 1634	306	Fetish	RO	4.0	3.9	2.4
House HH	Fill	WM/S 3008	304	Counter	WT	6.8	6.8	0.4
House PP	Fill	WM 2063	305	Fetish	Sh	2.3+	1.5+	0.3
House SS	Fill	WM/S 4237	305	Fetish	Sh	3.1+	2.4+	0.4
House AF	Fill	WM 2734	306	Fetish	WT	3.5+	3.9	3.2
House AF	Fill	WM 2739	305	Fetish	S	7.0	3.7	0.7
House AG	Fill	WM 2793	305	Fetish	WT	5.8	4.0	1.2
Burial 102	Extramural	WM 3091	304	Counter	Sh	5.0	4.8	0.3
Pit 31	Extramural	WM 1463	316	Counter	Ob	2.3	1.7	0.6
Block 13-C	Extramural	WM 599	305	Fetish	St	3.6	1.5	0.3
Block 38-A	Extramural	WM 1956	306	Fetish	A	3.8+	0.9	0.4

A = Alabaster, Ob = Obsidian, R = Ricolite, RO = Red Ocher, S = Sandstone, Sh = Shale, St = Steatite, WT = Welded Tuff.

FIGURE 8.8. Bone tubes and pipe stem. Left to right: WM 634, Reference No. 326, identified as a bird bone pipe stem, *Aquila chrysaetos* (refer to Figure 8.7); WM 2716, Reference No. 327, *Canis latrans*; WM 2038, Reference No. 327, *Mammalia* spp.; WM/B 145, unclassified; WM 365, Reference No. 327, identified as *Lepus californicus*. For context and dimensions, refer to Table 8.6 (Neg. No. WM 144–32A/L).

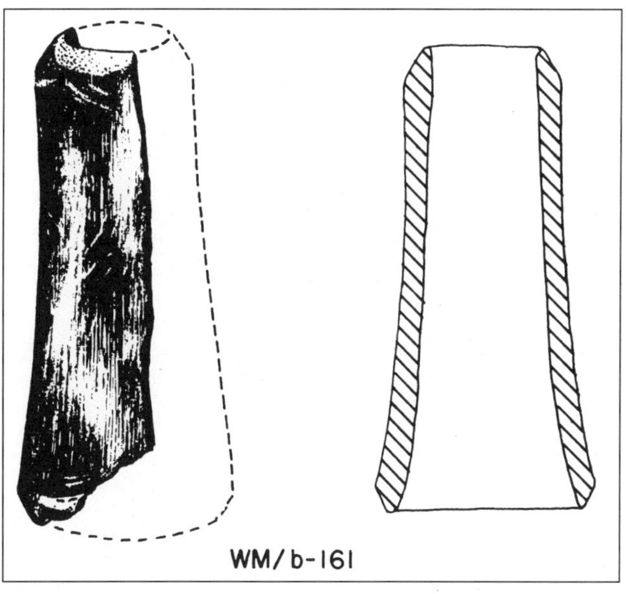

FIGURE 8.9. Bone tube fragment showing modification.

TABLE 8.8. Socioreligious Worked Sherds

Provenience	Context	Catalogue No.	Reference No.	Type	Material	Length (cm)	Width (cm)	Thickness (cm)
WM locus								
House DD	Fill	WM/C 482	338	E	Boldface	5.2+	3.7+	0.7
House AD	Fill	WM 2884	337	Z	Boldface	3.1+	1.9+	0.6
House AF	Fill	WM/C 1213	337	Z	AP	2.9+	2.1+	0.6
House AF	Fill	WM 2773	337	Z	SFR	3.3+	2.0	0.4
House AQ	Fill	WM 3030	338	E	AP	3.6	3.4	0.6
Block 21-D	Extramural	WM/C 611	337	Z	SFR	5.5+	3.1+	0.5
Block 26-A	Extramural	WM 384	337	Z	Boldface	2.8	2.0+	0.6
Block 28-A	Extramural	WM 695	338	E	SFR	4.7	3.2	0.6
Block 29-D	Extramural	WM/C 776	338	E	SFR	4.2+	2.5+	0.5
Block 60-B	Extramural	WM 2676	337	Z	B/W	3.3	2.0	0.4
RO locus								
House B	Fill	RO/C 7	337	Z	SFR	3.6+	2.7+	0.5

AP = Alma Plain, Boldface = Boldface Black-on-white, B/W = Indeterminate black-on-white, SFR = San Francisco Red, E = Eccentric, Z = Zoomorphic.

TABLE 8.9. Ceramic Cornucopias

Provenience	Context	Catalogue No.	Reference No.	Material	Length (cm)	Width (cm)	Thickness (cm)
WM locus							
House X	Fill	WM/C 613	328	AR	3.6+	2.7	0.8
Block 27-D	Extramural	WM 686	328	AR	3.8	2.5	0.3
Block 39-C	Extramural	WM/C 855	328	AP	2.5	2.5	0.4

AP = Alma Plain, AR = Alma Rough.

TABLE 8.10. Socioreligious Bone Artifacts

Provenience	Context	Catalogue No.	Reference No.	Type	Material	Length (cm)	Width (cm)	Thickness (cm)
WM locus								
House A	Fill	WM 28	320	Counter	O	4.6	2.4	0.5
House A	Fill	WM 40	320	Counter	O	4.8	2.0	0.5
House D	Fill	WM 142	320	Counter	O	3.5	2.0	0.6
House P2	Floor	WM 709	320	Counter	O	3.0	2.2	0.6
House T	Fill	WM 845	320	Counter	O	3.1	2.2	0.7
House X	Floor fill	WM/B 112	322	Thin section	O	5.8+	2.2+	0.2
House X	Fill	WM/B 74	322	Thin section	U	13.3+	3.2	0.3
House FF	Floor fill	WM 1762	320	Counter	O	3.5	2.2	0.8
House FF	Fill	WM/B 116	321	Counter	O	2.8+	1.6+	0.7
House GG	Fill	WM/B 138	318	Tube/Handle	O	6.0	4.2	2.0
House UU	Fill	WM 2319	320	Counter	O	2.0	2.0	0.6
House VV	Floor fill	WM/B 191	321	Counter	O	4.5	1.3+	0.4+
Room 9	Floor	WM 647	319	Rasp	Oh	26.8+	14.1	2.1
Block 10-D	Extramural	WM/B 16	323	Rasp	Oh	7.7+	2.3+	2.1+
Block 19-A	Extramural	WM 332	317	Rasp	Oh	16.0	2.6	1.6
Block 19-B	Extramural	WM 621	320	Counter	O	4.9+	1.4	0.5
Block 20-A	Extramural	WM/B 174	324	Rattle	Ch	3.4+	2.7+	0.5
Block 20-B	Extramural	WM 796	320	Counter	O	3.2	1.9	0.6
Block 30-A	Extramural	WM 1831	320	Counter	O	3.2	1.8	0.4

Ch = *Chelonia* spp., O = *Odocoileus* sp., Oh = *Odocoileus hemionus*, U = *Ursus americanus.*

FIGURE 8.10. Round and flat fetishes. Clockwise from upper left: WM 599, Reference No. 305; WM 1382, Reference No. 306; WM 2739, Reference No. 305; WM 1634, Reference No. 306. Such objects were thought to be personal amulets or charm stones. For context and dimensions, refer to Table 8.7 (Neg. No. WM 151–2L).

then north to the Hohokam, where artisans developed a highly evolved tradition of stone carving. The Hohokam subsequently introduced their techniques and certain designs into the Mogollon and Anasazi regions (Di Peso Wind Mountain files, Amerind Foundation). The Mogollon Chichimecs, given their proximity to turquoise sources, also begin to extract and work the colorful material. Turquoise, associated with Toltec gods, was believed to have captured the imagination of Mesoamericans whose traders moved into the northern reaches seeking the mineral after c. A.D. 950 (Di Peso 1974:205). From the Wind Mountain vicinity, for example, Di Peso proposed that raw turquoise procured from the White Signal Mine area was transported to Casas Grandes to be fashioned into jewelry by its artisans (1974:507–508, 695 n. 12).

Southern entrepreneurs were thought to have influenced Mogollon Chichimecs by introducing religious symbolism in the form of frogs, turtles, mountain lions, as well as macaws and other bird motifs (Di Peso 1974:490). Zoomorphic stone

TABLE 8.11. Stone Pendants

Provenience	Context	Catalogue No.	Reference No.	Type	Material	Length (cm)	Width (cm)	Thickness (cm)
WM locus								
House Q	Floor fill	WM 711	342	Tabular	C	2.5	3.0	0.3
House X	Floor fill	WM 1417	343	Effigy	R	3.2	1.6	0.4
House X	Fill	WM 1381	342	Tabular	BM	5.0	2.9	0.2
House X	Fill	WM 1635	342	Tabular	Tq	2.7	2.3	0.5
House X	Fill	WM/S 2376	345	Grooved	WT	3.2+	2.3	1.2
House Y	Fill	WM 1116	343	Effigy	WT	2.3	1.6	1.0
House AA	Floor fill	WM/S 1646	343	Effigy	Tq	1.0+	0.9+	0.3
House NN	Floor	WM 1872	343	Effigy	R	3.7	1.9	1.4
House OO	Floor fill	WM 2091	342	Tabular	Tq	1.4	1.2	0.3
House AD	Fill	WM 2706	342	Tabular	Tq	2.2	1.7	0.3
House AF	Fill	WM 2732	343	Effigy	R	2.9	2.5	0.6
House AL	Fill	WM 2915	343	Effigy	R	2.5+	2.0	1.1
House AL	Post hole 5	WM 2929	342	Tabular	Tq	0.8	0.6	0.2
Room 3	Floor fill	WM 247	342	Tabular	Tq	1.4	0.8	0.3
Room 4	Floor	WM 367	342	Tabular	Tq	2.7+	2.4+	0.5
Room 10	Floor	WM 2491	342	Tabular	Tq	0.7+	0.7	0.3
Burial 85	Extramural	WM 2280	343	Effigy	WT	1.6	1.0	0.5
Burial 97	Extramural	WM 2684	342	Tabular	Tq	1.3	1.0	0.3
Burial 101	Extramural	WM 2838	342	Tabular	Tq	2.7	2.3	0.6
Burial 102	Extramural	WM 3093	345	Grooved	Sta	4.2	2.1	1.2
Block 12-D	Extramural	WM 662	344	Notched	St	3.4	1.6	0.4
Block 19-B	Extramural	WM 606	343	Effigy	R	4.1	0.7	1.7
Block 21-D	Extramural	WM 1486	344	Notched	WT	1.9	3.9+	0.4
Block 27-C	Extramural	WM 527	343	Effigy	WT	2.4+	1.1	1.1
Block 36-C	Extramural	WM 763	342	Tabular	Tq	1.4	1.4	0.3
Block 44-B	Extramural	WM/S 959	345	Grooved	S	2.0+	1.3	0.9
Block 44-D	Extramural	WM 722	345	Grooved	Sh	11.7	3.3	0.7
Block 62-A	Extramural	WM/S 4035	342	Tabular	Tq	3.5+	3.1+	0.7
Block 62-A	Extramural	WM/S 4272	344	Notched	St	2.5+	1.8	0.4
Surface	Extramural	WM/S 3877	342	Tabular	Tq	0.5+	0.4+	0.2
Surface	Extramural	WM/S 4327	342	Tabular	Tq	0.7	0.5	0.2
Surface	Extramural	WM/S 5786	342	Tabular	Tq	0.5+	0.5	0.2

BM = Biotite Mica, C = Calcite, R = Ricolite, S = Sandstone, Sh = Shale, St = Steatite, Sta = Stalactite, Tq = Turquoise, WT = Welded Tuff.

pendants are not, of course, uncommon in either the southwestern (Haury 1976:298–299) or eastern United States (Ford 1969:61–66). In the Wind Mountain personal ornament assemblage, Di Peso identified carved effigy pendants with a Gran Chichimecan lapidary tradition whose symbolic and technological roots he firmly placed in the south (Figure 8.12). Di Peso drew comparisons between the ricolite zoomorphic pendant effigy at Wind Mountain and forms recovered at Casas Grandes (Di Peso 1974:506, Wind Mountain files, Amerind Foundation). He also felt the bird form in Tlatilco material culture (Lorenzo 1965:48–49), at Chupicuaro (Porter 1956:637), and in Amapa (Meighan 1976:387) to have similarities with Wind Mountain and Hohokam (Gladwin et al. 1937) carved examples. In the eastern United States, Di Peso compared bird motifs from Poverty Point (Ford 1969:61–66) to these but ultimately linked them all with Olmec/Tlatilco origins. He perceived many of these pendant carvings to have socioreligious meaning for their makers or owners.

In the case of mosaics or tesserae, the technology to produce them was identified with the Toltec (Di Peso 1974:506–509, 615–616), who were considered responsible for its introduction to other regions until it eventually appeared among the Hohokam. Mosaic work is also known in the Medio period of Casas Grandes (Di Peso 1974:742), at Pueblo Bonito (Judd 1954:104–106), at Aztec Ruin (Morris 1919:102–103), and from Basketmaker and Pueblo contexts (Woodbury 1954:150–151). Of the 177 turquoise tesserae recovered from the site, nine were scattered in fill, one came from Wind Mountain locus Burial 59, and the remaining 167 pieces were found under an Alma Rough jar accompanying Wind Mountain locus Burial 65.

FIGURE 8.11. Stone counter (WM 3091), Reference No. 304. Stone counters were suggested to have curing properties. Alternatively, they may have served as gaming pieces. For context and dimensions, refer to Table 8.7 (Neg. No. WM 151–3L).

FIGURE 8.12. Eccentric worked sherds. From left to right, upper to lower. Left: WM/C 769, WM 695; Center: WM 3030, WM/C 482, all Reference No. 338; Right: WM 2676, WM 2773, WM 384, all Reference No. 337. For context and dimensions, refer to Table 8.8 (Neg. No. WM 151–4L).

TABLE 8.12. Stone Beads

Provenience	Context	Catalogue No.	Reference No.	Type	Material	Length (cm)	Width (cm)	Thickness (cm)
WM locus								
House H	Fill	WM 229	346	Disk	Tq	0.6	0.6	0.2
House R	Floor fill	WM 748	346	Disk	Sh	0.5	0.5	0.2
House XX	Floor	WM 2677	346	Disk	Tq	0.6	0.6	0.4
House AF	Floor	WM 2833	347	Asymmetric	Tq	0.8	0.6	0.2
House AG	Post hole	WM 2860	347	Asymmetric	Tq	0.6	0.4	0.3
Burial 69	Extramural	WM 1891A	346	Disk	Sh	0.7	0.7	0.2
Burial 69	Extramural	WM 1891B	346	Disk	Sh	0.6	0.6	0.2
Burial 103	Extramural	WM 3107C	346	Disk	Tq	0.4+	0.7	0.1+
Work Area 3	Fill	WM 2314	346	Disk	Tq	0.6	0.6	0.2
Block 38-C	Extramural	WM 1895	347	Asymmetric	Tq	0.7	0.6	0.2
Block 54-A	Extramural	WM 2193	346	Disk	Sh	0.6	0.6	0.2
Block 60-D	Extramural	WM 2683	347	Asymmetric	Tq	0.6	0.5	0.3
Block 60-A	Extramural	WM 2708	346	Disk	Sh	1.0	1.0	0.7
Surface	Extramural	WM 15	347	Asymmetric	Tq	0.6	0.5	0.2
Surface	Extramural	WM 3102	346	Disk	Sh	0.6	0.6	0.2

Sh = Shale, Tq = Turquoise.

TABLE 8.13. Stone Ornament Blanks

Provenience	Context	Catalogue No.	Reference No.	Material	Length (cm)	Width (cm)	Thickness (cm)	Shape
WM locus								
House X	Fill	WM 1615	348	Sh	5.7	4.3	0.4	Asymmetric
House Z	Fill	WM 1062	348	Sh	4.4	4.0	0.7	Rectilinear
House EE	Fill	WM 1387	348	M	2.1	1.7	0.7	Rectilinear
House QQ	Fill	WM 2185	348	F	1.7	1.4	0.7	Asymmetric
House XX	Fill	WM 2513	348	Sh	3.9	2.9	0.2	Petaloid
House ZZ	Fill	WM 2505	348	WT	2.5	2.5	0.5	Square
House AD	Fill	WM 2996	348	Se	2.6	1.8	0.5	Rectilinear
House AF	Fill	WM 2733	348	Tq	3.2	1.9	0.7	Petaloid

F = Fluorite, M = Malachite, Se = Selenite, Sh = Shale, Tq = Turquoise, WT = Welded Tuff.

TABLE 8.14. Unclassified Stone Ornament Fragments

Provenience	Context	Catalogue No.	Reference No.	Material	Length (cm)	Width (cm)	Thickness (cm)
WM locus							
House B2	Floor	WM/S 240	349	CH	2.0+	1.8+	0.2
House B2	Floor fill	WM/S 235	349	C	1.7+	1.7+	0.7
House C	Fill	WM 116	349	R	3.1+	2.3	1.0
House H	Fill	WM/S 257	349	WT	4.1+	2.6+	1.3
House M	Floor	WM/S 795	349	Sh	3.9	2.0+	0.2
House M	Fill	WM/S 3626	349	R	3.2+	2.9+	0.7
House X	Fill	WM/S 1963	349	A	6.8+	2.9+	0.6
House GG	Fill	WM/S 2999	349	Sh	3.6+	2.9	0.2
House WW	Fill	WM/S 5798	349	M	1.4+	1.1+	1.1+
House AF	Fill	WM 2752	349	S	2.1+	3.2	0.5
Room 3	Fill	WM/S 269	349	St	3.4+	3.2+	0.2
Room 5/6	Fill	WM 460	349	Ch	3.9	2.2+	0.3
Block 28-D	Extramural	WM/S 882	349	Ch	2.1+	1.7+	0.6
Block 44-B	Extramural	WM/S 1119	349	Tq	1.9+	0.9+	0.4
Block 60-B	Extramural	WM/S 4680	349	R	2.5+	1.0+	0.4+
Block 61-C	Extramural	WM/S 2828	349	F	2.7+	2.5+	1.9
Block 62-A	Extramural	WM/S 4294	349	Sh	4.1+	2.9	0.4
RO locus							
House K	Floor fill	RO/S 231	349	S	4.6+	2.3+	0.6

A = Alabaster, C = Calcite, Ch = Chalcedony, CH = Compact Hematite, F = Fluorite, M = Malachite, R = Ricolite, S = Sandstone, Sh = Shale, St = Steatite, Tq = Turquoise, WT = Welded Tuff.

Neither tesserae nor stone beads constituted a large component of the Wind Mountain personal ornamentation inventory. Their size (mean dimension 6.5 mm x 6.0 mm x 2.6 mm for beads recovered) probably indicates that a majority of smaller pieces fell through the stock quarter inch screen used during the project and were, therefore, lost from the sample.

Ornaments of Shell

The vast majority of Wind Mountain shell consisted of various species of marine mollusca (95 percent), and a few fresh water gastropods (Figure 8.17). All shell species were identified by Di Peso. Ornaments were separated into modified pendants or arcs and whole beads that could be worn as pendants (n = 30, Reference Nos. 361, 362, 364–368, Table 8.15). Some unclassified shell ornaments were also counted (n = 5, Reference No. 363, Table 8.15). A second shell ornament class included disk beads of various sizes (Reference Nos. 350–352, Table 8.16; Figure 8.18). A third class was composed of bracelets and rings (n = 74, Reference Nos. 353–360, Table 8.17) manufactured from *Glycymeris gigantea* (Figure 8.19).

Wind Mountain shell was randomly distributed through-

FIGURE 8.13. Antler rasp (WM 647), Reference No. 319. The rasp, recovered from the floor of Room 9, was presumed to be a simple rhythm keeping instrument. For dimensions, refer to Table 8.10 (Neg. No. WM 143–29L).

FIGURE 8.14. Stone effigy pendants, Reference No. 343. Left to right: WM 1872 recovered from the floor of House NN; WM 2280 associated with Burial 85; WM 1116. For context and dimensions, refer to Table 8.11 (Neg. No. WM 143–34L).

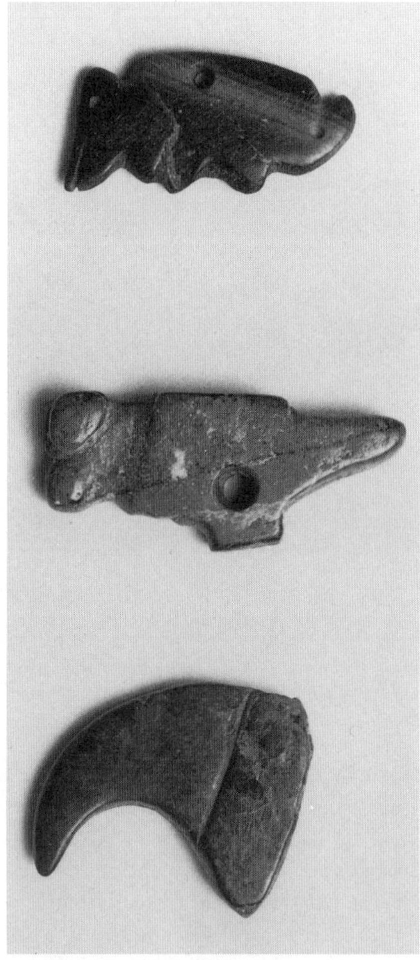

FIGURE 8.15. Stone effigy pendants, Reference No. 343. Upper to lower: WM 1417 recovered from the floor fill of House X; WM 606; WM 2732. WM 2732 appears to be a talon (Neg. No. WM 153–36L).

out the site, including floor, fill, burial, and extramural deposits. The largest concentrations of shell beads were recovered from burials (Table 9.2). Wind Mountain locus Burial 103 contained more than 1,100 beads, probably the remains of a necklace. Shell species used in the manufacture of Wind Mountain jewelry, as well as other artifact forms represented, parallel ornaments recovered from Mogollon Village and Harris Village (Haury 1936a:46, 46, 109), as well as with Hohokam materials (Haury 1976:306–307; Gladwin et al. 1937:135–146).

Unlike stone ornaments, however, most of which were

TABLE 8.15. Shell Objects of Personal Adornment

Provenience	Context	Catalogue No.	Reference No.	Type	Material	Length (cm)	Width (cm)	Thickness (cm)
WM locus								
House B	Floor fill	WM 43	361	Pendant	Gg	2.7+	0.4	0.3
House C	Fill	WM/SL 3	368	Bead	S	1.1+	1.6	0.5–1.2
House U	Fill	WM/SL 15	363	Unclassified	Gg	2.2+	0.7+	0.4+
House X	Floor	WM 3105	364	Bead	Os	0.9	0.9	0.3
House X	Fill	WM/SL 20	363	Unclassified	Gg	5.2+	0.4	0.4
House X	Fill	WM 1297	362	Arc	Gg	4.1	0.7	0.5
House PP	Floor fill	WM/SL 45	368	Bead	S	2.0	2.0	1.2
House AF	Fill	WM 2736	364	Bead	At	2.7+	1.5+	1.7+
House AI	Floor fill	WM 2835A	361	Pendant	Gg	3.7	0.8	0.4
House AI	Floor fill	WM 2835B	361	Pendant	Gg	3.8	0.7	0.3
Room 8	Floor	WM 518	361	Pendant	Gg	3.0+	0.2	0.6
Burial 4	Extramural	WM 250	364	Bead	Oi	2.6	1.2	0.1
Burial 11	Extramural	WM 369	361	Pendant	Ce	2.5	2.3	0.9
Burial 24	Extramural	WM 787A	366	Pendant	FP	2.5+	2.3	0.1
Burial 24	Extramural	WM 787B	366	Pendant	FP	2.1+	1.8+	0.1
Burial 102	Extramural	WM 3094	364	Bead	Os	1.4	1.3	0.1
Burial 103	Extramural	WM/SL 63	364	Bead	Od	1.2	0.6	0.1
Pit 63	Extramural	WM 2712	368	Bead	S	1.7	1.7	0.9
Block 10-B	Extramural	WM 216	364	Bead	At	3.4	1.6	0.2
Block 12-C	Extramural	WM 575	363	Unclassified	Pv	2.8+	2.1+	0.3
Block 18-C	Extramural	WM/SL 5	363	Unclassified	Gg	3.0+	1.6+	0.7+
Block 28-D	Extramural	WM/SL 9	367	Pendant	FP	2.8+	1.4	0.1
Block 29-B	Extramural	WM 1823	361	Pendant	Gg	3.5	0.4	1.2
Block 36-A	Extramural	WM/SL 22	363	Unclassified	Gg	2.9+	2.5+	1.9
Block 36-C	Extramural	WM 761	364	Bead	Od	1.6	0.7	0.1
Block 54-C	Extramural	WM 2542	361	Pendant	Gg	2.1	0.6	1.2
Surface	Extramural	WM 795	362	Arc	Gg	3.6	0.5	0.2
RO locus								
House C	Fill	RO/SL 2	368	Bead	S	1.5	1.5	0.7
Burial 1	Extramural	RO 218	364	Bead	Od	1.9	0.9	0.1
Burial 7	Extramural	RO/SL 8	367	Pendant	FP	1.5+	1.0	0.1
Burial 7	Extramural	RO 239	364	Bead	Od	1.5	0.7	0.1
Burial 7	Extramural	RO 240	361	Pendant	Ce	1.0	1.5	0.7
Burial 7	Extramural	RO 241	361	Pendant	Ce	1.3	0.8	0.5
Burial 10	Extramural	RO 224	365	Bead	Sg	8.1	3.3	1.0
Burial 13	Extramural	RO 225	361	Pendant	Ps	1.9	2.9	0.3

At = *Agaronia testacea,* Ce = *Chama echinata,* FP = Freshwater Pelecypod, Gg = *Glycymeris gigantea,* Od = *Olivella dama,* Oi = *Oliva incrassata,* Os = *Oliva spicata,* Ps = *Pteria sterne,* Pv = *Pectern vogdesi,* S = *Sonorella* spp., Sg = *Strombus galeatus.*

manufactured from locally available raw materials, shell objects embodied exotic resources that could only have been procured from distant sources via exchange networks. All of the Wind Mountain marine shell with the exception of abalone (*Haliotus* spp.) derived from the Gulf of California. Abalone is a cold water species native to the California coastline of the Pacific Ocean. All marine shell had to have been transported from either the warm Gulf or the cold Pacific waters into the Southwest.

Di Peso reported an early shell working tradition at Apatzingan in Michoacan (1974:162) that he hypothesized could have influenced shell artisans in the Gran Chichimeca. He also identified Boquillas on the northern Sonoran coast as a thriving center of shell production and redistribution (Di Peso 1974:162, 204–205). Because all but abalone were indigenous to the Guaymas coastal area, it seems likely that coastal Sonora and the Boquillas center actively participated in long distance shell trade. Conceivably, shell was transported north into the Hohokam region and from there along the Gila River into Mimbres Mogollon settlements (Haury 1936a:109). With the abundance of exotic shell artifacts throughout the Hohokam region and, to a somewhat lesser extent, in areas

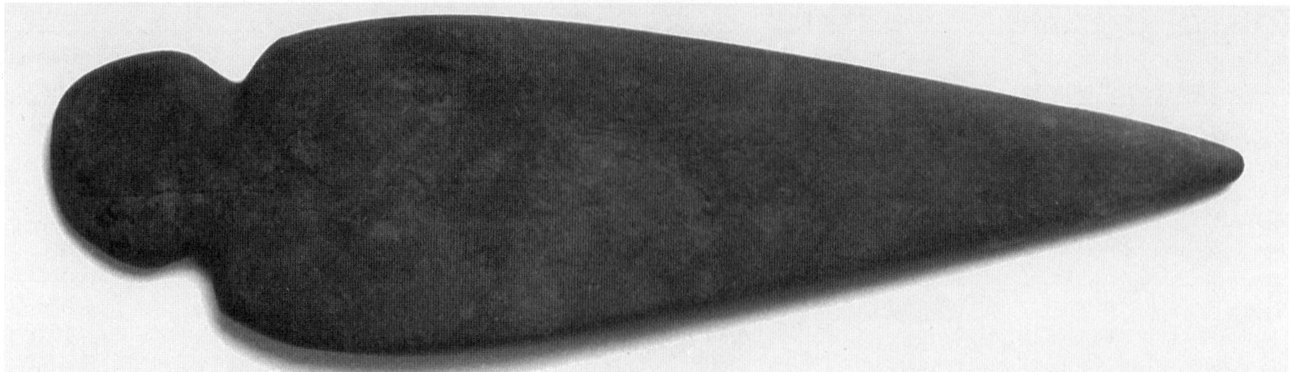

FIGURE 8.16. Identified as a grooved stone pendant (WM 722), Reference No. 345. For context and dimensions, refer to Table 8.11 (Neg. No. WM 153–36L).

of the Mogollon, an exchange network was clearly in effect from relatively early times. The precise nature of this network, including its intensity and exactly who distributed shell resources from where and along what route, remains unknown, but Wind Mountain was involved. Evidence indicating whether the residents of Wind Mountain traded for finished goods or raw shell is obscure but, in contrast to the stone inventory, no shell blanks or traces of ground shell for ornament making were recovered.

Miscellaneous Ornaments

A small collection of miscellaneous ornaments made of a variety of bone, ceramic, and wooden materials was recovered (n = 18, Reference Nos. 369–374, Table 8.18). The inventory included, among other items, a bone skewer (WM 1818) and perforated ceramic pendants. These sundry objects occurred in bulk fill and the extramural deposits of the site.

Raw Minerals and Stone

Presumably, the great appeal of the Wind Mountain settlement location to southern entrepreneurs was its proximity to mineral and stone resources (n = 3,876, Table 8.19). Not only were a variety of common lithic materials suited to the production of utilitarian tools easily available (e.g., welded tuff, shale, chalcedony, and sandstone), but the Big and Little Burro Mountains also contained valuable minerals. Di Peso maintained that turquoise, among other raw resources,

TABLE 8.16. Shell Disk Beads

Provenience	Context	Catalogue No.	Reference No.	Material	Diameter (cm)	Length (cm)	Width (cm)	Thickness (cm)
WM locus								
House X	Floor	WM 3104	350	Gg	0.5–0.6	–	–	0.1–0.2
House X	Fill	WM 1490	350	Ce	0.4	–	–	0.2
House NN	Floor fill	WM/SL 33	350	Gg	0.3	–	–	0.1
House PP	Floor fill	WM 2143	352	Gg	–	0.6	0.4	0.3
Burial 102	Extramural	WM 3095	350	Gg	0.7	–	–	0.2
Burial 102	Extramural	WM 3096	351	Gg	1.6	–	–	0.2
Burial 103	Extramural	WM 3107A	350	Gg	0.3–0.4	–	–	0.1–0.5
Burial 103	Extramural	WM 3107B	350	Ce	0.3–0.5	–	–	0.4–0.5
Block 36-C	Extramural	WM 762	350	Gg	0.1–0.3	–	–	0.4–0.6
Block 46-C	Extramural	WM/SL 48	351	H	1.2+	–	–	0.2
Surface	Extramural	WM 3103	350	Gg	0.5–0.6	–	–	0.1–0.2
RO locus								
Burial 13	Extramural	RO 226	350	Gg	0.5–0.7	–	–	0.1–0.3

Ce = *Chama echinata,* Gg = *Glycymeris gigantea,* H = *Haliotis* spp.

TABLE 8.17. Shell (*Glycymeris gigantea*) Bracelets/Rings

Provenience	Context	Catalogue No.	Reference No.	Diameter (cm)	Thickness (cm)	Band	Shape
WM locus							
House B2	Floor fill	WM/SL 2	356	5.0+	0.6	Plain	Triangular
House C	Fill	WM/SL 4	355	7.0+	0.5	Plain	Rectangular
House N	Floor	WM/SL 7	356	4.0+	0.6	Plain	Triangular
House T	Fill	WM/SL 12	356	5.0+	0.6	Plain	Triangular
House T	Fill	WM/SL 13	357	4.0+	0.5	Plain	Ovoid
House U	Fill	WM/SL 14A	353	4.9+	0.4	Plain	Rectangular
House U	Fill	WM/SL 14B	353	4.0+	0.4	Plain	Rectangular
House U	Fill	WM/SL 16	355	5.0+	0.5	Plain	Rectangular
House U	Fill	WM/SL 17	356	5.0+	0.5	Plain	Triangular
House V	Fill	WM/SL 18	355	6.0+	0.5	Plain	Rectangular
House X	Fill	WM/SL 19	353	4.0+	0.3	Plain	Rectangular
House X	Fill	WM/SL 24	356	6.0+	0.6	Plain	Triangular
House X	Fill	WM/SL 25	353	4.0+	0.3	Plain	Rectangular
House X	Fill	WM/SL 26	355	5.0+	0.5	Plain	Rectangular
House X	Fill	WM/SL 27	360	8.0+	0.7	Carved	Triangular
House X	Fill	WM 1043	355	5.6	0.5	Plain	Rectangular
House X	Fill	WM 1295	355	5.5	0.5	Plain	Rectangular
House X	Fill	WM 1296	355	5.7	0.5	Plain	Rectangular
House Y	Fill	WM/SL 21	355	7.1+	0.8	Plain	Rectangular
House FF	Fill	WM/SL 29	355	6.0+	0.5	Plain	Rectangular
House FF	Fill	WM/SL 30	356	6.0+	0.7	Plain	Triangular
House NN	Floor fill	WM/SL 32	355	6.0+	0.5	Plain	Rectangular
House OO	Floor fill	WM/SL 42	353	5.0+	0.3	Plain	Rectangular
House OO	Fill	WM/SL 34	355	5.0+	0.8	Plain	Rectangular
House OO	Fill	WM/SL 35	356	5.0+	0.5	Plain	Triangular
House OO	Fill	WM/SL 36	355	7.0+	0.6	Plain	Rectangular
House PP	Fill	WM/SL 37	356	7.0+	0.8	Plain	Triangular
House PP	Fill	WM/SL 38	355	6.0+	0.5	Plain	Rectangular
House PP	Fill	WM/SL 41	355	6.0+	0.5	Plain	Rectangular
House PP	Fill	WM/SL 43	357	7.0+	0.9	Plain	Ovoid
House PP	Fill	WM/SL 44	353	5.0+	0.3	Plain	Rectangular
House PP	Fill	WM/SL 56	357	6.0+	0.5	Plain	Ovoid
House UU	Fill	WM/SL 47	357	5.0+	0.6	Plain	Ovoid
House UU	Fill	WM/SL 49	356	5.0+	0.5	Plain	Triangular
House YY	Floor fill	WM/SL 53	357	7.0+	0.6	Plain	Ovoid
House ZZ	Floor fill	WM/SL 52	355	5.0+	0.6	Plain	Rectangular
House AG	Fill	WM 2781	359	3.0+	0.9	Carved	Rectangular
House AM	Floor fill	WM/SL 60	356	5.0+	0.6	Plain	Triangular
House AM	Fill	WM/SL 59	357	5.0+	0.6	Plain	Ovoid
House AQ	Floor	WM/SL 61	354	5.0+	0.3	Plain	Ovoid
Burial 4	Extramural	WM 187A	356	5.8+	0.3+	Plain	Triangular
Burial 4	Extramural	WM 187B	356	5.8+	0.3+	Plain	Triangular
Burial 4	Extramural	WM 187C	356	5.8+	0.3+	Plain	Triangular
Burial 4	Extramural	WM 187D	356	5.8+	0.3+	Plain	Triangular
Burial 59	Extramural	WM 1789	356	8.2	0.5	Plain	Triangular
Burial 103	Extramural	WM/SL 62	356	7.0+	0.5	Plain	Triangular
Burial 103	Extramural	WM 3082A	358	8.9	0.9	Plain	Ovoid
Burial 103	Extramural	WM 3082B	356	6.8+	0.4+	Plain	Triangular
Burial 103	Extramural	WM 3082C	356	6.8+	0.4+	Plain	Triangular
Burial 103	Extramural	WM 3082D	356	6.8+	0.4+	Plain	Triangular
Pit 55	Cache	WM/SL 40	354	4.0+	0.3	Plain	Ovoid

TABLE 8.17. *(continued)*

Provenience	Context	Catalogue No.	Reference No.	Diameter (cm)	Thickness (cm)	Band	Shape
Block 11-D	Extramural	WM/SL 46	355	7.0+	0.6	Plain	Rectangular
Block 17-D	Extramural	WM/SL 1	353	7.0+	0.3	Plain	Rectangular
Block 20-A	Extramural	WM/SL 8	353	6.0+	0.3	Plain	Rectangular
Block 25-D	Extramural	WM/SL 6	356	7.0+	0.5	Plain	Triangular
Block 36-C	Extramural	WM/SL 11	356	4.0+	0.5	Plain	Triangular
Block 38-D	Extramural	WM/SL 39	354	5.0+	0.3	Plain	Ovoid
Block 44-B	Extramural	WM/SL 10	356	6.0+	0.6	Plain	Triangular
Block 52-A	Extramural	WM/SL 23	356	6.0+	0.7	Plain	Triangular
Block 52-B	Extramural	WM/SL 31	356	6.0+	0.6	Plain	Triangular
Block 53-B	Extramural	WM/SL 54	355	8.0+	0.5	Plain	Rectangular
Block 54-D	Extramural	WM/SL 50	353	7.0+	0.3	Plain	Rectangular
Block 60-B	Extramural	WM/SL 55	355	4.7+	0.7	Plain	Rectangular
Surface	Extramural	WM/SL 28	357	5.0+	0.5	Plain	Ovoid
Surface	Extramural	WM/SL 51	353	5.0+	0.4	Plain	Rectangular
Surface	Extramural	WM/SL 64	354	1.5+	0.2	Plain	Ovoid
RO locus							
House A	Fill	RO/SL 1	356	6.0+	0.7	Plain	Triangular
House D	Fill	RO/SL 3	354	4.0+	0.3	Plain	Ovoid
House J	Fill	RO/SL 4	356	6.0+	1.0	Plain	Triangular
House K	Post hole	RO/SL 6	356	4.0+	0.5	Plain	Triangular
House K	Fill	RO/SL 5	357	5.0+	0.6	Plain	Ovoid
Burial 3	Extramural	RO/SL 7	356	7.0+	0.8	Plain	Triangular
Burial 13	Extramural	RO/SL 9A	355	6.0	0.6	Plain	Rectangular
Burial 13	Extramural	RO/SL 9B	355	5.2	0.5	Plain	Rectangular

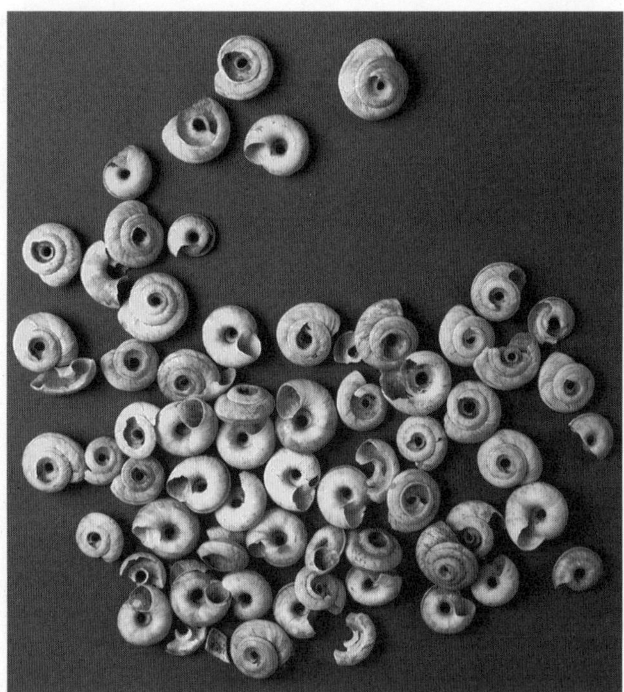

FIGURE 8.17. Freshwater gastropods (WM/SL 3). The shells, recovered from the fill of Wind Mountain locus House C, were perforated for stringing (Neg. No. WM 143–33L).

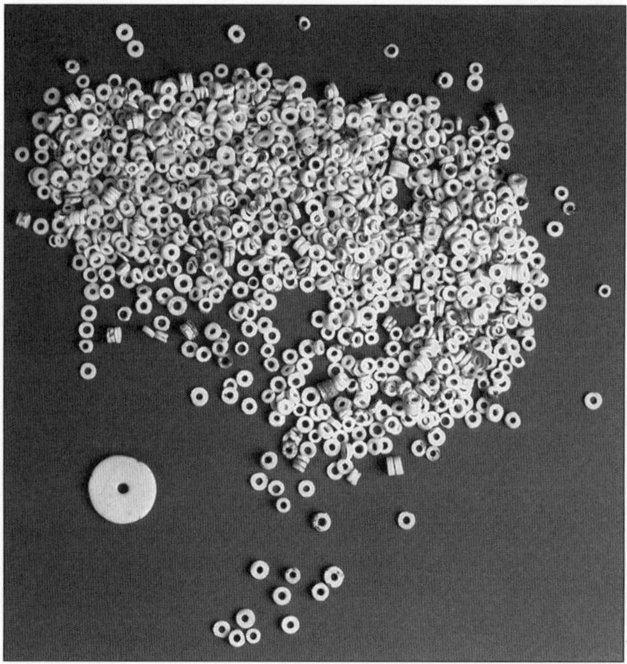

FIGURE 8.18. Shell disk beads. 1,192 small disk beads (WM 3107A), Reference No. 350, were recovered from Burial 103 and may represent a single necklace. The large disk bead (WM 3096), Reference No. 351, derived from Burial 102. All identified as *Glycymeris gigantea*. Refer to Table 8.16 for context and dimensions (Neg. No. WM 143–32L).

TABLE 8.18. Bone, Ceramic, and Wood Ornaments

Provenience	Context	Catalogue No.	Reference No.	Type	Material	Length (cm)	Width (cm)	Thickness (cm)	Edge
WM locus									
House F	Fill	WM 256	373	Bead	AP	2.1	2.1	0.7	–
House K	Fill	WM 376	374	Backing	W	2.3	1.8+	0.8	–
House DD	Fill	WM 1207	369	Ring	O	2.2	2.1	0.5	–
House HH	Fill	WM/C 735	372	Pendant	Bold B/W	2.7	1.7+	0.5	ground
House OO	Fill	WM/C 852	372	Pendant	Bold B/W	4.3+	2.8+	0.6	ground
House OO	Fill	WM 2041	372	Pendant	SFR	4.3	2.1	1.7	ground
House ZZ	Fill	WM/C 1185	372	Pendant	Bold B/W	4.3+	3.4	0.6	ground
House AD	Floor fill	WM 2774	372	Pendant	AP	3.8	2.3	0.5	ground
House AF	Fill	WM/C 1216B	372	Pendant	Bold B/W	5.1+	3.9+	0.6	ground
Pit 36	Extramural	WM 1818	371	Skewer	O	10.6	0.4	0.3	–
Block 13-A	Extramural	WM 580	372	Pendant	AP	4.5+	3.9	0.7	ground
Block 19-B	Extramural	WM 620	370	Unidentified	O	4.5	0.6	0.4	–
Block 20-A	Extramural	WM 665	372	Pendant	Bold B/W	3.8	3.4	0.6	ground
Block 30-C	Extramural	WM/C 1392	372	Pendant	M R/Br	3.0+	2.7+	0.5	ground
Block 36-C	Extramural	WM/C 303	372	Pendant	AP	2.4	2.3+	0.4	ground
Surface	Extramural	WM/C 177	372	Pendant	Bold B/W	2.8+	2.5	0.8	ground
RO locus									
House D	Fill	RO/C 58	372	Pendant	AP	2.8+	2.0+	0.7	chipped
House H	Fill	RO/C 51	372	Pendant	SFR	2.2+	2.9+	0.6	chipped

AP = Alma Plain, Bold B/W = Boldface Black-on-white, M R/Br = Mogollon Red-on-brown, O = *Odocoileus* sp., SFR = San Francisco Red, W = Wood.

enticed southern based merchants into the Mogollon Chichimec homeland in order to amass the materials required by craft specialists at centers such as Casas Grandes. The possible occurrence of White Signal Mine turquoise at Casas Grandes has already been noted. In fact, the Wind Mountain site was selected for excavation precisely because of its proximity to locally important turquoise mines, some of which were reportedly active during prehistoric times. For example, the Azure Mine was purported to contain a 40 foot deep prehistoric mine shaft (Northrop 1959:524). The nearby Parker Mine, too, showed evidence of prehistoric mining (Gillerman 1964:48–49). Traces of fire along a mineral vein suggest that turquoise was extracted by applying alternating heating and cooling techniques in order to crack open the rock that contained it.

Di Peso claimed that a variety of minerals, but principally turquoise, were procured by people associated with Wind Mountasin at least by c. A.D. 500 and possibly even earlier. He suggested an economic relationship (based on the presence of pottery at Wind Mountain which he identified as Negative A) between Wind Mountain and Zacatecas (Di Peso 1979a, 1979b). Di Peso postulated that Zacatecas and the important center of Alta Vista denoted an established mining area by c. A.D. 350, where chrysocolla was extracted for the markets of Teotihuacan (Di Peso Wind Mountain files, Amerind Foundation; Weigand 1968). Similarly, Wind Mountain was proposed to represent a far northern outpost (i.e., gleaning center) for the exploitation of various minerals. In addition to turquoise, other desirable minerals and stone surmised to serve the needs of southern artisans, but extracted by the residents of Wind Mountain, included hematite and limonite (red and yellow ocher), the lustrous specularite, azurite, kaolinite clay, malachite, and various colored crystals. All these resources were available within a 4 km (2.5 mile) radius of the site, with only ricolite occurring a greater distance in the Red Rock Valley to the west.

Though relatively few raw nodules and blocks were recovered from Wind Mountain deposits (e.g., 206.6 gm of unmodified turquoise), Di Peso nevertheless supported the idea that the site was a mineral procurement settlement under the sway of southern traders. He asserted that some minerals were imbued with such great value that they were treated with extraordinary care. For instance, since even small pieces of turquoise could be fashioned into tesserae, miscellaneous pieces were expected to occur randomly in site contexts on only rare occasions. In other words, if precious minerals such as turquoise were mined for transport to other localities where they were subsequently fashioned into finished products, large quantities of these materials might not commonly appear in the deposits of the procurement settlement.

TABLE 8.19. Raw Minerals and Stone Identified at the Wind Mountain Site

Reference No.		No. of Fragments
386	Red ocher	117
387	Abraded red ocher	69
388	Compact hematite	257
389	Abraded compact hematite	8
390	Compact hematite flakes	58
391	Compact hematite cores	9
392	Specularite	168
393	Abraded specularite	12
394	Kidney ore	1
395	Limonite	36
396	Abraded limonite	6
397	Kaolinite	7
398	Azurite	5
399	Malachite	250
400	Abraded malachite	26
401	Andesite	19
402	Aragonite	3
403	Biotite schist	8
404	Breccia	4
405	Calcite	8
406	Concretions	43
407	Copper	3
408	Dacite	3
409	Dolomite	6
410	Felsite slickenside	1
411	Fluorite	9
412	Fossils	7
413	Granite	34
414	Gypsum	8
415	Limestone	8
416	Muscovite mica	5
417	Biotite mica	80
418	Abraded biotite mica	6
419	Obsidian	15
420	Opaline	3
421	Pumice	3
422	Pyroxenite	1
423	Rock crystals	89
424	Amethyst	6
425	Milky quartz	25
426	Agate	5
427	Chalcedony	135
428	Chert	4
429	Flint	9
430	Jasper	3
431	Quartzite	43
432	Rhyolite	8
433	Ricolite	1
434	Sandstone	103
435	Shale	975
436	Steatite	9
437	Travertine	7
438	Tuff	1,045
439	Vein turquoise	4
440	Turquoise pebbles	78
441	Turquoise pebbles abraded	14
442	Turquoise incrustation	3
443	Vesicular basalt	4
Total		3,876

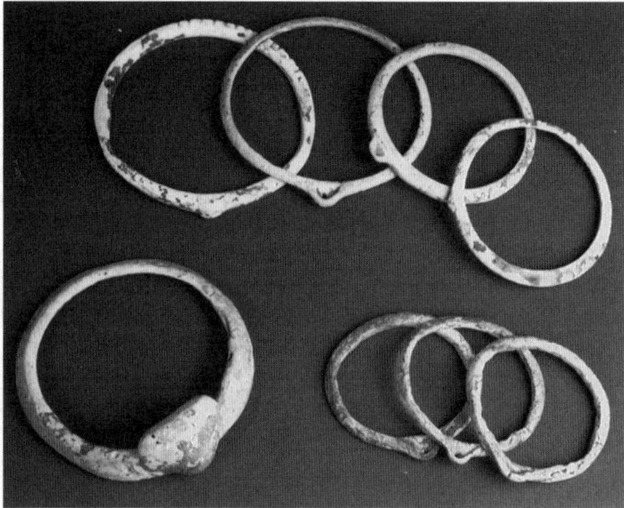

FIGURE 8.19. *Glycymeris gigantea* bracelets. Upper view left to right: WM 3082B, WM 1789, WM 3082C, WM 3082D, Reference No. 356. Lower left: WM 3082A, Reference No. 358. Lower right: WM 1296, WM 1043, WM 1295, Reference No. 355. Bracelets having accession numbers WM 3082A-D were recovered from Burial 103. For context and dimensions, refer to Table 8.17 (Neg. No. WM 143–30L).

In summary, Di Peso cited several artifact classes to support his thesis that a long distance mercantile system operated throughout the Gran Chichimeca. In this economic system, Wind Mountain represented a mineral gleaning or procurement settlement. Socioreligious artifact types were linked to Mesoamerican based symbolism, introduced by southern entrepreneurs who reorganized the indigenous Mogollon Chichimec settlement. Ornaments were thought to reflect the presence of more sophisticated merchant elements. Exotic marine shell illustrated the active reciprocal trade network that also brought commodities into the community. Valued minerals and stone, focus of entrepreneurial exploitation, were procured for redistribution to southern trade centers.

9

Wind Mountain Mortuary Data

In archaeological research, the humanity, those qualities that make a people human, is often submerged in sterile statistics. At Wind Mountain we know that a majority of the residents were right handed and the women averaged about 5' 1" in height and the men 5' 4". Many suffered from the litany of anticipated ailments, such as tooth abscesses and decay, broken bones, infections, and arthritis. Their expected life span may have been as short as 16 or 17 years (refer to Appendix 7). As sparse as this information is, when added to our findings of how the Wind Mountain inhabitants treated their dead, we discover the underlying human nature of the community. Their humanity is expressed in the interment of an elderly woman with corn (apparently a burial offering) or in the mystery of two small children buried together.

The Wind Mountain human burial population was extensive, consisting of 122 intact inhumations and two cremations, which were distributed throughout the structures and extramural contexts of the site (refer to Figure 4.1). A few burials were vandalized, chiefly those in the vicinity of visible architecture, whether pit structures or surface rooms (e.g., Wind Mountain locus Burials 11, 28, 34, and 35). Large numbers of miscellaneous human bone elements, particularly those belonging to infants and children, were also recovered from screened excavation blocks and structural fill. The analyses were, in part, encumbered by poor preservation of some bone, a situation not altogether uncommon and reported for other Mimbres Mogollon sites (e.g., Anyon and LeBlanc 1984:173; Lekson 1990:93–95). The human remains were not so deteriorated as to preclude interpretation. To date, the Wind Mountain sample constitutes the largest excavated burial population from the Upper Gila (for comparative Mogollon burial data, see Kelly 1940:88–93, 1943:250–251; Martin and Rinaldo 1947:376–378; Wheat 1955:66–71; Bussey 1972:259–268; Anyon and LeBlanc 1984:173–186; Ham 1989; Lekson 1990:93–95).

Initially, the Wind Mountain burials were studied to determine if the settlement's residents practiced any particularistic patterns for disposing of their dead. Even superficial examination of the Wind Mountain burial population clearly indicated that mortuary behavior was consistent throughout the lifetime of the community. Though treatment of the dead was apparently unchanging, the Wind Mountain burial sample was biased toward the Pit House period, the most extensive occupation of the site. Only four burials (Wind Mountain locus Burials 1, 24, 27, and 32) contained Mimbres Classic Black-on-white vessel accompaniments that could be positively associated with Mimbres phase occupations after c. A.D. 1000.

Burials were also scrutinized for any artifacts that might have served as purposeful funerary offerings. The possibility that elaborate grave goods might be found associated with some burials was carefully considered in light of Di Peso's belief in the presence of high status individuals, indicative of southern elites, at the site.

Lastly, an osteological study of the Wind Mountain burial population helped establish its demographic profile. Analyses included age and gender distributions, the condition of bone and dentition, as well as identifiable pathologies (refer to Appendix 7).

Inhumations

Inhumation was by far the most common method for disposing of the Wind Mountain dead. Extensive stripping of the site uncovered 80 burials in extramural contexts or excavation blocks, with another 42 inhumations recovered from structures or structure fill (Table 9.1). Only two cremations, discussed separately below, were noted. With the exception of two extended burials (Wind Mountain locus Burials 85 and 105), individuals were flexed or partially flexed, laid on their sides, or placed in a prone, supine, or seated position, and interred. Many individuals were contained in discrete burial pits (n = 66, or 54 percent), the dimensions of which were usually not much larger than the capacity required to accommodate the remains. Individual funerary pits were sometimes partially excavated into old house floors so that a portion of the body rested on or below a floor surface while the remainder extended upward into fill. Many of the dead were also buried entirely within the disturbed fill of abandoned structures. When individuals were placed in structural fill, the boundaries of pits were often not discernable. At Wind Mountain 53 inhumations (43 percent) were interred in an absence of a definable burial pit. Curiously, despite intensive probing, only three burials occurred in subfloor pits, all at the Wind Mountain locus, including an adult under Room 2 (Burial 1) and two infants, one under the floor of House TT (Burial 91) and the other under the floor of House AF (Burial 100). This positioning suggests a distinct and conscious desire for a physical separation between the living and dead of the settlement. Besides these three burials, no individual was buried in a structure still actively used.

In most cases, small burial pits were simply excavated with no additional elaborations. A few, however, exhibited a cobble lining or were covered with cobbles reminiscent of a cairn (e.g., Wind Mountain locus Burials 3, 24, and 45; Ridout locus Burials 1, 2, and 3). The cobble covering was sometimes substantial as observed atop Burial 24 (40 cm x 75 cm x 30 cm thick) and Burial 45 (30 cm x 50 cm x 25 cm thick). In Burial 68 at the Wind Mountain locus, cobbles were not used to seal the pit, but rocks were placed on the chest, head, and shoulders of the individual. Whether such cobble coverings were intended to protect the burials from disturbance or to protect the living from the restless dead will remain unknown.

Most inhumations contained a single interment, though some departures to this pattern were observed. Wind Mountain locus Burial 101 contained two children, but unfortunately the remains were greatly deteriorated and consisted solely of cranial fragments. In contrast, Burials 53 and 54, also from a single pit at the Wind Mountain locus, were well preserved. Two adult males were interred with their skulls touching and the right hand of one partially under the skull of the other. Apparently temporally unrelated, the fill of several structures also contained multiple interments. For example, three infants (Burials 26, 27, and 29) were recorded in House T, and several adult burials were recovered from Houses V, (Burials 30, 31, and 32), FF (Burials 47, 48, 50, and 51), and HH (Burials 59, 61, and 62) at the Wind Mountain locus as well as from House F (Burials 8, 9, and 13) at the Ridout locus.

Cremations

Burials 92 and 95, the two cremations discovered in extramural pits at the site, consisted of bone fragments and ash. Unlike cremation practices reported for the Hohokam, which involved the immediate disposal of individuals at death (Haury 1976:166), the Wind Mountain bones were not fresh or "green" when burned. Instead, the bodies seem to have been buried first, disinterred, and the remains collected for subsequent cremation. Although the occurrence of cremated remains interred in pits is anomalous in Mimbres Mogollon sites, it is by no means unknown (Bussey 1975:19; Creel 1989:309–313). Early excavations at Mogollon Village and Harris Village yielded three extramural cremations (Haury 1936a:24, 64; Wheat 1955:68–69). Some offerings were present in the cremations from both sites, although no funerary offerings accompanied the Wind Mountain cremation pit burials. Three Hohokam style inverted bowl cremations associated with the "Mangas phase/Mimbres period" deposits were described at the Saige-McFarland site (Lekson 1990:94). Haury (1936a:92) cited the occurrence of pit cremations in Mogollon sites as evidence of Mogollon and Hohokam contact during the Pit House period. Di Peso, too, believed the Wind Mountain cremations to be indications of interaction between the Hohokam and Mogollon Chichimecs. He dated the Wind Mountain cremations before c. A.D. 950, the period he suggested to reflect the greatest Hohokam influence. After c. A.D. 950 Di Peso (1974:141–142) felt that any Hohokam activities relating to Wind Mountain largely waned as Casas Grandes based merchants began to exert their economic dominance over the settlement.

Funerary Accompaniments

Material objects accompanied 48 (39 percent) of the 122 inhumations exposed at the Wind Mountain site (Table 9.2). Of all types of funerary offerings, ceramics occurred most frequently, as either whole vessels or sherds, appearing in 36 (30 percent) burials. The Alma series and San Francisco Red wares were most numerous, though Boldface Black-on-white (Style I and II) was relatively common, and Mimbres Classic Black-on-white (Style III) was noted. Three Circle Red-on-white and Mimbres Corrugated were rare. Neither Mogollon Red-on-brown, Three Circle Neck Corrugated, nor any intrusive pottery type was represented in the ceramic mortuary assemblage.

Objects of personal ornamentation adorned some of the dead or were placed with the human remains as they were

TABLE 9.1. Wind Mountain Burial Data

Burial No.	Provenience	Burial Pit Length (m)	Burial Pit Width (m)	Burial Pit Depth (m)	Body Position	Body Orientation	Head Facing	Age in Years	Sex
	WM locus								
1	Room 2 subfloor	.85	.38	1.50	F	N-S?	missing	26–39	nd
2	House A fill	N/A	N/A	nd	nd	nd	nd	I	nd
3	Block 2-D	1.50	.80	.95	PF,RS	E-W	N	25–35	F
4	Block 11-A	1.05	.80	.70	SE	nd	down	40+	M
5	Block 11-A	.37	.27	.17	F,S	N-S?	SW	3–4	nd
6	Block 10-A	.87	.80	.68	PF,S	E-W	ESE	26–39	nd
7	Pit 2	1.18	1.20	.55	F,S	nd	NE	I	nd
8	House G fill	N/A	N/A	1.00	PF,S	E-W	W	40+	M
9	Block 10-D	.98	nd	.30	F,RS	E-W	SE	40+	F
10	House J fill	.63	.22	.30	F,LS	E-W	N	I	nd
11a	Block 11-D	nd	nd	.60	F	nd	nd	40–45	F
11b	Block 11-D	nd	nd	.60	nd	nd	nd	A	nd
12	Block 26-A	.75	.65	.38	F?	E-W?	missing	26–39	F
13	Block 26-A	.90	.42	.82	F,S	E-W	down	26–39	F
14	Block 26-A	.85	.75	.45	F?	nd	nd	26–39	nd
15	Block 11-D	nd	.82	1.20	F,RS	nd	nd	26–39	M?
16	Block 12-D	N/A	N/A	.20	nd	nd	nd	26–39	M?
17	Block 27-B	.70	.55	.60	F?	nd	missing	26–39	nd
18	House N fill	1.40	.45	.95	nd	E-W	nd	26–39	nd
19	Block 13-C	.75	.50	.80	nd	nd	nd	26–39	M
20	Block 19-B	N/A	N/A	.80	F,S	S-W	missing	26–39	nd
21	Block 19-B	N/A	N/A	.70	F,S	E-W	missing	40+	M
22	Block 20-A	N/A	N/A	.55	F,LS	E-W	SE	50+	F
23	Block 20-A	N/A	N/A	.90	F,S	E-W	NE	40+	M
24	House Q fill	.90	.55	.95	F,RS	E-W	N	40+	M
25	Block 28-B	1.00	.97	.75	F	nd	nd	26–39	nd
26	House T fill	N/A	N/A	.60	nd	nd	nd	F	nd
27	House T fill	N/A	N/A	1.05	nd	nd	nd	I	nd
28	House S fill	N/A	N/A	.80	nd	nd	nd	26–39	nd
29	House T fill	N/A	N/A	.40	nd	nd	S	I	nd
30	House V fill	N/A	N/A	.95	F,LS	E-W	S	26–39	F
31	House V fill	N/A	N/A	1.10	PF,LS	E-W	down	40+	nd
32	House V fill	N/A	N/A	1.35	F?	nd	nd	A	nd
33	Block 43-B	.90	.50	1.20	F,SE	nd	missing	26–39	nd
34	House X fill	N/A	N/A	1.10	nd	nd	nd	4–6	nd
35	House Y fill	N/A	N/A	.95	F?	nd	nd	nd	nd
36	House Y fill	N/A	N/A	.80	F?	nd	nd	I	nd
37	Block 34-C	N/A	N/A	.35	nd	nd	nd	A?	nd
38	House Y fill	N/A	N/A	.90	F,S	E-W	E	45–50	F
39	Block 43-C	.60	.55	.55	F,SE	nd	N?	40+	nd
40	Block 29-A	1.05	1.05	.70	F,RS	E-W	N	15–25	M?
41	Block 29-A	.75	.70	.60	F,SE	nd	nd	26–39	nd
42	Block 21-A	N/A	N/A	.60	F,S	N-S	down	26–39	M
43	Block 22-D	1.30	1.00	.60	F,LS	N-W	N	26–39	M?
44	Block 36-D	.85	.48	.35	F,S	E-W	W	45–55	F
45	House X fill	N/A	N/A	1.05	PF,S	E-W	up	26–39	M
46	Block 43-C	.55	.50	.45	F,SE?	nd	nd	A?	nd
47	House FF fill	.65	.55	.70	F,SE	nd	down	26–39	M?
48	House FF fill	N/A	N/A	.75	F,LS	nd	ESE	26–39	nd
49	House X fill	N/A	N/A	.85	F,S	N-S	up	26–39	M
50	House FF fill	N/A	N/A	.65	F,RS	nd	nd	26–39	nd

TABLE 9.1. *(continued)*

Burial No.	Provenience	Burial Pit Length (m)	Width (m)	Depth (m)	Body Position	Body Orientation	Head Facing	Age in Years	Sex
51	House FF fill	N/A	N/A	1.10	F,SE	nd	nd	26–39	nd
52	Block 45-B	N/A	N/A	.65	PF,SE	E-W	down	16–18	F
53	Block 45-C	1.20	1.15	.85	F,P	N-S	W	26–39	M
54	Block 45-C	1.20	1.15	.85	F,S	N-S	NW	26–39	M
55	Block 52-B	N/A	N/A	.45	F,RS	nd	nd	26–39	nd
56	Blocks 37-A, 29-C	1.05	.75	.85	F,SE	E-W	NE	26–39	nd
57	Block 37-A	.75	.65	.68	F,SE?	nd	nd	26–39	nd
58	Block 30-B	N/A	N/A	.30	F?,S	N-S	missing	26–39	nd
59	House HH fill	.80	.72	1.05	F,SE	E-W	NW	40+	M?
60	Block 20-B	N/A	N/A	.60	nd	nd	nd	26–39	nd
61	Houses HH, JJ fill	.85	.50	1.05	F,S	E-W	missing	26–39	M
62	House HH fill	.65	.65	.90	F,SE?	nd	nd	26–39	nd
63	Block 30-D	N/A	N/A	.20	F	E-W	nd	45–55	F
64	Block 30-D	N/A	N/A	.50	F,S	nd	W	2.5–3.5	nd
65	Block 30-D	N/A	N/A	.38	PF,S	E-W	W	26–39	nd
66	Block 29-B	N/A	N/A	.40	nd	nd	nd	5–7	nd
67	Block 30-A	N/A	N/A	.45	nd	nd	missing	26–39	nd
68	Pit 40	1.60	1.45	.60	F,LS	N-S	E	26–39	M
69	Block 30-D	N/A	N/A	.50	F,S	E-W	W	50+	F
70	Block 30-D	N/A	N/A	.40	nd	nd	nd	0–3 mos.	nd
71	Block 29-D	.55	.55	.70	F,SE	nd	missing	26–39	nd
72	Blocks 29-D, 30-C, 37-B, 38-A	.60	.55	.55	F,LS	nd	nd	26–39	M?
73	Block 37-B	N/A	N/A	.40	nd	nd	nd	1–2	nd
74	Block 45-B	N/A	N/A	.10	SE	nd	NNE?	40+	nd
75	Block 38-A	N/A	N/A	.55	F,LS	nd	nd	4–6 mos.	nd
76	Block 38-A	N/A	N/A	.90	nd	nd	nd	26–39	nd
77	Block 46-D	.68	.55	.70	F,SE	E-W	down	17–18	M?
78	Block 45-D	N/A	N/A	.40	nd	nd	nd	F	nd
79	Block 55-C	.65	.60	.70	F,SE	nd	nd	26–39	M
80	House QQ fill	N/A	N/A	.70	F,S	nd	missing	26–39	nd
81	Block 63-C	N/A	N/A	.50	nd	nd	nd	50+	F
82	Block 62-C	N/A	N/A	.55	nd	nd	nd	C	nd
83	Block 62-D	N/A	N/A	.15	F,S?	nd	S	26–39	nd
84	Block 62-D	.65	.65	.40	F,S	E-W	SW	15–25	F
85	Block 62-D	.60	.35	.20	E,S?	nd	NE	2–3	nd
86	Block 62-D	.85	.50	.28	F,S	E-W	W	26–39	nd
87	Block 62-C	N/A	N/A	.25	nd	N-S	missing	26–39	M?
88	Blocks 62-A, 62-C	nd	nd	.95	nd	nd	nd	26–39	nd
89	Block 54-A	.75	.48	.55	F,S	E-W	SE?	26–39	nd
90	Block 62-B	nd	nd	nd	nd	nd	nd	26–39	nd
91	House TT sub-floor	.35	.30	1.30	nd	nd	nd	18 mos.	nd
92	Block 53-B	N/A	N/A	nd	nd	nd	nd	C	nd
93	Block 54-D	N/A	N/A	.90	nd	nd	nd	26–39	nd
94	House AC floor/fill	1.38	1.33	.38	F,SE	E-W	W	15–25	nd
95	Block 54-A	.47	.40	.52	nd	nd	nd	C	nd

Table 9.1. *(continued)*

Burial No.	Provenience	Burial Pit Length (m)	Burial Pit Width (m)	Burial Pit Depth (m)	Body Position	Body Orientation	Head Facing	Age in Years	Sex
96	House AB floor/fill	1.40	1.05	.56	F,LS	nd	E	26–39	nd
97	Block 53-B	1.00	.85	.55	nd	nd	nd	26–39	nd
98	Block 53-C	1.40	1.20	.75	PF	nd	nd	26–39	nd
99	House AE fill	.70	.60	.94	F,S	E-W	E	40+	M?
100	House AF subfloor	.62	.60	1.14	nd	nd	nd	N	nd
101	House AI floor/fill	N/A	N/A	.80	nd	nd	nd	4–5 and 5–6	nd
102	House AL fill	1.00	.42	.29	F	nd	N?	26–39	M
103	House AM fill	.90	.85	.60	F,SE	nd	W	26–39	M
104	House AM fill	1.75	1.10	1.70	F,SE	nd	W	26–39	M?
105	House AM fill	2.20	.80	.60	E	E-W	missing	40–45	F
106	Houses UU, VV fill	nd	nd	nd	nd	nd	nd	I	nd
Cremation 1	Block 29-D	1.75	.60	1.05	N/A	N/A	N/A	A	nd
Cremation 2	Block 53-D	1.00	.65	.15	N/A	N/A	N/A	A	nd
	RO locus								
1	Block E0E	1.00	.80	.10	F,SE	E-W	E	26–39	nd
2	Block E0E	1.20	.65	.25	F,P	E-W	missing	26–39	nd
3	Block E0W	1.65	.97	.23	F	E-W	E	26–39	nd
4	Block D2W	.93	.71	.53	F	E-W	E	26–39	M?
5	Block F0E	.80	.60	.30	F	E-W	W	40+	M
6	Block J1E	.90	.50	.20	F,S	N-S?	W?	26–39	nd
7	Block E0W	1.15	.90	.40	F	E-W	E	40+	M
8	House F floor	.70	.40	.90	F	nd	NW?	40+	F
9	House F floor/fill	.90	.80	.65	F	nd	S	26–39	nd
10	Block G0E	.50	.30	.25	nd	nd	E?	I	nd
11	Block G0W	.90	.90	.30	F,RS	nd	down	26–39	nd
12	Block G0W	N/A	N/A	.45	nd	nd	nd	I	nd
13	House F floor/fill	1.10	.80	1.05	F	nd	W?	26–39	nd
14	House I fill	.75	.75	.17	F	nd	W	1.5–2.5	nd
15	Block L3E	.80	.80	.15	F,RS	E-W	E	26–39	F
16	House K floor/fill	1.90	.55	1.01	E	E-W	up	26–39	F

Body Position: E = Extended, F = Flexed, LS = On left side, P = Prone, PF = Partly flexed, RS = On right side, S = Supine, SE = Seated; *Age:* A = Adult, C = Child (1.5–14 years), F = Fetus, I = Infant, N = Neonate; *Other:* nd = no data available.

interred. Shell jewelry (in eight burials) was recovered in the form of bracelets, pendants, ear bobs, and beads (Wind Mountain locus Burials 4, 24, 59, 102, 103; Ridout locus Burials 7, 10, 13). Jewelry was also fashioned from turquoise and other types of stone (six burials) into effigy style and simple pendants, beads, and tesserae (Wind Mountain locus Burials 65, 85, 97, 101, 102, 103). One bone shaft found under a skull may represent a hair pin (Wind Mountain locus Burial 13).

Utilitarian objects other than ceramics were also observed, but in relatively low numbers (10 burials for all classes of objects). These consisted of incidental manos, grinding slabs, core tools, projectile points, polishing stones, a stone bowl, and a bone awl (Wind Mountain locus Burials 3, 13, 14, 74, 97; Ridout locus Burials 2, 3, 6, 7, 13).

The remaining funerary items occurred only infrequently, sometimes as isolates in the total mortuary assemblage. Objects of possible ritual function, including two stone pipes

TABLE 9.2. Wind Mountain Burials and Associated Funerary Accompaniments

Burial No.	Catalogue No.	Funerary Accompaniment
WM locus		
1	WM 90	Mimbres Classic B/W (Style III) bowl
	WM 91	Mimbres Classic B/W (Style III) bowl
	WM 1952	Mimbres Corrugated jar
3	WM 198	Alma Plain jar
	WM 200	"Killed" Boldface B/W (Styles I/II) bowl behind skull
	WM 203	Hammerstone
4	WM 187A–D	*Glycymeris gigantea* bracelets on left arm
	WM 199	San Francisco Red bowl near right leg
	WM 250	*Oliva incrassata* beads (8) near pelvis
5	WM 202	San Francisco Red sherds
7	WM 1953	Alma Rough miniature bowl
8	–	San Francisco Red sherds near feet
10	–	San Francisco Red sherds
11	WM/C 898	Boldface B/W (Styles I/II) bowl sherds with charred corn kernels
12	WM/C 128	Alma Plain sherd inside WM 461
	WM 461	San Francisco Red bowl
13	WM/C 130	San Francisco Red sherds on right side of skull
	WM 391	Bone awl under WM 395
	WM 395	Mano at feet
	–	Bone shaft (hair pin?) behind skull
14	WM/C 129	Alma Plain sherd
	WM 393	Core
	WM 394	Flat slab; all artifacts clustered at center of pit
18	–	Boldface B/W (Styles I/II) and Mimbres Classic B/W (Style III) sherds
24	WM 716	Mimbres Classic B/W (Style III) bowl partially under skull
	WM 787A–B	Freshwater pelecypod adjacent skull
25	WM/C 332	Fragmentary Alma Rough miniature bowl
26	WM 805	San Francisco Red jar
27	WM 788	"Killed" Mimbres Classic B/W (Style III) bowl inverted over infant
30	WM 1162	Boldface B/W (Styles I/II) bowl over skull
32	WM/C 353	Boldface B/W (Styles I/II) sherd
	WM 962	Alma Plain bowl
	WM 963	Alma Plain miniature bowl placed inside WM 962
	WM 1163	Mimbres Classic B/W (Style III) bowl inverted over skull
	WM 1164	Mimbres Corrugated jar
35	WM 1208	Alma Plain bowl
40	WM/S 9	Ground red ocher on and under right arm
49	WM/C 643	Alma Plain sherd near left forearm
59	WM 1789	*Glycymeris gigantea* bracelet at left elbow
	WM 1790	San Francisco Red bowl over right forearm

TABLE 9.2. *(continued)*

Burial No.	Catalogue No.	Funerary Accompaniment
62	WM 1817	Alma Plain bowl adjacent left arm
65	WM 1890	Turquoise tesserae (167 pieces) under WM 1954
	WM 1922	San Francisco Red bowl
	WM 1923	Alma Incised jar adjacent left arm
	WM 1954	Alma Rough jar over left elbow
71	WM 1892	Fist–size nodule of malachite
74	WM 1924	Polishing stone adjacent skull
82	WM/C 918	Alma Plain miniature jar
	WM 919	Alma Plain miniature jar
	WM 920	San Francisco Red bowl
84	WM/S 4008	Mica flake on ribs
85	WM 2216	San Francisco Red bowl inverted over skull
	WM 2280	Stone animal effigy pendant at right side of jaw
86	WM/C 932	Alma Plain sherd between knees
	WM 2217	San Francisco Red miniature bowl near left shoulder
89	WM 2281	San Francisco Red bowl near left arm
94	WM 2777	San Francisco Red bowl over right knee
95	WM 2679	San Francisco Red bowl
96	WM 2669	Alma Plain bowl
	WM 2670	San Francisco Red bowl
97	WM 2684	Turquoise pendant
	WM/S 4774	Projectile point
	WM/S 4813	Drill
99	WM 2778	Alma Rough bowl and
	WM 2779	Three Circle R/W bowl at feet
101	WM 2836	Alma Plain bowl
	WM 2838	Turquoise pendant inside WM 2836
102	WM 3091	Shale counter
	WM 3092	Quartz crystal
	WM 3093	Stone (stalactite?) pendant
	WM 3094	*Oliva spicata* beads (14)
	WM 3095	*Glycymeris gigantea* disk bead
	WM 3096	*Glycymeris gigantea* disk bead
103	WM 3082	*Glycymeris gigantea* bracelets (4); two on each arm
	WM 3083	San Francisco Red bowl
	WM 3107	*Glycymeris gigantea* (1,192), *Chama echinata* (38), and turquoise (12) beads around body
	WM 3126	San Francisco Red bowl; WM 3083 was inverted over WM 3126
RO locus		
1	RO 208	Biotite schist pipe near pelvis
2	RO 209	Biotite schist pipe near pelvis
	RO 210	Limonite (yellow ocher) nodule
	RO 211	Chalcedony projectile point near feet

TABLE 9.2. *(continued)*

Burial No.	Catalogue No.	Funerary Accompaniment
3	RO 212	Shale slab with traces of red ocher
6	RO 213	Sandstone bowl or mortar
7	RO 223	Sandstone slab with ground malachite traces on one side, red ocher on the other
	RO 239	*Olivella dama* beads (12)
	RO 240	*Chama echinata* pendant
	RO 241	*Chama echinata* pendant
	RO/S 264	Malachite nodule
8	RO 217	Vesicular basalt tube
9	RO 219	San Francisco Red bowl
	RO 220	"Killed" San Francisco Red bowl
	RO 221	San Francisco Red bowl
	RO 222	San Francisco Red bowl
10	RO 224	Whole *Strombus galeatus* pendant inside RO 227
	RO 227	San Francisco Red bowl
	RO 228	San Francisco Red bowl
13	RO/SL 9a,b	*Glycymeris gigantea* bracelets (2) on arm
	RO 225	*Nacreous–Pteria sterna* pendant
	RO 226	*Glycymeris gigantea* beads (84); pendant and beads found in RO 229 part of one necklace
	RO 229	San Francisco Red bowl
	RO 230	Granite mano
	RO 231?	Andesite polishing stone

and a tube or "cloud blower," were encountered in three burials (Ridout locus Burials 1, 2, 8). A few minerals and crystals such as nodules or traces of ground hematite, limonite, and malachite were recovered in four burials (Wind Mountain locus Burials 40, 71; Ridout locus Burials 2, 7), as well as a large mica flake (Wind Mountain locus Burial 84), and a clear quartz crystal (Wind Mountain locus Burial 102). Quartz crystals have been identified as "special," nonutilitarian artifacts in certain contexts (McGuire 1987:67). The burial of an elderly woman (Wind Mountain locus Burial 11) yielded charred corn kernels, one of several examples of seeds associated with an interment at the site (Appendix 1). Evidence that plant material may have been placed in other burials is further indicated by pollen (Appendix 2). Two pollen clumps, possibly the remains of blossoms, were recovered from a vessel provided an adult (Wind Mountain locus Burial 65), and two vessels accompanying a young child (Wind Mountain locus Burial 101) contained corn pollen.

Wind Mountain Mortuary Patterns

As noted earlier, 39 percent of the 122 inhumations uncovered at the settlement exhibited objects in direct association with the human remains interred and are presumed to represent funerary offerings (Table 9.2). Out of a total of 95 adult burials—including young adults aged 15 to 25, middle adults aged 26 to 39, and old adults over the age of 40—37 contained mortuary materials (compare Table 9.1 and Appendix 7). In the adult inhumations with grave goods, gender could not be determined in 20 instances, but in the remaining burials, seven represented females (two women were old adults, in excess of 40 years) and 10 were males (six were old adults). In contrast to adults, infant and child burials occurred less frequently, although many scattered miscellaneous nonadult bone elements were collected from a variety of site contexts. Total infant (including fetuses) and child burials numbered 27 (15 infants and 12 children, one consisting of the double inhumation mentioned earlier, Wind Mountain locus Burial 101). Ten of these burials contained funerary accompaniments, divided evenly between five infant and five child interments. The bones of a final inhumation (Wind Mountain locus Burial 35), associated with artifacts, were too deteriorated to allow gender or age determinations.

Assessing the burials from Wind Mountain for content and quantity of mortuary remains revealed that 22 inhumations (Wind Mountain locus Burials 5, 7, 8, 10, 25, 26, 27, 30, 35, 40, 49, 62, 71, 74, 84, 89, 94, 95; Ridout locus Burials 1, 3, 6, 8) contained a sole object (fragments belonging to a single item were counted as one). Another 10 burials (Wind Mountain locus Burials 11, 12, 18, 24, 59, 85, 86, 96, 99,

101) included two objects, often ceramics or shell jewelry. Multiple funerary offerings, that is, three or more artifacts, were observed in 16 burials (Wind Mountain locus Burials 1, 3, 4, 13, 14, 32, 65, 82, 97, 102, 103; Ridout locus Burials 2, 7, 9, 10, 13). For example, Burial 32 at the Wind Mountain locus and Burial 9 at the Ridout locus each yielded four vessels. Other burials characterized by multiple mortuary accompaniments, such as Wind Mountain locus Burial 13, produced stone, bone, and ceramic objects, and Burial 65 contained vessels and 167 pieces of turquoise tesserae. Wind Mountain locus Burial 102 was noteworthy for its shell and stone ornaments as were two interments at the Ridout locus, Burial 2 with mineral pigment and stone tools and Burial 13 with pottery, shell jewelry, and stone implements.

Of infant or child burials with offerings (n = 10 individuals, Wind Mountain locus Burials 5, 7, 10, 26, 27, 82, 85, 101; Ridout locus Burial 10), six contained a single pottery vessel. In two burials, the young individual was accompanied by a vessel and some object of personal adornment. The child in Wind Mountain Burial 85, apparently wore a stone effigy pendant (WM 2280; refer to Figure 8.14). A turquoise pendant was placed in a bowl adjacent two children interred in Wind Mountain locus Burial 101. Two of the site's infant/child burials contained multiple offerings. In Wind Mountain locus Burial 82 a child was accompanied by three vessels. An infant in Ridout locus Burial 10 was provided with two vessels and a shell pendant.

Examining the total Wind Mountain burial population discloses an intriguing pattern in the distribution of funerary accompaniments. Of the 48 burials with grave goods, 21 percent (n = 10) represented juveniles (age 14 and younger) and 79 percent (n = 38) were adults (age 15 and older). However, if the site's total identifiable burial assemblage (26 juveniles and 95 adults, n = 121) is viewed as two discrete populations, 38.5 percent of the juveniles were provided with funerary offerings as compared with 40 percent of the adults. Consequently, despite possible variation in population size between the two groups, the actual percentage of grave goods is remarkably constant. In fact, the number of burials (n = 48) including all ages with mortuary objects equals 39.3 percent of the entire burial population. Again, the percentage is exceptionally uniform.

Interpreting the Wind Mountain funerary assemblage in the broader cultural context of the settlement raises additional interesting questions. Mortuary inclusions have been used to infer facets of prehistoric social organization, especially as regards status and role differentiation (Rothschild 1979). Yet it is impossible to know how the community's inhabitants weighted these accompaniments. The perceived value, for example, of a single Boldface Black-on-white bowl (Wind Mountain locus Burial 30) relative to one malachite nodule (Wind Mountain locus Burial 71) or a biotite schist pipe (Ridout locus Burial 1) is not known. The comparative worth of painted versus plainware pottery is a mystery. One cannot assume that a "cloud blower" tube or pipe had greater significance than, say, a mano based simply on a presumed religious function assigned to these nonutilitarian objects. One can only guess (and abstractly sympathize) at the symbolic gesture of three miniature ceramic vessels associated with a child burial (Wind Mountain locus Burial 82). Similarly, the distribution of shell as one component of the funerary assemblage may provide the window through which aspects of Wind Mountain social organization are glimpsed. Shell occurred only rarely in Wind Mountain burials. Of eight inhumations with shell ornamentation, all but one (the infant in Ridout locus Burial 10) were identified as adults—six males and one individual of indeterminate gender. Four of these adults represented individuals older than 40. One conjectures, albeit hesitantly, that this pattern of mortuary shell jewelry might be linked to social distinctions and distinguishes "leaders" in the Wind Mountain community. Such interpretations, though provocative, in an absence of corroborative data, must remain in the realm of speculation.

Funerary objects have also been categorized in terms of high or low cost investments (Peebles and Kus 1971; Braun 1979). Referring to degree of accessibility, high cost items are those more consumptive of time and energy to procure or produce, whereas low cost items describe those that are readily available. Shell, obtainable from the Gulf of California or Pacific Coast, was the only obvious high cost material recognized in the Wind Mountain mortuary inventory. No other exotics were observed as funerary inclusions since even turquoise, often cited as a high value material elsewhere, was locally available to the residents of Wind Mountain. Other imports noted in the total material inventory from the site that would have required transport to the settlement over some distance, either by direct procurement or trade, included obsidian, ricolite, and certain pottery types. None of these intrusives were found in burial contexts.

In addition to the composition of mortuary assemblages as indicative of prehistoric social or economic organization, investigators have examined differential mortuary behavior from the standpoint of the type of burial facility used, the placement of such facilities in sites, as well as methods for processing the dead (Goldstein 1981; McGuire 1987:108–109). Reviewing the interment practices at Wind Mountain, all discernable burial facilities consisted of simple pits. When human remains were interred in house fill or the loose deposits of the sloping settlement ridge, pit boundaries were not always visible. These burial pits were relatively homogeneous in both construction and size and, therefore, presumably necessitated about the same expenditure of labor and time to create. None seem to have been greatly consumptive of time or energy to construct.

Compared to such simple pits, the so-called cairn burials

constituted the only Wind Mountain burial facility requiring extra effort to build. But for the elaboration of their cobble coverings, these burials were not especially remarkable. One cairn contained an adult female with three ceramic vessels (Wind Mountain locus Burial 3), another included an old adult male with a bowl and freshwater shell (Wind Mountain locus Burial 24), and in a third an adult male was interred without accompanying artifacts. Wind Mountain locus Burial 68 was a variation on the cairn theme. Though the pit was not sealed by a cobble covering, stones had been positioned at various points on the corpse. Several other burials incorporated cobbles on top of or surrounding the individual interred (Ridout locus Burials 1, 2, and 3). Even these cairn burials, however, could not be considered particularly elaborate in their construction.

As previously mentioned, Wind Mountain burials appear to occur at random across the site. No formalized patterns were distinguished. The dead were evidently not welcomed as subfloor intrusions in structures that were occupied.

Preparation of the dead prior to burial was, for the most part, restricted to flexing or partially flexing the human remains. Traces of ground hematite suggest that some individuals may have been coated with pigment (Wind Mountain locus Burial 40). In general, however, individuals did not exhibit other, more specialized processing. The only exceptions to the practice of flexed interment included two cremations (at the Wind Mountain locus) and two extended inhumations (Wind Mountain locus Burial 105; Ridout locus Burial 16). These four burials contained no associated offerings.

To summarize Wind Mountain mortuary behavior, little energy, labor, or time was invested to construct the inconspicuous burial facilities scattered across the site. In the absence of evidence for prescribed postmortem processing, the preparation of human remains was simply achieved and commensurate regardless of age or gender. Burials were seldom provided with elaborate funerary offerings, and so-called high cost or status objects occurred infrequently. Locally made plain and painted ceramic wares were the most abundant form of grave goods, crosscutting gender and age. All stone and mineral mortuary inclusions were obtainable from nearby mountain sources. Shell, available through long distance procurement or exchange, was the only high cost material observed in the Wind Mountain funerary assemblage.

Based on attributes described above (i.e., type of burial facility employed, treatment of individual human remains, the nature and composition of the material accompaniments), Wind Mountain mortuary data does not support the existence of a rigidly ranked social or economic structure that served to organize a community. Nevertheless, in any social group, even so-called egalitarian communities, certain individuals are undoubtedly more influential than others. Greater influence does not automatically imply formalized status such as, for example, ascriptive hereditary ranking and associated wealth. A few Wind Mountain burials, notably those with shell, but perhaps also those that contained multiple ceramic vessels or objects of possible ritual function (e.g., Wind Mountain locus Burials 32 and 65; Ridout locus Burials 2 and 9), may represent individuals who were important within the context of their community. Alternatively, the offerings placed with these individuals, more simply, may reflect personal or familial devotion to loved ones. The fact that several infants (e.g., Wind Mountain locus Burials 82 and 85; Ridout locus Burial 10) were accompanied by numerous or somehow symbolically special objects may be significant but the evidence is too sparse to facilitate more comprehensive interpretations. In sum, the Wind Mountain burial population, its associated funerary assemblage, and presumed attendant mortuary behavior may properly describe the community by what has been termed as a "rather egalitarian" (Feinman 1991:466) social group.

Comparative Mogollon Mortuary Patterns

Treatment of the Wind Mountain dead corresponds with burial patterns reported for other Pit House period sites from not only the Upper Gila but elsewhere in the San Francisco/Reserve and Mimbres regions. The Pueblo period burials c. A.D. 950/1000 and later were so sparsely represented at Wind Mountain that one can only comment that the few interments with Mimbres Classic Black-on-white pottery were similar to those described from Mattocks Ruin (Nesbitt 1931), Swarts Ruin (Cosgrove and Cosgrove 1932), and the surface room block associations of Galaz Ruin (Anyon and LeBlanc 1984). Post-A.D. 1000 trends in which dramatic increases in the quantity and distribution of funerary accompaniments are reported at other sites do not occur at Wind Mountain. Nesbitt (1938), for instance, records that 52 burials from surface rooms at Starkweather Ruin exhibited an average of three vessels (range 1–15) per burial. Had Wind Mountain been more intensively occupied during the Mimbres phase, we might have expected a larger percentage of burials with a greater quantity of offerings.

Given the meager nature of the Wind Mountain Mimbres phase habitation, comparisons of mortuary practices are most appropriate for the pre-A.D. 950/1000 period, the time interval encompassing the majority of Wind Mountain burials. Survey of selected burial populations, including the Reserve area SU site (Martin 1940:93, 1943:251; Martin and Rinaldo 1947:376–378), Bear Ruin in the Forestdale Valley (Haury 1985:196–199), Mogollon Village along the banks of the San Francisco River (Haury 1936a:24), and Harris Village in the Mimbres Valley (Haury 1936a:64), demonstrates clear similarities in the mortuary behavior expressed by the residents of these Mogollon sites and the people of Wind Mountain. Saige-McFarland (Lekson 1990:93–95), even if its most extensive occupation was generally later than that reported for Wind Mountain, provides additional relevant burial data from another site in the Upper Gila.

At Bear Ruin (Forestdale phase; c. A.D. 563–702) some 40 burials were recovered from pits largely scattered throughout the site (Haury 1985:196, 377). The dead were interred in a partially flexed, reclining position in simple pits with no lining, cobble covering, or other elaboration. None of the Bear Ruin burials were placed under house floors, reminiscent of the Wind Mountain practice of separating the dead from the inhabited spaces of the living. Funerary objects occurred in all but four burials. Pottery was the most commonly encountered mortuary accompaniment. Besides ceramics, three burials contained shell jewelry, six had turquoise, and seven some form of mineral pigment. These disposal patterns, including the frequency of certain classes of mortuary inclusions, parallel trends observed at Wind Mountain.

Analogies in mortuary behavior were also evident at the SU site, where 54 burials were reported. At SU, 16 individuals were interred in simple, discrete extramural pits and the rest were placed in structures. Most human remains were buried in the fill of abandoned structures, though some were interred in subfloor pits that were then sealed over. These structures were presumably still in use (Wheat 1955:67). With the exception of one extended burial, all SU site inhumations consisted of flexed or partially flexed individuals placed in a seated or reclining position. As was the case for Wind Mountain, the SU funerary assemblage was dominated by pottery, smaller quantities of pigments, crystals, stone pipes, bone artifacts, and shell. A few SU site burials contained animal remains, including a dog skull and turkey bones. Mingling human and animal bone was also noted in certain Wind Mountain burials (refer to Appendix 7).

Burial practices at Mogollon Village and Harris Village duplicated these mortuary patterns, namely the most common method for disposing of the dead was interment of flexed individuals in simple pits. Pottery offerings were routinely provided, utilitarian objects were less frequent, and shell jewelry was relatively rare. Evoking Wind Mountain, both sites exhibited cremations, one at Mogollon Village and two at Harris Village.

Lastly, the 10 burials from Saige-McFarland compare well with the mortuary practices described above. Seven inhumations and three cremations were noted. Ceramics were the most commonly reported accompaniment, but some quartz crystals, shell jewelry, and turquoise were recovered. One Saige-McFarland inhumation (Burial 2, Feature 14) was remarkable for the 22 ceramic vessels it contained (Lekson 1990:44). Although the greatest number of vessels recovered from a single Wind Mountain burial was four, infant Burial 18 from Bear Ruin (Haury 1985:198) approached the sheer quantity of pottery observed in the Saige-McFarland inhumation with 17 jars and bowls. Rarely do the funerary offerings that accompany individual burials in Mogollon period settlements ever reach these amounts. By and large, individual Mogollon Pit House period burials contain either no funerary offerings or from one to half a dozen objects. Wind Mountain mortuary behavior reflects this pattern.

10

Animal Burials

The purposeful interment of animals in prehistoric settlements is known from many sites throughout the American Southwest and northern Mexico. At Wind Mountain, animal burials included dog, bear, turkey, golden eagle, hawk, mourning dove, and scarlet macaw (Table 10.1, Appendix 8). The underlying motivations compelling prehistoric peoples to inter certain animals remain enigmatic, but the archaeological context and associated artifacts of such burials, together with nineteenth and twentieth century ethnographic accounts and descriptive historical documents, provide some clues that the practice, at least in part, was related to ritual. It is equally likely, however, that certain animal burials denote pets given special treatment by their owners. The animal burials from the site were all recovered from the Wind Mountain locus; none were observed at the Ridout locus.

Dogs: *Canis* spp.

The majority of the Wind Mountain *Canis* burials (eight burials, 10 individuals) were identified as domestic dogs (Figure 10.1). A species level classification was not possible in several additional cases (four burials, six individuals). Two *Canis* burials contained two individuals, probably interred at the same time (Figure 10.2).

Domestic dog remains have great antiquity in Southwestern human habitation sites. They were reported from early Archaic deposits at Ventana Cave (Haury 1950:157–159) and from Basketmaker sites in the northern Southwest (Guernsey and Kidder 1921:44–45). The Wind Mountain burials, then, were a part of this long tradition of deliberate dog interment.

The precise role played by dogs during prehistoric times is somewhat more problematical. The hair of dogs is known to have been woven into cordage (Haury 1945b:35; Morris 1980:93). A more common use for dogs, perhaps, is their presumed assistance in hunting. If, as is highly likely, they were kept as pets, discovery of their remains in the burials of prehistoric settlements makes sense. At White Dog Cave, two dogs accompanying a human inhumation may indicate that these animals were killed and interred alongside their owner (Amsden 1949:62).

Moreover, the ritual sacrifice of dogs should not be discounted. McKusick (Wind Mountain files, Amerind Foundation) makes the following observations relating to Wind Mountain locus *Canis* Burials 7 and 8. She reported that one dog from Block 38–A exhibited a crushed right hind foot that healed with a fusion of the metatarsals and phalanges of the third and fourth digits. Its right fibula was fused to the tibia at the distal end. This young adult dog was killed by a shearing blow from the right side of the head across the frontals with an edged implement. The dog was buried with the head of another adult dog. McKusick saw similarities between this Wind Mountain *Canis* burial and another killed and skinned dog that had been interred with a turkey beneath the floor of Kiva M in Mound 7 at Gran Quivira, New Mexico (McKusick 1981:61). Both the Wind Mountain and Gran Quivira burials may represent the sacrifice and interment of dogs.

Dogs may have been consumed, but burial evidence in the form of intact remains argues against their primary use as a food source in the prehistoric Southwest. At Ventana Cave few dog remains were associated with trash, although they appeared throughout the cave deposits. In contrast, the bones of juvenile and adult coyotes were much broken and charred, suggesting that these animals were a food source (Haury 1950:155). Amsden (1949:65) also cited the lack of

TABLE 10.1. Animal Burials

Bird Burial No.	Provenience	Depth (cm)	Catalogue No.	Identification	No. of Individuals	Age
1	House D fill	60	WM/B 21	*Meleagris gallopavo*	1	A
2	Block 12-B	65	WM/B 112	*Meleagris gallopavo*	1	A
3	Block 20-A	40	WM/B 155	*Ara macao*	1	11–12 mo.
4	Block 20-B	45	WM/B 243	*Aquila chrysaetos*	1	A
5	Block 42-D	20–25	WM/B 471	*Meleagris gallopavo*	2	A
6	Block 39-A	15	WM/B 472	*Meleagris gallopavo*	1	A
7	House HH floor fill	60	WM/B 487	*Meleagris gallopavo*	1	J
8	House NN floor fill	45	WM/B 532	*Buteo* sp.	2	J
9	Block 63-C	25	WM/B 605	*Aquila chrysaetos*	1	A
10*	House F fill	0–80	WM/B 65	*Buteo* sp.	1	A
11*	House V fill	115–210	WM/B 280	*Zenaida macroura*	1	A
Canis Burial No.						
1	Block 13-A	90	WM/B 113	*Canis familiaris*	1	YA,M
2*	Block 12-C	48	WM/B 186	*Canis familiaris*	1	YA
3	House X fill	22	WM/B 416	*Canis familiaris*	1	A,M
4	House X fill	35	WM/B 417	*Canis familiaris*	1	A
5	Block 44-A; Room 1	50	WM/B 444	*Canis familiaris*	1	YA
6*	Block 38-B	30–100	WM/B 531	*Canis familiaris*	2	A
7–8	Block 38-A	20–25	WM/B 552	*Canis* sp. indet.	2	A
9	Block 47-C	50	WM/B 583	*Canis familiaris*	2	A
10	Block 46-D	40	WM/B 584	*Canis* sp. indet.	2	A,1M
11	House AC fill	19	WM/B 700	*Canis familiaris*	1	OA
13**	House PP fill	0–130	WM/B 574	*Canis* sp. indet.	1	J
14*	House X fill	30–120	WM/B 392	*Canis* sp. indet.	1	J
Animal Burial No.						
1	House AC fill	56	WM/B 728	*Ursus* sp. indet.	1	J

* Burial placement not precisely recorded.
**A break in the sequence; there is no *Canis* burial 12.
A = Adult, J = Juvenile, OA = Old adult, YA = Young adult, M = Male.

domestic dog bones in Basketmaker middens, albeit complete burials were often encountered in other site contexts. He thereby concluded that dogs in the prehistoric Southwest were not eaten frequently. A similar trend was observed at Wind Mountain, where domestic dogs occurred in intentional burials, not as disarticulated or charred and broken components of the settlement's trash.

Bear: *Ursus* sp.

One juvenile bear burial (*Ursus* sp.) was uncovered from the fill of House AC, 15 cm beneath the ground surface. Ethnographic accounts have recognized the bear as one of the most powerful symbols in Pueblo culture (Cushing 1883; Stephen 1969:307, 779, 860). Given the known importance of the bear to historic Southwestern peoples, one might speculate that the Wind Mountain cub reflects some analogous ceremonial significance. That prehistoric rituals actually incorporated bear symbolism is not entirely conjectural, because bear remains (e.g., claws, claw necklaces, skulls) have been observed in Southwest sites of varying age (Rodeck 1954:117). Notably at Casas Grandes, black and grizzly bear long bones were recovered as part of a trove attributed to religious functions postulated for the House of the Skulls (Di Peso et al. 1974:8:59, 251). Bear symbolism was also believed to relate to death practices at the site (Di Peso 1974:579).

The remaining animal burials exposed at the Wind Mountain settlement consist of several species of birds. Feathers, talons, and whole birds have been recovered from numerous dry caves and other protected contexts in prehistoric Southwestern sites (Haury 1945b, Plates 24 and 25; Martin 1959:100–101; Gifford 1980:207). Birds were un-

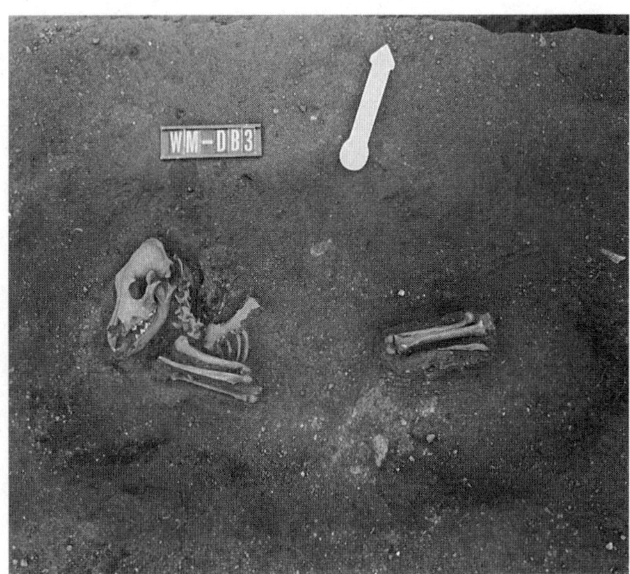

FIGURE 10.1. Domestic dog burial *(Canis familiaris, Canis* Burial 3) uncovered in the fill of House X at the Wind Mountain locus (Neg. No. WM 55–20F).

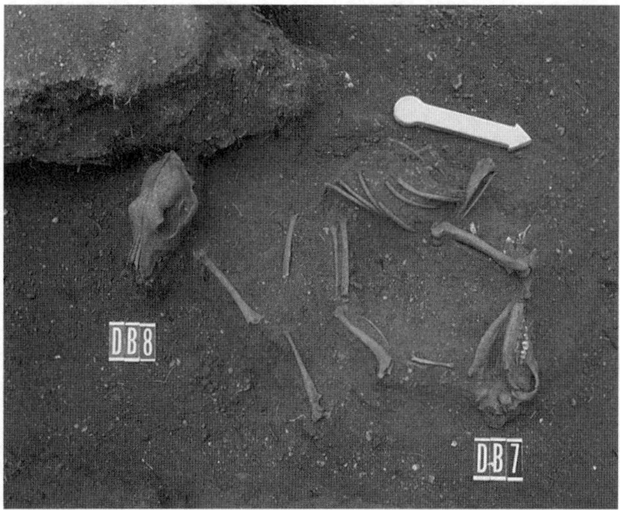

FIGURE 10.2. Double *Canis* burial (species indeterminate, *Canis* Burials 7 and 8) from Excavation Block 38–A at the Wind Mountain locus. Both animals were probably interred at the same time (Neg. No. WM 70–13F).

doubtedly eaten, but they were probably also taken for their feathers for both ritual as well as utilitarian purposes such as arrow fletching (Gifford 1980:94). Certain birds may have been kept as pets. Some or all of these uses most likely characterized the bird remains of Wind Mountain.

Turkeys: *Meleagris gallopavo*

Incidental turkey elements and actual burials appear as early as 500 to 300 B.C. at both Tularosa and Jemez caves (Schorger 1961:138–144, 1970:168–179; Heller 1976; Lang and Harris 1984). At Tularosa Cave, Hough (1914:5–6) described desiccated adult remains, poults, feathers, egg shell, and dung as indicative of turkey keeping, that is, these birds were domesticated, not wild (cited in Breitburg 1988:72). Recent evaluation of prehistoric remains from sites in the American Southwest and Mexico indicates that turkeys were domesticated in the former region and dispersed southward into the latter (Breitburg 1988, 1993). At Wind Mountain formalized interment of whole turkeys (five burials, six individuals), as well as the occurrence of random bones with butchering marks, intimates that birds not only had ritual function but were also butchered and possibly consumed by the settlement's residents.

Ritual use of turkeys during late prehistoric times, perhaps as sacrifices, is well established by the numerous burials, many of them headless, excavated at Medio period Casas Grandes (Di Peso 1974:469). Turkeys were raised for their feathers evidenced by both Basketmaker and Anasazi caves that contained the remains of turkey feather blankets (e.g., Haury 1945b). Ethnographic sources further document the importance of turkey feathers in ceremony. At Zuni, only golden eagle feathers were imbued with more power than turkey feathers for decorating prayer sticks and masks (Ladd 1963:92–92). Turkeys were often associated with the dead (Roediger 1941:71). The relatively common appearance of turkey burials at Wind Mountain supports the presumed longevity of the ritual and utilitarian roles played by turkeys in the cultures of prehistoric Southwestern peoples (Figure 10.3).

Golden Eagles: *Aquila chrysaetos*

Among historic Pueblo peoples, golden eagles were infused with extremely powerful symbolism (Stephen 1969:307; Ladd 1963:91–92). Their feathers were widely employed to embellish prayer sticks and ceremonial masks at Zuni, Hopi, and the Rio Grande Pueblos (Stephen 1969:392; Ladd 1963:87–88). At Zuni, eagles were also taken as nestlings and raised for years under semidomestic conditions (Ladd 1963:16, 87; Roediger 1941:75). When eagles died, they were never just thrown on the midden, but were carefully interred with corn pollen under a room floor or outside the village (Ladd 1963:16). At Hopi they were captured, sacrificed, and formally buried on an annual basis (Stephen 1969:568–569).

Of two golden eagle burials uncovered at Wind Mountain, one, Bird Burial 9, is of special interest because it con-

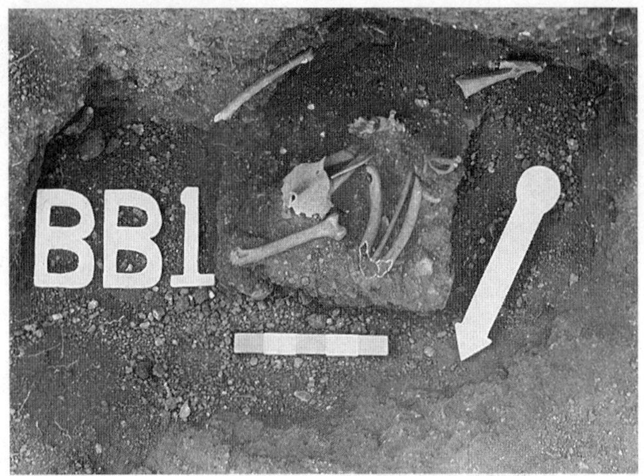

FIGURE 10.3. An adult turkey burial (*Meleagris gallopavo,* Bird Burial 1) recovered from the fill of House D at the Wind Mountain locus (Neg. No. WM 9–2F).

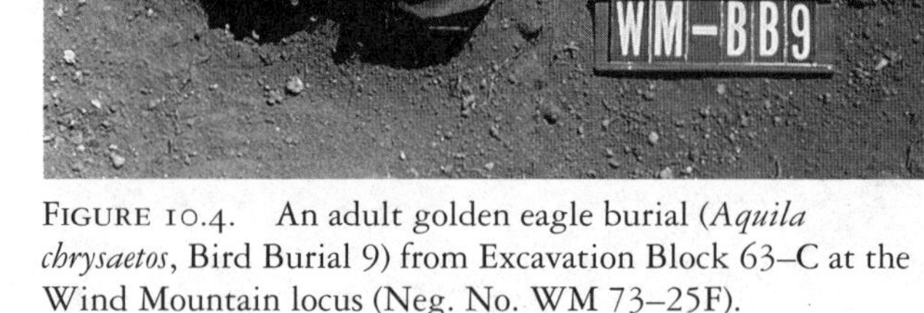

FIGURE 10.4. An adult golden eagle burial (*Aquila chrysaetos*, Bird Burial 9) from Excavation Block 63–C at the Wind Mountain locus (Neg. No. WM 73–25F).

tained all the bones of an adult bird except for the skull. Such treatment is reminiscent of the headless turkey burials described at Casas Grandes (Di Peso 1974:567, 602–603). The Wind Mountain eagles possibly reflect ceremonial use of birds, although the precise nature of such ritual remains unknown (Figure 10.4).

Hawks: *Buteo* spp.

Hawks are another bird used extensively for decorating ceremonial paraphernalia, including prayer sticks and masks (Ladd 1963:17, 85–87; Stephen 1969:76, 109, 248, 409). At Hopi, Hawk feathers were tied to horned water serpent images (Stephen 1969:316). In prehistoric contexts, Judd (1954) recovered hawk remains at Pueblo Bonito. The formalized burial of two hawks at Wind Mountain strongly supports their use in the ritual life of the community, not as sources of food.

Mourning Dove: *Zenaida macroura*

The mourning dove collected at Wind Mountain was identified as a discrete burial, but this cluster of disarticulated bones may simply represent the remains of a meal. Of all the Wind Mountain animal burials cited, only the dove appears to be a problematical interment. The use of dove feathers in Hopi ritual is known, but uncommon. For example, dove feathers decorated the Lalakon standard (Stephen 1969:833).

Scarlet Macaw: *Ara macao*

Wind Mountain produced a single intact macaw burial (Figure 10.5). Buried in the northern portion of the settlement ridge, the head of the macaw was covered with a two hand mano that exhibited traces of ground mineral pigment. The presence of scarlet macaw in the Wind Mountain deposits is significant because its prehistoric habitat is hundreds of kilometers to the south in the tropical lowlands of Mexico. Macaws appeared in Southwestern sites, perhaps, as early as A.D. 200 in the Hohokam (Haury 1976:346). Prehistoric trade with the south for live birds and feathers has been proposed for all three major Southwestern traditions—the Hohokam, Mogollon, and Anasazi. Hargrave (1970:1) cited Bandelier (1890:61), who had earlier reported that "parrot" (i.e., macaw) feathers were traded for green stones. The eighteenth century Pimas raised macaws for feathers (Wyllys 1931:129; cited in Hargrave 1970:1). Prehistorically, Casas Grandes was suggested to have imported birds from Oaxaca, then later breeding its own scarlet macaw population for redistribution into the northern Gran Chichimeca (Di Peso 1974:632). There is little doubt that, at least at certain times, Casas Grandes raised quantities of these brightly feathered birds (Di Peso 1974:599–601; Di Peso et al. 1974:8:181–182; Minnis et al. 1993). However, it must be remembered that there is absolutely no direct relationship between the scarlet macaw from Wind Mountain and Casas Grandes. The Wind Mountain settlement ridge was abandoned long before the emergence of the Medio period (see Chapter 11).

Macaw remains have appeared as formalized burials or as random occurrences of bone in Southwest sites. Only miscellaneous bone was recovered at Snaketown (Haury 1976:376). In contrast, at Pueblo Bonito, true macaw burials were uncovered (Pepper 1920:193–194). Comparable to the treatment of human remains, Hargrave (1933:26) reported that macaws were wrapped in rush matting prior to interment. An elaborate macaw burial was described at Galaz Ruin from Kiva 73 or the "Kiva of the Parrot." There, during the 1929–1931 field seasons, Jenks described a parrot burial (i.e., a macaw—possibly a military macaw) in which the specimen was found with 82 turquoise beads near its skull and more than 500 shell beads scattered around its legs (Jenks 1929–1931: unpublished notes). Other macaw burials have been reported at sites, including Cameron Creek c. A.D. 950–1000, Chaco Canyon c. A.D. 900, and, later, Winona Village c. A.D. 1150, Kiet Siel after c. A.D. 1250, and Freeman Ranch near Cliff c. A.D. 1300 (for an inventory of sites with macaws, see Hargrave 1970:28–54).

Historically, scarlet and military macaw feathers were described as important for decorating masks but not prayer sticks (Ladd 1963:16). Among the Tewa, runners were sent to southern locales to obtain the bright, iridescent feathers as well as live birds, especially scarlet macaws, in exchange for turquoise and skins (Roediger 1941:71). Macaw symbolism was said to be associated with rain ceremonies (Roediger 1941:71) and the Quetzalcoatl cult (Di Peso 1974:273). Wind Mountain inhabitants may also have procured the bird for its feathers and/or sacrifice.

Similar to shell material recovered from the settlement, the Wind Mountain macaw demonstrates that residents were involved in the procurement or exchange of a limited number of products over long distances. There is no doubt that tropical birds were exotics transported far beyond their points of origin.

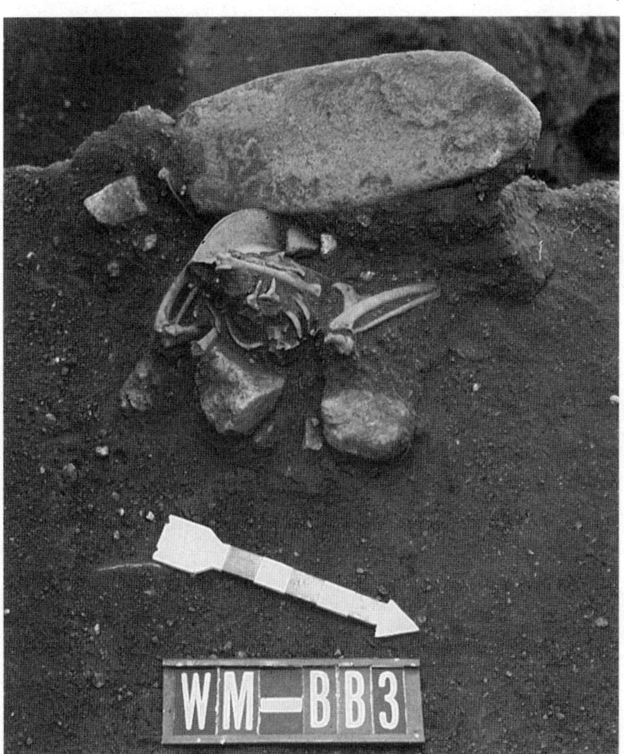

FIGURE 10.5. A scarlet macaw burial (*Ara macao,* Bird Burial 3) discovered in the northern portion of the Wind Mountain settlement ridge, Excavation Block 20–A. Its skull was covered with a two hand mano that showed traces of ground mineral pigment (Neg. No. WM 32–29F).

11

Closing Thoughts and Perspectives on Wind Mountain Prehistory

Wind Mountain was a Mimbres Mogollon site of prodigious time depth, occupying a narrow ridge top that supported multiple, succeeding settlements. Occupations spanned several centuries, possibly from A.D. 250 to 1150/1200, although first use of the ridge may have been even earlier (390 B.C.-A.D. 4). Throughout most of its history, the Wind Mountain site was a pit house village consisting of small clusters of domestic and community structures reflecting both the Early and Late Pit House periods. During the ensuing Pueblo period (A.D. 950/1000–1150/1200), substantial cultural change was apparent, if represented by only a few Mangas and Mimbres phase rooms.

Similar to many other early Mogollon site locations (Martin and Plog 1973:182), the hill top pit house dwellers who initially established Wind Mountain selected an upland locality that elevated them above the floodplain, afforded good visibility of their surroundings, a southeastern exposure, and adequate drainage appropriate to pit house construction. The site ridge was bordered by two intermittently flowing drainages that probably provided surface water for much of the year. In addition, its intermediate position between the adjacent higher mountains and floodplain floor ensured Wind Mountain favorable access to a broad base of resources. Forested uplands, riparian creek margins, and the nearby Mangas Valley furnished the residents of Wind Mountain with diverse foraging habitats. Dry farming could easily be conducted near the lower elevation drainages and on hillsides. The contribution of wild and domestic resources to the settlement's economy was demonstrated by the macrobotanical and faunal remains recovered from the site. Quantities of deer, rabbit, and rodent bone, charred and desiccated piñon nuts, corn kernels, beans, and squash rinds, provide direct evidence for a mixed subsistence base. Indirectly, an extensive, nonspecialized, multifunctional stone tool assemblage substantiates a broad spectrum exploitation pattern.

Wind Mountain was not merely advantageously positioned in terms of subsistence resources, but its inhabitants could avail themselves of numerous useful varieties of raw stone within a 4 km (2.5 mile) radius of the settlement. That Wind Mountain people did procure andesite, basalt, dacite, granite, quartzite, welded tuff, and much other stone material from the Big and Little Burro Mountains is evident by the presence of these materials as finished tools and debitage. Small task groups from the community, either formally or loosely organized, could easily travel to known source localities to collect stone. Certain stones, including chert and chalcedony, were available even closer at hand in the stream channels immediately below the ridge.

This rich physical setting with its proximity to diverse habitats and resources probably contributed to the longevity of the Wind Mountain site. The elevated ridge top also promoted community security by providing a measure of protection from potential intruders. These attributes may have been propitious to the various occupations throughout the Early and Late Pit House periods, even if the settlement did not progress significantly into the Pueblo period. The circumscribed ridge top location and lack of sufficient proximate arable land may have been an impediment to population growth, the capacity to increase food production, and the ability to expand the settlement. Consequently, Wind Mountain habitations, conspicuous in their great stability, even displaying a kind of a cultural redundancy until c. A.D. 950/1000, had apparently reached a maximum threshold during the Mimbres phase beyond which the site could not easily develop. The combination of physical and social circumstances that led to surface pueblos and population aggregation characteristic of Animas and Salado sites never transpired at Wind Mountain.

External Relationships

The residents of Wind Mountain did not live in isolation from other regions and peoples. Limited, but tangible evidence for contact with areas outside the Mangas drainage takes the form of intrusive ceramics. Late Basketmaker III and Pueblo I White Mound Black-on-white and Kiatuthlanna Black-on-white, as well as Pioneer period Snaketown Red-on-buff link the Wind Mountain Pit House period inhabitants with Northern Pueblo peoples (syn. Anasazi) to the north and the Hohokam of the Middle Gila. Based on the low frequency of intrusive sherds recovered, the nature and intensity of the relationship between these groups cannot be gauged precisely. Haury (1936b:27; 1985:405) has proposed Mogollon influence on the emerging ceramic tradition to the north (i.e., the Anasazi), especially in terms of design arrangement during the San Francisco phase.

Another group of slightly later occurring intrusive ceramic types, including Deadmans Black-on-red, Mancos Black-on-white, and Reserve Incised Corrugated, were discovered at the site. These wares, with approximate beginning dates between c. A.D. 800 to 900, represent contact with the Little Colorado/Chaco Canyon and Mesa Verde regions as well as the nearby San Francisco/Reserve. These imported wares, together with the earlier Anasazi and Hohokam types, correspond to the most extensive occupation at Wind Mountain.

A final component of trade ceramics consists of pottery types manufactured after c. A.D. 1100. The neighboring San Francisco/Reserve regions produced Tularosa Fillet Rim and Tularosa Patterned Corrugated. Widely distributed St. Johns Black-on-red and St. Johns Polychrome originated in the Little Colorado and Cibola areas. The southern Southwest is represented by El Paso Polychrome, Three Rivers Red-on-terracotta, and Chupadero Black-on-white.

The intrusive pottery assemblage, albeit recovered in small quantities, links Wind Mountain to other regions of the Southwest, particularly to the north before c. A.D. 1000. After that time, external contacts continue though ceramic exchange does not point to Chaco or Mesa Verde but to the more immediate Cibola and Little Colorado areas. The presence of El Paso Polychrome from the southern Southwest, including extreme southeastern Arizona and southern New Mexico, is not surprising given the extensive distribution of the type after c. A.D. 1150.

The limited number of these intrusives provides frustratingly little detailed information about the specific relationship between the Wind Mountain site and other regions. Although pottery obviously did not constitute a major trade commodity, exchange (i.e., interaction) is indicated even if by only a few exotic vessels. It is conceivable, for instance, that ceramics were introduced to Wind Mountain incidentally with other goods such as shell.

Economic Enterprise

Di Peso's belief that economic enterprise was the motivating factor effecting culture change at Wind Mountain specifically, and the Gran Chichimeca generally, is a theme repeated throughout this volume. He saw the culture patterns of indigenous Mogollon residents altered as pochteca merchants sought exploitable resources in the mineral rich Upper Gila. Intermittent but persistent exploratory incursions into the Upper Gila were suggested to begin c. A.D. 200, culminating in the dominance of Casas Grandes based entrepreneurs by at least c. A.D. 950. The intruders, or donors, characterized by their Mesoamerican roots, actively imposed sociopolitical, economic, and religious ideologies on the native, or passive recipient, Wind Mountain people. The logical consequence of these events was the reorganization of the Wind Mountain settlement into a gleaning or procurement satellite devoted to the exploitation of turquoise and other minerals and its integration into a larger southern based mercantile system.

To demonstrate the applicability of the donor-recipient culture conquest model to the Wind Mountain site, Di Peso looked to the material inventory. He predicted that Mogollon material culture would be transformed as southern merchants implanted new technologies, forms, and symbols. He expected the settlement to contain large quantities of exploitable raw and processed resources that represented community wealth and were the basis for its founding. The dominance of merchant entrepreneurs at Wind Mountain was suggested to translate into economic and social ranking in the community, discernable by the disproportionate quantities and unequal distribution of certain material classes at the site. The question must now be asked if the material assemblage supports these expectations.

There is no obvious proliferation of southern material imports or ideas. When examining the Wind Mountain ceramic assemblage, for example, most vessels were locally made, and the few intrusives are identifiable with nonsouthern, indeed mostly northern, sources. The scarlet macaw is the only object to have unequivocal southern origins in the entire material inventory. How *far* south or its actual point of origin remains unknown.

Di Peso placed special significance on the category of socioreligious objects and personal ornamentation as indicative of the reorganization of the indigenous Wind Mountain settlement by southern traders. Socioreligious artifacts were associated with the emergence of Mesoamerican cults, whereas personal ornamentation reflected the affluence of a newly arriving merchant class. But these artifact categories do not occur in notably large amounts, nor do they display definitively southern characteristics.

For instance, clay and stone figurines, effigies, and pipes, though not uncommon at Wind Mountain, are also reported from numerous other Mogollon sites. The Wind Mountain zoomorphic figurines often portrayed creatures native to the local environment and, consequently, familiar to site inhabitants. These, together with cloud blower pipes and tubes, may have ritual significance. Figurines, effigies, pipes, and tubes have pandemic spatial and temporal distribution across the New World, however, and their associated symbolism and function may be much more regionally varied than is expressed by the number of observable forms.

Objects of personal adornment occurred as shell, stone, and sometimes pottery beads, pendants, bracelets, and rings. Ornaments were randomly distributed in burials, on house floors, and in the bulk fill of the site. No great elaboration is apparent in either the quantity or quality of the Wind Mountain jewelry collection. Specific contexts such as burials, structures, or pits failed to contain large caches of ornaments that would suggest differential socioeconomic status (in other words, formalized ranking) among members of a Wind Mountain community. Similar to figurines and pipes, personal ornamentation and so-defined socioreligious artifacts have an extensive ancestry in the Southwest, certain forms originating during the Archaic. Both material categories are viewed as typical contributors expected in the developing Mimbres Mogollon material inventory.

Raw, unmodified stone and mineral fragments, blocks, and nodules were also recovered randomly from the settlement. The point has previously been made that Wind Mountain residents made use of the diverse lithic materials available in nearby mountains as demonstrated by the variety of stone represented as finished tools. No evidence indicates, however, that turquoise or any other mineral was considered of extraordinarily high value. Moreover, there is no confirmation of lithic stockpiling, storehouses, or specialized lapidary work areas that would corroborate that local stone or minerals were exploited for external (i.e., southern) redistribution. Employing the Wind Mountain material data to demonstrate a link between the north and south fails to argue persuasively in favor of such an economic connection.

Addressing the issue of southern (generic Mesoamerica) political domination through economic exploitation over the north (here, the Wind Mountain Mogollon) has always included the role played by Casas Grandes. The possible relationship between the two sites must be explored, not only using the Wind Mountain data specifically, but from the broader perspective of Casas Grandes and northern Mexico. As indicated in the Introduction to this volume, Di Peso felt that there was a causal relationship between the Perros Bravos phase of the Viejo period and the Pueblo period (Mimbres phase) of the Wind Mountain site. A review of data from the Casas Grandes publication (Di Peso 1974:179, Di Peso et al. 1974:8:127, 132) that might lend support to this assumption is not, however, forthcoming. The Perros Bravos phase, defined by a single radiocarbon date (date range A.D. 870–1250) offers little assistance in setting the temporal boundaries for the phase or for establishing a link with Wind Mountain. Di Peso felt that the Viejo period was "the time of first Puchteca contacts" (Di Peso 1974:105), though scant quantifiable data support this conclusion. Indeed, the intrusive ceramics associated with the Viejo period numbered upward of 338 sherds; however, only 19 sherds could be directly associated with a Perros Bravos phase assemblage (Di Peso et al. 1974:8:131–132). Of ceramic types stemming from northern cultural affiliations, four sherds were identified as Boldface Black-on-white, 11 sherds as Mimbres Classic Black-on-white, two as Dragoon Red-on-brown, and one sherd as Reserve Black-on-white. Only a single fragment was attributed to a southern source, an Aquaruto Exterior Incised sherd, assumed to originate from the area of Culiacan, Sinaloa. It should be noted that of the excavations undertaken by Di Peso in Chihuahua, the only occupations of possible affiliate nature with Wind Mountain probably occurred during the Convento phase of the Viejo period. However, a preponderance of pit houses and red or brown plainware ceramics that aid in describing the phase simply suggest a generalized Mogollon cultural expression. Such broad characteristics apply across much of the American Southwest and northern Mexico without indicating direct contacts or relationships among various regions.

The Casas Grandes donor-Wind Mountain recipient relationship in which the latter was a gleaning satellite linked to the former center for purposes of resource exploitation was the crux of Di Peso's original hypothesis (and the primary rationale for excavating Wind Mountain). Recent chronometric analysis of the dendrochronological sequence from Casas Grandes (Dean and Ravesloot 1993) enables detailed evaluation of a possible Casas Grandes-Wind Mountain relationship. Results of this tree-ring study revise the Medio period (currently separated into questionable Buena Fe, Paquime, and Diablo phases) upward in time. The Medio period, especially the Paquime phase, identified with the presumed political and economic dominance of the site, is firmly placed in the fourteenth century. The beginning of the Medio period (the Buena Fe phase) dates no earlier than A.D. 1200 but is probably more securely placed after A.D. 1250. The ramifications of the chronological reanalysis are significant, and any interpretation of a direct mercantile association between Casas Grandes and Wind Mountain is now untenable. The final occupation of Wind Mountain at c. A.D. 1150 (abandonment is suggested to occur no later than A.D. 1200) predates the earliest possible onset of the Medio period (Buena Fe phase). It certainly predates the florescence of the Medio period (Paquime phase) with earliest dates c. A.D. 1280s, which is predominantly a phenomenon of the A.D. 1300s. By reasoning, the Wind Mountain site could not, therefore, have participated in a southern based economic enterprise the proposed center of which had not yet developed (see also Woosley and Olinger 1993).

Although the data were not forthcoming to support the existence of a formal mercantile system, there is every indication that Wind Mountain was involved in an exchange network that distributed Gulf of California shell. This exchange was not operated by the mechanisms of a sophisticated pochteca style southern merchant class but as nonaligned informal transient procurement, either directly or indirectly, through the Hohokam.

Hohokam and Wind Mountain Contacts

Several clues point to contact between the Wind Mountain Mogollon and the Hohokam. First, there is the presence of Gulf of California shell. Perhaps, because shell constituted an exotic long distance trade commodity, it was more highly valued for personal adornment than any other material used by the residents of Wind Mountain. Unlike turquoise, which was apparently considered just one of many locally available resources, exotic shell occurred much more frequently as personal ornamentation. The entire turquoise collection from Wind Mountain consisted of less than 400 pieces (total weight: 268 gm, or 9.45 oz), whereas the single category of shell disk beads numbered in excess of 10,000 objects. Because there is no evidence of shell working at the site, shell ornaments (primarily bracelets and beads) were in all likelihood transported to Wind Mountain in the form of finished goods.

The long established Hohokam shell industry is the feasible source of Wind Mountain shell. Rather than engaging in direct shell procurement of their own, Wind Mountain inhabitants probably depended on trade with the Hohokam, who were located between the Gulf Coast and their settlement on Mangas Creek in the Upper Gila. The Hohokam themselves may have relied on groups living along the Sonoran coast between Boquillas and Guaymas to actually obtain shell, which they (i.e., the Hohokam) then redistributed eastward along the Gila River to Wind Mountain. Parenthetically, shell beads distributed east into the Mimbres Valley has been reported as manufactured by the Hohokam and presumably traded by them (Emil W. Haury, personal communication 1990). Other supplementary data in the form of material culture and burial practices also intimate that the Hohokam were the conduit of shell to Wind Mountain.

For example, the Wind Mountain and Hohokam connection is supported by the obvious familiarity of the former with the latter. Only a few Gila Basin Snaketown Red-on-buff sherds were recovered, but Wind Mountain potters were accustomed to Hohokam ceramics, imitating certain of their designs. Additionally, Hohokam palettes, including one example made of Pinal schist and another adorned with a carved lizard border, may represent direct imports, whereas others are probably local reproductions. Wind Mountain residents constructed at least one house (House AK) in the style of the Hohokam Pioneer period. The Hohokam practice of disposing of the dead by cremation may have influenced two cremation burials at Wind Mountain. The shell assemblage, together with these ancillary data supporting Hohokam contact, provide the most extensive body of information associating the residents of Wind Mountain with another identifiable prehistoric group or region.

Though Mogollon and Hohokam trade emphasized shell products, other commodities may have been introduced. Perhaps, the scarlet macaw entered the Wind Mountain settlement as an incidental by-product of the shell trade.

The Evolution of Mimbres Mogollon Culture

The Pit House Period

The Wind Mountain site traces the evolution of Mimbres Mogollon culture, if not from its origins, at least from c. A.D. 250 to Mimbres times. Throughout its long history Wind Mountain was an intermittently occupied habitation settlement. The material inventory reflects the multiplicity of tasks related to procuring, preparing, and storing food, providing shelter, obtaining raw materials for manufacturing tools and containers and, less explicitly, the ceremonial dimension of the lives of its residents. The whole of the occupational sequence was characterized by great stability and relatively little cultural change to c. A.D. 950/1000. For the most part, material assemblages including chipped and ground stone remained technologically and morphologically consistent. Diversity is apparent in the variety of raw materials used to create tools rather than in manufacturing techniques or forms. Continuity is apparent in subsistence practices that were characterized by hunting and foraging combined with farming in the same proportions throughout all habitations, including the Mimbres phase.

Some variations in the Mimbres Mogollon material culture are discernable in the ceramic tradition with the addition of two painted types to the earlier brown and red, plain or textured wares. The Wind Mountain ceramic assemblage demonstrates a strong developmental relationship in terms of design elements, their arrangement, and technological execution and morphology from Mogollon Red-on-brown to Three Circle Red-on-white and early Boldface Black-on-white (Style I). Even with the appearance of new painted types, however, for several hundred years, until c. A.D. 950, Mogollon ceramics are basically comprised of two principal types—the Alma series and San Francisco Red—to which two painted wares, Mogollon Red-on-brown and Three Circle Red-on-white, are added in only small amounts.

Gradual change is also evident in the Mogollon architectural progression as pit structures shift from round to rectangular floor plans and community houses are built as companion additions to domestic residences. That these alterations were never dramatic and that stability was maintained, is substantiated by the perpetuation of older structure types even as new types developed and became integrated into the architectural complex. Moreover, as house styles altered, the settlement composition of loosely organized clusters of domestic and community houses stayed the same.

The Pueblo Period

Transformation of the Mimbres Mogollon culture pattern that persisted in essentially the same configuration—characterized by dispersed pit structures centered around community structures, broad spectrum exploitation, and a stable material inventory—began to give way after c. A.D. 950. At Wind Mountain, contiguous surface room blocks appear, but pit structures continue to be built. Black-on-white wares become the favored painted pottery as compared with the earlier Wind Mountain ceramic assemblage, and low frequencies of Mogollon Red-on-brown and Three Circle Red-on-white may persist. Corrugated decorations supplant other textured surface treatments. Boldface Black-on-white (Styles I and II) is the preferred new type, but Mimbres Classic Black-on-white (Style III) begins to be observed in small quantities.

These taxonomic attributes constituted the basis for proposing a transitional stage, called the Mangas phase, between the Late Pit House period and the Mimbres phase of the Pueblo period. Wind Mountain during its post-A.D. 950 occupation appears as a small, architecturally mixed settlement whose residents fancied Boldface Black-on-white above other painted wares. We suggest that these changes in material culture including architectural forms and internal settlement organization reflect interaction with Northern Pueblo groups. Some investigators reject Anasazi influences on the Mogollon and propose that pueblo development was part of a natural, and evidently internal, Mogollon continuum (LeBlanc 1986:302–303). It seems more likely, however, that over time and through a process of adoption and adaptation, not characterized by cultural "swamping" but perhaps simply slow accretion, long-lived culture patterns were ultimately transformed by both internal and external means (see Haury 1986:451–456).

Similarly, though the existence of a discrete Mangas phase is disputed for the Mimbres Valley (Anyon and LeBlanc 1984; LeBlanc 1986:303), small pueblos displaying the above described attributes do occur in the Upper Gila. Wind Mountain, together with Saige-McFarland (Lekson 1990:91), Lee Village, Black's Bluff, and Villareal II (Fitting et al. 1982b:62) appear to establish the viability of a Mangas phase for this region of Mogollon adaptations. The limited Wind Mountain pueblo or surface village existed until c. A.D. 1150, possibly persisting a little later based on the presence of small quantities of El Paso Polychrome, Chupadero Black-on-white, and St. Johns Polychrome sherds, although never growing into a large Mimbres site. It is worth noting, as Lekson points out (1992:16–17), that the average Mimbres phase site was 10 rooms or less, in 66 to 75 percent of sites known; Wind Mountain easily correlates with this "average" Mimbres phase site. The truly dramatic changes associated with large Mimbres pueblos including, for example, internally formalized arrangements of room blocks in conjunction with plaza/courtyards and ceremonial structures, agricultural intensification, and material culture diversification did not develop and eventually the ridge top was abandoned.

Broad-based Mogollon Interaction

Di Peso's provocative ideas concerning active donor and passive recipient exchange based on economic expansion by pochteca merchants are not supported by evidence recovered from Wind Mountain. It is equally apparent that the isolated development of Mogollon patterns out of the earlier Archaic does not fully account for the origin and nature of Mogollon cultural expressions. Instead, the excavations at Wind Mountain reveal a data base that not only reflects internal development but also contributes clues indicative of interaction with other regions. Tangible evidence in the form of intrusive ceramics, changes in architectural forms, and possibly settlement configuration links Wind Mountain with Northern Pueblo peoples. Interaction with the Hohokam to the west is indicated by Gulf of California shell and material culture, including ceramics, architecture, and stone palettes. Despite not functioning as a significant component of a southern mercantile system, Wind Mountain may be linked to the south in terms of a geographically widespread ceramic tradition that ultimately had roots in Mexico.

The marked similarities in the technology and designs shown by numerous localized ceramic traditions from the central mountains of Arizona and New Mexico, and extending southward into Durango and Zacatecas are inescapable. The general consensus of the antiquity of pottery manufacture in Mexico intimates that this knowledge was transmitted northward, where it was accepted by Southwestern peoples, including the Mogollon. Unfortunately, the southern sources that contributed to the establishment of Mogollon ceramic making have never been identified. Nevertheless, in the case of Wind Mountain, its redwares display affinity with many as yet undescribed ceramic types of western Mexico, with Convento Red from Chihuahua, as well as the Dragoon complex of southern Arizona among others. In addition, Mogollon Red-on-brown from Wind Mountain is reminiscent of Anchondo Red-on-brown and Fernando Red-on-brown from Chihuahua and the earlier pottery from the

Morett site of Colima. Although these pottery traditions cannot be linked to actual contact, the resemblances among them denote comparable intent or preference on the part of ceramists who were producing red-on-brown wares.

Other aspects of Mogollon cultural developments, too, suggest southern influences. In architecture, the gabled roof form is proposed to be transmitted from a southern source into the Mogollon region via the Hohokam. The primary cultigens (corn and beans) together with the agricultural technology to sustain them were disseminated from the south. The list of probable imports and transmitted ideas from south to north is lengthy. The lines of communication have usually been described as "yet to be identified," though Braniff (1993) has recently reevaluated and proposed specific routes and sources between central and northern Mexico and the Southwestern United States.

Before leaving the topic of the Gran Chichimeca, reflection on the suitability of the term, from a geographical as well as a philosophical perspective, is in order. The geographic area encompassed is too broad to be functional. There is little cultural homogeneity characterizing the inhabitants of a region bounded by the Pacific Ocean on the west, the Tropic of Cancer to the south, the 38th parallel to the north, and the 97th western longitude to the east. Moreover, there is no demonstrable evidence for homologous economic, political, or social relationships among them. There are no logical grounds, consequently, for equating a discrete geographic expanse with the name. Perhaps of even greater importance is the negative connotation that Chichimec carries for the native peoples of North America (Nahuatl for "Sons of the Dog"; Wolf 1959:9), a pejorative label that generally defined peoples of the north as barbarous. Gran Chichimeca has taken on an almost "poetic" association and is finding its way more frequently into archaeological literature (e.g., Riley and Hedrick 1978; Mathian and McGuire 1986; Woosley and Ravesloot 1993). The term has an explicitly derisive and derogatory meaning and, for that reason alone, should be reassessed when referring to prehistoric Native Americans.

Wind Mountain, then, is viewed as an intermittently occupied settlement developing not in a vacuum but in a larger region of cultural sharing and adaptation. Cultural transformations are not explained in terms of models of economic determinism throughout a Gran Chichimeca or as locally isolated developments atop a ridge in the Mangas Valley of the Upper Gila. Rather, Wind Mountain, as a Mimbres Mogollon settlement, is seen to exist in a complex interaction sphere in which the transfer of information and goods was sporadic, of varying intensity, relatively unstructured, and probably multidirectional. The Mogollon people, including the residents of Wind Mountain, were clearly influenced by numerous other regions and cultures, although the precise timing, intensity, and mechanism of the contacts, whether direct or indirect, remain unknown.

The Wind Mountain data base facilitates an interpretation of Mogollon trends generally, as well as cultural developments specific to the Upper Gila. These interpretations are possible because of the extensive time depth, c. A.D. 250–1150/1200, during which the site was actively used, a longevity or intensity as yet unequalled by any other excavated Mimbres Mogollon site.

The people of Wind Mountain forged a series of slowly evolving communities adapted to the local mountainous setting but open to the influences of neighboring regions. Through their settlement, they elucidate the history of Mimbres Mogollon culture in the Upper Gila.

Appendices

Appendix 1

Wind Mountain Macrobotanical Plant Remains

CHARLES H. MIKSICEK AND PATRICIA L. FALL

Situated 1,730 m (5,680 feet) above sea level, Wind Mountain is located in the upper Sonoran life zone. Today, the broad floodplain below the site is dominated by weedy, pioneer species of the types described as "increasers" by range management people, because such plants thrive under overgrazed conditions. *Datura meteloides* (sacred datura), *Chrysothamnus nauseosus* (rabbitbrush), *Croton texanum* (doveweed), *Agremone* (prickly-poppy), *Mentzelia* (blazing star), *Cucurbita foetidissima* (buffalo gourd), *Yucca eleta* (narrow leaf yucca), and *Opuntia imbricata* (cholla) abound on the floodplain. Above the site, where the watercourses become narrower and more canyon-like, vegetation is more truly riparian. *Quercus oblongifolia* (Mexican blue oak), *Quercus emoryi* (Emory oak), *Quercus turbinella* (shrub live oak), *Acer negundo* (box elder), *Chilopsis linearis* (desert willow), *Juniperus depeana* (alligator juniper), *Artemisia ludoviciana* (threadleaf sage), *Brickellia* (brickellia or brickle bush), and *Juglans major* (walnut) dominate this assemblage. In contrast, *Pinus ponderosa* (ponderosa pine) and *Vitis arizonica* are found in more mesic locales. Shrubby species such as *Haplopappus tennuisectus* (burroweed), *Halopappus laricifolius* (turpentine bush), *Lycium pallidum* (wolfberry), *Senecio longilobus* (threadleaf groundsel), *Gutierrezia sarothrae* (snakeweed), *Yucca bacata* (banana yucca), narrow leaf yucca, *Opuntia phaeacantha* (prickly pear), *Nolina microcarpa* (bear grass), *Rhus trilobata* (skunkbush), datura, Emory oak, and *Cercocarpus brevifolia* (mountain mahogany) are common on the ridge immediately around the site and on the slopes above the washes. Trees such as *Prosopis glandulosa* (Texas mesquite), *Pinus edulis* (piñon pine), alligator juniper, and Mexican Blue oak also cover the slopes.

The distribution of three plants, one species of *Opuntia* and two of *Agave*, is interesting. *Opuntia imbricata* (cholla) grows densely on the slope immediately below the prehistoric trash midden but is sparsely represented elsewhere. In the Cibola area of west-central New Mexico, this species of cholla seems to occur almost exclusively on archaeological sites. Two century plant populations (*Agave palmerii* and *Agave chrysophila*) also grow downslope from the Wind Mountain midden. These are the only agaves evident in the vicinity of the site. Paul Minnis and Stephen Plog (1976) noted that populations of agave in the Chevlon area of eastern Arizona, disjunct from their normal range, were found only on archaeological sites. These clumps of cholla and agave may represent the remains of cholla buds or agave hearts brought to the Wind Mountain site for food. Modern plants may have been started from seeds or vegetative propagules discarded on the trash midden.

Archaeological Sampling

In order to learn more about prehistoric environment and subsistence at the Wind Mountain and Ridout loci, soil samples were collected during excavation for flotation. These were processed by standard water separation techniques, dried, and analyzed in the Southwestern Archaeo-Botanical Labs (SABL) at the University of Arizona. Seeds and plant fragments were identified by comparison with material in the comparative collections of SABL and the Tumamoc Hill Geochronology Labs. Sufficiently large fragments of charcoal were fractured to give a fresh transverse section and identified under a dissecting scope at 30x. Macrofossils such as maize, beans, twigs, and nuts were examined and identified at low power. Beans and maize remains were measured using standard metric variables discussed in Nickerson (1953), Kaplan (1965), and Bird (1970). The results of the flotation analyses are summarized (Appendix 1: Tables 1–5). Maize data is also presented (Appendix 1: Table 6).

Wood Remains

The selection of wood for construction, fuel, and tools is determined by its availability in the local environment, culturally defined preferences, and its mechanical properties including hardness, density, heat value, resin content, and tensile strength. Analysis of wood charcoal provides information about a variety of uses.

Wood Used in House Construction

Charcoal found on the floors of pit structures reflects a mixture of wood types used in both construction (the charred remains of posts and cross beams of the house) and as fuel (traces of hearth spillage). To distinguish between wood used as fuel or for building, the proportions of tree species identified from floor samples are expected to be significantly different from those observed in hearth samples.

At Wind Mountain, cottonwood, juniper, and piñon pine appear to be the most commonly encountered building materials. Smaller amounts of oak, ash, box elder, walnut, and ponderosa pine were also found. Most types are indicative of trees growing in the Mangas drainage. The few fragments of Douglas fir probably came from either the nearby Gila Mountains or Deadman Canyon.

Without tree-ring dates to verify the Wind Mountain chronology, it is difficult to establish any temporal trends in wood use. It is, however, possible to discuss certain attributes of particular wood types as potential building materials. Cottonwood and pine, used as upright supports and roof beams in pit structures, were favored perhaps because they are soft woods easily cut with stone axes. Juniper was also frequently used as upright supports and beams. Its high resin content rendered it resistant to insect damage and decay, an ideal property for a construction material. In addition, oak, box elder, walnut, and ponderosa pine apparently also served as major beams and supports though in lesser amounts. Smaller twigs, branches, and leaves of these trees, together with yucca leaves, agave stalks, and reed stems, were used to fill in the roofs of pit structures. Presumably, pit structures were then weatherproofed with a final layer of earth.

Fuel Wood

If hearths or fire pits were cleaned at intervals, any charcoal recovered from such contexts represents the last few uses of these features. Sweepings were discarded on middens, in abandoned rooms, or wherever else trash was thrown. Juniper, cottonwood, piñon, oak, and box elder, the same trees used in construction, apparently also served as fuel; all were recovered from hearths. All except rapidly burning cottonwood would make efficient fuels because they are dense woods with high heat values. Cottonwood would have made good kindling. Cottonwood was the predominant fuel or charcoal identified in pit ovens or roasting pits (Appendix 1: Table 4).

The most distinctive wood charcoal assemblage, characterized by juniper, oak, and cottonwood, was associated with two cremations on the Wind Mountain locus (Appendix 1: Table 5). Visitors to modern Southwestern pueblos are familiar with the fragrance of burning juniper. This trait may have been desirable when a human body was cremated at Wind Mountain. In any event, the combination of resinous juniper and oak would have produced an extremely hot, long lasting fire causing the virtual total reduction of human remains.

Plant Food Remains

Maize

Fragments of cobs and kernels of *Zea mays* were the most commonly recovered plant remains, occurring in over half the samples analyzed. Interestingly, no maize was recovered in Ridout locus flotation samples, though kernels were found on the floor of House J (Appendix 1: Table 6). The Ridout maize belongs to a flinty race of corn known as Onaveno. It exhibits a high proportion of eight-rowed kernels (48 percent) for pure Onaveno, which suggests a possible admixing with an eight-rowed flint variety. Onaveno was ubiquitous throughout the Southwest between 300 B.C. and Spanish Contact times. It is still grown to a limited extent by both Tohono O'odham (Papago) and Hopi as well as in northern Mexico.

Most of the Wind Mountain maize consisted of shelled kernels stored off the cob. The largest concentration came from the floor of House R. At least three types of maize were represented in a six liter measure of kernels. In the subsample studied intensively, 63 percent of the kernels were identified as a Pueblo Flour variety; 20 percent were Harinoso de Ocho, the large kernel eight-rowed flour corn; and 17 percent belonged to a high row number variety having some denting. Coincidentally, these proportions show an almost perfect Mendelian ratio for a dihybrid cross—9:3:3:1. The two dominant genes in this case would be floury endosperm (with dented endosperm recessive) and a modifier gene for high row number (with the recessive eight-rowed cobs).

True dents are rare in archaeological collections of maize from the Southwest, but dented forms of Pueblo Flour corn are relatively common. Dent corn is usually limited to Fremont Basketmaker sites in southern Utah. Pueblo Flour corn has been recovered from Alder Wash, a Salado site in the San Pedro River valley of southern Arizona. Pueblo Flour varieties are occasionally seen in post-A.D. 1050 Anasazi maize collections. Harinoso de Ocho is known from several sites in

APPENDIX 1: TABLE 1. Wind Mountain Locus House X Macrobotanical Stratigraphic Profile

Depth (cm)	Sample Volume (l)	Sample Weight (gm)	Wood Charcoal							Nuts, Berries								Quelites (Greens)									
			Acer negundo	Diffuse Porous–*Populus*/*Salix*	*Juniperus* sp.	*Pinus* piñon–type	*Pinus ponderosa*	*Quercus* sp.	*Zea mays*	*Celtis* sp.	*Juglans major*	*Juniperus* sp.	*Lycium*/*Physalis*–type	Platyopuntia	*Pinus* piñon–type	*Prunus virginiana*	Rosaceae	*Amaranthus* sp.	*Atriplex* sp.	*Chenopodium* Rough–seeded	*Chenopodium* Smooth–seeded	*Cleome*/*Polanisia*–type	Cruciferea	*Lepidium*–type	*Mullago verticilata*	*Portulaca* sp.	Other taxa
0–4	1	4.7	–	–	–	–	–	–	–	–	–	–	–	–	–	–	–	2	–	55	7	–	–	–	28	17	2 *Argemone* seeds, 1 Compositae seed, 1 *Echinocereus* sp. seed, 7 *Echinocereus aeroles* seeds, 22 *Oryzopsis hymenoides* seeds
4–24	1	1.4	–	–	–	–	–	–	4	–	–	–	–	–	–	–	–	–	–	–	–	–	–	–	–	–	
34–44	1	1.0	–	–	–	–	–	–	–	–	–	–	–	–	–	–	–	–	–	1	–	–	–	–	–	–	
54–64	1	2.3	–	–	–	–	–	1	3	–	–	–	–	–	–	–	–	3	–	6	2	–	–	–	–	–	
74–84	1	3.4	–	1	2	–	–	–	6	–	–	5	–	–	–	–	–	1	–	–	–	–	–	–	2	–	
94–104	1	2.6	–	1	1	1	–	–	6	–	–	–	–	–	–	–	–	–	–	–	–	–	–	–	–	–	
114–124	1	9.9	–	–	–	24	–	–	4	–	1	–	–	–	–	–	–	–	–	–	1	–	–	–	–	–	
134–144	1	5.5	–	1	1	1	–	–	5	–	5	1	–	–	–	–	–	–	–	–	–	–	–	–	–	–	1 *Phaseolus acutifolius* (Tepary bean)
Floor/ West ½	1	1.9	–	–	–	–	–	–	–	–	–	–	–	–	–	–	–	–	–	–	–	–	–	–	–	–	1 Gramineae seed and 1 unknown

Appendix 1: Table 2. Selected Macrobotanical Remains Recovered from Houses

Structure	Type	Context	Sample Volume (l)	Sample Weight (gm)	Wood Charcoal						Nuts, Berries										Quelites (Greens)									
					Acer negundo	Diffuse Porous–*Populus/Salix*	*Juniperus* sp.	*Pinus* piñon–type	*Pinus ponderosa*	*Quercus* sp.	*Zea mays*	*Celtis* sp.	*Juglans major*	*Juniperus* sp.	*Lycium/Physalis*–type	Platyopuntia	*Pinus* piñon–type	*Prunus virginiana*	Rosaceae	*Amaranthus* sp.	*Atriplex* sp.	*Chenopodium* Rough–seeded	*Chenopodium* Smooth–seeded	*Cleome/Polanisia*–type	Cruciferae	*Lepidium*–type	*Mullago verticilata*	*Portulaca* sp.	Other taxa
WM-GG	I	Floor	4	12.3	–	4	1	–	–	–	–	–	–	–	–	–	–	–	–	6	–	6	–	4	–	–	4	1	1 Gramineae seed, 1 Labiatae seed
WM-HH	I	Floor	4	9.3	–	4	–	–	–	–	2	–	–	1	–	–	–	–	–	11	–	7	2	–	–	–	–	–	
WM-II	I	Floor	4	9.7	–	1	–	–	–	–	3	–	–	3	–	–	–	–	–	16	1	17	12	2	–	–	1	2	1 Gramineae seed
WM-JJ	I	Floor	4	1.0	–	1	–	–	–	–	4	–	–	1	–	–	–	–	–	3	–	5	3	–	–	–	–	6	
WM-LL	I	Floor	4	6.3	–	2	–	–	–	–	8	–	–	–	–	–	–	–	–	1	–	2	1	–	–	–	–	2	
WM-Q	II	Floor	1	1.2	–	–	–	1	–	–	–	–	–	–	–	–	–	–	–	–	–	–	–	–	–	–	–	1	
WM-R	II	Floor	1	3.4	–	–	1	–	–	–	84	–	–	–	–	–	–	–	–	–	–	–	–	–	–	–	–	–	
WM-S	II	Floor	1	1.6	–	2	–	1	–	–	1	–	–	–	–	–	–	–	–	1	–	3	5	–	–	–	3	2	
WM-T	II	Floor	1	2.8	–	–	–	–	–	–	2	–	–	–	–	–	–	–	–	–	–	–	5	–	–	–	–	–	
WM-KK	II	Floor	4	6.5	–	–	–	–	–	–	14	–	–	1	–	1	–	–	–	–	–	4	8	–	–	2	3	3	
WM-KK	II	Hearth	3	3.5	–	1	1	–	–	–	12	–	–	–	–	–	–	–	–	1	–	1	–	–	–	1	–	–	
WM-QQ	II	Floor	4	21.7	–	6	3	–	1	–	94	–	–	1	–	–	–	–	–	–	–	–	1	–	–	–	–	–	
WM-RR	II	Floor	2	4.0	–	–	–	–	–	–	2	–	–	1	–	–	–	–	–	–	–	–	1	–	–	–	–	–	
WM-NN	III	Floor	4	5.6	–	–	–	–	–	–	–	–	–	6	–	–	–	–	–	–	–	1	–	–	–	–	–	–	
WM-NN	III	Hearth	1	2.6	–	–	–	–	–	–	–	–	–	1	–	–	–	–	–	–	–	–	–	–	–	–	–	–	
WM-WW	III	Floor	4	40.2	–	–	3	–	–	–	17	–	–	2	–	–	–	–	–	–	–	2	5	–	–	–	8	–	2 Gramineae seeds
WM-B	IV	Floor	1	.5	–	–	–	–	–	–	–	–	–	–	–	–	–	–	–	1	–	2	–	–	–	–	–	–	
WM-C	IV	Floor	1	2.0	–	–	–	–	–	–	–	–	–	–	–	–	–	–	–	3	–	18	–	3	–	–	18	–	
WM-D	IV	Floor	1	2.2	–	–	–	–	–	–	3	–	–	–	–	–	–	–	–	1	–	5	–	–	–	–	–	–	1 *Panicum*–type grass
WM-G	IV	Floor	1	1.7	–	–	–	–	–	–	–	–	–	–	–	–	–	–	–	–	–	1	1	–	–	–	–	–	
WM-H	IV	Floor	1	3.4	–	–	2	–	–	–	–	–	–	–	–	–	–	–	–	1	–	1	–	–	–	–	–	–	
WM-K	IV	Floor	1	2.0	–	–	–	–	–	–	3	–	–	–	–	–	–	–	–	–	–	–	–	–	–	–	1	–	1 *Argemone* seed
WM-L	IV	Floor	1	1.2	–	–	–	1	–	–	–	–	–	–	–	–	–	–	–	1	–	1	1	–	–	–	–	–	1 Compositae (sunflower)
WM-L	IV	Floor Vessel	–	7.7	–	–	–	–	–	–	6	–	–	–	–	–	–	–	–	–	–	–	1	–	–	–	–	–	
WM-L	IV	Floor Vessel	–	1.5	–	–	–	–	–	–	12	–	–	–	–	–	–	–	–	–	–	–	–	–	–	–	–	–	
WM-W	IV	Floor	1	1.4	–	2	1	–	–	–	1	–	–	–	–	1	–	–	–	1	–	–	1	–	–	–	–	1	

APPENDIX 1: TABLE 2. *(continued)*

					Wood Charcoal							Nuts, Berries								Quelites (Greens)									
Structure	Type	Context	Sample Volume (l)	Sample Weight (gm)	*Acer negundo*	Diffuse Porous–*Populus*/*Salix*	*Juniperus* sp.	*Pinus* piñon–type	*Pinus ponderosa*	*Quercus* sp.	*Zea mays*	*Celtis* sp.	*Juglans major*	*Juniperus* sp.	*Lycium*/*Physalis*–type	Platyopuntia	*Pinus* piñon–type	*Prunus virginiana*	Rosaceae	*Amaranthus* sp.	*Atriplex* sp.	*Chenopodium* Rough–seeded	*Chenopodium* Smooth–seeded	*Cleome*/*Polanisia*–type	Cruciferae	*Lepidium*–type	*Mullago verticilata*	*Portulaca* sp.	Other taxa
WM-Z	IV	Floor	1	1.4	–	–	–	–	–	–	–	–	–	–	–	–	–	–	–	–	–	–	1	–	–	–	–	–	
WM-AA	IV	Floor	1	2.7	–	–	–	–	–	–	3	–	–	–	–	–	–	–	–	–	–	7	–	–	–	–	325	–	
WM-BB	IV	Floor	1	1.3	1	1	–	1	–	–	–	–	–	–	–	–	–	–	–	–	–	1	1	–	–	–	–	–	1 *Cucurbita* rind fragment
WM-DD	IV	Floor	1	6.6	–	1	1	15	1	2	9	–	–	–	–	–	–	–	–	1	–	4	1	–	–	–	–	–	
WM-DD	IV	Floor	3	15.4	–	–	–	2	–	1	48	–	1	13	–	–	3	–	–	2	–	8	1	1	–	–	–	1	2 *Chenopodium berlandieri* seeds (large size)
WM-DD	IV	Hearth	1	11.1	–	6	5	1	–	–	–	–	–	–	3	–	–	–	1	10	1	9	6	2	–	–	8	–	5 Gramineae seeds, 1 Labiatae seed
WM-DD	IV	Hearth	1	16.1	–	4	–	–	–	1	3	–	–	1	–	1	–	–	–	1	–	4	1	1	–	–	–	–	
WM-FF	IV	Hearth	1	3.6	–	–	–	–	–	–	2	–	–	1	–	–	–	–	–	–	–	2	1	1	–	–	–	–	
WM-OO	IV	Floor	4	32.0	–	6	9	3	2	–	5	–	–	6	–	–	–	–	–	1	–	9	6	5	1	–	–	–	1 *Phragmites* (reed) fragment
WM-PP	IV	Floor	4	37.1	–	5	5	2	–	8	14	–	3	7	–	2	3	3	–	6	–	10	–	–	–	–	–	2	
WM-PP	IV	Hearths	2	9.9	–	5	1	–	–	–	–	–	–	4	–	–	–	–	–	–	–	–	–	–	–	–	–	–	
WM-SS	IV	Floor	4	23.3	–	2	–	–	–	–	102	–	–	1	–	–	4	–	–	10	–	20	12	3	–	–	6	–	
WM-SS	IV	Hearth	2	8.7	–	–	–	–	–	–	–	–	–	1	–	–	–	–	–	1	–	1	2	–	–	–	–	2	
WM-SS	IV	Metate	–	10.9	–	–	6	–	–	–	2	–	–	–	–	–	–	–	–	–	–	–	–	–	–	–	–	–	
WM-TT	IV	Floor	4	13.5	–	–	–	7	–	–	18	–	4	1	–	–	1	–	–	5	–	6	10	–	–	–	–	1	
WM-TT	IV	Hearth	2	7.4	–	–	–	–	–	–	–	–	–	–	–	–	–	–	–	1	–	–	4	–	–	–	–	–	1 *Phragmites* (reed) fragment
WM-UU	IV	Floor	4	7.2	–	7	2	–	–	1	–	–	–	–	–	–	–	–	–	1	1	2	1	–	–	–	4	–	1 Gramineae seed
WM-VV	IV	Floor	4	34.2	–	–	–	–	–	–	155	–	6	4	–	–	–	–	–	5	–	8	4	–	–	–	–	3	2 Gramineae seeds
WM-VV	IV	Hearth	2	11.2	–	15	3	1	–	1	4	–	–	4	–	–	–	–	–	–	–	4	–	–	–	–	–	1	
RO-C	IV	Floor	–	8.9	–	–	1	–	–	1	–	–	2	–	–	–	–	–	–	–	–	1	–	–	–	–	–	–	1 *Agave* stem, 6 fragments *Phragmites communis* stems, 1 *Pseudotsuga menzesii*, and 3 *Pinus edulis* charcoal and 1 nut fragment
RO-C	IV	Floor	–	8.9	–	–	2	–	–	–	–	–	1	–	–	–	–	–	–	–	–	–	–	–	–	–	–	–	2 *Fraxinus velutina* charcoal fragments
WM-4	V	Floor	1	2.7	–	–	–	–	–	–	–	–	–	–	–	–	–	–	–	–	–	1	–	–	–	–	3	–	
WM-8	V	Floor	1	.5	–	–	–	–	–	–	–	–	–	–	–	–	–	–	–	–	–	–	1	–	–	–	7	–	
WM-16	V	Floor Vessel	–	29.3	–	–	–	–	–	–	2,400	–	–	–	–	–	–	–	–	2	–	7	7	–	–	–	1	–	1 Gramineae seed
WM-YY	VI	Floor	–	17.6	1	–	–	–	–	3	–	–	56	1	–	–	–	–	–	–	–	–	–	–	–	–	–	–	14 *Quercus* acorns, 1 *Euphorbia* seed, 1 *Oryzopsis* seed, 5 wood charcoal fragments of *Juglans major*, 2 wood charcoal fragments of *Pinus edulis*

APPENDIX 1: TABLE 3. Selected Macrobotanical Remains Recovered from Community Structures

Structure	Type	Context	Sample Volume (l)	Sample Weight (gm)	Wood Charcoal							Nuts, Berries								Quelites (Greens)									
					Acer negundo	Diffuse Porous–*Populus*/*Salix*	*Juniperus* sp.	*Pinus* piñon–type	*Pinus ponderosa*	*Quercus* sp.	*Zea mays*	*Celtis* sp.	*Juglans major*	*Juniperus* sp.	*Lycium*/*Physalis*–type	Platyopuntia	*Pinus* piñon–type	*Prunus virginiana*	Rosaceae	*Amaranthus* sp.	*Atriplex* sp.	*Chenopodium* Rough–seeded	*Chenopodium* Smooth–seeded	*Cleome*/*Polanisia*–type	Cruciferae	*Lepidium*–type	*Mullago verticilata*	*Portulaca* sp.	Other taxa
WM-X	B	Hearth	1	.3	–	–	–	–	–	–	–	–	–	–	–	–	–	–	–	1	–	–	–	–	–	–	–	–	
WM-U	C	Floor	1	.8	–	–	–	–	–	–	1	–	–	–	–	–	–	–	–	–	–	1	1	–	–	–	–	–	
WM-U	C	Hearth	–	.2	–	–	–	–	–	–	2	–	–	–	–	–	–	–	–	1	–	3	3	–	–	–	20	–	
WM-Y	C	Floor	1	.5	–	–	–	–	–	–	3	–	–	–	–	–	–	–	–	1	–	–	–	–	–	–	5	–	
WM-XX	C	Storage Pit	–	10.5	1	–	1	–	–	3	2	–	5	4	–	–	–	–	–	1	–	–	2	–	–	–	–	3	3 wood charcoal fragments of *Platanus wrightii*, 1 fragment each *Juglans major* and *Fraxinus velutina*
WM-XX	C	Ash Pit	–	9.5	3	–	8	–	–	–	–	–	–	1	–	–	–	–	–	–	–	2	–	–	–	–	1	–	4 wood charcoal fragments *Pinus edulis*
WM-XX	C	Ash Pit	–	8.3	3	–	7	–	–	7	–	–	1	–	–	–	–	–	–	–	–	–	1	–	–	–	–	–	1 seed each *Euphorbia*, Gramineae, *Sporobolus*, 2 *Populus* wood charcoal fragments
WM-7	E	Floor	1	.3	–	–	–	–	–	–	–	–	–	–	–	–	–	–	–	1	–	2	2	–	–	–	1	4	
WM-V	F	Floor	1	1.7	–	–	–	–	–	–	–	–	–	2	–	–	–	–	–	–	–	13	–	–	–	–	10	3	
WM-3	G	Floor	1	1.6	–	–	–	–	–	–	–	–	–	–	–	–	–	–	–	1	–	–	4	–	–	–	–	–	
WM-15	G	Hearth	2	4.2	–	1	–	–	–	–	3	–	–	–	–	–	–	–	–	–	–	–	2	–	–	–	–	1	

APPENDIX 1: TABLE 4. Selected Macrobotanical Remains Recovered from Extramural Features

			Wood Charcoal							Nuts, Berries									Quelites (Greens)									
Pit	Sample Volume (l)	Sample Weight (gm)	*Acer negundo*	Diffuse Porous–*Populus/Salix*	*Juniperus* sp.	*Pinus* piñon–type	*Pinus ponderosa*	*Quercus sp.*	*Zea mays*	*Celtis* sp.	*Juglans major*	*Juniperus* sp.	*Lycium/Physalis*–type	Platyopuntia	*Pinus* piñon–type	*Prunus virginiana*	Rosaceae	*Amaranthus* sp.	*Atriplex* sp.	*Chenopodium* Rough–seeded	*Chenopodium* Smooth–seeded	*Cleome/Polanisia*–type	Cruciferae	*Lepidium*–type	*Mullago verticilata*	*Portulaca* sp.	Other taxa
WM-3	1	2.0	–	–	–	–	–	–	–	–	–	1	–	–	–	–	–	–	–	–	2	–	–	–	–	–	
WM-33	1	2.3	–	–	–	–	–	–	3	–	–	–	–	–	–	–	–	–	–	1	4	–	–	–	1	–	
WM-34	1	1.8	–	2	–	–	–	–	5	–	–	–	–	–	–	–	–	–	–	1	1	–	–	–	–	1	1 *Mentzelia* seed
WM-35	1	2.6	–	–	–	–	–	–	2	–	–	–	–	–	–	–	–	1	–	–	–	–	–	–	–	–	
WM-36	2	3.5	–	1	–	–	–	–	4	–	–	–	–	–	1	–	–	–	1	3	3	–	–	1	–	1	
WM-37	1	2.0	–	–	–	–	–	–	3	–	–	–	–	–	–	–	–	–	–	–	1	–	–	–	–	–	
WM-38	2	2.4	–	–	–	–	–	–	2	–	–	–	–	–	–	–	–	–	–	5	3	–	1	–	1	–	1 *Chenopodium berlandieri* sub sp. berlandieri
WM-39	2	2.3	–	–	–	–	–	–	5	–	–	2	–	–	–	–	–	–	–	–	2	–	–	–	–	–	
WM-40	1	2.9	–	1	–	–	–	–	–	–	–	–	–	–	–	–	–	–	–	–	–	–	–	–	–	–	
WM-41	1	3.0	–	–	–	–	–	–	–	–	–	–	–	–	–	–	–	–	–	–	–	–	–	–	–	–	1 Compositae seed
WM-44	2	4.6	–	–	–	–	–	–	–	–	–	1	–	–	–	–	–	–	–	–	–	–	–	–	–	–	
WM-51	1	2.8	–	–	–	–	–	–	2	–	–	1	–	–	–	–	–	–	–	–	–	–	–	–	–	–	
WM-57	–	6.0	–	–	–	–	–	1	1	–	–	1	–	–	–	–	–	–	–	–	–	–	–	–	–	1	2 fragments of *Celtis* wood charcoal, 1 fragment of *Juglans major* wood charcoal

APPENDIX 1: TABLE 4. *(continued)*

			Wood Charcoal							Nuts, Berries								Quelites (Greens)									
Pit	Sample Volume (l)	Sample Weight (gm)	*Acer negundo*	Diffuse Porous–*Populus/Salix*	*Juniperus* sp.	*Pinus* piñon–type	*Pinus ponderosa*	*Quercus* sp.	*Zea mays*	*Celtis* sp.	*Juglans major*	*Juniperus* sp.	*Lycium/Physalis*–type	Platyopuntia	*Pinus* piñon–type	*Prunus virginiana*	Rosaceae	*Amaranthus* sp.	*Atriplex* sp.	*Chenopodium* Rough–seeded	*Chenopodium* Smooth–seeded	*Cleome/Polanisia*–type	Cruciferae	*Lepidium*–type	*Mullago verticilata*	*Portulaca* sp.	Other taxa
WM-58	–	5.5	4	–	–	–	–	1	1	–	2	–	–	–	–	–	–	–	–	–	–	–	–	–	–	–	1 fragment each of *Fraxinus velutina*, *Celtis* wood charcoal
WM-66	–	5.5	–	–	1	–	–	5	–	–	–	–	–	–	–	–	–	–	–	–	–	–	–	–	1	–	
Pit Oven																											
WM-1	1	5.3	–	8	–	–	–	1	2	–	–	–	–	–	–	–	–	–	–	–	–	–	–	–	–	1	
WM-2	1	8.7	–	2	1	–	–	–	–	–	–	–	–	–	–	–	–	–	–	–	–	–	–	–	–	–	
WM-3	1	6.9	–	2	–	–	–	–	–	–	–	1	–	–	–	–	–	–	–	2	–	–	–	–	1	–	1 Polygonaceae seed, 1 Euphorbiaceae seed
WM-4	1	10.3	–	10	–	–	–	–	3	–	–	–	–	–	–	–	–	2	–	2	–	–	–	–	–	–	
WM-5	2	2.5	–	–	–	–	–	–	5	–	–	1	–	–	–	–	–	1	–	2	–	–	–	–	–	–	
WM-6	1	2.8	–	–	–	–	–	–	2	–	–	–	–	–	–	–	–	–	–	–	5	–	–	–	–	1	
WM-7	1	1.8	–	–	–	–	–	–	–	–	–	1	–	–	–	–	–	–	–	–	2	–	–	–	–	–	
WM-8	1	2.9	–	–	–	–	–	–	–	–	–	–	–	–	–	–	–	1	–	–	1	–	–	–	–	–	
WM-9	1	3.0	–	–	–	–	–	–	2	–	–	–	–	–	–	–	–	–	–	2	19	–	–	–	–	7	1 Euphorbiaceae seed
WM-10	2	2.2	–	2	–	–	–	–	–	–	–	–	–	–	–	–	–	–	–	2	–	–	–	–	–	1	
WM-12	1	1.2	–	–	–	–	–	–	–	–	–	1	–	–	–	–	–	–	–	–	–	–	–	–	–	–	
WM-18	–	5.4	1	–	–	–	–	3	–	–	–	–	–	–	–	–	–	–	–	–	–	–	–	–	–	–	fragment *Fraxinus velutina*, *Agave* stem, fragment *Platanus wrightii*

APPENDIX 1: TABLE 5. Selected Macrobotanical Remains Recovered from Burials and Cremations

Burial	Sample Volume (l)	Sample Weight (gm)	Wood Charcoal							Nuts, Berries								Quelites (Greens)									
			Acer negundo	Diffuse Porous–*Populus*/*Salix*	*Juniperus* sp.	*Pinus* piñon–type	*Pinus ponderosa*	*Quercus* sp.	*Zea mays*	*Celtis* sp.	*Juglans major*	*Juniperus* sp.	*Lycium*/*Physalis*–type	Platyopuntia	*Pinus* piñon–type	*Prunus virginiana*	Rosaceae	*Amaranthus* sp.	*Atriplex* sp.	*Chenopodium* Rough–seeded	*Chenopodium* Smooth–seeded	*Cleome*/*Polanisia*–type	Cruciferae	*Lepidium*–type	*Mullago verticilata*	*Portulaca* sp.	Other taxa
WM-1	–	.7	–	–	–	–	–	–	–	–	–	–	–	–	–	–	–	1	–	–	1	–	–	–	–	–	
WM-3	1	5.3	–	–	–	–	–	–	–	–	–	1	–	–	–	–	–	–	–	1	–	–	–	–	1	–	
WM-3	1	1.8	–	3	–	–	–	–	10	–	1	–	–	–	–	–	–	–	–	3	–	1	–	–	–	–	
WM-3	1	1.2	–	2	–	–	–	–	–	–	–	–	–	–	–	–	–	1	–	–	–	–	–	–	–	–	6 *Phragmites* reed fragments
WM-3	1	1.9	–	–	–	–	–	–	12	–	–	–	–	–	–	–	–	–	1	5	–	–	–	–	–	–	
WM-3	1	1.1	–	–	–	–	–	–	–	–	–	1	–	–	1	–	–	–	–	1	–	–	–	–	–	–	1 *Phaseolus acutifolius* (Tepary bean)
WM-4	1	3.0	–	–	–	–	–	–	4	–	–	–	–	–	–	–	–	–	–	–	–	–	–	–	–	–	
WM-7	–	.6	–	–	–	–	–	–	–	–	–	–	–	–	–	–	–	1	–	–	–	–	–	–	–	–	
WM-9	1	1.6	–	–	–	–	–	–	–	–	–	–	–	–	–	–	–	2	–	1	1	–	–	–	–	–	1 *Yucca* seed
WM-12	1	1.4	–	–	–	–	–	–	–	–	–	–	–	–	–	–	–	–	–	–	–	–	–	–	–	–	300 Polygonaceae (?) seeds
WM-24	1	1.3	–	–	–	–	–	–	1	–	–	–	–	–	–	–	–	–	–	–	1	–	–	–	–	–	
WM-32	1	2.3	–	–	–	–	–	–	2	–	1	2	–	–	–	–	–	–	–	–	–	–	–	–	–	–	
WM-53/54	1	6.1	–	2	3	–	–	–	–	–	–	–	–	–	–	–	–	4	1	–	–	–	–	–	–	–	
WM-65	–	4.0	–	–	–	–	–	–	8	–	2	–	–	–	–	–	–	–	–	2	–	–	–	–	–	–	1 *Sporobolus* seed
WM-99	–	7.7	5	–	2	–	–	6	–	–	–	1	–	–	–	–	–	–	–	–	–	–	–	–	–	–	3 fragments each of *Populus* and *Pinus edulis* wood charcoal
RO-3	–	5.3	–	–	4	–	–	–	–	–	–	–	–	–	–	–	–	–	–	–	–	–	–	–	–	–	1 fragment each of *Pseudotsuga menziesii* and *Fraxinus velutina* wood charcoal
RO-4	–	8.4	–	–	–	–	–	3	–	–	–	–	–	–	–	–	–	–	–	–	–	–	–	–	–	–	1 fragment each of *Pinus edulis* and *Fraxinus velutina* wood charcoal
Cremation																											
WM-1	2	2.9	1	3	5	1	–	–	1	–	–	–	–	–	–	–	–	–	–	–	–	–	–	–	1	–	
WM-2	–	4.8	1	–	4	–	–	–	–	–	–	–	–	–	–	–	–	–	–	–	–	–	–	–	–	–	1 seed each *Yucca bacata* and *Sporobolus*
WM-2	–	4.6	2	–	1	–	–	–	–	–	–	–	–	–	–	–	–	1	–	–	–	–	–	–	6	1	

Appendix 1: Table 6. Carbonized Maize Recovered from the Wind Mountain and Ridout Loci

Sample No.	Provenience	Type of Maize	Sample Size	Mean Row No.	Percent Cobs or Kernels per Row No. 8	10	12	14	16
	WM locus								
4	Work Area 1, Vessel 3		1 cob	10					
5	House L, Central Post hole	Pima-Papago	1 cob	10					
6	House E	Pima-Papago	1 cob	8					
7	Block 25-B	Harinoso de Ocho	1 cob	8					
10	House R		6 liters of kernels						
		Harinoso de Ocho	20%	8	100				
		Pueblo Flour	63%	10.5	31	35	21	8	6
		Dent	17%	13.1		14	28	43	14
15	House DD	Harinoso de Ocho	1 cob	8					
17	Work Area 1	Harinoso de Ocho	750 ml kernels	8	100				
	RO locus								
37	House J, floor	Onaveno	200 ml kernels	9.8	48	19	28	5	
45	House J, floor	Onaveno	50 ml kernels	10.7					

southern Arizona that postdate A.D. 700. The maize from House R is more similar to modern Pueblo Flour varieties from Hopi and Zuni than it is to those from the Rio Grande Pueblos.

The Wind Mountain maize data provide important clues for unraveling the genealogy of maize types in the prehistoric Southwest (Appendix 1: Table 6). The earliest type of maize in the Southwest was Chapalote, with 10 to 12 rows of golden brown, flinty kernels. Chapalote dating to at least 912 B.C. was recovered from Bat Cave in southwestern New Mexico (Yarnell 1976). By at least 300 B.C., a related popcorn known as Reventador with up to 22 rows of pearly, white kernels was introduced from northern Mexico. At about the same time Onaveno, an early representative of the Pima-Papago complex, also reached the Southwest. The Pima-Papago complex, or suprarace as defined by Anderson (1942), also includes Mais Blando de Sonora, Harinoso de Ocho, and an eight-rowed flinty race. Two genes, flint versus flour endosperm and eight-row versus higher row number, seem to account for most of the racial differences in this complex. The ratios of kernel types from House R suggest that a second complex of maize races, referred to here as the Pueblo complex, was possibly derived from floury forms of the Pima-Papago complex (Mais Blando and Harinoso de Ocho) through a selection for larger ears and the addition of a third gene controlling the dented endosperm. Another gene or set of genes that control anthocyanins would account for the blue, purple, and red flour corns characteristic of the Hopi, Zuni, and Rio Grande Pueblos. This Puebloid complex would include the Pueblo Flour corns and the Southern and Southwestern Dents (including Fremont Dent) and would share Harinoso de Ocho with the Pima-Papago complex. The trend for an increase in cob length would account for the very large ears with big butts characteristic of the Navajo and Rio Grande Pueblos.

Beans

Beans are relatively rare at Wind Mountain as they are at most Southwestern sites. This is a function of preservation rather than a lack of importance to prehistoric economy and diet. Several common bean (*Phaseolus vulgaris*) cotyledons were found in Houses R and WW as well as in Work Area 1 at the Wind Mountain locus and in House A and Burial 7 at the Ridout locus. The cotyledons were all approximately the same size and probably represent the same cultivar. Several beans from House A had intact seed coats with faint longitudinal stripes suggesting either a pinto or purple-striped Zuni variety. Based on this striped trait and the size of the cotyledons, these beans could represent types C^{11} or C^{13} as defined by Kaplan (1956), grown by both modern Hopi and Zuni but not previously identified for the prehistoric Mogollon.

Wind Mountain farmers also cultivated tepary beans. Two *Phaseolus acutifolius* var. *latifolius* cotyledons were identified in House X as well as in Burial 3.

Squash

The only evidence for the third member of the New World triad of cultivated plants is a *Cucurbita* sp. rind fragment from the floor of House BB (Appendix 1: Table 1). Squash remains,

Appendix 1: Table 6 *(continued)*

Mean Cupule Width (mm)	Mean Grain Thickness (mm)	Cob Diameter (mm)	Rachis Diameter (mm)	Cob/ Rachis Index	Mean Kernel Width (mm)	Mean Kernel Thickness (mm)	Mean Kernel Height (mm)
7.7	3.9						
6.9	4.2	11.4	8.3	1.37			
6.4	3.6	12.5	8.5	1.47			
7.5	4.9						
					10.6	5.9	8.8
9.3	4.0				9.2	5.6	9.0
					9.2	5.9	9.7
9.2	4.1	15.1	11.9	1.27			
					9.4	5.6	7.6
					7.4	5.2	6.8
					7.9	5.7	7.6

like beans, tend to be underrepresented in many archaeological sites.

Nuts

Several types of carbonized nuts were identified at both the Wind Mountain and Ridout loci. Walnuts (possibly modern intrusives) and piñon nuts were the most common, but a few acorns were also recovered from House XX (Appendix 1: Table 3). These nuts could be gathered in early fall and all are good sources of carbohydrates and oils. They are especially useful dietary supplements in years of poor maize harvests.

Agave

Stem, fiber, and heart fragments belonging to a species of *Agave,* or century plant, were recovered from Houses R and DD and Pit Oven 18 at Wind Mountain and House C at the Ridout locus. These remains together with two species of *Agave* from a Wind Mountain midden indicate that agave was an important food plant. Agave hearts were probably collected and roasted in numerous pit ovens or roasting pits uncovered throughout the site.

Fruits or Berries

Various berries and fleshy fruits added variety and essential nutrients to the prehistoric Wind Mountain diet. Wolfberries (*Lycium* sp.), prickly pear tunas (*Opuntia phaeacantha*), banana yucca fruits (*Yucca bacata*), and hedgehog cactus fruits (*Echinocereus triglochidiatus*) ripened from mid– to late summer, when cultivated crops were still immature. Hackberries (*Celtis reticulata*), chokeberries (*Prunus virginiana*), and alligator juniper berries (*Juniperus depeana*) could be gathered in early fall.

Seeds and Greens

The quantities of macrobotanical remains of plants with edible seeds and greens indicates the importance of wild plant collecting to the prehistoric inhabitants of Wind Mountain. Some plants were exploited for their carbohydrate-rich seeds: sunflower, *Helianthus* sp.; sacaton grass, *Sporobolus* sp.; Indian ricegrass, *Oryzopsis hymenoides;* panic grass, *Panicum* sp.; and blazing star, *Mentzelia* sp. Other plants provided both greens early in the growing season and seeds later as they matured: beeweed, *Cleome* sp.; pigweed, *Amaranthus* sp.; an annual saltbush, *Atriplex* sp.; purslane, *Portulaca* sp.; carpetweed, *Mollugo verticilata; Trianthema* sp.; tansy mustard, *Descurainia* sp.; and at least three distinct types of goosefoot, *Chenopodium* spp.

Because these plant species produce copious quantities of seed and thrive on disturbed ground, including archaeological sites, only carbonized remains were considered relevant to this analysis. Uncarbonized seed were considered to be part of the background or naturally occurring seed rain of the site and its immediate environs.

Carbonized seeds were most frequently encountered on house floors and hearths, suggesting that much processing and parching was conducted within structures. For example, pigweed was recovered from 57 percent of the floor samples and 40 percent of hearth samples. The relatively high percentage of pigweed seeds observed in burials (31 percent) may represent hearth and floor sweepings combined in the fill containing the human remains—rather than purposeful inclusion of seeds during inhumation.

The *Chenopodium* seeds from the Wind Mountain site are particularly interesting. As mentioned above, at least three taxa are represented. Most of the smooth-seeded type are probably *Chenopodium fremontii* or a closely related species. The reticulate or rough-seeded group most likely represents *C. berlandieri.* Three seeds, however, two from the floor of House DD and one from Pit 38, fall outside the size range for *C. berlandieri.* Although the expected seed diameter for this species is about 1.0 mm, these seeds averaged 1.7 mm in diameter. Upon further examination they were identified as *Chenopodium berlandieri* spp. *berlandieri* (Hugh Wilson, personal communication 1979). A larger sample is required to determine if this size variation is significant. The seeds may merely represent the extreme range for a wild population. Alternatively, intentional human selection of large seeds, or even incipient cultivation of *C. berlandieri* may be indicated.

Several other large seeded *C. berlandieri* individuals were recovered from Castle Peak, a rock shelter near the Salt River Canyon in Arizona. A subspecies of *C. berlandieri,* spp. *nuttalliae* was domesticated in Mexico. *Nuttalliae* belongs to the same subdivision of the genus *Chenopodium* that includes the South American domesticates *C. quinoa* and *C. pallidicaule.* Abnormally large *Chenopodium* seeds from dry rock shelters in the eastern United States have been suggested to be forms of local species or the introduced Mexican cultivar *C. nuttalliae.* Nancy and David Asch (1977) have, however, reexamined these collections together with a number of wild populations of *Chenopodium* spp. and conclude that most seeds belong to native species and fall within the expected size range for wild populations. Weedy species adapted to disturbed habitats show a great deal of phenotypic polymorphism and plasticity, often ignored in taxonomic studies. This variability was undoubtedly noted by prehistoric horticulturists, who intentionally selected large seeded types. This selectivity could easily produce shifts in the size ranges of plant populations associated with man.

Nonedible Seeds

Several types of nonedible seeds were recovered for which there is no ethnographic evidence for human consumption: *Argemone* sp., prickly poppy; members of the Euphorbiaceae, spurge family; Labiatae, mint family; Polygonaceae, buckwheat family; and Compositae, sunflower family. These plants contain alkaloids and other secondary compounds. Many are known to have medicinal properties and may, therefore, represent herbal medicines used by the inhabitants of Wind Mountain.

Environmental Changes during the Prehistoric Occupation

Early in the settlement of the area around the confluence of Whitewater Draw and Deadman Canyon (c. A.D. 325) population density was probably relatively low and there was little disruption of the local environment for agriculture. Subsistence included some maize agriculture, but depended heavily on wild foods. Dry farming was probably practiced which is suggested by the drought resistant maize (Onaveno and possibly an eight-rowed flint) that was grown.

During the middle of the site's occupation, the population presumably rose, and the introduction of at least three new types of maize (Pueblo Flour, Harinoso de Ocho, and Dent) implies an increasing emphasis on agriculture. Areas of the floodplain were probably cleared for farm fields, as suggested by the high proportion of cottonwood charcoal. These agricultural activities must have impacted the local environment, perhaps following the same pattern reported for the Mimbres Valley (Minnis 1978). The relatively poor recovery of material from flotation samples from the last components suggests that this occupation was comparatively short, probably, in part, due to the deterioration of the local environment for farming. This degradation may have been serious enough to cause abandonment of the Mangas drainage (Van Asdall et al. 1982).

Historic Changes in the Local Environment

Not until the introduction of cattle in the late 1800s was the local environment again as markedly impacted. Overgrazing caused dramatic increases in the variety of unpalatable shrubs (e.g., datura, rabbitbrush, snakeweed, burroweed, turpentine bush, buffalo gourd, and prickly pear). Texas mesquite, *Prosopis glandulosa,* which both produces edible pods and works as an efficient fuel, was observed in the area around the site. Because no mesquite remains were present in the Wind Mountain flotation sample, it must be assumed that it was not present in the pre-Hispanic flora of the Mangas drainage, but, as in many areas of the Southwest, was introduced alongside the expansion of cattle grazing.

Appendix 2

Palynology, Prehistoric Environment, and Plant Use at Wind Mountain

GERALD K. KELSO

The Wind Mountain and Ridout loci have been well sampled for pollen data. This analysis of the pollen samples was undertaken to recover information about the nature of the plants used by the site's inhabitants, the effect of environment on the economy of the occupation period, and the impact of human activities on the local vegetation.

Major Pollen Sources

The pollen spectra of archaeological sites contain at least two major components. One of these, the "ethnobotanical" component, is derived from plants imported by the former occupants and reflects active human selection of species among the local flora. The "background" or "environmental" pollen constitutes the second component. This pollen is derived from the natural vegetation, as well as from plants adapted to disturbed soils and inevitably attend the human presence. Environmental data and information about the human impact on native flora are derived from the latter component. These components may be statistically demonstrated (Fall et al. 1981) or empirically observed.

The Ethnobotanical Component

The ethnobotanical component consists of cultigens and wild or semicultivated plants. Corn, beans, and squash are the three most important plants grown by prehistoric Southwesterners. The pollen grains of each (*Zea mays, Phaseolus* spp., and *Cucurbita* spp.) are not widely dispersed by natural mechanisms and are generally easy to identify. Unlike other wind-pollinated plant species that produced vast quantities of pollen dispersed over wide areas (Erdtman 1969:63), corn pollen travels only short distances from point of origin (Martin 1963:50; Raynor et al. 1972:420). Common beans are self-pollinating, and squash is insect-pollinated. Both produce small amounts of pollen. The presence of a few pollen grains belonging to these cultigens, therefore, is significant and may suggest farming.

Many wild plants were also important for dietary, medicinal, or ritual purposes. If the pollen of low-producing, limited dispersing plants appears in the botanical record, their presence may indicate their use by prehistoric people. In contrast, if the pollen from widely distributed, abundant producers (a wind-pollinated plant) is found, it may be more difficult to assign conclusively a prehistoric use, even though ethnographic data shows that a number of wind-pollinated plants were important during the recent past.

The Background Component

The majority of pollen taxa comprising the background component consists of wind transported types, primarily trees. Of these, pine (*Pinus* spp.) is the most prominent arboreal pollen type represented in Southwestern pollen records. It has been employed as an indicator of environmental change. Martin (1963) relied on pine pollen frequencies to interpret post-Pleistocene alterations. Schoenwetter (1962, 1964) and Hevly (1964) emphasized the ratio of arboreal pollen (mostly pine) to nonarboreal pollen (mostly Chenopodiaceae to *Amaranthus* spp.) in archaeological sites. Schoenwetter (1970) also developed an effective moisture curve for the Colorado Plateau based on pine to Cheno-Am ratios. Tree pollen, especially pine, may be a good environmental indicator when recovered from natural deposits, but its value becomes problematical in cultural contexts subjected to human interference, including farming and land clearing.

Land Use versus Environment

Human land-use practices, particularly the result of agriculture, contribute greatly to the background pollen component. Pollen work in both Europe (Iversen 1941; Mitchell 1956; Hyde 1959) and North America (Butler 1959; M. B. Davis 1959; R. B. Davis 1967) demonstrates the proliferation of weedy plant pollen at the expense of tree pollen to be associated with agriculture. In the American Southwest, the occurrence of such pollen may also result from land clearance as sites were constructed.

Many of the weedy plants that favor disturbed soils, such as the low-spine Compositae or ragweeds and members of the Chenopodiaceae or goosefoot family, are prolific producers whose pollen disperses widely. The pollen of these plants occurs frequently in samples recovered from archaeological sites. An interesting pattern of arboreal versus weedy plant pollen emerges as weedy taxa are poorly represented in prehabitation strata, increase dramatically during occupation as cultural deposits are laid down, and decrease with site abandonment. In addition, pollen percentages of arboreal types (conspicuously pine) often form a mirror image of the weedy plant profile (Schoenwetter 1964: Figure 25). Martin and Byers (1965:133) first commented on this phenomenon in Pueblo III pollen counts from Mug House on Wetherill Mesa at Mesa Verde. They considered an environmental interpretation but preferred to attribute the postoccupational rise in arboreal pollen to be the result of secondary plant succession, that is, reforestation of abandoned site areas.

The disturbed soil plant versus arboreal pollen profile phenomenon also appears in Profile B at Grasshopper Ruin (c. A.D. 1300–1385), east-central Arizona. Here, the decline in the Cheno-Am pollen frequencies and the rise of arboreal pollen types began within 15 cm of the disappearance of potsherds from the profile that marked site abandonment (Kelso 1982:106). At Casas Grandes, Chihuahua, similar changes take place in the Reservoir 2 profile, coincident with the depth at which a change in sediment color marks abandonment of the site (Kelso in Di Peso et al. 1974:4:36). In the c. A.D. 850–900 profile from LA 3427, Navajo Reservoir region (Schoenwetter 1964:36), changes in the pine and Cheno-Am curves match precisely the cultural events of occupation and subsequent abandonment recorded in the fill.

The occurrence of the weedy plant versus arboreal pollen percentage curve in a number of Southwest sites widely separated by time and space supports Martin and Byers's (1965:133) original interpretation of a cultural, not environmental, cause and effect. The influence of prehistoric Southwestern populations on the plant communities growing near their settlements is clear.

Wind Mountain Pollen Analysis

One hundred twelve pollen samples taken from floors, fill profiles, vessels and milling stones at the Wind Mountain and Ridout loci were analyzed in the palynology laboratory of the Boston University Department of Archaeology. Following Adam and Mehringer (1975), a surface sample, composed of a series of subsamples taken in a transect across the Wind Mountain site, was examined for modern comparative data. Mehringer's (1967) mechanical/chemical extraction method was employed. Resulting pollen residues were mounted in glycerol. Two hundred pollen grains were initially tabulated for all samples. This first count was followed by a second count of 50 to 200 pollen grains, depending upon the pollen concentration in individual samples. Cheno-Ams were excluded from this second count in order to clarify the relative contributions of other, less abundant types.

Pollen was identified with a compound transmitted-light microscope at 430x. Problematical pollen grains and all pine pollen grains were examined under oil immersion at 970x. Identification of pollen types is based on comparison with the laboratory's pollen reference collection. The numbers of grains too badly eroded to be identified were recorded to aid in assessing degree of pollen preservation; they were not incorporated in pollen sums. Terminology follows Mehringer (1967).

Specific raw pollen taxa identifications and frequencies derived from the modern surface correlated with stratified profiles (Appendix 2: Table 1), from domestic Type I, II, and III houses (Appendix 2: Table 2), from domestic Type IV houses (Appendix 2: Table 3), from Type V surface rooms (Appendix 2: Table 4), from community structures (Appendix 2: Table 5), and from secondary architectural features and burial associations (Appendix 2: Table 6) are presented following the discussion.

Results of the Pollen Analysis

Pollen recovered from the Wind Mountain and Ridout loci is somewhat degraded. Due to the presence of massive quantities of Cheno-Am pollen in most modern samples, all but a few first counts exceed 2,000 grains per gram—a normal condition in exposed Southwestern archaeological sites. Pollen types other than Cheno-Ams are, however, present in small quantities. In contrast, only four of 112 prehistoric samples contained 2,000 or more non-Cheno-Am pollen grains per gram. Floor counts were as low as 82 pollen grains per gram, while profile counts were as low as 62 grains per gram. These counts are undoubtedly distorted by the destruction of more fragile types, and any interpretation of such samples must be approached with caution due to the small quantities of observable pollen. Special care must be

Appendix 2: Table 1. Taxa and Frequencies Representing the Modern Wind Mountain Pollen Rain Correlated with Stratified Pollen Profiles from Wind Mountain Locus House X and Ridout Locus House F

																		Compositae								Cactaceae							
Provenience	*Pinus*	*Pseudotsuga*	*Juniperus*	*Quercus*	*Populus*	*Prosopis*	*Juglans*	*Salix*	*Alnus*	*Tamarix*	*Fraxinus*	*Celtis*	*Acacia*	*Mimosa*	Cheno-Ams	*Sarcobatus*	*Tidestromia*	*Artemisia*	Low-Spines	High-Spines	Liguliflorae	*Cirsium*	Gramineae	*Zea mays*	*Cucurbita*	*Cereus*-type	Cylindropuntia	Platyopuntia	Liliaceae	Umbelliferae	Cruciferae	Caryopyllaceae	Ranunculaceae
Modern Surface Transect	19	–	24	27	5	7	1	–	1	–	–	1	2	–	80	–	–	2	68	6	–	–	8	–	–	–	–	3	–	1	1	–	–
WM House X																																	
.00 - .04m	9	–	26	8	–	1	1	–	–	–	–	–	–	–	145	–	1	7	68	8	–	2	23	–	–	–	–	–	–	1	1	–	–
.09 - .14m	5	–	8	1	–	–	–	–	–	–	–	–	–	–	169	–	–	7	50	3	–	–	4	–	–	–	–	–	–	1	–	–	–
.19 - .24m	4	–	6	4	–	–	–	3	–	–	–	–	–	–	175	–	–	7	44	–	–	–	6	–	–	–	3	–	–	2	1	–	–
.29 - .34m	1	–	2	3	1	–	–	–	–	–	–	–	–	–	173	–	–	6	55	5	–	–	5	–	–	1	–	–	–	–	–	–	–
.39 - .44m	3	–	7	9	–	–	–	–	–	–	–	–	–	–	337	–	–	13	174	13	2	–	14	1	–	–	2	–	–	1	2	–	–
.49 - .54m	1	–	4	5	–	–	–	–	–	–	–	–	–	–	181	–	–	6	40	5	–	–	4	1	–	–	–	5	–	5	–	–	–
.59 - .64m	2	–	4	1	–	–	–	–	–	–	–	–	–	–	172	–	–	4	44	2	1	–	8	3	–	–	–	6	–	2	–	–	–
.69 - .74m	1	–	5	5	–	–	–	–	–	–	–	–	–	–	185	–	–	4	47	2	–	–	6	2	–	–	–	2	–	1	–	–	1
.79 - .84m	1	–	2	–	–	–	–	–	–	–	–	–	–	–	193	–	–	3	63	1	–	–	3	2	–	–	3	4	–	2	–	–	–
.89 - .94m	2	–	1	2	–	–	–	–	–	–	–	–	–	–	195	–	–	5	61	1	3	–	3	1	–	–	–	10	–	1	–	–	–
.99 - 1.04m	3	–	6	3	–	–	–	–	–	–	–	–	–	–	187	–	–	7	56	–	–	1	8	–	–	–	–	2	–	–	–	–	–
1.09 - 1.14m	6	–	1	4	–	–	1	–	–	–	–	–	–	–	181	–	–	9	45	3	–	–	4	–	–	1	–	5	–	–	–	–	–
1.19 - 1.24m	7	–	4	3	–	–	–	–	–	–	–	–	–	–	169	–	–	3	39	2	–	–	11	6	–	–	–	4	–	–	2	–	–
1.29 - 1.34m	4	–	–	3	–	–	–	–	–	–	–	–	–	–	144	–	–	12	44	1	–	–	10	4	–	–	–	7	–	1	–	–	–
1.39 - 1.44m	4	–	5	6	–	–	–	–	–	–	–	–	–	–	163	–	–	13	29	3	–	–	12	5	–	1	–	–	–	3	–	–	–
Floor																																	
West ½ of Floor	11	–	1	3	1	–	–	–	–	–	–	–	–	–	156	–	–	10	33	4	–	–	10	4	–	–	–	1	–	2	–	–	–
RO House F																																	
.00 - .10m	2	–	29	4	–	3	–	–	–	5	–	–	–	–	161	–	–	12	100	5	2	–	11	–	–	2	–	–	–	2	–	–	–
.11 - .20m	6	–	26	9	1	–	2	–	–	–	–	–	–	–	83	–	–	6	91	8	–	–	25	–	–	–	1	–	–	–	–	–	–
.21 - .30m	7	–	21	18	3	–	1	–	–	–	–	–	–	–	104	1	1	2	102	11	–	–	4	–	–	–	2	–	–	–	–	–	–
.31 - .40m	7	–	25	11	–	–	–	–	–	–	–	–	–	–	114	–	–	5	101	12	–	–	9	–	–	–	–	–	–	–	–	–	–
.41 - .50m	–	–	9	3	–	–	1	–	–	–	–	–	–	–	167	–	–	1	52	5	–	–	5	–	–	–	–	–	–	1	–	–	–
.51 - .60m	2	–	–	1	–	–	–	–	–	–	–	–	–	–	189	–	1	1	36	–	–	–	3	–	–	–	–	–	–	–	–	–	–
.61 - .70m	–	–	9	2	–	–	–	–	–	–	–	–	–	–	180	–	–	10	123	4	–	–	12	5	–	–	1	–	–	–	–	–	–
.71 - .80m	–	–	–	3	–	–	–	–	–	–	–	–	–	–	191	–	–	3	24	2	–	–	3	3	–	–	1	–	–	–	–	–	–
.81 - .90m	1	–	–	3	–	–	–	–	–	–	–	–	–	–	178	–	–	5	60	3	–	–	10	6	–	–	–	–	–	–	–	–	–
.91 - 1.00m	2	–	2	2	–	–	–	–	–	–	–	–	–	–	170	–	–	10	39	9	–	–	13	3	–	–	–	–	–	–	–	–	–
1.01 - 1.10m	–	–	1	–	–	–	–	–	–	–	–	–	–	–	175	–	–	11	15	3	–	–	–	3	–	–	–	–	–	1	–	–	–
Floor																																	

APPENDIX 2: TABLE 1. *(continued)*

Provenience	Convolvulaceae	Leguminosae	Nyctaginacae	Malvaceae	Rosaceae	Onagraceae	Solanaceae	Saxifragaceae	Labiatae	Rutaceae	Martyniaceae	*Polygonum Periscoria*-type	*Eriogonum*	*Cleome*	*Plantago*	*Euphorbia*	*Rhamnus*	*Kallstromia*	*Ribes*	*Polygala*	*Gilia*	*Berberis*	*Ephedra* *Nevadensis*-type	*Ephedra* *Torreyana*-type	Cyperaceae	*Typha*-monads	Undetermined	Undeterminable	Raw Sum-1st Count	Raw Sum-2nd Count	Influx per Gram 1st Count	Influx per Gram 2nd Count	*Pinus* Sub-Genus Haploxlon	*Pinus* Sub-Genus Diploxlon	*Pinus* Sub-Genus Undetermined
Modern Surface Transect	–	2	–	–	1	–	1	–	–	–	–	–	3	–	–	7	–	–	–	–	–	–	–	–	–	–	10	4	200	200	6,395	3,029	17	2	1
WM House X																																			
.00 - .04m	–	13	–	–	2	–	2	–	–	–	–	–	1	–	–	1	–	–	–	–	–	–	–	1	2	–	20	61	200	200	8,106	2,432	4	1	4
.09 - .14m	–	10	–	–	1	–	–	–	–	–	–	–	–	–	1	1	–	–	–	–	–	–	–	–	1	–	7	26	200	100	22,930	2,639	1	2	2
.19 - .24m	–	6	–	–	–	–	1	–	–	–	–	–	–	2	–	–	–	–	–	–	–	–	–	1	–	–	10	46	200	100	12,128	1,271	3	–	1
.29 - .34m	–	8	–	1	–	–	1	–	–	–	–	–	–	1	–	–	–	–	–	–	–	–	–	–	1	–	9	25	200	100	30,157	2,512	–	1	–
.39 - .44m	–	18	–	1	2	–	1	–	–	–	–	–	2	–	–	2	–	–	–	–	–	–	–	1	–	–	33	67	400	300	12,579	1,255	–	–	3
.49 - .54m	–	6	–	–	1	–	–	–	–	–	–	–	–	–	–	–	–	–	–	–	–	–	1	1	–	–	15	24	200	100	21,216	1,375	1	–	–
.59 - .64m	–	6	–	–	1	–	–	–	–	–	–	–	–	1	1	–	–	–	–	–	–	–	–	1	–	–	13	31	200	100	16,534	1,210	–	2	–
.69 - .74m	–	4	–	–	1	–	–	–	–	–	–	–	1	–	–	1	–	–	–	–	–	–	–	–	–	–	17	25	200	100	11,325	2,535	–	1	–
.79 - .84m	–	4	–	–	–	–	–	–	–	–	–	–	–	1	–	2	–	–	–	–	–	–	–	–	–	–	9	36	200	100	27,747	570	1	–	–
.89 - .94m	–	3	–	–	–	–	–	–	–	–	–	–	–	–	–	–	–	–	–	–	–	–	–	–	–	–	7	20	200	100	12,128	515	1	–	1
.99 - 1.04m	–	2	–	–	1	–	–	–	–	–	–	–	–	–	–	1	–	–	–	–	–	–	–	–	1	–	8	24	200	100	4,637	178	1	1	1
1.09 - 1.14m	–	4	–	–	2	–	–	–	–	–	–	–	–	–	–	–	–	–	–	–	–	–	–	–	–	–	15	38	200	100	2,494	185	3	–	3
1.19 - 1.24m	–	6	–	–	–	–	–	–	–	–	–	–	–	1	–	1	–	–	–	–	–	–	–	–	–	–	11	52	200	100	1,545	400	2	3	2
1.29 - 1.34m	–	3	–	2	–	–	–	–	–	–	–	–	–	1	–	–	–	–	–	–	–	–	–	–	–	–	8	65	200	100	990	264	1	2	1
1.39 - 1.44m Floor	–	5	–	1	–	–	–	–	–	–	–	–	–	–	–	–	–	–	–	–	–	–	–	1	–	–	12	87	200	100	574	88	3	–	1
West ½ of Floor	–	1	–	1	2	–	–	–	–	–	–	1	–	–	4	–	–	–	–	–	–	–	–	1	1	–	9	55	200	100	1,311	347	5	4	2
RO House F																																			
.00 - .10m	–	2	–	–	–	–	4	–	–	–	1	1	–	–	–	–	–	–	–	–	–	–	–	1	–	–	16	71	200	200	7,238	1,185	–	1	1
.11 - .20m	–	9	–	1	–	–	1	–	–	–	–	2	–	–	2	–	–	–	–	–	–	–	–	–	1	–	10	40	200	200	3,865	2,241	1	3	2
.21 - .30m	–	7	–	–	3	1	2	–	–	–	2	2	–	–	–	–	–	–	–	–	–	–	–	–	–	–	10	59	200	200	4,181	1,472	4	3	–
.31 - .40m	–	3	–	–	4	–	1	–	–	–	2	2	–	–	1	–	–	–	–	–	–	–	–	2	1	–	14	64	200	200	2,885	784	5	2	–
.41 - .50m	–	5	–	1	1	–	1	–	–	–	–	–	–	–	1	–	–	–	–	–	–	–	–	2	–	–	12	60	200	100	4,714	803	–	–	–
.51 - .60m	–	–	–	–	–	–	1	–	–	–	–	–	1	–	–	–	–	–	–	–	–	–	–	–	–	–	4	45	200	50	914	62	2	–	–
.61 - .70m	–	7	–	1	2	–	–	–	–	–	–	–	1	–	1	–	–	–	–	–	–	–	–	1	–	–	21	33	200	200	6,418	752	–	–	–
.71 - .80m	–	–	–	–	–	–	3	–	–	–	–	3	1	–	–	–	–	–	–	–	–	–	–	1	–	–	3	40	200	50	11,713	694	–	–	–
.81 - .90m	–	5	–	–	–	1	–	–	–	–	–	–	–	–	–	–	–	–	–	–	–	–	–	–	–	–	6	48	200	100	14,733	766	1	–	–
.91 - 1.00m	–	4	–	1	2	–	–	–	–	–	–	–	–	–	–	–	–	–	–	–	–	–	–	–	–	–	13	43	200	100	12,303	1,137	–	2	1
1.01 - 1.10m Floor	–	4	–	–	–	–	2	–	–	–	–	–	3	–	–	–	–	–	–	–	–	–	–	–	–	–	7	48	200	50	10,971	824	–	–	–

APPENDIX 2: TABLE 2. Pollen Taxa and Frequencies Derived from Type I, II, and III House Floors and Associated Vessels

	Provenience																			Compositae								Cactaceae									
Type	House	Context	*Pinus*	*Pseudotsuga*	*Juniperus*	*Quercus*	*Populus*	*Prosopis*	*Juglans*	*Salix*	*Alnus*	*Tamarix*	*Fraxinus*	*Celtis*	*Acacia*	*Mimosa*	Cheno-Ams	*Sarcobatus*	*Tidestromia*	*Artemisia*	Low-Spines	High-Spines	Liguliflorae	*Cirsium*	Gramineae	*Zea mays*	*Cucurbita*	*Cereus*-type	Cylindropuntia	Platyopuntia	Liliaceae	Umbelliferae	Cruciferae	Caryopyllaceae	Ranunculaceae	Convolvulaceae	Leguminosae
I	WM-GG	Floor	1	–	1	1	–	–	–	–	–	–	–	–	3	–	179	–	–	18	46	3	–	–	8	–	–	–	–	–	–	–	1	–	–	–	2
I	WM-HH	Floor	2	–	2	5	–	–	–	–	–	–	–	–	2	–	182	–	–	6	48	–	1	–	1	6	–	–	–	9	–	–	–	–	–	–	5
I	WM-II	Floor	5	–	5	9	–	–	–	–	–	–	–	–	–	–	184	–	–	10	46	1	–	–	6	1	–	–	–	3	–	–	–	–	–	–	8
I	WM-JJ	Floor	2	–	1	5	–	–	–	–	–	–	–	–	1	–	184	–	–	14	41	2	–	–	6	3	–	–	1	–	–	–	–	–	–	–	6
I	WM-LL	Floor	6	–	2	2	–	–	–	–	–	–	–	–	–	–	182	–	–	2	55	1	1	2	7	1	–	–	–	4	–	2	1	–	–	–	4
I	RO-E	Floor	1	–	1	–	–	–	–	–	–	–	–	–	–	–	175	–	–	14	13	57	–	–	6	–	–	–	2	–	–	–	–	–	–	–	2
I	RO-I	White plaster	–	–	–	–	–	–	–	–	–	–	–	–	–	–	–	–	–	–	–	–	–	–	–	–	–	–	–	–	–	–	–	–	–	–	–
II	WM-Q	Floor	3	–	–	3	–	–	–	–	–	–	–	–	1	–	137	–	–	5	29	1	–	–	6	40	–	–	–	3	–	3	–	–	–	–	–
II	WM-R	Floor	4	–	2	5	–	–	–	–	–	–	–	–	–	–	182	–	–	6	39	1	–	–	6	10	–	–	–	7	–	–	–	–	1	–	3
II	WM-S	Floor	7	–	2	1	–	–	–	–	–	–	–	–	–	–	186	–	–	2	7	1	–	–	9	4	–	–	–	5	–	–	–	–	–	–	2
II	WM-T	Floor	4	–	1	2	–	–	–	–	–	–	–	–	–	–	102	–	–	13	14	3	–	–	5	43	–	–	–	4	–	–	–	–	–	–	–
II	WM-QQ	Floor	2	–	3	–	1	–	–	–	–	–	–	–	–	–	185	–	–	9	31	6	1	–	4	2	–	–	–	26	–	–	–	–	–	–	3
II	WM-RR	Floor	3	–	–	1	–	–	–	–	–	–	–	–	–	–	179	–	–	11	47	–	1	–	12	6	–	–	–	4	–	3	–	–	–	–	2
III	WM-WW	Vessel 1	2	–	2	1	–	–	–	–	–	–	–	–	–	–	180	–	–	1	24	–	–	–	4	2	–	–	–	2	–	1	–	–	–	–	3
III	WM-WW	Vessel 2	–	–	–	–	–	–	–	–	–	–	–	–	–	–	175	–	–	1	28	2	–	–	–	–	2	–	–	–	–	–	–	–	–	–	–
III	WM-WW	Vessel 10	4	–	–	1	–	–	–	–	–	–	–	–	2	–	191	–	–	–	20	–	1	–	2	4	–	–	–	12	–	–	–	–	–	–	–
III	WM-WW	Vessel 11	162	1	–	–	–	–	–	–	–	–	–	–	–	–	111	–	–	6	29	8	–	–	2	5	–	–	–	7	–	–	–	–	–	–	–
III	WM-WW	Vessel 13	1	–	–	1	–	–	–	–	–	–	–	–	–	–	180	–	–	–	20	2	–	–	4	10	–	–	–	5	–	1	–	–	1	–	–
III	WM-WW	Floor	2	–	1	1	1	–	–	–	–	–	–	–	–	–	175	–	–	1	46	1	–	–	2	15	–	–	–	9	–	1	–	–	–	–	8

Appendix 2: Table 2. *(continued)*

Provenience																							*Ephedra*										*Pinus* Sub-Genus		
Type	House	Context	Nyctaginaceae	Malvaceae	Rosaceae	Onagraceae	Solanaceae	Saxifragaceae	Labiatae	Rutaceae	Martyniaceae	*Polygonum Periscoria*-type	*Eriogonum*	*Cleome*	*Plantago*	*Euphorbia*	*Rhamnus*	*Kallstromia*	*Ribes*	*Polygala*	*Gilia*	*Berberis*	*Nevadensis*-type	*Torreyana*-type	Cyperaceae	*Typha*-monads	Undetermined	Undeterminable	Raw Sum-1st Count	Raw Sum-2nd Count	Influx per Gram 1st Count	Influx per Gram 2nd Count	Haploxlon	Diploxlon	Undetermined
I	WM-GG	Floor	–	–	1	–	–	–	–	–	–	–	–	–	–	–	–	–	–	–	–	–	–	1	–	–	12	44	200	100	8,542	1,045	–	–	1
I	WM-HH	Floor	–	1	1	–	2	–	–	–	–	–	–	–	–	–	–	–	–	–	–	–	1	1	–	–	7	21	200	100	17,647	621	2	–	–
I	WM-II	Floor	–	–	–	–	–	–	–	–	–	–	–	–	–	1	–	–	–	–	–	–	–	–	–	–	5	31	200	100	11,514	728	2	1	2
I	WM-JJ	Floor	–	–	1	–	2	–	–	–	–	–	–	–	–	–	–	–	–	–	–	–	–	1	1	1	12	32	200	100	19,908	1,025	2	–	–
I	WM-LL	Floor	–	–	1	–	–	–	–	–	–	–	–	1	–	–	–	–	–	–	–	–	–	2	–	–	6	37	200	100	72,267	937	4	–	2
I	RO-E	Floor	–	–	9	–	–	–	–	–	–	–	1	–	–	–	–	–	–	–	–	–	–	–	–	–	1	1	200	116	622	97	–	–	1
I	RO-I	White plaster	–	–	–	–	–	–	–	–	–	–	–	–	–	–	–	–	–	–	–	–	–	–	–	–	–	–	–	–	–	–	–	–	–
II	WM-Q	Floor	–	1	–	–	–	–	–	–	1	–	–	–	1	–	–	–	–	–	–	–	–	–	1	–	3	85	200	100	1,231	324	2	–	1
II	WM-R	Floor	–	–	1	1	–	–	–	–	–	–	1	2	–	–	–	–	–	–	–	–	–	1	3	–	7	51	200	100	3,392	253	2	1	1
II	WM-S	Floor	1	–	–	–	–	–	–	–	–	–	–	–	–	–	–	–	–	–	–	–	–	–	–	–	9	46	200	50	3,912	215	7	–	–
II	WM-T	Floor	–	–	2	–	–	–	–	–	–	–	–	1	1	–	–	–	–	–	–	–	1	–	–	–	6	30	200	100	645	315	2	–	2
II	WM-QQ	Floor	1	–	–	–	–	–	–	–	–	–	–	–	–	2	–	–	–	–	–	–	–	–	–	–	9	16	200	100	27,174	1,842	2	–	–
II	WM-RR	Floor	–	–	–	–	1	–	–	–	–	–	–	–	–	–	–	–	–	–	–	–	–	–	2	–	7	19	200	100	25,161	249	3	–	–
III	WM-WW	Vessel 1	–	–	3	–	–	–	–	–	–	–	–	–	–	–	–	–	–	–	–	–	–	–	–	–	5	37	200	50	–	–	1	–	1
III	WM-WW	Vessel 2	–	–	2	–	–	–	–	–	–	–	–	–	–	–	–	–	1	–	–	–	–	–	1	–	13	38	200	50	–	–	–	–	–
III	WM-WW	Vessel 10	–	–	–	–	–	–	–	–	–	1	–	–	–	–	–	–	–	–	–	–	–	–	–	–	3	27	200	50	–	–	2	–	2
III	WM-WW	Vessel 11	–	–	44	1	–	–	–	–	–	–	–	–	–	–	–	–	–	–	–	–	–	–	–	–	3	12	200	268	–	–	1	130	32
III	WM-WW	Vessel 13	–	–	–	–	–	–	–	–	–	–	–	–	–	–	–	–	–	–	–	–	–	–	–	–	4	51	200	51	–	–	–	–	1
III	WM-WW	Floor	–	–	2	–	–	–	–	–	–	–	1	–	–	2	–	–	–	–	–	–	–	–	–	–	7	16	200	100	5,805	123	2	–	–

Appendix 2: Table 3. Pollen Taxa and Frequencies Derived from Type IV House floors, Associated Features, and Artifacts

Provenience																			Compositae								Cactaceae									
House	Context	*Pinus*	*Pseudotsuga*	*Juniperus*	*Quercus*	*Populus*	*Prosopis*	*Juglans*	*Salix*	*Alnus*	*Tamarix*	*Fraxinus*	*Celtis*	*Acacia*	*Mimosa*	Cheno-Ams	*Sarcobatus*	*Tidestromia*	*Artemisia*	Low-Spines	High-Spines	Liguliflorae	*Cirsium*	Gramineae	*Zea mays*	*Cucurbita*	*Cereus*-type	Cylindropuntia	Platyopuntia	Liliaceae	Umbelliferae	Cruciferae	Caryopyllaceae	Ranunculaceae	Convolvulaceae	Leguminosae
WM-A	Vessel	2	–	1	–	–	–	–	–	–	–	–	–	–	–	154	–	–	1	16	1	–	–	5	17	–	–	2	–	–	–	–	–	–	–	1
WM-B	Floor	5	–	4	2	–	–	–	–	–	–	–	–	–	–	183	–	–	1	47	5	–	–	8	2	–	–	–	1	–	1	–	–	–	–	7
WM-B	Metate	2	–	3	2	–	–	–	–	–	–	–	–	–	–	174	–	–	2	44	3	1	–	10	5	–	–	–	–	–	1	–	–	1	–	6
WM-C	Floor	1	–	3	–	–	–	–	–	–	–	–	–	–	–	176	–	–	11	44	3	–	–	10	1	–	–	–	3	–	2	–	–	–	–	4
WM-D	Floor	4	–	3	1	–	–	–	–	–	–	–	–	–	–	178	–	–	2	43	–	–	–	10	–	1	–	1	3	–	12	–	–	–	–	9
WM-E	Floor	12	–	7	3	–	–	–	–	1	–	–	–	–	–	167	–	–	4	110	6	–	–	15	1	–	–	–	3	–	1	–	–	–	–	8
WM-G	Floor	5	–	1	–	–	–	–	–	–	–	–	–	–	–	185	–	–	5	42	1	–	–	5	6	–	–	6	12	–	3	–	–	–	–	4
WM-H	Floor	2	–	2	5	–	–	–	–	–	–	–	–	–	–	180	–	–	5	41	–	–	–	14	10	–	–	–	8	–	–	–	–	–	–	3
WM-J	Floor	6	–	3	4	1	–	–	–	–	–	–	–	–	–	189	–	–	8	45	5	–	1	3	3	1	–	–	2	–	2	–	–	–	–	4
WM-K	Metate 9	4	–	1	2	–	–	–	–	–	–	–	1	–	–	176	1	–	2	27	3	1	–	10	2	–	–	–	4	–	–	–	–	–	–	2
WM-K	Floor	6	–	4	3	–	–	–	–	–	–	–	–	–	–	189	–	–	3	34	6	–	–	12	8	–	–	–	3	–	2	–	–	–	–	4
WM-L	Floor	5	–	4	3	–	–	–	–	–	–	–	–	–	–	182	–	–	2	47	2	–	–	7	–	–	–	–	6	–	2	–	–	–	–	8
WM-N	Floor	1	–	1	2	–	–	–	–	1	–	–	–	–	–	195	–	–	3	50	2	–	–	5	–	–	–	–	11	–	1	–	–	–	–	6
WM-W	Floor	1	–	1	–	–	–	–	–	–	–	–	–	2	–	168	–	–	4	53	3	–	–	8	3	–	–	–	4	–	–	–	–	–	–	2
WM-Z	Floor	1	–	4	3	–	–	–	2	–	–	–	–	–	–	182	–	–	5	58	3	–	–	5	–	–	–	–	3	–	2	–	–	–	–	5
WM-AA	Floor	18	–	2	2	–	–	–	–	–	–	–	–	–	–	165	–	–	5	36	1	–	–	3	9	–	–	–	8	–	–	–	–	1	–	2
WM-BB	Floor	4	–	–	2	–	–	–	–	–	–	–	–	–	–	179	–	–	3	62	10	–	–	4	2	–	–	–	3	–	1	–	–	–	–	4
WM-DD	Floor	3	–	5	6	–	–	–	–	–	–	–	–	–	–	177	–	–	8	32	1	–	–	17	3	–	–	–	5	–	–	–	–	–	–	6
WM-OO	Floor	3	–	1	2	–	–	1	–	–	–	–	–	–	–	192	–	–	7	58	1	–	–	3	2	–	–	–	4	–	2	–	–	–	–	5
WM-PP	Vessel 1 in Floor Pit 3	14	–	–	–	–	–	–	–	–	–	–	–	–	–	4	–	–	2	2	–	–	–	5	61	1	–	–	2	–	–	–	–	–	–	1
WM-PP	Floor	19	–	–	2	–	–	1	–	–	–	–	–	–	–	190	–	–	10	29	5	–	–	3	12	–	–	–	8	–	–	–	–	–	–	2
WM-SS	Floor	21	–	2	2	–	–	–	–	–	–	–	–	–	–	157	–	–	7	14	3	–	–	12	15	–	–	–	9	–	1	–	–	–	–	3
WM-TT	Floor	4	–	–	6	–	–	–	–	–	–	–	–	–	–	184	–	–	1	54	3	1	–	8	1	–	–	–	–	–	2	–	–	–	–	–
WM-UU	Floor	1	–	–	4	–	–	–	–	–	–	–	–	–	–	181	–	–	5	53	2	–	–	6	2	–	–	–	–	–	2	–	–	–	–	12
WM-UU	Vessel in SE Quad	–	–	2	–	3	–	–	–	–	–	–	–	–	–	174	–	–	5	15	18	–	–	4	–	–	–	–	18	–	–	–	–	–	–	2
WM-VV	Floor	4	–	–	3	–	–	–	–	–	–	–	–	1	–	183	–	–	7	35	7	1	–	8	6	–	–	2	6	–	4	–	–	–	–	6
WM-AD	Vessel 1, floor	–	–	–	–	–	–	–	–	–	–	–	–	–	–	80	–	–	6	5	10	–	–	1	4	–	–	–	–	–	–	–	–	–	–	3
WM-AE	Vessel in Feature 1	5	–	2	–	–	–	–	–	–	–	–	–	–	–	178	–	–	3	9	2	1	–	4	15	–	–	2	–	–	–	–	–	–	–	2
WM-AI	Vessel 3, floor	2	–	–	3	–	–	–	–	–	–	–	–	–	–	177	–	–	1	14	4	–	–	3	3	–	–	–	5	–	–	–	1	–	–	1
WM-AI	Vessel 4, floor	3	–	2	–	–	–	–	–	–	–	–	–	–	–	136	–	–	4	10	15	–	–	6	9	–	3	1	–	–	–	1	–	–	1	13
RO-C	Floor, under Artifact No. 10	4	–	–	–	–	–	–	–	–	–	–	–	–	–	183	–	–	24	42	18	–	–	19	–	–	–	–	4	–	4	–	–	3	–	4
RO-C	Floor, under Metate No. 29	7	–	14	2	–	–	–	–	–	–	–	1	–	–	151	–	–	9	85	14	–	–	17	2	–	–	–	5	–	6	–	–	–	–	7
RO-C	Floor, NE corner	9	–	14	1	–	–	1	–	–	–	–	–	–	–	147	–	–	19	61	5	1	–	21	1	–	–	–	1	–	–	–	–	–	–	4
RO-D	Floor	7	–	6	3	1	–	–	–	–	–	–	–	–	–	121	–	–	8	93	29	1	–	5	–	–	–	–	1	–	1	–	–	1	–	16
RO-E	Floor	1	–	1	–	–	–	–	–	–	–	–	–	–	–	175	–	–	14	13	57	–	–	6	–	–	–	2	–	–	–	–	–	–	–	2
RO-H	Floor, SW corner	4	–	–	–	–	–	–	–	–	–	–	–	–	–	179	–	–	82	40	68	1	–	6	–	–	–	–	–	–	–	–	–	–	–	7
RO-K	Floor, under Metate No. 5	–	–	1	2	–	–	–	1	–	–	–	–	–	–	168	–	–	3	63	11	–	–	3	–	–	–	–	1	–	3	–	–	–	–	1
RO-K	Floor, SW corner	4	–	3	3	–	–	–	–	–	–	–	–	–	–	179	–	–	8	85	10	–	–	15	4	–	–	–	10	–	1	1	–	–	–	10

APPENDIX 2: TABLE 3. *(continued)*

Provenience																						*Ephedra*										*Pinus* Sub-Genus		
House	Context	Nyctaginaceae	Malvaceae	Rosaceae	Onagraceae	Solanaceae	Saxifragaceae	Labiatae	Rutaceae	Martyniaceae	*Polygonum Periscoria*-type	*Eriogonum*	*Cleome*	*Plantago*	*Euphorbia*	*Rhamnus*	*Kallstromia*	*Ribes*	*Polygala*	*Gilia*	*Berberis*	*Nevadensis*-type	*Torreyana*-type	Cyperaceae	*Typha*-monads	Undetermined	Undeterminable	Raw Sum-1st Count	Raw Sum-2nd Count	Influx per Gram 1st Count	Influx per Gram 2nd Count	Haploxlon	Diploxlon	Undetermined
WM-A	Vessel	–	–	1	–	–	–	–	–	–	–	–	2	–	–	–	–	–	–	–	–	–	1	–	–	1	40	200	50	13,739	3,135	1	–	1
WM-B	Floor	–	–	1	–	2	–	–	–	–	–	–	9	–	–	–	–	–	–	–	–	–	–	–	–	5	27	200	100	7,836	533	2	2	1
WM-B	Metate	–	–	2	–	–	–	–	–	–	–	2	6	–	–	–	–	–	–	–	–	–	1	3	–	6	40	200	100	–	–	2	–	–
WM-C	Floor	–	–	4	–	–	–	–	–	–	–	–	–	–	–	–	–	–	–	–	–	–	1	–	–	13	13	200	100	14,168	1,123	1	–	–
WM-D	Floor	–	–	–	–	1	–	–	–	–	–	–	4	–	–	–	–	–	–	–	–	–	–	–	–	11	47	200	105	12,019	654	–	4	–
WM-E	Floor	–	–	4	–	–	–	–	–	–	–	–	4	–	–	–	–	–	–	–	–	–	–	1	–	20	19	200	200	6,741	732	8	–	4
WM-G	Floor	–	–	–	–	4	–	–	–	–	–	–	3	–	–	–	–	–	–	–	–	–	–	–	–	3	25	200	100	4,348	589	3	1	1
WM-H	Floor	–	–	2	–	2	–	–	–	–	–	–	–	–	–	–	1	–	–	–	–	–	–	–	–	5	50	200	100	4,166	317	–	1	1
WM-J	Floor	–	–	3	–	–	–	–	–	–	–	–	2	–	–	–	–	–	–	–	–	–	3	–	–	4	29	200	100	11,081	611	4	1	1
WM-K	Metate 9	–	–	28	–	8	–	–	–	–	–	–	–	–	–	–	–	–	–	–	–	–	–	2	–	2	23	200	100	2,888	424	3	1	–
WM-K	Floor	–	–	–	–	–	1	–	–	–	–	1	2	–	–	–	–	–	–	–	–	–	1	2	–	8	56	200	100	3,850	309	2	4	–
WM-L	Floor	–	–	3	–	3	–	–	–	–	–	–	2	–	–	–	–	–	–	–	–	1	–	–	–	10	59	200	105	14,985	692	3	1	1
WM-N	Floor	–	–	1	–	–	–	–	–	–	–	1	2	–	–	–	–	–	–	–	–	–	–	–	–	13	25	200	100	25,252	628	–	1	–
WM-W	Floor	–	–	1	–	–	–	–	–	–	–	–	1	3	1	–	–	–	–	–	–	–	–	2	–	12	22	200	100	2,379	397	–	–	1
WM-Z	Floor	–	–	1	–	1	–	–	–	–	–	–	–	–	–	–	–	–	–	–	–	–	–	–	–	7	22	200	100	9,191	919	–	–	1
WM-AA	Floor	–	–	1	2	1	–	–	1	–	–	–	–	–	–	–	–	–	–	–	–	–	1	–	–	7	21	200	100	3,010	469	7	8	3
WM-BB	Floor	–	–	1	–	1	–	–	–	–	–	–	–	–	–	–	–	–	–	–	–	–	–	–	–	3	28	200	111	2,116	280	2	–	2
WM-DD	Floor	–	–	4	–	–	–	–	–	–	–	–	–	–	6	–	–	–	–	–	–	–	–	–	–	4	30	200	100	33,898	1,033	1	–	2
WM-OO	Floor	–	–	–	–	–	–	–	–	–	–	–	–	–	1	–	–	–	–	–	–	1	–	–	–	9	20	200	100	14,620	657	2	–	1
WM-PP	Vessel 1 in Floor Pit 3	–	–	3	–	–	–	–	–	–	–	–	–	–	–	–	–	–	–	–	5	–	–	3	–	1	14	100	100	185	180	4	6	4
WM-PP	Floor	–	–	–	1	–	–	–	–	–	–	–	–	–	–	–	–	–	–	–	–	–	1	–	–	7	28	200	100	1,513	477	14	4	1
WM-SS	Floor	–	2	1	–	–	–	1	–	–	–	–	–	–	–	–	–	–	–	–	–	–	–	4	–	3	5	200	100	999	268	17	–	4
WM-TT	Floor	–	1	1	–	1	–	–	–	–	–	–	2	–	–	–	–	–	–	–	–	–	–	1	–	14	40	200	100	10,480	82	3	–	–
WM-UU	Floor	–	–	–	–	–	–	–	–	–	–	–	2	–	1	–	–	–	–	–	–	–	–	–	–	9	20	200	100	16,234	108	–	1	–
WM-UU	Vessel in SE Quad	–	1	–	–	–	–	–	–	–	–	2	–	–	2	–	–	–	–	–	–	–	–	–	–	3	3	200	78	–	–	–	–	–
WM-VV	Floor	–	–	1	–	–	–	–	–	–	–	–	1	–	–	–	–	–	–	–	–	–	–	2	–	6	17	200	100	5,594	380	2	1	1
WM-AD	Vessel 1, floor	–	–	12	–	–	–	–	–	–	–	–	–	–	1	–	–	–	–	–	–	–	–	–	–	8	39	100	50	3,123	487	–	–	–
WM-AE	Vessel in Feature 1	–	2	–	–	–	–	–	–	–	–	–	1	–	–	–	–	–	–	–	–	–	–	–	–	2	53	100	50	–	–	2	1	1
WM-AI	Vessel 3, floor	–	–	1	–	2	–	–	–	–	–	–	4	–	–	–	–	–	–	–	1	–	1	–	–	4	23	200	50	2,440	274	1	–	1
WM-AI	Vessel 4, floor	–	6	–	–	13	–	–	–	–	–	–	1	–	–	–	–	–	–	1	5	–	1	1	–	4	34	200	100	2,387	760	2	–	1
RO-C	Floor, under Artifact No. 10	–	–	10	–	–	–	–	–	–	–	2	–	–	–	–	–	–	–	–	–	–	1	–	–	27	6	200	222	2,203	260	–	3	1
RO-C	Floor, under Metate No. 29	–	–	1	–	1	–	–	–	–	–	–	3	–	1	–	–	–	–	–	–	–	–	2	–	23	49	200	200	4,382	764	2	1	4
RO-C	Floor, NE corner	–	1	9	–	1	–	–	–	–	–	1	–	–	2	–	–	–	–	–	1	–	–	1	–	10	24	200	164	426	127	4	2	3
RO-D	Floor	–	–	4	–	2	–	–	–	–	–	–	5	2	1	–	–	–	–	–	–	–	–	2	–	12	43	200	200	4,575	1,450	3	–	4
RO-E	Floor	–	–	9	–	–	–	–	–	–	–	1	–	–	–	–	–	–	–	–	–	–	–	–	–	1	1	200	116	622	97	–	–	1
RO-H	Floor, SW corner	–	–	–	–	–	–	–	1	–	–	1	1	–	–	–	–	–	–	–	–	–	–	–	–	9	3	200	220	2,365	339	–	4	–
RO-K	Floor, under Metate No. 5	–	1	1	–	–	–	–	–	–	–	1	–	–	–	–	–	–	–	–	–	–	–	–	–	8	35	200	100	3,797	678	–	–	–
RO-K	Floor, SW corner	–	–	2	–	1	–	–	–	–	–	1	2	–	–	–	–	–	–	–	–	–	3	10	–	27	24	200	200	5,527	588	1	–	3

APPENDIX 2: TABLE 4. Pollen Taxa and Frequencies Derived from Type V Room Floors and One Associated Vessel

Provenience																		Compositae								Cactaceae									
Room	Context	*Pinus*	*Pseudotsuga*	*Juniperus*	*Quercus*	*Populus*	*Prosopis*	*Juglans*	*Salix*	*Alnus*	*Tamarix*	*Fraxinus*	*Celtis*	*Acacia*	*Mimosa*	Cheno-Ams	*Sarcobatus*	*Tidestromia*	*Artemisia*	Low-Spines	High-Spines	Liguliflorae	*Cirsium*	Gramineae	*Zea mays*	*Cucurbita*	*Cereus*-type	Cylindropuntia	Platyopuntia	Liliaceae	Umbelliferae	Cruciferae	Caryophyllaceae	Ranunculaceae	Convolvulaceae	Leguminosae
WM-2	Floor	1	–	–	–	–	–	–	–	–	–	–	–	–	–	180	–	–	5	28	1	–	–	3	–	–	–	–	–	–	4	–	–	–	–	12
WM-3	Floor	21	–	17	1	–	–	–	–	–	–	1	–	1	–	188	–	–	1	19	1	–	–	18	–	–	–	–	3	–	2	–	–	–	–	1
WM-4	Floor	3	–	–	2	–	–	–	–	–	–	–	–	–	–	183	–	–	3	39	–	–	–	6	3	–	–	–	15	–	5	–	–	–	–	7
WM-7	Floor	1	–	8	4	–	–	1	–	–	–	–	–	–	–	171	–	–	6	46	3	–	–	7	–	–	–	–	–	–	1	–	–	–	–	4
WM-8	Floor	–	–	3	2	–	–	–	–	–	–	–	–	–	–	185	–	–	4	53	–	–	–	9	1	–	–	–	2	–	2	–	–	–	–	4
WM-14	Vessel No. 2 in sub-floor pit	4	–	1	–	–	–	–	–	–	–	–	–	1	–	182	–	–	8	16	–	–	–	6	2	–	–	–	5	–	–	–	–	–	–	2

APPENDIX 2: TABLE 4. *(continued)*

Provenience: Room	Provenience: Context	Nyctaginaceae	Malvaceae	Rosaceae	Onagraceae	Solanaceae	Saxifragaceae	Labiatae	Rutaceae	Martyniaceae	*Polygonum Periscoria*-type	*Eriogonum*	*Cleome*	*Plantago*	*Euphorbia*	*Rhamnus*	*Kallstromia*	*Ribes*	*Polygala*	*Gilia*	*Berberis*	*Ephedra*: *Nevadensis*-type	*Ephedra*: *Torreyana*-type	Cyperaceae	*Typha*-monads	Undetermined	Undeterminable	Raw Sum-1st Count	Raw Sum-2nd Count	Influx per Gram 1st Count	Influx per Gram 2nd Count	*Pinus* Sub-Genus: Haploxlon	*Pinus* Sub-Genus: Diploxlon	*Pinus* Sub-Genus: Undetermined
WM-2	Floor	1	–	–	–	3	–	–	–	–	–	1	19	–	–	–	–	–	–	–	–	–	1	3	–	18	36	200	100	12,445	1,190	1	–	–
WM-3	Floor	–	–	–	–	2	–	–	–	–	–	–	3	–	–	–	–	–	–	–	–	1	–	–	–	8	45	200	100	13,321	672	13	4	4
WM-4	Floor	–	–	–	–	2	–	–	–	–	–	–	9	–	–	–	–	–	–	–	–	–	–	–	–	6	63	200	100	15,153	1,320	–	2	1
WM-7	Floor	–	–	2	–	–	–	–	–	–	–	–	5	–	–	1	–	–	1	–	–	–	1	1	–	8	41	200	100	5,079	787	1	–	–
WM-8	Floor	–	–	–	2	–	–	–	–	–	–	–	9	–	–	–	–	–	–	–	–	–	–	–	–	9	41	200	100	12,539	1,026	–	–	–
WM-14	Vessel No. 2 in sub-floor pit	–	–	–	–	–	–	–	–	–	–	–	–	–	–	–	–	–	–	–	–	–	–	–	–	5	43	200	50	–	–	3	–	–

APPENDIX 2: TABLE 5. Pollen Taxa and Frequencies Derived from Floors and Associated Artifacts of Community Structures

Provenience																				Compositae								Cactaceae									
Community Structure Type	WM Locus	Context	*Pinus*	*Pseudotsuga*	*Juniperus*	*Quercus*	*Populus*	*Prosopis*	*Juglans*	*Salix*	*Alnus*	*Tamarix*	*Fraxinus*	*Celtis*	*Acacia*	*Mimosa*	Cheno-Ams	*Sarcobatus*	*Tidestromia*	*Artemisia*	Low-Spines	High-Spines	Liguliflorae	*Cirsium*	Gramineae	*Zea mays*	*Cucurbita*	*Cereus*-type	Cylindropuntia	Platyopuntia	Liliaceae	Umbelliferae	Cruciferae	Caryopyllaceae	Ranunculaceae	Convolvulaceae	Leguminosae
C	House U	Floor	1	–	3	3	–	–	–	–	–	–	–	–	–	–	182	1	–	2	29	2	–	–	18	4	–	3	–	10	–	2	–	–	–	–	8
C	House Y	Floor	9	–	2	2	–	–	–	–	–	–	–	–	–	–	159	–	–	7	42	7	2	–	11	9	–	–	–	2	1	–	–	–	–	–	1
F	House V	Floor	4	–	3	1	–	–	–	–	–	–	–	–	–	–	186	–	–	6	59	3	–	–	2	–	–	–	–	3	–	1	–	–	–	–	7
G	Room 15	Floor, Mano No. 1	4	–	2	–	–	–	–	–	–	–	–	–	–	–	182	–	–	–	25	1	–	–	4	–	–	–	–	4	–	–	–	–	–	–	1
G	Room 15	Floor, Metate No.1	1	–	–	–	–	–	–	–	–	–	–	–	–	–	178	–	–	–	32	–	–	–	4	–	–	–	–	4	–	2	–	–	–	–	3

Appendix 2: Table 5. *(continued)*

Community Structure Type	Provenience WM Locus	Context	Nyctaginaceae	Malvaceae	Rosaceae	Onagraceae	Solanaceae	Saxifragaceae	Labiatae	Rutaceae	Martyniaceae	*Polygonum Periscoria*-type	*Eriogonum*	*Cleome*	*Plantago*	*Euphorbia*	*Rhamnus*	*Kallstromia*	*Ribes*	*Polygala*	*Gilia*	*Berberis*	*Ephedra* *Nevadensis*-type	*Ephedra* *Torreyana*-type	Cyperaceae	*Typha*-monads	Undetermined	Undeterminable	Raw Sum-1st Count	Raw Sum-2nd Count	Influx per Gram 1st Count	Influx per Gram 2nd Count	*Pinus* Sub-Genus Haploxlon	*Pinus* Sub-Genus Diploxlon	*Pinus* Sub-Genus Undetermined
C	House U	Floor	–	–	–	–	4	–	–	–	–	–	1	–	–	–	–	–	–	–	–	–	–	–	1	1	6	25	200	100	11,056	2,246	–	–	1
C	House Y	Floor	–	–	–	–	–	–	–	–	–	–	–	–	–	–	–	–	–	–	–	–	–	1	–	–	4	43	200	100	1,985	237	6	1	2
F	House V	Floor	–	1	–	–	–	–	–	–	–	–	–	3	–	–	–	–	–	–	–	–	–	–	–	–	7	37	200	100	9,441	522	1	1	2
G	Room 15	Floor, Mano No. 1	–	–	1	1	2	–	–	–	–	–	–	–	–	–	–	–	–	–	–	–	–	–	–	–	5	29	200	50	–	–	2	–	–
G	Room 15	Floor, Metate No.1	–	–	–	–	–	–	–	–	–	–	–	–	–	1	–	–	–	–	–	–	–	–	–	–	3	24	200	50	–	–	–	–	–

APPENDIX 2: TABLE 6. Pollen Taxa and Frequencies Derived from Secondary Architectural Features, One Extramural Vessel, and Artifacts Associated with Burials

Provenience																			Compositae								Cactaceae									
Feature	Context	*Pinus*	*Pseudotsuga*	*Juniperus*	*Quercus*	*Populus*	*Prosopis*	*Juglans*	*Salix*	*Alnus*	*Tamarix*	*Fraxinus*	*Celtis*	*Acacia*	*Mimosa*	Cheno-Ams	*Sarcobatus*	*Tidestromia*	*Artemisia*	Low-Spines	High-Spines	Liguliflorae	*Cirsium*	Gramineae	*Zea mays*	*Cucurbita*	*Cereus*-type	Cylindropuntia	Platyopuntia	Liliaceae	Umbelliferae	Cruciferae	Caryopyllaceae	Ranunculaceae	Convolvulaceae	Leguminosae
WM Work Area 1	Vessel 4	1	–	1	1	–	–	–	–	–	–	–	–	–	–	180	–	–	1	25	5	–	–	4	1	–	–	–	3	–	–	–	–	–	–	–
WM Work Area 1	Vessel 2	–	–	–	–	–	–	–	–	–	–	–	–	–	–	177	–	–	2	36	1	–	–	1	2	–	–	–	2	–	–	–	–	–	–	–
WM Pavement 4	Slab floor	5	–	19	6	–	–	1	1	–	–	–	–	–	–	121	–	–	10	105	9	1	–	14	–	–	–	–	–	–	–	–	–	–	–	12
WM Pit 3	Floor	5	–	6	–	–	–	–	–	–	–	–	–	–	–	180	–	–	6	38	4	–	–	11	6	–	–	–	4	–	1	–	–	–	–	11
WM Pit 19	Floor	1	–	–	2	–	–	–	–	–	–	–	–	–	–	179	–	–	8	14	–	–	–	13	5	–	–	–	–	–	–	–	–	–	–	1
WM Pit 31	Floor	3	–	2	6	–	–	–	–	–	–	–	–	1	–	181	–	–	24	17	2	–	–	15	11	–	–	–	1	–	–	–	–	–	–	4
WM Pit 36	Floor	–	–	4	–	–	–	–	–	–	–	–	–	–	–	184	–	–	10	51	–	1	1	4	3	–	–	–	4	–	1	–	–	–	–	4
WM Pit 38	Floor	3	–	2	2	–	–	–	–	–	–	–	–	–	–	188	–	–	8	54	3	–	–	7	–	–	–	–	–	–	2	–	–	–	–	10
WM Pit 39	Floor	2	–	4	8	2	–	–	–	–	–	–	–	–	–	188	–	–	11	32	2	1	–	8	5	1	–	–	–	–	1	–	–	–	–	4
WM Pit 40	Floor	7	–	7	1	–	–	–	–	–	–	–	–	1	–	186	–	–	6	43	2	–	–	5	–	–	–	–	1	–	2	–	–	–	–	5
WM Pit 41	Metate	22	–	–	–	–	–	–	1	–	–	–	–	–	1	145	–	–	7	10	33	1	–	9	5	–	–	–	–	1	1	–	–	–	–	5
WM Burial 1	Vessel 3	3	–	–	–	–	–	–	–	–	–	–	–	–	–	90	–	–	36	8	12	–	–	12	7	–	–	1	–	–	–	–	–	–	–	19
WM Burial 7	Vessel 1	–	–	–	–	–	–	–	–	1	–	–	–	–	–	75	–	–	11	23	14	–	–	7	–	–	–	–	–	–	–	–	–	–	–	4
WM Burial 65	Vessel 2	1	–	3	1	2	–	–	–	2	–	–	–	–	–	177	–	–	–	24	1	–	–	4	1	–	–	1	–	–	2	–	–	–	–	2
WM Burial 101	Vessel 1	2	–	–	2	1	–	–	–	–	–	–	–	–	–	170	–	–	2	21	3	–	–	6	3	–	–	–	1	–	–	–	–	–	–	4
WM Burial 101	Vessel 2	7	–	–	1	1	–	–	–	–	–	–	–	–	–	155	–	–	2	19	9	–	–	12	24	1	–	–	1	–	–	–	–	–	–	8
RO Burial 1	Pipe assoc. with skeleton	1	–	–	–	–	–	–	–	–	–	–	–	–	–	86	–	–	2	4	11	–	–	9	5	–	–	–	4	1	–	–	–	–	–	1
WM Block 30	SW corner, 15 cm BGS, * vessel	1	–	–	–	–	–	–	–	–	–	–	–	–	–	184	–	–	35	34	21	–	–	2	–	–	–	–	–	95	–	–	–	–	–	6

* BGS = Below ground surface.

APPENDIX 2: TABLE 6. *(continued)*

Provenience: Feature	Context	Nyctaginaceae	Malvaceae	Rosaceae	Onagraceae	Solanaceae	Saxifragaceae	Labiatae	Rutaceae	Martyniaceae	*Polygonum Periscoria*-type	*Eriogonum*	*Cleome*	*Plantago*	*Euphorbia*	*Rhamnus*	*Kallstromia*	*Ribes*	*Polygala*	*Gilia*	*Berberis*	*Ephedra*: *Nevadensis*-type	*Ephedra*: *Torreyana*-type	Cyperaceae	*Typha*-monads	Undetermined	Undeterminable	Raw Sum-1st Count	Raw Sum-2nd Count	Influx per Gram 1st Count	Influx per Gram 2nd Count	*Pinus* Sub-Genus: Haploxlon	*Pinus* Sub-Genus: Diploxlon	*Pinus* Sub-Genus: Undetermined
WM Work Area 1	Vessel 4	–	–	1	–	–	–	–	–	–	–	1	1	–	–	–	–	–	–	–	–	–	–	–	–	5	45	200	50	–	–	1	–	–
WM Work Area 1	Vessel 2	–	–	–	–	–	–	–	–	–	–	–	2	–	–	–	–	–	–	–	–	–	–	2	–	2	27	200	50	–	–	–	–	–
WM Pavement 4	Slab floor	–	–	–	–	1	–	–	–	–	–	1	1	–	–	–	–	–	–	–	–	1	1	–	–	12	41	200	200	3,034	946	–	3	2
WM Pit 3	Floor	–	–	–	–	–	–	–	–	–	–	–	1	–	–	–	–	–	–	–	–	–	–	–	1	6	59	200	100	6,024	542	1	3	1
WM Pit 19	Floor	–	–	1	–	–	–	–	–	–	–	–	–	–	–	–	–	–	–	–	–	–	1	–	–	4	70	200	50	865	101	–	–	1
WM Pit 31	Floor	–	–	–	–	–	–	–	–	–	–	–	1	–	–	–	–	–	–	–	–	–	–	–	–	13	57	200	100	2,309	137	3	–	–
WM Pit 36	Floor	–	–	2	–	–	–	–	–	–	–	–	1	–	–	–	–	–	–	–	–	–	–	–	–	14	38	200	100	13,915	663	–	–	–
WM Pit 38	Floor	–	–	–	–	–	–	–	–	–	–	–	–	–	–	–	–	–	–	–	–	–	–	1	–	8	39	200	100	21,186	770	1	–	2
WM Pit 39	Floor	–	–	–	–	–	–	–	–	–	–	–	–	–	–	–	–	–	–	–	–	–	2	3	–	14	40	200	100	11,641	783	1	–	1
WM Pit 40	Floor	–	–	1	–	–	–	–	–	–	–	–	4	–	–	–	–	–	–	–	–	–	–	3	–	12	50	200	100	8,260	405	3	3	1
WM Pit 41	Metate	–	–	37	–	4	–	–	–	–	–	–	3	–	–	–	–	–	–	–	–	–	–	–	–	16	153	200	159	–	–	–	20	1
WM Burial 1	Vessel 3	–	–	61	–	–	–	–	–	–	–	–	15	–	–	–	–	–	–	–	–	–	99	–	–	5	–	177	278	–	–	–	3	–
WM Burial 7	Vessel 1	–	–	26	–	–	–	–	–	–	–	–	–	–	–	–	–	–	–	–	–	–	–	–	–	4	–	100	91	–	–	–	–	–
WM Burial 65	Vessel 2	–	–	3	1	–	–	–	–	–	–	–	–	–	–	–	–	–	–	–	–	–	–	–	–	2	50	200	50	–	–	1	–	–
WM Burial 101	Vessel 1	–	1	1	–	–	–	1	–	–	–	–	–	–	–	–	–	–	–	–	–	–	–	–	–	2	42	200	50	1,773	206	–	1	1
WM Burial 101	Vessel 2	1	–	3	–	4	–	–	–	–	–	–	1	–	–	–	–	–	–	1	–	–	–	1	–	4	37	200	100	2,397	522	5	–	2
RO Burial 1	Pipe assoc. with skeleton	–	–	40	–	–	–	–	–	–	–	–	–	–	–	–	–	–	–	–	–	–	1	–	–	6	–	100	86	8,549	79	–	1	–
WM Block 30	SW corner, 15 cm BGS,* vessel	–	–	3	–	–	–	–	–	–	–	–	5	–	–	–	–	–	–	–	–	–	–	2	–	11	3	200	215	–	–	–	–	1

* BGS = Below ground surface.

exercised in assigning significance to changes in pollen representation if consistently low relative frequencies are evident. Only one sample, the white plaster from House I at the Ridout locus, proved to be completely devoid of pollen.

Arboreal Pollen Types

Pinus sp. Pine pollen was recovered in relatively low quantities in all but 13 of the 112 Wind Mountain and Ridout loci samples. Pines are prolific pollinators (Wodehouse 1971:5), so low pollen counts suggest no notable populations in the Wind Mountain vicinity at any time represented by the samples. A few pine pollen counts exceed that of the modern surface transect (10 percent). The majority of these counts are derived from floors and might reflect abandonment during the period of pine anthesis (spring). In most instances, they also correspond to lower than normal low-spine Compositae counts and could be statistical phenomenon. The depressed contribution of weedy plant pollen amplifies the pine pollen amount. One would expect other arboreal pollen types (e.g., juniper and oak) to be more prominent, but they are not.

At least some of the pollen may reflect prehistoric utilization of pine. The best case for such use comes from a vessel in House WW in which 162 grains were identified. All belong to the Diploxlon type, probably derived from ponderosa pines. On the basis of pollen, it is impossible to ascertain the form, whether cones or needles, of pine remains that were placed in the vessel. Experiments show that pollen grains do not adhere to piñon nuts (Bohrer 1972). No studies have been conducted with ponderosa pine seeds. If not purposeful, accidental intrusion of pollen contained within the pot is also possible. The remaining prominent pine pollen frequencies are based on smaller sums and are, with the exception of Wind Mountain locus Room 3 and House SS, derived from a mixture of Haploxlon and Diploxlon grains. They are probably contributors to the natural pollen rain.

One trend evident from the Wind Mountain locus House X profile shows relatively high pine percentages in floor and fill samples below 104 cm. Between 104 cm and 29 cm, the pine pollen counts drop off, but rise once again between 24 cm and the present ground surface. Juniper (*Juniperus* sp.) frequencies rise together with those of pine in the upper fill, while Cheno-Am and low-spine Compositae counts are high in the middle fill where pine counts are depressed. This pattern conforms to the previously discussed arboreal versus weedy plant pollen curves (Schoenwetter 1964: Figure 25) and suggests that the lower counts observed between 104 cm and 24 cm depth are a function of prehistoric occupation in which trees were reduced for land clearance and wood procurement. Coincidentally, weedy plants expanded with the expansion of farm fields. The upper three samples from the profile with increasing pine pollen counts reflect a resurgence of trees following abandonment of the site.

Juniperus sp. The distribution of juniper pollen frequencies generally equates the pine pollen trend. Juniper percentages are low in most of the occupation period samples but increase in the upper portion of the Wind Mountain locus House X profile. However, neither the high percentages of pine pollen deep in the House X profile nor the scattered high pine counts among the dated matrices have clear parallels among the juniper counts. This suggests that the inhabitants of the site made considerable inroads on the local juniper population quite early in the occupation. The one notable juniper count (Wind Mountain locus Room 3, floor) attributable to the Mimbres occupation occurs late in the life of the site. It is accompanied by high grass and pine pollen counts and is probably attributable to either secondary plant succession or to statistical release due to the low quantity of low-spine Compositae pollen in the same sample. At the Ridout locus, juniper counts begin to rise as corn pollen drops out and the Cheno-Am pollen contribution begins to decline (House F Profile). The upper five samples of the profile are clearly postabandonment in date. Pine pollen does not, however, increase significantly in these samples and the higher juniper frequencies are probably not entirely due to the decline in the weed pollen contribution. Junipers tend to migrate faster than pines, and it is probable that this contrast between the juniper and pine counts is due to reforestation, with the room fill accumulated before many pines came back into the area. At the Ridout locus, the highest juniper counts among the dated samples came from the earliest floors. When combined with the postoccupation profile samples, these give us the predicted arboreal pollen sequence: high arboreal pollen in early samples, low arboreal pollen during the major occupation, and high arboreal pollen in late and postabandonment samples.

Quercus sp. Oak pollen is a fairly common component of the surface transect pollen spectrum and reflects the modern proximity of oak trees to the site. The oak pollen contribution to the counts of the older samples is considerably less and is entirely absent in 23 of the 112 prehistoric pollen samples. This absence may be due to depressed populations of parent trees during the occupation of the site.

Minor Arboreal Pollen Types

Small quantities of pollen taxa representing 10 other trees and shrubs appear in the Wind Mountain and Ridout loci pollen spectra. These include seven wind-pollinated types—Douglas fir (*Pseudotsuga* sp.), cottonwood (*Populus* sp.), walnut (*Juglans* sp.), willow (*Salix* sp.), alder (*Alnus* sp.), hackberry (*Celtis* sp.), and tamarisk (*Tamarix* sp.) and three insect-pollinated types—mesquite (*Prosopis* sp.), acacia (*Aca-*

cia sp.), and sensitive plant (*Mimosa* sp.). Mesquite, a recent invader (Appendix 1) and tamarisk, a historic import from the Near East, are observed only in the surface and near-surface samples. The distribution of the other minor types seem to have little significance. For example, the highest cottonwood counts from both loci do not exceed the modern surface sample representation by more than one percent. Cottonwood and walnut pollen in the Ridout House F profile is also concentrated in the postoccupation sediments.

Nonarboreal Pollen Types—Cultigens

Zea mays sp. Corn is wind-pollinated, but its pollen is not widely dispersed. For analytical purposes, it may be treated much as an insect-pollinated plant, that is, in cultural contexts where corn pollen is found, some human agent served to concentrate it. The association between cultural activity and corn pollen is immediately evident in the Wind Mountain locus House X and Ridout locus House F profiles. Here, corn pollen is a regular component of the counts from the deeper fill of both houses but disappears from the pollen spectra just before the decline of weedy plants and the resurgence of the arboreal pollen types that mark postabandonment secondary plant succession.

Corn pollen was present in 59 of the 79 Wind Mountain floor, feature, and artifact samples as well as four of the nine Ridout locus samples. Each of these occurrences indicates that some form of corn was utilized in each locality by a human agent at least once. A number of Wind Mountain locus counts (House T floor, House Q floor, House PP Pit 2 vessel 2, House AA fill vessel, House WW vessel 10, and Burial 101 vessel 2) are high enough to imply either repeated use or the presence of large quantities of corn.

The distribution of corn pollen may also be chronologically significant. As noted within the profiled structures, corn pollen counts are significantly higher in the deeper fill, then declining or disappearing toward the surface strata. This will be discussed further in the section dealing with *Cleome* sp.

Cucurbita sp. Considerable quantities of squash pollen have been reported from prehistoric Southwestern feces (Martin and Sharrock 1964:177; Kelso 1976: Figures 13, 24), though it is not often found in the deposits of archaeological sites. Its presence in feces has been attributed to the consumption of blossoms. Its absence in other deposits is probably due to its limited dispersal as an insect-pollinated plant as well as its imperfect preservation in most exposed archaeological sites. Squash plants produce little pollen, some of which would be brought in, adhering to fruit harvested long after anthesis. Squash pollen grains, although large, are thin and apparently fragile and may not survive where other types do. Suggesting degradation of squash pollen, detached *Cucurbita* sp. operculi (pore covers) were noted in some samples that did not contain the rest of the grain.

The presence of squash pollen in six of the Wind Mountain locus floor, feature, and fill samples indicates that squashes were elements in the local prehistoric economy, but counts are insufficient to establish any trends in their utilization. The absence of this type from most samples is not meaningful.

It is also possible that at least some *Cucurbita* spp. pollen does not represent cultivated plants. The pollen of buffalo gourd (*C. foetidissima*), which grows in the area today, is not readily distinguishable from that of squash.

Wind-Pollinated Herbs

Cheno-Ams. Pollen contributed by members of the goosefoot family (Chenopodiaceae) and by pigweed (*Amaranthus* sp.) combined by convention under the term Cheno-Ams, dominates the first counts from the Wind Mountain and Ridout loci. Presumably large numbers of these plants grew in the vicinity during prehistoric occupation. With one exception (Ridout locus House D) in floor and vessel samples, this taxa is depressed where it is statistically forced down by a large influx of economic taxa. The Cheno-Am counts are significantly low only in postoccupational sediments.

In the Wind Mountain locus House X profile, Cheno-Am counts are relatively low in the deeper sediments where pine pollen frequencies are comparatively high. The Cheno-Am contribution increases in the center of the fill, peaking between 89 and 94 cm, where the pine pollen counts are low, and decreasing in the upper fill as the arboreal pollen types recover. This distribution confirms the status of the weedy Cheno-Ams as soil disturbance indicators at the Wind Mountain locus. In the Ridout locus House F profile, Cheno-Am pollen is even more closely associated with agricultural soil disturbance. Here, the decline of this type in the upper fill closely follows the disappearance of corn from the profile and is paralleled by a rise in juniper pollen that probably reflects reforestation. The high Cheno-Am count of the near-surface sample is aberrant and may be the product of localized recent soil disturbance by livestock.

The consumption of Chenopodiaceae and *Amaranthus* spp. is well documented for the historic Zuni, Hopi, Navajo, and Tewa-speaking Pueblos (Stevenson 1915:66; Robbins et al. 1916:53; Whiting 1939:73–74; Elmore 1944:44–45). Seeds of plants producing Cheno-Am type pollen have also been recovered in significant quantities from prehistoric human feces in the Southwest (Callen and Martin 1969:239; Kelso 1976: Table 8). Amaranths were cultivated in Mexico at the time of the Spanish *entrada* (Wolf 1959:53–54), and an introduced *Amaranthus cruentus* achieved a semicultivated status among the Hopi (Whiting 1939:23).

Chenopodium sp. pollen adheres to seed in abundant quantities (Bohrer 1972: Table 7), and it is probable that some grains were transported to sites on whole plants. Unfortunately, this pollen type is wind carried hundreds of yards from its source (Raynor et al. 1973: Figure 4), and its use by humans is indistinguishable from its massive contribution as a farming-attendant weed. The weeds themselves may have, in some cases, been considered valuable resources. For example, pollen data indicates that the inhabitants of Dead Valley, Arizona during the Pueblo II period were either semicultivating or selectively weeding in favor of plants producing Cheno-Am type pollen (Kelso 1980:365, 370).

Artemisia sp. Sagebrush pollen frequencies in the profiles at both loci are variable, highest in the deeper samples, declining toward the middle deposits, and increasing somewhat in postoccupation sediments. Its distribution parallels the pine pollen trend and runs opposite that of the weedy, soil disturbance indicators such as the Cheno-Ams and low-spine Compositae. Sagebrush counts continue to decline in the House F profile as the arboreal types rise. *Artemisia* sp. pollen counts from prehistoric contexts are higher than those observed in postoccupation samples. This suggests that some form of sagebrush was brought to the site. The 32 percent on the House H floor as well as the 22 percent on the House F floor, both at the Ridout locus, are probably of cultural origin. Wind Mountain locus *Artemisia* sp. counts that seem especially prominent occur on the floor of Pit 31, in the contents of vessel 2 from Room 14, the floor of House GG, the floor of Pit 19, the contents of vessel 1 from House AD, and the surface of a metate from Pit 41. The failure of sagebrush pollen to regain its abundance in the postoccupational counts suggests that exploitation of the plant may have proceeded to the point where it could not completely recover its former habitat even with the elimination of human pressure.

The portion of the plant utilized is not known from pollen alone, but ethnographic information shows that sagebrush seeds were eaten by the Zuni (Stevenson 1915:64). The Great Basin Shoshone (Fry 1969:8) and the Hopi (Whiting 1939:94) ate its leaves and used it in internal and external medicine (Stevenson 1915:42; Whiting 1939:94). Miksicek and Fall (Appendix 1) do not, however, identify sagebrush macrofossils in Wind Mountain samples. Thus, it is possible that the depression of the sagebrush population and the concentrations of its pollen at given loci are incidental to agricultural land use.

Low-spine Compositae. The wind-pollinated members of the Compositae family, here subsumed under low-spine Compositae, produce massive quantities of pollen that are easily distributed over considerable distances (Raynor et al. 1973: Figure 4). These plants are well known pioneer species in soils denuded of the normal native vegetation and are common agricultural weeds throughout North America. During the pre-Columbian era, their distribution was apparently more restricted due to an inability to compete with perennial plant species as topsoil began to form on naturally disturbed sediments (Wodehouse 1971:162). Because these plants invade disturbed soils, low-spine Compositae are common elements in the pollen spectra of many Southwestern archaeological sites.

The distribution of the low-spine Compositae pollen types is not as predictable as that of the Cheno-Ams. At Grasshopper Ruin near Cibecue, Arizona (Kelso 1982:109), for instance, their representation, along with that of the Cheno-Ams, increases in occupation period deposits and declines in postoccupation sediments. At other sites, for example, AZ:Q:12:13 near Springerville, Arizona (Kelso 1980:365), and a number of localities in the Navajo Reservoir region (Schoenwetter 1964), they follow the arboreal pollen types, declining in occupation sediment profiles and resurging after site abandonment. In nonprofile samples at AZ:Q:12:13, low-spine Compositae percentages are often more variable than Cheno-Ams, suggesting that the pollen rain of the former type does not so uniformly blanket the site as the latter.

No clear distributional pattern of low-spine Compositae has yet emerged. Possibly they cannot compete with the Cheno-Ams in areas of lower water tables and alkaline soils (Martin 1963:49). Something as simple as the distance to the nearest population of wind-pollinated Compositae could be the answer in certain cases, since the majority of the grains shed are deposited within a few meters of the parent plants (Raynor et al. 1973: Figures 6, 9). Human exploitation may also affect them. At least one plant producing this pollen type, *Dicoria* sp., was apparently eaten by the historic Hopi (Whiting 1939:96). Martin and Sharrock (1964:75) inferred consumption of another, *Oxtenia* sp., from prehistoric feces at Wetherill Mesa. Alternatively, prehistoric peoples may have weeded out these plants in favor of the Chenopodiaceae—a known food resource.

Low-spine Compositae pollen was present in all of the Wind Mountain and Ridout loci samples. Its distribution in the House X and House F profiles conforms to the predicted soil disturbance plant pattern reflected in the Cheno-Am counts. There is no firm evidence for the exploitation of the wind-pollinated members of the Compositae family at either locus.

Gramineae. Grass pollen was present in every Ridout locus sample and all but two of Wind Mountain locus samples. Grass pollen percentages decline toward the middle of both sample series, then rise in a single sample toward the top of each profile. This generally conforms to the predicted pattern of a natural contributor to the background pollen component and suggests that up to 13 percent of this type in other samples might be normally produced by grasses growing in the vicinity of the site. The fairly uniform quantities of grass pollen associated with burial artifacts at the Ridout locus suggest that this level of naturally derived grass pollen may not be unreasonable. As a rule, the New World grasses are not prolific pollen producers (Wodehouse 1971:46).

Five grass pollen counts from nonprofile samples at Wind Mountain locus significantly exceed 13 percent. The highest of these, the 23 percent count observed in a sample from the bottom of Pit 19, suggests either that grass seed was stored or that the pit was lined with grass. The remaining distinctive counts (Houses S, W, DD, and Room 3) derive from floors and could reflect processed grass seed, matting, bedding, or any number of plant forms.

Ephedra sp. Two morphological varieties of joint-fir pollen were recovered, *E. torreyana* and *E. nevadensis*. In modern surface samples, *E. nevadensis* is more common in the northwestern portions of the Southwest, where winter precipitation dominates, whereas *E. torreyana* is concentrated in southeastern areas characterized by summer rainfall.

This distribution permits comment on the environmental regimen. The Wind Mountain and Ridout loci currently lie in the region of summer rainfall. In all the prehistoric samples, *E. torreyana* is clearly the more important of the two varieties, both in total number of pollen grains and in the number of samples in which these types appear. While admittedly dealing with low frequencies, it appears that there may not have been a shift in the seasonal distribution of rainfall during occupation of the site.

Joint-fir is a prolific pollen producer, and its pollen is known to be wind carried over considerable distances (Maher 1964:392). At the Wind Mountain and Ridout loci the pollen from these plants does not, with one exception, exceed 3 percent. Consequently, *Ephedra* sp. probably did not figure prominently in nearby vegetation. One sample, a vessel from Burial 1, contains 36 percent joint-fir pollen. An apparent lack of a significant local joint-fir population might argue that a human agent was responsible for depositing *Ephedra* sp. pollen/blossoms in the burial. But human plant utilization is generally defined in terms of a pattern of occurrences, not a single instance, especially for wind-pollinated taxa. An isolated high count may, therefore, represent a fluke of pollen dispersal. The burial, whatever the source of its associated joint-fir pollen, probably took place during the spring when the plants were blooming (Kearney and Peebles 1951:60).

Ethnographic accounts show that joint-fir was widely used in beverages (usually medicinal) by the aboriginal inhabitants of the Southwest. The Zuni (Stevenson 1915:49) boiled the plant without its root and drank the resulting brew as a medicate for venereal disease. The Navajo (Elmore 1944:24) and the Hopi (Whiting 1939:63) used a joint-fir concoction for similar purposes, but the former also prescribed it for kidney ailments and general stomach problems. Joint-fir tea is a pleasant drink in its own right. It is possible that the inhabitants of the site attributed pharmaceutical value to these plants but data are insufficient to firmly establish such use.

Minor Wind-Transported Nonarboreal Pollen Types

Small quantities of pollen from four other wind-pollinated plants are scattered through the Wind Mountain and Ridout loci pollen spectra. Two of these, cattail (*Typha* sp.) and sedge (Cyperaceae), are normally associated with aquatic or marsh conditions. Both plants produce large amounts of pollen. Cattail pollen can be transported several miles from its originating source (Wodehouse 1971:43, 70). In contrast, sedge pollen apparently does not blow more than a few meters from its parent plant (Meyer 1973:988). The occasional manner in which cattail pollen occurs, three instances of two grains each, suggests that it is derived from the natural vegetation and that its point of origin cannot have been very near the site. Sedge pollen is more common, appearing in five Ridout locus samples and 24 Wind Mountain locus floor, feature, and artifact samples. In view of the short distances sedge pollen seems to travel, it may have been carried to the site by its inhabitants in containers filled with water or on plants used for matting and in construction. No sedge appears as macrobotanical remains.

The two remaining wind transported, nonarboreal pollen types, greasewood (*Sarcobatus* sp.) and *Tidestromina* sp., are produced by plants belonging to the Chenopodiaceae and Amaranthaceae respectively. Both produce massive amounts of pollen. They are present in such small quantities that they must be derived from natural populations that were either limited or located some distance from the site.

Insect-Pollinated Herbs

High-spine Compositae. By Martin's (1963:49) definition, the high-spine Compositae category incorporates those members of the family that are insect-pollinated. These plants are apparently imperfectly adapted to entomophily, and at least some seem to produce more pollen than is carried away by insects. At some Southwestern localities, high-spine Compositae pollen comprises 30 to 50 percent of the natural pollen rain (Martin and Sharrock 1964:174). Like their wind-pollinated relatives, plants producing these pollen types have an affinity for disturbed soils. Sunflowers (*Helianthus* sp.), for instance, are prominent weeds in agricultural fields and grow along road sides. At Grasshopper Ruin (Kelso 1982:109), the pattern of high-spine pollen Compositae pollen was typical of plants invading disturbed soils and paralleled the low-spine Compositae and Cheno-Ams.

A number of plants producing high-spine Compositae pollen possess considerable potential for human exploitation. Ethnographic data indicates that sunflowers were a minor cultigen among the historic Hopi (Whiting 1939:10) and Navajo (Elmore 1944:87). Domestication of sunflowers might predate European contact (Whiting 1939:12). Sunflower seed hulls have also been recovered from a number of prehistoric human feces (Kelso 1976:89).

The combination of documented economic potential, preference for disturbed soils, and partial wind dispersal complicates the interpretation of high-spine Compositae counts. Compositae pollen was present in all Ridout locus samples except the 60 cm level of the profile, and in all but 15 Wind Mountain locus samples. In profiles, counts are consistently low. They decline slightly where the primary soil-disturbance indicators (Cheno-Ams and low-spine Compositae) are high and recover when the influence of these types weakens in the upper fill. None of these counts is sufficiently distinctive to suggest that they originated in organic trash. The parent plants were undoubtedly growing around the site, and their normal contribution to the occupation period pollen rain was apparently less than 10 percent. At the Ridout locus, the typical high-spine Compositae range seems to be 4 to 15 percent.

Pollen counts in several samples exceed expected percentages produced solely by high-spine Compositae plants contributing to the background pollen component. For example, in floor samples from Ridout locus Houses E, H, and C, counts reach 49 percent, 40 percent, and 35 percent, respectively. Such counts strongly suggest human exploitation of high-spine Compositae plants.

The evidence for economic processing of high-spine Compositae plants in Wind Mountain locus samples is not so clear cut. Differences in counts between artifact samples (vessels in Houses UU, AD, and AE, as well as a metate in Pit 41) and the profile are not significantly higher. These lower frequencies reflect both natural and cultural processes whereby high-spine Compositae pollen was deposited in the site.

Cactaceae. Three morphological varieties of cactus pollen, prickly pear (Platyopuntia-type), cholla (Cylindropuntia-type), and *Cereus* sp. (under which most other Southwestern cacti are subsumed), were observed in the Wind Mountain and Ridout loci pollen spectra. Hevly and others (1965: Figure 12) report up to 8 percent *Cereus*-type in surface samples recovered from the Tucson Mountains dominated by saguaro (*Cereus giganteus*), but the pollen of cacti, like that of most insect-pollinated plants, is usually rare under natural conditions of deposition (Martin and Sharrock 1964:171; Bryant 1974:413). The infrequent representation of Playtopuntia pollen at 1.5 percent in the surface sample from the Wind Mountain site is not inconsistent with the presence of significant populations of both prickly pear and cholla in the vicinity of the site. By way of comparison, in Tucson Mountain surface transects, where these cacti were prominent elements in the vegetation, the highest pollen counts of both types combined was only 2.25 percent (Hevly et al. 1965: Figure 12).

Prickly pear is the most prominent of the three cactus pollen types recovered at the Wind Mountain settlement. It was present in all but one of the Ridout locus samples and in 53 of the 77 Wind Mountain locus floor, feature, and artifact samples. All but a few counts exceed percentages for the type observed in the surface transect. The House QQ floor, the House UU vessel, the Room 4 floor, and the House WW vessel 11 (all Wind Mountain locus contexts) counts were significantly higher. In the Wind Mountain locus House X profile, prickly pear is well represented in samples from the deeper fill but drops out above 49 cm. In the Ridout locus House F profile, it does not appear at all.

This distribution suggests that the prickly pear pollen in the House X profile is derived from organic trash tossed into the pit, and its absence from the postoccupation sediments indicates that most of the pollen from floor, feature, and artifact samples is humanly derived. Not all profile samples devoid of prickly pear pollen postdate prehistoric occupation. Possibly use of cactus resources declined late in the occupation. Alternatively, trash containing cactus pollen was simply dumped elsewhere. It is worth noting that there are no really high prickly pear pollen percentages among the Ridout samples. In general, its representation is lower at the Ridout locus.

Neither *Cereus*-type nor cholla pollen appears in the Wind Mountain surface transect. They do not appear in nearly as many prehistoric samples as does prickly pear pollen. In samples where they were observed, their percentages are also generally lower than those of prickly pear. No *Cereus*-type was seen in any of the Ridout locus samples. These contrasts could be due to differential pollen production, season of collection, processing method, or the nature of the plant product exploited. Comparisons drawn between the pollen contributions of different species are tenuous at best. It is not certain that cholla and cacti producing *Cereus*-type pollen were exploited at Wind Mountain, but if they were, they seem to have been used in small quantities. The only cactus macrofossils reported from the settlement include *Echinocereus* sp. seed and areoles from high in the House X profile.

Part of the prickly pear harvest probably took place during the flowering season to produce the quantities of pollen observed in samples. Precisely the form of the plant product used remains unknown. Cactus pollen adheres to the fruit in small quantities (Bohrer 1972). The Hopi (Whiting 1939:85) and the Navajo (Vestal 1952:37) ate the fruits of hedgehog cactus (*Echinocereus* spp.), as well as the fruits and roasted joints of several species of prickly pear. Stevenson (1915:69) reports that the Zuni ate cholla joints raw or stewed and dried them for winter use. The fruits were also dried, ground, and incorporated in mush.

Leguminosae. A number of morphological varieties of pollen attributable to undetermined members of the pea family, here combined as Leguminosae, were observed at levels approaching 10 percent in most samples analyzed. Several Wind

Mountain locus floor (House UU, Room 2), feature (Pit 3), and artifact (vessel 4 in House AI) counts were somewhat higher but probably not in sufficiently abundant amounts to indicate the Leguminosae pollen was humanly concentrated. Most, perhaps all, of the Leguminosae pollen identified represent the background pollen rain.

The presence of this pollen is nevertheless difficult to interpret. Legumes are considered primarily, if not entirely, insect-pollinated (Wodehouse 1971:131), and some members of the family are self-pollinating. Small quantities of Leguminosae pollen have been noted in samples from other Southwestern sites. In the profile from Rattlesnake Ruin, north-central New Mexico (Kelso n.d.), the pollen was consistently distributed, but at usually lower frequencies than is the case for Wind Mountain. The comparatively small quantity of Leguminosae in the Wind Mountain surface transect and the near-surface sample (6.5 percent) from Ridout locus House F suggests that parent plants were encouraged by the disturbed soil conditions during occupation. The disparity between modern and prehistoric Leguminosae frequencies, however, could also be the result of modern overgrazing.

Umbelliferae. Another insect-pollinated pollen type that appears consistently in the pollen spectra was contributed by members of the parsley family. With one exception, quantities of this pollen are low and may reflect the background component of the local pollen rain.

One count (Wind Mountain locus House D floor) reaches 12 percent, but a single, slightly higher percentage among so many low ones is insufficient to demonstrate normal exploitation on the part of Wind Mountain residents. Interestingly, the sample was recovered from the vessel in Burial 65 in which two pollen clumps, one consisting of 40 and the other of 30 grains, were identified. These concentrations may represent flowers placed in the vessel accompanying the burial.

Liliaceae. Pollen contributed by some members of the lily family appears in two Wind Mountain locus samples and was found in a pipe sample from Burial 1 at the Ridout locus. The pollen is probably produced by yucca plants. Narrow leaf yucca (*Yucca elata*) grows near the site today.

A few grains of Liliaceae pollen were caught in atmospheric traps on the San Augustín Plains of New Mexico (Potter and Rowley 1960: Table 1). Hevly and others (1965: Table 3) recovered one or two grains in four stations of their Tucson Mountain surface transect. *Yucca* spp. is not common in natural deposits because it is pollinated by a moth (*Tegiticula yuccasella*) that transfers a putty-like lump of pollen inside individual flowers (Faegri and Van der Pijl 1971:210).

The 44 percent Liliaceae pollen in one Wind Mountain locus vessel (found in Excavation Block 30) is probably of cultural origin, but presents the same perplexing interpretive problems encountered when trying to explain the single high joint-fir pollen count. It is unlikely that a high concentration of an insect-pollinated taxa could be concentrated without human assistance. On the other hand, the vessel was once exposed and, when excavated, was uncovered only 15 cm below the present ground surface. No other pollen evidence for use of the parent *Yucca* sp. plants was found, although a few seeds were recovered.

The ethnobotanical record details the exploitation of yucca roots, leaves, and stems, but Bryant's (1974:412) experiments in washing sotol (*Dasylirion* sp.), a related plant in the lily family, indicate that little pollen is retained on plant parts. This sample probably represents flowers, but their use is not known.

Rosaceae. The origin of rose family pollen, represented in low frequencies under 2 percent in Wind Mountain and Ridout loci profile samples, is less problematical. Rose pollen is present, normally, in the 2–6 percent range, in 43 of the 77 Wind Mountain locus prehistoric samples, and is recorded, for the most part in frequencies under 8 percent, in 10 of the 11 Ridout locus samples. The roses, although insect-pollinated, produce a relatively large amount of pollen (Wodehouse 1971:127) and, therefore, contribute to the natural pollen rain. One rose family pollen grain was noted in the Wind Mountain surface transect, and three grains were tabulated in each of the two most shallow House X profile samples.

At least some of the rose family pollen is probably derived from the background pollen component, but a number of counts from the Wind Mountain locus (metate 9 in House K, metate in Pit 41, vessel 3 in Burial 1, vessel 1 in Burial 7, vessel 1 in House AD, and vessel 11 in House WW) as well as one from the Ridout locus (a pipe from Burial 1) contrast so sharply with the expected norm that they indicate a cultural origin.

The Hopi, the Navajo, and the Rio Grande Tewa used many species of the rose family for food and medicinal purposes (Robbins et al. 1916:45, 47–48; Whiting 1939:78; Elmore 1944:52–55; Vestal 1952:30–31). Pollen evidence from coprolites indicates that the prehistoric inhabitants of Great Basin caves consumed plants belonging to the rose family (Kelso 1970:258). Clearly the inhabitants of the Wind Mountain settlement were doing the same.

Solanaceae. The pollen of the members of the potato family is insect-transported, but data from the Tucson Mountains in Arizona indicate that a few grains of this type may be expected in natural deposits (Hevly et al. 1965: Table 3). The single grain of Solanaceae pollen identified in the Wind Mountain surface transect and the up to 2 percent of the type recovered from the postoccupational samples of the Wind Mountain and Ridout loci profiles concur with this prediction. The Solanaceae pollen percentages in seven of the 23 Wind Mountain locus floor, feature and artifact samples, and in two of the Ridout locus House F profile occupational samples, show somewhat higher counts, implying either that there were once more parent plants growing in the site vicinity or that pollen was artificially concentrated as a result of human exploitation practices. The 9 percent Solanaceae pollen on metate 9 from Wind Mountain locus House K and the 13 percent in vessel 4 from Wind Mountain locus House AI argue for a cultural interpretation. Unfortunately, two somewhat higher counts out of 30 occupation period samples cannot be considered conclusive.

The genus and species of plants that contributed Solanaceae pollen could not be determined, but a few seeds of *Lycium* sp. or *Physalis* sp. were recovered from Wind Mountain pit house DD (Appendix 1: Table 2), suggesting that wolfberry or ground cherry were potential sources. Sacred datura (*Datura meteloides*), which presently grows near the site, is another possibility.

Cleome sp. Rocky Mountain beeweed is another potential plant resource whose pollen is rarely recovered from natural sediments (Martin and Sharrock 1964:176). At Inscription House, where the fecal specimens were dominated by beeweed pollen, only one grain of this type was found in a surface sample from the floodplain below the site (Kelso 1976:79).

Beeweed pollen is absent from the Wind Mountain surface samples and the upper samples of both Wind Mountain and Ridout loci profiles. In occupational samples, it only reaches 2 percent. These data indicate that beeweed is not a significant contributor to the site area pollen rain. Some of the beeweed counts from the 37 Wind Mountain locus floor, feature, and artifact samples contain higher amounts than might be expected from the background component. Several samples (House B floor, vessel 3 in House AI, Room 8 floor, Room 7 floor, Room 4 floor, and Room 2 floor) suggest that beeweed was utilized by the site inhabitants. There seems to be a concentration of beeweed pollen in the surface structures. Possibly, beeweed exploitation increased during the later stages of the occupation. At the Ridout locus beeweed pollen was present in five of the 11 samples, but its representation was too low, not exceeding 3 percent, to confidently equate the counts with human utilization of plants.

Beeweed seed was eaten by the Navajo (Elmore 1944:51) and the Zia (White 1962:107), but the ethnographic records of most native Southwestern people emphasize the consumption of greens, indicating a preference for young shoots and leaves. Plants were both eaten fresh and stored for winter consumption (Stevenson 1915:69; Robbins et al. 1916:58; Whiting 1939:77; Elmore 1944:50; White 1962:107). The Hopi insured a yearly beeweed supply by permitting plants to go to seed (Whiting 1939:58). Among the Hano-Tewa beeweed was of sufficient economic importance to be named in songs along with corn, pumpkin and cotton (Robbins et al. 1916:58).

Under conditions of environmental stress, native plants may prove to be more reliable resources than introduced crops, especially when the desired product is the green parts of the plant rather than mature seed heads. It is to such resources that subsistence farmers often turn during times of scarcity. Elmore (1944:54) reports that beeweed prevented starvation among the Navajo on several occasions.

Corn and *Cleome* sp. pollen seem to be mutually exclusive in floor samples. Corn is concentrated in the Late Pit House period, *Cleome* sp. in the surface rooms. This suggests that the surface occupation may have been under some economic stress. It is also possible that the separation of the two types reflect differences in the functions of structures. Perhaps more corn was stored in pit houses than in rooms. Room dwellers may have utilized other, exterior storage pit facilities.

Minor Insect-Pollinated Herbs

Small quantities of pollen from 22 other insect-pollinated plants were noted. Eleven of these taxa: pink family (Caryophyllaceae), unicorn plant family (Martyniaceae), mustard family (Cruciferae), buckthorn family (Rhamnaceae), convolvulus family (Convolvulaceae), four-o'clock family (Nyctaginaceae), mallow family (Malvaceae), evening primrose family (Onograceae), mint family (Labiatae), rue family (Rutaceae) and the close relatives of chicory (Liguliforae), could only be identified to the family level. The remaining 11 taxa: thistle (*Cirsium* sp.), lady's-thumb type (*Polygonum Persicaria*-type), wild buckwheat (*Eriogonum* sp.), plantain (*Plantago* sp.), spurge (*Euphorbia* sp.), milkwort (*Polygala* sp.), buckthorn (*Rhamnus* sp.), Mexican poppy (*Kallstromia* sp.), currant (*Ribes* sp.), gilia (*Gilia* sp.), and barberry (*Berberis* sp.) were identified to the genus level.

The ethnobotanical record makes reference to plants producing virtually all of these pollen types, and it is possible, since most of the parent plants produce very little pollen, that the presence of some of them represents human activities. Certain occurrences reach 6 percent, but among such scattered counts the patterns of distribution required to establish a pollen taxa as reflecting exploitation of the parent plants cannot be demonstrated. It is best to simply state that the plants were growing nearby and were available to the Wind Mountain inhabitants.

Summary and Conclusions

Pollen data from the Wind Mountain site indicate that corn and squash agriculture was practiced and that a number of wild (or possibly semicultivated) resources were exploited. Plants for which there is good evidence for prehistoric use include some insect-pollinated member or members of the Compositae family, one or more grasses, prickly pear cactus, joint-fir, sagebrush, Rocky Mountain beeweed and some member or members of the rose, sunflower, and lily families.

Plants that were probably utilized but where the evidence is more problematical are: cholla cactus and other cacti, as well as some member or members of the parsley and potato families. The local population of goosefoot was very likely exploited, but any firm evidence is submerged in the profuse pollen production of such plants accompanying agricultural soil disturbance.

Finally, mututally exclusive distributions of corn and *Cleome* sp. pollen in pit houses and surface structures may suggest that corn agriculture was more important in the Late Pit House period. The importance of Rocky Mountain beeweed in later structures may indicate that the surface occupation was a time of some economic stress.

Appendix 3

Summary of Archaeomagnetic Work at Wind Mountain

Robert S. Sternberg and Randall H. McGuire

Archaeomagnetic research has been going on in the southwestern United States for more than 30 years (beginning c. 1962–1963), primarily carried out by Dr. R. L. DuBois of the University of Oklahoma (Watanabe and DuBois 1965; Dubois 1975b). Only in the last few years have other laboratories begun to pursue this work: Sternberg, McGuire, and Butler at the University of Arizona, Eighmy and students at Colorado State University, and Wolfman at the Arkansas Archaeological Survey and later at the Archaeomagnetic Dating Laboratory at the Museum of New Mexico. Archaeomagnetism has proved productive as a dating tool for archaeology, and might be useful in probing other archaeological problems (Eighmy et al. 1980). It is also of interest to geophysicists who would like to have a detailed record of temporal changes in the regional geomagnetic field prior to the establishment of observatories early in this century. Revisions to the original archaeomagnetic curve proposed by DuBois (1975b) have recently been proposed (Eighmy et al. 1982; Sternberg and McGuire 1990).

Data for the archaeomagnetic features at Wind Mountain is summarized (Appendix 3: Table 1). Only the results after demagnetization are presented; presumably, unstable secondary components of magnetization have been erased, and the remaining magnetization is due to the last intense firing of the hearths. For the N samples used per feature, the mean direction of magnetization in geographic coordinates is specified by I, the dip with respect to horizontal, and D, the azimuth with respect to geographic north. The direction specified by I and D can be represented as a vector in spherical coordinates and plotted as a point on a stereographic projection. Thus $\alpha95$ is the spherical analog of two standard deviations; it is the angle subtended by the cone of uncertainty (two standard deviations) about the mean direction. The intersection of this cone of uncertainty with the sphere (or stereonet) is a circle of uncertainty about the mean direction. To enable comparisons between results from different sites, the mean direction is transformed to a virtual geomagnetic pole (VGP) position. This transformation is purely mathematical, yielding the location of the boreal magnetic pole that will provide the given direction at the given site. The circle of confidence is transformed to an oval of confidence specified by DM, the semimajor axis, and DP, the semiminor axis. DP is measured along a great circle between the site and the mean pole position, and DM is measured perpendicular to this direction. The VGPs and ovals of confidence can also be plotted in stereographic projection. The polar transformation assumes the morphology of Earth's magnetic field is dipolar. To a first approximation this is true, but second order differences between the shape of the real geomagnetic and that of a magnetic dipole is the reason why separate archaeomagnetic master curves are required for different regions. Further information on the above paleomagnetic and statistical procedures is presented by Eighmy et al. (1980) and in references provided by Irving (1964) and McElhinny (1973).

The number of samples used in computing feature averages is not always equal to the total number of samples collected (Appendix 3: Table 1). The samples not averaged are considered "outliers," which are unrepresentative of the statistical population being sampled. This is the first project in which the outlier problem has been rigorously considered. The general problem for Gaussian distributions is clearly outlined by Grubbs (1969). Selection of outliers inevitably depends upon the judgment of the experimenter. There is always a certain probability that a random sample of a statistical population will contain an observation far removed from the population mean. Glibly rejecting samples as outliers merely because they do not obviously agree with other measurements will lead to spuriously high precision. Thus, in an optimal

Appendix 3: Table 1. Summary of Wind Mountain Archaeomagnetic Results

Feature	N_c/N	Demag (Oersteds)	I (deg)	D (deg)	α95 (deg)	PLAT (deg)	PLONG (deg)	DM (deg)	DP (deg)
WM001	8/7	H 250	55.80	329.77	2.2	64.93	178.49	3.18	2.38
WM002	11/8	H 150	52.43	2.04	2.4	88.25	329.62	3.36	2.31
WM003	9/9	H 150	52.40	354.07	2.0	85.00	166.87	2.70	1.86
WM004	9/8	H 150	53.88	354.03	1.2	84.73	182.45	1.64	1.15
WM005	9/7	H 300	36.33	355.39	3.0	76.85	90.05	3.51	2.04
WM006	9/8	H 150	58.95	346.68	2.4	77.18	198.60	3.59	2.68
WM007	10/9	H 150	56.80	342.28	2.0	74.77	184.54	2.89	2.10
WM008	9/9	H 150	59.40	355.55	2.0	81.66	227.50	3.02	2.26
WM009	10/10	H 150	49.63	1.09	1.9	87.60	48.55	2.56	1.71
WM010	9/8	H 150	49.81	3.53	2.8	86.36	15.00	3.74	2.50
WM011	12/11	H 150	58.73	351.59	1.8	80.40	208.97	2.67	1.99
WM012	9/9	H 150	57.25	342.94	2.7	75.17	186.80	3.88	2.83
WM013	9/8	H 150	59.54	343.32	5.4	74.58	196.26	8.06	6.06
WM014	9/9	H 150	52.50	6.65	2.1	84.40	335.57	2.86	1.97
WM015	12/12	H 150	45.53	4.38	1.5	83.16	36.74	1.96	1.25
WM016	9/9	H 150	48.90	3.58	2.2	85.81	23.75	2.95	1.94
WM017	10/9	H 100	52.97	358.32	2.9	88.35	193.37	4.05	2.80
WM018	8/7	H 150	43.29	352.11	2.6	79.84	116.37	3.23	2.01
WM019	8/8	H 150	46.43	1.93	2.8	84.78	52.47	3.57	2.29
WM020	8/8	H 150	46.61	357.74	3.0	84.81	94.34	3.90	2.51
WM021	8/6	H 150	52.22	6.59	4.9	84.46	338.30	6.79	4.66
WM022	8/8	H 150	45.20	2.96	1.3	83.52	47.53	1.70	1.08
WM023	8/8	H 300	39.48	351.02	10.6	77.00	111.49	12.68	7.59
WM024	8/8	H 150	42.95	0.65	2.6	82.26	67.21	3.26	2.02
WM025	8/7	H 150	47.42	351.93	4.3	81.93	132.97	5.60	3.63
WM026	8/7	H 150	54.33	8.77	7.6	82.40	322.53	10.65	7.49
WM027	8/8	H 300	54.48	348.53	7.6	80.20	178.52	10.78	7.60
WM028	7/7	H 200	44.22	15.68	4.7	74.78	3.80	5.96	3.74
WM029	7/6	H 200	51.42	1.05	3.5	88.93	15.45	4.82	3.28
WM030	8/7	H 150	56.23	1.27	3.3	85.77	265.51	4.78	3.44
WM031	8/8	H 150	51.93	12.68	14.2	79.33	338.82	19.40	13.26
WM032	8/7	H 200	50.20	25.14	7.8	68.62	339.40	10.47	7.01
WM033	6/6	H 200	53.83	11.48	11.7	80.29	328.47	16.31	11.40
WM034	8/8	H 150	52.33	2.94	3.0	87.52	334.94	4.08	2.81
WM035	8/8	H 150	43.73	11.65	5.1	77.59	13.61	6.31	3.94
WM036	8/8	H 150	57.99	7.73	2.9	81.34	295.83	4.24	3.12
WM037	8/8	H 150	52.26	0.56	3.7	89.49	320.12	5.10	3.50
WM038	8/8	H 150	47.29	3.14	4.0	84.98	38.22	5.19	3.36
WM039	8/8	H 150	57.51	352.23	7.7	81.64	204.57	11.27	8.25
WM040	8/8	H 150	31.23	7.56	19.7	72.77	46.45	22.08	12.36
WM041	6/5	H 150	45.70	357.79	5.0	84.13	91.18	6.40	4.08
WM042	8/8	H 150	47.03	8.96	17.3	81.09	9.27	22.38	14.46
WM043	8/7	H 150	48.25	355.83	1.9	85.05	118.97	2.54	1.66
WM044	8/8	H 400	13.50	4.73	46.1	63.79	60.91	47.12	24.06

N is the number of samples needed to compute feature averages; N_c is the number of samples collected in the field; Demag is the peak alternating field used for magnetic cleaning; I and D are the mean paleomagnetic inclination and declination; α95 is the angle subtended by the cone of uncertainty about I and D; PLAT and PLONG are the latitude and longitude of the virtual geomagnetic pole position; DP is the uncertainty in the VGP along a great circle passing through the site and the VGP; DM is the uncertainty in the VGP perpendicular to this great circle. Site coordinates used are 32.687° N, 108.407° E with a current magnetic declination of 12.07° E.

situation, outliers would not be selected unless some reason could be determined why that observation was anomalous. In archaeomagnetic sampling such reasons would include a sample that had moved during collection, a poorly fired sample, a sample that contained extraneous material such as roots or pebbles, a sample that was spatially separated from others, a weakly demagnetized sample, or a sample that demonstrated unstable demagnetization behavior. For the 44 Wind Mountain features, 26 had no outliers, 15 had one outlier, two had two outliers, and one feature had three outliers. In most instances, outliers were only selected if the sample was anomalous in one of the above respects. However it is possible that the above conditions may not be noted or that errors are made in sample collection or laboratory measurement. For such cases it is useful to have a test to check on (quasi) statistical grounds alone whether or not a sample is an outlier. Such a test should be judiciously and stringently applied. Testing for detection of single outliers is as follows: (1) the sample direction (D,I) that makes the largest angle with the feature average is located; (2) a new mean direction for the feature is calculated, omitting the tentative outlier; (3) the probability is calculated that the suspected outlier is a member of the distribution corresponding to the revised average (McFadden 1980); (4) if this probability is less than 0.5 percent, the sample is considered a bona fide outlier and the revised average is accepted. The probability that 10 samples will be within the 0.5 percent limit is $.995^{10}$, or 95 percent. Thus, this test will falsely detect outliers only about one time in twenty. The test may be reapplied for detection of further outliers. If this test does not warrant rejection of a single outlier, but it appears that there may be multiple outliers in the data set, another test is used. The precision parameter k (similar to $\alpha 95$) is calculated before and after deletion of the suspected samples. Only if the precision has increased at the 0.5 percent level according to the F-test of Watson (see Irving 1964:63; McElhinny 1973:80) will these samples be considered possible outliers. This test does not seem as powerful as the one above and was used with caution. Only once was a pair of samples rejected primarily as a result of this test.

A chronological interpretation of Southwestern archaeomagnetic data is possible using DuBois's "polar data representation curves" for A.D. 600–900 (DuBois 1975a; Wolfman 1979) and A.D. 900–1500 (DuBois 1975a, 1975b). These curves are termed virtual geomagnetic pole paths in keeping with the usual paleomagnetic terminology. Neither the raw archaeomagnetic data nor the information on associated archaeological dates used to reconstruct DuBois's curves have been published in much detail. Recently, Eighmy et al. (1982) have proposed revisions of DuBois's curve from A.D. 600 to 960, and Sternberg and McGuire (1990) have proposed revisions for the time period A.D. 1000 to 1500. Dating interpretations for the Wind Mountain samples are presented using these revisions (Appendix 3: Table 2).

The data needed to make archaeomagnetic chronological interpretations are the virtual pole position specified by PLAT and PLONG and the error in estimating the position, DM and DP. Assuming no systematic errors, there is a 95 percent chance that the true VGP lies within the oval specified by these parameters. In using the polar plot method to interpret a date, the oval for each feature should be overlain on the VGP curve (drawn to the same scale). Ideally, calculating a date is simply a matter of noting where the path of the curve cuts through the oval of confidence. This procedure is not recommended, as it only incorporates imprecisions in the VGP and does not include imprecisions in the calibration of the curve. A new (Arizona) method for calculating archaeomagnetic dates has been developed that includes all sources of imprecision. Needless to say, this method usually produces dates with a wider range than the polar plot method (Sternberg and McGuire 1990).

No matter which procedure is used it is quite possible for the oval to intersect the curve for more than one age range because the curve loops back over itself. If the oval intersects the curve for two distinct age ranges (four times) there are two possible dates (age ranges), and for six intersections there are three possible interpretations. In such cases, there is no way to determine from the archaeomagnetic data which is the correct date. Furthermore, in some cases the oval of confidence will be so large that any date derived will cover such a range of time as to be useless.

Several of the hearths collected at Wind Mountain were expected to date before A.D. 600. No archaeomagnetic curves have been published for the Southwest that extend back into this period. It is not presently possible to infer pre-600 dates from archaeomagnetic data. If such early curves become available, the Wind Mountain data might be used to see if pre-600 dates could be interpreted. It should be noted that due to the vermicular path of the VGP curve, a hearth that was fired pre-600 might yield an apparent post-600 archaeomagnetic date. If the pre-600 curves were available, multiple interpretations would then result that would not be resolvable based solely on the archaeomagnetic evidence. Thus a post-600 interpreted date does not preclude the possibility that a feature might date to an earlier period.

Archaeomagnetic dates have traditionally been reported in a format similar to radiocarbon dates as a "best" date ± standard deviation. This has been determined to be a misleading procedure for interpreting archaeomagnetic dates. In the case of a radiocarbon date, the plus-minus factor is usually a one standard deviation counting error, and the error in age is normally distributed. This is not the case in an archaeomagnetic date as the VGP curve may pass through an oval lengthwise, across its width or even make a turn within the oval. For these reasons, the distribution of error in ages will not be normal.

Appendix 3: Table 2. Interpretation of Archaeomagnetic Dating at Wind Mountain

Lab No.	Provenience	Interpretation (all dates A.D.)
	WM locus	
WM-001	Hearth in front of House B entry	plotted off curve
WM-002	Hearth on floor, House N	630–720 or 870–1030
WM-003	Hearth on floor, House E	620–700 or 900–1070
WM-004	Hearth on floor, House H	620–720 or 900–1070
WM-005	Plastered floor, House G	plotted off curve
WM-006	Hearth on floor, House M	1000–1190
WM-007	Hearth on floor, Room 7	1040–1130
WM-008	Hearth on floor, House W	(?)–690 or 1300–1390
WM-009	Hearth on floor, House BB	640–760 or 820–940
WM-010	Hearth on floor, House AA	640–780 or 810–930
WM-011	Hearth on floor, House V	970–1080 or 1180–1350
WM-012	Hearth on floor, Room 15	1030–1150
WM-013	Plastered floor, Room 16	1000–1260
WM-014	Plastered floor, House EE	650–720
WM-015	Hearth on floor, House X	800–870
WM-016	Plastered floor, House X	650–780 or 810–940
WM-017	Plastered floor, House DD	620–720 or 810–1070
WM-018	Plaster on wall, House AJ	plotted off curve
WM-019	Hearth on floor, House AF	650–790 or 820–940
WM-020	Plastered floor, House AK	640–780
WM-021	Hearth on floor, House HH	640–730 or 820–960
WM-022	Plaster on wall, House SS	630–770 or 800–860
WM-023	Hearth on floor, House AC	Alpha-95 too great
WM-024	Cremation pit #2	670–860
WM-026	Hearth on floor, House AB	620–730 or 820–940
WM-027	Hearth on floor, House XX	Alpha-95 too great
WM-028	Plaster on wall, House AH	plotted off curve
WM-029	Plaster on wall, House AG	620–740 or 820–960
WM-036	Plaster on wall, House AM	plotted off curve
WM-037	Plaster on wall, House AL	620–720 or 830–1070
WM-038	Plaster on wall, House AQ	700–950
WM-043	Hearth on floor, House AD	640–720 or 820–990
WM-044	Plaster on wall, House WW	Alpha-95 too great
	RO locus	
WM-025	Hearth on floor, House B	plotted off curve
WM-030	Hearth on floor, House F	620–710, 880–1070 or 1350–1450
WM-031	Hearth on floor, House C	Alpha-95 too great
WM-032	Hearth on floor, House H	Alpha-95 too great
WM-033	Hearth on floor, House J	Alpha-95 too great
WM-034	Hearth on floor, House I	640–730 or 820–1020
WM-035	Plaster on wall, House G	plotted off curve
WM-039	Plaster on wall, House G	Alpha-95 too great
WM-040	Plaster on wall, House E	710–940
WM-041	Hearth on floor, House D	640–870
WM-042	Plaster on wall, House C	Alpha-95 too great

These interpretations were derived from the data in the appendix and Eighmy et al.'s (1982) VGP path for the time period A.D. 600–960 and Sternberg and McGuire's (1990) VGP path for the time period A.D. 1000–1500. The Arizona method of interpreting dates was used (Sternberg and McGuire 1990).

Also, if dates were given in a plus-minus format the error factor would often be asymmetrical; the plus factor would be the range of time from the "best" date to the most recent point of intersection, and the minus factor would be the range of time from the "best" date to the oldest path of intersection. An archaeomagnetic date is, therefore, best represented by the time range of the curve contained within the oval of confidence. Using a two standard deviation oval of confidence seems appropriate considering the several possible sources of error in the curve and dated feature and the unpredictable way in which these factors interact. The resultant age range is probably more equivalent to ± one standard deviation.

The approach here is similar to that suggested for the calibration of radiocarbon dates by the "Workshop on Calibration of the Radiocarbon Time Scale" held at the University of Arizona early in 1979 (Klein et al. 1980). The general interpretational procedure of archaeomagnetic dating is quite similar to the problem of radiocarbon calibration: an experimentally determined quantity (magnetic direction or radiocarbon age) must be compared with a master curve (VGP curve or radiocarbon versus calendar years). Both the measurement and the curves contain errors. However, archaeomagnetism deals with vector rather than scalar quantities. The calibration workshop concluded that calibrated radiocarbon ages should be presented as ranges and that the interpretation should be conservative and consider the uncertainty inherent in the calibration curve. Presentation of archaeomagnetic dates as ranges, then, is consistent with the latest procedures in radiocarbon dating. Alternative methods of archaeomagnetic interpretation are currently being explored that will allow consideration of the uncertainty in the VGP curve.

As should be apparent from this brief discussion, the interpretation of an archaeomagnetic date is not a mathematically rigorous procedure. Different interpretations can easily vary by 10 to 20 years. However, current research indicates (Eighmy et al. 1980) that the practical limit in precision for an archaeomagnetic date is a range of 40 years (± 20 years).

Appendix 4

The Orientation of Wind Mountain Structures in the Late Pit House Period
A Statistical Test for Nonrandomness

Allan J. McIntyre and Edward J. Pasahow

The observation that Mogollon structures of the Late Pit House period tend to orient in an easterly direction is not new. Among others, Wheat (1955), Bullard (1962), and Martin (1979) make passing reference to this phenomenon. However, little data has been presented that attempts to quantify or rationalize this trend, an apparently ubiquitous pattern in the Mimbres Mogollon culture sphere.

A brief review of the Wind Mountain site plan (Figures 4.1 and 4.2) presents a picture of a settlement that developed slowly over time. The site never supported continuous long-term occupation, but throughout an estimated 700– to 900–year period (c. A.D. 250/550–1150/1200) became a favored, intermittent-habitation locality. Wind Mountain best evidences recurrent occupation during the Late Pit House period (c. A.D. 550–950/1000). It was during this time that the site supported a series of residents who, with human imprecision and inconsistency, constructed and oriented their pit houses in a nonrandom manner. Within this nonrandomness, a tendency for an easterly orientation was established.

Statistical Tests and Results

In anticipation of statistical analysis, 61 substantially complete Wind Mountain structures were segregated into one of three typological categories: (1) community structures (n = 6), (2) Type II structures (n = 9), and (3) Type IV structures (n = 46). To better understand the orientation of these pit houses, diagrams (Appendix 4: Figures 1, 2, and 3) were formulated. Each figure represents the lateral entrance alignments for a given structure type. To evaluate the hypothesis that entry orientation occurred nonrandomly, the product of mixed cultural and environmental variables, a series of statistical tests were conducted (Freund 1971; Bruning and Kintz 1968).

The first observation drawn from the data (Appendix 4: Table 1) is that the means of all three structure types fall into a southeasterly orientation (*southeasterly* refers to the range between 90° and 179° off true north). Secondly, the ranges of one standard deviation on either side of the mean generally occur in an easterly direction (*easterly* refers to the range between 1° and 179° off true north) with the exception of Type II structures in which the southern range varied as much as 205.52° (25.52° west of due south).

To evaluate the data, it was felt that statistical hypothesis testing might refine our initial observations. To do so, three sets of statistical tests were conducted: Tests of One Mean, Tests Concerning Variances, and Tests for Differences between Means.

Tests of One Mean

This test asks whether we can accept or reject the null hypothesis for a given mean azimuth for the entrances in each set. Specifically, we asked, can we reject the null hypothesis that the mean of the entrances was 180° and 90° for each of the sample sets? The answer to this question should provide us with a solution as to whether the entrances were or were not randomly aligned.

Tests Concerning Variances

The test of variance is an intermediate step in our analysis. At this stage we require that the two population variances be equal before a two sample t-test is valid. Checking the reliability of that assumption is our rationale for this test.

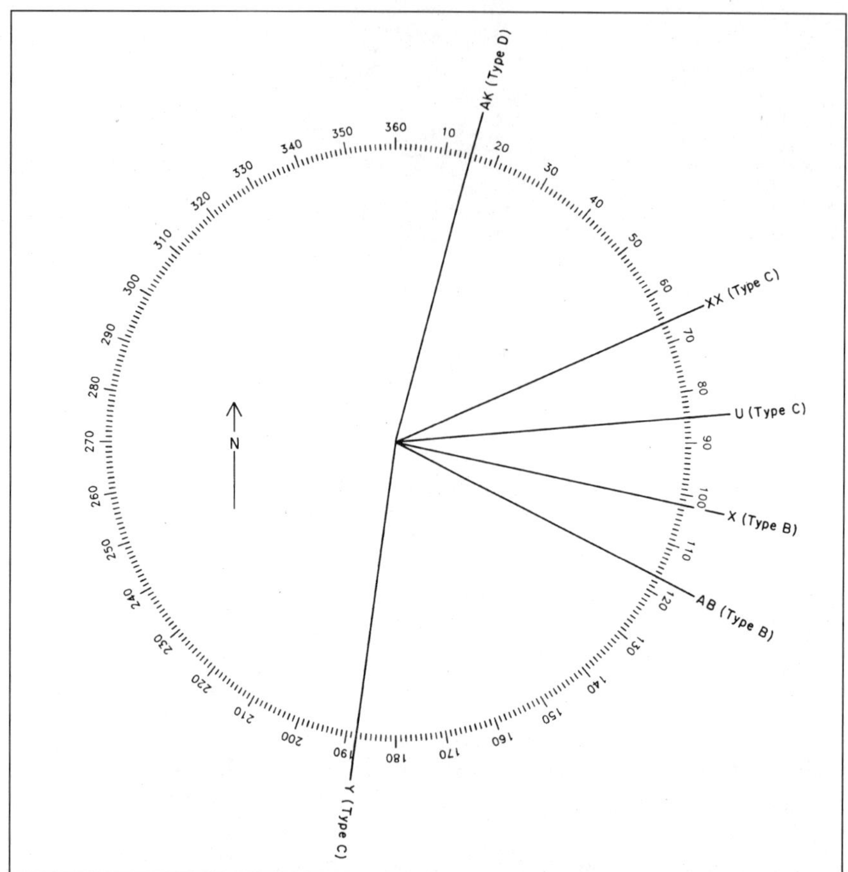

Appendix 4: Figure 1. Orientations of community structures (n = 6).

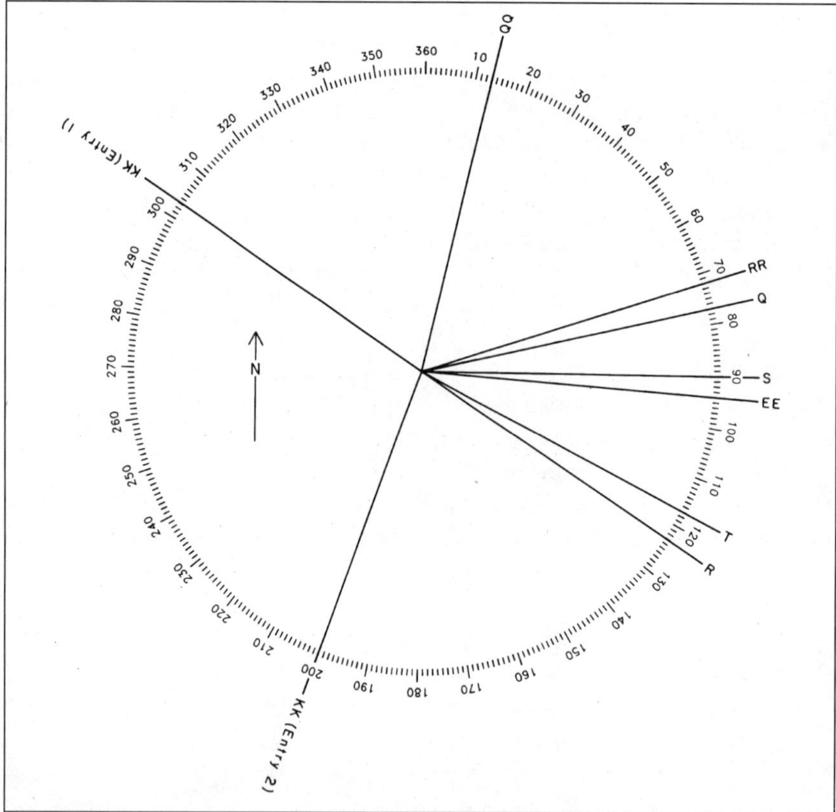

Appendix 4: Figure 2. Orientations of Type II structures (n = 9).

Tests for Differences between Means

The purpose of this, our final test, is to determine whether or not the three sample populations have the same mean azimuth. Based on statistical data, are we justified in concluding that the entrances to all three structure classes tend to be oriented in the same direction.

Our first test, the Test of One Mean, to establish whether we can reject the hypothesis for a mean alignment of 180°, was rejected for both community and Type IV structures. In the case of Type II structures, the hypothesis was accepted. The hypothesis for a mean alignment of 90° was accepted for all three structure types.

Test: Two-tailed t-test, where n<30. The level of significance was 95 percent.

$$t = \frac{\bar{x} - \mu_0}{\frac{s}{\sqrt{n}}}$$

Hypothesis:
Community Structures
H_o: Azimuth = 180°
H_1: Azimuth ≠180°

t = -3.60
t 0.025, 5 = -2.571

Therefore we reject H_o

Hypothesis:
Community Structures
H_o: Azimuth = 90°
H_1: Azimuth ≠ 90°

t = 0.23
t 0.025, 5 = 2.571

Therefore we accept H_o

The assumption of a mean azimuth for community structures was rejected at 180°, but accepted at 90°.

Hypothesis:
Type II Structures
H_o: Azimuth = 180°
H_1: Azimuth ≠ 180°

t = -2.10
t 0.025, 8 = -2.306

Therefore we accept H_o

Hypothesis:
Type II Structures
H_o: Azimuth = 90°
H_1: Azimuth ≠ 90°

t = 1.09
t 0.025, 8 = 2.306

Therefore we accept H_o

Our hypothesis was accepted for Type II structures in which both 180° and 90° azimuth points were confirmed.

To test the Type IV structures, a large sample z-score was chosen.

Test: Large sample z-score, where n = 46. The level of significance was 95 percent.

$$z = \frac{\bar{x} - \mu_0}{\frac{s}{\sqrt{n}}}$$

Hypothesis:
Type IV Structures
H_o: Azimuth = 180°
H_1: Azimuth ≠ 180°

APPENDIX 4: TABLE 1. Statistical Data of Orientation by Structure Class

Structure Classes	n	Mean Azimuth Orientation	s	s^2	Range of 1 Std. Dev. either Side of Mean
Community structures	6	95.50°	57.48°	3303.95	38.02° – 152.98°
Type II	9	120.89°	84.63°	7162.44	36.26° – 205.52°
Type IV	46	110.61°	69.73°	4862.27	40.88° – 180.34°

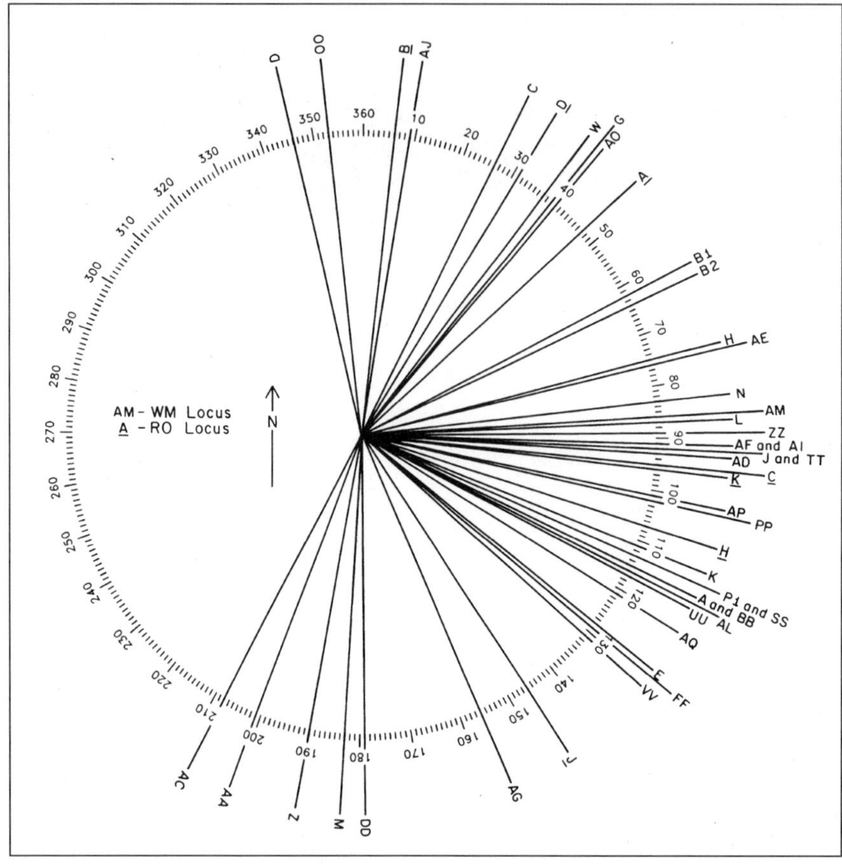

APPENDIX 4: FIGURE 3. Orientations of Type IV structures (n = 46).

z = -6.75
z 0.025 = -1.96

Therefore we reject H_o

Hypothesis:
Type IV Structures
H_o: Azimuth = 90°
H_1: Azimuth ≠ 90°

z = 1.95
z 0.025 = 1.96

Therefore we accept H_o

The assumption of a mean azimuth for Type IV structures was rejected at 180°, but accepted at 90°.

To test for variability in the data set, our samples were compared in pairs: (1) Type II Houses and Community Structures, (2) Type II and Type IV Houses, (3) Type IV Houses and Community Structures. In all instances, we concluded that the variability of the data samples was the same.

Test: Comparison of Variances (F distribution or ratio) is required to compute a two-sample t-test, which follows. In this test, each pair of data is compared, either accepting or rejecting the null hypothesis. The level of significance was 98 percent.

$$F = \frac{s_1^2}{s_2^2}$$

Hypothesis:
H_o: $\sigma 1 = \sigma 2$
H_1: $\sigma 1 = \sigma 2$

Comparison of Type II structure variance (a) with community structure variance (b).

$$\frac{s_a^2}{s_b^2} = 2.17$$

$F_{0.01, 8, 5} = 10.3$

Therefore we accept H_o

Comparison of Type II structure variance (a) with Type IV structure variance (c).

$$\frac{s_a^2}{s_c^2} = 1.47$$

$F_{0.01, 8, 45} = 2.93$

Therefore we accept H_o

Comparison of Type IV structure variance (c) with community structure variance (b).

$$\frac{s_c^2}{s_b^2} = 1.47$$

$F_{0.01, 45, 5} = 9.29$

Therefore we accept H_o

Our final test for differences between paired measurements consisted of a two sample t-test of the difference between means. This test is commonly used as a way of dealing with the problem of samples that are not independent. It should be pointed out that this could occur if the azimuth orientation of entrances were dependent upon cultural preferences.

Test: Tests for the Differences Between Means (two sample t-test). The level of significance was 95 percent.

$$t = \frac{\bar{x}_1 - \bar{x}_2 - \sigma}{\sqrt{\frac{(n_1-1)\,s_1^2 + (n_2-1)\,s_2^2}{n_1+n_2-2}}\sqrt{\frac{1}{n_1}+\frac{1}{n_2}}}$$

Hypothesis:
H_o: $\mu_1 = \mu_2$ ($\sigma = 0$)
H_1: $\mu_1 = \mu_2$ ($\sigma \neq 0$)

Comparison of community structures with Type II structures.
$t = -0.63$

APPENDIX 4: FIGURE 4. View from the Wind Mountain locus looking southeast toward the Big Burro Mountains (Neg. No. WM 4–14F).

$t_{0.025, 13} = -2.16$
Therefore we accept H_o

Comparison of Type II structures with Type IV structures.
$t = 0.40$
$t_{0.025, 53} = 2.007$

Therefore we accept H_o

Comparison of community structures with Type IV structures.
$t = 0.51$
$t_{0.025, 50} = 2.010$

Therefore we accept H_o

Discussion

In summary, though there was a differences of 25° between the means of the community and Type II structures, our tests indicate that the hypothesis for no difference in the means cannot be rejected. The equivalence of the means may be due to chance, small sample size, or indicates a deliberate attempt by pit house builders to orient entrances in a southeasterly direction.

To substantiate the assumption that house orientation was deliberate and not the product of poor sample size or chance, additional data was compiled. Early in our study we assumed that house entry alignment toward the east was due to either direct sunrise alignment or general sunrise orientation. If we are to assume that Wind Mountain residents had the opportunity to randomly orient their houses (at Wind Mountain there is no reason to speculate otherwise) we would expect to

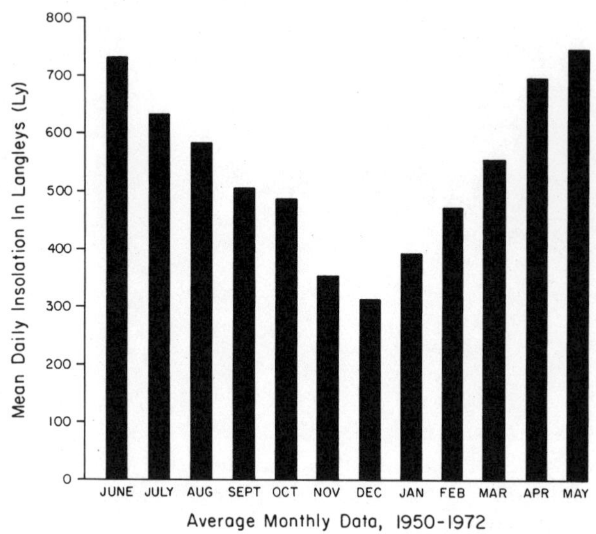

APPENDIX 4: FIGURE 5. Solar insolation in Langleys recorded near Silver City, New Mexico (after Tuan et al. 1973).

find structures dispersed about the entire range of a circular arc, n = 359. However, as is apparent in Appendix 4: Figures 1, 2, and 3, house orientation did not occur at random but instead was heavily biased towards the east. We reason that winter sunrise must have been a primary determinant in the orientation of structures, and that the low and open eastern and southeastern horizon at Wind Mountain (Appendix 4: Figure 4) presented an opportunity to receive both early morning daylight and warmth. To support an assumption that sunlight (and its associated warmth) equated with house orientation, we drew on data pertaining to solar radiation intensity.

The reception of solar radiation by a given body is measured in Langleys (Ly), one Ly = 3.68 BTU/cubic ft. A Langley is comprised of all forms of sun energy expressed as direct or diffuse radiation (a Langley does not include infrared wave lengths). Using data collected near Silver City, New Mexico, Bennett (in Tuan et al. 1973:157–184) provides computations of solar radiation intensity in the vicinity of Wind Mountain. As we would expect, the lowest number of Lys (range 313–488) were recorded during the months of October through February (Appendix 4: Figure 5), compared with the highest numbers (range 509–744) occurring March through September.

If morning warmth was a determining factor, the position of the sun on the eastern horizon should correlate with house entry orientation. Appendix 4: Table 2 presents data on all solstice and equinox sunrises and sunsets charted over five centuries at the Wind Mountain site (Latitude 32°40'20" N, Longitude 108°24'26" W) from A.D. 500 to A.D. 1000. The variation in movement for sunrise solstice localities changed little during this 500 year period, occurring between 60° to the north (summer solstice, range 60°56'-61°01') and 118° to the south (winter solstice, range 117°45'-117°49').

APPENDIX 4: TABLE 2. Azimuths of Solstices and Equinoxes at Wind Mountain

	Equinox	Solstice	Equinox	Solstice
	Spring	*Summer*	*Fall*	*Winter*
A.D. 500	3/18	6/20	9/21	12/19
Sunrise	89° 36'	60° 56'	89° 31'	117° 49'
Sunset	270° 09'	299° 03'	270° 42'	242° 10'
	Spring	*Summer*	*Fall*	*Winter*
A.D. 600	3/18	6/19	9/20	12/18
Sunrise	89° 15'	60° 58'	89° 24'	117° 48'
Sunset	270° 31'	299° 01'	270° 49'	242° 11'
	Spring	*Summer*	*Fall*	*Winter*
A.D. 700	3/17	6/18	9/19	12/17
Sunrise	89° 21'	60° 58'	89° 17'	117° 47'
Sunset	270° 24'	299° 00'	270° 56'	242° 12'
	Spring	*Summer*	*Fall*	*Winter*
A.D. 800	3/16	6/18	9/19	12/17
Sunrise	89° 27'	60° 59'	89° 39'	117° 46'
Sunset	270° 18'	299° 00'	270° 34'	242° 13'
	Spring	*Summer*	*Fall*	*Winter*
A.D. 900	3/15	6/17	9/18	12/16
Sunrise	89° 33'	61° 01'	89° 33'	117° 45'
Sunset	270° 12'	298° 58'	270° 40'	242° 14'
	Spring	*Summer*	*Fall*	*Winter*
A.D. 1000	3/14	6/16	9/17	12/15
Sunrise	89° 39'	61° 01'	89° 26'	117° 45'
Sunset	270° 06'	298° 58'	270° 47'	242° 14'

Note: Azimuths computed for a level horizon. Precession and refraction corrections were incorporated.

Using simple percentages, computations were made to test for the influence that the morning sun and heliacal movement might have had on structure orientation. Appendix 4: Table 3 illustrates the tendency for entry orientation to occur between summer and winter solstices as well as those concentrated toward winter sunrises (i.e., between equinoxes). The range of sunrise movement along the eastern horizon, averaging between 60° to the north and 118° to the south, represents a heliacal migration of 58°, or 16 percent of the entire range of possibilities in an arc. Fifty-six percent of all structure entries were oriented within this range. Of that data marking the period of time and segment of arc occurring between the fall and spring equinoxes, the equinox sunrise occurs at a position of approximately 90°, whereas the winter solstice occurs at an angle of about 118°. Within this particular 28° segment, 23 entrance orientations were documented. Consequently, during the winter months 38 percent of our sample was found to occur within 8 percent of the entire range of possibilities.

APPENDIX 4: TABLE 3. Structures Oriented Between Summer and Winter Solstices

Structure Classes	n	Number of Structures Oriented between 60° and 118°	Percent of Total	Number of Structures Oriented between 90° and 118°	Percent of Total
Community structures	6	4	67	3	50
Type II	9	5	56	3	33
Type IV	46	25	54	17	37
Totals	61	34	56	23	38

House orientations may have implications for the timing of construction activities at the site. The study suggests that a preponderance of pit houses may have been constructed during months coincident with fall and winter (for further discussion, see Farwell 1987).

In the Silver City area, the first killing frost after summer is usually anticipated between 20 and 30 October (range 30 September to 10 November). The last killing frost is expected between 10 and 20 April (range 26 March to 20 May; Tuan et al. 1973). We suspect that these intervals coincide with intensified construction episodes at the settlement. Thus, cold weather would create, or increase, the need to build or repair shelters. Alternatively, it seems reasonable to assume that the inhabitants of Wind Mountain, a people inextricably joined to the landscape, would have a rudimentary but intimate folk knowledge of astronomical and climatic information. This awareness of their surroundings, gained experientially and perpetuated through oral tradition, could have easily enabled them to predict the onset of winter and its associated cooler temperatures. The design of structures, their placement, orientation, and construction could all have been established well in advance of winter.

It is speculated that the orientation of houses at Wind Mountain in the Late Pit House period were not positioned randomly, but were preferentially placed. An easterly (n = 52 or 85 percent), and particularly southeasterly (n = 30 or 49 percent) orientation was probably determined through a combination of intertwined cultural dictates, personal needs, and environmental factors.

Appendix 5

Di Peso's Classification System

The following tables represent Di Peso's efforts to classify Wind Mountain (and Mogollon) material culture. The rationale underlying this taxonomic construct has been discussed (Chapter 5). Di Peso never elaborated in written form how he conceived of and developed his classification system. What survives is the literal system itself, with only infrequent cursory comments dispersed throughout a few rough notes.

The broad, functionally based object classes are presented first (Appendix 5: Table 1). These provide the framework that outlines the detailed, descriptive hierarchical attributes that define specific artifact types. Incidentally, this classification represents the only comprehensive analysis of any set of Wind Mountain data Di Peso completed before his death. He strongly believed that archaeologists should, as a matter of course, bring intense detail to object classification. Di Peso devised the scheme not merely for use at the Wind Mountain site, but for other material data bases. He fully intended for the complete classification to be included in the Wind Mountain publication in its entirety.

The second table (Appendix 5: Table 2) furnishes artifact summary descriptions and complex type notations correlated with reference numbers. Di Peso felt such numbers would simplify his classification scheme by supplying shorthand designations to be used as reference aids.

In addition to artifact classes, primary and secondary architectural forms were ordered according to structure and hearth types. The third table (Appendix 5: Table 3) defines the principal structure types including domestic structures, community houses, and surface room units (refer to Chapters 4 and 5). Identified as ancillary architectural features, hearth types are presented (Appendix 5: Table 4).

As can be inferred from the four tables, the material inventory from Wind Mountain consists not only of the portable objects such as stone tools or ceramic vessels that were recovered, but also includes the site's architecture. Taken together, these tables identify the individual elements (i.e., types) that comprise Di Peso's classification system.

APPENDIX 5: TABLE 1. Di Peso Classification System of Wind Mountain Material Culture

I. Utilitarian Tool Morphology
A. Stone tools
1. Pecked and/or ground manufacture
a. Two piece fitted pulverizer with coincident parts in contact
(1). Reciprocal action
(a). Flat surfaced
1'. ≥ 30 cm arm stroke (nether stone); slab metate
a'. Boulder
b'. Slab
2'. Handstone (upper stone); mano
a'. One hand (<16 cm long)
1". Taper cross section
a". Uniface
b". Biface
2". Block cross section
a". Uniface
3". Loaf cross section
a". Uniface
b'. Two hand (≥16 cm long)
1". Taper cross section
a". Uniface
b". Biface
2". Block cross section
a". Uniface
b". Biface
3". Loaf cross section
a". Uniface
3'. <30 cm arm stroke (nether stone); grinding slab
a'. Boulder
1". Unshaped
b'. Slab
1". Unshaped
2". Shaped
c'. Unclassified
4'. Handstone (upper stone) <13 cm long; rubbing stone
a'. Unshaped
1". Circular
a". Uniface
b". Biface
2". Rectangular
a". Uniface
b". Biface
b'. Shaped
1". Circular
a". Uniface
b". Biface
2". Rectangular
a". Uniface
b". Biface
3". Unclassified
(b). Trough
1'. ≥ 30 cm arm stroke (nether stone); trough metate
a'. One end open
1". Boulder
2". Slab
b'. Two ends open
1". Boulder
2". Slab

Appendix 5: Table 1. *(continued)*

2'. Handstone (upper stone); mano
  a'. One hand - < 16 cm long
    1". Taper cross section
      a". Uniface
      b". Biface
    2". Block cross section
      a". Uniface
      b". Biface
    3". Loaf cross section
      a". Uniface
  b'. Two hand - ≥16 cm long
    1". Taper cross section
      a". Uniface
      b". Biface
    2". Block cross section
      a". Uniface
      b". Biface
    3". Loaf cross section
      a". Uniface

(2). Rotary action; basin metate
  (a). <30 cm arm stroke (nether stone)
    1'. Boulder
    2'. Slab
  (b). One hand handstone (upper stone); mano
    1'. Taper cross section
      a". Uniface
    2'. Block cross section
      a". Uniface
    3'. Loaf cross section
      a". Uniface

(3). Unclassified two piece fitted pulverizer fragment (nether stone); unidentified metate
  (a). Boulder
  (b). Slab

(4). Unclassified two piece fitted pulverizer fragment (upper stone); unidentified mano

(5). Pounding and/or rotary action
  (a). Pebble receptacle pulverizer (nether stone), 1–15 cm diameter (long axis); mortar/bowl
    1'. Rectangular
      a". Unshaped
      b". Shaped
    2'. Circular
      a". Unshaped
      b". Shaped
  (b). One hand pounding handstone (upper stone) 1–10 cm long; pestle
    1'. Rectangular
      a". Unshaped
    2'. Circular
      a". Unshaped
      b". Shaped
    3'. Elongated
      a". Unshaped
  (d). One hand pounding handstone (upper stone) ≥ 10 to 15 cm long; pestle
    1'. Rectangular
      a". Unshaped
      b". Shaped
    2'. Circular
      b". Shaped

Appendix 5: Table 1. *(continued)*

3'. Elongated
a". Unshaped
(e). Boulder receptacle pulverizer (nether stone) >30 cm diameter (long axis); mortar
1'. Rectangular
b". Shaped
(g). Two hand pounding handstone (upper stone)
15 cm long; pestle
3'. Elongated
a". Unshaped
b. One piece nether pulverizer (object to be pulverized is held in hand and rubbed against nether stone)
(1). Reciprocal action - abrader/whetstone
(a). Concave grinding surface
1'. Pebble
a'. Unshaped
b'. Shaped
2'. Slab
a'. Unshaped
b'. Shaped
(b). Grooved grinding surface
1'. Pebble
a'. Unshaped
2'. Slab
a'. Unshaped
b'. Shaped
(2). Rotary action
(a). Concave grinding surface
2'. Slab
a'. Unshaped; protopalette
b'. Shaped; protopalette
c'. Bordered; palette
c. One piece unhafted reciprocal action pulverizer (handstone; tool held against object to be pulverized or shaped); abrader
(1). Pebble (<15 cm diameter)
(a). Unshaped
(2). Slab
(a). Unshaped
(b). Shaped
d. One piece unhafted rotary action pulverizer (handstone); polishing stone
(1). Pebble (<15 cm)
(a). Unshaped
(b). Shaped
e. One piece hafted pounding action pulverizer (upper stone)
(1). Cutting edge parallel to haft; axe
(b). Full groove
(c). Double three-quarter groove
(2). Pounding edge parallel to haft; maul
(a). Three-quarter groove
(b). Full groove
(3). Incomplete hafted pounding action handstone; fragment
(a). Cutting edged tool
1'. Bit
2'. Body
3'. Poll
(b). Pounding surface tool
2'. Body
f. Centrally perforated disk; spindle whorl
(1). Chipped edges
(2). Ground edges

Appendix 5: Table 1. *(continued)*

2. Percussion and/or flaked manufacture
a. One piece unhafted pulverizer; hammerstone
(1). Rounded
(a). Multidirectional
(b). Unidirectional
(c). Unclassified
b. Unhafted unshaped cutting and perforating tool
(1). Core; scraper, chopper
(a). Raw
(b). Utilized (edge damage and/or ground)
(c). Marginal retouch
1'. Unimarginal
(2). Flake; scraper, graver, perforator, knife
(a). Raw
(b). Utilized (edge damage and/or ground)
(c). Marginal retouch
1'. Unimarginal
2'. Bimarginal
(3). Shatter; knife, graver, scraper, perforator
(a). Raw
(b). Utilized (edge damage and/or ground)
(c). Marginal retouch
1'. Unimarginal
2'. Bimarginal
c. Hafted unshaped cutting tool; knife
d. Hafted shaped bifacially retouched cutting and perforating tool; projectile point, drill, knife
(1). Stemless
(a). Leaf shaped
1'. Convex base
a'. Expanded blade
2'. Straight base
a'. Expanded blade
(b). Triangular
1'. Convex base
a'. Expanded blade
2'. Straight base
a'. Expanded blade
b'. Restricted blade
(2). Stemmed
(a). Stem wider than blade
1'. Obtuse notch
a'. Convex base
1". Expanded blade
b'. Concave base
1". Expanded blade
2'. Lateral notch
a'. Convex base
1". Expanded blade
2". Restricted blade
b'. Straight base
1". Expanded blade
c'. Concave base
2". Restricted blade
3'. Oblique notch
a'. Convex base
2". Restricted blade
(b). Stem narrower than blade

Appendix 5: Table 1. *(continued)*

1'. Parallel sided stem
  a'. Obtuse notch
    1". Convex base
      a". Expanded blade
    2". Straight base
      a". Expanded blade
  b'. Lateral notch
    1". Convex base
      a". Expanded blade
    2". Straight base
      a". Expanded blade
  c'. Oblique notch
    2". Straight base
      a". Expanded blade
2'. Expanding stem
  a'. Obtuse notch
    1". Convex base
      a". Expanded blade
    2". Straight base
      a". Expanded blade
    3". Concave base
      a". Expanded blade
  b'. Lateral notch
    1". Convex base
      a". Expanded blade
    2". Straight base
      a". Expanded blade
    3". Concave base
      a". Expanded blade
  c'. Oblique notch
    1". Convex base
      a". Expanded blade
    2". Straight base
      a". Expanded blade
    3". Concave base
      a". Expanded blade
(c). Unclassified fragment
  1'. Expanded blade
  2'. Restricted blade

B. Bone tools
  1. Pointed piercing tools
    a. Complete artiodactyl metatarsus (distal); awl
      1'. Complete
      2'. Fragment
    b. Split artiodactyl metatarsus (distal); awl
      1'. Complete
      2'. Fragment
    c. Split artiodactyl metapodial (proximal); awl
      1'. Complete
      2'. Fragment
    d. Ulna; awl
      1'. Complete
      2'. Fragment
    e. Artiodactyl splinter; awl
      1'. Complete
      2'. Fragment
    f. Artiodactyl femur; awl

Appendix 5: Table 1. *(continued)*

- 1'. Complete
- 2'. Fragment

g. Leporid piercing tools (originally Aves)
- 1'. Complete
- 2'. Fragment

h. Unclassified fragment; awl
- 1'. Tip
- 2'. Shaft

2. Spatula tip tools; planting tools, spatulas, knives, scrapers

a. Ulna
- 1'. Complete
- 2'. Fragment

b. Artiodactyl costa
- 1'. Complete
- 2'. Fragment

c. Artiodactyl splinter
- 1'. Complete
- 2'. Fragment

d. Unclassified fragment

3. Antler tines

a. Faceted tip
- 1'. Complete
- 2'. Fragment

C. Ceramic tools

1. Finger manipulated hollow formed receptacles

a. Jar
- 1'. Standard (>165 ml)
- 2'. Miniature (<165 ml)

b. Bowl
- 1'. Standard (>165 ml)
- 2'. Miniature (<165 ml)

c. Effigy
- 1'. Standard (>165 ml)

d. Ladle
- 1'. Miniature (<165 ml)

e. Unclassified
- 1'. Miniature (<165 ml)

2. Sherd tools

a. Unperforated disk; gaming piece, jar cover
- 1'. Chipped edge
- 2'. Ground edge

b. Perforated disk; spindle whorl, bead
- 1'. Chipped edge
- 2'. Ground edge

c. Unperforated rectanguloid (<30 cm^2); scoop, scraper, spoon, ladle, potter's tool
- 1'. Chipped edge
  - b'. No edge wear
- 2'. Ground edge
  - a'. Beveled edge wear

d. Unperforated rectanguloid (>30 cm^2)
- 1'. Chipped edge
  - a'. Beveled edge wear
- 2'. Ground edge
  - a'. Beveled edge wear
  - b'. No edge wear

e. Unperforated trapezoid (<30 cm^2)

APPENDIX 5: TABLE 1. *(continued)*

- 2'. Ground edge
  - b'. No edge wear
- f. Unperforated trapezoid (>30 cm^2)
  - 2'. Ground edge
    - a'. Beveled edge wear
- g. Unperforated trianguloid (<30 cm^2)
  - 2'. Ground edge
    - a'. Beveled edge wear
    - b'. No edge wear
- h. Unperforated ovoid (<30cm^2)
  - 2'. Ground edge
    - a'. Beveled edge wear
    - b'. No edge wear
- i. Unperforated ovoid (>30 cm^2)
  - 1'. Chipped edge
    - b'. No edge wear
  - 2'. Ground edge
    - a'. Beveled edge wear
    - b'. No edge wear
- j. Unperforated free form (<30 cm^2)
  - 1'. Chipped edge
    - a'. Beveled edge wear
    - b'. Bi-beveled edge wear
  - 2'. Ground edge
    - b'. Bi-beveled edge wear
- k. Unperforated free form (>30 cm^2)
  - 1'. Chipped edge
    - b'. Bi-beveled edge wear
- l. Unclassified
  - 1'. Chipped edge
    - b'. No edge wear
  - 2'. Ground edge
    - a'. Beveled edge wear
    - b'. No edge wear
- 3. Solid modeled forms; fire dog, pot support, lid cover
  - a. Loaf shaped
  - b. T-shaped

II. Socioreligious Tool Morphology
- A. Stone
  - 1. Pecked and/or ground stone
    - a. Disk
      - 1'. Chipped edge
      - 2'. Ground edge
    - b. Carved fetish
      - 1'. Flat
      - 2'. Round
    - c. Straight, perforated tube; pipe
      - 1'. Plain tube
        - a'. Biconically drilled
        - b'. Conically and hollow stem drilled
        - c'. Biconically and hollow stem drilled
      - 2'. Incised tube
        - a'. Biconically drilled
        - b'. Conically and hollow stem drilled
        - c'. Biconically and hollow stem drilled

Appendix 5: Table 1. *(continued)*

- 3'. Incised, collared tube
  - a'. Biconically drilled
- 4'. Unfinished tube
2. Percussion and/or flaked stone
   - a. Cruciform; stone counter

B. Bone
1. *Odocoileus* antlers
   - a. Notched tine; rasp
   - b. Hollow core; pipe/handle
   - c. Y-shaped; musical rasp
2. Artiodactyl femurs; gaming piece, dice, scraper
   - a. Beveled rectanguloid
   - b. Thin walled section
   - c. Red pigment stained
3. Artiodactyl scapula; musical rasp
   - a. Notched
4. *Chelonia* plastron; rattle fragment?
   - a. Perforated
5. Aves femurs; bead, smoking pipe/sucking tube
   - a. Tube
   - b. Pipe form

C. Ceramic
1. Unperforated solid modeled figurines
   - a. Zoomorphic
   - b. Human
2. Unperforated sherd figurines
   - a. Zoomorphic
   - b. Eccentric
3. Finger manipulated ceramics
   - a. Cornucopia
   - b. Straight perforated tube; pipe
     - 1'. Single piece, long straight stem
     - 2'. Single piece, open barrel; tube
     - 3'. Single piece, biconical barrel
     - 4'. Two piece, side perforated barrel
     - 5'. Two piece, short blunt stem
     - 6'. Unclassified

III. Personal Ornamentation Morphology

A. Stone
1. Pecked and/or ground manufacture
   - a. Unperforated bevel edged rectilinear chip; tessera
   - b. Proximal perforated petaloid shaped bevel edge; pendant
   - c. Perforated carved effigy; effigy pendant
   - d. Proximal perforated incised edge (flat); pendant (sunburst)
   - e. Proximal incised suspension with beveled edges; pendant
   - f. Centrally perforated disk; disk bead
   - g. Centrally perforated asymmetrical shaped; odd shaped bead
   - h. Unfinished blank; ornament blank
   - i. Unclassified fragment; broken pendant

B. Shell
1. Marine mollusc
   - a. Perforated pelecypod disk; disk bead
     - 1'. Centrally perforated
       - a'. <1 cm diameter
       - b'. >1 cm diameter
   - b. Marginally perforated pelecypod bilobe; bilobe bead
   - c. Solid pelecypod circlet; bracelet

APPENDIX 5: TABLE 1. *(continued)*

1'. Thin (<0.5 cm) plain band with abraded umbo
a'. Rectanguloid section
b'. Ovoid section
2'. Medium (0.5–1.0 cm) plain band with abraded umbo
a'. Rectanguloid section
b'. Ovoid section
c'. Trianguloid section
3'. Medium (0.5–1.0 cm) plain band with shaped umbo
a'. Ovoid section
4'. Medium (0.5–1.0 cm) carved band, umbo missing
a'. Rectanguloid section
b'. Trianguloid section
d. Unshaped gastropod; whole bead
1'. Spire ground for horizontal suspension
2'. Marginally perforated for vertical suspension
e. Shaped pelecypod; pendant and earring
1'. Marginal perforation for vertical suspension
2'. Unperforated
f. Unclassified pelecypod fragment
2. Freshwater mollusc
a. Unshaped gastropod; whole bead
1'. Spire ground for horizontal suspension
b. Shaped pelecypod; pendant and earring
1'. Marginal perforation for vertical suspension
2'. Unperforated
C. Bone
1. Artiodactyl femurs
a. Solid circlet; ring
b. Rectanguloid rod
c. Skewer
D. Ceramic
1. Edge perforated sherd suspension; pendant
a. Chipped edge
b. Ground edge
2. Perforated modeled sphere; bead
a. Chipped edge
b. Ground edge

IV. Architectural Elements Morphology
A. Architectural stone element
1. Pecked and/or ground
a. Shaped rectangular paving slab
b. Shaped rectangular hearth slab; nether pulverizer
e. Cooking slab
1'. Unshaped
2'. Shaped
f. Shaped step element
g. Unclassified building element
1'. Slab
b'. Shaped
2'. Pebble (1–15 cm diameter)
b'. Shaped
3'. Cobble (15–30 cm diameter)
b'. Shaped
4'. Boulder (>30 cm diameter)
b'. Shaped

APPENDIX 5: TABLE 1. *(continued)*

B. Architectural ceramic element
1. Jacal casts
a. House wall/roof framing
b. Matting
c. Wall plaster

V. Raw Material Morphology
A. Raw stone/mineral material
1. Paint pigments; mineral
a. Red
1'. Red ocher
a'. Unworked
b'. Abraded
2'. Compact hematite
a'. Unworked (shatter or nodule)
b'. Abraded
c'. Percussion flake
d'. Percussion core
3'. Specularite
a'. Unworked (shatter or pebble/cobble)
b'. Abraded
4'. Kidney ore
a'. Unworked
b. Yellow
1'. Limonite ocher
a'. Unworked
b'. Abraded
c. White
1'. Kaolinite
a'. Unworked
d. Azure blue
1'. Azurite
a'. Unworked
e. Grass green
1'. Malachite
a'. Unworked
b'. Abraded
2. Andesite
3. Aragonite
4. Biotite schist
5. Breccia
6. Calcite
7. Concretion
8. Copper
9. Dacite
10. Dolomite
11. Felsite slickenside
12. Fluorite
13. Fossil
14. Granite
15. Gypsum
16. Limestone
17. Mica
a. White
1'. Muscovite
a'. Unworked
b. Brown

Appendix 5: Table 1. *(continued)*

- 1'. Biotite
  - a'. Unworked
  - b'. Ground edges
- 18. Obsidian
- 19. Opaline
- 20. Pumice
- 21. Quartz
  - a. Crystallized phenocrystalline
    - 1'. Rock crystal
    - 2'. Amethyst
    - 3'. Milky quartz
  - b. Cryptocrystalline
    - 1'. Agate
    - 2'. Chalcedony
    - 3'. Chert
    - 4'. Flint
    - 5'. Jasper
  - c. Crystalline
    - 1'. Quartzite
- 22. Rhyolite
- 23. Ricolite
- 24. Sandstone
- 25. Shale
- 26. Slag
- 27. Steatite
- 28. Travertine
- 29. Tuff
- 30. Turquoise
  - a. Greenish blue
    - 1'. Vein
      - a'. Unworked
    - 2'. Pebble
      - a'. Unworked
      - b'. Abraded facet
    - 3'. Incrustation
      - a'. Unworked
- 31. Vesicular basalt

B. Raw bone material
- 1. Artiodactyl femur
- 2. Artiodactyl metapodial
- 3. Artiodactyl costa
- 4. Artiodactyl cranium
- 5. Aves femur

C. Raw ceramic material
- 1. Fillet; rod
- 2. Modeled clay lump
- 3. Incised sherd
- 4. Sawed sherd

Appendix 5: Table 2. Artifact Type Concordance

Reference No.	Di Peso Type Designation	Type Description
1	IA1a(1a)1'a'	Metate, slab, from boulder
2	IA1a(1a)1'b'	Metate, slab, from slab
3	IA1a(1a)2'a'1"a"	Mano for slab, one hand, taper cross section, uniface, rectangular plan
4	IA1a(1a)2'a'1"a"	Mano for slab, one hand, taper cross section, uniface, oval plan
5	IA1a(1a)2'a'1"a"	Mano for slab, one hand, taper cross section, uniface, petaloid plan
6	IA1a(1a)2'a'1"b"	Mano for slab, one hand, taper cross section, biface, circular plan
7	IA1a(1a)2'a'1"b"	Mano for slab, one hand, taper cross section, biface, rectangular plan
8	IA1a(1a)2'a'1"b"	Mano for slab, one hand, taper cross section, biface, oval plan
9	IA1a(1a)2'a'2"a"	Mano for slab, one hand, block cross section, uniface, circular plan
10	IA1a(1a)2'a'2"a"	Mano for slab, one hand, block cross section, uniface, rectangular plan
11	IA1a(1a)2'a'2"a"	Mano for slab, one hand, block cross section, uniface, petaloid plan
12	IA1a(1a)2'a'2"a"	Mano for slab, one hand, block cross section, uniface, trapezoid plan
13	IA1a(1a)2'a'3"a"	Mano for slab, one hand, loaf cross section, uniface, oval plan
14	IA1a(1a)2'a'3"a"	Mano for slab, one hand, loaf cross section, uniface, petaloid plan
15	IA1a(1a)2'b'1"a"	Mano for slab, two hand, taper cross section, uniface, rectangular plan
16	IA1a(1a)2'b'1"a"	Mano for slab, two hand, taper cross section, uniface, oval plan
17	IA1a(1a)2'b'1"a"	Mano for slab, two hand, taper cross section, uniface, petaloid plan
18	IA1a(1a)2'b'1"a"	Mano for slab, two hand, taper cross section, uniface, trapezoid plan
19	IA1a(1a)2'b'1"b"	Mano for slab, two hand, taper cross section, biface, rectangular plan
20	IA1a(1a)2'b'1"b"	Mano for slab, two hand, taper cross section, biface, oval plan
21	IA1a(1a)2'b'1"b"	Mano for slab, two hand, taper cross section, biface, asymmetric plan
22	IA1a(1a)2'b'2"a"	Mano for slab, two hand, block cross section, uniface, circular plan
23	IA1a(1a)2'b'2"a"	Mano for slab, two hand, block cross section, uniface, rectangular plan
24	IA1a(1a)2'b'2"a"	Mano for slab, two hand, block cross section, uniface, asymmetric plan
25	IA1a(1a)2'b'2"b"	Mano for slab, two hand, block cross section, biface, rectangular plan
26	IA1a(1a)2'b'3"a"	Mano for slab, two hand, loaf cross section, uniface, rectangular plan
27	IA1a(1a)2'b'3"a"	Mano for slab, two hand, loaf cross section, uniface, oval plan
28	IA1a(1a)3'a'1"	Grinding slab, from boulder, unshaped
29	IA1a(1a)3'b'1"	Grinding slab, from slab, unshaped
30	IA1a(1a)3'b'2"	Grinding slab, from slab, shaped
31	IA1a(1a)3'c'	Grinding slab, unclassified
32	IA1a(1a)4'a'1"a"	Rubbing stone, unshaped, uniface, circular plan
33	IA1a(1a)4'a'1"b"	Rubbing stone, unshaped, biface, circular plan
34	IA1a(1a)4'a'2"a"	Rubbing stone, unshaped, uniface, rectangular plan
35	IA1a(1a)4'a'2"b"	Rubbing stone, unshaped, biface, rectangular plan
36	IA1a(1a)4'b'1"a"	Rubbing stone, shaped, uniface, circular plan
37	IA1a(1a)4'b'1"b"	Rubbing stone, shaped, biface, circular plan
38	IA1a(1a)4'b'2"a"	Rubbing stone, shaped, uniface, rectangular plan
39	IA1a(1a)4'b'2"b"	Rubbing stone, shaped, biface, rectangular plan

APPENDIX 5: TABLE 2. *(continued)*

Reference No.	Di Peso Type Designation	Type Description
40	IA1a(1a)4'b'3"	Rubbing stone, unclassified
41	IA1a(1b)1'a'1"	Metate, closed trough, from boulder
42	IA1a(1b)1'a'2"	Metate, closed trough, from slab
43	IA1a(1b)1'b'1"	Metate, through trough, from boulder
44	IA1a(1b)1'b'2"	Metate, through trough, from slab
45	IA1a(1b)2'a'1"a"	Mano for trough, one hand, taper cross section, uniface, circular plan
46	IA1a(1b)2'a'1"a"	Mano for trough, one hand, taper cross section, uniface, rectangular plan
47	IA1a(1b)2'a'1"a"	Mano for trough, one hand, taper cross section, uniface, oval plan
48	IA1a(1b)2'a'1"a"	Mano for trough, one hand, taper cross section, uniface, petaloid plan
49	IA1a(1b)2'a'1"a"	Mano for trough, one hand, taper cross section, uniface, asymmetric plan
50	IA1a(1b)2'a'1"b"	Mano for trough, one hand, taper cross section, biface, circular plan
51	IA1a(1b)2'a'1"b"	Mano for trough, one hand, taper cross section, biface, rectangular plan
52	IA1a(1b)2'a'1"b"	Mano for trough, one hand, taper cross section, biface, oval plan
53	IA1a(1b)2'a'2"a"	Mano for trough, one hand, block cross section, uniface, circular plan
54	IA1a(1b)2'a'2"a"	Mano for trough, one hand, block cross section, uniface, rectangular plan
55	IA1a(1b)2'a'2"a"	Mano for trough, one hand, block cross section, uniface, oval plan
56	IA1a(1b)2'a'2"a"	Mano for trough, one hand, block cross section, uniface, petaloid plan
57	IA1a(1b)2'a'2"a"	Mano for trough, one hand, block cross section, uniface, asymmetric plan
58	IA1a(1b)2'a'2"b"	Mano for trough, one hand, block cross section, biface, circular plan
59	IA1a(1b)2'a'2"b"	Mano for trough, one hand, block cross section, biface, oval plan
60	IA1a(1b)2'a'3"a"	Mano for trough, one hand, loaf cross section, uniface, rectangular plan
61	IA1a(1b)2'a'3"a"	Mano for trough, one hand, loaf cross section, uniface, oval plan
62	IA1a(1b)2'a'3"a"	Mano for trough, one hand, loaf cross section, uniface, petaloid plan
63	IA1a(1b)2'b'1"a"	Mano for trough, two hand, taper cross section, uniface, circular plan
64	IA1a(1b)2'b'1"a"	Mano for trough, two hand, taper cross section, uniface, rectangular plan
65	IA1a(1b)2'b'1"a"	Mano for trough, two hand, taper cross section, uniface, oval plan
66	IA1a(1b)2'b'1"a"	Mano for trough, two hand, taper cross section, uniface, petaloid plan
67	IA1a(1b)2'b'1"a"	Mano for trough, two hand, taper cross section, uniface, asymmetric plan
68	IA1a(1b)2'b'1"a"	Mano for trough, two hand, taper cross section, uniface, trapezoid plan
69	IA1a(1b)2'b'1"b"	Mano for trough, two hand, taper cross section, biface, rectangular plan
70	IA1a(1b)2'b'1"b"	Mano for trough, two hand, taper cross section, biface, oval plan
71	IA1a(1b)2'b'1"b"	Mano for trough, two hand, taper cross section, biface, petaloid plan
72	IA1a(1b)2'b'2"a"	Mano for trough, two hand, block cross section, uniface, circular plan
73	IA1a(1b)2'b'2"a"	Mano for trough, two hand, block cross section, uniface, rectangular plan
74	IA1a(1b)2'b'2"a"	Mano for trough, two hand, block cross section, uniface, oval plan
75	IA1a(1b)2'b'2"a"	Mano for trough, two hand, block cross section, uniface, asymmetric plan
76	IA1a(1b)2'b'2"a"	Mano for trough, two hand, block cross section, uniface, trapezoid plan
77	IA1a(1b)2'b'2"b"	Mano for trough, two hand, block cross section, biface, circular plan
78	IA1a(1b)2'b'2"b"	Mano for trough, two hand, block cross section, biface, rectangular plan
79	IA1a(1b)2'b'3"a"	Mano for trough, two hand, loaf cross section, uniface, rectangular plan
80	IA1a(1b)2'b'3"a"	Mano for trough, two hand, loaf cross section, uniface, oval plan

Appendix 5: Table 2. *(continued)*

Reference No.	Di Peso Type Designation	Type Description
81	IA1a(2a)1'	Metate, basin, from boulder
82	IA1a(2a)2'	Metate, basin, from slab
83	IA1a(2b)1'a"	Mano for basin, one hand, taper cross section, uniface, circular plan
84	IA1a(2b)2'a"	Mano for basin, one hand, block cross section, uniface, circular plan
85	IA1a(2b)2'a"	Mano for basin, one hand, block cross section, uniface, oval plan
86	IA1a(2b)2'a"	Mano for basin, one hand, block cross section, uniface, petaloid plan
87	IA1a(2b)3'a"	Mano for basin, one hand, loaf cross section, uniface, oval plan
88	IA1a(3a)	Metate, from boulder, unclassified
89	IA1a(3b)	Metate, from slab, unclassified
89A	—	Metate, unclassified
90	IA1a(4)	Mano, unclassified
91	IA1a(5a)1'a"	Mortar/bowl, from pebble, unshaped, rectangular plan
92	IA1a(5a)1'b"	Mortar/bowl, from pebble, shaped, rectangular plan
93	IA1a(5a)2'a"	Mortar/bowl, from pebble, unshaped, circular plan
94	IA1a(5a)2'b"	Mortar/bowl, from pebble, shaped, circular plan
95	IA1a(5b)1'a"	Pestle for pebble mortar, one hand, unshaped, rectangular plan
96	IA1a(5b)2'a"	Pestle for pebble mortar, one hand, unshaped, circular plan
97	IA1a(5b)2'b"	Pestle for pebble mortar, one hand, shaped, circular plan
98	IA1a(5b)3'a"	Pestle for pebble mortar, one hand, unshaped, elongated plan
99	IA1a(5d)1'a"	Pestle for cobble mortar, one hand, unshaped, rectangular plan
100	IA1a(5d)1'b"	Pestle for cobble mortar, one hand, shaped, rectangular plan
101	IA1a(5d)2'b"	Pestle for cobble mortar, one hand, shaped, circular plan
102	IA1a(5d)3'a"	Pestle for cobble mortar, one hand, unshaped, elongated plan
103	IA1a(5e)1'b"	Mortar, from boulder, shaped, rectangular plan
104	IA1a(5g)3'a"	Pestle for boulder mortar, two hand, unshaped, elongated plan
105	IA1b(1a)1'a'	Whetstone/abrader, pebble size, unshaped
106	IA1b(1a)1'b'	Whetstone/abrader, pebble size, shaped
107	IA1b(1b)1'a'	Whetstone/abrader, pebble size, unshaped, grooved
108	—	Whetstone/abrader, cobble size, unshaped
109	IA1b(1a)2'a'	Lapstone/whetstone/abrader, slab, unshaped
110	IA1b(1a)2'b'	Lapstone/whetstone/abrader, slab, shaped
111	IA1b(1b)2'a'	Abrader, unshaped, grooved, slab
112	IA1b(1b)2'b'	Abrader, shaped, grooved, slab
113	IA1b(2a)2'a'	Proto-palette, unshaped
114	IA1b(2a)2'b'	Proto-palette, shaped
115	IA1b(2a)2'c'	Palette, bordered
116	IA1c(1a)	Abrading/rubbing stone, unshaped, pebble size
117	IA1c(2a)	Abrading stone/rasp, unshaped, slab
118	IA1c(2b)	Abrading stone/rasp, shaped, slab
118A	—	Abrader, flat, unclassified
119	IA1d(1a)	Polishing stone, unshaped
120	IA1d(1b)	Polishing stone, shaped
121	IA2a(1a)	Hammerstone, multidirectional use wear
122	IA2a(1b)	Hammerstone, localized use wear

APPENDIX 5: TABLE 2. *(continued)*

Reference No.	Di Peso Type Designation	Type Description
123	IA2a(1c)	Hammerstone, unclassified
124	IA1e(1b)	Axe, full grooved
125	IA1e(1c)	Axe, double, 3/4 grooved
126	IA1e(3a)1'	Axe, bit fragment
127	IA1e(3a)2'	Axe, body fragment
128	IA1e(3a)3'	Axe, poll fragment
129	IA1e(2b)	Maul, full grooved
130	IA1e(2a)	Maul, 3/4 grooved
131	IA1e(3b)2'	Maul, body fragment
132	—	Axe/maul, fragment, unclassified
133	IA1f(1)	Spindle whorl, chipped edge
134	IA1f(2)	Spindle whorl, ground edge
135	IA2b(1a)	Core, raw
136	IA2b(1b)	Core tool, chopper, utilized, convex cutting edge
137	IA2b(1b)	Core tool, scraper, utilized, straight cutting edge
138	IA2b(1b)	Core tool, scraper, utilized, concave edge
138A	IA2b(1b)	Core tool, utilized, unclassified
139	IA2b(1c)1'	Core tool, chopper, unifacial edge retouch, convex cutting edge
140	IA2b(1c)1'	Core tool, scraper, unifacial edge retouch, convex edge
141	IA2b(1c)1'	Core tool, scraper, unifacial edge retouch, two cutting edges
141A	—	Core tool, unclassified
142	IA2b(2a)	Flake, raw – debitage
143	IA2b(2b)	Flake tool, knife/scraper, utilized, convex edge
144	IA2b(2b)	Flake tool, knife/scraper, utilized, straight edge
145	IA2b(2b)	Flake tool, scraper, utilized, concave edge
146	IA2b(2b)	Flake tool, knife/scraper with tip, utilized, convex edge
147	IA2b(2b)	Flake tool, knife/scraper with tip, utilized, straight edge
148	IA2b(2b)	Flake tool, scraper with tip, utilized, concave edge
149	IA2b(2b)	Flake tool, knife/scraper, utilized, two parallel edges
150	IA2b(2b)	Flake tool, graver/chisel/perforator/drill, utilized
151	IA2b(2b)	Flake tool, knife/scraper, utilized, two converging straight edges
152	IA2b(2b)	Flake tool, scraper, utilized, two concave edges
153	IA2b(2b)	Flake tool, utilized, unclassified
154	IA2b(2c)1'	Flake tool, knife/scraper, unifacial edge retouch, convex edge
155	IA2b(2c)1'	Flake tool, knife/scraper, unifacial edge retouch, straight edge
156	IA2b(2c)1'	Flake tool, scraper, unifacial edge retouch, concave edge
157	IA2b(2c)1'	Flake tool, knife/scraper with tip, unifacial edge retouch, convex edge
158	IA2b(2c)1'	Flake tool, knife/scraper with tip, unifacial edge retouch, straight edge
159	IA2b(2c)1'	Flake tool, scraper with tip, unifacial edge retouch, concave edge
160	IA2b(2c)1'	Flake tool, knife/scraper, unifacial edge retouch, two parallel edges
161	IA2b(2c)1	Flake tool, graver/chisel/perforator/drill, unifacial edge retouch
162	IA2b(2c)1'	Flake tool, knife/scraper, unifacial edge retouch, two converging straight edges
163	IA2b(2c)1'	Flake tool, scraper, unifacial edge retouch, two concave edges
164	IA2b(2c)1'	Flake tool, unifacial edge retouch, unclassified

APPENDIX 5: TABLE 2. *(continued)*

Reference No.	Di Peso Type Designation	Type Description
165	IA2b(2c)2'	Flake tool, knife/scraper, bifacial edge retouch, convex edge
166	IA2b(2c)2'	Flake tool, knife/scraper, bifacial edge retouch, straight edge
167	IA2b(2c)2'	Flake tool, scraper, bifacial edge retouch, concave edge
168	IA2b(2c)2'	Flake tool, knife/scraper with tip, bifacial edge retouch, convex edge
169	IA2b(2c)2'	Flake tool, knife/scraper with tip, bifacial edge retouch, straight edge
170	IA2b(2c)2'	Flake tool, scraper with tip, bifacial edge retouch, concave edge
171	IA2b(2c)2'	Flake tool, knife/scraper with tip, bifacial edge retouch, two parallel edges
172	IA2b(2c)2'	Flake tool, graver/chisel/perforator/drill, bifacial edge retouch
173	IA2b(2c)2'	Flake tool, knife/scraper, bifacial edge retouch, two converging straight edges
174	IA2b(2c)2'	Flake tool, scraper, bifacial edge retouch, two concave edges
175	IA2b(2c)2'	Flake tool, bifacial edge retouch, unclassified
175A	—	Flake tool, unclassified
176	IA2b(3a)	Shatter, raw - debitage
177	IA2b(3b)	Shatter tool, knife/scraper, utilized, convex edge
178	IA2b(3b)	Shatter tool, knife/scraper, utilized, straight edge
179	IA2b(3b)	Shatter tool, scraper, utilized, concave edge
180	IA2b(3b)	Shatter tool, knife/scraper with tip, utilized, convex edge
181	IA2b(3b)	Shatter tool, knife/scraper with tip, utilized, straight edge
182	IA2b(3b)	Shatter tool, scraper with tip, utilized, concave edge
183	IA2b(3b)	Shatter tool, scraper, utilized, two concave edges
184	IA2b(3b)	Shatter tool, utilized, unclassified
185	IA2b(3c)1'	Shatter tool, knife/scraper, unifacial edge retouch, convex edge
186	IA2b(3c)1'	Shatter tool, knife/scraper/grass knife/hoe, unifacial edge retouch, straight edge
187	IA2b(3c)1'	Shatter tool, scraper, unifacial edge retouch, concave edge
188	IA2b(3c)1'	Shatter tool, knife/scraper with tip, unifacial edge retouch, convex edge
189	IA2b(3c)1'	Shatter tool, knife/scraper with tip, unifacial edge retouch, straight edge
190	IA2b(3c)1'	Shatter tool, scraper with tip, unifacial edge retouch, concave edge
191	IA2b(3c)1'	Shatter tool, knife/scraper, unifacial edge retouch, two converging straight edges
192	IA2b(3c)1'	Shatter tool, scraper, unifacial edge retouch, two concave edges
193	IA2b(3c)1'	Shatter tool, unifacial edge retouch, unclassified
194	IA2b(3c)2'	Shatter tool, knife/scraper, bifacial edge retouch, convex edge
195	IA2b(3c)2'	Shatter tool, knife/scraper/grass knife/hoe, bifacial edge retouch, straight edge
196	IA2b(3c)2'	Shatter tool, scraper, bifacial edge retouch, concave edge
197	IA2b(3c)2'	Shatter tool, knife/scraper, bifacial edge retouch, two parallel edges
198	IA2b(3c)2'	Shatter tool, knife/scraper, bifacial edge retouch, two converging straight edges
199	IA2b(3c)2'	Shatter tool, scraper, bifacial edge retouch, two concave edges
200	IA2c	Shatter tool, knife, stemmed, bifacial edge retouch, broad, shallow side notches, convex base
201	IA2d(1a)1'a'	Projectile point/knife/drill, stemless, leaf shaped, convex base
202	IA2d(1a)2'a'	Projectile point/knife, stemless, leaf shaped, straight base
203	IA2d(1b)1'a'	Projectile point/knife/drill, stemless, triangular, convex base
204	IA2d(1b)2'a'	Projectile point/knife/drill, stemless, triangular, straight base
205	IA2d(1b)2'b'	Drill, stemless, triangular, straight base
206	IA2d(2a)1'a'1"	Projectile point/knife, stemmed, obtuse notches, wide, convex base

APPENDIX 5: TABLE 2. *(continued)*

Reference No.	Di Peso Type Designation	Type Description
207	IA2d(2a)1'b'1"	Projectile point/knife, stemmed, obtuse notches, wide, concave base
208	IA2d(2a)2'a'1"	Projectile point/knife, stemmed, lateral notches, wide, convex base
209	IA2d(2a)2'a'2"	Drill, stemmed, lateral notches, wide, convex base
210	IA2d(2a)2'b'1"	Projectile point/knife, stemmed, lateral notches, wide, straight base
211	IA2d(2a)2'c'2"	Drill, stemmed, lateral notches, wide, concave base
212	IA2d(2a)3'a'2"	Drill, stemmed, oblique notches, wide, convex base
213	IA2d(2b)1'a'1"a"	Projectile point/knife, straight stem, obtuse notches, narrow, convex base
214	IA2d(2b)1'a'2"a"	Projectile point/knife, straight stem, obtuse notches, narrow, straight base
215	IA2d(2b)1'b'1"a"	Drill, straight stem, lateral notches, narrow, convex base
216	IA2d(2b)1'b'2"a"	Projectile point/knife/drill, straight stem, lateral notches, narrow, straight base
217	IA2d(2b)1'c'2"a"	Projectile point/knife/drill, straight stem, oblique notches, narrow, straight base
218	IA2d(2b)2'a'1"a"	Projectile point/knife, stemmed, obtuse notches, narrow, convex base
219	IA2d(2b)2'a'2"a"	Projectile point/knife, stemmed, obtuse notches, narrow, straight base
220	IA2d(2b)2'a'3"a"	Projectile point/knife, stemmed, obtuse notches, narrow, concave base
221	IA2d(2b)2'b'1"a"	Projectile point/knife, stemmed, lateral notches, narrow, convex base
222	IA2d(2b)2'b'2"a"	Projectile point/knife, stemmed, lateral notches, narrow, straight base
223	IA2d(2b)2'b'3"a"	Projectile point/knife, stemmed, lateral notches, narrow, concave base
224	IA2d(2b)2'c'1"a"	Projectile point/knife, stemmed, oblique notches, narrow, convex base
225	IA2d(2b)2'c'2"a"	Projectile point/knife, stemmed, oblique notches, narrow, straight base
226	IA2d(2b)2'c'3"a"	Projectile point/knife, stemmed, oblique notches, narrow, concave base
227	IA2d(2c)1'	Bifacial tool, expanded blade, unclassified, fragment
228	IA2d(2c)2'	Bifacial tool, restricted blade, unclassified, fragment
229	IB1a1',IB1a2'	Bone awl, artiodactyl metatarsal, unsplit
230	IB1b1',IB1b2'	Bone awl, artiodactyl metatarsal, split
231	IB1c1',IB1c2'	Bone awl, artiodactyl metapodial, split
232	IB1d1',IB1d2'	Bone awl, ulna
233	IB1e1',IB1e2'	Bone awl, artiodactyl splinter
234	IB1f1',IB1f2'	Bone awl, femur
235	IB1g1'	Bone awl, leporid tibia complete
235A	IB1g2'	Bone awl, split tibia
236	IB1h1'	Bone awl, tip, unclassified, fragment
237	IB1h2'	Bone awl, shaft, unclassified, fragment
238	IB2a1',IB2a2'	Bone spatulate tool, ulna chisel/polisher/scraper/planting tool
239	IB2b1',IB2b2'	Bone spatulate tool, artiodactyl rib flesher
239A	—	Bone spatulate tool, artiodactyl vertebra flesher
240	IB2c1',IB2c2'	Bone spatulate tool, artiodactyl splinter flesher
241	IB2d	Bone spatulate tool, unclassified, fragment
242	IB3a1',IB3a2'	Antler tine tool, flaker/punch
243	IC1a1'	Alma Plain jar
244	IC1a2'	Alma Plain miniature jar
245	IC1b1'	Alma Plain bowl
246	IC1b2'	Alma Plain miniature bowl
247	IC1d1'	Alma Plain miniature ladle
248	IC1e1'	Alma Plain unclassified miniature

APPENDIX 5: TABLE 2. *(continued)*

Reference No.	Di Peso Type Designation	Type Description
249	IC1a1'	Alma Plain Finger Indented jar
250	IC1a1'	Alma Rough jar
251	IC1a2'	Alma Rough miniature jar
252	IC1b1'	Alma Rough bowl
253	IC1b2'	Alma Rough miniature bowl
254	IC1d1'	Alma Rough miniature ladle
255	IC1e1'	Alma Rough unclassified miniature
256	IC1a1'	Alma Scored jar
257	IC1a1'	Alma Neck Banded jar
258	IC1a1'	Alma Pattern Incised jar
259	IC1b2'	Alma Pattern Incised miniature bowl
260	IC1e1'	Alma Pattern Incised unclassified miniature
261	IC1a1'	Alma Tool Punched jar
262	IC1a1'	Alma Tool Punched miniature jar
263	IC1b1'	Alma Black Burnished bowl
264	IC1a1'	Three Circle Neck Corrugated jar
265	IC1a2'	Mimbres Corrugated miniature jar
266	IC1a1'	Mimbres Rubbed Corrugated jar
267	IC1b1'	Mimbres Rubbed Corrugated bowl
268	IC1a1'	San Francisco Red jar
269	IC1a2'	San Francisco Red miniature jar
270	IC1b1'	San Francisco Red bowl
271	IC1a1'	Wind Mountain Red jar
272	IC1b1'	Wind Mountain Red bowl
273	IC1b2'	Wind Mountain Red miniature bowl
274	IC1b1'	Mogollon R/Br bowl
275	IC1c1'	Mogollon R/Br effigy
276	IC1b1'	Three Circle R/W bowl
277	IC1a1'	Wind Mountain B/W jar
278	IC1a2'	Wind Mountain B/W miniature jar
279	IC1b1'	Wind Mountain B/W bowl
280	IC1b2'	Wind Mountain B/W miniature bowl
281	IC1b1'	Mangas B/W bowl
282	IC1b2'	Mangas B/W miniature bowl
283	IC1b1'	Mimbres B/W bowl
284	IC1b2'	Mimbres B/W miniature bowl
285	IC1a1'	Gila Plain jar
286	IC1b1'	Red Mesa B/W bowl
287	IC1b1'	Unidentified polychrome bowl
288	IC2a1',IC2a2'	Worked sherd, jar cover/counter
289	IC2b1',IC2b2'	Worked sherd, spindle whorl/bead
290	IC2c1'b',IC2c2'a'	Worked sherd, rectanguloid spoon/scraper/eccentric
291	IC2d1'a',IC2d2'a',IC2d2'b'	Worked sherd, rectanguloid scoop/scraper

APPENDIX 5: TABLE 2. *(continued)*

Reference No.	Di Peso Type Designation	Type Description
292	IC2e2'b'	Worked sherd, trapezoidal spoon/eccentric
293	IC2f2'a'	Worked sherd, trapezoidal scraper
294	IC2g2'a',IC2g2'b'	Worked sherd, trianguloid scraper/eccentric
295	IC2h2'a',IC2h2'b'	Worked sherd, ovoid spoon/scraper/eccentric
296	IC2i1'b',IC2i2'a', IC2i2'b'	Worked sherd, ovoid scoop/scraper
297	IC2j1'a',IC2j1'b', IC2j2'b'	Worked sherd, irregular spoon/scraper
298	IC2k1'b'	Worked sherd, irregular scoop/scraper
299	IC2l1'b',IC2l2'a', IC2l2'b'	Worked sherd, unclassified fragment
300	IC3a	Jar cover and plug, loaf shaped
301	IC3b	Plug, t-shaped
302	IC2b1'	Spindle whorl, disk shaped, chipped edge
303	—	Wood awl
304	IIA1a1',IIA1a2'	Stone counter, ground and pecked, disk-shaped
305	IIA1b1'	Stone fetish, flat
306	IIA1b2'	Stone fetish, round
307	IIA1c1'a'	Stone pipe, plain, biconically drilled
308	IIA1c1'c'	Stone pipe, plain, biconically and hollow stem drilled
309	IIA1c1'b'	Stone pipe, plain, conically and hollow stem drilled
310	IIA1c2'a'	Stone pipe, incised, biconically drilled
311	IIA1c2'c'	Stone pipe, incised, biconically and hollow stem drilled
312	IIA1c2'b'	Stone pipe, incised, conically and hollow stem drilled
313	IIA1c3'a'	Stone pipe, incised, collared, biconically drilled
314	IIA1c4'	Stone pipe, unfinished
315	—	Stone pipe, unclassified, fragment
316	IIA2a	Stone counter, chipped, cruciform
317	IIB1a	Antler rasp, notched tine
318	IIB1b	Antler tube/handle
319	IIB1c	Antler rasp, forked
320	IIB2a	Bone counter, plain, rectangular plan
321	IIB2c	Bone counter, painted, rectangular plan
322	IIB2b	Bone, thin walled sections
323	IIB3a	Bone rasp, artiodactyl scapula
324	IIB4a	Turtle shell, rattle fragment
325	IIB5a	Bird bone tube
326	IIB5b	Bird bone pipe stem
327	IIB6a	Mammal bone tube
327A	IIB6b	Mammal bone pipe stem
328	IIC3a	Ceramic cornucopia
329	IIC3b1'	Ceramic pipe, tapered, long, straight stem hole
330	IIC3b1'	Ceramic pipe, funnel shaped, long, straight stem hole

Appendix 5: Table 2. *(continued)*

Reference No.	Di Peso Type Designation	Type Description
331	IIC3b5'	Ceramic pipe, tapered, short, blunt stem hole
332	IIC3b4'	Ceramic pipe, tapered, ventilated, short, blunt stem hole
333	IIC3b2'	Ceramic tube
334	IIC3b3'	Ceramic pipe, tapered, biconical bowl-stem hole
335	IIC3b1'	Ceramic pipe, incised
336	IIC3b6'	Ceramic pipe/tube, unclassified, fragment
337	IIC2a	Worked sherd, zoomorphic
338	IIC2b	Worked sherd, eccentric
339	IIC1a	Ceramic figurine, zoomorphic
340	IIC1b	Ceramic figurine, anthropomorphic
341	IIIA1a	Stone tessera, rectilinear
342	IIIA1b	Stone pendant, tabular
343	IIIA1c	Stone pendant, effigy
344	IIIA1d	Stone pendant, notched
345	IIIA1e	Stone pendant, grooved
346	IIIA1f	Stone bead, disk
347	IIIA1g	Stone bead, asymmetrical
348	IIIA1h	Stone ornament blank
349	IIIA1i	Stone ornament, unclassified, fragment
350	IIIB1a1'a'	Marine shell bead, small (<1 cm)
351	IIIB1a1'b'	Marine shell bead, large (>1 cm)
352	IIIB1b	Marine shell bead, bilobe
353	IIIB1c1'a'	Marine shell bracelet, thin (<0.5 cm), plain band, rectanguloid section
354	IIIB1c1'b'	Marine shell bracelet/ring, thin (<0.5 cm), plain band, ovoid section
355	IIIB1c2'a'	Marine shell bracelet, medium (0.5 - 1.0 cm), plain band, rectanguloid section
356	IIIB1c2'c'	Marine shell bracelet, medium (0.5 - 1.0 cm), plain band, trianguloid section
357	IIIB1c2'b'	Marine shell bracelet, medium (0.5 - 1.0 cm), plain band, ovoid section
358	IIIB1c3'a'	Marine shell bracelet, medium (0.5 - 1.0 cm), plain band, shaped umbo, ovoid section
359	IIIB1c4'a'	Marine shell bracelet, medium (0.5 - 1.0 cm), carved band, rectanguloid section
360	IIIB1c4'b'	Marine shell bracelet, medium (0.5 - 1.0 cm), carved band, trianguloid section
361	IIIB1e1'	Marine shell pendant, marginal perforation
362	IIIB1e2'	Marine shell arc, unperforated
363	IIIB1f	Marine shell ornament, unclassified, fragment
364	IIIB1d1'	Marine shell bead, whole, spire ground for horizontal suspension
365	IIIB1d2'	Marine shell bead, whole, marginally perforated for vertical suspension
366	IIIB2b1'	Fresh water shell pendant, marginal perforation
367	IIIB2b2'	Fresh water shell pendant/tessera, unfinished
368	IIIB2a1'	Fresh water shell bead, spire ground for horizontal suspension
369	IIIC1a	Bone ring
370	IIIC1b	Bone rod ornament, unidentified
371	IIIC1c	Bone skewer
372	IIID1a,IIID1b	Ceramic pendant
373	IIID2a,IIID2b	Ceramic bead
374	—	Wood ornament backing

APPENDIX 5: TABLE 2. *(continued)*

Reference No.	Di Peso Type Designation	Type Description
375	IVA1a2'	Architectural element, paving slab, shaped
376	IVA1b2'	Architectural element, grinding slab, shaped
377	IVA1e1'	Architectural element, cooking slab, unshaped
378	IVA1f	Architectural element, step tread, shaped
379	IVA1g1'b'	Architectural element, slab, shaped
380	IVA1g2'b'	Architectural element, pebble (1–15 cm diameter), shaped
381	IVA1g3'b'	Architectural element, cobble (15–30 cm diameter), shaped
382	IVA1g4'b'	Architectural element, boulder (>30 cm diameter), shaped
383	IVB1a	Architectural element, framing cast
384	IVB1b	Architectural element, matting cast
385	IVB1c	Architectural element, wall plaster
386	VA1a1'a'	Red ocher
387	VA1a1'b'	Red ocher, abraded
388	VA1a2'a'	Compact hematite
389	VA1a2'b'	Compact hematite, abraded
390	VA1a2'c'	Compact hematite, flake
391	VA1a2'd'	Compact hematite, core
392	VA1a3'a'	Specularite
393	VA1a3'b'	Specularite, abraded
394	VA1a4'a'	Kidney ore
395	VA1b1'a'	Limonite
396	VA1b1'b'	Limonite, abraded
397	VA1c1'a'	Kaolinite
398	VA1d1'a'	Azurite
399	VA1e1'a'	Malachite
400	VA1e1'b'	Malachite, abraded
401	VA2	Raw material, stone, andesite
402	VA3	Raw material, stone, aragonite
403	VA4	Raw material, stone, biotite schist
404	VA5	Raw material, stone, breccia
405	VA6	Raw material, stone, calcite
406	VA7	Raw material, stone, concretion
407	VA8	Raw material, stone, copper
408	VA9	Raw material, stone, dacite
409	VA10	Raw material, stone, dolomite
410	VA11	Raw material, stone, felsite slickenside
411	VA12	Raw material, stone, fluorite
412	VA13	Raw material, stone, fossil
413	VA14	Raw material, stone, granite
414	VA15	Raw material, stone, gypsum
415	VA16	Raw material, stone, limestone
416	VA17a1'a'	Raw material, stone, muscovite mica
417	VA17b1'a'	Raw material, stone, biotite mica

Appendix 5: Table 2. *(continued)*

Reference No.	Di Peso Type Designation	Type Description
418	VA17b1'b'	Raw material, stone, biotite mica, abraded
419	VA18	Raw material, stone, obsidian
420	VA19	Raw material, stone, opaline
421	VA20	Raw material, stone, pumice
422	—	Raw material, stone, pyroxenite
423	VA21a1'	Raw material, stone, rock crystal
424	VA21a2'	Raw material, stone, amethyst
425	VA21a3'	Raw material, stone, milky quartz
426	VA21b1'	Raw material, stone, agate
427	VA21b2'	Raw material, stone, chalcedony
428	VA21b3'	Raw material, stone, chert
429	VA21b4'	Raw material, stone, flint
430	VA21b5'	Raw material, stone, jasper
431	VA21c1'	Raw material, stone, quartzite
432	VA22	Raw material, stone, rhyolite
433	VA23	Raw material, stone, ricolite
434	VA24	Raw material, stone, sandstone
435	VA25	Raw material, stone, shale
436	VA27	Raw material, stone, steatite
437	VA28	Raw material, stone, travertine
438	VA29	Raw material, stone, tuff
439	VA30a1'a'	Raw material, stone, vein turquoise
440	VA30a2'a'	Raw material, stone, turquoise pebble
441	VA30a2'b'	Raw material, stone, turquoise pebble, abraded
442	VA30a3'a'	Raw material, stone, turquoise incrustation
443	VA31	Raw material, stone, vesicular basalt
444	VB1	Raw material, bone, mammal femur
445	VB2	Raw material, bone, mammal long bone
446	VB3	Raw material, bone, mammal rib
447	VB4	Raw material, bone, mammal cranium
448	VB5	Raw material, bone, bird femur
449	VC3	Raw material, ceramic, sherd, incised
450	VC4	Raw material, ceramic, sherd, sawed
451	VC1	Raw material, ceramic, fillet
452	VC2	Raw material, ceramic, lump

Appendix. 5: Table 3. House Types

Secular Domestic Houses (<30 m^2)

Type I - Round/circular-oval pit house with no side entry.
I - Round/circular-oval pit house with side entry.
III - Rectangular/square pit house with no side entry.
IV - Rectangular/square pit house with side entry.
V - Rectangular/square contiguous surface room.
VI - Unclassified domestic house.

Community Houses

Type A - Round community pit house with no side entry (>30 m^2).
B - Round community pit house with side entry (>30 m^2).
C - Rectangular community pit house with side entry (>30 m^2).
D - Rectangular community pit house with four central post pattern with side entry (>30 m^2).
E - Rectangular contiguous surface community room house (>30 m^2).
F - Rectangular subterranean community pit house with roof entry and ventilator shaft (<30 m^2).
G - Rectangular community pit house with roof entry and ventilator shaft (<30 m^2).

House or Room Units

Unit 1 - Rooms 1-3 (Rooms 1 and 2 domestic, Room 3 community).
2 - Rooms 4-13 (all rooms are domestic except Room 7).
3 - Rooms 14-16 (Rooms 14 and 16 domestic, Room 15 community).

Appendix. 5: Table 4. Hearth Types

I. Irregular
- A. Clay-lined
  - 1. with edge rock
  - 2. with smaller, deeper depression
  - 3. with smaller, deeper depression and edge rock
- B. Unlined
  - 1. with edge rock
  - 2. with edge rock and smaller, deeper depression

II. Round/Oval
- A. Clay-lined
  - 1. with edge rock
  - 2. collared
  - 3. double
- B. Unlined
  - 1. with edge rock
- C. Stone-lined
  - 1. clay-lined (or set in clay)
  - 2. unlined

III. Rectangular
- A. Clay-lined
  - 1. collared
- B. Stone-lined
  - 1. clay-lined (set in clay)
  - 2. unlined

IV. Unclassified

Appendix 6

Petrographic Observations of Selected Sherds from Wind Mountain

JAMES B. STOLTMAN

Twenty painted and unpainted sherds from the Wind Mountain site were selected for petrographic analysis. Following procedures outlined in Stoltman (1989), each thin section was subjected to both qualitative and quantitative observation. Quantitative data were based upon a point-count procedure in which the total area of each thin section was observed at 1 mm intervals. An estimate of the relative proportions of mineral constituents (i.e., clay matrix, silt, sand, and temper) was thus compiled as a percentage of the total counts per thin section. The number of counts per thin section (excluding voids) ranged from 135 to 317, with a mean of 190 ± 39. Through this procedure, four basic properties of the sherds were observed: (1) paste exclusive of temper, (2) kind of temper, (3) temper amount, and (4) temper size.

The 20 sherds analyzed derive equally from the two major periods of occupation at the site and include nine painted bowls, one painted jar and 10 unpainted jars. Representing the Late Pit House period (c. A.D. 550–950/1000) are three Boldface Black-on-white (Style I), two Mimbres Transitional Black-on-white (Style II), four Three Circle Neck Corrugated, and one Alma Neck Banded sherds. Representing the Mimbres (c. A.D. 1000–1150) are five Mimbres Classic Black-on-white (Style III), two Mimbres Corrugated, and three Mimbres Rubbed Corrugated sherds. These sherds were selected to express the full range of ceramic variation observed at the site, but the extent to which they may be representative of the site as a whole is presently unknown. In order to place this sample in a larger context, comparison is made between the present sample and a sample of 52 thin sections analyzed from elsewhere in the Mimbres region. These latter thin sections derive from seven sites, six in the Mimbres Valley proper (represented by 32 vessels) and one (the Anderson site) located on the eastern flanks of the Black Range northeast of the Mimbres Valley (represented by 20 vessels). All 52 thin sections derive from Mimbres vessels, 32 from brownware jars and 20 from Mimbres Classic Black-on-white bowls.

Paste

All 20 of the Wind Mountain sherds were manufactured from clays that are relatively low in natural mineral inclusions in the silt and sand size ranges (i.e., .004–.0625 mm and .0625–2.0 mm, respectively). As can be seen from Appendix 6: Table 1, the amount of sand in the pastes of the 20 sherds ranges from 1 to 9 percent. However, in order to get a more accurate indication of the character of the raw clays, it is necessary to remove temper, a demonstrable human additive, from the tabulations. After deleting temper from the point count tabulations, the pastes of the sherds were observed to have from 1 to 19 percent silt-sized particles (mean = 7.8 mm ± 4.0%) and from 1 to 12 percent sand-sized particles (mean = 4.0 mm ± 3.1%). In none of the 20 vessels did the combined silt-sand percentage exceed 23 percent; that is, all vessels had pastes comprised of a minimum of 77 percent clay, excluding temper and voids. In this regard it should also be noted that an undetermined number of the particles identified as silt and sand (i.e., as natural inclusions) could actually be tiny fragments of temper that were misidentified. Accordingly, the silt and sand percentages must be regarded as maximum estimates.

One other property of the paste merits mention. In a number of cases a "clouding over" of the clay matrix was observed. Although not yet finally confirmed, this property may reflect the onset of vitrification of the clay, presumably due to high firing temperatures. Support for this view may be seen in the apparent nonrandom distribution of this property among the 20 sherds here examined. Among the 10 cor-

APPENDIX 6: FIGURE 1. Photomicrograph of thin section No. 29–32, a Mimbres Corrugated sherd with Granite 1 temper. The largest grain is dominated by microcline, with its characteristic tartan twining, along with lesser amounts of quartz (untwined). The maximum diameter of the largest grain is 2.25 mm. Photograph taken at 40x with crossed polars (courtesy James B. Stoltman).

rugated jars, only one showed evidence of this property; whereas among the 10 painted vessels, seven showed such evidence, including all five of the Mimbres Classic Black-on-white bowls. Based upon these data, it can be suggested that the firing of painted bowls involved special steps and hotter temperatures than was normally used in the firing of the utilitarian jars. It seems reasonable to infer that Mimbres bowls and jars were fired independently at Wind Mountain.

Kind of Temper

In all instances vessels observed in this analysis had fragments of crushed igneous rock added as temper. In terms of texture the igneous rocks used as temper by the potters at Wind Mountain were both phaneritic (i.e., the minerals can be distinguished with the naked eye) and aphanitic (i.e., the mineral constituents are too small to be identified with the naked eye). Compositionally, the phaneritic rocks used as temper are granitic, whereas the aphanitic rocks range from rhyolite to trachyte to latite to andesite. In addition one Mimbres Classic Black-on-white bowl was tempered with volcanic glass.

The most common rock used as temper in this sample is granite, which was observed in nine of the 20 sherds. Moreover, it is possible that at least three different rocks of granitic composition were utilized. The most common type, referred to as Granite 1 (Appendix 6: Table 1), is marked by the presence of microcline as one of its key alkali feldspars (Appendix 6: Figure 1), whereas microcline is absent from Granites 2 and 3. Granite 3, which occurs only in the Mimbres Transitional Black-on-white jar (No. 29–45), was distinguished from Granite 2 by the high degree of angularity and clarity, that is, lack of alteration, of its feldspars.

Granites were apparently the preferred temper used in jars

APPENDIX 6: TABLE 1. Petrographic Observations for Selected Wind Mountain Site Sherds

	Type	Thin Section	Temper	Matrix (%)	Sand (%)	Grit (%)
1	Alma Neck Banded	29–50	Trachyte/latite	69	2	29
2	Three Circle Neck Corrugated	29–46	Rhyolite	60	1	39
3	Three Circle Neck Corrugated	29–47	Granite 1	59	1	40
4	Three Circle Neck Corrugated	29–48	Granite 2	66	1	33
5	Three Circle Neck Corrugated	29–49	Granite 1	62	2	36
6	Mimbres Transitional B/W	29–44	Trachyte/andesite	64	1	35
7	Mimbres Transitional B/W	29–45	Granite 3	79	5	16
8	Boldface B/W	29–41	Rhyolite	58	4	38
9	Boldface B/W	29–42	Trachyte	65	7	28
10	Boldface B/W	29–43	Granite 1	67	6	27
11	Mimbres Corrugated	29–31	Trachyte	72	2	26
12	Mimbres Corrugated	29–32	Granite 1	56	2	42
13	Mimbres Rubbed Corrugated	29–38	Granite 1	67	5	28
14	Mimbres Rubbed Corrugated	29–39	Granite 1	59	2	39
15	Mimbres Rubbed Corrugated	29–40	Granite 2	71	2	27
16	Mimbres Classic B/W	29–33	Glass	77	5	18
17	Mimbres Classic B/W	29–34	Rhyolite	67	1	32
18	Mimbres Classic B/W	29–35	Trachyte	78	1	21
19	Mimbres Classic B/W	29–36	Trachyte	67	1	32
20	Mimbres Classic B/W	29–37	Trachyte	62	9	29

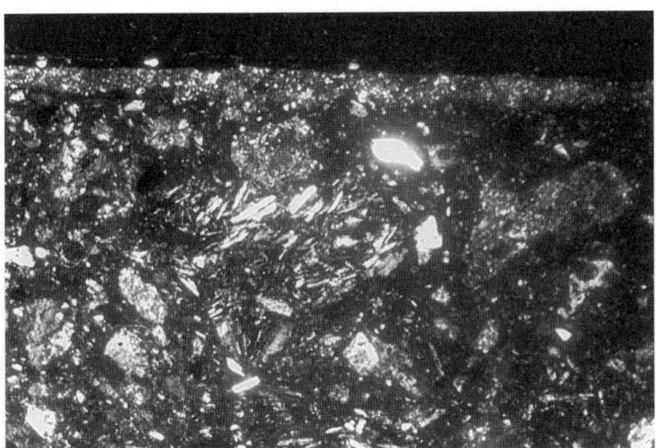

APPENDIX 6: FIGURE 2. Photomicrograph of thin section No. 29–37, a Mimbres Classic Black-on-white bowl sherd with latite and trachyte temper. Both are fine-grained igneous rocks dominated by mafic minerals and feldspars and lacking quartz. The largest grain near the center (with the characteristic plagioclase laths) is latite; most of the smaller grains are trachyte (orthoclase more abundant than plagioclase). Note the white slip underlying black paint at the top of the photograph. The large latite grain measures 1.375 mm in maximum diameter. Photograph taken at 40x under crossed polars (courtesy James B. Stoltman).

during both Late Pit House and Mimbres times at Wind Mountain. Three of the four Three Circle Neck Corrugated and four of the five Mimbres Corrugated/Rubbed Corrugated jars had granitic temper. By contrast, only two of the black-on-white vessels had granitic temper, one each from the two Late Pit House period types. It is noteworthy that none of the five Mimbres Classic Black-on-white bowls had granitic temper.

A similar pattern of using rocks of granitic composition preferentially as temper for utilitarian jars is also evident in the Mimbres Valley and at the Anderson site. In a sample of 22 brownware jars from six Mimbres Valley sites, 14 had granitic temper, and among 10 such jars from the Anderson site, one had granitic temper. By contrast, 20 Mimbres Classic Black-on-white bowls, 10 from the Mimbres Valley, and 10 from the Anderson site all lacked granite temper. From these data, it would appear that during Mimbres times potters throughout the Mimbres region, whenever they used granitic temper, did so exclusively in the manufacture of utilitarian jars.

Following granite, the most commonly used temper at Wind Mountain was a fine-grained igneous rock of trachytic composition (Appendix 6: Figure 2). Trachytes are characterized by a predominance of alkali feldspars (e.g., orthoclase) and the absence of quartz, except in accessory amounts; sodic feldspars (e.g., plagioclase) may be absent or present in small amounts. Seven vessels had trachytic temper, including the single Alma Neck Banded vessel, two Late Pit House period black-on-white bowls, one Mimbres Corrugated jar, and three Mimbres Classic Black-on-white bowls (Appendix 6: Table 1). In two of these vessels, fragments of a second igneous rock, either latite or andesite, were also observed. Both of the latter are basically quartz-free, aphanitic rocks in which sodic feldspars either equal (latite) or totally replace (andesite) alkali feldspars. In addition rhyolite (a fine-grained igneous rock in which quartz is present and alkali feldspar exceeds sodic feldspar) was used as temper in three vessels, one each of the following types: Three Circle Neck Corrugated (No. 29–46), Boldface Black-on-white (No. 29–41), and Mimbres Classic Black-on-white (No. 29–34). All of these aphanitic rocks were also used as temper at the Anderson and Mimbres Valley sites, where they constitute the sole tempers in the painted bowls.

Because none of the 25 Mimbres Classic Black-on-white bowls from eight different sites analyzed so far shows evidence of granite temper, it can be suggested that Mimbres potters had come to prefer fine-grained igneous rocks as the primary temper for their bowls while using granite for many of their utilitarian jars. Presumably, this reflects an awareness on the part of the Mimbres potters that the kind of temper used could alter or improve the functional properties of specific vessel forms. Because there is no reasonable doubt in this case that different tempers were being utilized within the same community of potters, we have here an important "cautionary tale" for archaeologists: temper differences can connote more than temporal or spatial variation in cultural practices.

Temper Amount

The estimated amount of temper added by the Wind Mountain potters ranges from 16 to 42 percent (Appendix 6: Table 1, Figure 3). When the sample is subdivided into painted versus unpainted vessels, a clear trend in the differential amount of temper is evident.

	Unpainted	*Painted*
Mean % Grit, Total Site Sample (n=20)	33.9±6.0	27.6±7.2
Mean % Grit, Late Pit House (n=10)	35.4±4.5	28.8±8.5
Mean % Grit, Mimbres (n=10)	32.4±7.5	26.4±6.5

As can be seen from the above data, the greater amount of temper used in vessels that are unpainted (all jars) as opposed to those that are painted (nine bowls and one jar) is characteristic not only of the entire site sample, but of each of the two major periods of occupancy as well. A t-test for the total site sample indicates that the observed differences between

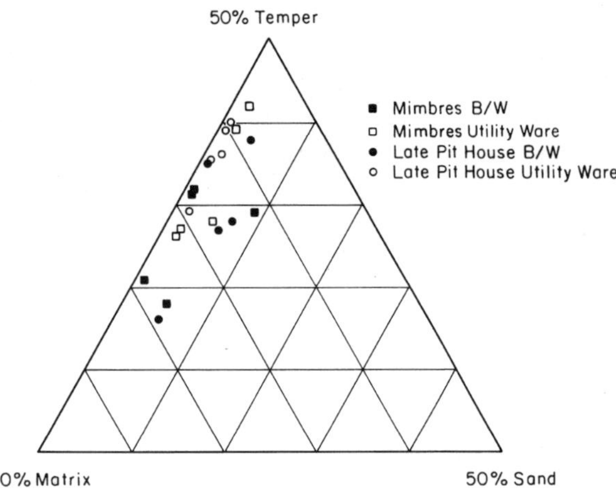

APPENDIX 6: FIGURE 3. Ternary diagram plotting the relative percentages of temper, sand, and matrix (i.e., silt and clay) for the 20 sherds analyzed. Note the tendency for utility vessels to have higher percentages of temper than painted vessels.

painted and unpainted vessels are significant at the .05 level, but comparable t-tests for Late Pit House period and Mimbres samples are not significant. Presumably, however, these latter results are due to the smallness of the samples, only five each for painted and unpainted vessels in each period.

Support for the view that potters tended to regulate carefully the amount of temper added to different vessel forms may be seen when the Wind Mountain data are viewed in a larger regional perspective. In both the Mimbres Valley sites and at the Anderson site, there is a clear tendency for unpainted jars to contain more temper than bowls:

	Jars	*Bowls*
Mean % Grit, 6 Mimbres Valley sites (n=32)	29.2±9.4	20.0±8.0
Mean % Grit, Anderson Site (n=20)	30.8±5.1	24.8±6.3

In both of the above two cases t-tests reveal that the difference between the amount of temper in the bowls as contrasted with the jars is statistically significant at the .03 level of probability. These data suggest the existence of a widespread tendency among Mimbres potters to add greater amounts of temper to their cooking/storage vessels (i.e., unpainted jars) than to their bowls, presumably to enhance vessel functions.

Temper Size

Not only were potters apparently varying the amount of temper added depending upon vessel form, but they also seem to have varied temper coarseness for similar reasons. The basic data from which this inference is drawn are presented below in the form of mean indices of grit coarseness:

	Brownware Jars	*B/W Vessels*
Late Prehistoric period (n=10)	2.24±.40	2.12±.25
Mimbres (n=10)	2.22±.27	1.78±.38

These indices were computed for each thin section based upon the sum of size values for each temper grain counted and weighted according to a simple ordinal scale as follows:

1 = fine (.0625 mm-.25 mm)
2 = medium (.25 mm-.50 mm)
3 = coarse (.50 mm-1.0 mm)
4 = very coarse (1.0 mm-2.0 mm)
5 = gravel (>2.0 mm)

These data indicate that temper size in jars was similar in both Late Pit House and Mimbres times and that black-on-white vessels of the earlier period were only slightly finer grained than the unpainted jars. By contrast, black-on-white Mimbres bowls display a notable reduction in temper coarseness. The difference between the indices for Mimbres black-on-white bowls and unpainted jars is significant at the .07 level and would certainly exceed the .05 level if the sample was larger. Whether or not this apparent temporal trend is regional in scope, or characteristic only of Wind Mountain, cannot presently be ascertained because comparable size data are currently not available from other sites.

Possible Trade Vessels

Based in large part upon the presence of unique tempers, but also upon other paste qualities as well, three vessels in the current sample of 20 from Wind Mountain can be identified as possible intrusives. The first, a Mimbres Transitional Black-on-white jar (No. 29–45), not only has a unique granitic temper (Granite 3), but its fine, uniform clay matrix is also characterized by two distinctive, apparently natural, inclusions in the silt and fine sand size range—biotite and brown isotropic grains of an unidentified material—that further accentuate its uniqueness. The second, a Mimbres Classic Black-on-white bowl (No. 29–33), is similarly distinctive, although very different from both No. 29–45 and No. 29–35. It is tempered with finely crushed fragments of volcanic glass, the only such sherd observed not only in the Wind Mountain sample, but also among the larger Mimbres area sample. The third possibly intrusive vessel is No. 29–35, a second Mimbres Classic Black-on-white bowl. Its temper has been tentatively identified as a trachyte, but it is highly distinctive in that it has a glassy matrix and angular feldspar phenocrysts that are clear and unaltered. It is noteworthy that each of these three vessels can unambiguously be identified by the uniqueness of their tempers and at the same time are also quantitatively distinctive. As can be seen from Appendix 6: Table 1, these three vessels are the only ones among the 20 from Wind Mountain to have less than 26 percent grit. Because at the present time an external source for these three vessels cannot be demonstrated, it would be premature to conclude that they actually *are* intrusive vessels, but this possibility certainly deserves serious consideration.

Conclusions

A petrographic thin section analysis of 20 pottery vessels from the Wind Mountain site, when viewed in a larger comparative context of 52 thin sectioned vessels from seven other sites in the Mimbres region, is the basis for offering the following two main conclusions. These conclusions rest upon the tentative and yet unconfirmed supposition that the current sample of thin sections is representative of the site and the region.

First, the pottery manufacturing practices observed during both Wind Mountain site Late Pit House period and Mimbres occupations conform to a wider, pan-regional tradition that seems to be characteristic of the Mimbres region as a whole. The hallmarks of this technological tradition are: a) the use of crushed igneous rocks, principally trachytes and granites, for temper in ceramic vessels and b) the differential use of temper types, sizes and densities depending upon vessel form.

Second, the potters at the Wind Mountain site, as elsewhere in the Mimbres region, had attained a high level of technological sophistication in pottery manufacture to accompany their undeniable artistic virtuosity. The data suggest that granite was the preferred temper used in the manufacture of brownware jars, but trachytes, rhyolites and other fine grained igneous rocks were the preferred tempers for bowls. Two exceptions to this pattern were observed in the current data set. At Wind Mountain granite temper was observed in two Late Pit House period bowls (the only bowls so tempered out of 30 examined in this study), though at the Anderson site only one jar out of ten had granite temper. In the former case, sample size is especially inadequate, because at no other sites have thin sections of Late Pit House period vessels been analyzed, whereas in the latter case local inaccessibility of granite sources may be indicated. Besides varying temper type with vessel form, it also appears that Mimbres potters consciously varied the amount and the size of temper according to vessel form and/or function. The data in this study suggest that unpainted Mimbres jars tend to have both greater amounts and larger sizes of temper inclusions than do bowls. It is suggested here that the observed covariation of vessel form with type, amount, and size of temper at Wind Mountain, as well as in the Mimbres region generally, is indicative of sophisticated "ceramic engineering" practices on the part of Mimbres potters, whose objective was to maximize the performance characteristics of the bowl and jar forms that predominate in their ceramic assemblages.

Appendix 7

Wind Mountain Osteological Analysis

MADELEINE J. M. HINKES

Osteological analysis was performed on approximately 124 skeletons, including two cremations, and much miscellaneous bone (refer to Chapter 9). Each of the 122 numbered burials submitted contained the remains of one or more individuals (Appendix 7: Table 1; Table 9.1). The bones, for the most part, were in only fair condition. Many were fragmented and fragile; several long bone shafts were filled with small gravel and sand. There was only minimal evidence of rodent gnawing activity.

Techniques of Analysis

Following procedures to stabilize the samples, bones and teeth within each burial were inventoried, and any anomalies, pathologies, or duplication of skeletal elements that indicated the presence of more than one individual noted. Measurements were taken of intact adult long bones in order to estimate living stature using the formulae of Genoves (1967). Complete human skeletal inventory sheets are on file both at the Arizona State Museum and the Amerind Foundation. Miscellaneous bones, that is, those not belonging to a particular burial, were similarly inventoried. Nonhuman bone was separated for analysis by researchers in the Arizona State Museum faunal lab (refer to Chapter 10, Appendix 8).

An attempt was made to observe 50 cranial and postcranial discrete traits on each individual skeleton, including the presence or absence of sutural ossicles of various types, mandibular tori, vastus notches on patellae, and bridging of cervical vertebral transverse foramina. The genetic heritability of these traits is complex (see, for example, Berry 1968) and should be interpreted only within and among large skeletal series. All recorded nonmetric (discrete) traits are on file at the Central Identification Laboratory, Fort Kamehameha, Hawaii.

The ages of individuals in the Wind Mountain series range from fetal/newborn to old adult. Subadults were aged more precisely by means of dental eruption patterns (Schour and Massler 1944), long bone lengths (Johnston 1962), and skeletal maturation (*Gray's Anatomy* 1973). The best method for aging adult material is by visual inspection of changes in the pubic bones, according to the standards of McKern and Stewart (1957). However, only 10 of the 79 adults from the Wind Mountain locus and one adult from the Ridout locus had one or both pubic bones. The majority of the adults could therefore be classified only as young adult (15–25 years), middle adult (26–39 years), or old adult (40+ years), based on dental wear and degenerative bony changes. Cranial suture closure as an aging criterion was not applicable because crania were fragmentary.

Determination of sex in adults was based on differences in pelvic and cranial morphology and general robusticity (Krogman 1962; Phenice 1969). Sexing of subadults was not attempted here, because there are few reliable means of doing so (Appendix 7: Table 2).

The Wind Mountain Locus Skeletal Series

Despite the apparent quantity of burials, relatively little skeletal material was analyzed, as nearly three-fourths of the skeletons are represented by less than half the normal complement of bones (Appendix 7: Table 3). There are, however, skeletal remains of other individuals besides those in numbered burials (i.e., the 800+ miscellaneous bone bags; Appendix 7: Tables 4 and 5). Several of these bags contained more complete individuals than did some of the burials,

Appendix 7: Table 1. The Wind Mountain Skeletal Series

Burial No.	Age/Sex	Estimated Completeness (%)	Dentition	Metrics	Pathologies Anomalies
WM locus					
1	MA/?	0–25			
2	Infant	0–25			
3	25–35 yrs./F	75–100	*	*	*
4	OA/M	25–50	*		
5	3–4 yrs.	75–100	*	*	
6	MA/?	25–50	*		
7	Infant	25–50			
8	OA/M	50–75			*
9	OA/F	50–75	*		*
10	Infant	25–50			
11A	40–45 yrs./F	75–100		*	*
11B	Adult	0–25			*
12	MA/F	0–25			
13	MA/F	50–75	*		
14	MA/?	0–25			
15	MA/M?	0–25			
16	MA/M?	0–25			
17	MA/?	0–25			*
18	MA/?	0–25	*		
19	MA/M	0–25	*		*
20	MA/?	25–50			
21	OA/M	50–75			*
22	50+ yrs./F	75–100	*	*	*
23	OA/M	50–75	*	*	
24	OA/M	75–100	*	*	
25	MA/?	0–25			
26	Fetus	25–50			
27	Infant	25–50			
28	MA/?	0–25			
29	Infant	0–25			
30	MA/F	25–50	*		
31	OA/?	25–50	*		*
32	A?/?	0–25			
33	MA/?	25–50	*		
34	4–6 yrs.	25–50	*		
35	?	0–25			
36	Infant	50–75			
37	A/?	0–25			
38	45–50 yrs./F	50–75	*		*
39	OA/?	0–25	*		
40	YA/M?	25–50	*		
41	MA/?	25–50	*		
42	MA/M	50–75	*		
43	MA/M?	0–25	*		
44	45–55 yrs./F	75–100	*	*	*
45	MA/M	50–75	*		
46	A?/?	0–25	*		
47	MA/M?	50–75	*	*	
48	MA/?	25–50	*		*

Appendix 7: Table 1 *(continued)*

Burial No.	Age/Sex	Estimated Completeness (%)	Dentition	Metrics	Pathologies Anomalies
WM locus					
49	MA/M	50–75	*		*
50	MA/?	0–25			
51	MA/?	0–25	*		
52	16–18 yrs./F	25–50	*		*
53	MA/M	50–75	*	*	
54	MA/M	25–50	*		*
55	MA/?	0–25			
56	MA/?	0–25	*		
57	MA/?	0–25			
58	MA/?	0–25			
59	OA/M?	50–75	*	*	
60	MA/?	0–25			
61	MA/M	50–75	*		
62	MA/?	0–25	*		
63	45–55 yrs./F	50–75	*		
64	2.5–3.5 yrs.	50–75	*		
65	MA/?	25–50	*	*	
66	5–7 yrs.	0–25			
67	MA/?	0–25			
68	MA/M	50–75	*	*	
69	50+ yrs./F	50–75	*	*	*
70	0–3 mos.	0–25			
71	MA/?	0–25			
72	MA/M?	25–50	*		
73	1–2 yrs.	0–25			
74	OA/M?	25–50			
75	4–6 mos.	25–50			
76	MA/?	0–25			
77	17–18 yrs./M?	25–50	*		
78	Fetus	0–25			
79	MA/M	0–25			*
80	MA/?	0–25			
81	50+ yrs./F	25–50	*		
82	Child	0–25			
83	MA/?	0–25	*		
84	YA/F	50–75	*	*	*
85	2–3 yrs.	25–50	*		
86	MA/?	50–75	*		
87	MA/M?	0–25			
88	MA/?	0–25			
89	MA?	25–50	*		
90	MA/?	0–25		*	*
91	Infant	75–100			
92	Child	0–25			
93	MA/?	0–25			
94	YA/?	25–50	*		
95	Child	0–25			
96	MA/?	25–50	*		
97	MA/?	0–25			
98	MA/?	0–25			

Appendix 7: Table 1 *(continued)*

Burial No.	Age/Sex	Estimated Completeness (%)	Dentition	Metrics	Pathologies Anomalies
WM locus					
99	OA/M?	25–50	*		*
100	Neonate	75–100	*	*	
101	2 children: 1, 4–5 yrs.; 2, 5–6 yrs.	Cranial fragments only			
102	MA/M	0–25			
103	MA/M	25–50	*		
104	MA/M?	25–50	*		
105	40–45 yrs./F	25–50			
106	Infant	0–25			
RO locus					
1	MA/?	0–25	*		
2	MA/?	0–25			
3	MA/?	25–50			
4	MA/M?	25–50	*		
5	OA/M	50–75	*	*	
6	MA/?	0–25			
7	OA/M	50–75	*		*
8	OA/F	0–25	*		
9	MA/?	0–25	*		
10	Infant	0–25			
11	MA/?	0–25	*		
12	Infant	0–25			
13	MA/?	0–25			
14	1.5–2.5 yrs.	50–75	*		
15	MA/F?	25–50	*	*	
16	MA/F	75–100	*	*	*

*These measurements/observations were able to be taken and are discussed in the text.
Note: YA = Young adult (15–25 yrs.), MA = Middle adult (26–39 yrs.), OA = Old adult (40+ yrs.), F = Female, M = Male.

especially those with infant material. Fifteen of the numbered burial remains contained one or more bones not attributable to the primary burial. Most of the miscellaneous bones were in better condition than were those from designated burials.

Cremations

Two cremations included with the Wind Mountain material were identified in the field as primary cremations. The bones within each are very fragmentary.

Cremation 1 contained 14 long bone fragments, one talus fragment, one odontoid process, and nine miscellaneous fragments. These could all belong to a single adult. Most fragments were calcined, although a lesser number are heavily charred. Because the bones are so fragmentary, it was difficult to determine the condition of the body when burned. However, the bone pieces do not appear to be warped, nor do they exhibit the heavy checking characteristic of a bone burned "green" or fresh (Baby 1954). Thus, they were probably burned when in a dry state.

Cremation 2 contained over 30 long bone fragments (mostly tibia), five cranial fragments, one anterior tooth root, two cervical vertebra fragments, and one talus fragment. All are well calcined and could belong to a single adult. It would appear that these bones were also burned when dry.

From an osteological standpoint, no statement can be made as to how these cremations relate to the rest of the burial series from Wind Mountain. The cremations were found in the same excavation blocks as were interments. It may be that the skeletalized bodies were subsequently disinterred for cremation, which could explain the dry state of the bones when burned. Conversely, the incineration may have been unintentional. There is no osteological evidence to support or disprove either of these theories.

Appendix 7: Table 2. Age and Sex at Death

Estimated Age	Female	Male	Indeterminate	Total (n)	Total (%)
		WM locus			
Infant, Fetus–18 mos.	–	–	13	13	12.1
Child, 1.5–14 yrs.	–	–	11	11	10.3
Young Adult, 15–25 yrs.	2	2	1	5	4.7
Middle Adult, 26–39 yrs.	4	18	37	59	55.1
Old Adult, 40+ yrs.	9	8	2	19	17.8
Total	15	28	64	107*	100.0
		RO locus			
Infant, Fetus–18 mos.	–	–	2	2	12.5
Child, 1.5–14 yrs.	–	–	1	1	6.3
Young Adult, 15–25 yrs.	–	–	–	0	0.0
Middle Adult, 26–39 yrs.	2	1	7	10	62.5
Old Adult, 40+ yrs.	1	2	–	3	18.7
Total	3	3	10	16	100.0

*One individual (Burial 35) was too incomplete and fragmentary to age.

Population Profile

The mortality profile based on age at death reveals 24 juveniles (22 percent) and 83 adults (78 percent). Child mortality was not particularly high, considering the greater susceptibility to disease, unhygienic conditions and the many vectors of infection to which children must have been exposed (Kraus 1954; Moore et al. 1972). Nineteen adults (18 percent) were classified as "old," (i.e., over 40 years of age), which is close to the proposed longevity of prehistoric groups (Blakely 1971).

These oldest individuals seem to have been well cared for. With their extremely worn or absent teeth and their fragile osteoporotic bones, the elderly residents of Wind Mountain would have had a difficult time fending for themselves. Males appear to outnumber females in the adult sector, but as nearly half of the adult skeletons were unsexable, the apparent male majority may not be real.

Based on osteological evidence, this group was generally healthy, except as will be noted below. No evidence of violent death was discovered and, in fact, there was little indication of the causes of death. The dentition exhibited much wear and antemortem loss but few caries.

Appendix 7: Table 3. Estimated Completeness of Skeletal Remains

Estimated Completeness (%)	No. of Individuals	Percent of Series
WM locus		
0–25	50	46.30
25–50	30	27.80
50–75	20	18.50
75–100	8	7.40
Total	108	100.00
RO locus		
0–25	9	56.25
25–50	3	18.75
50–75	3	18.75
75–100	1	6.25
Total	16	100.00

Stature

Fourteen adults have one or more complete long bones, the lengths of which could be measured to estimate living stature. Included are six males, six females, and two unsexable individuals (Appendix 7: Table 6).

Female stature ranges from 147.2 to 160.8 cm, with a mean of 155.7 cm (61.3 inches). The male mean is 163.1 cm (64.2 inches), with a range of 154.0 to 169.0 cm. Each sex showed about equal variation. The two "unsexable" individuals (Burials 65 and 90), then, would fit with either sex in terms of stature.

It is interesting to note that in the five individuals who have measurable long bones from both arms, the right arm bones are consistently 1 to 5 mm longer than the left. This discrepancy in length may indicate greater muscle-bone development due to more frequent use of the preferred side. Measurements of corresponding scapulae and clavicles might have supported this observation, but most are fragmentary or

Appendix 7: Table 4. Miscellaneous Human Bone

Sample No.	
WM locus	
1.	infant cervical vertebra neural arch; House A, fill
10.	rib; Block 18-C
16.	charred cervical vertebra fragment; Block 18-C
19.	3 long bone fragments; 2nd right metatarsal; House D, fill
24.	infant humerus fragment; Block 18-D
30.	infant left humerus; House G, fill
34.	ilium fragment; Block 11-A
35.	phalange; Block 11-A
38.	phalange; Block 3-C/D
40.	child parietal fragment, mandible fragment; phalange; Block 11-B
47.	fetal left ilium, right femur; House H, fill
48.	cranial fragment; House H, fill
58.	distal humerus fragment; 2 phalanges; Block 18-B
64.	2nd or 3rd metacarpal; House F, fill
70.	fetal right femur, left tibia; House I, floor fill
72.	basi-occipital fragment; 1 misc. cranial fragment; 1 hand phalange; House L, fill
83.	tibia fragment; Room 4, fill
86.	2 femur fragments, phalange; juvenile humerus fragment; House K, fill
87.	2 juvenile cranial fragments; 2 ribs; distal humerus; right talus; 2 phalanges; 1 metatarsal head; House K, fill
96.	right clavicle; House J, fill
98.	juvenile cranial, rib, long bone pieces; radius, femur fragments; left 4th metacarpal, Block 19-B
101.	left 3rd metatarsal and phalange; Block 26-A, Burial 13, fill
102.	child clavicle, 3 ribs; atlas fragment, thoracic vertebral body, 2 tarsal fragments; Pit 6, fill
104.	child right ulna fragment, adult ulna fragment; left 3rd cuneiform; House L, fill
105.	long bone fragments, phalange; Block 26-A
106.	2 vertebra fragments; House L, fill
114.	right 3rd metatarsal; right 2nd metatarsal; 3 phalanges; Pit 6, fill
115.	phalange; House K, floor fill
116.	phalange; House L, fill
118.	2 phalanges; 1 vertebra; right temporal; 2 incomplete metatarsal; House L, fill
123.	2 ilium fragments; 1 cranial; left malar; 1 phalange; left 5th metacarpal; metatarsal head; House L, fill
125.	ulna fragment; rib fragment; Block 4-C
131.	rib; House L, floor
132.	humerus shaft; long bone fragments; Room 4, subfloor
136.	phalange; worn tooth; Room 7, fill
138.	left humerus; left distal radius; 1 phalange; 1st lumbar vertebra; Block 12-D
141.	rib fragment; Room 7, floor fill
146.	2 rib fragments; phalange; Room 9, floor fill
150.	incomplete metatarsal or carpal; House N, fill
151.	calcined cranial fragments; House N, fill
153.	rib fragment; House N, fill
158.	smoked femur fragments; House N, fill
160.	phalange; House N, fill
162.	right talus; navicular fragment; 1 phalange; juvenile ilium, long bone, meta-; House N, fill
167.	rib fragment; Block 13-A
168.	2 rib fragments; Block 13-A
170.	fibula shaft; Block 13-C
171.	tibia, femur, humerus, ulna shafts; navicular; left scapula; 3 ribs; cranial fragment; Block 13-C

APPENDIX 7: TABLE 4. *(continued)*

Sample No.	
173.	tibia shaft fragment; rib fragment; cranial fragment; Block 13-D
175.	mandible shaft, infant proximal left femur; Block 19-B
176.	ulna and humerus fragments; 3 rib fragments; 10 cranial; 4 phalanges; left 1st metacarpal; left 5th metacarpal; left capitate; right hamate; Block 19-B
177.	hyoid body; Block 19-B
178.	10 ribs; 5 cranial; left maxilla; right patella; right talus; misc. thoracic vertebra; left vertebra; phalange; right hamate; right 1st metatarsal; right 2nd metatarsal; right 3rd metacarpal; left 5th metacarpal; Block 19-B
179.	infant femur; Block 20-B
180.	rib; right 5th metacarpal; left 1st metacarpal; Block 20-B
187.	left 2nd metacarpal; 4th metatarsal; Block 12-C
189.	right radius; 3 rib fragments; 2 phalanges; misc. thoracic vertebra; 1 cranial; 1 long bone fragment; Block 12-D
190.	2 humerus; ulna; radius; ribs; misc. thoracic vertebra; 6 phalanges; 2 calcaneus; left scapula; cuneiform; 2 right 1st metatarsals; left 1st metacarpal; right 2nd metacarpal; right 2nd metatarsal; 7 cranial fragments including temporal, mandible. 2 adults represented that are not Burial 21; Block 19-B
191.	infant left ulna and femur fragments; Block 19-B
192.	fetal right ulna; Block 20-A
194.	1st cervical vertebra; misc. thoracic vertebra; left talus; 2 phalanges; right 4th metatarsal; left 4th metatarsal; Block 20-A
195.	infant cranial fragments; right scapula; Block 20-A
196.	rib; 3 phalanges; Block 20-A
197.	infant cranial fragment; Block 20-C
198.	rib; cranial fragment; long bone fragment; Block 20-C
199.	juvenile tibia fragment; Block 20-D
200.	3 cranial fragments; Block 20-D
203.	juvenile cranial fragment; Block 20-D
205.	left 1st metatarsal; misc. shaft fragment; Block 27-B
208.	1 cranial fragment; Block 28-A
216.	2 rib fragments; 1 phalange; right 2nd metacarpal; House P, fill
217.	capitulum; House P, floor fill
218.	left talus; House P, floor fill
220.	left 5th metatarsal; 2 vertebra fragments; 1 rib fragment; 4th metatarsal; right navicular; House Q, fill
221.	infant femur; long bone fragment; House Q, fill
223.	1 rib fragment; Room 11, fill
226.	6th cervical vertebra; Block 13-D
227.	right humerus shaft; Block 35-B
228.	juvenile ulna shaft; Block 36-A
229.	fragments: parietal, femur, clavicle, phalange, vertebra; Block 44-B
230.	cranial fragments; Block 44-B
232.	rib fragment; radius fragment; navicular; Block 44-B
237.	cranial fragment; rib fragment; phalange; scapula fragment; House R, fill
24–.	left 3rd metacarpal; Block 36-A
242.	1 rib fragment; 2 cranial fragments; 2 innominate fragments; Block 36-B
244.	11 shaft fragments; 1st metatarsal head; rib fragment; calcaneus fragment; Block 36-B
245.	cranial fragment; Block 36-C
246.	1st metacarpal head; Block 44-B
247.	calcaneus fragment; Block 44-B
249.	cranial fragment; right ulna and radius – 2 children; Block 44-D
250.	rib fragment; Block 44-D
253.	phalange; House Q, floor fill/floor
254.	sphenoid fragment; House Q, floor
256.	juvenile ilium, petrous, malar, centrum, metatarsal shaft; right mandible – children; Block 20-B
257.	juvenile right 4th metatarsal; Block 44-A
258.	infant distal femur; House S, fill
259.	left talus; 2 phalanges; 1 immature; House S, fill
260.	juvenile clavicle fragment; House S, floor fill

APPENDIX 7: TABLE 4. *(continued)*

Sample No.	
261.	rib, long bone fragments; 2 phalanges; femur head; left calcaneus; cuneiform; right 1st and 4th metatarsals; House S, floor fill
262.	fetal right tibia, right femur; child left ulna, occipital, scapula fragment, cranial fragment; House T, fill
263.	3 rib fragments; 3 phalanges; 1 cranial fragment; right 5th metatarsal; House T, fill
265.	proximal ulna; proximal tibia; House T, floor fill
267.	1 phalange; 1 rib fragment; 2 meta-shafts; House U, fill
268.	clavicle?; Pit 8, fill
269.	atlas fragment; child right pubis, fibula fragment; fetal right humerus; Block 44-B
270.	juvenile right maxilla; Block 44-B
272.	large left calcaneus; cranial fragment; poss. Burial 28?; House S, fill
274.	6 phalanges; 4 rib fragments; 2 cranial fragments; 4 meta-shafts; House U, fill
277.	humerus shaft; House U, floor fill
279.	5 phalanges; House V, fill
281.	2 vertebra fragments; 1 temporal fragment; House V, fill
282.	child right femur; House V, floor fill
288.	right malar; House W, fill
295.	shaft—fibula?; Pit 21
299.	1 cranial fragment; Block 43-D
302.	rib; acromion; House Y, fill
313.	juvenile pubis; Room 14, fill
316.	parietal fragment; Room 13, fill
317.	infant: fragments of cranium, sphenoid, clavicle, right ilium, 3 meta-?; House X, fill
318.	adult & juvenile cranial fragments; juvenile ribs, vertebra, meta-shafts, mandible, maxilla, teeth; adult ulna; juvenile long bone fragments (numerous); House X, fill
320.	shaft fragment; 3 phalanges; 4 cranial fragments; left malar; House Y, floor fill
323.	2 cranial fragments—2 individuals; House BB, fill/floor fill
329.	juvenile femur fragment; right calcaneus fragment; Block 29-A
330.	3 cranial fragments, 1 coracoid; Block 29-A
335.	infant femur fragment; long bone fragment; Block 52-A
336.	6 long bone fragments; 1 cranial fragment; rib fragment; Block 52-A
338.	3 cranial fragments; 2 ilium fragments; 1 phalange; House DD, fill
345.	infant distal right humerus; cranial fragment; Block 21-C
346.	innominate fragment; 2 phalanges; Block 21-C
349.	1 phalange; Block 22-C
355.	rib fragment; foot phalange; House EE, fill
357.	calcined fragment; Block 36-A
358.	cranial fragment; Block 36-A
364.	right 1st metatarsal; 2 long bone fragments; 1 clavicle fragment; 1 orbit fragment; Block 21-D
367.	vertebra fragment; right hamate; phalange; metacarpal; House X, floor fill
372.	coracoid; House X, Strata 1, Level 4
376.	3 rib fragments; House X, Strata 1, Level 7
378.	phalange; House X, Strata 1, Level 8
382.	tooth root; Room 15, floor fill/floor
384.	juvenile left femur, rib; Pit 31
387.	clavicle fragment; phalange; right 4th metatarsal; metatarsal head; House X, entry fill, N. block, Level B
389.	phalange; left upper molar; vertebra; long bone fragments; House X, entry fill, N. block, Level C1
390.	infant left femur; House X, entry fill, C. block, Level A
391.	2 rib fragments; House X, entry fill, C. block, Level A
392.	juvenile caudal sacrum; House X, entry fill, C. block, Level B
393.	juvenile cranial; 1 rib; 2 phalanges; 1 unerupted molar; mandible fragment; House X, entry fill, C. block, Level B
394.	infant cranial fragment; House X, entry fill, C. block, Levels A-B
395.	fetal right femur; 2 rib fragments; House X, entry fill, C. block, Level C1
396.	7 rib fragments; hyoid; juvenile cranial; right cuboid; House X, entry fill, C. block, Level C1

Appendix 7: Table 4. *(continued)*

Sample No.	
399.	phalange; Block 21-C
401.	phalange; unident. fragment; House X, entry fill, S. block, Level A
402.	infant left radius; House X, entry fill, S. block, Level B
403.	infant innominate; left mandible; House X, entry fill, S. block, Level B
404.	left ulna and right fibula fetal; House X, entry fill, S. block, Level C1
406.	2 rib fragments; 1 phalange; House X, floor fill
408.	2 frontal fragments; House X, floor fill
411.	long bone fragment; House DD, floor fill
412.	long bone fragment; House FF, fill
413.	cranial, long bone fragments; 1 phalange; House FF, fill
415.	cranial, long bone fragments; phalange; right malar; House FF, fill
418.	left mandibular condyle; Work area 2, fill
420.	infant mandible fragment; adult cranial fragment; Block 37-A
421.	infant right petrous; House X, entry fill, N. block, Level C2
422.	infant right petrous; House X, entry fill, C. block, Level C2
423.	2 rib fragments; phalange, House X, entry fill, C. block, Level C2
426.	left mandible condyle (odd); House X, entry fill
427.	cranial fragment; 2 rib fragments; 1 long bone fragment; House X, entry fill
428.	2 juvenile ribs; House X, floor fill
429.	juvenile right radius shaft; House X, floor fill
432.	4 cranial fragments; 1 rib; House FF, fill
446.	right patella; Block 45-C
451.	8 cranial fragments; some long bone fragments; House FF, fill
454.	talus; 3 cranial fragments; right distal fibula; metatarsal fragment; House FF, floor fill
456.	2 long bone fragments; 6 cranial fragments; 1 rib fragment; 1 vertebra fragment; Block 29-C
459.	1 juvenile cranial fragment; Block 45-B
461.	rib fragments; cranial fragments; left 4th metacarpal; Block 45-B
465.	cervical vertebra; cranial fragments; rib fragments; 1 phalange; Block 52-B
474.	long bone fragment; 2 lower molars; Block 44-C
477.	calcined cranial fragment; House GG, fill
478.	3 rib fragments; 4 cranial fragments; House GG, fill
480.	10 cranial fragments; 3 long bone fragments; 1 meta-fragment; House HH, fill
481.	distal humerus fragment; House HH, floor fill
482.	2 cranial fragments; 1 vertebra fragment; right 5th metatarsal; meta-fragment; House HH, floor fill
484.	4 cranial fragments; metatarsal head; House HH, floor
486.	phalange; House II, floor fill
491.	phalange; House GG, floor fill
493.	juvenile cranial fragment; House LL, floor fill
497.	long bone fragment; Pit Oven 5
498.	hyoid horn; Burial 59, fill
500.	shaft fragment; Block 21-C/D
503.	infant scapula; Block 29-B
504.	calcaneus fragment; clavicle fragment; 1 molar; Block 29-B
506.	4 rib fragments; 44 long bone fragments; 2 cranial; left petrous; 1st metatarsal; 2nd metatarsal; 4th left metatarsal; acetabulum fragment; scapula fragment; Block 30-A
508.	femur shaft fragment; 1st metacarpal fragment; B. 30-B
509.	2nd cervical vertebra fragment; Block 30-C
510.	cranial, long bone fragments; right 1st metatarsal; 2 left talus; 1 phalange; Block 30-C
517.	2 humerus fragments; 7 rib fragments; 5 long bone fragments; 5 cranial fragments (1 cremated), malar fragment; clavicle fragment; 1 hand phalange, Block 29-D
521.	long bone fragment; Pit 43
522.	infant cranial; Pit 44
524.	calcined cranial fragment; Pit 45
529.	part of Burial 72; Burial 72, fill
531.	infant cranial; Block 38-B

Appendix 7: Table 4. *(continued)*

Sample No.	
534.	rib fragment; Block 30-D, Block 38-B, Pit 41
535.	left mandible with 4 teeth; coracoid; rib fragments; right 3rd metacarpal; phalange; Block 30-D, Block 38-B, Pit 41
536.	infant fragments: cranial, ilium; maxilla; proximal right ulna, left ulna; femur, tibia shafts, fibula, radius? shafts – 1+ children; Block 37-B
537.	many cranial, long bone fragments; incisor; mandible with 2 molars; 3 shafts; phalange; Block 37-B
539.	cranial fragment; House NN, floor fill
541.	infant right lateral occipital; Block 37-D
542.	2 sample bags. #1: 2 cranial fragments; phalange. #2: left talus; 3 meta-shafts; 1 incisor; phalange; cranial fragments; Block 37-D
544.	cranial and related fragments; Block 45-B
550.	rib fragment; unident. fragment; phalange, Burial 72, fill
558.	left scapular spine; 9 rib fragments; radius; 4 calcined cranial fragments; calcaneus; 2 phalanges; 2 long bone fragments; 9 vertebra fragments; 1 ulna; right 4th metatarsal; 2 metatarsals; Block 38-A
563.	2 cranial fragments; 1 rib fragment; Block 47-C
565.	right mandible (deciduous molars); adult phalange; cranial fragment; metatarsal shaft; Block 47-C
569.	2 rib fragments; 1 long bone shaft; left 1st metatarsal; upper right molar; Block 46-D
572.	fragments—tarsal, 2nd cervical vertebra; House OO, fill
573.	2 radius fragments; 1st metatarsal; phalange; manubrium; 1 rib; 1 vertebra fragment; 2 cranial fragments; 2 juvenile cranial fragments; 1 unerupted tooth; House OO, fill
575.	right scapula; phalange; meta-shafts, long bone shaft fragments; few vertebra, rib fragments; House PP, fill
578.	right humerus; right 1st metatarsal; right 1st metacarpal; 3 shaft fragments; canine; Block 38-D
580.	left 5th metatarsal; Block 39-C
586.	2 vertebra fragments; Block 54-B
588.	3 long bone fragments; 1 cranial; scapula fragment; vertebra body fragment; Block 55-A
590.	2 rib fragments; 1 cranial fragment; phalange; House OO, floor fill
592.	rib fragment; House PP, Strata 1, Unit A
594.	upper molar; calcaneus fragment; House PP, Strata 1, Unit B
596.	temporal fragment; Pit 29
598.	30 cranial fragments; 16 rib fragments; 1 long bone fragment; 5 phalanges; juvenile metatarsal, left 1st metatarsal; left 2nd metacarpal; left 4th metatarsal; coracoid; left 2nd metatarsal; House QQ, fill
600.	1 rib, left 2nd metatarsal; phalange; 2 cranial fragments; Block 55-C
602.	rib fragment; House PP, floor fill
607.	tibia fragment; 14 long bone fragments; 2 rib fragments; right malar-maxilla; clavicle fragment; Block 54-B
609.	right radius; 3 rib fragments; left 5th metatarsal; left 3rd metacarpal; right scapula spine; vertebra fragment; Block 63-A
616.	rib fragment; radius head; phalange fragment; Block 70-C
619.	distal ulna; cuneiform; phalange; left upper incisor; Block 11-D (House K, entry subfloor)
621.	7 cranial fragments; 5 long bones; 4 ribs; juvenile vertebra, right upper molar; left 2nd, 3rd and 5th metatarsal; right 5th metacarpal; 4 meta-shafts; House SS, fill
626.	infant cranial, misc. cervical vertebra, 2 long bone fragments; cuneiform; fragment of thoracic vertebra; House UU, fill
630.	right humerus shaft; tibia shaft; 4 rib fragments; left 3rd metacarpal; left 4th metatarsal; left navicular; phalange; infant ilium; clavicle; Block 62-A
632.	fibula shaft; Block 62-D
637.	3 cremated cranial fragments; right maxilla fragment; House WW, fill/floor fill
641.	8 juvenile cranial fragments; Block 53-B
645.	cranial fragment; epiphysis; House WW, floor fill
652.	phalange; House SS, Strata Level 4
655.	humerus fragment; ulna fragment; phalange; 1 rib fragment; 12th thoracic vertebra; House SS, floor fill
659.	phalange; House VV, floor
661.	left talus; right mandible, right orbit; left malar arch; right malar; radius fragments; left 5th metacarpal;1st metatarsal; right clavicle; right 1st metacarpal; molar; 2 femur shaft fragments; 24 long bone fragments; 47 cranial fragments; 9 ribs; 9 vertebra fragments; 4 scapula fragments; 3 phalanges; Block 54-D

APPENDIX 7: TABLE 4. *(continued)*

Sample No.	
663.	ulna shaft fragment; cranial fragment; left 2nd metatarsal; phalange; vertebra fragment; calcaneus fragment; Block 62-A
668.	rib fragment; House VV, Pit 1
670.	rib fragment; Block 52-B
681.	cranial fragment; 1 meta-fragment; House ZZ, floor fill
685.	infant metacarpal; Block 53-D
687.	long bone fragments; right patella; Block 54-A
690.	2 cranial fragments; long bone fragment; Block 54-C
694.	right 1st metatarsal; phalange; House AB, fill
696.	long bone shafts and fragments; phalange; House AC, fill
698.	3 long bone fragments; House AC, fill
705.	long bone fragment; Pit 66
708.	long bone, cranial fragments; Block 53-C
713.	long bone fragments; Block 61-B
730.	juvenile cranial; left 4th metatarsal; House AC, entry fill
732.	cuneiform; long bone fragment; calcined cranial fragment; House AC, floor fill
734.	talus; calcaneus fragment; long bone fragment; House AC, hearth
739.	long bone fragments; 2 rib fragments; House AD, floor fill
741.	rib fragment; House AD, floor
743.	cranial fragment; House AD, entry fill
746.	femur fragments; phalange; House AF fill
767.	juvenile left 4th metatarsal; cranial fragments; Block 61-A
769.	2 cranial fragments; long bone fragment; metatarsal; Block 61-A
782.	vertebra fragment; worn tooth; House SS, fill
798.	ulna shaft; smoked long bone fragments; cranial fragments; unerupted lower molar; House AI, fill
800.	juvenile shaft fragment; House AI, posthole 2
RO locus	
850.	left, right femur; left, right humerus; left ulna, radius, scapula; 3 cranial fragments; 1 clavicle—all from same individual (child); House G, fill

missing. However, an index of robusticity could be computed for three individuals, comparing right and left humeri from each (Appendix 7: Table 7). Results are not conclusive, but the suggestion of right hand dominance is a tempting one, at least for the two old women from Burials 22 and 44.

Dentition

The jaws and/or teeth of 54 individuals (49 adults and five children) were available for observation. However, the dental sample itself is small and consists of 493 adult and 62 deciduous teeth. The adult sample is 31 percent of the potential maximum total (49 mouths x 32 teeth = 1,568). The other teeth were either lost antemortem (n = 163) or were not recovered due to postmortem loss (n = 912). There are few complete maxillae or mandibles, and many teeth were cracked or chipped after death.

All dentitions exhibit the Mongoloid characteristics of shovel-shaped maxillary incisors and buccal pits on the lower molars (Dahlberg 1963). The dentition in general is extremely worn, with a low incidence of oral pathologies.

Tooth Wear

The extreme attrition so common to Southwest agriculturists is largely due to a high grit level in the diet, derived from limestone and granitic grinding tools. Advanced tooth wear, in turn, can contribute to other dental conditions such as caries, alveolar abscesses with and without cementum hyperplasia, and antemortem tooth loss, all of which are present in the Wind Mountain remains.

Tooth wear was scored according to Hrdlicka's five categories (Stewart 1952:53). A score of 1 signifies minimal wear on cusps, and a score of 5 indicates that the crowns have been completely worn away, exposing the pulp chamber. Incisors and molars show the heaviest wear. There are at least 40 root stubs representing anterior dentition in stage 5 wear. Wear patterns within each mouth are uneven, being heavier lin-

Appendix 7: Table 5. Miscellaneous Human Bone Associated with Burials

Sample No.	Context	
WM locus		
901.	Burial 52	right talus; distal right fibula; right navicular; cranial fragment; atlas fragment; 3 shaft fragments; left 2nd metacarpal, phalange; Block 45-B
902.	Burial 42	juvenile right femur; Block 21-A
903.	Burial 60	infant distal femur; Block 20-B
904.	Burial 53–54	juvenile right mandible; Block 45-C
905.	Burial 6	adult mandible fragments; burned fragment; Block 10-A
906.	Burial 14	infant long bone fragment; Block 26-A
907.	Burial 28	juvenile shaft, meta-?; House S, fill
908.	Burial 73	fragments; Block 37-B
909.	Burial 12	unerupted anterior tooth; Block 26-A
910.	Burial 71	rib; Block 29-D
911.	Burial 5	glabella; Block 11-B/D
912.	Burial 85	long bone fragments; lower premolar; deciduous lower molar; Block 62-D
913.	Burial 9	shaft; distal femur fragment; Block 10-D
914.	Burial 94	right foot navicular; right 2nd metacarpal; House AC
915.	Burial 91	fetal right radius, ulna, femur; left tibia; maxilla fragment; House TT, subfloor
RO locus		
916.	Burial 2	fetal left ilium, cranial fragment; Block E1E (E0E)
917.	Burial 3	child long bone shaft fragment; Block C2E (E0W)
918.	Burial 11	left temporal, 6 cranial fragments – child; Block G0W

Note: These elements, though recovered from burial pits, do not belong to the primary interment.

gually on the upper dentition and buccally on the lower. This is the normal pattern derived from the mechanics of chewing.

Antemortem Loss

Thirteen incidences of alveolar abscess were noted in the adult dental sample in upper first molars, premolars, canines, and incisors. Abscessing is a common sequitur to exposure of the pulp chamber caused by heavy occlusal wear of caries. Tooth loss is the usual result of such infections. In the Wind Mountain series, the teeth most frequently lost during life were the six lower molars (n = 69; 42 percent of total antemortem loss), although there were examples of antemortem loss in all 32 teeth. When the jaw itself was present, the alveolar bone usually showed good resorption, indicating that tooth loss occurred well before death.

Two difficulties were encountered when observing antemortem tooth loss. First, as a result of alveolar resorption and tooth migrations, it was not always possible to determine which teeth were originally present. Secondly, if a tooth were lost shortly or immediately before death, it would be difficult to determine whether the empty socket represented antemortem or postmortem loss. Therefore, the suggested total of 163 teeth lost before death must be considered an estimate.

Cementum Hyperplasia

Cementum hyperplasia (hypercementosis) is frequently associated with extreme attrition and/or apical abscessing. Cementum is a thin hard tissue covering the tooth roots that aids in anchoring them in the periodontal membrane. Hypercementosis refers to the deposition of excessive amounts of cementum (Brothwell 1963:282). Cementum increases in thickness with age, and there is some evidence that it also increases to compensate for the natural wear shortening of chewing surfaces (Garfield 1969). Sixteen molars (in seven individuals) in this series exhibited hypercementosis. Most of these teeth showed stage 3–4 wear.

Caries

The incidence of dental caries was relatively low. Thirty-nine caries of six different types are noted. Eighteen of these are in just three individuals (remains from Burials 24, 44, and 45, all middle to old adults). There is little information on the etiology of caries formation in primitive societies, but the carbohydrate content of the diet, the nature of the saliva, faults in the enamel, and dental hygiene are all important contributory factors (Brothwell 1963).

Occlusal caries are the most common (n = 17), occurring in upper and lower molars and in one upper second premolar. Most caries are small, but three extend interproximally. Five mesial and one distal interproximal caries were observed in second premolars and first molars. Seven cervical caries were seen on the distal aspect of upper incisors and upper and lower first and second molars. There are six crowns (canines and premolars) that have been decayed completely. Finally, three incidences of caries invading the pulp cavities of very worn incisors were observed.

Enamel Hypoplasia

Four individuals exhibited macroscopic enamel hypoplasia, seen as pits or transverse grooves in the tooth enamel. This condition likely results from a systematic and possibly recurrent disturbance during tooth formation (Brothwell 1963:380), although both environmental and genetic factors may be involved. Knowledge of the calcification rate of the teeth may suggest the individual's age at the time that the insult occurred. Repeated episodes can sometimes be documented (Brothwell 1963; Sweeney et al. 1969; White 1978).

The dentition from Burial 24 is hypoplastic in 11 of the 18 teeth present: upper and lower canines and lateral incisors, upper central incisors, and a lower premolar (most molars are not present). The remains from Burial 42 have the defect in eight of nine teeth: all the upper molars and the upper left canine and premolar. The entire crowns of the two third molars are hypoplastic and discolored. The jaws from Burial 45 are hypoplastic in six of 27 teeth: three canines both lower lateral incisors, and a lower premolar. Finally, the Burial 83 skeleton has three affected teeth out of 12, all the lower left molars (the right molars are missing). None of the deciduous teeth are hypoplastic, suggesting that the event(s) producing the enamel defect occurred postnatally and in early childhood rather than intrauterine.

Anomalies

Anomalous dental features include malpositioning, torsion, and a supernumerary tooth. The maxillae of Burial 84 are notable in this respect: on the right side the mesial surface of the canine is turned labially, possibly due to the presence of a captured deciduous first molar, as evidenced by the remnant of a root still imbedded in the alveolus. In the left maxilla, the canine is malpositioned anterior to the lateral incisor. The canine borders the central incisor distally with the lateral incisor lingual to it. There is a small alveolar indentation just mesial to the first premolar, which may represent a captured deciduous crown, possibly lost postmortem.

APPENDIX 7: TABLE 6. Stature Estimates

Burial No.	Age/Sex	Bone Used	Mean, Metric*	Mean, Inches
WM locus				
3	YA/F	Tibia	156.2 ± 3.51	61.5 ± 1.5
11A	OA/F	Tibia	156.5 ± 3.51	61.6 ± 1.5
22	OA/F	Tibia	156.7 ± 3.51	61.7 ± 1.5
44	MA/F	Tibia	160.8 ± 3.51	63.3 ± 1.5
69	OA/F	Humerus	157.0**	61.8
84	YA/F	Tibia	147.2 ± 3.51	57.9 ± 1.5
23	OA/M	Radius	169.0**	66.5
24	OA/M	Humerus	166.5**	65.5
47	MA/M	Ulna	167.0**	65.7
53	MA/M	Radius	162.5**	63.9
59	OA/M	Fibula	159.5**	62.8
68	MA/M	Femur	154.0 ± 3.42	60.6 ± 1.5
65	MA/?	Humerus	157.0–158.5***	61.8–62.4
90	MA/?	Fibula	158.0–160.5***	62.2–63.2
	Females (6) Range: 147.2–160.8 cm Mean: 155.7 cm (61.3 inches)		Males (6) Range: 154.0–169.0 cm Mean: 163.1 cm (64.2 inches)	
RO locus				
6	OA/M	Tibia	159.6 ± 2.81	62.8 ± 2.0
15	MA/F?	Radius	151.5**	59.6
16	MA/F	Tibia	150.1 ± 3.51	59.1 ± 2.0

* Stature formulae, Tables 12, 13, 14 in Genovés (1967).
** No standard deviations given with these tables.
***Range includes female mean and male mean.
YA = Young adult (15–25 yrs.), MA = Middle adult (26–39 yrs.), OA = Old adult (40+ yrs.), F = Female, M = Male.

APPENDIX 7: TABLE 7. Robusticity Indices as Computed from Paired Humeri

Burial No.	Maximum Length (mm) Left	Maximum Length (mm) Right	Least Circumference (mm) Left	Least Circumference (mm) Right	Robusticity Index Left	Robusticity Index Right
WM locus						
11A	295	301	50	51	16.95	16.94
22	293	294	53	55	18.09	18.71
44	310	313	52	54	16.77	17.25

Note: Humeral Robusticity Index = $\frac{\text{Least circumference x 100}}{\text{Maximum Length}}$ (Bass 1971:115).

In the maxillae from Burial 45, both first premolars exhibit mesial-lingual torsion (i.e., the mesial surface of the tooth is turned lingually). There is also an isolated supernumerary tooth from this individual. The remains from Burial 13 show mesial-labial torsion in the right upper lateral incisor. The other three upper incisors are absent, lost after death. Dahlberg (1963) sees mesial rotation of lateral incisors as an American Indian trait.

The individual in Burial 94 exhibits crowding in the area of the mandibular incisors. The third lower molar of this same individual, although not completely erupted, bears an enameloma (enamel pearl) at the bifurcation of the roots on the buccal surface. Enamelomas are harmless miniature tumors composed entirely of enamel, and, although rare in the general population, occur more frequently in individuals of Mongoloid ancestry (Tratman 1950).

Deciduous Dentition

The deciduous teeth are unremarkable for the most part. One child (Burial 5) has two caries, an occlusal in an upper left second molar and an interproximal distal in a lower right first molar.

Health and Disease

There are a variety of disease and age-related processes that left observable evidence in the skeletons of the Wind Mountain population, although nothing that could be construed as cause of death. Most of the diseases that result in mortality in an aboriginal population, such as many gastrointestinal and respiratory infections, leave no marks on the bones. None of the juveniles in this series and only 16 adult skeletons show bony evidence of disease.

Pathologies

The pathologies in this series can be divided into three types: trauma, including fractures and miscellaneous bone wounds, which involved eight individuals; infection, involving a single individual; and arthritis, involving 12 individuals. The skeletons from Burials 11A, 24, and 60 fit into two of the three types, and the skeleton from Burial 22 bears evidence of all three types of pathology.

There are three healed fractures among adults in the collection. The left radius from Burial 24 sustained a Colles' fracture, a transverse break in the distal end of the radius just above the wrist. If not properly set, as in this individual, it heals with a displacement of the hand backward and outward. This type of fracture is often the result of a forward or backward fall onto an outstretched arm and hand.

The individual in Burial 54 had a fracture in the shaft of the left fourth metacarpal. It healed with some shortening of the bone due to overlapping of the broken edges. In the remains from Burial 79, the right femur was fractured. The break occurred in the upper half of the diaphysis and shows good consolidation with a remaining palpable callous. Because the femur is incomplete, it was not possible to determine if shortening of the limb took place.

The final bone trauma observed is scars of parturition (birth scars) found on the dorsal surface of the female pubic bone. The scarring is due to tearing the pelvic tendons and ligaments during childbirth. Observations on modern females of known parity (Stewart 1970; Suchey et al. 1979) indicate that although there is a correlation between number of delivered births and size of scars, it is not a strong one. Even some known nulliparous woman have had significant scarring of the pubic bones. Age of the mother appears to be an important factor, as is possibly the size of the baby(s). Among the 10 female skeletons in this series who have one or both pubic bones, four (Burials 3, 11A, 22, 69) bear such scars of parturition.

There is one example of osteomyelitis, a nonspecific bone infection, in the left tibia from Burial 22. This disease entity refers especially to an inflammation of the marrow, caused by a pathogenic organism spread via a hematogenous (blood borne) route. The presence (or absence) of a draining abscess, which would indicate a chronic infection, could not be documented in this particular case due to poor preservation of the bone.

Two types of arthritis were seen in this series: osteoarthritis and vertebral osteophytosis. Osteoarthritis (degenerative joint disease) is a chronic disease of weight bearing synovial joints, usually associated with increasing age. The disease process involves destruction of articular cartilage and bony overgrowth in the form of lipping and spurring, which leads to impaired function. Two frequent sites of occurrence are the hips and knees.

In the Wind Mountain series, the predominant manifestation of osteoarthritis is in the patellae. These exhibit the bony changes consistent with chondromalacia, a softening and wearing away of the articular cartilage. The affected individuals are from Burials 11, 21, 24, and 69. The individual in Burial 11A shows a corresponding bony alteration in the proximal head of the right fibula. Another area of involvement is the left first metatarsal, as seen in the material from Burials 84 and especially 49. As the joint capsule deteriorates, the inferior surface of the metatarsal head is polished from rubbing directly on the two sesamoid bones normally found on the bottom surface of the bony foot.

The articular facets of the vertebrae are also synovial joints, and in two cases these show osteoarthritic changes. In the skeleton from Burial 31, two lower cervical vertebrae have fused along their articular joints. In the Burial 11A remains, it is two upper thoracic vertebrae that have fused. These two examples may be contrasted with the "pseudo-pathology" observed in bones from Burials 17 and 48. In each of these, it appeared that the left talus and calcaneus had fused; in actuality, the bones are locked together as the result of stubborn "caliche" (calcium carbonate) deposits.

Vertebral osteophytosis refers to bony excrescences that develop along the borders of the vertebral bodies in response to degeneration of the intervertebral discs. These outgrowths can be so extensive as to fuse two vertebral bodies together. Milder forms are seen in the skeletal material from Burials 8, 9, 11A, 44, and 90. The sacro-iliac joints from Burial 22 were also affected.

Age-Related Changes

Concomitant with increasing age, several other nonarthritic degenerative changes occur in the skeleton, possibly in response to endocrinal changes. One of these is an ossification of the costal cartilage, which attaches the ribs to the sternum, as seen in the Burial 11A skeletal material. Another observed change is hyperostosis of the cranial vault which may appear as cranial bone thickened through a widening of the diploic space or as an increase in the width of inner tables. The frontal and parietal bones (although incomplete) from Burial 28 are hyperostotic. The rest of the skeleton undergoes a loss of bone density—osteoporosis—and becomes very lightweight. The long bones from Burials 11B, 24, 31, 38, and 99 are good examples.

Anomalies

Three anomalous conditions can be cited from the Wind Mountain locus skeletal collection. The skulls in Burials 22 and 44 (the only nearly complete skulls in the collection) exhibit an occipital type of cranial deformation. This is a mild flattening of the back of the skull, probably the result of an infancy spent strapped to a cradleboard.

The individual from Burial 44 also has a fifth lumbar vertebra with spondylolysis, a lateral arch fissure which separates the inferior articular processes, the posterior arch, and spinous process from the rest of the bone. Movement is not impaired unless the vertebral body slips forward onto the sacrum (spondylolisthesis). The remains in Burial 99 may have this same condition, but because the vertebra in question is broken, diagnosis is uncertain.

A third type of anomaly can be seen in the left parietal bone from Burial 19. There is a small hole, approximately 1 cm in diameter, located near the lambdoidal suture. Examination of bone density and vascularization surrounding the hole does not indicate an infectious process, nor does it appear to be merely an enlarged parietal foramen. Radiographic evaluation of the hole gives no indication that this might be an old healing wound to the head. Consequently, no diagnosis can be made, although this parietal can be contrasted with the left parietal from Burial 44. The two small punched-in areas in this bone are easily diagnosed as postmortem damage to the skull by an archeologist's excavation tool.

The Ridout Locus Skeletal Series

The skeletal sample from the Ridout locus is limited to 16 individuals, most of which are incomplete (Table 9.1). The bones from Burial 11 had been charred, either from purposeful incineration or accidental exposure to fire. Seven cranial fragments from a child (Burial 12) were also found in this burial. Only one bag of miscellaneous bone was attributed to the Ridout locus, and it contained the partial skeletal remains of a child.

Population Profile

Only a very limited profile can be constructed on the basis of 16 fragmentary individuals (Appendix 7: Table 3), but the overall picture seems similar to that of the Wind Mountain locus. Three juveniles and 13 adults are represented, with most adults dying between 26 and 39 years of age (a "normal" mortality expectation, according to Blakely 1971). The adult sex ratio (Appendix 7: Table 2) is inconclusive because more than half the skeletons were unsexable.

Although this series has its share of pathologies, there is nothing in the bones to indicate cause of death.

Stature

Estimates of living stature could be computed for only the three individuals from Burials 6, 15, and 16 (Appendix 7: Table 6). The Ridout estimates compare favorably with the Wind Mountain locus ranges.

Dentition

Ten adults and one child retained teeth that were examined, for a total count of 190 permanent and 17 deciduous teeth. Burial 9 contains only two root stubs as dentition. The Burial 8 remains contain an edentulous mandible with the alveolus totally resorbed, indicating some passage of time because the teeth were lost. Burials 2, 5, 10, and 13 contain no teeth. It was estimated that among the adults, approximately 180 teeth were lost postmortem and at least 35 were lost before death. The four deciduous teeth observed in the child in Burial 14 were unremarkable.

Tooth wear was advanced, with scores of 3, 4, and 5 (Stewart 1952:53) common. As is the case with Wind Mountain locus remains, the heavy wear is probably attributable in large part to grit incorporated into the diet. Also, as in Wind Mountain material, the remains from the Ridout locus show a low incidence of abscessing and cementum hyperplasia, which are often associated with heavy chewing stresses and wear. The left maxilla from Burial 6 exhibits cementum hyperplasia in the upper second molar.

Eight cases of dental caries were observed in four individuals. The mandible in Burial 7 has an alveolar abscess in the area of the lower right canine; all that remains of the carious tooth is a portion of a root. The Burial 6 skeleton has mesial and distal interproximal caries in the lower right first molar and second premolar respectively. This individual also has a pulp-invasive caries on an extremely worn, lower left first premolar. The mandible from Burial 11 has occlusal caries in the lower right and left third molars; similarly, the mandible from Burial 15 has occlusal caries in the lower right second and third molars.

The three upper central incisors present are shovel shaped. There were no dental anomalies observed in this sample.

Pathologies

Three different pathologies, with one manifestation of each, are displayed in the Ridout sample. These are pathologies often associated with old age. At least one individual (Burial 16) was afflicted with osteoarthritis, especially at the knee joint where the patella shows the characteristic bony changes of degenerative joint disease. The lumbar vertebrae in Burial 7 show osteophytic lipping at the peripheries of the centra. The individual in Burial 8 (an old female) has a lightweight osteoporotic skeleton, often seen in postmenopausal women.

Conclusion

In terms of numbers, the skeletal sample recovered from Wind Mountain is good—122 burials. How characteristic this sample is of the actual populations who lived at the site is uncertain. The larger the mortuary sample, however, the more likely it is to have the same age and sex configuration as the corresponding living group. Unfortunately, less than 8 percent of the individuals represented can be classified as "complete" (i.e., 75–100 percent estimated completeness). Soil pH and moisture content, manner of excavation, or a combination of these and other postexhumation factors may have been responsible for the poor condition of the remains. Many infant interments may not have been recognized as such in the field, and consequently are represented only by scattered skeletal elements.

There are many similarities in demography and disease patterns between the Wind Mountain and Ridout loci. Child deaths comprise 22 percent (n = 27) of the skeletal sample (excluding miscellaneous bone). This is a low proportion when compared to Indian Knoll with 41 percent children (Johnston and Snow 1961) or Grasshopper Pueblo with 66 percent children (Hinkes 1983). But then these two series are much larger, nearly 900 and 700 individuals respectively, and special effort was made to recover immature material. At Pecos Pueblo, in contrast, little effort was made, because it was felt that "the skeletons of young subjects are of comparatively little anthropological value" (Hooton 1930:15). A growing number of researchers feel that juvenile material *is* important for the growth and development studies that might yield a clearer reconstruction of prehistoric lifeways.

Only 4 percent (n = 5) of the Wind Mountain site skeletal sample represents young adults, whereas 18 percent (n = 22) represents old adults. Apparently, if one survived that first critical year or two, his/her chances of living a relatively long life were good, a not uncommon situation among prehistoric as well as modern Indian groups (Blakely 1971; Johnston and Snow 1961; Moore et al. 1972).

The individuals within these burials show no bony indication as to cause of death. The children are particularly notable in this respect: the only pathology seen is one instance of dental caries. But the respiratory and gastrointestinal infections that, without antibiotic therapy, cause high child mortality (Kraus 1954; Moore et al. 1972) do not affect bones. The old adults show only degenerative changes (arthritis, osteoporosis). The remaining adults show very few serious pathological conditions, and it is likely that they also succumbed to common acute infectious diseases that leave no trace (Kraus 1954).

Appendix 8

An Analysis of Faunal Remains from Wind Mountain*

SANDRA L. OLSEN AND JOHN W. OLSEN

The archaeological faunal material collected during the excavation of the Wind Mountain locus contained much valuable information regarding diet, hunting and food preparation, ceremonial use of animals, and the paleoenvironment. The collection was well preserved, and aside from a negligible amount of rodent and carnivore gnawing and weathering, there was little evidence of adverse taphonomic conditions affecting the osteological sample.

Methodology

Identification of the faunal specimens was conducted by the 1978–1980 Zooarchaeology Laboratory classes, in the Anthropology Department of the University of Arizona, under the direction of Professor Stanley J. Olsen and the assistance of Felipe C. Jacome. Comparative osteological collections belonging to S. J. Olsen and the National Park Service were consulted. Data recorded included provenience, taphonomic identification, element, side (right or left), portion of element, aging criteria (epiphyseal fusion or dental eruption), sexing criteria, cultural modification (charring, butchering, and artifact manufacture), natural modification (rodent and carnivore gnawing, weathering, and root etching), and pathologies.

The taxa identified, showing the number of fragments in each taxonomic category and the percentage of the total faunal assemblage represented by each taxon, are presented (Appendix 8: Table 1). During the course of human osteological analysis, a small quantity of nonhuman material was found to be incorporated into the human burial remains (Appendix 8: Table 2). This list demonstrates the considerable variety of fauna used by the prehistoric people occupying this site, and gives the relative frequency with which each taxon was used.

The distribution of each taxonomic group by pit house (Appendix 8: Table 3), surface room (Appendix 8: Table 4), burial (Appendix 8: Table 5), and pit or pavement (Appendix 8: Table 6), showing clustering of some of the rarer species and a more even dispersal of the common food animals, such as rabbits and deer, is also recorded. Each taxon will be discussed below, highlighting its importance as a food resource, ceremonial symbol, environmental indicator, or source of nonfood products.

Class Osteichthyes

Family Catostomidae, genus and species indeterminate. A single fish vertebra, belonging to the family of freshwater suckers (Minckley 1973:145) was collected at the Wind Mountain locus. In light of the singular occurrence of fish remains in the sample, it is difficult to state that fish served as more than an incidental source of protein.

*Appendices 8 and 9 represent the faunal material recovered from the Wind Mountain site, accounting for a total of 17,459 fragments. Excavations at the Wind Mountain locus yielded 16,577 pieces, and the Ridout locus 882. Appendix 8 presents the faunal analysis for the following locations: Wind Mountain locus Houses A through SS, surface Rooms 1 through 16, as well as burials and cremations, pits, and pavements. Raw data from the Olsen and Olsen study is on file (Wind Mountain files, Amerind Foundation). Appendix 9 provides basic identification of miscellaneous faunal material from various deposits. It includes utilitarian and socioreligious artifacts, personal ornaments, and raw animal bone.

Appendix 8: Table 1. Taxonomic List Describing Faunal Remains Recovered from the Wind Mountain Site

Taxon	No. of Fragments
Class Osteichthyes	
Order Cypriniformes	
Family Catostomidae, gen. et sp. indet.	1
Class Amphibia	
Order Salientia	
Family Bufonidae	
Bufo sp. indet.: toad	6
Class Reptilia	
Order Chelonia	
Family Testudinidae	
Gopherus agassazi: desert tortoise	2
Terrapene ornata: western box turtle	1
Family Chelyridae	
Kinosternon sp. indet.: mud turtle	5
Order Squamata	
Family Crotalidae	
Crotalus sp. indet.: rattlesnake	1
Class Aves	
Order indet.	96
Order Pelecaniformes	
Family Pelecanidae	
Pelecanus erythrorhynchos: white pelican	1
Order Anseriformes	
Family Anatidae	
Anas sp. indet.: surface duck	1
Order Falconiformes	
Family Cathartidae	
Cathartes aura: turkey vulture	4
Family Accipitridae, gen. et sp. indet.	4
Accipiter cooperi: Cooper's hawk	4
Buteo sp. indet.: hawk	122
Aquila chrysaetos/Haliaeetus leucocephalus: golden or bald eagle	2
Aquila chrysaetos: golden eagle	74
Falco sparverius: sparrow hawk	1
Order Galliformes	
Family Phasianidae, gen. et sp. indet.	1
Lophortyx gambelii: Gambel's quail	4
Family Meleagrididae	
Meleagris gallopavo: turkey	178
Order Columbiformes	
Family Columbidae	
Columba fasciata: band-tailed pigeon	3
Zenaida macroura: mourning dove	19
Order Psittaciformes	
Family Psittacidae	
Ara macao: scarlet macaw	119

Appendix 8: Table 1 *(continued)*

Taxon	No. of Fragments
Order Cuculiformes	
Family Cuculidae	
Geococcyx californianus: roadrunner	2
Order Strigiformes	
Family Strigidae	
Bubo virginianus: great horned owl	2
Order Caprimulgiformes	
Family Caprimulgidae	
Chordeiles sp. indet.: nighthawk	1
Order Passeriformes	
Family Corvidae	
Corvus corax: common raven	8
Cyanocitta stelleri: Steller's jay	1
Family Icteridae, gen. et sp. indet.	1
Class Mammalia	
Order indet.	6,024
Order Lagomorpha	
Family Leporidae, gen. et sp. indet.	141
Sylvilagus sp. indet.: cottontail	1,294
Lepus sp. indet.: jackrabbit	1,522
Lepus cf. *L. californicus*: ?black-tailed jackrabbit	24
Lepus californicus: black-tailed jackrabbit	215
Lepus cf. *L. gaillardi*: ?Gaillard's jackrabbit	17
Lepus gaillardi: Gaillard's jackrabbit	4
Order Rodentia	
Family indet.	46
Family Sciuridae, gen. et sp. indet.	17
Spermophilus spilosoma: spotted ground squirrel	8
Spermophilus variegatus: rock squirrel	78
Spermophilus variegatus/*Cynomys ludovicianus*: rock squirrel or black-tailed prairie dog	23
Cynomys ludovicianus: black-tailed prairie dog	7
Family Geomyidae, gen. et sp. indet.	12
Geomys arenarius: desert pocket gopher	7
Thomomys umbrinus: southern pocket gopher	73
Family Heteromyidae	
Dipodomys sp. indet.: kangaroo rat	2
Family Cricetidae, gen. et sp. indet.	2
Peromyscus sp. indet.: mouse	1
Neotoma sp. indet.: wood rat	36
Sigmodon sp. indet.: cotton rat	3
Family Erethizontidae	
Erethizon dorsatum: porcupine	1
Order Carnivora	
Family indet.	14
Family Canidae	
Canis sp. indet.: dog or coyote	354
Canis cf. *C. familiaris*: ?dog	18
Canis familiaris: dog	144

Appendix 8: Table 1 *(continued)*

Taxon	No. of Fragments
Canis latrans: coyote	2
Vulpes macrotis: kit fox	1
Vulpes macrotis/Urocyon cinereoargenteus: kit fox or gray fox	6
Urocyon cinereoargenteus: gray fox	8
Family Ursidae	
Ursus sp. indet.: bear	70
Ursus americanus: black bear	5
Family Mustelidae	
?*Taxidea taxus*: ?badger	1
Taxidea taxus: badger	16
Mephitis sp. indet.: skunk	2
Mephitis macroura: hooded skunk	1
Family Felidae	
Lynx rufus: bobcat	14
Felis sp. indet.: mountain lion or jaguar	1
Order Artiodactyla	
Suborder Ruminantia	
Family indet.	1,170
Family Cervidae	
Cervus canadensis: wapiti	3
Odocoileus sp. indet.: deer	881
Odocoileus cf. *O. hemionus*: ?mule deer	106
Odocoileus hemionus: mule deer	293
Odocoileus cf. *O. virginianus*: ?white-tailed deer	20
Odocoileus virginianus: white-tailed deer	40
Family Antilocapridae	
Antilocapra americana: pronghorn	82
Family Bovidae	
Bos taurus/Bison bison: cattle or bison	13
Bos taurus: cattle	1
Ovis canadensis: bighorn	12
Kingdom Animalia, class indet.	2
Total number of fragments:	13,501

Class Amphibia

Six elements were identified as toad, *Bufo* sp. indet. Several species of toad occur in the site area, including: *B. woodhousei*, Woodhouse's toad; *B. cognatus*, the Great Plains toad; *B. debilis*, the green toad; and *B. punctatus*, the red-spotted toad. The ecozones occupied by these numerous species are varied, making these six specimens inadequate for environmental reconstruction. Toads may survive in relatively arid climates, requiring stands of water for only short intervals to produce their young. Breeding usually occurs in spring or summer after rains (Stebbins 1966:59). It is likely that the cluster of five fragments of toad bones in House FF represent one individual and is intrusive.

Class Reptilia

Kinosternon sp. indet. Five carapace fragments of mud turtle were identified. Today, there are two species with ranges approaching the vicinity of the Wind Mountain site. The yellow mud turtle, *K. flavescens*, inhabits permanent and intermittent streams in semiarid grasslands and open woodlands, rarely leaving the water (Stebbins 1966:82). More restricted to higher elevations is the Sonora mud turtle, *K. sonoriense*. This species occupies ponds, streams, and springs in woodlands of oak, piñon, juniper, pine, and fir. The close proximity these species maintain to aquatic environs provides evidence that the occupants of the Wind Mountain site exploited riparian or other fresh water resources. The turtles

APPENDIX 8: TABLE 2. Miscellaneous Faunal Material from the Wind Mountain Locus.

Sample No.	
WM Locus	
94.	Deer tooth (*Odocoileus hemionus*); House J, fill
129.	Turkey phalange (*Meleagris gallopavo*); Block 12-B
216.	2 unidentified phalanges; House P, fill
245.	Unidentified femur; Block 36-C
315.	Pigeon bone (*Columba fasciata*); House T, floor
352.	Rabbit bone (*Sylvilagus* sp.) and antelope bone (*Antilocapra americana*); House CC, floor fill
446.	Bear metatarsal (species unidentified); Block 45-C
463.	Bear bone (*Ursus americanus*); Block 52-A
531.	Dog Burial 6, 15 elements; Block 38-B
565.	Unidentified phalange; Block 47-C
675.	Bear phalange (*Ursus americanus*); House ZZ, fill
827.	Deer bone (*Odocoileus hemionus*); Pit Oven 18, fill
Total number of fragments: 28	

Note: Faunal material identified during human osteological analysis. Identifications made by the Arizona State Museum Faunal lab.

were most likely collected for their meat, and perhaps to use their shells for leg rattles and ornaments. Remains of this genus were found in Houses N, X, and NN, and Cremation 1.

Terrapene ornata. The western box turtle was identified by one carapace fragment. This species of land turtle inhabits treeless grasslands and occasionally appears in open woodlands (Stebbins 1966:86). It is active from March to November, during which time it is most accessible for exploitation.

Gopherus agassazi. Two fragments of desert tortoise plastron were found in House U. This terrestrial species, common to the arid Southwest, requires firm soil for burrowing; grass, cactus, or other low plant growth for food; and a minimum of ground moisture for its eggs and young (Stebbins 1966:87). The terrain occupied by desert tortoises includes washes, slopes, rocky areas, and edges of rivers. Like the mud turtle and western box turtle, the desert tortoise may have been captured for its meat or the use of its shell. Their habit of hibernating in long burrows during the winter makes this species relatively difficult to collect except in the warmer months of the year.

Crotalus sp. indet. Several species of rattlesnake are present in the area around Wind Mountain today. These include: *C. molossus,* the black-tailed rattlesnake; *C. lepidus,* the rock rattlesnake, *C. viridus,* the western rattlesnake, and *C. atrox,* the western diamondback. A single vertebra, the only specimen identified as rattlesnake from Wind Mountain, is inadequate for species determination. The wide range of ecozones inhabited by this genus means that one vertebra cannot be used as an environmental indicator. Their habit of occupying rodent burrows leads to intrusive skeletal remains. However, rattlesnake meat is of excellent quality and may have served as an occasional source of protein. All species of *Crotalus* are venomous and present a significant danger to humans.

Class Aves

Pelecanus erythrorhynchos. The white pelican, not a regular visitor to New Mexico today, was recognized from a radius in House Q. White pelicans form breeding colonies on lakes in the central and western states (Robbins et al. 1966:30), and migrate to California, central Arizona and the Gulf States, south to Mexico and Guatemala (American Ornithologists' Union 1975:29). Like other large birds, this rare visitor may have been used for food, or its feathers and bones may have been used as ornaments and tools.

Anas sp. indet. Numerous species of surface-feeding ducks pass through this area of New Mexico, so it is not possible to identify the single coracoid, recovered in House P, to the specific level. Surface-feeding ducks are aquatic and prefer ponds, lakes, marshes, and slow-moving streams.

Cathartes aura. The turkey vulture is a common North American scavenger that occupies a full range of environs wherever carrion is available. Turkey vultures occur occasionally in archaeological contexts in the Southwest. Like raptorial birds, vultures may have been captured or killed so that their feathers could be collected for ceremonial use. Two of the four vulture elements were found in Pit 34, and a third came from House NN. All were wing bones: a right coracoid, a right humerus, and the left first phalanx of digit II.

Accipiter cooperi. Four elements of Cooper's hawk were collected at Wind Mountain. Pit 34 contained a left fibula; Pit 45 yielded a left tibiotarsus. Uncommon today, this hawk normally dwells in open woodlands and along the edges of woods (Robbins et al. 1966:68). Its striated plumage may have been used in ceremonies or for personal adornment.

Buteo sp. indet. This genus of hawks is represented by several species in the Wind Mountain area, including the ferruginous hawk, *B. regalis;* the red-tailed hawk, *B. jamaicensis;* Swainson's hawk, *B. swainsoni;* and the zone- tailed hawk, *B. albonotatus.* Osteologically, these species are very difficult to distinguish, particularly when the archaeological specimens are fragmentary or immature. Hawk remains were second in quantity to one other bird, the turkey. At least three individual hawks were buried purposefully, including two juveniles recovered from a common pit. The third, a fully mature adult, was represented by 13 elements in the fill of House F. These hawk burials, and the miscellaneous elements distributed throughout the site, may indicate a strong reliance on hawks and their feathers in religious ceremonies. Simmons (1950) discusses the use of hawks by the Hopis. They are tethered on rooftops and their feathers plucked for

Appendix 8: Table 3. Distribution of Taxa in Wind Mountain Houses

Taxa\Provenience	A	B	C	D	E	F	G	H	I	J	K	L	M	N	O	P	Q	R	S	T	U	V	W	X	Y	Z
Bufo sp.																								1		
Gopherus agassazi																					2					
Kinosternon sp.														1										2		
Aves						1															1	1		1		
Pelecanus erythrorhynchos																	1									
Anas sp.																1										
Buteo sp.						13*		1				1										3		3		
Aquila/Haliaeetus																2										
Aquila chrysaetos														1										1		
Falco sparverius																					1					
Meleagris gallopavo				41*							3													2	6	
Lophortyx gambelii																								2		
Zenaida macroura																						19*				
Geococcyx californianus																								1		
Corvus corax																2								1		
Leporidae																					2	116		2	7	
Sylvilagus sp.	5	6	11	3	1	2	2	3		4	29	26	2	5	1	6	3	15	1	5	72	244	7	229	30	15
Lepus sp.	14	5	15	2	1	11	3	9	1		29	23	1	13		1		5	11		168	402	14	113	31	13
Lepus cf. *L. californicus*																				9						
Lepus californicus													4			3	4	1		1	55	9		45		
Lepus cf. *L. gaillardi*																							1	1		
L. gaillardi																								2		
Rodentia			1																	2	1			10		
Sciuridae			1									1									1	2		1		
Spermophilus spilosoma			1																		2					
S. variegatus											3	2							1			12		19	2	
Spermophilus/Cynomys								1									1					1		6	1	
Geomyidae																								7		
Geomys arenarius																				1				1		
Thomomys umbrinus	2	2			2						5	2		1							1	7		16		
Dipodomys sp.																						1				
Peromyscus sp.		1																								
Neotoma sp.						1						1									1	9		5		1
Sigmodon sp.																								1		
Carnivora																								9		
Canis sp.											1	2								1				35*	2	1

Appendix 8: Table 3 *(continued)*

Taxa\Provenience	A	B	C	D	E	F	G	H	I	J	K	L	M	N	O	P	Q	R	S	T	U	V	W	X	Y	Z
Canis cf. *C. familiaris*												1					7							9		
C. *familiaris*																								3		
Vulpes/Urocyon												2												1	1	
Urocyon cinereoargenteus											1													2	2	
Ursus sp.																								7		
?*Taxidea taxus*																					1					
Taxidea taxus																						14*?				
Lynx rufus											1													2		
Artiodactyla	1		2		3	6		1		4	38	4	2	5	7		4	5	9	9	32	40		246	17	1
Odocoileus sp.	6	1		1	1		2	5			16	38		14	2		2	3	4	7	27	28	3	166	37	6
Odocoileus cf. *O. hemionus*						2							1				2			1	5			18		
Odocoileus hemionus						6						3		7	2		1				1	1	7	72		1
Odocoileus cf. *O. virginianus*																				1				3		
Odocoileus virginianus															1									8		
Antilocapra											2			1						1	1			36	10	
Ovis canadensis																					1			2		
Bos/Bison																								2		
Bos taurus																								1		
Indeterminate mammal	35	7	23	24	2	30	9	42	1	4	151	156	3	58	-1	46	27	31	30	33	164	245	23	632	18	23

Taxa\Provenience	AA	AC	AD	AF	AG	AH	AI	AJ	BB	DD	EE	FF	GG	HH	II	JJ	NN	OO	PP	SS
Bufo sp.												5								
Kinosternon sp.																	1			
Aves		1	1				1						2	2	1		2			1
Cathartes aura																	1			
Buteo sp.									1								3	1	1	
Meleagris gallopavo													1		1			1		
Lophortyx gambelii												1								
Columba fasciata																			1	
Bubo virginianus												2								
Chordeiles sp.		1																		
Corvidae												1								
Cyanocitta stelleri																			1	
Leporidae										1		1								
Sylvilagus sp.	10	23	4	27	16		3			15	1	34	11	4	1		8	19	11	1

Appendix 8: Table 3 *(continued)*

Taxa\Provenience	AA	AC	AD	AF	AG	AH	AI	AJ	BB	DD	EE	FF	GG	HH	II	JJ	NN	OO	PP	SS
Lepus sp.	9	3	3	20	7	2	2		2	12		18	3	3	2			35	74	2
Lepus californicus					4					2		7		3			9			
Lepus cf. *L. gaillardi*		1		1										1						
Sciuridae					1															
Spermophilus spilosoma																			4	
S. variegatus	1	2	1	1	1		1				1	4	1							
Spermophilus/Cynomys					1															
Cynomys ludovicianus																		2		
Thomomys umbrinus				2			1				1							12	5	
																		7 skulls		
Neotoma sp.				3	1													2	3	
Carnivora																	1			
Canis sp.		1		2			1										1	5	11*?	
Vulpes/Urocyon										1									1	
Ursus sp.		61*																		
Ursus americanus											1						2			
Mephitis macroura									1											
Lynx rufus																		1		
Artiodactyla	6	14	7	82	11	2	2		1	13		5	12	10	1	1	6	21	21	
Cervus canadensis																		1		
Odocoileus sp.	5	1	1	65	8		2		4	5	4	4	5	10	1		3	27	33	1
Odocoileus cf. *O. hemionus*		3		3	2			3		1								14	5	1
O. hemionus	8	1		19	1						10		3	7	4			3	1	2
Odocoileus cf. *O. virginianus*				2																
O. virginianus	9			1					1								1			
Antilocapra americana				1						1			3					3		1
Ovis canadensis																	1			
Indeterminate mammal	32	104	27	335	83	1	69	4	8	35	2	42	22	49	14	1	42	184	269	24
Animalia							1													

*Purposeful burial.

Appendix 8: Table 4. Distribution of Taxa in Wind Mountain Surface Rooms

Taxa\Provenience	1	2	3	4	5	7	8	9	10	11	12	13	14	15	16
Geococcyx californianus			1												
Leporidae			2											1	
Sylvilagus sp.	1	2	15	1	2	5		1	1	3	6		2	2	2
Lepus sp.		4	21	9	5	5	1	5	1	2			6	2	
L. californicus										1	3			1	1
Lepus cf. *L. gaillardi*										1					
Sciuridae						1									
Spermophilus variegatus				2											
Spermophilus/Cynomys			1												
Cynomys ludovicianus						1					1				
Geomyidae				1											
Thomomys umbrinus															1
Dipodomys sp.					1										
Neotoma sp.						1								1	
Canis sp.													1		
Artiodactyla		1		1	1	1		2		1	8			2	1
Cervus canadensis			1												
Odocoileus sp.			1	1							4		2		
O. hemionus		1			1	1									1
Ovis canadensis										1					
Indeterminate mammal		5	3	17	16	10	4	3	2	6	9	2	7	3	5

ceremonies. After their ceremonial use is completed, they are "sent home," that is, killed and buried in a sacred manner (Simmons 1950:64–65). One element of a hawk was charred, suggesting that hawks may have also been eaten or were disposed of in a fire.

Aquila chrysaetos. The golden eagle, a frequent component of Southwestern archaeological faunal assemblages, was present at Wind Mountain chiefly in the form of two bird burials. Bird Burial 9 from Excavation Block 63–C contained 66 elements representing all the body parts, except the skull, of a fully-adult eagle. A partial burial in Excavation Block 20–B contained six elements from the legs, trunk, and wing of an adult eagle. Two isolated bones, a right tarsometatarsus from House N and a right jugal from House X, were also recovered. Two fragments from House P, the distal end of tarsometatarsus and a distal phalanx, were identified simply as *Aquila/Haliaeetus,* golden or bald eagle. The bald eagle, *Haliaeetus leucocephalus,* very rare today, may have been present in the area during prehistoric times. Its major requisite is the presence of streams supporting freshwater fish, its chief food source. Both genera of eagles are highly regarded by the Hopi, Pueblo, and Zuni Indians. Today these tribes keep golden eagles in cages to be plucked prior to festivals (Tyler 1979). After the ceremonies, like hawks, the eagles are sacrificed and buried. The presence of eagle burials at the Wind Mountain site indicates the religious importance of this species.

Falco sparverius. A single left humerus of a sparrow hawk was collected in House U. This small species of falcon is very common in the area today. The feathers of sparrow hawks may have been collected for ornamental or ceremonial use.

Meleagris gallopavo. With 178 fragments, turkeys were the most common species of bird observed at the Wind Mountain locus. It is likely that turkeys were used both for food and for their feathers. A left femur from Excavation Block 25–B exhibited transverse knife cuts on the shaft, indicating that it was butchered. Turkey burials at Wind Mountain suggest that this bird was important for more than just its meat (Table 10.1). House D contained a cluster of 41 bones, representing the whole body of an adult turkey. Bird Burial 5, in Excavation Block 42–D, contained the wings and legs of two adults. Bird Burial 7 consisted of 35 bones identified as turkey and eight other fragments recorded as large Aves, order indeterminate. All of these elements except a left tarsometatarsus probably represent a single juvenile. Eight miscellaneous elements from one or more adult turkeys were designated as Bird Burial 2. A cache of six elements from a mature turkey, collected in Excavation Block 39–A (Bird Burial 6), may or may not represent an intentional burial. Other scattered turkey bones include: three from House K, two from House X, six from House Y, one each from Houses GG, HH, and OO, and Burial 39.

Turkeys were domesticated in the Southwest as early as Basketmaker III times, c. A.D. 450–750 (S. J. Olsen 1968a:107). It is likely from the presence of numerous immature bones in the Wind Mountain faunal collection that

Appendix 8: Table 5. Distribution of Taxa in Wind Mountain Burials

Taxa\Provenience	Inhumation																																	
	3	7	8	9	13	18	20	21	33	38	39	40	41	42	45	50	51	52	53–54	56	57	59	61	68	71	72	74	77	89	94	97	100	101	1*
Kinosternon sp.																																		1
Aves																					1													
Meleagris gallopavo											1																							
Lophortyx gambelii																																	1	
Sylvilagus sp.		1	1		1											1	1		7	2									2	2				1
Lepus sp.		1			1	3			1				2						8					2		1		1					1	1
L. californicus		1														1											1							
Spermophilus/Cynomys																			1												1			
Geomys arenarius				1																														
Neotoma sp.																															1			
Canis sp.														2																				
Artiodactyla	2	1			1		1	2														1	1	1		1		2		1	2		1	2
Odocoileus sp.		1			1							2										2									1			
O. hemionus																			1												2			1
Antilocapra americana																									1									
Indeterminate mammal	4	16		1	16	2		5		1	1				1			2	2			9	1	3		2	2	6		5	21	2	2	4

*Cremation.

APPENDIX 8: TABLE 6. Distribution of Taxa in Wind Mountain Pits and Pavements

Taxa\Provenience	Pit																													
	3	4	6	11	19	20	21	24	25	26	27	31	32	33	34	37	38	39	41	43	44	45	46	47	49	51	68	69	70	1*	4*
Aves																							2				1				
Cathartes aura															2																
Accipiter cooperi															1							1									
Buteo sp.														1																	
Leporidae											4		1																		
Sylvilagus sp.			2		1		1	1	1		8	8	2	2				1			1			1							
Lepus sp.	2		2			1	1	1	2	2	1	2		1		1				2	2	1			1			3		1	
L. californicus												5	3		1			1													
Lepus cf.																															
L. gaillardi												1																			
Spermophilus/Cynomys															2																
Carnivora												1																			
Canis sp.												1																			
Urocyon cinereoargenteus												1																			
Artiodactyla							2				2	3			2	1					2	5	2	2				1	1		
Odocoileus sp.	1		3		1		6			2	1	2															2				1
O. hemionus							1					1					1					1									
O. virginianus																					2										
Indeterminate mammal	8	4	12	1		1	9		2	1	2	8		4	2		1	1	2	4	9		1		2	3	13	5	1	3	

*Pavement.

Appendix 8: Table 7. Deer Dentition Identified in the Wind Mountain Faunal Assemblage

Taxon	Catalogue No.	Teeth (presence/eruption/wear)	Approximate Age
Odocoileus sp. indet.	WM/B 210	Rt. p^4	Under 1.5 years
Odocoileus sp. indet.	WM/B 386	Lt. P_{2-4}, heavily worn	Old Adult
Odocoileus sp. indet.	WM/B 402	Rt. P_{2-3}, worn	Adult
Odocoileus sp. indet.	WM/B 541	Rt. P_{2-4}, M_{1-3}, heavily worn	Old Adult
Odocoileus sp. indet.	WM/B 541	Rt. M^{1-2}, heavily worn	Old Adult
Odocoileus cf. *O. hemionus*	WM/B 167	Lt. P^{3-4}, M^{1-3}	Adult
Odocoileus cf. *O. hemionus*	WM/B 430	Lt. M_3	Adult
Odocoileus hemionus	WM/B 458	Rt. P_{3-4}, M_{1-3}	Adult
Odocoileus hemionus	WM/B 541	Rt. P^{2-4}, heavily worn	Adult
Odocoileus hemionus	WM/B 541	Lt. P^3, heavily worn	Adult

Lt. = Left; Rt. = Right; M = Molar; p = Deciduous premolar; P = Permanent molar.

turkeys were domesticated at this site, but no poults or egg shell were reported and osteological evidence of domestication was not observed.

Intentional interment of turkey remains may be evidence of religious significance attached to this bird. Its feathers were probably used in ceremonies and for cloaks, blankets and arrow fletching.

Lophortyx gambelii. Gambel's quail, a common gallinaceous bird in the arid Southwest, is best adapted to areas with thick shrubs and herbaceous plants, low precipitation, and mild winters (Johnsgard 1975:74). This species was represented by four bones: a left and a right femur from House X, a right femur from House FF, and a sternum from Burial 101. Quail is still a desirable game bird, and probably served as an occasional source of protein for the people of Wind Mountain.

Ara macao. A total of 119 bone fragments of scarlet macaw were found in Bird Burial 3, Excavation Block 20–A (Table 10.1). The body was buried intact, because even the tracheal rings were present. This individual was newly fledged and approximately 11 to 12 months of age when it died. Macaws were important trade items in northern Mexico at such late period trade centers as Casas Grandes, Chihuahua (Di Peso 1974:272), and were traded as far north as Kiet Siel Pueblo in northern Arizona (Hargrave 1970:29). The peak of this trade seems to have occurred between A.D. 1100 and 1375 (Hargrave 1970:35). Their brightly colored feathers were plucked from the captive birds for ceremonial purposes. The Zunis continue to use macaw feathers in their ceremonies today (Judd 1954:263).

The importance of this macaw burial at Wind Mountain is in the indication that there was trade, directly or indirectly, with cultures in Mexico. It also demonstrates the presence of a shared cultural trait found among the Anasazi, Sinagua, Mogollon, Hohokam, and Rio Grande area. Macaws have been found at Cameron Creek Village and the Galaz Ruin in the Mimbres area (Hargrave 1970:48).

Columba fasciata. Three bones of the band-tailed pigeon were collected. Little can be said about this species except that it frequents western oak and pine woodlands (Robbins et al. 1966:154), nests in wooded canyon slopes, and consumes acorns, nuts, berries, and some grain (Johnsgard 1975:148–150). Band-tailed pigeons were probably occasionally hunted as a food resource.

Zenaida macroura. One adult mourning dove was found in House V. All of the body parts were represented in the 19 fragments recovered. Whether this was an intentional burial, or merely the scraps of a meal is not indicated by the remains. Because of its ubiquitous geographic distribution from forests to deserts, and its flexible diet and nesting habits (Johnsgard 1975:154–155), this species does not serve as an environmental indicator.

Geococcyx californianus. The roadrunner is a relatively common resident of the sagebrush flats of the arid Southwest up to about 2,135 m (7,000 feet) elevation in some places (Tyler 1979:257). This ground-dwelling cuckoo is a symbol of war to the Zuni Indians, who use its feathers in the ceremony of the scalps and in conjunction with many curing ceremonies (Tyler 1979:258–264). Roadrunners are identified at Wind Mountain by a left carpometacarpus from House X and a right humerus of an immature individual from Room 3.

Bubo virginianus. The great horned owl was represented by two bones from House FF, a right humerus and a left ulna. This large raptor is distributed over most of North America from northern Alaska to Mexico and from coast to coast. Today, wing and tail feathers of great horned owls are used on ceremonial masks and rosettes by the Zuni (Tyler 1979:183).

Chordeiles. sp. indet. A single left humerus of a nighthawk was collected from House AC. Both the common nighthawk,

C. minor, and the lesser nighthawk, *C. acutipennis,* are in the area today, and on this particular element, the two cannot be distinguished. Nighthawk feathers, especially the primaries, are used by the Zuni for prayer sticks relating to war or hunting in the Scalp Ceremony (Tyler 1979:178). Feathers are also offered at the dedication of a new cornfield.

Corvus corax. Eight elements of the common raven were identified. House P yielded a sacrum and a left carpometacarpus, and the fill of House X contained a left humerus. The remaining five bones were collected in open areas external to structures. All Pueblo Indians associate mythological characteristics with ravens and crows. Their jet black feathers often symbolize dark rain clouds (Tyler 1979:199). Feathers of ravens are used on Zuni kachina masks; and a Hopi War Dance described by Stephen mentions the carrying of a long pole with a raven's body impaled on the end (Tyler 1979:209). This scavenger is generally not eaten by Southwestern Indians.

Cyanocitta stelleri. One right humerus of a Steller's jay was found in House PP. The bright blue feathers of this species are used by both the Hopi and Zuni Indians to symbolize the cardinal direction West, and also function in various ceremonies (Tyler 1979:256). Steller's jays commonly reside in coniferous forests (Robbins et al. 1977:208).

Class Mammalia

Sylvilagus sp. indet. Two species of cottontail occur in the vicinity of the Wind Mountain site: *S. floridanus,* the eastern cottontail, and *S. audubonii,* the desert cottontail. The eastern cottontail has a vast range and inhabits ecozones from the Canadian Life-zone to the Tropical Life-zone. In New Mexico, this species occupies the upland, more wooded elevations, especially in the ponderosa zone and higher (Findley et al. 1975:83), whereas the desert cottontail inhabits piñon-juniper woodlands and lower, more arid altitudes.

Cottontail bones, numbering 1,294, were second in quantity only to jackrabbits. Of the total faunal assemblage, cottontail elements constituted about 9.6 percent. Bones of this genus, similar to jackrabbits, were distributed throughout the entire site. Twenty-nine fragments were charred and two tibiae exhibited butcher cuts on their shafts. Two innominates were worked in an unusual manner that resulted in the crest of the ilium being diagonally cut off (Appendix 8: Figure 1). This practice was noted on several jackrabbit ilia as well.

Traditionally, large numbers of cottontails are hunted communally by encircling them, constricting the circle until men can club or strangle the rabbits to death, or they are flushed out by controlled burning (Pennington 1963:90). Individual rabbits are pulled out of a burrow by entangling their fur in a barbed stick. Preparation of the carcass usually consists of skinning, eviscerating, and roasting. In addition to providing a ready meat source, rabbits have fine pelts that can be made into twisted rope blankets.

APPENDIX 8: FIGURE 1. Modified innominate of jackrabbit (stippled area of ilium indicates the area removed).

Lepus sp. indet. Two species of jackrabbit inhabit the area around Wind Mountain. The black-tailed jackrabbit, *L. californicus,* prefers sparse ground cover in cactus desert and mesquite grasslands, except on occasion, when individuals have been spotted in the open ponderosa forest (Findley et al. 1975:93). Gaillard's jackrabbit *L. gaillardi,* resides in mesquite grasslands and creosote desert, where vegetation is denser than the black-tailed jackrabbit's habitat. Because both forms fall within the same size range and no distinct morphological characteristics are apparent in their postcranial skeleton, these species are extremely difficult to distinguish.

About 13.2 percent of the Wind Mountain locus faunal collection consisted of jackrabbit bones. Of these 1,782 elements, 123 were charred and 13 were butchered. Seven innominates were modified by cutting off the crest of the ilium. This was done by means of the groove-and-snap technique. Similar artifacts have been reported from Mound 7 at Gran Quivira (Hayes et al. 1981:147–148) and from NAN Ruin (Shaffer 1990:7–14) in Grant County, New Mexico. Unlike the innominate tools from the NAN Ruin, those from the Wind Mountain locus did not exhibit use wear in the form of striations. Two humeri, one radius, one ischium, and two tibiae bore shallow knife cuts from butchering.

Jackrabbits were probably hunted communally in drives, as they have been for centuries by the Southwestern Indians. Unlike cottontails, jackrabbits do not dwell in burrows, so hunting generally involves a chase. Throwing sticks and bows and arrows were the likely weapons used in this pursuit. Preparation of the carcass would have been about the same as for cottontails.

Spermophilus spilosoma. Eight fragments of bone were identified as the spotted ground squirrel. This species inhabits open woodland, grassland, scattered brush (Burt and Grossenheider 1976:103) and deserts of New Mexico (Findley et al. 1975:121). Their habit of burrowing in sandy soil below rocks and shrubs makes them prime candidates as intrusives, that is, animals entering the archaeological record during postoccupational times. However, there is good evidence that the larger rock squirrels and prairie dog were common food items in the Southwest, so it is also possible that the much smaller spotted ground squirrel may have also been used. Remains of the spotted ground squirrel were recovered from Houses C, U, and PP.

Spermophilus variegatus. The rock squirrel was represented by 78 fragments, mostly cranial. This large ground squirrel occupies rocky canyons and slopes. As the name implies, it lives in dens hollowed out under boulders. Rock squirrels are found in a wide range of elevations in New Mexico, from the Sandia Crest to open lowland deserts with arroyos in which they may burrow (Findley et al. 1975:125).

The meat of rock squirrels is of good quality and is equivalent to a small cottontail in volume. These animals may be caught much like cottontails and prairie dogs, by pulling them from their burrow with sharp sticks, flushing them out with controlled burning, or by collapsing their tunnels.

Postcranially, the prairie dog and rock squirrel are very similar in skeletal morphology. For this reason, 23 elements were designated simply as *Spermophilus variegatus/Cynomys ludovicianus.* One of these fragments was charred.

Cynomys ludovicianus. Only seven elements were positively identified as black-tailed prairie dog. These consisted of mostly partial skulls and mandibles. Distributed within the living structures were: a left mandible and a right humerus in House OO, a right mandible in Room 7, and a left mandible in Room 12. One bone of this species was charred.

The black-tailed prairie dog resides in short grass prairies, and is marginally found in open woodland and semidesert landscapes (Findley et al. 1975:130–131). The once densely populated colonies of prairie dogs have been severely depleted in New Mexico and Arizona, as a result of the intensive eradication programs of the twentieth century.

Prairie dogs were probably hunted for their meat, using the same techniques employed when hunting cottontails and rock squirrels. Nooses and snares may also be used to capture these creatures. The Navajo often lure prairie dogs from their tunnels by dangling a mirror in the entrance so that sunlight is reflected into their eyes, dazzling them (Hill 1938:171–172). Prehistorically, a shiny object such as a quartz crystal could have been employed. It is likely that prehistoric farmers found prairie dogs and other rodents quite harmful to their crops, further motivating them to eliminate these pests.

Geomys arenarius. Desert pocket gophers have been identified by seven elements, including an incisor from House T, a partial skull from House X and a left mandible from Burial 9. Known to burrow in sandy and loamy soils (Findley et al. 1975:152), pocket gophers are probably intrusive agents in the archaeological faunal assemblage. The desert pocket gopher has not been recorded as far west as the Wind Mountain site in recent times, although it has been sighted near Deming, New Mexico (Findley et al. 1975:153).

Thomomys umbrinus. The southern pocket gopher, represented by 73 elements, is very similar in behavior and postcranial skeletal morphology to *Geomys arenarius.* These animals prefer loose loamy soil, but are also found in rocky areas. Pocket gophers are serious pests to the farmer, eating his crops from below the ground surface. The cornfields of prehistoric Wind Mountain farmers were most likely plagued by this rodent. A cache of seven skulls and five other elements of *T. umbrinus* was found in House OO and may represent human actions rather than merely natural intrusion.

Dipodomys sp. indet. Only two elements of kangaroo rat were identified: a left innominate from House V, and a partial skull from Room 5. Three species are found in southwestern New Mexico today: *D. ordii,* Ord's kangaroo rat; *D. spectabilis,* the banner-tailed kangaroo rat; and *D. merriami,* Merriam's kangaroo rat (Hall and Kelson 1959:513–531). Because the two archaeological specimens were not identifiable to the specific level, they cannot be used as environmental indicators. Ord's kangaroo rat dwells in a wide range of habitats below the mid-woodland zone in loose soils. The other two species prefer firm soil in grasslands and desert zones (Findley et al. 1975:180–183).

Peromyscus sp. indet. A single basicranium from House B was classified as belonging to this genus. Six species of *Peromyscus* inhabit southwestern New Mexico today: *P. eremicus,* the cactus mouse; *P. maniculatus,* the deer mouse; *P. leucopus,* the white-footed mouse; *P. boylii,* the brush mouse; *P. truei,* the piñon mouse; and *P. nasutus,* the rock mouse (Hall and Kelson 1959). Whatever the species collected at Wind Mountain, it is improbable that it was culturally significant.

Neotoma sp. indet. Thirty-six bone fragments from woodrats were observed. Structures and features containing elements of this genus include: Houses F, L, U, V, X, Z, AF, AG, OO, and PP; Rooms 7 and 15; and Burial 97. There are four species of woodrat found in the region today: *N. micropus,* the southern plains woodrat; *N. albigula,* the white-throated woodrat; *N. mexicana,* the Mexican woodrat; and *N. stephensi,* Stephen's woodrat. Together, these species cover most ecozones from grasslands to coniferous forests (Findley et al. 1975:238–247). Without a species determination, *Neotoma* sp. cannot be used for environmental reconstruction at the Wind Mountain site. The Zuni Indians are reported to have eaten woodrats by roasting their bodies, pounding the meat and bones into a pulp, and making a salty broth referred to as "rat brine" (Cushing 1920:599–600). Although none of the woodrat bones from the site were charred or butchered, it is likely that these plump rodents were occasionally eaten. However, the woodrat's fondness for woodpiles and rocky places and its habit of collecting curious objects would make it a likely intrusive agent during the occupation and postoccupation of a site.

Sigmodon sp. indet. A total of three elements were attributed to this genus. Disagreement exists as to the ranges and classifications of the species of cotton rats. According to Findley et al. (1975:233–237), the hispid cotton rat, *S. hispidus,* and the tawny-bellied cotton rat, *S. fulviventer,* are distributed throughout the southwestern corner of New Mexico. However, Hall and Kelson (1959:673–678) show *S. minimus,* the least cotton rat, as the only species in the area. Regardless of the species, cotton rats prefer grasslands and agricultural fields as their habitat. Consequently, they may have been a serious nuisance to prehistoric farmers.

Erethizon dorsatum. A single porcupine element was recovered. Bones of this large quill-bearing rodent are occasionally found in prehistoric sites, presumably representing food refuse. The porcupine feeds mainly on parts of trees (the twigs, buds, needles and cambium layer of the trunk) and forbs (Hall and Kelson 1959:780). Their range includes grasslands, rocky areas, and arroyos, but, because of their diet, their preferred habitat is the montane forest.

Canis sp. indet., *C. familiaris,* and *C. latrans.* Domestic dogs were common in the Wind Mountain faunal collection. The numerous *Canis* burials are of particular interest, and their distribution throughout the site is charted (Table 10.1). Five burials contain clearly distinguishable domestic dogs, and three interments consist of either dogs or coyotes. Numerous elements of immature *Canis* sp. indet. were recovered. A young puppy, less than five months old, was buried in the fill of House PP (CB 13). Another puppy, about four months of age, came from the fill of House X (CB 14). A total of 47 bone fragments of *Canis* sp. indet. were found in the fill of House X, representing at least two puppies and one fully mature adult. House X contained large quantities of faunal material in general, including a wide range of genera. Dog burials have been reported sporadically from a few prehistoric sites in the Southwest (Guernsey and Kidder 1921; S. J. Olsen 1968b; Emslie 1978; J. W. Olsen 1980), but are probably much more common than the literature indicates. Although there may be religious significance attached to the interment of dogs, it is also likely that the fondness of a child for his pet sometimes may have led to the special funerary practice.

Only two elements are positively identified as coyote, *C. latrans.* Coyotes are well distributed over the entire western United States and most of Mexico. These creatures play a more active and colorful role in North American Indian mythology than any other animal. Coyotes were killed, perhaps, because they destroy new corn and other edible plants, or because they are general pests that scavenge garbage.

Dogs, and possibly coyotes, were very likely eaten by the people of Wind Mountain. Five bone fragments of *Canis* sp. indet. were charred; one rib and a tibia show butchering marks.

One right maxilla of a dog or coyote showed evidence of a healed injury in the palatine process.

Vulpes macrotis. The kit fox was represented by a single element. This small desert-dwelling carnivore prefers sandy soil and low vegetation (Burt and Grossenheider 1976:75). This species is relatively uncommon in prehistoric sites in comparison to the gray fox.

Urocyon cinereoargenteus. Eight elements of the gray fox were recovered. This fairly common species prefers chaparral, broken woodlands of piñon, juniper, and oak, and rocky areas (Burt and Grossenheider 1976:76; Findley et al. 1975:289). Gray fox bones were frequently used as raw material for bone artifacts, especially fine awls and tubular beads (S. L. Olsen 1979, 1980). Their pelts are also suitable for sewing. Four fragments of fox bones (two *Vulpes/Urocyon* and two *Urocyon cinereoargenteus*) were burned. Remains of gray fox were distributed in Houses K, X, and Y, and Burial 31.

Ursus sp. indet. and *Ursus americanus.* Both the black bear, *U. americanus,* and the grizzly, *U. horribilis,* have been reported from this area of New Mexico. Many of the elements found at Wind Mountain were too immature or fragmentary to be diagnostic to the species level. This is the case with a young cub buried in House AC (Table 10.1). The cub was represented by 61 elements. Whether the bear cub was sacrificed as a part of a religious ceremony, or simply a pet found on a hunting expedition, is difficult to determine. In any case, the purposeful interment of a bear cub is a rare practice in the Southwest.

Bears are assigned considerable mythological importance by Pueblo Indians. Some groups consider the bear a god, others that he is really a man. Although bear meat is eaten by many groups, the skin and certain organs, such as the heart, are treated as sacred. Skulls are often buried under rocks, and bones are either thrown in a river or placed in shrines (Tyler 1975:191).

In addition to the bear cub burial, seven bones of *Ursus* sp. indet. were found in House X, and two more were collected outside the structures. Five elements were positively identified as black bear. Charring was found on eleven bones, suggesting that the people of Wind Mountain consumed bear meat.

Taxidea taxus. Sixteen badger bones were collected, 14 from House V fill. This possible burial consists of limb bones, an innominate, and the atlas of an immature badger. The right humerus of this individual and another isolated badger bone were charred. House U contained a single epiphysis of a right femur that was tentatively identified as *Taxidea taxus.*

The badger plays a significant role in the mythologies of many Southwestern tribes. The various Pueblo groups regard it as a clan symbol. Badgers are important in healing ceremonies, winter ceremonies of the sun, and other religious rituals among the Pueblo Indians (Tyler 1975:3–29).

Badgers prefer grasslands and the desert of Sonoran zones, but many occasionally migrate to the Transitional zone and even higher during the summer months where they have been spotted in alpine meadows (Tyler 1975:5; Findley et al. 1975:308). The unusual practice of badgers hunting rabbits in conjunction with coyotes has been the impetus for many Indian folk tales. In addition to their important role in Southwestern Indian mythology, badgers are sometimes eaten and skinned for their pelts.

Mephitis sp. indet. and *Mephitis macroura.* Both the striped skunk, *M. mephitis,* and the hooded skunk, *M. macroura,* are found in southwest New Mexico today. Two elements, of indeterminate species, were found outside the structures. One of these was charred. A partial skull from House BB was identified as a hooded skunk. This species dwells predominantly in the Lower Sonoran zone, but has been found as high as the ponderosa pine forests in New Mexico (Findley et al. 1975:313). The striped skunk, which may or may not have been present at the Wind Mountain site, inhabits open prairie, brush land, or mixed woods (Burt and Grossenheider 1976:65). Both species remain fairly close to fresh water sources.

Lynx rufus. Fourteen elements were identified as bobcat. House X yielded a cervical vertebra and a right femur. Houses K and OO produced a left tibia and a right humerus. Though not abundant, bobcat remains often occur in Southwestern prehistoric faunal assemblages. The appearance of this species may be attributed to several reasons. Bobcats are known to be minor pests to farmers because they will dig up young corn plants and eat squash in the same way coyotes will. They also kill domestic turkeys and may, therefore, have been eradicated themselves. The pelt of the bobcat is very fine, and is, therefore, desirable. Their bones and claws are frequently modified into tools and ornaments (S. L. Olsen 1979, 1980). It is possible that the meat of bobcats was eaten on occasion.

Felis sp. indet. A single element of a large cat was found. Jaguars, *F. onca,* were reported in New Mexico as recently as 1904 (Findley et al. 1975:317), but have always been rare in historic times. The mountain lion, *F. concolor,* on the other hand, is still relatively plentiful in western New Mexico, particularly in the mountains and areas of rough terrain (Findley et al. 1975:317). Their bones occur sporadically in small numbers in archaeological assemblages in the Southwest, whereas jaguar remains are extremely rare north of Mexico. The mountain lion plays an important part in Pueblo mythology and may have been hunted so that its pelt, teeth, and claws could be worn as ceremonial paraphernalia.

Suborder Ruminantia.

Based on the proportion of identified fragments (19.3 percent), ruminants (deer, pronghorn, or bighorn) constitute the second largest category of animals used by the people of Wind Mountain. Although there were more rabbit bones, by pounds of usable meat, the ruminants were clearly the more important source of protein. Ruminants would have provided hides for clothing, bags, and other necessities, sinew thread, and bone for the manufacture of tools and ornaments. The cervids would have also yielded antler for the manufacture of tools.

Cervus canadensis. Three elements were identified as wapiti. One is a proximal phalanx from House OO, and another, from Room 3, is a cervical vertebra. Their prehistoric geographic range is poorly known, especially as wapiti were extirpated from so many areas in New Mexico during the nineteenth century and were artificially replenished in the twentieth century. Wapiti apparently prefer montane grasslands in this region (Findley et al. 1975:328). It seems, from the scarcity of this excellent source of protein in prehistoric faunal assemblages, that wapiti were not common even prior to the influx of cattle and European sportsmen.

Odocoileus sp. indet., *O. hemionus,* and *O. virginianus.* As for most Southwestern Indians, deer were clearly a major dietary resource for the Wind Mountain people. The mule deer, *O. hemionus,* is found in the whole range of habitats and elevations in western New Mexico. Although the mule deer requires browse plants such as twigs and shrubs, it will also graze on grasses and herbs during the rainy season (Burt and Grossenheider 1976:216; Hall and Kelson 1959:1004). White-tailed deer, *O. virginianus,* prefer rough terrain, such as the chaparral-covered mountains of southwestern New Mexico (Findley et al. 1975:332). This species is more strongly riparian than the mule deer, and adheres more closely to thick vegetation for protection. The local subspecies, *O. virginianus couesi,* or desert white-tailed deer, is much smaller than the eastern white-tailed deer, *O. v. texanus* (Findley et al. 1975:332), so most adult bones are readily distinguishable from the even larger mule deer.

There was considerable evidence of food preparation in the form of butchering marks on deer bones. Evidence from such processing marks indicates the methods by which carcasses were sectioned (Appendix 8: Figure 2). According to the limited collection of mandibles and maxillae of deer, most were slaughtered as mature adults (Appendix 8: Table 7).

A mule deer proximal phalanx from House X exhibited exostosis around the distal condyle caused by osteoarthritis or some other inflammatory ailment.

Antilocapra americana. Pronghorns were represented by 82 elements. The largest cluster, consisting of 36 bones, was derived from House X. One proximal phalanx may have been drilled to remove the marrow, and 28 bone fragments were charred. Although pronghorns were not as common as deer in the faunal assemblage, they were no doubt an important dietary supplement.

This strictly North American species once roamed the open grasslands in large numbers, but the herds have been severely depleted by hunting and overgrazing by domestic animals. Preferring to browse on sagebrush, rabbitbrush, and buckbrush (Hall and Kelson 1959:1022), pronghorns usually do not range into heavily wooded areas.

Ovis canadensis. As in most Southwestern faunal assemblages, bighorns were much less common than the other ruminants of similar size. Only 12 elements were positively identified as mountain sheep. The scarcity of bighorns in archaeological sites is probably related to the fact that they inhabit the rocky cliffs of desert mountain ranges where the terrain is difficult for any predator, including human hunters, to negotiate. Leopold (1972:526) reports that their numbers were never as great as those of the mule deer or pronghorn, because their habitats are so restricted. The remains of this species were found in Houses U, X, and NN, and Room 11. Six fragments were charred.

Bos taurus/Bison bison. Thirteen elements were derived from large bovids the size and proportions of either cattle or bison. Two were found in House X, and the remaining bones were distributed outside the structures and features. Remains of bison have been found as far west as Point of Pines (Stein 1963:215), Snaketown (Gladwin et al. 1937:156), and Bear Ruin (Haury 1940:15) in Arizona. In prehistoric times this species probably would have been available to the people of Wind Mountain. In historic times, however, bison were not recorded west of the Rio Grande (Findley et al. 1975:335).

There is evidence that pothunters had disturbed the cultural layers in House X. This would account for the presence of a complete adult mesial phalanx identified as *Bos taurus,* domestic cattle.

Taphonomic Conditions of the Faunal Collection

The general condition of the faunal material from Wind Mountain is very stable. Only 19 bone fragments showed clear evidence of weathering. Eighty-two were rodent gnawed and 29 were gnawed by carnivores. Although most of the bones were broken, breakage was not extensive enough to severely hamper identification. The percentages of fragments that were unidentifiable below the level of class were 15 percent for birds and 47 percent for mammals. This is a relatively low proportion of indeterminate fragments in comparison to other archaeological faunal assemblages.

Environmental Reconstruction

The range of ecozones in the region around the Wind Mountain site includes the Lower Sonoran through the Canadian zones. The maximum elevation on Big Burro Peak is about 2,450 m (8,035 feet) above sea level. Much of the ecological variation is dependent upon the altitudinal differentiation within this area. Riparian vegetation and fauna were also in close proximity with the nearby Mangas Creek headwaters. The faunal collection further demonstrates the wide variety of animals occupying different ecozones that were utilized by the prehistoric people.

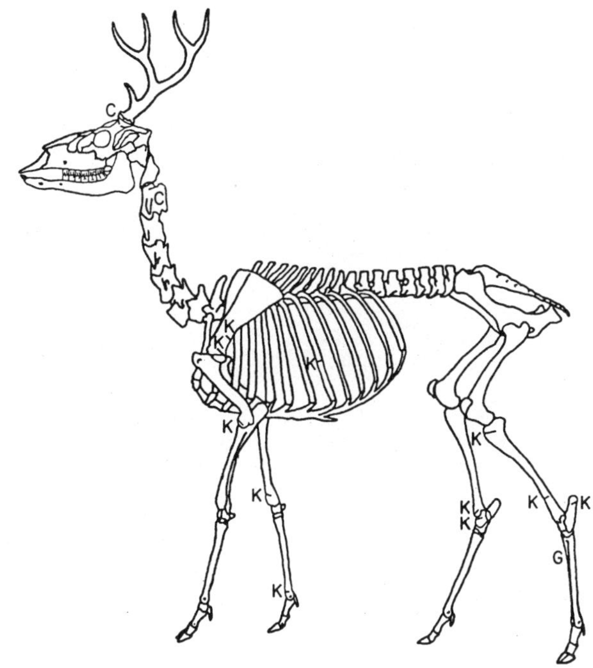

Appendix 8: Figure 2 Locations of butchering marks on deer elements. K = knife cuts; C = chop marks; G = grooved.

The presence of a single fish vertebra, mud turtle carapace fragments, and a coracoid of a surface-feeding duck (*Anas* sp. indet.) is evidence that riparian resources were exploited. Other taxa, such as the white pelican, the black bear, and skunk are also closely associated with freshwater sources.

Remains of Desert tortoise, Gambel's quail, roadrunner, and kit fox represent utilization of desert fauna from the Upper and Lower Sonoran zones.

Much of the faunal remains were derived from species that inhabit grasslands and open woodlands. These include: the western box turtle, Cooper's hawk, spotted ground squirrel, black-tailed prairie dog, cotton rat, skunk, and pronghorn.

Several species, which habitually dwell in rocky terrain, such as rock squirrels, the felids, white-tailed deer, and at the extreme, bighorn sheep, were also exploited.

A number of other taxa observed extend into montane woodlands, but only a few offer concrete evidence that these zones were used by prehistoric cultures. The band-tailed pigeon generally inhabits oak and pine woodlands and subsists on acorns, nuts, and berries. Steller's jay lives in coniferous forests. The porcupine, because of its diet, prefers montane forests, but does occur at lower elevations. Bighorns are fairly restricted to mountain ranges today because of the safety that rough terrain provides them, although this may have been less so in the past.

It appears that there was a preference for hunting animals in the grasslands and open woodlands around Wind Mountain, but that occasional excursions into both lower or higher elevations brought the site's inhabitants an ample variety of meat sources. Among the chief protein contributors were deer, cottontails, and jackrabbits.

Ceremonial Utilization

Several species of bird and at least two of mammals probably had religious significance to the Wind Mountain people. It is very likely that the feathers of birds, especially raptors, turkeys, and macaws, were used as ornamentation, for prayer sticks, and for other ceremonial objects. In particular, the macaw was sufficiently important to be traded in from the rain forests of southern Tamaulipas, its native habitat. Interment of hawks, golden eagles, turkeys, a mourning dove, and a macaw signify the importance endowed these species.

The large number of dog burials may be interpreted in two ways. Either the dogs were family pets, or they had ceremonial significance. The bear cub burial may represent an adopted orphan that was taken as a temporary companion, but bears are also important as clan symbols among many Southwestern tribes. Many other animals identified at Wind Mountain may have served religious functions. Indian mythology encompasses most local wildlife to varying degrees.

Summary and Conclusions

Detailed faunal analyses from the Mimbres area are a recent occurrence, though previous reports record the most commonly observed species such as deer, pronghorn, bighorn, jackrabbit, cottontail, dog, turkey, eagle, and hawk (Cosgrove and Cosgrove 1932:5; Graybill 1975:40–42). Additionally, bison were identified at the Harris site (Haury 1936a) and at Swarts Ruin (Cosgrove and Cosgrove 1932:5). Bison herds were probably within range of hunting expeditions from the Wind Mountain site. Prehistoric bison bones were also reported further west, just into Arizona, in the Point of Pines region (Stein 1963:215). Elk remains were also found at Swarts Ruin, providing further evidence that their prehistoric range included the Mimbres area. Mogollon and Mimbres sites other than Wind Mountain contain macaw burials (Cameron Creek Village and Galaz Ruin in the Mimbres River drainage). Hargrave reported a scarlet macaw (*Ara macao*) buried with a man, and another macaw burial (*Ara* sp. indet.) from Cameron Creek village (Hargrave 1970:48). Galaz Ruin contained the only military macaw (*Ara militaris*) found north of Mexico and three scarlet macaws (Hargrave 1970:49).

Because of the quantity of well preserved bones collected there, the Wind Mountain site demonstrates the wide variety of fauna used by the prehistoric peoples of the area. In addition to providing dietary, ceremonial, and trade information, the faunal assemblage informs us about the hunting practices, which must have led these people into a range of ecozones from Lower Sonoran to ponderosa pine habitats.

Appendix 9

An Analysis of Miscellaneous Faunal Materials from the Wind Mountain Locus and Analyses of Ridout Locus Faunal Materials

CHARMION R. MCKUSICK

The analysis of faunal material in Appendix 9 completes identification of miscellaneous fauna from the Wind Mountain locus (3,048 specimens) and the total faunal remains recovered from the Ridout locus (882 specimens). Analysis was conducted at the Southwest Bird Laboratory in Globe, Arizona. The Western Archeological Conservation Center in Tucson arranged the loan of comparative pronghorn skeletal material, and Zane Poor, Jr. provided an elk skeleton. Methods of faunal identification and recording were similar to those of the Olsens (Appendix 8).

The faunal collection from the Ridout locus and the miscellaneous material from the Wind Mountain locus generally consisted of small, but well-preserved, fragments of bone (Appendix 9: Table 1). Some evidence of limited postoccupation rodent gnawing was noted.

The faunal samples from the Wind Mountain and Ridout loci provide a picture of an economy in which mule deer was the protein mainstay. A need for fat, as suggested by the fracturing of bones to obtain bone fat and the probable hunting of does during prelactation (when they are at their fattest), is consistent with evidence from other sites. Mule deer may be hunted by a solitary person, but "surround" hunting of pronghorn would necessitate the cooperative efforts of a large group. The apparent stress placed upon the lagomorph population at Wind Mountain may simply reflect overhunting, or may be evidence for a communal activity such as a rabbit drive.

Taxonomic List of Faunal Material Described

Note: following the common name of each species is a locus identifier; WM = Wind Mountain, RO = Ridout. The identifier indicates that at least one related specimen was found at that locus and is identified here.

Class Amphibia
- Order Salientia
  - *Scapiopus holbrooki:* spade footed toad. WM.

Class Reptilia
- Order Chelonia
  - *Terrapene ornata:* western box turtle. WM.

Class Aves
- Order Falconiformes
  - *Accipitridae* sp.: hawk (?). WM.
  - *Aquila chrysaetos:* golden eagle. WM.
  - *Buteo jamaicensis:* red-tailed hawk. WM.
- Order Galliformes
  - *Meleagris gallopavo:* turkey. WM/RO.
- Order Columbiformes
  - *Columba fasciata:* band-tailed pigeon. WM.
- Order Passeriformes
  - *Corvus corax:* comman raven. WM.
  - *Corvus cryptoleucus:* white-necked raven. RO.
  - *Icterus* (?). RO.
- Order Strigiformes
  - *Tyto alba:* barn owl. WM.

Class Mammalia
- Order Lagomorpha
  - *Sylvilagus* sp.: cottontail. WM/RO.
  - *Sylvilagus floridanus* (?): eastern cottontail. RO.
  - *Lepus californicus:* black-tailed jackrabbit. WM/RO
- Order Rodentia
  - *Citellus variegatus* (cf. Appendix 8, *Spermophilus variegatus*): rock squirrel. WM/RO.
  - *Thomomys bottae* (cf. Appendix 8, *Thomomys* varieties): valley pocket gopher. WM/RO.
  - *Neotoma albigula:* wood rat. WM/RO.
- Order Carnivora
  - *Canis familiaris:* dog. WM.
  - *Canis latrans:* coyote. WM/RO.
  - *Urocyon cinereoargenteus:* gray fox. WM.
  - *Ursus americanus:* black bear. WM.

Lynx rufus: bobcat. WM.
Order Artiodactyla
Odocoileus hemionus: mule deer. WM/RO.
Odocoileus virginianus: white-tailed deer. RO.
Antilocapra americana: pronghorn. WM/RO.
Bos taurus/Bison bison: cattle or bison. WM.

Utilitarian and Worked Bone

Utilitarian bone tools are divided into three categories of awls, spatulate tools, and antler tine implements (Reference Nos. 229–242; Appendix 9: Tables 2 and 3). Most of the 273 tools from Wind Mountain consisted of awls (86 percent), with smaller numbers of spatulate tools (10 percent) and antler tine tools (4 percent). Bone tools are primarily represented by deer (96 percent), and rarely antelope (1 percent), rabbits (1 percent), and miscellaneous species (1 percent). The frequency of utilitarian tools manufactured from deer bone corresponds to its abundance as a material used for the manufacture of socioreligious objects including items of personal adornment such as beads and pendants.

Worked bone consisted primarily of femurs and other long bones of deer (92 percent) (Reference Nos. 444–448; Appendix 9: Tables 4 and 5). Smaller quantities of jackrabbit (3 percent) and unspecified mammal (2 percent) femurs were identified, as well as turkey femurs (3 percent). Again, the high frequency of deer in this category is also reflected in the range of socioreligious artifacts made of bone.

Appendix 9: Table 1. Analysis of Miscellaneous Fauna from the Wind Mountain Locus and the Faunal Component Recovered from the Ridout Locus.

WM locus

Houses and Rooms

House B
Sample 8 (Floor fill)
Canis familiaris, cranium; dentaries. Adult, nonspecific gender.

House D
Sample 216 (Fill)
Aquila chrysaetos, pes 4:3. Adult female.

House J
Sample 94 (Fill)
Odocoileus hemionus, left P^3. Nonspecific age or gender.

House K
Sample 86 (Fill)
Odocoileus hemionous, left M^1, right P^2. Adult male.

House N
Sample 162 (Fill)
Odocoileus hemionus, right tibia, proximal epiphysis. Immature, nonspecific gender.

House T
Sample 315 (Floor)
Columba fasciata, right tarsometatarsus. Adult female.

House CC
Sample 352 (Floor fill)
Antilocapra americana, rib. Adult female.
Sylvilagus sp., left dentary. Immature, nonspecific gender.

House FF
Sample 476 (Pit 1)
Ursus americanus, metapodial; metatarsal (?). Adult male.

House KK
Sample 513 (Floor fill)
Sylvilagus sp., right innominate. Immature, nonspecific gender.
Antilocapra americana, phalanx No. 1, proximal fragment. Adult female.

APPENDIX 9: TABLE 1. *(continued)*

House PP
Sample 575 (Fill)
Odocoileus hemionus, right auditory bulla. Adult male.

Sample 593 (Strata Test fill)
Sylvilagus sp., sacrum; right innominate; left dentary. Adult, nonspecific gender.
Sylvilagus sp., right calcaneum; metatarsal. Immature, nonspecific gender.

Sample 601 (Floor fill)
Tyto alba, right tibia, shaft fragment with fibular crest. Young adult female.
Sylvilagus sp., left tibia, distal end; metacarpal; fragments of right and left dentaries; vertebra fragment. Adult female.
Sylvilagus sp., right dentary. Adult male.
Lepus californicus, left dentary fragment; left innominate fragment; right maxilla with alveoli; left radius, proximal shaft fragment; metatarsal. Adult female.
Thomomys bottae, right dentary.
Odocoileus hemionus, right acetabulum; ilium fragment; right calcaneum fragment; phalanx No. 2; rib fragments (2); long bone shaft fragments; left radius, proximal head; metapodial, proximal fragment; left scapula fragment; vertebra fragment. Young adult male.
Odocoileus hemionus, phalanx No. 2. Adult female.

House QQ
Sample 597 (Fill)
Meleagris gallopavo, cervical vertebra fragment. Adult, nonspecific gender.
Corvus corax, left humeri (2), 1 right and 2 left ulnae; left carpometacarpus; right and left scapulae. Two individuals, both immature and nonspecific as to gender.
Sylvilagus sp., right innominate fragment; left tibia, distal articulation; left femur, distal articulation. Adult male.
Sylvilagus sp., left innominate fragment; left femur; right radius minus proximal articulation. Adult female.
Sylvilagus sp., metapodial minus distal epiphysis; 2 vertebrae, diaphysis of centrum. Immature, nonspecific gender.
Lepus californicus, right tibia, distal shaft fragment; left tibia, partial distal articulation; right femur, distal articulation; right dentary, partial transverse ramus. Adult female.
Neotoma albigula, left femur minus distal diaphysis. Immature, nonspecific gender.
Odocoileus hemionus, right metacarpal, proximal articulation and shaft fragment; pedal phalanges, 3 No. 3, 2 No. 2; right metatarsal, partial distal articulation. Adult male.
Odocoileus hemionus, metapodial, fragmentary distal articulation. Old adult male.
Odocoileus hemionus, right humerus, shaft fragmant; pedal phalanx, 2 No. 1; left metatarsal, distal articulation and shaft; fragmentary sternum; vertebrae fragments (4); carpal; partial right scapula. Adult female.
Artiodactyla sp., left radius, shaft fragment with nutrient foramen. Nonspecific age or gender.
Antilocapra americana, left radius, distal shaft; ulna. Adult male.

House RR
Sample 603 (Fill)
Buteo jamaicensis, left coracoid; 1 vertebra. Adult male.
Lepus californicus, right radius minus distal articulation; right dentary (2 fragments); right innominate fragment. Adult male.
Odocoileus hemionus, right metacarpal, distal articulation and shaft; left humerus, distal shaft fragment; rib fragment; left radius, partial proximal shaft. Young adult female.
Odocoileus hemionus, right naviculocuboid. Adult male.

Sample 604 (Floor fill)
Sylvilagus sp., left tibia, proximal diaphysis. Immature, nonspecific gender.
Lepus californicus, right ulna minus distal shaft. Adult male.
Odocoileus hemionus, left radius, partial proximal articulation and shaft fragments. Adult female.
Antilocapra americana, right metacarpals, diaphyses. Neonate.

House SS
Sample 620 (Fill)
Meleagris gallopavo, tarsometatarsal, posterior shaft. Young adult male.

APPENDIX 9: TABLE 1. *(continued)*

Mammalia sp., modern domestic animal (?), unidentifiable element, gnawed by carnivore. Nonspecific age or gender.
Sylvilagus sp., (unidentifiable fragments of three individuals). Immature female; immature, nonspecific gender; adult male.
Lepus californicus, lumbar vertebra—adult female; left humerus, distal articulation; left femur minus distal articulation—adult male; left acetabulum—immature, nonspecific gender.
Rodentia sp., left femur. Immature, nonspecific gender.
Citellus variegatus, left femur; cranium. Immature, nonspecific gender.
Canis familiaris (?), left maxilla; right and left humeri; left radius; left tibia; left scapula. Over 4 weeks, under 4 months.
Canis familiaris, right dentary with C_1, P_2, P_3, P_4, M_1. Old adult, probably male.
Odocoileus hemionus, (fragments of three individuals) humeri (4); ilium (1); scapulae (5); vertebrae (15); carpals (7); antler (6) with partial cranium; calcanea (2); astragalus (1); metatarsals (10); femurs (4); ribs (6); tibiae (2); phalanges (12); left ulna (1). Immature, nonspecific gender; immature female; adult male.
Scapiopus holbrooki (?), major elements.

House TT
Sample 622 (Fill)
Sylvilagus sp., left maxilla. Adult male.
Lepus californicus, right dentary, fragment; right tibia, proximal articulation and central shaft; left femur, central shaft. Adult female.
Citellus variegatus, left dentary. Adult, nonspecific gender.
Artiodactyla sp., right scapula, proximal fragment. Neonate.
Odocoileus hemionus, right femur, distal articulation, gnawed by carnivore; left radius, partial proximal articulation; long bone shaft fragmants; burned fragment of phalanx No. 2. Adult female.

Sample 623 (Fill)
Sylvilagus sp., right femur fragments (2). Two immature individuals, both nonspecific as to gender.
Lepus californicus, left humerus, diaphysis. Immature, nonspecific gender.
Thomomys bottae, right dentary, ascending ramus. Adult, nonspecific gender.
Odocoileus hemionus, right femur, distal shaft; rib fragment. Adult male.

Sample 624 (Fill)
Lepus californicus, right femur minus distal articulation; right innominate. Adult male.

Sample 625 (Fill)
Buteo jamaicensis, right ulna, proximal head (fractured and healed with malunion). Adult female.
Sylvilagus sp., (unidentifiable fragments of four individuals). Adult female; adult male; and two immature individuals both nonspecific as to gender.
Lepus californicus, eight unidentifiable fragments. Immature female.
Citellus variegatus, left ulna. Immature, nonspecific gender.
Odocoileus hemionus, (fragments of three individuals) cranium, opened posterior to antler bases; antler (10); tooth, unerupted (1) – adult male; scapulae (13); vertebrae (4); metacarpal (1); metapodial (1); calcaneum (1); pedal phalanx, 2 No. 1; 4 No. 2; radius (5); ribs (4); tibiae (6); ulnae (2); innominate (9); humeri (3) – young adult male and adult female.
Antilocapra americana, phalanx No. 1; innominate; right humerus, distal articulation; astragalus. Adult female.

House ZZ
Sample 675 (Fill)
Ursus americanus, phalanx. Adult female.

Room 2
Sample 7
Lepus californicus, left humerus, distal end of diaphysis. Immature male.
Canis familiaris, major elements. Nonspecific age or gender.

PITS AND PIT OVENS

Pit 36
Sample 488 (Fill)
Artiodactyla sp., long bone shaft fragment. Adult, nonspecific gender.

Pit 64
Sample 703 (Fill)
Odocoileus hemionus, left ischium, partial acetabulum. Adult male.

APPENDIX 9: TABLE 1. *(continued)*

Pit Oven 18
Sample 827 (Fill)
Odocoileus hemionus, left humerus, proximal epiphysis. Immature, nonspecific gender.

BURIAL CONTEXTS

Burial 11
Sample 855 (Fill)
Artiodactyla sp., unfused metapodial. Neonate.
Odocoileus hemionus, epiphysis of centrum of vertebra; right astragalus; rib; tibia. Immature male.

Burial 31
Sample 857 (Fill)
Odocoileus hemionus, fragmentary patella. Adult female.

Burial 38
Sample 859 (Fill)
Artiodactyla sp., rib. Nonspecific age or gender.

Burial 41
Sample 861
Odocoileus hemionus, metatarsal. Nonspecific age or gender.

Burial 44
Sample 862
Ocodoileus hemionus, caudal vertebra. Adult, nonspecific gender.

Burial 49
Sample 856 (Fill)
Odocoileus hemionus, patella. Adult male.

Burials 53–54
Sample 860
Lepus californicus, right humerus, distal articulation with fragmentary shaft. Adult male.
Odocoileus hemionus, right humerus, partially fragmented; metapodial shaft fragment. Adult male.

Burial 59
Sample 853 (Fill)
Odocoileus hemionus, partial proximal articulation and shaft of unidentifiable element. Adult male.

Burial 74
Sample 854 (Fill)
Odocoileus hemionus, pedal phalanx No. 2. Adult male.
Artiodactyla sp., unidentifiable elements (surface and ends of bones destroyed by rodents). Immature, nonspecific gender.

Burial 76
Sample 863
Canis latrans, right humerus, distal articulation. Adult female.

Burial 90
Sample 864
Lepus californicus, left innominate, fragment of acetabulum. Adult female.

Burial 94
Sample 851
Canis latrans, cranium, right lateral section. Immature, nonspecific gender.

Burial 99
Sample 852
Artiodactyla sp., femur, shaft fragment. Nonspecific age or gender.

Appendix 9: Table 1. *(continued)*

Burial 100
Sample 858
Sylvilagus sp. right ilium; pedal phalanx; cervical vertebra; partial cranium. Immature, nonspecific gender.

Excavation Blocks

Block 11-D
Sample 618 (House K, subfloor)
Sylvilagus sp., right femur, distal articulation and shaft fragment; left dentary, partial transverse ramus; metatarsal. Adult female.
Lepus californicus, calcaneum; right dentary, partial transverse ramus; left tibia, fibular stub with shaft fragment. Adult female.
Lynx rufus, right humerus, distal shaft. Immature, nonspecific gender.
Odocoileus hemionus, right femur, capitum with fragmentary shaft; right ilium; tooth fragments (2); phalanx No. 2; 1 femur partially fragmented. Adult male.
Artiodactyla sp., left radius, shaft fragment; right acetabulum, ischial. Immature, nonspecific gender.

Block 12-B
Sample 129 (Fill)
Meleagris gallopavo merriami (?). Adult male.

Block 19-B
Sample 178 (Fill)
Canis latrans (?), basioccipital. Immature, nonspecific gender.

Block 36-C
Sample 245 (Fill)
Lepus californicus, distal articulation and shaft. Adult male.

Block 47-C
Sample 565 (Fill)
Bos taurus/*Bison bison*, pedal phalanx No. 1 (surface destroyed by rodents). Immature, nonspecific gender.

Block 52-A
Sample 336 (Fill)
Odocoileus hemionus, left ulna; rib; long bone fragment. Adult male.

Sample 463 (Fill)
Ursus americanus, metapodial; metatarsal?, proximal articulation with fragmented shaft. Adult female.

Sample 462 (Fill)
Terrapene ornata (?), pleural of carapace.
Sylvilagus sp., left innominate. Young adult male.
Lepus californicus, left humerus minus distal end. Adult male.
Antilocapra americana, left humerus, distal articulation with fragmented shaft; left metatarsal, proximal articulation. Adult female.

Block 52-B
Sample 464 (Fill)
Buteo jamaicensis, right femur shaft fragment. Adult female.
Sylvilagus sp., innominate; left dentary. Immature, nonspecific gender.
Sylvilagus sp., left tibia minus distal end; ilia (2); left dentary. Two adult males.
Sylvilagus sp., femur, proximal articulation with shaft; tibia, distal end. Adult female.
Thomomys bottae, cranium. Immature, nonspecific gender.
Odocoileus hemionus, left humerus, distal shaft and head; pedal phalanx No. 3. Adult male.
Odocoileus hemionus, carpal. Adult female.
Antilocapra americana, right tibia, shaft fragment and distal epiphysis; pedal phalanx, proximal epiphysis. Immature female.
Lepus californicus, left dentary. Adult, nonspecific gender.
Lepus californicus, left dentary. Immature, nonspecific gender.

Block 53-C
Sample 708 (Fill)
Canis latrans, thoracic vertebra, dorsal spine. Adult, nonspecific gender.

Appendix 9: Table 1. *(continued)*

Block 54-A
Sample 612 (Fill)
Mammalia sp., unknown element, shaft fragment. Immature, nonspecific gender.
Sylvilagus sp., right femur, proximal half. Immature, nonspecific gender.
Lepus californicus, right innominate; right humerus, distal fragment. Immature female.
Odocoileus hemionus, left tibia, partial fibular crest; left metacarpal, 3/4's proximal articulation intact; calcaneum fragment; phalanx No. 2; rib, proximal articulation; long bone fragment, unidentifiable. Young adult male.
Odocoileus hemionus, right tibia, partial shaft; calcaneum fragment; left metacarpal No. 4, proximal head; long bone shaft fragment; left ulna, proximal articulation. Adult male.

Block 54-B
Sample 585 (Fill)
Odocoileus hemionus, right radius fragment; left tibia, distal end; left astragalus; right metatarsals, proximal articulation. Adult female.

Sample 606 (Fill)
Sylvilagus sp., right dentary; right tibia; right innominate (all fragments). Adult female.
Lepus californicus, left tibia, shaft fragment. Immature, nonspecific gender.
Lepus californicus, left humerus, distal end; sacrum; left radius minus proximal articulation. Adult female.
Lepus californicus, left radius, distal articulation. Adult male.
Thomomys bottae, cranium fragment; left dentary. Immature, nonspecific gender.
Ursus americanus, metapodial, distal end. Old adult female.
Odocoileus hemionus, left radius, partial distal articulation; left astragalus fragment; left humerus, distal articulation; right tibia, partial proximal shaft, partial distal shaft; left humerus, distal shaft; phalanx, 2 No. 3; left ulna, proximal head with fragmentary shaft. Adult female.
Antilocapra americana, phalanx No. 1, distal end. Adult male.

Block 61-D
Sample 628 (Fill)
Sylvilagus sp., left tibia, diaphysis; innominate (2 fragments). Immature, nonspecific gender.
Lepus californicus, right tibia, partial proximal articulation; right humerus, partial proximal articulation; vertebra C-1. Adult female.
Odocoileus hemionus, right femur, partial distal shaft; right tibia, partial proximal diaphysis. Immature, nonspecific gender.
Odocoileus hemionus, left radius, proximal articulation (2 fragments). Adult female.
Antilocapra americana, left metatarsal, fragmentary proximal shaft. Adult male.

Block 62-A
Sample 629 (Fill)
Buteo jamaïcensis, left ulna minus proximal shaft. Adult male.
Urocyon cinereoargenteus, left auditory bulla and temporal fragment. Immature, nonspecific gender.
Canis familiaris, metacarpal No. 4. Nonspecific age or gender.
Antilocapra americana, metapodial, distal epiphysis; rib fragment. Immature, nonspecific gender.

Sample 630 (Fill)
Accipitridae sp., *Buteo*-sized hawk, pedal phalanx. Immature, nonspecific gender.

Block 62-C
Sample 613 (Fill)
Lepus californicus, rib, proximal articulation. Adult, nonspecific gender.
Canis latrans, right dentary with carnassial; left radius, diaphysis. Nonspecific age or gender.
Odocoileus hemionus, right radius fragments; rib fragment. Immature, nonspecific gender.

Block 62-D
Sample 631 (Fill)
Odocoileus hemionus, right scapula minus distal blade. Adult male.
Odocoileus hemionus, right tibia, distal articulation; thoracic vertebra; ischium fragment (burned); antler tine; phalanx No. 3 (burned). Adult male.
Antilocapra americana, phalanx No. 1. Adult female.

APPENDIX 9: TABLE 1. *(continued)*

Block 63-A
Sample 608 (Fill)
Corvus corax, right coracoid, central shaft fragment. Immature, nonspecific gender.
Sylvilagus sp., right tibia, proximal articulation. Adult female.
Odocoileus hemionus, right dentary fragment; right femur, partial proximal shaft. Adult male.
Odocoileus hemionus, right dentary minus ascending ramus. Old adult female.
Odocoileus hemionus, thoracic vertebra; metacarpal, distal articulation; left scapula, partial head and proximal blade with spine fragment. Young adult.
Artiodactyla sp., right femur, shaft fragment. Neonate.

RO locus

House A
Sample 1 (Fill)
Odocoileus hemionus, left metatarsal, distal shaft fragment (burned); right acetabulum; innominate fragment; left humerus, shaft fragment with nutrient foramen. Adult female.

Sample 2 (Fill)
Odocoileus hemionus, right tibia, anterior shaft fragment (calcined); miscellaneous long bone fragments (9). Adult male.
Odocoileus hemionus, right humerus, distal fragment; right ischium, burned fragments (2); rib (burned). Nonspecific age or gender.

Sample 3 (Fill)
Artiodactyla sp., long bone shaft fragment.

Sample 4 (Fill)
Odocoileus hemionus, left metatarsal, 3/4's of the distal articulation (burned), long bone shaft fragment (burned). Adult male.

Sample 5 (Floor fill)
Lepus californicus, metatarsal. Adult female.

Sample 6 (Floor)
Artiodactyla sp., long bone shaft fragment.

Sample 7 (Floor — Posthole 2)
Sylvilagus sp., right and left femurs; right dentary, partial transverse ramus; right tibia, proximal epiphysis. Immature adult.

Sample 80 (Fill)
Antilocapra americana, right ulna, partial proximal articulation; long bone shaft fragments. Adult female.

House B
Sample 8 (Fill)
Thomomys bottae, right dentary.

Sample 9 (Fill)
Odocoileus hemionus, right metatarsal No. 3, distal head and partial shaft fragment (burned); Lumbar vertebra minus epiphyses. Immature adult male.

Sample 10 (Fill)
Sylvilagus sp., left tibia; fragmentary fibula shaft; innominate fragment. Adult female.
Odocoileus hemionus, left tibia, distal end; right ulna, proximal articulation and shaft fragment; left metacarpal, partial proximal head and shaft fragment; innominate fragment; vertebra fragment; rib fragment; unidentifiable long bone shaft fragments. Nonspecific age or gender.
Odocoileus hemionus, right ulna, proximal articulation and shaft fragment. Adult female.

Sample 11 (Floor)
Lepus californicus, metatarsal. Adult male.
Lepus californicus, lumbar vertebra. Immature female.
Sylvilagus floridanus (?), cranium fragment.
Artiodactyla sp., long bone shaft fragment; rib fragment.

Sample 12 (Fill)
Lepus californicus, lumbar vertebra. Adult female.
Sylvilagus sp., left tibia, distal diaphysis. Immature, nonspecific gender.
Odocoileus hemionus, phalanx No. 2. Young adult, female (?).

APPENDIX 9: TABLE 1. *(continued)*

Sample 75 (Fill)
Odocoileus hemionus, left tibia, proximal articulation (burned). Adult female.

House C
Sample 13 (Fill)
Lepus californicus, right tibia shaft fragment; fragmentary fibula. Adult female.
Odocoileus hemionus, right humerus, distal articulation and shaft fragment; rib fragment. Adult female.

Sample 14 (Fill)
Lepus californicus, femur fragment, proximal articulation and shaft. Adult male.
Sylvilagus sp., left tibia fragment, proximal articulation and shaft. Adult male.
Sylvilagus sp., left tibia shaft fragment. Adult male.
Odocoileus hemionus, left humerus, proximal articulation; phalanx No. 1; right scapula, proximal articulation (burned); left tibia, shaft fragment; left scapula, proximal articulation. Adult female.
Odocoileus hemionus, metapodial, fragment of distal diaphysis. Immature, nonspecific gender.

Sample 15 (Fill)
Sylvilagus sp., right femur, articulation surface. Adult female.
Odocoileus hemionus, left radius, distal shaft fragment (burned); fragmentary ribs (3); phalanx No. 2; long bone shaft fragments. Adult female.
Lepus californicus, metatarsal; left dentary; cranium fragment. Adult female.

Sample 16 (Fill)
Lepus californicus, left dentary fragment; left ulna, proximal articulation; right radius, proximal articulation. Adult male.
Sylvilagus sp., right humerus, proximal articulation; metatarsals (5); right and left tibia fragments; left innominate.
Rodentia sp., right innominate fragment.
Odocoileus hemionus, left humerus, distal articulation; left metatarsals No. 3 and No. 4, fragments of proximal shafts (burned); rib; long bone shaft fragment. Adult male.
Odocoileus hemionus, vertebra, T-5 (?) fragment. Young adult male.

Sample 17 (Floor fill)
Artiodactyla sp., scapula, blade fragment (burned).

Sample 18 (Floor)
Artiodactyla sp., long bone shaft fragment.

Sample 19 (Floor – Posthole 8)
Mammalia sp., unknown element.

Sample 20 (Floor fill)
Sylvilagus sp., left dentary fragment with 1 tooth, transverse ramus. Immature, nonspecific gender.

Sample 21 (Floor)
Sylvilagus sp., right ulna. Adult male.

Sample 22 (Floor)
Lepus californicus, dentary 3 right and 1 left plus 29 fragments from one individual; dentary 2 left and 1 right plus 1 fragment from a second individual; right ulna (2) plus fragments; right innominate; right humerus; metatarsals (3), fragmentary cranium; calcanea (2); lumbar vertebra fragment; left humerus, distal fragment. Two adult females, 1 adult male.
Sylvilagus sp., femurs 1 right and 2 left; right innominates (2); maxillae (2); dentary 5 right and 1 left; metatarsals (6); scapula 1 right and 1 left; right tibia (2); lumbar vertebra (1). Five adult males.
Thomomys bottae, right dentary.
Thomomys bottae, right dentary fragment.
Odocoileus hemionus, left scapula, neck and blade fragment (burned); tibia fragment, distal end; ribs (2); cranium fragment; long bone fragments (7). Adult female.
Odocoileus virginianus, metatarsals No. 3 and No. 4 (burned). Young adult male.

Sample 23 (Floor – Posthole 3)
Lepus californicus, femur, shaft fragment. Adult.
Odocoileus hemionus, metatarsals No. 3 and No. 4, distal articulation fragments; scapula blade fragments (4). Adult female.

APPENDIX 9: TABLE 1. *(continued)*

Sample 24 (Floor – Posthole 13)
Thomomys bottae, right dentary.

Sample 25 (Floor – Posthole 15)
Sylvilagus sp., calcaneum; metatarsal. Adult male.

Sample 26 (Floor – Posthole 20)
Odocoileus hemionus, left femur, distal shaft fragment. Adult male.
Sylvilagus sp., lumbar vertebra. Immature female.

House D
Sample 27 (Fill)
Odocoileus hemionus, right dentary, anterion end and nutrient foramen. Adult male.

Sample 28 (Fill)
Odocoileus hemionus, femur, shaft fragment; rib fragment; thoracic vertebra fragment. Adult female.

Sample 29 (Fill)
Odocoileus hemionus, antler fragment; right metacarpal, proximal shaft fragment; tibia, shaft fragment; left femur. Adult female.
Lepus californicus, left femur. Adult female.

Sample 30 (Floor fill)
Meleagris gallopavo, right ulna, proximal head. Adult female.
Lepus californicus, metatarsal. Adult male.
Thomomys bottae, cranium fragment.
Odocoileus hemionus, left humerus, shaft fragment; phalanx fragments; femur shaft fragment. Adult female.
Odocoileus hemionus, phalanx No. 1. Adult male.

Sample 31 (Floor)
Meleagris gallopavo, left ulna, shaft fragment. Adult female.
Odocoileus hemionus, right scapula, proximal blade fragment. Young adult male.

Sample 32 (Floor)
Icterus (?) Comment: larger than Red-winged Blackbird. left carpometacarpus – very fragmentary.
Sylvilagus sp., metatarsals (2); right dentary fragments (2); metacarpal. Adult female.
Neotoma albigula (?), left innominate.

Sample 36 (Fill)
Artiodactyla sp., long bone shaft fragment.

Sample 74 (Fill)
Odocoileus hemionus, right femur, proximal shaft, posterior face. Adult.

Sample 79 (Fill)
Antilocapra americana, right humerus, proximal shaft (burned). Adult male (?).

House E
Sample 33 (Fill)
Meleagris gallopavo, tarsometatarsus, shaft fragment. Young adult male.
Mammalia sp., dentary. Fetal or neonate.
Lepus californicus, astragalus; left tibia. Adult male.
Sylvilagus, left scapula. Adult male.
Thomomys bottae, left dentary.
Odocoileus hemionus, phalanx No. 1; cranium fragment; vertebra fragment; rib fragments (3). Immature, nonspecific gender.
Odocoileus hemionus, left tibia, distal end; rib; vertebrae; right and left dentaries; calcaneum; carpals (2); phalanx, 3 No. 1; phalanx, 3 No. 3. Adult female.

Sample 34 (Fill)
Lepus californicus, rib. Adult.
Canis latrans, right ulna, proximal diaphysis. Immature, nonspecific gender.
Odocoileus hemionus, cranium and antler fragment; rib fragments (4); right calcaneum. Adult male.

Appendix 9: Table 1. *(continued)*

Sample 35 (Fill)
Odocoileus hemionus, right metatarsal No. 4, proximal articulation. Adult female.
Antilocapra americana, right ulna, proximal head. Adult female.

Sample 37 (Fill)
Thomomys bottae, cranium.
Artiodactyla sp., long bone shaft fragments.

Sample 77 (Fill)
Artiodactyla sp., long bone shaft fragment; rib fragment; partial phalanx. Adult.

Sample 81 (Fill)
Odocoileus hemionus, phalanx No. 3; long bone shaft fragment. Adult.
House F

Sample 38 (Fill)
Canis latrans, right ulna, proximal head; right C and M^1. Adult male.
Antilocapra americana, left humerus, distal end. Adult female.

Sample 39 (Fill)
Odocoileus hemionus, right tibia, proximal shaft fragment; phalanx No. 3, right ulna, proximal articulation and shaft fragment; 2 fragments caudal vertebra (burned). Adult female.

Sample 40 (Fill)
Mammalia sp., long bone shaft fragment. Adult.
Odocoileus hemionus, right metatarsal No. 3 and No. 4, proximal shaft fragment with partial head (burned). Adult.

Sample 41 (Fill)
Mammalia sp., caudal vertebra (burned).
Odocoileus hemionus, left femur, proximal shaft; right tarsal fragment. Adult male.
Antilocapra americana, right femur, diaphysis. Neonate.

Sample 42 (Floor fill)
Lepus californicus, right femur, distal trochanter; left tibia minus distal shaft; pedal phalanx. Adult female.
Thomomys bottae, left femur.

Sample 43 (Posthole 4)
Lepus californicus, right tibia minus distal shaft. Adult female.
Artiodactyla sp., long bone shaft fragment.

Sample 44 (Posthole 5)
Artiodactyla sp., long bone shaft fragment (burned).

House G
Sample 45 (Fill)
Mammalia sp., long bone shaft fragment (calcined). Adult.
Odocoileus hemionus, left radius, proximal shaft; vertebra T-6. Adult female.
Antilocapra americana, left tibia, proximal medial shaft fragment. Adult female.

Sample 46 (Fill)
Corvus cryptoleucus, left humerus, distal end. Adult female.
Artiodactyla sp., left scapula, proximal blade fragment. Neonate.
Odocoileus hemionus, right ilium fragment; right tibia, distal shaft fragment. Adult male.
Antilocapra americana, left scapula, proximal blade fragment; phalanx No. 1. Adult male.

Sample 47 (Fill)
Thomomys bottae, cranium. Immature, nonspecific gender.
Odocoileus hemionus, right metatarsal No. 4, distal condyle (burned); rib. Adult male.
Lepus californicus, vertebra fragment. Adult male.

Sample 69 (Fill)
Antilocapra americana, phalanx No. 1. Adult female.

Appendix 9: Table 1. *(continued)*

Sample 76 (Fill)
Odocoileus hemionus, left ulna, proximal articulation and shaft fragment; long bone shaft fragment. Adult male.

House H
Sylvilagus sp., right femur, distal end and shaft fragment. Adult male.
Artiodactyla sp., long bone fragment, cranium fragment.
Odocoileus hemionus, right humerus, shaft fragment. Adult female.

Sample 50 (Fill)
Citellus variegatus, right and left humeri; right and left scapulae; right and left dentaries; right and left ulnae; vertebrae (9). Adult.
Odocoileus hemionus, left radius, partial proximal articulation with shaft fragment; antler fragment; 2 pedal phalanges; rib fragment; right femur shaft fragment. Adult male.
Antilocapra americana, left M^3. Adult male.
Sample 51 (Floor fill)
Artiodactyla sp., long bone shaft fragment.

Sample 52 (Doorway)
Mammalia sp., unknown elements.
Sylvilagus sp., left dentary, transverse ramus.
Lepus californicus, right dentary minus ascending ramus. Adult female.
Citellus variegatus, right femur, proximal articulation head. Adult.

Sample 63 (Fill)
Citellus variegatus, cranium. Adult.

Sample 82 (Fill)
Artiodactyla sp., scapula, blade fragment; long bone shaft fragment.

House I
Sample 53 (Fill)
Sylvilagus sp., left ischium. Immature, nonspecific gender.
Thomomys bottae, cranium.
Odocoileus hemionus, cranium fragment; right radius, distal end; right metatarsal, distal end. Adult male.
Antilocapra americana, right metatarsal, proximal head and shaft fragment; left tibia, proximal shaft and head (burned); left ulna, proximal head; phalanx No. 1; phalanx No. 3. Adult male.

Sample 54 (Floor fill)
Odocoileus hemionus, right dentary. Old adult female.
Odocoileus hemionus, left metacarpals; lumbar vertebra and epiphyses. Immature, nonspecific gender.
Odocoileus hemionus, antler tine; left tibia, shaft fragment with nutrient foramen. Adult male.
Sample 85 (Floor fill)
Odocoileus hemionus, left femur, distal shaft. Adult.

House J
Sample 55 (Fill)
Sylvilagus sp., left femur, proximal head; metatarsal. Adult male.
Odocoileus hemionus, right femur, proximal shaft; antler fragment (burned); right rib, proximal articulation. Adult male.
Odocoileus hemionus, right tibia, partial proximal shaft fragment (burned). Immature, nonspecific gender.

Sample 64 (Fill)
Sylvilagus sp., right humerus, shaft fragment. Adult male (?).
Lepus californicus, left humerus, distal shaft fragment (burned). Adult female.
Odocoileus hemionus, left ulna, articulation head and shaft fragment; left metatarsal No. 3, proximal head and shaft fragment; left dentary, partial transverse ramus.

Sample 65 (Floor fill)
Thomomys bottae (?), cranium fragment, anterior.

Sample 70 (Floor fill)
Odocoileus hemionus, right metatarsal No. 4, distal end (burned). Adult female.

Appendix 9: Table 1. *(continued)*

Sample 71 (Doorway fill)
Odocoileus hemionus, left metatarsal No. 3, proximal shaft fragment (burned). Adult male.

Sample 78 (Fill)
Artiodactyla sp., long bone shaft fragment. Adult.

House K
Sample 66 (Fill)
Odocoileus hemionus, right ulna, proximal head fragment (burned); metapodial, partial distal head (burned); phalanx No. 1. Adult female.

Sample 67 (Fill)
Odocoileus hemionus, right metatarsal No. 4, distal articulation head (burned). Adult male.
Antilocapra americana, right ulna, proximal articulation head and shaft fragment. Adult male.

Sample 68 (Floor fill)
Sylvilagus sp., left scapula fragment. Adult male.
Odocoileus hemionus, right and left calcanea; phalanx No. 1; left metatarsal No. 4, distal shaft (burned); right and left tibiae fragments; right ischium; left femur, shaft fragment; vertebra fragment; right radius shaft fragments (2). Adult male.

Sample 72 (Fill)
Odocoileus hemionus, right maxilla, P^3 - M^3 + P^2; left femur with fragmentary shaft and nutrient foramen. Adult, female (?).

Sample 86 (Floor)
Artiodactyla sp., long bone shaft fragment. Adult.

Faunal Material in Association with Ridout Burials

Burial 3
Sample 61 (Fill)
Odocoileus hemionus, right astragalus; right femur, medial shaft fragment. Adult female.

Burial 5
Sample 83 (Fill)
Artiodactyla sp., long bone shaft fragment.

Burial 5
Sample 88
Sylvilagus sp., right femur, distal articulation and shaft fragment. Adult male.

Burial 7
Sample 62 (Fill)
Artiodactyla sp., long bone shaft fragment. Adult.

Burial 7
Sample 84 (Fill)
Artiodactyla sp., scapula fragment.

Burial 7
Sample 89
Odocoileus hemionus, left ulna, proximal head (burned). Adult male.

Burial 8
Sample 90 (Floor)
Lepus californicus, right femur, distal articulation and shaft fragment. Adult male.
Odocoileus hemionus, right femur, medial shaft fragment. Adult female.

Excavation Blocks

Block E2W
Sample 56 (Fill)
Antilocapra americana, left metatarsals No. 3 and No. 4, distal ends and shaft fragments, partial proximal articulation surfaces.

Appendix 9: Table 1. *(continued)*

Block E2W
Sample 58 (Trench)
Odocoileus hemionus, right acetabulum; ischium; ilium. Adult female.

Block G
Sample 57 (Fill)
Odocoileus hemionus, cranium fragment; long bone shaft fragment; rib fragment.

Surface

Sample 87
Lepus californicus, left dentary. Adult female.

APPENDIX 9: TABLE 2. Utilitarian Bone Tools

Reference No.			*Antilocapra americana*	Artiodactyla	Aves	*Canis* spp.	*Felis concolor*	*Lepus* spp.	*Lynx rufus*	*Odocoileus* spp.	*Odocoileus hemionus*	*Odocoileus virginianus*	*Sylvilagus* spp.	Total
229	Awls	Artiodactyl metatarsal awls, unsplit									1	1		2
230		Artiodactyl metatarsal awls, split	1								41			42
231		Artiodactyl metapodial awls, split								6	35	1		42
232		Ulna awls							1		2			3
233		Artiodactyl splinter awls	1	1						15	11			28
234		Femur awls					1				2			3
235		Rabbit tibia awls						1					1	2
235A		Split tibia awls	1							1	2			4
236		Unclassified awl tips		35	1						4			40
237		Unclassified awl shafts		66							3			69
238		Ulna chisels/ Polishers/ Scrapers/ Plaiting tools	1			1				1	6			9
239		Artiodactyl rib fleshers		1						2				3
239A	Spatulate tools	Artiodactyl vertebra fleshers								3				3
240		Artiodactyl splinter								3	1	1		5
241	Fleshers	Unclassified spatulate tools								8				8
242	Antler tine tools	Flakers/ Punches								10				10
Total			4	103	1	1	1	1	1	49	108	3	1	273

APPENDIX 9: TABLE 3. Utilitarian and Worked Bone

Utilitarian Bone

No.	Overall Measurements Wt. (gm)	L. (cm)	W. (cm)	Th. (cm)	Tip Measurements L. (cm)	W. (cm)	Th. (cm)	Material	Provenience	Remarks
Reference No. 229 – Type IB1a2'										
Complete Artiodactyla Metatarsus (Distal) Piercing Tools—Fragments										
WM 588	36.2+	11.7+	3.4	2.0	–	–	–	*O. hemionus*	Block 13–B, fill	Dorsal split
WM 1184	23.0+	11.6+	3.0	1.8				*O. virginianus*	House X, fill	Dorsal split, broken edge reused
Reference No. 230 – Type IB1b1'										
Split Artiodactyla Metatarsus (Distal) Piercing Tools—Complete										
WM 324	5.2+	5.8+	2.1	1.1	–	–	–	*O. hemionus*	House D, fill	Burned
WM 359	9.2	7.5	2.3	1.6	2.4	0.8	0.5	*O. hemionus*	House H, fill	Shouldered
WM 1204	8.8	8.0	2.2	1.7	1.9	1.0	0.6	*O. hemionus*	House AA, floor fill	
WM 1206	6.4	6.2	2.1	1.4	1.1	0.8	0.6	*O. hemionus*	House BB, floor	
WM 1744	11.2	15.4	2.2	1.5	0.7	0.2	0.2	*O. hemionus*	House DD, floor fill	
WM 2054	9.2+	6.5+	2.2	1.5	–	–	–	*O. hemionus*	House PP, fill	
WM 2055	10.4	8.1	2.3	1.6	0.5	0.5	0.4	*O. hemionus*	House PP, fill	Shouldered
WM 2056	9.8	16.1	2.0	1.4	1.0	0.4	0.4	*O. hemionus*	House PP, fill	Shouldered
WM 2270	13.6	13.5	2.2	1.6	1.2	0.4	0.4	*O. hemionus*	House UU, fill	Shouldered
WM 2415	8.6	8.7	2.1	1.5	1.5	0.4	0.4	*O. hemionus*	House UU, floor fill	Shouldered
WM 2767	11.4	9.8	2.2	1.6	1.4	0.6	0.5	*O. hemionus*	House AF, floor fill	Shouldered
WM 2921	7.4	6.2	2.1	1.6	0.9	0.5	0.5	*O. hemionus*	House AM, fill	Burned, shouldered
WM 3021	4.8	7.6	3.1	2.0	1.0	0.4	0.4	*O. hemionus*	House AO, fill	Burned
WM/B 214& 239	11.8	11.1	2.3	1.6	1.0	0.3	0.3	*O. hemionus*	Block 61–A, fill	Shouldered
RO 237	9.8	7.8	2.1	1.6	0.7	0.3	0.3	*O. hemionus*	Block K1E, fill	Shouldered
RO/B 13& 14	18.2	21.1	2.3	1.8	1.7	0.4	0.4	*O. hemionus*	House F, floor fill	Shouldered
Reference No. 230 – Type IB1b2'										
Split Artiodactyla Metatarsus (Distal) Piercing Tools—Fragments										
WM/B 6	6.8+	5.6+	2.2	1.6	–	–	–	*O. hemionus*	House H, fill	Burned
WM/B 20	5.0+	4.2+	2.2	1.5	–	–	–	*O. hemionus*	House H, fill	Burned, shouldered

APPENDIX 9: TABLE 3. *(continued)*

No.	Overall Measurements Wt. (gm)	L. (cm)	W. (cm)	Th. (cm)	Tip Measurements L. (cm)	W. (cm)	Th. (cm)	Material	Provenience	Remarks
WM/B 21	9.6+	7.0+	2.2	1.7	–	–	–	*O. hemionus*	House H, fill	Shouldered
WM/B 26	3.2+	2.4+	2.0	1.4	–	–	–	*O. hemionus*	Block 11–D, fill	Burned
WM/B 27	6.8+	5.5+	2.3	1.3	–	–	–	*O. hemionus*	House K, fill	Burned
WM/B 40& 99	11.2+	10.0+	2.1	1.6	–	–	–	*O. hemionus*	House EE, fill Block 13–A, fill	Shouldered, immature
WM/B 56	4.8+	3.6+	1.7	1.2	–	–	–	*O. hemionus*	Block 28–C, fill	Burned
WM/B 78	9.6+	8.1+	2.0	1.5	–	–	–	*O. hemionus*	House Y, fill	Burned
WM/B 95	3.2+	3.7+	2.0	1.4	–	–	–	*O. hemionus*	House DD, fill	Burned
WM/B 100	4.8+	3.9+	2.1	1.5	–	–	–	*O. hemionus*	Block 21–D, fill	Burned
WM/B 107	4.0+	2.8+	2.1	1.9	–	–	–	*O. hemionus*	House X, fill	Burned
WM/B 108	3.4+	2.5+	2.3+	1.5	–	–	–	*O. hemionus*	House X, entry fill	Burned
WM/B 113	3.4+	2.4+	2.0	1.5	–	–	–	*O. hemionus*	House X, floor fill	Burned
WM/B 117	4.8+	5.1+	1.9	1.3	–	–	–	*O. hemionus*	House FF, fill	Burned, shouldered
WM/B 118	6.8+	8.0+	1.9	1.3	–	–	–	*O. hemionus*	House FF, fill	Burned
WM/B 124	5.2+	3.6+	2.2	1.6	–	–	–	*O. hemionus*	House DD, fill	Burned
WM/B 125	7.2+	4.9+	2.4	1.8	–	–	–	*O. hemionus*	House DD, floor	Burned, shouldered
WM/B 150	3.8+	2.3+	2.2	1.5+	–	–	–	*O. hemionus*	House PP, fill	Immature
WM/B 178	5.0+	3.7+	2.0	1.4	–	–	–	*O. hemionus*	House UU, fill	Burned, shouldered
WM/B 183	2.4+	1.9+	1.9	1.2	–	–	–	*A. americana*	House SS, fill	Burned
WM/B 192	7.0+	7.4+	2.2	1.7	–	–	–	*O. hemionus*	Block 54–D, fill	Shouldered
WM/B 193	7.4+	4.1+	2.3	1.6	–	–	–	*O. hemionus*	Block 62–A, fill	Shouldered
WM/B 200	1.6+	1.8+	2.1+	1.0+	–	–	–	*O. hemionus*	Block 54–A, fill	Burned
WM/B 206	8.0+	4.9+	2.2	1.7	–	–	–	*O. hemionus*	House AC, fill	Shouldered
WM/B 243	6.0+	6.5+	2.2	1.3+	–	–	–	*O. hemionus*	Burial 101	
RO/B 16	4.5+	2.8+	2.0	1.5	–	–	–	*O. hemionus*	House C, floor fill	
Reference No. 231 – Type IB1c' Split Artiodactyla Metapodia (Proximal) Piercing Tools—Complete										
WM 391	11.0	11.2	1.7	0.9	1.0	0.3	0.3	*O. hemionus*	Burial 13	R. metacarpal no. 4
WM 506	10.6	18.4	1.5	1.1	1.5	0.3	0.3	*O. hemionus*	Block 12–D, fill	R. metatarsal no. 3
WM 605	9.4	14.6	1.2	0.8	1.1	0.4	0.4	*O. virginianus*	Block 19–B, fill	R. metatarsal no. 4
WM 715	11.6	17.8	1.0	0.8	1.2	0.4	0.4	*O. hemionus*	House Q, fill	R. metatarsal no. 4

Appendix 9: Table 3. *(continued)*

No.	Overall Measurements Wt. (gm)	L. (cm)	W. (cm)	Th. (cm)	Tip Measurements L. (cm)	W. (cm)	Th. (cm)	Material	Provenience	Remarks
WM 929	5.6	11.6	1.4	0.9	0.9	0.4	0.4	*O. hemionus*	House V, fill	R. metatarsal no. 4
WM 1675	13.2	16.2	1.5	0.9	0.7	0.4	0.4	*O. hemionus*	House FF, fill	
WM 1798	6.4	8.0	1.6	0.8	0.4	0.3	0.3	*O. hemionus*	House DD, floor	
WM 1804	13.4	20.7	1.3	0.8	0.9	0.4	0.4	*O. hemionus*	House GG, fill	
WM 1815	9.4	14.9	1.2	0.7	0.9	0.3	0.3	*O. hemionus*	House II, floor fill	L. metatarsal no. 4
WM 1886	8.2	10.3	1.3	1.0	0.6	0.3	0.3	*Odocoileus* sp.	Pit 41, fill	
WM 1893	3.6	7.8	1.1	0.9	0.7	0.3	0.3	*Odocoileus* sp.	Block 30–C, fill	
WM 1898	8.6+	10.6	1.6+	0.9	1.1	0.4	0.4	*Odocoileus* sp.	House KK, fill	
WM 2271	4.8	6.5	1.5	1.1	0.6	0.4	0.4	*O. hemionus*	House UU, fill	R. metacarpal no. 4
WM 2339	17.6	17.3	1.8	1.0	1.1	0.3	0.3	*O. hemionus*	Block 53–B, fill	L. metatarsal no. 4
WM 2832	11.2	20.4	1.5	0.9	1.4	0.3	0.3	*O. hemionus*	House AF, floor	Artifact 2
WM 3005	6.6	13.5	0.9	0.7	1.1	0.3	0.3	*O. hemionus*	House AP, fill	L. metatarsal no. 3
WM/B 158	10.8+	9.8	1.8	1.3	0.9	0.4+	0.4+	*O. hemionus*	House PP, fill	
RO 154	10.4	10.3	1.7	0.8	0.7	0.4	0.4	*O. hemionus*	House H, floor	Artifact 1
RO 170	8.6	17.6	1.2	0.7	0.5	0.2	0.2	*O. hemionus*	House J, fill	Burned, L. metatarsal no. 4

Reference No. 231 – Type IB1c2'
Split Artiodactyla Metapodia (Proximal) Piercing Tools—Fragmentary

No.	Wt. (gm)	L. (cm)	W. (cm)	Th. (cm)	Tip L. (cm)	Tip W. (cm)	Tip Th. (cm)	Material	Provenience	Remarks
WM 27	8.4	9.2+	1.8	1.3	–	–	–	*O. hemionus*	House A, fill	
WM 619	7.2+	7.7+	1.6	0.9	–	–	–	*O. hemionus*	Block 19–B, fill	
WM/B 2	2.8+	3.1+	1.7	1.2	–	–	–	*O. hemionus*	House B, fill	
WM/B 3	4.6+	3.8+	1.9	1.4	–	–	–	*Odocoileus* sp.	House G, fill	Burned
WM/B 32	14.2+	15.9+	1.4	0.9	–	–	–	*O. hemionus*	Burial 11, fill	Metatarsal no. 3
WM/B 43	3.0+	3.1+	1.4	1.2	–	–	–	*O. hemionus*	Block 19–B, fill	
WM/B 60	4.8+	4.0+	1.8	0.8	–	–	–	*O. hemionus*	House Q, fill	Burned
WM/B 61	14.2+	12.2+	1.6	1.2	–	–	–	*O. hemionus*	Block 35–B, fill	Metatarsal no. 3
WM/B 62	6.4+	8.6+	1.2	0.7	–	–	–	*O. hemionus*	Block 44–B, fill	
WM/B 67	1.8+	2.0+	1.6	0.9	–	–	–	*O. hemionus*	House U, fill	Burned
WM/B 72	9.6+	8.3+	1.5	1.0	–	–	–	*O. hemionus*	House W, fill	
WM/B 96	3.6+	4.9+	1.2	0.8	–	–	–	*O. hemionus*	House DD, fill	Burned
WM/B 101	2.8+	4.4+	1.7	0.8	–	–	–	*O. hemionus*	House X, fill	

APPENDIX 9: TABLE 3. *(continued)*

	Overall Measurements				Tip Measurements					
No.	Wt. (gm)	L. (cm)	W. (cm)	Th. (cm)	L. (cm)	W. (cm)	Th. (cm)	Material	Provenience	Remarks
WM/B 114	5.6+	6.6+	1.7+	0.9+	–	–	–	*Odocoileus* sp.	House DD, floor fill	
WM/B 129	4.6+	8.3+	1.2	0.8	–	–	–	*O. hemionus*	House DD, floor fill	Burned
WM/B 147	2.4+	3.8+	1.4	0.5	–	–	–	*O. hemionus*	Block 37–D, fill	
WM/B 149	2.2+	3.0+	1.4	1.0	–	–	–	*O. hemionus*	House PP, fill	Burned
WM/B 167	3.0+	3.8+	1.6	0.8	–	–	–	*O. hemionus*	House QQ, fill	Burned
WM/B 199	2.0+	3.5+	1.4	0.8	–	–	–	*O. hemionus*	Block 53–D, fill	Burned
WM/B 202	4.8+	7.9+	1.2+	0.6+	–	–	–	*Odocoileus* sp.	Block 54–C, fill	
WM/B 234	2.8+	5.3+	1.1	0.9	–	–	–	*O. hemionus*	House AJ, fill	Burned
WM/B 251	3.8+	7.7+	1.0	0.2	–	–	–	*O. hemionus*	Pit Oven 18	
RO/B 12	6.4+	8.2+	1.5	0.8	–	–	–	*O. hemionus*	House F, floor fill	Side–notched
Reference No. 232 – Type IB1d1' Ulnae Piercing Tools—Complete										
WM 205	8.8+	11.6+	1.9	1.3	–	–	–	*L. rufus*	House G, fill	Immature
WM 341	18.4	11.2	3.8	2.2	0.5	0.8	0.3	*O. hemionus*	House D, floor	Artifact 18, immature
WM 1237	27.8	11.5	3.8	1.9	0.9	0.5	0.4	*O. hemionus*	House AA, floor	
Reference No. 233 – Type IB1e1' Artiodactyla Splinter Piercing Tools—Complete										
WM 42	16.2+	12.0+	1.8	1.4	–	–	–	*O. hemionus*	House B, floor	L. tibia
WM 249	5.6	8.9	1.0	0.5	1.3	0.5	0.5	*O. hemionus*	Pit 3, fill	Metatarsal
WM 459	4.6	8.2	0.8	0.6	1.3	0.4	0.4	*O. hemionus*	House L, floor fill	Metatarsal
WM 604	3.8	11.4	0.8	0.5	2.5	0.3	0.3	*Odocoileus* sp.	Block 19–B, fill	
WM 770	14.8	16.4	1.6	0.8	2.2	0.8	0.5	*O. hemionus*	Room 12, floor	R. metatarsal no. 4
WM 782	4.2+	8.7+	0.8	0.6	–	–	–	*Odocoileus* sp.	House S, fill	Burned
WM 879	5.4	7.9	1.6	0.8	1.4	0.7	0.4	*Odocoileus* sp.	Block 44–C, fill	Metapodial
WM 1148	2.0	6.3	1.3	0.7	1.5	0.5	0.3	*Odocoileus* sp.	House AA, fill	
WM 1178	8.0	9.9	1.3	0.7	0.9	0.4	0.3	*O. hemionus*	House X, fill	Metatarsal
WM 1867	6.2	10.5	1.4	0.8	1.4	0.4	0.3	*O. hemionus*	House GG, floor fill	Metatarsal no. 3/4
WM 2230	8.6	9.4	1.6	0.9	0.7	0.4	0.2	*A. americana*	Block 62–C, fill	L. tibia
WM 2585	8.6	10.8	1.5	0.7	1.5	0.5	0.4	*O. hemionus*	House AC, fill	Burned, R. metatarsals no. 3/4
WM 2747	3.4	6.2	1.8	0.6	0.7	0.5	0.3	*Odocoileus* sp.	House AF, fill	
WM/B 51	7.0+	10.8	1.7	0.8	1.4	0.7	0.5	*O. hemionus*	House M, floor fill	R. metatarsal no. 4
WM/B 130	7.4	9.7	1.7	0.8	1.1	0.5	0.4	*O. hemionus*	House DD, floor fill	R. tibia, burned
WM/B 229	3.6	7.9	0.9	0.5	0.9	0.5	0.4	*Odcoileus* sp.	House AG, fill	

APPENDIX 9: TABLE 3. *(continued)*

No.	Overall Measurements Wt. (gm)	L. (cm)	W. (cm)	Th. (cm)	Tip Measurements L. (cm)	W. (cm)	Th. (cm)	Material	Provenience	Remarks
WM/B 244C	0.8+	4.0+	0.8+	0.6+	–	–	–	*Artiodactyla* sp.	House AI, fill	Burned, rib
RO/B 15	5.0+	7.9+	1.0	0.7	0.3+	0.2	0.2	*Odocoileus* sp.	House G, fill	Burned
RO/B 20	3.8+	6.5	1.2+	1.0	1.0	0.5	0.4	*O. hemionus*	House J, floor fill	Burned, metatarsal
RO/B 22	3.2	5.9	1.1	0.5	1.0	0.5	0.4	*Odocoileus* sp.	House K, floor fill	
Reference No. 233 – Type IB1e2' Artiodactyla Splinter Piercing Tools—Fragments										
WM/B 79	3.8+	4.0+	1.3	1.1	–	–	–	*O. hemionus*	House Y, fill	Burned, antler
WM/B 122	4.6+	7.4+	1.0	0.8	–	–	–	*Odocoileus* sp.	House DD, floor fill	
WM/B 135	4.2+	7.2+	1.0	0.6	–	–	–	*Odocoileus* sp.	Block 29–C, fill	
WM/B 212	1.8+	5.1+	0.9	0.5	–	–	–	*Odocoileus* sp.	House AB, fill	
WM/B 216	2.6+	5.4+	1.2	0.5	–	–	–	*Odocoileus* sp.	House AF, fill	
WM/B 254	3.8+	4.6+	1.3	0.9	–	–	–	*Odocoileus* sp.	Pit Oven 18	Burned
RO/B 10	3.0+	3.8+	1.5	0.5	–	–	–	*Odocoileus* sp.	House F, fill	
RO/B 24	2.4+	4.6+	1.1	0.7	–	–	–	*Odocoileus* sp.	House K, floor fill	
Reference No. 234 – Type IB1f1' Artiodactyla Femur Piercing Tools—Complete										
WM 344& WM/B 18	37.2	21.7	2.4	0.4	1.0	0.8	0.4	*F. concolor*	House D, floor	L. femur
WM 325	12.4+	12.5+	1.3+	0.9+	1.2	0.9	0.5	*O. hemionus*	House D, fill	L. metatarsals, central shaft
WM 343	30.4+	15.1+	2.6	1.7				*O. hemionus*	House D, floor	L. tibia, distal articular head w/part of shaft
Reference No. 235 – Type 1B1g1' Leporid Tibia Piercing Tools										
WM 29	1.8	7.5	1.1	1.9	1.1	0.4	0.4	*S. lepus*	Room 2, fill	R. tibia
WM/B 176	2.6+	9.7+	0.7	0.5	1.1	0.6	0.3	*Lepus* sp.	House TT, fill	L. tibia
Reference No. 235A – Type IB1g2' Split Tibia Awls										
WM 3023	31.2+	19.2+	2.6	1.2	1.2	1.0	0.5	*Odocoileus* sp.	House AP, floor	R. tibia, proximal shaft
WM/B 75	11.0+	6.8+	2.3	1.5	–	–	–	*O. hemionus*	Block 43–B, fill	Burned, R. tibia
WM/B 85	12.6+	8.9+	2.1	0.8	2.2	2.1	0.8	*A. americana*	House X, fill	Tibia

APPENDIX 9: TABLE 3. *(continued)*

	Overall Measurements				Tip Measurements					
No.	Wt. (gm)	L. (cm)	W. (cm)	Th. (cm)	L. (cm)	W. (cm)	Th. (cm)	Material	Provenience	Remarks
WM/B 98	3.6+	3.8+	1.7+	1.4+	–	–	–	*O. hemionus*	House EE, fill	Burned, tibia
Reference No. 236 – Type IB1h1' Unclassified Piercing Tool Tip—Fragments										
WM 1203	4.2+	8.2+	1.0	0.5	1.3	0.6	0.4	*Artiodactyla* sp.	House AA, floor fill	
WM 2772	0.4+	3.1+	0.5	0.3	0.7	0.4	0.3	*Artiodactyla* sp.	House AF, floor	Burned
WM 3037	7.0+	10.6+	1.6	1.7	1.0	0.4	0.4	*O. hemionus*	House AQ, fill	Metatarsals no. 3/4
WM/B 5	1.8+	4.1+	0.9+	0.7	0.7	0.4	0.3	*Artiodactyla* sp.	House G, floor fill	Burned
WM/B 7	3.6+	5.5+	1.5+	0.9	0.2+	0.3	0.2	*Artiodactyla* sp.	Room 4, fill	
WM/B 28&	7.0+	10.7+	1.1	0.8	1.2	0.5	0.3	*O. hemionus*	House K, fill	Radius
WM/B 47										
WM/B 35	3.0+	5.7+	1.1	1.0	0.8	0.4	0.4	*Artiodactyla* sp.	House E, fill	
WM/B 44	1.2+	4.6+	0.8+	0.5	1.1	0.4	0.3	*Artiodactyla* sp.	Block 19–B, fill	
WM/B 66A	1.8+	4.1	0.9+	0.9+	1.4+	0.4	0.4	*Artiodactyla* sp.	House U, fill	Burned
WM/B 66B	1.0+	3.5+	0.9+	0.4+	1.9+	0.6	0.4	*Artiodactyla* sp.	House U, fill	Burned
WM/B 91	3.8+	9.7+	0.7+	0.5	1.4	0.5	0.4	*Artiodactyla* sp.	House BB, floor fill	
WM/B 94	2.4+	4.0+	1.3+	0.8+	0.9	0.5	0.4	*Artiodactyla* sp.	House DD, fill	
WM/B 109	1.2+	4.4+	0.7+	0.4+	0.9	0.5	0.3	*Artiodactyla* sp.	House X, entry fill	Burned
WM/B 119&	2.8+	7.2+	1.0+	0.4+	0.8+	0.4	0.3	*Artiodactyla* sp.	House FF, fill	Burned
WM/B 120									Room 16, fill	
WM/B 126	0.6+	2.5+	0.7+	0.4+	0.5+	0.3	0.3	*Artiodactyla* sp.	House WW, floor fill	Burned
WM/B 136	2.2+	2.7+	1.2+	0.8+	–	–	–	*Artiodactyla* sp.	Block 52–B, fill	Burned
WM/B 137	1.6+	4.6+	1.2+	0.6+	0.7	0.5	0.3	*Artiodactyla* sp.	House GG, fill	
WM/B 144	3.2+	5.6+	1.3+	0.8+	0.8	0.4	0.3	*Artiodactyla* sp.	Block 30–A, fill	
WM/B 146	5.0+	9.0+	1.3+	0.7+	–	–	–	*Artiodactyla* sp.	Block 30–C, fill	
WM/B 157	2.0+	4.7+	1.1+	0.5+	0.7	0.6	0.4	*Artiodactyla* sp.	House PP, fill	
WM/B 163	0.3+	1.8+	0.6+	0.6+	–	–	–	*Artiodactyla* sp.	House QQ, fill	Burned
WM/B 168	6.8+	8.0+	1.8	0.7	0.8	0.6	0.4	*Artiodactyla* sp.	House QQ, fill	
WM/B 173	2.2+	6.0+	0.7	0.5	0.7	0.3	0.3	*Artiodactyla* sp.	House SS, fill	
WM/B 179	1.2+	3.1+	1.4+	0.6+	0.9	0.5	0.4	*Artiodactyla* sp.	House UU, fill	Burned
WM/B 182	8.6+	10.9+	1.4	0.7	1.1	0.3	0.3	*O. hemionus*	Block 53–A, fill	Metatarsals no. 3/4
WM/B 185	2.0+	6.2+	0.6	0.5	0.7	0.5	0.4	*Artiodactyla* sp.	House SS, fill	Burned
WM/B 186	1.4+	3.9+	0.7+	0.7	0.7	0.4	0.4	*Artiodactyla* sp.	House SS, fill	Burned
WM/B 188	4.2+	12.5+	0.9+	0.5+	1.4	0.5	0.3	*O. hemionus*	House UU, fill	Ulna
WM/B 189	1.2+	3.5+	1.1	0.4	0.5	0.5	0.3	*Artiodactyla* sp.	House UU, floor fill	Burned
WM/B 190	1.6+	3.8+	0.9+	0.5+	0.4	0.3	0.3	*Artiodactyla* sp.	House VV, floor fill	
WM/B 204	5.0+	6.5+	1.2+	0.8+	0.9	0.4	0.4	*Artiodactyla* sp.	House ZZ, floor	

APPENDIX 9: TABLE 3. *(continued)*

No.	Overall Measurements Wt. (gm)	L. (cm)	W. (cm)	Th. (cm)	Tip Measurements L. (cm)	W. (cm)	Th. (cm)	Material	Provenience	Remarks
WM/B 215	0.3+	2.2+	0.7+	0.4+	–	–	–	*Artiodactyla* sp.	House AF, fill	Burned
WM/B 219	1.6+	5.8+	0.9+	0.4+	0.9	0.4	0.2	*Artiodactyla* sp.	House AF, fill	
WM/B 235	0.4+	2.5+	0.6+	0.4+	–	–	–	*Aves* sp.	House AJ, floor	Burned
WM/B 236	4.2+	6.7+	1.4+	0.6+	0.9	0.5	0.3	*Artiodactyla* sp.	Pit 68, fill	Burned
WM/B 245	3.8+	4.6+	1.0+	0.8+	0.4	0.3	0.3	*Artiodactyla* sp.	House TT, floor fill	
WM/B 247	6.4+	11.0+	1.1+	0.6+	0.8	0.5	0.4	*Artiodactyla* sp.	House AL, floor fill	
RO/B 1	1.2+	4.1+	0.8+	0.5+	0.6	0.3	0.3	*Artiodactyla* sp.	House A, fill	
RO/B 5	3.4+	6.8+	0.8+	0.5+	0.5	0.3	0.3	*Artiodactyla* sp.	House C, floor	
RO/B 7	1.0+	2.9+	0.8+	0.5+	0.7	0.3	0.3	*Artiodactyla* sp.	House D, floor fill	Burned
Reference No. 237 – Type IB1h2' Unclassified Piercing Tool Shaft Fragments										
WM/B 13	1.6+	3.8+	0.6+	0.6+	–	–	–	*Artiodactyla* sp.	House D, fill	Burned
WM/B 22	4.2+	7.5+	1.8+	0.6+	–	–	–	*Artiodactyla* sp.	House H, fill	
WM/B 24	7.6+	9.4+	1.4	0.9+	–	–	–	*Artiodactyla* sp.	Block 11–D, fill	
WM/B 25	2.6+	3.4+	1.4+	0.9+	–	–	–	*Artiodactyla* sp.	Block 11–D, fill	Burned, shouldered
WM/B 29	1.2+	4.8+	0.7+	0.4+	–	–	–	*Artiodactyla* sp.	House K, fill	
WM/B 31	3.0+	2.8+	1.6	0.7	–	–	–	*Artiodactyla* sp.	House K, fill	Burned
WM/B 34	2.8+	6.3+	1.1	0.5	–	–	–	*Artiodactyla* sp.	Block 12–D, fill	
WM/B 39	4.0+	5.8+	1.3	0.6	–	–	–	*Artiodactyla* sp.	Block 13–A, fill	
WM/B 41	3.8+	4.3+	1.2+	0.7+	–	–	–	*Artiodactyla* sp.	Block 13–C, fill	
WM/B 46	6.0+	7.1+	1.7+	0.9+	–	–	–	*Artiodactyla* sp.	Block 19–B, fill	
WM/B 48	0.8+	2.7+	1.0+	0.2	–	–	–	*Artiodactyla* sp.	Block 19–B, fill	
WM/B 53	1.2+	4.1+	0.8+	0.5+	–	–	–	*Artiodactyla* sp.	Block 12–D, fill	
WM/B 64	2.0+	3.1+	1.3+	0.8+	–	–	–	*Artiodactyla* sp.	House R, floor fill	Burned
WM/B 73	1.6+	3.2+	0.8+	0.5+	–	–	–	*Artiodactyla* sp.	House W, fill	Burned
WM/B 82	1.4+	3.0+	0.8+	0.6+	–	–	–	*Artiodactyla* sp.	House Z, floor fill	Burned
WM/B 84	5.6+	6.9+	1.3+	0.7+	–	–	–	*Artiodactyla* sp.	House X, fill	Burned
WM/B 90	5.0+	9.9+	1.1+	0.8+	–	–	–	*Artiodactyla* sp.	House AA, floor fill	Burned
WM/B 104	3.8+	3.9+	1.6+	0.7+	–	–	–	*Artiodactyla* sp.	House X, floor fill	
WM/B 111	3.2+	7.8+	0.9+	0.6+	–	–	–	*Artiodactyla* sp.	House X, entry fill	
WM/B 123	5.0+	7.2+	1.2+	0.9+	–	–	–	*Artiodactyla* sp.	House DD, floor fill	Burned
WM/B 127	3.0+	7.2+	1.1+	0.5+	–	–	–	*Artiodactyla* sp.	House DD, floor fill	Burned
WM/B 128	1.4+	3.2+	1.3+	0.4+	–	–	–	*Artiodactyla* sp.	House DD, floor fill	Burned
WM/B 140	1.2+	2.7+	0.8+	0.6+	–	–	–	*Artiodactyla* sp.	House DD, floor fill	Burned
WM/B 141	2.0+	5.6+	1.3+	0.8+	–	–	–	*Artiodactyla* sp.	Block 29–D, fill	Burned
WM/B 142	4.4+	5.3+	1.3+	0.8+	–	–	–	*Artiodactyla* sp.	Block 29–D, fill	

Appendix 9: Table 3. *(continued)*

No.	Overall Measurements Wt. (gm)	L. (cm)	W. (cm)	Th. (cm)	Tip Measurements L. (cm)	W. (cm)	Th. (cm)	Material	Provenience	Remarks
WM/B 151	1.2+	3.7+	0.7+	0.6+	–	–	–	*Artiodactyla* sp.	House PP, fill	Burned
WM/B 152	6.6+	7.4+	1.4	0.8	–	–	–	*Artiodactyla* sp.	House PP, fill	Burned
WM/B 155	5.2+	4.8+	1.8+	0.8+	–	–	–	*Artiodactyla* sp.	House OO, floor fill	Burned
WM/B 166	1.6+	3.6+	0.9+	0.5+	–	–	–	*Artiodactyla* sp.	House PP, floor fill	Burned
WM/B 172	3.2+	3.4+	1.7+	1.4+	–	–	–	*Artiodactyla* sp.	House SS, fill	Burned
WM/B 184A	1.8+	3.7+	0.8+	0.8+	–	–	–	*Artiodactyla* sp.	House SS, fill	Burned
WM/B 184B	2.4+	3.5+	1.5+	0.5+	–	–	–	*Artiodactyla* sp.	House SS, fill	Burned
WM/B 187	8.4+	13.9+	1.1+	0.6+	–	–	–	*Artiodactyla* sp.	House SS, fill	
WM/B 194	2.0+	2.7+	1.3+	0.6+	–	–	–	*Artiodactyla* sp.	House VV, floor fill	Burned
WM/B 195A	1.2+	3.8+	0.7+	0.6+	–	–	–	*Artiodactyla* sp.	House YY, floor	Burned
WM/B 195B	0.4+	1.7+	0.5+	0.5+	–	–	–	*Artiodactyla* sp.	House YY, floor	Burned
WM/B 198	4.4+	6.7+	1.2+	0.8+	–	–	–	*Artiodactyla* sp.	House YY, floor fill	
WM/B 203	1.4+	3.3+	1.6+	0.5+	–	–	–	*Artiodactyla* sp.	Block 54–C, fill	Burned
WM/B 207	1.0+	3.7+	0.6+	0.5+	–	–	–	*Artiodactyla* sp.	House AC, fill	Burned
WM/B 208	2.2+	3.2+	1.1+	0.8+	–	–	–	*Artiodactyla* sp.	House AC, fill	
WM/B 209	4.0+	6.3+	1.2+	0.7+	–	–	–	*Artiodactyla* sp.	Block 53–C, fill	
WM/B 210	1.2+	2.4+	1.0+	0.6+	–	–	–	*Artiodactyla* sp.	Block 60–B, fill	
WM/B 213	0.8+	2.8+	0.7+	0.4+	–	–	–	*Artiodactyla* sp.	Block 60–B, fill	Burned
WM/B 217A	5.0+	3.8+	1.6+	1.0+	–	–	–	*O. hemionous*	House AF, fill	Burned
WM/B 217B	1.6+	2.2+	1.4+	0.6+	–	–	–	*Artiodactyla* sp.	House AF, fill	Burned
WM/B 217C	0.6+	2.6+	0.5+	0.6+	–	–	–	*Artiodactyla* sp.	House AF, fill	Burned
WM/B 218	6.4+	6.4+	1.3+	0.9+	–	–	–	*Artiodactyla* sp.	House AF, fill	Burned
WM/B 220	0.6+	2.4+	0.8+	0.6+	–	–	–	*Artiodactyla* sp.	House AF, fill	Burned
WM/B 221A	10.4+	6.1+	2.0+	0.7+	–	–	–	*O. hemionus*	House AF, floor fill	Burned, R. metatarsals no. 3/4
WM/B 221B	4.2+	3.4+	2.4+	1.7+	–	–	–	*O. hemionus*	House AF, floor fill	Burned, L. metatarsal
WM/B 222	0.4+	1.1+	1.2+	0.4+	–	–	–	*Artiodactyla* sp.	House AF, floor fill	Burned
WM/B 223	1.6+	3.4+	0.8+	0.6+	–	–	–	*Artiodactyla* sp.	House AF, fill	Burned
WM/B 224	2.8+	5.5+	1.4+	0.7+	–	–	–	*Artiodactyla* sp.	House AF, fill	
WM/B 226	0.5+	2.3+	1.0+	0.5+	–	–	–	*Artiodactyla* sp.	House AG, fill	Burned
WM/B 228	1.6+	3.8+	0.7+	0.5+	–	–	–	*Artiodactyla* sp.	House AG, fill	
WM/B 237	11.2+	10.4+	1.9+	0.7+	–	–	–	*Artiodactyla* sp.	House AK, entry fill	Tibia, tarsals no. 3/4
WM/B 240	22.8+	9.7+	2.6+	2.2	–	–	–	*Artiodactyla* sp.	House AI, floor fill	Burned
WM/B 241	0.8+	2.4+	0.7+	0.5+	–	–	–	*Artiodactyla* sp.	House AI, floor fill	Burned
WM/B 242	0.6+	1.5+	0.9+	0.8+	–	–	–	*Artiodactyla* sp.	House AI, floor fill	Burned
WM/B 244A	3.4+	10.9+	0.6+	0.6+	–	–	–	*Artiodactyla* sp.	House AI, fill	Burned

APPENDIX 9: TABLE 3. *(continued)*

	Overall Measurements				Tip Measurements					
No.	Wt. (gm)	L. (cm)	W. (cm)	Th. (cm)	L. (cm)	W. (cm)	Th. (cm)	Material	Provenience	Remarks
WM/B 244B	2.8+	4.8+	1.1+	0.7+	–	–	–	*Artiodactyla* sp.	House AI, fill	Burned
WM/B 244D	2.2+	6.8+	0.7+	0.5+	–	–	–	*Artiodactyla* sp.	House AI, fill	Burned
WM/B 246	2.5+	2.8+	1.4+	0.7+	–	–	–	*Artiodactyla* sp.	Surface	Burned
WM/B 253	1.8+	3.4+	1.0+	0.5+	–	–	–	*Artiodactyla* sp.	Pit Oven 18, fill	
RO/B 2	0.8+	2.0+	0.9+	0.4+	–	–	–	*Artiodactyla* sp.	House A, floor	Burned
RO/B 3	0.8+	3.0+	0.7+	0.4+	–	–	–	*Artiodactyla* sp.	House B, fill	Burned
RO/B 4	1.6+	4.2+	0.7+	0.6+	–	–	–	*Artiodactyla* sp.	House B, fill	
RO/B 6	6.8+	12.4+	0.9+	0.7+	–	–	–	*Artiodactyla* sp.	House D, floor fill	
RO/B 8	1.2+	4.1+	0.7+	0.6+	–	–	–	*Artiodactyla* sp.	House F, fill	
Reference No. 238 – Type IB2a1' Complete Ulnae Spatula Tools										
WM 887	15.6	13.1	3.4	2.0	3.0	1.2	0.2	*O. hemionus*	House U, fill	
WM 917	19.8+	13.0+	3.9	2.2	3.2	1.3	0.4	*O. hemionous*	House U, fill	
WM/B 76	21.6+	11.7+	2.5	1.6	1.4+	1.3	0.4	*O. hemionus*	Block 43–B, fill	
WM/B 77	18.0+	9.9+	3.3	2.3	0.9+	1.1	0.3	*A. americana*	Block 43–B, fill	
WM/B 175	14.0+	8.5+	4.0	0.7	1.5	1.7	0.5	*O. hemionus*	Block 61–D, fill	Ulna
WM/B 181	2.4+	4.1+	1.7+	1.5+	–	–	–	*O. hemionus*	House WW, floor fill	Burned, ulna
RO 188	13.6	12.6	2.6	1.9	2.8	1.1	0.4	*Canis* sp.	House K, floor fill	
RO 234	13.2	13.6	2.6	1.0	4.2	1.1	0.3	*O. hemionus*	Block E2W	Ulna
RO/B 23	1.6+	3.9+	1.2+	0.4	3.1	1.2+	0.4	*Odocoileus* sp.	House K, floor fill	Ulna
Reference No. 239 – Type IB2b2' Artiodactyla Costa Spatula Tools—Fragments										
WM 368	8.4+	12.0+	2.4	0.5	1.5+	1.5	0.6	*Odocoileus* sp.	Room 4, floor	Artifact 2, rib
WM/B 15	3.8+	6.4+	1.6	0.5	1.4+	1.3	0.3	*Odocoileus* sp.	Room 4, fill	Rib
WM/B 156	1.8+	3.0+	1.6+	0.6+	–	–	–	*Artiodactyla* sp.	House OO, floor fill	Burned, rib
Reference No. 239A Artiodactyl Vertebra Fleshers										
WM/B 9	3.6+	4.0+	1.9+	0.7+	1.2+	1.3	0.3	*Odocoileus* sp.	Pit 3, fill	Vertebra, lateral spine or process
WM/B 14	2.2+	5.6+	1.3	0.4	1.3+	1.3	0.4	*Odocoileus* sp.	House F, fill	Vertebra, lateral process

Appendix 9: Table 3. *(continued)*

No.	Overall Measurements Wt. (gm)	L. (cm)	W. (cm)	Th. (cm)	Tip Measurements L. (cm)	W. (cm)	Th. (cm)	Material	Provenience	Remarks
RO/B 19	2.2+	4.2+	1.5	0.5	3.1	1.5	0.5	*Odocoileus* sp.	House J, fill	Burned, vertebra, lateral process
Reference No. 240 – Type IB2c1' Artiodactyla Splinter Spatula Tools—Complete										
WM 521	16.6	14.4	2.2	1.0	2.5	1.8	0.3	*O. hemionus*	House N, fill	Femur
WM 1112	13.6+	12.2+	1.6	1.0	2.1	1.2	0.4	*O. virginianus*	House Y, fill	L. metatarsal no. 4, distal shaft
WM 1149	4.6	13.8	1.0	0.5	1.2	0.7	0.3	*Odocoileus* sp.	House AA, fill	
WM 1745	19.0	15.3	2.0	1.0	1.5	1.2	0.3	*Odocoileus* sp.	House DD, floor fill	Burned, R. metatarsal no. 3/4
WM 2233	7.8+	12.6+	1.4+	0.6	2.0	0.9	0.3	*Odocoileus* sp.	House SS, fill	Metatarsal
Reference No. 241 – Type IB2d Unclassified Spatula Tip Tool Fragments										
WM/B 45	1.4+	3.8+	0.8	0.5	2.0+	0.8	0.5	*Odocoileus* sp.	Block 19–B, fill	
WM/B 54	3.0+	4.6+	1.4	0.5	2.5	1.4	0.5	*Odocoileus* sp.	Block 20–A, fill	
WM/B 55	1.4+	4.2+	1.1	0.3	2.7	1.1	0.3	*Odocoileus* sp.	Block 27–D, fill	
WM/B 68	1.4+	5.0+	1.0+	0.3	3.4	1.0	0.3	*Odocoileus* sp.	House U, floor fill	
WM/B 86	1.2+	3.5+	1.0+	0.5	1.2+	1.0+	0.5	*Odocoileus* sp.	House X, fill	
WM/B 160	1.4+	2.8+	1.4+	0.4	2.8+	1.4+	0.4	*Odocoileus* sp.	House PP, fill	
WM/B 162	3.6+	4.1+	1.9	0.5	0.9+	1.9	0.5	*Odocoileus* sp.	House PP, fill	
WM/B 225	4.2+	5.7+	1.2	0.5	3.2	1.2	0.5	*Odocoileus* sp.	House AD, floor fill	

No.	Overall Measurements Wt. (gm)	L. (cm)	W. (cm)	Th. (cm)	Facet Measurements L. (cm)	W. (cm)	Th. (cm)	Material	Provenience	Remarks
Reference No. 242 – Type IB3a1' Faceted Antler Tine Tools—Complete										
WM 771	10.0+	8.4+	1.8	1.5	0.5	0.6	–	*Odocoileus* sp.	Room 12, floor	2 facets
WM 1773	19.2+	11.1	2.3	2.0	0.6	0.6	–	*Odocoileus* sp.	Block 29–C, fill	
WM 2340	5.6+	6.6+	1.7	1.3	0.9	0.5	–	*Odocoileus* sp.	Block 53–B, fill	
WM/B 19	4.2	6.6	1.2	1.1	0.2	0.2	–	*Odocoileus* sp.	House D, floor	Artifact 22
WM/B 58	14.8+	11.0+	1.7+	1.5+	0.5	0.5	–	*Odocoileus* sp.	House P, floor	

APPENDIX 9: TABLE 3. *(continued)*

No.	Overall Measurements Wt. (gm)	L. (cm)	W. (cm)	Th. (cm)	Facet Measurements L. (cm)	W. (cm)	Th. (cm)	Material	Provenience	Remarks
WM/B 59	4.2+	7.3+	1.5+	1.1	1.5	0.6	–	*Odocoileus* sp.	House P, floor	2 facets
WM/B 97	1.6+	3.8+	1.1+	0.9+	0.6	0.3	–	*Odocoileus* sp	House X, fill	
WM/B 232	1.6+	3.0+	1.1+	1.0+	0.4	0.3	–	*Odocoileus* sp.	House AG, fill	
WM/B 249A	1.4+	2.8+	1.6+	1.0+	0.4	0.4	–	*Odocoileus* sp.	House AM, fill	Burned
WM/B 249B	4.0+	4.5+	1.4+	1.3+	0.6	0.3	–	*Odocoileus* sp.	House AM, fill	Burned

Socioreligious Bone

No.	Overall Measurements Wt. (gm)	L. (cm)	W. (cm)	Th. (cm)	Notch Measurements L. (cm)	W. (cm)	Th. (cm)	Material	Provenience	Remarks
Reference No. 317 – Type IIB1a Antler—Notched Tine Rasp										
WM 322	24.6	16.0	2.6	1.6	1.0	0.1	0.1	*O. hemionus*	Block 19–A, fill	15notches, 0.5 cm apart
Reference No. 318 – Type IIb1b Antler—Tube/Handle										
WM/B 138	36.2	6.0	4.2	2.0	6.0	2.3	1.3	*Odocoileus* sp.	House GG, fill	
Reference No. 319 – Type IIB1c Antler—Forked Rasp(?)										
WM 647	146.6+	26.8+	14.1	2.1	–	–	–	*O. hemionus*	Room 9, floor	
Reference No. 320 – Type IIB2a Artiodactyla Femur—Plain Rectangular Counters										
WM 28	7.4	4.6	2.4	0.5	–	–	–	*Odocoileus* sp.	House A, fill	
WM 40	5.1	4.8	2.0	0.5	–	–	–	*Odocoileus* sp.	House A, fill	
WM 142	1.5	3.5	2.0	0.6	–	–	–	*Odocoileus* sp.	House D, fill	
WM 621	2.8+	4.9+	1.4	0.5	–	–	–	*Odocoileus* sp.	Block 19–B, fill	
WM 638	2.0	2.0	1.7	0.5	–	–	–	*Odocoileus* sp.	Block 20–B, fill	
WM 709	4.2	3.0	2.2	0.6	–	–	–	*Odocoileus* sp.	House P, floor	
WM 796	4.0	3.2	1.9	0.6	–	–	–	*Odocoileus* sp.	Block 20–B, fill	
WM 845	3.8	3.1	2.2	0.7	–	–	–	*Odocoileus* sp.	House T, fill	
WM 1762	6.0	3.5	2.2	0.8	–	–	–	*Odocoileus* sp.	House FF, floor fill	

Appendix 9: Table 3. *(continued)*

No.	Overall Measurements Wt. (gm)	L. (cm)	W. (cm)	Th. (cm)	Tip Measurements L. (cm)	W. (cm)	Th. (cm)	Material	Provenience	Remarks
WM 1831	2.0	2.2	1.8	0.4	–	–	–	*Odocoileus* sp.	Block 30–A, fill	
WM 2319	1.8	2.0	2.0	0.6	–	–	–	*Odocoileus* sp.	House UU, fill	
Reference No. 321 – Type IIB2c Artiodactyla Femur—Painted Rectangular Counters										
WM/B 116	2.4+	2.8+	1.6+	0.7	–	–	–	*Odocoileus* sp.	House FF, fill	
WM/B 191	2.2+	4.5	1.3+	0.4+	–	–	–	*Odocoileus* sp.	House VV, floor fill	
Reference No. 322 – Type IIB2b Thin Walled Sections										
WM/B 74	13.4+	13.3+	3.2	0.3	–	–	–	*Ursus* cf. *americanus*	House X, fill	Polished, femur, large adult male
WM/B 112	2.6+	5.8+	2.2+	0.2	–	–	–	*Odocoileus* sp.	House X, floor fill	Innominate

No.	Overall Measurements Wt. (gm)	L. (cm)	W. (cm)	Th. (cm)	Notch Measurements L. (cm)	W. (cm)	Th. (cm)	Material	Provenience	Remarks
Reference No. 323 – Type IIB3a Artiodactyla Innominate—Notched										
WM/B 16	7.0+	7.7+	2.3+	2.1+	0.5	0.2	0.1	*O. hemionus*	Block 10–D, fill	5+ notches, 0.5 cm apart, R. ilium

No.	Overall Measurements Wt. (gm)	L. (cm)	W. (cm)	Th. (cm)	Perforation Measurements L. (cm)	W. (cm)	Th. (cm)	Material	Provenience	Remarks
Reference No. 324 – Type IIB4a Turtle Shell Plastron—Perforation										
WM/B 174	2.2+	3.4+	2.7+	0.5	–	0.8	0.8	*Chelonia* sp.	Block 20–A, fill	Conical perforation
Reference No. 325 – Type IIB5a Bird Bone Tubes										
WM 1746	1.2	2.9	1.2	1.0	–	0.7	0.6	*M. gallopavo*	House DD, floor fill	Ulna
WM 1777	1.6	2.2	1.7	1.3	–	1.5	1.1	*Aves* sp.	Block 45–B, fill	

Appendix 9: Table 3. *(continued)*

No.	Overall Measurements Wt. (gm)	L. (cm)	W. (cm)	Th. (cm)	Perforation Measurements L. (cm)	W. (cm)	Th. (cm)	Material	Provenience	Remarks
WM/B 4	0.01+	1.2+	0.8	0.1	–	0.5	0.4	*Aves* sp.	Burial 9	
WM/B 231	2.4+	7.5+	0.9+	0.4	–	0.3	0.3	*Aves* sp.	House AG, fill	

No.	Overall Measurements Wt. (gm)	L. (cm)	Diam. (cm)	Stem Measurements D. (cm)	OD. (cm)	ID. (cm)	Material	Provenience	Remarks
Reference No. 326 – Type IIB5b Bird Bone Pipe Stem									
WM 634	7.8	7.5	1.0	7.5	1.0	0.5	*A. chrysaetos*	Block 20–A, fill	Adult female, distal (0–1.9m) shaft, ulna, bi incision

No.	Overall Measurements Wt. (gm)	L. (cm)	W. (cm)	Th. (cm)	Bowl Measurements D. (cm)	OD. (cm)	ID. (cm)	Material	Provenience	Remarks
Reference No. 327 – Type IIB6a Mammal Bone Tubes										
WM 365	3.4	6.1	0.9	0.8	–	0.3	0.2	*L. californicus*	House H, floor fill	
WM 1812	1.5	3.8	0.8	0.7	–	0.5	0.5	*L. californicus*	House HH, floor fill	Tibia
WM 2038	1.6	3.6	0.9	0.8	–	0.6	0.4	*Mammalia* sp.	House OO, fill	
WM 2716	2.2	4.0	1.1	0.8	–	0.8	0.6	*C. latrans*	House AD, entry	Radius
WM/B 80	1.6	3.1	1.4+		3.1	1.4+	1.0+	*Artiodactyla* sp.	House Y, fill	Femur; lip L=0.3 cm (0–90 cm) external
WM/B 93	8.0+	6.9	2.5+	6.9	2.5+	–	2.0+	*Artiodactyla* sp.	Block 34–C, fill	Femur; lip L=0.3 cm (0–40 cm) internal/externa
WM/B 106	2.6+	5.7	2.5+	–	5.7	2.5+	2.0+	*Artiodactyla* sp.	House X, fill	Femur; lip L=0.3 cm external
WM/B 121	1.8+	4.6+	1.0	0.2	–	0.3	0.3	*L. californicus*	House X, floor fill	Tibia
WM/B 143	0.9+	4.0	0.9+	0.2	–	0.4	0.3	*L. californicus*	Pit 44, fill	Tibia
WM/B 161	9.8+	5.9	3.5+	5.9	3.5+	–	3.0+	*O. hemionus*	House PP, fill	Femur; lip L=0.3 cm external

APPENDIX 9: TABLE 3. *(continued)*

No.	Overall Measurements Wt. (gm)	L. (cm)	Diam. (cm)	Stem Measurements D. (cm)	OD. (cm)	ID. (cm)	Material	Provenience	Remarks
Reference No. 327A – Type IIB6b Mammal Pipe Stem									
WM/B 145	2.4+	5.5	0.8	5.5	0.8	0.5	*Lepus* sp.	Block 30–C, fill (0–50 cm)	Tibia, bit incision
Reference No. 369 – Type IIIC1a Artiodactyla Femur—Ring									
WM 1207	1.5	2.2	2.1	0.5	1.3	–	*Odocoileus* sp.	House DD, fill	
Reference No. 370 – Type IIIC1b Artiodactyla Femur—Unidentified Ornament									
WM 620	0.8	4.5	0.6	0.4	–	–	*Odocoileus* sp.	Block 19–B, fill	
Reference No. 371 – Type IIIC1c Artiodactyla Femur—Skewer									
WM 1818	1.4	10.6	0.4	0.3	–	–	*Odocoileus* sp.	Pit 36, fill	

Note; D = Depth, OD = Outside Diameter, ID = Inside Diameter.

APPENDIX 9: TABLE 4. Utilization of Primary Bone Types for Tool Production Compared with Animal Species Exploited

Species	Reference Nos. 444 Mammal Femurs	445 Other Mammal Long Bones	446 Mammal Costal	447 Mammal Crania	448 Bird Femurs	Total
Lepus californicus	2					2
Mammalia spp. indet.	1					1
Meleagris gallopavo					2	2
Odocoileus spp. indet.	29	15	1	2		47
Odocoileus hemionus	3	9				12
Odocoileus virginianus		1				1
Total	35	25	1	2	2	65

Appendix 9: Table 5. Bone Raw Material

No.	Wt. (gm)	L. (cm)	W. (cm)	Th. (cm)	Sawed	Split	Ground	Material	Provenience	Remarks
Reference No. 444 – Type VBI Raw Material, Mammal Femur										
WM 342c	11.4+	10.2+	1.8+	0.4+	X	X	X	*Odocoileus* sp.	House D, floor	
WM/B 1	2.0+	4.7+	1.2+	0.3			X	*Odocoileus* sp.	Block 18-D	
WM/B 8	1.2+	4.3+	1.2+	0.2		X	X	*Odocoileus* sp.	Pit 3, fill	
WM/B 11	0.3+	3.3+	0.5+	0.2+			X	*Mammalia* sp.	Block 18-B	
WM/B 12	0.5+	3.2+	1.0+	0.3+	X		X	*Odocoileus* sp.	Block 18-B	
WM/B 38	3.4+	4.1	1.8+	0.7	X	X	X	*Odocoileus* sp.	House N, floor	
WM/B 50	4.0+	3.1+	2.5+	0.4	X	X	X	*Odocoileus* sp.	House M, fill	Burned
WM/B 69	4.9+	4.0+	2.0+	0.9+	X	X	X	*Odocoileus* sp.	House U, floor fill	
WM/B 70	6.0+	5.3+	2.2+	0.8	X	X	X	*Odocoileus* sp.	House V, fill	
WM/B 83	4.7+	4.8+	2.4+	1.0+	X	X	X	*Odocoileus* sp.	Block 35-D	
WM/B 89	2.0+	4.5+	0.8+	0.6+			X	*Odocoileus* sp.	House AA, floor fill	Burned
WM/B 92	2.6+	4.7+	1.7	0.6	X		X	*L. californicus*	Block 29-A	
WM/B 105	2.7+	4.5+	1.3+	0.6	X	X	X	*Odocoileus* sp.	House X, floor fill	
WM/B 115a	4.2+	3.8+	2.1+	0.5+	X	X	X	*Odocoileus* sp.	House FF, fill	
WM/B 115b	2.8+	3.5+	1.7+	0.4+	X	X	X	*Odocoileus* sp.	House FF, fill	
WM/B 131 & 133	6.8+	5.9+	2.0	0.5+	X		X	*Odocoileus* sp.	House FF, floor fill	
WM/B 132	4.2+	4.4+	2.0+	0.6+		X		*Odocoileus* sp.	House FF, floor fill	
WM/B 134	3.9+	3.2+	1.7+	0.6+	X		X	*Odocoileus* sp.	House FF, floor fill	
WM/B 153	4.1+	3.0+	2.7+	1.0+	X		X	*O. hemionus*	House PP, fill	
WM/B 154	91.8+	18.3	6.2+	4.2	X		X	*O. hemionus*	Block 55-A	
WM/B 159	2.4+	2.1+	2.0+	0.5+	X		X	*Odocoileus* sp.	House PP, fill	Burned
WM/B 165	2.4+	3.3+	1.7+	0.9+	X		X	*Odocoileus* sp.	House PP, floor fill	Burned
WM/B 170	2.9+	3.4+	1.9+	0.6+			X	*Odocoileus* sp.	Block 54-B	Burned
WM/B 177	0.5+	4.3+	0.7+	0.3+	X		X	*L. californicus*	House AL, floor fill	
WM/B 196a	3.0+	3.8+	1.2+	0.7+	X		X	*Odocoileus* sp.	House ZZ, floor fill	
WM/B 196b	6.4+	5.5+	2.0+	1.1+	X			*O. hemionus*	House ZZ, floor fill	
WM/B 201	1.0+	1.6+	1.7+	0.6	X		X	*Odocoileus* sp.	Block 54-A	
WM/B 205	2.0+	2.4+	1.9+	0.6+	X			*Odocoileus* sp.	House AC, fill	
WM/B 211	3.4+	4.7+	1.7+	0.5+	X	X	X	*Odocoileus* sp.	House AC, fill	
WM/B 230	6.2+	8.6+	1.3+	0.4+	X		X	*Odocoileus* sp.	House AG, fill	
WM/B 238	0.8+	2.2+	1.0+	0.5			X	*Odocoileus* sp.	Pit 70, fill	Burned
WM/B 250	2.6+	3.8+	1.5+	0.2+	X		X	*Odocoileus* sp.	House AM, fill	
WM/B 255	0.2+	1.9+	1.1+	0.3+			X	*Odocoileus* sp.	House AQ, fill	Burned
WM/B 256	0.2+	1.9+	0.9+	0.3+			X	*Odocoileus* sp.	House AF, floor	
RO/B 18	7.2+	6.8+	1.8+	0.3+	X		X	*Odocoileus* sp.	House J, fill	

Appendix 9: Table 5. *(continued)*

No.	Wt. (gm)	L. (cm)	W. (cm)	Th. (cm)	Sawed	Split	Ground	Material	Provenience	Remarks
Reference No. 445 - Type VB2 Raw Material, Other Mammal Long Bones										
WM 342a&b	18.0+	12.1+	2.1+	0.7+		X	X	*O. hemionus*	House D, floor	Tibia
WM 342d&e	44.8+	20.9+	2.8+	1.2+		X	X	*O. hemionus*	House D, floor	Tibia
WM 592	13.8+	11.8+	1.9	0.6		X	X	*O. hemionus*	Block 13-C	Metapodial
WM 1888	37.6	20.1	2.9	1.3	X	X	X	*O. virginianus*	Pit 41, floor	
WM/B 10	3.8+	3.6+	1.5+	0.2		X	X	*Odocoileus* sp.	Burial 7	
WM/B 30	1.8+	3.7+	1.1+	0.6+			X	*Odocoileus* sp.	House K, fill	Burned
WM/B 33	7.4+	5.1+	2.5+	1.5			X	*O. hemionus*	House L, fill	
WM/B 52	23.5+	13.0+	2.4+	1.4+	X		X	*O. hemionus*	Burial 21, fill	Notched?
WM/B 63	0.3+	1.9+	0.7+	0.4+	X		X	*Odocoileus* sp.	House R, fill	
WM/B 71	3.4+	6.8+	0.8+	0.6+			X	*Odocoileus* sp.	House V, fill	
WM/B 88	0.5+	3.2+	0.6+	0.2+			X	*Odocoileus* sp.	House AA, floor fill	
WM/B 110	5.6+	5.6+	2.2+	1.6+	X			*O. hemionus*	House X, fill	Ulna
WM/B 139	10.7+	10.8+	1.7+	1.0+			X	*Odocoileus* sp.	House HH, floor fill	
WM/B 148	10.4+	9.0+	2.3+	0.9			X	*O. hemionus*	Block 38-A	Tibia
WM/B 164	1.0+	3.5+	0.7+	0.4+	X		X	*Odocoileus* sp.	House PP, floor fill	Metatarsal
WM/B 169	1.1+	4.3+	0.7+	0.5+			X	*Odocoileus* sp.	House RR, fill	Ulna
WM/B 180	6.4+	3.8+	2.0+	0.7+	X	X	X	*Odocoileus* sp.	House UU, fill	Tibia
WM/B 197	2.3+	3.4+	1.2+	0.8+	X		X	*Odocoileus* sp.	House XX, fill	
WM/B 227	1.6+	5.1+	1.0+	0.6+			X	*O. hemionus*	House AG, fill	Burned, metapodial
WM/B 233	4.2+	6.9+	1.3+	0.5+			X	*O. hemionus*	House AG, floor fill	Radius
WM/B 252	0.6+	1.8+	1.1+	0.4+			X	*Odocoileus* sp.	Pit 70, fill	Burned
RO/B 9&11	2.6+	4.2+	1.3+	0.5			X	*Odocoileus* sp.	House F, fill	Metapodial
RO/B 17	6.9+	3.7+	2.9+	2.3+	X		X	*O. hemionus*	House G, fill	Humerus
RO/B 21	0.4+	2.2+	0.9+	0.5+			X	*Odocoileus* sp.	House J, floor fill	Burned
RO/B 25	4.8+	9.7+	1.0+	0.6	X		X	*Odocoileus* sp.	House G, fill	Metatarsal
Reference No. 446 - Type VB3 Raw Material, Artiodactyla Costae										
WM 2144	3.7+	10.5+	1.2+	0.5+			X	*Odocoileus* sp.	House PP, floor fill	Rib, 14 cut marks

Appendix 9: Table 5. *(continued)*

No.	Wt. (gm)	L. (cm)	W. (cm)	Th. (cm)	Sawed	Split	Ground	Material	Provenience	Remarks
Reference No. 447 - Type VB4 Raw Material, Artiodactyla Crania										
WM/B 65	8.0	5.1	4.1	0.6	X			*Odocoileus* sp.	Block 44-B	
WM/B 103	2.4+	3.0+	2.5+	0.6+	X			*Odocoileus* sp.	House X, fill	
Reference No. 448 - Type VB5 Raw Material, *Aves* sp. Femur										
WM/B 102	1.8+	4.8+	1.3+	0.4+	X		X	*M. gallopavo*	House X, fill	
WM/B 248	4.2+	11.4+	1.2+	0.3	X		X	*M. gallopavo*	House AL, floor fill	

Bibliography

Accola, R. M.
1981 Mogollon Settlement Patterns in the Middle San Francisco River Drainage, West-Central New Mexico. *The Kiva* 46:155–168.

Adam, D. P., and P. J. Mehringer, Jr.
1975 Modern Pollen Surface Samples—An Analysis of Subsamples. *Journal of Research, U.S. Geological Survey* 3:733–736.

Ahlstrom, R.
1985 *The Interpretation of Archaeological Tree-Ring Dates.* Ph.D. dissertation, Department of Anthropology, University of Arizona, Tucson.

American Ornithologists' Union
1975 *Checklist of North American Birds.* American Ornithologists Union, Baltimore.

Amsden, C. A.
1949 *Prehistoric Southwesterners from Basketmaker to Pueblo.* Southwest Museum, Los Angeles.

Anderson, E.
1942 Races of *Zea mays:* Their Recognition and Classification. *Annals of the Missouri Botanical Garden* 29:69–88.

Anyon, R.
1980 The Late Pithouse Period. In *An Archeological Synthesis of South-Central and Southwestern New Mexico,* edited by S. A. LeBlanc and M. E. Whalen, pp. 142–204. Office of Contract Archeology, University of New Mexico, Albuquerque.

Anyon, R., and S. A. LeBlanc
1980 The Architectural Evolution of Mogollon-Mimbres Communal Structures. *The Kiva* 45:253–277.
1984 *The Galaz Ruin: A Prehistoric Mimbres Village in Southwestern New Mexico.* University of New Mexico Press, Albuquerque.

Anyon, R., P. A. Gilman, and S. A. LeBlanc
1981 A Reevaluation of the Mogollon-Mimbres Archaeological Sequence. *The Kiva* 46:209–225.

Asch, D. L., and N. B. Asch
1977 Chenopod as Cultigen: A Re-evaluation of Some Prehistoric Collections from Eastern North America. *Mid-Continental Journal of Archaeology* 2:3–45.

Baby, R. S.
1954 *Hopewell Cremation Processes.* Papers in Archaeology 1. Ohio Historical Society, Columbus.

Baker, G. S.
1971 *The Riverside Site, Grant County, New Mexico.* Southwestern Research Reports 5. Department of Anthropology, Case Western Reserve University, Cleveland.

Bandelier, A. F.
1890 *Contributions to the History of the Southwestern Portion of the United States.* Papers of the Archaeological Institute of America, American Series 5. Peabody Museum of American Archaeology and Ethnology, Harvard University, Cambridge.
1892 *Final Report of Investigations among the Indians of the Southwestern United States, Carried on Mainly in the Years from 1880 to 1885.* Part II. Papers of the Archaeological Institute of America, American Series 4. Peabody Museum of American Archaeology and Ethnology, Harvard University, Cambridge.

Berman, M. J.
1989 *Prehistoric Abandonment of the Upper San Francisco River Valley, West-Central New Mexico: An Economic Case Study.* Ph.D. dissertation, Department of Anthropology, State University of New York, Binghamton.

Berry, R. J.
1968 The Biology of Non-metrical Variation in Mice and Men. In *The Skeletal Biology of Earlier Human Populations,* vol. 8, edited by D. R. Brothwell, pp. 103–133. Symposia of the Society for the Study of Human Biology, Pergamon Press, New York.

Binford, L. R., and G. I. Quimby
1963 *Indian Sites and Chipped Stone Materials in the Northern Lake Michigan Area.* Fieldiana: Anthropology 36(12).

Bird, R. M.
1970 *Maize and its Cultural and Natural Environment in the Sierra of Huanoco, Peru.* Ph.D. dissertation, University of California, Berkeley.

Blake, M., S. A. LeBlanc, and P. E. Minnis
1986 Changing Settlement and Populations in the Mimbres Valley, S. W. New Mexico. *Journal of Field Archaeology* 13:439–464.

Blakely, R. L.
1971 Comparison of the Mortality Profiles of Archaic, Middle Woodland, and Middle Mississippian Skeletal Populations. *American Journal of Physical Anthropology* 34:43–54.

Bluhm, E. A.
1960 Mogollon Settlement Patterns in Pine Lawn Valley, New Mexico. *American Antiquity* 25:538–546.

Bohrer, V. L.
1972 *Paleoecology of the Hay Hollow Site, Arizona.* Fieldiana: Anthropology 63(1):1–30.

Bowen, T.
1976 *Seri Prehistory, the Archaeology of the Central Coast of Sonora, Mexico.* Anthropological Papers of the University of Arizona 27. Tucson.

Bradfield, W.
1931 *Cameron Creek Village: A Site in the Mimbres Area in Grant County, New Mexico.* Reprinted. El Palacio Press, Albuquerque. Originally published 1929, The School of American Research, Monograph 1, Santa Fe.

Bradfield, W., and L. B. Bloom
1928 A Preliminary Survey of the Archaeology of Southwestern New Mexico. *El Palacio* 24(6):98–112.

Braniff, C. B.
1975 *La Estratigrafia Arqueologica de Villa de Reyes, S. L. P.—Un Sition en la Frontera de Mesoamerica.* Instituto Nacional de Antropologia e Historia, Centro Regional del Noroeste, Cuadernos de los Centros 17.
1993 The Mesoamerican Northern Frontier and the Gran Chichimeca. In *Culture and Contact: Charles C. Di Peso's Gran Chichimeca,* edited by A. I. Woosley and J. C. Ravesloot, pp. 65–82. Amerind Foundation New World Studies Series 2. Amerind Foundation, Dragoon, Arizona, and University of New Mexico Press, Albuquerque.

Braun, D. P.
1979 Illinois Hopewell Burial Practices and Social Organization: A Reexamination of the Klunk-Gibson Mound Group. In *Hopewell Archaeology, the Chillicothe Conference,* edited by D. S. Brose and N. M. B. Greber, pp. 66–79. Kent State University Press, Kent, Ohio.
1980 Experimental Interpretation of Ceramic Vessel Use on the Basis of Rim and Neck Formal Attributes. Appendix I, In *The Navajo Project,* edited by D. C. Fiero, R. W. Munson, M. T. McClain, S. M. Wilson, and A. H. Zier, pp. 171–231. Research Paper 11. Museum of Northern Arizona, Flagstaff.
1983 Pots as Tools. In *Archaeological Hammers and Theories,* edited by A. S. Keene and J. A. Moore, pp. 107–134. Academic Press, New York.

Breitburg, E.
1988 *Prehistoric New World Turkey Domestication: Origins, Developments, and Consequences.* Ph.D. dissertation, Department of Anthropology, Southern Illinois University, Carbondale.
1993 The Evolution of Turkey Domestication in the Greater Southwest and Mesoamerica. In *Culture and Contact: Charles C. Di Peso's Gran Chichimeca,* edited by A. I. Woosley and J. C. Ravesloot, pp. 153–172. Amerind Foundation New World Studies Series 2. Amerind Foundation, Dragoon, Arizona, and University of New Mexico Press, Albuquerque.

Brew, J. O.
1946 *Archaeology of Alkali Ridge, Southeastern Utah.* Papers of the Peabody Museum of American Archaeology and Ethnology 21. Harvard University, Cambridge.

Brothwell, D. R.
1963 The Macroscopic Dental Pathology of Some Earlier Human Populations. In *Dental Anthropology,* vol. 5, edited by D. R. Brothwell, pp. 271–288. Symposia for the Study of Human Biology. Pergamon Press, New York.

Bruning, J. L., and B. L. Kintz
1968 *Computational Handbook of Statistics.* Scott, Foresman, Glenview, Illinois

Bryan, B.
1931a Excavation of the Galaz Ruin, Mimbres Valley, N. M. *Art and Archaeology* 32(1):35–42.
1931b Excavation of the Galaz Ruin, Mimbres Valley, N. M. *Masterkey* 4(6):179–189.
1931c Excavation of the Galaz Ruin, Mimbres Valley, N. M. *Masterkey* 4(7):221–226.

Bryant, V. M., Jr.
1974 Prehistoric Diet in Southwest Texas: The Coprolite Evidence. *American Antiquity* 39:407–420.

Bullard, W. R., Jr.
1962 *The Cerro Colorado Site and Pithouse Architecture in the Southwestern United States Prior to A.D. 900.* Papers of the Peabody Museum of Archaeology and Ethnology 44(2). Harvard University, Cambridge.

Burns, P. E.
1972 *The Heron Ruin, Grant County, New Mexico.* Southwestern New Mexico Research Reports 7. Department of Anthropology, Case Western Reserve University, Cleveland.

Burt, W. H., and R. P. Grossenheider
1976 *A Field Guide to the Mammals.* Houghton Mifflin, Boston.

Bussey, S. D.
1972 *Late Mogollon Manifestations in the Mimbres Branch, Southwest New Mexico.* Ph.D. dissertation, University of Oregon, Eugene.

1975 *The Archaeology of Lee Village.* Center of Anthroplogial Study, Monograph Series 2. COAS Publishing and Research, Las Cruces.

Butler, P.
1959 Palynological Studies of Barstable Marsh, Cape Cod, Massachusetts. *Ecology* 40:735–737.

Callen, E. O., and P. S. Martin
1969 Plant Remains in Some Coprolites from Utah. *American Antiquity* 34:325–331.

Carlson, R. L.
1970 *White Mountain Redware: A Pottery Tradition of East-Central Arizona and Western New Mexico.* Anthropological Papers of the University of Arizona 19. Tucson.

Chapman, R. C., C. W. Gossett, and W. J. Gossett
1985 *Class II Cultural Resource Survey, Upper Gila Supply Study, Central Arizona Project.* Bureau of Reclamation. Deuel and Associates, Albuquerque.

Colton, H. S., and L. L. Hargrave
1937 Handbook of Northern Arizona Pottery Wares. *Museum of Northern Arizona Bulletin* 11:87–91.

Cosgrove, C. B.
1947 *Caves of the Upper Gila and Hueco Areas in New Mexico and Texas.* Papers of the Peabody Museum of American Archaeology and Ethnology 24(2). Harvard University, Cambridge.

Cosgrove, H. S., and C. B. Cosgrove
1932 *The Swarts Ruin: A Typical Mimbres Site in Southwestern New Mexico.* Papers of the Peabody Museum of American Archaeology and Ethnology 15(1). Harvard University, Cambridge.

Crabtree, D. E.
1972 *An Introduction to Flintworking.* Occasional Papers 28. Idaho State University Museum, Pocatello.

Creel, D.
1989 A Primary Cremation at the NAN Ranch Ruin, with Comparative Data on Other Cremations in the Mimbres Area, New Mexico. *Journal of Field Archaeology* 16:309–329.

Cummings, B.
1940 *Kinishba: A Prehistoric Pueblo of the Great Pueblo Period.* Hohokam Museums Association and University of Arizona, Tucson.

Cushing, F. H.
1883 Zuñi Fetiches. *Bureau of American Ethnology, Second Annual Report, 1880–81.* pp. 3–45. Washington, D.C.
1920 *Zuñi Breadstuff.* Indian Notes and Monographs 8. Museum of the American Indian, Heye Foundation, New York.

Dahlberg, A. H.
1963 Analysis of the American Indian Dentition. In *Dental Anthropology,* edited by D. R. Brothwell, pp. 149–177. Symposia for the Study of Human Biology 5. Pergamon Press, New York.

Danson, E. B.
1957 *An Archaeological Survey of West Central New Mexico and East Central Arizona.* Papers of the Peabody Museum of Archaeology and Ethnology 44(1). Harvard University, Cambridge.

Davis, M. B.
1959 Three Pollen Diagrams from Central Massachusetts. *American Journal of Science* 256:540–570.

Davis, R. B.
1967 Pollen Studies of Near-Surface Sediments in Maine Lakes. In *Quaternary Paleoecology,* edited by E. J. Cushing and H. E. Wright, Jr., pp. 143–173. Yale University Press, New Haven.

Dean, J. S.
1991 Thoughts on Hohokam Chronology. In *Exploring the Hohokam: Prehistoric Desert Peoples of the American Southwest,* edited by G. J. Gumerman, pp. 61–149. Amerind Foundation New World Studies Series 1. Amerind Foundation, Dragoon, Arizona, and University of New Mexico Press, Albuquerque.

Dean, J. S., and J. C. Ravesloot
1993 The Chronology of Cultural Interaction in the Gran Chichimeca. In *Culture and Contact: Charles C. Di Peso's Gran Chichimeca,* edited by A. I. Woosley and J. C. Ravesloot, pp. 83–103. Amerind Foundation New World Studies Series 2. Amerind Foundation, Dragoon, Arizona, and University of New Mexico Press, Albuquerque.

Di Peso, C. C.
1951 *The Babocomari Village Site on the Babocomari River, Southeastern Arizona.* Amerind Foundation Publications 5. Dragoon, Arizona.
1956 *The Upper Pima of San Cayetano del Tumacacori.* Amerind Foundation Publications 7. Dragoon, Arizona.
1968a Casas Grandes: A Fallen Trading Center of the Gran Chichimeca. *Masterkey* 42(1):20–37.
1968b Casas Grandes and the Gran Chichimeca. *El Palacio* 75(4):45–61.
1974 *Casas Grandes: A Fallen Trading Center of the Gran Chichimeca.* Amerind Foundation Publications 9, vols. 1–3. Dragoon, Arizona.
1977 Amerind Mimbres Project. Grant Proposal. National Science Foundation No. BNS76–82545. Ms. on file, Amerind Foundation, Dragoon, Arizona.
1979a Amerind Mimbres Project. Part II. National Science Foundation No. BNS76–82545. Ms. on file, Amerind Foundation, Dragoon, Arizona.
1979b Progress Report: Amerind Mimbres Project. National Science Foundation No. BNS76–82545. Ms. on file, Amerind Foundation, Dragoon, Arizona.
1979c *Gran Chichimeca.* Instituto Panamericano de Geografica de Historia, Caracas, Venezuela. Unpublished English version on file at the Amerind Foundation, Dragoon, Arizona.
1983a The Northern Sector of the Mesoamerican World System. In *Forgotten Places and Things,* edited by A. E. Ward,

pp. 11–22. Contributions to Anthropological Studies 3. Center for Anthropological Research, Albuquerque.

1983b *Las Sociedades No Nucleares de Norteamerica: La Gran Chichimeca.* Historica General de America, Periodo Indigena. Academia Nacional de la Historia de Venezuela, Caracas.

Di Peso, C. C., J. B. Rinaldo, and G. J. Fenner

1974 *Casas Grandes: A Fallen Trading Center of the Gran Chichimeca.* Amerind Foundation Publications 9, vols. 4–8. Dragoon, Arizona.

Dozier, E. P.

1970 The Pueblo Indians of North America. Holt, Rinehart, and Winston, New York.

Dubois, R. L.

1975a Development of an Archaeomagnetic Chronology. Research Proposal Submitted to the National Science Foundation.

1975b Secular Variation in Southwestern United States as Suggested by Archaeomagnetic Studies. In *Takesi Nagata Conference—Magnetic Fields: Past and Present,* edited by R. M. Fischer, M. Fuller, V. A. Schmidt, and P. J. Wasilewski, pp. 133–144. Goddard Space Flight Center, Greenbelt, Maryland.

Eighmy, J. L., J. H. Hathaway, and A. E. Kane

1982 Extension of the Southwest Virtual Geomagnetic Pole Curve (A.D. 700–900) Based on Dolores Archaeological Project Results 1978–1980. Paper presented at the annual meeting of the Society for American Archaeology, Minneapolis.

Eighmy, J. L., R. S. Sternberg, and R. F. Butler

1980 Archaeomagnetic Dating in the American Southwest. *American Antiquity* 45:507–517.

Elmore, F. H.

1976 *Shrubs and Trees of the Southwest Uplands.* Southwest Parks and Monuments Association, Globe, Arizona.

Elmore, F. W.

1944 *Ethnobotany of the Navajo.* University of New Mexico Press, Albuquerque.

Emslie, S. D.

1978 Dog Burials from Mancos Canyon, Colorado. *The Kiva* 43:167–182.

Erdtman, G.

1969 *Handbook of Palynology.* Hafner Publishing, New York.

Faegri, K., and L. Van der Pijl

1971 *The Principles of Pollination Ecology.* Pergamon Press, New York.

Fall, P. L., G. K. Kelso, and V. Markgraf

1981 Paleoenvironmental Reconstruction at Canyon del Muerto, Arizona, Based on Principal-Component Analysis. *Journal of Archaeological Science* 8:297–307.

Farwell, R. Y.

1987 Pit Houses: Prehistoric Energy Conservation. *El Palacio* 87(3):43–47.

Feinman, G. M.

1991 Hohokam Archaeology in the Eighties: An Outside View. In *Exploring the Hohokam: Prehistoric Desert Peoples of the American Southwest,* edited by G. J. Gumerman, pp. 461–483. Amerind Foundation New World Studies Series 1. Amerind Foundation, Dragoon, Arizona, and University of New Mexico Press, Albuquerque.

Fewkes, J. W.

1912 Casa Grande, Arizona. *Bureau of American Ethnology, 28th Annual Report* 55:25–180.

1914 *Archeology of the Lower Mimbres Valley, New Mexico.* Smithsonian Institution, Smithsonian Miscellaneous Collections 63(10). Washington, D.C.

Findley, J. S., A. H. Harris, D. E. Wilson, and C. Jones

1975 *Mammals of New Mexico.* University of New Mexico Press, Albuquerque.

Fish, P. R., and S. K. Fish

1991 Hohokam Political and Social Organization. In *Exploring the Hohokam: Prehistoric Desert Peoples of the American Southwest,* edited by G. J. Gumerman, pp. 151–175. Amerind Foundation New World Studies Series 1. Amerind Foundation, Dragoon, Arizona, and University of New Mexico Press, Albuquerque.

Fitting, J. E.

1971 *Excavations at MC 110, Grant County, New Mexico.* Southwestern Research Reports 2. Department of Anthropology, Case Western Reserve University, Cleveland.

1972a *Chipped Stone from the 1967 Mimbres Area Survey, Parts I and II.* Southwestern New Mexico Research Reports 8. Department of Anthropology, Case Western Reserve University, Cleveland.

1972b Four Archaeological Sites in the Big Burro Mountain: A Preliminary Report. U.S. Forest Service, Gila Center. Ms. on file, Amerind Foundation, Dragoon, Arizona.

1973a An Early Mogollon Community: A Preliminary Report on the Winn Canyon Site. *The Artifact* 11(1–2).

1973b *Four Archaeological Sites in the Big Burro Mountains of New Mexico.* Center of Anthropological Study, Monograph No. 1. COAS Publishing and Research, Las Cruces.

1974 The Preceramic Eaton Site. *American Philosophical Society Yearbook,* 1972:578–579.

Fitting, J. E., J. L. Ross, and B. T. Gray

1971 *Preliminary Report on the 1971 Intersession Excavations at the Saige-McFarland Site.* Southwestern Research Reports 4. Department of Anthropology, Case Western Reserve University, Cleveland.

Fitting, J. E., C. B. Hemphill, and D. R. Abbe

1982a *Cultural Resources of the Upper Gila Water Supply Study Area. February.* Hemphill Associates, Springfield, Oregon.

1982b *The Upper Gila Water Supply Study. A Class I Cultural Resources Overview. April.* Hemphill Associates, Springfield, Oregon.

Flint, T. (editor)

1984 *The Personal Narrative of James O. Pattie of Kentucky.* University of Nebraska, Lincoln.

Ford, J. A.

1938 A Chronological Method Applicable to the Southeast. *American Antiquity* 3:260–264.

1969 *A Comparison of Formative Cultures in the Americas, Diffusion of the Psychic Unity of Man.* Smithsonian Contributions to Anthropology 11. Smithsonian Institution, Washington, D.C.

Freund, J. E.

1971 *Mathematical Statistics.* 2d ed. Prentice-Hall, Englewood Cliffs, New Jersey.

Fry, G.

1969 Preliminary Analysis of the Hogup Cave Coprolites. Paper presented at the annual meeting of the Society for American Archaeology, Milwaukee.

Fulton, W. S.

1941 *A Ceremonial Cave in the Winchester Mountains, Arizona.* Amerind Foundation Publications 1. Dragoon, Arizona.

Furst, P. T.

1974 Hallucinogens in Precolumbian Art. *Texas Tech University, The Museum, Special Publications* 7:55–101.

Garfield, S.

1969 *Teeth, Teeth, Teeth.* Simon and Schuster, New York.

Genovés, S.

1967 Proportionality of the Long Bones and their Relation to Stature among Mesoamericans. *American Journal of Physical Anthropology* 26:67–78.

Gifford, J. C. (editor)

1980 *Archaeological Explorations in Caves of the Point of Pines Region, Arizona.* Anthropological Papers of the University of Arizona 36. Tucson.

Gillerman, E.

1964 *Mineral Deposits of Western Grant County, New Mexico.* State Bureau of Mines and Mineral Resources Bulletin 83. State Bureau of Mines and Mineral Resources and New Mexico Institute of Mining and Technology, Socorro.

1970 Mineral Deposits and Structural Pattern of the Big Burro Mountains, New Mexico. In *Guidebook of the Tyrone-Big Hatchet Mountains-Florida Mountains Regions,* edited by L. A. Woodward, pp. 115–121. New Mexico Geological Society Field Conference Guidebook 21. State Bureau of Mines and Mineral Resources and New Mexico Institute of Mining and Technology, Socorro.

Gladwin, H.

1943 *A Review and Analysis of the Flagstaff Culture.* Medallion Papers 31. Gila Pueblo, Globe.

Gladwin, H. S., E. W. Haury, E. B. Sayles, and N. Gladwin

1937 *Excavations at Snaketown. Vol. I. Material Culture.* Medallion Papers 25. Gila Pueblo, Globe.

Gladwin, W. J., and H. S. Gladwin

1931 *Some Southwestern Pottery Types, Series II.* Medallion Papers 10. Gila Pueblo, Globe.

1934 *A Method for Designation of Cultures and their Variations.* Medallion Papers 15. Gila Pueblo, Globe.

Goldstein, L.

1981 One-dimensional Archaeology and Multidimensional People: Spatial Organization and Mortuary Analysis. In *The Archaeology of Death,* edited by R. Chapman, I. Kinnes, and K. Randsborg, pp. 39–52. Cambridge University Press, Cambridge.

Gossett, W. J.

1985 Chronological Trends Among Ceramic Phases in the Upper Gila and San Francisco River Valleys. In *Class II Cultural Resource Survey, Upper Gila Water Supply Study, Central Arizona Project,* by R. C. Chapman, C. W. Gossett, and W. J. Gossett, pp. 137–168. Deuel and Associates, Albuquerque.

Graybill, D. A.

1973a *Prehistoric Settlement Pattern Analysis in the Mimbres Region, New Mexico.* Ph.D. dissertation, University of Arizona, Tucson.

1973b Prehistory and Locational Analysis in the Mimbres Region, New Mexico. Paper presented at the annual meeting of the Society for American Archaeology, San Francisco.

1975 *Mimbres-Mogollon Adaptations in the Gila National Forest, Mimbres District, New Mexico.* Archeological Report 9. USDA Forest Service, Southwestern Region, Albuquerque.

Gray's Anatomy

1973 29th ed. Lea and Febiger, Philadelphia.

Gregory, D. A., and F. L. Nials

1985 Observations Concerning the Distribution of Classic Period Hohokam Platform Mounds. In *Proceedings of the 1983 Hohokam Conference,* edited by A. E. Dittert and D. E. Dove, pp. 373–388. Arizona Archaeological Society Occasional Paper 2. Tucson.

Grubbs, F. E.

1969 Procedures for Detecting Outlying Observations in Samples. *Technometrics* 11:1–21.

Guernsey, S. J., and A. V. Kidder

1921 *Basketmaker Caves of Northeastern Arizona, Report on the Explorations, 1916–17.* Papers of the Peabody Museum of American Archaeology and Ethnology 8(2). Harvard University, Cambridge.

Hall, E. R., and K. R. Kelson

1959 *The Mammals of North America.* 2 vols. Ronald Press, New York.

Ham, E.

1989 *Analysis of the NAN Ruin Burial Patterns: An Examination of Mimbres Social Structure.* Master's thesis, Texas A & M University, College Station, Texas.

Hammack, L. C., S. D. Bussey, and R. Ice; A. E. Dittert (assemblers)

1966 The Cliff Highway Salvage Project. Ms. on file, Laboratory of Anthropology, Museum of New Mexico, Santa Fe.

Hard, R. J.

1986 *Ecological Relationships Affecting the Rise of Farming Economies: A Test from the American Southwest.* Ph.D. dissertation, University of New Mexico, Albuquerque.

1990 Agricultural Dependence in the Mountain Mogollon. In *Perspectives on Southwestern Prehistory,* edited by P. E. Minnis and C. L. Redman, pp. 135–149. Westview Press, Boulder, Colorado.

Hargrave, L. L.

1933 *The Museum of Northern Arizona Archaeological Expedition, 1933; Wupatki National Monument.* Museum Notes 6(5). Museum of Northern Arizona, Flagstaff.

1970 *Mexican Macaws: Comparative Osteology and Survey of Remains from the Southwest.* Anthropological Papers of the University of Arizona 20. Tucson.

Haury, E. W.

1936a *The Mogollon Culture of Southwestern New Mexico.* Medallion Papers 20. Gila Pueblo, Globe.

1936b *Some Southwestern Pottery Types, Series IV.* Medallion Papers 19. Gila Pueblo, Globe.

1940 *Excavations in the Forestdale Valley, East-Central Arizona.* University of Arizona, Bulletin 11(4); Social Science Bulletin 12. Tucson.

1945a *The Excavation of Los Muertos and Neighboring Ruins in the Salt River Valley, Southern Arizona.* Papers of the Peabody Museum of American Archaeology and Ethnology 24(1):63–80. Harvard University, Cambridge.

1945b *Painted Cave, Northeastern Arizona.* Amerind Foundation Publications 3. Dragoon, Arizona.

1950 *The Stratigraphy and Archaeology of Ventana Cave, Arizona.* Reprinted in 1975, University of Arizona Press, Tucson.

1976 *The Hohokam: Desert Farmers & Craftsmen, Excava tions at Snaketown, 1964–1965.* University of Arizona Press, Tucson.

1983 Foreword; and Concluding Remarks. In *The Cochise Cultural Sequence in Southeastern Arizona,* by E. B. Sayles, pp. ix, 158–166. Anthropological Papers of the University of Arizona 42. Tucson.

1985 *Mogollon Culture in the Forestdale Valley, East-Central Arizona.* University of Arizona Press, Tucson.

1986 Mogollon and Anasazi. In *Emil W. Haury's Prehistory of the American Southwest,* edited by J. J. Reid and D. E. Doyel, pp. 451–456. University of Arizona Press, Tucson.

1988 Recent Thoughts on the Mogollon. *The Kiva* 53:195–196.

Hawley, F. M.

1936 *Field Manual of Prehistoric Southwestern Pottery Types.* University of New Mexico Bulletin, Anthropological Series 1(4).

Hayes, A. C., J. H. Young, and A. H. Warren

1981 *Excavation of Mound 7, Gran Quivira National Monument, New Mexico.* Publications in Archeology 16. National Park Service, Washington, D.C.

Heller, M. M.

1976 *Zooarchaeology of Tularosa Cave, Catron County, New Mexico.* Master's thesis, Biological Sciences, University of Texas at El Paso.

Hemphill, C. B.

1983 *The Eaton Site: Late Archaic in the Upper Gila.* Master's thesis, Department of Anthropology, University of Oregon, Eugene.

Hevly, R. H.

1964 *Pollen Analysis of Quaternary Archaeological and Lacustrine Sediments from the Colorado Plateau.* Ph.D. dissertation, University of Arizona, Tucson.

Hevly, R. H., P. J. Mehringer, Jr., and H. G. Yocum

1965 Modern Pollen Rain in the Sonoran Desert. *Journal of the Arizona Academy of Science* 3:123–135.

Hewett, E. L.

1958 *Geology and Mineral Deposits of the Northern Big Burro Mountains-Redrock Area, Grant County, New Mexico.* State Bureau of Mines and Mineral Resources Bulletin 60. State Bureau of Mines and Mineral Resources and New Mexico Institute of Mining and Technology, Socorro.

Hill, W. W.

1938 *The Agricultural and Hunting Methods of the Navajo Indians.* Publications in Anthropology 18. Yale University, New Haven.

Hinkes, M. J.

1983 *Skeletal Evidence of Stress in Subadults: Trying to Come of Age at Grasshopper Pueblo.* Ph.D. dissertation, University of Arizona, Tucson.

Hodge, F. W.

1920 *Hawikuh Bonework.* Indian Notes and Monographs 3(3). Museum of the American Indian, Heye Foundation, New York.

Hooton, E. A.

1930 *The Indians of Pecos Pueblo.* Yale University Press, New Haven.

Hough, W.

1907 *Antiquities of the Upper Gila and Salt River Valleys in Arizona and New Mexico.* Bureau of American Ethnology, Bulletin 35. Washington, D.C.

1914 *Culture of the Ancient Pueblos of the Upper Gila River Region, New Mexico and Arizona.* U.S. National Museum Bulletin 87. Washington, D.C.

Hyde, A. H.

1959 Atmospheric Pollen in Relation to Land Use. *Nature* 1:1694–1695.

Irving, E.

1964 *Paleomagnetism.* John Wiley & Sons, New York.

Iverson, J.

1941 Landnam; Danmarks Stenalder. *Danmarks Geol. Unders.,* Ser. II, 66:1–68.

Janes, J. B., and W. D. Rogers

1974a Birds of the Gila National Forest and Immediate Area: Preliminary Field Checklist. U.S. National Forest Service, Gila National Forest.

1974b Mammals of the Gila National Forest and Immediate Area: Preliminary Field Checklist. U.S. National Forest Service, Gila National Forest.

1974c Reptiles, Amphibians, and Fishes of the Gila National Forest and Immediate Area: Preliminary Field Checklist. U.S. National Forest Service, Gila National Forest.

Jenks, A. E.

1929–1931 Galaz Ranch Site. Unpublished field notes. Original on file, University of Minnesota, Minneapolis. Copy on file, Amerind Foundation, Dragoon, Arizona.

Johnsgard, P. A.

1975 *North American Game Birds of Upland and Shoreline.* University of Nebraska Press, Lincoln.

Johnston, F. E.

1962 Growth of the Long Bones of Infants and Young Children at Indian Knoll. *American Journal of Physical Anthropology* 20:249–254.

Johnston, F. E., and C. E. Snow

1961 The Reassessment of the Age and Sex of the Indian Knoll Population. *American Journal of Physical Anthropology* 19:237–244.

Jones, F. A.

1904 *New Mexico Mines & Minerals.* New Mexico Printing, Santa Fe.

Judd, N. M.

1954 *The Material Culture of Pueblo Bonito.* Smithsonian Miscellaneous Collections 124. Washington, D.C.

Kaplan, L.

1956 The Cultivated Beans of the Prehistoric Southwest. *Annals of the Missouri Botanical Garden* 43:189–251.

Kearney, T. H., and R. H. Peebles

1951 *Arizona Flora.* University of California Press, Berkeley and Los Angeles.

Kelley, J. C.

1966 Mesoamerica and the Southwestern United States. In *Archaeological Frontiers and External Connections,* vol. 4, edited by G. F. Eckholm and G. R. Willey, pp. 95–110. Handbook of Middle American Indians, R. Wauchope, general editor. University of Texas Press, Austin.

Kelley, J. C., and E. A. Kelley

1975 An Alternative Hypothesis for the Explanation of Anasazi Culture History. In *Collected Papers in Honor of Florence Hawley Ellis,* edited by T. R. Frisbie, pp. 178–223. Papers of the Archaeological Society of New Mexico 2. Santa Fe.

Kelly, M.

1940 Appendix: Report on the Skeletal Material. In *The SU Site: Excavations at a Mogollon Village, Western New Mexico,* by P. S. Martin, pp. 88–93. Anthropological Series 32(1). Field Museum of Natural History, Chicago.

1943 Report on the Skeletal Material. In *The SU Site: Excavations at a Mogollon Village, Western New Mexico: Second Season, 1941,* by P. S. Martin, pp. 250–251. Anthropological Series 32(2). Field Museum of Natural History, Chicago.

Kelly, R. L.

1985 *Hunter-Gatherer Mobility and Sedentism: A Great Basin Study.* Ph.D. dissertation, University of Michigan, Ann Arbor.

Kelso, G. K.

1970 Hogup Cave, Utah: Comparative Pollen Analysis of Coprolites and Cave Fill. In *Hogup Cave,* edited by C. M. Aikens, pp. 251–262. University of Utah Anthropological Papers 93, Salt Lake City.

1976 *Absolute Pollen Frequencies Applied to the Interpretation of Human Activities in Northern Arizona.* Ph.D. dissertation, University of Arizona, Tucson.

1980 Palynology and Human Paleoecology at Dead Valley. In *Prehistory in Dead Valley, East-Central Arizona: The TG&E Springerville Report,* edited by D. E. Doyle and S. S. Debowski, pp. 349–370. Archaeological Series 44. Arizona State Museum, Tucson.

1982 Two Pollen Profiles from Grasshopper Ruin. In *Multidisciplinary Research at Grasshopper Ruin,* edited by W. A. Longacre, pp. 106–109. Anthropological Papers of the University of Arizona 40. Tucson.

n.d. Pollen Analysis of Rattlesnake Ruin Reservoir Sediments. Ms. in possession of the author.

Kessell, J. L.

1971 Campaigning on the Upper Gila, 1756. *New Mexico Historical Review* 46(2):133–160.

Kidder, A. V.

1932 *The Artifacts of Pecos.* Papers of the Southwest Expedition 6. Department of Archaeology, Phillips Academy. Yale University Press, New Haven.

Klein, J., J. C. Lerman, P. E. Damon, and T. Linick

1980 Radiocarbon Concentrations in the Atmosphere: 8,000 Year Record of Variations in Tree-Rings. First Results of the USA Workshop. *Radiocarbon* 22:950–961.

Klinger, T. C., and S. H. Lekson

1973 A Bead Cache from Saige-McFarland, a Mimbres Site in Southwestern New Mexico. *The Artifact* 11(4):66–68.

Kohler, T. A.

1993 News from the Northern American Southwest: Prehistory on the Edge of Chaos. *Journal of Archaeological Research* 1:267–321.

Kraus, B. S.

1954 *Indian Health in Arizona.* 2nd Annual Report of the Bureau of Ethnic Research. University of Arizona Press, Tucson.

Krogman, W. M.

1962 *The Human Skeleton in Forensic Medicine.* Charles C. Thomas, Springfield, Illinois.

Ladd, E. J.

1963 *Zuni Ethno-ornithology.* Master's thesis, University of New Mexico, Albuquerque.

Lancaster, J. W.

1983 *An Analysis of Manos and Metates from the Mimbres Valley, New Mexico.* Master's thesis, University of New Mexico, Albuquerque.

1984 Groundstone Artifacts. In *The Galaz Ruin: A Prehistoric Mimbres Village in Southwestern New Mexico,* by R. Anyon and S. A. LeBlanc, pp. 247–262. University of New Mexico Press, Albuquerque.

1986 Ground Stone. In *Short-Term Sedentism in the American Southwest: The Mimbres Valley Salado,* edited by B. A. Nelson and S. A. LeBlanc, pp. 177–190. University of New Mexico Press, Albuquerque.

Lang, R. W., and A. H. Harris

1984 *The Faunal Remains from Arroyo Hondo, New Mexico: A Study in Short-term Subsistence Change.* Arroyo Hondo Archaeological Series 5. School of American Research Press, Santa Fe.

Lange, H. C., and C. L. Riley (editors and annotators)

1970 *The Southwestern Journals of Adolph F. Bandelier 1883–1884.* University of New Mexico Press, Albuquerque.

Laumbach, K. W.

1980 *Emergency Survey and Excavation in Southwestern New Mexico.* Cultural Resources Management Division, New Mexico State University Report 354. Las Cruces.

LeBlanc, S. A.

1980 The Post-Mogollon Periods in Southwestern New Mexico: The Animas/Black Mountain Phase and the Salado Period. In *An Archeological Synthesis of South-Central and Southwestern New Mexico,* edited by S. A. LeBlanc and M. E. Whalen, pp. 271–316. Office of Contract Archeology, University of New Mexico, Albuquerque.

1982a The Advent of Pottery in the Southwest. In *Southwestern Ceramics: A Comparative Review,* edited by A. H. Schroeder, pp. 27–51. Arizona Archaeologist 15. Arizona Archaeological Society, Phoenix.

1982b Temporal Change in Mogollon Ceramics. In *Southwestern Ceramics: A Comparative Review,* edited by A. H. Schroeder, pp. 107–127. Arizona Archaeologist 15. Arizona Archaeological Society, Phoenix.

1983 *The Mimbres People.* Thames and Hudson, London.

1986 Development of Archaeological Thought on the Mimbres Mogollon. In *Emil W. Haury's Prehistory of the American Southwest,* edited by J. J. Reid and D. E. Doyel, pp. 297–304. University of Arizona Press, Tucson.

LeBlanc, S. A., and M. E. Whalen (editors)

1980 *An Archeological Synthesis of South-Central and Southwestern New Mexico.* Office of Contract Archeology, University of New Mexico, Albuquerque.

Lekson, S. H.

1978a *Settlement Patterns in the Red Rock Valley, Southwestern New Mexico.* Master's thesis, Department of Anthropology, Eastern New Mexico University, Portales.

1978b The Villareal Sites, Grant County, New Mexico: Documentation of the 1972 & 1973 Season. Ms. on file, National Park Service, Albuquerque.

1984 Dating Casas Grandes. *The Kiva* 50:55–60.

1986 The Mimbres Region. In *Mogollon Variability,* edited by C. Benson and S. Upham, pp. 147–155. University Museum, Occasional Papers 15. New Mexico State University, Las Cruces.

1988 The Mangas Phase in Mimbres Archaeology. *The Kiva* 53:129–145.

1990 *Mimbres Archaeology of the Upper Gila, New Mexico.* Anthropological Papers of the University of Arizona 53. Tucson.

1992 The Surface Archaeology of Southwestern New Mexico. *The Artifact* 30(3):1–36.

Lekson, S. H., and T. C. Klinger

1973a A Mimbres Stone Effigy Vessel. *The Artifact* 11(4):5–7.

1973b Villareal II: Preliminary Notes on an Animas Phase Site in Southwestern New Mexico. *Awanyu* 1(2):33–38.

Leopold, A. S.

1972 *Wildlife of Mexico.* University of California Press, Berkeley and Los Angeles.

Lightfoot, K. G., and G. M. Feinman

1982 Social Differentiation and Leadership Development in Early Pithouse Villages in the Mogollon Region of the American Southwest. *American Antiquity* 47:64–86.

Lister, R. H.

1946 Survey of Archaeological Remains in Northwestern Chihuahua. *Southwestern Journal of Anthropology* 2(4):433–453.

1958 Archaeological Excavations in the Northern Sierra Madre Occidental, Chihuahua and Sonora, Mexico. *University of Colorado Studies, Series in Anthropology 9.*

Lorenzo, J. L.

1965 *Tlatilco, los artefactos.* Institutos Nacional de Antropologia e Historia, Investigaciones 7.

Lyon, L.

1988 Tewa Red and Tewa Black Pottery. *Pottery Southwest* 15(1):4–5.

McElhinny, M. W.

1973 *Paleomagnetism and Plate Tectonics.* Cambridge University Press, Cambridge.

McFadden, P. L.

1980 Determination of the Angle in a Fisher Distribution Which Will be Exceeded with a Given Probability. *Geophysical Journal of the Royal Astronomical Society* 60:391–396.

McGuire, R. H.

1987 *Death, Society and Ideology in a Hohokam Community: Colonial and Sedentary Period Burials from La Cuidad.* Arizona State University, Office of Cultural Resource Management Report 58. Tempe.

McKern, T. W., and T. D. Stewart

1957 *Skeletal Age Changes in Young American Males.* Technical Report EP-45, Quartermaster Research and Development Center, U.S. Army, Natick, Massachusetts.

McKern, W. C.

1939 The Midwestern Taxonomic Method as an Aid to Archaeological Study. *American Antiquity* 4:301–313.

McKusick, C. R.

1981 The Faunal Remains of Las Humanas. In *Contributions to Gran Quivira Archeology: Gran Quivera National Monument, New Mexico,* by A. C. Hayes, pp. 39–65. Publications in Archeology 17. National Park Service, Washington, D.C.

Maher, L. J., Jr.
1964 Ephedra Pollen in Sediments of the Great Lakes Region. *Ecology* 45:391–395.

Martin, Paul Schultz
1963 *The Last 10,000 Years.* University of Arizona Press, Tucson.

Martin, Paul S., and William Byers
1965 Pollen and Archaeology at Wetherill Mesa. In *Contributions of the Wetherill Mesa Project,* assembled by D. Osborne, pp. 122–135. Society for American Archaeology Memoirs 19. Society for American Archaeology, Washington, D.C.

Martin, Paul S., and F. W. Sharrock
1964 Pollen Analysis of Prehistoric Human Feces: A New Approach to Ethnobotany. *American Antiquity* 30:168–180.

Martin, Paul Sidney
1940 *The SU Site: Excavations at a Mogollon Village, Western New Mexico, 1939.* Anthropological Series 32(1). Field Museum of Natural History, Chicago.
1943 *The SU Site, Excavations at a Mogollon Village, Western New Mexico: Second Season, 1941.* Anthropological Series 32(2). Field Museum of Natural History, Chicago.
1959 *Digging into History: A Brief Account of Fifteen Years of Archaeological Work in New Mexico.* Chicago Natural History Museum Press, Chicago.
1979 Prehistory: Mogollon. In *Southwest,* vol. 9, edited by A. Ortiz, pp. 61–74. Handbook of North American Indians, W. C. Sturtevant, general editor. Smithsonian Institution, Washington, D.C.

Martin, Paul S., and F. T. Plog
1973 *The Archaeology of Arizona: A Study of the Southwest Region.* Doubleday/Natural History Press, Garden City, New York.

Martin, Paul S., and J. B. Rinaldo
1947 *The SU Site, Excavations at a Mogollon Village, Western New Mexico: Third Season, 1946.* Anthropological Series 32(3). Field Museum of Natural History, Chicago.
1950a *Turkey Foot Ridge Site: A Mogollon Village, Pine Lawn Valley, Western New Mexico.* Fieldiana: Anthropology 38(2).
1950b *Sites of the Reserve Phase, Pine Lawn Valley, Western New Mexico.* Fieldiana: Anthropology 38(3).

Martin, Paul S., J. B. Rinaldo, and E. R. Barter
1957 *Late Mogollon Communities: Four Sites of the Tularosa Phase, Western New Mexico.* Fieldiana: Anthropology 49(1).

Martin, P. S., J. B. Rinaldo, E. A. Bluhm, and H. C. Cutler
1956 *Higgins Flat Pueblo, Western New Mexico.* Fieldiana: Anthropology 45.

Martin, P. S., J. B. Rinaldo, E. A. Bluhm, H. C. Cutler, and R. Grange, Jr.
1952 *Mogollon Cultural Continuity and Change: The Stratigraphic Analysis of Tularosa and Cordova Caves.* Fieldiana: Anthropology 40.

Mathien, F. J., and R. H. McGuire (editors)
1986 *Ripples in the Chichimec Sea: New Considerations of Southwestern-Mesoamerican Interactions.* Southern Illinois University Press, Carbondale.

Mehringer, P. J., Jr.
1967 Pollen Analysis of the Tule Springs Area, Nevada. In *Pleistocene Studies in Southern Nevada,* edited by H. M. Wormington and D. Ellis, pp. 120–200. Nevada State Anthropological Papers 13. Nevada State Museum, Carson City.

Meighan, C. W.
1981 Personal Communication. Letter to Charles C. Di Peso, dated 1 May 1981. Amerind Foundation, Dragoon, Arizona.

Meighan, C. W. (editor)
1976 *The Archaeology of Amapa, Nyarit.* Monumenta Archaeologica 2.

Meighan, C. W., and G. S. Russell
1981 *Obsidian Dates III. A Compendium of the Obsidian Hydration Determinations Made at the UCLA Obsidian Hydration Laboratory.* Institute of Archaeology Monograph XVI. University of California, Los Angeles.

Mera, H. P.
1931 *Chupadero Black-on-White.* Laboratory of Anthropology Technical Series, Bulletin 1, Santa Fe.

Mera, H. P., and W. S. Stallings, Jr.
1931 *Lincoln Black-on-Red.* Laboratory of Anthropology Technical Series, Bulletin 2, Santa Fe.

Meyer, E. R.
1973 Late-Quaternary Paleoecology of the Cuatro Cienegas Basin, Coahuila, Mexico. *Ecology* 54:982–995.

Mills, J. P., and V. M. Mills
1972 The Dinwiddie Site: A Prehistoric Salado Ruin on Duck Creek, Western New Mexico. *The Artifact* 10(2):i-iv, 1–50.

Minckley, W. L.
1973 *Fishes of Arizona.* Arizona Game and Fish Department, Phoenix.

Minnis, P. E.
1978 Paleoethnobotanical Indicators of Prehistoric Environmental Disturbance: A Case Study. In *Nature and Status of Ethnobotany,* edited by R. I. Ford, pp. 347–366. University of Michigan Museum of Anthropology Papers 67. Ann Arbor.

Minnis, P. E., and S. Plog
1976 A Study of the Site Specific Distribution of *Agave parryi* in East-Central Arizona. *The Kiva* 41:299–308.

Minnis, P. E., M. E. Whalen, J. H. Kelley, and J. D. Stewart
1993 Prehistoric Macaw Breeding in the North American Southwest. *American Antiquity* 58:270–276.

Mitchell, G. F.
1956 Post-Boreal Pollen Diagrams from Irish Raised Bogs. *Proceedings of the Royal Irish Academy of Science* 57:185–251.

Moore, W. M., M. M. Silverberg, and M. S. Read
1972 *Nutrition, Growth and Development in North American Indian Children.* Department of Health, Education, and Welfare, Publication No. (NIH) 72–26, Washington, D.C.

Morris, D. H.
1990 Changes in Groundstone Following the Introduction

of Maize into the American Southwest. *Journal of Anthropological Research* 46(2):177–194.

Morris, E. A.

1980 *Basketmaker Caves in the Prayer Rock District, Northeastern Arizona.* Anthropological Papers of the University of Arizona 35. Tucson.

Morris, E. A., and V. H. Jones

1962 Seventh Century Evidence for the Use of Tobacco in Northern Arizona. *Atken des 34, Internationalen Amerikanistenkongresses* 34:306–309.

Morris, E. H.

1919 The Aztec Ruin. *Anthropological Papers of the American Museum of Natural History* 26(5):259–420.

1927 *The Beginnings of Pottery Making in the San Juan Area: Unfired Prototypes and the Ware of the Earliest Ceramic Period.* Anthropological Papers of the American Museum of Natural History 28(2).

Murdock, G. P.

1967 *Ethnographic Atlas.* University of Pittsburgh, Pittsburgh.

Neely, J. A.

1978a The Archaeology of the WS Ranch Site, West-Central New Mexico: The 1977 Season. Paper presented at the annual meeting of the Society for American Archaeology, Tucson.

1978b Field Report, 1978 Season of the WS Ranch Site Project. Report submitted to the Center for Field Research and the Earthwatch Programs, Belmont, Massachusetts.

Nelson, B. A., and S. A. LeBlanc

1986 *Short-Term Sedentism in the American Southwest: The Mimbres Valley Salado.* University of New Mexico Press, Albuquerque.

Nelson, M. C.

1981 *Chipped Stone Analysis in the Reconstruction of Prehistoric Subsistence Practices: An Example from Southwestern New Mexico.* Ph.D. dissertation, Department of Anthropology, University of California at Santa Barbara.

1986 Chipped Stone Analysis: Food Selection and Hunting Behavior. In *Short-Term Sedentism in the American Southwest: The Mimbres Valley Salado,* by B. A. Nelson and S. A. LeBlanc, pp. 141–176. University of New Mexico Press, Albuquerque.

Nelson, M. C., and H. Lippmeier

1993 Grinding-Tool Design as Conditioned by Land-Use Pattern. *American Antiquity* 58:286–305.

Nesbitt, P. H.

1931 *The Ancient Mimbreños: Based on Investigations at the Mattocks Ruin, Mimbres Valley, New Mexico.* Logan Museum Bulletin 4. Beloit, Wisconsin.

1938 *Starkweather Ruin: A Mogollon-Pueblo Site in the Upper Gila Area of New Mexico, and Affiliative Aspects of the Mogollon Culture.* Logan Museum Bulletin 6. Beloit, Wisconsin.

Nickerson, N. H.

1953 Variation in Cob Morphology among Certain Archaeological and Ethnological Races of Maize. *Annals of the Missouri Botanical Garden* 40:79–111.

Northrop, S. A.

1959 *Minerals of New Mexico.* Rev. ed. University of New Mexico, Albuquerque.

Olsen, J. W.

1980 *A Zooarchaeological Analysis of Vertebrate Faunal Remains from the Grasshopper Pueblo, Arizona.* Ph.D. dissertation, University of California, Berkeley.

Olsen, S. J.

1968a *The Osteology of the Wild Turkey.* Papers of the Peabody Museum of Archaeology and Ethnology 56(2). Harvard University, Cambridge.

1968b Canid Remains of Grasshopper Ruin. *The Kiva* 34:33–40.

Olsen, S. L.

1979 A Study of Bone Artifacts from Grasshopper Pueblo, AZ P:14:1. *The Kiva* 44:341–373.

1980 Bone Artifacts from Kinishba Ruin: Their Manufacture and Use. *The Kiva* 46:39–67.

Ortiz, A.

1969 *The Tewa World: Space, Time, Being, and Becoming in Pueblo Society.* University of Chicago Press, Chicago.

1972 Ritual Drama and the Pueblo World View. In *New Perspectives on the Pueblos,* edited by A. Ortiz, pp. 135–161. University of New Mexico Press, Albuquerque.

Parham, T. L., R. Paetzold, and C. E. Souders

1983 *Soil Survey of Grant County, New Mexico Central and Southern Parts.* USDA Soil and Conservation Service and Forest Service, Albuquerque.

Parsons, E. C.

1970 *Taos Pueblo.* Johnson Reprint, New York and London. Reprinted from 1936 edition. George Banta Publishing, Menasha, Wisconsin.

Paul, J. R.

1938 Report to the Secretary of the Smithsonian Institution Describing Some Preliminary Archeological Explorations Carried Out during May and June, 1938, in and near the Gila National Forest, Grant County, New Mexico. Ms. on file with the Smithsonian Institution. Washington, D.C.

Paz, O.

1993 The Art of Mexico: Material and Meaning. In *Essays on Mexican Art,* translated by Helen Lane, pp. 29–43. Harcourt Brace, New York.

Peckham, S.

1990 *From this Earth: The Ancient Art of Pueblo Pottery.* Laboratory of Anthropology/Museum of Indian Arts and Culture, Museum of New Mexico Press, Santa Fe.

Peckham, S., F. Wendorf, and E. N. Ferdon, Jr.

1956 Excavations near Apache Creek, New Mexico. In *Highway Salvage Archaeology,* vol. 2, edited by F. Wendorf, pp. 17–86. New Mexico State Highway Department and Museum of New Mexico, Santa Fe.

Peebles, C. S., and S. M. Kus
1977 Some Archaeological Correlates of Ranked Societies. In *Essays on Archaeological Problems,* edited by B. Fagan and B. Voorhies. *American Antiquity* 42:421–448.

Pennington, C. W.
1963 *The Tarahumar of Mexico: Their Environment and Material Culture.* University of Utah Press, Salt Lake City.

Pepper, G. H.
1920 *Pueblo Bonito.* Anthropological Papers of the American Museum of Natural History 27. New York.

Phenic, T. W.
1969 A Newly Developed Visual Method of Sexing the *Os Pubis. American Journal of Physical Anthropology* 30(2):297–301.

Plog, F.
1974 *The Study of Prehistoric Change.* Academic Press, New York.

Porter, M. N.
1956 *Excavations at Chupicuaro, Guanajuato, Mexico.* Transactions of the American Philosophical Society N.S. 46(5).

Potter, L. D., and J. Rowley
1960 Pollen Rain and Vegetation, San Augustín Plains, New Mexico. *Botanical Gazette* 122(1):1–25.

Raynor, G. S., J. V. Hayes, and E. C. Ogden
1972 Dispersion and Deposition of Corn Pollen from Experimental Sources. *Journal of Agronomy* 64:420–427.
1973 Dispersal of Pollens from Low-level Cross Wind Line Sources. *Agricultural Meteorology* 9:175–195.

Rice, G. E.
1975 *A Systematic Explanation of a Change in Mogollon Settlement Patterns.* Ph.D. dissertation, University of Washington, Seattle.
1980 What Happened in the Prehistory of Corduroy Creek? In *Studies in the Prehistory of the Forestdale Region, Arizona,* edited by G. E. Rice, pp. 462–475. Anthropological Field Studies 1. Office of Cultural Resource Management, Arizona State University, Tempe.

Riley, C. L.
1993 Charles C. Di Peso: An Intellectual Biography. In *Culture and Contact: Charles C. Di Peso's Gran Chichimeca,* edited by A. I. Woosley and J. C. Ravesloot, pp. 11–22. Amerind Foundation New World Studies Series 2. Amerind Foundation, Dragoon, Arizona, and University of New Mexico Press, Albuquerque.

Riley, C. L., and B. C. Hedrick (editors)
1978 *Across the Chichimec Sea: Papers in Honor of J. Charles Kelley.* Southern Illinois University Press, Carbondale.

Rinaldo, J. B., and E. A. Bluhm
1956 *Late Mogollon Pottery Types of the Reserve Area.* Fieldiana: Anthropology 36(7).

Robbins, C. S., B. Bruun, and H. S. Zim
1966 *Birds of North America.* Golden Press, New York.

Robbins, W. W., J. P. Harrington, and B. Freire-Marreco
1916 *Ethnobotany of the Tewa Indians.* Bureau of American Ethnobotany, Bulletin 55. Smithsonian Institution, Washington, D.C.

Roberts, F. H. H., Jr.
1930 *Early Pueblo Ruins in the Piedra District Southwestern Colorado.* Bureau of American Ethnology, Bulletin 96. Smithsonian Institution. Washington, D.C.

Roberts, F.
1931 *The Ruins at Kiatuthlanna.* Bureau of American Ethnology, Bulletin 100. Smithsonian Institution, Washington, D.C.

Rodeck, H. G.
1954 Animal and Bird Bones from the Durango Sites. In *Basket Maker II Sites near Durango, Colorado,* edited by E. H. Morris and R. F. Burgh, pp. 117–121. Publication 604. Carnegie Institution, Washington, D.C.

Roediger, V. M.
1941 *Ceremonial Costumes of the Pueblo Indians: Their Evolution, Fabrication, and Significance in the Prayer Drama.* University of California Press, Berkeley and Los Angeles.

Rothschild, N. A.
1979 Mortuary Behavior and Social Organization at Indian Knoll and Dickson Mounds. *American Antiquity* 44:658–675.

Russell, F.
1908 The Pima Indians. *Bureau of American Ethnology, Twenty-Sixth Annual Report,* pp. 3–389. Smithsonian Institution. Washington, D.C.

Sahagun, B., O. F. M.
1963 *Earthly Things. Florentine Codex: General History of the Things of New Spain,* translated and annotated by C. E. Dibble and A. J. O. Anderson, Book II. School of American Research and Museum of New Mexico, Monograph 14 (XII).

Sanburg, D., Jr.
1976 LA5356: An Introduction and Discussion of the Ceramic Materials. Paper presented at the Society for California Archeology-Southwestern Anthropology Association Meetings, San Diego.

Sayles, E. B.
1936 *Some Southwestern Pottery Types, Series V.* Medallion Papers 21. Gila Pueblo, Globe.
1945 *The San Simon Branch: Excavations at Cave Creek and in the San Simon Valley. Part I, Material Culture.* Medallion Papers 34. Gila Pueblo, Globe.

Scantling, F. H.
1940 *Excavation at the Jackrabbit Ruin, Papago Indian Reservation, Arizona.* Master's thesis, Department of Anthropology, University of Arizona, Tucson.

Schlonger, S. H.
1991 On Manos, Metates, and the History of Site Occupations. *American Antiquity* 56:460–474.

Schoenwetter, J.
1962 Pollen Analysis of Eighteen Archaeological Sites in Arizona and New Mexico. In *Chapters in the Prehistory of Ari-*

zona, edited by P. S. Martin, pp. 168–209. Fieldiana: Anthropology 55. Field Museum of Natural History, Chicago.

1964 The Palynological Research. In *Alluvial and Palynological Reconstruction of Environments: Navajo Reservoir District,* edited by J. Schoenwetter and F. W. Eddy, pp. 63–107. Museum of New Mexico Papers in Anthropology 13. Museum of New Mexico, Santa Fe.

1970 Archaeological Pollen Studies of the Colorado Plateau. *American Antiquity* 35:35–47.

Schorger, A. W.

1961 An Ancient Pueblo Turkey. *Auk* 78:133–144.

1970 A New Subspecies of *Meleagris gallopavo. Auk* 87:168–170.

Schour, I., and M. Massler

1944 *Chart - Development of the Human Dentition.* 2d ed. American Dental Association, Chicago.

Schultes, R. E.

1972 An Overview of Hallucinogens in the Western Hemisphere. In *Flesh of the Gods: The Ritual Use of Hallucinogens,* edited by P. T. Furst, pp. 3–54. Praeger, New York and Washington.

Scott, C. J.

1983 The Evolution of Mimbres Pottery. In *Mimbres Pottery: Ancient Art of the American Southwest,* by J. J. Brody, C. J. Scott, and S. A. LeBlanc, pp. 39–67. Hudson Hills Press, New York.

Shafer, H. J.

1982 Classic Mimbres Phase Households and Room Use Patterns. *The Kiva* 48:17–37.

1983 *NAN Ranch Archaeological Project: 1982 Season.* Anthropology Laboratory, Texas A & M University, College Station.

1986 *The NAN Ranch Archaeology Project: 1985 Interim Report.* Special Report 7, Anthropology Laboratory, Texas A & M University, College Station.

1987 *Explorations at the NAN Ruin (LA 15049): 1986 Interim Report.* Anthropology Laboratory, Texas A & M University, College Station.

1988 *Archaeology of the NAN Ranch Ruin: The 1987 Season.* Department of Anthropology, Texas A & M University, College Station.

1990 Archaeology at the NAN Ruin: 1984 Interim Report. *The Artifact* 28(4):5–27.

1991a Archaeology at the NAN Ruin (LA 15049): 1985 Interim Report. *The Artifact* 29(1):1–29.

1991b Archaeology at the NAN Ruin: 1986 Interim Report. *The Artifact* 29(2):1–42.

Shafer, H. J., and A. J. Taylor

1986 Mimbres Mogollon Pueblo Dynamics and Ceramic Style Change. *Journal of Field Archaeology* 13(1):43–68.

Shaffer, B. S.

1990 The Modified Rabbit Pelvis: A Newly Discovered Tool Type for the Mimbres. *The Artifact* 28(2):7–14.

Simmons, L. W. (editor)

1950 *Sun Chief: The Autobiography of a Hopi Indian.* Yale University Press, New Haven.

Spaulding, A. C.

1953 Statistical Techniques for the Discovery of Artifact Types. *American Antiquity* 18:305–313.

Stafford, C. R.

1980 A Consideration of Settlement-Subsistence Systems in the Forestdale Region. In *Studies in the Prehistory of the Forestdale Region, Arizona,* edited by G. E. Rice, pp. 41–75. Anthropological Field Studies 1. Office of Cultural Resource Management, Department of Anthropology, Arizona State University, Tempe.

Stebbins, R. C.

1966 *A Field Guide to Western Reptiles and Amphibians.* Houghton Mifflin, Boston.

Stein, W. T.

1963 Mammal Remains from Archaeological Sites in the Point of Pines Region, Arizona. *American Antiquity* 29:213–220.

Stephen, A. M.

1969 *Hopi Journal.* AMS Press, New York. Reprinted from 1936 edition, Columbia University Press, New York.

Sternberg, R. S., and R. H. McGuire

1990 Techniques for Constructing Secular Variation Curves and for Interpreting Archaeomagnetic Dates. In *Archaeomagnetic Dating,* edited by J. L. Eighmy and R. S. Sternberg, pp. 106–134. University of Arizona Press, Tucson.

Sterrett, D. B.

1908 Turquoise [in] New Mexico. *U.S. Geological Survey, Mineral Resources, 1907* 2:828–832.

Stevenson, M. C.

1915 Ethnobotany of the Zuni Indians. *Bureau of American Ethnology, Thirtieth Annual Report,* pp. 35–102. Smithsonian Institution, Washington, D.C.

Stewart, T. D.

1952 *Hrdlicka's Practical Anthropometry.* 4th ed. Wistar Institute, Philadelphia.

1970 Identification of the Scars of Parturition in the Skeletal Remains of Females. In *Personal Identification in Mass Disasters,* edited by T. D. Stewart. National Museum of Natural History, Washington, D.C..

Stoltman, J. B.

1989 A Quantitative Approach to the Petrographic Analysis of Ceramic Thin Sections. *American Antiquity* 54:147–160.

Stuiver, M., and P. J. Reimer

1987 *CALIB: Radiocarbon Calibration Program 1987.* Quaternary Isotope Laboratory, University of Washington, Seattle.

Suchey, J. M., D. V. Wiseley, and T. T. Noguchi

1979 Analysis of Dorsal Pitting in the *Os Pubis* in an Extensive Sample of Modern American Females. *American Journal of Physical Anthropology* 51:517–540.

Sweeney, E. A., J. Cabrera, J. Urrutia, and L. Mata

1969 Factors Associated with Linear Hypoplasia of Human Deciduous Incisors. *Journal of Dental Research* 48:1275–1279.

Taylor, A. J.

1984 *An Analysis of Form and Function of Mimbres Mogollon Bowls.* Master's thesis, Texas A & M University, College Station.

Tratman, E. K.

1950 A Comparison of the Teeth in People. *Yearbook of Physical Anthropology* 6:272–314.

Tuan, Yi-Fu, C. E. Everard, J. G. Widdison, and I. Bennett

1973 *The Climate of New Mexico.* State Planning Office, Santa Fe.

Tuthill, C.

1947 *The Tres Alamos Site on the San Pedro River, Southeastern Arizona.* Amerind Foundation Publications 4. Dragoon, Arizona.

Tyler, H. A.

1975 *Pueblo Animals and Myths.* University of Oklahoma Press, Norman.

1979 *Pueblo Birds and Myths.* University of Oklahoma Press, Norman.

Van Asdall, W., P. Fall, and C. H. Miksicek

1982 Corn, Chenopodium and Century Plant: Mogollon Subsistence in the Mangas Valley. In *Mogollon Archaeology: Proceedings of the 1980 Mogollon Conference,* edited by P. H. Beckett and K. Silverbird, pp. 167–178. Acoma Press, Ramona, California.

Vestal, P. A.

1952 *Ethnobotany of the Ramah Navajo. Report of the Ramah Project No. 4.* Papers of the Peabody Museum of American Archaeology and Ethnology 40(4). Harvard University, Cambridge.

Wallerstein, I.

1974 *The Modern World System I.* Academic Press, New York.

Watanabe, N., and R. L. Dubois

1965 Some Results of an Archaeomagnetic Study on the Secular Variation in the Southwest of North America. *Journal of Geomagnetism and Geoelectricity* 17:395–397.

Watson, E. L.

1927 Interior of Cave Dwellings at Gila Cliff National Monument. *El Palacio* 23(7–8):174–234.

1929 Caves of the Upper Gila River, New Mexico. *American Anthropologist* 31(2):299–306.

Webster's New World Dictionary, Encyclopedic Edition

1952 World Publishing, Cleveland.

Weigand, P. C.

1968 The Mines and Mining Techniques of the Chalchihuites Culture. *American Antiquity* 33:45–61

Wheat, J. B.

1955 *Mogollon Culture Prior to A.D. 1000.* American Anthropological Association, Memoirs 82; Society for American Archaeology, Memoirs 10; American Antiquity 20(4) part 2.

White, L. A.

1962 *The Pueblo of Sia.* Bureau of American Ethnology, Bulletin 184. Smithsonian Institution, Washington, D.C.

White, T. D.

1978 Early Hominid Enamel Hypoplasia. *American Journal of Physical Anthropology* 49(1):79–84.

Whiting, A. F.

1939 *Ethnobotany of the Hopi.* Museum of Northern Arizona Bulletin 15. Museum of Northern Arizona, Flagstaff.

Wilcox, D. R., and C. Sternberg

1983 *Hohokam Ballcourts and their Interpretation.* Arizona State Museum Archaeological Series 160. Tucson.

Wills, W. H.

1988 Early Agriculture and Sedentism in the American Southwest: Evidence and Interpretations. *Journal of World Prehistory* 2(4):455–488.

Wilson, C. D.

1992 Implications of a Ceramic Resource Survey in the Northern Mogollon Country. Paper presented at the 7th Mogollon Conference, Las Cruces.

Wilson, C. D., E. Blinman, J. M. Skibo, and M. B. Schiffer

1993 The Designing of Southwestern Pottery: A Technological and Experimental Approach. Revised version of a paper presented at the 1992 Third Southwest Symposium, Tucson.

Wilson, E. D.

1962 *A Resume of the Geology of Arizona.* Arizona Bureau of Mines, Bulletin 171. University of Arizona Press, Tucson.

Wodehouse, R. P.

1971 *Hayfever Plants.* Hafner Publishing, New York.

Wolf, E. R.

1959 *Sons of the Shaking Earth.* University of Chicago Press, Chicago.

Wolfman, D.

1979 Archaeomagnetic Dating in Arkansas. *Archaeo-Physika* 10:522–533.

Woodbury, R. B.

1954 *Prehistoric Stone Implements of Northeastern Arizona.* Papers of the Peabody Museum of American Archaeology and Ethnology 34. Harvard University, Cambridge.

Woosley, A. I.

1980a Agricultural Diversity in the Prehistoric Southwest. *The Kiva* 45:317–335.

1980b *Taos Archaeology.* Fort Burgwin Research Center, Southern Methodist University, Dallas.

1986 Puebloan Prehistory of the Northern Rio Grande: Settlement, Population, Subsistence. *The Kiva* 51:143–164.

Woosley, A. I., and B. Olinger

1993 The Casas Grandes Ceramic Tradition: Production and Interregional Exchange of Ramos Polychrome. In *Culture and Contact: Charles C. Di Peso's Gran Chichimeca,* edited by A. I. Woosley and J. C. Ravesloot, pp. 105–131. Amerind Foundation New World Studies Series 2. Amerind Foundation, Dragoon, Arizona, and University of New Mexico Press, Albuquerque.

Woosley, A. I., and J. C. Ravesloot (editors)
1993 *Culture and Contact: Charles C. Di Peso's Gran Chichimeca.* Amerind Foundation New World Studies Series 2. Amerind Foundation, Dragoon, Arizona, and University of New Mexico Press, Albuquerque.

Wyllys, R. K.
1931 Padre Luis Velarde's *Relación* of Pimeria Alta, 1716. *New Mexico Historical Review* 6(2):111–157.

Yarnell, R. A.
1976 Early Plant Husbandry in Eastern North America. In *Cultural Change and Continuity: Essays in Honor of James Bennett Griffin,* edited by C. Cleland, pp. 265–273. Academic Press, New York.

Index

DATE DUE